# Statistics for Criminology and Criminal Justice

## FOURTH EDITION

*This book is dedicated to our son, John Bachman-Paternoster,*
*and John would like to dedicate this book to our wonder-dog, Mickey.*

# Statistics for Criminology and Criminal Justice

## FOURTH EDITION

**Ronet D. Bachman**
*University of Delaware*

**Raymond Paternoster**
*University of Maryland*

Los Angeles | London | New Delhi
Singapore | Washington DC

Los Angeles | London | New Delhi
Singapore | Washington DC

FOR INFORMATION:

SAGE Publications, Inc.
2455 Teller Road
Thousand Oaks, California 91320
E-mail: order@sagepub.com

SAGE Publications Ltd.
1 Oliver's Yard
55 City Road
London EC1Y 1SP
United Kingdom

SAGE Publications India Pvt. Ltd.
B 1/I 1 Mohan Cooperative Industrial Area
Mathura Road, New Delhi 110 044
India

SAGE Publications Asia-Pacific Pte. Ltd.
3 Church Street
#10-04 Samsung Hub
Singapore 049483

Publisher: Jerry Westby
Associate Editor: Jessica Miller
eLearning Editor: Nicole Mangona
Editorial Assistant: Laura Kirkhuff
Production Editor: David C. Felts
Copy Editor: Sheree Van Vreede
Typesetter: C&M Digitals (P) Ltd.
Proofreader: Jen Grubba
Indexer: Michael Ferreira
Cover Designer: Michael Dubowe
Marketing Manager: Amy Lammers

Printed in the United States of America

*Library of Congress Cataloging-in-Publication Data*

Names: Bachman, Ronet, author. | Paternoster, Raymond, author.
Title: Statistics for criminology and criminal justice / Ronet Bachman, Ray Paternoster.
Description: Fourth edition. | Thousand Oaks, California : SAGE, [2017] | Includes bibliographical references and index.
Identifiers: LCCN 2015038682 |
ISBN 978-1-5063-2610-8 (pbk. : alk. paper)
Subjects: LCSH: Criminal statistics.
Classification: LCC HV6208 .B33 2017 | DDC 364.01/5195—dc23 LC record available at http://lccn.loc.gov/2015038682

This book is printed on acid-free paper.

18 19 20 10 9 8 7 6 5 4 3

# Brief Contents

About the Authors                                                                                          xi

Preface                                                                                                    xii

Chapter 1.    The Purpose of Statistics in the Criminological Sciences                                     1

PART I. UNIVARIATE ANALYSIS: DESCRIBING VARIABLE DISTRIBUTIONS                                             23

Chapter 2.    Levels of Measurement and Aggregation                                                        24

Chapter 3.    Understanding Data Distributions: Tabular and Graphical Techniques                           42

Chapter 4.    Measures of Central Tendency                                                                 81

Chapter 5.    Measures of Dispersion                                                                       105

PART II. MAKING INFERENCES IN UNIVARIATE ANALYSIS:
GENERALIZING FROM A SAMPLE TO THE POPULATION                                                               145

Chapter 6.    Probability, Probability Distributions, and an Introduction to Hypothesis Testing           146

Chapter 7.    Point Estimation and Confidence Intervals                                                    185

Chapter 8.    From Estimation to Statistical Tests: Hypothesis Testing for
              One Population Mean and Proportion                                                           208

PART III. BIVARIATE ANALYSIS: RELATIONSHIPS BETWEEN TWO VARIABLES                                          241

Chapter 9.    Testing Hypotheses With Categorical Data                                                     242

Chapter 10.   Hypothesis Tests Involving Two Population Means or Proportions                               273

Chapter 11.   Hypothesis Tests Involving Three or More Population Means: Analysis of Variance              312

Chapter 12.   Bivariate Correlation and Regression                                                        342

PART IV. MUTLITIVARIATE ANALYSIS:
RELATIONSHIPS BETWEEN MORE THAN TWO VARIABLES                                                              391

Chapter 13.   Controlling for a Third Variable: Multiple OLS Regression                                    392

Chapter 14.   Regression Analysis With a Dichotomous Dependent Variable: Logit Models                      433

Appendix A. Review of Basic Mathematical Operations                                                        468

Appendix B. Statistical Tables                                                                             475

Appendix C. Solutions for Odd-Numbered Practice Problems                                                   485

Glossary                                                                                                   506

References                                                                                                 513

Index                                                                                                      516

# Detailed Contents

About the Authors    xi

Preface    xii

Chapter 1. The Purpose of Statistics in the
    Criminological Sciences    1
    Introduction    2
    Setting the Stage for Statistical Inquiry    3
    The Role of Statistical Methods in Criminology and
        Criminal Justice    4
    Case Study: Youth Violence    4
        *Descriptive Research*    5
    Case Study: How Prevalent is Youth Violence?    5
        *Explanatory Research*    6
    Case Study: What Factors Are Related to Youth
        Delinquency and Violence?    7
        *Evaluation Research*    8
    Case Study: How Effective Are Violence Prevention
        Programs in Schools?    8
    Populations and Samples    9
    How Do We Obtain a Sample?    10
    Probability Sampling Techniques    11
        *Simple Random Samples*    11
        *Systematic Random Samples*    11
        *Multistage Cluster Samples*    12
        *Weighted or Stratified Samples*    12
    Nonprobability Sampling Techniques    13
        *Availability Samples*    14
        *Quota Samples*    14
        *Purposive or Judgment Samples*    15
    Descriptive and Inferential Statistics    16
    Validity in Criminology Research    16
        *Measurement Validity*    17
        *Reliability*    18
        *Causal Validity*    19
    ■ SUMMARY    19
    ■ KEY TERMS    20
    ■ PRACTICE PROBLEMS    20
    ■ SPSS EXERCISES    20

PART I. UNIVARIATE ANALYSIS: DESCRIBING
VARIABLE DISTRIBUTIONS    23

Chapter 2. Levels of Measurement and
    Aggregation    24
    Introduction    25
    Levels of Measurement    26

        *Nominal Level of Measurement*    28
        *Ordinal Level of Measurement*    28
        *Interval Level of Measurement*    31
        *Ratio Level of Measurement*    32
        *The Case of Dichotomies*    33
        *Comparing Levels of Measurement*    33
    Ways of Presenting Variable    33
        *Counts and Rates*    34
    Case Study: The Importance of Rates for
        Victimization Data    35
        *Proportions and Percentages*    36
    Units of Analysis    38
    ■ SUMMARY    39
    ■ KEY TERMS    39
    ■ KEY FORMULAS    39
    ■ PRACTICE PROBLEMS    40
    ■ SPSS EXERCISES    41

Chapter 3. Understanding Data Distributions:
    Tabular and Graphical Techniques    42
    Introduction    43
    The Tabular and Graphical Display of Qualitative
        Data    44
        *Frequency Tables*    45
    Case Study: An Analysis of
        Hate Crimes Using Tables    45
        *Pie and Bar Charts*    46
    The Tabular and Graphical Display of
        Quantitative Data    50
        *Ungrouped Distributions*    50
    Case Study: Police Response Time    50
        *Histograms*    53
        *Line Graphs or Polygons*    54
        *Grouped Frequency Distributions*    56
    Case Study: Recidivism    56
        *Refinements to a Grouped Frequency
          Distribution*    63
    The Shape of a Distribution    66
    Time Plots    67
    Case Study: A Trend Analysis of Crime Rates    68
        *When Trend Data Are Erratic— Smoothing
          Techniques*    70
    Case Study: Executions in the United States    71
    ■ SUMMARY    75
    ■ KEY TERMS    75
    ■ KEY FORMULAS    75

- Practice Problems   76
- SPSS Exercises   78

## Chapter 4. Measures of Central Tendency   81

Introduction   81
The Mode   82
Case Study: The Modal Category of Hate Crime   82
Case Study: The Modal Number of Prior
   Arrests   84
   *Advantages and Disadvantages of the Mode*   86
The Median   87
Case Studies: The Median Police Response Time
   and Vandalism Offending   87
   *The Median for Grouped Data*   89
   *Advantages and Disadvantages of the Median*   91
The Mean   93
Case Study: Calculating the Mean Time Until
   Rearrest   93
Case Study: Calculating the Mean Police Response
   Time   95
   *The Mean for Grouped Data*   96
   *Advantages and Disadvantages of the Mean*   98
- Summary   100
- Key Terms   100
- Key Formulas   100
- Practice Problems   101
- SPSS Exercises   103

## Chapter 5. Measures of Dispersion   105

Introduction   106
Measuring Dispersion for Nominal- and
   Ordinal-Level Variables   107
   *The Variation Ratio*   107
Case Study: Types of Patrolling Practices   108
Measuring Dispersion for Internal- and Ratio-Level
   Variables   111
   *The Range and Interquartile Range*   111
Case Study: Calculating the Range of Sentence
   Lengths   111
Case Study: Calculating the Interquartile Range of
   the Number of Escapes by Prison   113
The Standard Deviation and Variance   116
Case Study: Calculating the Variance and
   Standard Deviation of Judges' Sentences   120
Case Study: Self-Control for Delinquent
   Youth   123
   *Calculating the Variance and Standard*
     *Deviation With Grouped Data*   125
Case Study: Time Until Rearrest for a
   Sample of Released Inmates   125
Computational Formulas for Variance and
   Standard Deviation   127

Graphing Dispersion With Exploratory
   Data Analysis (EDA)   131
   *Boxplots*   132
Case Study: Prisoners Sentenced to Death by
   State   132
Case Study: Constructing a Boxplot for
   Police Officers Killed   137
- Summary   140
- Key Terms   140
- Key Formulas   140
- Practice Problems   141
- SPSS Exercises   143

## PART II. MAKING INFERENCES IN UNIVARIATE ANALYSIS: GENERALIZING FROM A SAMPLE TO THE POPULATION   145

## Chapter 6. Probability, Probability Distributions, and an Introduction to Hypothesis Testing   146

Introduction   147
Probability. What Is It Good for? Absolutely
   Everything!   148
The Rules of Probability   149
   *What Is Independence?*   153
Probability Distributions   156
A Discrete Probability Distribution—
   The Binomial Distribution   157
Hypothesis Testing With the Binomial
   Distribution   160
Case Study: Predicting the Probability
   of a Stolen Car Recovered   160
A Continuous Probability Distribution—
   The Standard Normal Distribution   167
   *The Area Under the Normal Curve*   169
   *The Standard Normal Distribution and*
     *Standard Scores*   171
Samples, Populations, Sampling Distributions,
   and the Central Limit Theorem   174
Case Study: The Probability of a Stolen Car
   Recovered   177
- Summary   179
- Key Terms   180
- Key Formulas   180
- Practice Problems   181
- SPSS Exercises   183

## Chapter 7. Point Estimation and Confidence Intervals   185

Introduction   186
Making Inferences from Point Estimates:
   Cofidence Intervals   187

Properties of Good Estimates   190

Estimating a Population Mean From Large
Samples   190

Case Study: Estimating Alcohol Consumption
for College Students   192

Case Study: Probation Officer Behavior   194

Estimating Confidence Intervals for a Mean From
Small Samples   196

Case Study: Work-Role Overload
and Policing   198

Estimating Confidence Intervals for Proportions and
Percents With a Large Sample   201

Case Study: Estimating the Effects of
Community Policing   202

Case Study: Clearing Homicides   203

- SUMMARY   204
- KEY TERMS   205
- KEY FORMULAS   205
- PRACTICE PROBLEMS   205
- SPSS EXERCISES   206

**Chapter 8. From Estimation to Statistical
Tests: Hypothesis Testing for One
Population Mean and Proportion   208**

Introduction   209

Hypothesis Testing for Population Means
Using A Large Sample: The $Z$ Test   210

Case Study: Testing the Mean Reading Level
From a Prison Literacy Program   210

Case Study: Testing the Mean Sentence
Length for Robbery   219

Directional and Nondirectional
Hypothesis Tests   221

Case Study: Mean Socialization Levels of Violent
Offenders   225

Hypothesis Testing for Population Means
Using Small Samples: The $t$ Test   227

Case Study: Assets Seized by ATF   228

Case Study: Rate of Law Enforcement
Personnel   229

Hypothesis Testing for Population
Proportions and Percents Using Large
Samples   231

Case Study: Attitudes Toward Gun Control   232

Case Study: Random Drug Testing of Inmates   234

- SUMMARY   236
- KEY TERMS   236
- KEY FORMULAS   237
- PRACTICE PROBLEMS   237
- SPSS EXERCISES   238

**PART III. BIVARIATE ANALYSIS:
RELATIONSHIPS BETWEEN TWO
VARIABLES   241**

**Chapter 9. Testing Hypothesis With
Categorical Data   242**

Introduction   243

Contingency Tables and the Two Variable
Chi-Square Test of Independence   243

Case Study: Gender, Emotions, and
Delinqency   244

Case Study: Liking School and Delinquency   247

The Chi-Square Test of Independence   248

A Simple-to-Use Computational Formula for
the Chi-Square Test of Independence   252

Case Study: Socioeconomic Status of
Neighborhoods and Police Response Time   253

Measures of Association: Determining
the Strength of the Relationship
Between Two Categorical Variables   258

*Nominal-Level Variables*   258

Case Study: Gender and Police Officer Work   258

Case Study: Type of Counsel and Sentence   259

*Ordinal-Level Variables*   262

Case Study: Adolescents' Employment and Drug
and Alcohol Use   263

Case Study: Age of Onset for Delinquency and
Future Offending   264

- SUMMARY   266
- KEY TERMS   267
- KEY FORMULAS   267
- PRACTICE PROBLEMS   268
- SPSS EXERCISES   270

**Chapter 10. Hypothesis Tests Involving
Two Population Means or Proportions   273**

Introduction   274

Explaining the Difference Between
Two Sample Means   274

Sampling Distribution of Mean Differences   276

Testing a Hypothesis About the Difference Between
Two Means: Independent Samples   279

*Model 1: Pooled Variance Estimate ($\sigma_1 = \sigma_2$)*   279

Case Study: State Prison
Expenditures by Region   281

Case Study: Social Disorganization and
Crime   284

Case Study: Boot Camps and Recidivism   286

*Model 2: Separate Variance Estimate
($\sigma_1 \neq \sigma_2$)*   288

Case Study: Formal Sanctions and
    Intimate Partner Assault   289
Case Study: Gender and Sentencing   291
Matched-Groups or Dependent-Samples
    $t$ Test   293
Case Study: Problem-Oriented Policing and
    Crime   296
Case Study: Siblings and Delinquency   300
Hypothesis Tests for the Difference Between Two
    Proportions: Large Samples   303
Case Study: Education and Recidivism   305
- SUMMARY   307
- KEY TERMS   307
- KEY FORMULAS   307
- PRACTICE PROBLEMS   308
- SPSS EXERCISES   310

**Chapter 11. Hypothesis Testing Involving Three
or More Populaiton Means: Analysis of
Variance   312**
Introduction   313
The Logic of Analysis of Variance   313
    *The Problem With Using a* t *Test
    With Three or More Means*   313
Case Study: Police Responses to Intimate
    Partner Assault   314
Types of Variance: Total, Between-Groups, and
    Within-Group   316
Conducting a Hypothesis Test With ANOVA   321
After the $F$ Test: Testing the Difference Between Pairs
    of Means   324
    *Tukey's Honest Significance Difference (HSD)*   324
A Measure of Association Test With ANOVA   326
    *Eta Squared (Correlation Ratio)*   327
A Second ANOVA Example: Caseload Size and Success
    on Probation   328
A Third ANOVA Example: Region of the
    Country and Homicide   329
- SUMMARY   335
- KEY TERMS   336
- KEY FORMULAS   336
- PRACTICE PROBLEMS   337
- SPSS EXERCISES   339

**Chapter 12. Bivariate Correlation and
Regression   342**
Introduction   343
Graphing the Bivariate Distribution
    Between Two Quantitative Variables:
    Scatterplots   343

Case Study: Causes of State-Level Crime   350
The Pearson Correlation Coefficient   355
A More Precise Way to Interpret a Correlation:
    The Coefficient of Determination   362
The Least-Squares Regression Line and
    the Slope Coefficient   362
Case Study: Age and Delinquency   363
    *Using the Regression Line for Prediction*   369
Case Study: Predicting State Crime Rates   370
Comparison of $b$ and $r$   376
Testing for the Significance of $b$ and $r$   376
Case Study: Murder and Poverty   379
Case Study: Robbery Rates and Rural
    Population   379
Case Study: Robbery Rates and Divorce   380
The Problems of Limited Variation, Nonlinear
    Relationships, and Outliers in the Data   381
- SUMMARY   385
- KEY TERMS   386
- KEY FORMULAS   386
- PRACTICE PROBLEMS   387
- SPSS EXERCISES   389

**PART IV. MULTIVARIATE ANALYSIS:
RELATIONSHIPS BETWEEN MORE
THAN TWO VARIABLES   391**

**Chapter 13. Controlling for a Third
Variable: Multiple OLS Regression   392**
Introduction   393
What Do We Mean by Controlling for
    Other Important Variables?   393
    *Illustrating Statistical Control With Partial
    Tables*   395
Case Study: Boot Camps and Recidivism   395
The Multiple Regression Equation   396
Case Study: Predicting Delinquency   399
Comparing the Strength of a Relationship
    Using Beta Weights   404
Partial Correlation Coefficients   405
    *Multiple Coefficient of Determination,* $R^2$   407
    *Calculating Change in* $R^2$   408
Hypothesis Testing in Multiple Regression   411
Another Example: Prison Density, Mean Age, and Rate
    of Inmate Violence   416
Case Study: Using a Dichotomous Independent
    Variable: Predicting Murder Rates in
    States   423
- SUMMARY   427
- KEY TERMS   427

- KEY FORMULAS   427
- PRACTICE PROBLEMS   428
- SPSS EXERCISES   431

**Chapter 14. Regression With a Dichotomous Dependent Variable: Logit Models   433**
Introduction   434
Estimating an OLS Regression Model With
    a Dichotomous Dependent Variable—
    The Linear Probability Model   435
Case Study: Age at First Delinquent Offense and
    Adult Criminality   435
The Logit Regression Model With One Independent
    Variable   440
    *Predicted Probabilities in Logit Models*   443
    *Significance Testing for Logistic Regression
        Coefficients*   448
    *Model Goodness-of-Fit Measures*   449
Case Study: Race and Capital Punishment   450
Logistic Regression Models With
    Two Independent Variables   453
Case Study: Age at Which Delinquency
    First Occurs and Gender   453
Case Study: Race of Victim, the Brutality of a
    Homicide, and Capital Punishment   459
- SUMMARY   463
- KEY TERMS   464

- KEY FORMULAS   464
- PRACTICE PROBLEMS   464
- SPSS EXERCISES   465

**Appendix A. Review of Basic Mathematical
Operations   468**

**Appendix B. Statistical Tables   475**
    B.1 Table of Random Numbers   476
    B.2 Area Under the Standard
        Normal Curve (z Distribution)   478
    B.3 The *t* Distribution   479
    B.4 Critical Values of Chi-Square   480
    B.5 The *F* Distribution   481
    B.6 The Studentized Range Statistic, *q*   483

**Appendix C. Solutions for Odd-Numbered
Practice Problems   485**

**Glossary   506**

**References   513**

**Index   516**

# About the Authors

**Ronet D. Bachman, Ph.D.,** is a professor in the Department of Sociology and Criminal Justice at the University of Delaware. She is coauthor of *The Practice of Research in Criminology and Criminal Justice* 6th ed. (with Russell Schutt), coauthor of *Violence: The Enduring Problem* and *Murder American Style* (with Alexander Alvarez), coeditor of *Explaining Crime and Criminology: Essays in Contemporary Criminal Theory* (with Raymond Paternoster), and author of *Death and Violence on the Reservation: Homicide, Suicide and Family Violence in Contemporary American Indian Communities,* as well as author/coauthor of numerous articles that examine the epidemiology and etiology of violence, with a particular emphasis on women, the elderly, and minority populations. Her most recent federally funded research was a mixed methods study that investigated the long-term trajectories of offending behavior using official data of a prison cohort released in the early 1990s and then interviewed in 2011.

**Raymond Paternoster, Ph.D.,** is a professor in the Department of Criminology and Criminal Justice at the University of Maryland. He received his B.A. in sociology at the University of Delaware where he was introduced to criminology by Frank Scarpitti and obtained his Ph.D. at Florida State University under the careful and dedicated tutelage of Gordon Waldo and Ted Chiricos. He is coauthor of *The Death Penalty: America's Experience with Capital Punishment.* In addition to his interest in statistics, he also pursues questions related to offender decision making and rational choice theory, desistance from crime, and capital punishment. With funding from the National Institute of Justice (NIJ), he is currently working on research comparing the decision-making patterns and characteristics of a sample of serious adult offenders and a comparable group of community members.

# Preface

One of the most important aspects of teaching a statistics course is conveying to students the vital role that research and statistics play in the study of criminology and criminal justice. After years of teaching statistics courses, we have found that the best avenue for achieving this goal has been to link the teaching of "how to calculate and interpret statistics" with contemporary research examples from the field. By combining discussions of the "how to" in statistics with real data and research examples, students not only learn how to perform and understand statistical analyses but also to make the connection between how they are used and why they are so important.

In this new edition of *Statistics for Criminology and Criminal Justice* published by SAGE, our goal is to present a discussion of basic statistical procedures that is comprehensive in its coverage, yet accessible and readable for students. In view of this general goal, we have chosen to emphasize a practical approach to the use of statistics in research. We continue to stress the interpretation and understanding of statistical operations in answering research questions, be they theoretical or policy oriented in nature. Of course, this approach is at the expense of a detailed theoretical or mathematical treatment of statistics. Accordingly, we do not provide derivations of formulas nor do we offer proofs of the underlying statistical theory behind the operations we present in this text. As you will see, however, we have not sacrificed statistical rigor.

Given the title, it is clear that we had the student majoring in criminology and criminal justice particularly in mind as a reader of this text. This can easily be seen in the nature of the research examples presented throughout the book. What are the causes of violence? What is the nature of hate crimes in the United States? Do different types of police patrolling activities affect rates of crime? Is crime increasing or decreasing? These and many other research questions are examined in the examples provided in the book, which we believe not only makes the book more interesting to criminal justice students but also makes the statistical material easier to understand and apply. If this book communicates the excitement of research and the importance of careful statistical analysis in research, then our endeavor has succeeded. We hope that students will enjoy learning how to investigate research questions related to criminal justice and criminology with statistics and that many will learn how to do some research of their own along the way.

In this edition, we continue to use our basic approach of describing each statistic's purpose and origins as we go. To facilitate learning, we present statistical formulas along with step-by-step instructions for calculation. The primary emphasis in our coverage of each statistical operation is on its interpretation and understanding. This edition updates all crime data and includes many new research examples. Each chapter sets up case studies from the research literature to highlight the concepts and statistical techniques under discussion. There are hand calculation practice problems at the end of each chapter that include examples from contemporary research in the field. There are also SPSS exercises that correspond to the chapter material; these exercises use real data including subsets of data from the National Crime Victimization Survey, Monitoring the Future, the Youth Risk Behavior Survey, state-level crime data from the Uniform Crime Reports (UCR), and opinion data from the General Social Survey. In addition, answers to all practice problems and computer output for all IBM® SPSS® Statistics* exercises are available on the instructor's website, and the answers to odd questions are available to students in the back of the book.

## Organization of the Book

The book is organized sequentially into four parts. The first is titled "Univariate Analysis: Describing Variable Distributions" and begins with a basic discussion of research and data gathering. Chapters 1 and 2 discuss the research

---

*IBM® SPSS® Statistics was formerly called PASW® Statistics. SPSS is a registered trademark of International Business Machines Corporation.

enterprise, sampling techniques, ways of presenting data, and levels of measurement. Chapter 3 offers an overview of interpreting data through the use of such graphical techniques as frequency distributions, pie charts, and bar graphs for qualitative data, as well as histograms, frequency polygons, and time plots for quantitative data. Chapter 4 provides an overview of measures of central tendency, and Chapter 5 discusses the various statistical techniques for measuring the variability of a variable, including the standard deviation as well as the exploratory data analysis technique of boxplots.

From this discussion of descriptive statistics, we move into the second section, "Making Inferences in Univariate Analysis: Generalizing From a Sample to the Population." Chapter 6 outlines the foundation of inferential statistics, probability theory, and sampling distributions (the normal distribution). In Chapter 6, the concept of hypothesis testing using the binomial distribution is also introduced. The remainder of the book concerns issues related to hypothesis testing and the search for a relationship between one or more independent variables and a dependent variable. Chapter 7 begins the journey into inferential statistics with confidence intervals. The steps to formal hypothesis testing are systematically repeated in each of the subsequent chapters.

The third section focuses on hypothesis testing using one independent variable to predict one dependent variable and is called "Bivariate Analysis: Relationships Between Two Variables." Chapter 8 focuses on hypothesis tests for one population mean. Chapter 9 is concerned with hypothesis testing when both independent and dependent variables are categorical using cross-tabulation and chi-square. In Chapter 10, you will examine hypothesis tests involving two population means or proportions, including tests for independent and matched groups. Chapter 11 discusses hypothesis testing involving three or more means using analysis of variance techniques. In Chapter 12, bivariate correlation and ordinary least-squares (OLS) regression analysis will be introduced. This chapter discusses the essential framework of linear regression, including the notion of "least squares," the importance of scatterplots, the regression line, and hypothesis tests with slopes and correlation coefficients.

The book concludes by highlighting the importance of controlling for other independent variables through "Multivariate Analysis: Relationships Between More than Two Variables." Chapter 13 extends OLS regression to two independent variables and one dependent variable. Chapter 14 provides a discussion of the essential components of logistic regression models and includes a discussion of multiple logistic regression analyses. Although logistic regression is seldom included in introductory statistics texts, these models have become so prominent in social science research that we felt their omission would have done a great disservice to those who want some degree of comprehensiveness in their first statistics course.

## ▣ Learning Aids

Working together, the authors and editors have developed a format that makes *Statistics for Criminology and Criminal Justice* a readable, user-friendly text. In addition to all of the changes we have already mentioned, the Fourth Edition not only includes a host of new tables and figures to amplify text coverage, but it also features the following student learning aids:

- Step-by-step lists and marginal key term and key formula boxes are included in every chapter to make mastery of statistical concepts and procedures easier.

- Each chapter closes with traditional practice problems to give students plenty of hands-on experience with important techniques, which incorporate research questions from contemporary published research from the discipline. Solutions to all end-of-chapter problems are also provided to instructors.

- Each chapter includes SPSS exercises that provide students with the opportunity to obtain the statistics covered in each chapter using a computer software program.

# 🔳 Supplements

edge.sagepub.com/bachmansccj4e

As a full-service publisher of quality educational products, SAGE does much more than just sell textbooks. They also create and publish supplements for use with those textbooks. SAGE edge offers a robust online environment featuring an impressive array of tools and resources for review, study, and further exploration, keeping both instructors and students on the cutting edge of teaching and learning. SAGE edge content is open access and available on demand. Learning and teaching has never been easier!

**SAGE edge for Instructors** supports teaching by making it easy to integrate quality content and create a rich learning environment for students.

- **Test banks** provide a diverse range of pre-written options as well as the opportunity to edit any question and/or insert personalized questions to effectively assess students' progress and understanding

- **Sample course syllabi** for semester and quarter courses provide suggested models for structuring one's course

- Editable, chapter-specific **PowerPoint® slides** offer complete flexibility for creating a multimedia presentation for the course

- EXCLUSIVE! Access to full-text **SAGE journal articles** have been carefully selected to support and expand on the concepts presented in each chapter to encourage students to think critically

- **Web resources** include links that appeal to students with different learning styles

- **Extra practice tests and solutions**

- **Discussion group problems and solutions**

- **Extra practice exercises** for all chapters

- A **course cartridge** provides easy LMS integration

- **Downloadable Data from real data sets:** (1) a subset of the 2013 Monitoring the Future Survey, (2) a state-level data set that includes rates of homicide, burglary, and violent crime, along with demographic and social indicators such as poverty and social disorganization, (3) a subset of the 2013 Youth Risk Behavior Survey, and (4) a sample of violent victimizations from the National Crime Victimization Survey.

**SAGE edge for Students** provides a personalized approach to help students accomplish their coursework goals in an easy-to-use learning environment.

- Mobile-friendly **eFlashcards** strengthen understanding of key terms and concepts

- Mobile-friendly practice **quizzes** allow for independent assessment by students of their mastery of course material

- A customized online **action plan** includes tips and feedback on progress through the course and materials, which allows students to individualize their learning experience

- **Web resources** include links that appeal to students with different learning styles

- **SPSS Student Datasets** to enhance student learning and provide more integration with the content

- **Practice problems and solutions**

- **Practice tests and solutions**

- **Discussion group problems and solutions**

- **Learning objectives** reinforce the most important material

- EXCLUSIVE! Access to full-text **SAGE journal articles** that have been carefully selected to support and expand on the concepts presented in each chapter

## ▣ Acknowledgments

Many authors have good editors but not many have good editors who also turn out to be good friends. We are very lucky in having both with Jerry Westby, an editor extraordinaire and one of the most decent persons either of us have bumped into. We have cherished his Sage (☺) advice on editorial matters, but even more the close bond of friendship that we share. He's the best editor, and overall the best guy north or south of the Mason-Dixon Line, and the three of us know exactly where that is; we have pictures to prove it! We are also indebted to others on the SAGE team, including our associate editor, Jessica Miller, who provided invaluable pedagogical advice along with a very critical eye while shepherding the text through the publication process, Sheree Van Vreede, for her meticulous copyediting, and Laura Kirkhuff and David Felts, for their attention to the numerous issues related to the ancillaries and the production process that seemed to never end!

We owe a huge debt of gratitude to those who provided meticulous reviews and sage advice for this and earlier editions:

Viviana Andreescu
*University of Louisville*

Jeb A. Booth
*Northeastern University*

Sara Z. Evans
*University of West Florida*

David R. Forde
*University of Alabama*

David Holleran
*The College of New Jersey*

William E. Kelly
*Auburn University*

Thomas Petee
*Auburn University*

Andre Rosay
*University of Alaska*

Christina DeJong Schwitzer
*Michigan State University*

Stephen M. Schnebly
*Arizona State University*

Lenonore Simon
*Temple University*

Ni He
*University of Texas-San Antonio*

Wesley G. Jennings
*University of South Florida*

Brian Johnson
*University of Maryland*

Brian A. Lawton
*Sam Houston University*

Shelly A. McGrath
*University of Alabama at Birmingham*

Fawn T. Ngo
*University of South Florida Sarasota/Manatee*

Dan Powers
*University of Texas*

Hanna Scott
*University of Ontario Institute of Technology*

Christopher J. Sullivan
*University of Cincinnati*

Gary Sweeten
*Arizona State University*

Christine Tartaro
*The Richard Stockton College of New Jersey*

There also have been others who have used the book and have made corrections and invaluable suggestions; they include Marc Riedel, Jacques Press, Douglas Thomson, Bonnie Lewis, Alexis Durham, and especially Keith Marcus, who went through the 3rd edition with a microscope. (Keith, we're sorry we could not incorporate all of your suggestions into this edition!) In addition, our hats are off to two Ph.D. students: Theodore (Teddy) Wilson for his meticulous proofreading under pressure and for the end-of-chapter practice problems and to Matthew (Matt) Manierre for the creative end-of-chapter SPSS exercises. Teddy and Matt are both amazing methodologists and statisticians in their own right and put forth Herculean efforts for this text!

Of course, we continue to be indebted to the many students we have had an opportunity to teach and mentor over the years at both the undergraduate and graduate levels. In many respects, this book could not have been written without these ongoing and reciprocal teaching and learning experiences. To all of our students, past and future: You inspire us to become better teachers! And finally, for whom this book is dedicated, our son, John, for being you!

—Ronet D. Bachman and Ray Paternoster,
*Newark, Delaware*

# CHAPTER 1

# The Purpose of Statistics in the Criminological Sciences

"*You gain strength, courage, and confidence by every experience in which you really stop to look fear in the face.*

—Eleanor Roosevelt

*Fear is that little darkroom where negatives are developed.*

—Michael Pritchard

*Do not worry about your difficulties in Mathematics. I can assure you mine are still greater.*"

—Albert Einstein

## 🔳 Introduction

Most of you reading this book are probably taking a course in statistics because it is required to graduate, not because you were seeking a little adventure and thought it would be fun. Nor are you taking the course because there is something missing in your life and, thus, you think the study of statistics is necessary to make you intellectually "well rounded." At least this has been our experience when teaching statistics courses. Everyone who has taught a statistics course has probably heard the litany of sorrows expressed by their students at the beginning of the course—the "wailing and gnashing of teeth." "Oh, I have been putting this off for so long—I dreaded having to take this." "I have a mental block when it comes to math—I haven't had any math courses since high school." "Why do I have to learn this, I'm never going to use it?"

There are those fortunate few for whom math comes easy, but the rest of us experience apprehension and anxiety when approaching our first statistics course. Psychologists, however, are quick to tell us that what we most often fear is not real—it is merely our mind imagining the worst possible scenario. FEAR has been described as an acronym for False Expectations Appearing Real. In fact, long ago it was Aristotle who said, "Fear is pain arising from anticipation." But then, this may not comfort you either because it is not Aristotle who is taking the course—it's you!

Although it is impossible for us to allay all of the fear and apprehension you may be experiencing right now, it may help to know that virtually everyone can and will make it through this course, even those of you who have trouble counting change. This is not, of course, a guarantee, and we are not saying it will be easy, that it can be done without a lot of hard work. We have found, however, that persistence and tenacity can overcome even the most extreme mathematical handicaps. Those of you who are particularly rusty with your math, and those of you who just want a quick confidence builder, should refer to Appendix A at the back of this book. Appendix A reviews some basic math lessons. Our book also includes practice problems and, more important, the answers to those problems. After teaching this course for over two decades, we have found that every student who puts forth effort and time can pass the course! Our chapters are designed to provide step-by-step instructions for calculating the statistics with real criminal justice data and case studies so you will not only learn about statistics but also a little about research going on in our discipline.

We hope that after this course you will be able to understand and manipulate statistics for yourself and that you will be a knowledgeable consumer of the statistical material you are confronted with daily and, believe it or not, you may confront in your criminal justice career. Understanding how to manipulate data and interpret statistics will be a tremendous asset to you, no matter what direction you plan to take in your career. Virtually every job application, as well as applications to graduate school and law school, now asks you about your data analysis skills. We now exist in a world where programs to organize and manipulate data are everywhere. Many police academies now have training for data analysis because virtually every police department now uses crime mapping programs to monitor high crime areas known as "hot spots" for special prevention efforts.

In addition to the mathematical skills required to compute statistics, we also hope to leave you with an understanding of what different statistical tests or operations can and cannot do, and what they do and do not tell us about a given problem. The foundations for the statistics presented in this book are derived from complicated mathematical theory. You will be glad to know, however, that it is *not* the purpose of this book to provide you with the proofs necessary to substantiate this body of theory. In this book, we provide you with two basic types of knowledge: (1) knowledge about the basic mathematical foundations of each statistic, as well as the ability to manipulate and conduct statistical analysis for your own research, and (2) an ability to interpret the results of statistical analysis and to apply these results to the real world. We want you, then, to have the skills to both calculate and comprehend social statistics. These two purposes are not mutually exclusive but related. We think that the ability to carry out the mathematical manipulations of a formula and come up with a statistical result is almost worthless unless you can interpret this result and give it meaning. Therefore, information about the mechanics of conducting statistical tests and information about interpreting the results of these tests will be emphasized equally throughout this text.

Learning about statistics for perhaps the first time does not mean that you will always have to calculate your statistics by hand, with the assistance of only a calculator. Most, if not all, researchers do their statistical analyses with a computer and software programs. Many useful and "user-friendly" statistical software programs are available, including SPSS, SAS, STATA, and Minitab. Because learning to conduct statistical analyses with a computer is such an essential task to master, we provide a discussion of the computer software program SPSS on the student website for this book, along with data sets that can be downloaded. We have also included SPSS data analysis exercises at the end of each chapter; however, you can easily use these exercises for virtually any other statistical software program including the spreadsheet program Excel.

You may be wondering why you have to learn statistics and how to calculate them by hand if you can avoid all of this by using a computer. First, we believe it is important for you to understand exactly what it is the computer is doing when it is calculating statistics. Without this knowledge, you may get results, but you will have no understanding of the logic behind the computer's output and little comprehension of how those results were obtained. This is not a good way to learn statistics; in fact, it is not really learning statistics at all. Without a firm foundation in the basics of statistics, you will have no real knowledge of what to request of your computer or how to recognize if something is wrong. Despite its talent, the computer is actually fairly stupid; it has no ability to determine whether what it is told to do is correct—it will do pretty much anything it is asked, and it will calculate and spit out virtually anything you want it to, correct or not. Neither will the computer make sense of the results. That is your responsibility!

## ▣ Setting the Stage for Statistical Inquiry

Before we become more familiar with statistics in the upcoming chapters, we first want to set the stage for statistical inquiry. The data we use in criminology are derived from many different sources: from official government agency data such as the Federal Bureau of Investigation's (FBI) Uniform Crime Reports; from social surveys conducted by the government (the Bureau of Justice Statistics' National Crime Victimization Survey), ourselves, or other researchers; from experiments; from direct observation, as either a participant observer or an unobtrusive observer; or from a content analysis of existing images (historical or contemporary), such as newspaper articles or films. As you can see, the research methods we employ are very diverse.

Criminological researchers often conduct "secondary data analysis" (Riedel, 2012), which, simply put, means reanalyzing data that already exist. These data usually come from one of two places: Either they are official data collected by local, state, and federal agencies (e.g., rates of crime reported to police, information on incarcerated offenders from state correctional authorities, or adjudication data from the courts), or they are data collected from surveys sponsored by government agencies or conducted by other researchers. Virtually all of these data collected by government agencies and a great deal of survey data collected by independent researchers are made available to the public through the Inter-University Consortium for Political and Social Research (ICPSR), which is located at the University of Michigan.

The ICPSR maintains and provides access to a vast archive of criminological data for research and instruction, and it offers training in quantitative methods to facilitate effective data use. For example, data available online at ICPSR include the Supplementary Homicide Reports (SHR) provided by the U.S. Department of Justice, which contain information for each homicide from police reports, including such details as the relationship between victims and offenders, use of weapons, and other characteristics of victims and offenders; survey data from the National Crime Victimization Survey (NCVS), which interviews a sample of U.S. household residents to determine their experiences with both property and violent crime, regardless of whether the crimes were reported to police or anyone else; survey data from samples of jail and prison inmates; survey data from the National Youth Survey (NYS), a survey conducted annually by Delbert Elliot and his colleagues at the University of Colorado to monitor the extent of adolescent delinquency and the factors related to delinquent offending; and survey data from the National Opinion Survey of Crime and Justice, which asked adults for their opinion about a wide range of criminal justice issues. These are just a few examples of the immense archive of data made available at the ICPSR. Take a look at what is available by going on the website: www.icpsr.umich.edu.

## The Role of Statistical Methods in Criminology and Criminal Justice

Over the past few decades, statistics and numerical summaries of phenomena such as crime rates have increasingly been used to document how "well" or "poorly" a society is doing. For example, cities and states are described as relatively safe or unsafe depending on their respective levels of violent crime, and age groups are frequently monitored and compared with previous generations to determine their relative levels of deviancy based on criteria such as their drug and alcohol use.

Research and statistics are important in our discipline because they enable us to monitor phenomena over time and across geographic locations, and they allow us to determine relationships between phenomena. Of course, we make conclusions about the relationships between phenomena every day, but these conclusions are most often based on biased perceptions and selective personal experiences.

**Science:** A set of logical, systematic, documented methods for investigating nature and natural processes; the knowledge produced by these investigations.

In criminological research, we rely on scientific methods, including statistics, to help us perform these tasks. Science relies on logical and systematic methods to answer questions, and it does so in a way that allows others to inspect and evaluate its methods. In the realm of criminological research, these methods are not so unusual. They involve asking questions, observing behavior, and counting people, all of which we often do in our everyday lives. The difference is that researchers develop, refine, apply, and report their understanding of the social world more systematically.

## Case Study

### Youth Violence

The population of the United States all too frequently mourns the deaths of young innocent lives taken in school shootings. The deadliest elementary school shooting to date took place on December 14, 2012, when a 20-year-old man named Adam Lanza walked into an elementary school in Newtown, Connecticut, armed with several semiautomatic weapons and killed 20 children and 6 adults. On April 16, 2007, Cho Seung-Hui perpetrated the deadliest college mass shooting by killing 32 students, faculty, and staff and left over 30 others injured on the campus of Virginia Tech in Blacksburg, Virginia. Cho was armed with two semiautomatic handguns that he had legally purchased and a vest filled with ammunition. As police were closing in on the scene, he killed himself. The deadliest high-school shooting occurred on April 20, 1999, when Eric Harris and Dylan Klebold killed 12 students and a teacher before killing themselves at Columbine High School in suburban Colorado.

None of these mass murderers were typical terrorists, and each of these incidents caused a media frenzy. Headlines such as "The School Violence Crisis" and "School Crime Epidemic" were plastered across national newspapers and weekly news journals. Unfortunately, the media play a large role in how we perceive both problems and solutions. What are your perceptions of violence committed by youth, and how did you acquire them? What do you believe are the causes of youth violence? Many (frequently conflicting) factors have been blamed for youth violence in American society, including the easy availability of guns, the lack of guns in classrooms for protection, the use of weapons in movies and television, the moral decay of our nation, poor parenting, unaware teachers, school and class size, racial prejudice, teenage alienation, the Internet and the World Wide Web, anti-Semitism, violent video games, rap and rock music, and the list goes on.

Of course, youth violence is not a new phenomenon in the United States. It has always been a popular topic of social science research and the popular press. Predictably, whenever a phenomenon is perceived as an epidemic, numerous explanations emerge to explain it. Unfortunately, most of these explanations are based on the media and popular culture, not on empirical research. Unlike the anecdotal information floating around in the mass media, social scientists interested in this phenomenon have amassed a substantial body of findings that have refined knowledge about the factors related to the problem of gun violence, and some of this knowledge is being used to shape social policy. Research that relies on statistical analysis generally falls into three categories of purposes for social scientific research: Descriptive, Explanatory, and Evaluation.

## Descriptive Research

Defining and describing social phenomena of interest is a part of almost any research investigation, but **descriptive research** is the primary focus of many studies of youth crime and violence. Some of the central questions used in descriptive studies are as follows: "How many people are victims of youth violence?" "How many youth are offenders?" "What are the most common crimes committed by youthful offenders?" and "How many youth are arrested and incarcerated each year for crime?"

> **Descriptive research:** Research in which phenomena are defined and described.

## Case Study

## How Prevalent Is Youth Violence?

**Police reports:** One of the most enduring sources of information on lethal violence in the United States is the FBI's SHR. Data measuring the prevalence of nonlethal forms of violence such as robbery and assaults are a bit more complicated. How do we know how many young people assault victims each year? People who report their victimizations to police represent one avenue for these calculations. The FBI compiles these numbers in its **Uniform Crime Reports (UCR)** system, which is slowly being replaced by the **National Incident-Based Reporting System (NIBRS)**. Both of these data sources rely on state, county, and city law enforcement agencies across the United States to participate voluntarily in the reporting program. Can you imagine why relying on these data sources may be problematic for estimating prevalence rates of

> **Police reports:** Data used to measure crime based on incidents that become known to police departments.

**Uniform Crime Reports (UCR):** Official reports about crime incidents that are reported to police departments across the United States and then voluntarily reported to the Federal Bureau of Investigation (FBI), which compiles them for statistics purposes.

**National Incident-Based Reporting System (NIBRS):** Official reports about crime incidents that are reported to police departments across the United States and then voluntarily reported to the Federal Bureau of Investigation (FBI), which compiles them for statistics purposes. This system is slowly replacing the older UCR program.

**Surveys:** Research method used to measure the prevalence of behavior, attitudes, or any other phenomenon by asking a sample of people to fill out a questionnaire either in person, through the mail or Internet, or on the telephone.

violent victimizations? If victimizations are never reported to police, they are not counted. This is especially problematic for victimizations between people who know each other and other offenses like rape in which only a fraction of incidents are ever reported to police.

**Surveys:** Many, if not most, social scientists believe the best way to determine the magnitude of violent victimization is through random sample surveys. This basically means randomly selecting individuals in the population of interest and asking them about their victimization experiences via a mailed or Internet, telephone, or in-person questionnaire. The only ongoing survey to do this on an annual basis is the NCVS, which is sponsored by the U.S. Department of Justice's Bureau of Justice Statistics. Among other questions, the NCVS asks questions like, "Has anyone attacked or threatened you with a weapon, for instance, a gun or knife; by something thrown, such as a rock or bottle, include any grabbing, punching, or choking?" Estimates indicate that youth aged 12 to 24 years all have the highest rates of violent victimization, which have been declining steadily since the highs witnessed in the early 1990s, despite the recent increases observed in homicide rates for this age group in some locations.

Another large research survey that estimates the magnitude of youth violence (along with other risk-taking behavior such as taking drugs and smoking) is called the Youth Risk Behavior Survey (YRBS), which has been conducted every 2 years in the United States since 1990. Respondents to this survey are a national sample of approximately 16,000 high-school students in grades 9 through 12. To measure the extent of youth violence, students are asked a number of questions, including the following: "During the past 12 months, how many times were you in a physical fight?" "During the past 12 months, how many times were you in a physical fight in which you were injured and had to be seen by a doctor or nurse?" "During the past 12 months, how many times were you in a physical fight on school property?" and "During the past 12 months, how many times did someone threaten or injure you with a gun, knife, or club on school property?"

Of course, another way to measure violence would be to ask respondents about their offending behaviors. Some surveys do this, including the National Youth Survey (NYS) and the Rochester Youth Development Study (RYDS). The RYDS sample consists of 1,000 students who were in the seventh and eighth grades in the Rochester, New York, public schools during the spring semester of the 1988 school year. This project has interviewed the original respondents at 12 different times including the last interview that took place in 1997 when respondents were in their early 20s (Thornberry et al., 2008). As you can imagine, respondents are typically more reluctant to reveal offending behavior compared with their victimization experiences. However, these surveys have been a useful tool for examining the factors related to violent offending and other delinquency. We should also point out that although this discussion has been specific to violence, the measures we have discussed in this section, along with their strengths and weaknesses, apply to measuring all crime in general.

## Explanatory Research

**Explanatory research:** Research that seeks to identify causes and/or effects of social phenomena.

Many people consider explanation to be the premier goal of any science. **Explanatory research** seeks to identify the causes and effects of social phenomena, to predict how one phenomenon will change or vary in response to variation in some other phenomenon. Researchers adopted explanation as a goal when they began to ask such questions as "Are kids who participate in after school activities less likely to engage in delinquency?" and "Does the unemployment rate influence the frequency of youth crime?" In explanatory research, studies are often interested in explaining a **dependent variable** by using one or more independent variables. In research, the dependent variable is expected to vary or change depending on variation or change in the **independent variable**. In this causal type of explanation, the independent variable is the cause and the dependent variable the effect.

> **Dependent variable:** Variable that is expected to change or vary depending on the variation in the independent variable.

> **Independent variable:** Variable that is expected to cause or lead to variation or change in the dependent variable.

## Case Study

## What Factors Are Related to Youth Delinquency and Violence?

When we move from description to explanation, we want to understand the direct relationship between two or more things. Does *x* explain *y* or if *x* happens, is *y* also likely to occur? What are some of the factors related to youth violence? Using the South Carolina YRBS (described earlier), Robert MacDonald et al. (2005) examined whether constructs from General Strain Theory (GST) (Agnew, 1992) and Michael R. Gottfredson and Travis Hirschi's (1990) general theory of crime could predict youth violence. Testing hypotheses generated from theory is often a goal of explanatory research. A **theory** is a logically interrelated set of propositions about empirical reality. Examples of criminological theories include social learning theory, general strain theory, social disorganization theory, and routine activities theory. A **hypothesis** is simply a tentative statement about empirical reality, involving a relationship between two or more variables.

> **Theory:** Logically interrelated set of propositions about empirical reality that can be tested.

GST generally contends that strain, such as a disjunction or misfit between expectations and aspirations (e.g., wanting a good job but not being able to get one), increases the likelihood that individuals will experience negative emotions (e.g., anger and anxiety), which in turn increases the likelihood of antisocial or violent behavior. The general theory of crime claims that self-control, which is primarily formed by the relationship children have with their parents and/or guardians, is the

> **Hypothesis:** Tentative statement about empirical reality, involving the relationship between two or more variables.

motivating factor for all crime. Individuals with low self-control, the theory predicts, will be more likely to pursue immediate gratification, be impulsive, prefer simple tasks, engage in risky behavior, have volatile tempers, and so on.

Earlier we described how the YRBS measures violent offending. To measure life satisfaction, MacDonald et al. (2005) used six questions from the YRBS that asked respondents to report on general satisfaction or the degree to which they felt "terrible" or "delighted" about family life, friendships, school, self, residential location, and overall life. To measure self-control, the authors used the indicators of smoking and sexual behavior to represent risky behaviors that are not illegal since they "reflect impulsivity and short-run hedonism" (p. 1502). When predicting violent behavior, they also controlled for a number of other factors like employment, drug use, family structure, and religious participation, along with age, race, and gender.

Consistent with the general theory of crime, MacDonald et al. (2005) found that high-school students who reported more impulsive behaviors, indicative of low self-control, also reported greater participation in violent behavior. In addition, results indicated that students who were more satisfied with life were significantly less likely to have engaged in violence compared with their less satisfied peers. In this way, MacDonald and his colleagues (2005) were conducting explanatory research.

## Evaluation Research

**Evaluation research:** Research about social programs or interventions.

**Evaluation research** seeks to determine the effects of a social program or other types of intervention. It is a type of explanatory research because it deals with cause and effect. However, evaluation research differs from other forms of explanatory research because evaluation research considers the implementation and effects of social policies and programs. These issues may not be relevant in other types of explanatory research.

Evaluation research is a type of explanatory research, but instead of testing theory, it is most often used to determine whether an implemented program or policy had the intended outcome. To reduce violence and create a safer atmosphere at schools across the country, literally thousands of schools have adopted some form of violence prevention training. These programs generally provide cognitive-behavioral and social skills training on various topics using a variety of methods. Such programs are commonly referred to as conflict resolution and peer mediation training. Many of these prevention programs are designed to improve interpersonal problem-solving skills among children and adolescents by training children in cognitive processing, such as identifying interpersonal problems and generating nonaggressive solutions. There is limited evidence, however, that such programs are actually effective in reducing violence.

## Case Study

### How Effective Are Violence Prevention Programs in Schools?

As many school administrators will tell you, there are direct mail, email, and in-person direct sales efforts to sell them programs that reduce violence, increase empathy among students, promote a positive school environment, promote other forms of mental well-being, and on and on. Unfortunately, not many of these programs have been rigorously evaluated to ensure they actually do what they promise. One program that has been the target of rigorous evaluation is the Gang Resistance Education Training (G.R.E.A.T.), which is a school-based gang and violence prevention program. Designed in 1991, the cognitive-based program was intended to, among other things, teach students about crime and its effects on victims, how to resolve conflicts without violence, and how to improve individual responsibility through goal setting. The G.R.E.A.T. program addresses multiple risk factors for violent offending among three domains: school, peer, and individual. Because it is curriculum based in the school, it does not address risk factors present in the family or neighborhood. It is a 13-week program taught in sixth or seventh grade and attempts to affect several risk factors including school commitment and performance, association with conventional or delinquent peers, empathy, and self-control, among others.

Finn-Aage Esbensen and his colleagues (Esbensen, Osgood, Peterson, Taylor, & Carson, 2013) evaluated the long-term effects of the G.R.E.A.T. program in seven cities across the United States. Schools selected for the program randomly assigned some seventh-grade classrooms to get the treatment (experimental groups), while the other classrooms did not (control groups). This is called a **true experimental design**. It is an extremely strong research method for determining the effects of programs or policies because if groups are truly randomly assigned, there is a strong reason to believe that differences between the groups after program implementation, such as reduced violent offending, are because of the program and not some other factor that existed before the introduction of the treatment.

**True experimental design:** When two groups are randomly assigned with one group receiving the treatment or program (experimental group) while the other group (control group) does not. After the program or treatment, a post-test determines whether there is a change in the experimental group.

Both experimental and control group students in the Esbensen et al. (2013) study completed four follow-up surveys annually for four years. The researchers examined 33 outcome measures of general delinquency, violent offending, gang affiliation, associations with delinquent peers, empathy, impulsivity, problem solving, among others. The statistical methods employed by Esbensen and his colleagues are very complicated and beyond the scope of this text so we will simply highlight the general findings. When the data for all seven sites were combined, there were no differences in violent offending between experimental and control group students over the four-year period. Those students who participated in the G.R.E.A.T. program were, however, less likely to become members of gangs, had higher levels of altruism, less anger and risk taking, and have more favorable attitudes toward the police, among other things.

With these results, would you deem the G.R.E.A.T. program a success? These are the important questions evaluation research must address. Esbensen et al. (2013) agree that the program did not reduce general delinquency or violent offending but note that it was effective in reducing gang membership, which is also a risk factor for violent offending. Can these findings be generalized to all the seventh-grade students? That is the question to which we now turn.

## ▣ Populations and Samples

The words "population" and "sample" should already have some meaning to you. When you think of a population, you probably think of the population of some locality such as the United States, or the city or state in which you reside, or the university or college you attend. As with most social science research, samples in criminology consist of samples at different units of analysis including countries, states, cities, neighborhoods, prisons, schools, individuals, etc. Since it is too difficult, too costly, and sometimes impossible to get information on the entire population of interest, we must often solicit the information of interest from samples. **Samples** are simply subsets of a larger **population.**

> **Sample:** Subset of the population that a researcher must often use to make generalizations about the larger population.

Most official statistics collected by the U.S. government are derived from information obtained from samples, not from the entire population (the U.S. Census taken every 10 years is an exception). For example, the NCVS is a survey used to obtain information on the incidence and characteristics of criminal victimization in the United States based on a sample of the U.S. population. Every year, the NCVS interviews more than 100,000 individuals aged 12 years or older to solicit information on their experiences with victimization that were both reported and unreported to the police. Essentially, professional interviewers ask persons who are selected into the sample if they were the victim of a crime in the past 6 months, regardless of whether this victimization was reported to police.

> **Population:** Larger set of cases or aggregate number of people that a researcher is actually interested in or wishes to know something about.

You may be thinking right now, "Well, what if I am only interested in a small population?" Good question! Let's say we were interested in finding out about job-related stress experienced by law enforcement officers in your state. Although it would be easier to contact every individual in this population compared with every U.S. citizen, it would still be extremely difficult and costly to obtain information from every law enforcement officer, even within one state. In fact, in almost all instances, we have to settle for a sample derived from the population of interest rather than study the full population. For this reason, the "population" usually remains an unknown entity whose characteristics we can only estimate. The **generalizability** of a study is the extent to which it can be used to inform us about persons, places, or events that were *not* studied.

We usually make a generalization about the characteristics of a population by using information we have from a sample; that is, we make inferences from our sample data to the population. Because the purpose of sampling is to make these generalizations, we must be very meticulous when selecting our sample. The primary goal of sampling is to make sure that the sample we select is actually representative of the population we are estimating and want to generalize to. Think about this for a minute. What is representative? Generally, if the characteristics of a sample (e.g., age, race/ethnicity, and gender) look similar to the characteristics of

> **Generalizability:** Extent to which information from a sample can be used to inform us about persons, places, or events that were not studied in the entire population from which the sample was taken.

the population, the sample is said to be representative. For example, if you were interested in estimating the proportion of the population that favors the death penalty, then to be representative, your sample should contain about 50% men and 50% women because that is the makeup of the U.S. population. It also should contain about 85% Whites and 15% non-Whites because that is the makeup of the U.S. population. If your sample included a disproportionately high number of males or non-Whites, it would be unrepresentative. If, on the other hand, your target population was individuals older than 65 years of age, your sample should have a somewhat different gender distribution. To reflect the gender distribution of all individuals in the United States older than 65, a sample would have to contain approximately 60% women and 40% men since this is the gender distribution of all individuals older than age 65 in the United States as defined by the Census Bureau.

In sum, the primary question of interest in sample generalizability is as follows: *Can findings from a sample be generalized to the population from which the sample was drawn?* Sample generalizability depends on sample quality, which is determined by the amount of **sampling error** present in your sample. Sampling error can generally be defined as the difference between the sample estimate and the population value that you are estimating. The larger the sampling error, the less representative the sample and, as a result, the less generalizable the findings are to the population.

**Sampling error:** The difference between a sample estimate (called a sample statistic) and the population value it is estimating (called a population parameter).

With a few special exceptions, a good sample should be representative of the larger population from which it was drawn. A representative sample looks like the population from which it was selected in all respects that are relevant to a particular study. In an unrepresentative sample, some characteristics are overrepresented and/or some characteristics may be underrepresented. Various procedures can be used to obtain a sample; these range from the simple to the complex as we will see next.

## ▣ How Do We Obtain a Sample?

**Probability sampling methods:** These methods rely on random selection or chance and allow us to know in advance how likely it is that any element of a population is selected for the sample.

From the previous discussion, it should be apparent that accuracy is one of the primary problems we face when generalizing information obtained from a sample to a population. How accurately does our sample reflect the true population? This question is inherent in any inquiry because with any sample we represent only a part—and sometimes a small part—of the entire population. The goal in obtaining or selecting a sample, then, is to select it in a way that increases the chances of this sample being representative of the entire population.

**Nonprobability sampling methods:** These methods are not based on random selection and do not allow us to know in advance the likelihood of any element of a population being selected for the sample.

One of the most important distinctions made about samples is whether they are based on a probability or nonprobability sampling method. Sampling methods that allow us to know in advance how likely it is that any element of a population will be selected for the sample are **probability sampling methods**. Sampling methods that do not let us know the likelihood in advance are **nonprobability sampling methods**.

**Random selection:** The fundamental aspect of probability sampling. The essential characteristic of random selection is that every element of the population has a known and independent chance of being selected for the sample.

The fundamental aspect of probability sampling is **random selection**. When a sample is randomly selected from the population, this means every element of the population (e.g., individual, school, or city) has a known, equal, and independent chance of being selected for the sample. All probability sampling methods rely on a random selection procedure.

Probability sampling techniques not only serve to minimize any potential bias we may have when selecting a sample, but also they allow us to gain access to probability theory in our data analysis, which you will learn more about later in this text. This body of mathematical theory allows us to estimate more accurately the degree of error we have when generalizing results obtained from known sample statistics to unknown population parameters. But don't worry about probability theory now. For now, let's examine some of the most common types of probability samples used in research.

Flipping a coin and rolling a set of dice are the typical examples used to characterize random selection. When you flip a coin, you have the same chance of obtaining a head as you do of obtaining a tail: one out of two. Similarly, when rolling a die, you have the same probability of rolling a 2 as you do of rolling a 6: one out of six. In criminology, researchers generally use random numbers tables, such as Table B.1 in Appendix B, or other computer-generated random selection programs to select a sample. Because they are based on random selection, probability sampling methods have no systematic bias; nothing but chance determines which elements are included in the sample. As a result, our sample also is more likely to be representative of the entire population. When the goal is to generalize your findings to a larger population, it is this characteristic that makes probability samples more desirable than nonprobability samples. Using probability sampling techniques serves to avoid any potential bias we might introduce if we selected a sample ourselves.

## ▣ Probability Sampling Techniques

### Simple Random Samples

Perhaps the most common type of probability sample to use when we want to generalize information obtained from the sample to a larger population is called a **simple random sample**. Simple random sampling requires a procedure that generates numbers or identifies cases of the population for selection strictly on the basis of chance. The key aspect of a simple random sample is random selection. As we stated earlier, random selection ensures that every element in the population has a known, equal, and independent chance of being selected for the sample. If an element of the population is selected into the sample, true simple random sampling is done by replacing that element back into the population so that, once again, there is an equal and independent chance of every element being selected. This is called sampling with replacement. However, if your sample represents a very small percentage of a large population (say, less than 4%), sampling with and without replacement generally produce equivalent results.

> **Simple random sample:** Method of sampling in which every sample element is selected only on the basis of chance through a random process.

Organizations that conduct large telephone surveys often draw random samples with an automated procedure called **random digit dialing (RDD)**. In this process, a computer dials random numbers within the phone prefixes corresponding to the area in which the survey is to be conducted. Random digit dialing is particularly useful when a sampling frame is not available. The researcher simply replaces any inappropriate numbers, such as those numbers that are no longer in service or numbers for businesses, with the next randomly generated phone number. Many surveys rely on this method and use both numbers for land lines and cell phones (Bachman & Schutt, 2017). For example, National Intimate Partner Violence and Sexual Victimization Surveys sponsored by The Centers for Disease Control and Prevention selects a random sample of adult males and females residing in the United States by using the RDD sampling technique.

> **Random digit dialing (RDD):** Random dialing by a machine of numbers within designated phone prefixes, which creates a random sample for phone surveys.

### Systematic Random Samples

Simple random sampling is easy to do if your population is organized in a list, such as from a phone book, registered voters list, court docket, or membership list. We can make the process of simple random selection discussed earlier a little less time-consuming by systematically sampling the cases. In **systematic random sampling**, we select the first element into the sample randomly, but instead of continuing with this random selection, we *systematically* choose the rest of

> **Systematic random sampling:** Method of sampling in which sample elements are selected from a list or from sequential files, with every kth element being selected after the first element is selected randomly within the first interval.

the sample. The general rule for systematic random sampling is to begin with a single element (any number selected randomly within the first interval, say the 10th) in the population and then proceed to select the sample by choosing every *k*th element thereafter (say, every 12th element after the 10th). The first element is the only element that is truly selected at random. The starting element can be selected from a random numbers table or by some other random method. Systematic random sampling eliminates the process of deriving a new random number for every element selected, thus, saving time.

For systematic sampling procedures to approximate a simple random sample, the population list must be truly random, not ordered. For example, we could not have a list of convicted felons ordered by offense type, age, or some other characteristic. If the list is ordered in any way, this will add bias to the sampling process, and the resulting sample is not likely to be representative of the population. In virtually all other situations, systematic random sampling yields what is essentially a simple random sample.

## Multistage Cluster Samples

There are often times when we do not have the luxury of a population list but still want to collect a random sample. Suppose, for example, we wanted to obtain a sample from the entire U.S. population. Would there be a list of the entire population available? Well, there are telephone books that list residents of various locales who have telephones; there are lists of residents who have registered to vote, lists of those who hold driver's licenses, lists of those who pay taxes, and so on. However, all these lists are incomplete (some people do not list their phone number or do not have telephones; some people do not register to vote or drive cars). Using these incomplete lists would introduce bias into our sample.

In such cases, the sampling procedures become a little more complex. We usually end up working toward the sample we want through successive approximations: by first extracting a sample from lists of groups or clusters that are available and then sampling the elements of interest from within these selected clusters. A cluster is a naturally occurring, mixed aggregate of elements of the population, with each element appearing in one and only one cluster. Schools could serve as clusters for sampling students, prisons could serve as clusters for sampling incarcerated offenders, neighborhoods could serve as clusters for sampling city residents, and so on. Sampling procedures of this nature are typically called **multistage cluster samples.**

**Multistage cluster sampling:** Sampling in which elements are selected in two or more stages, with the first stage being the random selection of naturally occurring clusters and the last stage being the random selection of multilevel elements within clusters.

Drawing a cluster sample is at least a two-stage procedure. First, the researcher draws a random sample of clusters (e.g., blocks, prisons, and counties). Next, the researcher draws a random sample of elements within each selected cluster. Because only a fraction of the total clusters from the population are involved, obtaining a list of elements within each of the selected clusters is usually much easier.

Many large surveys sponsored by the federal government use multistage cluster samples. The U.S. Justice Department's NCVS is an excellent example of a multistage cluster sample. Because the target population of the NCVS is the entire U.S. population, the first stage of sampling requires selecting a first-order sample of counties and large metropolitan areas called primary sampling units (PSUs). From these PSUs, another stage of sampling involves the selection of geographic districts within each of the PSUs that have been counted by the 2000 census. And finally, a probability sample of residential dwelling units are selected from these geographic districts. These dwelling units, or addresses, represent the final stage of the multistage sampling. Or in a cluster sample of students, a researcher could contact the schools selected in the first stage and make arrangements with the registrars to obtain lists of students at each school. Figure 1.1 displays the multiple stages of a cluster sample like this.

## Weighted or Stratified Samples

In some cases, the types of probability samples described earlier do not actually serve our purposes. Sometimes, we may want to make sure that certain segments of the population of interest are represented within our sample, and we do not

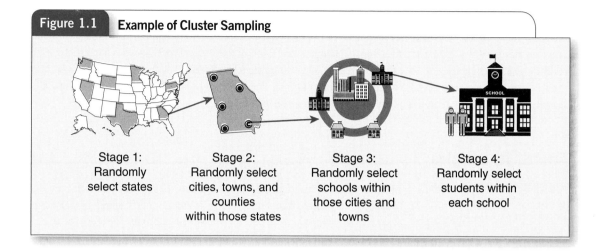

**Figure 1.1** Example of Cluster Sampling

Stage 1:
Randomly
select states

Stage 2:
Randomly select
cities, towns, and
counties
within those states

Stage 3:
Randomly select
schools within
those cities and
towns

Stage 4:
Randomly select
students within
each school

want to leave this to chance. Say, for example, that we are interested in incidents of personal larceny involving contact, such as purse snatching. We know from the National Crime Victimization Survey that Americans older than 65 years of age are as vulnerable to this type of crime as those who are younger than 65. We may be interested in whether there are differences in the victimization circumstances (e.g., place or time of occurrence and number of offenders) between two groups of persons: those younger than 65 and those older than 65. To investigate this, we want to conduct a sample survey with the entire U.S. population. A simple random sample of the population, however, may not result in a sufficient number of individuals older than 65 to use for comparison purposes because individuals older than 65 make up a relatively small proportion of the entire population (approximately 12%).

One way to achieve this goal would be to weight the elements in our population disproportionately. These samples are referred to as **stratified or weighted samples**. Instead of having an equal chance of being selected, as in the case of random samples, individuals would have a known but unequal chance of being selected. That is, some elements would have a greater probability of being selected into the sample than others. This would be necessary in our study of purse snatching because those older than 65 represent only about 12% of the total U.S. population. Because we want to investigate differences between the victimizations of those younger than and older than 65, we want to have more than this 12% proportion represented in our sample. To do this, we would disproportionately weight our sample selection procedures to give persons older than 65 a better chance of being selected. It is important to note that if we were going to make generalizations from a weighted sample to the population, then adjustments to our statistics would be necessary to take this sample weighting into account. This is a somewhat complicated procedure that is usually accomplished through the aid of computer technology.

> **Stratified or weighted sampling:**
> Method of sampling in which sample elements are selected separately from population strata or are weighted differently for selection in advance by the researcher.

## Nonprobability Sampling Techniques

As you can imagine, obtaining a probability sample such as those described in the previous section can be a very laborious, and sometimes costly, task. Many researchers do not have the resources, in either time or money, to obtain a probability sample. Instead, many rely on nonprobability sampling procedures. Unlike the samples we have already discussed, when samples are collected using nonprobability sampling techniques, elements within the target population do *not* have a known, equal, and independent probability of being selected. Because the chance of one element being selected versus another element remains unknown, we cannot be certain that the selected sample actually represents our target population. Since we are generally interested in making inferences to a larger population, this uncertainty can represent a significant problem.

Why, then, would we want to use nonprobability sampling techniques? Well, they are useful for several purposes, including those situations in which we do not have a population list. Moreover, nonprobability sampling techniques are often the only way to obtain samples from particular populations or for certain types of research questions, especially those about hidden or deviant subcultures. At other times when we are just exploring issues we may not need the precision (and added costs and labor) of a probability sample. We will briefly discuss three types of nonprobability samples in this section: availability, quota, and purposive or judgement samples.

## Availability Samples

**Availability sampling:** Sampling in which elements are selected on the basis of convenience.

The first type of sampling technique we will discuss is one that is perhaps too frequently used and is based solely on the availability of respondents. This type of sample is appropriately termed an **availability sample**. The media often pass availability samples off as probability samples. Popular magazines and Internet sites periodically survey their readers by asking them to fill out questionnaires, and those individuals inclined to respond make up the availability sample for the survey. Follow-up articles then appear in the magazine or on the site displaying the results under such titles as "What You Think about the Death Penalty for Teenagers." Even if the number of people who responded is large, however, these respondents only make up a tiny fraction of the entire readership and are probably unlike other readers who did not have the interest or time to participate. In sum, these samples are not representative of the total population—or even of the total population of all readers.

You have probably even been an element in one of these samples. Have you ever been asked to complete a questionnaire in class, say as a course requirement for a psychology class? University researchers frequently conduct surveys by passing out questionnaires in their large lecture classes. Usually, the sample obtained from this method consists of those students who voluntarily agree to participate or those who receive course credit for doing so. This voluntary participation injects yet another source of bias into the sample. It is not surprising that this type of sample is so popular; it is one of the easiest and least expensive sampling techniques available. But it may produce the least representative and least generalizable type of samples.

## Quota Samples

**Quota sampling:** Nonprobability sampling method in which elements are selected to ensure that the sample represents certain characteristics in proportion to their prevalence in the population or to oversampled segments of the population.

**Quota sampling** is intended to overcome availability sampling's biggest downfall: the likelihood that the sample will just consist of who or what is available, without any concern for its similarity to the population of interest. The distinguishing feature of a quota sample is that quotas are set to ensure that the sample represents certain characteristics in proportion to their prevalence in the population.

Quota samples are similar to stratified probability samples, but they are generally less rigorous and precise in their selection procedures. Quota sampling simply involves designating the population into proportions of some group that you want to be represented in your sample. Similar to stratified samples, in some cases, these proportions may actually represent the true proportions observed in the population. At other times, these quotas may represent predetermined proportions of subsets of people you deliberately want to oversample.

The problem is that even when we know that a quota sample is representative of the particular characteristics for which quotas have been set, we have no way of knowing if the sample is representative in terms of any other characteristics. Realistically, researchers can set quotas for only a small fraction of the characteristics relevant to a study, so a quota sample is really not much better than an availability sample (although following careful, consistent procedures for selecting cases within the quota limits always helps).

## Purposive or Judgment Samples

Another type of nonprobability sample that is often used in the field of crimi-nology is called a **purposive** or **judgment sample**. In general, this type of sample is selected based on the purpose of the researcher's study and on his or her judgment of the population. It is often referred to as judgment sampling because the researcher uses her or his own judgment about whom to select into the sample, rather than drawing sample elements randomly. Although this type of sample does not provide the luxury of generalizability, it can provide a wealth of information not otherwise attainable from a typical random sample.

Many noted studies in the field of criminology have been carried out by using a purposive or judgment sample. For example, in the classic book *The Booster and the Snitch: Department Store Shoplifting,* Mary Cameron (1964) tracked a sample of individuals who had been caught shoplifting by department store employees.

Another variation of a purposive sample is called a **snowball sample**. By using this technique, you identify one member of the population and speak to him or her, then ask that person to identify others in the population and speak to them, then ask them to identify others, and so on. The sample size increases with time as a snowball would rolling down a slope. This technique is useful for hard-to-reach or hard-to-identify interconnected populations where at least some members of the popu-lation know each other, such as drug dealers, prostitutes, practicing criminals, gang leaders, and informal organi-zational leaders. Figure 1.2 displays the process of snowball sampling.

> **Purposive or judgment sampling:** Nonprobability sampling method in which elements are selected for a purpose usually because of their unique position.

> **Snowball sample:** Type of purposive sample that identities one member of a population and then asks him or her to identify others in the population. The sample size increases as a snowball would rolling down a slope.

| Figure 1.2 | **Example of Snowball Sampling** |

Successive waves of sampling gradually produce a more representative sample than is typical of snowball sampling.

Instructions to respondents:
"We'll pay you $5 each for up to three names, but only one of those names can be somebody from your own town. The others have to be from somewhere else."

Peter St. Jean (2007) used snowball sampling for recruiting offenders in a Chicago neighborhood for interviews. After several years of participant observation within a Chicago community, St. Jean wanted to understand the logic offenders used for setting up street drug dealing and staging robberies. He explained his sampling technique as follows:

> I was introduced to the offenders mainly through referrals from relatives, customers, friends, and acquaintances who, after several months (sometimes years), trusted me as someone whose only motive was to understand life in their neighborhood. For instance, the first three drug dealers I interviewed were introduced by their close relatives. Toward the end of each interview, I asked for leads to other subjects, with the first three interviews resulting in eleven additional leads. (p. 26)

We believe it is fundamental to identify the types of samples that are used in research before beginning a course in statistics. All inferential statistics we will examine in this text assume that the data being examined were obtained from a probability sample. What are inferential statistics, you ask? Good question. We will answer this next.

## Descriptive and Inferential Statistics

**Descriptive statistics:** Statistics used to describe the distribution of a sample or population.

**Inferential statistics:** Mathematical tools for estimating how likely it is that a statistical result based on data from a random sample is representative of the population from which the sample was selected.

**Sample statistic:** Statistic (i.e., mean, proportion, etc.) obtained from a sample of the population.

**Population parameter:** Statistic (i.e., mean, proportion, etc.) obtained from a population. Since we rarely have entire population data, we typically estimate population parameters using sample statistics.

Traditionally, the discipline of statistics has been divided into descriptive and inferential statistics. In large part, this distinction relies on whether one is interested in simply describing some phenomenon or in "inferring" characteristics of some phenomenon from a sample to the entire population. See? An understanding of sampling issues is already necessary.

**Descriptive statistics** can be used to describe characteristics or some phenomenon from either a sample or a population. The key point here is that you are using the statistics for "description" only. For example, if we wanted to describe the number of parking tickets given out by university police or the amount of revenues these parking tickets generated, we could use various statistics, including simple counts or averages.

If, however, we wanted to generalize this information to university police departments across the country, we would need to move into the realm of **inferential statistics**. Inferential statistics are mathematical tools for estimating how likely it is that a statistical result based on data from a random sample is representative of the population from which the sample was selected. If our interest is in making inferences, a **sample statistic** is really only an estimate of the population statistic, called a **population parameter**, which we want to estimate. Because this sample statistic is only an estimate of the population parameter, there will always be some amount of error present. Inferential statistics are the tools used for calculating the magnitude of this sampling error. As we noted earlier, the larger the sampling error, the less accurate the sample statistic will be as an estimate of the population parameter. Of course, before we can use inferential statistics, we must be able to assume that our sample is actually representative of the population. And to do this, we must obtain our sample using appropriate probability sampling techniques. We hope the larger picture is beginning to come into focus!

## Validity In Criminological Research

Before we conclude this introductory chapter, it is important to cover two more concepts. In criminological research, we seek to develop an accurate understanding of empirical reality by conducting research that leads to valid knowledge about the world. But when is knowledge valid? In general, we have reached the goal of validity when our statements or conclusions about empirical reality are correct. If you look out your window and observe that it is raining, this is probably a valid observation. However, if you read in the newspaper that the majority of Americans favor the death penalty for adolescents who commit murder, this conclusion should be held up to stronger scrutiny because it is probably based on an interpretation of a social survey. There are two types of validity that we will examine here: measurement validity and causal validity.

## Measurement Validity

In general, we can consider **measurement validity** the first concern in establishing the validity of research results because if we haven't measured what we think we have measured, our conclusions may be completely false. To see how important measurement validity is, let's go back to the descriptive research question we addressed earlier: "How prevalent is youth violence and delinquency in the United States?"

> **Measurement validity:** When we have actually measured what we intended to measure.

Data on the extent of juvenile delinquency come from two primary sources: official data and surveys. Official data are based on the aggregate records of juvenile offenders and offenses processed by agencies of the criminal justice system: police, courts, and corrections. As noted earlier, one primary source of official statistics on juvenile delinquency is the UCR or the newer NIBRS produced by the FBI. However, the validity of these official statistics for measuring the extent of juvenile delinquency is a subject of heated debate among criminologists. Although some researchers believe official reports are a valid measure of serious delinquency, others contend that these data say more about the behavior of the police than about delinquency. These criminologists think the police are predisposed against certain groups of people or certain types of crimes.

Unquestionably, official reports underestimate the actual amount of delinquency. Obviously, not all acts of delinquency become known to the police. Sometimes delinquent acts are committed and not observed; other times they are observed and not reported, and if the official data include arrests, then even crimes that are observed and reported frequently do not result in anyone being arrested. In addition, there is evidence that UCR data often reflect the political climate and police policies as much as they do criminal activity. Take the U.S. "War on Drugs," which heated up in the 1980s. During this time, arrest rates for drug offenses soared, giving the illusion that drug use was increasing at an epidemic pace. However, self-report surveys that asked citizens directly about their drug use behavior during this same time period found that the use of most illicit drugs was actually declining (Regoli & Hewitt, 1994). In your opinion, then, which measure of drug use, the UCR or self-report surveys, was more valid? Before we answer this question, let's continue our delinquency example.

Despite the limitations of official statistics for measuring delinquency, these data were relied on by criminologists and used as a valid measure of delinquency for many decades. As a result, delinquency and other violent offending were thought to involve primarily minority populations and/or disadvantaged youth. In 1947, however, James Wallerstein and Clement Wyle surveyed a sample of 700 juveniles and found that 91% admitted to having committed at least one offense that was punishable by one or more years in prison and 99% admitted to at least one offense for which they could have been arrested had they been caught. In 1958, James Short and F. Ivan Nye reported the results from the first large-scale self-report study involving juveniles from a variety of locations. In their research, Short and Nye concluded that delinquency was widespread throughout the adolescent population and that youth from high-income families were just as likely to engage in delinquency as youth from low-income families. Contemporary studies using self-report data from the NYS indicate that the actual amount of delinquency is much greater than that reported by the UCR and that, unlike these official data where non-Whites are overrepresented, self-report data indicate that White juveniles report almost exactly the same number of delinquencies as non-Whites, but fewer of them are arrested (Elliott & Ageton, 1980).

This is just one example that highlights the importance of measurement validity, but it should convince you that we must be very careful in designing our measures and in subsequently evaluating how well they have performed. For example, how would you evaluate the measurement validity of the life satisfaction and self-control measures used by MacDonald et al. (2005) that we highlighted earlier? Do you think they validly capture life satisfaction or self-control for the adolescents in their sample? Can you think of other ways that may have improved on the measurement of these variables? The point we are trying to make is that we cannot just assume that the measures we use are measuring what we believe them to measure. Remember this as we use real data and case studies from the criminology and criminal justice literature throughout this book.

## Reliability

**Reliability:** Measure that is reliable when it yields consistent scores or observations of a given phenomenon on different occasions. Reliability is a prerequisite for measurement validity.

There are several types of reliability, but we are only going to concentrate on the basic concept here. **Reliability** means that a measure procedure yields consistent scores as long as the phenomenon being measured is not changing. For example, if we gave students a survey about alcohol consumption with the same questions, the measure would be reliable if the same students gave approximately the same answers six months later, assuming their drinking patterns had not changed much. Reliability is a prerequisite for measurement validity; we cannot really measure a phenomenon if the measure we are using gives inconsistent results. Figure 1.3 illuminates the difference between reliability and measurement validity.

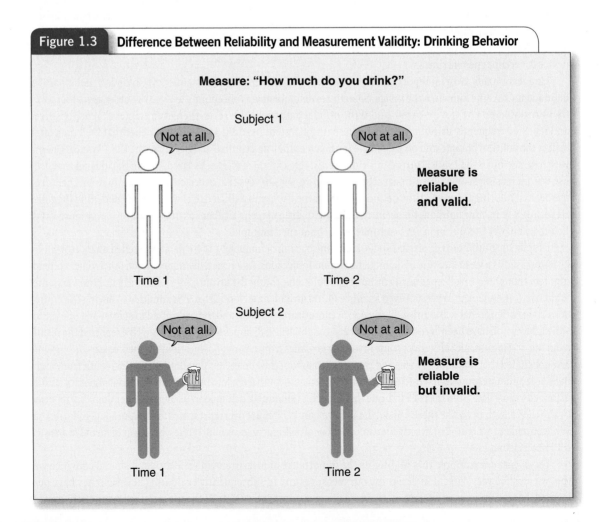

**Figure 1.3** — Difference Between Reliability and Measurement Validity: Drinking Behavior

## Causal Validity

**Causal validity**, also known as **interval validity**, is another issue of validity we are concerned with and has to do with the truthfulness of an assertion that an independent variable did, in fact, cause the dependent variable, or that *X* caused *Y*. Let's go back to the issue of violence prevention programs in schools. Imagine that we are searching for ways to reduce violence in high schools. We start by searching for what seems to be particularly effective violence prevention programs in area

> **Causal validity (internal validity):** When we can assume that our independent variable did cause the dependent variable.

schools. We find a program at a local high school—let's call it Plainville Academy—that a lot of people have talked about, and we decide to compare rates of violence reported to the guidance counselor's office in that school with those in another school, Cool School, that does not offer the violence prevention program. We find that students in the school with the special program have lower rates of reported violence, and we decide that the program caused the lower rates. Are you confident about the causal validity of our conclusion? Probably not. Perhaps the school with the special program had lower rates of reported violence even before the special program began. Maybe kids who go to Cool School are at a greater risk of violence because of where it is located.

This is the sort of problem that randomized experiments, like that used by Esbensen and his colleagues (2013), are designed to resolve. Randomly assigning students to either receive the G.R.E.A.T. curriculum or not made it very unlikely that youngsters who were more aggressive would be disproportionately represented in either group. In addition, causal conclusions can be mistaken because of some factor that was not recognized during planning for the study, even in randomized experiments. Statistical control of other factors thought also to explain or predict the phenomenon of interest is essential in determining causal validity. The final two multiple regression chapters in this book highlight the ways research uses statistical methods to control for many independent variables thought to affect a dependent variable.

## ▣ Summary

Our goal in this introductory chapter is to underscore the nature of the importance of statistics in criminology and criminal justice along with several fundamental aspects of the research process. We have set the stage for us to begin our exploration into the realm of statistics. Can't wait!

We have seen that, unlike observations we make in everyday life, criminological research relies on scientific methods. Statistical methods play a role in three types of research we conduct in our field: descriptive research, explanatory research, and evaluation research. The goal of all research is validity—for our statements or conclusions about empirical reality to be correct. Measurement validity exists when we have actually measured what we think we have measured. Causal or internal validity exists when the assertion that an independent variable causes a dependent variable, or that *X* causes *Y*, is correct. Generalizability, also known as external validity, exists when we can assume that results obtained from a sample can be generalized to the population.

Because it is almost never possible to obtain information on every individual or element in the population of interest, our investigations usually rely on data taken from samples of the population. Furthermore, because virtually all of the statistics we will examine in this text are based on assumptions about the origins of our data, we have provided a discussion of the most common types of samples used in our field of study. Samples generally fall within two categories: those derived from probability sampling techniques and those derived from nonprobability sampling techniques. The fundamental element in probability sampling is random selection. When a sample is randomly selected from the population, it means that every element (e.g., individual) has a known and independent chance of being selected for the sample.

We examined four types of probability samples: the simple random sample, the systematic random sample, the multistage cluster sample, and the weighted sample. In addition, we discussed three types of nonprobability samples: quota samples, purposive or judgment samples, and availability samples. We concluded the chapter with a brief discussion of descriptive and inferential statistics and highlighted the importance of measurement and causal validity.

## Key Terms

> Review key terms with eFlashcards. $SAGE edge™

availability sample   14
causal validity (internal validity)   19
dependent variable   7
descriptive research   5
descriptive statistics   16
evaluation research   8
explanatory research   6
generalizability   9
hypothesis   7
independent variable   7
inferential statistics   16
measurement validity   17
multistage cluster sample   12

National Incident-Based Reporting
  System (NIBRS)   5
nonprobability sampling methods   10
police reports   5
population   9
population parameter   16
probability sampling methods   10
purposive or judgment sample   15
quota sample   14
random digit dialing   11
random selection   10
reliability   18
sample   9

sample statistic   16
sampling error   10
science   4
simple random sample   11
snowball sample   15
stratified or weighted sampling   13
surveys   6
systematic random sample   11
theory   7
true experimental design   8
Uniform Crime Reports (UCR)   5

## Practice Problems

> Test your understanding of chapter content.
Take the practice quiz. $SAGE edge™

1. Obtain a list of students from the statistics or research methods course in which you are currently using this book. Using this list and the random numbers table in Appendix B, select a simple random sample of 15 students. What are the steps you performed in doing this? Comment on how well this sample represents the entire sophomore class. Now draw a systematic random sample from the same list. Are there any differences?

2. How can you approximate a simple random sample when you do not have a list of the population?

3. Discuss the importance of probability sampling techniques.

4. How does random selection ensure that we are obtaining the most representative sample possible?

5. If we wanted to make sure that certain segments of the population were represented and/or overrepresented within our sample, what are two types of sampling techniques we could use?

6. What is the danger in using nonprobability samples in research?

7. In what types of situations would nonprobability samples be the most appropriate?

## SPSS Exercises

> Explore additional data sets. $SAGE edge™

| Data for Exercise | |
|---|---|
| Dataset | Description |
| 2013 YRBS.sav | The 2013 YRBS, short for Youth Risk Behavior Survey, is a national study of high-school students. It focuses on gauging various behaviors and experiences of the adolescent population, including substance use and some victimization. |

1. SPSS introduction: SPSS, short for "Statistical Package for the Social Sciences," is a professional statistical analysis program that is used by universities, hospitals, and businesses. The exercises at the end of each chapter are intended to get you comfortable with the basics of SPSS. The first thing we've got to do is open some data:

   a. First, go to the website for this textbook (**edge.sagepub .com/bachmansccj4e** ) and download all the data sets somewhere you can access easily.

   b. **Opening a data set in SPSS:** After double clicking on the SPSS icon you'll see a spreadsheet in the background and a welcome screen pop up, asking what you want to do. Select "Open an existing data source" and "More Files." This will cause a Windows browser to open, at which point you must simply go to the folder you found and select the data set of interest; in this case, that is the 2013 YRBS.sav file.

   c. Alternately, if the welcome screen does not pop up, you can always select file->open->data from the menu bar to access your data set.

2. Navigating SPSS:

   a. SPSS uses two main screens through which you can view your data set. The buttons to switch between "views" are on the bottom left of the SPSS window. By default you open up to the **variable view** screen:

      i. **Variable View in SPSS:**

         1. Variable view in SPSS lets you look at information on each variable in the data set. Each numbered row corresponds to a different measure from the survey. Some of the information in the columns is not of interest to us for this book; instead, focus on the following:

            a. **Name:** The name of the variable. Double clicking allows you to edit this field.

            b. **Label:** A summary of what the variable tells us or how the question was asked. Double clicking allows you to edit this field.

            c. **Values:** This allows us to put labels on numeric values. For instance, we could tell SPSS that responses with a 1 should be labeled as "White." You can specify your own labels or view them by clicking the cell for a given row and clicking the " . . . " field.

            d. **Missing:** This tells us values that SPSS will treat as missing, excluding them from analyses. Many surveys code cases as −9 or a similar value rather than leaving them blank so it is important to make sure these are treated as missing. You can specify missing values by licking in the cell and pressing the " . . . " box.

      ii. **Variable View Exercises:**

         1. Identify the variable name, label, and value labels for the following variables:
            a. Row 2
            b. Row 4
            c. Row 23
            d. Row 45

         2. **Searching for variables:** If you know the variable name, you can search for it to make the process faster. Do this by pressing ctrl+F on your keyboard or selecting edit->find. Find the labels and values for the following variables:
            a. Qn43
            b. QhallucDrug
            c. Qnowt

         3. How many variables are in this data set?

      iii. **Data View:**

         1. In the bottom left you can click to switch to "data view." This changes you to a spreadsheet containing your raw data. Each column is a different variable. Each row corresponds to a respondent; it contains a person's specific responses to all the survey questions.

         2. You'll notice lots of "." marks; these are "system missing" responses. We just don't have data for that person for whatever reason! SPSS ignores these automatically.

         3. Clicking the ⬛ swaps numerical values to their value labels, making it easier for you to read at a glance.

      iv. **Data View Exercises:**

         1. What was respondent 1's (i.e., row 1) response to question q13? Flip back to variable view and explain what this response to this question tells us.

         2. What was respondent 71's race according to the variable race7?

         3. How many respondents do we have in this data set?

## STUDENT STUDY SITE

# $SAGE edge™

**WANT A BETTER GRADE?**

Get the tools you need to sharpen your study skills. Access practice quizzes, eFlashcards, data sets, and exercises at **edge.sagepub.com/bachmansccj4e**.

# Part I: Univariate Analysis

*Describing Variable Distributions*

# CHAPTER 2

# Levels of Measurement and Aggregation

*" Science cannot progress without reliable and accurate measurement of what it is you are trying to study. The key is measurement, simple as that.*

—Robert D. Hare

*When you can measure what you are speaking about, and express it in numbers, you know something about it.*

—Lord Kelvin *"*

## LEARNING OBJECTIVES

1. Summarize the role of variables in research.

2. Identify the four levels of measurement variables can have.

3. Describe the difference between variables that identify qualities compared with variables that identify quantities.

4. Explain the differences among raw frequencies, proportions, percentages, and rates.

5. Define the units of analysis in any particular data set.

# ▣ Introduction

In Chapter 1, we examined various sampling techniques that can be used for selecting a sample from a given population. Once we have selected our sample, we can begin the process of collecting information. The information we gather is usually referred to as "data" and in its entirety is called a "data set." In this chapter, we will take a closer look at the types of variables that can make up a data set.

This may be the first time you have been formally exposed to statistics, but we are sure each of you has some idea what a variable is even though you may not call it that. A **variable** is any element to which different values can be attributed. Respondents' gender is a variable with two values, male and female. Race/ethnicity is a variable with many values, such as American Indian, African American, Asian, Hispanic, and Caucasian. Age is another variable that can take on different values, such as 2, 16, or 55 years. As we noted in the last chapter, in explanatory research, we are interested in explaining a dependent variable by using one or more independent variables. In research, the dependent variable is expected to vary or change depending on variation or change in the independent variable. In this causal type of explanation, the independent variable is the cause and the dependent variable the effect or outcome. The entire set of values a variable takes on is called a **frequency distribution** or an **empirical distribution**. In a given data set, a frequency distribution, or empirical distribution, is a distribution (a list) of outcomes or values for a variable. It is referred to as an empirical distribution because it is a distribution of empirical (real and observed) data, and it is called a frequency distribution because it tells us how frequent each value or outcome is in the entire data set. For example, suppose we conducted a survey from a sample of 100 persons in your class at your university. In one question we asked for respondent's age. Suppose this "age" variable ranged from 18 to 42. There might be 15 people who were 18 years of age, 30 people who were 19 years of age, 17 people who were 20 years of age, only 1 person who was 42 years of age, and so on. An empirical, or frequency, distribution would tell you not only what the different ages were but also how many people of each age were represented in the entire distribution.

In contrast, a characteristic of your sample element that does not vary in a data set is called a **constant**. Unlike a variable, whose values vary or are different, a constant has only one value. For example, if you have a sample of inmates from a male correctional institution, the value for "respondent's gender" would be considered a constant—"male". Since all elements of the sample would be male, respondent's gender would not vary in that data set. Similarly, if you selected a sample of 20-year-olds from the sophomore class at a state university, age would be a constant rather than a variable in that sample because all members of the sample would be the same age (20 years).

Notice that a given characteristic, such as respondent's gender or age, is not always a variable or a constant. Under different conditions, it may be one or the other. For example, in a sample of male prisoners, gender is a constant, but age is a variable because the male inmates are likely to be different ages. In the sample of 20-year-old sophomore students from a university, age is a constant, and respondent's gender is a variable because some persons in the sample would be male and some would be female.

We can classify variables in many different ways and make several distinctions among them. First, there are differing levels of measurement that can be associated with variables. The next section of the chapter examines these measurement differences, beginning with the classification of variables as either continuous or categorical variables. We then examine the four measurement classifications within these two broad categories: nominal, ordinal,

> **Variable:** Characteristic or property that can vary or take on different values or attributes.

> **Frequency or empirical distribution:** Distribution of values that make up a variable distribution.

> **Constant:** Characteristic or property that does not vary but takes on only one value.

**Get the edge on your studies.**
edge.sagepub.com/bachmansccj4e

- Take a quiz to find out what you've learned.
- Review key terms with eFlashcards.
- Explore additional data sets.

**⑤SAGE edge™**

**Units of analysis:** Particular units or aggregations (e.g., people and cities) that constitute an observation in a data set.

interval, and ratio measurement. The second section of the chapter addresses the difference between independent and dependent variables and the different ways of reporting the features of variables. In the final section, you will learn how to identify the **units of analysis** in a research design so that you can state conclusions about the relationships between your variables in the appropriate units.

## 📑 Levels of Measurement

Recall that data generally come from one of three places: They are gathered by us personally, gathered by another researcher, or gathered by a government agency. Doing research on a previously collected data set is often referred to as "secondary data analysis" because the data already existed and had been analyzed before. No matter how they were collected, however, data sets are by definition simply a collection of many variables. For illustrative purposes, imagine that we were interested in the relationship between levels of student drinking and drug use and student demographic characteristics such as gender, age, religion, and year in college (freshman, sophomore, junior, senior). Table 2.1 displays the small data set we might have obtained had we investigated this issue by collecting surveys from 20 college students (a random sample, of course).

To measure the extent to which each student used alcohol and other drugs, let's say we asked them these questions: "How many drinks do you consume in an average month? By 'drinks' we mean a beer, a mixed drink, or a glass of wine." "How many times during an average month do you take drugs, such as ecstasy, marijuana, cocaine, or any other illegal drug?" Each of the other variables in the table relates to other information about each student in the sample. Everything listed in this table, including the respondent's identification number, is a variable. All of these variables combined represent our data set. The first thing you may notice about these variables is that some are represented by categories and some are represented by actual numbers. Gender, for example, is divided into two categories, female and male. This type of variable is often referred to as a **qualitative** or **categorical variable**, implying that the values represent qualities or categories only. The values of this variable have no numeric or quantitative meaning. Other examples in the data set of qualitative variables include college year and religion.

**Qualitative or categorical variables:** Values that refer to qualities or categories. They tell us what kind, what group, or what type a value is referring to.

The rest of the variables in our data set, however, have values that do represent numeric values that can be quantified—hence the name **quantitative or continuous variables**. The values of quantitative variables can be compared in a numerically meaningful way. Respondent's identification number, age, grade point average, number of drinks, and number of times drugs were used are all quantitative variables. We can compare the values of these variables in a numerically meaningful way. For example, from Table 2.1, we can see that respondent 1 has a lower grade point average than respondent 19. We can also see that respondents 7 and 16 have the highest levels of alcohol consumption in the sample.

**Quantitative or continuous variables:** Values that refer to quantities or different measurements. They tell us how much or how many.

In Table 2.1, it is relatively easy to identify which variables are qualitative and which are quantitative simply because the qualitative variables are represented by **alphanumeric data** (by letters rather than by numbers). Data that are represented by numbers are called **numeric data**. A good way to remember the distinction between these two types of data is to note that alphanumeric data consist of letters of the alphabet, whereas numeric data consist of numbers.

**Alphanumeric data:** Values of a variable that are represented by letters rather than by numbers.

It is certainly possible to include alphanumeric data in a data set, as we have done in Table 2.1, but when stored in a computer, as most data are, alphanumeric data take up a great deal of space, and alphanumeric data are difficult to statistically analyze. For this reason, these data are usually converted to or represented by numeric data. For example, females may arbitrarily be identified with the

**Numeric data:** Values of a variable that represent numerical qualities.

| Table 2.1 | Example of the Format of a Data Set from a Survey of 20 College Students | | | | | | |
|---|---|---|---|---|---|---|---|

| | | | | | Average Month | | |
|---|---|---|---|---|---|---|---|
| ID Number | Gender | Age | College Year | GPA | # Drinks | # Times Drugs Used | Religion |
| 1 | Female | 19 | Sophomore | 2.3 | 45 | 22 | Catholic |
| 2 | Male | 22 | Senior | 3.1 | 30 | 10 | Other |
| 3 | Female | 22 | Senior | 3.8 | 0 | 0 | Protestant |
| 4 | Female | 18 | Freshman | 2.9 | 35 | 5 | Jewish |
| 5 | Male | 20 | Junior | 2.5 | 20 | 20 | Catholic |
| 6 | Female | 23 | Senior | 3.0 | 10 | 0 | Catholic |
| 7 | Male | 18 | Freshman | 1.9 | 45 | 25 | Not religious |
| 8 | Female | 19 | Sophomore | 2.8 | 28 | 3 | Protestant |
| 9 | Male | 28 | Junior | 3.3 | 9 | 0 | Protestant |
| 10 | Female | 21 | Junior | 2.7 | 0 | 0 | Muslim |
| 11 | Female | 18 | Freshman | 3.1 | 19 | 2 | Jewish |
| 12 | Male | 19 | Sophomore | 2.5 | 25 | 20 | Catholic |
| 13 | Female | 21 | Senior | 3.5 | 2 | 0 | Other |
| 14 | Male | 21 | Junior | 1.8 | 19 | 33 | Protestant |
| 15 | Female | 42 | Sophomore | 3.9 | 10 | 0 | Protestant |
| 16 | Female | 19 | Sophomore | 2.3 | 45 | 0 | Catholic |
| 17 | Male | 21 | Junior | 2.8 | 29 | 10 | Not religious |
| 18 | Male | 25 | Sophomore | 3.1 | 14 | 0 | Other |
| 19 | Female | 21 | Junior | 3.5 | 5 | 0 | Catholic |
| 20 | Female | 17 | Freshman | 3.5 | 28 | 0 | Jewish |

number 1, rather than with the word "female," and males with the number 2. Assigning numbers to the categorical values of qualitative variables is called "coding" the data. Of course, which numbers get assigned to qualitative variables (for example, 1 for females and 2 for males) is arbitrary because the numeric code (number) assigned has no real quantitative meaning. Males could be given either a 1 or a 2, or a 0, with females coded either a 2 or a 1; it makes no difference.

Table 2.2 redisplays the data in Table 2.1 numerically as they would normally be stored in a computer data set. Because values of each variable are represented by numbers, it is a little more difficult to distinguish the qualitative variables from the quantitative variables. You have to ask yourself what each of the values really means. For example, for the variable gender, what does the "1" really represent? It represents the code for a female student and is therefore not numerically meaningful; it is a random code number given to all female students who filled out the questionnaire. Similarly, the number "1" coded for the religion variable represents those students who said they were Catholic, and the code "3" represents those students who said they were Jewish. There is nothing inherently meaningful about the numbers 1 and 3. They simply represent categories for the religion variable and we changed the letters of the alphabet for numbers. For the variable age, what does the number 19 represent? This is actually a meaningful value—it tells us that this respondent was 19 years of age, and it is therefore a quantitative variable.

In addition to distinguishing between qualitative and quantitative, we can differentiate among variables in terms of what is called their **level of measurement**. The four levels of measurement are (1) nominal, (2) ordinal, (3) interval, and (4) ratio. Figure 2.1 depicts the difference among these four levels of measurement.

> **Level of measurement:** Mathematical nature of the values for a variable.

## Nominal Level of Measurement

> **Nominal-level variables:** Values that represent categories or qualities of a case only.

Variables measured at the nominal level are exclusively qualitative in nature. The values of **nominal-level variables** convey classification or categorization information *only*. Therefore, the only thing we can say about two or more nominal-level values of a variable is that they are different. We cannot say that one value reflects more or less of the variable than the other. The most common types of nominal-level variables are gender (male and female), religion (Protestant, Catholic, Jewish, Muslim, etc.), and political party (Democrat, Republican, Independent, etc.), The values of these variables are distinct from one another and can give us only descriptive information about the type or label attached to a value. Notice we can say that males are different from females but not that they have more "gender." We can say that Protestants have a different religion than Catholics or Jews, but again, not that they have more "religion." The only distinction we can make with nominal-level variables is that their values are different.

Because they represent distinctions only of kind (one is merely different from the other), the categories of a nominal-level variable are not related to one another in any meaningful numeric way. This is true even if the alphanumeric values are converted or coded into numbers. For example, in Table 2.2, the values assigned to the variables gender and religion are given numeric values. Remember, however, that these numbers were simply assigned for convenience and have no numeric meaning. The fact that Catholics are assigned the code of 1 and Protestants are assigned the code of 2 does not mean that Protestants have twice as much religion as Catholics or that the Protestant religion is "more than" the Catholic religion. The only thing that the codes of 1 and 2 mean is that they refer to different religions. Because we cannot make distinctions of "less than" or "more than" with them, then, nominal-level variables do not allow us to rank-order the values of a given variable. In other words, nominal-level measurement does not have the property of order. It merely reflects the fact that some values are different from others. Consequently, mathematical operations cannot be performed with nominal-level data. With our religion variable, for example, we cannot subtract a 2 (Protestant) from a 3 (Jewish) to get a 1 (Catholic). Do you see how meaningless mathematical operations are with variables measured at the nominal level?

## Ordinal Level of Measurement

> **Ordinal-level variables:** Values that not only represent categories but also have a logical order.

The values of **ordinal-level variables** not only are categorical in nature, but the categories also have some type of relationship to each other. This relationship is one of order or transitivity. That is, categories on an ordinal variable can be rank-ordered from high (more of the variable) to low (less of the variable) even though they still cannot be exactly quantified. As a result, although we can know whether a value is more or less than another value, we do not know exactly *how much* more or less. The properties of ordinal-level measurement are clearer with an example.

Let's say that on a survey, we have measured income in such a way that respondents simply checked the income category that best reflected their annual income. The categories the survey provided are as follows:

1. Less than $20,000

2. $20,001 to $40,000

3. $40,001 to $60,000

4. More than $60,000

Now suppose that one of our respondents (respondent 1) checked the first category and that another respondent (respondent 2) checked the third category. We don't know the exact annual income of each respondent, but

| | | | | | Average Month | | |
| ID Number | Gender | Age | College Year | GPA | # Drinks | # Times Drugs Used | Religion |
|---|---|---|---|---|---|---|---|
| 1 | 1 | 19 | 2 | 2.3 | 45 | 22 | 1 |
| 2 | 2 | 22 | 4 | 3.1 | 30 | 10 | 6 |
| 3 | 1 | 22 | 4 | 3.8 | 0 | 0 | 2 |
| 4 | 1 | 18 | 1 | 2.9 | 35 | 5 | 3 |
| 5 | 2 | 20 | 3 | 2.5 | 20 | 20 | 1 |
| 6 | 1 | 23 | 4 | 3.0 | 10 | 0 | 1 |
| 7 | 2 | 18 | 1 | 1.9 | 45 | 25 | 5 |
| 8 | 1 | 19 | 2 | 2.8 | 28 | 3 | 2 |
| 9 | 2 | 28 | 3 | 3.3 | 9 | 0 | 2 |
| 10 | 1 | 21 | 3 | 2.7 | 0 | 0 | 4 |
| 11 | 1 | 18 | 1 | 3.1 | 19 | 2 | 3 |
| 12 | 2 | 19 | 2 | 2.5 | 25 | 20 | 1 |
| 13 | 1 | 21 | 4 | 3.5 | 2 | 0 | 6 |
| 14 | 2 | 21 | 3 | 1.8 | 19 | 33 | 2 |
| 15 | 1 | 42 | 2 | 3.9 | 10 | 0 | 2 |
| 16 | 1 | 19 | 2 | 2.3 | 45 | 0 | 1 |
| 17 | 2 | 21 | 3 | 2.8 | 29 | 10 | 5 |
| 18 | 2 | 25 | 2 | 3.1 | 14 | 0 | 6 |
| 19 | 1 | 21 | 3 | 3.5 | 5 | 0 | 1 |
| 20 | 1 | 17 | 1 | 3.5 | 28 | 0 | 3 |

**Table 2.2  Example of the Data Presented in Table 2.1 as They Would Be Stored in a Computer Data File**

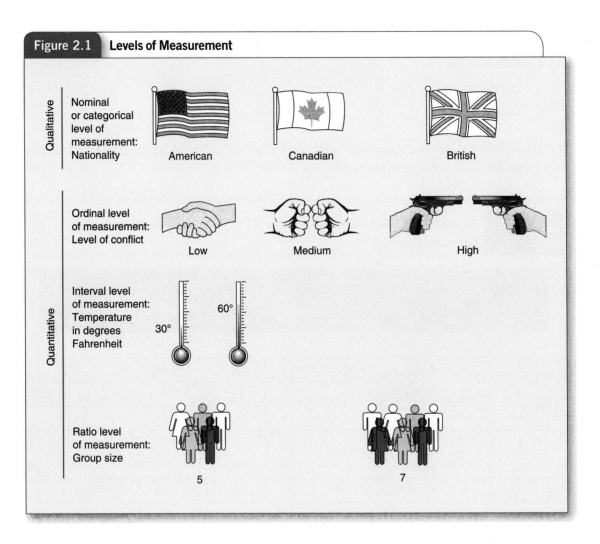

**Figure 2.1** **Levels of Measurement**

we do know that the second respondent makes more than the first. Thus, in addition to knowing that our respondents have different annual incomes (nominal level), we also know that one income is more than the other. In reality, respondent 1 may make anywhere between no money and $20,000, but because income was measured using ordinal categories, we will never know. Had we measured income in terms of actual dollars earned per year, we would be able to make more precise mathematical distinctions. Suppose we had a third person (respondent 3) who checked the response more than $60,000. The property of transitivity says that if respondent 1 makes less than respondent 2, and if respondent 2 makes less than respondent 3, then respondent 1 also makes less than respondent 3. The rank order is thus:

1. Less than $20,000 respondent 1

2. $20,001 to $40,000

3. $40,001 to $60,000 respondent 2

4. More than $60,000 respondent 3

Other examples of ordinal-level variables include the "Likert-type" response questions found on surveys that solicit an individual's attitudes or perceptions. You are probably familiar with this type of survey question. A typical one follows: "Please respond to the following statement by circling the appropriate number: '1' Strongly Agree, '2' Agree, '3' Disagree, '4' Strongly Disagree." The answers to these questions represent the ordinal level of measurement. Often these categories are displayed like this:

| 1 | 2 | 3 | 4 |
|---|---|---|---|
| Strongly Agree | Agree | Disagree | Strongly Disagree |

Response categories that rank-order attitudes in this way are often called *Likert* responses after Rensis Likert, who is believed to have developed them back in the 1930s. There are other ways to measure judgements using a Likert-type response. For example, the aggression questionnaires (AQs) in the literature are designed to measure an individual's propensity to feel anger and hostility (Buss & Warren, 2000). It consists of 34 items, such as "Given enough provocation, I may hit another person," "When people annoy me, I may tell them what I think of them," and "I have trouble controlling my temper." Individuals taking the AQ are asked to respond to the statements using a five-point Likert-type scale from "not at all like me," which is coded 0, to "completely like me," coded 5. Tracey Skilling and Geoff Sorge (2014) used the AQ to assess the validity of two other scales, one intended to measure criminal attitudes and another intended to measure antisocial attitudes. Using a sample of delinquent offenders in Canada, they found that all three measures were significantly related to each other, indicating that they were each measuring antisocial attitudes.

## Interval Level of Measurement

In addition to enabling us to rank-order values, **interval-level variables** allow us to quantify the numeric relationship among them. To be classified as an interval-level variable, the difference between adjacent values along the measurement scale must be the same at every two points. For example, the difference in temperature on the Fahrenheit scale between 40 degrees and 41 degrees is the same as the difference between 89 degrees and 90 degrees: one degree. Another characteristic of interval-level measurement is that the zero point is arbitrary. An arbitrary zero means that, although a value of zero is possible, zero does not mean the absence of the phenomenon. A meaningless zero is an arbitrary zero.

> **Interval-level variable:** In addition to an inherent rank order, a value's relationship to other values is known. There is an equal and constant distance between adjacent values. Therefore, the values can be added and subtracted.

For example, a temperature on the Fahrenheit scale of 0 degrees does not mean that there is no temperature outside, it simply means that it is cold! Zero degrees on the Fahrenheit scale is arbitrary. These characteristics allow scores on an interval scale to be added and subtracted, but meaningful multiplication and division cannot be performed. This level of measurement is represented in Figure 2.1 by the difference between two Fahrenheit temperatures. Although 60 degrees is 30 degrees hotter than 30 degrees, 60 in this case is not twice as hot as 30. Why not? Because heat does not begin at 0 degrees on the Fahrenheit scale.

Social scientists often treat indices (see the AQ earlier) that were created by combining responses to a series of variables measured at the ordinal level as interval-level measures. Another example of an index like this could be created with responses to the Core Institute's (2015) questions about friends' disapproval of substance use (see Table 2.3). The survey has 13 questions on the topic, each of which has the same three response choices. If Do Not Disapprove is valued at 1, Disapprove is valued at 2, and Strongly Disapprove is valued at 3, then the summed index of disapproval would range from 12 to 36. The average could then be treated as a fixed unit of measurement. So a score of 20 could be treated as if it were 4 more units than a score of 16 and so on.

## Ratio Level of Measurement

**Ratio-level variables:** Variables that we assume can be added and subtracted as well as multiplied and divided and that have true-zero points.

**Ratio-level variables** have all the qualities of interval-level variables, and the numeric difference between values is based on a natural, or true-zero, point. A true-zero point means that a score of zero indicates that the phenomenon is absent. For example, if people were asked how many hours they worked last month and they replied "zero hours," it would mean that there was a complete absence of work—they were unemployed that month. Ratio measurement allows meaningful use of multiplication and division, as well as addition and subtraction. We can therefore divide one number by another to form a ratio—hence the name of this level of measurement. Suppose we were conducting a survey of the victimization experiences of residents in rural areas and asked them to provide their annual income in dollars. This variable would be an example of the ratio-level of measurement because it has both a true-zero point and equal and known distances between adjacent values. For example, a value of no income, "zero dollars," has inherent meaning to all of us, and the difference between $10 and $11 is the same as that between $55,200 and $55,201.

There are a few variables in Table 2.2 that are measured at the ratio level. One is the number of drinks respondents had in an average month. Notice that there were a few respondents who had "0" drinks—this is an absolute zero! And a college student who drinks an average of 20 drinks a month has 10 more drinks than someone who

| Table 2.3 | Ordinal-Level Variables Can Be Added to Create an Index With Interval-Level Properties: Core Alcohol and Drug Survey | | |
|---|---|---|---|
| How Do You Think Your Close Friends Feel (or Would Feel) About You . . . (Mark One for Each Line) | Do Not Disapprove | Disapprove | Strongly Disapprove |
| a. Trying marijuana once or twice | | | |
| b. Smoking marijuana occasionally | | | |
| c. Smoking marijuana regularly | | | |
| d. Trying cocaine once or twice | | | |
| e. Taking cocaine regularly | | | |
| f. Trying LSD once or twice | | | |
| g. Taking LSD regularly | | | |
| h. Trying amphetamines once or twice | | | |
| i. Taking amphetamines regularly | | | |
| j. Taking one or two drinks of an alcoholic beverage (beer, wine, liquor) nearly every day | | | |
| k. Taking four or five drinks nearly every day | | | |
| l. Having five or more drinks in one sitting | | | |
| m. Taking steroids for bodybuilding or improved athletic performance | | | |

*Source:* Adapted from *Core Alcohol and Drug Survey: Long Form* © 2015 from the Core Institute.

has 10 drinks a month and 10 fewer drinks than someone who has an average of 30 drinks a month. We have not shown you how to calculate the mean yet, but imagine we calculate the average number of drinks a senior in college has from this table and find that it is 10.5 drinks. We then calculate the average number of drinks a first-year student has as 31.75. Because this is a ratio-level variable with an absolute zero, we could now take the ratio of drinks consumed by a first-year student compared with a senior to be (31.75 / 10.5 = 3.02) and say that first-year students consume about 3 times as much alcohol as seniors! Does this seem accurate to you? Because we can do this, the level of measurement is called "ratio."

For most statistical analyses in social science research, the interval and ratio levels of measurement can be treated as equivalent. In addition to having numerical values, both the interval and ratio levels also involve **continuous measures**: The numbers indicating the values of variables are points on a continuum, not discrete categories. Because of this, researchers often treat variables measured at the interval and ratio levels as comparable. They then refer to this as the **interval–ratio level of measurement**. In this text, we generally rely on this distinction.

## The Case of Dichotomies

**Dichotomies** are variables having only two values and are a special case from the standpoint of levels of measurement. Although variables with only two categories are generally thought of as nominally measured, we can also think of a dichotomy as indicating the presence or absence of an attribute. Suppose, for example, we were interested in differences between individuals who had never used illegal drugs in the last year and those who had used at least one illegal drug in the last year. We could create a variable that indicated this dichotomous distinction by coding those individuals who said they did not use any of the substances listed as 0 and all others as 1. Viewed in this way, there is an inherent order to the two values: In one group, the attribute of consuming illegal substances is absent (those coded 0), and in another, it is present (those coded 1). When we code variables like this as 0 or 1, they are often called **binary variables**.

## Comparing Levels of Measurement

Table 2.4 summarizes the types of comparisons that can be made with different levels of measurement, as well as the mathematical operations that are legitimate. All four levels of measurement allow researchers to assign different values to different cases. All three quantitative measures allow researchers to rank cases in order.

## ▣ Ways of Presenting Variables

In this section, we examine some of the most commonly used pieces of information you will confront in criminology: counts, rates, ratios, proportions, and percentages. These are simply different ways in which to present, describe, and compare variables.

---

**Four Types of Measurement**

**Nominal:** Values represent categories or qualities of a case only.

**Ordinal:** Values not only represent categories but also have a logical order.

**Interval:** In addition to an inherent rank order, a value's relationship to other values is known. There is an equal and constant distance between adjacent values.

**Ratio:** Not only can distances be determined between values, but these distances are based on a true-zero point.

---

**Continuous measure:** Measure with numbers indicating the values of variables as points on a continuum.

---

**Interval-ratio level of measurement:** Variables that we assume can be added and subtracted as well as multiplied and divided regardless of whether they have true-zero points.

---

**Dichotomy:** Variable having only two values.

---

**Binary variable:** Dichotomous variable that has been coded 0 or 1.

| Table 2.4 | **Properties of Measurement Levels** |
| | |

| Examples of Comparison Statements | Appropriate Math Operations | Relevant Level of Measurement | | | |
| --- | --- | --- | --- | --- | --- |
| | | Nominal | Ordinal | Interval | Ratio |
| A is equal to (not equal to) B | = (≠) | √ | √ | √ | √ |
| A is greater than (less than) B | > (<) | | √ | √ | √ |
| A is three more than (less than) B | + (−) | | | √ | √ |
| A is twice (half) as large as B | × (÷) | | | | √ |

## Counts and Rates

**Count or frequency:** Number of units in the sample that has a particular value in a variable distribution.

The most elementary way of presenting information is to present the counts or frequencies of the variable you are interested in. A **count** or **frequency** is simply the number of times that an event occurs in your data. The numbers of violent victimizations recorded by the National Crime Victimization Survey (NCVS), which includes rapes, robberies, and assaults, by age for 2013 are presented here:

| Age Group | Number of Victims (f) |
| --- | --- |
| 12–17 | 545,370 |
| 18–24 | 527,410 |
| 24–34 | 604,500 |
| 35–49 | 684,150 |
| 50–64 | 566,990 |
| 65 and older | 112,760 |

These numbers tell us exactly how many victims of violent crime there were in the United States in 2013 in each of the six age groups. Violent crimes include rapes, robberies, and assaults. We can see from these data that there were fewer victims in the age 65 and older group than in any other age group. The highest number of victims of violent crime appeared in the 35 to 49 age group (684,150 victims). Based on these counts, who has the greatest vulnerability to becoming a victim? Do those who are aged 35 to 49 have a greater risk of becoming the victim of violence compared with those aged 18 to 24, or those aged 12 to 17? The short answer is no. The long answer is that if we want to make comparisons across different categories, whether they be age categories, gender, race/ethnicity, city, year, or any other aggregation, it is not possible to produce conclusions of relative risk. Why? Because simple counts and frequencies do not take into consideration the size of the total at-risk population within each category. Although we may sometimes come to the same conclusion, using simple frequencies to make these comparisons most often leads to misleading conclusions.

**Rate:** Number of a phenomenon divided by the total possible, which is then multiplied by a constant such as 1,000, 10,000, or 100,000.

To make comparisons accurately across units with different population sizes, it is important to control for the size of the populations you are comparing. To do this, it is necessary to calculate the **rate** of an occurrence.

# Case Study

## The Importance of Rates for Victimization Data

Let's assume we want to assess how much risk a person across each age group has of experiencing a violent victimization. Table 2.5 presents the same violent victimization data along with the population counts for each age group. Rates are derived by dividing the observed number of occurrences or phenomena by the total number that could theoretically have been observed within the population of interest. In addition, rates are usually standardized according to some population base, such as a rate per 1,000, 10,000, or per 100,000 people:

$$\text{Rate} = \frac{\text{Number in subset}}{\text{Total number}} \times \text{Constant} (\text{e.g.}, 1,000) \tag{2-1}$$

As formula 2-1 shows, to derive the victim rate of violence within age categories, we must first divide the number of victims of violent crimes observed within an age group by the total number of potential victims within this age group. This latter number would be the entire population for this age group because, theoretically, everyone in the age group could have become a victim of a violent crime. We then multiply that by some population standard to get a rate per 1,000, or a rate per 10,000 population. What population standard you choose should be what is most meaningful.

Let's calculate the rate of violent crime for those aged 18 to 24 using the population standard of 1,000:

$$\left( \frac{527,410}{27,143,454} \right) = .0194 \times 1,000 = 19.4$$

We obtain a rate of violent crime for those aged 18 to 24 of 19.4 per 1,000 of those aged 18 to 24. When we calculate the victimization rates for each age category displayed in Table 2.5, a very different picture of vulnerability emerges. After standardizing for the size of the at-risk population, we see that those between the ages of 12 and 17 have the highest risk of violent victimization compared with all other age categories. In fact, the risk of victimization for those in this age group is more than twice as great as for those who are 35–49 years of age.

| Table 2.5 | Violent Crime Victims, Total Population, and Violent Crime Rates per 1,000 by Age Group, 2013 | | |
|---|---|---|---|
| Age Group | Number of Victims | Total Population | Rate per 1,000 |
| 12–17 | 545,370 | 24,633,684 | 22.1 |
| 18–24 | 527,410 | 27,143,454 | 19.4 |
| 24–34 | 604,500 | 39,891,724 | 15.2 |
| 35–49 | 684,150 | 65,240,931 | 10.5 |
| 50–64 | 566,990 | 41,860,232 | 13.5 |
| 65 and older | 112,760 | 34,991,753 | 3.2 |

*Source:* Adapted from *Criminal Victimization, 2013* by Truman and Langton, 2014, from the Bureau of Justice Statistics, U.S. Department of Justice.

Let's look at another dramatic example of how a frequency count can mislead you because of differences in population size, whereas a rate will not. In 2013 there were 99 murders and non-negligent manslaughters in Kansas City, Missouri. In that same year, there were 49 of these same crimes in Baton Rouge, Louisiana. From the numbers, Kansas City is more dangerous to live in compared with Baton Rouge; in fact there were almost twice as many murders there. But before you pack your bags and move to Baton Rouge, stop and think about it. Can you compare these raw frequency counts? No. You can't compare relative risk by using simple frequency counts in this case! In fact, the population of Baton Rouge at the time was only 230,212, whereas the population in Kansas City was nearly a half-million (465,514). Now let's calculate the rate of homicide per 100,000 people in each city:

$$\text{Rate for Kansas City} = \left(\frac{99}{465,514}\right) = .000212 \times 100,000 = 21.2$$

$$\text{Rate for Baton Rouge} = \left(\frac{49}{230,212}\right) = .000212 \times 100,000 = 21.2$$

Amazing! The relative risk for becoming a murder victim in both Kansas City and Baton Rouge was the same in 2013. A final analogy that is often used to underscore the notion of relative risk will help cement this point. If you are like us, every time we are about to take off in an airplane, we get a bit nervous. In fact, when our son was very young, we occasionally took separate flights to ensure that if the airplane crashed, one of us would be alive to take care of him. Unfortunately, we weren't thinking very clearly because we both took the same taxi to the airport even when we were on different flights. The problem in this scenario is that we had a greater risk of being in an accident in the taxi on the way to and from the airport than we did on the flight. On average, flying kills about 200 people a year in the United States, whereas driving kills an average of 32,300 people (Motavalli, 2012). Let's assume a 2010 U.S. population of 308,745,538 and plug this number into a rate per 100,000 as we have done here:

$$\text{Rate of Death for Flying} = \left(\frac{200}{308,745,538}\right) = .00000064 \times 1,000,000 = .64$$

$$\text{Rate of Death for Driving} = \left(\frac{32,300}{308,745,538}\right) = .0001046 \times 100,000 = 104.6$$

Our thinking about taking separate flights but the same taxi to the airport was really flawed! Remember that a **ratio** is a number that expresses the relationship between two numbers and indicates their relative size. As you saw earlier, the ratio of $x$ to $y$ is determined by dividing $x$ by $y$. A ratio for the relative risk of dying while driving compared with flying is 104.6 / .064 = 1,634. Wow! This tells us that the risk of dying while driving is 1,634 times greater compared with flying. Think about that the next time you get behind the wheel of your car! Buckle up!

> **Ratio:** Expresses the relationship between two numbers and indicates their relative size.

## Proportions and Percentages

Two other common techniques used to present information about variables are **proportions** and **percentages**. These measures are really special kinds of ratios obtained by dividing the number of observations from a subset of your sample by the total number in your sample. In other words, a proportion is obtained by dividing the number of counts for a given event ($f$) by the total number of events ($n$). More specifically, proportions are obtained using the following formula:

> **Proportions:** Number of some value in a variable distribution that is divided by total possible scores.

$$\text{Proportion} = \frac{\text{Number in subset of sample}}{\text{Total number in sample}} = \frac{f}{n} \qquad (2\text{-}2)$$

A proportion may also be called a **relative frequency** because it expresses the number of cases in a given subset ($f$) relative to the total number of cases ($n$). In this text, we use the terms "proportion" and "relative frequency" interchangeably.

Percentages are obtained simply by multiplying a proportion by 100. This standardizes the numbers to a base of 100, which is generally easier for an audience to interpret:

$$\text{Percent} = \frac{f}{n} \times 100 = \text{Proportion} \times 100 \qquad (2\text{-}3)$$

> **Percentages:** Number of some value in a variable distribution that is divided by total possible scores and then is multiplied by 100.

> **Relative frequency:** See Proportions.

Let's go through an example. Using data from the NCVS for 2013, Table 2.6 presents the total number of each type of victimization, the total number of each that was reported to police, the proportion reported, and the percent reported to police. If we were attempting to understand the differences in reporting behavior across different types of crimes, comparing the number of crimes reported would not tell us anything about which crime was most likely to be reported. However, examining either the proportion or the percentage columns tells us a great deal. We can easily see that rape and sexual assaults (.35) are the least likely violent crimes to be reported to police. The crime most likely to be reported to police is motor vehicle theft. Still, it is quite interesting that almost 1/4 (100% – 76% = 24%) of motor vehicle thefts are never reported to police.

| Table 2.6 | **Total Number, Number Reported, Proportion, and Percentage of Crimes Reported to Police by Type of Crime (NCVS 2013)** | | | |
|---|---|---|---|---|
| *Type of Crime* | *Total Number (n)* | *Number Reported (f)* | *Proportion (f / n)* | *Percent (f / n) × 100* |
| **Violent Crime** | **3,041,170** | **1,398,938** | **.46** | **46** |
| Rape/Sexual Assault | 173,610 | 60,073 | .35 | 35 |
| Robbery | 369,070 | 250,967 | .68 | 68 |
| Assault | 2,600,920 | 1,118,395 | .43 | 43 |
| Aggravated | 633,090 | 405,177 | .64 | 64 |
| Simple | 2,046,600 | 777,708 | .38 | 38 |
| Domestic Violence | 589,140 | 335,809 | .57 | 57 |
| Intimate Partner | 369,310 | 210,506 | .57 | 57 |
| Stranger Violence | 1,244,560 | 609,834 | .49 | 49 |
| Violence w/Injury | 849,240 | 305,726 | .56 | 56 |
| **Property Crime** | **11,531,420** | **4,151,311** | **.36** | **36** |
| Burglary | 2,458,360 | 1,401,265 | .57 | 57 |
| Motor Vehicle Theft | 555,660 | 422,301 | .76 | 76 |
| Personal Theft | 9,070,680 | 2,630,497 | .29 | 29 |

*Source:* Adapted from Tables 4 and 6 of *Criminal Victimization, 2013* by Truman and Langton, 2014, from the Bureau of Justice Statistics, U.S. Department of Justice.

| Table 2.7 | Murder Rates by State per 100,000 Population (FBI, 2013a) | | |
|---|---|---|---|
| Alabama | 7.2 | Montana | 2.2 |
| Alaska | 4.6 | Nebraska | 3.1 |
| Arizona | 5.4 | Nevada | 5.8 |
| Arkansas | 5.4 | New Hampshire | 1.7 |
| California | 4.6 | New Jersey | 4.5 |
| Colorado | 3.4 | New Mexico | 6.0 |
| Connecticut | 2.4 | New York | 3.3 |
| Delaware | 4.2 | North Carolina | 4.8 |
| Florida | 5.0 | North Dakota | 2.2 |
| Georgia | 5.6 | Ohio | 3.9 |
| Hawaii | 1.5 | Oklahoma | 5.1 |
| Idaho | 1.7 | Oregon | 2.0 |
| Illinois | 5.5 | Pennsylvania | 4.7 |
| Indiana | 5.4 | Rhode Island | 2.9 |
| Iowa | 1.4 | South Carolina | 6.2 |
| Kansas | 3.9 | South Dakota | 2.4 |
| Kentucky | 3.8 | Tennessee | 5.0 |
| Louisiana | 10.8 | Texas | 4.3 |
| Maine | 1.8 | Utah | 1.7 |
| Maryland | 6.4 | Vermont | 1.6 |
| Massachusetts | 2.0 | Virginia | 3.8 |
| Michigan | 6.4 | Washington | 2.3 |
| Minnesota | 2.1 | West Virginia | 3.3 |
| Mississippi | 6.5 | Wisconsin | 2.8 |
| Missouri | 6.1 | Wyoming | 2.9 |

*Source:* Adapted from Table 4 of *Crime In the United States* 2013 from the Federal Bureau of Investigation.

# Units of Analysis

The final issue we discuss in this chapter is often referred to as the unit of analysis. The **units of analysis** is the particular unit or object we have gathered our data about and to which we apply our statistical methods. Stated differently, our unit of analysis is whatever constitutes an observation in our data set. For example, are our observations or data points made up of persons? Prisons? Court cases? States? Nations? In social research, we employ many different levels of aggregation for research. Sometimes we use questionnaires or interviews to obtain data from individuals. The NCVS, for example, interviews individuals in households from around the United States and asks them about their experiences with criminal victimization. In this particular research, the unit of analysis is the individual or person because the data are obtained from individual respondents, but these data can also be aggregated to the household level.

In other instances, the unit of analysis is a group or collectivity. Often, these data originally were collected from individuals and then combined, or aggregated, to form a collectivity. For example, the Federal Bureau of Investigation (FBI) collects information about the number of crimes reported by individuals to local police departments. However, the FBI aggregates this information, identifying what state the report came from and, in some cases, what city and/or county. Depending on what data you use, then, the unit of analysis may be states, counties, or cities.

As an example of data at the state level of analysis, Table 2.7 presents the homicide rate per 100,000 population for each state. This information is collected by each local law enforcement agency within a state, and then this information is aggregated to reflect the total number of people killed during this time period. Even though the information is based on small levels of aggregation (e.g., law enforcement agencies), the units of analysis in this case are the individual states, not the individual agencies.

This concept is important when making statistical interpretations from data as you will see in the next chapter. We can only make generalizations about the units of analysis for which our data represent. For example, if we have state-level data and we find that states that have higher rates of poverty also tend to have higher rates of murder, we can generalize this find to the states only not to

**Units of analysis:** Particular units or aggregations (e.g., people and cities) that constitute an observation in a data set.

counties or cities. Nor can we say that individuals who live under conditions of poverty are more likely to experience a homicide. Only if we were analyzing individual victims and offenders could we make statements about individual factors related to lethal violence. We will remind you of this throughout the book!

# Summary

We hope that you now have a better understanding of the differences between the many types of variables and the many levels of measurement used in criminological research. It is essential that you be fully familiar with these concepts so that you can understand their statistical applications. We have classified the two most general measurement levels of variables as being qualitative and quantitative. Qualitative variables tell us "what kind" or "what category" a variable's value denotes, and the values of quantitative variables give us numeric information regarding "how much" or the "quantity" a value contains. Within these two categories, we have also specified the conditions under which a variable can be defined as measured at the nominal, ordinal, interval, or ratio level. These levels are hierarchical in nature and can be thought of as a sort of quantitative hierarchy. Values of nominal-level variables only differ in kind or quality and have no numerical distinction. Ordinal variables have values with a rank order. In addition to an inherent rank order, the distance between categories of an interval-level variable has a known and constant value. And finally, not only can distances be determined between values of a ratio-level variable, but also these distances are based on a true-zero point. The remainder of the chapter examined the differences between simple counts of a phenomenon (referred to as frequencies) and rates, ratios, proportions, and percentages. The final section discussed the units of analysis used in research.

## Key Terms

➤ Review key terms with eFlashcards. **⑤SAGE** edge™

| | | |
|---|---|---|
| alphanumeric data 26 | frequencies 34 | qualitative variable 26 |
| binary variable 33 | frequency distribution 25 | quantitative variable 26 |
| categorical variable 26 | interval-level variable 31 | rate 34 |
| constant 25 | interval–ratio level of measurement 33 | ratio 36 |
| continuous measures 33 | level of measurement 28 | ratio-level variable 32 |
| continuous variable 26 | nominal-level variable 28 | relative frequency 37 |
| count 34 | numeric data 26 | units of analysis 38 |
| dichotomy 33 | ordinal-level variable 28 | variable 25 |
| distribution 25 | percentage 36 | |
| empirical distribution 25 | proportion 36 | |

## Key Formulas

Rate (equation 2-1):

$$\text{Rate} = \frac{\text{Number in subset}}{\text{Total number}} \times \text{Constant (e.g., 1,000)}$$

Proportions (equation 2-2):

$$\text{Proportion} = \frac{\text{Number in subset of sample}}{\text{Total number in sample}} = \frac{f}{n}$$

Percentages (equation 2-3):

$$\text{Percent} = \frac{f}{n} \times 100 = \text{Proportion} \times 100$$

## Practice Problems

➤ Test your understanding of chapter content.
Take the practice quiz. **⑤SAGE** edge™

1. For each of the following variables, define the level of measurement as either qualitative or quantitative and, further, as one of the four more distinct levels: nominal, ordinal, interval, or ratio:

   a. A convicted felon's age in years

   b. A driver's score on the breathalizer exam

   c. The fine for a parking ticket

   d. The specific offense code of a felony

   e. A defendant's gender

   f. Fines levied on industrial companies convicted of violating the Clean Air Act

2. What distinguishes a variable measured at the ordinal level from a variable measured at the interval level of measurement? What more does the ratio level of measurement add to this?

3. In a study examining the effects of arrest on convicted drunk drivers' future drunk-driving behavior, which is the independent variable and which is the dependent variable?

4. If we are interested in determining the extent to which males and females are more or less afraid to walk outside alone at night, which variable would we designate as our independent variable and which as our dependent variable?

5. To compute a rate of violent crime victimizations against people 14–18 years old, what would we use as the numerator and what as the denominator?

6. What are the advantages of rates over frequency counts? Give an example.

7. From the following table, compute the proportions and percentages of the household crime victimizations that were reported to the police by the loss value of the victimization:

|  | f | Proportion | % |
|---|---|---|---|
| Less than $10 | 16 |  |  |
| $10–$49 | 39 |  |  |
| $50–$99 | 48 |  |  |
| $100–$249 | 86 |  |  |
| $250–$999 | 102 |  |  |
| $1,000 or more | 251 |  |  |
|  | $n = 542$ |  |  |

8. Patrick Schnapp (2015) examined the effect of immigration on homicide rates in 146 U.S. cities. He found that rates of immigration in cities did not affect the homicide rates. In this study, what were the units of analysis? Another study by Jason Rydberg and Jesenia Pizarro (2014) examined the factors related to homicide clearance rates. They found that homicide cases in which the victims were more involved in deviant lifestyles took longer to be cleared by arrest compared with victims who were not engaged in deviance. In this study, what were the units of analysis?

9. To test the existence of a relationship between unemployment and crime, we use data from 50 states of the United States. What are the units of analysis? What would you select to be the independent variable? What would you deem to be the dependent variable?

10. Suppose we are interested in the amount of time police departments took to respond to reports of crime. We track response times for several police departments within large metropolitan areas to see whether there are any differences based on the location of the jurisdiction. In this study, what are the units of analysis?

## SPSS Exercises

➤ Explore additional data sets. $SAGE edge™

| Data for Exercise | |
|---|---|
| Data Set | Description |
| 2012 states data.sav | This data set compiles official statistics from various official sources, such as the census, health department records, and police departments. It includes basic demographic data, crime rates, and incidence rates for various illnesses and infant mortality for entire states. |
| Variables for Exercise | |
| Variable Name | Description |
| State | The state from which data were collected. |
| Murdercat | An indicator for the rate at which murders occur. |
| Perindpoverty | The proportion of individuals below the poverty line. |
| BurglaryRt | An indicator for the rate at which burglaries occur. |
| MedianIncome | The median income for a state. |

1. First, take a look at the description and variable information in "variable view" in the 2010 states data set. What is the unit of analysis for this data?

2. In variable view, find the following variables and look at the variable and value labels. For each variable, identify if it is a 1) quantitative or qualitative measure, 2) its level of measurement, and 3) if appropriate, the unit that it is measured in:

   a. State
   b. Murdercat
   c. Perindpoverty
   d. BurglaryRt
   e. MedianIncome

3. In data view, find Alabama and Alaska (rows 1 and 2). What is the burglary rate for each state? Can you think of any reason for the differences between the two states?

4. **Creating a frequency table in SPSS:** We want to create a frequency table for the variable Murdercat. To do this select analyze->descriptives->frequencies and put Murdercat into the box on the right. Looking at the output window, what proportion of states have 0–3 murders per 100,000? What proportion have fewer than 9 murders per 100,000?

   a. **Sorting data in SPSS:** Let's identify which state(s) have the highest murder rate by sorting the Murdercat variable. To do this, go into data view and scroll until you find the variable Murdercat. Right click on the variable name for Murdercat and select "sort descending," which will sort the data so high values are on top. You can also sort cases by selecting data->sort cases and then placing Murdercat in the box. Now scroll left. What state(s) have the highest murder rates?

## STUDENT STUDY SITE

## $SAGE edge™

**WANT A BETTER GRADE?**

Get the tools you need to sharpen your study skills. Access practice quizzes, eFlashcards, data sets, and exercises at **edge.sagepub.com/bachmansccj4e**.

CHAPTER 3

# Understanding Data Distributions

## Tabular and Graphical Techniques

 *Done any exciting sums lately?*

*I don't just sum, Miles told her. There's much more to my life than that.*

*Is there? Alicia asked, trying to sound interested.*

*Yes, said Miles. Sometimes I draw graphs.*

—Sarah Rees Brennan

*Often the most effective ways to describe, explore, and summarize a set of numbers—even a large set—is to look at pictures of those numbers.*

—Edward Tufte

---

**LEARNING OBJECTIVES**

1. Describe the purpose of frequency distributions to examine a variable.

2. Identify bar charts and pie charts and the types of variables for which they are used.

3. Explain the usefulness of a grouped frequency distribution for a quantitative variable.

4. Describe the difference between a histogram and a bar chart.

5. Describe the difference between a histogram and line graph.

6. Discuss the concept of cumulative frequencies and cumulative percentages.

7. Identify the shape of a distribution and determine types of skewness.

8. Describe time plots and the concept of smoothing data.

# ▣ Introduction

In general, the rate of gun violence in the United States has been decreasing steadily during the past two decades. In fact, the rate of both fatal and nonfatal gun violence has been *decreasing* (Truman & Langton, 2014). Despite this fact, most Americans believe that gun violence has *increased* in recent years (Cohn et al., 2013). With one glance, we can capture these two facts with a chart displaying gun violence rates along with attitudes toward gun violence, as done in Figure 3.1. From this figure, you can clearly see the difference between empirical reality and perceptions. Of course, we could have also displayed this information in table form with the actual numbers, but sometimes, a picture is worth a thousand words, to borrow a cliché!

The first step (and one of the most important steps) in any statistical analysis is having a clear understanding of the general characteristics or appearance of your data. Understanding the distributions of your variables is referred to as **univariate analysis** because it is examining the distribution of one variable. One theme that we emphasize throughout this text is that no matter how simple or complex your statistical analysis is, there is no substitute for first knowing the shape and characteristics of your variables: the number of different values each variable has, the frequency or number of cases for each value, whether your observations "bunch up" at a few values of a variable or are more evenly distributed across the different values, and whether your data are skewed or have outliers. All of this very valuable information should be known *before* you do any additional statistical analyses.

> **Univariate analysis:** Examining the distribution of one variable.

The purpose of this chapter is to provide you with some tabular and graphical tools for examining and describing the characteristics and patterns of your data. A tabular display of your data can show you exactly how many values your variable has, how many cases or observations you have for each value (and the percentage or proportion of the total that the frequency represents), how extreme your values are, and the extent to which the cases cluster around a few values or are more evenly spread across the different values. The graphical presentation of the distribution of a variable can display much of the same information in picture form, although usually with much less detail. One advantage that a graphical display of your data has over a tabular presentation, however, is that it immediately and vividly shows you what your data look like. What a graphical display of your data may lack in precision, then, it makes up for in clarity. In statistics a picture is frequently worth a thousand numbers! A glance at a graphical presentation of data can reveal some very important features of your data. As you will see, we strongly recommend using both tabular and graphical displays to get the complete picture of your data. You will also learn that preparing and communicating to others about the characteristics of your data is as much art as it is science and that the key question to ask when constructing tables and graphs from your data is, "Is this format effectively communicating the important characteristics of these variables?" In this chapter, we will treat nominal-level variables as qualitative and ordinal, and interval/ratio-level variables as quantitative.

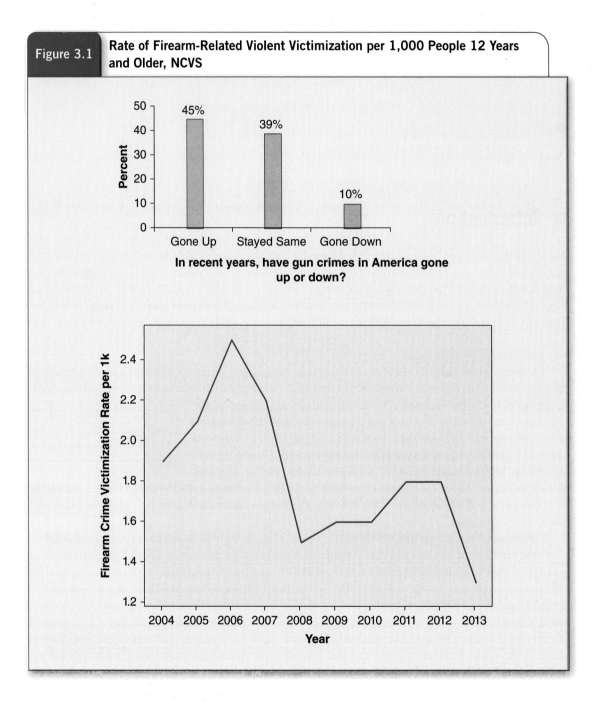

**Figure 3.1** Rate of Firearm-Related Violent Victimization per 1,000 People 12 Years and Older, NCVS

## The Tabular and Graphical Display of Qualitative Data

Recall from Chapter 2 that qualitative variables—those measured at the nominal level—capture differences *in kind* among the values only. That is, the values of a nominal-level variable differ in quality and not quantity, which is why they are referred to as qualitative data. To refresh your memory, gender is a qualitative variable with two values, male and female, that differ only in kind: Males are only different from females; they do not have more "gender" (even if we add a third value like "transgender," it is still a nominal-level variable). Unlike quantitative variables, whose values differ in degree, therefore, nominal variables differ only in kind. The only sort of comparative statement we can make about different values of a nominal-level variable is simply that they are not the same. One of the easiest ways to show a nominal-level variable is to report some descriptive information about the variable's values, such as the frequency of each value and the percentage or proportion of the total for each value. This is done in a descriptive table of the variable.

## Frequency Tables

### Case Study

### An Analysis of Hate Crimes Using Tables

In Table 3.1 we report descriptive information for a nominal-level variable, the types of hate crime incidents reported by law enforcement agencies in the year 2013. Hate crimes are criminal acts that are perpetrated in part or entirely by personal prejudice or animosity against others because of their race, religion, sexual preference, ethnicity or national background, or some real or perceived disability.

In the *Hate Crimes Statistics Act of 1990,* the U.S. Congress required the collection of nationwide information about criminal acts that were motivated by hate or prejudice. To comply with this act, the Federal Bureau of Investigation (FBI) began to compile data about crimes across the United States that were motivated by racial, religious, sexual, or ethnic/national origin, as well as by disability hatred. This information is collected in a yearly report, *Hate Crime Statistics.* As part of their reporting to the FBI's Uniform Crime Reports Program, federal, state, and local law enforcement agencies report crimes that they have determined are motivated by these different forms of hate or bias.

Table 3.1 provides four pieces of information for this nominal-level variable: the different values of the variable hate crime (the basis of hate), the frequency of each value for the variable, the relative frequency or the proportion of the total number of cases for each value, and the percentage of the total for each value. Recall from the previous chapter that a frequency $(f)$ is just a count of the number of times each value appears or occurs, the proportion is a relative frequency found by dividing the frequency of each value by the total number of values or observations (proportion $= f/n$), and the percentage is found by multiplying the proportion by 100 (percent $= f/n \times 100$) to create a frequency standardized by 100. This tabular presentation of descriptive data, then, describes a variable by displaying the frequency, proportion, and percentage for each of its values.

According to Table 3.1, in the year 2013 there were a total of 5,922 reported incidents of single-bias hate crimes motivated by racial, religious, sexual, or ethnic/national origin, as well as by disability bias. A single-bias hate crime is one that is motivated by one source of bias (bias against someone's religion or race but not both). Table 3.1 breaks these 5,922 incidents down by the specific basis or nature of the bias (the different values of the variable "hate crime"). The qualitative variable we are interested in for this example is "hate crime," which takes on seven different nominal-level values: racial hatred, religious hatred, sexual orientation hatred, hatred directed at the victim's race/national origin, hatred because of the victim's disability, hatred because of the victim's gender, and lastly, hatred directed at the victim's gender identity. You should be able to determine that this is a nominal or qualitative

| Table 3.1 | Types of Hate Crime Incidents Reported to Police in 2013 | | |
|---|---|---|---|
| *Basis of Hate* | *f* | *Proportion* | *%* |
| Race | 2,871 | .485 | 48.5 |
| Religion | 1,031 | .174 | 17.4 |
| Sexual orientation | 1,233 | .208 | 20.8 |
| Ethnicity/national origin | 655 | .111 | 11.1 |
| Disability | 83 | .014 | 1.4 |
| Gender | 18 | .003 | .3 |
| Gender identity | 31 | .005 | .5 |
| Total | 5,922 | 1.000 | 100.0% |

*Source:* Adapted from *Hate Crimes Statistics—2013* from the Federal Bureau of Investigation (2013b).

variable because these values differ only in kind or quality. We can only say that one value of the hate crime variable is simply different from another value, not that one such crime is "more" or "less" of a hate crime than the other. For example, a racially motivated hate crime differs from a sexually motivated hate crime but is not "more" of a hate crime or more hateful than one motivated by a victim's sexual orientation. The distinction among the different values of hate crimes, then, is simply qualitative.

We can see from this table that of the 5,922 hate crimes that were reported by law enforcement agencies in 2013, 2,871 of them were motivated by racial hatred. In other words, there was a frequency of 2,871 incidents of racially motivated hate crimes. This is the frequency or count of racial hate crimes for that year. We can also see that dividing this frequency by 5,922 (2,871 / 5,922), the total number of hate crime incidents for that year, we conclude that the proportion of hate crimes that were racially motivated was .485, or just under one half of the total number of hate crime incidents that year. Multiplying this by 100 to obtain the percentage, we see that racial hate crimes constituted 48.5% of the total number of hate crimes in 2013.

Looking at Table 3.1, we can see that there were 1,031 hate crimes that were motivated by religious bias in 2013. This is the frequency of religiously motivated hate crimes for that year, and the proportion of hate crimes that were religiously motivated was .174, or 17.4% of the total. A total of 1,233 hate crimes were motivated by hatred against another's sexual preference, and the corresponding proportion of the total number of hate crimes is .208, or 20.8%. The frequency of hate crimes motivated by bias against the victim's ethnicity or national origin was 655 with a corresponding proportion of .111, or 11.1%, of the total number of hate crimes. There were only 83 hate crimes motivated by the victim's disability in 2013, comprising .014, or a little more than 1%, of the total number of hate crimes reported in 2013. We will let you figure out the proportion and percentage of the total for the other two hate crimes—those resulting from gender and gender identity—and compare these with the figures in the table. Finally, you should note that the frequency column will sum to the total number of observations (5,922 hate crimes), the column of proportions will sum to 1.0 (unless there is some rounding error), and the column of percentages will sum to 100.0 (again, unless there is some rounding error).

## Pie and Bar Charts

Although this tabular presentation of frequency, proportion, and percentage information is helpful in seeing the makeup of the different sources of hate crimes, we would now like to provide a graphical representation of this descriptive data, which may be more illustrative. When we have qualitative data, such as we have here with "hate crimes," we can graphically present the frequency, proportion, and percentage data in either a pie chart or a bar chart.

**Pie chart/bar chart:** Graphical ways to display nominal- or ordinal-level variables. These charts can include frequencies, proportions, or percentages. Pie charts represent quantities as slices and bar charts represent quantities as bars.

A **pie chart** is exactly what the term implies. It consists of a round "pie" shape divided into parts, or "slices," where each slice represents a separate value of the variable. The size of each slice of the pie is proportionate to the frequency (or proportion or percentage of the total) for each value; that is, the greater the contribution that a given value makes to the total number of observations, the larger the slice of the pie for that value. The total area of the pie chart should equal the number of observations if you are graphing the frequencies, 1.0 if you are graphing proportions, and 100 if you are graphing percentages. Figure 3.2 shows what a pie chart would look like for the frequency distribution reported in Table 3.1.

This pie chart of the frequency data does a very nice job of clearly showing the characteristics of the hate crime data. First, it reports the frequency of each value, as did Table 3.1. It shows that there were 2,871 racially motivated hate crimes reported in 2013, which is the largest slice of the pie. It shows about equally sized slices for crimes motivated by religious hatred (1,031) and by sexual orientation (1,233); a much smaller slice for hate crimes committed because of the victim's ethnicity or national origin (655); and a very small, almost indiscernible slice of the pie for disability-based hate crimes (83) and hate crimes motivated by gender (18) or gender identity (31). The size of each pie slice vividly shows the relative contribution of each value to the total number of observations. The relative sizes of the slices clearly indicate that almost one half of the hate crimes reported by the police in 2013 were racially motivated, about an equal proportion were motivated by either religious or sexual prejudice, and relatively few were motivated by disability or gender-based bias.

Figure 3.3 provides the same frequency data in the form of a pie chart but adds the percentage for each value along with the frequency count. There is no reason why we could not have reported the proportion rather than the percentage in Figure 3.3, but it is more conventional to report percentages rather than proportions since they make more intuitive sense to most people. We do, however, think that it is very important to report both the frequency for each value in a pie chart and its corresponding percentage (or proportion), as we have done in Figure 3.3.

We will go through one final example of tabular data with a corresponding pie chart. Table 3.1 reveals that 1,031 hate crimes motivated by religious hatred were reported in 2013. Table 3.2 breaks these hate crimes down into more specific subtypes. As shown, most of these hate-related crimes were directed against those of perceived Jewish faith ($f = 625$; 60.6%). These incidents greatly surpassed anti-Catholic ($f = 70$; 6.8%), anti-Protestant ($f = 35$; 3.4%), and Anti-Islamic hate crimes ($f = 135$; 13.1%).

We take these frequency and percentage data and create a pie chart for graphical illustration, as shown in Figure 3.4. Unlike the previous pie chart, this one appears a bit cluttered, and although it is clear that most hate crimes motivated by religious bias are anti-Jewish, the other details are hard to discern.

When your pie chart of qualitative data looks a little messy and you think you are losing your ability to communicate the characteristics of your data, it is time to consider using a second graphical form to display the descriptive data at the nominal or ordinal level that we have been discussing: frequency counts, proportions, and percentages. Like the pie chart, the **bar chart** is appropriate for the graphical display of qualitative data only (nominal and ordinal). A bar chart represents the frequencies, proportions, or percentages of each value by a vertical or horizontal bar. The width of the bar is equal to 1.0, and the height (or length for a horizontal bar chart) is equal to the value's frequency, proportion, or percentage (it does

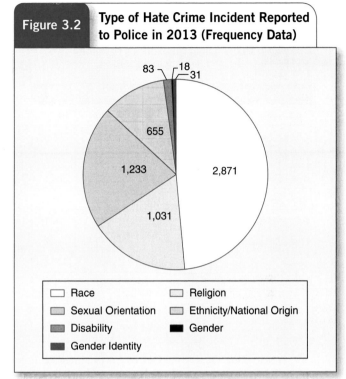

**Figure 3.2** Type of Hate Crime Incident Reported to Police in 2013 (Frequency Data)

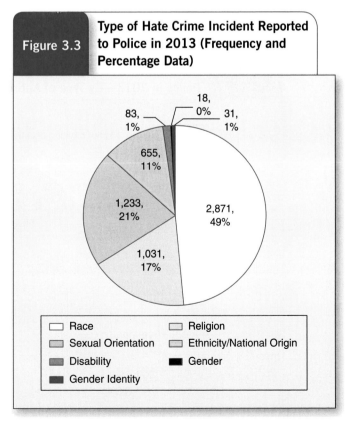

**Figure 3.3** Type of Hate Crime Incident Reported to Police in 2013 (Frequency and Percentage Data)

| Table 3.2 | Hate Crime Incidents Reported to Police in 2013 That Were Motivated by Bias Against the Victim's Religion | | |

| Type of Religious Hate | f | Proportion | % |
|---|---|---|---|
| Anti-Jewish | 625 | .606 | 60.6 |
| Anti-Catholic | 70 | .068 | 6.8 |
| Anti-Protestant | 35 | .034 | 3.4 |
| Anti-Islamic | 135 | .131 | 13.1 |
| Anti-Other-Religions | 117 | .113 | 11.3 |
| Anti-Multireligious Group | 42 | .041 | 4.1 |
| Anti-Agnostic/Atheist | 7 | .007 | .7 |
| Total | 1,031 | 1.00 | 100% |

*Source:* Adapted from *Hate Crimes Statistics—2013* from the Federal Bureau of Investigation (2013b).

not matter which because the shape will be the same regardless). When we make the width of the bar equal to 1 and the height (or length) equal to the value's frequency (or proportion or percentage), the total area of a bar in a bar chart corresponds to the area represented by the frequency (or proportion or percentage) of that value.

Figure 3.5 shows a bar chart for the frequency data reported in Table 3.2. This is a vertical bar chart because the variable's different values are represented along the $x$ (horizontal) axis and the frequency scale is represented along the $y$ (vertical) axis. Note that the height of each bar can be followed to the $y$ axis to determine the frequency count, but in this bar chart, the frequencies are provided above each bar for easy reading. Note also that the bars in a bar chart are not connected to each other but are separated along the $x$ axis by a space or gap. This is intentional. It reminds us that the measurement for this variable is not continuous, with one value moving meaningfully along the continuum of numeric measurement to the next, but, rather, is discrete and qualitative. Anti-Catholic sentiment in a hate crime is not "more" of a hate crime than anti-Jewish sentiment; it is simply different. We could just as easily and meaningfully have these bars switched in our table with anti-Catholic sentiment coming before anti-Jewish sentiment. The placements of the values of this and other

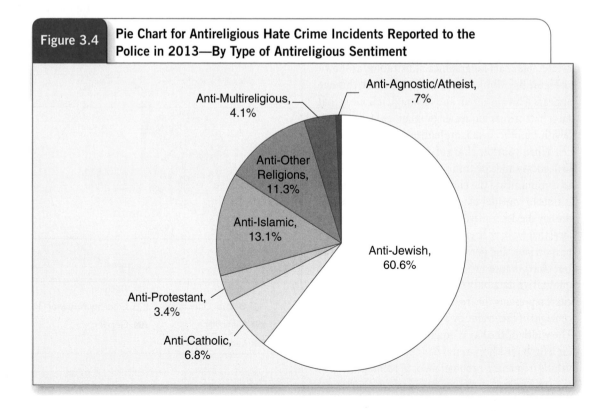

| Figure 3.4 | Pie Chart for Antireligious Hate Crime Incidents Reported to the Police in 2013—By Type of Antireligious Sentiment |

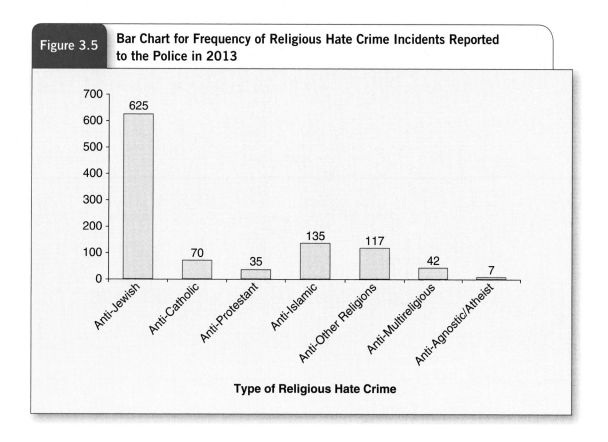

**Figure 3.5** Bar Chart for Frequency of Religious Hate Crime Incidents Reported to the Police in 2013

qualitative variables are simply distinctions in quality or kind, and their location along the x axis is arbitrary, which is why we can move their location around on the graph.

The bar chart in Figure 3.5 is more effective than the pie chart in communicating the distribution of these data because it appears less cluttered. We could just as easily have created a bar chart with the proportion data in Table 3.2 or the percentage data. Both pie charts and bar charts can be used for the graphical display of frequency counts, proportions, or percentages (or combinations of the three).

One advantage of a bar chart over a pie chart for graphing qualitative data is that you can create overlapping or double bar charts that employ more than one variable. Table 3.3 reports the percentage of arrests for violent, property, and total index offenses for both males and females for the year 2013. This simple tabular presentation of descriptive data reports only percentages and not raw frequencies or proportions, but a graph may help illustrate its features. The table shows that in the year 2013, males represented slightly less than 80% of the arrests for violent crimes in the United States, more than 60% of the property crimes, and almost 75% of the total index arrests.

These data are shown in a vertical bar chart in Figure 3.6. Note that in this figure we are graphing the percentage of the total for each value, not its frequency count. As you can see from this figure, the height of each bar corresponds to the percentage for that value. By tracing the height of each bar over to the y axis, you can determine the approximate percentage. Note, for

**Table 3.3** Percentage of Arrests for Violent Crimes, Property Crimes, and Total Index Crimes, by Gender—2013

| Crime Type | Percent Male | Percent Female |
|---|---|---|
| Violent Crimes | 79.9 | 20.1 |
| Property Crimes | 62.2 | 37.8 |
| Total Index Crimes | 73.5 | 26.5 |

*Source:* Adapted from Table 42 of *Crime In the United States* from the Federal Bureau of Investigation (2013a).

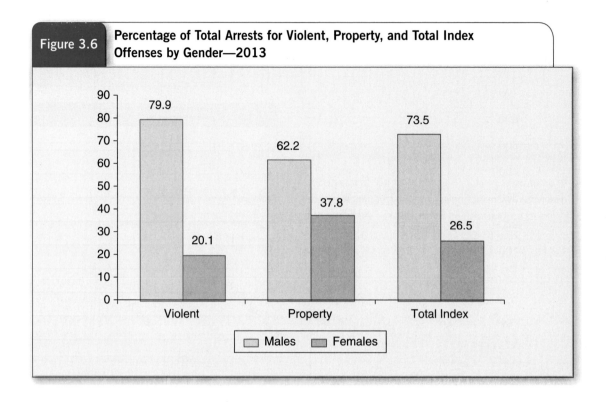

**Figure 3.6** Percentage of Total Arrests for Violent, Property, and Total Index Offenses by Gender—2013

example, by following the height of the bar for violent crimes, you can easily see that nearly 80% of the arrests for violent index crimes in 2013 were of men, 62% of all index property crimes were men, and approximately 74% of the arrests for all index crimes were of men. The data in Figure 3.6 are exactly the same as those in Table 3.3, but sometimes a figure is easier to interpret than a table.

## The Tabular and Graphical Display of Quantitative Data

### Ungrouped Distributions

Quantitative data are data measured at the ordinal, interval, or ratio level. The values of a quantitative variable express how much of the variable exists. As we learned in the previous chapter, ordinal-level variables consist of rank-ordered categories, whereas interval-level and ratio-level variables have values that consist of equidistant intervals that are continuous with either an arbitrary zero (interval scales) or an absolute zero (ratio scales). As with nominal-level data, we can present descriptive information for quantitative data in both tabular and graphical form.

## Case Study

### Police Response Time

We will start with a simple example consisting of ratio-level data. Table 3.4 shows the response time for a sample of fifty 911 calls (requests for police service) made to a local police department. The measurement unit is minutes, and each call time was rounded to the nearest minute. There is no ordering to these data; they simply appear in the order in which they occurred in the dispatcher's log sheet. Looking at these data does not provide much information about these response times because the information is disorganized and chaotic. This table is simply too difficult to read and comprehend. For example, it is not easy to locate the quickest and slowest response times, and we cannot easily determine whether the data tend to cluster around some typical response time.

We need to impose some order on these data so we can better understand them and know exactly what they suggest about police response times. The easiest way to organize these data is to create a table that includes descriptive information such as the frequency of each value, its proportion, and its percentage—just as we did with the qualitative data in the previous section. With quantitative data, however, we can provide even more information.

We begin the process of describing these data by first listing all values in the data in some meaningful order, either from lowest to highest (ascending order) or from highest to lowest (descending order). We list all values of the "911 response time" variable in ascending order in the first column of Table 3.5. In the second column, we report the frequency of each value ($f$), which is a count of the number of times each response time or value occurs in the data. In this case, each value represents the time it took the police to respond to a 911 call for police assistance. Table 3.5 is referred to as an **ungrouped frequency distribution**. It is an ungrouped distribution because we have recorded all values or the entire range of scores from the lowest to the highest with no score left out. The data values go from the lowest of 1 minute to the highest of 11 minutes, and all recorded times in between appear in the frequency distribution. An ungrouped frequency distribution, therefore, lists all of the values of the variable that exist in the data, along with how many times each value occurs.

We can see from Table 3.5 that the fastest the police responded to a 911 call was within 1 minute and that they did this 5 out of 50 times. The slowest police response time was 11 minutes, which occurred only once. You will note from the frequency column that the response times appear to cluster in the 2- to 6-minute range. It seems that most often the police responded to a 911 call in somewhere between 2 and 6 minutes. There are only a handful of very quick response times (a minute or less), and there were only a few responses after 7 minutes, with a diminished frequency at the longest response times. Finally, you can also see that the sum of the frequency column equals the number of scores or observations ($\sum f = n$). In these data, there were 50 recorded response times to 911 calls so the total number of cases is 50. As you can see, a frequency distribution for these data was relatively simple to

**Table 3.4 Hypothetical Response Times of the Police to a 911 Call (in Minutes)**

| 7 | 4 | 3 | 1 | 3 | 2 | 6 | 10 | 7 | 2 |
|---|---|---|---|---|---|---|---|---|---|
| 5 | 3 | 5 | 9 | 2 | 4 | 9 | 3 | 1 | 4 |
| 4 | 4 | 6 | 6 | 5 | 6 | 11 | 5 | 3 | 8 |
| 3 | 2 | 1 | 4 | 8 | 5 | 6 | 3 | 3 | 2 |
| 1 | 2 | 6 | 7 | 5 | 3 | 1 | 4 | 4 | 6 |

**Ungrouped frequency distribution:** Every value of a variable is displayed in contract to a grouped frequency distribution that displays intervals that correspond to the data values.

**Table 3.5 Ungrouped Frequency Distribution for 50 Police Response Times to a 911 Call for Service**

| Minutes | f | cf | p | cp | % | c% |
|---|---|---|---|---|---|---|
| 1 | 5 | 5 | .10 | .10 | 10 | 10 |
| 2 | 6 | 11 | .12 | .22 | 12 | 22 |
| 3 | 9 | 20 | .18 | .40 | 18 | 40 |
| 4 | 8 | 28 | .16 | .56 | 16 | 56 |
| 5 | 6 | 34 | .12 | .68 | 12 | 68 |
| 6 | 7 | 41 | .14 | .82 | 14 | 82 |
| 7 | 3 | 44 | .06 | .88 | 6 | 88 |
| 8 | 2 | 46 | .04 | .92 | 4 | 92 |
| 9 | 2 | 48 | .04 | .96 | 4 | 96 |
| 10 | 1 | 49 | .02 | .98 | 2 | 98 |
| 11 | 1 | 50 | .02 | 1.00 | 2 | 100% |
| Total | 50 | | 1.00 | | 100% | |

create, but it provides much more useful information, clarity, and organization than the data in Table 3.4. A simple frequency distribution has much to offer in helping you understand and communicate the important features of a quantitative variable.

---

**Cumulative frequency distribution:**
Frequency distribution reserved for ordinal or interval/ratio-level data made by starting with the lowest value of the variable (or the highest value) and cumulating (keeping a running tally or sum) the frequencies in each adjacent value until the highest value is reached (or the lowest value is reached).
The sum of a cumulative frequency distribution should be equal to the total number of cases (*n*).

---

In addition to a frequency distribution, Table 3.5 provides, in the third column, something called a **cumulative frequency distribution** (*cf*). The cumulative frequency distribution indicates how many scores were at or lower than a given value, or at a given value or higher, depending on how you tally the cumulative frequencies. You may have noticed that we did not report cumulative frequencies in the table from the previous section of this chapter, on qualitative data (Table 3.1). This is because qualitative data differ only in kind, not in degree. We cannot, therefore, speak of "more than" or "less than" or "lower than" with qualitative data.

The column of cumulative frequencies reported in Table 3.5 begins at the lowest value and cumulates until the highest value, and it is created in the following manner. In the first entry of the cumulative frequency column, enter the frequency for the first or lowest value. In this example, the first entry is 5, indicating that there were five instances where the police responded to a 911 call within 1 minute. Note that by subtracting this frequency of 5 from our total number of observations (50), we could also observe that there were 45 instances where the police took more than 1 minute in responding to a call. To continue with the cumulative frequency column, we add the frequency for the next value (2 minutes) to the first frequency. Thus, the second entry in the cumulative frequency column becomes 11. This tells us that there were 11 times when the police responded to a 911 call in 2 minutes or less (the five times they responded to a call in a minute or less and the six times they responded in between 1 and 2 minutes). We then proceed to the next value and note that there were nine instances when the police responded in between 2 and 3 minutes. Adding this to the cumulative frequency accumulated so far, we find that the next entry in the cumulative frequency column is 20 (5 + 6 + 9), indicating that the police responded to a 911 call within 3 minutes 20 times. We continue summing the frequencies for each value in succession. When we get to the last value of 11 minutes, the cumulative frequency is 50, telling us that the police responded to a 911 call in 11 minutes or less all 50 times. This should make intuitive sense because no call was responded to in more than 11 minutes and there were only 50 calls in our sample. The final entry in a cumulative frequency column should always equal the total number of observations, or *n*.

Cumulative frequencies like the one we just did where we start at the lowest value tell us how many observations were at or less than a given value (and by implication, how many were more than a given value). For example, Table 3.5 shows that 28 of the 50 calls for police assistance (more than one half) were responded to in 4 minutes or less. Therefore, slightly less than one half took more than 4 minutes to respond to. We also know that 44 of the 50 calls were responded to in 7 minutes or less. This implies that six calls took more than 7 minutes to respond to. We could also just as easily have calculated our cumulated frequency distribution in the opposite direction, starting with the highest value and cumulative frequencies in each adjacent lower value. Doing it this way is perfectly acceptable and would give us at any point the number of observations that were at a given value or greater.

Table 3.5 also reports other descriptive information about the variable "police response time," including the familiar column of proportions and percentages. Recall that a proportion is just a relative frequency that indicates the frequency of a given value relative to the total number of cases and is calculated as ($p = f / n$).

---

**Cumulative proportions:** Identical to a cumulative frequency distribution except that what is cumulated is the proportion at each value. The cumulative summing of proportions can go either from the lowest to the highest score or from the highest to the lowest score. The sum of a cumulative percentage distribution should be 1.0.

---

We can determine from Table 3.5 that .10 of the response times were within 1 minute, .12 of them were responded to in between 1 and 2 minutes, .18 were responded to in between 2 and 3 minutes, and .02 of them took 11 minutes to respond to. The column next to the proportion column consists of the **cumulative proportions** (*cp*). These cumulative proportions are calculated in the same manner as the cumulative frequencies.

Begin with the proportion of the first value, .10, which indicates that .10 (about 1 in 10) of the 911 calls were responded to in 1 minute or less. Since .12 of the calls were responded to in between 1 and 2 minutes, we add this to the

.10 and note that .22 (the second entry in the *cp* column) of the calls were responded to in 2 minutes or less. We continue summing the proportions for each successive value until we reach the last value of 11 minutes. Here we see that 1.0, or all, of the 911 calls were responded to within 11 minutes. The last entry in a column of cumulative proportions should be 1.0 (or close to that in the presence of rounding error). Cumulative proportions are useful in revealing the proportion of cases at a given value or less. For example, we can quickly see from Table 3.5 that slightly more than one half (.56) of the 911 calls were responded to within 4 minutes and more than 9 out of 10 (.92) within 8 minutes (implying that only .08, or 1 – .92, of the 911 calls took more than 8 minutes to respond to). As with our cumulative frequency column, we could have started at the highest value and cumulated proportions toward the lowest value.

The next column of numbers in Table 3.5 shows the percentage for each value. Recall that a percentage is simply a standardized frequency, standardized in units of 100, and is calculated as percent $= (f / n) \times 100$, or the proportion of a value multiplied by 100. We can determine from Table 3.5 that 10% of the 911 calls were responded to within 1 minute, 12% were responded to in between 1 and 2 minutes, nearly 20% (18%) were responded to in between 2 and 3 minutes, and only 4% took between 8 and 9 minutes to respond to.

The final column in Table 3.5 is a column of **cumulative percentages** (c%). These are generally more useful than cumulative proportions because they are easier for most people to comprehend. The cumulative percentages are calculated in exactly the same manner as the cumulative frequencies and cumulative proportions. For example, take the percentage of the first value, 10% of the calls were responded to within 1 minute, and add that to the percentage for the second value (12%). This reveals that 22% of the fifty 911 calls were responded to in 2 minutes or less. Now add the percentage for the third value, response times between 2 and 3 minutes, and we can see that 4 in 10 (40%) of the calls were responded to within 3 minutes. By subtraction, 60% of the calls took longer than 3 minutes to respond to. Finally, we can see that more than 9 in 10 of the 911 calls (92%) were responded to in 8 minutes or less. The final entry in a column of cumulative percentages should be 100%, or close to that if there is rounding error. Cumulative percentages can also be calculated in either direction. Table 3.5, then, provides a great deal of information about our sample of fifty 911 calls to the police. You will not be surprised, however, to learn that we can also display this information in a graphical display. The first we will examine is called a histogram.

> **Cumulative percentages:** Identical to a cumulative frequency distribution except that what is cumulated is the percentage at each value. The cumulative summing of percentages can go either from the lowest to the highest score or from the highest to lowest score. The sum of a cumulative percentage distribution should be 100%.

## Histograms

A **histogram** is very much like a bar chart. It is a graph of bars where the width of each bar on the *x* axis is equal to one (1.0) and the height of the bar on the *y* axis is equal to the value's frequency, percentage, or proportion. However, there are two important differences between a bar chart and a histogram. The first is that in the histogram, the bars are connected to one another, indicating that the underlying measurement continuum is continuous and quantitative. Recall that in a bar chart, the bars are separated by a space or gap to indicate that the underlying measurement is discrete and qualitative, rather than quantitative. Second, the bars on a histogram are placed on the graph from lowest score to highest score. In the bar chart, the placement of the values along the *x* axis is arbitrary.

> **Histogram:** Method of graphing the distribution of an interval/ratio-level variable. It consists of a series of bars at each value of a variable where the height of the bar reflects the frequency of a value, its proportion, or its percentage.

Figure 3.7 shows a histogram for the ungrouped frequency distribution reported in Table 3.5. In graphical form, it shows that the most frequent response time was 3 minutes and that the data cluster around the 3- to 6-minute response time values. You can also see that the reported response times fall off fairly substantially after 6 minutes. At least in this sample, the police do seem to respond to a 911 call within 6 minutes.

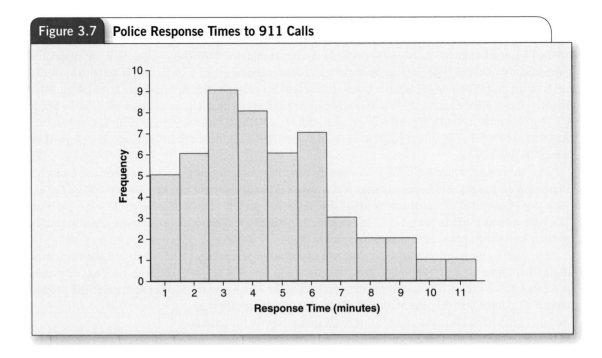

**Figure 3.7** | **Police Response Times to 911 Calls**

## Line Graphs or Polygons

**Line graph (polygon):** Method of graphing interval/ratio-level data.

If we have continuous data, we can also use other graphs to illustrate the frequency, proportion, or percentage distribution. One of these graphs is a **line graph** or **polygon** (frequency polygon, proportion polygon, or percentage polygon). The difference between a histogram and a polygon is that in a polygon, the frequency (or percentage or proportion) is represented by a point or dot above each score, rather than by a rectangular bar, where the height of the point corresponds to the magnitude of the frequency. The points or dots are then connected by a series of straight lines. Figure 3.8 illustrates the use of a frequency polygon for the 911 response call data in Table 3.5.

Like the histogram, this frequency polygon clearly shows that the response times to 911 calls in this sample cluster in the range of 3–6 minutes. It also clearly shows that there are far fewer response times that are 7 minutes or more. In other words, although there are some response times that are 8, 9, 10, and 11 minutes, there are not very many of them. Figure 3.9 illustrates that you could also create a polygon with the percentage data (or even the proportion data), and the story would be the same. The most likely response time (18% of the time) was 3 minutes, followed by 4 minutes, with a clustering of cases in the response time range of 3–6 minutes.

Finally, it is possible to graph the cumulative data as well—cumulative frequencies, cumulative percentages, and cumulative proportions—in the form of a line graph or polygon. Figure 3.10 shows a cumulative percentage polygon, but keep in mind that we could just as easily have graphed the cumulative frequencies or cumulative proportions. In the cumulative percentage polygon, the entry for each value of the variable corresponds to the percentage of cases or scores at that value or less. To interpret this cumulative percentage graph, simply move up from a value on the x axis until you hit the line, and then move over to the y axis to find the percentage of the cases that are at that value or less. For example, start at the value of 3 minutes, move up to hit the line and then over to the y axis, and you will discover that 40% of the response times for the police were in 3 minutes or less. Approximately 80% of the response times were within 6 minutes, and 90% were within 8 minutes. Of course, 100% of the calls were responded to in 11 minutes or less. You should know that since cumulative percentages are calculated by

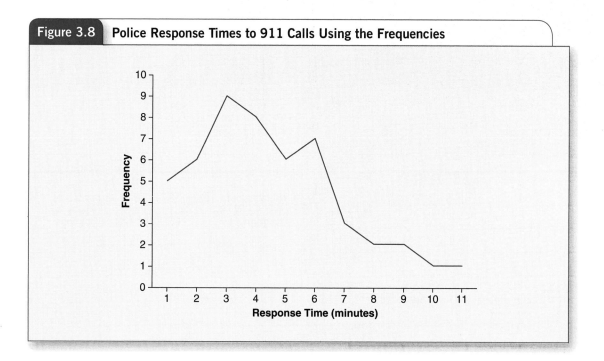

**Figure 3.8**   **Police Response Times to 911 Calls Using the Frequencies**

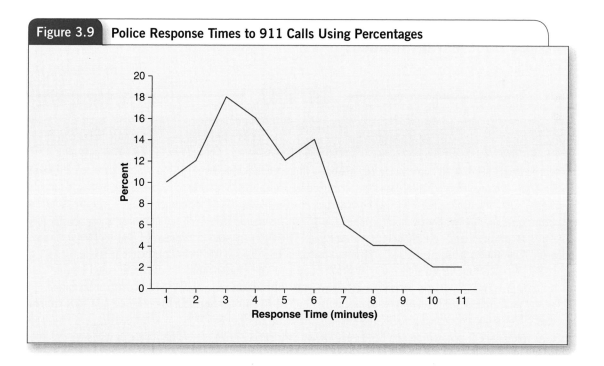

**Figure 3.9**   **Police Response Times to 911 Calls Using Percentages**

summing the successive percentages for each value, the line on a cumulative percentage polygon should never fall; it should always be either rising or flat. This holds true for graphs of cumulative frequencies and cumulative proportions as well.

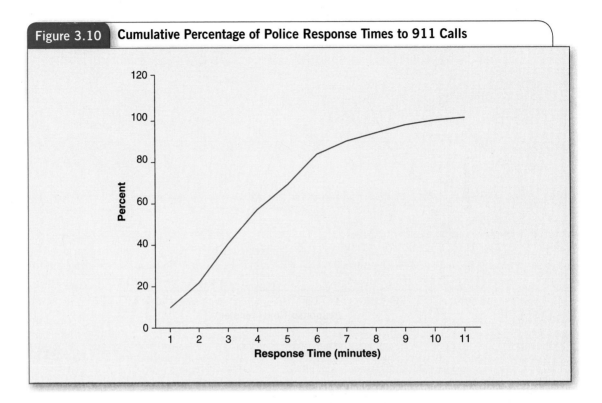

**Figure 3.10** | **Cumulative Percentage of Police Response Times to 911 Calls**

## Grouped Frequency Distributions

## Case Study

## Recidivism

From prison release data, we know that nearly two out of three people released from prison will be rearrested within one year. Table 3.6 presents hypothetical data from a sample of 120 male offenders released from a penitentiary and followed until they were arrested for a new offense. For each person, we have recorded the number of days he was free before he committed a new offense. The first value in the table, 25, implies that someone was out in the community for 25 days before he committed a new offense or arrested for a parole violation, the second value shows that another person was free for 37 days before he was rearrested, and the last person in Table 3.6 was free for 34 days before he was rearrested.

This variable is measured at the ratio level. Notice that all 120 released offenders were rearrested at some time. Criminologists sometimes refer to this variable as a "time until failure" variable (because a rearrest is considered a "failure" for corrections). Since our interest here is the time until failure, all 120 of the hypothetical offenders are rearrested. Of course, not everyone released from prison is arrested again!

As you can see, it is hard to comprehend a pattern with the data in Table 3.6. We cannot easily tell much about the time it took for the typical person to be rearrested. It is even difficult to determine very simple information, such as how quickly the first person was arrested and how long it was before the last offender was rearrested. The first thing we would like to do with our data, therefore, is to organize it. So far, we have learned how to organize data into an ungrouped frequency distribution.

Table 3.7 shows the ungrouped frequency distribution for these data. This ungrouped frequency distribution gives us some clarity but not very much. We can now see, for example, that one person was rearrested in 17 days,

| Table 3.6 | Number of Days Until Rearrest for Sample of 120 Released Offenders | | | | |
|---|---|---|---|---|---|
| 25 | 30 | 31 | 33 | 19 | 36 |
| 37 | 34 | 39 | 32 | 33 | 37 |
| 20 | 27 | 38 | 29 | 23 | 36 |
| 29 | 39 | 30 | 28 | 33 | 35 |
| 27 | 27 | 25 | 24 | 29 | 38 |
| 28 | 26 | 34 | 23 | 36 | 17 |
| 40 | 31 | 29 | 28 | 33 | 38 |
| 26 | 31 | 32 | 35 | 37 | 32 |
| 30 | 29 | 37 | 33 | 33 | 25 |
| 18 | 19 | 33 | 40 | 31 | 29 |
| 27 | 23 | 40 | 24 | 36 | 38 |
| 24 | 27 | 35 | 33 | 32 | 32 |
| 34 | 30 | 31 | 31 | 36 | 36 |
| 24 | 25 | 25 | 26 | 27 | 28 |
| 34 | 32 | 28 | 35 | 33 | 29 |
| 35 | 29 | 35 | 31 | 28 | 27 |
| 31 | 34 | 37 | 36 | 36 | 35 |
| 40 | 29 | 31 | 34 | 34 | 33 |
| 30 | 32 | 30 | 29 | 29 | 30 |
| 31 | 33 | 33 | 34 | 35 | 34 |

| Table 3.7 | Time Until Rearrest— Ungrouped Frequency and Percentage Distribution | | |
|---|---|---|---|
| Days Until Rearrest | f | % | c% |
| 17 | 1 | .8 | .8 |
| 18 | 1 | .8 | 1.6 |
| 19 | 2 | 1.7 | 3.3 |
| 20 | 1 | .8 | 4.1 |
| 21 | 0 | .0 | 4.1 |
| 22 | 0 | .0 | 4.1 |
| 23 | 3 | 2.5 | 6.6 |
| 24 | 4 | 3.3 | 9.9 |
| 25 | 5 | 4.2 | 14.1 |
| 26 | 3 | 2.5 | 16.6 |
| 27 | 7 | 5.8 | 22.4 |
| 28 | 6 | 5.0 | 27.4 |
| 29 | 11 | 9.2 | 36.6 |
| 30 | 7 | 5.8 | 42.4 |
| 31 | 10 | 8.3 | 50.7 |
| 32 | 7 | 5.8 | 56.5 |
| 33 | 12 | 10.0 | 66.5 |
| 34 | 8 | 6.7 | 73.2 |
| 35 | 8 | 6.7 | 79.9 |
| 36 | 8 | 6.7 | 86.6 |
| 37 | 6 | 5.0 | 91.6 |
| 38 | 4 | 3.3 | 94.9 |
| 39 | 2 | 1.7 | 96.6 |
| 40 | 4 | 3.3 | 99.9* |
| Total | n = 120 | 99.9* | |

*Does not sum to 100% because of rounding.

whereas four offenders lasted 40 days before they were rearrested. From the cumulative percentage column, we can also see that about one half (50.8%) of the 120 offenders were rearrested within 31 days. Although this ungrouped frequency distribution is somewhat helpful in organizing the data, it still looks a little cluttered. This is because we have so many different values to report—there are 24 different values reported for the variable—and with few exceptions, the frequency for each value is fairly low. We provide a histogram of these ungrouped data in Figure 3.11. This histogram is also not especially helpful for us to visualize the variable's patterns or features. There is simply too much information. We need to reorganize these data to make the picture a little clearer.

We will first create a **grouped frequency distribution**. Unlike an ungrouped distribution, which reports all scores in a distribution, a grouped distribution organizes the data by grouping scores into groups of values

**Grouped frequency distribution:**
Reports the values of a quantitative continuous variable in intervals or a range of values, rather than reporting every distinct value.

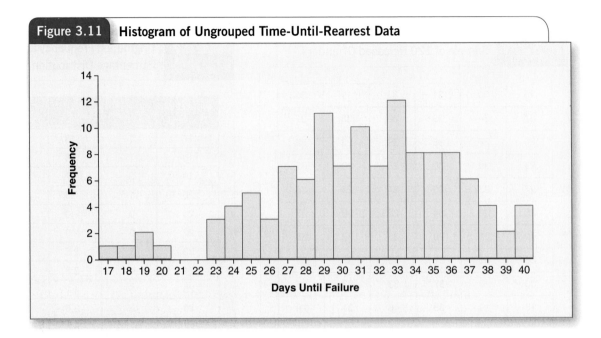

**Figure 3.11** Histogram of Ungrouped Time-Until-Rearrest Data

Frequency

Days Until Failure

**Class interval:** In creating a grouped frequency distribution, the class interval defines the range of values that are included in each interval.

or class intervals. Then it lists the frequency, proportion, and percentages associated with each class interval, rather than with each separate value. A **class interval** is simply a range of values for a variable. For example, rather than reporting the individual values 17, 18, 19, 20 . . . days until rearrest, in a grouped distribution, we may have a class interval that goes from 17 to 20 days. We would then determine the number or frequency of cases that fell within this interval and report that. What we are going to do is take the ungrouped distribution reported in Table 3.7 and construct a grouped distribution. Before we do this, however, we need to discuss some rules and guidelines for the construction of grouped frequency distributions.

But first, one general point needs to be made. The construction of a grouped frequency distribution is as much art as it is science. By this we mean you must keep in mind that your goal in creating a grouped distribution is to organize your data and communicate its important characteristics and features. A good grouped frequency distribution does this, and a poor one does not. Unfortunately, there is often not a single or "correct" way to organize data into a grouped distribution. What you have to do is make some tentative decisions about how to construct your grouped distributions, make the distribution in accordance with those decisions, and then look at the distribution you have made. You must then determine whether this distribution adequately conveys the features of your data (e.g., its shape or most typical score) or obscures them. If you think the grouped distribution you have made is inadequate or fails to show the features of your data, simply construct another one and go through the same process. Keep the grouped frequency distribution that you are convinced appropriately reveals the features of your data.

Several "hard-and-fast" rules apply to the creation of a grouped frequency distribution. These rules should never be broken:

1. Make your class intervals **mutually exclusive**. That is, be certain that each value falls into one and only one interval. Do not have overlapping intervals like, for example, 17–20 days and 20–24 days. Under this incorrect scheme, someone who was rearrested in 20 days could be placed in either the first or the second interval.

**Mutually exclusive intervals:** Class intervals must not overlap.

2. Make your class intervals **exhaustive**. In other words, make sure that each value falls into an interval. Do not make intervals that leave some values off. For example, in our time until rearrest data, do not have your first two intervals be 18–21 days and 22–25 days. Although these intervals are mutually exclusive, they are not exhaustive because you have a value of 17 days in your data, and it is not included in either interval.

> **Exhaustive intervals:** Class intervals must provide a place to count all original values of the variable distribution.

3. Make all your intervals the same width. The **interval width**, symbolized as $w_i$, is the number of values that the class interval contains. For example, a class interval of 17–20 days has an interval width of 4 because it includes four values: 17, 18, 19, and 20 days until rearrest. The class interval 21–29 days has an interval width of 9. You would not want to have a grouped distribution that has the two intervals 17–20 days and 21–29 days because these class intervals do not have the same width. Class intervals of different widths would distort the appearance of your distribution.

> **Interval width:** Number of different values that are contained within the class interval. For example, for the given interval 0 -5 arrests, the width is 6 because the interval contains the values 0, 1, 2, 3, 4, 5, or 6 arrests.

4. Make sure that your first class interval contains your lowest value and that your last class interval contains your highest value. In other words, do not make your first or last interval such that no cases fall into it. In the time-until-rearrest data, we would not want to make our first class interval 13–16 days and our second class interval 17–20 days. Although both class intervals have a width of 4 and they are mutually exclusive, with the data we have, the first interval would have a frequency of 0 since the earliest rearrest time was in 17 days. For the same reason, we would not want to have 41–44 days as our last class interval since it too would have a frequency of 0.

These rules for the construction of a grouped frequency distribution should be followed at all times and never violated. This is the science part, but beyond this, it becomes art.

Let us try to make a grouped frequency distribution from the rearrest time data shown in Table 3.7. There are really only three steps to follow in making a grouped frequency distribution. These three steps are as follows. As you perform them, keep the hard-and-fast rules in mind and follow them carefully.

**Step 1: Determine the Number of Class Intervals You Want.** Here we directly confront the "art" of creating grouped frequency distributions. There is no hard-and-fast rule about how many class intervals you should have; it depends entirely on your data. But there are some things you avoid as you decide how many intervals you want to have. You should not have so few intervals that you lose most of the information in your data. And you should not have too many intervals because you are trying to simplify, organize, and make sense of your data. A reasonable guide to follow is that at least at first you should have somewhere between 7 and 14 class intervals. After examining your data, determine what you think might be a good number of class intervals to begin the process. A good place to start if you are stuck is to say you want 10 class intervals. For our time-until-rearrest data, then, we will start with the decision to have 10 class intervals.

**Step 2: Determine the *Width* of the Class Interval.** Once you have determined the number of class intervals you want, you have to decide what your interval width should be. Keep in mind the hard-and-fast rule that each class interval must be the same width. To estimate an approximate interval width, the following simple routine is useful. First, find the range in your data, where the range is simply the arithmetic difference between your highest and lowest scores. In our time-until-rearrest data, the range is 23 days since the longest time until rearrest was 40 days and the shortest time was 17 days (Range = 40 − 17 = 23 days). With this, an estimate of the interval width can be obtained by taking the ratio of the range to the number of class intervals you selected in Step 1. The formula for the estimated interval width is:

$$w_i = \frac{\text{Range}}{\text{Number of intervals}}$$

(3–1)

In this example:

$$w_i = \frac{23}{10}$$
$$w_i = 2.3$$

Given the fact that our data consist of whole numbers, we would not really want to have an interval width with a decimal place. We could round down and have a class interval width of 2 or round up and have an interval width of 3. Again, this is the "art" part where there are no hard-and-fast rules to guide you. Because this is not mathematical precision and partly art, let's decide to round up. We now have two critical pieces of information to make our grouped frequency distribution. We know we would like to have approximately 10 class intervals, and we want each interval width to be 3.

**Step 3: Make Your Class Intervals.** Now we are ready to make our class intervals. With the understanding that they must be mutually exclusive, must be exhaustive, and must include the lowest score in the first interval and the highest score in the last interval, we want to approximate 10 class intervals, and each class interval will have a width of 3. In making our grouped frequency distribution with the time-until-rearrest data, we have to make sure that our first interval contains the value 17 days because that is our lowest score. One way we can ensure this is to have the first interval begin with 17. The score that defines the beginning of any class interval is called the *lower limit* of the interval. If the first interval begins with 17 days, what should the last value of this interval be? The last value of any class interval is the *upper limit* of the interval. Many students make the mistake of adding the interval width to the lower limit to determine what the upper limit of the interval should be. For example, if we did this, we would obtain an interval of 17–20 since 17 + 3 (the interval width) = 20. Unfortunately, this would give us an interval width of 4 rather than 3 since it contains the values 17, 18, 19, and 20 days until rearrest.

A helpful hint in making your class intervals is to do the following. First, select the lower limit of your first class interval. In this case, it is 17. Instead of figuring out what the upper limit is, leave it unknown for the moment.

Add your interval width to this lower limit, and this value becomes the lower limit of the next interval. In our case, the lower limit of the second class interval should be 20 (lower limit of first class interval + interval width = 17 + 3):

17 – ?

20 – ?

Since the lower limit of the second interval is 20 days, the upper limit of the first interval must be 19 days. The first class interval, then, is 17–19 days, and it contains three values: 17, 18, and 19 days. This is as it should be with an interval width of 3. You can complete your class intervals very easily now by adding the interval width to the lower limit of each class interval to find out what the lower limit of the next class interval should be. Repeat this procedure until you have a class interval that includes your highest score, and then you can stop.

For our time-until-rearrest data, the class intervals are shown for you in the first column of Table 3.8 under the heading "Stated Class Limits." The **stated class limits** define the range of values for each class interval in the grouped frequency distribution. As we mentioned, there are two components to any stated class interval, a lower class limit and an upper class limit. Remember that the first score in any class interval is the lower limit of the interval (LL), and the last score of the class interval is the upper limit of the interval (UL). For the first class interval, then, the lower limit is 17 days and the upper limit is 19 days. The lower limit of the second class interval is 20 days, and the upper limit is 22 days.

**Stated class limits:** Lowest value that is included in an interval and the highest value that is included in an interval.

| Table 3.8 | Grouped Distribution for Time-Until-Rearrest Data | | | | | |
|---|---|---|---|---|---|---|
| *Stated Class Limits* | *f* | *cf* | *p* | *cp* | *%* | *c%* |
| 17–19 days | 4 | 4 | .0333 | .0333 | 3.33 | 3.33 |
| 20–22 days | 1 | 5 | .0083 | .0416 | 0.83 | 4.16 |
| 23–25 days | 12 | 17 | .1000 | .1416 | 10.00 | 14.16 |
| 26–28 days | 16 | 33 | .1333 | .2749 | 13.33 | 27.49 |
| 29–31 days | 28 | 61 | .2333 | .5082 | 23.33 | 50.82 |
| 32–34 days | 28 | 89 | .2333 | .7415 | 23.33 | 74.15 |
| 35–37 days | 21 | 110 | .1750 | .9165 | 17.50 | 91.65 |
| 38–40 days | 10 | 120 | .0833 | .9998 | 8.33 | 99.98 |
| Total | 120 | | .9998* | | 99.98%* | |

*Does not sum to 1.0, or 100%, because of rounding.

Note that because we rounded up our estimated interval width from 2.3 to 3.0, we have 8 class intervals rather than the 10 we thought we were going to have according to Step 1. Had we rounded the estimated interval width down to 2.0, we would have had 12 class intervals rather than 10. Stay calm! This is the art part. For now, we will work with the 8 intervals and see if we like it. We have abided by our hard-and-fast rule that that each class interval has the same width; ours is 3, and that the intervals are mutually exclusive and exhaustive. The first interval contains the lowest score (17), and the last interval contains the highest score (40). Everything looks good so far.

Now that we have our class intervals created, we can make a frequency distribution by counting the number of cases that fall into each class interval. For example, by looking at the data in Table 3.8, you can determine that there are 4 offenders who were rearrested between 17 and 19 days, only 1 who was rearrested between 20 and 22 days, 12 who were rearrested between 23 and 25 days, and so on until you find that there are 10 people who were rearrested between 38 and 40 days. As was true with an ungrouped frequency distribution, the sum of the frequency column in a grouped frequency distribution should equal the total number of cases ($\sum f = n$)—in this example, 120. We can use these frequencies now to determine the proportions (*p*) and percentage of the total for each class interval, where $p = f / n$, and percentage $= p \times 100$. Since there were 4 offenders out of 120 who were rearrested between 17 and 19 days, they comprise .0333 of the total (4 / 120 = .0333), or 3.33%. Similarly, since there were 28 offenders who were rearrested between 29 and 31 days, they comprise .2333 of the total (28 / 120 = .2333), or 23.33%. We can also meaningfully calculate the cumulative frequencies, cumulative proportions, and cumulative percentages for each class interval.

One thing you should immediately notice about our grouped frequency distribution is that while our ungrouped data were measured at the interval/ratio level, by creating class intervals, we now have ordinal-level data. Our data values now consist of rank-ordered categories rather than of equally distanced values. In a sense, then, we "dumbed down" our data from interval/ratio to ordinal level.

To see this clearly, assume we take one hypothetical person from each of the first two class intervals. What we now know is that the person who falls into the first class interval (17–19 days) was rearrested sooner than the person who is in the second class interval (20–22 days)—"sooner" implies a rank order of time (sooner, rather than at the same time, or later). What we do not know, however, is *how much* sooner the first person was rearrested. Since we know only that he falls into the first interval and not the precise number of days until rearrest, we can use only words like "rearrested sooner" or "rearrested later" and not more precise words like "rearrested two days sooner" or "arrested twice as fast." With our original continuous data that measured the exact number of days until rearrest, we could calculate precise things like "how much more than" or "how much less than"—statements we cannot make with ordinal-level data. In creating a grouped frequency distribution from continuous data, then, we lose some precision in our measurement. What we will have to determine is how large a price we have to pay for creating a grouped frequency distribution. In other words, how much precision did we lose in going from interval/ratio to ordinal-level measurement? We will address this issue in later chapters.

Even though there is some loss of precision because we have created categories or class intervals rather than reporting every value, Table 3.8 shows the distribution of the data much better than the ungrouped distribution shown in Table 3.7. We can see here that not many people were immediately rearrested. There were no rearrests for 16 days and then only a handful until 23 days after release (5 rearrests, or less than 5% of the total). There were, however, a large number of people rearrested between 29 and 37 days; in fact, 77 cases, or nearly two thirds (64.17%) of the total, were rearrested within that range. By the 37th day after their release, 110 offenders of the 120 had been rearrested, and this consisted of more than 9 out of 10 released offenders, or greater than 90% of the total. By having constructed this grouped distribution, we will now construct a histogram of the grouped frequency data, shown for you in Figure 3.12.

This histogram of the grouped frequency distribution is a little more informative than that for the ungrouped data in Figure 3.11. We clearly see that few persons were rearrested very soon after release, that it was not until approximately 29 days after release when most offenders began to be rearrested, and that they then were rearrested at a fairly steady level until the 37th day. One

| | Grouped Distribution for |
|---|---|
| **Table 3.9** | **Time-Until-Rearrest Data Using Interval Width of 2** |

| Stated Class Limits | f | % |
|---|---|---|
| 17–18 | 2 | 1.7 |
| 19–20 | 3 | 2.5 |
| 21–22 | 0 | 0.0 |
| 23–24 | 7 | 5.8 |
| 25–26 | 8 | 6.7 |
| 27–28 | 13 | 10.8 |
| 29–30 | 18 | 15.0 |
| 31–32 | 17 | 14.2 |
| 33–34 | 20 | 16.7 |
| 35–36 | 16 | 13.3 |
| 37–38 | 10 | 8.3 |
| 39–40 | 6 | 5.0 |
| Total | 120 | 100.0 |

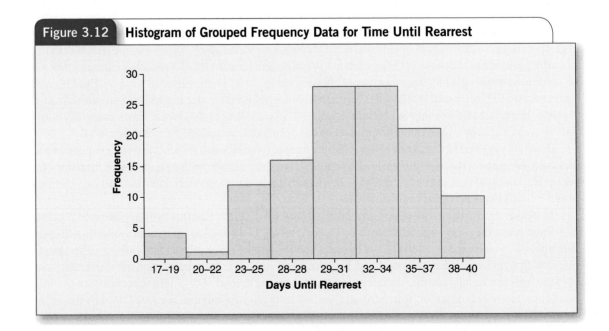

**Figure 3.12** **Histogram of Grouped Frequency Data for Time Until Rearrest**

is immediately struck by the fact that a large proportion of rearrests occurred between 29 and 34 days—approximately a month after release.

In case we were not satisfied with the grouped frequency distribution that has 8 class intervals and an interval width of 3, we might want to try constructing a different set of intervals. Rather than rounding the interval width up from 2.3 to 3.0, we will now round down and have class intervals with a width of 2. We go through the same procedures as before, and as practice you should stop reading any further and attempt to create this grouped frequency distribution on your own. Then check it with what we have done.

The grouped frequency distribution where the width of each class interval is 2 is shown in Table 3.9, along with the percentage distribution. The corresponding histogram for the grouped frequency distribution is given in Figure 3.13. Because the interval width is 2.0 rather than 3.0, there are now 12 rather than 8 class intervals. But the story provided by the table and graph are virtually the same as when the interval width was 3.0, and both sets of tables and graphs are very easy to read, interpret, and understand. One would be hard pressed to say that one set of tables/graphs is any better than the other. It looks as if they both are effective in showing the distribution of these time-until-rearrest data. You now have clear evidence that making a grouped frequency distribution does not have a clearly defined single answer, and that making such distributions is "as much art as it is science."

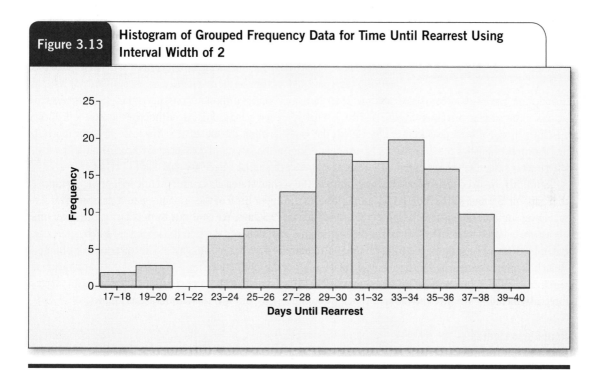

**Figure 3.13** Histogram of Grouped Frequency Data for Time Until Rearrest Using Interval Width of 2

## Refinements to a Grouped Frequency Distribution

Recall that we created our grouped frequency distribution in the previous section with data that were initially quantitative and continuous. The variable, Time Until Rearrest, was measured at the interval/ratio level as the number of days a released offender was out in the community before he was rearrested. We then collapsed this data into ordinal-level categories. We see this categorization in our stated class limits. We would like to show you the difference between continuous data and the ordinal-level categories of the class intervals. First the interval/ratio-level data measure time until rearrest in continuous increments of one day:

```
|----------|------------|---------|----------|----------|-----------|----------|----------------------------------------|
one          two          three      four       five       six         seven      eight...                            ...forty
days         days         days       days       days       days        days       days                                    days
```

This measurement of time until rearrest is continuous, and this continuity is seen in the gradual evolution of one day into two days into three days, and so on. When we collapsed the data into the ordinal categories of stated class intervals as in Table 3.8, however, our class intervals became discrete categories:

```
|-----------|    |------------|    |-----------|    |------------|    |-----------|    |-----------|    |----------|    |-----------|
17–19 days       20–22 days       23–25 days       26–28 days       29–31 days       32–34 days       35–37 days       38–40 days
```

There will be times, however, when we will want to maintain the continuous nature of our original interval/ratio measurement even though we have created ordinal-level categories. We do this by constructing something called **real class limits**. The creation of real class limits will both remind us that our underlying measurement is truly continuous and enable us to perform certain statistical operations on the data (discussed in later chapters), which we could not do if the data were truly ordinal.

> **Real class limits:** Real limits in a grouped distribution take into account the space between the adjacent intervals. For example, for an interval with stated limits of 0–5 and 6–11 prior arrests, the real limits are .5–5.5 and 5.5–11.5.

Constructing real class limits is very simple. Let's take as an illustration the first and second class intervals in Table 3.8. First, note that there is a one-unit "gap" between the upper limit of a given class interval and the lower limit of the next. For example, there is a one-unit (one-day) "gap" between the upper limit of the first stated class interval (19 days) and the lower limit of the next stated class interval (20 days). Note that this one-unit "gap" exists for each stated class limit, even the first class interval (the stated class interval 14–16 exists; we simply didn't use it because our first observed value is 17 days). What we are now going to do is extend the upper limit of the first stated class interval one half of the distance of this "gap." Since the "gap" is one unit, this means we will increase the upper limit of the first stated class limit by one half or .5 units. Now the upper limit of the first stated class interval will be .5 units closer to the lower limit of the next stated class interval. The real upper limit for the first class interval would then be 19.5 days.

Similarly, we need to decrease the lower limit of the second stated class interval one half of the distance of the "gap," or .5 units, so that now it is .5 units closer to the upper limit of the previous stated class interval. The real lower limit for the second class interval would then be 19.5 days. We continue by decreasing the lower limit of each stated class interval by .5 (half the distance of the "gap" between the stated class limits) and by increasing the upper limit of each state class interval by .5 (also half the distance of the "gap"). The lower real limit for our first class interval would be 16.5 because we are decreasing the lower stated limit of 17 by .5 units, and the upper real limit would be 19.5 because we are increasing the upper stated limit of 19 by .5 units. We do this for all class intervals, including the first and the last. When we complete this, our real class limits are as follows.

## Real Class Limits

16.5–19.5 days

19.5–22.5 days

22.5–25.5 days

25.5–28.5 days

28.5–31.5 days

31.5–34.5 days

34.5–37.5 days

37.5–40.5 days

Note that the upper real limit of each class interval is equal to the lower real limit of the next class interval. The intervals now merge together, reflecting the continuous nature of the underlying data. There are no "gaps" in this continuous data. Essentially, we have tried to recapture some of the measurement properties we lost when we created a grouped frequency distribution and made the originally continuous data categorical. What we are trying to remind ourselves, therefore, is that despite the fact that we created ordinal categories with our grouped frequency distribution, the underlying measurement of the original data was continuous. We illustrate this in the following diagram. With real class limits, we now have:

```
|---------------|
16.5–19.5 days
        |---------------|
        19.5–22.5 days
                |---------------|
                22.5–25.5 days
                        |---------------|
                        25.5–28.5 days
                                |---------------|
                                28.5–31.5 days
                                        |---------------|
                                        31.5–34.5 days
                                                |---------------|
                                                34.5–37.5 days
                                                        |---------------|
                                                        37.5–40.5 days
```

We will use these real limits in later chapters to do some simple statistical calculations that normally would require us to have interval/ratio-level data. You should note that we cannot use these real class limits to calculate our frequency, proportion, or percentage distributions for grouped data. Why not? Recall that one of the hard-and-fast rules in making a grouped frequency distribution is that the class intervals must be mutually exclusive. This means that a given score must fall in one and only one class interval. Real class limits violate this rule because the intervals overlap. Where, for example, would we place a score of 19 days? Would it go in the first or the second class interval?

Another piece of information we are now going to add to our grouped frequency distribution is something called the midpoint of the interval (the midpoint of a given class interval $i$ is given by $m_i$). We will use the interval midpoints in the next two chapters when we discuss measures of central tendency and dispersion. The **midpoint** of a class interval is exactly what the term implies; it is a score that lies exactly at the midpoint of the class interval, exactly one half of the distance between the lower limit and the upper limit of a given class interval.

> **Midpoints:** Exact middle value in an interval of a grouped frequency distribution. The midpoint is found by summing the lower and upper limits (stated or real) and dividing by 2.

Each class interval, therefore, has its own midpoint. The midpoint of a class interval is very easy to calculate. Simply take the sum of the lower limit and the upper limit of the interval and divide by 2. It does not matter whether you use the lower and upper limits of the stated class limits or of the real class limits; the result will be the same:

$$m_i = \frac{\text{Lower limit} + \text{Upper limit}}{2} \qquad \textbf{(3–2)}$$

| Table 3.10 | Stated Class Limits, Real Class Limits, and Midpoints for Grouped Frequency Distribution in Table 3.9 |

| Stated Class Limits | Real Class Limits | $m_i$ | f |
|---|---|---|---|
| 17–19 | 16.5–19.5 | 18 | 4 |
| 20–22 | 19.5–22.5 | 21 | 1 |
| 23–25 | 22.5–25.5 | 24 | 12 |
| 26–28 | 25.5–28.5 | 27 | 16 |
| 29–31 | 28.5–31.5 | 30 | 28 |
| 32–34 | 31.5–34.5 | 33 | 28 |
| 35–37 | 34.5–37.5 | 36 | 21 |
| 38–40 | 37.5–40.5 | 39 | 10 |
| | | | Total = 120 |

**Normal distribution:** Symmetrical distribution that has the greatest frequency of its cases in the middle of the distribution with fewer cases at each end or "tail" of the distribution. A normal distribution looks like a bell when drawn and it is often referred to as a "bell-shaped" distribution.

For example, with our grouped frequency distribution in Table 3.8, we can calculate the midpoint of the first interval as $(17 + 19) / 2 = 36 / 2 = 18$ using the stated limits or as $(16.5 + 19.5) / 2 = 36 / 2 = 18$ using the real class limits. Midpoints are always calculated for every class interval in a grouped frequency distribution. Table 3.10 shows the real limits and midpoints of each class interval for the grouped frequency distribution data in Table 3.8, where the width of each stated class interval was 3.0.

# ▣ The Shape of a Distribution

One important piece of information that a graph of continuous data can give you at a glance is the shape of your distribution. For statistical purposes, one important shape of a continuous distribution is normal. A **normal distribution** is a distribution that is symmetrical, which means that if you drew a line down the center of the distribution, the left half would look exactly like the right half. A normal distribution has a single peak in the middle of the distribution, with fewer and fewer cases as you move away from this middle. The ends of a distribution of continuous scores are often called the "tails" of the distribution. A distribution has both a left or negative tail and a right or positive tail.

A normal distribution is often referred to as a "bell-shaped curve" because it is shaped a bit like a bell. An example of a normal distribution is shown in Figure 3.14. We will discuss the normal distribution in great detail in Chapter 6 because many variables of interest in criminology and criminal justice are normally or approximately normally distributed, and many of the statistics we apply to our data depend on the assumption that they are normally distributed.

When a distribution departs, or *deviates*, from normality, it is said to be a **skewed distribution.** There are two forms of skewed distributions. Figure 3.15 shows a distribution where there is a long series of low scores with most of the scores at the high end of the distribution. Note that this distribution has a long left

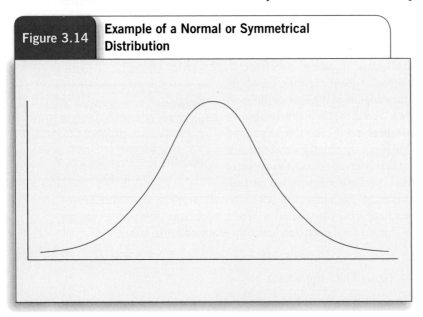

| Figure 3.14 | Example of a Normal or Symmetrical Distribution |

or negative tail. This type of skew is called a **negative skew** because the long tail of the distribution is to the left, and the left side of the number line moves toward negative numbers. In a distribution with a negative skew, then, most of the scores cluster at higher values of the variable and there is a long left tail, indicating that there are low values with few cases at each value. Figure 13.16 shows a distribution where there are series of low-frequency high scores with most of the scores clustered at the low end of the distribution. Note that this distribution has a long right or positive tail. This type of skew is called a **positive skew** because the long tail of the distribution is to the right, and the

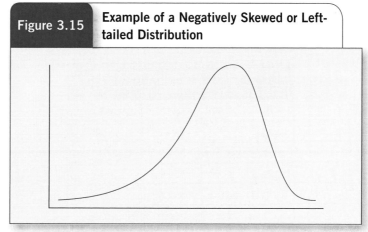

**Figure 3.15** Example of a Negatively Skewed or Left-tailed Distribution

right side of the number line moves toward positive numbers. In a distribution with a positive skew, therefore, most of the scores cluster at lower values of the variable and there is a long right tail, indicating that there are a lot of high values with few cases at each value. Remember that the skew is indicated by the direction where the tail is being pulled by a few low frequency scores, not by where the bulk of the data lie.

If you think of a very high or very low score as an **outlier**, then a negatively skewed distribution has outliers at the left tail of the distribution (the long tail), whereas a positively skewed distribution has outliers at the right tail of the distribution.

**Skewed distribution:** Non-normal (nonsymmetrical) distribution.

**Negatively skewed distribution:** Long "tail" is found on the left side of the distribution (toward the negative numbers).

**Positively skewed distribution:** Long "tail" is found on the right side of the distribution (toward positive numbers).

**Outlier:** Unusually high or low value or score for a variable.

## ▣ Time Plots

Frequently in criminology and other social sciences, we are interested in the extent to which events change or remain stable over time. In other words, the values of some of our variables may change over time, and we would like to have a convenient way to show this. We can do this in a table where we report the value of a variable at different time points—for example, every six months or every year. In addition to the tabular presentation of the value of a variable over time, we can graph the change in a time plot. A time plot is simply a graphical display of a variable's values over some unit of time (year, month, week, etc.). It is actually a type of line graph where the height of the line on the $y$ axis reflects some attribute of the value (a frequency or a percentage) and its length is marked off in units of time on the $x$ axis. In such a time plot, we can easily determine the value of the variable at any given point in time.

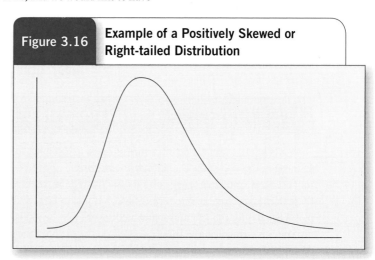

**Figure 3.16** Example of a Positively Skewed or Right-tailed Distribution

| Table 3.11 | Annual Rates (per 100,000) of Rape, Robbery, and Aggravated Assault Known to the Police and Reported to the FBI's Uniform Crime Reports Program: 1972–2013 |

| Year | Rape Rate | Robbery Rate | Aggravated Assault Rate | Year | Rape Rate | Robbery Rate | Aggravated Assault Rate |
|------|-----------|--------------|-------------------------|------|-----------|--------------|-------------------------|
| 1972 | 22.5 | 180.7 | 188.8 | 1993 | 41.1 | 256.0 | 440.5 |
| 1973 | 24.5 | 183.1 | 200.5 | 1994 | 39.3 | 237.8 | 427.6 |
| 1974 | 26.2 | 209.3 | 215.8 | 1995 | 37.1 | 220.9 | 418.3 |
| 1975 | 26.3 | 220.8 | 227.4 | 1996 | 36.3 | 201.9 | 391.0 |
| 1976 | 26.6 | 199.3 | 233.2 | 1997 | 35.9 | 186.2 | 382.1 |
| 1977 | 29.4 | 190.7 | 247.0 | 1998 | 34.5 | 165.5 | 361.4 |
| 1978 | 31.0 | 195.8 | 262.1 | 1999 | 32.8 | 150.1 | 334.3 |
| 1979 | 34.7 | 218.4 | 286.0 | 2000 | 32.0 | 144.9 | 323.6 |
| 1980 | 36.8 | 251.1 | 298.5 | 2001 | 31.8 | 148.5 | 318.6 |
| 1981 | 36.0 | 258.7 | 289.3 | 2002 | 33.1 | 146.1 | 309.5 |
| 1982 | 34.0 | 238.9 | 289.0 | 2003 | 32.3 | 142.5 | 295.4 |
| 1983 | 33.7 | 216.5 | 279.4 | 2004 | 32.4 | 136.7 | 288.6 |
| 1984 | 35.7 | 205.4 | 290.6 | 2005 | 31.8 | 140.8 | 290.8 |
| 1985 | 37.1 | 208.5 | 304.0 | 2006 | 30.9 | 149.4 | 287.5 |
| 1986 | 37.9 | 225.1 | 347.4 | 2007 | 30.1 | 155.7 | 292.6 |
| 1987 | 37.4 | 212.7 | 352.9 | 2008 | 29.4 | 154.0 | 281.6 |
| 1988 | 37.6 | 220.9 | 372.2 | 2009 | 28.9 | 139.6 | 268.3 |
| 1989 | 38.1 | 233.0 | 385.6 | 2010 | 27.8 | 122.7 | 255.5 |
| 1990 | 41.2 | 257.0 | 422.9 | 2011 | 26.8 | 117.1 | 243.5 |
| 1991 | 42.3 | 272.7 | 433.4 | 2012 | 26.7 | 116.3 | 246.5 |
| 1992 | 42.8 | 263.7 | 441.9 | 2013 | 23.1 | 112.9 | 233.7 |

*Source:* Adapted from Uniform Crime Reports 1990, 1995, 2000, 2005–2013 from the Federal Bureau of Investigation.

# Case Study

## A Trend Analysis of Crime Rates

Table 3.11 reports annual rates of crimes reported to the police for three "index offenses"—forcible rape, robbery, and aggravated assault—in the United States over the time period 1972–2013. There are, then, three variables—rape rates, robbery rates, and rates of aggravated assault—that are reported over more than a 40-year-period. We reproduce these rates for each of the three crimes as a time plot in Figure 3.17. Note that we have graphed all three crimes in one plot. The rates for robbery and aggravated assault use the *y* axis on the left side of the chart, but because the level of rape rates is so much lower, these rates rely on the *y* axis on the right side of the chart. You can see that the rates for the three violent index crimes trend closely together over time, although the level of their values is different. If we had plotted rape rates with the same axis values as the other two index crimes, the rates for rape would have appeared very flat over time and you would not be able to see the variation over time. Not that there was no variation over time, but you would not be able to see it. We plot the crime rates for the three index crimes using the same y axis in Figure 3.18 to illustrate. Unlike Figure 3.17, notice that in this figure, the time trend line for forcible rape is flat. Again, this is not because there is no variation over time in rape arrest rates, but it is lost because its absolute rate is much lower than the other two crimes. This example serves as a reminder to be aware of your measurements when making graphs and, more importantly, when examining graphs made by others!

Notice that the graphical display of the arrest rates allows us to see the variation over time much more quickly and clearly. As shown in Figure 3.17, crime rates for all three crimes started at a moderate level in the early 1970s, and there was a consistent increase in the rates of all three crimes until around 1980. After this increase, there was a slight decline in the rates of robbery and a fairly flat rate for aggravated assault and rape until the middle-to-late 1980s, and then a fairly steady increase until the early 1990s, when all three crime rates reached a peaked (rape and armed robbery in 1991 and aggravated assault in 1992). After the peak, there was a gradual decline over the next 25 years. A useful statistic that allows us to quantify the change in trends is called a **percent change score** Let us examine some percent change scores over different parts of the time trend. To calculate percent change scores, we perform the following calculations:

**Percent change score:** Score that quantifies the percent change of a score between two different time periods or other units.

$$\% \text{ Change} = \left( \frac{\text{End value} - \text{Start value}}{\text{Start value}} \right) \times 100 \qquad \textbf{(3-3)}$$

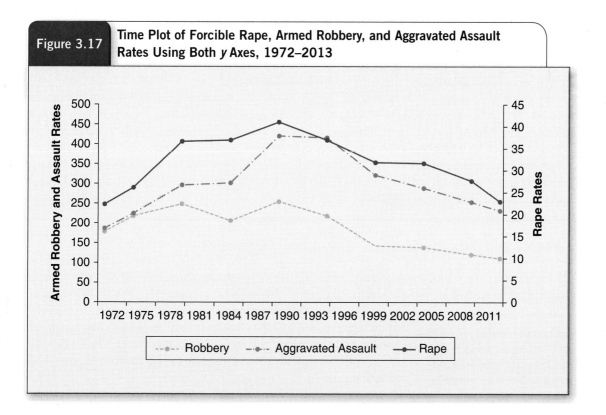

**Figure 3.17**  Time Plot of Forcible Rape, Armed Robbery, and Aggravated Assault Rates Using Both *y* Axes, 1972–2013

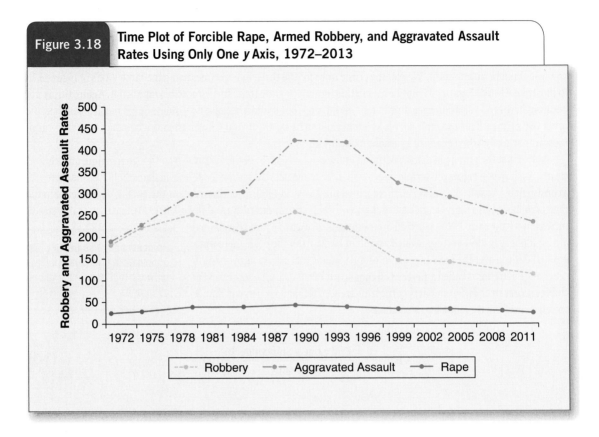

**Figure 3.18** Time Plot of Forcible Rape, Armed Robbery, and Aggravated Assault Rates Using Only One *y* Axis, 1972–2013

If we calculate the percent change in the crime rate from 1972 until the peak rate for each crime in the early 1990s, we can determine that rates of forcible rape increased 90% [(42.8 − 22.5) / 22.5 × 100 = 90.22%], while robbery rates increased only by about 51% [(272.7 − 180.7) / 180.7 × 100 = 50.9%] and rates of aggravated assault increased by 134% [(441.9 − 188.8) / 188.8 × 100 = 134.1%]. Thus, over the period from the early 1970s to the early 1990s, rates of forcible rape increased almost twice as much as rates of armed robbery. Now let's calculate the percent change in crime rates for each offense from its peak in the early 1990s until the end of the time period in 2013. When we do this, we see that rape rates declined by 46% [(23.1 − 42.8) / 42.8 × 100 = −46.0%], about the same as the decline in aggravated assault rates [(233.7 − 441.9) / 441.9 × 100 = −47.1%] but less than the decline in armed robbery rates [(112.9 − 272.7) / 272.7 × 100 = −58.6%].

## When Trend Data Are Erratic—Smoothing Techniques

Often, trend data show substantial fluctuations across the units of time used (e.g., years and months). In these cases, some researchers often elect to modify the data slightly so that any long-term trends can be made more apparent. This modification removes much of the severe short-term variability and appropriately is called **smoothing** the data. In smoothing, a new data point is created by taking what is called a moving average. A moving average is simply the average frequency at which an event occurred over some short-term time period.

**Smoothing:** Creating new data points for trend data to smooth out the short-term fluctuations to identify long-term trends.

# Case Study

## Executions in the United States

A good example of chaotic trend data is the number of executions that took place in the United States in our recent history. In Table 3.12, we report the number of executions that took place in the United States from 1977 until the end of 2014. In 1977, the execution in Utah of Gary Gillmore ended an unofficial moratorium of 10 years on the imposition of the death penalty in the United States. There are two things you might notice from this table: (a) The frequency of executions started out very low and then increased fairly steadily over time until it began to decline 2000, and (b) the frequency of executions has been very erratic and unstable from year to year. There were, for example, only 5 executions in 1983 and then 21 in 1984. Fourteen executions in 1991 increased to 31 in 1992, and 85 executions in 2000 declined to less than 40 in 2014. You can more clearly see both of these patterns in the execution data when you look at the time plot in Figure 3.19. This time plot very nicely illustrates the value of the graphical display of data.

**Table 3.12**  **Number of Executions in the United States: 1977–2014**

| Year | # of Executions | Year | # of Executions |
|------|-----------------|------|-----------------|
| 1977 | 1 | 1996 | 45 |
| 1978 | 0 | 1997 | 74 |
| 1979 | 2 | 1998 | 68 |
| 1980 | 0 | 1999 | 98 |
| 1981 | 1 | 2000 | 85 |
| 1982 | 2 | 2001 | 49 |
| 1983 | 5 | 2002 | 71 |
| 1984 | 21 | 2003 | 65 |
| 1985 | 18 | 2004 | 59 |
| 1986 | 18 | 2005 | 60 |
| 1987 | 25 | 2006 | 53 |
| 1988 | 11 | 2007 | 42 |
| 1989 | 16 | 2008 | 37 |
| 1990 | 23 | 2009 | 52 |
| 1991 | 14 | 2010 | 46 |
| 1992 | 31 | 2011 | 43 |
| 1993 | 38 | 2012 | 43 |
| 1994 | 31 | 2013 | 39 |
| 1995 | 56 | 2014 | 35 |

*Source:* Data taken from the Death Penalty Information Center at www.deathpenaltyinfo.org.

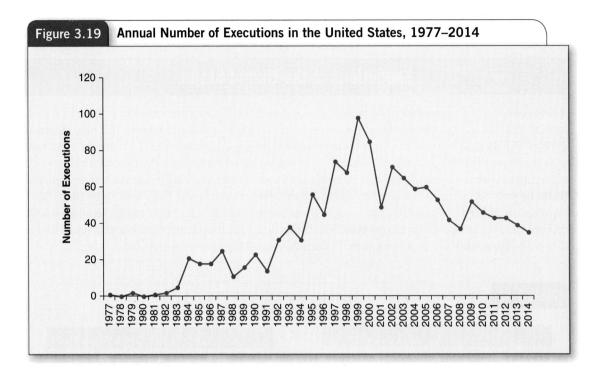

**Figure 3.19** **Annual Number of Executions in the United States, 1977–2014**

Because these execution frequency data show substantial year-to-year fluctuations, some researchers often elect to modify the data slightly so that any trends can be made more apparent. This modification removes much of the severe short-term variability so long-term trends can be revealed in the data. In these execution data, we are going to create a moving average of three years. In all smoothing techniques, the value of the first score and that of the last score in the time series remain the same. In our execution data, therefore, we would not smooth the number of executions that occurred in 1977 (1) or those that occurred in 2014 (35). Beginning with the year 1978, however, we create moving averages of three years. In this moving average of three years, we take the frequency of executions for each year, add to that number the frequency of executions for the year immediately before that year and the year immediately after that year, and then calculate the average of these three years by dividing this sum by 3. Thus, if $f_2$ is the frequency for the second year in the time series (recall that the first frequency $f_1$ is not smoothed) and $f_3$ is the frequency for the third year, the first new data point we would calculate would be an average of the first, second, and third frequencies as a moving average of three for $f_2 = (f_1 + f_2 + f_3) / 3$. So the value of our first smoothed data point would be for the year 1978, and it would be $(1 + 0 + 2) / 3 = 3 / 3 = 1.00$. This value is the average number of executions for three years—1977, 1978, and 1979. The value of our second smoothed data point would be for the year 1979; it would be the average number of executions for the years 1978, 1979, and 1980, $(0 + 2 + 0) / 3 = 2 / 3 = .67$. You then smooth each of the original frequency values for each year after this by taking the average of three data points (the year you are smoothing, the year before this, and the year after this) until you reach the last data point in the series, which you leave unsmoothed.

Table 3.13 shows the value of the original execution frequency, how the smoothing technique was used, and then the new value of each smoothed frequency. We graph these smoothed frequencies and the unsmoothed raw frequencies as a time plot in Figure 3.19. You should note that we decided to calculate a moving average of three years for these data; there is nothing sacred about a moving average of three. We could have calculated a moving average of two or four years, or even five years. Generally, the more years or data points that are included in the moving average, the more smoothed the data will be. In practice, your decision about how many years to include in the moving average should be based on the characteristics and appearance of your data; with more erratic data (ups and downs), you might want to use a larger moving average, and you might have to do a number of smooth time plots before you finally decide what the best moving average is. Again, this is the art part!

| Table 3.13 | Number of Executions in the United States: 1977–2014 After a Running Average of Three-Year Smoothing |
|---|---|

| Year | # of Executions | Smoothing Process | Smoothed # of Executions |
|---|---|---|---|
| 1977 | 1 | Endpoint remains | 1.00 |
| 1978 | 0 | (1 + 0 + 2) / 3 = 1.00 | 1.00 |
| 1979 | 2 | (0 + 2 + 0) / 3 = .67 | .67 |
| 1980 | 0 | (0 + 2 + 1) / 3 = 1.00 | 1.00 |
| 1981 | 1 | (0 + 1 + 2) / 3 = 1.00 | 1.00 |
| 1982 | 2 | (1 + 2 + 5) / 3 = 2.67 | 2.67 |
| 1983 | 5 | (2 + 5 + 21) / 3 = 9.33 | 9.33 |
| 1984 | 21 | (5 + 21 + 18) / 3 = 14.67 | 14.67 |
| 1985 | 18 | (21 + 18 + 18) / 3 = 19.00 | 19.00 |
| 1986 | 18 | (18 + 18 + 25) / 3 = 20.33 | 20.33 |
| 1987 | 25 | (18 + 25 + 11) / 3 = 18.00 | 18.00 |
| 1988 | 11 | (25 + 11 + 16) / 3 = 17.33 | 17.33 |
| 1989 | 16 | (11 + 16 + 23) / 3 = 16.67 | 16.67 |
| 1990 | 23 | (16 + 23 + 14) / 3 = 17.67 | 17.67 |
| 1991 | 14 | (23 + 14 + 31) / 3 = 22.67 | 22.67 |
| 1992 | 31 | (14 + 31 + 38) / 3 = 27.67 | 27.67 |
| 1993 | 38 | (31 + 38 + 31) / 3 = 33.33 | 33.33 |
| 1994 | 31 | (38 + 31 + 56) / 3 = 41.67 | 41.67 |
| 1995 | 56 | (31 + 56 + 45) / 3 = 44.00 | 44.00 |
| 1996 | 45 | (56 + 45 + 74) / 3 = 58.33 | 58.33 |
| 1997 | 74 | (45 + 74 + 68) / 3 = 62.33 | 62.33 |
| 1998 | 68 | (74 + 68 + 98) / 3 = 80.00 | 80.00 |
| 1999 | 98 | (68 + 98 + 85) / 3 = 83.67 | 83.67 |
| 2000 | 85 | (98 + 85 + 49) / 3 = 77.33 | 77.33 |
| 2001 | 49 | (85 + 49 + 71) / 3 = 68.33 | 68.33 |
| 2002 | 71 | (49 + 71 + 65) / 3 = 61.67 | 61.67 |
| 2003 | 65 | (71 + 65 + 59) / 3 = 65.00 | 65.00 |
| 2004 | 59 | (65 + 59 + 60) / 3 = 61.33 | 61.33 |
| 2005 | 60 | (59 + 60 + 53) / 3 = 57.33 | 57.33 |

*(Continued)*

| Table 3.13 | (Continued) | | |
|---|---|---|---|

| Year | # of Executions | Smoothing Process | Smoothed # of Executions |
|---|---|---|---|
| 2006 | 53 | (60 + 53 + 42) / 3 = 51.67 | 51.67 |
| 2007 | 42 | (53 + 42 + 37) / 3 = 44.00 | 44.00 |
| 2008 | 37 | (42 + 37 + 52) / 3 = 43.67 | 43.67 |
| 2009 | 52 | (37 + 52 + 46) / 3 = 45.00 | 45.00 |
| 2010 | 46 | (52 + 46 + 43) / 3 = 47.00 | 47.00 |
| 2011 | 43 | (46 + 43 + 43) / 3 = 44.00 | 44.00 |
| 2012 | 43 | (43 + 43 + 39) / 3 = 41.67 | 41.67 |
| 2013 | 39 | (43 + 39 + 35) / 3 = 39.00 | 39.00 |
| 2014 | 35 | Endpoint remains | 35.00 |

*Source:* Data taken from the Death Penalty Information Center at www.deathpenaltyinfo.org.

| Figure 3.20 | **Annual Number of Executions in the United States, Original and Smoothed Data, 1977–2014** |
|---|---|

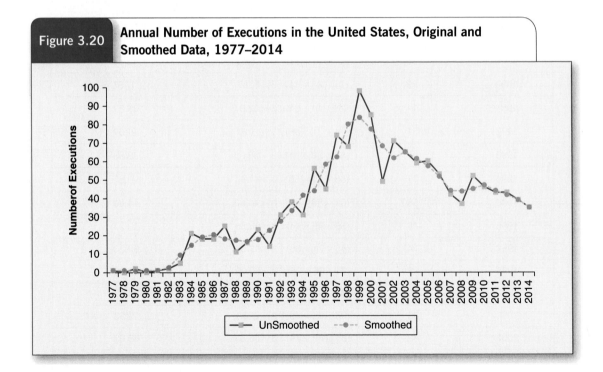

Note in Figure 3.20 that smoothing took out the "peaks" and "valleys" in these data as you would guess given the fact that the technique is called smoothing. Without the erratic fluctuations, the trend in the smoothed data is a little easier to discern. You can see that executions remained at a very low level until the early 1980s when they began to rise steadily until reaching a peak in 1999. The number of executions per year next shows a consistent downward trend from the peak in 1999 to the end of the shown time series in 2014.

# 🔲 Summary

In this chapter we covered some ways to present qualitative and quantitative data in tabular (or numeric) form and in graphs. An important point to take away from this chapter is that it is always a good idea to look at the appearance or distribution of your data before conducting any further statistical analyses. Qualitative data can be examined in both tabular and graphical form along with the calculation of some very simple descriptive information, such as the distribution of frequencies, proportions, and percentages. A frequency distribution displays the values that the qualitative variable takes and how many cases fall into each value. The proportions and percentages show the relative frequencies. Qualitative data can be graphed with either a pie chart or a bar chart.

Quantitative or continuous data can also be viewed in tabular or graphical form. With quantitative data there is a greater variety of descriptive information to report. With quantitative data we can meaningfully calculate relative and cumulative frequencies, proportions, and percentages. If every value of a quantitative variable is reported, along with its frequency, proportion, and/or percentage, the distribution is called an ungrouped frequency distribution. If the data are collapsed into ranges/intervals of values, the corresponding distribution is referred to as a grouped frequency distribution. Continuous data can be graphed with a histogram or one of several different kinds of line graphs or polygons. Frequently in criminology and criminal justice, we are interested in reporting the values of a variable over time. This information can also be displayed in a table or with a graph called a time plot. When there are sharp fluctuations in the data over a short period of time, it is often helpful to smooth the data before graphing the trend.

## Key Terms

➤ Review key terms with eFlashcards. ⑤SAGE edge™

bar chart   47
class interval   58
cumulative frequency distribution   52
cumulative percentages   53
cumulative proportions   52
grouped frequency distribution   57
exhaustive intervals   59
histogram   53
interval width   59

line graph (polygon)   54
midpoints   65
mutually exclusive
   intervals   58
negatively skewed distribution   67
normal distribution   66
outlier   67
percent change score   69
pie chart   46

positively skewed distribution   67
real class limits   64
skewed distribution   66
stated class limits   60
smoothing   70
ungrouped frequency distribution   51
univariate analysis   43

## Key Formulas

Estimated interval width (equation 3-1):

$$w_i = \frac{\text{Range}}{\text{Number of intervals}}$$

Midpoint of class limit (equation 3-2):

$$m_i = \frac{\text{Lower limit} + \text{Upper limit}}{2}$$

Percent change scores (equation 3-3):

$$\%\text{Change} = \left( \frac{\text{Finish value} - \text{Start value}}{\text{Start value}} \right) \times 100$$

## Practice Problems

➤ Test your understanding of chapter content.
Take the practice quiz. $SAGE edge™

1. Which of the following two grouped frequency distributions is more effective in displaying the data on the number of prior offenses? Why?

**Number of Prior Offenses for a Sample of Convicted Offenders**

| Stated Class Limits | f |
|---|---|
| 0–7 | 0 |
| 7–10 | 35 |
| 10–15 | 40 |
| 16–30 | 50 |
| Total | 125 |

**Number of Prior Offenses for a Sample of Convicted Offenders**

| Stated Class Limits | f |
|---|---|
| 7–9 | 5 |
| 10–12 | 25 |
| 13–15 | 15 |
| 16–18 | 20 |
| 19–21 | 10 |
| 22–24 | 5 |
| 25–27 | 10 |
| 28–30 | 5 |
| Total | 125 |

2. If you had data on a variable called "the number of offenders sentenced to death in the United States from 1977 to 2014" and wanted to graph the frequency distribution, which type of graph would you use?

3. Imagine that you took a sample of 150 persons in a large lecture class from your university and asked each student the following question: "During the past 12 months, how many times did you use marijuana, cocaine, or some other illegal drug?" The possible response options were "never," "a few times," "more than a few times but not a lot," and "a lot." You found that 30 people reported "never" using drugs in the past year, 75 reported that they had used drugs "a few times," 35 said they had used drugs "more than a few times but not a lot," and 10 reported using drugs "a lot."

   a. What is the level of measurement for your variable, "self-reported drug use?"

   b. What is the ratio of "users" to "nonusers?"

   c. What is the ratio of users who reported using drugs "more than a few times but not a lot" to those reporting "a lot?"

   d. Construct an ungrouped frequency distribution from your data, and include both the proportion and percentage.

   e. What percentage of your sample reported using drugs?

   f. What proportion of your sample reported using drugs "a lot?"

4. You are the director of a state's department of corrections. You have 20,751 inmates currently confined in four types of institutions: community correctional facilities ($n = 5,428$), minimum security institutions ($n = 3,285$), medium security institutions ($n = 1,733$), maximum security institutions ($n = 875$), and pretrial detention centers ($n = 9,430$).

   a. Construct a frequency distribution with these data, and include the percentage and proportion.

   b. What percentage of your inmates are housed in minimum security institutions?

   c. What proportion of your inmates are housed in maximum security institutions?

   d. What percentage of your inmates are housed in pretrial detention facilities?

   e. Graph these data with the appropriate graph.

5. As the head of a state's police academy, you give a final examination to each class of recruits. This 20-question examination covers things that a rookie police officer should know, such as safety rules, constitutional requirements in arrests, and other matters. The following table shows the scores received on this exam by the last class of recruits, which included 25 people. It also shows the gender of each recruit.

**Scores on the Police Officer Recruit Test**

| Number Correct | Gender |
|:---:|:---|
| 15 | Male |
| 16 | Female |
| 11 | Male |
| 10 | Male |
| 14 | Male |
| 15 | Male |
| 15 | Female |
| 11 | Female |
| 10 | Male |
| 10 | Male |
| 20 | Female |
| 15 | Female |
| 14 | Male |
| 16 | Male |
| 15 | Male |
| 19 | Female |
| 11 | Male |
| 13 | Male |
| 15 | Female |
| 13 | Female |
| 10 | Male |
| 20 | Male |
| 15 | Male |
| 16 | Female |
| 10 | Male |

a. Construct an ungrouped frequency distribution of the test scores. In the table, also include the proportions, percentages, cumulative frequencies, cumulative proportions, and cumulative percentages.

b. Construct a frequency distribution of the variable "gender," including both proportions and percentages.

c. If a score of 14 or higher constituted a "pass" on the exam, how many and what percentage of the recruits passed the test?

d. If a score of 18 or higher earned a rookie the distinction of "passing with honors," how many and what proportion of the class passed with honors?

e. If those who had a score of 13 or lower have to repeat their training, how many of this class will have to repeat it?

f. What were the proportions of males and females in this class?

g. Graph the frequency data for the test scores and the percentage data (with a pie chart) for the gender data.

h. Graph the cumulative frequency data for the test scores.

6. You have a sample of 75 adults and have asked them all to report the age at which they committed their first delinquent or criminal act. The responses are shown in the following table. With these data, construct a grouped frequency distribution. Make the lower limit of your first class interval be 6, and have an interval width of 5. Then make a frequency distribution that includes the proportions, percentages, cumulative frequencies, cumulative proportions, and cumulative percentages.

**Age at First Offense**

| | | | | |
|:---:|:---:|:---:|:---:|:---:|
| 17 | 22 | 13 | 24 | 15 |
| 12 | 30 | 17 | 27 | 16 |
| 21 | 14 | 12 | 13 | 18 |
| 18 | 27 | 19 | 18 | 25 |
| 11 | 19 | 11 | 26 | 30 |
| 28 | 28 | 23 | 14 | 35 |
| 8 | 13 | 26 | 22 | 21 |
| 17 | 20 | 15 | 39 | 15 |
| 26 | 24 | 16 | 30 | 31 |
| 31 | 25 | 24 | 23 | 6 |
| 15 | 32 | 29 | 38 | 36 |
| 34 | 16 | 12 | 34 | 12 |
| 20 | 12 | 33 | 35 | 34 |
| 7 | 21 | 11 | 37 | 19 |
| 11 | 21 | 20 | 43 | 35 |

Then answer the following questions:

a. What are the real limits of these class intervals?

b. What is the midpoint of each class interval?

c. How many of these persons committed their first offense before the age of 31?

d. What proportion committed their first offense between the ages of 11 and 15?

e. What percentage committed their first offense after age 20?

f. What percentage committed their first offense before the age of 16?

7. The data in the following table show the total property crime victimization rate from the National Crime Victimization Survey for the time period 1993–2013. Graph these data with a time plot. What time trend or trends do you detect in these data?

**National Crime Victimization Survey Property Crime Trends, 1993–2013**

| Victimization Year | Rate per 1,000 Households | Victimization Year | Rate per 1,000 Households |
|---|---|---|---|
| 1993 | 351.8 | 2004 | 167.5 |
| 1994 | 341.2 | 2005 | 159.5 |
| 1995 | 315.5 | 2006 | 169.0 |
| 1996 | 289.3 | 2007 | 154.9 |
| 1997 | 267.1 | 2008 | 142.6 |
| 1998 | 237.1 | 2009 | 132.6 |
| 1999 | 210.6 | 2010 | 125.4 |
| 2000 | 190.4 | 2011 | 138.7 |
| 2001 | 177.7 | 2012 | 155.8 |
| 2002 | 168.2 | 2013 | 131.4 |
| 2003 | 173.4 | | |

*Source:* Data taken from the Bureau of Justice Statistics at www.ojp .usdoj.gov/bjs/.

8. The following data represent the estimated number of arrests over the time period 1994–2012 for robberies among adults as determined by the FBI's Uniform Crime Reports. With these data, construct a time plot of the number of arrests with both the original data and then after smoothing the data with a three-year moving average.

| Year | Number of Arrests | Year | Number of Arrests |
|---|---|---|---|
| 1994 | 117,300 | 2004 | 83,700 |
| 1995 | 116,200 | 2005 | 85,600 |
| 1996 | 106,400 | 2006 | 90,800 |
| 1997 | 92,300 | 2007 | 92,400 |
| 1998 | 86,900 | 2008 | 94,200 |
| 1999 | 79,200 | 2009 | 95,000 |
| 2000 | 78,600 | 2010 | 85,100 |
| 2001 | 81,900 | 2011 | 82,900 |
| 2002 | 81,200 | 2012 | 82,200 |
| 2003 | 82,300 | | |

*Source:* Data taken from Easy Access to FBI Arrest Statistics at http://www.ojjdp.gov/ojstatbb/ezaucr/asp/ucr_display.asp.

## SPSS Exercises

➤ Explore additional data sets. $SAGE edge™

| Data for Exercise | |
|---|---|
| *Data Set* | *Description* |
| NCVS lone offender assaults 1992 to 2013.sav | These data are from the National Crime Victimization Survey (NCVS), a nationally representative study of individual's experience of criminal victimization. This particular data set contains responses from 1992 to 2013, allowing for larger numbers of uncommon offenses to be used in analyses. It also only includes data from respondents who reported either violent or nonviolent assault by a single offender. |
| **Variables for Exercise** | |
| *Variable Name* | *Description* |
| Year | The year in which the data were collected. Ranges from 1992 to 2013. |
| Maleoff | The sex of the offender where 1 = male and 0 = female. |

| Variables for Exercise | |
|---|---|
| *Variable Name* | *Description* |
| Injury | A binary variable indicating if the respondent was physically injured during the assault, where 1 = injured and 0 = uninjured. |
| Age_r | The age (in years) at which victimization occurred. This variable is cut off at 75. |
| V2129 | This is a three-category nominal indicator of where a person lives. This is based on metropolitan statistical area (MSA) classifications, but loosely speaking, 1 = lives in city, 2 = lives near city (e.g., suburbs and outskirts), 3 = lives in a rural area away from cities. |

1. **Creating Charts in SPSS:** Identify the level of measurement and which type of graph (histogram, pie chart, bar chart) is appropriate for each of the following variables. If it is helpful, feel free to make frequency tables to determine this. Then, create that chart in SPSS. To create the chart select Graphs->Legacy Dialogues->select bar, pie, or histogram. Then put the appropriate variable in the "category axis" or "variable" box:

   a. Injury

   b. Maleoff

   c. Age_r

      i. For this variable, also answer: Is this variable's distribution skewed? If so, in what direction? Is there evidence of any extreme outliers?

   d. V2129

2. Pick two of the variables and/or charts from question 1. Write an explanation for your results in a way that would be easily understood by a lay person that isn't familiar with statistics. What does it tell us about people who are assault victims?

3. What proportion of individuals were assaulted before they were 18? One way to see this is to look at a cumulative percentage table for the variable age_r. Create a frequency table for age_r as was described in chapter 1, but this time focus on the far right column. What proportion of individuals were younger than 18 when they were victimized?

4. The downside of the approach in question 3 is that you won't be able to easily make a graph of that finding. In this question we'll do a *recode* to allow for a graph of the age_r variable to make it easier to graph. Recoding typically involves grouping values of a variable in a way that simplifies them or makes useful distinctions:

   a. **Recoding Variables in SPSS:** Start with a plan. We want 0 to correspond to "younger than 18" and 1 to correspond to "older than 18."

   b. To begin the recoding process, select data->recode into *different* variables. Make sure you *don't* select "recode into same variables," which will overwrite your original variable!

   c. Put age_r in the box. Then under the field for "output variable," type the name "Vic18andover". Click "change."

   d. Select "old and new values." A new window will pop up. On the left side, you enter your original values; while on the right side, you specify a value that they will be recoded to. First, select "system or user missing" and select "system-missing" in the new value; then press "add." *This is an essential habit to get into as it will prevent you from unintentionally recoding missing values, which are treated as positive infinity by SPSS.*

   e. Use the "greater than" and "less than" options to tell SPSS the values that you want to use as a cut off; in this case, all values greater than 18 = 1, all values 17 or lower = 0. Be sure to hit "add" after each old and new value is specified.

   f. The new variable will appear at the bottom of variable view mode. Under the "values" column, select the cell for "Vic18andover" and click the " . . . " option. Then, copy the meaning for 0 and 1 specified in part 5a, selecting "add" for each one. This will make it so that output will show you what the categories you've created mean, rather than just showing the numbers 0 and 1.

   g. Create a frequency table of Vic18andover. Make sure that the proportion of individuals who were victimized younger than age 18 is the same as your answer for question 3. If it is not, double check your recode because you've made a mistake!

   h. Create a bar chart of your new variable, Vic18andover.

5. The NCVS has been conducted for many years using roughly the same measures. As such it is an excellent tool for tracking trends over time. To begin with, let's look at this theory: Some criminologists have suggested that as women enter the workforce and adopt more traditionally masculine roles, they will also engage in other more masculine behaviors. In particular, they will be more likely to commit crimes!

a. To test this assertion we'll look at whether assault victims report a male or a female offender at different rates over time. To do this, select graphs->legacy dialogues->line->simple. Then put the variable year in the "category axis" box. In the "line represents" area, select "other statistic" and add the variable maleoff into the box that lights up. Then select "ok":

i. What is the general trend over time? The *y* axis can be multiplied by 100 to get the % of offenders who are male.

ii. Do these results support the theory presented?

iii. Look carefully at the scale of your graph: How large are these changes that have occurred over time?

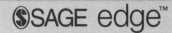

# CHAPTER 4

# Measures of Central Tendency

---

**LEARNING OBJECTIVES**

1. Describe the only measure of center appropriate for a nominal-level variable.

2. Identify the difference between the median and the mean.

3. Describe when the median may be a better measure of center compared with the mean.

4. Explain how to calculate and interpret all measures of center from both grouped and ungrouped data.

---

## 回 Introduction

What do you think about when you think about the average or typical prisoner released from state prisons today? Well, the most recent data available tell us that the typical state prisoner released is more likely to be a male who is 40 years of age or older, equally likely to be African American or White, and has an average of 4.9 prior convictions (Durose,

Cooper, & Snyder, 2014). We have conveyed a lot of information with concepts such as "typical" and "average," in this sentence, but in this chapter, you are going to learn more precise statistical concepts used to describe the most typical quality or value of a variable. In Chapter 3, we learned to describe our data using frequency distributions and graphical displays. These pieces of information are important, but they should be combined with summary statistics that also help describe our variable distribution. In this chapter, you will learn about summary statistics called **measures of central tendency**. Think of the two key words in this term and what they connote—central tendency—a tendency to be at the center of something, in this case, the center of data. Measures of central tendency capture the "typical," "average," or "most likely" score or value in a distribution of scores.

**Measures of central tendency:**
Summary statistics that capture the "typical," "average," or "most likely" score or value in a variable distribution.

We will discuss three different measures of central tendency in this chapter: the mode, the median, and the mean. Each measure captures a somewhat different notion of "central tendency," and you should not be surprised to learn that each requires a certain level of measurement.

## ▣ The Mode

**Mode:** Value of a variable that occurs more often than any other value.

The **mode** is one measure of central tendency. The mode conceptualizes "central tendency" in terms of what is the *most likely, most common, or most frequent* score in a distribution of scores. Another way to think of the mode is to note that it is the score or value that has the greatest probability of occurring. The mode can be calculated with data measured at the nominal, ordinal, or interval/ratio level. However, if you have nominal- or purely ordinal-level data (purely ordinal in the sense that the data are not continuous data that you have made ordinal by making class intervals or grouping your data), then the mode is the *only* appropriate measure of central tendency that you may legitimately use.

The mode is also very easy to calculate or determine. If the data are in numerical or tabular form, the mode can be identified by finding the score or value in a distribution that has (a) the greatest frequency, (b) the largest proportion, or (c) the highest percentage. If the data are in graphical form, the mode can be identified by finding the score or value in the graph that has (a) the largest slice in a pie chart, (b) the longest bar in a bar chart, or (c) the highest bar in a histogram. Thus, the way the mode "interprets" central tendency is that it is the most likely or probable or the most frequent score or value in a distribution of values. Since it is the most frequent score, if you divide the frequency by the total number of cases, you can see that the mode is also the score with the greatest probability of occurring. Think of the mode like this: If you had information on the type of different sentences for a sample of convicted offenders (probation, jail, a fine, prison) and you wanted to know which sentence was most often imposed, you would be asking about the mode.

## Case Study

### The Modal Category of Hate Crime

Let's go through a couple of examples. In Chapter 3, we presented data that showed the distribution of different kinds of hate crimes that were reported to the police in the year 2013 (Table 3.1); these data are reproduced in Table 4.1. A hate crime is defined as one that is intended to hurt and intimidate someone because of his or her race, ethnicity, national origin, religion, sexual preference, or disability. As you can see, there were 5,922 single-bias, hate-crime incidents reported to the Federal Bureau of Investigation (FBI) Uniform Crime Reports Program that year that fell into one of five distinct types based on the motivation or the type of hate that precipitated the crime. The variable "reported hate crime" is measured at the nominal level because the only distinction among the values of this variable are qualitative distinctions of "kind."

Looking at the distribution of scores in this table, we can discern that the most frequent type of hate crime in 2013, or the modal hate crime, was one motivated by racial hostility. We would conclude, therefore, that the mode for this variable is "racially motivated hate crime." There are a number of different ways we could come to this conclusion, each of which would converge on the same answer. First, we could look at the reported frequencies, discover that there were 2,871 racially motivated hate crimes, and note that this frequency is clearly greater than the frequency for all other kinds of reported hate crimes. Second, we could look at the column of proportions, find that nearly one half (.485) of all hate crimes that were reported were racially motivated, and note that this proportion is greater than the proportion for any other kind of hate crime. Third, we could examine the row of percentages, find that 48.5% of all hate crimes in 2013 were racially motivated hate crimes, and note that this percentage is greater than the percentage for any other type of hate crime. Finally, we could use the information we have about proportions to determine the probability of each type of hate crime and then draw a conclusion about what the mode is. Since the proportion or relative frequency of a value/score can also be understood as its expected chance or probability of occurring, we can see that if we were to select randomly 1 out of the 5,922 hate crimes in 2013, the probability that it would be a racially motivated hate crime would be .485, the probability that it would be motivated by religious prejudice would be .174, the probability of a sexually motivated hate crime would be .208, and so on. The greatest-probability event, therefore, is a racial hate crime—nearly 49 out of every 100 hate crimes reported in 2013 were racial hate crimes, a probability that exceeds that of all other possible outcomes. All of our different ways to capture the mode tell us that the modal type of hate crime was racially motivated hate crime.

Another way to determine what the mode is for a nominal- or ordinal-level variable is to examine the graph of the frequency data (or the graphed proportions or percentages). In Figure 4.1, we show the pie chart of

**Table 4.1**  Types of Hate Crime Incidents Reported to Police in 2013

| Basis of Hate | f | Proportion | % |
|---|---|---|---|
| Race | 2,871 | .485 | 48.5 |
| Religion | 1,031 | .174 | 17.4 |
| Sexual orientation | 1,233 | .208 | 20.8 |
| Ethnicity/national origin | 655 | .111 | 11.1 |
| Disability | 83 | .014 | 1.4 |
| Gender | 18 | .003 | .3 |
| Gender identity | 31 | .005 | .5 |
| Total | 5,922 | 1.000 | 100.0% |

*Source:* Adapted from *Hate Crimes Statistics—2013* from the Federal Bureau of Investigation (2013b).

**Figure 4.1**  Type of Hate Crime Incident Reported to Police in 2013

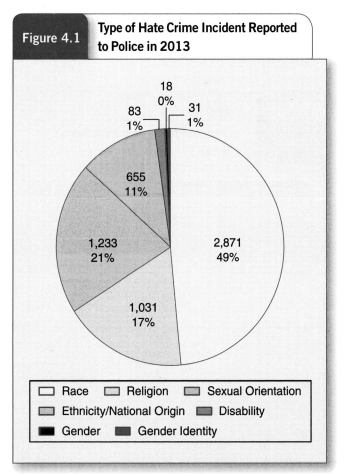

the data in Table 4.1 with both the frequency and the percentage of each value. Note that the largest slice in the pie is for the value "race hate crime." This is the modal hate crime for 2013.

The modal type of hate crime reported in 2013, then, is a racially motivated hate crime. Note that the mode is the *value* or *score* that is most frequent or most likely, not the actual numerical value of the frequency, proportion, or percentage. The mode for the variable "reported hate crime in the year 2013" is "racially motivated hate crime." The mode is not 2,871 or .485 or 48.5%. The mistake that students most frequently make when they are first learning statistics is that they conclude that the mode is some frequency, proportion, or percentage rather than the value of a given variable. To avoid making this mistake, just remember that the mode is the value, score, or outcome of a variable that is most likely or frequent, not the actual frequency of that value.

## Case Study

## The Modal Number of Prior Arrests

In Table 4.2, we report the frequency distribution (and percentages) of the number of prior arrests for a hypothetical sample of 150 armed robbery suspects. The data are in the form of an ungrouped frequency distribution, and the variable "number of prior arrests" is measured at the interval/ratio level. The histogram for the frequency data is shown in Figure 4.2. Note in the table that there are two values that are more frequent than all of the others: "0 prior arrests" and "1 prior arrest." The probability that a randomly selected armed robber from this sample would have exactly 0 prior arrests is .2533 ($f = 38$), and the probability of exactly 1 prior arrest is .2333 ($f = 35$). The two frequencies and probabilities for these values are very comparable and much greater than any of the other values. This corresponds to the height of the two largest rectangular bars in the histogram (Figure 4.3) for 0 and 1 prior arrest. Even though the frequencies for 0 and 1 prior arrests are not exactly equal, they are very comparable, and their frequencies are much greater than those of any other value. They are comparable enough that it might be misleading to say that there is one and only one distinct mode in these data. It would appear more appropriate, then, that for this variable, there are two distinct modes: a mode of 0 prior arrests and a mode of 1 prior arrest. Because there are two modes in the data, this distribution has a bimodal distribution. A **bimodal distribution** is a distribution that has two distinct values with the greatest frequency or the largest probability of occurring, even if their frequencies are not exactly equal. It tells us that there are two scores that are roughly the most typical or most likely scores in the distribution.

The strategy for identifying the mode when the data are in the form of a grouped frequency distribution is pretty much the same as what we have just discussed. Table 4.3 provides the grouped frequency distribution for the variable "time until rearrest" for a sample of 120 male inmates who were released from prison and who were rearrested at some point after release. We first presented these data in the previous chapter. Recall that each person's "score" reflects the number of days he was

> **Bimodal distribution:** Distribution that contains two distinct modes with the greatest frequency, even if the frequencies are not exactly equal.

| Table 4.2 | Number of Prior Arrests for a Sample of Armed Robbery Suspects | |
|---|---|---|
| Number | f | % |
| 0 | 38 | 25.33 |
| 1 | 35 | 23.33 |
| 2 | 10 | 6.67 |
| 3 | 9 | 6.00 |
| 4 | 14 | 9.33 |
| 5 | 7 | 4.67 |
| 6 | 11 | 7.33 |
| 7 | 8 | 5.33 |
| 8 | 10 | 6.67 |
| 9 | 5 | 3.33 |
| 10 or more | 3 | 2.00 |
| Total | n = 150 | 99.99%* |

*Percentages may not sum to 100% due to rounding.

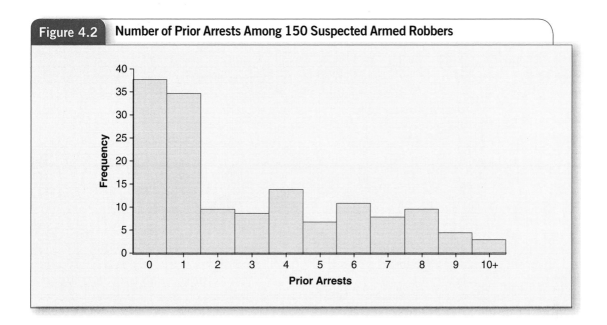

Figure 4.2 Number of Prior Arrests Among 150 Suspected Armed Robbers

out in the community after being released before he committed a new offense. The histogram for these data is shown in Figure 4.3, where the class intervals are shown on the $x$ axis. When we look at this frequency distribution, it is apparent that these are bimodal data. The two modes are represented by the class intervals 29–31 days and 32–34 days. For both of these class intervals, the frequency is higher than for any other class interval. Exactly 28 persons were arrested between 19 and 31 days after release and 28 persons were rearrested between 32 and 34 days (very close to one month) after their release from prison. The two modes also can be seen from the histogram as the two highest peaks in Figure 4.3.

**Table 4.3** Grouped Frequency Distribution for Time-Until-Rearrest Data for 120 Released Offenders

| Stated Limits | f | Midpoint |
|---|---|---|
| 17–19 days | 4 | 18 |
| 20–22 days | 1 | 21 |
| 23–25 days | 12 | 24 |
| 26–28 days | 16 | 27 |
| 29–31 days | 28 | 30 |
| 32–34 days | 28 | 33 |
| 35–37 days | 21 | 36 |
| 38–40 days | 10 | 39 |
| | n = 150 | |

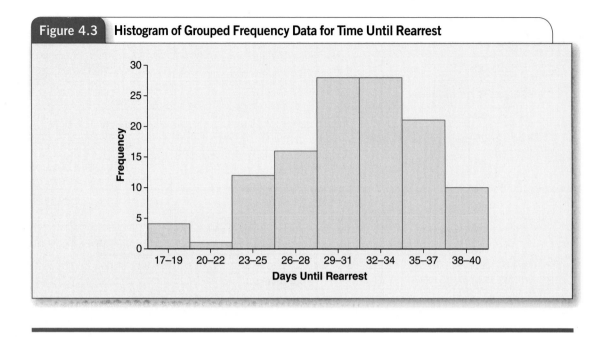

**Figure 4.3** Histogram of Grouped Frequency Data for Time Until Rearrest

## Advantages and Disadvantages of the Mode

As a measure of central tendency, the mode has both advantages and disadvantages relative to other measures. One advantage of the mode is that it is very simple to determine and appealing conceptually. It is the score or value that is the most frequent and that has the greatest probability of occurring in a distribution of scores. This simple elegance means that the mode is very easy for readers to comprehend and understand, which is a key quality that statistical measures should have. The mode is also very simple to "calculate." In fact, there is no real arithmetic calculation to determine the mode—nothing to add or subtract. We just identify the score with the greatest frequency (or proportion or percentage) in either a tabular presentation of data or a graph (find the tallest or longest bar or the largest slice of pie). Finally, the mode is a very general measure of central tendency since it can be determined for variables measured at any level. The mode is an appropriate measure of central tendency for data measured at the nominal, ordinal, and interval/ratio level.

The simplicity of understanding and determining the mode is offset by its disadvantage. Since the mode is based only on the most frequent score or scores, it does not take into account all or even most of the information available in a distribution. One thing statisticians do not like to do is ignore data or information, but that is exactly what the mode does; it ignores all information in the data except the values/scores with the highest frequency. By ignoring or throwing out information, the mode may at times give us a very misleading notion of the central tendency of our data. For example, Table 4.4 shows the number of subsequent

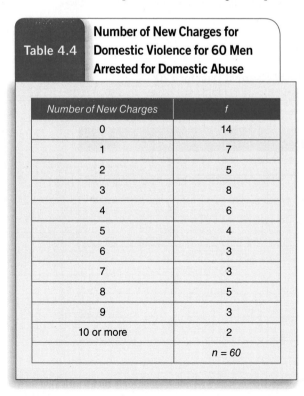

**Table 4.4** Number of New Charges for Domestic Violence for 60 Men Arrested for Domestic Abuse

| Number of New Charges | f |
|---|---|
| 0 | 14 |
| 1 | 7 |
| 2 | 5 |
| 3 | 8 |
| 4 | 6 |
| 5 | 4 |
| 6 | 3 |
| 7 | 3 |
| 8 | 5 |
| 9 | 3 |
| 10 or more | 2 |
| | n = 60 |

charges of domestic violence accumulated over a one-year period by a sample of 60 men who had been arrested for intimate partner assault. According to the table, the mode would be "0 new charges since arrest" since this value has the greatest frequency. Note, however, that the ease of identifying "0 new charges" as the mode comes at the price of ignoring the fact that many of the men in this sample *did* have numerous new charges of being abusive toward their partner after they were first arrested. Although it is technically correct that the modal number of new charges is zero, this is somewhat misleading and does not represent the entire distribution of values. Because of this deficiency with the mode, when we have interval/ratio-level data, we most often use an alternative measure of central tendency such as the median or the mean.

## 🖾 The Median

The **median** is an appropriate measure of central tendency for quantitative data measured at the interval/ratio level or for data that may have originally been measured at the interval/ratio level but now consist of grouped data (class intervals for grouped frequency distributions that have real limits). The easiest way to think of the median is that it is the value that is at the 50th percentile in a rank-ordered distribution of scores. The 50th percentile is also known as the second quartile when the data are divided into four quartiles.

> **Median:** Score at the 50th percentile in a rank-ordered distribution of scores. Thus, one half of a variable's values are less than the median and one half are greater than the median.

The median score, in other words, is the score in the exact middle of a rank-ordered distribution of quantitative scores such that the median is the point above which one half of the scores are and below which the other one half of the scores fall.

When the data are continuous (not grouped), the median value is very easy to find by following these two steps:

---

### Steps to Find the Median

**Step 1:** Rank-order all scores from lowest score to highest score.

**Step 2:** Find the position of the score ($x$) that is the median score by the following formula: Median position = $(n + 1) / 2$. This formula says that the *position* of the median score is found by adding 1 to the total number of scores and then dividing by 2. *This formula will not give you the value of the median but the position of the median score.* To find the value of the median, find the score in the position indicated by the formula in the rank-ordered array of scores.

---

When there are an odd number of scores, this formula is very easy to use.

## Case Study

## The Median Police Response Time and Vandalism Offending

Let us say that we have seven scores that represent the number of minutes it takes the police to respond to a 911 call for service: 9, 1, 3, 6, 12, 2, and 15. To find the median number of minutes it takes the police to respond, step 1 instructs us first to rank-order the scores from low to high:

| Rank | Score |
|------|-------|
| 1 | 1 minute |
| 2 | 2 minutes |
| 3 | 3 minutes |
| 4 | 6 minutes |
| 5 | 9 minutes |
| 6 | 12 minutes |
| 7 | 15 minutes |

Then we find the position of the median with our positional locator, $(n + 1) / 2$, which in this case is $(7 + 1) / 2 = 8 / 2 = $ 4th position. The median score is in the fourth position in our rank-ordered scores. Again, we emphasize that the median is not 4, but it put falls in the fourth position of our rank-ordered scores. The scores, therefore, must all be put in rank order before you can find the median. To find the value of the median, find the score in the fourth position. We can do this either by starting at the top of the rank-ordered scores (the lowest score) and counting down until we find the fourth score or by starting at the bottom (the highest score) and counting up until we find the fourth score. The result is the same; the score in the fourth position of our rank-ordered scores is 6 minutes. The median amount of time it took to respond to a 911 call for service, therefore, is 6 minutes. Note that exactly one half of the scores in this distribution are lower (1, 2, and 3 minutes) and exactly one half are higher (9, 12, and 15 minutes). The median score, then, sits in the exact middle of the distribution of rank-ordered scores. This is the way the median "interprets" central tendency—it is a positional measure. We can say that 50% of the scores in the distribution of police response time fall below 6 minutes and 50% fall above this value.

Now let us add one more call for service to these data. In this case it took the police 18 minutes to respond—the longest time so far. We now have a total of eight scores, and the rank order of these eight scores is:

| Rank | Score |
|------|-------|
| 1 | 1 minute |
| 2 | 2 minutes |
| 3 | 3 minutes |
| 4 | 6 minutes |
| 5 | 9 minutes |
| 6 | 12 minutes |
| 7 | 15 minutes |
| 8 | 18 minutes |

When we use our positional locator formula for the median, we find that the position of the median is $(8 + 1) / 2 = 9 / 2 = $ 4.5th score [notice we now have 8 data points so the numerator in our formula is 8). What does a position of 4.5 mean? It means that the median score is the score that is at the midpoint between the fourth and fifth scores in our rank-ordered distribution of scores. Since our fourth score (starting from the lowest score) is 6 minutes and our fifth score (again from the lowest score) is 9 minutes, the median score is the midpoint between these scores. Had we found the fourth and fifth scores by starting at the bottom or highest score and counted up, the two scores would still have been 9 and 6. To find the midpoint between our two scores, we have to add the two scores and then divide by 2.

The midpoint between 6 minutes and 9 minutes is $(6 + 9) / 2 = 15 / 2 = 7.5$ minutes. The median number of minutes it took the police to respond in this second set of scores, then, is 7.5 minutes. Note that one half of the scores are greater than this time and one half are less. The median measures central tendency as the score in the middle in a set of rank-ordered scores, or 50th percentile. That is what the median means.

Another way to identify the median in a set of continuous scores is to find the 50th percentile in a cumulative percentage distribution (you already learned how to make a cumulative percentage distribution, so this should be good practice). Table 4.5 reports the distribution of scores for a variable called "number of times committing vandalism" for a sample of 77 boys; the values range from 0 times to 10 or more times. The first column in Table 4.5 reports the value or score (the number of times a boy reported committing an act of vandalism), the second column shows the frequency for each value, the third column reports the cumulative frequency, the fourth column is the percentage for each value, and the fifth and final column compiles the cumulative percentages.

There are two ways to find the median number of acts of vandalism in this distribution. One is to use the formula for the position of the median we just learned. Since we have $n = 77$ total scores, the median is in the $(77 + 1) / 2 = 78 / 2 = 39$th position. To find the score at the 39th position, all we have to do is use the column of cumulative frequencies. We can see from this column that 30 scores are at the value of 2 or lower and that 41 scores are at

| Table 4.5 | Reported Number of Times Committing Vandalism for 77 Boys | | | |
|---|---|---|---|---|
| # of Times | f | cf | % | c% |
| 0 | 15 | 15 | 19 | 19 |
| 1 | 10 | 25 | 13 | 32 |
| 2 | 5 | 30 | 7 | 39 |
| 3 | 11 | 41 | 14 | 53 |
| 4 | 7 | 48 | 9 | 62 |
| 5 | 8 | 56 | 10 | 72 |
| 6 | 5 | 61 | 7 | 79 |
| 7 | 4 | 65 | 5 | 84 |
| 8 | 5 | 70 | 7 | 91 |
| 9 | 4 | 74 | 5 | 96 |
| 10 or more | 3 | 77 | 4 | 100 |
| Total | n = 77 | | 100 | |

the value of 3 or lower. If the 30th score is a 2, and that is the last 2 in the distribution, we have to go to the next value to find the next scores. This means that the 31st score is a 3, the 32nd score is a 3, . . . , the 39th score is a 3, and the 40th and 41st as well [the 42nd score is a 4]. Since the median score is the 39th score, the median must be "3 acts of vandalism." We could also have discovered this by looking at the column of cumulative percentages. Since the median is the 50th percentile, all we have to do is find the score at the 50th percentile. We can see that values of "2 acts of vandalism" are at the 39th percentile and that values of "3 acts of vandalism" go from the 40th to the 53rd percentile—the 50th percentile is contained here. The 50th percentile, then, is at the score of "3 acts of vandalism." In words, then, 50% of the boys in the sample committed 3 or fewer acts of vandalism and 50% of the boys committed 3 or more acts of vandalism.

## The Median for Grouped Data

What do we do when we have grouped data and want to find the median score? Things get a little more complicated, but with a formula and a little work, we can determine the median with grouped data as well. Table 4.6 reports the grouped frequency distribution for the example of 120 prison inmates who had served their sentences and were released into the community from whom we have the number of days they were "free" before they were rearrested. Note that this table reports the real limits of the class intervals. As you will see, you need to know the real limits when calculating the median for grouped data. The presence of real limits tells us that these ordinal-level data were once measured at the interval or ratio level permitting us to calculate a median. The procedure for determining the value of the median for these grouped data is comparable to that for ungrouped data.

First we have to rank-order the values of the variable. In Table 4.6, the values of the variable "time until rearrest" consist of class intervals, and they are already rank-ordered from low to high. Now that the class intervals are

| Table 4.6 | Grouped Frequency Distribution for Time-Until-Rearrest Data for 120 Inmates | | |
|---|---|---|---|
| Stated Limits | Real Limits | f | cf |
| 17–19 days | 16.5–19.5 days | 4 | 4 |
| 20–22 days | 19.5–22.5 days | 1 | 5 |
| 23–25 days | 22.5–25.5 days | 12 | 17 |
| 26–28 days | 25.5–28.5 days | 16 | 33 |
| 29–31 days | 28.5–31.5 days | 28 | 61 |
| 32–34 days | 31.5–34.5 days | 28 | 89 |
| 35–37 days | 34.5–37.5 days | 21 | 110 |
| 38–40 days | 37.5–40.5 days | 10 | 120 |
| | | n = 120 | |

rank-ordered, we need to find the interval that contains the median. We can use our positional locator $(n + 1) / 2$ and the column of cumulative frequencies to find the interval that contains the median. Since $n = 120$, the median is in the $(120 + 1) / 2 = 121 / 2 = 60.5$th position, or the score that is at the midpoint between the 60th and 61st scores. We now have to locate the class interval that has the median. The class interval 26–28 days contains the 18th to the 33rd score according to the column of cumulative frequencies ($cf$). The 34th score through the 61st score, then, can be found in the class interval 29–31 days (see the column of cumulative frequencies). This is the interval that contains the median since the median score is the midpoint between the 60th and 61st scores and the 60th and 61st scores are at the end of that interval. With this information we are now ready to calculate the actual value of the median. We can determine the value of the median (and not just the location in this case) with the following formula:

$$X_{median} = L + \left( \frac{\left( \frac{n+1}{2} \right) - cf}{f} \right) w_i \qquad \text{(4-1)}$$

where

$X_{median}$ = the value of the median

$L$ = the lower real limit of the class interval that contains the median

$cf$ = the cumulative frequency of the class interval just before the class interval that contains the median

$f$ = the frequency of the interval that contains the median

$w_i$ = the width of the class interval

$n$ = the total number of observations in the sample

Now let us calculate what the median number of days until rearrest is in these data:

$$X_{median} = L + \left( \frac{\left( \frac{n+1}{2} \right) - cf}{f} \right) w_i$$

$$X_{median} = 28.5 + \left( \frac{\left( \frac{120+1}{2} \right) - 33}{28} \right) 3$$

$$X_{median} = 28.5 + \left( \frac{60.5 - 33}{28} \right) 3$$

$$X_{median} = 28.5 + (.98)3$$

$$X_{median} = 28.5 + 2.94$$

$$X_{median} = 31.44 \text{ days until rearrest}$$

The median number of days until rearrest, then, is 31.44 days. In this distribution of grouped data, we can say that one half of the inmates were rearrested within 31.44 days, or about one month, and one half were arrested at 31.44 days or later. Remember that all of the people in this sample were eventually arrested.

## Advantages and Disadvantages of the Median

The median has a number of advantages as a measure of central tendency. First, unlike the mode that can have more than one value, there will always be only one median. Second, as the score in the exact middle of a rank-ordered distribution of scores, the median value has intuitive appeal—it is easy to understand. For example, if when you took the ACT or SAT test before college you found out that you scored at the 50th percentile, you knew that you were in the middle of the rank-ordered scores, that one half of the students taking the test the same time you did scored higher than you and one half scored lower than you. Third, the median is a useful measure of central tendency that is used in some graphical displays of data. In Chapter 5, for example, we will consider other ways to display graphically the distribution of a variable in something called a "box-and-whisker plot." In these graphs, the median is the measure of central tendency in the data that we will use. Finally, because the median does not use all of the scores in our data, it is not influenced by extremely high or extremely low scores. As we learned in the last chapter, extremely high or low scores in a distribution are referred to as outliers. Since the median locates the score in the middle of the distribution, or at the 50th percentile, it does not matter whether there are outliers in the data. Let us explain.

Table 4.7 records three columns of data. Each column represents the rate of forcible rape per 100,000 people for a sample of U.S. cities in 2013. There are seven cities in the first column, and the rape rates have already been rank-ordered. The position of the median in these data is the 4th score:

$$\left( \frac{7+1}{2} = 4 \right)$$

and the median rape rate for these seven cities is 28.1 rapes per 100.000. In the next column of cities we simply add one more city, Anchorage, Alaska, with a rape rate of 133.2 per 100,000. This is an extremely high rape rate, and adding it to this list of seven cities makes it a high outlier. What happens to the value of the median? Well, with eight cases now in the distribution, the median score is the midpoint between the 4th and 5th scores:

$$\left( \frac{8+1}{2} = 4.5 \right)$$

As such, we have to take the average of the scores in the 4th and 5th positions, which gives us:

$$\left( \frac{28.1 + 28.4}{2} = 28.25 \right) \text{ rapes per } 100,000$$

As you can clearly see, adding this very high outlier did not change the median rape rate much at all, only from 28.1 rapes per 100,000 to 28.25 rapes per 100,000. Despite the outlier, the median still gives a very accurate assessment of the central tendency of rape rates in these data. The median is sturdy or robust in the presence of a high outlier.

In the next set of cities, we remove Anchorage and substitute Goldsboro, North Carolina, which in 2013 had a rate of forcible rape of only 4.0 per 100,000, one of the lowest rape rates of all major U.S. cities [since these are rape rates, or the number of rapes per population, it does not matter that Goldsboro is a small town; Goldsboro has a population that is greater than Redmond, Oregon]. The rape rate for Goldsboro is an example of a low outlier. We once again find the median for these eight scores as the midpoint between the 4th and 5th scores:

$$\frac{28.0 + 28.1}{2} = 28.05 \text{ rapes per } 100,000$$

By comparing the three medians we calculated with seven cities, the median rape rate was 28.1 per 100,000. When we added Anchorage with a high outlier, the median rate was 28.25. And when we added Goldsboro with a low outlier, the median rape rate was 28.05. In each case, the measure of central tendency tells us that the median rape rate is around 28 per 100,000 population. Even when there are outlying scores, then, the median is a very stable measure of central tendency because it is defined as the 50th percentile and does not take the value of each and every score into account. This is an important advantage of the median as a measure of central tendency. One disadvantage of the median is that, like the mode, it uses only one or two pieces of information. The next measure of central tendency we will discuss, the mean, uses all the information in the data to determine its central tendency.

**Table 4.7**    **Rape Rates (per 100,000 people) for Selected U.S. Cities in 2013**

| Rank | City | Rate | Rank | City | Rate | Rank | City | Rate |
|------|------|------|------|------|------|------|------|------|
| 1 | Binghamton, NY | 22.2 | 1 | Binghamton, NY | 22.2 | 1 | Goldsboro, NC | 4.0 |
| 2 | Albany, GA | 23.5 | 2 | Albany, GA | 23.5 | 2 | Binghamton, NY | 22.2 |
| 3 | Redmond, OR | 28.0 | 3 | Redmond, OR | 28.0 | 3 | Albany, GA | 23.5 |
| 4 | Cedar Rapids, IA | 28.1 | 4 | Cedar Rapids, IA | 28.1 | 4 | Redmond, OR | 28.0 |
| 5 | Charleston, SC | 28.4 | 5 | Charleston, SC | 28.4 | 5 | Cedar Rapids, IA | 28.1 |
| 6 | Boston, MA | 33.8 | 6 | Boston, MA | 33.8 | 6 | Charleston, SC | 28.4 |
| 7 | Akron, OH | 38.4 | 7 | Akron, OH | 38.4 | 7 | Boston, MA | 33.8 |
|  |  |  | 8 | Anchorage, AK | 133.2 | 8 | Akron, OH | 38.4 |

*Source:* Adapted from *Crime In the United States* from the Federal Bureau of Investigation (2013a).

# ▣ The Mean

The third and final measure of central tendency that we will examine is the mean. Like the median, the mean requires that the data be measured at the interval/ratio level. However, it too can be calculated if you have ordinal data in the form of a grouped frequency distribution where you have taken continuous data and created class intervals. An example of this is the time until rearrest for the group of 120 released offenders that we have been discussing.

---

## Case Study

### Calculating the Mean Time Until Rearrest

The **mean** is defined as the arithmetic average of a group of scores and is calculated by summing all of the scores and then dividing by the total number of scores. You are already very familiar with the mean. Your college grade point average is a mean. For example, suppose you took five classes last semester and earned two A's, a B, a C, and one D (in math, of course). Let's assume that your college assigns 4.0 for an A grade, 3.0 for a B grade, 2.0 for a C grade, and 1.0 for a grade of D. Your GPA, or grade point *average,* for last semester, then, would be $(4 + 4 + 3 + 2 + 1) / 5 = 14 / 5 = 2.8$. This is the mean grade you received in all five of your classes. Your average would be almost a B, reflecting the fact that you did get two A's but also received a C and a D.

> **Mean:** Arithmetic average of a group of scores calculated as the sum of the scores divided by the total number of scores. The mean is an appropriate measure of central tendency for interval/ratio-level data.

Before we get some practice in calculating the mean, we need to distinguish between the mean of a population and the mean of a sample. Recall from our discussion in Chapter 1 that a population consists of the universe of cases we are interested in. For example, if we are interested in the relationship between IQ scores and delinquency among male youths between the ages of 12 and 18 in the United States, then our population would consist of all male youths between the ages of 12 and 18 who reside in the United States. The population we are interested in, then, is generally very large and both difficult and costly to study directly. Our population of male adolescents, for example, would number in the millions. A sample, you will remember, is a subset of the population. We select a sample from the population and study the sample with the intention of making an inference to the population based on what we know about the sample. The sample is much smaller than the population. We might, for example, take first a sample of states, then a sample of cities, and finally a sample of youths between the ages of 12 and 18 from those cities.

It would be possible (although it would involve a great deal of work and money) to calculate the mean of a population. The mean of a population, therefore, is unknown but knowable. In statistics, the mean of a population is denoted by the symbol $\mu$ (the Greek letter mu) and is defined as the sum of all scores in the population divided by the total number of observations in the population:

$$\mu = \frac{\sum_{i=1}^{N} X_i}{N} \tag{4-2}$$

where

$X_i =$ each $X$ score in the population

$N =$ the total number of observations in the population

To calculate the population mean, therefore, sum all scores in the population, starting with the first and ending with the last or $N$th, and then divide by the total number of observations ($N$). Note that the mean takes all scores into account since we have to sum all scores before calculating the mean.

When we have a sample and wish to calculate the mean of the sample, the formula we use is:

$$\overline{X} = \frac{\sum\limits_{i=1}^{n} x_i}{n}$$

(4-3)

where

$\overline{X}$ = the symbol used for the sample mean and is pronounced "$x$ bar"

$x_i$ = the $i$th raw score in a distribution of scores

$\sum\limits_{i=1}^{n} x_i$ = the instruction to sum all $x_i$ scores, starting with the first score $(i = 1)$ and continuing until the last score

$(i = n)$ $n$ = the total number of scores

This formula is telling you that to calculate the sample mean, you begin by summing all of the scores in your distribution, starting with the first score and ending with the last or $n$th score, and then divide this sum by the total number of scores in your sample. For example, if you had a distribution of 10 scores, you would calculate the mean of those scores by taking the sum of all 10 scores and then dividing by 10: $\overline{X} = (x_1 + x_2 + x_3 + \cdots + x_{10}) / 10$. Unlike the median, the mean is not a positional measure of central tendency. Since the mean takes into account all of your scores, you do not need to rank-order them beforehand; you can simply start summing numbers from the very first score.

As an example of calculating the mean, let's begin by calculating the mean rape rate for the seven cities that make up the first column of Table 4.7. The mean rate of forcible rape would be:

$$\overline{X} = \frac{\sum\limits_{i=1}^{n} x_i}{n}$$

$$\overline{X} = \frac{x_1 + x_2 + x_3 + x_4 + x_5 + x_6 + x_7}{7}$$

$$\overline{X} = \frac{22.2 + 23.5 + 28 + 28.1 + 28.4 + 33.8 + 38.4}{7}$$

$$\overline{X} = \frac{202.4}{7}$$

$$\overline{X} = 28.91 \text{ rapes per 100,000}$$

As practice, let's also calculate the mean rape rate per 100,000 for the second column of cities in Table 4.7:

$$\overline{X} = \frac{22.2 + 23.5 + 28 + 28.1 + 28.4 + 33.8 + 38.4 + 133.2}{8}$$

$$\overline{X} = \frac{335.6}{8}$$

$$\overline{X} = 41.95 \text{ rapes per 100,000}$$

Like the median, the mean also is a sort of balancing score. Rather than balancing the exact number of scores in a distribution as the median does, however, the mean exactly balances the distance of each score from the mean. If we were to subtract the mean of a distribution from each score in the distribution, the negative differences from the mean would exactly equal the positive differences. Let's take a simple example. We have a set of 5 scores (2, 4, 6, 8, and 10). We calculate the mean and find that:

$$\overline{X} = \frac{(2+4+6+8+10)}{5} = \frac{30}{5} = 6$$

We then subtract this mean from each score:

$$2 - 6 = -4$$

$$4 - 6 = -2$$

$$6 - 6 = 0$$

$$8 - 6 = 2$$

$$10 - 6 = 4$$

Subtracting the mean from each score yields what is called the *mean deviation*. Note that the sum of the negative differences is –6 and the sum of the positive differences is +6, so the sum of all differences from the mean is equal to zero. This will always be true. It is in this sense that the mean is a balancing score of the differences. The mean is the only measure of central tendency that has this characteristic. The sum of the differences of each score from the mean, then, will always be zero. In mathematical terms, this means that $\Sigma(x_i - \overline{X}) = 0$.

Formula 4-3 for calculating the sample mean is very simple and easy to use when there are only a few scores. When there are a large number of scores, however, this formula is a bit cumbersome. To calculate the mean when there are many scores in a frequency distribution, the following formula is easier to use:

$$\overline{X} = \frac{\Sigma x_i f_i}{n} \tag{4-4}$$

where

$\overline{X}$ = the mean

$x_i$ = the *i*th score

$f_i$ = the frequency for the *i*th score

$X_i f_i$ = the *x*th score multiplied by its frequency

$n$ = the total number of scores

Formula 4-4 may seem a bit complicated, so let's illustrate its use step by step with an example.

## Case Study

## Calculating the Mean Police Response Time

Table 4.8 shows an ungrouped frequency distribution of response times to 911 calls to the police for assistance. Each response time was rounded to the nearest minute. Just so there is no confusion here, note that there were five occasions when the police responded to a 911 call within 1 minute, six times when they responded within 2 minutes, 9 times when they responded within 3 minutes, and so on, concluding with one time when they responded to a call for assistance

| Table 4.8 | Response Times to 911 Calls for Police Assistance | |
|---|---|---|
| Minutes | $f_i$ | $x_i f_i$ |
| 1 | 5 | 5 |
| 2 | 6 | 12 |
| 3 | 9 | 27 |
| 4 | 8 | 32 |
| 5 | 6 | 30 |
| 6 | 7 | 42 |
| 7 | 3 | 21 |
| 8 | 2 | 16 |
| 9 | 2 | 18 |
| 10 | 1 | 10 |
| 11 | 1 | 11 |
| | $n = 50$ | $\Sigma = 224$ |

within 11 minutes. You may recall that we used these data in the last chapter. The first step in calculating the mean is to create a new column of scores where each entry in the column is the product of each.

The $x$ score is multiplied by its frequency $f$ [this column is labeled $(x_i f_i)$]. For example, the first entry in the $x_i f_i$ column is 5, which represents the fact that the police responded to a 911 call within 1 minute five times. Normally, to calculate the mean we would add these five scores of 1 by doing $1 + 1 + 1 + 1 + 1 = 5$. By taking the product of the score and its frequency $(x_i f_i)$ instead, we are simply taking advantage of the fact that $1 + 1 + 1 + 1 + 1 = 1 \times 5 = 5$. For the second entry of the third column we are taking advantage of the fact that $2 + 2 + 2 + 2 + 2 + 2 = 2 \times 6 = 12$. We take each $x_i$ score and multiply it by its frequency to form the column of $x_i f_i$. The second step in calculating the mean is to sum all of these products. The sum of the column of $x_i f_i$ in Table 4.8 is 224. This is what we would have obtained had we taken the first approach and summed all $x_i$ scores $(1 + 1 + 1 + 1 + 1 + \ldots + 7 + 7 + 7 + \ldots + 10 + 11 = 224)$. The third step in calculating the mean is to divide the sum of the product $x_i f_i$ by the total number of scores. In this case, since there were fifty 911 calls, we can calculate the mean or average response time to a 911 call as $\overline{X} = 224 / 50 = 4.48$ minutes. Since .48 minutes is equal to 28.8 seconds (.48 × 60 seconds), the average response time was 4 minutes and 28.8 seconds, or about 4 1/2 minutes.

---

### Steps to Calculate the Mean from an Ungrouped Frequency Distribution

**Step 1:** Multiply each $x_i$ score by its frequency $(f_i)$. This will give you a column of products $(x_i f_i)$.

**Step 2:** Sum the obtained products from step 1:

$$\Sigma(x_i f_i)$$

**Step 3:** Divide this by the total number of scores $(n)$:

$$\overline{X} = \frac{\Sigma(x_i f_i)}{n}$$

---

Remember that the total number of scores is $n$ and is the sum of the number of frequencies. Very often students will use the number of different scores in the frequency distribution, rather than the total number of scores, as the denominator for the mean. For example, rather than using 50 as the denominator in the earlier problem since there were 50 response times recorded, many students are tempted to use 11 because there are 11 different values. There may be only 11 values for the variable "police response time," but there were a total of 50 calls for police services, and this is the total number of observations.

---

## The Mean for Grouped Data

The procedures for calculating the mean when the data are in a grouped frequency distribution are very similar to that used when the data are in an ungrouped frequency distribution. The first thing you have to determine is that the underlying measurement of the data is continuous even though the data are grouped. If you are satisfied that the data are continuous and have been put into a grouped frequency distribution for convenience and clarification, then you may proceed. Keep in mind that since the data are in the form of a grouped frequency distribution, there are no individual $x_i$ scores. Rather, the data are now in the form of class intervals, and although we know which class interval a score falls into, we do not know the exact score. To calculate a mean with grouped data, then, we are going to have to make a simplifying assumption. *We must make the assumption that each score within a class interval is located exactly at its midpoint.* Once we make this assumption, we do not exactly have a distribution of $x_i$ scores, but we have a distribution of $m_i$ scores, where the $m_i$ refers to the midpoint of the $i$th class interval.

 Earlier in this chapter, Table 4.3 provided the grouped frequency distribution data for the time until arrest for a sample of 120 offenders released into the community. Recall that these data are a count of the number of days a released offender was in the community until he was rearrested. These are grouped data that were originally continuous, so we can legitimately calculate a mean. Our simplifying assumption is that each score within a class interval lies at its midpoint. So, for purposes of calculating the mean, we are going to assume that all four cases in the first class interval are at the midpoint of 18 days, the one score in the second class interval is at the midpoint of 21, the 12 scores in the third class interval are at the midpoint of 24, and so on. Recall that we need to make this assumption because to calculate a mean, we need to have a specific score (18 days, for example) rather than an interval within which a score lies (17–19 days). Since we are making this assumption, we are getting only an estimate of the mean for these data. This estimate is probably not going to be exactly what the value of the mean would be if we calculated it from the original continuous data. In a moment, we will check and see how accurate we are in making this assumption.

 Once we have made this assumption, we are ready to calculate our mean. Recall that when we have data in the form of a frequency distribution, we can use formula 4-4 to calculate the mean by taking the product of each $x$ score and its frequency ($x_i f_i$), summing these products over all $x_i$ scores, and then dividing by the total number of scores $\overline{X} = \Sigma x_i f_i / n$. We are going to modify this formula only slightly and use it to calculate a mean from grouped data. With grouped data, we do not have an individual $x_i$ score, but we do have $m_i$ scores since we are assuming that each score within its class interval lies at its midpoint ($m_i$). To calculate the mean from grouped data, then, we just substitute $m_i$ for $x_i$ in formula 4-4 and take the product of each midpoint and the number of scores that are assumed to lie at that midpoint:

$$\overline{X} = \frac{\Sigma m_i f_i}{n}$$

(4-5)

where

$\overline{X}$ = the mean

$m_i$ = the midpoint for the $i$th class interval

$f_i$ = the frequency for the $i$th class interval

$m_i f_i$ = the $m_i$ midpoint multiplied by its frequency

$n$ = the total number of scores

 In other words, to calculate the mean, we multiply the midpoint of each class interval by the frequency of that class interval. Once we have done this for each class interval, we sum these products over all intervals and then divide by the total number of scores. We will illustrate the use of the mean formula for grouped data with the time-until-rearrest data. Table 4.9 provides the information we need.

 The sum of each midpoint multiplied by its frequency is 3,723. Now, to calculate the mean all we have to do is divide this sum by the total number of scores or observations. The mean number of days free until rearrest is therefore:

$$\overline{X} = \frac{3,723}{120} = 31.02 \, \text{days}$$

| Table 4.9 | Calculating a Mean Using Grouped Data—Time Until Rearrest for 120 Inmates | | |
|---|---|---|---|
| Stated Limits | f | Midpoint | $m_i f_i$ |
| 17–19 days | 4 | 18 | 72 |
| 20–22 days | 1 | 21 | 21 |
| 23–25 days | 12 | 24 | 288 |
| 26–28 days | 16 | 27 | 432 |
| 29–31 days | 28 | 30 | 840 |
| 32–34 days | 28 | 33 | 924 |
| 35–37 days | 21 | 36 | 756 |
| 38–40 days | 10 | 39 | 390 |
| | $n = 120$ | | $\Sigma = 3{,}723$ |

On average, then, these offenders were free for 31.02 days before being rearrested and returned to prison. When you calculate the mean from grouped data using this method, make sure that you use the correct sample size for the denominator. The $n$ in the formula is the total number of observations or scores you have. In this example, our data consist of 120 observations.

---

***Steps to Calculate the Mean From a Grouped Frequency Distribution***

**Step 1:** Multiply each midpoint $(m_i)$ by its frequency $(f_i)$. This will give you a column of products $(m_i f_i)$.

**Step 2:** Sum the obtained products from step 1:

$$\Sigma(m_i f_i)$$

**Step 3:** Divide this by the total number of scores $(n)$:

$$\overline{X} = \frac{\Sigma(m_i f_i)}{n}$$

---

Recall that these time-until-rearrest data were originally measured at the interval/ratio level from which we created class intervals. In the previous example, we estimated the mean number of days an offender was free in the community based on the class interval scores. The question to answer now is whether we were accurate in our estimation of the mean using this grouped data. To determine our precision, let's calculate the mean number of days until rearrest from the original variable measured at the interval/ratio level and compare it with our estimate with formula 4-5. Table 4.10 gives the frequency distribution for the time-until-rearrest data in their original form, and we provide the necessary $(f_i x_i)$ column. Using the ungrouped data, then, we can calculate the mean as $\overline{X} = 3{,}729 / 120 = 31.075$ days. Our estimate of the mean with the grouped data was 31.02 days, so we were pretty close to the value of the mean had the data remained in its original interval/ratio form. In general, you will find that you will not lose much accuracy in estimating the mean when you use grouped rather than ungrouped data.

## Advantages and Disadvantages of the Mean

The mean has a number of advantages as a measure of central tendency. First, it is intuitively appealing. Everyone is familiar with an average. The mean also uses all of the information in a data set, and this is an advantage as long as there are no outliers in the data. The mean is also an efficient measure of central tendency. In other words, if we had a population of scores (with a mean and median), and from this population, we took many, many samples and calculated both the mean and the median for each sample, the medians of these samples would differ more from each other and the population median than the means would differ from each other and the population mean.

Because we usually draw only one sample from a population, we want to have the measure of central tendency that is the most precise. This is the mean. The one disadvantage of the mean is a by-product of one of its strengths: Because it takes every score into account, the mean may be distorted by high or low outliers. When we sum every score to calculate the mean, we may at times be adding uncharacteristically high or uncharacteristically low scores. When this happens, the value of the mean will give us a distorted sense of the central tendency of the data. To illustrate this point, let's return to Table 4.7, which provided three columns of rape rates per 100,000 for selected U.S.

cities. The first column consists of seven cities. Calculate the mean rape rate for these cities. You should have obtained a value of $\bar{X} = 202.4/7 = 28.91$ rapes per 100,000. What happens to the mean when we include the high outlier of Anchorage from the second column? The mean now is $\bar{X} = 335.6/8 = 41.95$ rapes per 100,000. Note what happened to the value of the mean when we included this high outlier. The magnitude of the mean increased dramatically, and it is now greater than 64 rapes per 100,000. The inclusion of a high outlier, then, had the effect of inflating our mean.

Now look at the third column of cities in Table 4.7. What happens to the mean when we drop the high outlier of Anchorage and add the low outlier of Goldsboro, with a rape rate of 4.0 per 100,000? The value of the mean is now $\bar{X} = 202.4/8 = 25.3$ rapes per 100,000. The mean has now declined slightly, although it does not distort the central tendency as much as our high outlier did. As you can see, however, the effect of a low outlier is to lessen the magnitude of the mean.

The purpose of this exercise is to show that sometimes the mean can provide a distorted sense of the central tendency in our data. Since the mean uses every score in our distribution, high outliers can inflate the mean, and low outliers can deflate the mean, relative to what the value of the mean would be without the outliers. For this reason, it is generally a good idea to report *both* the mean and median when you are discussing the central tendency in your data. With respect to Table 4.7, we saw how the mean moves up or down with the inclusion of outliers in the data. Remember that the median was much more stable, which further illustrates this point.

Reporting both the mean and the median can also tell us something important about the shape of our data. In Chapter 3, we illustrated the difference between symmetrical and skewed distributions. In Chapter 6, we will be discussing the normal or "bell-shaped" distribution, which is a very important theoretical probability distribution in statistics. A normal distribution has one mode (it has a single peak), and it is symmetrical. If a line were drawn down the center of the distribution, the left half would be a mirror image of the right half. In a symmetrical or normal distribution, the mean, median, and mode are all the same, located right at the center of the distribution. If a distribution is not normal, recall that it is said to be a skewed distribution. In a negatively skewed distribution, the mean is less than the median. This is because there are low outlying scores on the left of the distribution pulling the value of the mean down. Stated differently, in a negatively skewed distribution, the mean is lower in magnitude than the median because low outliers are deflating the mean. This is what we saw in the third column of Table 4.7. Thus, knowing that in a distribution of scores the mean is much lower than the

| Table 4.10 | Calculating a Mean Using Ungrouped Data—Time Until Rearrest for 120 Inmates | |
|---|---|---|
| $x_i$ | $f_i$ | $x_i f_i$ |
| 17 | 1 | 17 |
| 18 | 1 | 18 |
| 19 | 2 | 38 |
| 20 | 1 | 20 |
| 21 | 0 | 0 |
| 22 | 0 | 0 |
| 23 | 3 | 69 |
| 24 | 4 | 96 |
| 25 | 5 | 125 |
| 26 | 3 | 78 |
| 27 | 7 | 189 |
| 28 | 6 | 168 |
| 29 | 11 | 319 |
| 30 | 7 | 210 |
| 31 | 10 | 310 |
| 32 | 7 | 224 |
| 33 | 12 | 396 |
| 34 | 8 | 272 |
| 35 | 8 | 280 |
| 36 | 8 | 288 |
| 37 | 6 | 222 |
| 38 | 4 | 152 |
| 39 | 2 | 78 |
| 40 | 4 | 160 |
| | $n = 120$ | $\Sigma = 3{,}729$ |

median, we might suspect that the distribution has a negative skew. The greater the difference there is between the mean and the median, the greater the negative skew. Conversely, in a positively skewed distribution, the mean is greater than the median because high outliers are inflating the magnitude of the mean relative to the median, as we saw in the second column of Table 4.7.

## 🔲 Summary

In this chapter we focused on measures of central tendency. These measures of central tendency are used as summary indicators of the typical, usual, most frequent, or average score in a distribution of scores. There are three measures of central tendency: the mode, the median, and the mean.

The mode is the score or value with the highest frequency. It is therefore the score or value that has the greatest probability or likelihood of occurring. There may be more than one mode in a given distribution of scores. As a measure of central tendency, the mode is probably the easiest to obtain since it requires no real calculations and is an appropriate measure of central tendency for nominal, ordinal, or interval/ratio-level data.

The median is the score at the 50th percentile. Thus, it is the score or value that divides a rank-ordered distribution of scores into two equal halves. A characteristic of the median, then, is that one half of the scores will be greater than the median and one half will be less than it. The median requires continuous-level data (interval/ratio) or continuous-level data that have been made ordinal through the creation of a grouped frequency distribution. Since the median locates the score at the 50th percentile, it is not affected by outlying scores in a distribution. For this reason, it is a very good measure of central tendency when the data are skewed.

The mean is the arithmetic average of all scores. It is calculated by summing all scores and dividing by the total number of scores. Calculation of the mean requires the same level of measurement as does the median. Because the mean uses all of the scores, it can be substantially affected by the presence of outliers in the data. In a normal distribution, the mode, median, and mean are the same. In a negatively skewed distribution, the mean is less than the median, and in a positively skewed distribution, the mean is greater than the median. Because the presence of outliers may distort the mean as a measure of central tendency, it is generally a good policy to report both the median and the mean.

## Key Terms

> Review key terms with eFlashcards. **⑤SAGE edge™**

| | | |
|---|---|---|
| bimodal distribution  84 | measure of central tendency  82 | mode  82 |
| mean  93 | median  87 | |

## Key Formulas

Sample median for grouped data (equation 4-1):

$$X_{median} = L + \left( \frac{\left( \frac{n+1}{2} \right) - cf}{f} \right) w_i$$

where

$X_{median}$ = the value of the median

$L$ = the lower real limit of the class interval that contains the median

$cf$ = the cumulative frequency of the class interval just before the class interval that contains the median

$f$ = the frequency of the interval that contains the median

$w_i$ = the width of the class interval
$n$ = the total number of observations in the sample

Sample mean (equation 4-3):

$$\bar{X} = \frac{\sum_{i=1}^{n} x_i}{n}$$

where

$\overline{X}$ = the symbol used for the sample mean (pronounced "x bar")

$x_i$ = the "*i*th" raw score in a distribution of scores

$\sum_{i=1}^{n} x_i$ = the instruction to sum all $x_i$ scores, starting with the first score ($i = 1$) and continuing until the last score ($i = n$)

$n$ = the total number of scores

Sample mean for data in a frequency distribution (equation 4-4):

$$\overline{X} = \frac{\sum x_i f_i}{n}$$

where

$\overline{X}$ = the mean

$x_i$ = the *i*th score

$f_i$ = the frequency for the ith score

$x_i f_i$ = the xth score multiplied by its frequency

$n$ = the total number of scores

Sample mean for grouped data (equation 4-5):

$$\overline{X} = \frac{\sum m_i f_i}{n}$$

where

$\overline{X}$ = the mean

$m_i$ = the midpoint for the *i*th class interval

$f$ = the frequency for the *i*th class interval

$m_i f_i$ = the $m_i$ midpoint multiplied by its frequency

$n$ = the total number of scores

# Practice Problems

➤ Test your understanding of chapter content. Take the practice quiz. **$SAGE edge™**

1. As a measure of central tendency, the mode is the most common score. Consider the following information on a variable called "the number of delinquent friends that someone has." What is the mode for these data, and what does it tell you? Why can't you calculate the "mean number of delinquent friends"?

**Number of Delinquent Friends**

| X | f |
|------|------|
| None | 20 |
| Some | 85 |
| Most | 30 |
| All | 10 |

2. Say you asked a random sample of seven correctional officers what their annual salary was, and their responses were as follows:

$25,900

$32,100

$28,400

$31,000

$29,500

$27,800

$26,100

What is the median salary, and what is the mean salary for this sample?

3. The following data show the homicide rate per 100,000 people for 10 American cities. Given these data, which measure of central tendency would you use, and why?

| City | Homicide Rate |
|------|------|
| Boston, MA | 6.8 |
| Cincinnati, OH | 4.5 |
| Denver, CO | 6.0 |
| Las Vegas, NV | 8.8 |
| New Orleans, LA | 43.3 |
| New York, NY | 8.7 |

*(Continued)*

(Continued)

| City | Homicide Rate |
|------|---------------|
| Pittsburgh, PA | 10.5 |
| Salt Lake City, UT | 5.6 |
| San Diego, CA | 4.3 |
| San Francisco, CA | 7.7 |

4.  Rachel Sutherland and her colleagues (2015) have investigated the relationship between injection drug use and criminal activity. The hypothetical data that follow represent the number of crimes committed during a two-year period by 20 heroin addicts. Using ungrouped data, calculate the mean and the median for these 20 persons. Which measure of central tendency do you think best summarizes the central tendency of these data, and why?

| Person Number | Number of Crimes Committed | Person Number | Number of Crimes Committed |
|:---:|:---:|:---:|:---:|
| 1 | 4 | 11 | 4 |
| 2 | 16 | 12 | 11 |
| 3 | 10 | 13 | 10 |
| 4 | 7 | 14 | 88 |
| 5 | 3 | 15 | 9 |
| 6 | 112 | 16 | 12 |
| 7 | 5 | 17 | 8 |
| 8 | 10 | 18 | 5 |
| 9 | 6 | 19 | 7 |
| 10 | 2 | 20 | 10 |

5.  In a study of police interventions and mental illness in a large Canadian city, Yannick Charette, Anne Crocker, and Isabelle Billette (2014, p. 513) reported the following distribution of the reasons for police intervention when the subject was without mental illness:

| Request | Frequency |
|---------|-----------|
| Offense against person | 213 |
| Offense against property | 496 |
| Other criminal offense | 238 |
| Potential offense | 3,784 |
| Individual in distress | 139 |
| Noncriminal incident | 986 |

What is the measure of central tendency most appropriate for these data? Why? What does this measure of central tendency tell you about the "most typical" reason for a police intervention when the subject was without mental illness?

6.  The following hypothetical data show the distribution of the percentage of total police officers who do narcotics investigation in 100 American cities. Determine the mode, median, and mean.

**% of Force Doing Investigation**

| Narcotics Investigation (%) | Frequency |
|:---:|:---:|
| 0–9 | 5 |
| 10–19 | 13 |
| 20–29 | 26 |
| 30–39 | 38 |
| 40–49 | 14 |
| 50–59 | 2 |
| 60–69 | 2 |

7.  The following data represent the number of persons executed in the United States over the years 2007–2014.

| Year | # of Executions |
|:---:|:---:|
| 2007 | 42 |
| 2008 | 37 |
| 2009 | 52 |
| 2010 | 46 |
| 2011 | 43 |
| 2012 | 43 |
| 2013 | 39 |
| 2014 | 35 |

What were the mean number and the median number of executions over this time period? What happens to the median and mean when we add the year 2006, in which there were 53 executions? Which measure of central tendency would you use to describe the 2007–2014 distribution?

8.  One seemingly inconsistent finding in criminological research is that women have a greater subjective fear of crime than men even though their objective risk of being the victim of a crime

is lower. In one study, Jodi Lane and Kathleen Fox (2013) tried to explain this fact in part through the shadow of sexual assault thesis by suggesting that women are more afraid of crime because of their fear of sexual assault and the intense physical and emotional consequences they would face if raped. They suggest that women transfer this fear of sexual assault to a fear of crime generally. The hypothetical data that follow represent the responses of a sample of 200 women who were asked to report to an interviewer the number of times that they had been sexually assaulted within the previous five years. Using these data, calculate the mean, median, and mode.

| Number of Times Assaulted | Frequency |
| --- | --- |
| 0–1 | 85 |
| 2–3 | 70 |
| 4–5 | 30 |
| 6–7 | 15 |

9. Research reported by Adrian Raine, Annis Lai Chu Fung, Jill Portnoy, Olivia Choy, and Victoria Spring (2014) suggests that there is a link between low resting heart rates and aggression and psychopathic traits. They define those with resting heart

rates below 67 beats per minute as having low resting heart rates. In a random sample of 20 violent offenders currently incarcerated in a state penitentiary, the prison doctor finds the following resting heart rates. Calculate the mean and median for these data. Are the mean and median the same or different? Why do you think this is so?

| Person | Resting Heart Rate | Person | Resting Heart Rate |
| --- | --- | --- | --- |
| 1 | 59 | 11 | 60 |
| 2 | 62 | 12 | 55 |
| 3 | 69 | 13 | 52 |
| 4 | 62 | 14 | 70 |
| 5 | 64 | 15 | 52 |
| 6 | 70 | 16 | 57 |
| 7 | 54 | 17 | 53 |
| 8 | 66 | 18 | 61 |
| 9 | 51 | 19 | 64 |
| 10 | 56 | 20 | 63 |

# SPSS Exercises

➤ Explore additional data sets. ⑤SAGE edge™

| Data for Exercise | |
| --- | --- |
| Data Set | Description |
| Youth.sav | These data are from a random sample of students from schools in a southern state. Although not representative of the United States, it covers a variety of important delinquent behaviors and peer influences. |

| Variables for Exercise | |
| --- | --- |
| Variable Name | Description |
| V77 | A five-category ordinal measure asking respondents how wrong they think their friends think it is to steal. Responses range from 1 (always wrong) to 5 (never wrong). |
| V79 | A five-category ordinal measure asking respondents how wrong they think their friends think it is to drink. Response options are the same as V77. |
| Certain | A scale indicating how likely respondents feel it is that they will be punished for delinquent behavior. High values indicate high certainty. |
| Delinquency | A scale indicating the number of delinquent acts that respondents report participating in. |
| Gender | The gender of the respondents, where 1 = male and 0 = female. |
| Parnt2 | A scale indicating the amount of parental supervision that the respondents receive with values ranging from 2 to 8, with high values indicating more supervision. |

1. Use SPSS to construct a frequency table for the variable Parnt2. Based on that frequency table, derive the following with just the output. Any calculations should be done by hand with a calculator:

   a. The mean parental supervision score.

   b. The median parental supervision score.

   c. The modal parental supervision score

   d. For each of these points, write a sentence interpreting the value you receive in a way that a lay person would understand.

   e. Of these three measures of central tendency, which do you think is most appropriate for describing this distribution, and why? Be sure to consider whether skewness or outliers are a problem in your decision.

2. **Measures of Central Tendency in SPSS:** To do this, start off just like you were making a frequency table, but this time click "statistics." A new menu will pop up giving you lots of options. In the top right will be options for the mean, median, and mode; tick off all three. Have SPSS output the mean, median, and mode for the following variables:

   i. V77

   ii. V79

   iii. Certain

   iv. Gender

   b. First, what is the level of measurement for each variable? For each variable, identify which measures of central tendencies may be most appropriate.

   c. For the interval- and ratio-level variables of this list, use the mean and media to describe the variable's distribution; does it appear to be skewed? In what direction?

   d. Pick one measure of central tendency for each variable. Explain why you prefer this measure for this variable. Then, write a sentence interpreting the measure.

3. Create a histogram of the variable Delinquency. Looking at this distribution, what measure of central tendency will be most appropriate and informative? Will any be misleading? Use SPSS to calculate the appropriate measures of central tendency for this variable.

4. Gender is coded 0 = female and 1 = male. This specific coding scheme is called "dummy coding," and it is extremely common. Because it is both a binary variable and coded this way, the mean is actually still useful! It's your job to find out what this mean represents in this specific circumstance:

   a. Construct a frequency for the variable Gender. Make note of the proportion that is male and female.

   b. Take a look at the mean from question 2 or the mean "gender" here. Now consider that the value .47 is rounded; the actual value is 0.465409.

   c. What does the mean of a dummy coded variable actually tell us?

# CHAPTER 5

# Measures of Dispersion

> " *O*ne can state, without exaggeration, that the observation of and the search for similarities and differences are the basis of all human knowledge.
>
> –Alfred Nobel
>
> *R*esemblances are the shadows of differences.
>
> *D*ifferent people see different similarities and similar differences.
>
> –Vladimir Nabokov "

## LEARNING OBJECTIVES

1. Explain what measures of dispersion tell us about a variable distribution compared with measures of center.

2. Identify a measure of dispersion appropriate for nominal- or ordinal-level data.

3. Describe the difference between the range and the interquartile range.

4. Discuss the relationship between the variance and the standard deviation.

5. Calculate and interpret the standard deviation with both grouped and ungrouped data.

6. Construct and interpret a boxplot and understand how it can reveal virtually everything about a variable distribution including the measure of center, variability, shape, and outliers.

# 🖿 Introduction

At the beginning of Chapter 4, we told you that the average age of inmates in state correctional facilities across the United States was 40 years old. What if we told you that the age range of individuals housed in state prisons was from 17 to 82 years old? These numbers convey a different kind of information about the age of state prisoners. The range of ages captures the differences among scores within a group of scores. Unless all of the scores in a distribution are the same (that is, unless what we have is a constant and not a variable), the scores will be different from one another, and the magnitude of this difference is important to know. Measures that capture differences within a variable are called **measures of dispersion** or variability. Like the measures of central tendency we discussed in Chapter 4, measures of dispersion are summary measures that in one number reflect the differences among the values of a variable. In this chapter you will learn that there are different measures of dispersion, and like the case of measures of central tendency, which we use depends on the level of measurement of our variable. For nominal- and purely ordinal-level data, we will discuss a measure of dispersion called the variation ratio. With interval- and ratio-level variables, we can use four different measures including the range, the interquartile range, the variance, and standard deviation. The latter two measures of dispersion are particularly important, and we will use them frequently in later chapters. You will learn how to calculate and interpret the variance and standard deviation with both grouped and ungrouped data.

> **Measures of dispersion:** Capture how different the values of a variable are. The more dispersion there is in a variable, the more different the values are from each other or from some central tendency and the more heterogeneity in the data.

Measures of dispersion tell us about the heterogeneity in the data. Heterogeneity exists whenever scores are dissimilar. The opposite is homogeneity, which exists when all scores are very similar. Take the following group of five scores that are the number of crimes reported in five different neighborhoods over a two-year period:

$$103, 104, 102, 103, 103$$

You can see that these scores are very similar to each other and are not very different from the mean of 103 crimes (calculate this mean for yourself), so the homogeneity in the scores is high and the heterogeneity is low. Now consider the following five different neighborhood crime totals over two years:

$$74, 130, 80, 120, 111$$

The scores from these neighborhoods have the same mean number of crimes as the first group ($\overline{X} = 103$ crimes), but compared with the first group, these neighborhood crime levels are very different both to each other and to the mean of the scores. In this second group of scores, the homogeneity of these crime levels is low and the heterogeneity is high. Measures of dispersion capture this notion of the heterogeneity of scores.

As a more detailed illustration of the importance and kind of information a measure of dispersion provides, let's look at Table 5.1. This table reports the sentence length in years given by two different judges to 20 defendants convicted of armed robbery. The data have been rank-ordered and put into a frequency distribution, so it is pretty easy to calculate the mean and the median of the sentence lengths given by these two judges. Each judge sentenced 20 different convicted armed robbers. The median sentence length for both judges is 8.5 years, and they have the same mean sentence length of 9.0 years. As far as these two measures of central tendency are concerned, therefore, the two judges are similar in how they sentence armed robbery defendants. But does this convey all we need to know about the behavior of these two judges? No. Judge

1's sentencing behavior is clustered narrowly around the mean of 9 years and median of 8.5 years—her lowest sentence length is 5 years, and her highest sentence length is 14 years. Judge 2, however, seems "all over the map" when it comes to sentencing. Her sentences are not so tightly clustered around the mean and the median. Judge 2's sentences for armed robbery are as low as 1 year and as high as 20 years! You can see this very clearly in Figure 5.1, which shows the sentence lengths given by the two judges, along with their common mean (solid line) and median (dashed line) sentence lengths. Note that the line showing the sentences given by Judge 1 is much closer to the mean and median lines than is the line showing the sentences given by Judge 2. What the table and figure both show is that even though these judges have the same median and mean sentence length, Judge 2 exhibits much more flexible and diverse sentencing behavior than Judge 1.

What we need to do is indicate the amount of heterogeneity or dispersion in a variable in addition to a measure of central tendency. This is what measures of dispersion do; they are summary measures that capture the amount of dispersion or heterogeneity in a variable. Offering a measure of dispersion, then, in addition to a measure of central tendency, will help us understand our variables better. Just as there is more than one measure of central tendency, there is more than one measure of dispersion, and the appropriate measure of dispersion depends on the level of measurement of your variable.

| Table 5.1 | Number of Years of Prison Time for Armed Robbery Defendants | |
|---|---|---|
| | *Judge 1* | *Judge 2* |
| *Defendant* | *Sentence Given* | *Sentence Given* |
| 1 | 5 | 1 |
| 2 | 7 | 2 |
| 3 | 7 | 2 |
| 4 | 7 | 3 |
| 5 | 7 | 3 |
| 6 | 7 | 3 |
| 7 | 8 | 4 |
| 8 | 8 | 4 |
| 9 | 8 | 5 |
| 10 | 8 | 8 |
| 11 | 9 | 9 |
| 12 | 9 | 10 |
| 13 | 9 | 11 |
| 14 | 10 | 14 |
| 15 | 11 | 15 |
| 16 | 11 | 15 |
| 17 | 11 | 16 |
| 18 | 12 | 17 |
| 19 | 12 | 18 |
| 20 | 14 | 20 |
| $n = 20$ | $\Sigma = 180$ | $\Sigma = 180$ |
| | $\bar{X} = 9$ | $\bar{X} = 9$ |

# ▣ Measuring Dispersion for Nominal- and Ordinal-Level Variables

## The Variation Ratio

The **variation ratio** is a very simple measure of dispersion that you can use whenever you have data measured at the nominal or ordinal level. Recall from Chapter 4 that when we employ nominal or ordinal measurement, the only measure of central tendency we can use is the mode, which is the score or value with the greatest frequency. The measure of dispersion for this type of data, the variation ratio, is based on the mode. The variation ratio (VR) simply measures the extent to which the observations are *not* concentrated in the modal category of the variable. More specifically, it is the proportion of cases not in the modal category of the variable. The smaller the proportion of cases that are in the modal category, the larger the variation ratio will be. The greater the value of the variation ratio is, then the more variation or heterogeneity that will be found in the data. The formula for the variation ratio is:

**Variation ratio:** Appropriate measure of dispersion to use when variables are measured at the nominal or purely ordinal level. It measures the proportion of cases of a variable that are not in the modal value.

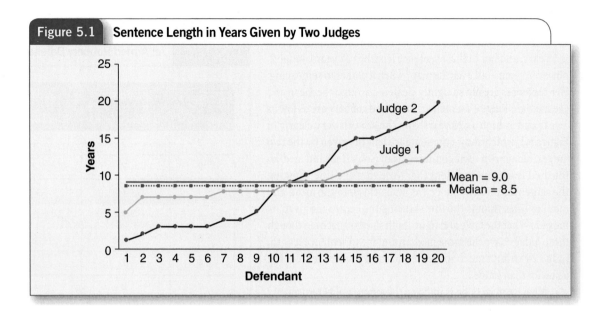

**Figure 5.1**  **Sentence Length in Years Given by Two Judges**

$$VR = 1 - \frac{f_{\text{modal}}}{n} \tag{5-1}$$

where

$f_{\text{modal}}$ = the frequency of cases in the modal category

$n$ = the total number of cases

The numerator of the fraction in equation 5-1, then, is the frequency in the modal category, and the denominator is the number of cases in the sample. Since the frequency of the modal category divided by $n$ is just a proportion—the proportion in the mode—1 is the proportion not in the mode.

Note that if all of the cases in the variable fell into one value or category, two things would be true: (1) There would be no variation or dispersion in the data since the "variable" would actually be a constant (all cases fall into only one value), and (2) the magnitude of the variation ratio would be zero since $f_{\text{modal}}$ would equal $n$, so $f_{\text{modal}}/n$ would be equal to 1.0, and thus, $1 - f_{\text{modal}}/n$ would be zero. So the lower limit of the variation ratio occurs when all cases fall into one and only one category of the nominal or ordinal variable and there is no variability at all—the variation ratio is equal to 0 (no variation). We will show you later in this section that the upper limit for the variation ratio is not so easily determined.

## Case Study

## Types of Patrolling Practices

Let's start with a simple example. In Table 5.2, we report the number of shifts in a given week for each of three types of patrolling practices used by a city police department. A shift is simply a block of time when officers are working—sometimes the shifts last 8 or 10 hours and sometimes 12 hours. So, for example, the first shift of the day might last from 7 am to 5 pm, a 10-hour shift. The variable "type of patrolling practice" is a nominal-level variable because its values differ only in kind or quality—patrolling on foot is different than police car patrolling; it is not more patrolling. We can see that there were 45 shifts where the police were doing neighborhood patrols, and in 5 of these, they did foot patrol only; in 30, they patrolled only by police car; and 10 shifts involved a mixture of foot and car patrol. The modal type of police patrolling is car patrol since it has the greatest frequency. The variation ratio is:

| Table 5.2 | **Type and Frequency of Patrolling Used in Police Shifts in One U.S. City** |
|---|---|
| | *f* |
| Foot Patrol Only | 5 |
| Car Patrol Only | 30 |
| Foot and Car Patrol | 10 |
| Total # of Shifts | 45 |

$$VR = 1 - \frac{30}{45}$$
$$VR = 1 - .67$$
$$VR = .33$$

The value of the variation ratio is, then, .33. About a third (33%) of all police patrols are not in the modal category of car patrol.

As another example, in Table 5.3, we present a nominal-level variable that we used in Chapters 3 and 4. The variable "type of hate crime" is a nominal-level variable because the values represent only qualitative distinctions; one type of hate crime is simply different from another, not "more" of a hate crime. We learned in the last chapter that the mode for this variable is "racial hate crime" since there were more of this kind of hate crime reported in 2013 than of any other kind. More specifically, .485 of the total number of hate crimes were racially motivated hate crimes. We can calculate the value of the variation ratio for this variable as:

$$VR = 1 - \frac{2,871}{5,922}$$
$$VR = 1 - .485$$
$$VR = .515$$

The variation ratio, then, is .515, which tells us that slightly more than one half of the cases (51.5% to be exact) are not in the modal category of racial hate crimes.

Table 5.4 lists some hypothetical data on hate crimes. There are still 5,922 reported hate crimes, but in this example, there are 4,975 cases in the category "racial hate crimes." Note that there is less dispersion or heterogeneity in these data than in Table 5.3 because there is a greater concentration of cases in one category (the mode, racially motivated hate crimes). Now when we calculate the variation ratio, we get:

| Table 5.3 | **Type of Hate Crime Incident Reported to Police in 2013** | | |
|---|---|---|---|
| *Basis of Hate* | *f* | *Proportion* | *%* |
| Race | 2,871 | .485 | 48.5 |
| Religion | 1,031 | .174 | 17.4 |
| Sexual orientation | 1,233 | .208 | 20.8 |
| Ethnicity/national origin | 655 | .111 | 11.1 |
| Disability | 83 | .014 | 1.4 |
| Gender | 18 | .003 | .3 |
| Gender Identity | 31 | .005 | .5 |
| Total | 5,922 | 1.0 | 100.0% |

$$VR = 1 - \frac{4,975}{5,922}$$
$$VR = 1 - .840$$
$$VR = .160$$

There are now only .160, or 16%, of the total number of cases not in the modal category. This means that 84% of

*Source:* Adapted from *Hate Crimes Statistics—2013* from the Federal Bureau of Investigation.

| Table 5.4 | Hypothetical Hate Crime Data | |
|---|---|---|
| Type of Hate | f | Proportion |
| Racial | 4,975 | .840 |
| Religious | 414 | .070 |
| Sexual orientation | 272 | .046 |
| Ethnicity/national origin | 148 | .025 |
| Disability | 53 | .009 |
| Gender | 30 | .005 |
| Gender Identity | 30 | .005 |
| Total | 5,922 | 1.000 |

the cases fall into the modal category, more than in our previous example with real data, indicating that there is *less* heterogeneity in these data than in those found in Table 5.3. This is reflected in a lower magnitude of the variation ratio for Table 5.4.

Now look at Table 5.5, which gives another set of hypothetical data. In this example, we still have 5,922 reported hate crimes, but now the cases are evenly distributed across the four values. In fact, there is no mode because every category has the same frequency. For Table 5.5, we calculate the magnitude of the variation ratio, we find it to be:

$$VR = 1 - \frac{846}{5,922}$$
$$VR = 1 - .143$$
$$VR = .857$$

Now .857, or about 86%, of the cases are not in the modal category, indicating that this distribution of hate crimes has more dispersion than the other two examples.

One problem with the variation ratio is that the maximum value it can attain is not some fixed value. The maximum amount of heterogeneity or the maximum value for the variation ratio for any table will be obtained when there is no mode and the cases therefore are equally distributed in each of the values, but it also depends on the *number of categories* the variable has. The maximum value of the VR will always be:

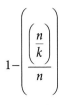

$$1 - \left( \frac{\left( \frac{n}{k} \right)}{n} \right)$$

| Table 5.5 | Hypothetical Hate Crime Data | |
|---|---|---|
| Type of Hate | f | Proportion |
| Racial | 846 | .143 |
| Religious | 846 | .143 |
| Sexual orientation | 846 | .143 |
| Ethnicity/national origin | 846 | .143 |
| Disability | 846 | .143 |
| Gender | 846 | .143 |
| Gender Identity | 846 | .143 |
| Total | 5,922 | 1.001* |

*Greater than 1.0 due to rounding.

where *k* is equal to the number of values or categories a variable has and *n* is the total number of cases. For the data we used in Tables 5.3 to 5.5, the maximum magnitude of the VR is .857, the value we calculated from the data in Table 5.5:

$$VR = 1 - \frac{\left( \frac{5,922}{7} \right)}{5,922}$$
$$VR = 1 - \frac{846}{5,922}$$
$$VR = 1 - .143$$
$$VR = .857$$

Another way to understand what the VR is telling us about the dispersion in a set of nominal/ordinal data is to take the ratio of the variation we observe over the maximum possible variation and then multiply by 100 to get the percentage of the maximum variation observed. For example, in Table 5.3, which is the real hate crime data from the Federal Bureau of Investigation's (FBI's) Uniform Crime Reports, the variation ratio was .515. Since we just calculated the maximum amount of variation we could possibly have in this data from Table 5.5 and we found that to be equal to .857, we can take the ratio of VR we observe to the maximum VR (.515 / .857) which is .60, and then multiply by 100 to get 60%. Now what we can conclude is that in Table 5.3 we have about 60% of the total possible amount of variation that could be observed. The important thing to keep in mind is that higher values of the variation ratio imply greater dispersion in the distribution of a nominal/ordinal-level variable or more heterogeneity in the data. If you think that the variation ratio is a very crude measure of dispersion since it captures only the proportion of cases not in the modal category, you are right. It is pretty crude and not greatly informative. But recall that the mode is a very simple and crude measure of central tendency, reflecting simply the value with the greatest number of cases.

## ▣ Measuring Dispersion for Interval- and Ratio-Level Variables

### The Range and Interquartile Range

Let's now consider the case where we have data measured at the interval/ratio level—in other words, data that can be considered continuous (continuous data that have been grouped). When we have continuous data, there are other, more precise, ways that we can characterize. The simplest measure of dispersion with continuous data is called the **range**. For ungrouped data, the range is the difference between the highest score in the distribution and the lowest score:

> **Range:** Measure of dispersion appropriate for interval/ratio-level data. It is calculated as the difference between the highest value or score and the lowest: Range = Highest value - Lowest value.

$$Range = highest\ value - lowest\ value$$

When we have data in a grouped frequency distribution, the range is the difference between the midpoint of the last class interval and the midpoint of the first class interval, or the difference between the highest and lowest midpoints.

## ═══ Case Study ═══

### Calculating the Range of Sentence Lengths

In Table 5.1, the range for Judge 1's sentences for armed robbery defendants is 9 years because the longest sentence she imposed was 14 years and the shortest sentence she imposed was 5 years (14 − 5 = 9 years). The range for Judge 2 is 19 years because her longest sentence was 20 years and her shortest was 1 year (20 − 1 = 19 years). Based on the calculation of the range, there is more dispersion or heterogeneity in the sentencing of Judge 2 than in that of Judge 1. Sometimes the range is expressed as the lowest and highest values rather than as the difference between these values. In these terms, the range for Judge 1 would be "between 5 and 14 years," and for Judge 2 it would be "between 1 and 20 years." No matter how it is expressed, the range in sentencing is greater for Judge 2 than it is for Judge 1—a fact expressed by the greater magnitude of the range for Judge 2.

Table 5.6 shows the grouped frequency distribution for the "time-until-rearrest" data of our 120 offenders released into the community—the same data that we have used in previous chapters. These were originally

| Table 5.6 | Grouped Frequency Distribution for Time-Until-Failure Data for 120 Inmates | |
|---|---|---|

| Stated Limits | f | Midpoint |
|---|---|---|
| 17–19 days | 4 | 18 |
| 20–22 days | 1 | 21 |
| 23–25 days | 12 | 24 |
| 26–28 days | 16 | 27 |
| 29–31 days | 28 | 30 |
| 32–34 days | 28 | 33 |
| 35–37 days | 21 | 36 |
| 38–40 days | 10 | 39 |
| | n = 120 | |

| Table 5.7 | Number of Years of Prison Time for Armed Robbery Defendants | | |
|---|---|---|---|

| Judge 1 | | Judge 2 | |
|---|---|---|---|
| Years Sentenced | f | Years Sentenced | f |
| 5 | 1 | 1 | 10 |
| 6 | 1 | 20 | 10 |
| 7 | 3 | | |
| 8 | 4 | | |
| 9 | 3 | | |
| 10 | 1 | | |
| 11 | 3 | | |
| 12 | 2 | | |
| 13 | 1 | | |
| 14 | 1 | | |
| | n = 20 | | n = 20 |

interval- and ratio-level data, which we made ordinal by creating a grouped frequency distribution. We have midpoints for our class intervals so we can calculate a range for the data. Since the midpoint of the last class interval is 39 days and the midpoint for the first class interval is 18 days, the range in these time until rearrest ordinal data is 39 − 18 = 21 days. We can also say that the range in the time until rearrest data is between 18 and 39 days.

The range is a very simple measure of dispersion to calculate and is very easy to understand. But as in every other dimension of life, "there is no such thing as a free lunch." The ease of calculating the range may come at a high price: With some data, the range may distort the amount of dispersion that exists in the data. Since the range includes only two scores in our data, the highest and lowest, it completely ignores the dispersion that may lie between these two values. If either or both of these two scores are unusual or extreme (in other words, an outlier), using the range as our only measure of dispersion may be misleading.

For example, let's look at Table 5.7, which shows the sentencing data of two different judges. In both cases the judges sentenced 20 armed robbery defendants, and just as in Table 5.1, the range in sentencing is 9 years for Judge 1 and 19 years for Judge 2. Using the range, then, we would get the impression that there is a great deal more dispersion or heterogeneity in the sentencing behavior of Judge 2 compared with Judge 1. Although the ranges of 9 and 19 years are technically correct, would it really be accurate to conclude that Judge 2 has a lot more dispersion in her sentencing than Judge 1? Judge 2 uses options of only 1 year or 20 years when she sentences armed robbery defendants, whereas Judge 1 is much more flexible in the sentences that she imposes. When we use the range in this example, therefore, we are somewhat misstating the amount of dispersion in the two judges' sentencing behavior. Fortunately, we have other measures of dispersion for continuous variables that take more information into account than just the highest and lowest scores.

One alternative to the range as a measure of dispersion is something called the **interquartile range** (IQR). In calculating the interquartile range, we still take the difference between two scores, but rather than taking the difference between the highest and lowest scores, in the IQR, we take the difference between the score at the 75th percentile (the third quartile or $Q_3$) and the score at the 25th percentile (the first quartile or $Q_1$). Note that since we are taking the range of scores between the 75th and 25th percentiles, this range covers the dispersion at the middle 50% of our distribution. In other words, one half of all our scores can be found between the 75th and 25th percentiles and the IQR measures the dispersion within those two boundaries.

Recall that we can divide our distribution in many different ways. One of these ways we already know. For example, we can divide our scores into percentiles, or units of 100, as we did in Table 5.8. We can then take these percentiles and group them into intervals of 10, or deciles. There are 10 deciles for 100 percentiles. The first 10 percentiles make up the first decile, the second 10 percentiles make up the second decile, and so on. We can also group our percentiles into intervals of 25%, or quartiles. Since the 100 percentiles are equally distributed into four quartiles, each quartile comprises 25 percentiles, or 25% of the data. The first 25 percentiles make up the first quartile ($Q_1$), and the second 25 percentiles make up the second quartile ($Q_2$). Recall that the median is the second quartile. The next 25 percentiles, from the 51st to the 75th percentile, are contained in the third quartile ($Q_3$), and the last 25% of the cases are in the fourth quartile ($Q_4$). This information on percentiles, deciles, and quartiles is shown in Table 5.8.

With this information we can see that the 25th percentile is the first quartile ($Q_1$) and that the 75th percentile is the third quartile ($Q_3$). To find the interquartile range, then, we are going to have to locate the score that lies at the 75th percentile ($x_{Q_3}$), locate the score that lies at the 25th percentile ($x_{Q_1}$), and then take the difference between these two scores:

$$IQR = x_{Q_3} - x_{Q_1}$$ (5–2)

> **Interquartile range:** Measure of dispersion appropriate for interval/ratio-level data. It measures the range of scores in the middle 50% of a distribution of continuous scores and is calculated as the difference between the score at the third quartile (the 75th percentile) and the score at the first quartile (the 25th percentile).

> **Q1:** First quartile or 25th percentile in a distribution of scores.
>
> **Q2:** Second quartile or the 50th percentile, also called the median, in a distribution of scores.
>
> **Q3:** Third quartile or 75th percentile in a distribution of scores.

As you can see, the interquartile range reflects the range in the data in between the 75th and 25th percentiles, or the middle 50% of the distribution, thereby ignoring the highest and lowest scores. The calculation of the IQR is pretty straightforward, and we will show you two different ways to calculate the IQR in the following Case Study.

---

## Case Study

### Calculating the Interquartile Range of the Number of Escapes by Prison

For this example, let's use the data in Table 5.9, which shows the hypothetical number of escapes from 20 correctional institutions in the prison system of two states, State A and State B. We can easily calculate the range in the number of escapes for the prisons in these two states. For State A, the range is 23 because the highest number of escapes was 23 and the lowest was 0. For State B, the range is 9 because there was a high of 10 escapes and a low of 1. Judging by the range, there seems to be substantially more dispersion in the number of escapes in State A. However, the range is greater for State A only because there was one prison that had an unusually high number of escapes (23 of them), and this outlier is distorting the true dispersion in the data. There are two different ways to calculate the IQR.

One way is first to rank-order the data in ascending order (lowest to highest). After the data are rank-ordered, we need to identify something called the *truncated median position* or TMP. The truncated median position is simply the position of the median in the data with the decimal place in the calculation truncated (*truncated* means that the decimal place is dropped or rounded down to the nearest integer). For example, we have 20 observations for each state in Table 5.9. Using our positional formula for the location of the median, we find that the median is in the $(20 + 1) / 2 = 10.5$th position. The truncated median position is 10, which was found by dropping the .5. With the value of the TMP, we can now identify where the third and first quartiles can be found, or the quartile positions (QPs):

$$QP = (TMP + 1) / 2$$

| Table 5.8 | The Relationship Among Percentiles, Deciles, and Quartiles | |
|---|---|---|

| Percentile | Decile | Quartile |
|---|---|---|
| 100th | 10th | |
| 99th | | |
| 98th | | |
| 90th | 9th | |
| . | | |
| 80th | 8th | |
| . | | |
| . | | |
| 75th | | 3rd ($Q_3$) |
| . | | |
| . | | |
| 60th | 6th | |
| . | | |
| . | | |
| 50th | 5th | 2nd ($Q_2$) |
| . | | |
| . | | |
| . | | |
| 30th | 3rd | |
| 29th | | |
| 28th | | |
| 25th | | 1st ($Q_1$) |
| . | | |
| . | | |
| 20th | 2nd | |
| . | | |
| 3rd | | |
| 2nd | | |
| 1st | | |

With a truncated median position of 10, we can determine that the position of the two quartiles ($Q_1$ and $Q_3$ or the 25th and 75th percentile) is $(10 + 1) / 2 = 5.5$th position (the truncated median position plus 1 divided by 2). The third and first quartiles, then, are at the midpoint of the 5th and 6th scores in the rank order of scores. More specifically, *in a rank-ordered distribution of scores,* the first quartile is the midpoint between the 5th and 6th *lowest* scores, and the third quartile is the midpoint between the 5th and 6th *highest* scores. In Table 5.10, we provide the number of escapes from each state in rank order, along with the position of the first ($Q_1$) and third ($Q_3$) quartiles. To find the first quartile, we start from the lowest score, identify what the 5th and 6th scores are, and find the average of those two scores. To find the third quartile, we start from the highest score, identify what the 5th and 6th scores are, and find the average.

The first quartile for State A is 2 because the scores at both the 5th and 6th positons are equal to 2 ($[2 + 2] / 2 = 2$), and the first quartile for State B is 3 ($[3 + 3] / 2 = 3$). The third quartile for both states is 6 because both states have 6 escapes at the 5th and 6th values down from the highest score ($[6 + 6] / 2 = 6$).

With this information, we can now calculate the interquartile range for both states:

$$\text{IQR State A} = 6 - 2 = 4 \text{ escapes}$$

$$\text{IQR State B} = 6 - 3 = 3 \text{ escapes}$$

Thus, the interquartile range for the two states is fairly comparable, indicating that in the middle 50% of the distributions of the number of escapes, there is about an equal amount of variation in the two states. This is a different picture of the dispersion in the data from the one we got when we calculated the range, which was influenced by the fact that one institution in State A experienced 23 escapes.

Another way to find the interquartile range without having to identify the truncated median position is to use cumulative percentages. Recall that the first quartile is the score at the 25th percentile, and the third quartile is the score at the 75th percentile. We can find the scores at the 25th and 75th percentiles by simply calculating a column of cumulative percentages. Table 5.11 provides the frequency, percentage, and cumulative percentage distribution of escapes for the two states. For State A, the score at the 25th percentile is 2 escapes. How do we know this? Note that 15% of the scores are either 0 or 1 and that 30% of the scores are 0, 1, or 2. This indicates that the scores at the 16th percentile, the 17th percentile, . . . and all the way to the 30th percentile are all 2s. The score at the 25th percentile, then, is a 2, or 2 escapes. For State A, the score at the 75th percentile is 6 escapes because 70% of the scores are 5 or lower, and 80% of the scores are 6 escapes or lower so this must mean that the scores at the 71st, 72nd. 73rd, 74th, 75th, and all the way to the 80th percentile are 6 escapes. The 75th percentile, then, is 6 escapes. For State A, the IQR is $6 - 2 = 4$ escapes. For State B, the score at the 25th percentile is 3 escapes because 20% of the scores are 2 escapes or lower and 40% of the scores are 3 escapes or lower. The score at the 25th percentile, then, is a 3. The score at the 75th percentile is 6 escapes since 70% of the scores are 5 escapes or lower and 80% of them are 6 escapes or lower. The score at the 75th percentile,

| Table 5.9 | Number of Escapes from 20 Correctional Institutions in Two States | |
|:---:|:---:|:---:|
| Institution | State A | State B |
| 1 | 3 | 3 |
| 2 | 2 | 4 |
| 3 | 4 | 1 |
| 4 | 9 | 2 |
| 5 | 2 | 3 |
| 6 | 5 | 6 |
| 7 | 6 | 5 |
| 8 | 4 | 3 |
| 9 | 1 | 4 |
| 10 | 3 | 4 |
| 11 | 4 | 5 |
| 12 | 5 | 2 |
| 13 | 2 | 3 |
| 14 | 0 | 5 |
| 15 | 7 | 8 |
| 16 | 1 | 1 |
| 17 | 7 | 6 |
| 18 | 6 | 8 |
| 19 | 9 | 9 |
| 20 | 23 | 10 |

| Table 5.10 | Rank-Ordered Number of Escapes from 20 Correctional Institutions in Two States from Table 5.9 | |
|:---:|:---:|:---:|
| Institution | State A | State B |
| 1 | 0 | 1 |
| 2 | 1 | 1 |
| 3 | 1 | 2 |
| 4 | 2 | 2 |
| 5 | 2 | 3 |
| 6 | 2 | 3 |
| 7 | 3 | 3 |
| 8 | 3 | 3 |
| 9 | 3 | 4 |
| 10 | 4 | 4 |
| 11 | 4 | 4 |
| 12 | 4 | 5 |
| 13 | 5 | 5 |
| 14 | 5 | 5 |
| 15 | 6 | 6 |
| 16 | 6 | 6 |
| 17 | 7 | 8 |
| 18 | 7 | 8 |
| 19 | 9 | 9 |
| 20 | 23 | 10 |

| Table 5.11 | Frequency Counts, Percentages, and Cumulative Percentages for Escape Data From Two States | | | | | | |
|:---:|:---:|:---:|:---:|:---:|:---:|:---:|:---:|

| STATE A # of Escapes | f | % | Cum % | STATE B # of Escapes | f | % | Cum % |
|:---:|:---:|:---:|:---:|:---:|:---:|:---:|:---:|
| 0 | 1 | 5 | 5 | 1 | 2 | 10 | 10 |
| 1 | 2 | 10 | 15 | 2 | 2 | 10 | 20 |
| 2 | 3 | 15 | 30 | 3 | 4 | 20 | 40 |
| 3 | 3 | 15 | 45 | 4 | 3 | 15 | 55 |

*(Continued)*

| Table 5.11 | (Continued) |

| STATE A # of Escapes | f | % | Cum % | STATE B # of Escapes | f | % | Cum % |
|---|---|---|---|---|---|---|---|
| 4 | 3 | 15 | 60 | 5 | 3 | 15 | 70 |
| 5 | 2 | 10 | 70 | 6 | 2 | 10 | 80 |
| 6 | 2 | 10 | 80 | 8 | 2 | 10 | 90 |
| 7 | 2 | 10 | 90 | 9 | 1 | 5 | 95 |
| 9 | 1 | 5 | 95 | 10 | 1 | 5 | 100 |
| 23 | 1 | 5 | 100 | | | | |
| | $n = 20$ | 100.0 | | | $n = 20$ | 100.0 | |

then, is 6 escapes. The IQR for State B is $6 - 3 = 3$ escapes. These are the same answers we got using the truncated median position formula and finding our quartiles that way. The next measures of dispersion we will cover provide yet a different way to measure a variable's dispersion!

# The Standard Deviation and Variance

Because the range and interquartile range estimate the amount of dispersion in the data by taking the difference between only two scores, they are somewhat limited. Recall that with interval- and ratio-level data, we can calculate a mean or arithmetic average as a measure of central tendency. Not surprisingly, there are measures of dispersion that use the mean as the reference point to measure dispersion. These measures are based on the notion that measuring how much heterogeneity there is for a variable is to determine how different a value is from the mean. The most common of these mean-based measures of dispersion are the variance and standard deviation.

Both the standard deviation and the variance measure dispersion by taking the difference, or deviation, of each score from the mean of a variable. Scores that are clustered very close to the mean are less disperse, or more homogeneous, than scores that are very far from the mean. The *distance from the mean or the deviation from the mean,* therefore, is another way to capture the amount of dispersion in a variable. The simple formula for taking the distance of a score from the mean is $x_i - \bar{X}$ where $x_i$ is the score for the $i$th score and $\bar{X}$ is the mean of the sample.

As we will see, using the distance or deviation from the mean as the basis for a measure of dispersion for continuous data will give us two pieces of information. First, the sign of the distance or deviation will tell us whether the score is less than or greater than the mean. Second, the magnitude of the deviation will tell us how far the score is—its distance—from the mean. Let's use this simple formula $(x_i - \bar{X})$ for the distance of a score from the mean, referred to as a **mean deviation score**, and determine how it applies to the notion of dispersion.

> **Mean deviation score:** Distance between a score and the mean of the group of scores: $(x_i - \bar{X})$.

Figure 5.2 shows two distributions of one variable. The mean of both distributions is 25. In the first distribution, shown in Figure 5.2(a), you can see that most of the values or scores are close to the mean. The farthest a score is away from the mean is 2 units (a score of 23 is −2 units from the mean, whereas a score of 27 is +2 units away). In other words, for this variable, the distance of each score from the mean is not great, indicating that the scores are not very different from the mean (or, by implication, from each other). There does not seem to be much dispersion or heterogeneity in this distribution, and this fact is reflected in the short distance of each score from the mean. However, in the second distribution shown

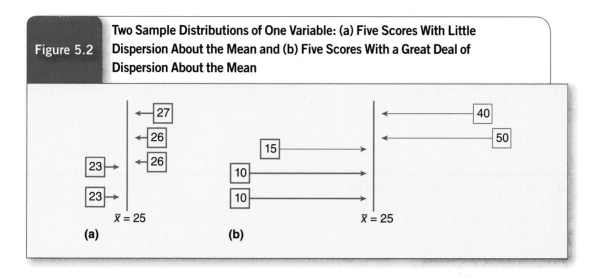

**Figure 5.2** Two Sample Distributions of One Variable: (a) Five Scores With Little Dispersion About the Mean and (b) Five Scores With a Great Deal of Dispersion About the Mean

in Figure 5.2(b), the scores are much more different from the mean than those in Figure 5.2(a), and this is indicated by the fact that there is a greater distance between each of these scores and the mean. Without doing any math, you should be able to determine that the distribution shown in Figure 5.2(b) has more dispersion (the scores are more different from the mean, or more heterogeneous) than the distribution of scores in Figure 5.2(a). In sum, the notion of distance from the mean, or mean deviation scores, is another way to capture the dispersion of a variable measured at the interval/ratio level.

Let's take this example one step further and calculate, for each score in Figure 5.2, the distance from the mean. We mentioned earlier that the distance of each score from the mean is also called a *deviation* from the mean.

As we mentioned, the deviation from the mean contains two pieces of information. Let's take the first $x$ score, 23, where the deviation from the mean is −2. The negative sign of the deviation tells us that a score of 23 is less than the mean, and the magnitude of 2 tells us that it is 2 units away from the mean. A negative mean deviation, then, indicates that the $x$ score is less than the mean, whereas a positive mean deviation indicates that the score is greater than the mean. Moreover, the greater the magnitude of the mean deviation, the greater the distance the $x$ score is from the mean. Finally, the greater the overall distance a distribution of scores are from the mean, the more dispersion or variability there is in the data. Knowing this, it's pretty easy to see that there is more dispersion in the

**For the Scores in Figure 5.2(a)**

| Score | Mean | Deviation from Mean |
|-------|------|---------------------|
| 23 | 25 | 23 − 25 = −2 |
| 26 | 25 | 26 − 25 = +1 |
| 23 | 25 | 23 − 25 = -2 |
| 27 | 25 | 27 − 25 = +2 |
| 26 | 25 | 26 − 25 = +1 |

**For the Scores in Figure 5.2(b)**

| Score | Mean | Deviation from Mean |
|-------|------|---------------------|
| 10 | 25 | 10 − 25 = −15 |
| 50 | 25 | 50 − 25 = +25 |
| 15 | 25 | 15 − 25 = −10 |
| 40 | 25 | 40 − 25 = +15 |
| 10 | 25 | 10 − 25 = −15 |

second set of scores, and this is reflected in the fact that when we take all of the scores into account, the magnitude of the deviations, regardless of their sign, is much greater in the second set of scores than in the first.

Rather than having all of these deviation scores (imagine how messy things would look if we had 20 scores or 100!), it might be nice to create a summary measure or one number that captures the *average distance* or deviation from the mean. That is, since we know that the mean is a good measure of central tendency, let's calculate the mean deviation score that would provide us with one number that indicates the average distance of each score from the mean. This number would then give us the average, or mean, of the deviations. This would be easy to do. Again, we know that the formula for the mean is:

$$\bar{X} = \frac{\sum_{i=1}^{n} x_i}{n}$$

and that it is calculated by adding up all the scores and dividing by the total number of scores. We can use this same formula for the mean here; the only difference is that our "score" is not an $x_i$ but a difference score: $(x_i - \bar{X})$. All we have to do is say $x_i = (x_i - \bar{X})$, and calculate our mean distance or mean deviation score as:

$$\bar{D} = \frac{\sum_{i=1}^{n}(x_i - \bar{X})}{n}$$

(just for now, let's let $\bar{D}$ be the symbol for the average deviation or distance score). This formula simply tells us to subtract score from the mean, then sum up these deviation scores, and divide by the total number of scores. For the scores in Figure 5.2(a), the average deviation would be:

$$\bar{D} = \frac{-2 + 1 - 2 + 2 + 1}{5}$$

$$\bar{D} = \frac{0}{5}$$

For the scores in Figure 5.2(b), the average deviation would be:

$$\bar{D} = \frac{-15 + 25 - 10 + 15 + 15}{5}$$

$$\bar{D} = \frac{0}{5}$$

We've hit a snag! The numerator of our formula for the average distance from the mean is zero; in fact, it will always be zero. The essence of the mean as a measure of central tendency is that it is a score that perfectly balances the negative and positive differences from it. In other words, the sum of the negative deviations from the mean is exactly equal to the sum of the positive deviations from the mean. As a result, when we add the negative deviations from the mean to the positive deviations from the mean, we are always left with a sum of zero. The way to state this property in words is to say that "the sum of the deviations around the mean is always zero" or in formula:

$$\sum_{i=1}^{n}(x_i - \bar{X}) = 0$$

Because of this property of the mean, we are stuck. One way to get unstuck would be to get rid of the negative signs for the scores. An easy way to do this would be to square the deviation scores, which would give us $(x_i - \bar{X})^2$. This squaring of deviations will ensure all positive values (since the square of a negative number is a positive number) in the numerator. Then we can take the mean of these squared deviations. Now, our formula for measuring dispersion looks like this:

$$\frac{\sum_{i=1}^{n}(x_i - \bar{X})^2}{n}$$

In words, this formula says to subtract each score from the mean (the "mean deviation score"), square this deviation for each score, sum all of these squared deviations, and finally divide by the total number of scores. Let's use this formula with our data in Figure 5.2(a) and (b).

**For the Scores in Figure 5.2(a)**

| Score | Mean | Deviation from Mean | Squared Deviation |
|-------|------|---------------------|-------------------|
| 23 | 25 | 23 − 25 = −2 | 4 |
| 26 | 25 | 26 − 25 = +1 | 1 |
| 23 | 25 | 23 − 25 = −2 | 4 |
| 27 | 25 | 27 − 25 = +2 | 4 |
| 26 | 25 | 26 − 25 = +1 | 1 |

The average squared deviation from the mean would be:

$$\bar{D} = \frac{4+1+4+4+1}{5} = \frac{14}{5} = 2.8$$

The average squared deviation from the mean would be:

$$\bar{D} = \frac{225+625+100+225+225}{5} = \frac{1,400}{5} = 280$$

**For the Scores in Figure 5.2(b)**

| Score | Mean | Deviation from Mean | Squared Deviation |
|---|---|---|---|
| 10 | 25 | 10 − 25 = −15 | 225 |
| 50 | 25 | 50 − 25 = 25 | 625 |
| 15 | 25 | 15 − 25 = −10 | 100 |
| 40 | 25 | 40 − 25 = 15 | 225 |
| 10 | 25 | 10 − 25 = −15 | 225 |

Now we have one number for each set of scores that measures the amount of dispersion in the data by taking the average squared deviation from the mean. By using this, we can see clearly that there is substantially more dispersion in the second set of scores than in the first, and that is exactly the impression we got from Figure 5.2.

**Variance:** Measures the average squared deviations from the mean for an interval/ratio variable.

Congratulations! What you have actually just done is to calculate the **variance**. The variance is the average squared difference of each score in a set of scores from the mean of those scores. The greater the magnitude of the variance, the more dispersion there is in the data. We now need to complicate things a little because we must distinguish between the variance of a population and the variance of a sample.

Recall from our discussion in Chapter 1 that a population consists of the universe of cases that we are interested in. For example, if we are interested in the relationship between IQ scores and delinquency among male youths between the ages of 12 and 18 years in the United States, our population consists of all male youths between the ages of 12 and 18 who reside in the United States. The population we are interested in, then, is generally very large and both difficult and costly to study directly. Our population of male adolescents, for example, would number in the millions. A sample, you will remember, is a subset of the population. We select a sample from the population and study the sample with the intention of making an inference to the population based on what we know about the sample. The sample is much smaller than the population, and it is the group that we actually study. We might, for example, first take a sample of states, then a sample of cities, and finally a sample of youths between the ages of 12 and 18 from those cities.

As was true for the mean, it would be entirely possible (although it would require a great deal of work and considerable money) to calculate the variance of most populations. As such, its value generally remains unknown. In statistics, the variance of a population is noted by the term $\sigma^2$ (the Greek letter sigma, squared) and is defined as the averaged squared deviation of each score in a population from the mean of that population:

$$\sigma^2 = \frac{\sum_{i=1}^{N}(x_i - \mu)^2}{N} \tag{5-3}$$

where $\mu$ is the population mean and $N$ is the total number of scores in the population.

If we do not have the entire population and have, instead, drawn a sample from that population, we have to estimate the unknown population value with our sample data. Recall that for the mean, we estimated $\mu$, the unknown population mean, with $\bar{X}$ the mean of the sample. Similarly, when we have sample data, we estimate the variance of the population with the variance of our sample data. The formula for the variance of the sample is:

$$s^2 = \frac{\sum_{i=1}^{n}(x_i - \bar{X})^2}{n-1} \tag{5-4}$$

There are two differences between the formula for the variance of a population (equation 5-3) and the formula for the variance of a sample (equation 5-4). In the variance of a population, we take the sum of the squared deviations of each score from the population mean ($\mu$) and divide by the population size ($N$). In the variance of a sample, we take the sum of the squared deviations of each score from the sample mean ($\overline{X}$) and divide by the number of scores in the sample ($n$) minus 1. The reason we use $n-1$ in the denominator of the sample variance is that it is a biased estimator of the population value $\sigma^2$. To correct for that bias, we divide by $n-1$ rather than by $n$ in our sample formula. Note that the practical effect of using $n-1$ is that we have a smaller denominator. This means that the estimate of the sample variance will be larger than if we simply used the sample size. It also means that the difference between $n-1$ and $n$ will be more substantial when the sample size is small. This should make sense to you because it means the bias is larger in smaller samples.

Note that to get rid of the negative signs in calculating the variance, we took the *squared* deviation of each score from the mean. The variance, therefore, measures dispersion in the awkward terminology of "average squared deviation from the mean."

The other measure of dispersion for interval- and ratio-level data that we will discuss, the standard deviation, adjusts for the squaring of the deviations about the mean. It does this by taking the square root of the variance (taking the square root of a value is the "opposite" operation to squaring it; 2 squared is 4, and the square root of 4 is 2). The symbol $\sigma$ is used to denote the population standard deviation, which has the formula:

$$\sigma = \sqrt{\frac{\sum_{i=1}^{N}(x_i - \mu)^2}{N}} \tag{5-5}$$

The symbol $s$ is used to denote the sample **standard deviation**, which has the formula:

$$s = \sqrt{\frac{\sum_{i=1}^{n}(x_i - \overline{X})^2}{n-1}} \tag{5-6}$$

Notice that:

$$\text{variance} = \text{standard deviation}^2$$

$$\text{standard deviation} = \sqrt{\text{variance}}$$

**Standard deviation:** Square root of the squared deviations about the mean.

The variance is the standard deviation squared, whereas the standard deviation is the square root of the variance. So if you calculate the sample variance, all you have to do to get the standard deviation is take the square root of that value to get the standard deviation. The variance and standard deviation are the two most frequently used measures of dispersion for interval- and ratio-level data. To summarize what we have covered in this section, Table 5.12 shows the population and sample formulas for the variance and the standard deviation.

## Case Study

## Calculating the Variance and Standard Deviation of Judges' Sentences

Let's practice using these sample formulas by calculating the variance and standard deviation for our two judges' sentencing data from Table 5.1. Since these are samples of 20 sentences from the population of sentences that these judges handed

| Table 5.12 | Definitional Formulas for Population and Sample Variance and Standard Deviation |
|---|---|

| Population | |
|---|---|
| Variance ($\sigma^2$) | $\sigma^2 = \dfrac{\Sigma(x_i - \mu)^2}{N}$ |
| Standard deviation ($\sigma$) | $\sigma = \sqrt{\dfrac{\Sigma(x_i - \mu)^2}{N}}$ |
| Sample | |
| Variance ($s^2$) | $s^2 = \dfrac{\Sigma(x_i - \overline{X})^2}{n-1}$ |
| Standard deviation ($s$) | $s = \sqrt{\dfrac{\Sigma(x_i - \overline{X})^2}{n-1}}$ |

| Table 5.13 | Calculations for the Variance and Standard Deviation in Judge 1's Sentencing, $n = 20$ |
|---|---|

| $x$ | $(x_i - \overline{X})$ | $(x_i - \overline{X})^2$ |
|---|---|---|
| 5 | $5 - 9 = -4$ | 16 |
| 7 | $7 - 9 = -2$ | 4 |
| 7 | $7 - 9 = -2$ | 4 |
| 7 | $7 - 9 = -2$ | 4 |
| 7 | $7 - 9 = -2$ | 4 |
| 7 | $7 - 9 = -2$ | 4 |
| 8 | $8 - 9 = -1$ | 1 |
| 8 | $8 - 9 = -1$ | 1 |
| 8 | $8 - 9 = -1$ | 1 |
| 8 | $8 - 9 = -1$ | 1 |
| 9 | $9 - 9 = 0$ | 0 |
| 9 | $9 - 9 = 0$ | 0 |
| 9 | $9 - 9 = 0$ | 0 |
| 10 | $10 - 9 = 1$ | 1 |
| 11 | $11 - 9 = 2$ | 4 |
| 11 | $11 - 9 = 2$ | 4 |
| 11 | $11 - 9 = 2$ | 4 |
| 12 | $12 - 9 = 3$ | 9 |
| 12 | $12 - 9 = 3$ | 9 |
| 14 | $14 - 9 = 5$ | 25 |
| | | $\Sigma = 96$ |

down to convicted defendants, we will use the sample formulas for the variance (equation 5-4) and standard deviation (equation 5-6). Let's calculate the variance first by using the following steps:

### Steps in Calculating the Sample Variance

**Step 1:** Calculate the mean.

**Step 2:** Subtract the mean from each score: $x_i - \overline{X}$.

**Step 3:** Square the deviation of each score from the mean: $(x_i - \overline{X})^2$.

**Step 4:** Sum the squared deviations for all scores, starting with the first score and continuing to the last score:

$$\sum_{i=1}^{n}(x_i - \overline{X})^2$$

This is called the sum of the squared deviations from the mean.

**Step 5:** Divide by the number of scores minus 1:

$$\frac{\sum_{i=1}^{n}(x_i - \overline{X})^2}{n-1}$$

This is the sample variance.

| Table 5.14 | Calculations for the Variance and Standard Deviation in Judge 2's Sentencing, $n = 20$ | |
|---|---|---|
| $x$ | $(x_i - \bar{X})$ | $(x_i - \bar{X})^2$ |
| 1 | $1 - 9 = -8$ | 64 |
| 2 | $2 - 9 = -7$ | 49 |
| 2 | $2 - 9 = -7$ | 49 |
| 3 | $3 - 9 = -6$ | 36 |
| 3 | $3 - 9 = -6$ | 36 |
| 3 | $3 - 9 = -6$ | 36 |
| 4 | $4 - 9 = -5$ | 25 |
| 4 | $4 - 9 = -5$ | 25 |
| 5 | $5 - 9 = -4$ | 16 |
| 8 | $8 - 9 = -1$ | 1 |
| 9 | $9 - 9 = 0$ | 0 |
| 10 | $10 - 9 = 1$ | 1 |
| 11 | $11 - 9 = 2$ | 4 |
| 14 | $14 - 9 = 5$ | 25 |
| 15 | $15 - 9 = 6$ | 36 |
| 15 | $15 - 9 = 6$ | 36 |
| 16 | $16 - 9 = 7$ | 49 |
| 17 | $17 - 9 = 8$ | 64 |
| 18 | $18 - 9 = 9$ | 81 |
| 20 | $20 - 9 = 11$ | 121 |
| | | $\Sigma = 754$ |

Now we will calculate the variance separately for each judge. First, the calculations for Judge 1 are shown in Table 5.13. We can see from Table 5.13 that the sum of the squared deviations is 96. To find the variance, we divide this by the number of scores ($n$) minus 1. The variance for Judge 1, therefore, is:

$$s^2 = \frac{96}{20 - 1}$$

$$s^2 = \frac{96}{19}$$

$$s^2 = 5.05$$

The calculations necessary to find the variance for Judge 2 are shown in Table 5.14. We can see from this table that the sum of the squared deviations about the mean for Judge 2 is 754. Again, to find the variance, we divide this by the number of scores ($n$) minus 1. The variance for Judge 2, therefore, is:

$$s^2 = \frac{754}{20 - 1}$$

$$s^2 = \frac{754}{19}$$

$$s^2 = 39.68$$

When we calculate the variance for Judge 1 and Judge 2, then, we find that the magnitude is much higher for Judge 2, confirming our suspicion that there is more dispersion, or heterogeneity, in this judge's sentencing behavior than in that of Judge 1. The interpretation of a sample variance is really only useful with reference to the sample mean. The interpretation for these sample variances would be as follows: For Judge 1, the sample of 20 sentences varied 5.05 squared deviation units around their mean of 9, and for Judge 2, the sample of 20 sentences varied 39.68 squared deviation units around their mean of 9. The problem, of course, is who can imagine what these squared deviation units actually mean? That's why the standard deviation is most often utilized to describe the variability in sample data, and we can easily calculate that now!

If you look at the formula for the sample standard deviation, you can see that all we have to do is take the square root of the variance. Thus there is only one more step involved in calculating the standard deviation. Since this is our first time calculating the standard deviation, however, we will give you each of the necessary steps:

---

### Steps in Calculating the Sample Standard Deviation

**Step 1:** Calculate the mean.

**Step 2:** Subtract the mean from each score: $x_i - \bar{X}$. This is called taking the deviation from the mean.

**Step 3:** Square the deviation of each score from the mean: $(x_i - \bar{X})^2$.

**Step 4:** Sum the squared deviations for all scores, starting with the first score and continuing to the last score:

$$\sum_{i=1}^{n}(x_i - \overline{X})^2$$

This is called the sum of the squared deviations from the mean.

**Step 5:** Divide the number of scores by $n$ minus 1:

$$\frac{\sum_{i=1}^{n}(x_i - \overline{X})^2}{n-1}$$

$$\sqrt{\frac{\sum_{i=1}^{n}(x_i - \overline{X})^2}{n-1}}$$

This is the sample standard deviation.

Since we already have the variances, let's quickly calculate the two standard deviations. First, for Judge 1:

$$s = \sqrt{s^2}$$
$$s = \sqrt{5.05}$$
$$s = 2.25$$

This value is measured in units that are consistent with the measurement units of the variable, in this case years sentenced. So we can interpret this by saying that the average variation around the sentences handed down by Judge 1 for this sample of 20 robbery defendants was 2.25 units (years) around the mean sentence length of 9 years. The standard deviation for Judge 2 is:

$$s = \sqrt{s^2}$$
$$s = \sqrt{39.68}$$
$$s = 6.30$$

For Judge 2, the average variation around the sentences handed down is 6.30 units (years) around the mean of 9 years. It should be noted that you should never compare standard deviation values across variables that are measuring the same thing. In this case, we have the same variables so the comparison makes sense. Because the standard deviation is much larger for Judge 2's sentences compared to those of Judge 1, we can say there is more dispersion or heterogeneity for Judge 2's sentencing practices.

## Case Study

## Self-Control for Delinquent Youth

Let's go through one more example of calculating the variance and standard deviation with ungrouped data before moving on to the grouped case. Michael Gottfredson and Travis Hirschi (1990) theorized that those individuals who

| Table 5.15 | Self-Control Scores for a Sample of 25 Incarcerated Youth | |
|---|---|---|
| $x$ | $(x_i - \bar{X})$ | $(x_i - \bar{X})^2$ |
| 85 | 85 − 91 = −6 | 36 |
| 100 | 100 − 91 = 9 | 81 |
| 87 | 87 − 91 = −4 | 16 |
| 93 | 93 − 91 = 2 | 4 |
| 78 | 78 − 91 = −13 | 169 |
| 103 | 103 − 91 = −12 | 144 |
| 88 | 88 − 91 = −3 | 9 |
| 94 | 94 − 91 = 3 | 9 |
| 94 | 94 − 91 = 3 | 9 |
| 101 | 101 − 91 = 10 | 100 |
| 94 | 94 − 91 = 3 | 9 |
| 92 | 92 − 91 = 1 | 1 |
| 83 | 83 − 91 = −8 | 64 |
| 70 | 70 − 91 = −21 | 441 |
| 110 | 110 − 91 = 19 | 361 |
| 87 | 87 − 91 = −4 | 16 |
| 91 | 91 − 91 = 0 | 0 |
| 79 | 79 − 91 = −12 | 144 |
| 84 | 84 − 91 = −7 | 49 |
| 88 | 88 − 91 = −3 | 9 |
| 90 | 90 − 91 = 1 | 1 |
| 104 | 104 − 91 = 13 | 169 |
| 100 | 100 − 91 = 9 | 81 |
| 98 | 98 − 91 =7 | 49 |
| 82 | 82 − 91 = −9 | 81 |
| | | Σ = 2,052 |

had low self-control would be at greater risk for engaging in crime, delinquency, and other self-destructive behaviors. Studies have indicated consistent support for this theory (Meldrum, Barnes, & Hay, 2015). In Table 5.15, we have a sample of males from a juvenile correctional facility. To measure their self-reported self-control, suppose we asked them a number of questions about risk-taking behavior, their ability to delay gratification, along with other questions intended to measure individual levels of self-control. The self-control scale has a low of 65 indicating very low self-control and a high of 150 indicating very high levels of self-control. We find in this sample of 25 youths that the mean self-control score is 91.00.

The second column of Table 5.15 presents the deviations from the mean, and the third column presents the squared deviations from the mean. If you were to sum the second column (the deviations from the mean), you should obtain

$$\sum_{i=1}^{n}(x_i - \bar{X}) = 0$$

The sum of the third column gives us the numerator for the sample variance, the sum of the squared deviations from the mean. In this example, the sum of the squared deviations is equal to 2,052. We can very easily obtain the sample variance by dividing this by $n-1$. The variance of these self-control scores, then, is equal to:

$$s^2 = \frac{2,052}{24}$$
$$s^2 = 85.50$$

The average squared distance of each self-control score from the mean of 91 is equal to 85.5. The standard deviation is equal to:

$$s = \sqrt{\frac{2,052}{24}}$$
$$s = \sqrt{85.50}$$
$$s = 9.25$$

The interpretation of this is more understandable: For this sample of incarcerated male adolescents, the average self-control score is 91 with an average variability around this mean of 9.25 units. In this case, we can only refer to the scores as units since they are not measured in any more understandable units such as years, dollars, convictions, and so on. Let's move on to calculate the variance and standard deviation from grouped data.

## Calculating the Variance and Standard Deviation With Grouped Data

In previous chapters, we have used continuous (interval/ratio) level data to create class intervals that transformed our variable into the ordinal level of measurement. As we did in the last chapter, we will make the assumption that each score in any given class interval falls at the midpoint of the interval so that we can calculate a mean and a deviation from the mean score. Once we calculate the deviation from the mean, we can easily calculate a variance and standard deviation. To calculate a variance and standard deviation with grouped data, we only need to make two minor modifications to our formulas. Here is the formula to calculate a sample variance with grouped data:

$$S^2 = \frac{\sum\limits_{i=1}^{k} f_i(m_i - \overline{X})^2}{n-1} \tag{5-7}$$

where

$k$ = the number of class intervals or categories

$m_i$ = the midpoint of the $i$th interval

$f_i$ = the frequency of the $i$th interval

$\overline{X}$ = the mean of the grouped frequency distribution

In words, here is what equation 5-7 is telling you to do. Start with the first class interval ($k = 1$) and subtract the mean from the midpoint of this interval. Square this difference or deviation, multiply that squared difference by the number of scores that are in that class interval, and then go to the next class interval and do the same thing, continuing until you do the last class interval. Finally, sum these values, and divide by the total number of scores minus 1.

There are two differences between this equation for the variance of grouped sample data and the equation for the variance of ungrouped sample data (equation 5-4). The first difference is that we do not have an $x_i$ score but an $m_i$ score since we use the midpoint of each class interval ($m_i$) as the score from which we subtract the mean. Second, we have to take into account that there may be more than one score in a given class interval—that, in fact, there are $f_i$ scores in each class interval, all of which are assumed to lie at the midpoint. Hence, rather than taking $(m_i - \overline{X})^2$ $f$ number of times (one for each case in the interval), we multiply $(m_i - \overline{X})^2$ by the number of scores in the interval. Once we have the variance of a sample of grouped data, we can very easily find the standard deviation by taking the square root of the variance just as we did with ungrouped data:

$$s = \sqrt{\frac{\sum\limits_{i=1}^{k} f_i(m_i - \overline{X})^2}{n-1}} \tag{5-8}$$

## Case Study

## Time Until Rearrest for a Sample of Released Inmates

Let's do an example of calculating the variance and standard deviation with grouped data.

Table 5.16 shows a very familiar data set. It is the time-until-rearrest data for our sample of 120 inmates released from a correctional institution and followed up until they were rearrested. Remember this is a sample in which all were eventually rearrested. Table 5.16 gives the stated class limits for each interval, the midpoint of the interval, and the frequency for each interval. In Chapter 4, we learned that the mean of this grouped data was 31.025 days. To make our calculations a little easier, let's calculate the variance and standard deviation with a mean of 31 days. You can refer back to Chapter 4 for the steps involved in calculating the mean with grouped data.

---

### Steps in Calculating the Sample Variance and Standard Deviation With Grouped Data

**Step 1:** Determine the midpoint of each class interval ($m_i$).

**Step 2:** Calculate the mean ($\overline{X}$) from the grouped data.

**Step 3:** Subtract the mean from the midpoint $(m_i - \overline{X})$ of the first interval.

**Step 4:** Square the deviation of the midpoint from the mean: $(m_i - \overline{X})^2$.

**Step 5:** Multiply the squared deviation of the midpoint from the mean by the frequency for the class interval: $f_i(m_i - \overline{X})^2$.

**Step 6:** Repeat Steps 2–4 for each class interval, starting with the first and ending with the last.

**Step 7:** Sum the $f_i(m_i - \overline{X})^2$ for all class intervals.

**Step 8:** Divide the result in Step 7 by the number of scores minus 1:

$$\frac{\left(\sum_{i=1}^{k} f_i\left(m_i - \overline{X}\right)^2\right)}{n-1}$$

This is the variance for grouped data.

**Step 9:** Take the square root of this:

$$\sqrt{\frac{\left(\sum_{i=1}^{k} f_i\left(m_i - \overline{X}\right)^2\right)}{n-1}}$$

This is the sample standard deviation for grouped data.

---

**Table 5.16** Stated Class Limits, Midpoints, and Frequencies for Grouped Frequency Distribution of Time-Until-Rearrest Data, $n = 120$

| Stated Class Limits | Midpoints $m_i$ | f |
|---|---|---|
| 17–19 | 18 | 4 |
| 20–22 | 21 | 1 |
| 23–25 | 24 | 12 |
| 26–28 | 27 | 16 |
| 29–31 | 30 | 28 |
| 32–34 | 33 | 28 |
| 35–37 | 36 | 21 |
| 38–40 | 39 | 10 |

We show the necessary calculations to calculate the variance for these grouped data in Table 5.17. The sum of the squared deviations about the mean for these grouped data is equal to 2,925. Now we are ready to calculate the variance:

$$s^2 = \frac{\left(\sum_{i=1}^{k} f_i(m_i - \overline{X})^2\right)}{n-1}$$

$$s^2 = \frac{2,925}{119}$$

$$s^2 = 24.58$$

The average squared distance of each score from the mean, then, is 24.58 days. Since we have the variance, the standard deviation would be:

| Table 5.17 | Calculations for Variance and Standard Deviation for Time-Until-Rearrest Data, $n = 120$ |
|---|---|

| Midpoint of Class Interval | $(m_i - \bar{X})$ | $(m_i - \bar{X})^2$ | $f_i$ | $f_i(m_i - \bar{X})^2$ |
|---|---|---|---|---|
| 18 | $18 - 31 = -13$ | 169 | 4 | $4(169) = 676$ |
| 21 | $21 - 31 = -10$ | 100 | 1 | $1(100) = 100$ |
| 24 | $24 - 31 = -7$ | 49 | 12 | $12(49) = 588$ |
| 27 | $27 - 31 = -4$ | 16 | 16 | $16(16) = 256$ |
| 30 | $30 - 31 = -1$ | 1 | 28 | $28(1) = 28$ |
| 33 | $33 - 31 = 2$ | 4 | 28 | $28(4) = 112$ |
| 36 | $36 - 31 = 5$ | 25 | 21 | $21(25) = 525$ |
| 39 | $39 - 31 = 8$ | 64 | 10 | $10(64) = 640$ |
| | | | | $\Sigma = 2{,}925$ |

$$s^2 = \sqrt{\frac{\left( \sum_{i=1}^{k} f_i (m_i - \bar{X})^2 \right)}{n-1}}$$

$$s^2 = \sqrt{\frac{2{,}925}{119}}$$

$$s^2 = 4.96$$

In words, the average time until rearrest for this sample of offenders is 31 days with an average variability around this mean of 4.96 units (about 5 days).

You may be wondering how much precision we lost by categorizing the original interval- and ratio-level time-until-rearrest data into ordinal-level class intervals. Recall from Chapter 4 that the mean with the time-until-rearrest data when measured at the interval/ratio level was 31.075 days (and 31.025 days when the data were grouped). For the grouped data, we learned in the previous paragraph that the variance was 24.58 days and the standard deviation was 4.96. When these 120 observations were kept at their original interval/ratio level of measurement, the variance was 24.81 and the standard deviation was 4.98. Clearly, in this case we have not lost much precision in our data by grouping the values into class intervals.

## Computational Formulas for Variance and Standard Deviation

In the last two sections, we provided you with what are called definitional formulas for the variance and standard deviation because they clearly show what these measures of dispersion capture. By taking the term $(x_i - \bar{X})^2$ (or $m_i$ for grouped data), you can quickly see that they are based on the squared distance of each score from the mean of the scores. Although these formulas are useful because we can see exactly how dispersion is being measured, some students find them a little difficult to use, and all the calculations provide opportunities for error. In this section, we will provide several computational formulas that you might find easier to use in calculating the variance and standard deviation. We will then use these formulas with data from earlier in the chapter to show that we get the same result no matter which formula we use.

When we have ungrouped data, the computational formulas for the variance and standard deviation are:

$$\text{Variance} = s^2 = \frac{\Sigma(x_i^2) - \frac{(\Sigma x_i)^2}{n}}{n-1} \tag{5-9}$$

$$\text{Standard deviation} = s = \sqrt{\frac{\Sigma(x_i^2) - \frac{(\Sigma x_i)^2}{n}}{n-1}} \tag{5-10}$$

where

$\Sigma x_i^2$ = the sum of each squared $x$ score

$\Sigma(x_i)^2$ = the sum of the $x$ scores squared

$n$ = the total number of scores

These computational formulas for ungrouped data require that we obtain three quantities. The first of these quantities is the sum of the squared $x$, scores [$\Sigma(x_i^2)$]. To get this, we take each $x_i$ score, square it ($x_i^2$), and then sum across all scores ($x_1^2 + x_2^2 + x_3^2 + \cdots + x_n^2$). The second quantity is the sum of the $x_i$ scores squared. This is obtained by first summing across all $x$ scores and then squaring that sum ($x_1 + x_2 + x_3 + \cdots + x_n)^2$. The third quantity is simply the number of scores or $n$. As measures of dispersion, these computational formulas may not make as much intuitive sense to you as the definitional formulas, but they may be easier to use because they involve fewer calculations. Rather than taking the square of each score from the mean, all you have to do with the computational formula is to take the squares of the raw scores and the sum of the raw scores squared.

Let's practice one problem with these computational formulas before moving on to the computational formulas for grouped data. Let's use the sentencing data from the two judges we reported in Table 5.1. We reproduce these data along with the squared $x$ scores in Table 5.18. Using the computational formula for Judge 1, we have the following estimates of the variance and standard deviation:

$$s^2 = \frac{\Sigma(x_i^2) - \frac{(\Sigma x_i)^2}{n}}{n-1}$$

$$s^2 = \frac{1,716 - \frac{(180)^2}{20}}{19}$$

$$s^2 = \frac{1,716 - 1,620}{19}$$

$$s^2 = 5.05 \text{ this is the variance}$$

$$s = \sqrt{5.05}$$

$$s = 2.25 \text{ this is the standard deviation}$$

### Steps for Using Computational Formulas for Variance and Standard Deviation With Ungrouped Data

**Step 1:** Square each of the $x_i$ scores and sum these squared values: $\Sigma(x_i^2)$.

**Step 2:** Add all of the $x$ scores, square this sum, and divide by the number of scores:

$$\frac{(\Sigma x_i)^2}{n}$$

**Step 3:** Subtract the results in Step 2 from the value in Step 1:

$$\Sigma(x_i^2) - \frac{(\Sigma x_i)^2}{n}$$

**Step 4:** Divide this by the number of scores minus 1:

$$\frac{\Sigma(x_i^2) - \frac{(\Sigma x_i)^2}{n}}{n-1}$$

This is the variance.

**Step 5:** Take the square root of Step 4:

$$\sqrt{\frac{\Sigma(x_i^2) - \frac{(\Sigma x_i)^2}{n}}{n-1}}$$

This is the standard deviation.

**Table 5.18** Data and Calculations for Variance and Standard Deviation (Judge Sentencing Data from Table 5.1)

| Judge 1 | | Judge 2 | |
| --- | --- | --- | --- |
| x | x² | x | x² |
| 5 | 25 | 1 | 1 |
| 7 | 49 | 2 | 4 |
| 7 | 49 | 2 | 4 |
| 7 | 49 | 3 | 9 |
| 7 | 49 | 3 | 9 |
| 7 | 49 | 3 | 9 |
| 8 | 64 | 4 | 16 |
| 8 | 64 | 4 | 16 |
| 8 | 64 | 5 | 25 |
| 8 | 64 | 8 | 64 |
| 9 | 81 | 9 | 81 |
| 9 | 81 | 10 | 100 |
| 9 | 81 | 11 | 121 |
| 10 | 100 | 14 | 196 |
| 11 | 121 | 15 | 225 |
| 11 | 121 | 15 | 225 |
| 11 | 121 | 16 | 256 |
| 12 | 144 | 17 | 289 |
| 12 | 144 | 18 | 324 |
| 14 | 196 | 20 | 400 |
| Σ = 180 | Σ = 1,716 | Σ = 180 | Σ = 2,374 |

For Judge 2, the variance and standard deviation are:

$$s^2 = \frac{\Sigma(x_i^2) - \frac{(\Sigma x_i)^2}{n}}{n-1}$$

$$s^2 = \frac{2,374 - \frac{(180)^2}{20}}{19}$$

$s^2 = 39.68$ this is the variance

$s = \sqrt{s^2}$

$s = 6.30$ this is the standard deviation

These results with the computational formula are exactly the same as the estimated variance and standard deviation we got when we used the definitional formulas earlier in the chapter. We also have computational formulas to use when we have grouped data. With grouped data, the computational formula for the variance and standard deviation are:

$$\text{Variance} = s^2 = \frac{\Sigma(m_i^2 f_i) - \dfrac{(\Sigma m_i f_i)^2}{n}}{n=1} \tag{5-11}$$

$$\text{Standard deviation} = s = \sqrt{\frac{\Sigma(m_i^2 f_i) - \dfrac{(\Sigma m_i f_i)^2}{n}}{n-1}} \tag{5-12}$$

where

$\left(\Sigma m_i^2 f_i\right)$ = the sum of each squared midpoint $(m_i)$ times the frequency of the class interval $(f_i)$

$\left(\Sigma m_i f_i\right)^2$ = the sum of the product of each midpoint $(m_i)$ multiplied by the frequency of the class interval $(f_i)$, with the sum then squared

$n$ = the total number of scores

These computational formulas for ungrouped data require that we obtain three quantities. The first of these quantities requires us to square the midpoint of each class interval $(m_i^2)$, multiply each squared midpoint by the frequency of that class interval $[f_i(m_i^2)]$, and then sum across all intervals $(\Sigma m_i^2 f_i)$. The second quantity is obtained by multiplying the midpoint of each class interval by the frequency of that interval $[f_i(m_i)]$, summing across all class intervals, and then squaring this sum $[(\Sigma m f_i)^2]$. The third quantity is simply the number of scores or $n$.

**Table 5.19** Calculations for Variance and Standard Deviation for Grouped Time-Until-Rearrest Data

| Midpoint | $mf$ | $f_i$ | $m_i^2 f_i$ | $mf_i$ |
|---|---|---|---|---|
| 18 | 324 | 4 | 1,296 | 72 |
| 21 | 441 | 1 | 441 | 21 |
| 24 | 576 | 12 | 6,912 | 288 |
| 27 | 729 | 16 | 11,664 | 432 |
| 30 | 900 | 28 | 25,200 | 840 |
| 33 | 1,089 | 28 | 30,492 | 924 |
| 36 | 1,296 | 21 | 27,216 | 756 |
| 39 | 1,521 | 10 | 15,210 | 390 |
| | | | $\Sigma = 118,431$ | 3,723 |

### Steps for Using Computational Formulas for Variance and Standard Deviation With Grouped Data

**Step 1:** Square each of the midpoints of the class intervals $(m_i)$, multiply each of these squared midpoints by the frequency of its class interval $(f_i)$, and then sum across all class intervals . $\left[\Sigma f_i(m_i^2)\right]$.

**Step 2:** Multiply each midpoint by the frequency of its class interval $(f_i m_i)$, sum across all class intervals, and square this sum:

$$\left[\Sigma(m_i f_i)\right]^2$$

**Step 3:** Subtract the results in Step 2 from the value in Step 1:

$$\Sigma(m_i^2 f_i) - \frac{(\Sigma m_i f_i)^2}{n}$$

**Step 4:** Divide this by the number of scores minus 1:

$$\frac{\Sigma(m_i^2 f_i) - \frac{\left(\Sigma m_i f_i\right)^2}{n}}{n-1}$$

This is the variance.

**Step 5:** Take the square root of Step 4:

$$\sqrt{\frac{\Sigma(m_i^2 f_i) - \frac{\left(\Sigma m_i f_i\right)^2}{n}}{n-1}}$$

This is the standard deviation.

Let's use these computational formulas for grouped data to calculate the variance and standard deviation of our time-until-rearrest data that appeared in Table 5.6. We reproduce those data and all the necessary calculations for the variance and standard deviation in Table 5.19. The variance and standard deviation are:

$$s^2 = \frac{\Sigma(m_i^2 f_i) - \frac{\left(\Sigma m_i f_i\right)^2}{n}}{n-1}$$

$$s^2 = \frac{118,431 - \frac{(3,723)^2}{120}}{119}$$

$$s^2 = \frac{118,431 - 115,506.075}{119}$$

$$s^2 = 24.58$$

$$s = \sqrt{s^2}$$

$$s = 4.96$$

These are exactly the same values for the variance and standard deviation that we obtained when we used the definitional formulas.

## ▣ Graphing Dispersion With Exploratory Data Analysis (EDA)

In this final section, we introduce a class of techniques that were originally developed by the statistician John W. Tukey in the late 1970s and are subsumed under the name exploratory data analysis (EDA). The name is fitting because this is what Tukey intended when he developed this type of analysis. The techniques of EDA enable us to "explore" the distributions of the variables in a data set; they facilitate our understanding of what our distributions look like, what abnormalities (such as outliers) might be present, and what secrets they might hold.

In this section, we focus exclusively on the most widely used EDA technique, the boxplot. It is difficult to categorize a boxplot as either numerical or graphical since it is really both. A boxplot offers a visual display of the data and, in addition, provides the analyst with numerical information about the distribution's center, spread, and outliers. The novelty of a boxplot, however, is that all of this information is available at a glance from a graph.

## Boxplots

**Boxplot:** Graphical technique to display the distribution of a variable that is part of the exploratory data analysis (EDA) family.

**Boxplots** were originally called box-and-whisker plots, and they are a technique in the EDA family used to convey information about the distribution and important characteristics of a variable. Boxplots provide a very illuminating picture of the shape, central data points, and variability of a distribution. At a glance, you can ascertain what the distribution looks like as a whole, how spread out the distribution is, where its center lies, and where any unusual data points (outliers) lie. They are quite simply an amazing way to visualize a variable distribution!

---

## Case Study

### Prisoners Sentenced to Death by State

Essentially, constructing a boxplot involves calculating particular values from your data and then forming a graph based on these values. The values primarily used in boxplot construction are the median, the quartiles, and the IQR, which we have already discussed. Figure 5.3 displays a boxplot with all possible values depicted; however, in reality, some variable distributions may not contain either mild or extreme outliers.

Let's illustrate these steps through an example by using the number of people sentenced to death for states where the death penalty was still used in 2015. These data are presented in Table 5.19, which lists both the state and the number of people sentenced to death in rank order.

If this variable distribution were not already rank-ordered, the first step would be to place the values in order. In Table 5.20, we ranked the data in order from lowest to highest, but you can do it either way. Because all other points necessary to construct a boxplot can be obtained by knowing the median and the first ($Q_1 = $ 25th percentile) and third ($Q_3 = $ 75th percentile) quartiles, the next step is to find these values from our data. We have already calculated these values in this text so we are going through these steps rather quickly. Since we have an even number of scores ($n = 35$), the median can be found at the 18th position, which is Arkansas with 35 people on death row. The median value is thus 35.

We can easily find the first and third quartiles ($Q_1$ and $Q_3$, respectively) by first finding the TMP. As you will recall, the TMP is the position of the median truncated at the decimal point. Since our median position has no decimal point, the TMP is 18. We can now find the position of the first and third quartile with the simple formula:

| Figure 5.3 | **Boxplot Containing All Possible Values** |

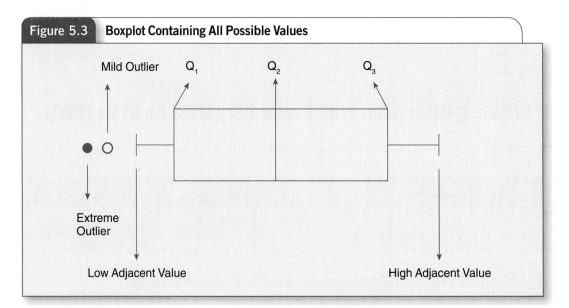

$$\text{Quartile Position} = \frac{TMP+1}{2}$$

$$\text{Quartile Position} = \frac{18+1}{2}$$

$$\text{Quartile Position} = \frac{19}{2} = 9.5$$

This tells us that the quartile position falls in the 9.5 position up from our lowest value and down from our highest value. In our rank-ordered list, $Q_1$ falls between Kansas and Utah, which both have 9 people on death row so the value of $Q_1$ is equal to (9 + 9 / 2 = 9). The value of $Q_3$ falls between Louisiana with 85 people on death row and Georgia with 86 people on death row, which gives us a $Q_3$ value of 85.5 (85 + 86 / 2 = 85.5).

By knowing the values of the quartiles and the median, we can calculate all the other values we need. To construct our boxplot, we must calculate the IQR. Remember that this is simply the difference between the scores at the first and third quartiles (IQR = $Q_3 - Q_1$). For our data, then, the IQR is 85.5 − 9 = 76.5. With this last piece of information,

| Table 5.20 | Number of People Sentenced to Death as of April 1, 2015, n = 35 States | | | | |
|---|---|---|---|---|---|
| Rank | State | Number on Death Row | Rank | State | Number on Death Row |
| 1 | Wyoming | 1 | 19 | Oregon | 36 |
| 2 | New Hampshire | 1 | 20 | South Carolina | 44 |
| 3 | Montana | 2 | 21 | Mississippi | 48 |
| 4 | New Mexico | 2 | 22 | Oklahoma | 48 |
| 5 | South Dakota | 3 | 23 | Federal System | 61 |
| 6 | Colorado | 3 | 24 | Tennessee | 73 |
| 7 | Virginia | 8 | 25 | Nevada | 78 |
| 8 | Washington | 9 | 26 | Louisiana | 85 |
| 9 | Kansas | 9 | 27 | Georgia | 86 |
| 10 | Utah | 9 | 28 | Arizona | 124 |
| 11 | Nebraska | 11 | 29 | Ohio | 145 |
| 12 | Idaho | 11 | 30 | North Carolina | 157 |
| 13 | Connecticut | 12 | 31 | Pennsylvania | 184 |
| 14 | Indiana | 14 | 32 | Alabama | 201 |
| 15 | Delaware | 17 | 33 | Texas | 271 |
| 16 | Missouri | 33 | 34 | Florida | 401 |
| 17 | Kentucky | 34 | 35 | California | 746 |
| 18 | Arkansas | 35 | | | |

*Source:* Adapted from Death Penalty Information Center © 2015.

we can construct the box part of our boxplot. Although a boxplot can be constructed either vertically or horizontally, computer programs usually display them with the axis running along the vertical axis. We like to construct them horizontally because it is easier to visualize a normal curve over the box this way.

The first element to be entered into our boxplot design is the horizontal axis. Along the side of the paper we construct a horizontal axis that will accommodate all of the data points for the death penalty data in Table 5.19. Because the range of these data is so huge, spanning a high in California of 746 and a low in Wyoming and New Hampshire of 1, we are going to place a break in the axis scale at the high end to accommodate all the possible values. A break is simply a place on the axis in which the chronicity of axis labeling is deviated from to accommodate a large range of values. Next, along this axis, we construct the first part of our boxplot by simply drawing a box the length of the IQR from our first quartile to the third quartile. In our example, the box would extend from 9 down to 85.5. Across this box, we place a line indicating where the median ($Q_2$) falls within the distribution. In our example, this line is drawn at 35. The box for the as-yet-unfinished boxplot from the death penalty data from Table 5.19 is shown in Figure 5.4.

The next step is to add what Tukey termed the "whiskers" to the box. These whiskers are actually lines that extend out from the box on both the upper and lower ends denoting how far the data extend up and down to a calculated value called a *fence*. There are four fences we must calculate from the following formulas:

*The Calculation of Fences*

Higher outer fence $= Q_3 + 3.0(\text{IQR})$

High inner fence $= Q_3 + 1.5(\text{IQR})$

Low inner fence $= Q_1 - 1.5(\text{IQR})$

Lower outer fence $= Q_1 - 3.0(\text{IQR})$

The inner fences, then, are placed at a distance one and one-half times the IQR above (high inner) and below (low inner) the edges of the box. The outer fences are placed at a distance three times the IQR above (higher outer) and below (lower outer) the edges of the box. Let's state this a different way. There are two inner fences in a boxplot, one coming out of the bottom of the box (the low inner fence) and one coming out of the top of the box (the high inner fence). These two inner fences extend a distance from the box equal to one and one-half times the value of the IQR [1.5(IQR)]. There are two outer fences, one coming out of the bottom of the box (the lower outer fence), and one coming out of the top of the box (the higher outer fence). These two outer fences extend a distance from the box equal to three times the value of the IQR, (3[IQR]). Note that the values for the two lower fences (low inner and lower outer) are found by *subtracting* 1.5(IQR) or 3.0(IQR) from the first quartile. We subtract because these fences

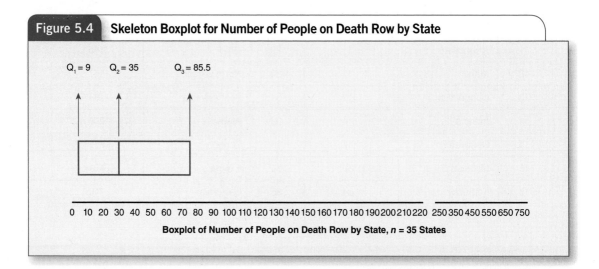

**Figure 5.4** Skeleton Boxplot for Number of People on Death Row by State

$Q_1 = 9$    $Q_2 = 35$    $Q_3 = 85.5$

0  10 20 30 40 50 60 70 80 90 100 110 120 130 140 150 160 170 180 190 200 210 220  250 350 450 550 650 750

**Boxplot of Number of People on Death Row by State, *n* = 35 States**

are found below the box and are therefore below or less than the first quartile and, therefore, the median as well. The values for the two upper fences (high inner and higher outer) are found by *adding* 1.5 (IQR) or 3.0(IQR) to the median because these fences are found above the box and are therefore above or greater than the third quartile and, therefore, the median as well. For our death penalty data, we would obtain the following fence values:

Higher outer fence (HOF) = [85.5 + 3.0(76.5)] = 85.5 + 229.5 = 315

High inner fence (HIF) = [85.5 + 1.5(76.5)] = 85.5 + 114.75 = 200.25

Low inner fence (LIF) = [9 − 1.5(76.5)] = 9 − 114.75 = −105.75

Lower outer fence (LOF) = [9 − 3.0(76.5)] = 9 − 229.5 = −220.5

Again, notice that the values for the low inner and lower inner fences are obtained by subtracting the distance of each fence from $Q_1$, whereas the values for the high outer and higher outer fences are obtained by adding the distance of each fence to $Q_3$. These fences are statistical fences and used only to identify the adjacent values and outliers that exist in our real data. As such, the values of the fences themselves *do not* get placed in the boxplot.

With these values, we can finish the boxplot by adding the whiskers. We use the values of our fences to determine the exact length of each whisker. There are two whiskers: a bottom one extending down from the bottom of the box (low end), and a top one extending up from the top of the box (high end). Before we can draw the whiskers from the box, however, we must find one more set of numbers. These are what are called the *adjacent values* in our distribution.

The adjacent values are the highest and lowest values in our variable distribution that do not fall beyond/outside either the low inner fence or the high inner fence. There are, then, two adjacent values, the *low adjacent value* and the *high adjacent value.* The low adjacent value is the lowest value in our distribution that does not fall outside our low inner fence. The lower inner fence value for our data is −105.75. We don't have any negative values in our actual death penalty data, so the low adjacent value would be equal to the lowest value in the distribution, which is 1. So our lower whisker line extends from the bottom of the box ($Q_1$) down to the value of the low adjacent value of 1.

The high adjacent value is the highest value in our distribution that does not fall beyond/outside the high inner fence. In our example, the value of this high inner fence is 200.25 and the value in our distribution that comes closest to that fence without going over/beyond it is Pennsylvania's 184. Alabama's number of death row inmates of 201 goes beyond the fence value of 200.25! So we extend the high whisker line from the top of the box from $Q_3$ all the way to our high adjacent value of 184. Draw a line from the middle of the box up to each of the adjacent values, and then make another small line the width of the box perpendicular to that first line. These whisker lines are added to our skeleton box in Figure 5.5.

The beautiful thing about boxplots is that they convey all of our data with one picture including abnormalities like outliers. Notice that the values of Alabama, Texas, Florida, and California are not yet displayed on our boxplot. This is because by statistical definition, they are considered outliers. In a boxplot, there are two types of outliers displayed: *mild outliers* and *extreme outliers.* As these terms imply, extreme outliers are even more unusual scores than mild outliers. Mild outliers, labeled with the symbol ○ are those values in the distribution that fall outside the calculated inner fences but do *not* fall outside the calculated outer fences. Extreme outliers, labeled with the symbol ●, are those values in the distribution that fall outside both the inner and outer fences.

So going back to our original data in Table 5.20, let's find the mild outliers. They are the values that fall beyond/outside the lower inner fence value of 200.25 but not beyond/outside the high outer fence value of 315. We see that both Alabama (201) and Texas (271) are mild outliers, so we must place an unfilled circle at those exact values on the horizontal axis. Both Florida (401) and California (746) have death row populations that exceed or go beyond the value of the high outer fence of 315, so they are considered extreme outliers and symbolized on the boxplot with filled circles. Our boxplot is now complete and displayed in Figure 5.6.

Now that we have created the masterpiece displayed in Figure 5.6, what can it tell us about our variable distribution? Think about it for a minute. Exactly what information makes up this boxplot? We know from looking at the display that the median in our distribution falls at 35 death row inmates. We also have the other quartile

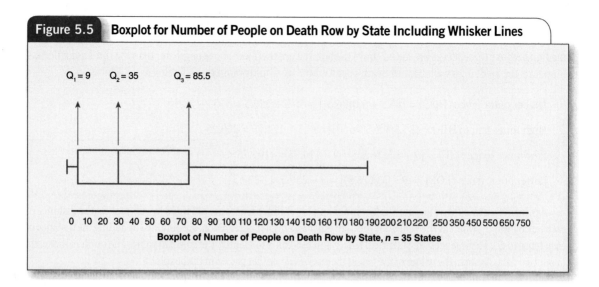

**Figure 5.5** Boxplot for Number of People on Death Row by State Including Whisker Lines

Boxplot of Number of People on Death Row by State, *n* = 35 States

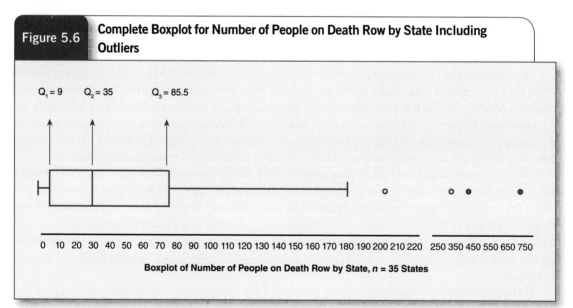

**Figure 5.6** Complete Boxplot for Number of People on Death Row by State Including Outliers

Boxplot of Number of People on Death Row by State, *n* = 35 States

information along specific values of outliers. It may help you see the shape of the distribution if you impose a bell-shaped curve over the box to help you visualize what the distribution looks like. A perfect symmetrical distribution would have the median line falling in the center of the box, both whisker lines would be the same length, and there would be no outliers. This is clearly not the case here. This is how we would interpret the variable distribution: The shape of this distribution of the number of people on death row for the 35 states that still use the death penalty is positively skewed. In words, that means that the majority of the states have relatively few people on death row, but there are a few states with a very high number of people on death row, and it is these states that are pulling the distributions tail to the positive or high side. In addition, we have four high outliers that pull the tail of the distribution out to the right even further, including two mild outliers (Alabama and Texas) and two extreme outliers (Florida and California). We know from our quartiles that 25% of the states have 9 ($Q_1$) or fewer people on death row and that 50% of the states have 35 ($Q_2$) or fewer people on death row. However, we also know from $Q_3$ that 25% of the states have 85.5 or more people on death row. A quick question: Would you guess the mean of this distribution would be higher than the median? If so, you are correct. The mean is 85.7, which is much higher than the median of 35. In fact, the mean is even higher than the third quartile of 85.5! This is further evidence of the positive skew in the distribution. An outline of the steps used for boxplot construction is given in Table 5.21.

To facilitate learning boxplots, let's go over another quick example.

| Table 5.21 | Steps for Boxplot Construction |
| --- | --- |

**Step 1:** Rank your data in ascending order.

**Step 2:** Find the following values:

Median [Median position = $(n + 1) / 2$]

$Q_1$ and $Q_3$ [Quartile position = $(TMP + 1) / 2$]

$IQR = Q_3 - Q_1$

**Step 3:** Draw a scale along a horizontal or vertical axis (it's your choice) to accommodate all data values.

**Step 4:** Draw a box indicating the width of the IQR from $Q_1$ to $Q_3$.

**Step 5:** Draw a line through the box indicating the median value.

**Step 6:** Find fences:

Higher outer fence = $Q_3 + 3.0(IQR)$

High inner fence = $Q_3 + 1.5(IQR)$

Low inner fence = $Q_1 - 1.5(IQR)$

Lower outer fence = $Q_1 - 3.0(IQR)$

**Step 6:** Find adjacent values (those values that are closest to the inner fences but do not fall outside/beyond them).

**Step 7:** Draw whisker lines to each adjacent value.

**Step 8:** Find the mild outliers (those values that fall outside the inner fences but not outside the outer fences). Mark them with the symbol o.

**Step 9:** Find the extreme outliers (those values that fall outside the outer fences). Mark them with the symbol •.

*Source:* Adapted from Death Penalty Information Center © 2015.

## Case Study

## Constructing a Boxplot for Police Officers Killed

Law enforcement officers die every day, not just being killed by their apprehending suspects, but from accidental deaths as well. Table 5.21 displays the number of police officers who died for all reasons from 1984 through 2014. The unit of analysis for these data would actually be a year. If you glance at the data, you can see that there is a very high outlier in 2001. This, of course, represents the high number of law enforcement officers that were killed during the 9/11 terrorist attacks. Since this was not a typical year, and we want to examine the typical distribution of law enforcement officer deaths during this time period, let's remove this year from our analysis. Table 5.22 displays the rank-ordered listing of law enforcement deaths without 2001. We can begin to calculate the values we need as follows:

Median position = $(n + 1) / 2 = (30 + 1) / 2 = 15.5$

Median value = $(161 + 162) / 2 = 161.5$

| Table 5.21 | Number of Law Enforcement Officer Deaths in the United States Including Accidents and Felonious Killings, 1984–2014 | | |
|---|---|---|---|

| Year | Number of All Cause Police Deaths | Year | Number of All Cause Police Deaths |
|---|---|---|---|
| 1984 | 193 | 2000 | 162 |
| 1985 | 183 | 2001 | 241 |
| 1986 | 176 | 2002 | 159 |
| 1987 | 179 | 2003 | 150 |
| 1988 | 183 | 2004 | 165 |
| 1989 | 196 | 2005 | 163 |
| 1990 | 159 | 2006 | 156 |
| 1991 | 148 | 2007 | 192 |
| 1992 | 161 | 2008 | 148 |
| 1993 | 158 | 2009 | 125 |
| 1994 | 179 | 2010 | 161 |
| 1995 | 183 | 2011 | 171 |
| 1996 | 140 | 2012 | 126 |
| 1997 | 172 | 2013 | 107 |
| 1998 | 171 | 2014 | 117 |
| 1999 | 144 | | |

*Source:* Adapted from "Officer Deaths by Year" © 2015 from the National Law Enforcement Officers Memorial Fund.

Quartile position $= (TMP + 1) / 2 = (15 + 1) / 2 = 8$

$Q_1 = 148$

$Q_3 = 179$

$IQR = (179 - 148) = 31$

Higher outer fence $= 179 + 3(31) = 272$

High inner fence $= 179 + 1.5(31) = 225.5$

Low inner fence $= 148 - 1.5(31) = 101.5$

Lower outer fence $= 148 - 3(31) = 55$

High adjacent value $= 196$

Low adjacent value $= 107$

No Outliers!

The final boxplot displaying the number of law enforcement officers killed during the 1984 to 2014 time period (excluding 2001) is presented in Figure 5.7. We can see that this distribution is slightly negatively skewed, indicating that a few years had a relatively low number of officers killed compared with the other years; however,

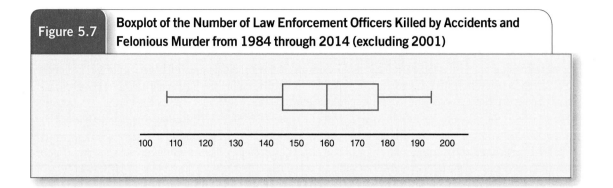

**Figure 5.7**   Boxplot of the Number of Law Enforcement Officers Killed by Accidents and Felonious Murder from 1984 through 2014 (excluding 2001)

**Table 5.22**   Number of Law Enforcement Officer Deaths in the United States Excluding 2001 in Ascending Order

| Rank | Number of Officer Deaths | Rank | Number of Officer Deaths |
|---|---|---|---|
| 1 | 107 | 16 | 162 |
| 2 | 117 | 17 | 163 |
| 3 | 125 | 18 | 165 |
| 4 | 126 | 19 | 171 |
| 5 | 140 | 20 | 171 |
| 6 | 144 | 21 | 172 |
| 7 | 148 | 22 | 176 |
| 8 | 148 | 23 | 179 |
| 9 | 150 | 24 | 179 |
| 10 | 156 | 25 | 183 |
| 11 | 158 | 26 | 183 |
| 12 | 159 | 27 | 183 |
| 13 | 159 | 28 | 192 |
| 14 | 161 | 29 | 193 |
| 15 | 161 | 30 | 196 |

it is fairly symmetrical. Interpreting the quartiles, we can say that for this time period, 25% of the years had 148.0 or fewer officers killed and 50% had 161.5 or fewer officers killed, but 25% of the years had 179.0 or more police officers killed.

We hope that you have become a convert to EDA and agree that these techniques are very effective methods for examining the shape of variable distributions. Researchers often forget this crucial step in statistical analysis and sometimes move on prematurely to more complicated inferential statistics, unaware that they may be working with variable distributions that are extremely skewed or have other abnormalities, such as outliers. If, in the initial phase of your research, you use the EDA techniques we have just gone over, you will avoid these mistakes.

## ▣ **Summary**

In this chapter, we learned about measures of dispersion that capture how different the values of a variable are from some reference point. Just as there are different measures of central tendency, and which one is appropriate depends on the level of measurement of a variable, different measures of dispersion also correspond to the levels of measurement. For variables measured at the nominal or ordinal level, a common measure of dispersion is the variation ratio. The variation ratio measures dispersion with reference to the mode and reflects the extent to which the observations do not cluster in the modal category. When we have data measured at the interval/ratio level (or can assume we have this level of measurement), there are more measures of dispersion to employ. The simplest is the range, which is merely the difference between the highest and lowest values of a variable. The interquartile range is the difference between the score at the third quartile (the 75th percentile) and the first quartile (the 25th percentile). Thus, the interquartile range captures the dispersion present in the middle 50% of a distribution of continuous scores. By far the most common measures of dispersion for continuous (interval/ratio)-level data are the variance and standard deviation. The variance and standard deviation use the mean as the reference point for measuring the amount of dispersion in a variable. Both are based on the deviation from the mean, which is the difference between a given score and the mean of its distribution.

We also learned that the boxplot, a technique under the rubric of exploratory data analysis, is a useful tool for displaying the dispersion of a variable. With one glance at a boxplot, you can determine the shape of a distribution, along with that distribution's center, its variability, and any abnormalities that may exist.

## Key Terms

➤ Review key terms with eFlashcards. ⑤SAGE edge™

boxplot   132
interquartile range (IQR)   112
mean deviation score   116
measures of dispersion   106

$Q_1$   113
$Q_2$   113
$Q_3$   113
range   111

standard deviation   120
variance   119
variation ratio   107

## Key Formulas

Variation ratio (equation 5-1):

$$VR = 1 - \frac{f_{\text{modal}}}{n}$$

Range:

$$\text{Highest } x_i \text{ score} - \text{Lowest } x_i \text{ score}$$

Interquartile range (equation 5-2):

$$IQR = XQ_3 - XQ_1$$

Variance of a population (equation 5-3):

$$\sigma^2 = \frac{\sum\limits_{i=1}^{N}(x_i - \mu)^2}{N}$$

Variance of a sample (equation 5-4):

$$s^2 = \frac{\sum\limits_{i=1}^{n}(x - \overline{X})^2}{n-1}$$

Standard deviation of a population (equation 5-5):

$$\sigma = \sqrt{\frac{\sum\limits_{i=1}^{N}(x_i - \mu)^2}{N}}$$

Standard deviation of a sample (equation 5-6):

$$s = \sqrt{\frac{\sum\limits_{i=1}^{n}(x - \overline{X})^2}{n-1}}$$

Variance of a sample with grouped data (equation 5-7):

$$s^2 = \frac{\sum\limits_{i=1}^{n} f_i (m_i - \bar{X})^2}{n-1}$$

Standard deviation of a sample with grouped data (equation 5-8):

$$s = \sqrt{\frac{\sum\limits_{i=1}^{n} f_i (m_i - \bar{X})^2}{n-1}}$$

Computational formula for sample variance with ungrouped data (equation 5-9):

$$s^2 = \frac{\sum (x_i^2) - \dfrac{(\sum x_i)^2}{n}}{n-1}$$

Computational formula for sample standard deviation with ungrouped data (equation 5-10):

$$s = \sqrt{\frac{\sum (x_i^2) - \dfrac{(\sum x_i)^2}{n}}{n-1}}$$

Computational formula for sample variance with grouped data (equation 5-11):

$$s^2 = \frac{\sum (m_i^2 f_i) - \dfrac{(\sum m_i f_i)^2}{n}}{n-1}$$

Computational formula for sample standard deviation with grouped data (equation 5-12):

$$s = \sqrt{\frac{\sum (m_i f_i^2) - \dfrac{(\sum m_i f_i)^2}{n}}{n-1}}$$

## Practice Problems

➤ Test your understanding of chapter content.
Take the practice quiz. ⓈSAGE edge™

1. What is the difference between the central tendency and the dispersion in a group of scores, and why is it important to know about and report both the central tendency and the dispersion of our variables?

2. A sample of 1,090 youth who had been arrested for one of four offenses (property, violent, drug, and status offense) were asked what type of crime they committed previous to this one. Below are the data. As you can see, of the 125 current property offenders, 75 of them last committed a property offense; of the 110 current violent offenders, 30 of them last committed a violent offense; of the 230 drug offenders, 110 last committed a drug offense; and of the 575 status offenders, 320 last committed a status offense. With these data, calculate the variation ratio for each type of current offense. Which type of current offense has the most variation/dispersion, and which has the least?

| | | Current Offense Is: | | | |
| --- | --- | --- | --- | --- | --- |
| | | Property | Violent | Drug | Status |
| Previous Offense Was: | Property | 75 | 50 | 40 | 120 |
| | Violent | 10 | 30 | 30 | 20 |
| | Drug | 20 | 10 | 110 | 115 |
| | Status | 20 | 20 | 50 | 320 |
| Total | | 125 | 110 | 230 | 575 |

3. A sample of 205 high-school males were asked to report the number of times in the past year that they had stolen something that was worth at least $25 in value. Their responses are shown in the following grouped frequency distribution. With these data, calculate the variance and standard deviation.

| Number of Thefts | f |
| --- | --- |
| 0–4 | 76 |
| 5–9 | 52 |

| Number of Thefts | f |
| --- | --- |
| 10–14 | 38 |
| 15–19 | 21 |
| 20–24 | 10 |
| 25–29 | 8 |

4. You take a random sample of 20 females from the population of female offenders incarcerated in a state prison system and find

out how many years of school they have completed. The data are shown as follows. Calculate:

a. The range

b. The interquartile range

c. The variance

d. The standard deviation

| Person | Years of Education | Person | Years of Education |
|--------|--------------------|--------|--------------------|
| 1 | 11 | 11 | 9 |
| 2 | 8 | 12 | 9 |
| 3 | 12 | 13 | 5 |
| 4 | 9 | 14 | 9 |
| 5 | 9 | 15 | 7 |
| 6 | 9 | 16 | 6 |
| 7 | 10 | 17 | 10 |
| 8 | 10 | 18 | 12 |
| 9 | 10 | 19 | 9 |
| 10 | 11 | 20 | 5 |

5. You have data on the race of the new inmates committed to a state's penitentiary for four years: 1980, 1990, 2000, and 2010. Is there a trend in the dispersion found in these data?

| Year | Race | f |
|------|------|---|
| 1980 | White | 852 |
| | Black | 675 |
| | Hispanic | 112 |
| | Asian | 25 |
| | Other | 59 |
| 1990 | White | 979 |
| | Black | 756 |
| | Hispanic | 262 |
| | Asian | 86 |
| | Other | 78 |
| 2000 | White | 1,211 |
| | Black | 925 |
| | Hispanic | 636 |
| | Asian | 310 |
| | Other | 120 |
| 2010 | White | 1,300 |
| | Black | 1,017 |
| | Hispanic | 750 |
| | Asian | 400 |
| | Other | 145 |

6. The following data show the 2012 arrest rates for robbery (per 100,000 persons) for a sample of 18 states. For these data, determine:

a. The range

b. The interquartile range

c. The variance

d. The standard deviation

| State | Robbery Arrest Rate | State | Robbery Arrest Rate |
|-------|---------------------|-------|---------------------|
| Arizona | 29 | New York | 70 |
| Arkansas | 22 | North Carolina | 41 |
| Colorado | 17 | North Dakota | 7 |
| Georgia | 32 | Oregon | 30 |
| Idaho | 6 | Pennsylvania | 51 |
| Kentucky | 29 | South Carolina | 32 |
| Maine | 17 | Texas | 25 |
| Maryland | 56 | Utah | 13 |
| Missouri | 33 | Wyoming | 5 |

*Source:* Adapted from Puzzanchera and Kang © 2014 from the Office of Juvenile Justice and Delinquency Prevention.

7. In the following table, homicide rates are presented by state and by the four regions of the United States for 2010. Construct separate boxplots for the regional distributions of murder. Compare and contrast how murder is distributed across the regions of the country.

**Murder Rates per 100,000 by Region, Rank-Ordered by State**

| State | Murder Rate | State | Murder Rate |
|-------|-------------|-------|-------------|
| SOUTH | | WEST | |
| Virginia | 3.8 | Idaho | 1.8 |
| West Virginia | 3.9 | Utah | 1.8 |
| Texas | 4.4 | Hawaii | 2.1 |
| Kentucky | 4.5 | Oregon | 2.4 |
| North Carolina | 4.9 | Wyoming | 2.4 |
| Florida | 5.2 | Montana | 2.7 |
| Oklahoma | 5.7 | Washington | 3 |
| Arkansas | 5.9 | Colorado | 3.1 |
| Georgia | 5.9 | Alaska | 4.1 |
| Tennessee | 6 | Nevada | 4.5 |
| Delaware | 6.2 | California | 5 |
| Maryland | 6.3 | Arizona | 5.5 |

| State | Murder Rate | State | Murder Rate |
|---|---|---|---|
| South Carolina | 6.9 | New Mexico | 5.6 |
| Alabama | 7.1 | | |
| Mississippi | 7.4 | | |
| Louisiana | 10.8 | | |
| District of Columbia | 13.9 | | |
| MIDWEST | | NORTHEAST | |
| Iowa | 1.5 | New Hampshire | 1.1 |
| Minnesota | 1.8 | Vermont | 1.3 |
| Kansas | 2.9 | Massachusetts | 1.8 |

| State | Murder Rate | State | Murder Rate |
|---|---|---|---|
| Nebraska | 2.9 | Maine | 1.9 |
| South Dakota | 3 | Rhode Island | 3.2 |
| Wisconsin | 3 | New York | 3.5 |
| North Dakota | 4 | Connecticut | 4.1 |
| Ohio | 4.3 | New Jersey | 4.4 |
| Indiana | 4.7 | Pennsylvania | 5.4 |
| Illinois | 5.8 | | |
| Missouri | 6.5 | | |
| Michigan | 7 | | |

*Source:* Adapted from the FBI Uniform Crime Reports as prepared by the National Archive of Criminal Justice Data.

# SPSS Exercises

➤ Explore additional data sets. ⑤SAGE edge™

| Data for Exercise | |
|---|---|
| **Data Set** | **Description** |
| Youth.sav | These data are from a random sample of students from schools in a southern state. Although not representative of the United States, they cover a variety of important delinquent behaviors and peer influences. |
| **Variables for Exercise** | |
| **Variable Name** | **Description** |
| V77 | A five-category ordinal measure asking respondents how wrong they think their friends think it is to steal. Responses range from 1 (always wrong) to 5 (never wrong). |
| V79 | A five-category ordinal measure asking respondents how wrong they think their friends think it is to drink. Responses are the same as V77. |
| Certain | A scale indicating how likely respondents feel it is that they will be punished for delinquent behavior. High values indicate high certainty. |
| Delinquency | A scale indicating the number of delinquent acts that respondents report participating in. |
| Parnt2 | A scale indicating the amount of parental supervision that the respondents receive, with high values indicating more supervision. |
| Moral_Cat | A categorical variable based on a scale that measured if respondents thought delinquency was morally wrong. Five response categories range from 1 = "1 through 4" to 5 = "17 through 20". |

1. One measure of dispersion covered in this chapter is the variation ratio, which reflects the proportion of cases that fall outside the modal category. For the variables that follow, construct a frequency table and then calculate the variation ratio by hand. Then, write a sentence or two explaining what that variation ratio tells us about the distribution of the variable:

   a. V77

   b. V79

2. Use frequency tables to calculate the range for the following variables:

a. Delinquency

b. V79

3. Use frequency tables for the variable Parnt2 to calculate the variance and standard deviation for this measure. The mean for this measure is 6.23.

4. Using a frequency table and the procedures outlined for calculating the variance and standard deviation for grouped data, calculate the standard deviation and variance for the variable Moral_cat.

5. **Getting Measures of Dispersion in SPSS:** These can be obtained under the "frequencies" menu. Select analyze-> descriptives->frequencies, and then click "statistics." In the bottom left, you will see a box labeled "dispersion." Check off "range" and "standard deviation":

a. What is the standard deviation and range for the variables:

   i. Fropinion

   ii. Delinquency

   iii. Certain

6. **Creating Boxplots in SPSS:** To do this, simply select graphs-> legacy dialogues->boxplot->; then tick off "simple" and "summaries of separate variables". Then, put your desired measures in the "boxes represent" space and click ok:

a. First, construct boxplots for the following variables. Note that you can put more than one variable in the "boxes represent" box to speed up the process:

   i. Fropinion

   ii. Delinquency

   iii. Certain

b. What do these boxplots tell us about:

   i. The median of each variable?

   ii. Its overall distribution?

c. Which variable has the most outliers? The most symmetrical distribution?

7. Following your boxplot from question 6, let's look at how standard deviations are influenced by skewness of a distribution and outliers. We'll use the variable Delinquency, which is a measure of the delinquent behaviors a student has participated in:

a. First, use the SPSS frequency dialogues to get the standard deviation for this variable, as described in question 5.

b. Then, return to your boxplot and see where the cut-off for the upper "fence" is (e.g., where the outliers begin to appear). Your best guess for the cut-off value will be sufficient here.

c. Now we'll tell SPSS to only conduct analyses on the cases that are not outliers. To do this, go to Data-> select cases, and select the "if" button. Then, enter Delinquency<=YOUR VALUE. This reads "select cases if delinquency is less than or equal to the value you identified based on your boxplot."

d. Now use the frequency dialogues to calculate the standard deviation of delinquency again. How has it changed? Which of the two standard deviations would you trust more in this case?

---

## STUDENT STUDY SITE

## $SAGE edge™

**WANT A BETTER GRADE?**

Get the tools you need to sharpen your study skills. Access practice quizzes, eFlashcards, data sets, and exercises at **edge.sagepub.com/bachmansccj4e**.

# Part II: Making Inferences in Univariate Analysis

*Generalizing From a Sample to the Population*

# CHAPTER 6

# Probability, Probability Distributions, and an Introduction to Hypothesis Testing

> "*In the long run, if you're lucky enough to be a dog on the beach, you're lucky enough!*
>
> —Mickey Bachman-Paternoster

> *[A]s we know, there are known knowns; there are things we know we know. We also know there are known unknowns; that is to say we know there are some things we do not know. But there are also unknown unknowns – the ones we don't know we don't know.*
>
> —Donald Rumsfeld
>
> *What did he just say?*
>
> —John Bachman-Paternoster "

## LEARNING OBJECTIVES

1. Explain the basic notion of probability of being in "the long run" compared with predictions of single cases.

2. Describe the notion of independence between variables.

3. Summarize the difference between probability distributions and empirical distributions.

4. Identify the rules of probability.

5. Describe how probability distributions are used to test hypotheses.

6. State the difference between a null and a research hypothesis.

7. Identify areas under the normal curve and how we can transform values from a variable distribution to $z$ scores and determine the probability of their occurrence.

8. Describe why probability theory is important for criminological and criminal-justice–related research.

# Introduction

Imagine you are a probation officer in charge of a new program called Honest Opportunity Probation and Enforcement (HOPE). This program was first implemented in Hawaii and is based on regular random drug testing and swift and certain sanctions to positive drug tests. In contrast to traditional probation where multiple violations of parole may be tolerated, probationers in the HOPE program know that if they commit another crime or fail a drug test, they will immediately be sent to jail. This may sound severe, but the difference is that instead of being sent to prison for an extended sentence, the sentence is short. As such, the sanction is swift but not severe. Although it may be swift and certain, the sanction is typically only a few days in jail. Although early evaluations of the HOPE program in Hawaii seemed to be successful in reducing parole violations, results of replications studies in other locations have not been consistent (Zajac, Lattimore, Dawes, & Winger, 2015). If you were a probation officer who wanted to determine whether your implementation of the HOPE project worked, you would need to conduct inferential statistics to do so. And to conduct inferential statistics, you would need a solid understanding of probability theory!

So far in this book, we have discussed the differences between samples and populations, along with how to organize, display, and summarize important features of your data. Statistical tools like frequency and percentage distributions, graphs and charts, measures of central tendency and dispersion, and the techniques of exploratory data analysis are all useful ways to describe variables. That is why this collection of statistical tools is often referred to as **descriptive statistics**. Descriptive statistics are useful in helping us understand what our data look like and in communicating the properties and characteristics of our data to others. Descriptive statistics do exactly what they say—they describe, usually they describe characteristics of our sample. In addition to describing our variables, however, we often wish to do other things, such as use the information we have collected from our sample to make an inference about some unknown population value or to make a decision about the relationship between two variables in a population based on the relationship we find in our sample data. A very important part of statistical work in criminology and criminal justice, therefore, does not consist of describing information gathered from a sample but of using the sample data to make inferences about some unknown population value. As we noted in Chapter 1, these statistics are called **inferential statistics**, and they will be the focus of our attention for the remainder of this book.

> **Descriptive statistics:** Statistics used to describe the distribution of a sample or population.

> **Inferential statistics:** Statistical tools for estimating how likely it is that a statistical result based on data from a random sample is representative of the population from which the sample has been selected.

**Get the edge on your studies.**
edge.sagepub.com/bachmansccj4e

- Take a quiz to find out what you've learned.
- Review key terms with eFlashcards.
- Explore additional data sets.

**$SAGE edge**™

An important set of tools you will learn in this book are the tools of inferential statistics. In inferential statistics, we have information that we have observed from our sample data, and with it, we wish to make an inference to a larger population. The foundation of inferential statistics, the link between our sample data and the population, is probability theory. You do not need to be an expert in probability theory to understand the statistical procedures in this book, but the background provided in this chapter should prove helpful. In this chapter, we will discuss two notions of probability: the chance that an event occurs in one trial, and the chance that an event occurs "over the long run." We will learn how to calculate the probability of events, including unconditional, conditional, and joint probabilities. To calculate these probabilities, you will learn some basic probability rules. With this basic knowledge of probability, we will apply these rules and learn about probability distributions, which are extremely important because we use these theoretical distributions to conduct hypothesis tests. There are two probability distributions that you will learn in this chapter: a distribution for events that only have two outcomes (binomial) and a continuous distribution (the standard normal distribution). The standard normal distribution is one of the most useful probability distributions because of a theorem in statistics called the central limit theorem, which is the foundation for many statistical tests you will learn in the remainder of the book.

## 🔳 Probability. What Is It Good for? Absolutely Everything!

The foundation of inferential statistics is probability theory. Probability theory can be a very difficult foundation to understand, but in this chapter, we will break it down into its most basic elements and rules. You no doubt already have some idea what probability is because you have likely asked yourself questions like the following: "What is the chance that I will pass a test if I go out partying the night before rather than studying?" "What is the likelihood that I will win the lottery if I buy one ticket today?" "How likely is it that I will get stopped for running this kind of a yellowish-red traffic light?" Questions like these are all about the probability of an event. The answers you had to these typical questions are typically along the lines of "not likely but I will try anyway" or "a snowball's chance in hell." In this chapter, we will teach you to be a little more precise about how you speak about probabilities.

Persons in the criminal justice system frequently have to respond to probability questions. For example, in criminal cases, a jury must determine whether a defendant is guilty "beyond a reasonable doubt" before it can convict the person. The term "beyond a reasonable doubt" implies that there must be a very great probability that the person accused actually committed the offense before he or she can be convicted, say, a probability of 95 or 99 out of 100. Wardens in correctional institutions often have to make a probability judgment as to how dangerous an inmate is before deciding whether he or she can live in the regular inmate population or will require some additional restriction or custody. Police officers make probability judgments about whether they should wear body armor on a given assignment, pull over a suspicious vehicle, and so on. The concept of probability also forms the foundation for research and statistical work in criminology and criminal justice. To consider more precisely the concept of probability and how it applies to research problems in our field, we must first discuss the mathematical notion of probability.

In mathematical terms, the probability of an event has a definite meaning. The probability of an event is defined as the number of times that a specific event can occur relative to the total number of times that any event can occur. The probability of an event (say, event $A$) is often written as $P(A)$, and the total number of times that any event can occur is often referred to as the number of trials. For simplicity's sake, let's think about the simple case of drawing an ace from a deck of cards. There are four aces in a standard deck of 52 cards. The probability of selecting one ace from the deck, then, is:

$$P(\text{Ace}) = \frac{4\,(\text{aces})}{52\,(\text{cards})} = .0769$$

since there are four possible ways of an ace occurring (an ace of hearts, diamonds, clubs, or spades) and there are 52 possible cards (52 possible outcomes) in the deck. Similarly, if we were to flip a coin, what is the probability that it would land heads? Since there are two and only two possible outcomes in one flip of a coin (either heads or tails), and we want to know the probability of one possible outcome (a head), the probability would be:

$$P(\text{Head}) = \frac{1(\text{head})}{2(\text{possible outcomes in one flip})} = .50$$

We need to maintain a distinction in this book between two related but different notions of the concept of the probability of an event. The first conception of probability is the one we have just discussed. The probability of an event is the number of times an event can occur in a given number of trials. In our coin-flipping example, the probability of a head in one flip of a coin is .5. This does not mean, however, that if we flip a coin 10 times, we will always get 5 heads and 5 tails even though the probability of a head (and that of a tail, of course) is .5. If you are not convinced of this, run an experiment in which you flip a coin 10 times, and do this several times. For each of the 10 trials, count the number of heads and tails. We are pretty sure that you will not get exactly 5 heads and 5 tails on every trial of 10 flips.

The second notion of probability—let's refer to this as the sampling notion of probability—tells us, however, that *in the long run, the most likely or most probable* outcome when you flip a coin 10 times is that you will get 5 heads and 5 tails. Sometimes, but rarely, you will observe 0 heads or 0 tails in 10 flips. Sometimes, but less rarely, you will observe 1 head or 1 tail, but the most likely or most probable outcome if you flip a coin 10 times will be 5 heads and 5 tails. If you were to repeat the coin flip experiment a large number of times (say 10,000 times), the outcome with the greatest frequency (and therefore the one with the greatest probability) would be 5 heads and 5 tails. To understand probability better, we need to learn some basic rules.

## ▣ The Rules of Probability

The first probability rule is called the bounding rule (Rule 1). Recall that the formula for determining a probability is:

$$P(A) = \frac{\text{Number of times event } A \text{ can occur}}{\text{Total number of possible events or trials}}$$

Let's designate the denominator, the total number of events, as $n$. Note that we can have no fewer than 0 events of $A$ out of $n$ trials, and no more than $n$ events of $A$ out of $n$ trials. This means that the minimum value of a probability is $0/n$, or zero, and the maximum value is $n/n$, or 1.0. The minimum probability occurs when event $A$ occurs 0 times out of $n$, and the maximum probability occurs when event $A$ occurs $n$ times out of $n$. This expresses the **bounding rule of probabilities**—the probability of any event is bounded by 0 and 1.0. Any probability can never be less than 0 or greater than 1.0. A probability of 0 means that event $A$ is impossible, probabilities close to 0 imply that event $A$ is unlikely to occur, probabilities close to 1.0 imply that there is a good chance that event $A$ will occur, and a probability of 1.0 implies that event $A$ will always occur.

The probability of an event *not* occurring is called the **complement of an event**. We have defined the probability of event $A$ occurring as $P(A)$. The probability of event $A$ not occurring, $P(\text{not-}A)$, is referred to as the complement of event $A$. Based on the bounding rule (since the maximum probability can only be 1.0), if the probability of event $A$ is $P(A)$, then the probability that $A$ will not occur, or the probability of its complement, must be $1 - P(A)$. For example, the probability of drawing one ace from a deck of cards is $4 / 52 = .0769$ because there are four aces in the deck of 52 cards. The probability of not drawing an ace, therefore (the probability of drawing any card but an ace), must be $48 / 52 = .9231$, or $1 - .0769$. The bounding rule tells us, therefore, that the sum of an event and its complement is 1.0.

**Bounding rule of probabilities:** Probability of any event can never be less than zero nor greater than 1.0. $0 \le P(A) \le 1.0$.

**Complement of an event:** Complement of event $A$ is the set of all outcomes of a sample space that are not $A$. It is calculated as $1 - P(A)$.

Notice one thing about the probability of an event and its complement—they cannot both occur at the same time. If the complement of event A consists of all occurrences that are not A, then we cannot have both A occurring and not-A occurring. For example, we cannot both select an ace from a deck of cards (event A) and select a card other than an ace (event not-A) in a single draw from the deck. In other words, an event and its complement are **mutually exclusive events**. The probability of two mutually exclusive events occurring at the same time, therefore, is zero.

> **Mutually exclusive events:** Events that cannot occur at the same time. In other words, there is no intersection of mutually exclusive events so their joint probability is equal to zero.

Let's use another example. For a single criminal trial with a single criminal charge, the events of conviction and acquittal on the charge are mutually exclusive events (let's forget about the possibility of a "hung jury" or some other disposition). At the end of this trial you cannot observe both a conviction and an acquittal for one criminal charge; they are mutually exclusive events. Figure 6.1 shows a Venn diagram that illustrates the notion of mutually exclusive events. Note that the areas covered by the probability of event A and event B never overlap or intersect. This means that their joint occurrence is impossible. They cannot both occur at the same time, so they are mutually exclusive events.

With our knowledge of mutually exclusive events, we can now discuss the second rule of probabilities—the addition rule of probabilities. The addition rule will help us answer the question, "What is the probability *of either event A or event B occurring*?" This rule is also known as the "or" rule because it allows us to calculate the probability of one event *or* the other event occurring. There are actually two forms of the addition rule for probabilities: a general version and a more restricted or limited version. The restricted version covers instances where we can assume that all events are mutually exclusive. In the general version, we cannot maintain this assumption. We call this the *general form* of the addition rule because you can also use this rule when events are or are not mutually exclusive. The restricted rule is a little simpler, so we will discuss it first.

> **Restricted addition rule of probabilities (Rule 2a):** If two events are mutually exclusive, the probability of event A occurring or event B occurring is equal to the sum of their separate probabilities: $P(A \text{ or } B) = P(A) + P(B)$.

The **restricted addition rule of probabilities (Rule 2a)** states that the probability of either of two mutually exclusive events occurring is equal to the sum of their separate probabilities. In other words, if event A and event B are mutually exclusive events, then the probability of event A or B occurring, which is written $P(A \text{ or } B)$, is equal to $P(A) + P(B)$.

What if we can't assume the events are mutually exclusive? Figure 6.2 shows a Venn diagram of two events, event A and event B, which are not mutually exclusive. Recall that non–mutually-exclusive events can occur at the same time. The possibility of their joint occurrence is illustrated in the Venn diagram by the intersection of the two events. The intersection of the two events shows the area where both event A and event B are occurring. The greater the area of the intersection of the two events is, the greater the probability of their joint occurrence.

> **General addition rule of probabilities (Rule 2b):** If two events are not mutually exclusive, the probability of event A occurring or event B occurring is equal to the sum of their separate probabilities minus their joint probability: $P(A \text{ or } B) = P(A) + P(B) - P(A \text{ and } B)$.

When two events are not mutually exclusive, we cannot use the restricted version of the addition rule and must apply the **general addition rule of probabilities (Rule 2b)**. We will see why in a moment. This form of the addition rule states that, for two non–mutually-exclusive events, events A and B, the probability of event A or event B occurring is equal to the sum of their separate probabilities minus the probability of their joint occurrence: $P(A \text{ or } B) = P(A) + P(B) - P(A \text{ and } B)$. The new part of the addition rule is the last term, $P(A \text{ and } B)$, and is the probability of event A and B occurring at the same time or simultaneously—that is, their *joint probability*. For example, the probability of drawing a heart from a deck of cards is 13 out of 52, and the probability of drawing a king is 4 out of 52. The joint probability of a heart and a king is the probability of drawing the king of hearts, or 1 out of 52. The probability of the king of hearts is the joint probability of a king

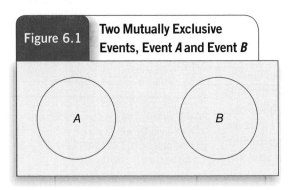

**Figure 6.1** Two Mutually Exclusive Events, Event *A* and Event *B*

and a heart occurring at the same time. When two events are not mutually exclusive, this joint probability must be subtracted from the sum of the two separate probabilities because as we will see, it is counted twice: once in determining the probability of event $A$ and again in determining the probability of event $B$.

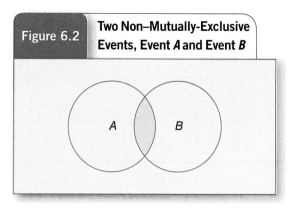

**Figure 6.2**   **Two Non–Mutually-Exclusive Events, Event *A* and Event *B***

Let's answer some probability questions that require the use of this general addition rule and find out why it is more general than the restricted rule. One prominent theory in criminology, *general strain theory,* maintains that participation in delinquent behavior is more likely when youths experience strain in the form of stressful or unpleasant stimuli. In Table 6.1, we show some data pertaining to two variables: whether a youth's parents were separated or divorced in the past year (a stressful event) and whether one of the children committed a delinquent act in the subsequent year.

1.  What is the probability that parents were divorced/separated or the child did not commit a delinquent act?

Note that these events are not mutually exclusive. How do we know this? To determine whether two events are mutually exclusive, ask yourself if it is possible for both events to occur simultaneously. In this case, is it possible that the parents could have experienced a separation or divorce and have a child who did not commit delinquent acts? By looking at Table 6.1, you should be able to see that the answer to that question is "yes"; in fact, there were 10 instances when there was both a separation/divorce and a nondelinquent child. There are instances, therefore, of separation/divorce and a child with no delinquent offenses. Since there is an intersection of the two events, separation/divorce and delinquency are not mutually exclusive. Thus, we cannot use the restricted form of the addition rule but must instead appeal to its general form. The probability of having separated/divorced parents and a nondelinquent child is equal to the probability of separated/divorced parents plus the probability of a nondelinquent child, minus the probability of both separated/divorced parents and a nondelinquent child:

$$P(\text{divorced / separated / or no delinquent acts}) = \frac{110}{310} + \frac{135}{310} - \frac{10}{310} = \frac{235}{310} = .76$$

Why do we have to subtract the joint occurrence of divorced/separated parents and no delinquent acts from the sum of the separate probabilities? Note that we included these 10 cases when we counted the number of divorced/separated parents and then again when we counted those with no delinquent acts. Since these 10 non–mutually-exclusive cases include those with both a divorced/separated parent and no delinquent acts, they are counted twice. The final term removes these cases that were counted twice.

2.  What is the probability of parents who are separated/divorced or a child with five or more delinquent acts?

These two events are not mutually exclusive events since there are 65 instances when there were divorced/separated parents and a child with five or more delinquent acts. The intersection of the two events is not zero, indicating that they are not mutually exclusive. To find the probability, then, we use the general version of the addition rule:

$$P(\text{divorced / separated or 5 + delinquent acts}) = \frac{110}{310} + \frac{80}{310} - \frac{65}{310} = \frac{125}{310} = .40$$

In our discussion of the addition rule of probabilities for events that are not mutually exclusive, we introduced the concept of joint probability, or the simultaneous occurrence of two events. Recall that non–mutually-exclusive events are

| Table 6.1 | Adolescents Delinquent Conduct by Family Status |

| Parents are Divorced/ Separated | Number of Delinquent Acts Committed | | | |
| --- | --- | --- | --- | --- |
| | 0 | 1–4 | 5 or More | Total |
| No | 125 | 60 | 15 | 200 |
| Yes | 10 | 35 | 65 | 110 |
| Total | 135 | 95 | 80 | 310 |

two or more events that can occur at the same time (see Figure 6.2), such as having divorced/separated parents (event A) and committing five or more delinquent acts (event B). We had to subtract the joint occurrence of two events from the sum of the separate probabilities in applying the general form of the addition rule (the "*or* rule"). What we did not discuss, however, was exactly how one calculates the joint probability of two or more events—that is, the probability of event A *and* event B both occurring.

The joint probability of two or more events is determined by applying the *multiplication rule of probabilities*. The multiplication rule of probabilities is often referred to as the "*and* rule" because with it we can determine the probability of both one event *and* another (or others) occurring. (Recall that the addition rule was used to determine the probability of one event *or* another occurring.) The application of the multiplication rule to two events is written as $P(A \text{ and } B)$. There are also two forms of the multiplication rule; one is more general in its application, and the other is used under more restricted conditions.

The **restricted multiplication rule of probabilities (Rule 3a)** concerns the case where the events are independent of one another. Two events are independent of each other when the occurrence of one event has no effect on (does not influence) the occurrence of another event. In other words, there is no relationship between independent events. For example, in two flips of a coin, the fact that the first flip resulted in a head does not affect the outcome of the second flip—a head is no more likely to follow a tail than to follow another head. Later in this section we will examine a more formal test for the independence of two events. If two or more events are independent, then the probability of their joint occurrence is equal to the product of their separate probabilities. For example, assuming that event A and event B are independent, the probability of both event A and event B occurring is equal to $P(A \text{ and } B) = P(A) \times P(B)$.

Let's take as our first example a coin toss. The probability of a head (or of a tail) on any given flip of a fair coin is .5. In two flips of a coin, the probability of getting two heads is $.5 \times .5 = .25$. In three flips of a coin, the probability of getting three heads is $.5 \times .5 \times .5 = .125$.

What do we do when we cannot assume events are independent? In this case, we cannot use the restricted form of the multiplication rule but must use a more *general form*. The **general multiplication rule of probabilities (Rule 3b)** states that the probability of two non-independent events, events A and B, occurring is equal to the probability of event A times the **conditional probability** of event B: $P(A \text{ and } B) = P(A) \times P(B|A)$. The last term of this formula, the conditional probability, is something new and is read, "the conditional probability of event B given event A." We will learn about this and about the general multiplication rule by revisiting Table 6.1.

Previously, when we were interested in calculating a probability, we used as our denominator the total number of events. For example, in Table 6.1, the probability that any child will have committed 1–4 delinquent acts was found by dividing the number of children who committed 1–4 delinquent acts (95) by the total number of children (310), the number who theoretically could have committed 1–4 delinquent acts in our sample. This probability is called an unconditional probability. When we are interested in conditional probabilities, however, we are saying that some other event occurs first.

> **Restricted multiplication rule of probabilities (Rule 3a):** If two events are independent of each other, the probability of event A occurring and event B occurring is equal to the product of their separate probabilities: $P(A \text{ and } B) = P(A) \times P(B)$.

> **General multiplication rule of probabilities (Rule 3b):** If two events are not independent of each other, the probability of event A occurring and event B occurring is equal to the product of the unconditional probability of event A and the conditional probability of event B given A: $P(A \text{ and } B) = P(A) \times P(B|A)$.

> **Conditional probability:** Probability of one event occurring (A) given that another event has occurred (B), written as $P(A|B)$.

The conditional probability of *B* given *A* asks, "What is the probability of event *B* occurring given that event *A* has already occurred?" In other words, the probability of *B* is now conditioned on *A*. In a conditional probability, the denominator is the number of events for event *A*, not the total number of events.

For example, in Table 6.1, the unconditional probability of 1–4 delinquent acts is .31, *P*(1–4 delinquent acts = 95 / 310). Now, what is the conditional probability of 1–4 delinquent acts *given that* there is a divorced or separated parent [*P*(1–4 acts| divorced/separated parent)]? Before we calculate the probability of *B* (1–4 delinquent acts), event *A* (divorced/separated parent) has to occur first. So now let's look only at the subgroup of observations involving divorced/separated parents. There are 110 divorced/separated parents, and since we are conditioning on this event, this becomes the denominator of our probability. Of these 110 divorced/separated parents, 35 have children who committed 1–4 delinquent acts. The conditional probability of 1–4 delinquent acts given divorced/separated parents, therefore, is 35 / 110 = .32. In this case, the conditional probability is not that much different from the unconditional probability, but this will not always be the case.

## What Is Independence?

We needed to learn about conditional probabilities in order to use the general version of the multiplication rule. Before we move on to this, however, we would like to discuss the notion of independence and its relationship to the multiplication rule. We have said that if we can assume that two events are independent of each other, then we can determine their joint probability, *P*(*A* and *B*), with the simpler, restricted version of the multiplication rule [*P*(*A* and *B*) = *P*(*A*) × *P*(*B*)]. If, however, our events are not independent, then we have to use the more restricted (and more complicated) general rule, [*P*(*A* and *B*) = *P*(*A*) × *P*(*B*|*A*)]. How do we know if two events are independent?

Remember that two events are **independent events** if one event occurring has no effect on the probability of the other event occurring. Our example of two independent events was flipping a coin two times—a heads on the second flip of a coin is no more or less likely to occur just because the first flip lands on heads. When two events are not independent, however, the outcome of one event influences the outcome of the other. If this is true, then knowing about the first event will help us predict the second event better. A more formal way to state this is to say that *if two events (A and B) are independent, then the unconditional probability of A will be equal to the conditional probability of A given B: P(A) = P(A|B)*. In this instance, knowing that event *B* has occurred does not change the probability of event *A*. If two events (*A* and *B*) are not independent, however, the unconditional probability of *A* will not be equal to the conditional probability of *A* given *B*: *P*(*A*) ≠ *P*(*A*|*B*). In this case, knowing that event *B* has occurred does alter the probability of *A* occurring.

> **Independent events:** Two events, *A* and *B*, are independent when the unconditional probability of *A* is equal to the conditional probability of *A* given *B*: *P*(*A*) = *P*(*A*|*B*). When two events are independent, knowledge of one event does not help predict the probability of the other event occurring.

Table 6.2 presents the joint distribution of two variables or events based on information collected from 100 youths. Variable or event *A* is whether the youth was right- or left-handed, and variable or event *B* is whether the youth committed a delinquent act in the previous year. Let's find out what the probability is that a youth will have committed a delinquent act. Since 50 of the 100 youths committed at least one delinquent act, this unconditional probability of delinquency is equal to .50.

Now let's find out if knowing whether someone is right- or left handed helps predict whether he or she will engage in delinquency. What is the conditional probability of at least one delinquent act given that a

| Table 6.2 | Joint Frequency Distribution for Right-Left-Handedness and Delinquency |

|  | Committed Delinquent Act Last Year? | | |
| --- | --- | --- | --- |
| Handedness | No | Yes | Total |
| Left-Handed | 25 | 25 | 50 |
| Right-Handed | 25 | 25 | 50 |
| Total | 50 | 50 | 100 |

| Table 6.3 | Joint Frequency Distribution for Impulsivity and Delinquency | | |
|---|---|---|---|
| | **Committed Delinquent Act Last Year?** | | |
| **Youth Impulsive?** | No | Yes | Total |
| No | 40 | 10 | 50 |
| Yes | 10 | 40 | 50 |
| Total | 50 | 50 | 100 |

youth was left-handed? Since there were 50 left-handed youths, and 25 of them had committed a delinquent offense in the past year, the conditional probability of delinquency given left-handedness is .50 (25 / 50). Now, what is the conditional probability of at least one delinquent act given that a youth was right-handed? Since there were 50 right-handed youths, and 25 of them had committed a delinquent offense in the past year, the conditional probability of delinquency given right-handedness is .50 (25 / 50). What we have discovered is that the unconditional probability of delinquency is equal to the conditional probability of delinquency given that the person is left-handed (and given the fact that the person is right-handed). Does knowing whether someone is left-handed help us predict the probability that this person will be delinquent? No, because the conditional probability of delinquency given left-handedness, .5, is the same as the unconditional probability of delinquency (.5).

Now let's look at Table 6.3 where we have the joint distribution of two events for the same 100 youths. As before, 50 youths committed a delinquent act in the past year and 50 did not. Instead of handedness, however, the other event is whether the youth was impulsive, according to a psychological test. Fifty of them were deemed to be impulsive, and 50 were not. As in Table 6.2, the unconditional probability that a youth committed a delinquent act is .50 since 50 out of 100 youths committed a delinquent act.

Now, does knowing whether a youth was not impulsive affect this probability of a delinquent act? The conditional probability of a delinquent act given the fact that a youth was not impulsive is $P(\text{delinquency}|\text{not impulsive}) = 10 / 50 = .20$. The conditional probability of delinquency for those who were not impulsive is much less than the unconditional probability of delinquency (.20 versus .50). Does knowing whether a youth was impulsive affect the probability of a delinquent act? The conditional probability of a delinquent act given the fact that a youth was impulsive is $P(\text{delinquency}|\text{impulsive}) = 40 / 50 = .80$. The unconditional probability of delinquency is not equal to the conditional probability of delinquency given being impulsive (.50 versus .80). It seems that a youth who is impulsive has a much greater risk of being delinquent, and one who is not impulsive has a much lower risk. Does knowing the level of a youth's impulsivity affect the probability that the youth will be delinquent? The answer is yes; he or she is at a greatly reduced risk of delinquency if the youth is not impulsive and at a greatly elevated risk of delinquency if he or she is impulsive. As such, knowing whether someone is impulsive *does* affect the outcome of delinquency, so we can say that the two events (delinquency and impulsivity) are not independent.

Now that we know about conditional probability and the independence of two events, we are ready to apply the more general form of the multiplication rule, which states that if two events, A and B, are not independent, then the probability of A and B occurring is equal to the probability of A times the probability of B given A: $P(A \text{ and } B) = P(A) \times P(B|A)$. Let's use this version of the multiplication rule to answer a few probability questions about Table 6.3. We already know that impulsivity and the commission of delinquent acts are not independent.

1. What is the probability that a youth has been rated not impulsive and has committed no delinquent acts?

The answer is found by determining the unconditional probability of being not impulsive times the conditional probability of having no delinquent acts given the fact that a youth was not rated impulsive: $P(\text{not impulsive}) = 50 / 100 = .50$, $P(\text{not delinquent}|\text{not impulsive}) = 40 / 50 = .80$. Therefore, $P(\text{not impulsive and not delinquent}) = .50 \times .80 = .40$.

2. What is the probability that a youth has been rated impulsive but has not committed a delinquent act?

The unconditional probability that a youth has been rated impulsive is $P(\text{impulsive}) = 50 / 100 = .50$, and the conditional probability that a youth has not committed a delinquent offense given that the youth has been rated impulsive is $P(\text{not delinquent}|\text{impulsive}) = 10 / 50 = .20$. Therefore, $P(\text{impulsive and not delinquent}) = .50 \times .20 = .10$.

3. What is the probability that a youth has been rated impulsive and has committed a delinquent act?

The unconditional probability that a youth has been rated impulsive is $P(\text{impulsive}) = 50 / 100 = .50$, and the conditional probability that a youth has committed a delinquent act given that the youth has been rated impulsive is $P(\text{delinquent}|\text{impulsive}) = 40 / 50 = .80$. Therefore, $P(\text{impulsive and delinquent}) = .50 \times .80 = .40$.

As you can see, the probability of event $A$ is very much affected by event $B$.

The conditional probability version of the multiplication rule (Rule 3b) is more general because we can use this version both when our events are independent and when they are not. We have summarized all of the probability rules we have discussed so far in Table 6.4.

| Table 6.4 | **Probability Rules** |
|---|---|

| **Rule 1: The Bounding Rule** |
|---|
| The probability of an event (event $A$) must always be greater than or equal to zero or less than or equal to 1.0. |
| $0 \leq P(A) \leq 1$ |

| **Rule 2: The Addition Rule** |
|---|
| ***Rule 2a: The Restricted Addition Rule for Mutually Exclusive Events*** |
| If two events (events $A$ and $B$) are mutually exclusive, the probability of either event $A$ or event $B$ occurring is equal to the sum of their separate probabilities. |
| $P(A \text{ or } B) = P(A) + P(B)$ |
| ***Rule 2b: The General Addition Rule*** |
| If two events (events $A$ and $B$) are not mutually exclusive, the probability of either event $A$ or event $B$ occurring is equal to the sum of their separate probabilities minus their joint probability. |
| $P(A \text{ or } B) = P(A) + P(B) - P(A \text{ and } B)$ |

| **Rule 3: The Multiplication Rule** |
|---|
| ***Rule 3a: The Restricted Multiplication Rule for Independent Events*** |
| If two events (events $A$ and $B$) are independent, the probability of event $A$ and event $B$ occurring simultaneously is equal to the product of their separate probabilities. |
| $P(A \text{ and } B) = P(A) \times P(B)$ |
| ***Rule 3b: The General Multiplication Rule*** |
| If two events (events $A$ and $B$) are not independent, the probability of event $A$ and event $B$ occurring simultaneously is equal to the product of the unconditional probability of $A$ and the conditional probability of $B$ given $A$. |
| $P(A \text{ and } B) = P(A) \times P(B|A)$ |

## ▣ Probability Distributions

We can now apply our knowledge about probability to understanding a critically important concept in inferential statistics—a probability distribution. We already know from our study of descriptive statistics what a frequency distribution is. A frequency distribution is a tally of the number of times *that we observe* the different values of a variable. A frequency distribution, then, captures what we actually have observed or measured. A **probability distribution** is

> **Probability distribution:** Distribution of all possible outcomes of a trial and the associated probability of each outcome.

not something we actually observe; rather, it is a theoretical distribution of what we *should* observe over the long run. In other words, in a probability distribution we do not have the probability that each outcome actually occurred, but the theoretical probability that it will occur over the long term. This may sound a bit confusing, and a quick example might help before we go on.

Let's say we are interested in the number of times we get a head when we flip a coin two times. To calculate a probability distribution, we first determine what the possible outcomes are. If we flip a coin two times, we could get:

1. A head followed by another head {H,H}—two heads

2. A head followed by a tail {H,T}—one head

3. A tail followed by a head {T,H}—one head

4. A tail followed by another tail {T,T}—no heads

So, on two flips of a coin, we could get zero, one, or two heads. Since flipping a coin once and then flipping it a second time are independent events, we can use the restricted multiplication rule to determine the probability of each of the four outcomes:

1. $P(\text{head and head}) = .5 \times .5 = .25$

2. $P(\text{head and tail}) = .5 \times .5 = .25$

3. $P(\text{tail and head}) = .5 \times .5 = .25$

4. $P(\text{tail and tail}) = .5 \times .5 = .25$

In Table 6.5, we show you the number of heads possible from flipping a coin twice and the probability of each outcome. Note that we had to use our addition rule to find the probability of getting one head since we could obtain one head by getting a head on the first flip and then a tail on the second flip *or* by getting a tail on the first flip and a head on the second: $P(\text{head and tail})$ or $P(\text{tail and head}) = .25 + .25 = .5$.

Table 6.5 is a probability distribution. This probability distribution is a theoretical distribution based on probability theory, and it shows us what we should expect to see over the long run if we flip a coin twice. The sum of the probabilities is equal to 1.0, indicating that we have listed all possible outcomes and correctly calculated their probabilities. It is important to understand that this distribution is completely theoretical, based on probability theory, and is not what we observe. If we actually flipped a coin twice and recorded the number of times we got a head, we would have a frequency distribution. We would like to do an experiment now. Take a coin and flip it twice, recording the number of heads you get. Then repeat this 10 times (for 10 trials). We did, and Table 6.6 shows what we obtained.

We observed zero heads five times, one head three times, and two heads twice. What we observed from 10 trials of flipping a coin twice

| Table 6.5 | Probability Distribution of the Number of Heads From Flipping a Coin Two Times |
|---|---|

| Number of Heads | P |
|---|---|
| 0 | .25 |
| 1 | .50 |
| 2 | .25 |

was a greater proportion of no heads than what we saw in Table 6.5. Based on probability theory, the probability of getting zero heads is .25, but one half, or .50, of our actual coin flips resulted in getting no heads. This shows you the difference between a frequency distribution (Table 6.6), which is observed, and a theoretical probability distribution (Table 6.5), which is based on probability theory.

There are different kinds of probability distributions for different kinds of events or outcomes. In the remainder of this chapter, we will discuss two important kinds of probability distributions. In the first, the event we are interested in has only two outcomes (heads or tails, guilty or innocent, rearrested or not rearrested). In the second, the event has a large number of possible outcomes (IQ scores, criminal propensity) and is a continuous probability distribution. These are not all of the possible probability distributions, but they do have wide applicability in criminology and criminal justice and they will help us transition to hypothesis testing in the upcoming chapters.

| Table 6.6 | Observed Results From the Flipping of a Coin Twice 10 Times | | |
| --- | --- | --- | --- |
| *Number of Heads* | | *f* | *P* |
| 0 | | 5 | .50 |
| 1 | | 3 | .30 |
| 2 | | 2 | .20 |
| Total | | 10 | 1.00 |

## A Discrete Probability Distribution—The Binomial Distribution

There are many instances in criminology and criminal justice research when we are interested in events that have only two outcomes. Examples include whether a defendant appears for trial, whether an accused gets a public defender or retains his or her own lawyer, and whether someone who is arrested tests positive or negative for the presence of drugs. In statistics, a process that generates only two outcomes is called a Bernoulli process. The probability distribution based on a Bernoulli process is referred to as the **binomial distribution**. Let's examine the binomial probability distribution in some detail.

> **Binomial distribution:** Probability distribution for which there are just two possible outcomes with fixed probabilities that sum to 1.0.

As our example, let's examine defendants who pay a cash bail after being arrested pending trial, and we are interested in the event that they appear (or fail to appear) for their trial. The event we are looking at, therefore, has two outcomes: The defendant either shows up for trial or fails to show up. The probability that he or she appears for trial is denoted as $p$, and the probability that he or she fails to show up for their trial is $1 - p$, or $q$. Let's assume that based on past research, we know that the probability of showing up for trial if he or she has been released on a cash bail is .80, and the probability of failing to show up, therefore, is .20. Let's say that we have five persons recently released on cash bail, and we want to calculate the probability distribution of the number of times that they would appear for trial. Let's use the term "success" for any defendant who shows up for trial and designate that with the letter $r$; we'll use the term "failure" for any defendant who fails to show up.

With five defendants, it is possible that either none, one, two, three, four, or all five of them would show up for trial. We will assume that the event of one defendant showing up for trial is independent of the others, so that we have independent events. By applying the restricted version of the multiplication rule, using knowledge that the probability of a success is .80 and the probability of a failure is .20, and letting $r$ be the number of successes (showing up for trial) and $n$ the total number of trials (therefore, $n - r$ is the number of failures or those who do not show up), we can use the following formula to calculate the probability of each outcome: $p^r q^{n-r}$. Let's use this formula to determine the probability that zero defendants will show up for trial (this means that we have no successes out of five defendants and five failures):

$$P(0 \text{ successes}) = (.8^0)(.2^5) = .2 \times .2 \times .2 \times .2 \times .2 = .0003$$

The probability that one defendant would show up for trial would be:

$$P(1 \text{ success}) = (.8^1)(.2^4) = .8 \times .2 \times .2 \times .2 \times .2 = .00128$$

Now we need to stop and point something out. The probability we calculated is the probability of one success followed by four failures. In other words, in this instance, the first person out on cash bail showed up for trial, but the next four did not. But there are other ways that we could observe one success in five trials, aren't there? The first case could fail, the second one could be a success, and the next three could be failures (that is, F,S,F,F,F). Or the first two could fail, the next could show up for trial (be a success), and the two after that could fail (F,F,S,F,F).

What we need to do is to figure out how to count all the different ways of having one success out of five trials. Fortunately, there is a very simple counting rule in probability that we can use to determine this. This is the counting rule for combinations, and the formula is:

$$\binom{n}{r} = \left( \frac{n!}{r!(n-r)!} \right)$$

The first expression:

$$\binom{n}{r}$$

is read as "$n$ choose $r$" and is the number of ways in which $r$ objects can be ordered out of $n$ objects without regard to order. The expression that it is equal to:

$$\left( \frac{n!}{r!(n-r)!} \right)$$

is read as "$n$ factorial" over "$r$ factorial times $n-r$ factorial." A *factorial* is just an operation where the number we are taking the factorial of is multiplied by every whole number less than itself and greater than zero. Thus 5! is equal to $5 \times 4 \times 3 \times 2 \times 1 = 120$. By convention, $0! = 1$.

Let's use this combination formula to calculate the number of ways in which we could get one success (defendant showing up for trial) out of five trials:

$$\frac{5!}{1!(5-1)!} = \frac{5!}{1!4!} = \frac{5 \times 4 \times 3 \times 2 \times 1}{1 \times 4 \times 3 \times 2 \times 1} = \frac{120}{24} = 5$$

We can verify this by noting that the success could appear in the 1st, 2nd, 3rd, 4th, or 5th case (the probability of each outcome is written next to it):

$$(S,F,F,F,F) \ P = (.8 \times .2 \times .2 \times .2 \times .2) = .8^1 \times .2^4 = .00128$$

$$(F,S,F,F,F) \ P = (.2 \times .8 \times .2 \times .2 \times .2) = .8^1 \times .2^4 = .00128$$

$$(F,F,S,F,F) \ P = (.2 \times .2 \times .8 \times .2 \times .2) = .8^1 \times .2^4 = .00128$$

$$(F,F,F,S,F) \ P = (.2 \times .2 \times .2 \times .8 \times .2) = .8^1 \times .2^4 = .00128$$

$$(F,F,F,F,S) \ P = (.2 \times .2 \times .2 \times .2 \times .8) = .8^1 \times .2^4 = .00128$$

Now, if we want to know the probability of getting one success out of five failures, we can do one of two things. We can use our addition rule and determine the probability of (S,F,F,F,F) or (F,S,F,F,F) or (F,F,S,F,F) or (F,F,F,S,F) or

(F,F,F,F,S), which would be .00128 + .00128 + .00128 + .00128 + .00128 = .0064. Or we could use our counting rule that we can get one success out of five trials five different ways. The probability of getting one success out of five trials in any order is .00128; multiplying the two together, we get 5 × .00128 = .0064. No matter which way we do it, we get the same result.

If we use the counting rule, we now have a general formula to determine the probability of getting $r$ successes out of $n$ trials, where the probability of a success is $p$ and the probability of failure is $q$ $(1 - p)$:

$$P(r) = \binom{n}{r} p^r q^{n-r}$$

**(6–1)**

$$P(r) = \left( \frac{n!}{r!(n-r)!} \right) p^r q^{n-r}$$

Equation 6-1 is known as the *binomial theorem*. The binomial theorem can be used to determine the probability of any number of successes, $r$, so long as there are only two outcomes—success ($p$) and failure ($q$).

We will use the binomial coefficient to calculate the probability of zero, one, two, three, four, and five successes, where success is defined as a defendant who posted a cash bail and who shows up for trial. We show both the calculations and the probabilities in Table 6.7, and we graph the probability distribution in Figure 6.3.

From Table 6.7, we can see that the probability of no defendant showing up for trial is quite small, as is the probability of only one or two of them appearing at their trial. Based on probability theory, we would expect to see three out of five appear for trial about 20% of the time, and about 40% of the time, four defendants would appear. Finally, if the probability of appearing at trial for a defendant released on ROR (release on recognizance) is .80, we would expect all five to show up about one third of the time ($p = .3277$).

Just like a frequency distribution, a probability distribution has both a mean and a standard deviation. For a binomial probability distribution, the mean is given by $np$ (the number of trials or observations multiplied by the probability of a success). The mean of a theoretical probability distribution is generally referred to as the expected value $E(x)$, so for a binominal distribution, $E(x) = np$. The formula for the variance of a binomial distribution is $\sigma^2 = npq$, and for the standard deviation, we simply take the square root of the variance, $\sigma = \sqrt{npq}$. The mean of the probability distribution in Table 6.7 is 5(.8) = 4.0. This means that if the probability of a success is .8, and we have five observations, the expected value of the number of observed successes is 4. Out of five persons who post cash bail, then, the average number who would be expected to appear at trial would be four. Note from both the probability distribution and the histogram in Figure 6.3, we see that the greatest expected probability corresponds to four successes. This means that "over the long run" we would

| Table 6.7 | Probability Distribution of Appearance at Trial, Where $p$ (success) = .8, $q$ (failure) = .2, and $n = 5$ |||

| Number of Successes | Calculation | P |
|---|---|---|
| 0 | $\left( \frac{5!}{0!(5-0)!} \right).8^0.2^5$ | .0003 |
| 1 | $\left( \frac{5!}{1!(5-1)!} \right).8^1.2^4$ | .0064 |
| 2 | $\left( \frac{5!}{2!(5-2)!} \right).8^2.2^3$ | .0512 |
| 3 | $\left( \frac{5!}{3!(5-3)!} \right).8^3.2^2$ | .2048 |
| 4 | $\left( \frac{5!}{4!(5-4)!} \right).8^4.2^1$ | .4096 |
| 5 | $\left( \frac{5!}{5!(5-5)!} \right).8^5.2^0$ | .3277 |
| | | Total 1.00 |

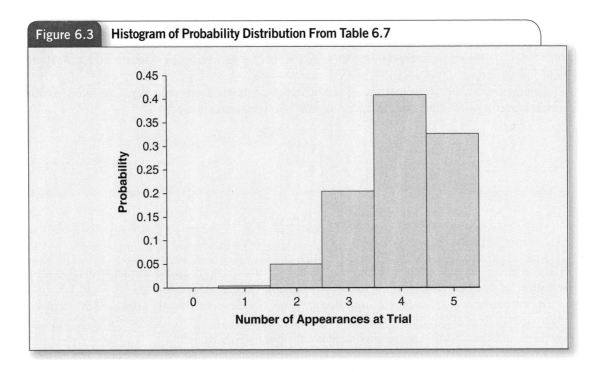

Figure 6.3 | **Histogram of Probability Distribution From Table 6.7**

expect to see, on average, four people out of five show up for their trials if they posted a cash bail. You can use these formulas to find that the variance of the probability distribution is .8 (5 × .8 × .2) and the standard deviation is .89 ($\sqrt{.8}$). Remember that this does *not* mean that we will obtain this result every time, but we should be more likely to obtain it *over the long run* compared with any other outcome.

## 🔲 Hypothesis Testing With the Binomial Distribution

So why is this important? One important use of probability distributions is that they enable us to make decisions under a situation of uncertainty. That is, they are critical in the testing of hypotheses. As we noted in Chapter 1, a *hypothesis* is simply a scientific "hunch" or assumption about the relationship between two variables that is tested empirically. In explanatory research, we start with a hypothesis, collect data or information that pertains to that hypothesis from a sample, and then, with the help of a known probability distribution, come to some decision about the hypothesis. Remember that to make inferences to a population, we must also be able to assume that the sample is representative of the population, and to do this, we must have used probability sampling techniques! What allows us to make that inference is probability theory. This is how we go about inferential statistical analysis! Let's go through a brief example.

──────────── **Case Study** ────────────

### Predicting the Probability of a Stolen Car Recovered

Let's say we recently purchased a car and we are concerned about the possibility of car theft. We hear from commercials that the car theft device "Lo-Jack" is effective in helping the police recover your car should it get stolen. The Lo-Jack device is a hidden transformer in your car that you activate when the car is stolen. The transformer sends out an electronic transmission that the police are able to monitor in order to locate your car. The company claims that with Lo-Jack, the police are better able to find and quickly recover stolen cars. You talk to the local police chief, and she claims that, based on 10 years' worth of evidence, the police department recovers about 40% of the stolen cars reported and returns them undamaged to the owner. You have a hunch that Lo-Jack might produce a recovery rate better than 40%. But you do not know that for a fact, and before you spend money installing Lo-Jack in your new car, you want to make sure that it will give you more protection from auto theft than the police working without the assistance of Lo-Jack. Here's what you do.

First, you collect information from people (your sample) who have Lo-Jack in their car and ask them (a) if they have ever had it stolen and (b) if so, whether it was returned undamaged. You find 10 people who have had their cars stolen and who had Lo-Jack, and you learn that 8 of those cars were returned undamaged within 24 hours. What you observe, therefore, is an 80% recovery rate. But this is just what you found in your sample, and you still do not know the recovery rate for all cars with Lo-Jack (your population). You wonder whether this means that Lo-Jack does result in a greater probability of recovery. Maybe the 8 people who had their cars returned quickly happened to be very lucky and are not typical of most car owners with Lo-Jack. Perhaps if you selected a different 10 people who had cars stolen with Lo-Jack you would find that only 2 had their cars returned undamaged. In other words, the 80% recovery rate you observed from your sample of 10 people may have been due to random sampling variation, not to the superiority of Lo-Jack in the overall population.

How do you decide whether Lo-Jack is better than the police alone for all Lo-Jack users (the population) and not just within your sample? One way to be more confident that you made the correct decision is to conduct a formal hypothesis test. There are a number of steps involved in a hypothesis test, and the basic framework of these steps will be the same throughout this book. In the remainder of this section, we will discuss these steps of a hypothesis test, but do not be alarmed if you do not understand them right away. We will be conducting hypothesis tests under different situations in every chapter, so you will have a chance to review this material regularly. For now, it is important to understand the basic process of hypothesis testing!

The first step in a hypothesis test is to make a few assumptions. In science, we always test an assumption that states there is no relationship between our variables. In this case, having Lo-Jack would be the independent variable (have it or not) and vehicle recovery is the dependent variable (recovered or not). The assumption that we test, therefore, states that Lo-Jack is no better than not having Lo-Jack in recovering stolen cars. Practically, this means that our starting assumption is that 40% of the stolen cars equipped with Lo-Jack will be recovered undamaged. In other words, we presume that Lo-Jack does not work, and our hypothesis test will involve disproving this assumption. Researchers call this assumption the **null hypothesis** because of the implication that there is no relationship—or, in our specific case, that Lo-Jack does not work any better than the police. This is how scientists work, not by proving something they may believe to be true (Lo-Jack is more effective in getting stolen cars returned), but by disproving the assumption that there is no relationship (having Lo-Jack does not get your car back faster).

> **Null hypothesis:** In a hypothesis test, the null hypothesis is the hypothesis that is initially assumed to be true. It is called the null hypothesis because it presumes that there is no relationship (null) between the variables being tested.

The null hypothesis is usually designated by $H_0$. Since our null hypothesis involves the assumption that Lo-Jack's recovery rate is no better than without it, this means that the expected probability of recovering a stolen Lo-Jack-equipped car is .40. Here, then, is our null hypothesis:

$H_0$: The probability of recovering a stolen car that has Lo-Jack is .40: $P(\text{recovery}) = .40$. In other words, Lo-Jack does not work.

In addition to making an assumption in the null hypothesis (assume Lo-Jack does not work), we also make an assumption about an alternative outcome. This assumption asks the question, "If the null hypothesis is not true, then what do we think is really going on?" This hypothesis is called the research or alternative hypothesis and is designated by $H_1$. It is called the alternative hypothesis because this is the alternative to the null hypotheses, and it's sometimes called the research hypothesis because it is usually based on the question motivating our research. In this case, does Lo-Jack work? There are two general ways of stating the alternative hypothesis. It can be stated as a directional (one-tailed) or as what is called a nondirectional (two-tailed) alternative hypothesis.

In our example with Lo-Jack, the null hypothesis states that the probability of recovering a stolen car with Lo-Jack is no greater than without Lo-Jack. Now, let's say we think that Lo-Jack is likely to increase the probability of recovering a stolen car undamaged because the company claims that the transmitting device will enable the police to find the stolen car easier. With this *a priori* knowledge (knowledge we have before we make our hypothesis), we can make the assumption in the alternative hypothesis that the probability of recovering a stolen car undamaged with Lo-Jack is greater than .40. We do not have to say exactly how much greater in our alternative hypothesis, just that we think it is greater than that assumed in the null hypothesis:

$H_1$: The probability of recovering a stolen car that has Lo-Jack is greater than .40: $P$(recovery) > .40.

This alternative hypothesis is basically saying that Lo-Jack works—if you have it in your car, and it gets stolen, the chances are greater that you will get it back than if you did not have it. This is a *directional alternative hypothesis* because we have assumed that the recovery rate with Lo-Jack is greater than .40 and therefore have stated a specific direction (greater than) for Lo-Jack's recovery probability.

Alternatively, we could have stated that the probability of recovery with Lo-Jack will be less than .40: $P$(recovery < .40). This too is a directional alternative hypothesis because we have stated a specific direction in our alternative with respect to the null hypothesis (it is less than that assumed in the null). To support this alternative assumption, we might have created a theory that the police might be "put off" when someone reports that they have Lo-Jack in their car and might be less than enthusiastic in recovering it. This seems very unlikely, however, and our alternative hypothesis of a greater probability of recovery seems more plausible.

And finally, we also could have created a *nondirectional alternative hypothesis*. In a nondirectional alternative hypothesis, we simply state that the expected outcome is different from that assumed in the null hypothesis—not that it is greater or less, just that it is different. So, for example, our nondirectional alternative would have been that the rate of recovery for cars with Lo-Jack is not equal to .40: $P$(recovery) ≠ .40. For our example we are satisfied with our alternative hypothesis that the probability of recovery for cars with Lo-Jack is greater than .40 so let's continue with that. We now have two hypotheses, a null hypothesis and a directional alternative hypothesis:

$H_0$: The probability of recovering a stolen car that has Lo-Jack is .40: $P$(recovery) = .40.

$H_1$: The probability of recovering a stolen car that has Lo-Jack is greater than .40: $P$(recovery) > .40.

It is very important to understand that in the process of hypothesis testing, *only the null hypothesis is tested*. We never directly test the alternative hypothesis. We are really asking how likely it is that the null hypothesis is true, that is, that there is no relationship, given what our sample data tell us.

Because we only test the null hypothesis, we make our decision by either rejecting the null hypothesis or failing to reject the null hypothesis. For example, if we discover that what is stated in the null hypothesis is "very unlikely" or is a "rare event" given our data (and we will discuss in a moment what we mean by "very likely" or a "rare event"), we will reject the null hypothesis. When we reject the null hypothesis, we no longer believe that the assumption it contains is true, and our faith in the truthfulness of the alternative hypothesis is strengthened (not proven, but strengthened). Therefore, although the alternative hypothesis is never directly tested, in rejecting the null hypothesis, we gain confidence in the alternative hypothesis.

A useful analogy for the idea of hypothesis testing is the task given to a jury in a criminal trial. The jury starts with the assumption or hypothesis that the defendant is innocent; the alternative hypothesis is that the defendant is guilty. It then tests this assumption of innocence (the null hypothesis) by looking at the data—in this case, the evidence presented by the prosecution and the defense. After examining this evidence, the jury makes a determination about how likely it is that the defendant is innocent in the face of the evidence. If it thinks that the evidence is consistent with the defendant's innocence, it acquits (it fails to reject the hypothesis of innocence). If, however, the jury thinks that the evidence raises grave suspicions about the defendant's innocence (meaning that it surpasses the burden of proof of "beyond a reasonable doubt"), then it rejects the null hypothesis, and the assumption of innocence is abandoned in favor of the alternative. The jury essentially says, "the person cannot be so unlucky that he is innocent and yet has all this evidence indicating guilt." The standard of "beyond a reasonable doubt," then, is like an implicit probability level. If the probability is very great that the person did the crime based on the evidence, the jury should reject its "null hypothesis" of innocence. If, however, the probability is not great, not "beyond a reasonable doubt," then the jury should not reject its null hypothesis and continue to assume that the defendant is innocent.

Notice one very important thing about the jury's decision (and our own decisions about null hypotheses). In making its decision, the jury almost never knows with absolute certainty that it is correct. That is, the jury will have a notion about how likely it is that the defendant is innocent, but it has no way of knowing for sure (only the defendant knows that). This means that the jury is making a decision under uncertainty, so, it might have been the wrong decision.

There are two types of wrong decisions or errors a jury may make. First, it could reject the null hypothesis of innocence when in fact the defendant is innocent. In this error the jury convicts an innocent person. The jury could also continue to accept the null hypothesis of innocence and acquit the defendant when, in fact, the accused is guilty. In this error the jury lets a guilty person go free. In our legal system, we generally think the first error is worse than the second. That is, we think it is worse to convict an innocent person than to acquit a guilty person. In an effort to ensure that we do not convict innocent people, the legal system makes the requirement of proof very great in criminal cases—the jury must believe "beyond a reasonable doubt" that the defendant is guilty before it may reject the null hypothesis of innocence. The phrase "beyond a reasonable doubt" means that the jury must determine that the null hypothesis of innocence is very, very unlikely before it may reject it.

| Table 6.8 | Decision Making in Hypothesis Tests | | |
|---|---|---|---|
| | | *Decision Regarding Null Hypothesis* | |
| *True State of Affairs* | | *Fail to Reject* | *Reject* |
| Null Hypothesis is true | | Correct decision | Type I error |
| Null Hypothesis is false | | Type II error | Correct decision |

In trying to answer our research question about car theft protection, we are very much like the jury. We will not know for sure whether Lo-Jack produces a higher recovery rate of stolen cars because we have information from only 10 owners of Lo-Jack, not from everyone who has installed it (our population). In other words, we have a sample of Lo-Jack owners, not the entire population, and the success rate we observed might be unique to our sample. When we make a decision about the null hypothesis, therefore, we (like the jury) are making it under uncertainty. Since we have incomplete information, we might error in making our decision about the null hypothesis. We could reject a null hypothesis that happens to be true, or we could fail to reject a null hypothesis that is false. These errors have names as shown in Table 6.8. Rejecting a null hypothesis that is true is referred to as a Type I error, and failing to reject a false null hypothesis is referred to as a Type II error.

It would be nice if we could minimize the risk of making both kinds of errors, but unfortunately, that is not possible. As we will learn, as we reduce the risk of making a Type I error, we simultaneously increase our risk of making a Type II error. Think about this for a moment with respect to the jury's decision. One way that it can minimize the risk of a Type I error (convicting an innocent person) would be to make the burden of proof even greater than beyond a reasonable doubt. Such a standard might be something like, "Do not convict someone unless you are 99.999% sure that they are guilty"—"way beyond a reasonable doubt." Although this will decrease the risk of convicting an innocent person, it will increase the risk that a truly guilty person will be found innocent (a Type II error). Similarly, minimizing the risk of making a Type II error (acquitting a truly guilty person) by lessening the standard of proof in criminal proceedings, say, to the standard that applies in civil court ("a preponderance of the evidence"), increases the risk of convicting an innocent person. What we have to do, therefore, is carefully balance the risks of making each type of error.

In research, we establish beforehand some level of risk we are willing to take that we will make a Type I error. This level of risk is called a level of **significance** or **alpha level**. Alpha and significance are interchangeable terms in research, and

**Significance or alpha level (α):** Risk we are willing to take in rejecting a true null hypothesis. For example, if we select an alpha level of .05, we are willing to be incorrect .05 or 5% of the time.

alpha is symbolized as α. For example, if we set $\alpha = .05$, we are saying that we are willing to risk rejecting a true null hypothesis 5 times out of 100, or 5% of the time. If we wanted to reduce that risk, we could adopt a significance level of .01 or even .001.

Recall that we begin our hypothesis test by assuming that the null hypothesis is true (that Lo-Jack is no better than not having it). We then say that we are going to continue to assume this is true unless our data (what we observe) tell us that the outcome we actually observed is "very unlikely" or "a rare event" given the null hypothesis. What we do, then, is maintain our belief in the null hypothesis until we are informed by the data that this belief is improbable given what we have observed. What we mean by "very unlikely" or "a rare event" is determined by the significance level. *What the significance level actually tells us is the probability of observing our data if the null hypothesis is true.* If this probability is very great, we have no reason to think our null hypothesis is false, and we continue to assume it is true and fail to reject it. If, however, the probability of observing what we did given that the null hypothesis is true is very low (where low is defined as less than or equal to our level of significance) or if what we observe is a "rare event" where how rare is defined by our significance level, then it seems to us more probable that the null hypothesis is false and we can reject it. This does not mean that we know the null hypothesis is wrong. It means only that the observed outcome is so unlikely that it's more likely that the null hypothesis is wrong or false than that it is correct. We are making a decision based on what we think is "most probable or likely," but we will never know for sure what is actually true. Before moving on, we also want to underscore why we can *never* accept a null hypothesis, we can only reject or fail to reject it. Why? Because we are dealing in the world of probability, and since we can never be 100% certain that our sample data reflect the population, we can only make generalizations with less than 100% certainty.

Let's say that with respect to our Lo-Jack example, we are willing to accept a 5% risk of making a Type I error, giving us a .05 level of significance or alpha. What we are saying is that we are assuming that the null hypothesis is true unless the outcome that we observe is unlikely, where "unlikely" now specifically means that it has a probability of occurring of .05 or less. If what we observe has a probability of occurring greater than .05, we continue to assume that the null hypothesis is true. If, however, what we observe has a probability of occurring less than or equal to .05, we reject the null hypothesis and conclude that it is false.

How, you may ask, do we know what the probability observing our actual data is? More specifically, what is the probability of having 8 out of 10 stolen cars with Lo-Jack recovered undamaged if the true probability of recovery is .40? This is an excellent question. This is where probability distributions enter, and we have the tools in our toolbox now to calculate that probability distribution.

In our null hypothesis, we are assuming that the probability of recovering a stolen car with Lo-Jack is no better than not having it. Specifically, the information from the chief of police tells us this probability is .40. So we assume that $P(\text{recovery with Lo-Jack}) = .40$, which is less than half the time. We now ask the following question: "If the probability of recovering a stolen car with Lo-Jack is .40, what is the probability that we would have observed 8 people out of 10 recovering their stolen car undamaged (this is what you observed, so these are your data)?" Actually, what we really want to know is this: Given a level of significance of .05, what are all the outcomes with a probability of .05 or less because those are the outcomes that would lead us to reject the null hypothesis? If 8 recovered cars is included among those outcomes, we reject the null hypothesis. If it is not included among those outcomes, we fail to reject the null hypothesis.

Note that the event of recovering a stolen car can be considered a Bernoulli event—the car either is recovered undamaged or it is not. With our binomial formula in equation 6-1, we can determine the probability of 0, 1, 2, . . . , 10 undamaged recoveries. Here is the binominal formula as it translates for this particular problem, where $n = 10$ (the number of trials or the number of people in our sample who had Lo-Jack when their car was stolen), $p = .40$ (the probability of recovery), and $q = .60$ ($1 - p$, or the probability of not getting the car recovered undamaged):

$$P(r) = \left( \frac{10!}{r!(10-r)!} \right)(4^r)(6^{10-r})$$

where $r$ = the number of successful recoveries of a stolen car. You should use this formula to calculate on your own the probability of 0 to 10 successful recoveries. We report the results for you in Table 6.9 and graph the probability distribution in Figure 6.4.

Note that if the null hypothesis is true [i.e., $P$(recovery) = .40], the probability of observing 8 successfully recovered cars out of 10 is .0106. By using our addition rule of probabilities, we can determine that the probability of 8 or 9 or 10 recoveries, $P$(8, or 9 or 10) is equal to .0123 (.0106 + .0016 + .0001). Understand what this means. It says that if the true probability of undamaged recovery is .40 (what we are assuming under the null hypothesis), then the probability that we would observe 8, 9, or 10 successful recoveries is .0123 or less—that is, 1% of the time or less.

Earlier we adopted a level of significance of .05. We said that we would reject the null hypothesis if what we observed was "very unlikely," which we defined as an event with a probability of .05 or less. We have just determined that the event of 8 or more undamaged recoveries out of 10 given a recovery probability of .40 has a probability of .0123. What we have observed, then, fits our definition of "very unlikely." We now have information that leads us to conclude that 8 out of 10 recoveries is very unlikely given a true recovery probability of .40, so we can reject the null hypothesis that $P$(recovery) = .40. In rejecting this, we can conclude that we believe the alternative hypothesis is more likely to be true in the population. As such, we can conclude that having a Lo-Jack will make it more likely that our car, if stolen, will be recovered by police compared with not having Lo-Jack. Keep in mind, however, that we might be wrong in rejecting the null hypothesis—that is, we might be committing a Type I error!

Note from Table 6.9 that with a significance level of .05, we would have rejected the null hypothesis had we observed 10 successful recoveries out of 10, 9 successful recoveries out of 10, or 8 successful recoveries out of 10. We know that the cumulative probability of each of these events is equal to .0123, which is less than .05. In research, we have a special name for these events. This is called the **critical region** of our probability distribution for any given test. The critical region defines all outcomes that will lead us to reject the null hypothesis. In our case, the three outcomes of 8, 9, and 10 successful recoveries will lead us to reject the null hypothesis because their cumulative probability is less than our .05 level of significance. Since the event that we observed (8 out of 10

| Table 6.9 | Probability Distribution of Recovering a Stolen Car With Lo-Jack Where $p$ (success) = .4, $q$ (failure) = .6, and $n$ = 10 |||
|---|---|---|
| *Number of Successes* | *Calculation* | *P* |
| 0 | $\left(\dfrac{10!}{0!(10-0)!}\right).4^0.6^{10}$ | .0060 |
| 1 | $\left(\dfrac{10!}{1!(10-1)!}\right).4^1.6^9$ | .0403 |
| 2 | $\left(\dfrac{10!}{2!(10-2)!}\right).4^2.6^8$ | .1209 |
| 3 | $\left(\dfrac{10!}{3!(10-3)!}\right).4^3.6^7$ | .2150 |
| 4 | $\left(\dfrac{10!}{4!(10-4)!}\right).4^4.6^6$ | .2508 |
| 5 | $\left(\dfrac{10!}{5!(10-5)!}\right).4^5.6^5$ | .2007 |
| 6 | $\left(\dfrac{10!}{6!(10-6)!}\right).4^6.6^4$ | .1115 |
| 7 | $\left(\dfrac{10!}{7!(10-7)!}\right).4^7.6^3$ | .0425 |
| 8 | $\left(\dfrac{10!}{8!(10-8)!}\right).4^8.6^2$ | .0106 |
| 9 | $\left(\dfrac{10!}{9!(10-9)!}\right).4^9.6^1$ | .0016 |
| 10 | $\left(\dfrac{10!}{10!(10-10)!}\right).4^{10}.6^0$ | .0001 |
| | | Total 1.00 |

undamaged car recoveries) falls into this critical region, our decision is to reject the null hypothesis. We show you the critical region for this specific problem in Figure 6.4.

Suppose we had observed 7 out of 10 successful recoveries, what would our decision have been at the same significance level? By using our addition rule and the information in Table 6.9, we can determine that the probability of

**Critical region of a probability distribution:** Defines the entire class of outcomes that will lead us to reject the null hypothesis. If the event we observe falls into the critical region, our decision will be to reject the null hypothesis.

7, 8, 9, or 10 successful recoveries is equal to .0548 (.0425 + .0106 + .0016 + .0001 = .0548). Since our definition of a "very unlikely" or "rare" event is an event with a probability of .05 or less, the event of 7 or more successful recoveries just misses being unlikely enough to lead us to reject the null hypothesis. Had we observed 7 out of 10 successful car recoveries, therefore, we would continue to assume that the null hypothesis is true and would not reject it because the event of 7 successful car recoveries does not fall into our critical region.

| Figure 6.4 | **Histogram of Probability Distribution of Stolen Car Recoveries** |

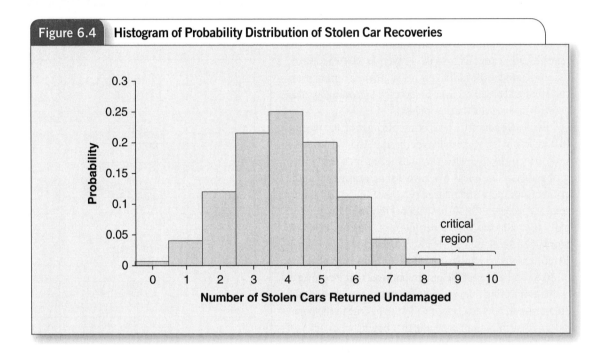

Now suppose that we had observed 8 out of 10 successful recoveries, but instead of a significance level of .05, we had decided earlier to adopt a significance level of .01. The selection of a significance level is adopted *before* the hypothesis test is conducted, but we are changing the rules of the game to make a point here. By lowering the level of significance, we are saying that what is to be considered a "very unlikely" event must now have an even less likely probability of occurring before we are willing to reject the null hypothesis. In other words, we are reducing the risk we are willing to take that we will make a Type I error from 5% to 1%. We know that the probability of observing 8, 9, or 10 successful car recoveries if $P$(recovery) = .40 is .0123. Since .0123 is greater than .01, our decision would have been to fail to reject the null hypothesis at a .01 level of significance. Note that by lowering our level of significance, we are making it more difficult to reject the null hypothesis. With a .01 level of significance, the critical region becomes 9 or 10 successful recoveries out of 10, whereas with a .05 alpha level, the critical region becomes 8, 9, or 10 successful recoveries.

The decision whether to fail to reject or to reject the null hypothesis is the final step of our hypothesis testing process. Before we move on, however, we want to highlight the relationship between significance/alpha and levels of confidence. If we adopt an alpha level of .05, that means we are willing to risk making an incorrect decision 5% of the time while desiring to be correct, or confident in our findings, 95% of the time. In science, typically this is the lowest level of confidence we are willing to accept. Similarly, if we adopt an alpha of .01, we can say we are 99% confident in our conclusion. Answer this: What is the confidence we would have if we adopted an alpha of .10? How about .001?

The following list reviews all the steps in that process. Make sure you understand each step because you will be seeing them again and again throughout this book.

*Steps of a Hypothesis Test*

**Step 1:** Formally state your null and alternative hypotheses.

**Step 2:** Determine what probability distribution you will use for your test.

**Step 3:** Define what you mean by a "very unlikely" event by selecting a level of significance (the alpha level).

**Step 4:** Calculate the probability of observing your sample data under the null hypothesis.

**Step 5:** Make a decision about the null hypothesis (reject or fail to reject), and interpret your results.

In this section of the chapter we have been concerned with events (called Bernoulli events) that have only two possible outcomes. The binomial probability distribution that characterizes these events is very useful because many interesting events in criminology and criminal justice have only two outcomes. But other interesting events are continuous, measured at the interval/ratio level and have many more than two possible outcomes. For example, we might be interested in continuous variables, like the number of years convicted homicide defendants are sentenced to prison. Unfortunately, we cannot use the binomial distribution to characterize continuous variables. We must learn another type of probability distribution—a continuous probability distribution.

## ▣ A Continuous Probability Distribution— The Standard Normal Probability Distribution

In this section we are going to investigate another kind of probability distribution that has wide applicability in criminology and criminal justice research—the normal probability distribution. The normal distribution is a probability distribution for continuous events and looks like a smooth curve (unlike the binomial probability distribution, which looks like a series of "steps"). Figure 6.5 is an example of what a normal probability distribution might look like. Note that the probability of an event occurring is greater in the center of the curve and declines for events at each of the two

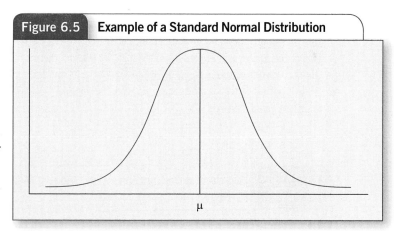

| Figure 6.5 | **Example of a Standard Normal Distribution** |

μ

ends, or "tails" of the distribution. A characteristic of the tails of the distribution is that they never touch the $x$ axis, meaning that they go to both positive and negative infinity. It makes sense that the tails extend to infinity if we keep in mind that the normal distribution is a theoretical probability distribution. Like the binomial, the normal distribution is defined by a mathematical equation, and although many characteristics can be assumed to be distributed as normal, the normal distribution is not an empirical distribution. There are some common features of any normal distribution. The normal distribution is a unimodal, symmetrical distribution and assumes the appearance of a bell-shaped curve. By a "symmetrical distribution" we mean that if we drew a line down the center of the curve, the left and right halves would be mirror images of each other. Compare this smooth curve to the histogram for a binomial probability distribution in Figure 6.4.

The mathematical formula for the normal distribution, or the normal probability density function, is:

$$f(x) = \frac{1}{\sigma\sqrt{2\pi}} e^{\frac{-(x-\mu)^2}{2\sigma^2}}$$

(6–2)

where

$\mu$ = the mean (expected value) of the continuous variable $x$

$\sigma^2$ = the variance of $x$

$\pi$ and $e$ = constants equal to 3.14 and 2.72, respectively

Any normal distribution is defined by its two parameters, its mean ($\mu$) or expected value, and its variance ($\sigma^2$). The mean defines the location of each normal distribution on the number line, and the variance defines its general shape. What this means is that there is not just one, but many, normal distributions, which vary in terms of their mean, their variance, or both. Figure 6.6 shows two normal distributions, each with a mean different from the other but the same variance. Figure 6.7 shows two normal distributions with equal means but different variances, and Figure 6.8 shows two normal distributions with different means and different variances. These figures illustrate that there is not one but a family of normal curves defined by $\mu$ and $\sigma^2$.

We could employ equation 6-2 and determine the probability distribution for any continuous variable. There is, however, one significant difference between determining the probability of a discrete variable and determining that of a continuous one. When we calculated the probability of a discrete variable by using the binomial probability distribution, we could employ the binomial formula to calculate the probability of a given event (i.e., the probability of recovering 8 or more stolen cars out of 10). A continuous distribution, however, comprises events that are theoretically infinite. For example, response time to a 911 call could theoretically be measured in millionths of a second or in even finer gradations. Continuous events by their very nature are not discrete events, and this is reflected in the fact that the continuous probability distribution is a smooth curve. What we are interested in, therefore, is a point on a smooth curve. Recall from your high-school or college geometry that the area of a point on a curve is zero—there is no area to a point; it is theoretically undefined. What we must do with continuous events, therefore, is determine the area between two points on a curve. For example, what we must do is calculate the probability that a 911 response time will be between 2 and 4 minutes [$P(2 \leq x \leq 4)$] or the probability that it will be more than 6 minutes [$P(x > 6)$].

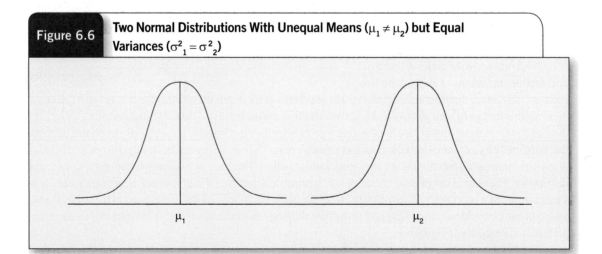

| Figure 6.6 | **Two Normal Distributions With Unequal Means ($\mu_1 \neq \mu_2$) but Equal Variances ($\sigma^2_1 = \sigma^2_2$)** |

## The Area Under the Normal Curve

Since the normal distribution is a probability distribution, the area under the curve is 1.0. In other words, all possible outcomes are included in the area under a normal curve. One of the most important properties of a normal probability distribution is that there is a fixed area or a fixed proportion of cases that lie between the mean and any number of standard deviations to the left or right of that mean. Moreover, based on mathematical theory, we can determine the exact proportion of cases between the mean and any point at a given number of standard deviations away

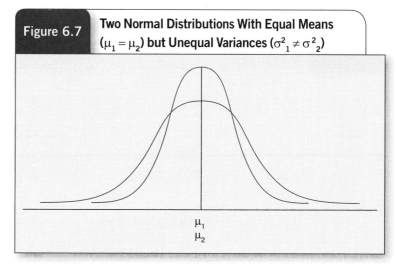

**Figure 6.7** Two Normal Distributions With Equal Means ($\mu_1 = \mu_2$) but Unequal Variances ($\sigma^2_1 \neq \sigma^2_2$)

from the mean. For example, we know that for every normal distribution, .3413 (34.13%) of the area of the curve lies between the mean and a point that is 1.0 standard deviation to the right of that mean ($\mu + 1\sigma$). In other words, if we drew a line through any normal curve at its mean and another line through the curve at 1.0 standard deviation to the right of the mean, the area between those two lines would be .3413 of the total area under the curve. This means that .3413 of the events in a normal probability distribution lie within 1.0 standard deviation to the right of the mean. We also know from mathematical theory that .4772 (or 47.72%) of the events of a normal probability distribution lie in an area from the mean to a point 2.0 standard deviations to the right of the mean and that .4987 (or 49.87%) of the cases lie within 3.0 standard deviations to the right of the mean. This property of the normal distribution is illustrated in Figure 6.9.

Combining this information with the fact that any normal distribution is symmetrical enables us to make some additional conclusions. If there is .3413 of the area of the normal curve from the mean to a point 1.0 standard deviation to the right of the mean, then since a normal distribution is symmetrical, .3413 of the area of the curve must also lie from the mean to a point 1.0 standard deviation to the *left* of the mean. We can conclude from this that .6826 (.3423 + .3413) of the area (or 68.26%) of any normal distribution must lie within ±1 standard deviation of the mean. Similarly, if .4772 of the area of any normal curve lies between the mean and a point 2.0 standard deviations to the right of the mean,

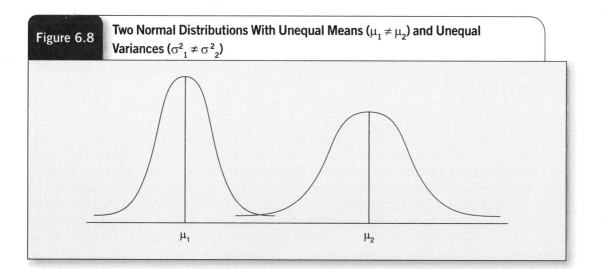

**Figure 6.8** Two Normal Distributions With Unequal Means ($\mu_1 \neq \mu_2$) and Unequal Variances ($\sigma^2_1 \neq \sigma^2_2$)

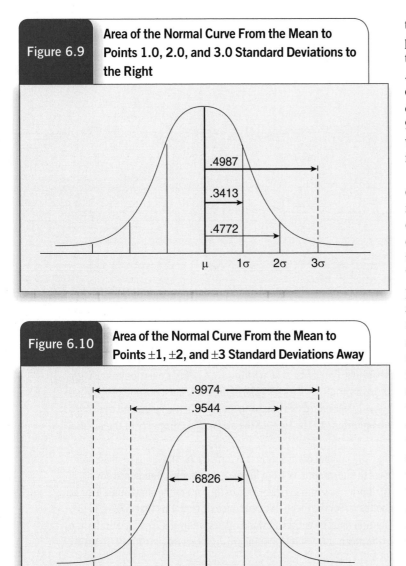

**Figure 6.9** Area of the Normal Curve From the Mean to Points 1.0, 2.0, and 3.0 Standard Deviations to the Right

.4987

.3413

.4772

$\mu$   $1\sigma$   $2\sigma$   $3\sigma$

**Figure 6.10** Area of the Normal Curve From the Mean to Points ±1, ±2, and ±3 Standard Deviations Away

.9974

.9544

.6826

$-3\sigma$   $-2\sigma$   $-1\sigma$   $1\sigma$   $2\sigma$   $3\sigma$

then .4772 also lies between the mean and a point 2.0 standard deviations to the left of the mean. We can conclude from this that .9544 (.4772 + .4772) of the area (or 95.44%) of any normal curve lies within ±2 standard deviations from the mean. Finally, .9974 (or 99.74%) of the area under any normal curve will lie within ±3 standard deviations away from the mean. See Figure 6.10.

By using these properties of normal distributions, we have some way of determining and understanding the probability of continuous events. With our knowledge of normal distributions and standard deviations, we can define a "very unlikely" or "rare" continuous event. For example, suppose we were told that a given continuous $x$ score was 2.4 standard deviations to the right of the mean. What would we conclude about its probability? Since we know that about 95% of all scores in a normal probability distribution lie within ±2 standard deviations of the mean, an $x$ score that is more than 2.0 standard deviations from the mean occurs with a probability less than .05 (less than 5% of the time). This can be considered a "very unlikely" or "rare" event. An $x$ score that is 3.0 standard deviations to the left of the mean is also a "very unlikely" event since we know that approximately 99% of all scores lie within ±3 standard deviations of the mean. An $x$ score that is only 1.0 standard deviation to the right of the mean would *not* be considered "very unlikely" because we now know that approximately 68% of the area of the normal curve lies within 1.0 standard deviation from the mean. We can

conclude from this, therefore, that "unlikely" or low probability scores are going to be those that are a number of standard deviations away from the mean, or out in the "tails" of the normal distribution.

With our knowledge about the relationship between the area under any normal curve and standard deviations, we can use equation 6-2 to calculate probabilities with any continuous variable $x$. There is one practical difficulty with this, however. In addition to some complex mathematics we would have to do, since normal distributions differ depending on the value of their two parameters, $\mu$ and $\sigma$, we would have to calculate new probabilities for virtually every problem we confronted. (The mean and standard deviation of response times, for example, would be different from the mean and standard deviations of sentence length, IQ, the number of self-reported offenses committed, and so on because each of these distributions would have a different mean and a different standard deviation.) It would be easier if we had only one normal probability distribution with known values of $\mu$ and $\sigma$ to use, wouldn't it? Luckily for us there is, and it is known as the *standard normal probability distribution* or the *z* distribution. Remember how having one normal distribution like this is making our work easier as we move along!

# The Standard Normal Distribution and Standard Scores

The standard normal distribution is a normal probability distribution that has a mean of 0 and a standard deviation of 1.0. To use the standard normal probability distribution, however, we need to convert the scores of a continuous variable $x$ into what is called a **standard score** or $z$ score. A $z$ score is simply a score for a continuous $x$ variable that has been converted into standard units—in this case, into standard deviation units rather than how the original variable was measured (i.e., months, years, or dollars). The formula for converting a raw $x$ score into a standard $z$ score is:

> **Standard score ($z$ score):** Score from the standard normal probability distribution that indicates how many standard deviation units a score is from the mean of zero.

$$z = \frac{x - \overline{X}}{s}$$

**(6–3)**

where

$x$ = a raw score for a continuous variable

$\overline{X}$ = the sample mean of the empirical distribution

$s$ = the standard deviation of the empirical distribution

Let's go through an example.

Suppose we have an empirical distribution of 10 scores. These 10 scores represent the number of prior offenses committed by a sample we took of persons arrested by our local police department in the past year. The level of measurement for this variable is interval/ratio, and the exact metric of measurement here is "number of arrests." This variable distribution is displayed in Table 6.10. The mean number of prior arrests for this sample is 5.1, and the standard deviation is 4.25. Let's convert the first raw score, 3, which is measured in units of "arrests," into a standardized $z$ score:

$$z = \frac{3 - 5.1}{4.25}$$

$$= -.49$$

There are two pieces of information we can get from any $z$ score: its sign and its magnitude. The sign of our $z$ score of −.49 is negative, telling us that it lies to the left of the mean of the standard normal distribution (remember that the mean of the standard normal distribution is 0). The magnitude of this $z$ score is .49, telling us that it is approximately one half of a standard deviation away from the mean (remember that the mean of the standard normal distribution is 1). The sign of a $z$ score, then, tells us whether it is to the left of (less than) or to the right of (greater than) the mean, and the magnitude tells us how many standard deviation units away from the mean the score is. For this distribution, then, a raw score of 3 tells us that it is equivalent to having a score that is .49 standard deviation units below the mean of 5.1. Note also that the difference between 3 and 5 prior arrests is 2, and this is approximately one half of the standard deviation of 4.25. So, a raw score of 3 arrests when converted into a $z$ score

| Table 6.10 | Number of Prior Arrests for Sample of 10 Persons Arrested in Past Year |
|---|---|

| Person | Number of Prior Arrests |
|---|---|
| 1 | 3 |
| 2 | 2 |
| 3 | 0 |
| 4 | 8 |
| 5 | 0 |
| 6 | 6 |
| 7 | 13 |
| 8 | 4 |
| 9 | 10 |
| 10 | 5 |

is equal to a score that is almost one half a standard deviation (.49) to the left (in the negative direction) of the mean of the *z* distribution of 0.

What is the corresponding *z* score for 13 prior arrests?

$$z = \frac{13 - 5.1}{4.25}$$

$$= 1.86$$

This tells us that a raw score of 13 prior arrests corresponds to a *z* score that is 1.86 standard deviation units above or to the right of the mean. In essence, what we are saying is that a raw score of 13 prior arrests corresponds to a score of 1.86 on the *z* scale.

Once we have converted our raw scores into *z* scores, we can begin to answer probability questions. Like the binomial distribution, the standard normal distribution is a known probability distribution. To answer probability questions, we need to refer to what is called a standard normal or *z* table. Table B.2 in Appendix B is such a *z* table, and we need to become very familiar with it because we will be using it a few more times in this book. Table B.2 provides you with the area or proportion of the standard normal curve that lies between the mean and some given *z* score. The *z* scores in this table are always reported to two decimal places. The *z* score can be located by using the first column of the table to the far left side, which lists the value of the one's digit and the first decimal place. The value of the second decimal place can be found in the row at the top of the table. The values reported in the body of the table are the proportions of the standard normal distribution (also called the *z* distribution) that lie between the mean and that *z* score. This is probably a little confusing, so let's do a couple of examples.

Suppose we had a *z* score of 1.47. The question then becomes, "How much of the standard normal curve lies between the mean and this *z* score?" To find out, we go down the first column of numbers until we reach the value 1.4 (1 is our units digit, and .4 is our first decimal place). Then we use the row of *z* scores at the top of the table until we find the value of the second decimal place, .07. Where the row of 1.4 intersects the column of .07 (our *z* score of 1.47), we see the table entry .4292. What this tells us is that .4292 (or 42.92%) of the area of the normal curve lies from the mean to a point 1.47 standard deviation units to the right. We show this for you in Figure 6.11. This means

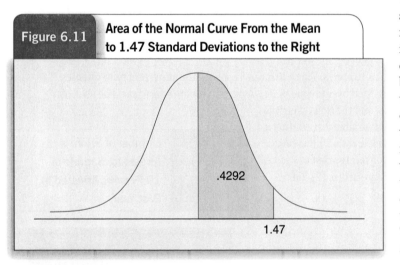

**Figure 6.11**  **Area of the Normal Curve From the Mean to 1.47 Standard Deviations to the Right**

.4292

1.47

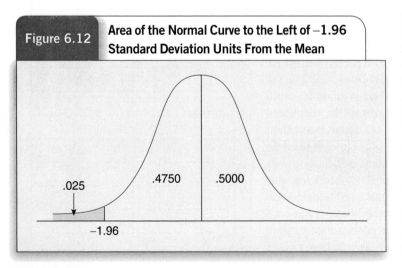

**Figure 6.12**  **Area of the Normal Curve to the Left of −1.96 Standard Deviation Units From the Mean**

.025

.4750  .5000

−1.96

that the probability that a z score is greater than or equal to zero and less than or equal to 1.47 is .4292: $P(0 \leq z \leq 1.47) = .4292$. Since the z distribution is symmetrical, we also know that .4292 of the normal curve lies between the mean and a z score of −1.47. By using this information, we can calculate that .8584 (or 85.84%) of the normal curve lies between a z score of −1.47 and a z score of +1.47.

What proportion of the normal curve lies between the mean and a z score of −1.96? To find this we follow the same procedure as earlier. Since the z distribution is symmetrical, we can ignore the minus sign. We go down the first column until we find the value 1.9, and then we use the z column at the top of the page until we find .06. At the convergence of the 1.9 row and the .06 column, we see the entry .4750, telling us that .4750 (or 47.50%) of the area of the normal curve lies between the mean and a z score of −1.96. Therefore, the probability that a z score is less than or equal to zero and greater than or equal to −1.96 is .4750: $P(−1.96 \leq z \leq 0) = .4750$.

What is the probability that a z score will be less than −1.96, that is, will fall below it? We know that .50 of the normal curve lies to the right of the mean. We also know that .4750 of the curve lies from the mean to a z score that is 1.96 standard deviation units to the left of the mean. By combining this knowledge, we know that .9750 (.50 + .4750)

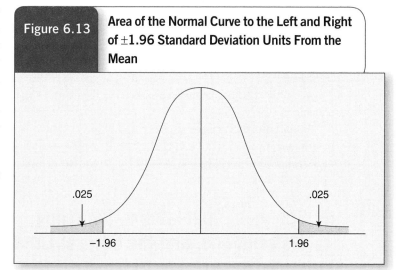

| Figure 6.13 | Area of the Normal Curve to the Left and Right of ±1.96 Standard Deviation Units From the Mean |

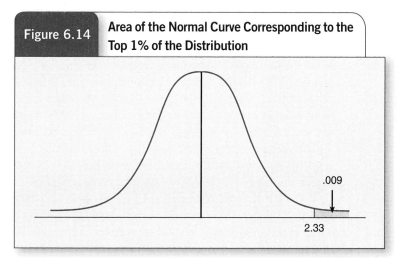

| Figure 6.14 | Area of the Normal Curve Corresponding to the Top 1% of the Distribution |

of the curve lies to the right of a z score of −1.96. Since the total area of the normal curve is 1.0, we can determine that 1 − .9750, or .025, of the curve lies to the left of $z = −1.96$. The probability that a z score is less than or equal to −1.96, therefore, is .025 (see Figure 6.12). A z score that is less than −1.96, then, can be considered a "rare" or low probability event since it occurs less than 3% of the time. Because the z distribution is symmetrical, a z score greater than or equal to 1.96 is also a low probability event because it occurs less than 3% of the time. Combining these two probabilities (.025 + .025) tells us that a z score that is less than −1.96 or greater than +1.96 is a low probability event because it occurs 5% of the time or less (see Figure 6.13).

Now let's answer the following probability question: "What z scores are so unlikely that they fall into the top 1% of the standard normal probability distribution?" We show you the approximate top 1% of the z distribution in Figure 6.14. Let's use what we know about the z distribution to solve this problem. First, we know that .50 of the curve lies to the left of the mean, telling us that the probability is .50 that a z score will be less than or equal to 0 (the mean). Since .50 of the normal curve lies to the left of the mean, we know we have to find .49 of the area to the right of the mean (which, with .50 to the left of the mean, will sum to .99). Go into the body of the z table (Table B.2) and try to find .4900.

You don't see .4900, but you should see .4901, which will be close enough. What we need, though, is not the area but the z score that corresponds to this area. To find the z score that corresponds to this area, work backward. First find the z score for this row (this will identify the digit and the first decimal place of your z score, and it will be 2.3). Then find the second decimal place by finding the column you are in (column .03). You now have a z score of 2.33. By combining all this information, you know that the probability that a z score will be less than 2.33 is .9901 (.50 + .4901). The probability that a z score will be greater than or equal to 2.33, therefore, is .009, or almost .01 (1%). Another way to state this is to say that a z score greater than 2.33 will fall in the upper 1% of the standard normal distribution, and as such, it is a low probability or "rare" event.

We will not show you here how to conduct hypothesis tests using the standard normal distribution because we will be doing that in several later chapters. We do, however, hope you see how we would conduct such a hypothesis test by defining in probability terms what a "very unlikely" or low probability event is based on our selected level of alpha, and then finding exactly what that means in terms of z scores. In the last section of this chapter, we want to discuss why the standard normal distribution is so important for our statistical work.

## ▣ Samples, Populations, Sampling Distributions, and the Central Limit Theorem

A good understanding of the properties of the normal distribution is very important for statistical analysis. At some point in your reading of this chapter, though, you may have wondered just why the normal distribution is so important. You may have thought that although there certainly are some variables that are normally distributed in the population, many others are not really normal. For example, population characteristics such as the number of crimes committed or convictions experienced by persons are not likely to be normally distributed (most people commit zero or only a few crimes, and there is a long right tail of the distribution where few offenders commit many crimes). If only a few variables are normally distributed in the population, the utility of the normal distribution surely must be rather restricted. Not so!

The normal distribution has wide applicability that makes it invaluable for research. The reason behind the generality of the normal distribution is based on one of the most important and remarkable theorems of statistics: the *central limit theorem*. It is because of the central limit theorem that we can employ the standard normal distribution in so much of our statistical work even if we do not have normal populations. Before we examine this theorem and its implications, however, we need to discuss some preliminary issues.

Recall that in conducting research, we typically draw a sample from a large population rather than studying the entire population. We draw a sample from our population and collect data on characteristics of the sample, with the intention of making an *inference* about the corresponding, but unknown, characteristics in the population. Thus, although we know a great deal about the characteristics of our sample (we know its mean, its standard deviation, the skew of the distribution, etc.), we know virtually nothing about the characteristics of the population. This is a problem because it is to the population that we want to generalize. Fortunately, through inferential statistics, we can make some estimate about the characteristics of populations from our knowledge of sample characteristics. The connection between sample information and population characteristics involves something called a **sampling distribution**.

**Sampling distribution:** Probability distribution of a sample statistic (e.g., mean or proportion) drawn from a very large number of samples from some given population.

As an example, let's assume that we are interested in the variable of height, and we want to know the mean height of persons in some population (the students at a university). In this problem, we collect data on the height of those selected into our random sample from which to estimate the height of our larger population. Let's also assume for the moment that the distribution of height in the population is normal. We draw a random sample of 100 persons, so our sample size is 100 ($n = 100$). Both our sample of 100 persons and the larger population from which it was drawn have a mean value. Recall that for our sample, the mean height is symbolized by $\overline{X}$, our *sample statistic*. The corresponding population value is called the *parameter* and is symbolized by $\mu$.

In our sample of 100 persons, some people are taller than the sample mean height, some are shorter, and some may actually be equal to the mean. We have, then, variation around our sample mean, which we measure with the sample standard deviation ($s$). Similarly, in our population, not everyone is the same height as the population mean, and this variation around the mean is measured in terms of the population standard deviation ($\sigma$). Keep in mind that although the population is normally distributed (we have assumed that this is true), our sample of 100 heights may not be normally distributed. The distribution of height from our sample may in fact be very skewed.

Now, instead of taking just one random sample of 100 people from our population, let's imagine taking 10,000 random samples of 100 people ($n = 100$). For each one of these 10,000 samples of 100, we can determine the mean $\left( \overline{X} \right)$. This would involve a huge amount of time and effort. We would draw a sample of 100 people and then calculate the mean of that sample $\left( \overline{X}_1 \right)$. We draw a second random sample of size 100 and determine the mean of that sample $\left( \overline{X}_2 \right)$. We continue drawing a random sample from a population 10,000 times, each of size 100, and calculate the mean of each sample $\left( \overline{X}_{10,000} \right)$. This would give us 10,000 sample means. Since these 10,000 sample means are not all alike (that is, the value of the mean will vary from sample to sample because different people are in each sample), there is a corresponding distribution of means and a corresponding mean and standard deviation of this distribution of means. The fact that we are referring to a very large number (10,000) of sample means should alert you to the fact that we are speaking about a theoretical distribution, not an empirical distribution that is based on real information. The distribution of these 10,000 sample means with a sample size of 100 is called a sampling distribution of means in this case, but more generally, it is just a sampling distribution.

In this sampling distribution of 10,000 sample means, although the value of each mean will vary from sample to sample, these values will still cluster around the mean of the population from which we sampled ($\mu$). The standard deviation of this distribution of 10,000 sample means will be equal to:

$$\frac{\sigma}{\sqrt{n}}$$

Based on this formula, you can see that the larger the size of the random sample we select from this normal population ($n$), the smaller the standard deviation of the sampling distribution will be because the larger $n$ becomes, the larger the denominator becomes, which decreases the value of $s$. As our sample size increases, then, variation around the mean of the sampling distribution decreases and therefore is more likely to cluster around the true population mean ($\mu$). Stated another way, the means will have less variation from sample to sample with a large sample size ($n$). *Therefore, we will have more faith that any given sample represents the population mean if we have a large sample size.* Since the mean of the sample is our best estimate of the unknown mean of the population, we can draw two conclusions: (1) There is a certain amount of error in using a known sample mean to estimate an unknown population mean since there is variation in the means from sample to sample, and (2) the amount of this error or imprecision decreases as the size of the sample ($n$) increases. Since it reflects the amount of error due to sampling variation, the standard deviation of the sampling distribution:

$$\left( \frac{\sigma}{\sqrt{n}} \right)$$

is generally referred to as the standard error; in this case, it is the *standard error of the mean*.

Figure 6.15 shows what happens to the standard deviation of the sampling distribution or the standard error when sample size is increased. Note that the distribution of the sample means is narrower than the population distribution (except, of course, when $n = 1$; then it is the same), and the larger the

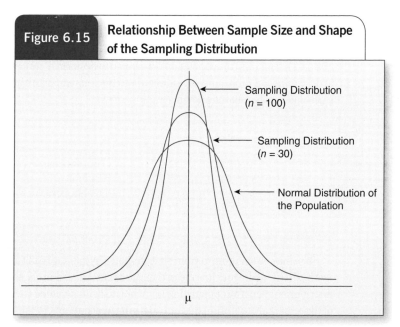

**Figure 6.15**  **Relationship Between Sample Size and Shape of the Sampling Distribution**

Sampling Distribution ($n = 100$)

Sampling Distribution ($n = 30$)

Normal Distribution of the Population

$\mu$

sample size ($n$), the more narrow that sampling distribution will be. As you can see, then, the larger the sample size, the more likely it will be that any particular randomly drawn sample of size $n$ will be close to the population mean ($\mu$). In other words, the larger the sample size, the less error there is in using our known sample statistic $\left(\overline{X}\right)$ to estimate our unknown population parameter ($\mu$). ***The general rule to remember is that larger samples are always better than smaller ones because they give more precise estimates.*** This should make intuitive sense; larger samples will more likely represent the population compared with smaller samples.

In addition to having a known mean and standard deviation ($\mu$ and $\sigma/\sqrt{n}$, respectively), according to one probability theorem, the distribution of these 10,000 sample means drawn from a normal population (the sampling distribution) will also be normal. We will state this theorem explicitly:

> If an infinite number of random samples of size $n$ are drawn from a normal population, with a mean equal to $\mu$ and standard deviation equal to $\sigma$, the sampling distribution of the sample means will itself be normally distributed with mean equal to $\mu$ and standard deviation equal to $\sigma/\sqrt{n}$.

In other words, the theoretical sampling distribution of the means of a very large number of random samples drawn from a normal population will have a normal distribution.

Before we introduce an even more useful and important statistical theorem, the central limit theorem, you need to remember that in the discussion earlier we referred to *three distinct distributions,* only two of which were normal. First, we have an empirical distribution of raw scores from a single random sample that we actually obtain. These scores are empirically observed and represent the heights of the individual persons in our random sample. The scores within our sample differ, so there is a distribution of sample scores with a mean $\left(\overline{X}\right)$ and standard deviation (s). The distribution of our sample values is *not* presumed to be normal. The characteristic of interest (mean height) is referred to as a sample statistic. The second distribution is the distribution of our population characteristic (height). The scores in this distribution vary one from the other and are presumed to be normally distributed with mean ($\mu$) and standard deviation ($\sigma$). The characteristic of interest in this distribution (mean height) is called the population parameter. The third distribution discussed is the sampling distribution, which is a theoretical distribution of a sample of means obtained from a very large number of random samples drawn from our normally distributed population. Based on the theorem provided earlier, this distribution is also assumed to be normally distributed, with a mean equal to the population parameter ($\mu$) and a standard deviation equal to $\sigma/\sqrt{n}$. These three distributions and their associated characteristics are summarized in Table 6.11.

You should keep in mind that these are three distinct distributions. The first is a distribution of sample scores (empirical), and the second is a distribution of population scores (empirical but not known). What connects these two is the third (theoretical) distribution, which in this case is a distribution of sample means. With our sampling distribution, we can determine the probability of obtaining our sample statistic. Since the sampling distribution of means is normal and the population is assumed to be normal, we can make use of the standard normal distribution to determine this probability regardless of whether our empirical sample data are normally distributed. This can be represented in the following flow diagram:

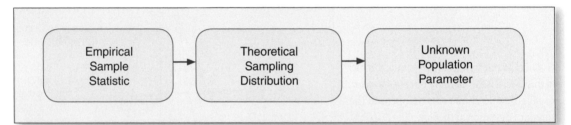

You may be thinking to yourself right now, "What if we can't assume that the population distribution is normally distributed? Does this mean that the normal distribution is inapplicable?" No. We can employ the normal distribution even if our population is not normally distributed (so long as we take a large sample). This is because of the remarkable nature of the **central limit theorem**:

*If an infinite number of random samples of size n are drawn from any population with mean μ and standard deviation σ, then as the sample size (n) becomes large, the sampling distribution of sample means will approach normality, with mean μ and standard deviation σ/√n, even if the population distribution is not normally distributed.*

The importance of this theorem is that the sampling distribution does not depend on normality in the population. No matter what the shape of the distribution in the population, the theoretical probability distribution of sample means will approximate a normal distribution as the sample size becomes large. The sampling distribution not only will be normal but also will have a mean equal to the population mean (μ) and a standard deviation equal to $\sigma/\sqrt{n}$. This is a very important theorem because it suggests that even if our population distribution is quite skewed (like the number of arrests in the population), we can still assume that our sampling distribution of means will be normal as the size of the sample becomes large. Since it is the sampling distribution that links our sample estimate to the population parameter, we can employ the normal probability distribution in instances where our population is not normal.

| Table 6.11 | **Characteristics of Three Types of Distributions** | | |
|---|---|---|---|
| | *Mean* | *Standard Deviation* | *Distribution* |
| Sample | $\bar{X}$ | S | Empirical and known |
| Population | μ | σ | Empirical but not known |
| Sampling distribution | μ | $\dfrac{\sigma}{\sqrt{n}}$ | Theoretical |

**Central limit theorem:** Statistical theorem that states that the sampling distribution of any statistic will approximate normality as the sample size increases.

The important and practical question to ask now is, "How large is large enough so we can relax the normality assumption and appeal to the central limit theorem?" A rough rule of thumb (although it is only a rule of thumb) is that the assumption of normality can almost always be relaxed when the sample size is 30 or more ($n \geq 30$). With sample sizes of less than 30, the normality assumption should not be made. In the case of small samples, statistics that do not appeal to the central limit theorem and normal distribution must be employed.

Before we leave this chapter, let's look at an example of the central limit theorem at work.

---

*Three Characteristics of the Sampling Distribution of the Mean Based on the Central Limit Theorem*

Whenever the sample size is large:

1. We can assume that the mean of the sampling distribution is equal to the population mean, μ.

2. We can assume that the standard deviation of the sampling distribution is equal to $\sigma/\sqrt{n}$.

3. We can assume the sampling distribution is normally distributed even if the population from which the sample was drawn is not.

---

## Case Study

## The Probability of a Stolen Car Recovered II

Earlier in this chapter we worked with an example involving car theft recovery with Lo-Jack. Under the null hypothesis, we assumed that the probability of getting a stolen car recovered undamaged was .40. You can see that having a stolen car returned without damage is definitely not a normally distributed event. In fact, it follows a binomial distribution. Let's take a sample of $n = 1$ and calculate the probability distribution for this size sample. Figure 6.16 illustrates this probability distribution, and we can see that this is a very non-normal distribution. There is a .60 probability that the car will not be returned undamaged and a .40 probability that it will. Now let's increase our sample size to 5. In this case, as shown in Figure 6.17, we take a random sample of 5 people who had Lo-Jack in their car when it was stolen and ask if it was recovered undamaged. We then calculate the probability of 0, 1, 2, 3, 4, or 5 undamaged car recoveries. This probability distribution is also not very normal in its appearance. In Figure 6.18, we increase the sample size to 10 and calculate the probability distribution. It too is non-normal, but you can see that even when the population distribution is very skewed, the probability distribution starts to approximate normality as we increase our sample size. Finally, in Figure 6.19, we have a sample size of $n = 50$, and this probability distribution is approximately normal. As we increased our sample size from 1 in Figure 6.16 to 50 in Figure 6.19, our sampling distribution came closer and closer to being normal. This is the central limit theorem at work!

**Figure 6.16** Probability Distribution of Stolen Car Recoveries Where $n = 1$

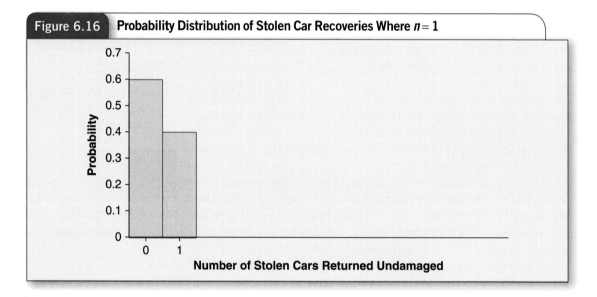

**Figure 6.17** Probability Distribution of Stolen Car Recoveries Where $n = 5$

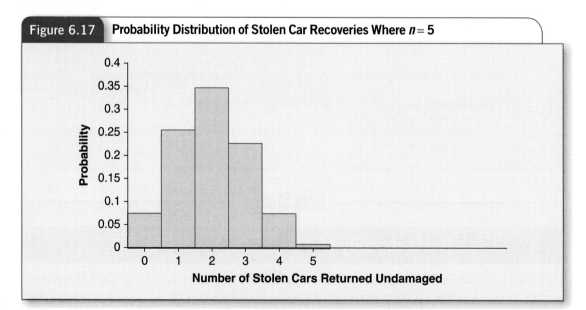

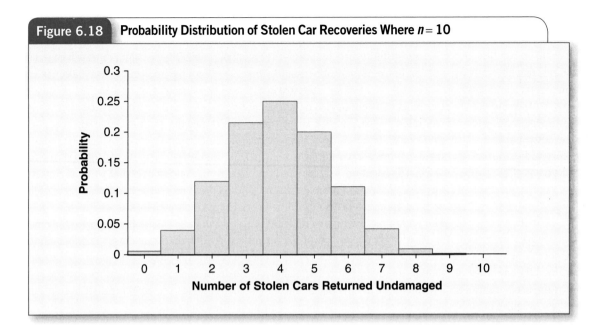

Figure 6.18   **Probability Distribution of Stolen Car Recoveries Where $n = 10$**

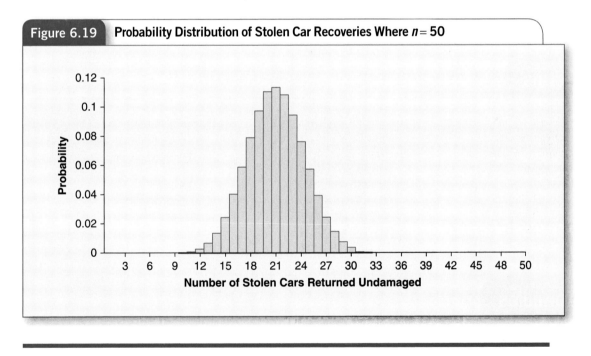

Figure 6.19   **Probability Distribution of Stolen Car Recoveries Where $n = 50$**

## 📖 Summary

We have covered a lot of important ground in this chapter, a discussion that will serve as the foundation for our discussion of inferential statistics, which makes up the remainder of this book. At the core of this foundation is the notion of probability. We have discussed two types of the probability: (1) the chance or likelihood that a single event will occur in a given trial, and (2) the chance of an event occurring over the long run with an infinite number of trials. We introduced the notion of the probability distribution—a theoretical distribution of outcomes determined by the laws of probability. One of these probability distributions is the binomial probability distribution, which governs events that have only two possible outcomes, called Bernoulli events. The binomial probability distribution is an important one for us since many of the events we are interested in have only two outcomes.

We then discussed a probability distribution that describes continuous events, the normal distribution. This unimodal, symmetrical distribution looked like a bell-shaped curve. We learned that there is a large family of normal distributions, which would make for some cumbersome probability calculations were it not for the standard normal distribution. The standard normal distribution is a normal distribution with a mean of 0 and a standard deviation of 1.0. To use the normal distribution to figure out the probability of continuous events, we must convert our raw x scores into what are called standard normal z scores. The z score is measured in standard deviation units. Once we have a z score, the determination of probabilities is relatively simple with the use of a z table.

Finally, we considered how a sample, a sampling distribution, and a population differ along with the relationship between them. We usually take one sample of size n from a single population and use the information from a sample to make an inference about some unknown population value using theoretical sampling distributions. Like any other distribution, a sampling distribution has a mean and a standard deviation. We also learned the important central limit theorem, which says that as our sample size increases, the sampling distribution will begin to approximate normality no matter what the shape of the population looks like.

## Key Terms

➤ Review key terms with eFlashcards. $\circledS$SAGE edge™

| | | |
|---|---|---|
| alpha level (level of significance)  163 | general addition rule of probabilities   150 | probability distribution   156 |
| binomial distribution   157 | | restricted addition rule of probabilities   150 |
| bounding rule of probabilities   149 | general multiplication rule of probabilities   152 | |
| central limit theorem   176 | | restricted multiplication rule of probabilities   152 |
| complement of an event   149 | independent events   153 | |
| conditional probability   152 | inferential statistics   147 | sampling distribution   174 |
| critical region   165 | mutually exclusive events   150 | standard score (z score)   171 |
| descriptive statistics   147 | null hypothesis   161 | |

## Key Formulas

The probability of success—the binomial theorem (equation 6-1):

$$P(r) = \binom{n}{r} p^r q^{n-r}$$

$$P(r) = \left( \frac{n!}{r!(n-r)!} \right) p^r q^{n-r}$$

The mathematical formula for the normal distribution (equation 6-2):

$$f(x) = \frac{1}{s\sqrt{2\pi}} e^{\frac{-(x-\mu)^2}{2s^2}}$$

Formula for converting a raw score into a z score (equation 6-3):

$$z = \frac{x - \bar{X}}{s}$$

## Practice Problems

➤ Test your understanding of chapter content.
Take the practice quiz. ⑤SAGE edge™

1. The following data consist of the starting salaries for police officers in 110 police departments in a northeastern state:

| Salary | f |
|--------|---|
| $25,000 | 6 |
| $26,000 | 8 |
| $27,500 | 9 |
| $28,000 | 10 |
| $30,000 | 16 |
| $31,500 | 19 |
| $32,000 | 12 |
| $32,500 | 15 |
| $34,000 | 8 |
| $35,000 | 7 |
| Total | 110 |

With this information, calculate:

a. The probability that a starting salary will be exactly $30,000.

b. The probability that a starting salary will be exactly $35,000.

c. Whether a starting salary of $30,000 and a starting salary of $35,000 are mutually exclusive events. Explain.

d. The probability that a starting salary will be at least $31,000.

e. The probability that a starting salary will be $30,000 or less.

f. The probability that a starting salary will be between $27,800 and $33,000.

g. The probability that a starting salary will be less than $25,000.

h. The probability that a starting salary will be $28,000, $32,000, or $35,000,

2. The probability of being acquitted in criminal court in Baltimore, Maryland, is .40. You take a random sample of the past 10 criminal cases where the defendant had a public defender and find that there were seven acquittals and three convictions. What is the probability of observing seven or more acquittals out of 10 cases if the true probability of an acquittal is .40? By using an alpha of .05, test the null hypothesis (that the probability of an acquittal is .40 for defendants with public defenders), against the alternative hypothesis that it is greater than .40.

3. Assume that you have a normal distribution of IQ scores with a mean of 100 and a standard deviation of 10.

a. What is the z score for a raw score of 115?

b. What is the z score for a raw score of 83?

c. What is the z score for a raw score of 70?

d. What proportion of the cases have an IQ score above 115?

e. What proportion of the cases have an IQ score between 90 and 110?

f. What is the probability that you would find an IQ score of 70 or below?

g. What is the probability that you would find an IQ score of 125 or above?

4. In a recent article, Thomas Loughran, Greg Pogarsky, Alex R. Piquero, and Raymond Paternoster (2012) examined the relationship between perceived certainty of punishment and self-reported offending. They found that the certainty of punishment deterred the criminal behavior only for those who believed the likelihood of getting caught for committing a crime was medium to great. Let's say you are interested in the same idea with the concept of impulsivity. That is, you think the impulsive cannot be deterred. You do some research and find the following joint distribution between impulsivity and whether someone was deterred by the certainty of punishment:

| Impulsivity | Was the Person Deterred? | | |
|-------------|-------------------------|-------------|-------|
| | Deterred | Not Deterred | Total |
| Not impulsive | 75 | 15 | 90 |
| Impulsive | 5 | 25 | 30 |
| Total | 80 | 40 | 120 |

a. What is the probability that someone was deterred?

b. Is this a conditional or an unconditional probability? Explain.

c. What is the probability that someone was not deterred?

d. What is the probability that someone was impulsive?

e. What is the probability that someone was impulsive or not deterred by punishment? Are these mutually exclusive events? Explain.

f. What is the conditional probability that someone was not deterred given that the person was impulsive?

g. What is the conditional probability that someone was deterred by punishment given that the person was not impulsive?

h. Are impulsivity and being deterred by punishment independent events? Explain.

i. What is the probability that someone was impulsive and not deterred?

j. What is the probability that someone was not impulsive and deterred?

5. The department of corrections in the state where you live has a policy whereby it accepts as correctional officers only those who score in the top 5% of a qualifying exam. The mean of this test is 80, and the standard deviation is 10.

   a. Would a person with a raw score of 95 be accepted?

   b. Would a person with a raw score of 110 be accepted?

   c. What is the minimum score you would have to have on the test in order to be accepted?

6. Explain how a sample, a sampling distribution, and a population differ. What are the means and standard deviations for each of these?

7. Draw a picture indicating what proportion (area) of the normal curve lies:

   a. To the right of a z score of 1.65

   b. To the left of a z score of –1.65

   c. Either to the left of a z score of –1.96 or to the right of a z score of 1.96

   d. To the right of a z score of 2.33

   e. Is a z score of –2.56 a rare or low probability score? Explain.

8. There has been some controversy about school violence and how to prevent it. To study measures that might prevent school violence, you take a random sample of 250 schools that differ in what they do to prevent school violence. You also collect information on the number of violent acts that were committed in each school during the previous school year. The information you have collected is shown as follows:

| Number of Violent Acts | Type of Preventive Measure | | | | Total |
| --- | --- | --- | --- | --- | --- |
| | No Measures | Metal Detectors Only | Guards Only | Guards and Metal Detectors | |
| None | 5 | 10 | 15 | 30 | 60 |
| 1–4 acts | 25 | 20 | 15 | 15 | 75 |
| 5+ acts | 50 | 30 | 25 | 10 | 115 |
| Total | 80 | 60 | 55 | 55 | 250 |

With these data, answer the following probability questions:

   a. What is the probability that a school had no violent acts last year?

   b. What is the probability that a school had guards only as part of its violence prevention measures?

   c. What is the probability that either metal detectors or guards were used, but not both?

   d. What is the probability that no measures were used?

   e. What is the probability that a school used both guards and metal detectors together or had 1–4 violent acts committed last year?

   f. What is the probability that a school used metal detectors only or had five or more acts of violence committed last year?

   g. What is the conditional probability of no violent acts in a school given that there were no preventive measures used?

   h. What is the conditional probability of no violent acts in a school given that some type of preventive measure was used?

   i. What is the conditional probability of five or more violent acts given that metal detectors only were used?

   j. What is the conditional probability of five or more violent acts given that both guards and metal detectors were used?

   k. Are the two events, type of preventive measure used and number of violent acts in the school, independent events? Explain.

   l. What is the probability of no violent acts and the presence of guards only as a preventive measure?

   m. What is the probability of no preventive measures and five or more violent acts?

   n. What is the probability of both guards and metal detectors together and 1–4 violent acts in the school?

9. A jail has an inmate population where the mean number of prior arrests is 6 and the standard deviation is 2.

   a. Would a new inmate with 9 prior arrests have an unusually high number, where unusual is in the top 5%?

   b. Would a new inmate with 11 prior arrests have an unusually high number, where unusual is in the top 5%?

   c. Would an inmate with 2 prior arrests have an unusually low number, where unusual is in the bottom 5%?

10. What is the central limit theorem? What does it enable us to assume about sampling distributions if we have a large enough sample?

# SPSS Exercises

➤ Explore additional data sets. ⑤SAGE edge™

| Data for Exercise | |
|---|---|
| Data Set | Description |
| NCVS lone offender assaults 1992 to 2013.sav | These data are from the National Crime Victimization Survey (NCVS), a nationally representative study of individual's experience of criminal victimization. This particular data set contains responses from 1992 to 2013, allowing for larger numbers of uncommon offenses to be used in analyses. It also only includes data from respondents who reported either violent or nonviolent assault by a single offender. |
| 2012 states data.sav | This state-level data set compiles official statistics from various official sources, such as the census, health department records, and police departments. It includes basic demographic data, crime rates, and incidence rates for various illnesses and infant mortality for entire states. |
| Variables for Exercise | |
| Variable Name (Dataset) | Description |
| Maleoff (NCVS) | The sex of the offender where 1 = male and 0 = female. |
| Victimreported (NCVS) | A binary variable indicating if respondents reported their victimization to the police. |
| Relationship (NCVS) | A four-category nominal measure that tells us the victim's relationship to the offender. 0 = total stranger, 1 = slightly known, 2 = casual acquaintance, 3 = well known. |
| V3018 (NCVS) | A respondent's sex where 1 = male, 2 = female. |
| MurderRt (States) | Number of murders in a state per 100,000. |
| BurglaryRt (States) | Number of burglaries in a state per 100,000. |

1. Do victims know their assailants, or is it mostly strangers? Estimate a frequency table for the variable Relationship, and use the output to find out! Use this output to do the following:

   a. Use the restricted addition rule to calculate the following probabilities:

      i. Pr(stranger)

      ii. Pr(well known)

      iii. Pr(slightly known, casual acquaintance, OR well known)

   b. Use the probabilities you calculated to calculate the odds of each event occurring.

   c. Write a sentence or two answering the question at the beginning of this question.

2. One of the most common methods for comparing two variables is to construct a cross tabulation. We'll make one of these that compares victim gender with their relationship to the assailant to practice using the general addition rule of probabilities. To do this, go to analyze-> descriptive statistics->crosstabs. Then, put gender in the row box and relationship in the columns. The output should look familiar—use Table 6.1 in the text and associated examples as a reference!

   a. Using this table, use the general addition rule to calculate the following probabilities:

      i. Pr(female OR stranger)

      ii. Pr(male OR stranger)

      iii. Pr(male OR well known)

   b. Now use the multiplication rule to calculate predicted probabilities—recall that this notation refers specifically to *conditional probabilities*:

      i. Pr(stranger | female)

      ii. Pr(stranger | male)

      iii. Pr(well known | female)

      iv. Pr(well known | male)

      v. Zoom out for a moment and think substantively about these results:

         1. Which gender has a greater probability of being assaulted by a stranger? A well-known acquaintance?

         2. Do women have a greater probability of being assaulted by a stranger or a well-known acquaintance?

3. Hypothesis tests are quick and easy in SPSS. Let's do a hypothesis test to answer the following research question: Are women more likely to assault another person than men?

a. First, write out the null and alternative hypotheses. In this case, no sex differences would be evidenced by an even probability of assault. That is, $p = .50$.

b. What probability distribution will be used to answer this question?

c. What alpha level will you use—typical values are .05, .01 and .001, with smaller alpha values reflecting more difficult criteria?

d. **Binomial Hypothesis Tests in SPSS:** Do this by clicking analyze->nonparametric tests->legacy dialogues->binomial. Put the variable "maleoff" into the "test variable list." Set "test proportion" to .50:

   i. The output you receive gives you two pieces of information: The "observed prop" is the probability of being in group 1 versus group 2." The "Exact Sig (2-tailed)" column will have a value in it. This is the exact value for "$p$" in this analysis; if it is equal to ".000", it is actually even smaller than .001.

e. Using the output from this model, what do you conclude about the null hypothesis? Substantively, what does this mean?

4. Let's do another hypothesis test to answer the following research question: Are victims more likely to report their own victimization than to have it be reported by someone else or another avenue?

   a. First, write out the null and alternative hypotheses. In this case, the probability that any victimization will be reported is .447.

   b. What probability distribution will be used to answer this question?

   c. What alpha level will you use—typical values are .05, .01 and .001, with smaller alpha values reflecting more difficult criteria?

   d. In SPSS, run the hypothesis test. Do this by clicking analyze->nonparametric tests->legacy dialogues->binomial. Put the variable "Victimreported" into the "test variable list." Set "test proportion" to .447.

   e. Using the output from this model, what do you conclude about the null hypothesis?

   f. Substantively, what does this mean? Explain the results of your hypothesis test in a way that a lay person could understand easily.

The remaining questions are answered using the 2010 states data.sav.

5. What does the distribution of homicide look like throughout the United States?

   a. First, create a histogram of the variable MurderRt. Describe the distribution. Is it relatively normally distributed or skewed?

   b. Use the frequency menu to get the standard deviation of MurderRt. Use it to answer the following:

      i. What range would you expect 68% of state's murder rates to fall within?

      ii. What range would you expect 95% of state's murder rates to fall within?

      iii. What range would you expect 99.7% of state's murder rates to fall within?

6. Repeat question 5 using the variable RobberyRt.

7. $z$ scores are easily obtained in SPSS and can then be used to answer a wide array of questions. Let's get $z$ scores for the murder rates across states. To do this, go to analyze->descriptive statistics->descriptives. Then, put MurderRt in the variable box and check off the "save standardized values as variables," option. A new variable called "ZMurderRt" will show up at the bottom of variable view:

   a. Look at the $z$ score for Alabama: What proportion of states are expected to have a *higher* murder rate?

   b. Look at the $z$ score for Alaska: What proportion of states are expected to have a *lower* murder rate?

   c. Now compare $z$ scores for Alabama and Alaska: What proportion of states are expected to have a murder rate *between* that of Alaska or Alabama?

8. The standard error of the sampling distribution is easily attained in SPSS. The easiest way to do so is to go to the frequency menu and select the "statistics" menu. Then, tick off "S.E. Mean":

   a. What is the standard error for the murder rate (MurderRt) in this case?

   b. What is the standard error for the burglary rate (BurglaryRt) in this data set?

# CHAPTER 7

# Point Estimation and Confidence Intervals

❝ *Confidence, like art, never comes from having all the answers; it comes from being open to all the questions.*

—Earl Gray Stevens ❞

---

**LEARNING OBJECTIVES**

1. State the difference between a point estimate and a confidence interval.

2. Describe how probability theory allows us to make generalizations from a point estimate to a population parameter.

*(Continued)*

(Continued)

3. Identify the relationship between levels of confidence and the precision of an interval at a given sample size.

4. Explain why different sampling distributions to make inferences from point estimates are necessary when using small versus large samples.

# ▣ Introduction

On June 17, 2015, 21-year-old Dylann Roof opened fire at a Bible study meeting at Emanuel African Methodist Episcopal Church in Charleston, SC, using an illegally obtained semi-automatic handgun. Nine people were killed at short range, all with multiple bullet wounds (Harlan, Brown, & Fisher, 2015). The Guardian notes that after mass shootings in the United States, the reaction is virtually always the same, "Gun control groups diagnose an epidemic, the president declares a crisis, and gun advocates prescribe more guns" (McCarthy & Gambino, 2015, p. 1), and this mass shooting resulted in little variation to this script. In addition to politicians making statements, television and newspaper articles frequently feature "person on the street" interviews that ask passersby to voice their opinions about the tragedy. These opinions are usually presented as if they are representative of something larger.

In Chapter 1, you learned that we cannot make generalizations from a sample to the population of interest unless we have collected a random sample that is representative of that population. Clearly, these "person on the street" interviews are not representative of any population. In research, if we want to have confidence in findings, including findings about attitudes, we have to examine the sample and data very systematically. For example, we know from professional opinion polls that have been conducted with random samples of the U.S. population (Pew Research Center, 2015) that a majority of Americans are in favor of certain forms of gun control including the following:

|  | *Favor* |
|---|---|
| Background checks for private and gun show sales | 85% |
| Preventing people with mental illness from purchasing guns | 80% |
| Federal database to track gun sales | 67% |
| Ban on semi-automatic weapons | 58% |
| Ban on high-capacity ammunition clips | 54% |

The margins of error that Pew calculated around these percentages were about plus or minus 4%. Therefore, the percentages displayed here are really just our best estimates of public sentiment about gun control legislation. Before we can make generalizations from these estimates to the population, we have to provide some level of statistical accuracy in our results. These statements of accuracy are usually made with regard to a "margin of error" or "sampling error," and they are usually found in the fine print of a story or in the final paragraph, but they must be provided if the results are to be believed. These estimates of error are created using inferential statistics.

In this chapter, we take our first step into the world of inferential statistics. We concentrate on two **sample statistics** in this chapter, the *mean* and the *proportion*. The estimates of the mean and proportion that we obtain from a sample are referred to as **point estimates** of the same values in the population. Think of these point estimates as our best guess, based on sample information, as to what the unknown **population parameters** are. Since our sample only gives us estimates, we have to construct what are called confidence intervals around them. These intervals enable us to make generalizations to the population with a known degree of certainty (i.e., confidence), and they are frequently used in the media as well as in scientific research. By the end of the chapter, you will be able to construct and interpret confidence intervals on your own. In addition, you will become more informed consumers of the point estimates that are presented in the media on a daily basis.

> **Point estimates:** Sample statistics such as the mean and proportion that are sample estimates of the same values in the population.

> **Sample statistic:** Statistic obtained from a sample.

> **Population parameter:** Statistic obtained from the population.

## ▣ Making Inferences From Point Estimates: Confidence Intervals

To reiterate, the objective of inferential statistics is to make inferences about an unknown population characteristic based on information we obtain from a sample. In this chapter, we examine different ways of estimating a population parameter based on a sample statistic. A population parameter is some unknown characteristic of a population. An example would be the mean reading level of inmates in all the prisons of a state correctional system. We do not know what this mean reading level is—that is our unknown population parameter ($\mu$)—but we would like to estimate what it is without giving reading tests to every single inmate. So let's say we select a random sample of 500 inmates from a state prison, give them a reading test, and determine that the mean grade level at which this sample can read is 8.3. This is our known sample statistic ($\overline{X}$). We use the sample statistic as our point estimate of the unknown population parameter. Estimation is a common interest to many researchers. "What is the average number of prior arrests for those convicted of armed robbery in a particular state?" "What proportion of the U.S. population agrees with the use of capital punishment instead of life in prison for those convicted of murder?" "How often do teenagers use alcohol or other drugs?" The answers to all these questions begin with estimation.

Our general goal is to evaluate how accurate our sample statistic (mean or proportion) is as an estimate of the true population parameter. To generalize these estimates to the entire population, we have to construct a margin of error around the point estimate that consists of a range of values or an interval into which we believe, with some established degree of confidence, the population value falls. This interval is called a **confidence interval**. Think of a confidence interval as an estimated interval that we are reasonably confident contains the true population value "over the long run." The confidence interval gives formal mathematical expression to the uncertainty we have in capturing the true population parameter with our sample statistic. To see this, think of a confidence interval as made up of two parts, a point estimate and a margin of error: confidence interval = point estimate ± margin of error.

> **Confidence interval:** Statistical interval around a point estimate (e.g., mean) that we can provide a level of confidence to for capturing the true population parameter.

Like the example of attitudes toward different types of gun control discussed earlier, you have undoubtedly heard about a statistical confidence interval without even being aware of it.

Figure 7.1 displays the results of a Gallup poll conducted in October 2014, asking respondents about the crimes they worry about the most (Gallup, 2014a). Typically, most news outlets (such as television reports and newspapers) focus primarily on the point estimates for each question. For example, they would typically report that 69% of Americans state that the crime they fear the most is identity theft of a credit card, whereas only 45% report that the crime they worry about the most is burglary of their home when they are not there, and only 31% say that it is being mugged. However, to be scientific, the confidence interval around this point estimate must also be noted somehow, usually at the end of a story. On its website, Gallup says the following about the sample and the confidence interval

| Figure 7.1 | Top Crime Worries of Americans |
| --- | --- |

*Crime Worries in U.S.*
How often do you, yourself, worry about the following things—frequently, occasionally, rarely or never? How about . . .

| | %Frequently or occasionally worry |
| --- | --- |
| Having the credit card information you have used at stores stolen by computer hackers | 69 |
| Having your computer or smartphone hacked and the informatian stolen by unauthorized persons | 62 |
| Having your home being burglarized when you are not there | 45 |
| Having your car stolen or broken into | 42 |
| Having a school-aged child physically harmed attending school | 31 |
| Getting mugged | 31 |
| Having your home being burglarized when you are there | 30 |
| Being the victim of terrorism | 28 |
| Being attacked while driving your car | 20 |
| Being a victim of a hate crime | 18 |
| Being sexually assaulted | 18 |
| Getting murdered | 18 |
| Being assaulted/killed by a coworker/employee where you work | 7 |

around the point estimates: "For results based on the total sample of national adults, the margin of sampling error is ±4 percentage points at the 95% confidence level." What this is really telling readers is that, to be 95% confident that the true population parameter (percent) is included in the estimate, you must add 4% to, and subtract 4% from, any point estimate to create an interval, which would then become a 95% confidence interval. For example, 42% reported that the crime they worried about the most was having their car broken into. This 42% is the point estimate. To make a generalization about how worried the population is of getting their car broken into, we have to create a margin of error around this estimate. Gallup did this and concluded that to be 95% confident in their estimation, it would be 42% ± 4%.

What does this tell us? Well, it says that we can be 95% confident that the true percentage of adults in the United States who worry most about having their car broken into is between 38% and 46%. What is important about this statement is that a level of confidence, 95%, accompanies it. Without creating a confidence interval around the point estimate of 42%, researchers would not be able to provide any confidence claims in their inferences. Also note that researchers had to start with a probability sample to do this in the first place! In addition, the correct technical interpretation of a 95% confidence interval is, if we repeated our sampling and point estimation an infinite number of times (or a very large number of times) and created a 95% confidence interval around each point estimate, 95% of those intervals would contain the true population parameter while the other 5% would not. In other words, we have confidence in our procedure of sample selection and estimation, not in our one sample statistic.

Figure 7.2 illustrates the concept of a 95% confidence interval graphically. It shows a hypothetical example in which 20 samples ($n = 100$) are drawn from the same population. From each sample, the mean number of times individuals from that sample ran a stop sign per month was calculated, and a 95% confidence interval was drawn around each mean. The horizontal lines across the figure represent these 95% confidence intervals, and the vertical line running down the middle of the figure represents the true population mean of stop sign violations. From Figure 7.2, you can see that 95% (19) of these confidence intervals actually contain the true population mean, whereas 5% (1) do not. Even though each of these confidence intervals varies from sample to sample, 95% of them nevertheless contain the true population parameter. You should also note that the true population parameter does not change but that the estimated interval does vary from sample to sample. This illustrates that what we are 95% confident about is the procedure, not the particular confidence interval we estimate with our sample data. That is, we should interpret our confidence interval as saying that over the long run, 95% of the confidence intervals we would estimate using this sample size and sampling procedure would include the true population parameter. This is the goal of inferential statistics: to make inferences to the target population with some degree of confidence.

Of course, in the real world, we never take repeated samples from the population and we never really know for sure whether we have contained the "true" population parameter within our confidence interval. However, if we have drawn our sample using probability sampling techniques (for example, a simple random sample), we can use both probability theory and what we know about probability distributions to estimate a population parameter from only one sample. And probability theory enables us to make numerical statements about the accuracy or the confidence we have in our estimates.

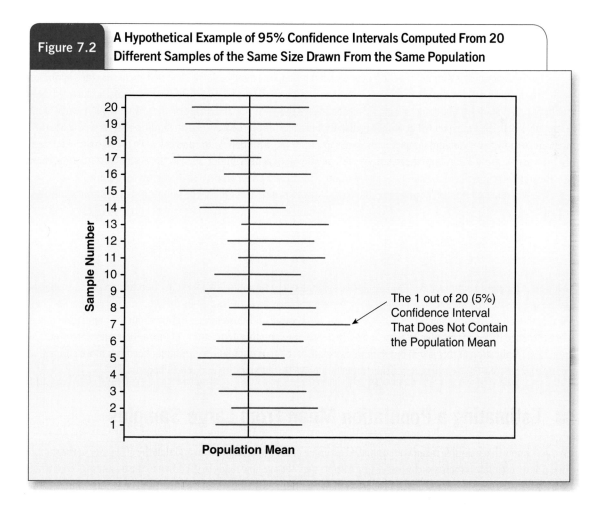

**Figure 7.2** A Hypothetical Example of 95% Confidence Intervals Computed From 20 Different Samples of the Same Size Drawn From the Same Population

In the sections that follow, we begin by examining the properties that any good estimate should have. We then examine confidence interval estimation procedures for sample means based on large samples ($n \geq 30$). We use the **z distribution** to do this. Next, we will introduce the **t distribution**, which is used for estimating means from small samples ($n < 30$). We will conclude the chapter by examining estimation procedures used for proportions and percentages.

**z distribution:** Statistical sampling distribution used in many statistical tests including for the construction of confidence intervals, for determining the difference between two means, and for calculating the number of standard deviations an observation is above or below the mean.

**t distribution (Student's t distribution):** Statistical sampling distribution used in many statistical tests including for the construction of confidence intervals and the difference between two means.

##  Properties of Good Estimates

The first parameter we are going to estimate is a population mean, which is symbolized by the Greek letter $\mu$. We are going to use the sample mean ($\overline{X}$) as our point estimate of the population mean. Why use the sample mean? Why not use the sample median or the average of the mean and the median value as our point estimator? The sample mean is chosen as our estimator because it is an *unbiased estimate* of the population mean. Any given estimate of a population parameter is unbiased if the mean of its sampling distribution is equal to the parameter being estimated. In the last chapter we learned that the mean of the sampling distribution of means (the mean of a distribution of a large number of sample means) is the population mean ($\mu$). Of course, one cannot conclude from this that any given sample mean ($\overline{X}$) will be equal to the population mean. Think of bias in the long run. With an infinite (or very large number) number of samples of size $n$ within which we calculate a mean for each sample, the mean of all the sample means will be equal to the population mean. We know this is probably a bit confusing, but it will become clear, we promise. What is important to know is that our estimate be unbiased. The sample mean and proportion are unbiased estimates of their respective population values. In addition to being unbiased, a second important property of an estimate is that it be efficient.

The efficiency of an estimate is the degree to which the sampling distribution is clustered about the true population value. In this case, an efficient estimate for the mean is one where the sampling distribution of means is clustered close to the population mean. The more the sample means cluster about the population mean, the greater the efficiency of the estimate. Recall from Chapter 6 that sampling distributions are simply theoretical distributions that we would obtain if we were to draw many random samples of the same size from the same population and calculate the statistic of interest. In this case we are talking about the mean. As with any theoretical distribution such as the normal distribution, there are theoretical properties of the sampling distribution of the mean. These properties are displayed in Table 7.1.

You will remember from the previous chapter that the standard deviation of the sampling distribution of means is equal to:

$$\frac{\sigma}{\sqrt{n}}$$

where $n$ is the size of your sample. The standard deviation of the sampling distribution, therefore, is in proportion to $n$, the sample size. As sample size increases, the standard deviation of the sampling distribution decreases. This tells us that the sample means themselves differ less from one another and cluster more tightly about the population mean. As we learned in the last chapter, as sample sizes increase, the sampling distribution of means becomes narrower. The practical implication of this is that our sample estimate of the true population parameter becomes more efficient as sample size increases. We will reiterate this important point throughout this and other chapters.

## Estimating a Population Mean From Large Samples

We now know that a sample mean is an unbiased estimate of the population mean and that the efficiency of the sample mean as an estimate is increased by increasing sample size. We are now ready to get down to the business of constructing confidence intervals. Based on the properties of the sampling distribution of the mean and on what we know about

| Table 7.1 | **Properties of the Sampling Distribution of $\bar{X}$** |
|---|---|

1. The mean of this sampling distribution of $\bar{X}$ is $\mu$.

2. The standard deviation of the sampling distribution of $\bar{X}$ is:

$$\sigma_{\bar{X}} = \frac{\sigma}{\sqrt{n}}$$

   where $\sigma$ is the standard deviation of the original population, $n$ is the sample size, and $\sigma_{\bar{X}}$ is used to denote the standard deviation of the sampling distribution. This entire term is called the **standard error of the mean.**

3. Because of the central limit theorem, when $n$ is large (safely, when $n \geq 30$), the sampling distribution of $\bar{X}$ is normally distributed regardless of the distribution of the population from which the sample was drawn.

4. As the sample size increases, the standard deviation of the sampling distribution (the standard error of the mean) decreases.

the normal distribution and probability theory, we can use the following formula to construct a confidence interval around a sample mean ($\bar{X}$), where we will assume that we have taken a large sample ($n \geq 30$) so we can invoke the central limit theorem and use the standard normal probability distribution or the $z$ distribution:

**Standard error of the mean:** Standard deviation of the sampling distribution of the mean.

$$\bar{X} \pm z_{\alpha}(\sigma_{\bar{X}}) = \bar{X} \pm z_{\alpha}\left(\frac{\sigma}{\sqrt{n}}\right) \tag{7–1}$$

where

$\bar{X}$ = the mean of our sample

$z_{\alpha}$ = the $z$ score corresponding to the level of alpha we are using to construct our interval (i.e., the level of confidence we will have in our estimate)

$\sigma_{\bar{X}}$ = the standard deviation of the sampling distribution (i.e., the standard error)

The confidence interval, then, is determined by going out in both a positive and a negative direction from the point estimate (the mean in equation 7-1) a specified multiple of standard errors ($\sigma/\sqrt{n}$) of the $z$ or standard normal distribution. How many standard errors we go out from the point estimate is a function of the **confidence level** we select.

The first order of business, then, is to select the degree of confidence we desire for our interval. Typically, researchers choose an alpha level of .05 or .01, which correspond to 95% or 99% confidence intervals respectively. In fact, most of the poll data you hear about in the media virtually always use a 95% confidence level.

**Confidence level:** Level of confidence (e.g., 95% or 99%) that is set for a statistical inference from the sample to the population.

If $\alpha$ = .05, we have a 95% confidence level. If $\alpha$ = .01, we have a 99% confidence level. A 95% confidence level means that over the long run, we are willing to be wrong only 5% of the time. A 99% confidence level means that over the long run, we are willing to be wrong only 1% of the time. Being wrong in this case means that the population mean will not fall within the boundaries established by the confidence interval. We will later see that the size of the confidence interval is a function of how confident we want to be *and* how large our sample is.

Let's begin with a 95% confidence interval. After we have selected our level of confidence, we must next determine the corresponding $z$ score from the $z$ distribution for that level of confidence. The $z$ score corresponding to an alpha of .05 (95% confidence) is 1.96 (see Appendix B, Table B.2). Why is it 1.96? With a 95% confidence interval, we are concerned with 5% of the tail of the standard normal distribution. Since, however, we do not know whether our sample statistic ($\bar{X}$) is less than or greater than the true population value ($\mu$), we are really concerned about

| Table 7.2 | Common Confidence Intervals and Their Corresponding Critical Values of *z* From the Sampling Distribution of *z* | |
|---|---|---|
| Confidence Level (%) | Alpha/Significance (α) | z Score |
| 90 | .10 | 1.65 |
| 95 | .05 | 1.96 |
| 99 | .01 | 2.58 |
| 99.9 | .001 | 3.27 |

both the left and right tails of the distribution. Hence, we divide our 5% into two equal halves (2.5%) and place them at each tail of the *z* distribution. The proportion of the standard normal curve that corresponds to an area under the curve of 2.5% is .025. Remember that in the standard normal curve, .50 of the area lies to the left of the mean and .50 of the area lies to the right of the mean. Since we have .025 in each tail where our alpha is, we find the area of the curve and then our *z* score by taking the difference .50 – .025 = .4750. So we must go into the body of the *z* table and find the area .4750 or as close as you can to .4750. The *z* score that corresponds to .4750 of the normal curve (.50 – .025) is 1.96 (from Table B.2 of Appendix B). To repeat, to find this *z* score, simply go into the body of the table until you see the proportion .4750; the *z* score for this proportion is 1.96. Since we are interested in both tails of the distribution, our *z* score is ±1.96. In Table 7.2, we provide a list of some common confidence intervals and their corresponding *z* scores.

You know from the previous chapter that the term ($\sigma_{\bar{X}}$) in formula 7-1 is the standard deviation of the sampling distribution, or the standard error. In cases where the standard deviation of the population is known, we can easily determine the standard error of the sampling distribution by dividing the population standard deviation by the square root of the sample size ($\sigma/\sqrt{n}$). When we know the population standard deviation, then, the standard error of the sampling distribution can be directly determined, and we can create our confidence intervals from formula 7-1.

It is rarely the case, however, that we know the standard deviation of our population. If we knew it, we would probably also be in a good position to know the mean, so our point estimate and confidence interval construction would be unnecessary. Most of the time, then, we do not know our population standard deviation, and the standard error of the sampling distribution must be estimated. If the sample size is large enough, we can use our sample standard deviation (*s*) to estimate the population standard deviation (σ) and then use the *z* distribution to obtain the critical value needed for our confidence interval. The sample estimate of the standard deviation of the sampling distribution is:

$$\frac{s}{\sqrt{n}}$$

and the formula for our confidence interval is:

$$\bar{X} \pm z_\alpha \left( \frac{s}{\sqrt{n}} \right) \tag{7-2}$$

Let's go through an example.

---

## Case Study

## Estimating Alcohol Consumption for College Students

Suppose that we conducted a survey from a random sample of 140 undergraduate university students from a state university, asking them about the number of drinks of alcohol they consumed during the last 30 days. One objective of the study was to estimate (make an inference about) the average number of drinks per month that undergraduate students attending this university ingests. The population we are interested in making an inference about is all undergraduate students at that university, but since that population is too large for us to study, we took a simple random sample of 140 students. The sample statistics we obtained were as follows:

$$\bar{X} = 12.4$$
$$s = 8.2$$
$$n = 140$$

The sample mean tells us that, on average, the students from our sample have an average of 12.4 alcoholic drinks per month. To remind you, this sample statistic ( $\bar{X}$ ) is referred to as our point estimate of the true population parameter ($\mu$). What does our sample mean tell us about the mean of the entire population of university students? This is the question we are really trying to answer. We don't think that the average number of alcoholic drinks an undergraduate has is exactly equal to 12.4, but it is our best guess, or our point estimate. We can't simply report that our best guess is 12.4 drinks per month without formally stating our level of confidence with a margin of error. To do this, we use formula 7-2 to construct a 95% confidence interval around the sample mean estimate of 12.4 using the critical value of $z$ of 1.96 obtained from Table 7.2 as follows:

**95% Confidence Interval (c.i.) of Drinks per Month for University Students 95%**

$$95\% \text{ c.i.} = 12.4 \pm 1.96 \left( \frac{8.2}{\sqrt{140}} \right)$$

$$95\% \text{ c.i.} = 12.4 \pm 1.96 \left( \frac{8.2}{11.83} \right)$$

$$95\% \text{ c.i.} = 12.4 \pm 1.96(.69)$$

$$95\% \text{ c.i.} = 12.4 \pm 1.35$$

To find the confidence interval for our mean, we simply subtract 1.35 from the mean of 12.4 to get what is called the lower limit of our confidence interval, and then add 1.35 to the mean of 12.4 to get our upper limit:

$$12.4 - 1.35 = 11.05$$

$$12.4 + 1.35 = 13.75$$

$$95\% \text{ c.i.} = 11.05 \text{ to } 13.75 \text{ alcoholic drinks per month}$$

What does this interval tell us? First of all, it tells us that our point estimate of the number of monthly drinks that undergraduate students in the population imbibe is 12.4 and the 1.35 drinks per month is our margin of error. Second, it tells us that, based on our sample data, we can be 95% confident that the mean number of drinks that university students in the population consume per month lies between 11.05 and 13.75. The correct interpretation is that if we had taken a large number of random samples from this same population (undergraduate students at this university) and calculated a 95% confidence interval around the mean obtained from each sample, approximately 95% of these intervals would include the true population mean ($\mu$) and 5% would not (this 5% of the intervals that would not contain our population parameter is our margin of error). Another way to express this confidence interval would be:

$$11.05 \leq \mu \leq 13.75 \text{ drinks per month}$$

Or, simply, (11.05,13.75).

We are 95% confident that the mean number of monthly drinks in the undergraduate university population is greater than or equal to 11.05 and less than or equal to 13.75.

To illustrate how levels of confidence affect the size of the confidence interval, let's create a 90% confidence interval around the same sample mean, rather than a 95% confidence interval. From Table 7.2 we see that the $z$ score corresponding to an alpha level ($\alpha$) of .10, or a 90% confidence interval, is 1.65. As before, using formula 7-2 and the same sample mean, standard deviation, and $n$, we construct our confidence interval as follows:

$$90\% \text{c.i.} = 12.4 \pm 1.65 \left( \frac{8.2}{\sqrt{140}} \right)$$

$$90\% \text{c.i.} = 12.4 \pm 1.65(.69)$$

$$90\% \text{c.i.} = 12.4 \pm 1.14$$

$$90\% \text{c.i.} = 11.26 \text{ to } 13.54 \text{ drinks per month}$$

$$11.26 \leq \mu \leq 13.54$$

This interval indicates that we are 90% confident that the true mean number of drinks per month in the population of undergraduate university students falls between 11.26 and 13.54 drinks. Note that the 90% confidence interval is slightly narrower than the 95% confidence interval, but the trade-off is that we are less confident (90% compared with 95% confident) that our true population mean falls into this interval. By lowering our level of confidence, we gained some precision in our estimate. We could reduce the width of our confidence interval even more, but we would have to pay the price in a lower level of confidence. Similarly, if we wanted to increase our confidence, say using a 99% confidence level, how would our confidence interval changed? If you thought it would have increased, you would be correct!

One way to decrease the width of our interval without compromising our level of confidence would be to increase our sample size. Why? Remember that a large standard error (like a large standard deviation) indicates that the mean varies a great deal from sample to sample, whereas a small standard error indicates that there is little variation from sample to sample. Intuitively, then, as the size of the standard error decreases, the level of confidence we have in any one sample estimate typically increases. The larger the sample size ($n$), the smaller the standard error will be (or our estimate of the standard error). Less sample-to-sample variation indicates that we can be more confident that our sample statistic represents the true population parameter.

Let us state this principle another way. If the standard error of the sampling distribution of means is small, then all samples drawn from a given population will have fairly similar means. The means from these samples will cluster tightly about the true population mean ($\mu$). In this case, any given sample mean will be a relatively good estimate of the population mean. We therefore will have a smaller (narrower) confidence interval. The smaller the sample size, the larger the standard deviation of the sampling distribution (the standard error) will be, and the larger the standard error, the larger the confidence interval. So if you want to increase your precision (decrease the width of your interval), but you do not want to change your level of confidence, acquiring a larger sample is the key. In fact, as you will see in the next section, when we have very small sample sizes (less than 30), we must use another sampling distribution to create confidence intervals. Since virtually every statistic we will cover in this text includes a term in the formula to quantify the standard error of its sampling distribution, we will return to this concept again and again and again. But it should make intuitive sense. With a large random sample compared with a small random sample, we are more likely to have captured the true population parameter!

## Case Study

## Probation Officer Behavior

Because repetition is the key to acquiring skill, let's go through another example from the literature. In an article in the journal *Justice Quarterly*, Joel Miller (2015) examined the role of community corrections officers who perform probation officer duties. More than 1,700 probation officers were sampled from the population of members of the American

Probation and Parole Association and completed a questionnaire. One item on the questionnaire asked how much they relied on reminding probationers of the legal consequences of their behavior. This item was designed to measure a component of the law enforcement duties that probation officers have, that is, to remind those under their supervision about the legal consequences of their behavior. The response options provided for the probation officers ranged on a seven point continuum from 0 (never) to 6 (always). The mean response for this item was 4.69 (much closer to "always" than "never") with a standard deviation of 1.34. Let's construct a 95% confidence interval around this sample mean but assume that the sample size was 200 ($n = 200$):

$$95\% \text{c.i.} = 4.69 \pm 1.96 \left( \frac{1.34}{\sqrt{200}} \right)$$

$$95\% \text{c.i.} = 4.69 \pm 1.96 \left( \frac{1.34}{14.14} \right)$$

$$95\% \text{c.i.} = 4.69 \pm 1.96(.095)$$

$$95\% \text{c.i.} = 4.69 \pm .186$$

$$95\% \text{c.i.} = 4.504 \text{ to } 4.876$$

$$4.504 \leq \mu \leq 4.876$$

How would you interpret this interval? As we explained at the beginning of this book, we believe that the ability to interpret statistical results is just as important as the ability to calculate them. So even though we have asked it before, the question "How would you interpret this?" is not merely rhetorical. This 95% confidence interval indicates that we can be 95% confident, based on our sample statistics, that in the population of all probation officers that are members of this professional organization, the mean number of times they remind those under their supervision about the legal consequences of their behavior is between 4.504 and 4.876 on a scale where 0 equals never and 6 equals always. This suggests that reminding their clients of the possible legal consequences of their actions is a fairly common strategy used by probation officers in their practice.

Let's now take the same data, and instead of constructing a 95% confidence interval, let's increase the confidence we have in our interval estimate by calculating a 99% interval. The only change that is necessary in the formula is the critical value of $z$. Because we have increased the level of confidence we wish to have about our point estimate ($\overline{X}$), the critical value of $z$ increases from 1.96 to 2.58 (Table 7.2). Using formula 7-2, the calculation of the 99% interval is:

$$99\% \text{c.i.} = 4.69 \pm 2.58 \left( \frac{1.34}{\sqrt{200}} \right)$$

$$99\% \text{c.i.} = 4.69 \pm 2.58 \left( \frac{1.34}{14.14} \right)$$

$$99\% \text{c.i.} = 4.69 \pm 2.58(.095)$$

$$99\% \text{c.i.} = 4.69 \pm .245$$

$$99\% \text{c.i.} = 4.445 \text{ to } 4.925$$

$$4.445 \leq \mu \leq 4.925$$

This 99% confidence interval indicates that we can be 99% confident, based on our sample statistics, that in the population of all probation officers that are members of this professional organization, the mean number of times they remind those under their supervision about the legal consequences of their behavior is between 4.445 and 4.925. Note that this 99% confidence interval is wider than that from the same data with only a 95% confidence interval. We wanted to be more confident that our interval contains the population mean with the 99% confidence interval, and this increased confidence comes at the price of a wider confidence interval. By now, this should be making sense to you. It suggests that if we want to be more confident that the true population mean falls in our estimated interval, we have to make the interval wider (everything else staying equal). To reiterate, greater confidence comes at a price, and the price we pay is the precision (width) of the confidence interval.

---

Think for a minute about this question: "If we want to be more confident without increasing the size of the interval, what can we do?" If your answer was to increase our sample size, you were right! A confidence interval will be smaller with a larger sample size because when the standard deviation of the sampling distribution (standard error) is reduced, the sample value is a more accurate estimate of the true population mean.

After all of this discussion of different confidence levels, you may be asking yourself, "When do we want to use a 99% confidence interval compared with a 95% interval or even a 90% interval? What guides us in selecting a level of confidence?" Unfortunately, there are no hard-and-fast rules for this. The decision you make is in part a judgment call that depends on the nature of your research and on the importance of having high confidence weighed against having a slightly larger confidence interval. Just remember that there is usually a trade-off between confidence and precision. Generally speaking, at a fixed sample size you will get a smaller interval, and therefore more precision, with lower levels of confidence. The lower your confidence, however, the less sure you are that your interval contains the true population mean. If you want greater confidence that your interval actually contains the population mean, increase your confidence level. The trade-off you make in doing this is a larger confidence interval (unless you increase your sample size). In general, however, the 95% level of confidence is fairly standard in the criminology and criminal justice literature as well as in the popular media.

## 🔲 Estimating Confidence Intervals for a Mean With a Small Sample

In constructing confidence intervals with formula 7-2, we used the sample standard deviation to estimate the population standard deviation. When our sample size is large (recall from Chapter 6 that when the sample size is at least 30, the assumption of a normal population can generally be relaxed), the sample standard deviation is a fairly good estimate of $\sigma$. This is not true, however, when our sample size is small. In the case of small sample sizes ($n < 30$), the sample standard deviation shows substantial variation from sample to sample. For small samples, therefore, the standard deviation of the sampling distribution (standard error) is greater than for large samples. The practical implication of this is that the $z$ distribution cannot be used for constructing confidence intervals when the sample size is small because the sampling distribution cannot be assumed to be approximately normal.

There are many times, however, when we must rely on small samples. In instances such as this, the assumptions we make about the normal distribution do not apply. Why? Well, recall that the properties of the central limit theorem (described in the last chapter) applied only to large samples. Therefore, if our sample is small, we must use statistics that do not invoke this "large sample" assumption.

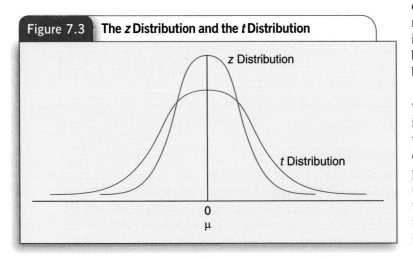

**Figure 7.3** The *z* Distribution and the *t* Distribution

z Distribution

t Distribution

0
μ

When our research dictates that we have no choice and must use a small sample, Student's $t$ distribution is typically used to make inferences from the sample mean, $\overline{X}$, to the population mean, $\mu$, instead of the $z$ distribution.

The theoretical sampling distribution called Student's $t$ was calculated by W. E. Gosset and published in 1908. Gosset was a statistician for the Guinness brewing company. Although Guinness did not usually allow its employees to publish their own work, Gosset was permitted to do so under the pen name of "Student." Hence, his distribution has been called Student's $t$ distribution.

The $t$ distribution is flatter and has a greater spread (fatter at the tails) than the $z$ distribution, which indicates that there is more sample-to-sample variability in the former. The two sampling distributions are shown in Figure 7.3. There is a different $t$ distribution for each sample size, and the smaller the sample size, the flatter the $t$ distribution is, compared with the normal distribution. Just like the standard normal distribution ($z$), the $t$ distribution has several known properties, which are listed in Table 7.3.

As noted in Table 7.3, there are actually many $t$ distributions, depending on the **degrees of freedom (df)** present in the sample. As the sample size (and $df$) becomes larger, the $t$ distribution more closely approximates the standard normal distribution ($z$ distribution). When $n > 120$, the two distributions are virtually identical, but the $t$ distribution will always be flatter and fatter at the tails than the $z$ distribution. The values of $t$ associated with these degrees of freedom at differ- ent levels of alpha ($\alpha$) and for one- and two-tailed hypothesis tests are displayed

> **Degrees of freedom (df):** Value necessary along with a given alpha value to determine the critical value and region for a null hypothesis test or for a confidence interval.

in Table B.3 in Appendix B. Remember that by definition, confidence intervals are two-tailed tests because we do not know whether our sample statistic is greater than or less than the true population value. For confidence intervals, then, we always use values of $t$ associated with a two-tailed test (see Table B.3) since we are creating an interval by going around a sample statistic and, therefore, using both tails of the sampling distribution.

Let's say we had a sample size of $n = 10$ and wanted to make an inference to the population mean at the 95% level. With this, we would go into the $t$ table using $\alpha = .05$ for a two-tailed test. We next have to find the degrees of freedom associated with our sample size, which in the case of confidence intervals is $n - 1$, giving us a $df$ equal to 9 ($10 - 1 = 9$). Going down the alpha column of $\alpha = .05$ for a two-tailed test to the row that lists 9 degrees of freedom, we would obtain a critical value of $t = 2.262$. That is the value that we would plug into the formula for our $t$-based confidence interval.

In Table B.3, note that when the sample size is greater than 100, the critical values of $t$ are about the same as those for $z$, and that when the sample size is greater than 120 (at the infinity symbol sign), they are identical. This reflects the fourth property listed in Table 7.3, which states that as the sample size approximates 120, the $t$ distribution begins to look more and more like the $z$ distribution. This should make intuitive sense to you based on our discussion in the last chapter.

The formula for calculating a confidence interval around a mean using the $t$ distribution is shown as follows. It looks almost exactly like that employed when calculating confidence intervals using the $z$ distribution, doesn't it? That's because it is the same except that we use the $t$ value from the $t$ table rather than the $z$ value from the $z$ table:

$$\overline{X} \pm t_\alpha(\sigma_{\overline{X}}) = \overline{X} \pm t_\alpha\left(\frac{s}{\sqrt{n}}\right) \tag{7-3}$$

---

**Table 7.3** **Properties of the Sampling Distribution of $t$**

1. The $t$ distribution is bell-shaped and symmetrical and centers around $t = 0$.

2. The $t$ distribution is flatter and has fatter tails than the $z$ distribution.

3. There are many different $t$ distributions based on the sample size. More specifically, the distribution of $t$ that we use for our statistical test is based on a parameter called the degrees of freedom ($df$). The number of degrees of freedom is different for different kinds of statistical problems. For confidence intervals, there are $n - 1$ degrees of freedom, where $n$ is the sample size.

4. With sample sizes of 120 or more, the $t$ distribution becomes virtually identical to the $z$ distribution.

## Case Study

## Work-Role Overload in Policing

Let's go through an example of making inferences about μ with a small sample using the *t* distribution. Linda Duxbury, Chris Higgins, and Michael Halinski (2015) developed a study to measure what they called "work-role overload" in policing. Work-role overload occurs when police officers experience stress and anxieties because of the demands of the different duties, obstacles, and organizational demands they face in their policing job. For example, police feel stress and overwhelmed because of the emotional demands of the job, the excessive paper work, unpredict-

| Police Officers' Overload Score in Our Sample |
|:---:|
| $\bar{X} = 31$ |
| $s = 3$ |
| $n = 14$ |

able work schedules, financial limitations, and the demands made by supervisors. The ultimate objective of the study was to design an instrument to measure this role overload.

Suppose we were interested in using this work-role overload data collection instrument in our own study of police in a large urban police department. The department has thousands of police officers (this is our population), and we take a random sample of 14 officers for our study. The mean score on the overload measure for our officers was 31, with a standard deviation of 3. Let's assume the actual overload measure has a low of 0, indicating no perceived overload, and a high of 50, indicating the maximum score possible on the overload scale. The point estimate for the average work overload from our sample of offic-

ers was 31, and to generalize this point estimate to the entire department, we want to build a 95% confidence interval around that estimate. Since we have such a small sample, we cannot invoke the central limit theorem and must use the *t* distribution for our confidence interval.

The first step involves calculating the degrees of freedom and finding the critical value of *t*. With a sample size of 14, our degrees of freedom are equal to 13 ($n - 1$). We first note that we look for a two-tailed *t* because all confidence intervals are two-tailed tests (we use a two-tailed test for the *t*, which is the same as dividing our alpha level by 2 as we did with the *z* table doing confidence intervals with a large sample), then we find our alpha level of .05 (since we have a 95% confidence interval), then we go down the rows until we find our degrees of freedom (13). Going down the appropriate column and across the appropriate row in the *t* table (Appendix B, Table B.3), you find the critical value needed is 2.160. Remember that the selection of the confidence level (and the corresponding critical value) is up to you. Once you have this, you can construct your confidence interval with formula 7-3:

$$95\% \text{ c.i.} = 31 \pm 2.160 \left( \frac{3}{\sqrt{14}} \right)$$

$$95\% \text{ c.i.} = 31 \pm 2.160 \left( \frac{3}{3.74} \right)$$

$$95\% \text{ c.i.} = 31 \pm 2.160(.80)$$

$$95\% \text{ c.i.} = 31 \pm 1.73$$

$$95\% \text{ c.i.} = 29.27 \text{ to } 32.73$$

$$29.27 \leq \mu \leq 32.73 \text{ overload score}$$

**Confidence limits:** Numerical lower and upper values that correspond to any given confidence interval around a point estimate from the sample.

As before, to find the lower and upper **confidence limits,** we add 1.73 to, and subtract 1.73 from, our sample mean of 31. This interval tells us that based on our sample data, we can be 95% confident that the mean work overload of police officers in the city police department is between 29.27 and 32.73. If we had taken a large number of random same-sized samples from this same population of police officers and calculated 95% confidence intervals around the means obtained from each sample, approximately 95% of these intervals would include the true population mean, μ, and 5% would not.

| Female Police Officers' Scores on Work Overload Test | Male Police Officers' Scores on Work Overload Test |
|---|---|
| $\bar{X} = 41.9$ | $\bar{X} = 32.5$ |
| $s = 7.8$ | $s = 9.3$ |
| $n = 15$ | $n = 15$ |

Note the difference between the critical value in this confidence interval for small samples and that for the same 95% confidence interval we calculated earlier for large samples. If we had had a larger sample in this case, we could have used the critical $z$ value of 1.96 instead of the larger $t$ value of 2.160 that was necessary here. To reiterate the reasoning behind this, remember that since the $t$ distribution is flatter than the $z$ distribution and fatter at the tails, we have to go farther out in the tail to find our critical region. At the same alpha level, with small sample sizes, the critical value of $t$ will be larger than the large sample $z$.

For the $t$ distribution, the relationships among confidence levels, sample sizes, and confidence intervals are still the same. At a fixed sample size, decreasing the confidence level will narrow the confidence interval, and increasing the confidence level will widen the confidence interval. The confidence interval can be narrowed (even when increasing the confidence level) by increasing the sample size.

Let's work with two more examples using the Duxbury et al. (2015) study. Let's assume that the police work overload test they developed ranged from a low of 0, meaning absolutely no work overload stress, to a maximum of 50, meaning that the different demands of police work are completely overwhelming. Let's also assume that we drew a sample of 15 male officers and 15 female officers from the same city police department and gave them the work overload instrument. It turned out that the mean score for the males was 32.5, with a standard deviation of 9.3, and the mean score of the females was 41.9, with a standard deviation of 7.8. Let's build a 99% confidence interval around each of these two estimates. First, the information for males and females is in the box above and to the right.

The first step in this procedure is to find our $t$ value. We go to the $t$ table in Appendix B (Table B.3) knowing that this is a two-tailed test; then we find our alpha level of .01, and we go down the row to find our degrees of freedom. With a sample size of 15, our degrees of freedom are equal to 14 ($n - 1$). Going down the appropriate column and across the appropriate row in the $t$ table (Appendix B, Table B.3), you find that the critical value needed is 2.977. The 99% confidence interval for female officers is:

$$99\% \text{ c.i.} = 41.9 \pm 2.977 \left( \frac{7.8}{\sqrt{15}} \right)$$

$$99\% \text{ c.i.} = 41.9 \pm 2.977 \left( \frac{7.8}{3.87} \right)$$

$$99\% \text{ c.i.} = 41.9 \pm 2.977(2.02)$$

$$99\% \text{ c.i.} = 41.9 \pm 6.01$$

$$99\% \text{ c.i.} = 35.89 \text{ to } 47.91$$

$$35.89 \leq \mu_{females} \leq 47.91$$

This interval tells us that based on our sample data, we can be 99% confident that the mean score for the females on the work overload scale is between 35.89 and 47.91. The female population mean is, therefore, estimated to be at the upper or overwhelmed end of the scale.

The 99% confidence interval for the male officers is:

$$99\% \text{ c.i.} = 32.5 \pm 2.977 \left( \frac{9.3}{\sqrt{15}} \right)$$

$$99\% \text{ c.i.} = 32.5 \pm 2.977 \left( \frac{9.3}{3.87} \right)$$

$$99\%\,\text{c.i.} = 32.5 \pm 2.977(2.40)$$
$$99\%\,\text{c.i.} = 32.5 \pm 7.14$$
$$99\%\,\text{c.i.} = 25.36 \text{ to } 39.64$$

$$25.36 \leq \mu_{\text{males}} \leq 39.64$$

This confidence interval tells us that based on our sample data, we can be 99% confident that the mean score for the males on the work overload scale is between 25.36 and 39.64. For both females and males, if we had taken a large number of random same-size samples from this same population of police officers and calculated 99% confidence intervals around the means obtained from each sample, approximately 99% of these intervals would include the true population mean $\mu$, and 1% would not.

Suppose we wanted to decrease our interval but did not want to gather more data. We would have to decrease our level of confidence to 95%. The degrees of freedom necessary to find the critical value of $t$ for a 95% confidence interval would still be 14 ($n - 1$), but we would select an alpha ($\alpha$) level of .05 instead of the .01 level of alpha we used for the 99% confidence interval earlier. From Table B.3, we see that the critical value of $t$ for this interval becomes 2.145 and the computation of the confidence interval for the female officers is as follows:

$$95\%\,\text{c.i.} = 41.9 \pm 2.145\left(\frac{7.8}{\sqrt{15}}\right)$$
$$95\%\,\text{c.i.} = 41.9 \pm 2.145\left(\frac{7.8}{3.87}\right)$$
$$95\%\,\text{c.i.} = 41.9 \pm 2.145(2.02)$$
$$95\%\,\text{c.i.} = 41.9 \pm 4.33$$
$$95\%\,\text{c.i.} = 37.57 \text{ to } 46.23$$

$$37.57 \leq \mu_{\text{females}} \leq 46.23$$

Note that the interval got narrower with this change from the 99% to the 95% level of confidence. The advantage of being less confident is to have more precision in our point estimate. Now we can say, however, that we are 95% confident that the population mean of female police officers on the work overload scale is between 37.57 and 46.23. We now have a 5% probability ($\alpha = .05$)—of not including the true population mean female workload scale in our confidence interval.

Let's now estimate this same 95% confidence level for the female officers and assume that we had a sample size of 30 rather than 15. To find the necessary critical value of $t$, we now enter Table B.3 with 29 degrees of freedom ($30 - 1 = 29$). The critical value necessary for this confidence interval is 2.045 ($df = 29$, $\alpha = .05$). The confidence interval in this case would be:

$$95\%\,\text{c.i.} = 41.9 \pm 2.045\left(\frac{7.8}{\sqrt{30}}\right)$$
$$95\%\,\text{c.i.} = 41.9 \pm 2.045\left(\frac{7.8}{5.48}\right)$$
$$95\%\,\text{c.i.} = 41.9 \pm 2.045(1.42)$$
$$95\%\,\text{c.i.} = 41.9 \pm 2.90$$
$$95\%\,\text{c.i.} = 39.00 \text{ to } 44.80$$

$$39.00 \leq \mu_{\text{females}} \leq 44.80$$

As shown, with a 95% confidence level and a sample size of 30, our confidence interval is 39.00 to 44.80. This interval is narrower than the interval at the same confidence level for an $n$ of 15. This is because the estimated standard deviation of the sampling distribution:

$$\frac{s}{\sqrt{n}}$$

gets smaller when the sample size is increased, and our value of $t$ from the $t$ table gets smaller. In the example with $n = 15$, the standard error was 2.02. When we increased our sample size to 30, the standard error was reduced to 1.42. The value of $t$ in our calculations went from 2.145 to 2.045. The confidence intervals for our female officers at each level of confidence and sample size were as follows:

$$n = 15, 95\% \text{ confidence interval} = 37.57 - 46.23$$

$$n = 15, 99\% \text{ confidence interval} = 35.89 - 47.91$$

$$n = 30, 95\% \text{ confidence interval} = 39.00 - 44.80$$

As you can see, when the sample size is the same, confidence intervals for 99% will be larger compared with those for 95%. To decrease the size of the interval at any level of confidence, you can increase your sample size!

---

## ▣ Estimating Confidence Intervals for Proportions and Percentages With a Large Sample

Compared with the confidence intervals around means that we have just examined, you are perhaps more familiar with confidence intervals constructed around proportions and percentages. The media bombard us with examples of these all the time. As we said earlier, results of opinion polls are usually quickly followed by a phrase such as "plus or minus 3%." This is one way of presenting a confidence interval to the public in a way they will better understand. The calculation of a confidence interval around a proportion when you have a large sample is done by using the $z$ distribution and the following formula:

$$\text{Confidence interval} = \hat{p} \pm z_\alpha (\sigma_p)$$

(7–4)

where

$$\hat{p} = \text{sample proportion}$$

$$\sigma_p = \sqrt{\frac{P(1-P)}{N}}$$

It is fairly easy to determine whether you have a large enough sample to use the $z$ probability distribution. If $\hat{p}$ is the sample proportion estimated from the data, and $\hat{q} = 1 - \hat{p}$, and $n$ is your sample size, then the following two conditions must both be true for you to use the $z$ probability distribution: $n\hat{p} > 5$ and $n\hat{q} > 5$. With a large sample, sample proportions have sampling distributions that are approximately normal with a mean equal to the true population proportion ($P$) and a standard deviation ($\sigma_p$) equal to:

$$\sigma_p = \sqrt{\frac{P(1-P)}{N}}$$

The latter term is referred to as the **standard error of the proportion**. The estimation of confidence intervals for a small sample is not that straightforward, so we will work only with proportions from large samples in this chapter.

In formula 7-4, the value of $\hat{p}$ in the confidence interval formula is the sample proportion. It is the sample point estimate ($\hat{p}$) of the unknown population parameter ($P$). As with the confidence interval for the mean with large samples, $z$ is the critical value of $z$ we obtain from the standard normal table. As before, the precise value of $z$ depends on the particular confidence level we select. Note, however, that the standard error of the proportion is based on the population proportion ($P$)—a quantity that we do not know and are in fact trying to estimate with our sample statistic ($\hat{p}$). Since $P$ is not known, it must be estimated, and consequently, the standard error of the proportion also must be estimated. We estimate it using the sample proportion ($\hat{p}$). In most instances when we have a large sample, this will be a reasonable solution, and the sample proportion will provide a good estimate of the population proportion. In sum, we simply substitute $\hat{p}$ for $P$ in the previous formula, substitute our sample size $n$ for the population size $N$, and proceed with construction of the confidence interval. In this approach, the estimated standard error of the proportion is:

$$\sigma_p = \sqrt{\frac{\hat{p}(1-\hat{p})}{n}}$$

where $\hat{p}$ = sample proportion and $n$ is the sample size. So, the formula for our large sample confidence interval for proportions is:

$$\text{Confidence interval} = \hat{p} \pm z_\alpha \left( \sqrt{\frac{\hat{p}(1-\hat{p})}{n}} \right) \tag{7-5}$$

## Case Study

## Estimating the Effects of Community Policing

Many police departments across the United States have adopted a policing innovation called "community oriented policing," or (naturally) COP for short. Community policing is designed to increase the frequency of police–citizen encounters, which is then expected to improve relationships between the police and community residents. Jihong Zhao and Ling Ren (2015) conducted a study of public attitudes toward the police with telephone surveys in Houston, Texas. Let's assume we conduct a similar study in a small Midwestern city and find that 33% of our sample of 100 ($n = 100$) are not satisfied with the police. The sample proportion of .33, then, would be our point estimate. Let's construct 95% and 99% confidence intervals around this sample estimate. First, let's verify we can use the $z$ probability distribution here and our large sample formula. Since $\hat{p} = .33$, $.33 \times 100 = 33$, which is greater than 5, and since $\hat{q} = .67$, $.67 \times 100$ is also greater than 5, we can use the large sample formula for proportions. Since we have large samples, we can use the critical value of $z$ at the $\alpha = .05$ and .01 levels. First, the calculations for the 95% confidence interval:

$$95\% \text{ Confidence interval} = \hat{p} \pm z_\alpha \left( \sqrt{\frac{\hat{p}(1-\hat{p})}{n}} \right)$$

$$95\% \text{ Confidence interval} = .33 \pm 1.96 \left( \sqrt{\frac{.33(.67)}{100}} \right)$$

$$95\% \text{ Confidence interval} = .33 \pm 1.96\left(\sqrt{.002}\right)$$

$$95\% \text{ Confidence interval} = .33 \pm 1.96(.045)$$

$$95\% \text{ Confidence interval} = .33 \pm .09$$

$$95\% \text{ Confidence interval} = .24 \text{ to } .42$$

$$.24 \le P \le .42$$

To find the lower limit of our confidence interval, we subtracted .09 from our point estimate of .33, and to find the upper limit, we added .09 to our point estimate. We then converted these proportions to percentages by multiplying each limit by 100. We have 95% confidence that the true proportion of the population in our city who are not satisfied with the police is between .24 and .42 or between 24% and 42%.

Now the calculations for a 99% confidence interval:

$$99\% \text{ Confidence interval} = \hat{p} \pm z_\alpha\left(\sqrt{\frac{\hat{p}(1-\hat{p})}{n}}\right)$$

$$99\% \text{ Confidence interval} = .33 \pm 2.58\left(\sqrt{\frac{.33(.67)}{100}}\right)$$

$$99\% \text{ Confidence interval} = .33 \pm 2.58\left(\sqrt{.002}\right)$$

$$99\% \text{ Confidence interval} = .33 \pm 2.58(.045)$$

$$99\% \text{ Confidence interval} = .33 \pm .12$$

$$99\% \text{ Confidence interval} = .21 \text{ to } .45$$

$$.21 \le P \le .45$$

By interpreting this interval, we can say we have 99% confidence that the true proportion of citizens who are not satisfied with the police is between .21 and .45 or between 21% and 45%. Again, notice that when we went from a 95% confidence interval to a 99% confidence interval with the same sample size, the width of our interval increased. The price to be paid by greater confidence is less precision.

---

## Case Study

## Clearing Homicides

Let's go through another quick example. Jason Rydberg and Jesenia M. Pizarro (2014) were interested in explaining the time it takes police to clear a homicide by an arrest. They had a theory, lifestyle theory, which hypothesized that if the victim were involved in a "deviant lifestyle," it would take the police longer to solve the homicide. The connection between being involved in a deviant lifestyle and a longer clearance rate for homicides was the expectation that law enforcement would in essence be more indifferent to solving the murder of a victim who may also have been less than lawful. This lifestyle theory had been used in the past to explain who is likely to become a homicide victim, but Rydberg and Pizarro were the first to use the theory to explain homicide clearances. By using data from the Newark, New Jersey Police Department's Homicide Unit, they found that the more indicators of a deviant lifestyle for a victim (for example, the victim was a gang member, drug dealer, or had a criminal history), the longer it took for the police to solve the homicide.

Let's assume we did a related study by examining a sample of gang-related homicides and finding the proportion of them that were cleared by an arrest within one year in a northeastern city. From our sample of 150 gang-related homicides, we find that 58% were cleared within one year. Our point estimate of the proportion of gang-related homicides in the northeastern city that were cleared by an arrest, then, would be .58. Let's build a 95% confidence interval around that point estimate:

$$95\% \text{ c.i.} = .58 \pm 1.96\sqrt{\frac{.58(1-.58)}{150}}$$

$$95\% \text{ c.i.} = .58 \pm 1.96\sqrt{\frac{.58(.42)}{150}}$$

$$95\% \text{ c.i.} = .58 \pm 1.96\sqrt{\frac{.24}{150}}$$

$$95\% \text{ c.i.} = .58 \pm 1.96\sqrt{.0016}$$

$$95\% \text{ c.i.} = .58 \pm 1.96(.04)$$

$$95\% \text{ c.i.} = .58 \pm .078$$

$$95\% \text{ c.i.} = .502 \text{ to } .658, \text{ or } 50.2\% \text{ to } 65.8\%$$

$$.502 \leq P \leq .658$$

To determine the lower limit of our confidence interval, we simply subtract .078 from the sample point estimate of .58, and to determine the upper limit, we add .078 to our point estimate of .58. Our 95% confidence interval of the proportion of gang-related homicides in this city cleared by an arrest is between .502 and .658, or between 50.2% and 65.8%. This is quite a large interval. How could we make our confidence interval narrower without losing any confidence? We hope your immediate answer was, "*Increase the sample size!*"

## 🔲 Summary

In this chapter we have examined the procedures for estimating population parameters using confidence intervals. To estimate confidence intervals around a $\overline{X}$ obtained from a large sample, we examined estimation procedures based on the $z$ distribution. We also examined the formula based on the $t$ distribution used to construct confidence intervals around means obtained from small samples. We concluded the chapter by examining the estimation procedures used to construct confidence intervals around proportions and percentages with a large sample.

Each type of interval could have been constructed using any level of confidence (e.g., 75%, 88%, 95%, etc.). However, we focused on confidence levels of 95% and 99% since these are the levels typically used in all disciplines including criminology and criminal justice. We discussed the trade-offs made when adopting particular levels of confidence: at the same sample size, higher levels of confidence (e.g., 99% compared with 95%) produce wider intervals. So while you gain confidence in your estimation, you also lose precision. Smaller samples always inflate the standard error of the sampling distribution you are working with, thereby increasing the width of a confidence interval. Thus, larger samples are more desirable than smaller ones because whether we are estimating a population mean or proportion, the larger the sample the more precise our sample statistic is.

# Key Terms

> Review key terms with eFlashcards. **$SAGE** edge™

confidence interval    187
confidence level    191
confidence limits    198
degrees of freedom (*df*)    197
point estimates    187

population parameter    187
sample statistic    187
standard error of the mean    191
standard error of the
    proportion    202

*t* distribution
    (Student's *t* distribution)    190
*z* distribution    190

# Key Formulas

Confidence interval around a sample mean with large samples (equation 7-2):

$$\bar{X} \pm z_\alpha(\sigma_{\bar{x}}) = z_\alpha\left(\frac{s}{\sqrt{n}}\right)$$

Confidence interval around a sample proportion with large samples (equation 7-5):

$$\hat{p} \pm z_\alpha(\sigma_p) = z_\alpha\sqrt{\frac{\hat{p}(1-\hat{p})}{n}}$$

Confidence interval around a sample mean with small samples (equation 7-3):

$$\bar{X} \pm t_\alpha(\sigma_{\bar{x}}) = \bar{X} \pm t_\alpha\left(\frac{s}{\sqrt{n}}\right)$$

# Practice Problems

> Test your understanding of chapter content.
> Take the practice quiz. **$SAGE** edge™

1. What is the purpose of confidence intervals?

2. Describe the differences between the *z* distribution and the *t* distribution. When is it appropriate to use the *z* distribution for estimation procedures?

3. A hypothetical study concerned with estimating th187e amount of marijuana use per year among a teenage population obtained a sample of 110 high-school students. With the following sample statistics, construct a 95% confidence interval around the mean number of times this sample uses marijuana in a given 6-month period:

$$\bar{X} = 4.5 \text{ times per year}$$

$$s = 3.2$$

$$n = 110$$

What does the interval you constructed tell us about marijuana use in the population? Interpret these results.

4. By using the same mean and standard deviations as in problem 3, change the sample size to 25 and construct a confidence interval around the mean using the appropriate procedures. How does the interval change? Provide an interpretation for your interval.

5. What does the standard deviation of the sampling distribution of the mean tell us? What affects the size of the standard error?

6. In a 2014 article, Evan McCuish, Raymond Corrado, Patrick Lussier, and Stephen D. Hart investigated the role of psychopathic traits in determining patterns of offending from adolescence into adulthood. They found those with psychopathic traits were far more likely to have more serious offending trajectories. Let's say you have a sample of 20 young males who have been in

juvenile institutions at least twice. The mean psychopathic trait score for these 20 males was 18 with a standard deviation of 4. Build a 99% confidence interval around this point estimate.

7. A mayor of a large city wants to know how long it takes the police in his city to respond to a call for service. In a random sample of 15 citizens who called the police for service, the mayor's research director found that the average response time was 560 seconds, with a standard deviation of 45 seconds. Construct a 95% confidence interval around your point estimate. What would you say to your mayor?

8. Wayne N. Welsh, Gary Zajac, and Kristofer Bucklen (2014) investigated the extent to which recidivism rates differed between convicted offenders who were assigned to a therapeutic

community (TC) drug treatment and those who were assigned to outpatient (OP) group counseling. Treatment was randomly assigned to the offenders toward understanding which treatment modality was more effective at curbing recidivism. Recidivism in this study was operationalized by computing the percentage of youths who had been reincarcerated for any crime within 36 months of their release from the programs. About .44 of the offenders assigned to TC ($n = 286$) were reincarcerated within 36 months, compared with .38 of the offenders assigned to the OP group ($n = 318$). Construct a 95% confidence interval around each of these sample proportions.

9. If you constructed a 99% confidence interval around the proportions in problem 8, how would this change the intervals? Why?

## SPSS Exercises

➤ Explore additional data sets. **⑤SAGE edge™**

| Data for Exercise | |
|---|---|
| Data Set | Description |
| 2012 states data.sav | This data set compiles official statistics from various official sources, such as the census, health department records, and police departments. It includes basic demographic data, crime rates, and incidence rates for various illnesses and infant mortality. |

| Variables for Exercise | |
|---|---|
| Variable Name | Description |
| State | ID for state the data are from. |
| AssaultRt | Number of assaults in a state per 100,000. |
| RobberyRt | Number of robberies in a state per 100,000. |
| MVTheftRt | Number of motor vehicle thefts in a state per 100,000. |
| Assault_bin | A binary recode of the assault rate where 0 = less than 200 assaults per 100,000 and 1 = more than 200 per 100,000. |

1. First, take a look at the 2010 state data set. Answer these questions:

   a. How many cases are in this data set?

   b. What does the variable "State" tell you if you look at a frequency?

   c. What unit of analysis should be used for these data?

   d. Assume that official records are accurately collected. Is this sample data or population data?

   e. Say we took an average of the murder rates in these data. What will that average tell us?

2. Take a look at the average assault rate for the United States by looking at descriptives for the variable AssaultRt (analyze-> descriptive statistics->frequencies->statistics):

   a. What do you find? Hang on to that mean!

   b. Consider the type of data you're working with, based on your answer to question 1. What does the standard deviation you've been given by SPSS reflect? Recall Table 6.12 in Chapter 6. What symbol is appropriate for this value?

3. If you decided in question 1 that this is *population* level data you'd be correct! Such data is rather rare, but we can use it to explore how close estimates from a *sample* from the population come to capturing the actual population mean. We'll do this taking a random sample of states, using it to generalize to the population as a whole with a confidence interval:

a. **Taking a random sample**: To select 25 states randomly, select data->select cases and then click "sample" under the "random sample of cases" option. In the pop-up menu, tell it to select 25 of 50 states randomly. Some rows should now be crossed off in data view.

b. Get the mean and standard deviation for this subsample. Use this information to calculate a standard error and 95% confidence interval for the variable AssaultRt:

    i. What is the appropriate *t* statistic for this confidence level?

c. Interpret the confidence interval in technical terms in a sentence. Then write another sentence that a lay person would be able to understand easily.

d. Return to your results from problem 2. Is your confidence interval able to capture the true population mean?

4. **Estimating a confidence interval in SPSS:** To get SPSS to give you a confidence interval, you must select analyze-> descriptives->explore. For this case we want to estimate value for the population mean robbery rate from our sample. The output you're interested is the mean and the confidence interval for the mean:

a. First, get the population mean for the robbery rate (RobberyRt)—all 50 states should be selected.

b. Now take a random sample of 25 states. Estimate a 95% confidence interval around the mean:

    i. Calculate the standard error of the mean by hand using the information in this output.

    ii. Write a sentence interpreting this confidence interval so a lay person could understand it.

    iii. Is the true population mean captured in this confidence interval? Why or why not?

c. Under the "explore" menu, click "statistics." Change the confidence interval for the mean to 90%:

    i. How has the confidence interval changed compared with 4b? Why has this change happened?

    ii. Is the true population mean captured in this confidence interval? Why or why not?

d. Under the "explore" menu, click "statistics." Change the confidence interval for the mean to 99%:

    i. How has the confidence interval changed compared with 4b and 4c? Why has this change happened?

    ii. Is the true population mean captured in this confidence interval? Why or why not?

e. Repeat parts 4b through 4d with a random sample of 10 states:

    i. How has the standard error of the mean changed? Why has this happened?

    ii. Explain the relationship among sample size, level of confidence, and the confidence intervals width.

5. Repeat parts 4a–4c with the variable MVTheftRt in a subsample of both 10 and 25 states.

6. SPSS does not allow for the automatic estimation of confidence intervals around a proportion. We can easily acquire the information needed to create this estimate by hand from a frequency table, however. Let's build a confidence interval around an estimate for the proportion of states with an assault rate higher than 200 assaults per 100k:

a. Create a frequency for the variable Assault_bin to get the population proportion; make sure you aren't looking at a random sample! Remember that this value is presented as a percentage in SPSS. You'll need to divide it by 100 to convert it into a proportion.

b. Create another frequency table for the same variable, this time using a random subsample of only 25 states.

c. Use the information provided in this table to calculate the standard error of the proportion and both 95% and 99% confidence intervals; you will need to look in the back of the book for the appropriate *t* statistic values.

d. For each confidence interval you estimate, write a sentence interpreting the result in a way that a lay person would be able to understand.

e. Do your confidence intervals capture the true population proportion? Why or why not?

# CHAPTER 8

# From Estimation to Statistical Tests

## *Hypothesis Testing for One Population Mean and Proportion*

> *It is, in fact, nothing short of a miracle that the modern methods of instruction have not entirely strangled the holy curiosity of inquiry.*
>
> —Albert Einstein

> *Non sunt multiplicanda entia sine necessitate. ("entities must not be multiplied beyond necessity") – Ockham's razor.*
>
> —William of Ockham

### LEARNING OBJECTIVES

1. Explain the purpose of hypothesis testing to determine the difference between a population mean and proportion and a sample mean and proportion.

2. Conduct and interpret the results of hypothesis tests for a sample mean and proportion.

3. Describe the difference between a directional (one-tailed) and nondirectional (two-tailed) null hypothesis test.

4. Evaluate the advantage of conducting a directional (one-tailed) hypothesis test compared to a nondirectional test.

5. Identify the appropriate sampling distribution to use for a one sample hypothesis test when the sample size is small.

# Introduction

Although research has examined sentence disparities between white collar crime and street crime, there is still a paucity of research that has investigated the sentencing disparities between types of white collar crime, especially for different subgroups of the population (e.g., by gender and race). Long ago, Edwin Sutherland defined white collar crime as a "crime by a person of high social-status and respectability in the course of his occupation" (Sutherland, 1949, p. 9). The pronoun "his" is likely attributable to the historical period in which this quote was taken! Kristy Holtfreter (2013) recently examined survey data collected by the Association of Certified Fraud Examiners (ACFE), which asked respondents to provide details about their most recently investigated closed case. She found that the mean sentence length in months given to the entire sample was 41.4. Suppose you wanted to determine whether white collar criminals convicted of fraud in your state received sentences that were similar to this national estimate, which you assume represents the population estimate of sentence length for people convicted of fraud. How would you answer this question? Luckily for you, this chapter will provide you with all you need to investigate these types of questions.

In this chapter, we are going to make an assumption or hypothesis about what the value of the unknown population parameter is and ask whether this assumption is realistic given a particular sample statistic we observed from our data. Our question in this chapter is, then, "Is it likely that the unknown population parameter (mean or proportion) is equal to what we have assumed or hypothesized it to be, given what we know about our sample value (our sample mean or proportion)?"

As we did in Chapter 6, when we performed a hypothesis test using the binomial distribution, in this chapter, we again compare information we have from our sample with what we assume to be true about our population. We use probability theory to help us decide the reasonableness of our assumption. The decision we make, however, is not without some risk of error. Recall the Lo-Jack car security issue from Chapter 6—no matter what we decide, there is always a chance that we have made the wrong decision. Probability theory permits us to understand in advance the probability of making the wrong decision. It lets us make our decision with some level of confidence.

Let's use a hypothetical thought exercise. Suppose you have been hired by the warden of a correctional institution to evaluate a literacy program in the prison. After reviewing all the records at the state department of corrections, you know that the average reading level for the population of incarcerated inmates in the state who have not been in a literacy program is 7.5 years. You take a random sample of 100 "graduates" of the literacy program and find that their mean reading level is 9.3 years, with a standard deviation of 2.2 years. You want to know whether the mean reading level for the sample of literacy program graduates is equal to the general population mean—that is, whether the population mean of literacy program graduates is equal to 7.5 years, the same as for the general population. The question you must ask yourself is, "Is it reasonable to assume that the population mean for program graduates is 7.5 years, given that my sample mean is 9.3 years?" Note that if you assume that the mean population reading level of your sample of graduates is no different from the mean reading level of incarcerated inmates of 7.5 years, you are assuming that your literacy program has no effect on increasing the reading level of those who complete the program. In other words, there is no "treatment effect" for being in a literacy program while in prison.

If, instead of a sample of 100 graduates, you had information about every graduate who had ever completed the program (the population of program graduates), you would be better able to

<table>
<tr><td colspan="2">**Figure 8.1**    **Formal Steps for Hypothesis Testing**</td></tr>
</table>

**Step 1.** Formally state your null ($H_0$) and research ($H_1$) hypotheses.

**Step 2.** Select an appropriate test statistic and the sampling distribution of that test statistic.

**Step 3.** Select a level of significance (alpha $= \alpha$), and determine the critical value and rejection region of the test statistic based on the selected level of alpha.

**Step 4.** Conduct the test: Calculate the obtained value of the test statistic and compare it to the critical value.

**Step 5.** Make a decision about your null hypothesis and interpret this decision in a meaningful way based on the research question, sample, and population.

answer your question. In this case, you could simply compute the average reading level for your population of program graduates and see whether it was equal to 7.5 years. Either it would be equal or not. You would have no doubt, and there would be no risk of error about your conclusion because you would have the information about the entire population. In the real world, however, we rarely have information about the entire population; instead, we must make inferences about the population from information we acquire from a sample of the population.

Of course, with sample information, we can never be 100% positive about whatever decision we make. Even if your sample mean is very different from the presumed value of the population mean, you cannot automatically conclude that your assumption about the value of that population mean was wrong. The difference between your sample mean and the presumed population mean might be due simply to **sampling variation** or chance. This is because the means of repeated samples taken from the same population are invariably different from the true population value. Enter probability theory! With the information provided by your sample and the presumed value of the population mean, you can determine the likelihood or probability of obtaining the sample mean if, in fact, the **null hypothesis** is true. We do this through the formal procedures of conducting a hypothesis test. Something to remember: We will not know with 100% certainty that we are correct no matter what we decide, only the probability that we are correct!

The remainder of this chapter examines the ways to test a hypothesis about a single population mean using both large and small samples, and about a population proportion using a large sample. We also examine the difference between **hypothesis testing** using **nondirectional (so-called two-tailed) tests** versus directional (one-tailed) tests. Before we begin this new section, however, let's refresh our memory from Chapter 6 about the steps involved in any hypothesis test by examining Figure 8.1. In the following sections, we consistently apply these five steps to the problem of testing first a hypothesis about a sample mean and then a hypothesis about sample proportion.

> **Sampling variation:** Differences between the sample and the population that are due to chance or sample variation.

> **Null hypothesis:** Hypothesis that is tested; it always assumes there is no relationship between the independent and dependent variables.

> **Nondirectional hypothesis test:** When a research/alternative hypothesis does not state the direction of difference; it only states that there is a relationship between the independent and dependent variables.

## Hypothesis Testing for Population Means Using a Large Sample: The *z* Test

### Case Study

### Testing the Mean Reading Level From a Prison Literacy Program

Let's begin our discussion of hypothesis testing using the example about reading levels for the sample of prison literacy program graduates and the general population of incarcerated inmates discussed earlier. We can summarize what we know about the two groups as follows:

|  | Population | Sample |
|---|---|---|
| Mean reading level | $\mu = 7.5$ | $\bar{X} = 9.3$ |
| Standard deviation | $\sigma$ = unknown | $s = 2.2$ |
|  | N = unknown | $n = 100$ |

What we know for sure, then, is that the mean reading level of our sample of 100 literacy program graduates ($\bar{X} = 9.3$) is different from the mean for the entire population of incarcerated inmates ($\mu = 7.5$). But is the mean reading level of the literacy program graduates really different from the population mean? In statistical terms, are the means *statistically significantly* different, or are they different merely because of sampling variation or chance? To conduct a formal hypothesis test to answer this question, we will initially assume that the population of literacy program graduates has the same mean reading level as the rest of the inmates—that is, 7.5 years. Remember, science is not about proving research hypotheses but about disproving null hypotheses. How valid is this assumption given the fact that our sample mean, 9.3 years, appears quite different from the presumed population mean of 7.5 years? Because we have only a *sample* of literacy program graduates, we can account for this apparent difference in one of two ways.

One explanation for the difference between our sample mean of 9.3 years and the population mean of 7.5 years is that the mean population reading level of literacy graduates is not really 7.5 years. This means that our initial assumption about the value of the population mean of 7.5 years is incorrect and that the true population mean for the literacy program graduates is actually different from this. The implication of this is that literacy program graduates come from a different population with a different mean than nonprogram inmates. By this we mean that our sample did not come from the population of all other incarcerated offenders but from another population, the population of literacy program graduates, which has a different mean reading level (hopefully a mean reading level that is higher than the general population's).

Figure 8.2 illustrates this explanation by showing the distribution of reading levels for the two populations. In Figure 8.2, the curve on the left is the population of incarcerated offenders with a mean reading level of 7.5 years ($\mu = 7.5$). The one on the right is a different population with a higher population mean ($\mu = 10$). One explanation for the difference between our sample mean (9.3 years) and what we have assumed is the true population mean (7.5 years) is that our sample was actually drawn from a different population. Perhaps our sample was drawn from the population on the right, where the population mean is 10 years rather than 7.5 years. If this is true, our assumption that the population mean reading level for literacy program graduates is 7.5 years is not correct and we would like to reject that assumption.

## Figure 8.2 Two Populations With Different Mean Reading Levels

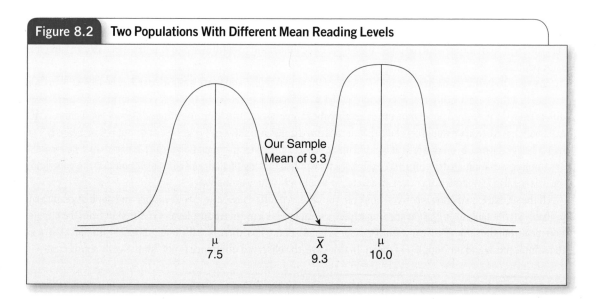

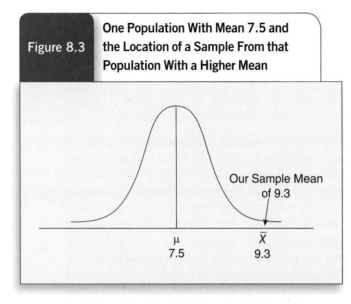

**Figure 8.3** One Population With Mean 7.5 and the Location of a Sample From that Population With a Higher Mean

A second explanation for the difference between the presumed population mean (7.5 years) and the observed sample mean (9.3 years) is based on sampling variation—that the difference in means is simply due to the fact that we just happened to select a sample with a high mean reading level even though the true population mean is really equal to 7.5 years. Figure 8.3 illustrates this possibility. If we assume that this explanation is true, we conclude that the population mean for both program graduates of the literacy program and nongraduates is, in fact, 7.5 years. We then conclude that there is only one population and that population has a mean reading level of 7.5 years. If this is true, our assumption that the population mean for literacy program graduates is 7.5 years is correct. Well, you may wonder, "If the true population mean is 7.5 years, why is our sample mean different?" This explanation is that the only reason the sample mean (9.3 years) is different from the presumed population mean (7.5) is that not every sample selected from a population will have a mean equal to that population's mean. Based on chance alone, we may have selected a sample that has a different mean than the true population mean has. It was just the "luck of the draw," so to speak, just like it is entirely possible to get 8 heads in 10 flips of a coin. There will always be variation in the proximity of the many sample means to the true population mean. In other words, simple sampling variation can account for the difference between a sample mean and the mean of the population from which that sample was drawn.

Recall from our discussion of the sampling distribution of the mean in Chapter 7 that if we take a very large or infinite number of samples of size $n$ from a population whose mean is $\mu$, the individual sample means will differ from one another and from the true population value ($\mu$), but the mean of the infinite number of sample means will still be $\mu$. Well, according to this second explanation, we have simply selected one of those samples from the population in which the sample mean just happens to be quite different from the population mean. In this case, the sample we have was drawn from a population with a mean reading level of 7.5 years, but the sample mean just happens to be quite different from that (9.3 years). The reason it is different, then, is not that the population means are actually different; rather, the reason is sampling variation—chance alone. This is the explanation that "stuff happens," where "stuff" really means chance. There is a standard deviation for the distribution of sample means, and it is called the standard error of the mean. Figure 7.2 in Chapter 7 illustrates this point. In that figure, confidence intervals were drawn around sample means taken from 20 different samples, all of which were different. In sum, it may be possible for a sample mean to be very different from the mean of the population from which the sample was drawn and still have been drawn from that same population.

As you can perhaps imagine, the implications of these two explanations are quite different. The first explanation implies that there are two different populations with two different population means. In this scenario, our sample mean differs from the presumed population mean because the sample was drawn from an entirely different population. If this explanation is correct, we would conclude that the observed difference between the sample and population means is "statistically significant." In other words, it is a difference due to a difference in population means, not to chance factors such as sampling variation. In drawing this conclusion, we would be saying that our initial assumption that the population mean is equal to 7.5 years was incorrect. In a word, we would *reject* this assumption.

If the second explanation is correct, however, the observed difference between our sample and population mean is probably attributable to our just happening to pick a sample whose mean reading level was different from the population mean, but the sample still came from this same population. Thus, there is really no significant difference between the sample mean and the population mean. In this case, the observed difference is not "statistically significant"—it is due not to a real difference between the two groups but instead simply to sampling variation. In drawing this conclusion, we have not rejected our initial assumption that the population mean is 7.5 years. Stated in statistical terms, we have *failed to reject* our initial assumption or hypothesis. We would continue to assume that the prison literacy program is not related to reading levels.

In sum, we have two possible and equally compelling explanations for the difference between our sample mean and population mean—but two explanations with very different implications. Which explanation is correct? Unfortunately, because we have sample data, not information from a population, we cannot know for certain which explanation is correct. Remember that we did not know what the mean reading level was in the population for the literacy program graduates; we only know the mean of a sample. We assumed that it was a given value, and we wondered how safe an assumption that was given what we observed our sample mean to be. Although we cannot know for certain which explanation is true, what we can do is set up a decision-making rule that will help us decide whether one of the two explanations described earlier is more likely than the other. This decision rule will also tell us how confident we can be in determining which explanation is "more likely." The basis of this decision rule is the subject matter of hypothesis testing.

In making a hypothesis test about our two explanations, we begin by assuming that the second explanation is correct—that is, that the sample actually was drawn from the population in question. We are assuming, then, that the population mean is a particular value—in our example, that the mean reading level in the population was equal to 7.5 years. We have suggested that this assumption implies that the literacy program graduates come from the same population as do nonprogram inmates. In essence, we assume that the two groups come from the same population. We want to be very conservative in our decision making and not jump to any conclusion that the two groups are different. We proceed, then, by initially assuming that they are not different and seeing whether that assumption can be maintained given the sample information. The one-population explanation is the one we assume at first because it is more parsimonious than the two-population explanation. This is in accordance with Ockham's razor stated at the head of the chapter.

The assumption that there is one population with a mean of 7.5 years constitutes our null hypothesis. The word "null" implies that there is nothing going on, that things are null, that any difference you see between sample and population characteristics is due to chance. We stated that the null hypothesis is the hypothesis of no difference between our sample mean and the assumed but unknown population mean. Our hypothesis that the population mean is 7.5 years is a null hypothesis because we are assuming that there is no "real" difference between the observed sample mean of 9.3 years and the population mean of 7.5 years. The difference is null or of no consequence because it is due simply to sampling variation or chance, not to any "real" difference between the sample and the population. "Real difference" in this case means that the treatment of having inmates in a literacy program "works" and increases the level at which they can read such that their population mean reading level is higher than those not in such a program. The starting point of the process of hypothesis testing, then, is an assumption of no differences—a null hypothesis. In a hypothesis test, we determine whether this assumption is reasonable given the evidence we have from our sample data.

In Chapter 6, we drew an analogy between the null hypothesis and the presumption of innocence in a criminal proceeding. Just as a defendant is presumed to be innocent, a null hypothesis is presumed to be true. Similarly, just as the state must present considerable evidence ("beyond a reasonable doubt") to overcome this presumption of innocence and convince the jury to convict the defendant, the research scientist must present considerable evidence to overcome the presumption that the null hypothesis is true. If there is enough evidence to suggest that the null hypothesis is probably not true, the scientist rejects it (*we never accept a null hypothesis; we simply fail to reject it*). Let us quickly remind you, however, that both the jury and the scientist can make an error in rejecting their initial presumption. The jury may convict an innocent person or let a guilty person go, and a researcher may reject a null hypothesis that in fact is true (Type I error) or fail to reject a null hypothesis that is false (Type II error). However, the legal procedures of the criminal trial and the methodological and statistical rigor of science are there to keep this risk of error small and, in the scientist's case, known.

In our research example, the null hypothesis is the hypothesis that the true population mean reading level for the population of literacy program graduates is equal to 7.5 years. It specifically refers to the fact that the sample mean and the population mean are not really (significantly) different. So our initial assumption or null hypothesis is:

$H_0$: The population mean is equal to 7.5 years. The sample mean is not significantly different from this population mean.

Since the null hypothesis is symbolized by a capital H with a subscript of zero (the zero symbolizes the null condition or no difference), there are actually two ways to state this symbolically:

$H_0$: $\mu = 7.5$ years

or

$H_0$: $\bar{X} - \mu = 0$

After stating this null hypothesis, we ask ourselves, "If this null hypothesis is not true, what is the alternative state?" We formally express this by stating the alternative hypothesis (sometimes called the research hypothesis because it is often our belief in this hypothesis that motivates us to do the research in the first place). The *alternative hypothesis* is the likely true state of affairs if the null hypothesis is not true. In the case at hand, one of three alternative states may be true:

$H_1$: The sample was drawn from a population whose mean reading level is less than 7.5 years:

$$\mu < 7.5 \text{ years.}$$

Substantively, this means that the literacy program made things worse and that those who completed the course read at a lower mean level than those who did not take the program.

OR

$H_1$: The sample was drawn from a population whose mean reading level is more than 7.5 years:

$$\mu > 7.5 \text{ years.}$$

Substantively, this means that the literacy program improved reading and that those who completed the course read at a higher mean level than those who did not take the program.

OR

$H_1$: The sample was drawn from a population whose mean reading level is different from 7.5 years:

$$\mu \neq 7.5 \text{ years.}$$

Substantively, this means that the literacy program made some difference, but we are not willing to say in advance whether the program made things worse or better.

For reasons that should now be easy to remember, the first two alternatives are called directional alternative hypotheses and involve a one-tailed hypothesis test, and the third is called a nondirectional alternative hypothesis and involves a two-tailed hypothesis test.

Having stated our null hypothesis ($\mu = 7.5$ years), then, we ask whether the assumption made in the null hypothesis is likely to be true. We ask, "What is the probability of getting the particular sample mean ($\bar{X} = 9.3$ years) if the sample were drawn from a population whose mean is stated in the null hypothesis ($\mu = 7.5$ years)." In other words, we want to know how likely it is that we would observe the value of our sample mean if the population mean is 7.5. In our specific example, we determine the probability of selecting a sample with a mean reading level of 9.3 years from a population whose mean is 7.5. If the null hypothesis is true, we can determine the probability of observing the given value of our sample mean. Moreover, we can state in advance that if this probability is very small (say 5 chances out of 100, which translates to an alpha level of

.05 [α = .05], or 1 chance out of 100, which translates to an alpha level of .01 [α = .01], we will conclude that the assumption behind the null hypothesis must be false. In other words, if it is very unlikely that we would have observed the sample mean that if the population mean were what we have presumed it to be under the null hypothesis, we will reject the null hypothesis. So, we will continue to assume that the null hypothesis is true unless the probability of our observing the sample data under this assumption is such a "rare event," an event with a probability of .05 or less or .01 or less, that it is more likely that the alternative hypothesis is true, and we must reject the null.

This is exactly the procedure we used in Chapter 6 with our hypothesis involving Lo-Jack. There, we determined that if the probability of getting your stolen car returned 8 out of 10 times were very unlikely or rare, we would reject the assumption that the return rate of stolen cars with Lo-Jack was different from that of stolen cars without Lo-Jack. Forgive our repetition, but we again remind you that because we are asking questions about a sample, there is no way of knowing for sure whether the decision we made regarding Lo-Jack was the correct one. What we *do* know when we reject the null hypothesis is that the outcome we have observed (in this case, the sample mean) is so unlikely that "chances are" it came from a different population. The risk that we are wrong is determined by the alpha level we set in our hypothesis test.

Although we have previously suggested that .05 and 01 are commonly selected levels of alpha, this is just conventional practice. There are at times compelling reasons to use a larger (.10) or much smaller alpha level (.001). Recall that in choosing a particular alpha level, we are selecting the risk we are willing to take of making a Type I error—that is, of rejecting a null hypothesis that is actually true. Sometimes the cost of a Type I error may be very great and we may want to be very, very sure before we reject the null hypothesis (say, with a probability of 1 out of 1,000). This is the situation in criminal trials, where the cost of a Type I error, convicting a person who in fact is innocent, is thought to be extraordinarily high. To avoid making this mistake, we set the bar of evidence very high, "beyond a reasonable doubt"—a probability that must be very, very low. In civil proceedings there is much less at stake since the defendant who loses usually forfeits only money rather than liberty. In this case, the cost of a Type I error of convicting an innocent person is lower, so the burden of proof required is also lower: "a preponderance of the evidence."

As scientists we have to do the same kind of balancing act and weigh the cost of making a Type I error against the cost of making a Type II error (failing to reject a null hypothesis that is in fact not true). There are some cases where the cost of a Type I error is very high and that of a Type II error is low. Suppose, for instance, that we have two treatment programs for those convicted of drunk driving. One of these programs is exceptionally expensive and involves a great deal of intrusion into a person's life (it involves random drug tests and surprise home visits), whereas the other treatment is very inexpensive and involves little in the way of intrusion. Before we decide to make convicted drunk drivers take the first treatment, we want to make sure that it is more effective than the second treatment. In this instance, we might set the risk of a Type I error at .001. If, however, we are comparing two treatments that cost about the same and involve the same loss of liberty, then we might want to increase our risk of a Type I error to .05 or even .10. The point you should remember is that *you need to think carefully about the cost of making a Type I and of making a Type II error before deciding what your alpha level is going to be.* In addition, you must remember that you cannot reduce the probability of both types of errors simultaneously. If you decrease the risk of making a Type I error (the probability of rejecting a null hypothesis that is in fact true) by setting alpha very low, you are increasing the risk of making a Type II error (the probability of failing to reject a null hypothesis that is in fact wrong). There is no such thing as a free lunch!

Let's get back to our literacy program example. There are a few remaining questions we must address before we begin the nitty-gritty work of hypothesis testing with one sample mean. One concerns how we determine the likelihood or probability of observing a particular sample mean $\bar{X}$ given an observed population with mean μ. For example, how do we know the likelihood of obtaining a sample mean of 9.3 if the true population mean is 7.5? We can determine this likelihood or probability based on what we know about the theoretical sampling distribution of means, the central limit theorem, and the standard normal distribution (the *z* distribution). From the central limit theorem, we know that with a large enough sample ($n \geq 30$), the sampling distribution of an infinite number of sample means from a population with mean μ and standard deviation σ will be normally distributed and have a mean of μ and a standard deviation of $\sigma_{\bar{X}}$, where:

$$\sigma_{\bar{X}} = \frac{\sigma}{\sqrt{n}}$$

We also know that if the sampling distribution of means is normally distributed with a known mean and standard deviation, we can convert our sample mean into a standard normal score called a $z$ score. With our given sample mean expressed as a $z$ score, we can then use our knowledge of the standard normal distribution (the $z$ distribution) and determine the probability of observing a mean of this value given the known population mean. If this probability is less than or equal to our selected alpha level, we will reject the null hypothesis. If the probability is greater than our selected alpha level, we will fail to reject the null hypothesis.

The only piece of information we lack now is how to translate our sample mean $\left( \overline{X} \right)$ into a $z$ score. We transformed a raw score into a $z$ score in Chapter 6 with the formula:

$$z = \frac{x - \overline{X}}{s} \qquad (8\text{–}1)$$

where

$x$ = our raw score

$\overline{X}$ = the mean for the sample

$s$ = the sample standard deviation

To transform our sample mean into a $z$ score, we need to slightly modify equation 8-1:

$$z = \frac{\overline{X} - \mu}{\sigma / \sqrt{n}} \qquad (8\text{–}2)$$

In this equation, our raw score $(x)$ is replaced by the sample mean $\left( \overline{X} \right)$, the sample mean in equation 8-1 is replaced by the mean of the sampling distribution (which is $\mu$, the population mean), and the standard deviation of the sample $(s)$ is replaced by the standard deviation of the sampling distribution of means, which is called the standard error:

$$\left( \frac{\sigma}{\sqrt{n}} \right)$$

As you should guess by now, however, the population standard deviation is often not known. If it is not known, and if our sample size is large $(n \geq 30)$, we can use the sample standard deviation $(s)$ to estimate the population standard deviation $(\sigma)$. Whenever $\sigma$ is not known and the sample size is large, then, the estimate for the standard deviation of the sampling distribution becomes:

$$\left( \frac{s}{\sqrt{n}} \right)$$

**z test:** Statistical test used to test several null hypotheses including the difference between two means.

The formula for the $z$ test when the population standard deviation is not known and our sample size is large enough, then, becomes:

$$z_{\text{obt}} = \frac{\overline{X} - \mu}{s / \sqrt{n}} \qquad (8\text{–}3)$$

We are now ready to conduct our hypothesis test with our hypothetical data about mean reading levels.

To refresh your memory, we have a sample of 100 graduates from a prison literacy program where the sample mean reading level was 9.3 years. The mean reading level for the population of incarcerated inmates was 7.5 years. We want to know whether our sample came from a population whose mean reading level is 7.5 years.

**Step 1:** We begin our hypothesis test by stating the null hypothesis and the research, or alternative, hypothesis.

$H_0$: The two means are equal $\bar{X} = \mu$. We could also state this null hypothesis by giving the value of the population parameter ($\mu = 7.5$). Our hypothesis test is whether the sample, whose mean we have observed, comes from a population with a mean of 7.5.

$H_1$: The two means are not equal $\bar{X} \neq \mu$.

Note that the alternative hypothesis ($H_1$) simply states that the two means are not equal. Remember that this is called a *nondirectional* (or two-tailed) *alternative hypothesis* because it does not state the directional difference between the means. It simply assumes that they are different. We will have more to say about directional and nondirectional tests later in this chapter.

**Step 2:** The next step in hypothesis testing is to select an appropriate test statistic and obtain the sampling distribution for that statistic. Because the population standard deviation is not known, we use the $z$ score formula in equation 8-3. Because we have a large sample, we use the standard normal distribution ($z$ distribution) as our sampling distribution. By calculating the test statistic $z$ with equation 8-3, what we are actually doing is obtaining a measurement of the distance in *standard error units* between the sample statistic (the sample mean, $\bar{X}$) and the hypothesized population parameter (the population mean, $\mu$). If, for example, we obtained a $z$ score of 1.5, this would indicate that our sample mean was 1.5 standard deviations above the population mean $\mu$. An obtained $z$ score of –2.3 would indicate that our sample mean was 2.3 standard deviations below $\mu$, and so on.

**Step 3:** The next step in formal hypothesis testing is to select a level of significance, termed our alpha level ($\alpha$), and identify the critical region. Remember that the alpha level we set determines our risk of making a Type I error—that is, of rejecting a null hypothesis that is really true. Also remember that the selection of an alpha level is a judgment call. By tradition, the usual alpha levels in criminology and most other social sciences are .05, .01, and .001, but there is nothing sacred about these values. Based on our selected level of alpha, we must then find the critical value of our $z$ statistic, which we refer to as $z_{crit}$. This critical value determines the rejection region for our hypothesis test.

For the sake of illustration, let's opt for an alpha level of .05 ($\alpha = .05$). Because we are testing a nondirectional hypothesis, we have to divide our selected alpha level into two equal halves and place one half in each tail of the distribution (hence, it is referred to as a two-tailed test). With an alpha level of .05, we are interested in identifying the $z$ score that corresponds to $.05 / 2 = .025$ of the area at each tail of the normal curve. This .025 of the area at each tail of the normal distribution defines our *critical region*. Since in the normal distribution .50 of the curve lies on each side of the mean, it will be easy to calculate the area that we need by subtraction. With critical region of .025 in each tail of the curve, the remaining area up to the mean is equal to $.50 – .025 = .4750$, so we need to find the $z$ score that corresponds to .4750 of the curve (an area equal to .025 lies to the right and left of this area, and these are our critical regions). We find this from the $z$ table in Table B.2 in Appendix B. Going into the body of the table until we find .4750, we can determine that the corresponding $z$ score is 1.96. Because the normal curve is symmetrical, we do the same thing for the other tail of the distribution, where the corresponding $z$ score is –1.96. The critical value of $z$ for a two-tailed test with an alpha level of .05, then, is ±1.96 ($z_{crit} = \pm1.96$). This means that for us to reject the null hypothesis at the .05 level based on our sample data, the value of $z$ we obtain from our test ($z_{obt}$) must fall 1.96 standard errors or more either above or below the population mean $\mu$. Stated another way, our decision rule is to reject the null hypothesis if $z_{obt} \leq$ –1.96 or $z_{obt} \geq$ +1.96 and to fail to reject the null hypothesis if $-1.96 < z_{obt} < 1.96$. For future reference, the critical values of $z$ that are used most often are provided in Table 8.1.

Now that we have our critical value of $z$, we can define the critical region in the sampling distribution. The critical region is the area of the sampling distribution that contains all unlikely or improbable sample outcomes (think of it as containing "rare events" where a rare event is defined by our alpha level), based on the selected alpha level.

| Table 8.1 | Alpha (α) Levels and Critical Values of *z* for One- and Two-Tailed Hypothesis Tests |
|---|---|

| Type of Hypothesis Test | Significance/Alpha Level | Critical Area in Each Tail | Critical z |
|---|---|---|---|
| Two-tailed | .10 | .05 | 1.65 |
| One-tailed | .10 | .10 | 1.29 |
| Two-tailed | .05 | .025 | 1.96 |
| One-tailed | .05 | .05 | 1.65 |
| Two-tailed | .01 | .005 | 2.58 |
| One-tailed | .01 | .01 | 2.33 |
| Two-tailed | .001 | .0005 | 3.27 |
| One-tailed | .001 | .001 | 3.08 |

We use the word "region" because the critical value of our test statistic defines the class of all obtained values that would lead us to reject the null hypothesis. For example, if we defined our critical value of *z* as ±1.96, one critical region would consist of all obtained *z* scores equal to or less than –1.96. The second critical region would consist of all obtained *z* scores equal to or greater than +1.96. The critical value of *z* at ±1.96 and the corresponding rejection regions are shown in Figure 8.4.

Because we selected an alpha level equal to .05 and are conducting a two-tailed hypothesis test, the critical region is equal to .025 (.05 / 2) of the area of the normal curve at each tail. If you are getting a little lost (and even a bit hysterical), no worries, just remain calm and continue through the entire example. The small pieces of the picture often become clear when we observe the picture in its entirety!

**Step 4:** The fourth step is to calculate the obtained test statistic, in this case $z_{obt}$, using the data we obtained from our sample. We have the sample size ($n = 100$), sample mean ($\overline{X} = 9.3$), and sample standard deviation ($s = 2.2$),

| Figure 8.4 | Critical *z* and Critical Region for Two-Tailed Test and Alpha = .05 |
|---|---|

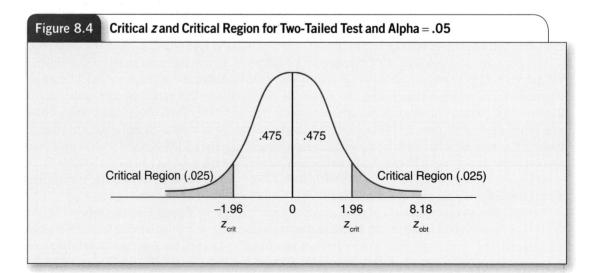

so we can simply plug them into equation 8-3. The value of $\mu$ that is used in our calculations is always the value of $\mu$ we are testing in the null hypothesis; in this case, it is 7.5. The calculation of the $z_{obt}$ statistic follows:

$$z_{obt} = \frac{\overline{X} - \mu}{s/\sqrt{n}}$$

$$z_{obt} = \frac{9.3 - 7.5}{2.2/\sqrt{100}}$$

$$z_{obt} = \frac{1.8}{2.2/10}$$

$$z_{obt} = \frac{1.8}{.22}$$

$$z_{obt} = 8.18$$

**Step 5:** The obtained value of $z$, then, is 8.18. The final step of our hypothesis-testing enterprise involves making a decision about the validity of the null hypothesis based on the results of our statistical test. We do this by comparing our critical value of $z$ ($z_{crit} = \pm 1.96$) with the value we obtain from our statistical test ($z_{obt} = 8.18$), or by seeing if our obtained statistic falls into one of our defined critical regions (see Figure 8.4). We see that the obtained $z$ value of 8.18 is greater than 1.96. In fact, it falls well into the critical region, more than 8 standard deviation units above the hypothesized $\mu$. Because $z_{obt} > 1.96$, we will reject the null hypothesis that the population mean is equal to 7.5. This observed sample outcome is highly unlikely if the null hypothesis is really true. Since our sample value of 9.3 years is very unlikely given our hypothesized population value, we are going to reject the null hypothesis; that is, we reject the assumption that our sample comes from a population whose mean reading level is 7.5 years. We will conclude instead that the sample of literacy program graduates comes from a population where the mean reading level is not equal to 7.5 years. In doing this, we can assume, based on our sample mean, that the mean reading levels of program graduates is higher than nongraduates and that the literacy program improves reading levels.

## Case Study

### Testing the Mean Sentence Length for Robbery

Let's do another example. Suppose we were interested in the mean length of the sentence given to convicted armed robbers in a state after the passage of a new firearms law. This new legislation provides for an automatic 3-year additional prison term for those convicted offenders sentenced for any felony in which a gun was used during the commission of a crime. What we really want to know is whether this new law has actually changed sentencing practices for armed robbery. We know that the mean sentence length given to convicted armed robbers in the 10 years before the new legislation was passed was 52.5 months. We will assume that this is our population mean $\mu$. We take a random sample of 110 armed robbers who were convicted under the new law and sentenced to prison. The mean sentence length given to these 110 offenders was 53.2 months, with a standard deviation of 6 months. The information we know, then, is as follows:

| Population Parameters for Armed Robberies before New Legislation | Sample Statistics for Armed Robberies after Legislation |
|---|---|
| $\mu$ = 52.5 months | $\overline{X}$ = 53.2 months |
| $\sigma$ = Unknown | $s$ = 6 |
| N = Unknown | $n$ = 110 |

We want to know whether our observed sample mean of 53.2 months is significantly different from the population mean assumed under the null hypothesis. Of course, we know that it is different since 53.2 months is not 52.5 months, but this difference can be due to sampling variation, not to the fact that sentences imposed after the law was passed are greater than those imposed thereafter. In other words, we want to know if we can reject chance and assume that the observed difference is *significantly* different. To find out, we must conduct a formal hypothesis test. Again, let's state each step along the way.

**Step 1:** The first step is to state our null and alternative hypotheses. Our null hypothesis in this example is that the mean sentence length for our sample of armed robbers sentenced under the new law is the same as the mean from the population of previously sentenced armed robbers. This is the same thing as saying that the new law had no effect on sentence lengths. Formally, the null hypothesis is that our sample is drawn from a population with a mean of 52.5 months:

$$H_0: \mu = 52.5$$

For our research or alternative hypothesis, we will state the nondirectional alternative that the population from which our sample was drawn has a mean that is not equal to 52.5. We are not stating direction in this research hypothesis because we do not know for sure whether the mean sentence length under the new law will be more than or less than the previous mean sentence. We are hesitant to predict direction because other things are working to affect the mean sentence length of armed robbers in addition to the new legislation. For example, the state may be experiencing tremendous prison overcrowding, and judges might respond to this by decreasing the average prison sentence they impose in all cases despite the new law. In addition, judges might not like the fact that the state legislators are "meddling" in their sentencing domain. They might respond to the automatic 3-year addition to a sentence length by taking off 3 years to what they normally would have imposed. Because of these countervailing effects, the only alternative hypothesis we feel comfortable asserting is that the mean sentence length for newly convicted armed robbers is not 52.5.

$$H_0: \mu \neq 52.5$$

**Step 2:** The second step requires that we select our test statistic and the sampling distribution of that statistic. In this example, our test statistic is the $z$ test and the sampling distribution is the standard normal ($z$) distribution. The population standard deviation ($\sigma$) is not known, so we will use equation 8-3.

**Step 3:** Our third step in hypothesis testing is to select a level of significance (alpha level, $\alpha$) and determine the critical value and critical region(s) of our test statistic. We select a .01 alpha level for this example. As we have stated, for a nondirectional research hypothesis, we place half of our selected alpha level (.01 / 2 = .005) in each tail of the $z$ distribution. With .005 in each tail, we look in the $z$ table for the area corresponding to .495. We find that the $z$ score

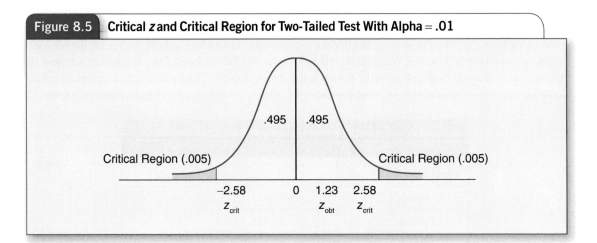

**Figure 8.5** **Critical *z* and Critical Region for Two-Tailed Test With Alpha = .01**

for this area is 2.58 (actually, ±2.58). You can also find this critical value in Table 8.1 These areas constitute our critical regions, and they are marked in Figure 8.5.

Any obtained $z$ score that falls into either of these two critical regions will lead us to reject the null hypothesis. Thus, our decision rule is to reject the null hypothesis if either $z_{obt} \leq -2.58$ or $z_{obt} \geq +2.58$ or to fail to reject the null hypothesis if $-2.58 < z_{obt} < 2.58$.

**Step 4:** Now that we have our critical value of $z$ ($z_{crit} = \pm 2.58$), we need to compute our test statistic ($z_{obt}$). Using equation 8-3, we can transform our sample mean into a $z$ score as follows:

$$z_{obt} = \frac{\overline{X} - \mu}{s/\sqrt{n}}$$

$$z_{obt} = \frac{53.2 - 52.5}{6/\sqrt{110}}$$

$$z_{obt} = \frac{.7}{6/10.49}$$

$$z_{obt} = \frac{.7}{.57}$$

$$z_{obt} = 1.23$$

**Step 5:** With our sample data, we have an obtained $z$ score of 1.23. Using this obtained value of $z$, our fifth and final step is to make a decision about our null hypothesis. Because our obtained $z$ score of 1.23 is less than our critical $z$ score of 2.58 ($z_{obt} < z_{crit}$) and more than our critical value of $-2.58$ ($z_{obt} > z_{crit}$), and does not fall into either critical region, we must fail to reject the null hypothesis. We conclude that the sample mean does, in fact, come from a population where the mean sentence length is 52.5 months. Thus, it appears that the sentencing enhancement (an additional 3 years for a gun during a felony) stipulated by the new law has not significantly increased the length of sentences for those convicted of armed robbery, compared with the population mean sentence length before the law was implemented. Remember, it is necessary not only to make a decision about your null hypothesis but also to interpret this decision based on the data and your research question.

## ▣ Directional and Nondirectional Hypothesis Tests

The choice between a *directional* and a *nondirectional hypothesis test* depends on the researcher's beliefs about the population from which the sample was drawn and how much *a priori* information (either from theory or prior research) he or she has about the question. **Directional hypothesis tests** are referred to as "one-tailed" statistical tests, and nondirectional hypothesis tests are called "two-tailed" statistical tests. In our one-sample-mean problems earlier, the null hypothesis stated that the observed sample mean came from a population with a known mean ($\mu$). The possibility that our sample came from the population whose mean is known and is expressed in the null hypothesis is one possible state of affairs. But there is another possibility— that the sample we drew came from a different population with a different mean. This other possible state of affairs is expressed in the alternative hypothesis. There are three possible versions of the alternative state of affairs:

> **Directional hypothesis test:** When a research/alternative hypothesis states the directional difference expected.

1. The sample was drawn from a population with a different mean. ($\overline{X} \neq \mu$)

2. The sample was drawn from a population with a higher mean. ($\overline{X} > \mu$)

3. The sample was drawn from a population with a lower mean. ($\overline{X} < \mu$)

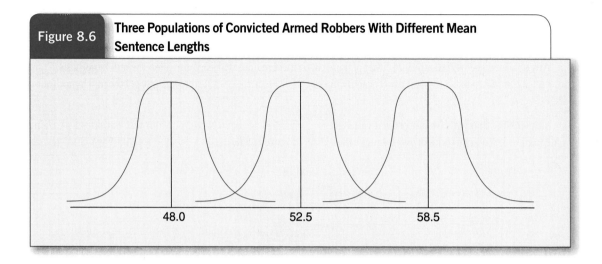

Figure 8.6 | Three Populations of Convicted Armed Robbers With Different Mean Sentence Lengths

The first possibility simply states a difference, but the latter two state a more specific direction of difference.

The first possibility is a nondirectional hypothesis. As we have seen, nondirectional hypotheses are tested by a two-tailed hypothesis test. The second two possibilities are variations of a directional research hypothesis. Directional hypotheses are tested with one-tailed hypothesis tests.

In the preceding two examples, the alternative hypothesis was stated as a nondirectional alternative. In both cases, although we did not think that our sample came from the null hypothesis population, we did not know whether the population from which the sample was drawn had a mean higher or lower than that stated in the null hypothesis. For example, in the most recent example, maybe the population of convicted armed robbers from which we drew our sample had a mean sentence length that was higher than 52.5 months, or maybe it had a mean sentence lower than that. These two possibilities are shown in Figure 8.6. You can perhaps see from this figure why we are interested in both tails of a sampling distribution when we have a nondirectional research hypothesis—we have to cover both possibilities.

Unlike this scenario, directional research hypotheses state a more precise relationship between the sample and the null hypothesis parameter (in this case, population mean). When we use directional hypotheses, we believe not only that the sample and population means are different but also that we can define the exact direction of that difference. For example, in the previous problem, if we had been more confident in our belief that the effect of the firearm law would be unequivocally to increase the prison term of those convicted of a felony involving a weapon, we could have stated our alternative hypothesis more specifically as $H_1: \mu > 52.5$. This is a directional alternative hypothesis because we are specifically stating what type of difference the population mean has from our sample mean. In this case, we are saying that our sample was drawn from a population whose mean is greater than the population mean expressed in the null hypothesis. This is illustrated in Figure 8.7, which shows two curves. The curve on the left is the curve for the population defined by the null hypothesis with a mean of 52.5. The curve to the right is an example of a possible population defined by the directional alternative hypothesis ($H_1: \mu > 52.5$). In this population, the mean is hypothesized to be greater than that for the population of the null hypothesis. Had our directional alternative hypothesis stated that the sample mean came from a population whose mean was less than 52.5 ($H_1: \mu < 52.5$), our two curves would look like those in Figure 8.8. Thus, when stating a directional alternative or research hypothesis, we are stating the direction in which, we believe, the population from which our sample was drawn lies: either above (Figure 8.7) or below (Figure 8.8) the mean specified by the null hypothesis.

You may be wondering what possible difference it makes whether we state our research hypothesis as nondirectional or directional. It does make a difference. If you can, it is to your advantage as a researcher to specify a direction for your alternative hypothesis. This does not mean that in the absence of prior knowledge or sound theory you should always make a directional research hypothesis—only that if you can, it is to your advantage to do so. Of course, this answer leads to another question: "Why is testing a directional rather than a nondirectional hypothesis

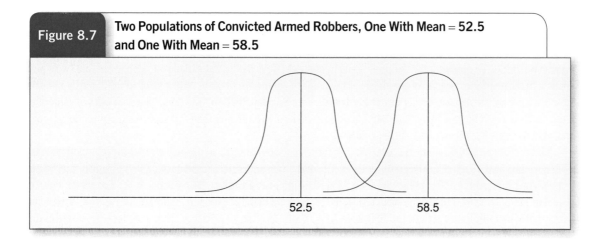

**Figure 8.7** Two Populations of Convicted Armed Robbers, One With Mean = 52.5 and One With Mean = 58.5

52.5          58.5

to my advantage?" Well, let's think about this for a minute. When we state a nondirectional research hypothesis, we hypothesize that our sample was drawn from a population with a mean that is different from that specified in the null hypothesis. We do not know, then, whether the population from which our sample was drawn has a mean that is larger or smaller than that stated in the null hypothesis. These two possibilities, and the null hypothesis, are illustrated in Figure 8.6. As you can see, in the nondirectional case, we are interested in both tails of the distribution for the null hypothesis. That is why we divide our alpha level into two equal halves and place one half in the right tail and one half in the left tail of the distribution. Note that when we divide our alpha level in half, we are also cutting the area of the critical region in the tail of the sampling distribution in half and going out further on the tail of the probability distribution. Instead of .05 of the area of the curve in one tail of the sampling distribution, we have .025 (.05 / 2) of the area in each tail. As we just said, because we are interested in a smaller area of the curve, the effect of this is to push the critical region farther out into the tail of the distribution. As you can see, it is not that our critical region is smaller in the two-tailed (nondirectional) research hypothesis; our critical area (alpha level) is still .05 of the curve. But this total area is now divided into two equal halves.

When we state a directional research hypothesis, however, we make the much more specific statement that we believe the population from which our sample was drawn has a mean that is higher (or lower) than that stated in the null hypothesis. Examples of a directional research hypothesis are shown in Figures 8.7 and 8.8. In these directional hypotheses, we are interested in only one tail of the sampling distribution. Figure 8.7 illustrates the case when we hypothesize that the sample comes from a population with a higher mean than that stated in the null hypothesis.

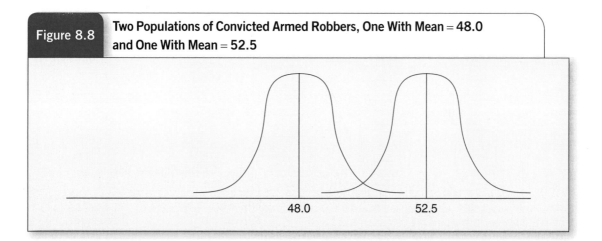

**Figure 8.8** Two Populations of Convicted Armed Robbers, One With Mean = 48.0 and One With Mean = 52.5

48.0          52.5

Because we suspect a higher population mean, our attention is directed at the right tail. Figure 8.8 illustrates the case when we hypothesize that the sample comes from a population with a lower mean than that stated in the null hypothesis. Now the critical region is only in the left tail of the distribution. Both instances are examples of one-tailed hypothesis tests. Unlike the case with the nondirectional hypothesis, we do not have to divide our alpha level into two equal halves. In the one-tailed case, all of our alpha level is in one tail of the distribution. When using a two-tailed hypothesis test, then, we are pushed out farther into the tail of the sampling distribution, which increases our critical value of $z$. As a result, to reject the null hypothesis, our obtained $z$ will have to be greater than that required in a directional (one-tailed) alternative hypothesis at the same alpha level.

Figures 8.9 and 8.10 illustrate this point. In Figure 8.9, we show the critical region for a two-tailed hypothesis test with an alpha of .05. Each critical region is equal to .025 of the area under the normal curve, and the critical value of $z$ is ±1.96. Thus, to reject the null hypothesis, we would need to obtain a $z$ score less than or equal to −1.96 or greater than or equal to +1.96. This two-tailed hypothesis test would correspond to the situation in Figure 8.6. In Figure 8.10, we have a one-tailed hypothesis test at the same alpha level ($\alpha = .05$). In this test, all .05 of our critical region is in one tail of the sampling distribution. You can see that the critical region in the right tail of Figure 8.10 is larger than that in Figure 8.9; in fact, it is twice as large. Because we do not have to go so far out into the right tail, our critical value of $z$ is only 1.65, compared with the 1.96 $z$ value for the nondirectional two-tailed test in Figure 8.9. The greater the absolute value of the critical value, the more difficult it is to reject the null hypothesis. The same principle applies when moving from a .05 alpha to a .01 alpha (for either a one- or two-tailed test); our critical value increases because we are going further out into the tail of the probability distribution, and our critical alpha will be greater for the .01 alpha than for an alpha of .05.

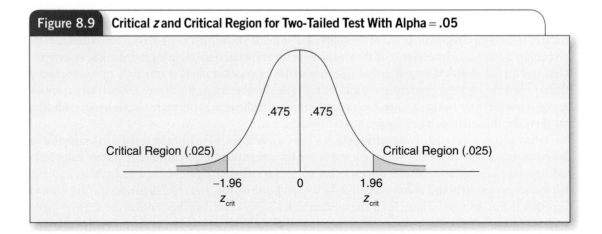

**Figure 8.9** | **Critical $z$ and Critical Region for Two-Tailed Test With Alpha = .05**

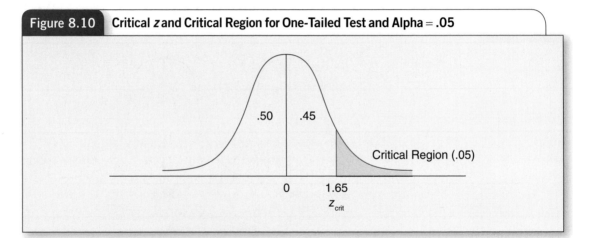

**Figure 8.10** | **Critical $z$ and Critical Region for One-Tailed Test and Alpha = .05**

As you can see, at any given level of alpha, we will need a smaller $z_{obt}$ to reject the null hypothesis in the one-tailed (directional) hypothesis test. Now you can see more clearly why it is to your advantage to specify a directional alternative hypothesis *if you can*. The critical $z$ values reported in Table 8.1 confirm that at each level of alpha, you will need a smaller value of $z_{obt}$ to reject the null hypothesis using a one-tailed than using a two-tailed test. Remember, though, that, no matter which type of test you are conducting, directional or nondirectional, the steps necessary to conduct a hypothesis test remain the same. Let's go through another example.

## Case Study

## Mean Socialization Levels of Violent Offenders

Some criminologists and psychologists have long contended that there are important and stable personality differences between criminal offenders and the nonoffending "normal" population. One of these supposed personality differences between offenders and nonoffenders is psychopathy—the degree to which persons act antisocial or lack any regard for the feelings of others. A frequently used psychological test that has been assumed to measure the trait of psychopathy is the Socialization (SO) scale of the California Psychological Inventory.[1] The SO scale measures such things as one's ability to form close social relationships, the extent to which one is concerned with the rights and feelings of others, and a tendency for deliberately planned rather than impulsive behavior. As a measure of healthy socialization, then, we would expect that adult criminal offenders might score lower on the SO scale than nonoffenders. When the scale was first designed, Edwin Megargee (1972) reported a mean SO scale score of 35.99 for a large group of working-class male adults. We will take this as our population value. Let's suppose that we collected a sample of 177 male prison inmates convicted of violence in California who had a mean SO scale score of 27.76 and a standard deviation of 6.03. We want to know whether our sample of California prison inmates came from the nonincarcerated population with a mean of 35.99. Because we expect the mean for the prisoners to be less than that for the nonincarcerated population, we can state a directional research hypothesis. We now explicitly go through our formal hypothesis test.

**Step 1:** Our null and alternative hypotheses are as follows:

$H_0: \mu = 35.99$

$H_1: \mu < 35.99$

Remember that the null hypothesis is always the same whether you state a directional or a nondirectional alternative hypothesis. In the directional research hypothesis, we are specifically stating that the true population mean for the incarcerated sample is less than 35.99, so we will conduct a one-tailed test. It is important to remember our substantive question, whether those who are incarcerated have lower socialization scores (or more psychopathy) than those not incarcerated.

**Step 2:** Our test statistic will be the $z$ statistic, and our sampling distribution will be the standard normal distribution ($z$ distribution).

**Step 3:** We will select .01 as our alpha level. The critical value of $z$ for an $\alpha = .01$ with a one-tailed test in this direction is $-2.33$ ($z_{crit} = -2.33$). The critical value of $z$ is negative because in our research hypothesis, we have predicted that the true population mean is less than the mean stated in the null hypothesis. We are therefore interested in the left tail of the sampling distribution. If it helps, think of the numerator of formula 8-3. When the sample mean $\overline{X}$ is less than the hypothesized population mean $\mu$, the value of the numerator will be negative. If you are making a directional hypothesis test stating this difference $\left( \overline{X} < \mu \right)$, the critical value of your test statistic should also be negative. For this example, then, the critical region will consist of all $z_{obt}$ scores less than or equal to $-2.33$. Our decision rule, therefore, is to reject $H_0$ if $z_{obt} \leq -2.33$.

**Step 4:** The value of $z_{obt}$ is:

$$z_{obt} = \frac{\bar{X} - \mu}{s / \sqrt{n}}$$

$$z_{obt} = \frac{27.76 - 35.99}{6.03 / \sqrt{177}}$$

$$z_{obt} = \frac{-8.23}{6.03 / 13.30}$$

$$z_{obt} = \frac{-8.23}{.45}$$

$$z_{obt} = -18.29$$

**Step 5:** Because the obtained value of $z$ falls inside the rejection region and $-z_{obt} < -z_{crit}$, we would reject the null hypothesis. This is illustrated in Figure 8.11. We would therefore conclude that the population of incarcerated offenders has a mean SO scale score that is less than 35.99. Based on this test, then, we can also conclude that incarcerated violent offenders demonstrate greater psychopathy than nonoffenders in the population.

Because hypothesis testing involves probabilities and not certainties, let us acknowledge yet another time that there is some known risk of error in rejecting the null hypothesis. Our alpha level of .01 serves notice that, in the long run, there is 1 chance in 100, or a 1% chance, that we could have observed a sample mean of 27.76 even if the true population mean were 35.99. Because the probability of that occurring is very small, however (it is what we have come to know as a "rare event"), we have opted to reject the null hypothesis in favor of the alternative. Nevertheless, there is no way of knowing for sure whether we are correct. Keep in mind that the risk of rejecting a true null hypothesis is always present and is equal to alpha.

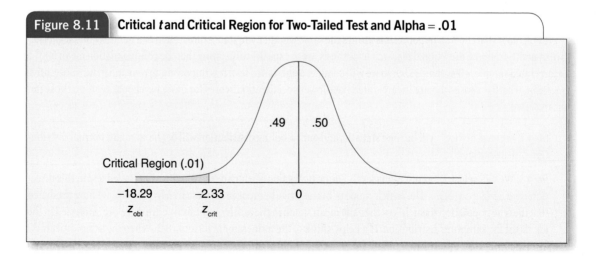

**Figure 8.11** | **Critical *t* and Critical Region for Two-Tailed Test and Alpha = .01**

# ▣ Hypothesis Testing for Population Means Using a Small Sample: The *t* Test

In the previous section we discussed hypothesis testing about one sample mean when our sample size was large enough so that we could invoke the central limit theorem, which states that when the sample size gets large (generally, $n \geq 30$), the distribution of an infinite number of sample means drawn from any population is approximately normal. This theorem enables us to use the *z* test and the *z* distribution as our probability distribution in order to conduct our hypothesis test. When we have small samples ($n < 30$), however, we cannot take advantage of the central limit theorem in this manner. As with the differences we observed between calculating confidence intervals when we have large and small samples, the techniques we use when testing a hypothesis about a population mean also are a little bit different when we are using a small sample. With small samples the appropriate test statistic is the *t* test we used in Chapter 7 with confidence intervals. Our sampling distribution, then, is Student's *t* distribution.

> **t test:** Statistical test used to test several null hypotheses including the difference between two means.

As we discussed in Chapter 7, the *t* distribution is somewhat different from the *z* distribution. The *t* distribution is flatter than the *z* distribution, and it is much flatter when the sample size is small, and is fatter at the tails. This means that the critical value of *t* at a given alpha level will be greater than the comparable critical value of *z* and can be much greater when *n* is very small. As an example, you know that the critical value of *z* for a one-tailed test at $\alpha = .05$ is 1.65. Let's take the same alpha level and find the critical value of *t* with an *n* of 10. As before, to find the critical value of *t*, go to the table of *t* values in Table B.3 of Appendix B. You first locate the appropriate alpha (significance) level and type of test (one- or two-tailed) at the top of the table. Then you must determine the correct degrees of freedom (*df*), where *df* is equal to $n - 1$ in this problem. With a sample size of 10, therefore, we have 9 degrees of freedom. Keep in mind that unlike the *z* table, the numbers in the body of the *t* table correspond to critical values of *t*, not to areas under the curve. We can see from the *t* table that the critical value of *t* for a one-tailed test and an alpha of .05 with 9 degrees of freedom is 1.833. This is greater than the critical value of *z* at the same alpha level (1.65).

As an exercise, stay in the same column of *t* and move down the page. Note what happens when the size of the sample increases. The size of critical *t* decreases. At a sample size of 121 (120 degrees of freedom), the critical value of *t* (1.658) is almost the same as the critical value of *z* (1.65). Therefore, you can see that as the sample size increases, the more the *t* distribution more closely approximates the shape of the *z* distribution. When our sample size has reached about 100, the two distributions are virtually identical.

The formula for the *t* test used to conduct a hypothesis test about a population mean using small samples is identical to the formula used for the *z* test when the population standard deviation is unknown:

$$t_{obt} = \frac{\overline{X} - \mu}{s / \sqrt{n}} \tag{8-4}$$

The steps involved in conducting a hypothesis test with *t* are the same as in the previous section with the *z* test; the only difference is that we use the *t* probability distribution and the *t* table rather than the standard normal (*z*) probability distribution and table. We first state the null and alternative hypotheses. We then determine our test statistic and sampling distribution. We next select an alpha level, and based on this, we determine the critical value of our test statistic ($t_{crit}$) and the critical region of our sampling distribution. We calculate our test statistic ($t_{obt}$) and compare it with the critical value. Finally, we make a decision about our null hypothesis and interpret this decision in a way that is meaningful to the research question at hand. The main difference between hypothesis testing using the *t* test and using the *z* test lies in these statistics' respective sampling distributions and, consequently, in the critical values and rejection regions for a given level of alpha. Let's go through an example.

## Case Study

### Assets Seized by ATF

The Federal Bureau of Alcohol, Tobacco, Firearms and Explosives (ATF) routinely seizes the assets of arrested drug dealers. In a given year with thousands of cases, the average dollar amount seized by the ATF is $75,200 per case. We are going to assume that this is our population value as the average dollar amount of asset seizures in drug cases for that year. In the state in which we live, our local police department began seizing the assets of the drug dealers it arrested, and in one year with 14 cases, it seized an average dollar amount of $71,500, with a standard deviation of $3,900. Our research question is, "Does our state seize more or less than the average dollar amount in the population?" The statistical information we have, then, is:

| National Sample of Asset Seizures in Dollars from ATF | Sample of 14 Asset Seizures in Our State in Dollars |
|---|---|
| μ = $75,200 | $\bar{X}$ = $71,500 |
| σ = Unknown | s = $3,900 |
| N = Unknown | n = 14 |

**Step 1:** With these data we want to test the null hypothesis that the population mean dollar amount seized by our police department is equal to the average compiled by the ATF ($75,200). In other words, we want to test the hypothesis that our sample of 14 asset seizures came from the overall ATF population. Our alternative hypothesis states that μ is not equal to $75,200. Since we are not stating the direction of this difference, our alternative hypothesis is nondirectional or a two-tailed test. Formally, these hypotheses would be stated like this:

$H_0$: μ = $75,200

$H_1$: μ ≠ $75,200

**Step 2:** Because we have a small sample ($n = 14$), we will use the $t$ statistic and the sampling distribution of the $t$ to perform the hypothesis test.

**Step 3:** We decide to adopt an alpha level of .01 to test the null hypothesis. The next step is to find the critical value of $t$ and map out our critical regions. We know that we are conducting a nondirectional test using α = .01, but we also need to calculate how many degrees of freedom we have in our sample. Remember that in this problem the degrees of freedom is equal to $n - 1$ (14 – 1), which gives us 13 degrees of freedom. From Table B.3 of Appendix B, we find that for a two-tailed test with an alpha of .01 and 13 degrees of freedom, our critical value of $t$ is 3.012. Recall that when doing a nondirectional test, we are interested in both tails of our sampling distribution. In a nondirectional test, then, the critical value corresponds to both positive and negative values. Our critical value of $t$, therefore, is $t_{crit} = \pm 3.012$. Our decision rule will be to reject the null hypothesis if $t_{obt}$ is less than or equal to –3.012 or greater than or equal to +3.012. Stated differently, we must fail to reject the null hypothesis if $-3.012 < t_{obt} < 3.012$.

**Step 4:** We are now ready to compute our test statistic:

$$t_{obt} = \frac{\bar{X} - \mu}{s / \sqrt{n}}$$

$$t_{obt} = \frac{71,500 - 75,200}{3,900 / \sqrt{14}}$$

$$t_{obt} = \frac{-3,700}{3,900 \,/\, 3.74}$$

$$t_{obt} = \frac{-3,700}{1042.78}$$

$$t_{obt} = -3.55$$

**Step 5:** The value of *t* we obtained from our statistical test was –3.55. Figure 8.12 shows the obtained value of *t* relative to the critical regions of the sampling distribution. Because our obtained test statistic falls into the critical region on the left side of the sampling distribution (negative end), and because $t_{obt} < t_{crit}$, we must reject the null hypothesis that the dollar amount seized from drug dealers in our state is the same as the ATF average. It seems that there is a significant difference between our sample mean and the population mean. From our sample data, we can conclude that our state seizes significantly less compared to the national average.

| Figure 8.12 | Critical *t* and Critical Region for Two-Tailed Test and Alpha = .01 |

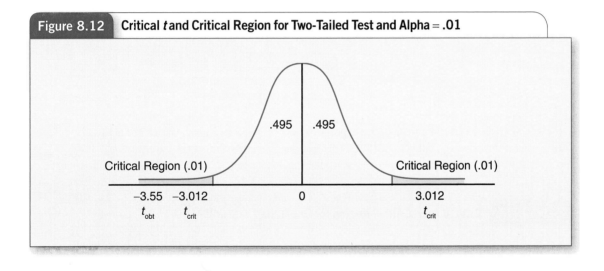

---

## Case Study

## Rate of Law Enforcement Personnel

Let's go through another quick example. You should have the steps down fairly well now, so we will not go into any great detail, but make a mental note as we take each step. The Federal Bureau of Investigation (FBI) has reported that the average number of law enforcement officers per 1,000 inhabitants in recent years was generally around 3.3. That is, there were an average of 3.3 police officers for every 1,000 inhabitants in cities and townships. We are going to assume this is our population mean. Let's suppose that we represent a group of small-town mayors who want to challenge this figure to demonstrate that rural towns have a lower number of officers to serve their population compared to the United States as a whole. To investigate this, we collect information about the number of sworn officers from a sample of 9 rural communities (*n* = 9). From this sample of rural police departments, we find that the average number of police officers per 1,000 inhabitants is 2.9 with a standard deviation of .8.

To determine whether this mean is significantly different from the population mean, we must conduct a formal hypothesis test. The null and alternative hypotheses are:

$H_0: \mu = 3.3$

$H_1: \mu < 3.3$

For this test, we decide that an alpha level of .05 is sufficient. Because we are stating a directional research hypothesis, we will be conducting a one-tailed test, and our concern is with the left tail of the probability distribution (the negative end). Given this information, along with our sample statistics, we next define our critical value of $t$ to be equal to $-1.86$ ($df = 8$, $\alpha = .05$, one-tailed test). The critical region is any $t$ value equal to or less than $-1.86$. Our decision rule is to reject $H_0$ if $t_{obt} \leq -1.86$. Our critical value of $t$ is $-1.86$ because in our alternative hypothesis, we have specifically hypothesized that the sample comes from a population with a lower mean than that expressed in the null hypothesis. Stated differently, we are hypothesizing that our sample was drawn from a population with a mean that is less than 3.3 officers per 1,000 population. If this is correct, we should obtain a negative value of $t$. If $t_{obt}$ is positive, we will fail to reject the null hypothesis even if it is greater than the absolute value of $t_{crit}$ because it is in the wrong direction from that stated in the alternative hypothesis. Next we calculate the test statistic as follows:

$$t_{obt} = \frac{2.9 - 3.3}{.8 / \sqrt{9}}$$

$$t_{obt} = \frac{-.4}{.8 / 3}$$

$$t_{obt} = \frac{-.4}{.267}$$

$$t_{obt} = -1.50$$

Since we stated a directional alternative hypothesis, we are interested only in the left tail of the $t$ distribution and in negative values of $t_{obt}$. The obtained $t$ value of $-1.50$ does not fall within our stated critical region, $t_{obt} > t_{crit}$. In Figure 8.13, we illustrate the critical value of $t$ and the rejection region relative to the value of $t$ we obtained in our test.

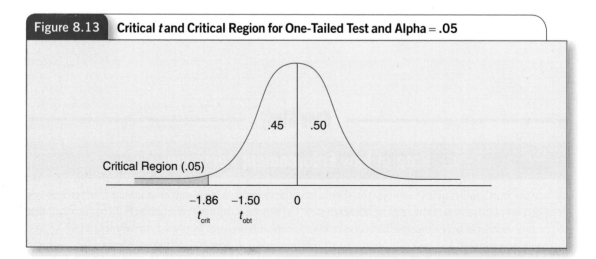

**Figure 8.13** **Critical *t* and Critical Region for One-Tailed Test and Alpha = .05**

We must therefore fail to reject the null hypothesis and conclude that the mean number of law enforcement officers per 1,000 persons in rural areas (2.9) is not significantly different from 3.3, the population mean number of police officers per capita for the United States as a whole. Contrary to the mayors' contention, then, there is no statistical evidence that rural communities have lower levels of police protection per capita than other areas of the country.

So far, we have talked about hypothesis tests for population means only. We have conducted hypothesis tests for a population mean μ using data from both large samples (z test) and small samples (t test). Before we move on to hypothesis tests for proportions, let us summarize the types of tests that we can use when conducting hypothesis tests about a single population mean μ. The accompanying text box displays the three combinations of hypothesis tests that can be conducted when making an inference from a sample to the population about μ.

---

*Formal Statements of the Null and Research/Alternative Hypotheses for Both Nondirectional (Two-Tailed) and Directional (One-Tailed) Tests with a Hypothetical Population Mean of 5*

Nondirectional hypotheses for a population mean:

$H_0: \mu = 5$

$H_1: \mu \neq 5$

Directional hypotheses for a larger population mean:

$H_0: \mu = 5$

$H_1: \mu > 5$

Directional hypotheses for a smaller population mean:

$H_0: \mu = 5$

$H_1: \mu < 5$

---

## Hypothesis Testing for Population Proportions and Percentages Using Large Samples

Very frequently we find that our data consist of a proportion or percentage rather than a mean. These data include such things as the percentage of the American public that support the death penalty, the percentage that own firearms, the proportion of arrested defendants who test positive for drugs, and the proportion of arrested defendants who plead guilty in exchange for a lesser charge. Even though we have percentage and proportion data, we still may be interested in the kind of problem we have been examining thus far in the chapter: testing the difference between a sample statistic and an unknown population parameter. In this case, however, our sample statistic is a proportion or percentage, as is the unknown population parameter. The question is, "Can we still conduct a hypothesis test about a population parameter if that parameter is a proportion or percentage?" The answer to that question is yes, and it is very simple to do.

The general procedure used to conduct a hypothesis test about a single population proportion is virtually identical to that used for a population mean, so we will not need to go into great detail here. As in the last chapter, we use $p$ to denote the proportion obtained from our sample data and $P$ to denote the population proportion. In this chapter, we focus exclusively on tests used for proportions obtained from a large sample. With a large sample, we can invoke the central limit theorem and use our familiar z test. The general rule regarding sample size in tests of proportions is that the normal approximation (standard normal or z distribution) can be used when both $n(\hat{p}) \geq 5$ and $n(\hat{p}-1) \geq 5$. For example, if $\hat{p} = .5$, we would need a sample size of at least 10 to conduct a z test because $10(.5) \geq 5$. If $\hat{p} = .10$, we would need a sample size of at least 50 $[50(.10) \geq 5]$.

To perform a hypothesis test about a population proportion using large samples, we again use the z test as our test statistic and the z distribution as our sampling probability distribution. The formula used to conduct a z test for proportions is comparable with the formula for hypothesis tests with a mean:

$$(8\text{-}5)$$

$$z = \frac{\hat{p} - P}{\sigma_{\hat{p}}}$$

where

$$\sigma_{\hat{p}} = \sqrt{\frac{PQ}{n}}$$

$\hat{P}$ = the sample proportion

$P$ = the population proportion assumed under the null hypothesis

$Q = 1 - P$

The numerator of this formula simply is the difference between the sample proportion and the assumed population proportion. This represents the distance between the sample statistic and the hypothesized population parameter. The denominator:

$$\sigma_{\hat{p}} = \sqrt{\frac{PQ}{n}}$$

is an estimate of the standard deviation of the sampling distribution, which is called the standard error of the proportion and should be very familiar to you by now. This is the standard deviation of the distribution of an infinite or very large number of samples of size $n$ where we have calculated the sample proportion $(\hat{p})$ for each sample. Notice that in the formula for the estimated standard error of the proportion we have the population parameter for the proportion $P$ and $Q\,(1 - P)$. Normally, we do not know the value of a population parameter, and here we do not know what it is, but *we are assuming a value of $P$ in the null hypothesis* and that is the value we use.

---

## Case Study

## Attitudes Toward Gun Control

Let's go through the procedures of conducting a hypothesis test for a population proportion. Since 1990, the Gallup Polling Organization has included in one of its polls this question: "In general, do you feel that the laws covering the sale of firearms should be made more strict, less strict, or kept as they are now?" In 2014, the proportion of the total population who believed that the sale of firearms should be made "more strict" was .47 (Gallup, 2014b). This will be used as the population parameter in this example. Let's say that we believe that such attitudes regarding a law like this vary significantly by community. For example, we believe that individuals residing in communities such as Newtown, Connecticut, who have experienced traumatic mass murders (such as the killings at the Sandy Hook Elementary School where 20 children lost their lives) will be much more likely on average to favor such a law.

**Step 1:** To test our hypothesis, we collect a random sample of 107 individuals from communities that have experienced some form of mass murder where the killings were perpetrated with a gun. As all good researchers do, we formally state our hypotheses (we use a directional or one-tailed research hypothesis in this case) before conducting the statistical test. Our hypotheses are:

$$H_0 : P = .47$$

$$H_1 : P > .47$$

**Step 2:** Since we have an appropriately large number in our sample, we will use the $z$ test along with the corresponding $z$ sampling distribution.

**Step 3:** We next specify the level of alpha at .05 and determine the critical region. The critical value of $z$ with $\alpha = .05$ using a directional hypothesis is equal to 1.65 (Table 8.1). The critical value is positive in this case because we believe the proportion of residents who live in a community that has experienced a firearm-related traumatic incident will be much more likely to favor a gun control law. What we are saying is that our sample was drawn from a population where the proportion of those who favor restrictive hand gun laws is greater than .47. The critical region includes all values of $z_{obt}$ that are equal to or greater than 1.65. We will reject the null hypothesis, then, if $z_{obt} \geq 1.65$.

**Step 4:** The results of our sample indicate that 66 of the 107 individuals from our sample believe that the sale of firearms should be made stricter. Remember that to obtain the proportion, we simply divide the frequency of interest—in this case, those in favor of the law—by the total number in the sample ($f / n = 66 / 107$), which gives us a sample proportion of $\hat{p} = .62$. With this information, we calculate the obtained test statistic of $z$:

$$z_{obt} = \frac{\hat{P} - P}{\sqrt{\dfrac{P(1-P)}{n}}}$$

$$z_{obt} = \frac{.62 - .47}{\sqrt{\dfrac{.47(1-.47)}{107}}}$$

$$z_{obt} = \frac{.15}{\sqrt{\dfrac{.47(.53)}{107}}}$$

$$z_{obt} = \frac{.15}{\sqrt{\dfrac{.249}{107}}}$$

$$z_{obt} = \frac{.15}{\sqrt{.0023}}$$

$$z_{obt} = \frac{.15}{.048}$$

$$z_{obt} = 3.12$$

The value of $z$ we obtain from our statistical test indicates, just as all $z$ scores do, that if the null hypothesis were true, the sample proportion $\hat{p} = .62$ would fall about 3.12 standard errors above the hypothesized population proportion $P$ of .47. Since the obtained $z$ of 3.12 is greater than the critical value of 1.65, it falls within the rejection region. The obtained value of $z$ relative to the critical value of $z$ is displayed in Figure 8.14. Because $z_{obt} > z_{crit}$, we can reject the null hypothesis and conclude that among residents of communities who have experienced gun trauma, the true proportion who favor stricter regulation of the sale of guns is significantly greater than .47. We can state this in terms of percentages by simply multiplying the proportions by 100. Based on our hypothesis test, then, we can conclude that among people who reside in communities that have experienced a mass shooting, the percentage of residents favoring stricter gun sales is higher than the national percentage.

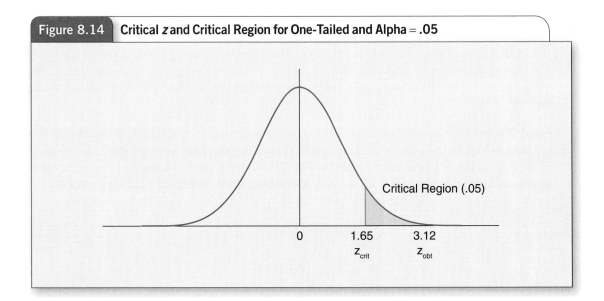

**Figure 8.14** **Critical _z_ and Critical Region for One-Tailed and Alpha = .05**

# Case Study

## Random Drug Testing of Inmates

Let's do another example, this time using percentages. Imagine that you have passed your statistics course with flying colors, have received your degree, and are now the research specialist for a municipal jail. During the course of your duties, you notice that in a random drug test of 100 new pretrial detainees, 36 of them (36%) tested positive for some form of cocaine. You begin to wonder whether the population of pretrial detainees contains a higher-than-normal percentage of cocaine users. You do a little background research and discover that, according to the National Survey on Drug Use and Health conducted in 2013, approximately 12% of young adults (aged 18–25 years) have used cocaine at some time in their lives. By using this as your population parameter, you decide to test the hypothesis that the percentage of cocaine use among your pretrial detainees is significantly higher than the 12% found in the general population.

You have the following information:

| Population | Sample |
|:---:|:---:|
| $P$ = 12% | $\hat{p}$ = 36% |
| | $n$ = 100 |

With your well-honed statistical skills, you identify this as a call for a hypothesis test of a one-sample proportion and go through the following steps in order.

**Step 1:** You state the null and research hypothesis:

$H_0: P = .12$, or 12%

$H_1: P > .12$, or 12%

Because you suspect that the sample of pretrial detainees comes from a population where the percentage of cocaine use is greater than 12%, you state a directional research hypothesis.

**Step 2:** Because you have a large sample ($n = 100$), you select the $z$ test for proportions as your statistical test and the $z$ distribution as your sampling distribution.

**Step 3:** You select an alpha level of .01. With a one-tailed test, the critical level of $z$ at this level of alpha is 2.33. The critical region is composed of all $z_{obt}$ values greater than or equal to 2.33. Your decision rule, therefore, is to reject the null hypothesis if $z_{obt} > 2.33$.

**Step 4:** For ease of calculation, you convert the percentages back into proportions by simply dividing them by 100. You calculate the obtained value of your test statistic, $z_{obt}$:

$$z_{obt} = \frac{.36 - .12}{\sqrt{\frac{.19(1 - .19)}{100}}}$$

$$z_{obt} = \frac{.24}{\sqrt{\frac{.19(.81)}{100}}}$$

$$z_{obt} = \frac{.24}{\sqrt{\frac{.15}{100}}}$$

$$z_{obt} = \frac{.24}{\sqrt{.0015}}$$

$$z_{obt} = \frac{.24}{.04}$$

$$z_{obt} = 6.00$$

**Step 5:** The location of the obtained value of $z$ relative to the critical value and the critical region are illustrated in Figure 8.15. Because $z_{obt} > 2.33$ and falls into the critical region, you would reject the null hypothesis, knowing that there is 1 chance in 100 that you are making the wrong decision (Type I error). From this hypothesis test, you can conclude that the percentage of your pretrial detainees who have ever used cocaine is significantly greater than the percentage who have used cocaine in the general population of young adults.

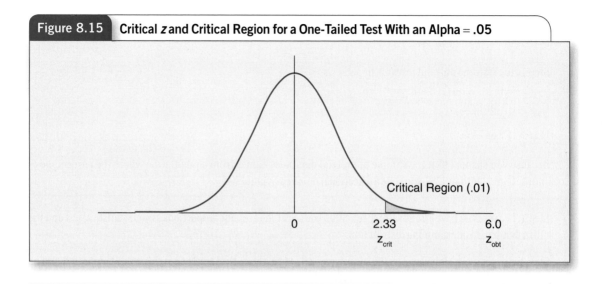

**Figure 8.15** | **Critical *z* and Critical Region for a One-Tailed Test With an Alpha = .05**

## ▣ Summary

In this chapter, we have examined the procedures used to make inferences about two population parameters: inferences from an observed sample mean ($\overline{X}$) about an unknown population mean ($\mu$), and inferences from an observed sample proportion ($\hat{p}$) to an unknown population proportion ($P$). We used a $z$ test when making inferences about both sample means and sample proportions when we had large samples. When working with small samples, we demonstrated the steps necessary for hypothesis testing involving a mean using a $t$ test. Each of these hypothesis tests involved a series of decisions. The first one is whether to state a directional or a nondirectional alternative hypothesis. If there are sound reasons to state your research hypothesis as a directional one, you should do so. The second decision to make concerns which test statistic and which corresponding sampling distribution to use. The third decision pertains to which level of significance (the alpha level) to use in conducting your hypothesis test. This is one of the most important decisions you will make in hypothesis testing because the alpha level determines the risk you accept of rejecting a null hypothesis that is really true (i.e., the risk of making a Type I error). Finally, the last and easiest decision you have to make is whether to fail to reject or to reject your null hypothesis. This is the easiest decision because if you have properly conducted the hypothesis test and followed the steps in order, this last decision will have essentially been made for you. Once you have chosen your alpha level and found the critical value and critical region, all you need to do is to determine whether the obtained value of your test statistic falls in the critical region. If it does, you reject the null hypothesis; if it does not, you fail to reject the null hypothesis. What could be easier?

## Key Terms

➤ Review key terms with eFlashcards. **⑤SAGE edge™**

directional
    hypothesis test   221
hypothesis testing   210
nondirectional
    hypothesis test   210

null hypothesis   210
one-tailed hypothesis
    test   221
sampling variation   210
$t$ test   227

two-tailed
    hypothesis test   210
$z$ test   216

# Key Formulas

To find a $z$ score (equation 8-3):

$$z_{obt} = \frac{\bar{X} - \mu}{s/\sqrt{n}}$$

To find a $t$ score (equation 8-4):

$$t_{obt} = \frac{\bar{X} - \mu}{s/\sqrt{n}}$$

To conduct a hypothesis test for proportions (equation 8-5):

$$z = \frac{\hat{p} - P}{\sigma_{\hat{p}}}$$

where

$$\sigma_{\hat{p}} = \sqrt{\frac{P(Q)}{n}}$$

$\hat{p}$ = the sample proportion

$P$ = the population proportion under the null hypothesis

$Q = 1 - P$

# Practice Problems

> Test your understanding of chapter content.
> Take the practice quiz. $SAGE edge™

1. When is it appropriate to use a $t$ test for hypothesis testing instead of a $z$ test?

2. We are interested in the average dollar amount lost by victims by burglary. The National Insurance Association has reported that the mean dollar amount lost by victims of burglary is $2,222. Assume that this is the population mean. We believe that the true population mean loss is different from this. Formally state the null and research hypotheses we would test to investigate this question. What if we believed the dollar amount to be higher?

3. The Internal Revenue Service has claimed that the mean number of times the average U.S. citizen has cheated on taxes in the last 10 years is 4.6 times. Assume that this is your population value. We believe the actual population mean ($\mu$) of the number of times individuals cheat on their taxes is higher than this. We collect a random sample of 61 tax-paying citizens and find the following sample statistics: $\bar{X} = 6.3, s = 1.9$. Perform all of the procedures necessary for conducting a hypothesis test based on our assumption. Set your alpha level at .01. What do you conclude?

4. A major research study concluded that the mean number of times that adolescents had engaged in vandalism during the previous 12 months was 3.5 times. We believe the true population mean to be less than this. After collecting our own sample of 29 adolescents, we find that the mean number of times they have vandalized property during a 1-year period was $\bar{X} = 2.9$ with a standard deviation equal to .7. Perform all of the procedures

necessary for conducting a hypothesis test based on our assumption. What do you conclude? Set your alpha level at .05.

5. Over a 20-year period, the average sentence given to defendants convicted of aggravated assault in the United States was 25.9 months. Assume this to be your population mean. Because you think it might be different in your home state, you conduct a little study to examine this question. You take a random sample of 175 jurisdictions in your home state and find that the mean sentence for aggravated assault is 27.3 months, with a standard deviation of 6.5. Test the null hypothesis that the mean sentence length in your state is 25.9 months against the alternative hypothesis that it is different from that. Set your alpha level at .01.

6. A study conducted by Research Institute of America has concluded that the average number of hours inmates at state correctional facilities spend in their cells during a day is 15. We believe the population mean number of hours to be different from this. We contacted a sample of 15 state correctional facilities and inquired about the mean number of hours that inmates housed in these facilities spent in their cells. We came up with the following sample data:

| Facility Number | Hours Spent in Cells |
|---|---|
| 1 | 16.3 |
| 2 | 21.1 |

*(Continued)*

(Continued)

| Facility Number | Hours Spent in Cells |
|:---:|:---:|
| 3 | 14.9 |
| 4 | 13.5 |
| 5 | 22.2 |
| 6 | 15.3 |
| 7 | 18.1 |
| 8 | 19.0 |
| 9 | 14.2 |
| 10 | 9.3 |
| 11 | 10.1 |
| 12 | 21.1 |
| 13 | 22.3 |
| 14 | 15.4 |
| 15 | 13.2 |

Calculate the mean number of hours inmates spend in their cells from the sample data. Test the null hypothesis that the mean number of hours inmates spend in their cells is 15 against the null hypothesis that it is different from that. Set your alpha level at .05. *Hint:* You will also have to calculate the standard deviation. Remember, practice makes perfect! What do you conclude?

7. You are on the police force in a small town. During an election year, a candidate for mayor claims that fewer police are needed because the average police officer makes only four arrests per year. You think the population mean is much higher than that, so you conduct a small research project. You ask 12 other officers how many arrests they made in the past year. The average for this sample of 12 is 6.3, with a standard deviation of 1.5. With your sample evidence, test the null hypothesis that the population mean is four arrests against the alternative that it is greater than four. Set your alpha level at .01.

8. The American Bar Association reports that the mean length of time for a hearing in juvenile court is 25 minutes. Assume that this is your population mean. As a lawyer who practices in the juvenile court, you think that the average hearing is much shorter than this. You take a sample of 20 other lawyers who do juvenile work and ask them how long their last case in juvenile court was. The mean hearing length for this sample of 20 was 23 minutes, with a standard deviation of 6. Test the null hypothesis that the population mean is 25 minutes against the alternative that it is less than 25. Set your alpha level at .05.

9. A spokesperson for the National Rifle Association (NRA) states that 45% of the households in the United States contain at least one firearm. Assume that this is your population value. You take a random sample of 200 homes and find that about 23% of them contain a firearm. Test the null hypothesis that the population proportion is 45% against the alternative that it is less than that. Set your alpha level at .01.

10. A friend of yours claims that 20% of the people in your neighborhood have been the victim of a crime. Take this as your population value. You take a random sample of 60 homes and find that about 31% of the homes reported some kind of crime. Test the null hypothesis that the population proportion is 20% against the alternative that it is different from 20%. Set your alpha level at .05.

11. A public opinion study concluded that the proportion of Americans agreeing with the statement, "Prisons should be for punishment, not rehabilitation" was .31. You believe the true population proportion agreeing with this statement is actually higher than that. After collecting your own sample of 110 individuals and asking them the same question, you find that .46 agree with the statement. Test the null hypothesis that the population proportion is .31 against the alternative that it is more than this. Set your alpha level at .05.

# SPSS Exercises

➤. Explore additional data sets. ⑤SAGE edge™

| Data for Exercise | |
|:---|:---|
| **Data Set** | **Description** |
| Youth.sav | These data are from a random sample of students from schools in a southern state. While not representative of the United States, it covers a variety of important delinquent behaviors and peer influences. |

| Variables for Exercise | |
| --- | --- |
| Variable Name | Description |
| Certain | A scale indicating how likely respondents feel it is that they will be punished for delinquent behavior. High values indicate high certainty. |
| Delinquency | A scale indicating the number of delinquent acts that respondents report participating in. |
| Moral | A scale that measures if respondents thought delinquency was morally wrong. High values indicate that delinquency is viewed as morally wrong. |
| Parnt2 | A scale indicating the amount of parental supervision that respondents receive with values ranging from 2 to 8, with high values indicating more supervision. |

1. **A fictional example with real data:** Imagine that you are a school official working to reduce delinquency within the student body. You and your staff members implemented a wide array of programs trying to fix your delinquency problem:

   a. A meeting was held explaining to students that it was very likely that they would be caught if they were bad.

   b. You held a session explaining why delinquent behaviors were harmful to people other than themselves and therefore wrong.

   c. You contacted students' parents and told them it was very important that they monitor their children's behavior and engagement in school.

2. You measured student delinquency and student attitudes about deviance both before and after the intervention. To begin with, you want to see if the students view punishment as being more certain than the original test, which had a mean of 10.40:

   a. Formally write your statistical hypotheses.

   b. Use the frequencies dialogue menu to get the standard deviation, mean, and sample size for the variable "certain."

   c. What is the appropriate test statistic and sampling distribution for this case? Will you do a one-tailed or a two-tailed test. Why?

      i. What is the appropriate value for the test statistic for your one/two-tailed test when:

         1. $\alpha = .05$
         2. $\alpha = .01$
         3. $\alpha = .001$

   d. By using the mean and standard deviation, calculate your test statistic by hand; recall that your comparison "population" value is 10.40.

   e. What do you conclude about your hypotheses? Is the conclusion the same at all levels of significance?

      i. If you ran a one-tailed test, now compare with a two-tailed test. Likewise, if you started with a two-tailed test, compare with a one-tailed test. Are your findings the same?

   f. Write a few sentences summarizing these results to your boss. Be sure to include mention of the type of test you used, what the result was, and the highest level at which the results were significant, if at all. Also write a sentence about the "so what" of your results: What does this mean for your intervention, and how large was the change produced?

3. You quickly realize that doing these tests by hand will take quite some time. Fortunately, SPSS allows us to conduct $z$ tests very quickly, although the option is labeled as a $t$ test. In reality this function does both; $t$ and $z$ statistics are equivalent when your sample is greater than 120. With this knowledge in mind, you move on to the possibility that students view crime as more wrong following the intervention, a key element of social bond theories. The original survey of students found that they had a mean score of 16.5:

   a. Formally write your statistical hypotheses.

   b. What is the appropriate test statistic and sampling distribution for this case? In this case, assume a two-tailed test will be used.

   c. Determine an alpha level that you will use. You do not need to find the critical value.

   d. Using SPSS to perform a one-sample $z$ or $t$ test: Select analyze-> compare means->one sample $t$ test. Put the variable "moral" in the "test variable" box, and set your test value to the comparison mean, 15.2:

      i. The output SPSS provides gives several key pieces of information, most of which are intuitively labeled. In this case, the "$t$" statistic provided is actually a $z$ statistic due to your sample size. The main box to notice is labeled "sig (2-tailed)," which contains the exact $p$ value, which is compared against your specified alpha. Value of .000 means your $p$ value is actually something like .000001— certainly significant at $\alpha = .001$.

   e. What do you conclude about your hypotheses? Is the conclusion the same at all levels of significance?

f.  Write a few sentences summarizing these results to your boss. Be sure to include mention of the type of test you used, what the result was, and the highest level at which the results were significant, if at all. Also write a sentence about the "so what" of your results: What does this mean for your intervention, and how large was the change produced?

4.  You receive a call with some very bad news. Your research assistant jumped the gun and destroyed a lot of your surveys before they had been fully entered! At the end of the day, you now have only 7% of the data that you thought you had for the delinquency and parent supervision measures. You decide to push on with what you've got—only 81 responses instead of 1272! Your next task is to see if parents were more engaged in supervising their children than in the original test, which has a mean score of *6.1*. Your research assistant also broke SPSS so you'll have to do this one by hand:

a.  Select a random sample of 7% of your data by selecting Data->select cases and selecting "sample", "approximately 7% of cases."

b.  Formally write your statistical hypotheses.

c.  Use the frequencies dialogue menu to get the standard deviation, mean, and sample size for the variable "parnt2."

d.  What is the appropriate test statistic and sampling distribution for this case? Will you do a one-tailed or a two-tailed test? Why?

   i.  How many degrees of freedom do you have?

   ii.  What is the appropriate value for the test statistic for your one/two-tailed test when:

      1.  $\alpha = .05$

      2.  $\alpha = .01$

      3.  $\alpha = .001$

e.  By using the mean and standard deviation, calculate your test statistic by hand; recall that your comparison "population" value is 6.1.

f.  What do you conclude about your hypotheses? Is the conclusion the same at all levels of significance?

i.  If you ran a one-tailed test, now compare with a two-tailed test. Likewise, if you started with a two-tailed test, compare with a one-tailed test. Are your findings the same?

g.  Write a few sentences summarizing these results to your boss. Be sure to include mention of the type of test you used, what the result was, and the highest level at which the results were significant, if at all. Also write a sentence about the "so what" of your results: What does this mean for your intervention, and how large was the change produced?

5.  You are finally ready to move on to your final outcome: whether students are engaging in less delinquent behaviors. SPSS is working again so we'll do this analysis with software. Before the interventions you found students reported a mean of 38 delinquent activities:

a.  Select a random sample of 7% of your data (see 3a).

b.  Formally write your statistical hypotheses.

c.  What is the appropriate test statistic and sampling distribution for this case? In this case, assume a two-tailed test will be used.

d.  Determine an alpha level that you will use. You do not need to find the critical value.

e.  Use SPSS to perform the hypothesis test. Do this by selecting analyze->compare means->one sample *t* test. This process and associated output is explained in question 2d, and this time your comparison value is 38.

f.  What do you conclude about your hypotheses? Is the conclusion the same at all levels of significance?

g.  Write a few sentences summarizing these results to your boss. Be sure to include mention of the type of test you used, what the result was, and the highest level at which the results were significant, if at all. Also write a sentence about the "so what" of your results: What does this mean for your intervention, and how large was the change produced?

6.  Step back and look at all the results from questions 1 through 4. If you had to advocate for the use of just *one* intervention, which one seems to be most effective, and why?

## STUDENT STUDY SITE

**⑤SAGE edge**™

### WANT A BETTER GRADE?

Get the tools you need to sharpen your study skills. Access practice quizzes, eFlashcards, data sets, and exercises at **edge.sagepub.com/bachmansccj4e**.

# Part III: Bivariate Analysis

*Relationships Between Two Variables*

# CHAPTER 9

# Testing Hypotheses With Categorical Data

> *There are two possible outcomes: if a result confirms the hypothesis, then you've made a measurement. If the result is contrary to the hypothesis, then you've made a discovery.*
>
> —Enrico Fermi

> *The TV scientist who mutters sadly, "The experiment is a failure; we have failed to achieve what we had hoped for," is sufferening mainly from a bad script writer. An experiment is never a failure solely because it fails to achieve predicted results.*
>
> —Robert M. Pirsig

## LEARNING OBJECTIVES

1. Identify the appropriate sampling distribution to use for a hypothesis test when both the independent and dependent variables are measured at the nominal or ordinal levels.

2. Identify the components of a cross-tabulation table.

3. Explain how to calculate and interpret the appropriate cell percentages in a cross-tabulation table when you want to determine whether the independent variable affects the dependent variable.

4. Conduct and interpret the results of a hypothesis test for the bivariate relationship between a nominal/ordinal independent and dependent variable.

5. Describe what a measure of association tells us compared with the chi-square hypothesis test.

6. Calculate and interpret measures of association appropriate for both nominal- and ordinal-level variables.

# Introduction

This first step in all research is identifying bivariate relationships, that is, identifying a relationship between one independent variable (IV) and one dependent variable (DV). You will later learn that this does not allow us to establish causal relationships between variables, only associations. Why did the homicide rate drop substantially in the past two decades, and why has it significantly increased in the past few years in some cities? Do programs like CompStat, which indicates where crimes are clustering in cities, affect crime rates? Do tougher gun control policies reduce gun-related crimes? Each of these are research questions that begin understanding bivariate relationships. In this chapter, you will learn about the chi-square statistic and how it is used to test whether there is a relationship between two categorical variables—variables measured at the nominal or ordinal level. When we have two categorical variables, the chi-square statistic enables us to test the null hypothesis that the two variables are independent. This assumption of independence implies that there is no relationship between the variables. Whether a relationship exists between two categorical variables can be seen by inspecting a contingency table, which may also be referred to as a cross-tabulation table. A contingency table shows the joint distribution of two categorical variables. With a contingency table, we can look for the presence of a relationship between the two variables by comparing percentage differences on the dependent variable and by looking at relative risks. Finally, we will examine measures of association for the relationship between two variables. Although the chi-square statistic can tell us whether there is a relationship between two categorical variables in the population, it tells us nothing about the possible strength of the relationship. Telling us about the strength of a relationship is the job of a measure of association.

In this chapter, we will be concerned with testing hypotheses and exploring relationships with categorical variables. Categorical variables are measured at either the nominal or the ordinal level, and the values of these variables consist of distinct categories. One example of a categorical nominal-level variable would be whether a teenager most frequently plays violent video games or sports video games. An example of a categorical ordinal-level variable would be "number of delinquent acts committed in the past year," with the values "none," "1–5 acts," "6–10 acts," and "11 or more delinquent acts." Using a chi-square test ($\chi^2$), pronounced like "ki" (as in *kite*), where $\chi$ is the Greek letter chi, we can test the null hypothesis that two variables are independent or that they are not statistically related to each other. If we determine that the two variables are not independent but that, in fact, there is a relationship or association between them, we then ask how strongly they are related to each other. These tests are often referred to as *tests of independence.*

# Contingency Tables and the Two-Variable Chi-Square Test of Independence

When we are examining the relationship between two variables, we can usually distinguish between the independent variable and the dependent variable. Recall that an independent variable is a variable that we think has an influence on another variable, called the dependent variable. When we use causal language, we refer to the independent variable as the "cause" and to the dependent variable as the "effect." In the rest of this chapter, we are going to be interested in determining two things: (1) whether the independent and dependent variables are related to one another when both of the variables are nominal or ordinal, and (2) if so, how strongly they are related. You may remember from Chapter 6 that two events (the values of two variables) are independent if the outcome of one variable has no effect or influence on the outcome of another. Similarly, our job in this chapter is to determine whether our variables are independent of each other. With categorical variables, the tool we use to determine this is the

**Get the edge on your studies.**
edge.sagepub.com/bachmansccj4e

- Take a quiz to find out what you've learned.
- Review key terms with eFlashcards.
- Explore additional data sets.

**$SAGE edge**™

**Chi-square test of independence:** Tests the null hypothesis that two nominal- or ordinal-level variables are independent.

chi-square test of independence. Before we get to the chi-square test, however, we need to examine what the two-categorical-variable problem looks like and exactly how we are going to attack it.

---

## Case Study

## Gender, Emotions, and Delinquency

One of the most persistent facts in criminology is that males are more antisocial and engage in more violence than females. The question is why. There are several theoretical explanations for this, but one that has received a great deal of attention is general strain theory (GST) (Agnew, 1992). The main idea with GST is that when people experience strain, they then experience negative emotions such as anger or depression. These negative emotions may be alleviated through particular coping measures like substance abuse or aggressive outbursts. The way in which males and females process these emotional reactions to strain may be one reason why males are more aggressive compared with females. The empirical evidence is mixed with some research finding that males and females respond similarly to strain (Jennings, Piquero, Gover, & Perez, 2009; Piquero, Fox, Piquero, Capowich, & Mazerolle, 2010), whereas others find that males are more likely to experience anger in response to strain while females are more likely to experience depression (DeCoster & Zito, 2010; Francis, 2014).

Let's assume we are conducting research to examine the relationship between gender and emotions among a sample of adolescents. Our independent variable is gender (male or female), and our dependent variable is how the individuals experience negative emotions (high versus low negative emotions). The first step in exploring the relationship between these two categorical variables is to examine their **joint frequency distribution**. The joint frequency distribution of two variables is simply a distribution that shows how the values of the two variables occur simultaneously or jointly. In Table 9.1, we show the frequency distribution of these two variables for a sample of 120 adolescents. Of the 120 adolescents, the frequency distribution for gender shows that there are 60 males and 60 females. The 120 persons in Table 9.1 were given a personality test, and the frequency distribution for that variable shows that 90 of them were found to have "low" negative emotions and 30 had "high" negative emotions. Both of these variables are categorical variables; gender is a nominal-level variable, and negative emotions is an ordinal-level variable. Note also that each variable has two values (male and female; low and high negative emotions).

**Joint frequency distribution:** For two categorical variables, the intersection of two values or categories.

The third distribution (the contingency table) is actually the joint frequency distribution of the two variables–gender and negative emotions. A joint frequency distribution of two variables shows the number of cases for each value of one variable at each value of the second variable. For example, there are 46 females who have low negative emotions. This is the joint distribution of the value "female" for the variable "gender" and the value "low negative emotions" for the variable "negative emotions." There are 14 females who have high negative emotions. This is the joint distribution of the value "female" and the value "high negative emotions." There are also 44 males with low negative emotions and 16 males with high negative emotions. Since there are two values of gender and two values of negative emotions, their joint distribution will result in four possible outcomes: (1) female and low negative emotions, (2) female and high negative emotions, (3) male and low negative emotions, and (4) male and high negative emotions. Since both variables have two levels (male/female and low/high emotions), the joint distribution has four possible outcomes: male and low negative emotions, male and high negative emotions, female and low negative emotions, and female and high negative emotions. All four of these joint outcomes and the frequency of each are shown in Table 9.1.

**Contingency table:** Shows the joint distribution of two categorical variables. A contingency table is defined by the number of rows and the number of columns it has. A contingency table with 3 rows and 2 columns is a "3 by 2" contingency table. Also called a cross-tabulation table.

A joint frequency distribution of categorical variables like that in Table 9.1 is called a contingency table, sometimes referred to as a cross-tabulation table. **Contingency tables** are generally defined by the number of rows and columns that they have. Table 9.1 is called a 2 × 2 (read, 2 "by" 2) contingency table because there are two rows (female and male) and two columns (low and high negative emotions). Generally, contingency tables are referred to as $R \times C$ tables, where $R$ is the number of rows and $C$ is the number of columns. A contingency table with three rows and two columns, then, would be a $3 \times 2$ contingency table. The rows and columns refer to the number of levels or values of each categorical variable. The product of the number of rows in a contingency table and the number of columns is equal to the number of "cells." The number of cells corresponds to the total number of possible outcomes of the joint distribution of the two variables. For example, in Table 9.1, there are two rows and two columns, for a total of four ($2 \times 2 = 4$) cells. These four cells of the contingency table correspond to the four possible outcomes of the joint distribution of the two variables.

Table 9.2 provides important information that is contained in a contingency table. First there are the row ($R_1$ and $R_2$) and **column marginals** ($C_1$ and $C_2$). The **row marginals** correspond to the number of cases in each row of the table, and the column marginals correspond to the number of cases in each column of the table. In the contingency table in Table 9.1, for example, the row marginals are 60 females and 60 males. The column marginals are 90 persons low in negative emotions and 30 persons high in negative emotions. The sum of the row marginals should equal the sum of the column marginals, and these should equal the total number of cases ($R_1 + R_2 = C_1 + C_2 = n$). For example, in Table 9.1, the sum of the two row marginals ($60 + 60$) is equal to the sum of the two column marginals ($90 + 30$), which is equal to the total number of cases, 120.

One reason for looking at a joint frequency distribution is that it can provide us with information about the relationship between the two variables. Recall that our research question is, "Are males more likely to experience negative emotions than females?" In hypothesizing that there is a relationship between gender and negative emotions, we presume that gender is the independent variable and the experience of negative emotions is the dependent variable. Our null hypothesis would be that there is no relationship between gender and negative emotions, and our alternative hypothesis would be that males are more likely than females to experience such negative emotional states. Later in this chapter we will learn about the chi-square test for independence, which is a formal hypothesis test, but first we will learn what a reading of the contingency table alone can tell us about the relationship between two variables.

Because our hypothesis is that one's gender has an impact or influence on the kinds of emotional experiences one is likely to have, what we would like to know is the extent to which males are more likely than females to have negative emotions. In other words, if gender varies, does the tendency to have negative emotions vary? One way to answer this question is to

| Table 9.1 | Distribution of Gender and Negative Emotionality, and Joint Distribution of Gender and Negative Emotionality in Contingency Table |

| *Gender* | *f* |
|----------|-----|
| Female | 60 |
| Male | 60 |

| *Negative Emotionality* | *f* |
|------------------------|-----|
| Low | 90 |
| High | 30 |

*Contingency Table of Observed Joint Frequency Distribution*

| *Gender* | Negative Emotionality | | |
|----------|------|------|-------|
| | *Low* | *High* | *Total* |
| Female | 46 | 14 | 60 |
| Male | 44 | 16 | 60 |
| Total | 90 | 30 | 120 |

**Column marginal, or column frequency:** Total frequencies for the variable displayed on the column of a cross-tabulation table.

**Row marginal:** Total frequencies for the categories of a variable displayed in the rows of a cross-tabulation table.

| Table 9.2 | Labeling a 2 × 2 Contingency Table |

| *Number of Rows* | Number of Columns | | Row Marginals |
|------------------|-----|-----|---------------|
| | *1* | *2* | |
| 1 | A* | B* | $R_1$ |
| 2 | C* | D* | $R_2$ |
| Column Marginals | $C_1$ | $C_2$ | N |

*Cell frequencies.

examine the percentage of males who have negative emotions and compare that with the percentage of females. This implies that in examining percentages in contingency tables, we look at the percentage of cases for *different levels* of the independent variable for *the same level* of the dependent variable. This means that we calculate our percentages using the marginals of the independent variable (IV) and compare percentages on the dependent variable (DV). That is, the marginal frequencies for our independent variable are the denominator we use in calculating these percentages, and this is true whether the independent variable is your row variable or the column variable. Because you never know where someone will place the independent variable on a contingency table, we think it is extremely important that you understand how to calculate the appropriate percentages wherever the IV happens to be! Let's go through an example.

In the contingency table shown in Table 9.1, gender is our IV. To calculate the appropriate cell percentages, we use the row marginals as the denominators for our percentage calculations because gender is on the row of the table. In this way, the percentages should sum to 100% at the end of each row or each value of the independent variable. After calculating these, we find 77% of females are low in negative emotions [(46 / 60) × 100], and that 23% of females are high in negative emotions [(14 / 60) × 100]. Now, let's calculate the percentage of males who are low in negative emotions: 73% of the males are low in negative emotions [(44 / 60) × 100], and 27% of males are high in negative emotions [(16 / 60) × 100]. Again, it is important to use the marginals for the independent variable to calculate our percentages. The relevant percentages for this contingency table are reported in Table 9.3.

**Percentage differences:** One way to examine the bivariate relationship in a contingency table. The rule is to calculate the percentages based on the marginals of the independent variable and compare different levels of the independent variable at the same level or category of the dependent variable.

Having calculated our percentages on the independent variable, we will now compare them at a fixed level of the dependent variable. Notice that we have labeled the cells A through D for ease of discussion. We want to know whether gender affects negative emotions so we must make comparisons *across* gender categories *within* a category of emotions. In cell C, we find that 23% of the females have high negative emotions *compared with* 27% of the males (cell D). We could have compared gender percentages across the low negativity cells just as easily. The rule is that we must compare **percentage differences** found in different categories of the independent variable (female and male) at the same category level of the dependent variable (high negative emotions) because in doing this notice that

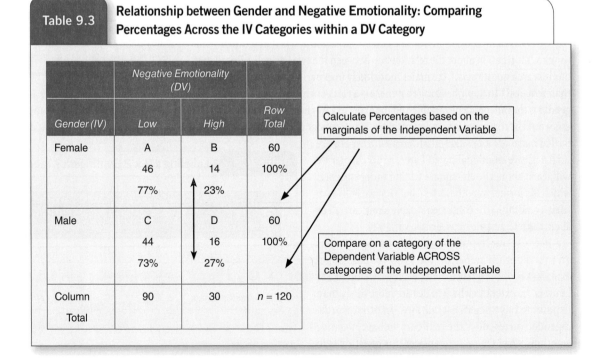

**Table 9.3** — Relationship between Gender and Negative Emotionality: Comparing Percentages Across the IV Categories within a DV Category

| Gender (IV) | Negative Emotionality (DV) Low | High | Row Total |
|---|---|---|---|
| Female | A 46 77% | B 14 23% | 60 100% |
| Male | C 44 73% | D 16 27% | 60 100% |
| Column Total | 90 | 30 | n = 120 |

Calculate Percentages based on the marginals of the Independent Variable

Compare on a category of the Dependent Variable ACROSS categories of the Independent Variable

we are varying the independent variable (female vs. male) and seeing if there is variation between them on the dependent variable. Instead of using percentages, you could have left your calculations as proportions. Some people call this the relative risk of the dependent variable occurring. For example, the relative risk of having high negative emotions is .23 for females and .27 for males; the relative risk of having low negative emotions is .77 for females and .73 for males. Regardless of which category of the dependent variable you use (high or low negative emotions), you will come to the same conclusion. It seems that males are only slightly more likely to have high negative emotions than are females.

What can we conclude as to whether males are more likely to have higher negative emotions than females? Well, a percentage difference of 4% is not very impressive. Is a 4-percentage-point difference enough for us to conclude that a relationship exists between gender and negative emotions? How large should the percentage difference be before we could with confidence conclude that there is a relationship? Five percent? Ten percent? What if the 4% difference we observed is due only to random sampling variation, and the true difference is 0%? What if the 4% difference was actually a real difference between males and females, but the relationship was just very weak? What we need is a formal hypothesis test of this difference of percentages with a known sampling distribution, and a measure of association to tell us about the strength of the relationship. First we will work on the formal hypothesis test. The chi-square test gives us that formal hypothesis test. Before we discuss this two-variable chi-square test, however, let's look at another example of a contingency table.

---

## Case Study

### Liking School and Delinquency

Social control theory predicts that adolescents who are more committed to school and who like school will be less likely to engage in delinquency (Hirschi, 1969). Table 9.4 shows the joint distribution between two variables, whether the respondent said that he or she "liked school" and the number of delinquent acts he or she reported committing in the past year. This information was collected from a sample of 450 youths. We are interested in this joint distribution because we think that adolescents who like school are less likely to commit delinquent acts than those who dislike school. A positive attitude toward school, we hypothesize, is a positive social bond that we think will inhibit an inclination to commit delinquency. In this example, attitude toward school is our independent variable, and the number of delinquent acts is the dependent variable. Note that in this contingency table, our independent variable is in the column variable, not the row variable. In determining whether there is a relationship between attitude toward school and number of delinquent acts committed, we will look at percentage differences and relative risks.

Why is it necessary to compute percentages before we examine the relationship between the variables? This answer is related to our discussion of raw numbers and rates in Chapter 1. In Table 9.4, attitude toward school is our independent variable, so we want to compare information at different categories of this variable at a fixed category of the dependent variable. Let's fix the category of the dependent variable at "2+ delinquent acts." If we were to compare raw frequencies, we would say that 70 youths who liked school committed 2 or more delinquent acts in the past year and 60 youths who disliked school committed 2+ delinquent acts. It would seem, therefore, that those who disliked school

| Table 9.4 | Relationship Between Attitudes Toward School and Self-Reported Delinquency, Observed Frequencies | | |
|---|---|---|---|
| DV: Number of Self-Reported Delinquent Acts | IV: Do You Like School? | | |
| | Like | Dislike | Total |
| 0 | 140 | 25 | 165 |
| 1 | 105 | 50 | 155 |
| 2+ | 70 | 60 | 130 |
| Total | 315 | 135 | 450 |

**Table 9.5** Relationship Between Attitudes Toward School and Self-Reported Delinquency, Observed Frequencies With Percentages and Making Comparisons Across the IV Categories

| DV: Number of Self-Reported Delinquent Acts | IV: Do You Like School? | | |
| --- | --- | --- | --- |
| | Like | Dislike | Total |
| 0 | 141 45% | 25 19% | 166 |
| 1 | 104 33% | 50 37% | 174 |
| 2+ | 70 22% | 60 44% | 150 |
| Total | 315 100% | 135 100% | 450 |

were less likely to commit a lot of delinquent acts than those who were neutral and those who liked school—a finding counter to our hypothesis. But note that there are only 135 students out of 450 who disliked school. Because the marginal frequencies for attitude toward school are so different ($C_1 = 315$, $C_2 = 135$), we can't simply compare raw frequencies. We must standardize these column marginals by calculating percentages. Remember that percentages are standardized frequencies that show the frequency per 100 observations.

Remember that we must calculate our percentages *based on the marginal frequencies of the independent variable*, regardless of whether it is the column or the row. Since the independent variable (liking school) in Table 9.5 is the column variable, we will use the column marginals to calculate the percentages (calculate down). Our percentages, then, should sum to 100% at the end of each column. Table 9.5 reports both the cell frequencies and the cell percentages for Table 9.4. When we compare percentages, we now come to a different conclusion. Of those who reported that they liked school, only 22% committed two or more delinquent offenses in the past year compared with 44% of those who disliked school. If you dislike school, then, you are twice as likely to have committed two or more delinquent acts. Note that we compared percentages for different values of the independent variable at one category of the dependent variable (2+ delinquent offenses).

This should make intuitive sense to you because what we are doing is examining the variation in the independent variable to determine whether this variation is related to different percentages on the dependent variable. If there is a relationship between our two variables, there will be variation; if there is no relationship, then the percentage differences will be small or close to zero. This table seems to indicate that there is a relationship between attitude toward school and number of delinquent acts committed. As we said earlier, those who dislike school are twice as likely to report committing two or more delinquent acts compared with those who liked school (22% vs. 44%). More specifically, it looks like there is a negative relationship between liking school and delinquency. Having a positive attitude toward school does seem to restrain the commission of delinquent acts.

Although we have a larger percentage difference across different values of the independent variable in Table 9.5 than we did in Table 9.3, we still cannot be confident that this difference is a "real" one and not due to sampling variation or chance. To dismiss the probability of random sampling variation producing our observed results, we need to perform a formal hypothesis test involving a test statistic that has a known sampling distribution. Fortunately, we have one, and it is called the chi-square test of independence.

## The Chi-Square Test of Independence

The chi-square test of independence tests the null hypothesis that two categorical variables are independent of each other. In hypothesizing that they are independent, we are making the assumption that they are not related to one another—in causal terms, that the independent variable does not affect or influence the dependent variable. Recall from Chapter 6 that events are independent when they do not influence or affect the outcome of each other. If we can reject this null hypothesis, then we can presume that they are related at least at our stated level of confidence. If, however, we fail to reject the null hypothesis of independence, we must assume that they are not related to each other.

The definitional formula for the chi-square test of independence is the following:

$$\chi^2 = \sum_{i=1}^{k} \frac{(f_o - f_e)^2}{f_e} \qquad (9-1)$$

where

$f_o$ = the observed cell frequencies from our sample data

$f_e$ = the expected cell frequencies we should get under the null hypothesis

$k$ = the number of cells in the table

Note that in describing this formula we are referring to the cells of a contingency table. More specifically, the chi-square test of independence is based on the cell frequencies. The frequencies we must calculate ourselves are the "expected," where "expected" means the frequency we would expect to find in each cell if the two variables were, in fact, independent or not related to each other (which is the assumption of our null hypothesis). What we have, then, is a contingency table of observed cell frequencies and another contingency table of expected cell frequencies. For each cell, we take the difference between the observed and expected cell frequencies, square that difference, divide this squared difference by the **expected frequency**, and sum across all cells. What we do not know yet is where the values of expected cell frequencies come from. We need to explore this in a little detail before proceeding to our hypothesis test.

> **Expected frequencies of a contingency table:** Joint frequency distribution we would expect to see if the two categorical variables were independent of each other. The expected frequencies, therefore, are calculated under the assumption of the null hypothesis—or no relationship between the two variables.

Let's return to our example involving gender and negative emotions. In the contingency table in Table 9.1, we have two categorical variables, a person's gender and whether that person scored "low" or "high" on a measure of negative emotionality. The easiest way to calculate the expected cell frequencies is using the following formula:

$$\text{Expected cell frequency of cell } f_e = \frac{RM_i \times CM_j}{n} \qquad (9-2)$$

where

$RM_i$ = the row marginal frequency for row $i$

$CM_j$ = the column marginal frequency for column $j$

$n$ = the total number of cases

> **Observed frequencies of a contingency table:** Joint distribution of two categorical variables that we actually observed in our sample data.

In words, to find the expected frequency of a given cell, multiply the frequency at the end of the row for this cell times the frequency at the bottom of the column for this cell, and divide this product by the total number of cases, and then do this for each cell in the table. By applying this simple formula to our **observed frequencies** in Table 9.1, we can calculate the expected cell frequencies (expected under the null hypothesis of independence) as:

$$\text{Female and low negative emotions} = \frac{60 \times 90}{120} = 45$$

$$\text{Female and high negative emotions} = \frac{60 \times 30}{120} = 15$$

$$\text{Male and low negative emotions} = \frac{60 \times 90}{120} = 45$$

$$\text{Male and high negative emotions} = \frac{60 \times 30}{120} = 15$$

| Table 9.6 | Observed Cell Frequencies and Expected Cell Frequencies for Relationship Between Gender and Negative Emotionality | | |

| Gender | Negative Emotionality | | Row Total |
| | Low | High | |
|---|---|---|---|
| Female | A<br>46<br>$f_e = 45$ | B<br>14<br>$f_e = 15$ | 60 |
| Male | C<br>44<br>$f_e = 45$ | D<br>16<br>$f_e = 15$ | 60 |
| Column Total | 90 | 30 | $n = 120$ |

We now have two tables of frequencies for gender and negative emotions. Table 9.6 displays both the original observed frequencies along with these calculated expected frequencies. We have also labeled the cells A through D for easier reference. The *expected frequencies* tell us what the joint frequency distribution of gender and negative emotions should look like if, in fact, the two variables were independent. This is what we should see if our two categorical variables are not related to each other. Notice that the row and column marginals and the total number of cases is the same in both the observed and expected tables; the only thing that differs is their joint distribution, which is found in the cells of the table.

The chi-square test of independence answers this question: "Are the observed frequencies significantly different from the expected frequencies?" More specifically, the chi-square test takes the difference between the observed and expected cell frequencies for each cell in the table. If the observed frequencies are equal to the expected frequencies (i.e., if the difference between them is zero), then we would be confident in concluding that the two variables are independent and not related. In fact, if the difference between the observed and expected cell frequencies is zero, the chi-square test will also be zero. As the difference between the observed and expected cell frequencies increases, the value of chi-square increases, and our assumption of independence becomes less likely. Of course, the difference between the expected and observed cell frequencies is generally not going to be exactly zero even when the two variables are independent. In other words, even if the two variables are independent, we would still expect to find a nonzero value of the chi-square statistic. What we have to determine, therefore, is how large a difference we must find between the observed and expected cell frequencies, or how large a chi-square we demand before we are willing to reject the null hypothesis of independence. How large a difference the difference must be is determined by the chi-square probability distribution.

The answer to this question is that the observed value of the chi-square statistic must be equal to or greater than the critical value of chi-square we obtain from our chi-square table at a given alpha level (our selected level of significance) and degrees of freedom. We need to set our alpha level, determine our degrees of freedom, and then go to the chi-square table and identify our critical value and the critical region of the chi-square probability distribution.

To determine our level of significance, we simply weigh the costs of making a Type I and a Type II error. Let's say we have done this and have decided that an alpha level of .05 is reasonable for our current problem. The determination of the number of degrees of freedom in a chi-square test of independence is based on the following formula:

$$\text{Degrees of freedom} = (\text{\# of rows} - 1) \times (\text{\# of columns} - 1)$$

$$\text{Degrees of freedom} = (R - 1) \times (C - 1)$$

In the chi-square test of independence, then, the degrees of freedom are equal to the number of rows minus one times the number of columns minus one. In Table 9.6, we have two rows and two columns, so there is $(2 - 1)(2 - 1) = 1$ degree of freedom. As you will see in the next chapters, degrees of freedom are usually based on the sample size. However, for chi-square, they are based on the table size for a good reason. Recall that a degree of freedom refers to a value that is free to vary, which means that it is not fixed and can assume any number. In Table 9.7, we have question marks in each cell of our contingency table, with the row and column marginals provided. Which cell frequencies are free to vary given the observed row and column marginals?

In determining how many degrees of freedom we have, the row and column marginals or frequencies are given, they are not free to vary. What are free to vary are the four cell frequencies that correspond to the joint distribution of the two variables. Let's start in cell A of Table 9.8 (female and low negative emotions) and ask what value this frequency can be, restricted only by the row and column marginals. Theoretically, this cell can have any frequency as long as we can still get sums of 60 for the row and 90 for the column. Although we could use any number, let's use the number 46 in that cell. Let's now move to cell B. What value can this cell frequency be and still have a row total of 60 and a column total of 30? There is only one number that this cell frequency can be, and that is 14. A cell frequency of 14 and only 14 will make the row marginal equal to 60. As such, this cell frequency is not free to vary because it can only equal 14. How about cell C? Is this cell frequency free to vary? No. The column marginal must sum to 90, and the row marginal must sum to 60. The only way that this can happen is if the cell frequency was 44. It is fixed, then, and not free to vary, as is the cell just to the right of this one (male and high negative emotions). It is not free to vary either because the row marginal must sum to 60 and the column marginal must sum to 30. The only value this frequency can be is 16. In sum, in a 2 × 2 table, there is only one cell frequency that is free to vary, and once that cell frequency is determined, all the other cell frequencies are fixed (i.e., they can be only one value). That is what the concept of degrees of freedom means with respect to contingency tables.

| Table 9.7 | Row and Column Marginals for Gender and Negative Emotions Data Found in Table 9.6 |
|---|---|

| Gender | Negative Emotionality | | |
| | Low | High | Total |
|---|---|---|---|
| Female | ? | ? | 60 |
| Male | ? | ? | 60 |
| Total | 90 | 30 | 120 |

| Table 9.8 | Determining Degrees of Freedom in a 2 × 2 Table, Fixing the Frequencies for the First Cell |
|---|---|

| Gender | Negative Emotionality | | |
| | Low | High | Total |
|---|---|---|---|
| Female | A<br>46 | B<br>? | 60 |
| Male | C<br>? | D<br>? | 60 |
| Total | 90 | 30 | 120 |

We now have all the information we need to conduct our formal hypothesis test. The null hypothesis is that the two variables are independent, and the alternative hypothesis is that they are not independent, and there is a relationship between them. We will test this hypothesis with an alpha of .05.

With an alpha of .05 and 1 degree of freedom, we can go to our chi-square probability distribution table (Table B.4 in Appendix B) and find our critical value of the chi-square statistic. By looking at the table, we see that the critical value of chi-square is 3.841, and since all values of chi-square are positive, the critical region is any chi-square value that is greater than or equal to 3.841. We are now ready to conduct our formal hypothesis test, one step at a time.

**Step 1:**

$H_0$: Gender and negative emotions are independent of each other. If they are independent, we would expect the value of our obtained chi-square statistic to be zero: $\chi^2 = 0$.

$H_1$: Gender and negative emotions are not independent of each other. If they are not independent, we would expect the value of our obtained chi-square statistic to not be equal to zero: $\chi^2 > 0$.

The chi-square distribution is a positive distribution in that we will never have an obtained value that is less than zero. That is because we square the difference between the observed and expected frequencies.

The chi-square test of independence, therefore, will always be a directional or one-tailed test with the alternative stated as $\chi^2 > 0$.

**Step 2:** Our test statistic is the chi-square test of independence. The chi-square test has a chi-square distribution with $(R-1) \times (C-1)$ degrees of freedom.

**Step 3:** We selected an alpha level of .05 and have 1 degree of freedom in our $2 \times 2$ table. We discovered that the critical value of chi-square is 3.841. The critical region is defined as any chi-square greater than or equal to 3.841 (a chi-square is always positive so the hypothesis test will be whether the obtained chi-square is greater than or equal to the critical chi-square).

**Step 4:** We have our table of observed and expected frequencies in Table 9.6. The definitional formula for the chi-square test of independence is:

$$\chi^2 = \sum_{i=1}^{k} \frac{(f_o - f_e)^2}{f_e}$$

where $k$ = the number of cells. What this formula tells us to do is to subtract the expected cell frequency from the observed cell frequency, square this difference, divide this squared difference by the expected cell frequency, repeat the procedure for every cell in the table, and sum the results over all cells. This is our obtained value of the chi-square statistic. The calculations for the independence of gender and negative emotions are shown in Table 9.9, and we have an obtained chi-square of .178.

**Step 5:** Since our obtained chi-square ( $\chi^2_{obt} = .178$ ) is less than our critical chi-square ( $\chi^2_{crit} = 3.841$ ) and does not fall into the critical region, our decision is to fail to reject the null hypothesis. Our conclusion, therefore, is that gender and negative emotions are independent; that is, there is no relationship between them in the population. Our data do not support the hypothesis that males are more likely than females to experience high negative emotions.

| Table 9.9 | Calculation of the Chi-Square Statistic for the Null Hypothesis That Gender and Negative Emotions Are Independent |

| $f_o$ | $f_e$ | $f_o - f_e$ | $(f_o - f_e)^2$ | $\frac{(f_o - f_e)^2}{f_e}$ |
|---|---|---|---|---|
| 46 | 45 | 1 | 1 | .022 |
| 14 | 15 | −1 | 1 | .067 |
| 44 | 45 | −1 | 1 | .022 |
| 16 | 15 | 1 | 1 | .067 |
| | | | | $\chi^2_{obt} = .178$ |

## 🔲 A Simple-to-Use Computational Formula for the Chi-Square Test of Independence

You may find the definitional formula for the chi-square statistic in equation 9-2 some what cumbersome. There is an alternative, computational formula you can use to calculate your observed chi-square statistic, which you might find easier to use since it involves fewer computations. The computational formula for the chi-square test of independence is:

$$\chi^2 = \sum_{i=1}^{k} \left( \frac{f_o^2}{f_e} \right) - n \qquad (9\text{--}3)$$

In this computational formula, the observed frequency for each cell is first squared, and then each squared observed frequency is divided by the expected cell frequency. This is done for each cell in the contingency table. Next these values are summed, and the total number of cases is subtracted from that sum. In steps:

**Step 1:** Square the observed frequency for each cell in your table.

**Step 2:** Divide each squared observed frequency by its expected frequency.

**Step 3:** Perform this operation on each cell in your contingency table, and then sum over all cells.

**Step 4:** Subtract the sample size from this sum. This is your obtained chi-square statistic.

Let's use this computational formula to calculate the chi-square statistic for our gender and negative emotions data in Table 9.6. We show the necessary calculations in Table 9.10. The value of our obtained chi-square statistic is .178, which is exactly the same as what we obtained when we used the definitional formula.

---

## Case Study

## Socioeconomic Status of Neighborhoods and Police Response Time

Table 9.11 gives the joint distribution for two categorical variables: (1) the socioeconomic status of a neighborhood and (2) the swiftness of police response time to a 911 call for assistance. Both variables are measured at the ordinal level. Based on the literature, we think that the affluence of the neighborhood influences police response time and that the police respond faster to calls for assistance made from higher status neighborhoods. In this case study, therefore, neighborhood socioeconomic status is the independent variable and police response time is the dependent variable.

Our independent variable, neighborhood socioeconomic status, has three levels or categories ("low status," "medium status," and "high status"), and the dependent variable, police response time, is also a three-category, ordinal-level variable, with values "less than 3 minutes," "between 3 and 7 minutes," and "more than 7 minutes." Table 9.11 is a 3 × 3 (again, 3 "by" 3) contingency table because there are three rows and three columns. Each cell in this table represents the joint occurrence of neighborhood status and police response time. With three rows and three columns, there are a total of nine cells, with each cell constituting one possible outcome of the joint occurrence of the two variables. Again, we have labelled the cells A through I for ease of discussion. In cell A, we see that there are 11 cases where there is a low-status neighborhood and a police response time of less than 3 minutes. This cell reflects the simultaneous occurrence of two events: a low-status neighborhood and a police response time of less than 3 minutes. Cell B indicates that there were 17 cases where there was a low-status neighborhood and a police response time of between 3 and 7 minutes.

Note that there are a total of 191 cases, which is our total sample size. Note also that there are 63 low-status neighborhoods, 53 medium-status

| Table 9.10 | Calculations for Chi-Square Statistic on Gender and Negative Emotions Data Using the Computational Formula |

| $f_o$ | $f_o^2$ | $f_e$ | $\dfrac{f_o^2}{f_e}$ |
|---|---|---|---|
| 46 | 2,116 | 45 | (2,116 / 45) = 47.022 |
| 14 | 196 | 15 | (196 / 15) = 13.067 |
| 44 | 1,936 | 45 | (1,936 / 45) = 43.022 |
| 16 | 256 | 15 | (256 / 15) = 17.067 |
| | | | $\Sigma = 120.178$ |
| | | | $\chi^2 = 120.178 - 120 = .178$ |

| Table 9.11 | Joint Distribution of Neighborhood Socioeconomic Status and Police Response Time to a 911 Call for Assistance | | | |
|---|---|---|---|---|
| | Police Response Time | | | |
| Neighborhood Socioeconomic Status | Less than 3 minutes | 3–7 Minutes | More than 7 Minutes | Total |
| Low | A<br>11 | B<br>17 | C<br>35 | 63 |
| Medium | D<br>16 | E<br>24 | F<br>13 | 53 |
| High | G<br>48 | H<br>20 | I<br>7 | 75 |
| Total | 75 | 61 | 55 | 191 |

neighborhoods, and 75 high-status neighborhoods in our data. Recall that these numbers (63, 53, and 75) are referred to as the row marginals because they tell us the total number of cases that fall into each row of our table. Similarly, our column marginals tell us that there were 75 times the police responded to a 911 call in less than 3 minutes, 61 times they responded to a call between 3 and 7 minutes, and 55 times they responded to a call in more than 7 minutes. The sum of the row marginals should equal the sum of the column marginals, and these should both equal the total number of cases or observations we have ($63 + 53 + 75 = 75 + 61 + 55 = 191$).

We are now going to test the hypothesis that neighborhood status and police response time are independent events. In other words, the null hypothesis we are testing assumes that the socioeconomic status of the neighborhood is not related to how quickly the police respond to a 911 call for assistance. Before we conduct a formal hypothesis test, however, let's examine the appropriate percentages across values of the independent variable for a fixed value of the dependent variable. Recall that we need to examine how variation in the independent variable affects variation in the dependent variable. Since the socioeconomic status of the neighborhood is the independent variable, we will use the row marginals as the denominator for our percentages. Practically, this means that our percentages will sum to 100% at the end of the rows. We calculate these percentages in Table 9.12.

Let's examine the value of the dependent variable at a response time of more than 7 minutes. From Table 9.12 we can see that 56% of the time the police responded to a 911 call for assistance in a low-status neighborhood in more than 7 minutes. This drops to 25% of the time in medium-status neighborhoods, and it drops still further to only 9% of the time in high-status neighborhoods. As the social status of the neighborhood varies from low to high, then, it becomes less likely that the police will take longer than 7 minutes to respond to a 911 call. In other words, police respond faster in high status than either medium- or low-status neighborhoods. We reach the same substantive conclusion when we examine the value of the dependent variable at a quick police response time—less than 3 minutes. Police responded quickly only 17% of the time in a low-status neighborhood, 30% of the time in a medium-status neighborhood, and 64% of the time in a high-status neighborhood. From these percentage differences, it looks like there is a relationship between the socioeconomic status of the neighborhood and how quickly the police respond to a 911 call; they are more likely to respond quickly, and less likely to respond slowly, in more affluent neighborhoods.

Examining how these two variables co-vary is only the first indicator, however, in determining whether a relationship exists between the two variables. The problem with using the calculation of percentage differences is that there is no probability distribution associated with these statistics. Without a known probability distribution, there is no way to determine whether the difference in percentages we observed in our sample data is due to a

| Table 9.12 | Relationship Between Neighborhood Socioeconomic Status and Police Response Time to a 911 Call for Assistance: Examining Percentages | | | |
|---|---|---|---|---|
| | *Police Response Time* | | | |
| *Neighborhood Socioeconomic Status* | *Less than 3 Minutes(%)* | *3–7 Minutes (%)* | *More than 7 Minutes (%)* | *Total* |
| Low | 11 | 17 | 35 | 63 |
| | 17% | 27% | 56% | 100% |
| Medium | 16 | 24 | 13 | 53 |
| | 30% | 45% | 25% | 100% |
| High | 48 | 20 | 7 | 75 |
| | 64% | 27% | 9% | 100% |
| Total | 75 | 61 | 55 | 191 |

relationship between the two variables in our population or to random sampling variability. A formal hypothesis test avoids this ambiguity, and that is why we use the chi-square test for independence.

The first step in conducting a chi-square test of independence is to determine what the expected frequencies would be if the two variables were in fact independent. Let's use the formula to calculate the expected frequencies:

$$\left( \frac{RM_i \times CM_j}{n} \right)$$

Here is what you should obtain:

Low status and less than 3 minutes response time: $\frac{63 \times 75}{191} = 25$

Low status and 3–7 minutes response time: $\frac{63 \times 61}{191} = 20$

Low status and more than 7 minutes response time: $\frac{63 \times 55}{191} = 18$

Medium status and less than 3 minutes response time: $\frac{53 \times 75}{191} = 21$

Medium status and 3–7 minutes response time: $\frac{53 \times 61}{191} = 17$

Medium status and more than 7 minutes response time: $\frac{53 \times 55}{191} = 15$

High status and less than 3 minutes response time: $\frac{75 \times 75}{191} = 29$

$$\text{High status and 3–7 minutes response time: } \frac{75 \times 61}{191} = 24$$

$$\text{High status and more than 7 minutes response time: } \frac{75 \times 55}{191} = 22$$

The expected cell frequencies under the null hypothesis that neighborhood socioeconomic status and police response time are independent of each other are given along with the original observed cell frequencies in Table 9.13. Remember that the expected cell frequencies tell us the joint distribution of neighborhood status and police response time we would *expect to see* if these two variables were not related to each other, that is, if they were independent.

We next need to select an alpha level and calculate our degrees of freedom. Let's use an alpha of .01 for this hypothesis test. By using our formula for the correct degrees of freedom in a contingency table $[df = (R - 1) \times (C - 1)]$, we can see that we have $(3 - 1) \times (3 - 1)$ or 4 degrees of freedom. With an alpha level of .01 and 4 degrees of freedom, we can now go to our chi-square probability distribution table (Table B.4 in Appendix B) and find our critical value of the chi-square statistic. By looking at the table, we see that the critical value of chi-square is 13.277. The critical region for rejecting the null hypothesis, then, is any chi-square value that is greater than or equal to 13.277. We are now ready to conduct our formal hypothesis test, one step at a time:

**Step 1:**

$H_0$: Neighborhood socioeconomic status and police response time are independent of each other. Our obtained value of chi-square should not be significantly different from zero: $\chi^2 = 0$.

$H_1$: Neighborhood socioeconomic status and police response time are not independent of each other; neighborhood status and police response time are related to each other. Our obtained value of chi-square should be significantly greater than zero: $\chi^2 > 0$.

**Step 2:** Our test statistic is the chi-square test of independence. The chi-square test has a chi-square distribution.

**Step 3:** We selected an alpha level of .01 and have 4 degrees of freedom in our 3 × 3 table $((3 - 1)(3 - 1) = 4)$. The critical value of chi-square is 13.277. The critical region is defined as any chi-square greater than or equal to 13.277.

| Table 9.13 | Observed and Expected Cell Frequencies under the Null Hypothesis of Independence | | | |
|---|---|---|---|---|
| | Police Response Time | | | |
| Neighborhood Socioeconomic Status | Less than 3 Minutes | 3–7 Minutes | More than 7 Minutes | Total |
| Low | 11 $f_e = 25$ | 17 $f_e = 20$ | 35 $f_e = 18$ | 63 |
| Medium | 16 $f_e = 21$ | 24 $f_e = 17$ | 13 $f_e = 15$ | 53 |
| High | 48 $f_e = 29$ | 20 $f_e = 24$ | 7 $f_e = 22$ | 75 |
| Total | 75 | 61 | 55 | 191 |

**Step 4:** We have both our observed and expected cell frequencies in Table 9.13, and we will use the computational formula to calculate the chi-square statistic:

$$\chi^2 = \sum_{i=1}^{k} \left( \frac{f_o^2}{f_e} \right) - n$$

The calculations for this problem are shown for you in Table 9.14, and our obtained chi-square is 52.04.

**Step 5:** Since our obtained chi-square $\chi_{obt}^2 = 52.04$ is greater than our critical chi-square $\left( \chi_{crit}^2 = 13.277 \right)$ and falls into the critical region, our decision is to reject the null hypothesis. Our conclusion, therefore, is that neighborhood socioeconomic status and police response time are not independent; they are related to one another in the population. We can also conclude the direction of this relationship. We can generalize that in the population, neighborhoods with higher socioeconomic status are more likely to get quicker police response times than neighborhoods with lower socioeconomic status.

Although the chi-square statistic enables us to reject the null hypothesis of independence in favor of the alternative hypothesis, it does not tell us anything about the magnitude or strength of the relationship. Two variables may be related to each other in the population, but the relationship may be very weak, it may be of moderate strength, or it may be very strong. To determine the strength of the relationship between two categorical variables, we need to learn about something called measures of association. We will do this in the next section.

**Table 9.14**

**Computational Formula: Calculation of the Chi-Square Statistic for the Null Hypothesis that Neighborhood Socioeconomic Status and Police Response Time Are Independent**

| $f_o$ | $f_o^2$ | $f_e$ | $\dfrac{f_o^2}{f_e}$ |
|---|---|---|---|
| 11 | 121 | 25 | 4.84 |
| 17 | 289 | 20 | 14.45 |
| 35 | 1,225 | 18 | 68.06 |
| 16 | 256 | 21 | 12.19 |
| 24 | 576 | 17 | 33.88 |
| 13 | 169 | 15 | 11.27 |
| 48 | 2,304 | 29 | 79.45 |
| 20 | 400 | 24 | 16.67 |
| 7 | 49 | 22 | 2.23 |
| | | | $\Sigma = 243.04$ |
| | | | $\chi_{obt}^2 = 243.04 - 191$ |
| | | | $\chi_{obt}^2 = 52.04$ |

## 🔲 Measures of Association: Determining the Strength of the Relationship Between Two Categorical Variables

The chi-square statistic enables us to determine whether two categorical variables (nominal or ordinal) are independent or are related to each other in the population, but it tells us nothing about the strength of the relationship if in fact one exists. Throughout this text, you will continually be reminded that a significant relationship does not always indicate that two variables have a strong relationship. In fact, with a large enough sample size, many relationships can attain significance but be only weakly related. When we are interested in understanding the strength of the relationship between our variables, we need to be acquainted with something called measures of association. A **measure of association** is a summary measure that captures the magnitude or strength of the relationship between two variables. There are different kinds of measures of association, depending on the level of measurement for our variables.

> **Measures of association:** Statistics that inform us about the strength, or magnitude, as well as the direction of the relationship between two variables.

### Nominal-Level Variables

## Case Study

## Gender and Police Officer Work

Let's start with a very simple problem. In this problem we have a 2 × 2 contingency table with nominal-level data. For example, in Table 9.15, we have the joint distribution of two nominal-level variables, the gender of a police officer (male/female), and the type of job that officer does (desk job/patrol). We believe that male and female police officers may be given very different assignments. In this scenario, gender is our independent variable, and work assignment is the dependent variable. When we calculate the percentages in the table, by using the row marginals as the denominators because the independent variable is on the row, we see that 67% of female police officers work in desk jobs, compared with only 36% of male officers. If we were to conduct a hypothesis test of the independence of these two variables, we would obtain a chi-square of 12.25. With 1 degree of freedom, we would reject the null hypothesis of independence at either a .05 or a .01 level of significance. We would conclude that in the population, female police officers are more likely to be in desk jobs compared with patrol jobs.

A measure of association we could use in this problem to gauge the strength of the relationship is the phi-coefficient. The phi-coefficient ($\phi$) is appropriate when we have nominal-level variables and a 2 × 2 table. The phi-coefficient is very simple to calculate and uses the obtained value of our chi-square coefficient along with the sample size:

$$\phi = \sqrt{\frac{\chi^2_{obt}}{n}} \qquad (9\text{--}4)$$

| Table 9.15 | Joint Distribution of Gender of Police Officer and Type of Work Performed | | |
|---|---|---|---|
| Gender | Desk Job | Patrol | Total |
| Male | 45 36% | 80 64% | 125 100% |
| Female | 30 67% | 15 33% | 45 100% |
| Total | 75 | 95 | 170 |

The formula tells us to take the ratio of the obtained chi-square statistic to the number of cases in the sample, and then take the square root. The phi-coefficient has a finite range between 0 and 1; it will equal 0 when there is no relationship and will attain a maximum value of 1.0 with a perfect relationship. The phi-coefficient will always be positive, and the magnitude of the relationship will tell us how strongly the two nominal-level variables are related. Magnitudes of phi near zero indicate a very weak relationship, and those near 1.0 indicate a very strong relationship. A helpful rule of thumb to follow with the phi-coefficient (and any other measure of association) is that relationships between 0 and ±.29 can be considered "weak," relationships between ±.30 and ±.59 can be considered "moderate," and relationships between ±.60 and ±1.00 can be considered "strong." However, this is only an informal guide. For the data in Table 9.15, we would have a phi-coefficient of:

$$\phi = \sqrt{\frac{12.25}{170}}$$
$$\phi = .27$$

A phi-coefficient of .27 tells us that there is only a weak relationship between gender and type of assignment on the police force.

The phi-coefficient cannot be used for nominal variables that have more than two levels or categories. One measure of association for tables that are larger than $2 \times 2$ is the **contingency coefficient (C)**. Like phi, the contingency coefficient is based on the obtained value of the chi-square statistic. The formula for $C$ is:

> **Contingency coefficient (C):** Statistical measure of association that quantifies the strength or magnitude of a relationship between two nominal-level variables.

$$C = \sqrt{\frac{\chi^2_{obt}}{n + \chi^2_{obt}}} \qquad (9\text{--}5)$$

Let's do an example.

| Table 9.16 | Joint Distribution for Type of Lawyer and Type of Sentence Received | | | |
|---|---|---|---|---|
| | *Type of Sentence Received* | | | |
| *Type of Lawyer* | *Probation* | *Fine Only* | *Fine and Jail Time* | *Total* |
| Court-Appointed | 5 | 10 | 40 | 55 |
| | 9% | 18% | 73% | 100% |
| Public Defender | 15 | 20 | 30 | 65 |
| | 23% | 31% | 46% | 100% |
| Private | 25 | 10 | 5 | 40 |
| | 63% | 25% | 12% | 100% |
| Total | 45 | 40 | 75 | 160 |

## Case Study

## Type of Counsel and Sentence

Table 9.16 shows you the joint distribution of two nominal-level variables: (1) the type of lawyer a criminal defendant had and (2) the type of sentence that criminal received after conviction. We think that the type of lawyer a defendant has affects the kind of sentence received, so type of lawyer is the independent variable and type of sentence is the dependent variable. When we examine the joint percentage distributions within the dependent variable category "receiving a fine and jail time," we see that 73% of those who had a court-appointed lawyer received this sanction, compared with only 46% of those who had a public defender and only 12% of those who had a private attorney. It seems that having a private attorney gives you an advantage at sentencing. By looking at the least severe sanction of probation, we see that 63% of those who had private attorneys received a probation only sentence compared with 9% of court-appointed lawyers and 23% of those who had public defenders. When we conduct a chi-square test of independence at an alpha level of .01 and 4 $df$, we can reject the null hypothesis because $\chi^2_{\text{crit}} = 13.277$ and $\chi^2_{\text{obt}} = 44.94$. We conclude from this that there is a relationship in the population between these two variables, although we do not know the strength of the relationship. We can use the contingency coefficient to tell us that:

$$C = \sqrt{\frac{44.94}{160 + 44.94}}$$

$$C = .47$$

A contingency coefficient of .47 informs us that there is a moderately strong relationship between the type of lawyer one has and the type of sentence one receives when convicted.

Although it is easy to calculate, one disadvantage of the contingency coefficient is that a perfect relationship is not always anchored by a maximum value of 1.0. Depending on the size of the table, a perfect relationship may be lower than 1.0, although it will never be greater than 1.0. A measure of association for nominal-level variables that does not have this disadvantage is known as **Cramer's V**. Cramer's $V$ can also be used with nominal-level data and with tables that are larger than $2 \times 2$. Like $C$ and the phi-coefficient, it is based on chi-square, and it ranges in magnitude from 0 to 1.0. The formula for calculating $V$ is:

> **Cramer's V:** Statistical measure of association that quantifies the strength or magnitude of a relationship between two nominal-level variables.

$$V = \sqrt{\frac{\chi^2_{\text{obt}}}{n(k-1)}} \tag{9-6}$$

where $k$ = the number of rows or the number of columns, whichever is smaller. For Table 9.16, the value of $V$ would be:

$$V = \sqrt{\frac{44.94}{160(3-1)}}$$

$$V = .37$$

We would conclude from this that there is a moderately strong association between type of lawyer and type of sentence.

Still another measure of association with nominal-level data is **lambda ($\lambda$)**. Lambda can be used on tables that are larger than $2 \times 2$, and it is known as a proportionate reduction in error (PRE) measure of association. Recall that when two variables are independent, knowledge of one variable will not help us predict the occurrence of the other. When two variables are related to one another, however (that is, when they are not independent), knowing something about one variable should help us predict the other. A **proportionate reduction in error (PRE)** measure will tell us exactly how much better we will be in predicting one variable from knowledge of the other. The calculation of lambda requires that we identify beforehand which variable is the independent variable and which is the dependent variable because its magnitude will be different depending on this identification. Because of this fact, lambda is known as an *asymmetric* measure of association.

> **Lambda ($\lambda$):** Statistical measure of association that quantifies the strength or magnitude of a relationship between two nominal-level variables.

> **Proportionate reduction in error (PRE) measure:** Statistics that tell us how much we can reduce prediction errors by knowing the value of an independent variable.

The magnitude of our lambda coefficient will vary between 0 and 1.0. A value of 0 means that we do not reduce our errors at all in predicting the dependent variable from knowledge of the independent variable, and a value of 1.0 means that we can reduce all of our errors—that is, that knowledge of the independent variable will allow us to predict with perfect accuracy the value of the dependent variable. Magnitudes of lambda close to 0 suggest that the relationship between the variables is weak, and the strength of the relationship increases as the observed lambda value approaches 1.0. An easy way to interpret lambda is to multiply the obtained value by 100 to obtain the percentage amount that we are able to reduce our prediction errors in the dependent variable by having information about the independent variable. For example, if we have an obtained lambda of .70, when we multiply this value by 100 (.70 × 100 = 70%), we can claim that we can reduce our prediction errors in the dependent variable by 70% with knowledge of the independent variable. For an obtained lambda of .15, we have reduced our prediction errors by only 15% and so on. The whole notion of prediction errors and reducing these errors may be a bit vague, so let's carefully go through an example.

Let's use the data in Table 9.16. Suppose that without any other information, we have to predict what the sentence would be for each of these 160 criminal defendants. What would our best guess be? Our best guess for each case would be the mode of the dependent variable—a fine and jail time ($n = 75$). That would be our best guess because absent any other information, the mode of the dependent variable is the outcome with the greatest probability. If we predicted that each of the 160 defendants would be sentenced to pay a fine and serve some jail time, we would be correct 75 times (the actual number who received this sentence) and would have made 85 prediction errors (the 45 who received probation plus the 40 who received a fine only). With 75 correct predictions out of 160, we would have a 47% correct rate of prediction. The question now is whether we can improve this rate of prediction by having some knowledge of the independent variable.

In the calculation of lambda, we ask the following question: "If I use the modal response *for each level or category of the independent variable* to predict the dependent variable, how many prediction errors will I make?" Among defendants who had court-appointed lawyers, the mode is a fine with jail time. By using this mode to predict the dependent variable for defendants with court-appointed lawyers, you would accurately predict 40 cases (because 40 defendants with court-appointed lawyers received a fine with jail time) and make 15 prediction errors (because you predicted they would get a fine and jail time, but 5 received probation and 10 received a fine only). The mode for those with public defenders is also a fine with jail time. If you predicted that all 65 of these cases would receive a fine with jail, you would be correct 30 times and make 35 prediction errors. The mode for those defendants with private lawyers is probation. If you predicted that all 40 defendants with private lawyers received probation, you would be correct 25 times and would make 15 prediction errors. By using the mode of each level of the independent variable to predict the category of the dependent variable, then, you would make a total of 15 + 35 + 15 = 65 prediction errors. Recall that if you did *not* use knowledge of the independent variable to predict the dependent variable but used only the mode of the dependent variable for all cases, you would have made 85 errors. The formula for the lambda coefficient is:

$$\lambda = \frac{\begin{array}{c}\text{Number of errors} \\ \text{using mode of} \\ \text{dependent variable}\end{array} - \begin{array}{c}\text{Number of errors using mode} \\ \text{of dependent variable within} \\ \text{categories of the independent} \\ \text{variable}\end{array}}{\text{Number of errors using mode of dependent variable}} \qquad (9\text{--}7)$$

In our example with type of counsel as the independent variable and type of sentence as the dependent variable (Table 9.16), the observed value of lambda is:

$$\lambda = \frac{85 - 65}{85}$$
$$\lambda = .24$$

By multiplying this by 100, we can conclude that we are able to reduce our errors in predicting the dependent variable (type of sentence received) by 24% when we use the independent variable. To see why we have a proportionate reduction in errors of 24%, remember that when we just used the mode of the dependent variable to predict sentence type, we made 85 errors out of 160 predictions, for an error rate of 53%. When we used knowledge of the independent variable to predict the type of sentence, we made 65 errors out of 160 predictions, for an error rate of 41%. The percentage difference in the error rates of 53% (without using the independent variable) and 41% (error rate when using the independent variable) is 12%. Twelve percent is equal to 24% of our error rate of 53% obtained when we did not use the independent variable. Hence, the proportionate reduction in error is 24%—this is the value of our lambda statistic.

There is also a computational formula for lambda that is very easy to use:

$$\lambda = \frac{(\Sigma f_i) - f_d}{n - f_d} \tag{9-8}$$

where

$f_i$ = the largest cell frequency in *each* category of the independent variable

$f_d$ = the largest marginal frequency of the dependent variable

$n$ = the total number of cases

For the data in Table 9.16, the largest cell frequency for court-appointed lawyers is 40, for public defenders it is 30, and for private counsel it is 25. The largest marginal frequency for the dependent values is 75, for the value "fine and jail time." With this information we can calculate the value of lambda:

$$\lambda = \frac{(40 + 30 + 25) - 75}{160 - 75}$$
$$\lambda = .24$$

As you can see, this is the same value as we obtained using the definitional formula.

---

## Ordinal-Level Variables

When our variables are measured at the ordinal level, phi, the contingency coefficient, Cramer's *V,* and the lambda coefficient are no longer appropriate measures of association. With ordinal-level variables, one of the most popular measures of association in the literature is **Goodman and Kruskal's gamma**. Like lambda, gamma ($\gamma$) is a proportionate reduction in error measure, which takes on a minimum value of 0 (when there is no relationship between the two ordinal variables) and maximum values of $\pm 1.0$ (for a perfect positive and a perfect negative relationship). As we noted with respect to the phi-coefficient, a helpful rule of thumb to follow with any measure of association—although it is only an informal guide—is that relationships between 0 and $\pm .29$ can be considered "weak," relationships between $\pm .30$ and $\pm .59$ can be considered "moderate," and relationships between $\pm .60$ and $\pm 1.00$ can be considered "strong." Unlike lambda, gamma is a symmetric measure of association, which means that it does not matter which variable we designate as the independent and which as the dependent variable.

> **Goodman and Kruskal's gamma:**
> Statistical measure of association that quantifies the strength or magnitude of a relationship between two ordinal-level variables. **Also called Yule's Q** with a 2 X 2 table.

In the special case of a $2 \times 2$ table (a table with two rows and two columns), gamma is often referred to as **Yule's Q**. With the four cells labeled as follows:

| A | B |
|---|---|
| C | D |

Yule's Q or gamma for a $2 \times 2$ table is defined as:

$$Q = \frac{(f_{cellA} \times f_{cellD}) - (f_{cellB} \times f_{cellC})}{(f_{cellA} \times f_{cellD}) + (f_{cellB} \times f_{cellC})} \tag{9-9}$$

To calculate the $Q$ coefficient, then, all you do is take the product of the frequency in cell A times the frequency in cell D (called the cross-product), and the product of the frequency in cell B and the frequency in cell C (the other cross-product). In the numerator of $Q$, we take the difference between these two values, and in the denominator, we take the sum.

Let's use this formula to calculate the value of $Q$ for our two variables in Table 9.3, which showed the joint distribution of gender and negative emotions. Recall that we failed to reject the null hypothesis when we conducted our chi-square test of independence. The value of $Q$ for these data is:

$$Q = \frac{(46 \times 16) - (44 \times 14)}{(46 \times 16) + (44 \times 14)}$$
$$Q = \frac{120}{1,352}$$
$$Q = .09$$

The value of Yule's $Q$ here is very small—not that much different from zero—confirming our chi-square test result that there is no relationship in the population between gender and negative emotions.

--- **Case Study** ---

## Adolescents' Employment and Drug and Alcohol Use

Let's try another example. Table 9.17 shows the joint distribution of two variables. One variable is the number of hours that a youth spends working during the school year, and the second is the number of times during the year that he or she reports using drugs or alcohol. In this example, we will take the number of working hours as the independent variable and the level of drug/alcohol use as the dependent variable. Since the independent variable is located on the rows, that is how the percentages are calculated. We can see that 80% of those adolescents who work 20 hours or less a week have used alcohol or drugs on two or more occasions compared to only 33% of those who worked more than 20 hours a week. When we conduct a chi-square test of independence, we obtain a chi-square value of 31.85, which with 1 degree of freedom is significant at either a .05 or a .01 level. Therefore, we reject the null hypothesis of independence and conclude that there is a relationship between the two variables. In the population, we can conclude that students who work more are less likely to engage in drug and alcohol use compared with those who work less. We can then determine the strength of the relationship with Yule's $Q$:

$$Q = \frac{(15 \times 20) - (40 \times 60)}{(15 \times 20) - (40 \times 60)}$$
$$Q = \frac{-2,100}{2,700}$$
$$Q = -.78$$

We have a Yule's $Q$ of −.78, implying that there is a fairly strong negative relationship between working while in school and substance use. What does a negative relationship imply here?

In a **negative relationship**, increasing the level of one variable has the effect of decreasing the level of the other, whereas in a **positive relationship**, increasing the level of one variable has the effect of increasing the level of the other. Note that in Table 9.17, the two variables are arranged in

> **Negative relationship between two variables:** An increase in one variable is related to a decrease in the other.

**Table 9.17** Joint Distribution of Number of Hours Worked per Week During the School Year and Number of Times a Youth Has Used Drugs or Alcohol

| Number of Hours Worked | Number of Times Used Drugs/Alcohol | | Total |
|---|---|---|---|
| | 0 | 1 or More | |
| Less than 20 | 15 | 60 | 75 |
| | 20% | 80% | 100% |
| 20 or more | 40 | 20 | 60 |
| | 67% | 33% | 100% |
| Total | 55 | 80 | 135 |

**Positive relationship between two variables:** An increase in one variable is related to an increase in the other.

increasing order in the sense that drug/alcohol use increases from left to right (from no use to using it one or more times), and working increases from less than 20 hours per week in the top row to working 20 or more hours per week in the lower row. A negative relationship between two ordinal-level variables means that increasing the independent variable decreases the dependent variable. In this case, increasing the level of working from less than 20 hours per week to 20 or more hours has the effect of decreasing the level of the dependent variable from one or more times using drugs/alcohol to not using. Had we obtained a $Q$ coefficient of +.78, we would have concluded that increasing the level of working from less than 20 to more than 20 hours per week increases the risk of drug/alcohol use from zero times to one or more times.

In contingency tables that are larger than $2 \times 2$, we cannot use Yule's $Q$ but must use a more general formula for Goodman and Kruskal's gamma that can be used on any table. The formula for gamma is:

$$\gamma = \frac{CP - DP}{CP + DP} \tag{9–10}$$

where

$CP$ = the number of concordant pairs of observations

$DP$ = the number of discordant pairs of observations

Before we get to the application of the gamma coefficient, we need to understand exactly what a concordant pair and a discordant pair of observations are. We are not going to calculate the value of gamma by hand, but it is important for you to understand what it is actually measuring.

## Case Study

### Age of Onset for Delinquency and Future Offending

Let's begin with two variables measured from a sample of adult offenders. Both variables are measured at the ordinal level and have three levels or categories. The independent variable is the age at which adults first engaged in delinquent offending:

**Variable 1 ($V_1$): Age of First Delinquent Act**

Level 1: 8–10 years old

Level 2: 11–13 years old

Level 3: 14–16 years old

The dependent variable is the number of years into adulthood that the person offends:

## Variable 2 ($V_2$): Years of "Criminal Career"

Level 1: 1–4 years

Level 2: 5–8 years

Level 3: 9 years or more

Since these two variables are measured at the ordinal level, those at a higher level or category have more of the variable than those at a lower level. Let's now take five people from our sample who fall into different categories of the two ordinal variables. The following table shows the level, or "score," on both variables for each of these five people.

| Person Number | Level on $V_1$ | Level on $V_2$ |
|:---:|:---:|:---:|
| 1 | 1 | 2 |
| 2 | 2 | 3 |
| 3 | 3 | 2 |
| 4 | 3 | 3 |
| 5 | 3 | 2 |

Two pairs of observations are said to be *concordant* when the scores on the two variables are consistently higher or consistently lower. For example, let's take person 1 and person 2. In comparing person 1 and person 2 on the two variables, we see that the second person scores higher on both $V_1$ and $V_2$ (2 vs. 1 on $V_1$ and 3 vs. 2 on $V_2$). This pair of persons or pair of observations, then, is concordant because person 2 scores consistently higher on both variables compared with person 1. Person 4 is concordant with person 1 also because that person also scores higher on both variables (3 vs. 1 on $V_1$ and 3 vs. 2 on $V_2$). Now let's compare person 2 and person 3. Person 2 is lower on $V_1$ compared with person 3 (2 vs. 3) but higher on $V_2$ (3 vs. 2). Person 2 is not, therefore, consistently higher (or lower) on both variables than person 3 but, rather, is higher on one variable and lower on another. Pairs of observations like these, where one case is higher on one variable but lower on another, are called a *discordant pair*. Think of discordant pairs of cases as those where the scores on the two variables are dissimilar. A person is higher than the other person on one variable but lower than that person on the other. Person 5 is also discordant with person 2. Now let's compare person 3 with person 4. In this pair of observations, persons 3 and 4 are tied on $V_1$ and person 4 is higher than person 3 on $V_2$. Person 4 is also tied with person 2 on the second variable ($V_2$). Person 3 is tied with person 5 on both variables. These three comparisons are neither concordant nor discordant; they are referred to as *tied* pairs of observations because they have the same score on at least one variable.

In comparing a pair of cases, then, there are three possible outcomes: concordant, discordant, or tied pairs. In a given contingency table, if concordant pairs outnumber discordant pairs, we will find a positive relationship because the predominance of concordant pairs implies that as one variable increases, so does the other. If we have instead a predominance of discordant pairs, then we will find a negative relationship between the two variables because this implies that as one variable increases, the other decreases. If there are approximately the same number of concordant as discordant pairs, then our variables are not related to one other or not related very strongly. Now that we know what concordant and discordant pairs are, we can reintroduce the gamma coefficient and apply it to a few of our problems.

The formula for gamma is:

$$\gamma = \frac{CP - DP}{CP + DP}$$

Gamma, therefore, simply takes the ratio of the difference between the number of concordant pairs of cases (*CP*) and the number of discordant pairs (*DP*) to the sum of the concordant and discordant pairs.

| Table 9.18 | Grades in School and Self-Reported Acts of Petty Theft | | | |
|---|---|---|---|---|
| | Self-Reported Theft | | | |
| Grades in School | 0 | 1–5 | 6+ | Total |
| Mostly Ds and Fs | 23 | 19 | 20 | 62 |
| Mostly Cs | 307 | 157 | 123 | 587 |
| Mostly Bs | 762 | 345 | 155 | 1,262 |
| Mostly As | 418 | 166 | 56 | 640 |
| Total | 1,510 | 687 | 354 | 2,551 |

Like Yule's Q, gamma ranges in magnitude from 0 to ± 1.0, with 0 indicating no relationship between our ordinal-level variables, –1.0 indicating a perfect negative relationship, and +1.0 indicating a perfect positive relationship. As you can perhaps see from the formula, gamma takes into account only concordant and discordant pairs of cases; it ignores all those pairs that are tied on one or both of the variables. Note also that when $CP > DP$, gamma will be positive, and when $CP < DP$, gamma will be negative. Finally, note that the magnitude of gamma will increase as the number of $CP$ or $DP$ cases increases relative to the other. Now, the only issue remaining is how we go about calculating gamma. As you might imagine, calculating the value of gamma by hand can be quite time consuming. Those of you interested can go to the website to find out how to calculate the value of gamma by hand for the data in Table 9.18. This table shows the joint distribution for a high-school sample of 2,551 students and the independent variable of grades in school and the dependent variable of self-reported thefts in the past year. For the rest of you, we are simply going to give you the number of concordant and discordant pairs! The number of concordant pairs is 472,657, and the number of discordant pairs is 699,336. This results in the value of gamma for Table 9.18 as follows:

$$\gamma = \frac{472,657 - 699,336}{472,657 + 699,336}$$

$$\gamma = -.19$$

If we calculated the value of chi-square for these data, we would have been able to reject the null hypothesis and would have concluded that in the population, students with higher grades were less likely to engage in property crime. The gamma coefficient of –.19 tells us that there is only a weak negative relationship between school grades and self-reported theft. This should be a reminder that just because we reject the null hypothesis and conclude that there is a relationship between two variables in the population that the relationship is a strong one. Here, we reject the null, but the relationship happens to be weak. Recall that the presence of a negative relationship means that an increase in the independent variable is associated with a decrease in the dependent variable. By looking at Table 9.18, this means that as a student's grades "increase" (that is, improve by going from Ds and Fs to As), the student is less likely to commit acts of theft. In other words, having good grades decreases the probability that high-school students will engage in property crime.

## ▣ Summary

In this chapter, we learned how to test a null hypothesis when both the independent and dependent variables are measured at the nominal or ordinal level using a chi-square ($\chi^2$) test. Because testing the significance of a relationship is different than determining the strength of a relationship, we also examined measures of association, which capture information about the strength of the relationship between two categorical variables. The appropriate measure of association depends on the level of measurement of our variables.

## Key Terms

> Review key terms with eFlashcards. **$**SAGE edge™

chi-square test of independence   244
column marginal, or column
   frequency   245
contingency coefficient (C)   259
contingency table   244
Cramer's V   260
expected frequencies   249

Goodman and Kruskal's
   gamma (γ)   262
joint frequency distribution   244
lambda (λ)   260
measure of association   258
negative relationship   263
observed frequencies   249

percentage differences   246
positive relationship   263
proportionate reduction in error
   measure (PRE)   260
row marginal, or row frequency   245
Goodman and Kruskal's gamma   262

## Key Formulas

Definitional formula for chi-square statistic (equations 9–1 and 9–2):

$$\chi^2 = \sum_{i=1}^{k} \frac{(f_o - f_e)^2}{f_e}$$

Computational formula for expected cell frequencies:

$$\frac{RM_i \times CM_i}{n}$$

Computational formula for chi-square statistic (equation 9–3):

$$\chi^2 = \sum_{i=1}^{k} \left( \frac{f_o^2}{f_e} \right) - n$$

Phi-coefficient (equation 9–4):

$$\phi = \sqrt{\frac{\chi^2_{obt}}{n}}$$

Contingency coefficient (equation 9–5):

$$C = \sqrt{\frac{\chi^2_{obt}}{n + \chi^2_{obt}}}$$

Cramer's V (equation 9–6):

$$V = \sqrt{\frac{\chi^2_{obt}}{n(k-1)}}$$

Lambda (equation 9–7):

$$\lambda = \frac{\begin{array}{c}\text{Number of errors}\\ \text{using mode of}\\ \text{dependent variable}\end{array} - \begin{array}{c}\text{Number of errors using mode}\\ \text{of dependent variable within}\\ \text{categories of the independent}\\ \text{variable}\end{array}}{\text{Number of errors using mode of dependent variable}}$$

Computational formula for lambda (equation 9–8):

$$\lambda = \frac{(\Sigma f_i) - f_d}{n - f_d}$$

Yule's Q (equation 9–9):

$$Q = \frac{(f_{cellA} \times f_{cellD}) - (f_{cellB} \times f_{cellC})}{(f_{cellA} \times f_{cellD}) + (f_{cellB} \times f_{cellC})}$$

Gamma (equation 9–10):

$$\gamma = \frac{CP - DP}{CP + DP}$$

## Practice Problems

1. The following contingency table describes the joint distribution of two variables: (1) the type of institution a correctional officer works in and (2) whether the officer reports being satisfied with the job. Your hypothesis is that those who work in medium-security facilities will be more satisfied with their job:

| Type of Institution | Satisfied with Job? | | Total |
|---|---|---|---|
| | No | Yes | |
| Medium Security | 15 | 30 | 45 |
| Maximum Security | 100 | 40 | 140 |
| Total | 115 | 70 | 185 |

a. What is the independent and what is the dependent variable?

b. How many observations or cases are there?

c. What are the column marginals?

d. What are the row marginals?

e. What is the size of this contingency table?

f. How many correctional officers are in medium-security facilities and are satisfied with their job?

g. How many correctional officers are in maximum-security facilities and are not satisfied with their jobs?

h. How many degrees of freedom are there in this table?

i. Calculate the relative risk of not being satisfied with one's job for each of the two types of facilities. What does this suggest?

j. Test the null hypothesis that the two variables are independent. Use an alpha level of .05, and state each step of your hypothesis test. If you reject the null hypothesis, how strongly are the two variables related?

2. Social disorganization theorists have argued that neighborhoods that lack the capacity to solve their own problems (i.e., are socially disorganized) have higher rates of crime and other social problems than neighborhoods that are organized. To test this hypothesis, you take a random sample of 250 communities and determine whether they are socially organized or disorganized and whether they have low or high crime rates. Here are your data:

| Type of Institution | Social Organization | | Total |
|---|---|---|---|
| | Socially Organized | Socially Disorganized | |
| Low Crime Rate | 90 | 98 | 188 |

| Type of Institution | Social Organization | | Total |
|---|---|---|---|
| | Socially Organized | Socially Disorganized | |
| High Crime Rate | 10 | 52 | 62 |
| Total | 100 | 150 | 250 |

a. What is the independent and what is the dependent variable?

b. How many observations or cases are there?

c. What are the column marginals?

d. What are the row marginals?

e. What is the size of this contingency table?

f. How many socially disorganized neighborhoods have a high crime rate?

g. How many socially organized neighborhoods have a low crime rate?

h. How many degrees of freedom are there in this table?

i. Calculate the relative risk of a high neighborhood crime rate for both socially organized and socially disorganized communities. What does this suggest?

j. Test the null hypothesis that the two variables are independent. Use an alpha level of .01, and state each step of your hypothesis test. If you reject the null hypothesis, how strongly are the two variables related?

3. You think that there is a relationship between where a defendant's case is tried and the type of the sentence the defendant received. To test this hypothesis, you collect data on 425 defendants convicted in rural, suburban, and urban courts in your state. Here are your data:

| Type of Sentence Received | Where Defendant Was Tried | | | Total |
|---|---|---|---|---|
| | Rural Court | Suburban Court | Urban Court | |
| Jail Only | 18 | 30 | 94 | 142 |
| Fine and Jail | 22 | 37 | 36 | 95 |
| Less 60 Days of Jail Time | 24 | 38 | 50 | 112 |

| Type of Sentence Received | Where Defendant Was Tried | | | |
|---|---|---|---|---|
| | Rural Court | Suburban Court | Urban Court | Total |
| 60 or More Days of Jail Time | 16 | 20 | 40 | 76 |
| Total | 80 | 125 | 220 | 425 |

a. What is the independent and what is the dependent variable?

b. How many observations or cases are there?

c. What are the column marginals?

d. What are the row marginals?

e. What is the size of this contingency table?

f. How many defendants from suburban courts received a sentence of less than 60 days of jail time?

g. How many defendants from rural courts received a sentence of a fine and jail time?

h. How many degrees of freedom are there in this table?

i. Calculate the relative risk of getting a sentence of 60 or more days of jail time for defendants from different court jurisdictions. What does this suggest?

j. Test the null hypothesis that the two variables are independent. Use an alpha level of .01, and state each step of your hypothesis test. If you reject the null hypothesis, how strongly are the two variables related?

4. You think that there might be a relationship between race and the number of property crimes a defendant has committed. To test this hypothesis, you take a random sample of 360 defendants convicted of a crime, examine their criminal records, and count the number of property crimes they have committed. Here are your data:

| Race | Number of Property Crimes | | |
|---|---|---|---|
| | 0–4 | 5 or More | Total |
| Non-White | 77 | 33 | 110 |
| White | 180 | 70 | 250 |
| Total | 257 | 103 | 360 |

a. What is the independent and what is the dependent variable?

b. How many observations or cases are there?

c. What are the column marginals?

d. What are the row marginals?

e. What is the size of this contingency table?

f. How many non-White offenders have committed 5 or more property offenses?

g. How many White offenders have committed 0–4 property offenses?

h. How many degrees of freedom are there in this table?

i. Calculate the relative risk of having 5 or more property crime arrests for each race. What does this suggest?

j. Test the null hypothesis that the two variables are independent. Use an alpha level of .05, and state each step of your hypothesis test. If you reject the null hypothesis, how strongly are the two variables related?

5. Daniel Mears, Xia Wang, and William Bales (2014) argued that employment and labor market conditions influence reentry experiences and the likelihood of recidivism. Let's say you were interested in this notion and studied the post-release behavior of random samples of three groups of formerly incarcerated offenders: those who had a stable and satisfying job, those with intermittent or sporadic employment, and those unable to find a job. For each group, you were able to determine how many had been rearrested within three years of their release from prison. Here is what you found:

| Number of Arrests Within Three Years | Stable Employment | Sporadic Employment | Unemployed | Total |
|---|---|---|---|---|
| None | 30 | 14 | 10 | 54 |
| One or More | 15 | 16 | 30 | 61 |
| Total | 45 | 30 | 40 | 115 |

a. What is the independent and what is the dependent variable?

b. How many observations or cases are there?

c. What are the column marginals?

d. What are the row marginals?

e. What is the size of this contingency table?

f. How many persons with sporadic employment had one or more arrests within three years?

g. How many persons who were unemployed had no arrests within three years?

h. How many degrees of freedom are there in this table?

i. Calculate the relative risk of having one or more arrests for those with different types of post-release employment. What does this suggest?

j. Test the null hypothesis that the two variables are independent. Use an alpha level of .05, and state each step of your hypothesis test. If you reject the null hypothesis, how strongly are the two variables related?

6. Wesley Jennings, Bryanna Hahn Fox, and David Farrington (2014) investigated the relationship between tattoos and crime to determine whether the two were positively related. To test the notion people with tattoos commit more crime, you take a random sample of 320 adults currently on probation. You determine whether they have tattoos and then get a count of the number of crimes they have committed as adults. Here are your data:

| Tattoo Status | 0–4 Adult Offenses | 5–9 Adult Offenses | 10–14 Adult Offenses | 15 or More Adult Offenses | Total |
|---|---|---|---|---|---|
| No Tattoos | 78 | 56 | 34 | 15 | 183 |
| Has Tattoos | 15 | 22 | 37 | 63 | 137 |
| Total | 93 | 78 | 71 | 78 | 320 |

a. What is the independent and what is the dependent variable?

b. How many observations or cases are there?

c. What are the column marginals?

d. What are the row marginals?

e. What is the size of this contingency table?

f. How many offenders with tattoos have 10–14 adult offenses?

g. How many offenders without tattoos have 15 or more adult offenses?

h. How many degrees of freedom are there in this table?

i. Calculate the relative risk of having only 0–4 adult offenses for both tattoo statuses. What does this suggest?

j. Calculate the relative risk of having 15 or more adult offenses for both tattoo statuses.

k. Test the null hypothesis that the two variables are independent. Use an alpha level of .01, and state each step of your hypothesis test. If you reject the null hypothesis, how strongly are the two variables related?

## SPSS Exercises

➤ Explore additional data sets. **⑤SAGE** edge™

| Data for Exercise | |
|---|---|
| Data Set | Description |
| NCVS lone offender assaults 1992 to 2013.sav | These data are from the National Crime Victimization Survey (NCVS), a nationally representative study of an individual's experience of criminal victimization. This particular data set contains responses from 1992 to 2013, allowing for larger numbers of uncommon offenses to be used in analyses. It also only includes data from respondents who reported either violent or nonviolent assault by a single offender. |

| Variables for Exercise | |
|---|---|
| Variable Name | Description |
| V2129 | This is a three-category indicator of where a respondent lives. This is based on metropolitan statistical area (MSA) classifications, but loosely speaking, 1 = lives in city, 2 = lives near city (suburbs, outskirts), 3 = lives in a rural area away from cities. |
| V3023 | The race of the respondent, where 1 = White, 2 = Black, 3 = Native American, 4 = Asian. |
| V3018 | A respondent's sex where 1 = male, 2 = female. |
| Maleoff | The sex of the offender (attacker) where 1 = male, 2 = female. |
| Relationship | A four-category nominal measure that tells us the victim's relationship to the offender. 0 = total stranger, 1 = slightly known, 2 = casual acquaintance, 3 = well known. |

1. Are people from different races more likely to be assaulted if they live inside or outside of cities? For instance, perhaps Whites are more likely to be assaulted in the city than non-Whites? We can examine this question with a contingency table in SPSS and then calculate the appropriate cell proportions:

   a. In this case, what is your independent variable?

   b. Constructing a contingency table (i.e., cross tabulation) in SPSS: First, select analyze->descriptives->cross tabs. Place your two variables, V2129 and V3023, into the row and column boxes. Only put one variable per box; pay close attention to whether the independent variable is placed along rows or columns.

   c. Calculate cell percentages for this table, using the appropriate marginal to allow for comparisons across the categories of your independent variable.

   d. Looking at the proportions you've calculated, what do your results tell you about the relationship between geographic region and race of victim? What is the relative risk of a Black person being assaulted in the city versus a rural area (not SMSA)?

   e. Can you think of any reasons as to why you've found what you did; why might this crime be unequally distributed by geography?

2. Who hurts whom? Are men (or women) more likely to assault a member of a different sex or the same sex?

   a. Write a hypothesis about this question; this does not need to be a formal hypothesis yet.

   b. First, we must set up our data so we are only looking at assaults that result in injury. To do this we will run analyses on only individuals who reported being injured. Under data->select cases, click the "if" button. Enter the expression "injured = 1" into the field. You will know this worked if you calculate a frequency of the variable injured and see that it always equals 1.

   c. **Getting cell percentages from SPSS:** First, select analyze->descriptives->cross tabs, as usual. Then, put one variable in the row slot and the other variable in the column slot; your variables are named maleoff and V3018 this time. Then, click the "cells" button and look for the "percentages" section of the menu that pops up. If your independent variable was in the "rows" box, tick off the "rows" option, and if your independent variable is in the "columns" box, tick off the "columns" option. This make's it so that percentages adding up along either rows/columns are provided, allowing for easy comparisons of categories of the independent variables.

   d. Interpret the results of the cross-tabulation fully. What are the implications of these results for our understanding of victimization?

3. Using the cross-tabulation from question 2, calculate the chi square test of independence:

   a. Formally state your research hypothesis, statistical distribution, alpha level, and critical values.

   b. What is your $\chi^2$ test statistic?

   c. What do you conclude about your hypotheses?

4. Now let's assess the strength of the association from part 3: Of this list, choose and calculate the appropriate measure of association by hand: Phi, Gamma, Cramer's *V*. Also calculate Lambda:

   a. What do these statistics tell us? Write a sentence or two assessing the strength of the association.

   b. Take another look at your results from questions 2 through 4. Consider the following assertion: "Women inflict violence against men at the same rate as men inflict violence against women." Based on all of your results, defend or critique this statement. Be sure to discuss the results of your hypothesis test and the strength of the associations that you found.

5. One common idea in our culture is that we need to be wary of strangers, as we never know which one may actually be a rapist, attacker, or robber. On the other hand, people who know are characterized as safe, trustworthy, and predictable. This idea was touched on in Chapter 6, but now let's expand on those results and add hypothesis tests. Put briefly, the idea of "stranger danger" would lead us to hypothesize that most attackers in a violent crime are unknown:

   a. (If you haven't already, select only assault cases that resulted in injury to the victim as described in question 2b.)

   b. Construct a frequency table for the variable Relationship. What does this tell us about the perpetrators in violent assaults?

   c. Perhaps strangers are of a particular threat to just women as compared with men? To investigate this, do the following:

      i. Create a cross-tab for the variables V3018 and Relationship. Be sure to put your independent variable in the "column" box and to select the column percentage option in the cellmenu.

      ii. Conduct a chi-square hypothesis test in SPSS. To do this, go to the cross-tab dialog and then select "statistics." Tick off "chi square":

         1. The output provided gives the chi-square test statistic and its associated *p* value (labeled "sig"). For now only focus on the "Pearson's Chi Square" row.

         2. Write a few sentences interpreting the hypothesis test; be sure to note your alpha level, the value of your chi-square statistic, and your conclusions about the null hypothesis.

iii. **Using SPSS to estimate categorical measures of association**: In this case, Lambda and Cramer's *V*. These can be found under the same menu that you located the chi-square test:

1. Write a few sentences explaining what these results suggest about the strength of the association.

d. Based on these analyses, what would you conclude about the idea of stranger danger in the case of violent assault? Is it accurate to caution that strangers should be feared and well-known acquaintances are safe? Be sure to use all the details from your analysis to back up your argument.

## STUDENT STUDY SITE

### WANT A BETTER GRADE?

Get the tools you need to sharpen your study skills. Access practice quizzes, eFlashcards, data sets, and exercises at **edge.sagepub.com/bachmansccj4e**.

# CHAPTER 10

# Hypothesis Tests Involving Two Population Means or Proportions

> *Basic research is what I am doing when I don't know what I'm doing.*
>
> —Wernher Von Braun
>
> *What a weak barrier is truth when it stands in the way of a hypothesis!*
>
> —Mary Wollstonecraft

## LEARNING OBJECTIVES

1. Identify the appropriate sampling distribution to use for a hypothesis test for large samples when you have a two-category independent variable and an interval- or ratio-level dependent variable.

2. Explain why you must use a slightly different hypothesis test when you cannot assume the variances for two groups are equal.

3. Describe the difference between independent groups and matched groups.

4. Conduct a hypothesis for the difference between means using the three variations of the *t* test, and interpret the results.

5. Conduct a hypothesis for the difference between proportions, and interpret the results.

# ▣ Introduction

Imagine you are working for a state prison system and are in charge of testing a new batterer intervention program (BIP) designed to reduce recidivism for those convicted of intimate partner assaults. You have several individuals in the prison who were convicted of assaulting their intimate partners whom you randomly assign to either get the new BIP (called an experimental group) or be in a control group, whose group members do not receive the program. To measure individuals' approval of using violence to settle conflicts, you give all participants a survey both before the treatment (called a pretest) and after the treatment (called a posttest). To determine whether the BIP actually decreased the participants' approval of violence, you would have to conduct a hypothesis test between mean approval ratings for the pretest and posttest. In this case, the dependent variable would be the approval of violence scores and the independent variable would be a two-category variable indicating whether individuals were in the BIP program or the control group. Luckily for you, you will be an expert on these types of tests after reading this chapter!

In this chapter, we examine the statistical procedures that enable us to test hypotheses about the differences between two population means ($\mu_1 - \mu_2$) and two population proportions ($P_1 - P_2$). We will examine two different types of mean difference tests: one for independent samples and one for dependent or matched samples. The independent-samples test is designed to measure mean differences between *two* samples that are independent of each other or *two* subsets within the same sample (i.e., males and females). The key here is that we have two samples that are assumed to be independent. There are two different statistical tests for the difference between two independent samples; the appropriate one to use depends on what assumption we can make about the population variances. In contrast, the matched-groups or dependent-samples test is designed to measure the difference between means obtained for the same sample at two points in time or between two samples that are matched on certain characteristics so as to be as much alike as possible. This is the scenario we presented at the beginning of this section regarding the BIP treatment program. We also examine a test for the difference between two proportions in this chapter, which is a special case of a test for mean differences. In this chapter, we may use the terms "sample" and "group" interchangeably. Let's get started.

# ▣ Explaining the Difference Between Two Sample Means

The hypothesis tests in this chapter are appropriate for the following variables: The independent variable (IV) is a two-level or binary categorical variable, and the dependent variable is continuous (interval/ratio). For example, one of the most persistent findings in criminology is the relationship between gender and the number of delinquent offenses committed. Consistently, males report having committed more delinquent acts than females. In a random sample of young males and females, then, the mean number of delinquent acts committed by the males is expected to be greater than the mean for females. In the language of causal analysis, gender is the independent variable that is predicted to "cause" high levels of delinquency, the dependent variable. In this example, gender is the dichotomous independent variable (male/female) and the number of committed delinquent acts is the dependent variable. Let's follow this example through to illustrate the kinds of problems we will encounter in this chapter.

If we were to take a random sample of 70 young males from some population, independently select an equal number of young females, and then ask each youth to self-report the number of times in the past year that he or she committed each of four delinquent offenses (theft, vandalism, fighting, and use of drugs), we would have two means: a mean for the sample of young men ($\bar{X}_{men}$) and a mean for the sample of young women ($\bar{X}_{women}$). We also would have two population means: one from the population of men ($\mu_{men}$) and one from the population of women ($\mu_{women}$) that we have not directly measured. Both the sample and the population also have standard deviations (remember, the sample standard deviation is $s$ and the population standard deviation is $\sigma$). To keep these different components of samples and populations straight, we show each and their respective notations in Table 10.1.

Let's say that, consistent with previous research, the mean number of delinquent offenses committed for the sample of young males in the samples is greater than the mean for the sample of young females ($\bar{X}_m > \bar{X}_w$). As we learned in Chapter 9, we can account for the difference between these two sample means in two very different ways.

One possible explanation for the difference between the male and female sample means is that there really is a difference between the rate at which young men and young women offend. What this explanation implies is that males and females come from different offending populations with different population means (Figure 10.1). This means that there are two

| Table 10.1 | Characteristics and Notations for Two-Sample Problems |  |
| --- | --- | --- |
| | *Population 1* | *Population 2* |
| Population mean | $\mu_1$ | $\mu_2$ |
| Population standard deviation | $\sigma_1$ | $\sigma_2$ |
| Sample mean | $\bar{X}_1$ | $\bar{X}_2$ |
| Sample standard deviation | $s_1$ | $s_2$ |
| Sample size | $n_1$ | $n_2$ |

distributions of the rate of delinquent offending: one for females, on the left, and one for males, on the right. The population mean for the number of delinquent acts committed is greater for men ($\mu_m = 20$) than it is for women ($\mu_w = 10$). Note that if this is true, then when we randomly select a sample of men and record their mean, and randomly select a sample of women and record their mean; more frequently than not, the sample mean for men will be greater than the sample mean for women.

A second explanation for the observed difference in sample means between young men and women is that the two population means are equal ($\mu = 17$), and it was just by chance that we happened to select a sample of males with a higher mean of delinquent offending than our female mean. This is illustrated in Figure 10.2, which shows two distributions of offending: one for the population of males and one for the population of females. Although they may differ in some respects (their respective standard deviations may be different, for example), the two population means are the same implying that the mean level of offending is the same for both genders. If this explanation is true, when we draw random samples from both populations, the two sample means will sometimes differ by chance alone, with the male mean sometimes the larger of the two and other times the female mean the larger of the two, and sometimes the two means will be equal. Over a large number of mean differences, the mean or average of those differences will be zero. The important point is that if the two population means are equal, the two sample means we obtained in this sample are different because of random sample variation and chance alone.

These two explanations have very different substantive implications. If the first explanation is true, then we will conclude that the mean number of delinquent offenses committed by males is significantly different from the mean number of offenses committed by females. Because the frequency of committing delinquent acts is significantly different between males and females, we will say that there is a "statistically significant" relationship between the IV of gender and DV of delinquency. What

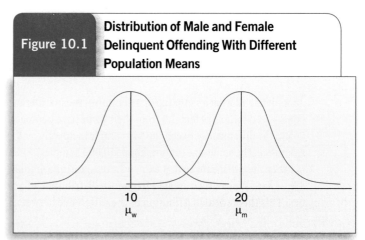

| Figure 10.1 | Distribution of Male and Female Delinquent Offending With Different Population Means |

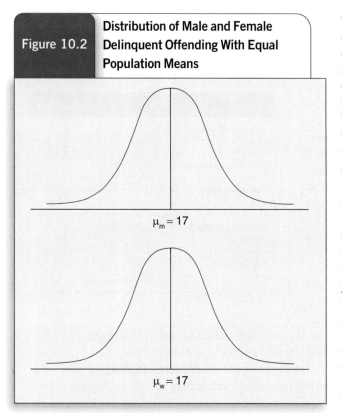

**Figure 10.2** Distribution of Male and Female Delinquent Offending With Equal Population Means

$\mu_m = 17$

$\mu_w = 17$

we are saying here is that the difference between the male and female sample means is so large that "chances are" the samples came from different populations. In a sense, this means that the sample difference is "real" (a real population difference). On the other hand, if the second explanation is true, then we will conclude that the observed difference between the male and female means is no greater than what we would expect to observe by chance alone, despite that the sample means are different. In this case, the sample difference does not reflect a real difference in the population—it's due to luck or chance or random sampling variation, whatever you want to call it.

In sum, because we have sample data, not population data, any difference we actually observe in our sample means may be due to "real differences" between males and females in how frequently they commit delinquent acts, or just due to chance/sampling variability. Enter probability theory! With the help of probability theory, we can determine which explanation is *more likely* to be true. In deciding which of these two possible explanations is more likely, we will proceed exactly as we have in the last two chapters when we have conducted formal hypothesis tests.

We will begin by assuming that there is no difference between the two population means. That is, we will begin with the null hypothesis that assumes the populations from which each of the two samples were drawn have equal means ($\mu_m = \mu_w$). This is the simplest explanation, consistent with Ockham's razor. With the use of probability theory and a new kind of sampling distribution, we will then ask, "Assuming that the population means are equal, how likely is it that we would have observed the difference between the two sample means that we actually observed?" If it is a likely event, where likely is defined by our alpha level, then we will conclude that our assumption of equal population means cannot be rejected. If, however, we find that the difference between our sample means is an unlikely or a very rare event (say, an event with a probability of .05, or .01, or .001), we will instead conclude that our assumption of equal population means is not likely true, and we will reject the null hypothesis.

In this chapter, we are interested in something called the *sampling distribution of sample mean differences*. We illustrate the process of hypothesis testing with two sample means in Figure 10.3.

## ▣ Sampling Distribution of Mean Differences

To understand what a sampling distribution of mean differences is, imagine that we take a sample of males and an equal-sized sample of females from their respective populations, compute a mean for each sample, and then calculate the difference between the two sample means ($\overline{X}_1 - \overline{X}_2$). Imagine that we do this for an infinite number of samples of the same size (or how about 10,000 samples), calculating the mean for each group and the difference between the two means so that we now have an infinite number (or 10,000) of values of these mean difference scores ($\overline{X}_1 - \overline{X}_2$). We can then create a frequency distribution of an infinite number (or 10,000) of mean difference values. This theoretical distribution of the difference between an infinite number (or 10,000) of sample means is

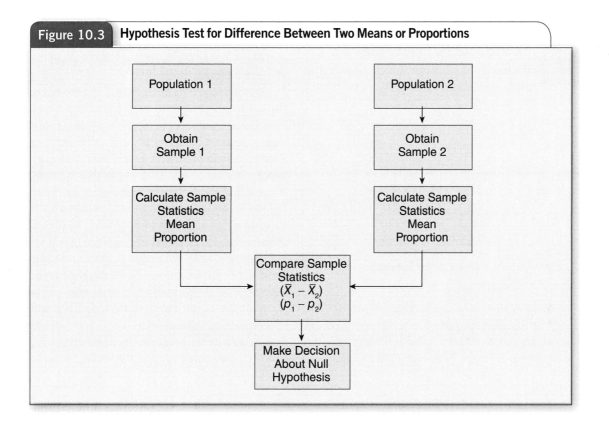

**Figure 10.3** Hypothesis Test for Difference Between Two Means or Proportions

our **sampling distribution of sample mean differences.** We illustrate what this distribution might look like in Figure 10.4 and provide a summary of the characteristics of this sampling distribution here:

1. The mean of the sampling distribution of the difference between two means, $\mu_1 - \mu_2$, is equal to the difference between the population means.

2. The standard deviation of the sampling distribution of the difference between two means $\left(\sigma_{\bar{X}1-\bar{X}2}\right)$ is called the standard error of the difference between two means, and it reflects how much variation exists in the difference from sample to sample. In other words, it is the standard deviation of the large number of sample mean differences.

> **Sampling distribution of sample mean differences:** Theoretical distribution of the difference between an infinite number of sample means.

This sampling distribution of mean differences is analogous to the sampling distribution of the mean that we discussed in Chapter 9. What changes is that the sampling distribution in Figure 10.4 is composed of the *difference* between two sample means rather than the distribution of a single mean. In addition, the distribution of mean differences is centered about the difference between the two population means $(\mu_1 - \mu_2)$, not around a single population mean $(\mu)$.

The mean of this distribution of mean differences is determined by the difference between the two population means. If the two population means are equal $(\mu_m = \mu_w)$ as in Figure 10.2, the mean of the sampling distribution of mean differences will be 0 $(\mu_1 - \mu_2 = 0)$. As we stated earlier, even if the means in the population are equal, not every sample mean difference is expected to be equal to zero. Sometimes the male mean will be greater than the female mean, sometimes the female mean will be greater than the male mean, and sometimes they will be equal. What will be

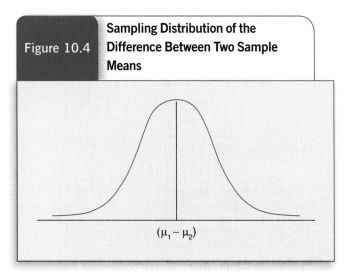

**Figure 10.4** Sampling Distribution of the Difference Between Two Sample Means

$(\mu_1 - \mu_2)$

true, however, is that with an infinite or very large number of samples, the mean of the distribution of sample differences (the mean difference of the infinite number of sample differences) will be zero.

If the two population means are different, however, as they are in Figure 10.1 with the population mean for men being greater than that for women ($\mu_m > \mu_w$), then most of the sample mean differences $\bar{X}_m - \bar{X}_w$ will be positive. This will be true because in most of the sample comparisons, the male mean will be greater than the female mean. In this case, the mean of the sampling distribution of differences will be greater than zero. More specifically, the mean of the sampling distribution will be equal to the difference between the two population means ($\mu_m - \mu_w$).

Up to now, we have repeatedly stated that no matter what the value of the means for the two populations, when repeated random samples are taken, means calculated, and differences between sample means taken, not every mean difference will be exactly the same. There will, then, be dispersion about the mean of the sampling distribution of differences. You can see the spread about the mean of the sampling distribution of differences in Figure 10.4. This dispersion is measured by the standard deviation of sample mean differences or otherwise known as the standard error of the difference ($\sigma_{\bar{X}_1 - \bar{X}_2}$), which is defined as:

$$\sigma_{\bar{X}_1 - \bar{X}_2} = \sqrt{\frac{\sigma_1^2}{n_1} + \frac{\sigma_2^2}{n_2}} \qquad (10\text{--}1)$$

where

$\sigma_1$ = the standard deviation of the first population

$\sigma_2$ = the standard deviation of the second population

Not only do we know the mean and standard deviation of the sampling distribution of differences, we also are in a position to know its shape. An important statistical theorem states the following: If two independent random samples of size $n_1$ and $n_2$ are drawn from normal populations, then the sampling distribution of the difference between the two sample means $(\bar{X}_1 - \bar{X}_2)$ will be normally distributed.

We now can use the central limit theorem to generalize this to include any population whenever the sample sizes are large. That is, no matter what the shape of the two populations, if independent random samples of size $n_1$ and $n_2$ are drawn, the sampling distribution of the difference between the two sample means will approximate a normal distribution as $n_1$ and $n_2$ become large (both sample sizes greater than 30). With normal populations or with large enough samples from any population, then, the sampling distribution of differences between sample means will approximate normality.

This should sound very familiar to you because it is similar to what we did in Chapter 8. An appropriate statistical test for the difference between two sample means is either a z test or t test. Therefore, an appropriate sampling distribution would be either a z or a t distribution. The z test for two means is appropriate whenever the two population variances ($\sigma_1, \sigma_2$) are known. If these values are unknown, the t test for two means is the appropriate statistical test. Since we are seldom in a position to know the value of the population variances, the t test is more frequently applied. Keep in mind, however, that when the sample size gets large, the t and z distributions start to look the same. For that reason, we will discuss only *t* tests for the difference between two means in this chapter. Now, let's go through some examples of different types of hypothesis tests involving two population means.

## 🔲 Testing a Hypothesis About the Difference Between Two Means: Independent Samples

In this section, we will discuss the case of hypothesis tests for the difference between two *independent* sample means. In the case of **independent random samples**, we have two samples whose elements are randomly and independently selected. Random and independent selection occurs whenever there is a known probability of any element being selected into a sample, and the selection of an element into one sample has no effect on the selection of any element into the other sample. In other words, both samples are randomly selected and are independent of each other.

> **Independent random samples:** Samples that are randomly and independently selected.

In our example, independence would occur if the selection of a male into one sample had no effect on the selection of a female into the other sample. The independence assumption is violated in the case of matched groups or dependent samples, where an element is deliberately selected into a sample or when the same observations are found in both samples. We will review the special case of hypothesis testing presented by matched groups and dependent samples later in this chapter.

The statistical test we will conduct here is different from the *t* test we used in Chapter 8 in three ways: (1) Our sample statistic is not a single sample mean but the difference between two sample means $(\overline{X}_1 - \overline{X}_2)$; (2) the mean of the sampling distribution is not the population mean ($\mu$) but the difference between two population means $(\mu_1 - \mu_2)$; and (3) the estimated standard deviation of the sampling distribution is the estimated standard deviation of the sampling distribution of the difference between sample means $(\sigma_{\overline{X}_1 - \overline{X}_2})$. The general formula for the *t* test involving the difference between two sample means can be expressed as:

$$t_{\text{obt}} = \frac{\overline{X}_1 - \overline{X}_2}{\hat{\sigma}_{\overline{X}_1 - \overline{X}_2}} \tag{10–2}$$

This *t* test requires that the two samples be independent random samples and that the dependent variable be measured at the interval or ratio level.

As you can see from equation 10–2, the *t* statistic is obtained by dividing the difference between the two sample means by the estimated standard deviation of the sampling distribution (the standard error of the difference). There are, however, two versions of the *t* test between two means. In one test we can assume that the unknown population standard deviations are equal ($\sigma_1 = \sigma_2$); in the second case, we cannot make that assumption ($\sigma_1 \neq \sigma_2$). The importance of this is that our estimate of the standard error of the difference $(\hat{\sigma}_{\overline{X}_1 - \overline{X}_2})$ is different for the two cases. We will examine the *t* test for both of these cases separately.

### Model 1: Pooled Variance Estimate ($\sigma_1 = \sigma_2$)

If we can assume that the two unknown population standard deviations are equal ($\sigma_1 = \sigma_2$), we estimate the standard error of the difference using what is called a *pooled variance estimate*. Because the population standard deviations are not known, the decision of whether they are equal is based on the equality of the sample standard deviations ($s_1$ and $s_2$). Something called an *F* test is the appropriate test for the significance of the difference between the two sample standard deviations. Without going into too much detail here, the *F* test tests the null hypothesis that $\sigma_1^2 = \sigma_2^2$. If we fail to reject this null hypothesis, we can assume that the population standard deviations are equal and the that $t$ test we will discuss in this section for the difference between two population means is the right test. If, however, we are led to reject this null hypothesis, we cannot make the assumption that the two population standard deviations are equal $\sigma_1^2 \neq \sigma_2^2$, and we must estimate the standard error of the difference using what is called a *separate variance estimate*, which we will discuss later as Model 2—Separate Variance Estimate. Since the $F$ test has not yet been discussed, we will simply provide the information for you whether you can assume that the population standard deviations are equal (Model 1) or whether you cannot make that assumption (Model 2).

We will continue in this section under the assumption that the population standard deviations are equal ($\sigma_1 = \sigma_2$) and demonstrate the use of a pooled variance estimate of the standard error of the difference. Recall from formula 10–1 that the standard error of the difference was:

$$\sigma_{\bar{X}_1 - \bar{X}_2} = \sqrt{\frac{\sigma_1^2}{n_1} + \frac{\sigma_2^2}{n_2}}$$

If we can assume that the two population standard deviations are equal ($\sigma_1 = \sigma_2$), then we have a common value of $\sigma$ since $\sigma_1 = \sigma_2$. Using the common value of the population standard deviations, we can then rewrite the formula from earlier as:

$$\sigma_{\bar{X}_1 - \bar{X}_2} = \sqrt{\frac{\sigma_1^2}{n_1} + \frac{\sigma_2^2}{n_2}}$$

$$\sigma_{\bar{X}_1 - \bar{X}_2} = \sigma \sqrt{\frac{1}{n_1} + \frac{1}{n_2}}$$

$$\sigma_{\bar{X}_1 - \bar{X}_2} = \sigma \sqrt{\frac{n_1 + n_2}{n_1 n_2}}$$

We must, of course, find an estimate of this common standard deviation ($\sigma$). Since we are assuming that the two population standard deviations are equal, we can obtain an estimate of the common standard deviance by pooling or combining the two sample standard deviations. By combining the two sample values, we get a better estimate of the common population standard deviation. However, since in many instances the samples are of unequal size, we must weight each sample standard deviation by its respective degrees of freedom ($n - 1$) because we are going to give more weight to the standard deviation that is based on the larger sample size (because a larger sample means more information). Since we are still using the sample standard deviation to estimate the population value, we will continue to employ the degrees of freedom ($n - 1$) in the denominator. Our pooled sample estimate of the common population standard deviation, then, becomes:

$$\sigma = \hat{\sigma}$$

$$\hat{\sigma} = \sqrt{\frac{(n_1 - 1)s_1^2 + (n_2 - 1)s_2^2}{n_1 + n_2 - 2}}$$

As the formula illustrates, our estimate of the population standard deviation of mean differences ($\hat{\sigma}$) uses the weighted average of the two sample standard deviations. More weight is therefore given to larger samples. You should also note that our pooled estimate ($\hat{\sigma}$) will be in between the two sample values of $s_1$ and $s_2$. Now that we have our estimate of the common population standard deviation ($\hat{\sigma}$), we can multiply it by:

$$\sigma \sqrt{\frac{n_1 + n_2}{n_1 n_2}}$$

to obtain our pooled variance estimate of the standard error of the difference:

$$\hat{\sigma}_{\bar{X}_1 - \bar{X}_2} = \sqrt{\frac{(n_1 - 1)s_1^2 + (n_2 - 1)s_2^2}{n_1 + n_2 - 2}} \sqrt{\frac{n_1 + n_2}{n_1 n_2}}$$

For the grand finale, the formula for our pooled variance $t$ test then becomes:

$$t_{obt} = \frac{\bar{X}_1 - \bar{X}_2}{\sqrt{\dfrac{(n_1 - 1)s_1^2 + (n_2 - 1)s_2^2}{n_1 + n_2 - 2}} \sqrt{\dfrac{n_1 + n_2}{n_1 n_2}}} \qquad (10\text{–}3)$$

As we have done with other hypothesis tests, once we have our obtained value of $t$ ($t_{obt}$), we will compare it with our critical value ($t_{crit}$) taken from our probability distribution (the $t$ distribution) and make a decision about the null hypothesis. The critical value of $t$ is based on our chosen alpha level, whether we have a one- or two-tailed test, and our degrees of freedom and is obtained from the $t$ table (Table B.3 of Appendix B). You will remember from Chapter 8 that before using the $t$ table, we need to determine the appropriate degrees of freedom in addition to our selected alpha level. When we are testing the difference between two sample means, the degrees of freedom are equal to ($n_1 + n_2 - 2$) in the independent-samples two-sample case for the $t$ test. Once we have determined our degrees of freedom, we can go to the $t$ table with our chosen alpha level and a one- or two-tailed test and find our critical value.

Let's go through an example of a formal hypothesis test using the $t$ test. In this example, we will assume that we have conducted our $F$ test and have failed to reject the null hypothesis about equal population standard deviations. Because we can assume that the population standard deviations are equal, then, we can use the pooled variance estimate of the standard error of the difference (Model 1).

---

## Case Study

## State Prison Expenditures by Region

Suppose that we are interested in regional differences in the cost of housing state prison inmates. Table 10.2 displays data from state prisons for two regions in the United States (West and Northeast). The dependent variable of interest is the cost per inmate per day, which is measured at the interval or ratio level. Let's say we believe that the average annual cost to house an inmate in state prisons will differ between the West and the Northeast, but we cannot say in which region it will be more costly. In this scenario, region would be the two-category independent variable (West vs. Northeast), and cost would be the dependent variable. We have reviewed the steps necessary to conduct a hypothesis test in Table 10.3. We will go through each of these steps using this example.

**Step 1**: Since we have no real idea about the nature of the relationship between region of the country and prison costs, a nondirectional (two-tailed) hypothesis test is appropriate. The null hypothesis ($H_0$) will state that the mean annual cost to house prison inmates in the West is equal to the mean cost in the Northeast. The alternative hypothesis ($H_1$) will represent our belief that the regional means are not equal to each other. These hypotheses are formally stated as:

| Table 10.2 | Prison Expenditures per Inmate per Day by State and Region—2011 |
|---|---|

| State | Daily Mean State Prison Operating Expenditures per Inmate |
|---|---|
| **West** | |
| Nevada | 56.59 |
| Idaho | 53.55 |
| Arizona | 67.96 |
| Montana | 82.81 |
| Colorado | 83.22 |
| California | 129.92 |
| Washington | 128.48 |
| Utah | 80.41 |

Sample Statistics for the West

$\bar{X}_1 = 85.37$

$s_1 = 29.33$

$n_1 = 8$

| Northeast | |
|---|---|
| New Hampshire | 93.37 |
| Pennsylvania | 116.00 |
| New York | 164.59 |
| New Jersey | 150.32 |
| Vermont | 135.62 |
| Connecticut | 137.70 |
| Maine | 127.13 |
| Rhode Island | 134.61 |

Sample Statistics for the Northeast

$\bar{X}_2 = 132.42$

$s_2 = 21.45$

$n_2 = 8$

*Source:* Adapted from *The Cost of Prisons: What Incarceration Costs Taxpayers* © 2012 from the Vera Institute of Justice.

$H_0$: No Relationship between region and prison costs OR $\mu_{West} = \mu_{Northeast}$

$H_1$: There is a relationship between region and prison costs OR $\mu_{West} \neq \mu_{Northeast}$

**Step 2**: To determine the validity of this null hypothesis, we will rely on the *t* statistic, along with its corresponding sampling distribution. Because we can assume that the unknown population standard deviations are equal, we can estimate the standard error of the difference using a pooled variance estimate (Model 1).

**Step 3**: Let's adopt an alpha level equal to .05 ($\alpha = .05$). With this level of alpha, using a nondirectional test and ($8 + 8 - 2 = 14$) degrees of freedom, the critical value of *t* is equal to ± 2.145 ($t_{crit} = \pm 2.145$). Since we have a nondirectional alternative hypothesis, the value of *t* we obtain from our statistical test must be equal to or greater than 2.145 or equal to or less than −2.145 to reject the null hypothesis of equal means. In other words, the obtained *t* value must be greater in absolute terms than 2.145 regardless of the sign. We show the two critical values and critical regions in Figure 10.5.

**Step 4**: Since we are assuming that the population standard deviations are equal, we can use a pooled variance estimate of the standard error of the difference. The calculation of $t_{obt}$ from these sample data is presented in the following discussion. Please notice that in the preceding data, we have given you the sample standard deviation; to get the variance that the formula calls for, you will have to square the standard deviation. Sometimes we will provide the standard deviation, and sometimes the variances; you will have to be on your toes and alert as to which one you are given:

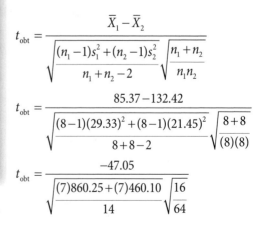

$$t_{obt} = \frac{\bar{X}_1 - \bar{X}_2}{\sqrt{\dfrac{(n_1 - 1)s_1^2 + (n_2 - 1)s_2^2}{n_1 + n_2 - 2}}\sqrt{\dfrac{n_1 + n_2}{n_1 n_2}}}$$

$$t_{obt} = \frac{85.37 - 132.42}{\sqrt{\dfrac{(8-1)(29.33)^2 + (8-1)(21.45)^2}{8 + 8 - 2}}\sqrt{\dfrac{8 + 8}{(8)(8)}}}$$

$$t_{obt} = \frac{-47.05}{\sqrt{\dfrac{(7)860.25 + (7)460.10}{14}}\sqrt{\dfrac{16}{64}}}$$

$$t_{obt} = \frac{-47.05}{\sqrt{\dfrac{6,021.75+3,220.7}{14}}\sqrt{.25}}$$

$$t_{obt} = \frac{-47.05}{\sqrt{660.18}\sqrt{.25}}$$

$$t_{obt} = \frac{-47.05}{25.69(.50)}$$

$$t_{obt} = \frac{-47.05}{12.85}$$

$$t_{obt} = -3.66$$

| Table 10.3 | **Steps Taken When Conducting a Hypothesis Test** |
|---|---|

**Step 1:** Formally state your null ($H_0$) and research ($H_1$) hypotheses.

**Step 2:** Select an appropriate test statistic and the sampling distribution of that test statistic.

**Step 3:** Select a level of significance (alpha = $\alpha$), and determine the critical value and rejection region of the test statistic based on the selected level of alpha and degrees of freedom.

**Step 4:** Conduct the test: Calculate the obtained value of the test statistic, and compare it with the critical value.

**Step 5:** Make a decision about your null hypothesis, and interpret this decision in a meaningful way based on the research question, sample, and population.

| Figure 10.5 | **Critical *t* and Critical Region for Alpha = .05 (*df* = 14) and a Two-Tailed Test** |
|---|---|

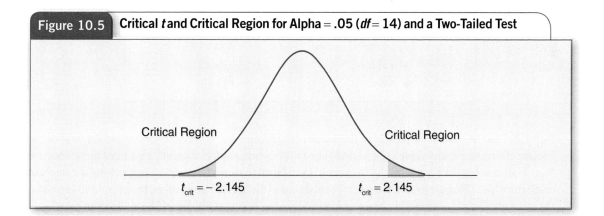

Critical Region     Critical Region

$t_{crit} = -2.145$       $t_{crit} = 2.145$

**Step 5**: The obtained value of $t$ ($t_{obt} = -3.66$) falls into the critical region since $-3.66 < -2.145$ (or is greater in absolute terms of the 2.145 needed!). The data obtained from our sample, then, provide enough evidence for us to reject the null hypothesis that the population means are actually equal. We conclude that there is a significant relationship between region and annual cost to house prison inmates. The results of our test indicate that region—at least the West versus the Northeast—does affect the cost of incarcerating offenders housed in state prisons. In addition, the direction of this difference seems to be that it is significantly more expensive to house prison inmates in the Northeast than in the West. Let's go through another example.

# Case Study

## Social Disorganization and Crime

Ever since the days of the Chicago School in the 1920s, criminologists have postulated that states of social disorganization within a residential community increase the likelihood of various kinds of social problems, including unemployment, mental illness, and criminal victimization. One indicator that has been used to measure social disorganization within communities is the extent to which people move in and out of the community. Communities wherein very few families move in and move out are considered more stable and more organized than those where there is a great deal of population "turnover" in the neighborhood. This is because in communities with relatively little turnover, residents live in the same place for a long time and get to know their neighbors, and as a result, a sense of community becomes established. It is hypothesized that this sense of community and the network of social relationships between community members is responsible for the lower crime rates in these kinds of stable neighborhoods. In this hypothesis, the population turnover in a community is the independent variable, and the rate of crime is the dependent variable.

Suppose we wanted to investigate the relationship between social disorganization and household crime. To do so, we collect a random sample of residents in a neighborhood and ask them how many times something has been stolen from or around their home (including their automobile) within the last six months (household theft). In addition, we ask them how long they have lived at their present address. From this survey, we divide our sample into two groups according to the length of time they have resided at their address: (1) those who have resided at their current address for less than one year, whom we will term "transient," and (2) those who have resided there for more than one year, whom we will term "stable." These two categories are our independent variable. We then calculate the mean number of times each group experienced a household theft, which is our dependent variable. For this hypothetical example, we obtain the following sample statistics:

| Less than One Year | More than One Year |
|---|---|
| $\bar{X}_1 = 22.4$ | $\bar{X}_2 = 16.2$ |
| $s_1^2 = 4.3$ | $s_2^2 = 4.1$ |
| $n_1 = 49$ | $n_2 = 53$ |

**Step 1**: Because we have some idea about the nature of the relationship between residential stability and risk of household victimization, we adopt a directional (one-tailed) hypothesis test. Since we believe that those who have lived in an area less than one year (the "transients") will be more vulnerable to becoming victims of household crime than those who have lived in the neighborhood longer (the "stables"), our alternative hypothesis states that the mean number of household victimizations experienced by residents who have lived at their current address less than one year will be greater than the mean for those who have lived in their residences more than one year. Both the null and the alternative hypothesis are formally stated as follows:

$H_0: \mu_{\text{less than 1 year}} = \mu_{\text{more than 1 year}}$

$H_1: \mu_{\text{less than 1 year}} > \mu_{\text{more than 1 year}}$

**Step 2**: To determine the validity of the null hypothesis, we will rely on the $t$ statistic, along with its corresponding sampling distribution. Because we can assume that the unknown population standard deviations are equal, we can estimate the standard error of the difference using a pooled variance estimate.

**Step 3**: For this test, let's select an alpha level of .01. With $\alpha = .01$, using a directional test and degrees of freedom equal to $(n_1 + n_2 - 2) = (49 + 53 - 2 = 100)$, the critical value of $t$ that defines the rejection region can be found in

Table B.3 of Appendix B. By using the degrees of freedom of 120 listed in the table (since that is the closest value we have to 100), we see that the critical value of $t$ that defines the lower limit of the rejection region is 2.358. Therefore, to reject the null hypothesis, we must obtain a $t$ value equal to or greater than 2.358. We use a positive value of $t$ in this case because our alternative hypothesis states that the value of the first mean (for the "transients") will be greater than the value of the mean for the second group (the "stables"); the obtained value of $t$ is therefore predicted to be positive. If we obtain a negative value of $t$, no matter how large it is, we must fail to reject the null hypothesis. We show the critical value of $t$ and the critical region for this problem in Figure 10.6.

**Step 4**: The next step of our hypothesis test is to convert the difference between our sample means into a $t$ value. Notice that you have been given the sample variances in this problem so there is no need to square the terms again! We're just making sure you are paying attention!

$$t_{obt} = \frac{22.4 - 16.2}{\sqrt{\frac{(49-1)4.3 + (53-1)4.1}{49+53-2}} \sqrt{\frac{49+53}{(49)(53)}}}$$

$$t_{obt} = \frac{6.2}{\sqrt{\frac{(48)4.3 + (52)4.1}{100}} \sqrt{\frac{102}{2,597}}}$$

$$t_{obt} = \frac{6.2}{\sqrt{\frac{206.4 + 213.2}{100}} \sqrt{.039}}$$

$$t_{obt} = \frac{6.2}{\sqrt{\frac{419.6}{100}} \sqrt{.039}}$$

$$t_{obt} = \frac{6.2}{\sqrt{4.2} \sqrt{.039}}$$

$$t_{obt} = \frac{6.2}{(2.049)(.198)}$$

$$t_{obt} = \frac{6.2}{.406}$$

$$t_{obt} = 15.27$$

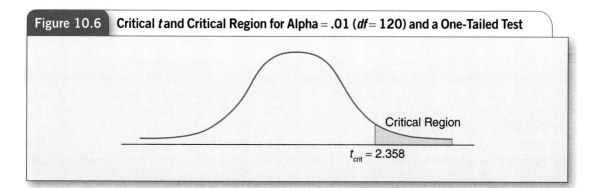

**Figure 10.6** **Critical $t$ and Critical Region for Alpha = .01 ($df$ = 120) and a One-Tailed Test**

Critical Region

$t_{crit} = 2.358$

**Step 5:** The *t* value we obtained of 15.27 is substantially greater than the critical value of *t* (2.358) that was needed in order to reject the null hypothesis—it falls into the critical region. Since $t_{obt} > t_{crit}$, we will reject the null hypothesis that the population means are equal. This suggests that the observed sample mean difference is too large to be attributed to chance or sampling variation, and we can therefore assume that the mean rate of household victimization experienced by those who have recently moved to a neighborhood is greater than the mean rate experienced by those who have lived in their places of residence for 1 year or more. The results of our statistical test lend support to one of the premises of social disorganization theory; we have found that individuals who have just recently been in a state of transiency (e.g., have moved within the last year) are more likely to become victims of household crime than are those who have been more residentially stable (e.g., have not moved within the last year).

## Case Study

### Boot Camps and Recidivism

When crime rates in the United States were high in the mid-1980s to the early 1990s, a correctional program called correctional boot camps (sometimes called shock incarceration programs) became very popular in both state and federal prison systems. Although they were rapidly put in place, it was not always clear whether they reduced recidivism any better than regular correctional facilities. Despite their increased popularity, there have been only a few really rigorous attempts to evaluate their efficacy in reducing recidivism. Perhaps some of the most ambitious evaluations of boot camps have been conducted by Professor Doris MacKenzie and her colleagues, who have compared graduates from boot camps to individuals sentenced for the same crimes but sent to prison (for review, see MacKenzie, 2013).

Suppose we want to conduct our own experiment on the issue. We get the help of a local judge and randomly select, from a group of young adult offenders convicted of a felony offense, those who will go to a military style boot camp and those who will be sent to the state prison for regular correctional programming. After their release, individuals are followed for two years. To collect information on offending behavior, we conduct interviews with the individuals and obtain official arrest data. Mean levels of offending behavior (for all crimes, including violent, property, and drug offenses) are calculated for both groups as follows:

| Boot Camp Group | Prison Group |
|---|---|
| $\bar{X}_1 = 15.2$ offenses | $\bar{X}_2 = 15.9$ offenses |
| $s_1^2 = 4.7$ | $s_2^2 = 5.1$ |
| $n_1 = 32$ | $n_2 = 29$ |

In this example, the type of custody (boot camp vs. prison) is our independent variable and the number of offenses committed is our dependent variable. To determine whether there is a significant difference in the mean rates of offending between the boot camp graduates and those released from prison, we must conduct a formal hypothesis test about the difference between two means. To help you learn the steps of formal hypothesis testing, we ask that you check off each step as we go through them.

Because there has been so little research on the efficacy of boot camps, and because the research that does exist is inconsistent, it would be hard to predict in advance which type of programming is more effective in reducing recidivism so let's select a nondirectional alternative hypothesis. The formal hypothesis statements are as follows:

$$H_0: \mu_{\text{boot camps}} = \mu_{\text{prison}}$$

$$H_1: \mu_{\text{boot camps}} \neq \mu_{\text{prison}}$$

The $t$ test, along with its corresponding sampling distribution, is an appropriate statistical test for our data. Let's select an alpha level of .05. With a nondirectional hypothesis test, $\alpha = .05$, and 59 degrees of freedom ($32 + 29 - 2 = 59$), we will use the critical value of $t$ for 60 degrees of freedom because that is the closest value in Table B.3. We will reject the null hypothesis if our obtained $t$ is either less than or equal to $-2.00$ or greater than or equal to $+2.00$. The critical values and corresponding critical regions are displayed in Figure 10.7. The obtained value of $t$ is calculated as follows:

$$t_{\text{obt}} = \frac{15.2 - 15.9}{\sqrt{\dfrac{(32-1)4.7 + (29-1)5.1}{32 + 29 - 2}} \sqrt{\dfrac{32 + 29}{(32)(29)}}}$$

$$t_{\text{obt}} = \frac{-.7}{\sqrt{\dfrac{(31)4.7 + (28)5.1}{59}} \sqrt{\dfrac{61}{928}}}$$

$$t_{\text{obt}} = \frac{-.7}{\sqrt{\dfrac{145.7 + 142.8}{59}} \sqrt{.066}}$$

$$t_{\text{obt}} = \frac{-.7}{\sqrt{\dfrac{288.5}{59}} \sqrt{.066}}$$

$$t_{\text{obt}} = \frac{-.7}{\sqrt{4.89} \sqrt{.066}}$$

$$t_{\text{obt}} = \frac{-.7}{(2.21)(.26)}$$

$$t_{\text{obt}} = \frac{-.7}{.57}$$

$$t_{\text{obt}} = -1.23$$

| Figure 10.7 | **Critical $t$ and Critical Regions for Alpha $= .05$ ($df = 60$) and a Two-Tailed Test** |

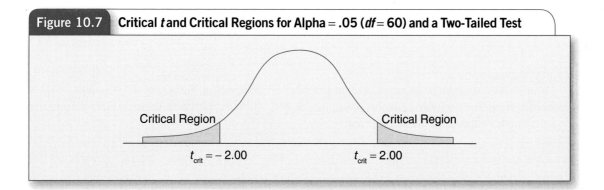

Our statistical test results in an obtained $t$ value of $-1.23$. An obtained $t$ of $-1.23$ does not lie within the critical region, so we must fail to reject the null hypothesis. Because we failed to reject the null hypothesis, we must conclude that the mean offending rates after release for boot camp and regular prison inmates are not significantly different from one another. This would be in line with much of the research to date on boot camps, which has shown that the core elements of boot camp programs—military-style discipline, hard labor, and physical training—do not reduce offender recidivism any better than regular prison (MacKenzie, 2013).

## Model 2: Separate Variance Estimate ($\sigma_1 \neq \sigma_2$)

In the previous examples, we have assumed that the two population standard deviations were equal. Under this assumption, we can take advantage of this equality and use a common estimate of the population standard deviation ($\hat{\sigma}$) to calculate a pooled variance estimate for the standard error of the difference ($\sigma_{\bar{X}_1 - \bar{X}_2}$). Unfortunately, it will not always be possible for us to make this assumption about equal population standard deviations. In many instances, our $F$ test will lead us to *reject* the null hypothesis that $\sigma_1 = \sigma_2$ and we must conclude that the two population standard deviations are different. When this happens, we cannot use a pooled variance estimate of the standard error of the difference. Instead, we must estimate what is called a separate variance estimate of the standard error of the difference. The formula for this estimate is:

$$\sigma_{\bar{X}_1 - \bar{X}_2} = \sqrt{\frac{s_1^2}{n_1 - 1} + \frac{s_2^2}{n_2 - 1}}$$

With a separate variance estimate of the standard error of the difference, the formula for our $t$ test now becomes:

$$t_{\text{obt}} = \frac{\overline{X}_1 - \overline{X}_2}{\sqrt{\dfrac{s_1^2}{n_1 - 1} + \dfrac{s_2^2}{n_2 - 1}}} \qquad (10-4)$$

The steps necessary to conduct a hypothesis test remain exactly the same as before, except for determining the degrees of freedom. The correct degrees of freedom for the separate variance $t$ test are not as easy as $n_1 + n_2 - 2$. In fact, the formula to calculate the degrees of freedom for a $t$ test using the separate variance estimate is quite a bit more complicated. The following formula has been suggested to obtain the appropriate degrees of freedom for this test (Blalock, 1979; Hays, 1994):

$$df = \left[ \frac{\left( \dfrac{s_1^2}{n_1 - 1} + \dfrac{s_2^2}{n_2 - 1} \right)}{\left( \dfrac{s_1^2}{n_1 - 1} \right)^2 \left( \dfrac{1}{n_1 + 1} \right) + \left( \dfrac{s_2^2}{n_2 - 1} \right)^2 \left( \dfrac{1}{n_2 + 1} \right)} \right] - 2 \qquad (10-5)$$

Wow! And you thought the degrees of freedom were relatively unimportant! The results of this formula should be rounded to the nearest integer to obtain the approximate degrees of freedom. Let's go through two examples using the separate variance estimate approach for the $t$ test.

———————————————— **Case Study** ————————————————

## Formal Sanctions and Intimate Partner Assault

In 1981, the first large-scale experiment to test the deterrent effects of arrest on domestic batterers, called the Minneapolis Domestic Violence Experiment, was conducted by Lawrence Sherman and Richard Berk (1984a, 1984b). The theoretical impetus for this experiment was guided by notions of specific deterrence. The primary research question driving the study was as follows: "Does arresting a man who has assaulted his partner decrease the probability that he will assault her in the future compared to less punitive interventions which are typically used, such as separating the parties?" From their study, the researchers concluded that arrest provided the strongest deterrent to future violence and consequently was the preferred police response to domestic violence. This led to many jurisdictions implementing mandatory arrest policies for intimate partner assault.

To test the validity of experimental findings, an important canon of science is *replication*. Accordingly, the National Institute of Justice funded replication experiments of the Minneapolis experiment in six other cities. Unlike the original Minneapolis experiment, the published findings from these replications, which became known as the Spouse Assault Replication Program (SARP), did not uniformly find that arrest is an effective deterrent in spouse assault cases.[3] The effect of arrest on intimate partner assault was revisited recently by Lawrence Sherman and Heather Harris (2015), who examined death rates among the original victims of domestic violence 23 years after the first study in Minneapolis. They found that victims whose abusers were arrested were more likely to die prematurely than those victims whose abusers were simply warned. Clearly, this latest study calls into further question the effectiveness of mandatory arrest policies.

Let's say we attempted to conduct our own study on a much smaller scale about the effects of an arrest policy on future domestic violence. By working with a police department, we would randomly assign arrested suspects who had assaulted their intimate partner to either short-term (no more than three hours) or long-term (four or more hours) detention in jail after their arrest. We would then follow these offenders and victims for a 120-day period and record the number of new victimizations their partners reported to interviewers, along with the number of calls to police during that period. The independent variable is the type of detention and the dependent variable is the number of intimate partner assaults perpetrated postrelease. The hypothetical mean number of postdetention- assaults, along with other sample statistics for each group, are as follows:

| Short-Term Detention | Long-Term Detention |
|---|---|
| $\bar{X}_1 = 6.4$ | $\bar{X}_2 = 8.1$ |
| $s_1 = 2.2$ | $s_2 = 3.9$ |
| $n_1 = 14$ | $n_2 = 42$ |

We would like to test the null hypothesis that the population means for the two groups are equal. In saying this, we are suggesting that the length of detention after an arrest has no effect on the frequency with which intimate partner assault is committed in the immediate future. Suppose also that, based on an $F$ test, we rejected the null hypothesis that the population standard deviations are equal, and therefore, we must assume they are significantly different and use the separate variance $t$ test as our statistical test.

**Step 1**: Because the literature on the efficacy in deterring intimate partner assault with stiff penalties is unclear, we will conduct a nondirectional (two-tailed) alternative hypothesis that states the two population means are simply different. Our null hypothesis states that the two population means are equal or, stated in words, that there is no relationship between the type of detention experienced by arrested suspects and rates of intimate partner assault post release. Both hypotheses are formally stated as follows:

$H_0$: $\mu_{\text{short detention}} = \mu_{\text{long detention}}$

$H_1$: $\mu_{\text{short detention}} \neq \mu_{\text{long detention}}$

**Step 2**: As mentioned earlier, our statistical test will be the separate variance $t$ test, and our sampling distribution will be the $t$ distribution.

**Step 3**: We will select an alpha level of .01. To find our critical value of $t$ and the critical region, we first need to determine the appropriate degrees of freedom. Based on formula 10–4, we can approximate our degrees of freedom as equal to:

$$df = \left[ \frac{\left( \dfrac{4.84}{14-1} + \dfrac{15.21}{42-1} \right)^2}{\left( \dfrac{4.84}{14-1} \right)^2 \left( \dfrac{1}{14+1} \right) + \left( \dfrac{15.21}{42-1} \right)^2 \left( \dfrac{1}{42+1} \right)} \right] - 2$$

$$df = \left[ \frac{\left( \dfrac{4.84}{13} + \dfrac{15.21}{41} \right)^2}{\left( \dfrac{4.84}{13} \right)^2 \left( \dfrac{1}{15} \right) + \left( \dfrac{15.21}{41} \right)^2 \left( \dfrac{1}{43} \right)} \right] - 2$$

$$df = \frac{(.37 + .37)^2}{(.37)^2 (.07) + (.37)^2 (.02)} - 2$$

$$df = \frac{(.74)^2}{.010 + .003} - 2$$

$$df = \frac{.55}{.013} - 2$$

$$df = 42.3 - 2$$

$$df = 40.3$$

$$df = 40$$

With 40 degrees of freedom and an alpha of .01 for a two-tailed test, our critical values of $t$ are ±2.704 (Table B.3, Appendix B). Because we are doing a two-tailed or nondirectional test, our critical region will consist of any $t_{\text{obt}}$ less than or equal to −2.704 or greater than or equal to 2.704. We show the critical values and critical region in Figure 10.8.

We now calculate our obtained value of $t$ as shown here (notice that we have given you the sample standard deviations rather than the variances):

$$t_{\text{obt}} = \frac{\overline{X}_1 - \overline{X}_2}{\sqrt{\dfrac{s_1^2}{n_1 - 1} + \dfrac{s_2^2}{n_2 - 1}}}$$

$$t_{obt} = \frac{6.4 - 8.1}{\sqrt{\dfrac{(2.2)^2}{14-1} + \dfrac{(3.9)^2}{42-1}}}$$

$$t_{obt} = \frac{6.4 - 8.1}{\sqrt{\dfrac{4.84}{14-1} + \dfrac{15.21}{42-1}}}$$

$$t_{obt} = \frac{-1.7}{\sqrt{\dfrac{4.84}{13} + \dfrac{15.21}{41}}}$$

$$t_{obt} = \frac{-1.7}{\sqrt{.37 + .37}}$$

$$t_{obt} = \frac{-1.7}{.86}$$

$$t_{obt} = -1.98$$

| Figure 10.8 | Critical *t* and Critical Region for alpha = .01 (*df* = 40) and a Two-Tailed Test |

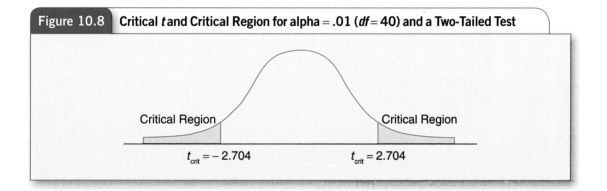

Critical Region      Critical Region

$t_{crit} = -2.704$      $t_{crit} = 2.704$

Our obtained *t* statistic is −1.98. Because this does not fall below the critical negative value of *t* (and, therefore, it does not fall into the critical region), we fail to reject the null hypothesis. Our conclusion, based on our sample results, is that there is no significant difference between the mean number of postdetention assaults for those who were given short-term detention versus those who were given long-term detention in the population. Thus, it seems that there is no significant relationship between detention time and an arrested batterer's propensity to commit acts of violence in the future. Note that we also had to square the standard deviation that was provided to obtain the variance! Let's go through another quick example.

## Case Study

## Gender and Sentencing

An area that has received a great deal of research in criminology and criminal justice revolves around the idea of gender disparity in sentencing in both state and federal courts (Daly, 1987; Engen, Gainey, Crutchfield, & Weis, 2003; Starr, 2015; Steffensmeier, Kramer, & Streifel, 1993).

Controversy still exists over whether disparity in sentencing truly exists or whether observed gender differences in sentencing are due to legal characteristics of the offense or the offender. Some research has found that female defendants were sentenced for shorter prison terms than males (Spohn & Spears, 1997; Starr, 2015), whereas others have found little or no evidence of gender disparity (Daly, 1994; Rapaport, 1991; Steffensmeier et al., 1993). Steffensmeier and his colleagues, for example, have gone so far as to conclude, "When men and women appear in (contemporary) criminal court in similar circumstances and are charged with similar offenses, they receive similar treatment" (Steffensmeier et al., 1993, p. 411). You should have immediately recognized that gender in this scenario is the independent variable (a two-category, nominal-level variable) and the length of the sentence received is the continuous dependent variable.

Let's assume that we have a random sample of 50 male and 25 female defendants who were found guilty of burglary and sentenced to some time in prison. The mean sentence length received for male and female defendants, along with their respective standard deviations and sample sizes, are as follows:

| Male Defendants | Female Defendants |
|---|---|
| $\bar{X}_1 = 12.02$ | $\bar{X}_2 = 3.32$ |
| $s_1 = 72.68$ | $s_2 = 11.31$ |
| $n_1 = 50$ | $n_2 = 25$ |

**Step 1**: Let's say we believe that males will be sentenced more harshly than females. Accordingly, we state a directional (one-tailed) alternative hypothesis that the population mean sentence length is greater for male defendants than for female defendants. The null hypothesis is that the population means are equal:

$H_0: \mu_{males} = \mu_{females}$

$H_1: \mu_{males} > \mu_{females}$

**Step 2**: Our test statistic is the separate variance $t$ test, and our sampling distribution is the $t$ distribution.

**Step 3**: We will choose an alpha level of .05 ($\alpha = .05$). Based on formula 10–10, we determine that the approximate degrees of freedom is 56. (We will not show the work here, but it would be a good idea to compute this for yourself just for practice.) With 56 degrees of freedom, $\alpha = .05$, and a one-tailed test, we can see from the $t$ table that our critical $t$ value is 1.671 (actually, this $t$ score corresponds to 60 degrees of freedom, but it is the closest value we have to 56 $df$ in the table). Since we have predicted that the population mean for males will be greater than the

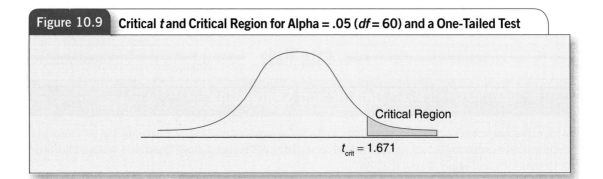

**Figure 10.9**  **Critical *t* and Critical Region for Alpha = .05 (*df* = 60) and a One-Tailed Test**

Critical Region

$t_{crit} = 1.671$

population mean for females, we will reject the null hypothesis if $t_{obt} \geq 1.671$, and we will fail to reject the null hypothesis if $t_{obt} < 1.671$. We show the critical value and the critical region in Figure 10.9.

**Step 4**: We will now calculate our obtained $t$ value, using the separate variance estimate, as shown:

$$t_{obt} = \frac{12.02 - 3.32}{\sqrt{\dfrac{(72.68)^2}{50-1} + \dfrac{(11.31)^2}{25-1}}}$$

$$t_{obt} = \frac{8.7}{\sqrt{107.80 + 5.33}}$$

$$t_{obt} = \frac{8.7}{\sqrt{113.13}}$$

$$t_{obt} = \frac{8.7}{10.64}$$

$$t_{obt} = .82$$

Note that we again had to square the standard deviation to obtain the variance! Our obtained $t$ score of .82 is considerably less than the critical $t$ of 1.671 and does not fall into the critical region. Our decision, then, will be to fail to reject the null hypothesis that there is no difference in the population means. We will conclude that, based on our sample data, there is not a significant relationship between sentence length received for burglary and gender of defendant in the population. Thus, the sentences handed down by judges for males convicted of robbery do not seem to be greater than the sentences received by females convicted of the same offense in the population. You may be thinking that the vast difference between the means should certainly have produced a significant result. However, remember that the test is also greatly influenced by the variation in each group—note the huge standard deviation around the mean sentence length for males!

So far, we have examined ways of comparing means across two independent samples or groups of cases. In the next section, we will examine a procedure called the matched-groups $t$ test that is used to compare two means within the same or a comparable group or sample. In this case, we cannot assume that we have two independent samples.

## 🔲 Matched-Groups or Dependent-Samples *t* Test

In our application of the $t$ test for the difference between two means in the previous section, we assumed that the two samples were independent of each other. That is, we assumed that the selection of the elements of one sample had no effect on the selection of the elements of the other. There are times when this assumption is deliberately violated. One instance of this lack of independence occurs when we have a "treatment" group and a "control" group. To make sure that the two groups are comparable with one another in as many ways as possible, each observation in one group is sometimes "matched" with an observation in the other group on relevant characteristics. Matching of samples can be done whenever it is not practical or ethical to randomly assign the "treatment." Matching subjects is done so that the only thing that differentiates the two groups is that one group received a certain type of treatment or was exposed to some phenomenon and the other group was not.

For example, one way to determine the effect of counseling on future delinquency would be to collect data from two samples that are very similar to each other with the exception that one has received counseling (treatment group) and the other has not (control group). In such a study, an 18-year-old White male who lives in an urban area and has no criminal history might be placed in a sample that is to receive treatment (counseling) while another 18-year-old White male who lives in an urban area and has no criminal history might be "matched" to this treatment male but placed in a sample that is to receive no treatment (no counseling). In this case, the two subjects are matched with respect to five characteristics: age (they are both 18 years old), ethnicity (they are both White), gender (both males), residence (both urban dwellers), and criminal history (both have no criminal history). If the members of the two groups are effectively matched on important characteristics that are related to the dependent variable (such as age, minority status, gender, location of residence, and criminal history), then any observed differences between the two groups on the dependent variable after treatment (future delinquency) are unlikely to be due to these demographic characteristics. Rather, they are more likely to be due to the treatment, which in this example is counseling. The important point here is that by matching someone in one sample with a counterpart in a second sample, we have violated our assumption that the two samples are independent and so cannot use either of our two independent samples $t$ tests.

> **Matched or dependent samples:**
> Samples in which individuals are either dependent or matched on several characteristics (i.e., age, race, gender, etc.) or before-and-after samples of the same people.

A second common use of **matched or dependent samples** occurs with "before–after" research designs, more generally referred to as pre–post designs. In this type of study, there is only one sample, but measures of the dependent variable are taken at two different points in time, "before" some intervention or treatment and again "after." For example, suppose we have access to only one group of arrested delinquents and all of them are going to receive counseling. In this case, we would have access to the individuals before and after they received counseling. In this case, we might use self-report or official arrest data before and after counseling to determine whether counseling actually decreased rates of offending. However, this type of sample also violates our assumption of independence since the same persons appear in both groups. The subjects before the intervention cannot be independent of those after the intervention since they are the same people.

It should be clear to you that the two previously described $t$ tests would not be appropriate because we would not have independent samples because the elements of each sample were deliberately selected to be alike or, in fact, are the same people. In both the matched-groups and the pre–post design, the independent observation is actually a *pair of cases*, not two independent groups. If we now consider *each pair* as an independent observation, we can conduct a statistical test based on the difference between the scores for each pair. In other words, we will make a pair-by-pair comparison by obtaining a difference score for each pair. Unlike the $t$ test for independent samples that tests for the difference between two sample means ($\overline{X}_2 - \overline{X}_1$), the matched-groups or dependent samples $t$ test calculates the difference between the scores for each pair of subjects ($x_2 - x_1$), where a pair is either a pair of subjects that have been matched on some characteristics or where it is the same person measured at two different points in time. In this example, one population consists of one of the matched groups or the group before the treatment, whereas the second population consists of the other matched group or the group after the treatment.

In the null hypothesis of the $t$ test for matched groups or dependent samples, we will assume that the two populations are equal, which implies that the treatment or intervention has no effect. If this is true, the scores for the two groups will on average be equal, so the difference between them will be 0. If, under the null hypothesis, we take the difference between each pair of observations, each difference is expected to be zero, and the mean of the differences will be zero. The null hypothesis, then, presumes that the population mean of group differences will be zero. We will symbolize the mean of the population of group differences as $\mu_D$ with the subscript $D$ indicating that this is the difference between the two populations. The statistical test in a dependent-samples $t$ test, then, is really a single-sample test of the hypothesis that $\mu_D = 0$ (the sample statistic is $\overline{X}_D$ the mean of the difference between each pair of scores in the sample).

Our procedure will be to determine the difference between each pair of scores ($X_D = x_2 - x_1$) in the sample, calculate the mean of these differences ($\overline{X}_D$), and then test whether this sample mean difference is equal to the expected population mean difference ($\mu_D$) of zero. If the null hypothesis is true, then most of these $X_D$ differences will be close to zero, as will the mean of the differences $\overline{X}_D$. If, however, the null hypothesis is not true, then the two scores will tend to be different from each other, and the mean difference score will be greater than or less than zero. The greater the difference between each pair of scores, the greater the mean difference will be, and the more likely we will be to reject the null hypothesis.

The formula for the $t$ test with dependent samples is:

$$t = \frac{\overline{X}_D - \mu_D}{s_D / \sqrt{n}} \tag{10-6}$$

Remember that we have drawn an analogy between the $t$ test for matched samples and a hypothesis test involving a single population mean. In the $t$ test in Chapter 8, where we dealt with one-population problems, we subtracted the population mean from the sample mean and divided by the standard deviation of the sampling distribution. This is exactly what we do in the independent-samples or matched-groups $t$ test in formula 10−6. We subtract the population mean ($\mu_D$) from the sample mean ($\overline{X}_D$), where the sample mean is the mean of the differences between each pair of scores in the sample, and we divide by the estimated standard deviation of the sampling distribution, which is the standard deviation of the observed difference scores. Note that the dependent-samples $t$ test is based solely on the difference scores $X_D$ (where $X_D = x_2 - x_1$) and the standard deviation of the difference scores ($s_D$).

Since the null hypothesis assumes that the population mean is zero ($\mu_D = 0$), we can drop that term from the numerator and the formula for the dependent-samples $t$ test can be reduced to:

$$t_{obt} = \frac{\overline{X}_D}{s_D / \sqrt{n}} \tag{10-7}$$

where

$$s_D = \sqrt{\frac{\Sigma(x_D - \overline{X}_D)^2}{n-1}}$$

or

$$s_D = \sqrt{\frac{\left(\Sigma D^2 - \frac{(\Sigma D)^2}{n}\right)}{n-1}}$$

The term $s_D$ in equation 10−7 is just our old friend the standard deviation, and we gave you two ways to calculate it that you should recognize from Chapter 5 as the definitional and computational formulas for the standard deviation respectively.

Once we have our obtained the $t$ value, we do the same thing we have done with any $t$ test discussed thus far. We compare $t_{obt}$ with $t_{crit}$ and make a decision about our null hypothesis. We even go to the same $t$ table as for independent samples $t$ tests (Table B.3 of Appendix B). The difference is that in the case of matched groups or dependent samples, since we have only $n$ pairs of independent observations (rather than $n_1 + n_2$ observations as in the case of independent samples), we have $n - 1$ degrees of freedom, where $n$ is equal to the number of *pairs* of observations. If this sounds a bit confusing right now, no worries. A couple of examples will help illustrate what is going on here. In each example we will conduct a formal hypothesis test.

---

## Case Study

### Problem-Oriented Policing and Crime

Several recent studies have found that more than half of all crimes in a city are committed in only a few places. Some criminologists have called these places "hot spots" (Braga et al., 1999; Caplan, Kennedy, & Piza, 2013; Kennedy, Caplan, & Piza, 2013; Sherman, Gartin, & Buerger, 1989). Even within the most crime-ridden neighborhoods, it has been found that crime clusters at a few locations while other areas remain relatively free of crime. The clustering of violent crime at particular locations suggests that there are important features of, or key dynamics at, these locations that give rise to frequent violence. Thus, focused crime prevention efforts have recently sought to modify these "criminogenic" conditions and reduce violence.

Problem-oriented policing strategies (similar to community policing) are increasingly used by urban jurisdictions to reduce crime in these high-activity or "hot spot" crime places. Problem-oriented policing challenges officers to identify and analyze the causes of problems behind a string of criminal incidents. Once the underlying conditions that give rise to crime problems are known, police officers can then develop and implement appropriate responses to reduce crime. For example, strategies include using community members as information sources to discuss the nature of the problems the community faces, the possible effectiveness of proposed responses, and the assessment of implemented responses. Other strategies target the social disorder problems inherent in these neighborhoods, such as cleaning up the environment of the place and making physical improvements, securing vacant lots, or removing trash from the street.

Suppose we are interested in the efficacy of these policing strategies in reducing acts of violence in neighborhoods plagued by high rates of crime. We target 20 neighborhoods within a city and send out teams of community police officers to implement problem-oriented policing strategies in these neighborhoods. Before the program begins, we obtain the number of arrests for violent offenses that were made in each neighborhood within the 60 days prior to program implementation. After the program has been in place, we again obtain the number of arrests for violent offenses that were made in each neighborhood for a 60-day period. In this case, the program of having problem-oriented policing in the community is the independent variable, and the number of violent offenses is the dependent variable. Notice that we have the same neighborhoods here; we have the number of crimes before and after the introduction of problem-oriented policing. We want to know whether the average number of violent arrests increased or decreased after the policing program was implemented. The hypothetical numbers of arrests for each time point are reported in the second and third columns of Table 10.4. We now are ready to conduct our hypothesis test.

**Step 1:** First, we state our null and research hypotheses. Our null hypothesis is that the mean difference score in the population is equal to zero. This implies that the problem-oriented policing had no effect on the number of violent arrests within neighborhoods. Since we are unsure what the exact effect of our problem-oriented policing strategy will be (maybe it will make things better, but maybe with more police it may make things worse or more crime will simply be seen), we will opt for a nondirectional alternative hypothesis stating our belief that, on average, the number of arrests in neighborhoods after the new policing strategy will be different from the number of arrests before problem-oriented policing was implemented. Both the null and research hypotheses are formally stated as follows:

$H_0: \mu_D = 0$ This implies that the same number of crimes were committed before and after the policing program was put in place.

$H_1: \mu_D \neq 0$ This implies that there is some effect of the policing program on crime, but we cannot state in advance if it decreases or increases crime.

**Step 2:** The next step is to state our test statistic and the sampling distribution of that test statistic. Because we have dependent samples (the same community is used before and after the policing program was introduced), we use the dependent-samples $t$ test as the statistical test and the $t$ distribution as our sampling distribution.

**Step 3**: The third step is to select our alpha level and determine the critical value and region. Let's select an alpha level of .01 ($\alpha = .01$) for this example. Because we have 20 pairs of observations ($n = 20$), we have $20 - 1$, or 19, degrees of freedom. We go to Table B.3 of Appendix B and find that for a two-tailed hypothesis test, $\alpha = .01$, and 19 degrees of freedom, the critical value of $t$ is $\pm 2.861$. We will therefore reject the null hypothesis if $t_{obt}$ is less than or equal to $-2.861$ or if $t_{obt}$ is greater than or equal to 2.861. We illustrate this for you in Figure 10.10.

**Step 4**: The fourth step of our hypothesis-testing procedure is to calculate the test statistic and compare it with our critical value.

For our first example of a matched-groups $t$ test, we illustrate the calculations in detail. From equation 10–6, we see that we need to determine the mean of the difference scores and the estimated standard deviation of the difference scores. In Table 10.4, we report that the sum of the difference scores is equal to $-48$ ($\Sigma X_D$ or $\Sigma (x_2 - x_1) = -48$). Note how these difference scores are created. For each neighborhood, we subtract the first score

**Table 10.4** Number of Violent Arrests in Neighborhoods Before (First Score) and After (Second Score) Implementation of Problem-Oriented Policing

| Pair Number | First Score $x_1$ | Second Score $x_2$ | $(x_2 - x_1)$ | $(x_2 - x_1)^2$ |
|:---:|:---:|:---:|:---:|:---:|
| 1 | 25 | 21 | −4.00 | 16 |
| 2 | 29 | 25 | −4.00 | 16 |
| 3 | 32 | 32 | .00 | 0 |
| 4 | 42 | 39 | −3.00 | 9 |
| 5 | 21 | 25 | 4.00 | 16 |
| 6 | 29 | 25 | −4.00 | 16 |
| 7 | 33 | 29 | −4.00 | 16 |
| 8 | 35 | 36 | 1.00 | 1 |
| 9 | 32 | 29 | −3.00 | 9 |
| 10 | 36 | 35 | − 1.00 | 1 |
| 11 | 39 | 40 | 1.00 | 1 |
| 12 | 25 | 21 | −4.00 | 16 |
| 13 | 27 | 25 | −2.00 | 4 |
| 14 | 41 | 35 | −6.00 | 36 |
| 15 | 36 | 35 | − 1.00 | 1 |
| 16 | 21 | 23 | 2.00 | 4 |
| 17 | 38 | 31 | −7.00 | 49 |
| 18 | 25 | 21 | −4.00 | 16 |
| 19 | 29 | 25 | −4.00 | 16 |
| 20 | 25 | 20 | − 5.00 | 25 |
| | | | $\Sigma = -48$ | $\Sigma = 268$ |
| | | | $\bar{X}_D = -2.40$ | |

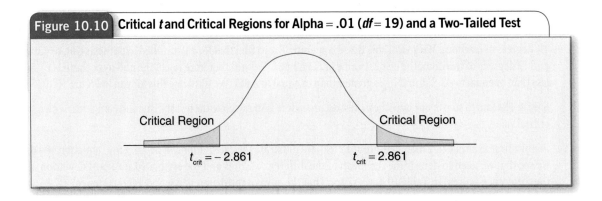

Figure 10.10 Critical *t* and Critical Regions for Alpha = .01 (*df* = 19) and a Two-Tailed Test

(before the policing program) from the second (after the policing program was implemented). For example, the first pair of cases had 21 arrests after the problem-oriented policing strategy was implemented and 25 arrests before. The difference, then, is $21 - 25 = -4$, or a reduction by 4 crimes. We do this for each neighborhood (each pair), sum across the pairs, and then divide by the number of pairs to obtain a mean difference score. All scores are added in calculating this mean difference score, including zeros and scores with negative signs. With 20 pairs of scores, the mean difference score for these data is $-48/20$, or $-2.40$ ($\bar{X}_D = -2.40$).

We now calculate the estimated standard deviation of the difference scores. This is just like calculating the standard deviation for any other group of scores, except that the raw data are the difference scores and the mean is the mean of the difference scores. First, we will use the definitional formula for the standard deviation. We subtract the mean difference score from each difference score, square this difference, sum these squared differences, divide by the number of pairs minus one, and then take the square root. This is equal to the standard deviation of the difference scores. To get the standard error or the standard deviation of the sampling distribution, divide this standard deviation by the square root of the sample size. The calculations necessary to find this are shown in Table 10.5.

We can place this into our definitional formula for the standard deviation (Chapter 5):

$$s_D = \sqrt{\frac{\Sigma(X_D - \bar{X}_D)^2}{n-1}}$$

The standard deviation of the difference scores is symbolized as $s_D$ and, for this example, is calculated using the earlier standard deviation formula: 152.80:

$$s_D = \sqrt{\frac{152.80}{19}}$$
$$s_D = \sqrt{8.042}$$
$$s_D = 2.836$$

Now that we have the standard deviation of the difference scores, we can calculate our test statistic:

$$t_{obt} = \frac{\bar{X}_D}{s_D / \sqrt{n}}$$

$$t_{obt} = \frac{-2.40}{2.836 / \sqrt{20}}$$

$$t_{obt} = \frac{-2.40}{2.836 / 4.472}$$

$$t_{obt} = \frac{-2.40}{.634}$$

$$t_{obt} = -3.785$$

| Table 10.5 | Standard Deviations of the Sampling Distribution for the Number of Neighborhood Violent Arrests Before (First Score) and After (Second Score) Problem-Oriented Policing Implementation | |
|---|---|---|

| *Pair* | $(x_D - \bar{X}_D)$ | $(x_D - \bar{X}_D)^2$ |
|---|---|---|
| 1 | −4 − (−2.4) = − 1.60 | 2.56 |
| 2 | −4 − (−2.4) = − 1.60 | 2.56 |
| 3 | 0 − (−2.4) = 2.40 | 5.76 |
| 4 | −3 − (−2.4) = −.60 | .36 |
| 5 | 4 − (−2.4) = 6.40 | 40.96 |
| 6 | −4 − (−2.4) = − 1.60 | 2.56 |
| 7 | −4 − (−2.4) = − 1.60 | 2.56 |
| 8 | 1 − (−2.4) = 3.40 | 11.56 |
| 9 | −3 − (−2.4) = −.60 | .36 |
| 10 | − 1 − (−2.4) = 1.40 | 1.96 |
| 11 | 1− (−2.4) = 3.40 | 11.56 |
| 12 | −4 − (−2.4) = − 1.60 | 2.56 |
| 13 | −2 − (−2.4) = .40 | .16 |
| 14 | −6 − (−2.4) = −3.60 | 12.96 |
| 15 | − 1 − (−2.4) = 1.40 | 1.96 |
| 16 | 2− (−2.4) = 4.40 | 19.36 |
| 17 | − 7 − (−2.4) = −4.60 | 21.16 |
| 18 | −4 − (−2.4) = − 1.60 | 2.56 |
| 19 | −4 − (−2.4) = − 1.60 | 2.56 |
| 20 | −5 − (−2.4) = −2.60 | 6.76 |
| $n = 20$ | | $\Sigma (X_D - \bar{X}_D)^2 = 152.80$ |

**Step 5**: Finally, we compare our obtained value of $t$ (−3.785) with our critical value (±2.861) and the critical region. Since $t_{obt}$ falls within the critical region (−3.785 < −2.861), we can reject the null hypothesis that the mean of the differences is equal to zero. We will conclude that the number of postarrests for violence is significantly different from the number of prearrests. The implementation of problem-oriented policing within our sample of neighborhoods seems to have had a significant impact in reducing the number of violent arrests made within neighborhoods in the population.

---

# Case Study

## Siblings and Delinquency

One of the most comprehensive studies ever undertaken on the causes of delinquent behavior was reported more than 60 years ago by Sheldon and Eleanor Glueck (1950). The Gluecks compared 500 institutionalized chronic delinquents with a matched group of 500 nondelinquents. Among their findings, the Gluecks reported that members of the delinquent group were more likely than the nondelinquents to come from broken homes and economically disadvantaged families, to have friends who were also delinquents, and to have parents who were cruel and erratic in their discipline.

Let's presume that, like the Gluecks, we have a group of 15 nondelinquents and a group of 15 delinquents, who are matched with respect to social class, gender, age, race, and whether both parents are in the home. For each youth, we also have the number of siblings who he or she reports have been arrested for a crime. What we want to know is whether the delinquent youth have more delinquent siblings than the nondelinquents. In this scenario, whether a youth has been arrested for delinquency is the independent variable and the number of delinquent siblings is the dependent variable. The data from the two groups are reported in the second and third columns of Table 10.6.

| Table 10.6 | Number of Delinquent Siblings for 15 Delinquent Youths and a Matched Group of 15 Nondelinquent Youths, and the Calculations Necessary for a Matched Group $t$ Test |
| --- | --- |

| Pair | Nondelinquent Score $x_1$ | Delinquent Score $x_2$ | $x_D$ $(x_2 - x_1)$ | $x_D^2$ $(x_2 - x_1)^2$ | $x_D - \bar{X}_D$ | $\left(x_D - \bar{X}_D\right)^2$ |
| --- | --- | --- | --- | --- | --- | --- |
| 1 | 1 | 3 | 2 | 4 | 2 − 1.40 = .60 | .36 |
| 2 | 0 | 2 | 2 | 4 | 2 − 1.40 = .60 | .36 |
| 3 | 0 | 1 | 1 | 1 | 1 − 1.40 = −.40 | .16 |
| 4 | 1 | 4 | 3 | 9 | 3 − 1.40 = 1.60 | 2.56 |
| 5 | 2 | 1 | −1 | 1 | −1 − 1.40 = −2.40 | 5.76 |
| 6 | 0 | 3 | 3 | 9 | 3 − 1.40 = 1.60 | 2.56 |
| 7 | 2 | 2 | 0 | 0 | 0 − 1.40 = −1.40 | 1.96 |
| 8 | 1 | 4 | 3 | 9 | 3 − 1.40 = 1.60 | 2.56 |
| 9 | 0 | 1 | 1 | 1 | 1 − 1.40 = −.40 | .16 |
| 10 | 0 | 2 | 2 | 4 | 2 − 1.40 = .60 | .36 |
| 11 | 0 | 0 | 0 | 0 | 0 − 1.40 = −1.40 | 1.96 |
| 12 | 1 | 2 | 1 | 1 | 1 − 1.40 = −.40 | .16 |
| 13 | 0 | 2 | 2 | 4 | 2 − 1.40 = .60 | .36 |
| 14 | 1 | 3 | 2 | 4 | 2 − 1.40 = .60 | .36 |
| 15 | 0 | 0 | 0 | 0 | 0 − 1.40 = −1.40 | 1.96 |
| n = 15 | | | $\Sigma x_D = 21$ $\bar{X}_D = 21/15 = 1.40$ $\Sigma x_D^2 = 51$ | | | $\Sigma(x_D - \bar{X}_D)^2 = 21.60$ $s_D = \sqrt{\dfrac{21.60}{15-1}} = 1.24$ |

**Step 1:** Our null hypothesis is that the number of delinquent siblings is not different between the two matched groups. In other words, we are assuming that the population mean for the difference between the pair of scores is zero. Based on our knowledge of the delinquency literature, we will make the directional (one-tailed) alternative hypothesis that the delinquent group will have more siblings who have violated the law than the nondelinquent group. Our prediction, therefore, is that if the number of law-violating siblings for the nondelinquent group is the first score and the number of law-violating siblings for the delinquent group is the second score, then the difference scores $(x_2 - x_1)$ will generally be positive and the population mean for the differences will be greater than zero. Both hypotheses are formally stated as follows:

$H_0: \mu_D = 0$

$H_1: \mu_D > 0$

**Step 2:** Our test statistic will be the dependent-samples $t$ test, and the sampling distribution will be the $t$ distribution.

**Step 3:** For our hypothesis test, we will choose an alpha level of .05. Since our alternative hypothesis stated that the true population mean was greater than zero, our critical region will lie in the right tail of the sampling distribution. With $n - 1$ or 14 degrees of freedom, $\alpha = .05$, and a one-tailed test, we can find in the $t$ table (Table B.3) that $t_{crit} = 1.761$. The critical region consists of all obtained $t$ scores that are greater than or equal to 1.761. We will therefore fail to reject the null hypothesis if $t_{obt} < 1.761$. We show the critical $t$ value and critical region in Figure 10.11.

Step 4: The second and third columns of Table 10.6 show the calculations necessary to determine both the mean and the standard deviation of the difference scores. We use the definitional formula for the standard deviation of the difference scores, but you would have obtained the same value with the computational formula! The value of $t_{obt}$ is calculated as follows:

$$t_{obt} = \frac{\bar{X}_D}{\sqrt{\dfrac{\Sigma(D - \bar{X}_D)^2}{n-1}} / \sqrt{n}}$$

$$t_{obt} = \frac{1.40}{\sqrt{\dfrac{21.60}{14}} / \sqrt{15}}$$

$$t_{obt} = \frac{1.40}{\sqrt{1.54} / \sqrt{15}}$$

$$t_{obt} = \frac{1.40}{1.24 / 3.87}$$

$$t_{obt} = \frac{1.40}{.32}$$

$$t_{obt} = 4.375$$

**Step 5:** The obtained value of our test statistic is 4.375. Because $t_{obt} > t_{crit}$, we can reject the null hypothesis that the mean population difference is zero. We conclude that there is a significant relationship between delinquency and the number of delinquent siblings a youth has. In the population, we can assume delinquents have significantly more siblings who have violated the law than nondelinquents.

In this and the previous two sections of this chapter, we have examined several different types of statistical tests to test a hypothesis about two population means. This must present a somewhat bewildering picture, and we admit that it might seem a bit overwhelming right now. In selecting the appropriate test statistic for the two-sample mean problem, however, a good deal of confusion can be eliminated if you remember that you only need to answer a few fundamental questions

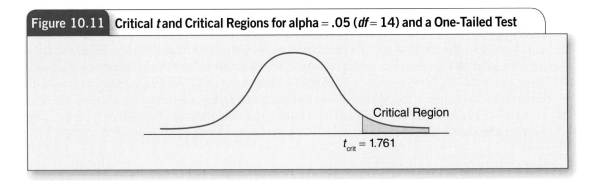

**Figure 10.11** Critical *t* and Critical Regions for alpha = .05 (*df* = 14) and a One-Tailed Test

Critical Region

$t_{crit} = 1.761$

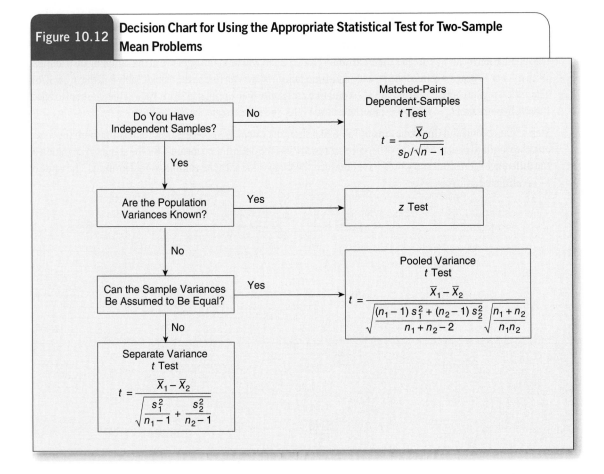

**Figure 10.12** Decision Chart for Using the Appropriate Statistical Test for Two-Sample Mean Problems

Do You Have Independent Samples? — No →

Matched-Pairs Dependent-Samples *t* Test

$$t = \frac{\bar{X}_D}{s_D/\sqrt{n-1}}$$

Yes ↓

Are the Population Variances Known? — Yes →

*z* Test

No ↓

Can the Sample Variances Be Assumed to Be Equal? — Yes →

Pooled Variance *t* Test

$$t = \frac{\bar{X}_1 - \bar{X}_2}{\sqrt{\frac{(n_1-1)\,s_1^2 + (n_2-1)\,s_2^2}{n_1 + n_2 - 2}}\sqrt{\frac{n_1 + n_2}{n_1 n_2}}}$$

No ↓

Separate Variance *t* Test

$$t = \frac{\bar{X}_1 - \bar{X}_2}{\sqrt{\frac{s_1^2}{n_1-1} + \frac{s_2^2}{n_2-1}}}$$

before deciding which test is appropriate for your problem. Figure 10.12 summarizes these decisions. Think of this figure as a road map in deciding which statistical test you should use for two-sample mean problems. In the next section, we will examine hypothesis tests about the difference between two sample proportions.

# ▣ Hypothesis Tests for the Difference Between Two Proportions: Large Samples

In this section, we will examine a statistical test for the significance of the difference between two population *proportions* ($P_1$ and $P_2$). Think of the difference of proportions test as a special case of the difference of means test. There are many cases in our discipline where this test is applicable.

Let's say we have a random sample of 100 persons and we asked each of them whether they favor the death penalty for those who commit first-degree murder. We arbitrarily assign a score of "0" for those who say no and "1" for those who say yes. Let's assume that 89 of the 100 said they approved of the death penalty under that circumstance and 11 said they did not. Since there are only two values (0 = no and 1 = yes), we can treat this variable as being measured at the interval level. We can determine the mean of this variable by counting the number of "1" scores (or "0" scores) and dividing by *n*. Since we have 89 "1" scores, the mean would be 89 / 100, or .89. The mean for a binary variable (a variable with only two values coded as "0" and "1"), then, is the proportion of "1" scores—in this case, the proportion of our sample that was in favor of the death penalty. The mean, therefore, is actually the proportion of "1" scores. Even though the population is dichotomous (it is made up of zeros and ones), we know from the central limit theorem that with a large enough sample, the distribution of sample means and the difference between two sample means will be approximately normal. Hence, we can use a *z* test and the *z* distribution to test hypotheses about the difference between two proportions.

In this chapter, we will consider only tests appropriate for data obtained from large independent samples. If $n\hat{p} \geq 5$ *and* $n\hat{q} \geq 5$ for each of the two samples (where $\hat{p}$ is the sample proportion and $\hat{q} = 1 - \hat{p}$), the sampling distribution of the difference between proportions will be approximately normal, and we can use a *z* test as our test statistic.

In calculating the test statistic for the *t* test for two sample means, we subtracted one sample mean from the other and divided by the standard error of the difference between means. We will conduct the same procedure in our test for the difference between two proportions. In our *z* test for two proportions, we will subtract the two sample proportions ($\hat{P}_1 - \hat{P}_2$) and divide by the standard deviation of the sampling distribution of the difference between proportions ($\sigma_{p1-p2}$). This standard deviation is also referred to as the standard error of the difference between proportions. The *z* test for the difference between proportions is:

$$z_{obt} = \frac{\hat{P}_1 - \hat{P}_2}{\sigma_{P_1 - P_2}} \tag{10–8}$$

where

$\hat{P}_1$ = the sample proportion for the first sample

$\hat{P}_2$ = the sample proportion for the second sample

$\sigma_{P_1-P_2}$ = the standard error of the difference between proportions.

The two sample proportions ($\hat{p}_1$ and $\hat{p}_2$) are both known, and the only remaining unknown is the denominator, the standard error of the difference between two proportions. Since the null hypothesis states that there is no difference between the two population proportions, we can assume that $P_1 = P_2$. We have already seen in Chapter 8 that the standard deviation of a population proportion ($\sigma_p$) is equal to $\sqrt{PQ/n}$ (where $Q$ is $= 1 - P$). If, by the null hypothesis,

$P_1 = P_2$, then it will be true that $\sigma_1 = \sigma_2$ because $\sqrt{P_1 Q_1} = \sqrt{P_2 Q_2}$. In the difference of proportions test, then, we can assume that the population standard deviations are equal, and we can simplify our hypothesis test by using a pooled variance estimate for the standard error of the difference between proportions. The formula for the pooled standard error is:

$$\sigma_{p_1 - p_2} = \sigma \sqrt{\frac{n_1 + n_2}{n_1 n_2}}$$

where

$$\sigma = \sqrt{PQ}$$

However, because the population proportion ($P$) is unknown, we need to estimate the pooled standard deviation ($\sigma = \sqrt{PQ}$) by calculating a pooled estimate of P ($\hat{p}$). The formula for our pooled estimate of the population proportion $P$ is:

$$\hat{p} = \frac{n_1 \hat{p}_1 + n_2 \hat{p}_2}{n_1 + n_2} \tag{10–9}$$

where

$\hat{p}$ = the estimate of the pooled population proportion

$\hat{p}_1$ = the sample proportion for the first sample

$\hat{p}_2$ = the sample proportion for the second sample

Notice that this $p$ does not have a subscript. That is because it is our estimate of $P$ we obtain from pooling our sample estimates, $\hat{p}_1$ and $\hat{p}_2$. Once we have found $\hat{p}$, we can determine $\hat{q}$ by subtraction, since $\hat{q} = 1 - \hat{p}$. Our estimate of the standard error of the difference between two proportions can then be calculated from the formula:

$$\sigma_{p_1 - p_2} = \sqrt{\hat{p}\hat{q}} \sqrt{\frac{n_1 + n_2}{n_1 n_2}} \tag{10–10}$$

Our obtained value of $z$ can now be estimated using the following formula:

$$z_{\text{obt}} = \frac{\hat{p}_1 - \hat{p}_2}{\sqrt{\hat{p}\hat{q}} \sqrt{\frac{n_1 + n_2}{n_1 n_2}}} \tag{10–11}$$

Again, notice that the terms $p$ in the numerator have a subscript because they come from our two samples, whereas the $p$ term in the denominator does not have a subscript because it is our pooled estimate of our sample proportion $P$. Just as with all of the preceding hypothesis tests, once we have obtained the test statistic, we compare our $z_{\text{obt}}$ with $z_{\text{crit}}$ and make a decision about the null hypothesis. Let's go through an example.

# Case Study

## Education and Recidivism

One of the primary questions in the correctional literature is to determine what programs within the correctional setting decrease inmates' rates of recidivism once they are released. Recently, Ryang Kim and David Clark (2013) examined recidivism rates between inmates who participated in prison-based college programs and those who did not. Not surprisingly to some, they found that the proportion of inmates who had participated in the college program were lower than the recidivism rate for those who did not participate.

Let's say we have independent random samples of 120 inmates from a correctional institution; 60 inmates in this group have received either their associate or their baccalaureate degree while in prison, and the remaining 60 inmates have received no educational curriculum whatsoever. Of the 60 who had received an education, 18% ($\hat{p}_1 = .18$) were rearrested within one year of their release from prison. Of the 60 who had not received any education, 38% ($\hat{p}_2 = .38$) were rearrested within the same time period. We wonder whether there is a significant difference between the percentage of released inmates who were rearrested (our measure of recidivism) for those who received an education in prison compared with those who did not. To answer this question, we need to conduct an explicit hypothesis test.

**Step 1:** Our null hypothesis is that the two samples came from populations with the same proportion of inmates who were rearrested after release. In other words, receiving an education while in prison had no effect on the likelihood of recidivating in the year after release. To be on the safe side, we test a nondirectional (two-tailed) alternative hypothesis that the two proportions are simply different from each other. These hypotheses are stated as follows:

$H_0: P_1 = P_2$

$H_1: P_1 \neq P_2$

**Step 2:** To test these hypotheses, we select as our test statistic the $z$ test for a difference of proportions. Since we have a large sample size, the $z$ distribution will be our sampling distribution.

**Step 3:** We will select an alpha level of .01. For a two-tailed test, the critical level of $z$ at $\alpha = .01$ is $z_{crit} = \pm 2.58$ (see Table B.2 in Appendix B or Table 8.1 in Chapter 8 for the critical values of $z$ for common levels of alpha). Since this is a two-tailed test, the critical region lies in both tails of the $z$ distribution and consists of all obtained $z$ scores less than or equal to $-2.58$ or greater than or equal to 2.58. We will reject the null hypothesis if $z_{obt}$ is less than or equal to $-2.58$ or greater than or equal to $+2.58$. Figure 10.13 shows the two critical regions and the critical $z$ values.

**Step 4:** To make the calculations more manageable, we will find our obtained value of $z$ in a series of steps.

*Step 4.1:* We find the estimated value of the pooled population proportions:

$$\hat{p} = \frac{(60)(.18) + (60)(.38)}{60 + 60}$$

$$\hat{p} = \frac{10.8 + 22.8}{120}$$

$$\hat{p} = \frac{33.6}{120}$$

$$\hat{p} = .28$$

*Step 4.2:* We find the standard error estimate of the difference between population proportions:

$$\sigma_{p_1-p_2} = \sqrt{\hat{p}\hat{q}}\sqrt{\frac{n_1+n_2}{n_1 n_2}}$$

$$\sigma_{p_1-p_2} = \sqrt{(.28).72}\sqrt{\frac{60+60}{60(60)}}$$

$$\sigma_{p_1-p_2} = \sqrt{.20}\sqrt{\frac{120}{3,600}}$$

$$\sigma_{p_1-p_2} = (.45)\sqrt{.033}$$

$$\sigma_{p_1-p_2} = (.45)(.18)$$

$$\sigma_{p_1-p_2} = .081$$

*Step 4.3:* Finally, plugging our sample proportions into the numerator and this standard error estimate into the denominator of formula 10–11, we calculate the value of our obtained *z* test:

$$z_{obt} = \frac{\hat{p}_1 - \hat{p}_2}{\sqrt{\hat{p}\hat{q}}\sqrt{\frac{n_1+n_2}{n_1 n_2}}}$$

$$z_{obt} = \frac{.18-.38}{.081}$$

$$z_{obt} = \frac{-.2}{.081}$$

$$z_{obt} = -2.47$$

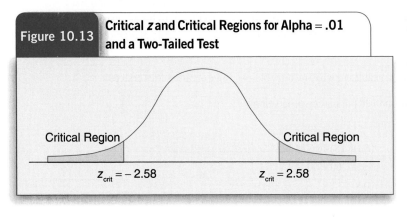

**Figure 10.13** **Critical *z* and Critical Regions for Alpha = .01 and a Two-Tailed Test**

Critical Region

Critical Region

$z_{crit} = -2.58$

$z_{crit} = 2.58$

**Step 5:** Our obtained *z* statistic is −2.47. This value of $z_{obt}$ just misses falling into our rejection region. Since it does not lie within the critical region, we must fail to reject the null hypothesis. We cannot conclude, based on our sample data, that in the population the proportion of inmates who recidivate is significantly different between those inmates who receive education in prison and those who do not. To test yourself, conduct the same null hypothesis using an alpha of .05 (α = .05). What do you conclude?

# ▣ Summary

In this chapter, we have examined techniques used to perform hypothesis tests to determine the difference between two means and two proportions. With unknown population variances, the statistical test for the difference between two means is conducted with a *t* test. If the test involves two independent random samples, we can choose from two different kinds of *t* tests. The first type is called a pooled variance *t* test. This test for two-sample means is appropriate when we can assume that the population standard deviations are equal. When we cannot maintain that assumption, the correct *t* test to use is the separate variance *t* test.

In addition to these tests for independent samples, we also examined a *t* test for matched groups or dependent samples. In this kind of *t* test, we are less interested in the difference between two means as in testing whether the difference between two sets of scores is equal to zero.

Finally, we learned how to test for the significance of the difference between two proportions and discovered that it was a special instance of the two-sample mean test.

## Key Terms

> ➤ Review key terms with eFlashcards. **⑤SAGE** edge™

independent random samples   279
matched or dependent samples   294

sampling distribution of sample
   mean differences   277

## Key Formulas

Pooled variance *t* test (equation 10–3):

$$t_{obt} = \frac{\bar{X}_1 - \bar{X}_2}{\sqrt{\dfrac{(n_1 - 1)s_1^2 + (n_2 - 1)s_2^2}{n_1 + n_2 - 2}}\sqrt{\dfrac{n_1 + n_2}{n_1 n_2}}}$$

Separate variance *t* test (equation 10–4):

$$t_{obt} = \frac{\bar{X}_1 - \bar{X}_2}{\sqrt{\dfrac{s_1^2}{n_1 - 1} + \dfrac{s_2^2}{n_2 - 1}}}$$

Degrees of freedom for separate variance *t* test (equation 10–5):

$$df = \left[ \frac{\left( \dfrac{s_1^2}{n_1 - 1} + \dfrac{s_2^2}{n_2 - 1} \right)^2}{\left( \dfrac{s_1^2}{n_1 - 1} \right)^2 \left( \dfrac{1}{n_1 + 1} \right) + \left( \dfrac{s_2^2}{n_2 - 1} \right)^2 \left( \dfrac{1}{n_2 + 1} \right)} \right] - 2$$

Dependent-samples *t* test (equation 10–7):

$$t_{obt} = \frac{\bar{X}_D}{s_D / \sqrt{n}}$$

Difference between proportions $z$ test (equation 10–11):

$$z_{obt} = \frac{\hat{p}_1 - \hat{p}_2}{\sqrt{\hat{p}\hat{q}}\sqrt{\frac{n_1 + n_2}{n_1 n_2}}}$$

## Practice Problems

➤ Test your understanding of chapter content.
Take the practice quiz. **⑤SAGE** edge™

1. Explain the difference between independent and dependent variables. If you think that low self-control affects crime, which is the independent and which is the dependent variable?

2. When is it appropriate to use an independent-samples $t$ test, and when is it appropriate to use a $t$ test for dependent samples or matched groups?

3. John Worrall and colleagues (2014) found that the fear of losing the good opinion of one's family and peers kept people from driving home drunk. Let's say we have two independent random samples of people: those who think that their peers would disapprove of them for driving drunk, and those who think that their peers would either not care or approve of their driving drunk. We ask each person in each group to self-report the number of times that he or she has driven drunk in the past 12 months. Here are the results:

| Would Not Approve of Driving Drunk | Would Approve of Driving Drunk |
| --- | --- |
| $n_1 = 40$ | $n_2 = 25$ |
| $\bar{x}_1 = 2.1$ | $\bar{x}_2 = 8.2$ |
| $s_1 = 1.8$ | $s_2 = 1.9$ |

Test the null hypothesis that the two population means are equal against the alternative hypothesis that the group whose peers would not approve of driving drunk has a lower mean rate of driving drunk. In your hypothesis test, assume that the unknown population standard deviations are equal, and use an alpha level of .01.

4. The use of monetary fines as a criminal sanction is being considered as one possible solution to the problem of prison overcrowding. Supporters of the use of fines contend that it would be both an effective deterrent to crime and a way to punish even moderately severe crimes without imprisonment. Critics argue that giving criminal offenders fines only increases their motivation to commit more crimes in order to pay their fine. You want to test the effect of fines versus incarceration on criminal behavior. You take a random sample of 150 convicted offenders who have been given a fine as punishment and follow them up for three years. You take a second independent random sample of 110 offenders recently released from prison and follow them up for three years. At the end of the three-year follow-up period, you find that 33% of those given a fine had been rearrested and 38% of those given a prison sentence had been rearrested. Test the null hypothesis that the proportions rearrested in the two groups are equal against the alternative hypothesis that they are different. Use an alpha level of .05.

5. Jason Ingram and William Terrill (2014) have conducted some research on the perceptions that female and male police officers have of their roles, the public, and their departments. They concluded that female and male police officers do not view their jobs very differently. Let's say that we wanted to continue their work and were interested in how female and male police officers view one component of police work: the handling of domestic disputes. To do this research, we have created a scale that measures how important settling domestic disputes is and whether it is perceived as part of "police work." Those who score high on this scale think that the fair settling of domestic disturbances is of high priority and that it should be an important part of a police officer's duties. We have then taken two random samples. One is a sample of 50 male police officers, and a second is an independent random sample of 25 female police officers. We give each officer a questionnaire that includes our domestic dispute scale. The mean score for female officers is 21.3 (with a standard deviation of 3.0). The mean score for male officers is 18.8 (with a standard deviation of 4.5). Test the null hypothesis that the two population means are equal against the alternative hypothesis that the male mean is lower than the female mean. In your hypothesis test, *do not* presume that the population standard deviations are equal, and use an alpha level of .05.

6. Capital punishment law is among the most complex bodies of law in our legal system. As a result, judges make frequent errors in capital cases in terms of their rulings regarding a change of venue, the decision to sequester jurors, questions of *voir dire*, suppression of evidence, and so on. When these errors are made, cases are often won on appeal and have to be retried or have a second penalty phase hearing. The Trial Judges Association thinks that only judges who have received special training should sit on capital cases because these judges would commit fewer errors and there would be fewer cases lost on appeal. You decide to test this hypothesis. You take a random sample of 15 judges who have received extensive training in capital punishment law. You match these judges with 15 other judges who have not received such training but are matched in terms of their number of years on the bench, experience as trial lawyers, gender, and age. You want the two groups of judges to be alike in every way except the experience of capital punishment law training. The data on your matched groups of judges are as follows:

**Number of Cases Lost on Appeal**

| Judge | Untrained | Trained |
|:-----:|:---------:|:-------:|
| 1 | 3 | 0 |
| 2 | 1 | 3 |
| 3 | 2 | 4 |
| 4 | 7 | 4 |
| 5 | 5 | 2 |
| 6 | 4 | 5 |
| 7 | 6 | 1 |
| 8 | 2 | 1 |
| 9 | 7 | 0 |
| 10 | 5 | 6 |
| 11 | 3 | 4 |
| 12 | 4 | 2 |
| 13 | 5 | 5 |
| 14 | 6 | 3 |
| 15 | 2 | 1 |

Test the null hypothesis that the mean difference in the number of cases lost on appeal for the two groups of judges is zero against the alternative hypothesis that the untrained judges lose more cases on appeal. Use an alpha level of .01.

7. In a recent book, Adrian Raine (1994) discusses some research in biological criminology that suggests that children with criminal parents are more likely to be criminals themselves than are children with noncriminal parents. Suppose you conduct a study on a random sample of 100 delinquent youths confined in a correctional institution and a random sample of 75 nondelinquent youths. You find that 43% of the delinquent youths have at least one criminal parent but that only 17% of the nondelinquent youths have a criminal parent. Test the null hypothesis that the two population proportions are equal against the alternative hypothesis that the delinquent group has a greater proportion of criminal parents. Use an alpha level of .01.

8. It is common wisdom to believe that dropping out of high school leads to delinquency. For example, Travis Hirschi's (1969) control theory might predict that those with little or no commitment to education are delinquent more often than those with strong educational commitments. In his general strain theory, however, Robert Agnew (1992) might predict that dropping out of school would lower one's involvement in delinquency because it would get youths out of an aversive and painful environment. You want to examine the relationship between dropping out of high school and delinquency. You have a random sample of 11 students. You have the number of delinquent offenses that each student reported committing in the year before dropping out of school and the number of offenses that each reported in the year after dropping out of school. Here are those data:

**Number of Delinquent Acts**

| Person | Before | After |
|:------:|:------:|:-----:|
| 1 | 5 | 7 |
| 2 | 9 | 5 |
| 3 | 2 | 3 |
| 4 | 7 | 7 |
| 5 | 8 | 11 |
| 6 | 11 | 13 |
| 7 | 8 | 4 |
| 8 | 8 | 10 |
| 9 | 5 | 7 |
| 10 | 2 | 1 |
| 11 | 9 | 3 |

Test the null hypothesis that the mean difference between the two sets of scores is zero against the alternative hypothesis that it is different from zero. Use an alpha level of .05.

## SPSS Exercises

➤ Explore additional data sets. **⑤SAGE edge™**

| Data for Exercise | |
|---|---|
| *Data Set* | *Description* |
| Youth.sav | These data are from a random sample of students from schools in a southern state. Although not representative of the United States, it covers a variety of important delinquent behaviors and peer influences. |

| Variables for Exercise | |
|---|---|
| *Variable Name* | *Description* |
| D1 | A binary variable based on the number of delinquent acts a respondent reported. A 0 indicates that the respondent reported 1 or fewer acts, whereas 1 indicates 2 or more. |
| Lowcertain_bin | Binary indicator of whether respondents felt there was certainty that they'd be punished for delinquent behaviors. 1 = low certainty, 0 = high certainty. |
| Gender | The gender of the respondent, where 1 = male and 0 = female. |
| V2 | Age of the respondent, in years. |
| Moral | A scale that measures if respondents thought delinquency was morally wrong. High values indicate that delinquency is viewed as more wrong. |
| Delinquency | A scale indicating the number of delinquent acts that an individual reports participating in. |
| Studyhard | Binary indicator of studying behavior of respondents, where 0 = studies 8 or fewer hours a week and 1 = studies 8 or more hours a week. |

1. Are delinquent teens more likely to be older than teens that don't report delinquency? One way to look at this question is with a *t* test. In this case, we'll compare the mean age for delinquent students with the mean age of non-delinquent students:

   a. State research and null hypotheses for this topic.

   b. What type of test should you use: an independent samples *t* test or a matched-group test?

   c. For this analysis, use an alpha of .001 for your significance level.

   d. **Conducting an independent samples *t* test in SPSS:** To run a *t* test in SPSS, select analyze->compare means-> independent-samples t-test. Put the variable V2 (age) in the "test variable" box. Click "define groups" and enter 0 in one box and 1 in the other. Then, put our grouping variable, D1, in the "grouping variable" box. Select Ok:

      i. The output for this needs some explanation. The first box that comes out tells you the number of cases in each group (*n*) and the means and standard deviations for each group. The second box has two rows that correspond to *t* tests

   conducted with equal or unequal variances assumed. Levene's test for equality of variances is an *F* test comparing group variances that will be addressed in a later question. You are interested in the columns labeled "T" and "sig. 2-tailed"; these are your test statistic and its exact *P* value. Also of interest is the "mean difference" box, which contains the value for the mean of group 1 minus the mean of group 2.

   e. Assume that a difference of .15 in standard deviations is evidence that you have unequal variances. After looking at the standard deviations for either group, do you conclude that these groups have equal or unequal variances?

   f. By using the appropriate variance assumptions, what do you conclude about the null hypothesis?

   g. Write a sentence explaining what this result tells us about delinquency in substantive terms.

2. Are students who spend lots of time studying likely to also view delinquency as wrong? Some theorists would suggest this should be the case as high adherence to social roles (student, good kid) means that the penalties for delinquency will have a higher social cost. Let's investigate with a *t* test:

a. State research and null hypotheses for this topic.

b. What type of test should you use: an independent samples *t* test or a matched-group test?

c. For this analysis, use alphas of both of .05 and .001 for your significance level.

d. Conduct the independent samples *t* test in SPSS (described earlier). In this case, use the variables "moral" as the dependent variable and "studyhard" as the independent variable.

e. **Levene's test for equality of variances:** The easiest way to determine whether we should assume equal variances in our *t* test is to use an *F* test comparing the variances of both groups. The two columns for Levene's Test for Equality of Variances do just that. The output shows an *F* test and its associated *p* value. The null hypothesis in this case is that variances are equal, whereas the research hypothesis is that they are unequal. In other words, a significant test means we should use the "equal variances no assumed" test row:

   i. What is your decision about the null hypothesis in Levene's test? What assumptions should you use for your *t* test?

f. What is your conclusion regarding the null and research hypotheses?

g. Substantively, do these results support the theory described earlier, or do they contradict it? Use your data to explain why.

3. Do boys commit more delinquent acts, on average, than girls? Perform an independent samples *t* test with the variables Gender and Delinquency to test this question. Use questions 1 and 2 to guide you through this process; be sure to check your *F* test in determining the appropriate test to use. After the test, provide a criminological or sociological explanation for why you found what you did.

4. Just before being hauled off to jail, TV show villains often say, "I would have gotten away with it if it wasn't for you meddling kids!" The underlying statement is that they committed the crime because they thought they could get away with it. We could ask, then, are individuals who think they won't get punished more likely to commit delinquent acts? Conduct an independent hypothesis test between the variables lowcertain_bin and delinquency. Be sure to go through all steps of the hypothesis testing process. After the analysis, write a few sentences about the practical implications of this result.

5. "But I didn't know it was wrong!" is a common statement made by children when they have been caught doing something bad. Perhaps the belief that their behaviors just aren't so wrong might lead to more delinquency? To research this, conduct a *t* test of the variables moral and delinquency. You may notice that the variable "moral" is not binary; when defining groups in the *t* test menu, use the value 16 as a cut point. This will compare individuals with scores that are greater than or equal to 16 against those that score less than 16. What do you conclude about the null hypothesis? What is the practical significance of this result?

# CHAPTER 11

# Hypothesis Tests Involving Three or More Population Means

## *Analysis of Variance*

" *The analysis of variance is not a mathematical theorem, but rather a convenient method of arranging the arithmetic.*

*To call in the statistician after the experiment is done may be no more than asking him to perform a post-mortem examination: he may be able to say what the experiment died of.* "

—Sir Ronald Fisher

---

**LEARNING OBJECTIVES**

1. Explain why multiple *t* tests are not appropriate when an independent variable has more than two categories.

2. Describe the importance of the variance in testing the difference between means.

3. Identify and interpret the total, between, and within group sum of squares and their relationship to testing the difference between means.

4. Conduct a hypothesis for the difference between three or more group means, and interpret the results.

5. Describe the purpose of John Tukey's Honest Significance Difference (HSD) test.

6. State the difference between measures of association and the analysis of variance (ANOVA) hypothesis test.

# Introduction

In Chapter 10, we were interested in the relationship between an independent variable that has only two values or levels and a continuous dependent variable. There will be many times, however, when our independent variable is a categorical variable that has more than two values. For example, suppose we were interested in finding out whether the sentence given to armed robbers (measured in months) varied by the race of the defendant. Suppose also that our independent variable (race of defendant) consisted of the following categories: White, Black, Hispanic, and Asian. Here we have a continuous dependent variable, and our independent variable has four values. In this chapter, we will examine cases like this where we have an independent variable with three or more levels or categories and a continuous (interval/ratio) dependent variable. Just as in the last chapter, we are also interested in the difference between the means of different groups. In this chapter, however, we have three or more groups, and for reasons we will explain, applying the *t* test to more than two groups is not appropriate. In this chapter you will learn about a technique called analysis of variance, or ANOVA for short, which relies on the *F* probability distribution. In addition, because we have more than two means, the results of a null hypothesis that three or more population means are equal can only tell us that at least one pair of the means may be different from each other, but it does not tell us which pair or pairs. You will also learn how to conduct a test called John Tukey's Honest Significant Difference (HSD) test to determine which of your group means are significantly different from each other. What neither the *F test* nor Tukey's HSD test can do, however, is tell us about the *strength* of the relationship between our independent and dependent variable. Therefore, we will conclude our discussion by learning how to calculate something called eta squared ($\eta^2$), which measures the strength of the relationship between an independent and a dependent variable in an analysis of variance.

# The Logic of Analysis of Variance

## The Problem With Using a *t* Test With Three or More Means

To illustrate the problem with using the *t* test we learned in the last chapter when we have more than two means, let's go back to our scenario of examining the difference between the sentence received for armed robbery for a sample of White, Black, Hispanic, and Asian defendants. With the tools we now have in our tool box, we might be tempted just to do a series of pairwise *t* tests. That is, we could use our *t test* for independent samples and conduct the hypothesis test at some level of significance (say, $\alpha = .05$)

that each pair of population means is equal, against the alternative hypothesis that each pair is not equal. Note that if we did this, we would have a lot of pairwise *t tests* to perform. With four groups, we would have to do six different *t tests*:

$$\mu_{\text{white}} - \mu_{\text{black}}; \mu_{\text{white}} - \mu_{\text{Hispanic}}; \mu_{\text{white}} - \mu_{\text{Asian}}; \mu_{\text{black}} - \mu_{\text{Hispanic}}; \mu_{\text{black}} - \mu_{\text{Asian}}; \mu_{\text{Hispanic}} - \mu_{\text{Asian}}$$

We would therefore have a lot of work to do. That's not the real problem with this strategy, however. The main problem in doing a series of *t tests* with the same data is that the significance level of our hypothesis test assumes that the sample means are independent. When we use the same sample means for multiple significance tests (note that the White group mean in the preceding example is used in three separate hypothesis tests), this assumption of independence is violated. The problem with doing these multiple *t tests* with our one set of data, therefore, is that our alpha level increases with each hypothesis test. That is, although our first *t test* hypothesis test is done with an alpha level of .05, the next hypothesis test using one of same samples has an alpha higher than .05 because the assumption of independence is violated. What this means is that for our six separate hypothesis tests, the probability of making a Type I error in rejecting a true null hypothesis is not .05 but greater than that, sometimes much greater. In conducting multiple means tests with the same data, therefore, we do not have a consistently true alpha level.

**Analysis of variance (ANOVA):**
Statistical model used to test the differences between three or more group means.

Because of this, we need a tool where we can compare multiple population means and maintain a consistently true alpha level. This tool, which we will learn in this chapter, is called the **analysis of variance**, or **ANOVA** for short. The analysis of variance test is to be used when we are interested in conducting a hypothesis test where we have a continuous (interval/ratio) dependent variable and an independent variable that is categorical (nominal or ordinal) with three or more values.

Let's assume we have three population means whose equality we are testing ($\mu_1 = \mu_2 = \mu_3$). Our hypothesis test is called the analysis of variance because in testing this hypothesis, we are not going to examine the means directly; rather, we are going to examine the variances. That is why the test is called an analysis of *variance*. Now, it may seem very odd to do a hypothesis test about population means by examining variances, so allow us to explain with an example.

## Case Study

### Police Responses to Intimate Partner Assault

The example we are going to use to illustrate ANOVA examines the differential effect of three different kinds of police response to an intimate partner assault call: (1) simply separate the couple and do nothing else, (2) separate the couple and require counseling for the offender, or (3) arrest the offender. The outcome we are interested in is the number of times in the following year that the police are called back to the address on another domestic violence call involving the same offender. Our nominal-level independent variable is the police response to domestic violence, and there are three values or categories: separate, counsel, and arrest. Our interval- and ratio-level dependent variable is the number of return calls to the address against the same offender. Let's assume that we have a sample of 100 persons in each group, for a total sample size of 300, and that after a year we calculate the mean number of return visits to the house for each group.

Figure 11.1(a) shows a hypothetical distribution of the number of times the police have to return to the house for each of the three groups. Note that the three group means are very different. The mean number of return visits is highest for the separate-only group, next highest for the counsel group, and lowest for the arrest group. Note also that although the three group means are very different from each other, the scores within each group are not that different from their own unique group mean. In other words, each score within each group clusters fairly tightly around its

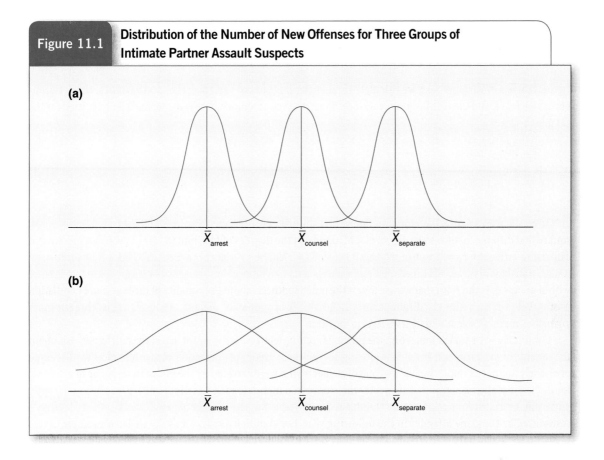

**Figure 11.1** Distribution of the Number of New Offenses for Three Groups of Intimate Partner Assault Suspects

(a)

$\bar{X}_{arrest}$   $\bar{X}_{counsel}$   $\bar{X}_{separate}$

(b)

$\bar{X}_{arrest}$   $\bar{X}_{counsel}$   $\bar{X}_{separate}$

group mean. In sum, scores do not vary that much within groups, but the mean scores vary a great deal across the three groups. Based on this figure and our "eye-ball test," we would be tempted to conclude that how the police respond to a domestic violence call does indeed make a difference in terms of the effect on the suspect, that is, that there is a "treatment effect." Suspects who have been arrested seem least likely to repeat their offense in the subsequent year compared with those counseled and those separated, and the counseled group of suspects seems to do better than those who are simply told to leave the scene. In fact, the latter group has the highest number of new offenses. In other words, it looks as if $\bar{X}_{arrest} \neq \bar{X}_{counsel} \neq \bar{X}_{separate}$. If we think in terms of population means rather than sample means, it looks as if $\mu_{arrest} \neq \mu_{counsel} \neq \mu_{separate}$.

Figure 11.1(b) shows a different set of hypothetical distributions for the same data. In this hypothetical case, even though the three group means are the same as in Figure 11.1(a), there is much greater variability within each group. The scores within each group no longer cluster tightly about the group mean but are highly variable, overlapping sometimes with the scores from another group. It looks like there is more variability within a group than there is between groups. In this set of distributions, we are less tempted to conclude that there is a clear "treatment effect" due to the different police responses to domestic violence. Now it looks like $\bar{X}_{arrest} = \bar{X}_{counsel} = \bar{X}_{separate}$ or again with respect to the population that we want to generalize to $\mu_{arrest} = \mu_{counsel} = \mu_{separate}$. We came to this tentative conclusion by comparing the variability within each group with that across the three groups. This comparison of within-group to between-group or across-group variability is at the heart of the analysis of variance. All we have to do is change the word "variability" to "variance" and we can see that an analysis of variance is based on comparing the variance within groups with the variance between groups to draw a conclusion about the equality of group means.

# ▣ Types of Variance: Total, Between-Groups, and Within-Group

In the analysis of variance test, we calculate three different types of variance: the total variance, the between-groups variance, and the within-group variance. To refresh your memory, here is the formula we have used for the sample variance:

$$S^2 = \frac{\Sigma(x - \bar{X})^2}{n-1} \tag{11–1}$$

To calculate a variance, therefore, we simply take the difference between a score and the mean of those scores, square that difference, sum over all scores, and divide by the degrees of freedom ($n - 1$). As you can see, we can calculate a variance for any group of scores; all we need to calculate a variance is a mean. Technically, the statistical test in an analysis of variance is called the *F test*, which is actually a ratio of the variance between groups to the variance within groups. It is the *F test* that we use to test the null hypothesis about the equality of three or more population means. Let's first examine the different sorts of variability or sources of variance we have in this "three or more population mean" problem, and then we'll get to the *F* test.

Continuing with our example from the previous section, let's assume we want to test the null hypothesis about the equality of the mean number of new offenses for our three groups of domestic violence offenders we discussed previously. In that example, we had a group of suspects who were arrested by the police in response to a 911 call for domestic violence, a group of suspects who were given mandatory counseling, and a group who were only physically separated from their victim. Our dependent variable was the number of new domestic violence offenses committed by the same offender in the following year. For simplicity's sake, let's say we have a sample of five offenders in each of our three groups. The number of new offenses for each offender and the mean for each group are shown in Table 11.1.

You can see that the mean number of new offenses differs across the three groups. Those arrested have on average one new subsequent offense, those counseled committed on average five new offenses, and those merely separated had an average of nine new offenses in the year that followed. We cannot, of course, conclude on the basis of this sample data that the way the police respond affects the number of new offenses in the population. That is, we cannot automatically conclude from these different sample means that $\mu_{arrest} \neq \mu_{counseled} \neq \mu_{separated}$ because our observed sample means may differ from each other by chance alone. That is, sampling variation, instead of a real difference between the population means, may be accounting for the observed differences in our sample means. Our decision to rule out the possibility of sampling variation is going to be based on a formal hypothesis test using the analysis of variance.

For the data in Table 11.1, we can calculate a couple of different means. The first mean we will calculate is the mean number of new offenses for each group separately—that is, a mean number of new offenses for each of the arrested, counseled, and separated treatment groups. We have already done this in Table 11.1, and the three means are reported at the bottom of each

| Table 11.1 | Number of New Offenses for Suspects Arrested, Counseled, or Separated by Police in Response to a 911 Call for Intimate Partner Assault |
|---|---|

| Arrested | Counseled | Separated |
|---|---|---|
| 0 | 6 | 8 |
| 2 | 4 | 10 |
| 1 | 4 | 9 |
| 1 | 6 | 10 |
| 1 | 5 | 8 |
| $\bar{X}_{arrest} = 1.0$ | $\bar{X}_{counsel} = 5.0$ | $\bar{X}_{separate} = 9.0$ |

group. Let's call these three means the within-group means. Now let's calculate another mean by ignoring the fact that someone belongs in a particular group. We will add together all 15 scores, ignoring group membership, and divide by 15. Let's call this mean the "grand mean" because it is the overall mean for all the scores. The grand mean is calculated as:

$$\overline{X}_{grand} = \frac{0+2+1+1+1+6+\ldots+9+10+18}{15}$$

$$\overline{X}_{grand} = 5$$

Ignoring the group that someone falls in, then, the average number of new domestic offenses for these 15 offenders is 5. Let's calculate a third mean this time by summing the three group means and then dividing by three, and we'll call this the between-groups mean:

$$\overline{X}_{between} = \frac{1+5+9}{3}$$

$$\overline{X}_{between} = 5$$

The between-groups mean is the same as the grand mean whenever there are the same number of observations in each group, as is the case here.

So now we have three different means: (1) a unique mean for each of our three groups; (2) a mean for the entire set of scores, ignoring the group that the score came from; and (3) a mean for the three groups. With these means we are now going to calculate a couple of different measures of *variability,* where variability is defined as the difference between a given score and the mean of those scores. First, we are going to calculate a measure of **total variability**, which is the difference between an individual score ($x_i$) and the grand mean or the mean of all the scores $(x_i - \overline{X}_{grand})$. This total variability can be divided into two separate components. One component of the total variability is the difference between an individual score and the mean of the group to which an individual belongs $(x_i - \overline{X}_k)$, where $\overline{X}_k$ is the mean for the $k$th group (in our example here, $k = 3$). This is a measure of *within-group variability*. There is variation within a group not because the people within it received a different treatment by the police (because all persons within a group received the same treatment), but for other reasons, reasons we have not measured. In other words, within-group variability measures how different the scores are from the mean of the group.

The second component of the total variability is the difference between the group mean and the grand mean $(\overline{X}_k - \overline{X}_{grand})$. This is a measure of **between-groups variability**. There is variation between groups because offenders in different groups received a different "treatment" (police response). In other words, there is a group "treatment effect." For example, there are on average a different number of offenses committed between the groups because offenders in a case of domestic violence respond to being arrested differently than they do to being counseled or separated. Between-groups variability measures how different the group means are from the overall mean. By separating the two types of variability, we can determine which type contributes more to the total variability.

Let's illustrate this with our data. The total variability for the first case in the arrested group is equal to $(0 - 5) = -5$. This person has five fewer offenses than the overall average number of offenses (the grand mean, $\overline{X}_{grand}$). We will now break this variability down into two components. First is the within-group variability, which is the difference between the individual score and the group mean. Since the mean of the first group (the arrested group) is 1, this component is equal to $-1$ ($0 - 1 = -1$). Part of the total variability for person 1, then, is because the number of new offenses for this person is 1 less than the average for the group that person is in (the arrested group). The between-groups variability is the difference between the mean of the group to which the person belongs and the grand mean or $-4$ ($1 - 5 = -4$). Most of the total variability for this person is due to the fact that those in the arrested group have fewer new offenses than the overall average. To illustrate:

| Total Variability | | Within-Group Variability | | Between-Groups Variability |
|---|---|---|---|---|
| $(x_i - \bar{X}_{grand})$ | = | $(x_i - \bar{X}_k)$ | + | $(\bar{X}_k - \bar{X}_{grand})$ |
| $(0 - 5)$ | = | $(0 - 1)$ | + | $(1 - 5)$ |
| $-5$ | = | $-1$ | + | $-4$ |
| $-5$ | = | $-5$ | | |

Another way to describe this is (Individual score – Grand mean) = (Individual score – Group mean) + (Group mean – Grand mean).

Let's now do the same thing for the first case in the counseled group. We will divide the total amount of variability (the difference between the individual's score and the grand mean) into both within-group (the difference between the individual's score and the mean of the group they are in) and between-groups variability (the difference between the mean of the group they are in and the grand mean) sources:

| Total Variability | | Within-Group Variability | | Between-Groups Variability |
|---|---|---|---|---|
| $(x_i - \bar{X}_{grand})$ | = | $(x_i - \bar{X}_k)$ | + | $(\bar{X}_k - \bar{X}_{grand})$ |
| $(6 - 5)$ | = | $(6 - 5)$ | + | $(5 - 5)$ |
| $1$ | = | $1$ | + | $0$ |
| $1$ | = | $1$ | | |

In this case, all of the variability is due to within-group variability. Finally, let's take the first person in the separated group and decompose that person's total variability into its two components:

| Total Variability | | Within-Group Variability | | Between-Groups Variability |
|---|---|---|---|---|
| $(x_i - \bar{X}_{grand})$ | = | $(x_i - \bar{X}_k)$ | + | $(\bar{X}_k - \bar{X}_{grand})$ |
| $(8 - 5)$ | = | $(8 - 9)$ | + | $(9 - 5)$ |
| $3$ | = | $-1$ | + | $4$ |
| $3$ | = | $3$ | | |

The total variability for this person is a +3, and most of this is because this person's group (suspects separated by police) has a higher mean number of new offenses than the other two groups (i.e., it's due to variability between groups).

What the analysis of variance does, therefore, is calculate the overall or total variability for each observation and then partition it into the "within" and "between" components. You should be able to see that if the lion's share of this total variability for these domestic violence data is due to variability within groups and the variability between groups is relatively small (see Figure 11.1[b]), we are not so likely to conclude that the group means are different and, thus, not so likely to conclude that the population means are different from each other. If, however, most of the total variability is due to that between groups, and the variability within groups is relatively small (see Figure 11.1[a]), then we suspect that there really is a group "treatment effect" and that the population means really are different from each other. Although we have been talking about variability, the analysis of variance *F test* is really based on two types of *variance* that we will demonstrate next.

First, we are going to take each of our three sources of variability, total, within-group, and between-groups, and square them. These different components are called the *sum of squares*. For example, let's take the simple formula we used for total variability $(x_i - \overline{X}_{grand})$ and do two things to it: (1) Square the difference, and (2) require that we take this squared difference for every score or observation. If we do this, the squared difference between each score and the grand mean is given a special term; it is called the **total sum of squares**, or $SS_{total}$. This formula is:

> **Total sum of squares:** Measures the total variability in the sample for an ANOVA.

$$SS_{total} = \sum_i \sum_k (x_{ik} - \overline{X}_{grand})^2 \qquad \textbf{(11–2)}$$

where *i* refers to the individual *x* score and *k* refers to the group. This formula says that the total sum of squares is obtained by subtracting the grand mean from each score ignoring group membership, squaring that difference, and then summing over all scores (the summation signs $\sum_i \sum_k$ instruct us to start with the first *i* score in the first of *k* groups, and continue until we have done the last *i* score in the last of *k* groups). Note that this total sum of squares looks a lot like the numerator of an estimate of the variance that we see in equation 11-1; it's a squared difference of some score from the mean.

We are now going to take our within-group variability and with it derive an estimate of the squared difference of each score in a group from the mean of that group. This squared difference of each score from the mean of the group is called the **within-group sum of squares**, or ($SS_{within}$):

> **Within-group sum of squares:** Measures the variability within a group for an ANOVA.

$$SS_{within} = \sum_i \sum_k (x_{ik} - \overline{X}_k)^2 \qquad \textbf{(11–3)}$$

In words, this formula tells us to start with the first group ($k = 1$) and take the first person in this group ($i = 1$), subtract the group mean from this $x_i$ score, square this difference, repeat this for each person in the first group, and then sum the squared differences. Then, go to the first person in the second group ($k = 2$) and do the same thing for each person in this group. Continue until you have squared the difference between the score for the last person in the last group and that group mean. Note that this within-group sum of squares also looks a lot like the numerator of an estimate of the variance in equation 11-1. Like the total sum of squares, it too is a squared difference of the mean from some score.

Finally, we are going to take our measure of the variability between groups and derive an estimate of the squared difference of each group mean from the grand mean. This squared difference of each group mean from the grand mean is called the **between-groups sum of squares**, or ($SS_{between}$):

> **Between-groups sum of squares:** Measures the variability between groups for an ANOVA.

$$SS_{between} = \sum_i \sum_k (\overline{x}_k - \overline{X}_{grand})^2 \qquad \textbf{(11–4)}$$

In words, this formula tells us to take the first group mean and subtract the grand mean from that and square the difference, then do the same for each of the *i* persons in that group, and sum over the number of cases in that group.

Then do the same thing for each of the other $k$ groups and sum over groups. Note that this between-groups sum of squares also looks a lot like the numerator of an estimate of the variance in equation 11-1. Like the total and within-group sums of squares, the sum of squares between groups also is a squared difference of the mean from some score. The three sum of squares have this property:

$$SS_{total} = SS_{within} + SS_{between}$$

Accordingly, we only need to calculate two sources of the sum of squares, and the third can be found by subtraction (i.e., $SS_{total} - SS_{within} = SS_{between}$) or addition ($SS_{within} + SS_{between} = SS_{total}$).

We now have three sum of squares measures, total, within-group, and between-groups sum of squares. Each of these sum of squares is the numerator of an estimate of a source of variance, total variance, within-group variance, and between-group variance. Looking at equation 11-1, to complete our formulas for each of these three variances, we need to divide each sum of squares by its respective degrees of freedom. Just as there are three different sums of squares, there are three corresponding degrees of freedom:

**Total degrees of freedom** $= df_{total} = n - 1$

**Within-group degrees of freedom** $= df_{within} = n - k$

**Between-groups degrees of freedom** $= df_{between} = k - 1$

where

$n$ = total number of observations

$k$ = number of groups

As with the sum of squares:

$$df_{total} = df_{within} + df_{between}$$

So we have to calculate only two sources of degrees of freedom and then can obtain the third by subtraction or addition.

We now have three different variance estimates:

$$\textbf{Total variance} = \frac{SS_{total}}{df_{total}} = \frac{\sum_i \sum_k (x_{ik} - \overline{X}_{grand})^2}{n-1} \tag{11-5}$$

$$\textbf{Within - group variance} = \frac{SS_{within}}{df_{within}} = \frac{\sum_i \sum_k (x_{ik} - \overline{X}_k)^2}{n-k} \tag{11-6}$$

$$\textbf{Between - groups variance} = \frac{SS_{between}}{df_{between}} = \frac{\sum_i \sum_k (\overline{X}_k - \overline{X}_{grand})^2}{k-1} \tag{11-7}$$

The *F test* that is the test statistic for the analysis of variance is simply the ratio of the between-groups to the within-group variance:

$$F = \frac{SS_{\text{between}}/df_{\text{between}}}{SS_{\text{within}}/df_{\text{within}}} = \frac{\text{Variance Between Groups}}{\text{Variance Within Groups}} \qquad (11\text{–}8)$$

Note that this $F$ statistic will become larger as the variance between groups becomes larger relative to the variance within groups. This corresponds to Figure 11.1(a). Large values of the $F$ statistic, then, lead us to reject the null hypothesis of equal population means. What we do not yet know, however, is how large our obtained $F$ must be in order for us to reject the null hypothesis of equal population means. We do know that even if the three population means are the same, our sample means will be different due simply to sample variation or chance. By now, it should be no surprise that we need to conduct a formal hypothesis test to rule out chance.

Like any test statistic we have discussed (the $t$, $z$, or chi-square test, for example), to conduct our hypothesis test, we need to select a level of significance, or alpha level, and then find a critical value of our test statistic from the appropriate probability distribution. In this case, involving a hypothesis test of three or more population means, we know that our test statistic is the analysis of variance $F$ test. The $F$ statistic follows an $F$ *distribution*. Critical values of $F$ can be obtained from Table B.5 in Appendix B. There are two $F$ tables here: one table in which the alpha level is .05 and another for a .01 level of significance. To find the critical value of $F$ at some alpha level, we also need to know two types of degrees of freedom. The between-groups degrees of freedom are found at the top of each of the two tables, forming columns, and the within-group degrees of freedom are found down the left side of the tables, forming rows. To find the correct critical value of $F$, then, you need to know your alpha level, identify the column corresponding to your between-groups degrees of freedom, and finally identify the correct row corresponding to your within-group degrees of freedom. The value of $F$ found at the convergence of that column and that row is your critical $F$ for a given alpha level. Since the obtained $F$ statistic is based on a *sum of squares* (deviations from some mean, squared), we will have only positive values of $F$. The $F$ statistic can never be negative. Our decision, then, will always be to reject the null hypothesis when our obtained $F$ is greater than or equal to our critical $F$.

Since we have all the necessary tools to do an analysis of variance, we should now move on and actually test a hypothesis about equal population means. Let's use data in Table 11.1, which reported the number of new offenses for three groups of offenders who were given different treatments by the police responding to a 911 call for intimate partner assault.

## 🔲 Conducting a Hypothesis Test With ANOVA

In an analysis of variance, the hypothesis test involves the equality of three or more population means. In our example, we want to know whether the mean number of new offenses for the arrested, counseled, and separated populations is equal. The null hypothesis is expressed as $\mu_{\text{arrest}} = \mu_{\text{counsel}} = \mu_{\text{separate}}$. When we fail to reject the null hypothesis, therefore, we are assuming that the population means are equal. This conclusion implies that the different "treatments," or police responses to intimate partner assault, make no difference in terms of the number of new offenses committed, that arrest is no better than counseling or separating offenders in reducing the number of new offenses. The alternative hypothesis in an analysis of variance always states that the population means are simply different from each other (i.e., that they are not equal): $\mu_{\text{arrest}} \neq \mu_{\text{counsel}} \neq \mu_{\text{separate}}$. When we reject the null hypothesis, therefore, we are concluding that at least two of the population means are different. There is no directional alternative hypothesis test in an analysis of variance; the alternative hypothesis is always that the population means are not equal. When we reject the null hypothesis, the only thing we know for sure is that at least one population mean is significantly different from at least one other population mean. We do not know from the analysis of variance test which specific population means are different from each other. This will require an additional step, which we will get to later in the chapter. Let's now do our hypothesis test with the data on police response to domestic violence. As always, we do it in a series of five steps.

**Step 1:**

$H_0$: $\mu_{arrest} = \mu_{counsel} = \mu_{separate}$. In other words, the different police responses to intimate partner assault have no effect on the number of new offenses.

$H_1$: $\mu_{arrest} \neq \mu_{counsel} \neq \mu_{separate}$. The alternative or research hypothesis states that the type of response the police make to a call for an intimate partner assault does make a difference in the number of new offenses.

**Step 2:** Since we are testing a hypothesis about the equality of more than two population means, we recognize this as an analysis of variance test. Our test statistic is the *F test*, and we use the *F* probability distribution.

**Step 3:** For this problem we are going to select an alpha level of .05. To find our critical value of *F*, we need to determine our two degrees of freedom: within-group and between-groups.

The within-group degrees of freedom is equal to $n - k$, where $n$ is the total number of observations and $k$ is the number of groups. In our problem, $n = 15$ and $k = 3$, so the within-group degrees of freedom is equal to $15 - 3 = 12$. The between-groups degrees of freedom is equal to $k - 1$. With three groups, the between-groups degrees of freedom for this problem is equal to $3 - 1 = 2$. We can now go to the appropriate *F* table, with an alpha of .05, and 12 within-group and 2 between-groups degrees of freedom. We use the 2 between-groups degrees of freedom in Table B.5 to find the correct column, and we use the 12 within-group degrees of freedom to find the correct row. We can see that with an alpha of .05, and 2 and 12 degrees of freedom, the critical value of *F* is 3.88. The critical region consists of all values of *F* equal to or greater than 3.88, and our decision rule is to reject the null hypothesis when $F_{obtained} \geq 3.88$.

**Step 4:** We now need to calculate our obtained value of *F*. To do this we need to calculate our three sources of variance. We will do this in a series of steps as well. Our first step will be to find the three sums of squares. We show all the calculations in Table 11.2. We provide the calculations to obtain all three sums of squares, but recall we could have calculated only two and obtained the third by subtraction or addition.

For example, we could have calculated the total and within-group sums of squares and then subtracted these two to get the between-groups sum of squares:

$$SS_{total} - SS_{Within} = SS_{between}$$
$$170 - 10 = 160$$

Or we could have calculated the between-groups and within-group sums of squares and obtained the total sum of squares by addition:

$$SS_{between} + SS_{Within} = SS_{total}$$
$$10 + 160 = 170$$

We recommend that you calculate all three sources of sum of squares until you are completely comfortable with doing an analysis of variance.

Now that we have our sum of squares from Table 11.2, we need to determine the degrees of freedom:

$df_{within} = n - k = 15 - 3 = 12$ within-group degrees of freedom

$df_{between} = k - 1 = 3 - 1 = 2$ between-groups degrees of freedom

$df_{total} = n - 1 = 15 - 1 = 14$ total degrees of freedom

### Figure 11.2 — Calculations of Sum of Squares for Analysis of Variance Test

| Total Sum of Squares | |
|---|---|
| $(X_i - \bar{X}_{grand})$ | $(X_i - \bar{X}_{grand})^2$ |
| $(0 - 5) = -5$ | 25 |
| $(2 - 5) = -3$ | 9 |
| $(1 - 5) = -4$ | 16 |
| $(1 - 5) = -4$ | 16 |
| $(1 - 5) = -4$ | 16 |
| $(6 - 5) = 1$ | 1 |
| $(4 - 5) = -1$ | 1 |
| $(4 - 5) = -1$ | 1 |
| $(6 - 5) = 1$ | 1 |
| $(5 - 5) = 0$ | 0 |
| $(8 - 5) = 3$ | 9 |
| $(10 - 5) = 5$ | 25 |
| $(9 - 5) = 4$ | 16 |
| $(10 - 5) = 5$ | 25 |
| $(8 - 5) = 3$ | 9 |
| | $\Sigma = 170$ |

| Within-Group Sum of Squares | |
|---|---|
| $(X_i - \bar{X}_k)$ | $(X_i - \bar{X}_k)^2$ |
| $(0 - 1) = -1$ | 1 |
| $(2 - 1) = -1$ | 1 |
| $(1 - 1) = 0$ | 0 |
| $(1 - 1) = 0$ | 0 |
| $(1 - 1) = 0$ | 0 |
| $(6 - 5) = 1$ | 1 |
| $(4 - 5) = -1$ | 1 |
| $(4 - 5) = -1$ | 1 |
| $(6 - 5) = 1$ | 1 |
| $(5 - 5) = 0$ | 0 |
| $(8 - 9) = -1$ | 1 |
| $(10 - 9) = 1$ | 1 |
| $(9 - 9) = 0$ | 0 |
| $(10 - 9) = 1$ | 1 |
| $(8 - 9) = -1$ | 1 |
| | $\Sigma = 10$ |

| Between-Groups Sum of Squares | |
|---|---|
| $(\bar{X}_k - \bar{X}_{grand})$ | $(\bar{X}_k - \bar{X}_{grand})^2$ |
| $(1 - 5) = -4$ | 16 |
| $(1 - 5) = -4$ | 16 |
| $(1 - 5) = -4$ | 16 |
| $(1 - 5) = -4$ | 16 |
| $(1 - 5) = -4$ | 16 |
| $(5 - 5) = 0$ | 0 |
| $(5 - 5) = 0$ | 0 |
| $(5 - 5) = 0$ | 0 |
| $(5 - 5) = 0$ | 0 |
| $(5 - 5) = 0$ | 0 |
| $(9 - 5) = 4$ | 16 |
| $(9 - 5) = 4$ | 16 |
| $(9 - 5) = 4$ | 16 |
| $(9 - 5) = 4$ | 16 |
| $(9 - 5) = 4$ | 16 |
| | $\Sigma = 160$ |

We can verify that these are correct because the sum of the within-group and between-groups degrees of freedom should equal the total degrees of freedom, and the total degrees of freedom is equal to 1 less than the total number of observations.

Now we are ready to calculate the estimates of our within-group variance and between-groups variance, which goes into the *F* statistic. Recall that the estimate of each source of variance is obtained by dividing the sum of squares by its respective degrees of freedom. We will put this information into what is frequently called an *F test*

| Table 11.3 | Summary *F* Table for Police Response to Domestic Violence Data | | | |
|---|---|---|---|---|
| Source | Sum of Squares | df | Variance | F |
| Between-groups | 160 | 2 | 80.00 | 96.39 |
| Within-group | 10 | 12 | .83 | |
| Total | 170 | 14 | | |

summary table. This summary table shows the sum of squares, the degrees of freedom, the estimated variance, and the obtained *F* statistic. For our example, we provide this *F* table in Table 11.3. The value of the *F* statistic reported in Table 11.3 is obtained by taking the ratio of the between-groups variance to the within-group variance (80 / .83 = 96.39).

**Step 5**: Since $F_{obtained} > F_{critical}$ (96.39 > 3.88), our obtained *F* statistic falls into the critical region so our decision is to reject the null hypothesis in favor of the alternative. We would conclude, then, that $\mu_{arrest} \neq \mu_{counsel} \neq \mu_{separate}$. We are saying two things in making this conclusion. First, we are saying that the independent variable, type of police response to intimate partner assault, is related to the number of new domestic violence acts an offender subsequently commits. However, the only thing we can conclude is that some combination of these population means is not equal to the others. In other words, we know that the three populations of arrested, counseled, and separated suspects have different means, but we do not know which specific population means are different. We could be rejecting the null hypothesis because $\mu_{arrest} \neq \mu_{counsel} \neq \mu_{separate}$, because $\mu_{arrest} \neq \mu_{counsel}$, because $\mu_{arrest} \neq \mu_{separate}$, or because $\mu_{counsel} \neq \mu_{separate}$. We simply don't know, on the basis of our *F test* which of these is true or if all are true (since we rejected the null hypothesis, however, we know that at least one of these inequalities is true). To decide which particular population means are different, we have to do some more calculations.

# After the *F* Test: Testing the Difference Between Pairs of Means

## Tukey's Honest Significance Difference (HSD) Test

Once we have rejected the null hypothesis in an analysis of variance, our attention turns next to the question: "Which means are significantly different from which other means?" We will answer this question by conducting a statistical test about the difference between two population means. There are several different statistical tests in the literature that can do this, each appropriate under different situations. For our purposes here, we will learn one of the most frequently used tests, **Tukey's Honest Significant Difference (HSD) test**. Tukey's HSD test requires that we calculate something called the **critical difference (CD) score**:

**Tukey's Honest Significant Difference (HSD) test:** Tests the difference between a series of group mean combinations after the null hypothesis from an ANOVA has been rejected.

**Critical difference (CD) score:** Calculated by Tukey's Honest Significant Difference (HSD) test to determine the significant difference between a series of group mean combinations after the null hypothesis from an ANOVA has been rejected.

$$CD = q\sqrt{\frac{\text{Within Group Variance}}{n_k}} \quad \text{(11–9)}$$

where

$n_k$ = the number of cases in each of the *k* groups

$q$ = the studentized range statistic

Values of the studentized range statistic can be found in Table B.6 in Appendix B. You need three pieces of information to find the correct value of $q$ to use in equation 11-9: your selected alpha level ($\alpha$), your degrees of freedom within groups ($df_{within}$), and the number of groups you have ($k$). What the critical difference gives us is the minimum absolute value of the difference between two sample means that would lead us to reject the null hypothesis of their equality. Now this last sentence, although accurate, is entirely too cryptic to be helpful. We can best explain things by going through an example using the HSD test.

In our analysis of variance in the last section, we rejected the null hypothesis that $\mu_{arrest} = \mu_{counsel} = \mu_{separate}$ in favor of the alternative hypothesis that $\mu_{arrest} \neq \mu_{counsel} \neq \mu_{separate}$. We now want to know which of these three population means is significantly different from which others. To find out, we will use our sample means and conduct a Tukey HSD test of *each pair* of sample means. That is, we will examine the difference between our sample means to make an inference about the equality of the unknown population means. Unlike a series of independent sample $t$ tests, however, Tukey's HSD will give us an honest level of significance or alpha for each of our sample mean comparisons (that's why it's called Tukey's *Honest* Significant Difference test).

First, we will list our null and alternative hypotheses for each population mean comparison (notice that these three hypotheses constitute all possible two-mean comparisons:

$H_0$: $\mu_{arrest} = \mu_{counsel}$

$H_1$: $\mu_{arrest} \neq \mu_{counsel}$

$H_0$: $\mu_{arrest} = \mu_{separate}$

$H_1$: $\mu_{arrest} \neq \mu_{separate}$

$H_0$: $\mu_{counsel} = \mu_{separate}$

$H_1$: $\mu_{counsel} \neq \mu_{separate}$

Second, we will calculate the value of the critical difference (CD) using equation 11-9. In Tukey's HSD test, we use the same level of significance we employed in the analysis of variance $F$ test ($\alpha = .05$ in the preceding example). To calculate CD, we need to get the value of $q$, or the studentized range statistic, and to obtain this, we need to go to Table B.6 in Appendix B with our alpha level (.05), the within-group degrees of freedom ($df_{within} = 12$), and the number of groups ($k = 3$). With this information, we can see that the value of $q$ is equal to 3.77. We can now put this value into equation 11-9 for the CD with the other values (the within-group variance and the number of people in each group):

$$CD = 3.77\sqrt{\frac{.83}{5}}$$
$$CD = 1.54$$

We have a critical difference score of 1.54. This means that the absolute value of the difference between any two sample means that we test must be greater than or equal to 1.54 for us to reject the null hypothesis of equal population means. Keep in mind that what we need to compare the CD score with is the *absolute value* of the difference between two sample means.

With our critical difference score of 1.54, let's calculate the absolute value of the difference between each of the three pairs of sample means. First, the difference in the mean number of new offenses between the arrested group and the counseled group:

$$\begin{array}{r} 1 \\ -5 \\ \hline |4| \end{array}$$

Since the absolute value of the difference between these two sample means is greater than the critical difference score of 1.54, we can conclude that the two population means are significantly different from each other. We will decide, therefore, that $\mu_{arrest} \neq \mu_{counsel}$ and that the population of offenders who are arrested for domestic violence have significantly fewer new offenses on average than those who are counseled. Second, let's calculate the absolute value of the difference in the mean number of new offenses between the arrested group and the separated group:

$$
\begin{array}{r}
1 \\
-9 \\
\hline
|8|
\end{array}
$$

Since the absolute value of the difference between these two sample means is greater than our critical difference score of 1.54, we will conclude that these two population means are also significantly different from each other. We will decide that $\mu_{arrest} \neq \mu_{separate}$ and that domestic violence offenders who are arrested have significantly fewer new offenses on average than those who are separated from their partners. Finally, let's calculate the absolute value of the difference between the mean number of new offenses for the counseled group and the separated group:

$$
\begin{array}{r}
5 \\
-9 \\
\hline
|4|
\end{array}
$$

Since the absolute value of the difference between these two sample means is greater than the critical difference score of 1.54, we will conclude that the population mean number of new offenses is significantly different for those offenders who are counseled and those who are separated from their partners. It seems that counseling offenders of domestic violence is more effective in reducing the number of new offenses than merely separating the couple.

In sum, the analysis of variance test and the series of Tukey Honest Significant Difference tests tell us that how the police respond to an incident of domestic violence does make a difference. At least in terms of reducing the number of new offenses committed by the same offender is concerned, arrest leads to the fewest new offenses on average, counseling leads to significantly more new offenses than arrest but to significantly fewer offenses than just separating the couple, and a police response of separating the pair is the least effective in curbing future acts of intimate partner assault. In this particular example, all three sample means were significantly different from each other, but please remember that this will not always be the case, and you will have to interpret your results accordingly.

## ▣ A Measure of Association With ANOVA

In the previous sections, we conducted the *F test* of an analysis of variance and Tukey's HSD test to assess the relationship between the type of police response to domestic violence and the number of new offenses committed by an offender. When we rejected the null hypothesis in the analysis of variance, we concluded that there was a relationship between the type of response the police make to domestic violence and the number of new offenses subsequently committed. What neither the *F test* nor Tukey's HSD test told us, however, was the *strength* of the relationship between our independent and dependent variables. As we have learned in previous chapters, concluding that there is a relationship between two variables gives no clue as to the magnitude or strength of the relationship between them. To assess the strength of a relationship between two variables, we must use an appropriate measure of association.

Recall that in the analysis of variance, we calculated three different sum of squares: total, between-groups, and within-group. The total sum of squares measures the total amount of variability that exists among the scores. The between-groups variability measures the amount of variability due to group membership. This variability reflects the extent to which the groups differ from each other on the dependent variable, and it captures a "treatment" effect.

If there is a substantial amount of this variability, then it would seem that the group membership matters, at least as far as the dependent variable is concerned. Finally, the within-group variability measures the amount of variability that is unaccounted for by group membership. Since everyone within a group shares the same group membership, they cannot differ because of different group effects. In fact, since they have the same level of the independent variable, we do not know exactly why the scores within a group are different, so this variability is unexplained or unaccounted for (it's just "noise" or error). With this in mind, think of the total sum of squares as consisting of total variability, the between-groups sum of squares as consisting of explained variability (variability explained by membership in the group), and the within-group sum of squares as consisting of unexplained variability.

Recall also that the sum of the between-groups and within-group sum of squares is equal to the total sum of squares. The total variability in the scores, or the total sum of squares, then, is equal to two components: an explained component (the between-groups sum of squares) and an unexplained component (the within-group sum of squares). If we take the ratio of the between-groups to the total sum of squares, then, we have a ratio of explained to total variability, and from this, we get an estimate of the proportion of the total variability that is explained. The greater the amount of the total variability that is explained or due to variation in the independent variable, the stronger the relationship there is between it and the dependent variable. Fortunately, we have a way to quantify this that we explain next.

## Eta Squared (Correlation Ratio)

This discussion of explained, unexplained, and total variability is the conceptual basis behind one measure of association with ANOVA called **eta squared** or the **correlation ratio**:

> **Eta squared:** Describes the ratio of variance explained in the dependent variable by an independent variable.

$$\eta^2 = \frac{SS_{\text{between}}}{SS_{\text{total}}}$$

(11–10)

Eta squared measures the strength of the relationship between an independent and a dependent variable in an analysis of variance. More specifically, it measures the amount of variability in the dependent variable that is explained by the independent variable. Eta squared can range from 0, indicating no relationship between the independent and dependent variables, to 1.0, indicating a perfect relationship between the two. A perfect relationship means that all of the variability (you are explaining all of variance in the dependent variable with the independent variable) among the scores is due to differences in group membership, and there is no within-group variability. What we are saying here is that all our variability is due to treatment and nothing is due to noise or error. A zero relationship means that none of the variability (you are explaining none of variance in the dependent variable with the independent variable) among the scores is due to differences in group membership, and everything is due to within-group variability (noise or error). In between these values, we can follow our old rule of thumb about measures of association and state that values of eta squared between 0 and .29 can be interpreted as a "weak" relationship, values between .30 and .59 indicate a "moderate" relationship, and values greater than .60 reflect a "strong" relationship.

Let's use our data on police response to intimate partner assault as an example and calculate the value of eta squared:

$$\eta^2 = \frac{160}{170}$$
$$\eta^2 = .94$$

We have a very strong relationship between type of police response and the number of subsequent offenses. Multiplying eta squared by 100 tells us that 94% of the variability in the number of offenses committed is due to differences in police response.

## ▣ A Second ANOVA Example: Caseload Size and Success on Probation

In our second example, we are interested in the relationship between the number of cases that a probation officer has to supervise and how successful probation is in terms of the number of probation infractions or new offenses committed by a probationer. There has been some controversy in the criminal justice literature about this issue. Some studies have found that smaller caseload sizes for probation officers are more effective in reducing new offenses or probation violations, whereas other studies have indicated that the number of cases a probation officer has to supervise has no effect on success. This is an important issue because we would like to reduce the number of probation violations, but reducing probation supervision size costs money. To examine the relationship between the caseload size a probation officer has and success on probation, we take a sample of women who were convicted by a court and sentenced to four years of probation each. Ten of these women were randomly assigned to probation officers who had "low" caseloads (fewer than 25 cases), ten were randomly assigned to probation officers who had "moderate" caseloads (between 25 and 50 cases), and ten were randomly assigned to probation officers who had "heavy" caseloads (more than 50 cases to supervise). For each of these women, we identify the number of probation inf ractions or new crimes they committed while they were on probation over the four-year period. The data are shown in Table 11.4.

We want to test the null hypothesis that $\mu_{low} = \mu_{moderate} = \mu_{heavy}$ against the alternative hypothesis that $\mu_{low} \neq \mu_{moderate} \neq \mu_{heavy}$. We will use an alpha of .01 for this hypothesis test, and all of the steps are shown as follows.

| Table 11.4 | Size of Probation Officer Caseload and Number of Crimes and Violations Committed on Release |
| --- | --- |

| Caseload Supervision Size | | |
| --- | --- | --- |
| Low | Moderate | Heavy |
| 7 | 10 | 11 |
| 12 | 14 | 8 |
| 13 | 8 | 7 |
| 5 | 7 | 10 |
| 8 | 9 | 9 |
| 11 | 11 | 9 |
| 10 | 13 | 7 |
| 14 | 12 | 8 |
| 9 | 8 | 3 |
| 6 | 8 | 3 |
| $\bar{X}_{low} = 9.5$ | $\bar{X}_{moderate} = 10.0$ | $\bar{X}_{heavy} = 7.5$ |

**Step 1:**

$H_0: \mu_{low} = \mu_{moderate} = \mu_{heavy}$

$H_1: \mu_{low} \neq \mu_{moderate} \neq \mu_{heavy}$

**Step 2**: This is a problem involving the equality of three population means, so the correct statistical test is the *F test* of an analysis of variance. The *F test* has an *F* probability distribution.

**Step 3**: We will use an alpha of .01. Our within-group degrees of freedom $(n - k)$ is equal to 27 (30 total subjects and 3 groups), and our between degrees of freedom $(k - 1)$ is equal to 2. With 2 and 27 degrees of freedom, our critical value of *F* with $\alpha = .01$ is 5.49, and the critical region comprises all *F* values greater than or equal to 5.49. Our decision rule is to reject the null hypothesis if $F_{obtained} \geq 5.49$.

**Step 4:** The calculations for the total, between-groups, and within-group sums of squares are shown in Table 11.5. With the sum of squares, and degrees of freedom, we can then calculate the between-groups and within-group variance and the *F* statistic. The analysis of variance summary table is shown in Table 11.6.

**Step 5:** We have an obtained *F* value of 2.374. Since this is less than our critical value of $F_{critical} = 5.49$, our decision is to fail to reject the null hypothesis. We

| Table 11.5 | Calculations for Caseload Size and Probation Success |
| --- | --- |

| Total Sum of Squares | | Within-Group Sum of Squares | | Between-Groups Sum of Squares | |
| --- | --- | --- | --- | --- | --- |
| $(X_i - \bar{X}_{grand})$ | $(X_i - \bar{X}_{grand})^2$ | $(X_i - \bar{X}_k)$ | $(X_i - \bar{X}_k)^2$ | $(\bar{X}_k - \bar{X}_{grand})$ | $(\bar{X}_k - \bar{X}_{grand})^2$ |
| 7 − 9 = −2 | 4 | 7 − 9.5 = −2.5 | 6.25 | 9.5 − 9 = .5 | .25 |
| 12 − 9 = 3 | 9 | 12 − 9.5 = 2.5 | 6.25 | 9.5 − 9 = .5 | .25 |
| 13 − 9 = 4 | 16 | 13 − 9.5 = 3.5 | 12.25 | 9.5 − 9 = .5 | .25 |
| 5 − 9 = −4 | 16 | 5 − 9.5 = −4.5 | 20.25 | 9.5 − 9 = .5 | .25 |
| 8 − 9 = −1 | 1 | 8 − 9.5 = −1.5 | 2.25 | 9.5 − 9 = .5 | .25 |
| 11 − 9 = 2 | 4 | 11 − 9.5 = 1.5 | 2.25 | 9.5 − 9 = .5 | .25 |
| 10 − 9 = 1 | 1 | 10 − 9.5 = .5 | .25 | 9.5 − 9 = .5 | .25 |
| 14 − 9 = 5 | 25 | 14 − 9.5 = 4.5 | 20.25 | 9.5 − 9 = .5 | .25 |
| 9 − 9 = 0 | 0 | 9 − 9.5 = −.5 | .25 | 9.5 − 9 = .5 | .25 |
| 6 − 9 = −3 | 9 | 6 − 9.5 = −3.5 | 12.25 | 9.5 − 9 = .5 | .25 |
| 10 − 9 = 1 | 1 | 10 − 10 = 0 | 0.00 | 10 − 9 = 1 | 1.00 |
| 14 − 9 = 5 | 25 | 14 − 10 = 4 | 16.00 | 10 − 9 = 1 | 1.00 |
| 8 − 9 = −1 | 1 | 8 − 10 = −2 | 4.00 | 10 − 9 = 1 | 1.00 |
| 7 − 9 = −2 | 4 | 7 − 10 = −3 | 9.00 | 10 − 9 = 1 | 1.00 |
| 9 − 9 = 0 | 0 | 9 − 10 = −1 | 1.00 | 10 − 9 = 1 | 1.00 |
| 11 − 9 = 2 | 4 | 11 − 10 = 1 | 1.00 | 10 − 9 = 1 | 1.00 |
| 13 − 9 = 4 | 16 | 13 − 10 = 3 | 9.00 | 10 − 9 = 1 | 1.00 |
| 12 − 9 = 3 | 9 | 12 − 10 = 2 | 4.00 | 10 − 9 = 1 | 1.00 |
| 8 − 9 = −1 | 1 | 8 − 10 = −2 | 4.00 | 10 − 9 = 1 | 1.00 |
| 8 − 9 = −1 | 1 | 8 − 10 = −2 | 4.00 | 10 − 9 = 1 | 1.00 |
| 11 − 9 = 2 | 4 | 11 − 7.5 = 3.5 | 12.25 | 7.5 − 9 = −1.5 | 2.25 |
| 8 − 9 = −1 | 1 | 8 − 7.5 = .5 | .25 | 7.5 − 9 = −1.5 | 2.25 |
| 7 − 9 = −2 | 4 | 7 − 7.5 = −.5 | .25 | 7.5 − 9 = −1.5 | 2.25 |
| 10 − 9 = 1 | 1 | 10 − 7.5 = 2.5 | 6.25 | 7.5 − 9 = −1.5 | 2.25 |
| 9 − 9 = 0 | 0 | 9 − 7.5 = 1.5 | 2.25 | 7.5 − 9 = −1.5 | 2.25 |
| 9 − 9 = 0 | 0 | 9 − 7.5 = 1.5 | 2.25 | 7.5 − 9 = −1.5 | 2.25 |

*(Continued)*

(Continued)

| Total Sum of Squares | | Within-Group Sum of Squares | | Between-Groups Sum of Squares | |
|---|---|---|---|---|---|
| $(X_i - \bar{X}_{grand})$ | $(X_i - \bar{X}_{grand})^2$ | $(X_i - \bar{X}_k)$ | $(X_i - \bar{X}_k)^2$ | $(\bar{X}_k - \bar{X}_{grand})$ | $(\bar{X}_k - \bar{X}_{grand})^2$ |
| $7 - 9 = -2$ | 4 | $7 - 7.5 = -.5$ | .25 | $7.5 - 9 = -1.5$ | 2.25 |
| $8 - 9 = -1$ | 1 | $8 - 7.5 = .5$ | .25 | $7.5 - 9 = -1.5$ | 2.25 |
| $3 - 9 = -6$ | 36 | $3 - 7.5 = -4.5$ | 20.25 | $7.5 - 9 = -1.5$ | 2.25 |
| $3 - 9 = -6$ | 36 | $3 - 7.5 = -4.5$ | 20.25 | $7.5 - 9 = -1.5$ | 2.25 |
| | $\Sigma = 234$ | | $\Sigma = 199$ | | $\Sigma = 35$ |

| Table 11.6 | **Summary *F* Table for the Relationship Between Caseload Size and Success on Probation** |
|---|---|

| Source | Sum of Squares | df | Variance | F |
|---|---|---|---|---|
| Between-groups | 35 | 2 | 17.50 | 2.374 |
| Within-group | 199 | 27 | 7.37 | |
| Total | 234 | 29 | | |

will conclude that $\mu_{low} = \mu_{moderate} = \mu_{heavy}$ and that the intensity of the probation officer's caseload has no effect on the success of her or his clients. Since we failed to reject the null hypothesis, we do not need to examine our individual pairs of sample means with Tukey's HSD. The HSD test is appropriate only after we reject the null hypothesis in an analysis of variance. We can, however, calculate eta squared:

$$\eta^2 = \frac{35}{234}$$

$$\eta^2 = .15$$

A magnitude of .15 is small, strengthening our conclusion that caseload size is not related to success on probation.

## 🔲 A Third ANOVA Example: Region of the Country and Homicide

Let's work on one more example of an analysis of variance. In this last example, our independent variable is the region of the country, and our dependent variable is the homicide rate. We have information on the homicide rate for 36 states, and we have classified each state as belonging to one of four regions of the country: Northeast, Midwest, South, and West. There are nine states that fall into each region, and we calculate the average homicide rate per 100,000 population in each of the four regions. These data are shown in Table 11.7. You can see that the sample means indicate that the homicide rate is lowest in northeastern states, that midwestern and western states have comparable rates of homicide on average, and that southern states have the highest average homicide rate. We will test the hypothesis that the population mean homicide rates for the four regions are the same, and we will use an alpha of .05 in our hypothesis test. As always, we follow a series of five steps.

**Step 1:**

$H_0: \mu_{Northeast} = \mu_{Midwest} = \mu_{South} = \mu_{West}$

$H_1: \mu_{Northeast} \neq \mu_{Midwest} \neq \mu_{South} \neq \mu_{West}$

**Step 2**: Since this is a test involving the equality of three or more population means, the correct statistical test is the analysis of variance $F$ test. The $F$ test has an $F$ probability distribution.

**Step 3**: We will use an alpha of .05. We have 32 within-group degrees of freedom ($n - k$; $36 - 4 = 32$), and we have 3 between-groups degrees of freedom ($k - 1$; $4 - 1 = 3$). There is no row for 32 within-group degrees of freedom in Table B.5, so we will use 30 degrees of freedom. With 30 within and 3 between degrees of freedom and an alpha of .05, our critical value of $F$ is 2.92. The critical region consists of all values of $F$ equal to or greater than 2.92. Our decision rule is to reject the null hypothesis if $F_{obtained} \geq 2.92$.

**Step 4:** The calculations necessary to find the total, within-group, and between-groups sum of squares are recorded in Table 11.8. With the sum of squares and degrees of freedom, we can also calculate the between-groups and within-group variance and the $F$ statistic. The analysis of variance summary table is shown in Table 11.9.

**Step 5:** We have an obtained $F$ value of 5.08. Since this is greater than our critical value of $F_{critical} = 2.92$ and so our obtained $F$ falls into the critical region, our decision is to reject the null hypothesis that $\mu_{Northeast} = \mu_{Midwest} = \mu_{South} = \mu_{West}$ in favor of the alternative hypothesis that there is a statistically significant difference in the rate of homicide across some regions of the United States ($\mu_{Northeast} \neq \mu_{Midwest} \neq \mu_{South} \neq \mu_{West}$). We will now use Tukey's HSD test to determine which pair or pairs of population means are significantly different from each other

We first need to determine the value of CD, the critical difference score:

$$CD = q \sqrt{\frac{\text{Within} - \text{group variance}}{n_k}}$$

To find the value of $q$, the studentized range statistic, we consult Table B.6 in Appendix B. With an alpha of .05, 30 within-group degrees of freedom (there is no row for 32 degrees of freedom in this table either), and 4 groups ($k = 4$), we find that $q = 3.84$. We are now ready to find our critical difference score:

$$CD = 3.84 \sqrt{\frac{4.75}{9}}$$
$$CD = 2.79$$

Our critical difference score is 2.79. This means that when we compare each pair of our regional sample means, the absolute value of the difference between the two means must be 2.79 or greater for us to reject the null hypothesis that they are equal.

Let's state explicitly each null hypothesis and its alternative, and then we will do the necessary hypothesis test for Tukey's HSD. Since we have four groups, there are six different mean comparisons to make [with $k$ groups, there will be $\frac{k(k-1)}{2}$ comparisons to make].

$$H_0 : \mu_{Northeast} = \mu_{Midwest}$$
$$H_1 : \mu_{Northeast} \neq \mu_{Midwest}$$
$$3.23$$
$$-5.01$$
$$\overline{|1.78|}$$

| Table 11.7 | Rate of Murders and Non-Negligent Manslaughters (per 100,000) by Four Regions of the United States |
|---|---|

| Northeast | Rate | Midwest | Rate | South | Rate | West | Rate |
|---|---|---|---|---|---|---|---|
| Connecticut | 3.3 | Illinois | 7.7 | Florida | 5.7 | Arizona | 8.0 |
| Maine | 2.2 | Indiana | 6.6 | Georgia | 7.5 | Idaho | 2.0 |
| Massachusetts | 2.2 | Michigan | 7.0 | North Carolina | 7.2 | Montana | 2.6 |
| New Hampshire | 1.5 | Ohio | 3.5 | South Carolina | 6.6 | Nevada | 9.1 |
| Rhode Island | 3.6 | Wisconsin | 3.4 | Virginia | 5.7 | New Mexico | 9.8 |
| Vermont | 2.9 | Iowa | 1.5 | Alabama | 7.9 | California | 6.0 |
| New Jersey | 3.5 | Kansas | 6.0 | Louisiana | 10.7 | Oregon | 2.7 |
| New York | 5.0 | Minnesota | 2.8 | Texas | 6.1 | Washington | 3.0 |
| Pennsylvania | 4.9 | Missouri | 6.6 | Mississippi | 7.7 | Utah | 2.1 |
| $\bar{X}_{\text{Northeast}} = 3.23$ | | $\bar{X}_{\text{Midwest}} = 5.01$ | | $\bar{X}_{\text{South}} = 7.23$ | | $\bar{X}_{\text{West}} = 5.03$ | |

| Table 11.8 | Calculations for Region of the Country and Rates of Murder |
|---|---|

| Total Sum of Squares | | Within-Group Sum of Squares | | Between-Groups Sum of Squares | |
|---|---|---|---|---|---|
| $(X_i - \bar{X}_{\text{grand}})$ | $(X_i - \bar{X}_{\text{grand}})^2$ | $(X_i - \bar{X}_k)$ | $(X_i - \bar{X}_k)^2$ | $(\bar{X}_k - \bar{X}_{\text{grand}})$ | $(\bar{X}_k - \bar{X}_{\text{grand}})^2$ |
| 3.3 − 5.13 = −1.83 | 3.35 | 3.3 − 3.23 = .07 | .005 | 3.23 − 5.13 = −1.90 | 3.61 |
| 2.2 − 5.13 = −2.93 | 8.58 | 2.2 − 3.23 = −1.03 | 1.06 | 3.23 − 5.13 = −1.90 | 3.61 |
| 2.2 − 5.13 = −2.93 | 8.58 | 2.2 − 3.23 = −1.03 | 1.06 | 3.23 − 5.13 = −1.90 | 3.61 |
| 1.5 − 5.13 = −3.63 | 13.18 | 1.5 − 3.23 = −1.73 | 2.99 | 3.23 − 5.13 = −1.90 | 3.61 |
| 3.6 − 5.13 = −1.53 | 2.34 | 3.6 − 3.23 = .37 | .14 | 3.23 − 5.13 = −1.90 | 3.61 |
| 2.9 − 5.13 = −2.23 | 4.97 | 2.9 − 3.23 = −.33 | .11 | 3.23 − 5.13 = −1.90 | 3.61 |
| 3.5 − 5.13 = −1.63 | 2.66 | 3.5 − 3.23 = .27 | .07 | 3.23 − 5.13 = −1.90 | 3.61 |
| 5.0 − 5.13 = −.13 | .02 | 5.0 − 3.23 = 1.77 | 3.13 | 3.23 − 5.13 = −1.90 | 3.61 |
| 4.9 − 5.13 = −.23 | .05 | 4.9 − 3.23 = 1.67 | 2.79 | 3.23 − 5.13 = −1.90 | 3.61 |

| Total Sum of Squares | | Within-Group Sum of Squares | | Between-Groups Sum of Squares | |
|---|---|---|---|---|---|
| $(X_i - \overline{X}_{grand})$ | $(X_i - \overline{X}_{grand})^2$ | $(X_i - \overline{X}_k)$ | $(X_i - \overline{X}_k)^2$ | $(\overline{X}_k - \overline{X}_{grand})$ | $(\overline{X}_k - \overline{X}_{grand})^2$ |
| 7.7 − 5.13 = 2.57 | 6.60 | 7.7 − 5.01 = 2.69 | 7.24 | 5.01 − 5.13 = −.12 | .01 |
| 6.6 − 5.13 = 1.47 | 2.16 | 6.6 − 5.01 = 1.59 | 2.53 | 5.01 − 5.13 = −.12 | .01 |
| 7.0 − 5.13 = 1.87 | 3.50 | 7.0 − 5.01 = 1.99 | 3.96 | 5.01 − 5.13 = −.12 | .01 |
| 3.5 − 5.13 = −1.63 | 2.66 | 3.5 − 5.01 = −1.51 | 2.28 | 5.01 − 5.13 = −.12 | .01 |
| 3.4 − 5.13 = −1.73 | 2.99 | 3.4 − 5.01 = −1.61 | 2.59 | 5.01 − 5.13 = −.12 | .01 |
| 1.5 − 5.13 = −3.63 | 13.18 | 1.5 − 5.01 = −3.51 | 12.32 | 5.01 − 5.13 = −.12 | .01 |
| 6.0 − 5.13 = .87 | .76 | 6.0 − 5.01 = .99 | .98 | 5.01 − 5.13 = −.12 | .01 |
| 2.8 − 5.13 = −2.33 | 5.43 | 2.8 − 5.01 = −2.21 | 4.88 | 5.01 − 5.13 = −.12 | .01 |
| 6.6 − 5.13 = 1.47 | 2.16 | 6.6 − 5.01 = 1.59 | 2.53 | 5.01 − 5.13 = −.12 | .01 |
| 5.7 − 5.13 = .57 | .32 | 5.7 − 7.23 = −1.53 | 2.34 | 7.23 − 5.13 = 2.10 | 4.41 |
| 7.5 − 5.13 = 2.37 | 5.62 | 7.5 − 7.23 = .27 | .07 | 7.23−5.13 = 2.10 | 4.41 |
| 7.2 − 5.13 = 2.07 | 4.28 | 7.2 − 7.23 = −.03 | .001 | 7.23 − 5.13 = 2.10 | 4.41 |
| 6.6 − 5.13 = 1.47 | 2.16 | 6.6 − 7.23 = −.63 | .40 | 7.23−5.13 = 2.10 | 4.41 |
| 5.7 − 5.13 = .57 | .32 | 5.7 − 7.23 = −1.53 | 2.34 | 7.23 − 5.13 = 2.10 | 4.41 |
| 7.9 − 5.13 = 2.77 | 7.67 | 7.9 − 7.23 = .67 | .45 | 7.23−5.13 = 2.10 | 4.41 |
| 10.7 − 5.13 = 5.57 | 31.02 | 10.7 − 7.23 = 3.47 | 12.04 | 7.23 − 5.13 = 2.10 | 4.41 |
| 6.1 − 5.13 = .97 | .94 | 6.1 − 7.23 = −1.13 | 1.28 | 7.23−5.13 = 2.10 | 4.41 |
| 7.7 − 5.13 = 2.57 | 6.60 | 7.7 − 7.23 = .47 | .22 | 7.23 − 5.13 = 2.10 | 4.41 |
| 8.0 − 5.13 = 2.87 | 8.24 | 8.0 − 5.03 = 2.97 | 8.82 | 5.03−5.13 =− .10 | .01 |
| 2.0 − 5.13 = −3.13 | 9.80 | 2.0 − 5.03 = −3.03 | 9.18 | 5.03 − 5.13 = −.10 | .01 |
| 2.6 − 5.13 = −2.53 | 6.40 | 2.6 − 5.03 = −2.43 | 5.90 | 5.03 − 5.13 = −.10 | .01 |
| 9.1 − 5.13 = 3.97 | 15.76 | 9.1 − 5.03 = 4.07 | 16.56 | 5.03 − 5.13 = −.10 | .01 |
| 9.8 − 5.13 = 4.67 | 21.81 | 9.8 − 5.03 = 4.77 | 22.75 | 5.03 − 5.13 = −.10 | .01 |
| 6.0 − 5.13 = .87 | .76 | 6.0 − 5.03 = .97 | .94 | 5.03 − 5.13 = −.10 | .01 |
| 2.7 − 5.13 = −2.43 | 5.90 | 2.7 − 5.03 = −2.33 | 5.43 | 5.03 − 5.13 = −.10 | .01 |
| 3.0 − 5.13 = −2.13 | 4.54 | 3.0 − 5.03 = −2.03 | 4.12 | 5.03 − 5.13 = −.10 | .01 |
| 2.1 − 5.13 = −3.03 | 9.18 | 2.1 − 5.03 = −2.93 | 8.58 | 5.03 − 5.13 = −.10 | .01 |
| | Σ = 224.51 | | Σ = 152.11 | | Σ = 72.40 |

| | Summary *F* Table for the Relationship between Region of the Country and Homicide Rates | | | | |
|---|---|---|---|---|---|
| **Table 11.9** | | | | | |
| Source | Sum of Squares | df | Variance | F | |
| Between-groups | 72.40 | 3 | 24.13 | 5.08 | |
| Within-group | 152.11 | 32 | 4.75 | | |
| Total | 224.51 | 35 | | | |

This absolute difference in sample means is not greater than or equal to the CD score of 2.79, so we conclude that the population mean homicide rate for the northeastern states is not significantly different from that for the midwestern states. We would fail to reject that null hypothesis:

$$H_0 : \mu_{Northeast} = \mu_{South}$$
$$H_1 : \mu_{Northeast} \neq \mu_{South}$$
$$3.23$$
$$-7.23$$
$$\overline{|4.00|}$$

This absolute difference in sample means is greater than the CD score of 2.79, so we conclude that the population mean homicide rate for the northeastern states is significantly different from that for the southern states. We would reject that null hypothesis. On average, the southern states have significantly higher average homicide rates than northeastern states:

$$H_0 : \mu_{Northeast} = \mu_{West}$$
$$H_1 : \mu_{Northeast} \neq \mu_{West}$$
$$3.23$$
$$-5.03$$
$$\overline{|1.8|}$$

This absolute difference in sample means is not greater than or equal to the CD score of 2.79, so we conclude that the population mean homicide rate for the northeastern states is not significantly different from that for the western states. We would fail to reject that null hypothesis:

$$H_0 : \mu_{Midwest} = \mu_{South}$$
$$H_1 : \mu_{Midwest} \neq \mu_{South}$$
$$5.01$$
$$-7.23$$
$$\overline{|2.22|}$$

This absolute difference in sample means is not greater than or equal to the CD score of 2.79, so we conclude that the population mean homicide rate for the midwestern states is not significantly different from that for the southern states. We would fail to reject that null hypothesis:

$$H_0 : \mu_{Midwest} = \mu_{West}$$
$$H_1 : \mu_{Midwest} \neq \mu_{West}$$
$$5.01$$
$$-5.03$$
$$\overline{|0.02|}$$

This absolute difference in sample means is not greater than or equal to the CD score of 2.79, so we conclude that the population mean homicide rate for the midwestern states is not significantly different from that for the western states. We would fail to reject that null hypothesis:

$$H_0 : \mu_{South} = \mu_{West}$$
$$H_1 : \mu_{South} \neq \mu_{West}$$
$$7.23$$
$$-5.03$$
$$\overline{|2.20|}$$

This absolute difference in sample means is not greater than or equal to the CD score of 2.79, so we conclude that the population mean homicide rate for the southern states is not significantly different from that for the western states. We would fail to reject that null hypothesis. In sum, we rejected the analysis of variance null hypothesis of equal population mean homicide rates for the northeastern, midwestern, southern, and western states only because the homicide rates in the northeastern states are significantly different from those in the southern states. None of the other mean comparisons were significantly different from each other.

Finally, we can calculate the value of eta squared to determine how strongly region of the country and homicide rates are related:

$$\eta^2 = \frac{72.40}{224.51}$$
$$\eta^2 = .32$$

This value of eta squared, when multiplied by 100 tells us that 32% of the variability in homicide rates can be explained by regional location. This indicates a moderate relationship between region of the country and homicide rates.

## ▣ Summary

In this chapter, we studied the analysis of variance. Although this statistical technique is called an analysis of *variance*, it is used to test a hypothesis about the equality of three or more population *means*. In an analysis of variance, we have an independent variable that is measured at the nominal or ordinal level and has three or more values, or levels, and a continuous (interval/ratio) dependent variable. The test statistic is the $F$ statistic and is the ratio of the variability that exists between groups to that which exists within groups. The variability between groups reflects differences due to "treatment" or the independent variable, whereas variability within groups reflects noise or error. A high $F$ statistic means that there is more between-groups than within-group variance, a finding that would lead us to reject the null hypothesis of equal population means.

When we reject the null hypothesis in an analysis of variance, we conclude that some of the population means are not equal, although we do not know which specific ones are different on the basis of the $F$ test alone. To identify which population means are significantly different, we used Tukey's HSD test. Finally, we learned about a measure of association in an analysis of variance, eta squared. Eta squared measures the amount of variability in the dependent variable that is explained by the independent variable. The larger the magnitude of eta squared, the stronger the relationship between the independent and dependent variables.

## Key Terms

➤ Review key terms with eFlashcards. $SAGE edge™

analysis of variance
  (ANOVA)   314
between-groups sum of
  squares   319

critical difference
  (CD) score   324
eta squared   327
total sum of squares   319

Tukey's Honest Significant
  Difference (HSD) test   324
within-group sum of
  squares   319

## Key Formulas

Total sum of squares ($SS_{total}$) (equation 11-2):

$$SS_{total} = \sum_i \sum_k (x_{ik} - \overline{X}_{grand})^2$$

Within-group sum of squares ($SS_{within}$) (equation 11-3):

$$SS_{within} = \sum_i \sum_k (x_{ik} - \overline{X}_k)^2$$

Between sum of squares ($SS_{between}$) (equation 11-4):

$$SS_{between} = \sum_i \sum_k (\overline{X}_k - \overline{X}_{grand})^2$$

Formulas to estimate the three types of variance (equations 11-8 through 11-0):

$$\text{Total variance:} \frac{SS_{total}}{df_{total}} = \frac{\sum_i \sum_k (x_{ik} - \overline{X}_{grand})^2}{n-1}$$

$$\text{Within-group variance:} \frac{SS_{within}}{df_{within}} = \frac{\sum_i \sum_k (x_{ik} - \overline{X}_k)^2}{n-k}$$

Between-groups variance : $\dfrac{SS_{between}}{df_{between}} = \dfrac{\sum_i \sum_k (\overline{X}_k - \overline{X}_{grand})^2}{k-1}$

Formula for calculating $F$ (equation 11-8):

$$F : \frac{SS_{between}/df_{between}}{SS_{within}/df_{within}} = \frac{\text{Variance between groups}}{\text{Variance within group}}$$

Turkey's Honest Significant Difference Test:
Critical difference score (equation 11-9):

$$CD = q\sqrt{\frac{\text{Within-group variance}}{n_k}}$$

Eta squared or the correlation ratio (equation 11-10):

$$\eta^2 = \frac{SS_{between}}{SS_{total}}$$

## Practice Problems

> Test your understanding of chapter content.
> Take the practice quiz. **⑤SAGE** edge™

1. When is it appropriate to perform an analysis of variance with our data? What type of variables do we need?

2. What statistical technique should we use if we have a continuous dependent variable and a categorical independent variable with only two categories?

3. Why do we call this statistical technique an analysis of *variance* when we are really interested in the difference among population *means*?

4. What two types of variance do we use to calculate the $F$ ratio?

5. How do we determine the $df_{total}$, $df_{between}$, and $df_{within}$?

6. Meagan Tucker and Christina Rodriguez (2014) published a paper in which they argued that stress contributes directly toward increased risks for physical child maltreatment. Let's say you want to test this hypothesis. You have a random sample of 30 women with small children living at home. Based on questions about their home life and possible sources of stress, you are able to place them into one of three groups: "high stress," "medium stress," and "low stress." You then ask each of the women how many times she has physically punished her children in the past month. You think that stress might be related to the use of physical punishment. The following are the data from your sample:

**Number of Times Physical Punishment Used Last Month**

| Level of Stress | | |
|---|---|---|
| High | Medium | Low |
| X | X | X |
| 4 | 2 | 3 |
| 6 | 4 | 1 |
| 12 | 5 | 2 |
| 10 | 3 | 0 |
| 5 | 0 | 2 |
| 9 | 3 | 2 |

| 8 | 2 | 4 |
|---|---|---|
| 11 | 5 | 1 |
| 10 | 5 | 0 |
| 8 | 4 | 1 |

With these data, do the following:

a. Identify the independent and dependent variables.

b. Calculate the total, between-groups, and within-group sums of squares.

c. Determine the correct number of degrees of freedom, calculate the ratio of sum of squares to degrees of freedom, and determine the $F$ ratio.

d. With an alpha of .05, test the null hypothesis that the three population means are equal against the alternative hypothesis that some of them are different.

e. If appropriate, conduct a mean comparison for each pair of means using Tukey's HSD test.

f. Calculate the value of eta squared, and make a conclusion about the strength of the relationship between a mother's stress level and the frequency with which she punishes her child.

7. One of the most pressing social problems is the problem of drunk driving. Drunk driving causes untold human suffering and has profound economic effects. States have tried various things to inhibit drunk driving. Some states have tried to cut down on drunk driving within their borders by "getting tough" with drunk drivers. One way to do this is to suspend their driver's licenses and impose heavy fines, as well as jail and prison sentences, on those convicted of drunk driving. Other states have tried a "moral appeal" by mounting public relations campaigns that proclaim the harm and injury produced by drunk driving. You want to determine the effectiveness of these strategies. You calculate the rate of drunk driving per 100,000 residents for each of the 50 states, and you classify each state into one of three categories: a "get tough" state, a "moral appeal" state, or a "control" state. The latter states do nothing special to those who get caught drinking and driving. Your summary data look like the following:

| Get Tough States | Moral Appeal States | Control States |
|---|---|---|
| $n_1 = 15$ | $n_2 = 15$ | $n_3 = 15$ |
| $\bar{X}_1 = 125.2$ | $\bar{X}_2 = 119.7$ | $\bar{X}_3 = 145.3$ |

Part of the summary $F$ table looks like this:

| | Sum of Squares | df | SS/df | F |
|---|---|---|---|---|
| Between-groups | 475.3 | | | |
| Within-group | 204.5 | | | |
| Total | 679.8 | | | |

With these summary data, do the following:

a. Identify the independent and dependent variables.

b. Determine the correct number of degrees of freedom, calculate the ratio of sum of squares to degrees of freedom, and determine the $F$ ratio.

c. With an alpha of .01, test the null hypothesis that the three population means are equal against the alternative hypothesis that some of them are different.

d. If appropriate, conduct a mean comparison for each pair of means using Tukey's HSD test.

e. Calculate the value of eta squared, and make a conclusion about the strength of the relationship between sanction policy and the rate of drunk driving.

8. In a 2014 article, Nancy Steinmetz and Mark Austin suggested that there are areas of a college campus that might be characterized as evoking a greater fear of crime. These "fear spots" are defined geographical areas where people feel vulnerable to criminal victimization. As a research project, you want to find out why particular areas are feared more than others. You think it is because people's perceptions of their risk of criminal victimization are strongly related to their actual risks of being the victim of a crime. Let's say that you identified five geographical areas in your city that vary in terms of how much fear people felt when going into those areas ("high fear" spot to "very low fear" spot). You then went into each of those areas and asked a random sample of 50 people how many times they had been the victim of a crime in the last five years. You found the following mean numbers of victimizations for these areas:

| | Very High Fear Spot | High Fear Spot | Medium Fear Spot | Low Fear Spot | Very Low Fear Spot |
|---|---|---|---|---|---|
| Mean | 14.5 | 14.3 | 14.7 | 13.4 | 13.9 |
| n | 50 | 50 | 50 | 50 | 50 |

Part of your summary $F$ table looks like this:

| | Sum of Squares | df | SS/df | F |
|---|---|---|---|---|
| Between | 12.5 | | | |
| Within | 616.2 | | | |
| Total | 628.7 | | | |

With these summary data, do the following:

a. Identify the independent and dependent variables.

b. Determine the correct number of degrees of freedom, calculate the ratio of sum of squares to degrees of freedom, and determine the $F$ ratio.

c. With an alpha of .05, test the null hypothesis that the four population means are equal against the alternative hypothesis that some of them are different.

d. If appropriate, conduct a mean comparison for all pairs of means using Tukey's HSD test.

e. Calculate the value of eta squared, and make a conclusion about the strength of the relationship between fear spot and number of actual criminal victimizations.

9. In their study of the influence of delinquent peers, Constance Chapple, Jamie Vaske, and Meredith Worthen (2014) have suggested that females who have more friends are at greater risk for receiving delinquent peer pressure. To test their notion, you take a random sample of girls and classify them into one of three groups: those who (1) "have a lot of friends," (2) those who "have some friends," and (3) those who "have a few friends." You then ask each girl to self-report the number of delinquent offenses her friends had encouraged her to do. The following table shows the number of delinquent acts encouraged by friends for each female:

Number of Delinquent Acts Committed

| How Many Friends Each Female Has: | | |
|---|---|---|
| A Lot | Some | Few |
| 5 | 7 | 2 |
| 8 | 5 | 3 |
| 9 | 4 | 0 |
| 4 | 9 | 3 |
| 7 | 6 | 1 |
| 10 | 4 | 3 |
| 6 | 7 | 2 |

With these data, do the following:

a. Identify the independent and dependent variables.

b. Calculate the total, between-groups, and within-group sum of squares.

c. Determine the correct number of degrees of freedom, calculate the ratio of sum of squares to degrees of freedom, and determine the $F$ ratio.

d. With an alpha of .05, test the null hypothesis that the three population means are equal against the alternative hypothesis that some of them are different.

e. If appropriate, conduct a mean comparison for each pair of means using Tukey's HSD test.

f. Calculate the value of eta squared, and make a conclusion about the strength of the relationship between the number of friends a girl has and the number of crimes she is encouraged to do by her peers.

## SPSS Exercises

➤ Explore additional data sets. **⑤SAGE** edge™

| Data for Exercise | |
|---|---|
| Data Set | Description |
| Monitoring the future 2013 grade 10.sav | This data set contains variables from the 2013 Monitoring the Future (MTF) study. These data cover a national sample of 10th graders, with a focus on monitoring substance use and abuse. |

| Variables for Exercise | |
|---|---|
| Variable Name | Description |
| V1070 | A student's race, where 1 = Black, 2 = White, and 3 = Hispanic. |
| Schoolskip | A count of the number of days a student has skipped school or classes. |
| V7253 | An ordinal measure asking whether the student has any friends who have dropped out of school, where 1 = none, 2 = a few, 3 = some, and 4 = most if not all. |
| LowParentEduc | A three-category summary of both parent's education, where 0 = both parents have high-school degrees, 1 = one parent has less than a high-school education, 2 = both parents have less than a high-school degree. |
| V7214 | An ordinal measure asking students the number of hours they are home alone after school on a typical day. Responses range from 1 = 0 hours to 6 = 5 or more hours. |
| Smokedrink | A continuous index measuring the quantity and frequency of smoking and drinking self-reported by respondents. |

1. Are students of different races more likely to skip out on school? Criminologists are interested in this question because school acts as a form of social control; if you're at school, you won't have as many chances to engage in crime or interact with the justice system! We can test this question using a one-way ANOVA in SPSS with the variables SchoolSkip and V1070:

   a. First, state the null and research hypotheses for this ANOVA.

   b. Second, determine the critical value of $F$ you will need for your results to be significant at $p < .01$. You will need to calculate your within- and between-groups degrees of freedom in this case; in this case, $n = 10,216$ and $k = 3$.

   c. **Estimating an ANOVA model in SPSS:** Doing this by hand would take weeks, but SPSS does it in seconds. To do this, select "analyze->compare means->one-way ANOVA." Place the variable V1070 in the "factor" slot and SchoolSkip in the dependent list:

      i. Output provided gives the sum of squares within and between groups, your degrees of freedom, and $F$ statistics. It also provides the $p$ value for your specific $F$ statistic.

   d. What is your $F$ statistic? What do you conclude about the null hypothesis in this case?

2. You may have noticed that an ANOVA test on its own isn't a very precise assessment of our research question. Let's follow this up by estimating the difference between pairs of means and the strength of the association:

   a. **Post Hoc Tests in ANOVA:** In the one-wave ANOVA menu, you will notice an option to "post-hoc" tests. Click that button and select "Tukey," which will give you an estimation of Tukey's Honest Significant Difference:

      i. The output provided compares one racial category with all the others, providing the statistical significance of each difference. So, for instance, the first row compares Blacks against Whites and shows that difference between the means for Blacks and Whites is .449 days skipped.

      ii. Interpret the remaining differences between racial groups. Are all groups significantly different from one another? Which group means closest/furthest from one another?

      iii. What new information does this test add to our ANOVA interpretation?

   b. By using the ANOVA sum of squares output, calculate $\eta^2$ by hand:

      i. What new information does this statistic tell us?

      ii. Consider the difference between statistical and substantive significance. Do we have both in this case?

3. Do students who hang out with individuals who drop out of school also tend to skip out on school themselves? Run a one-way ANOVA test with pairwise comparisons and estimate $\eta^2$ (by hand) using the variables V7253 and SchoolSkip:

   a. Conduct the hypothesis test fully, stating your null hypotheses and identifying test statistics ($n = 12,449$ and $k = 4$ in this case). What do you conclude about the null hypothesis?

   b. What do the pairwise comparisons in this case tell you? What groups are most prone to skipping school?

   c. What does $\eta^2$ tell us in this case; what proportion of the variability in school skipping can be explained by one's peer network?

   d. By thinking substantively, what does this tell us about the role of peer networks? Do you think it might relate to other areas of deviant behavior as well?

4. Are kids that have lots of unsupervised time more likely to use alcohol or drugs than other kids? Use variables SmokeDrink and V7214 to test this hypothesis. Also estimate pairwise comparisons and $\eta^2$:

   a. Conduct the hypothesis test fully, stating your null hypotheses and identifying test statistics ($n = 12,169$ and $k = 6$ in this case). What do you conclude about the relationship?

   b. What do the pairwise comparisons in this case tell you? Use an alpha of .001 for this test. Are any groups not statistically different? It may help visually rank each group against one another in a diagram.

   c. What does $\eta^2$ tell us in this case?

   d. Given your results, what are your policy recommendations?

5. Often researchers talk about the importance of socioeconomic status in producing heightened risk for criminal and delinquent activity. The education of a student's parents is one way to look at this difference. Let's see whether the variable LowParentEduc is associated with higher levels of student smoking and drinking:

   a. Conduct a hypothesis test to examine whether there is a relationship between parent education and child alcohol and tobacco use. Fully state your null hypotheses and identifying test statistics ($n = 10,726$ and $k = 3$ in this case). What do you conclude about the relationship?

b.  What do the pairwise comparisons in this case tell you? Use an alpha of .001 for this test. Are any groups not statistically different from one another?

c.  What does $\eta^2$ tell us in this case?

d.  Take a moment to consider the "why" part of this result; what mechanisms might explain why the results you have found might lead to delinquent behaviors?

# CHAPTER 12

# Bivariate Correlation and Regression

"

*There's absolutely no correlation between qualifying for the Open and playing in the Open, other than it gets you here. I would rather shoot under par at the Open than 59 screwing around at home.*

—Olin Browne

*One of the first things taught in introductory statistics textbooks is that correlation is not causation. It is also one of the first things forgotten.*

"

—Thomas Sowell

**LEARNING OBJECTIVES**

1. Describe the difference between a positive and a negative relationship between two continuous (interval/ratio) level variables.

2. Conduct and interpret a scatterplot between two continuous (interval/ratio) level variables.

3. Calculate and interpret the correlation coefficient and the coefficient of determination.

4. Describe how the ordinary least-squares (OLS) regression equation is different from the correlation coefficient and why they are both useful.

5. Calculate and interpret the OLS regression equation, and interpret the intercept and slope coefficient.

6. Explain how to use the OLS regression equation for prediction.

7. Conduct and interpret null hypothesis tests for both the correlation and slope coefficients.

# Introduction

You have probably heard the adage that "correlation is not causation," but you have probably never known the true meaning of correlation. Although we have discussed several different statistics to test the significance of bivariate relationships already, in this chapter, we will introduce you to the correlation coefficient along with its counterpart, the ordinary least-squares (OLS) regression coefficient. Whenever both an independent and a dependent variable are measured at the interval/ratio level, the strength of the association or relationship between them is usually referred to as the correlation between two variables. And when we have only one independent variable, the relationship is referred to as a **bivariate correlation**. In this chapter, you first will learn how to construct a scatterplot graphically depicting the relationship between a quantitative independent variable and a quantitative dependent variable. You will then learn about the statistics that

> **Bivariate correlation:** Measures the linear relationship between two variables.

quantify this relationship, including the correlation coefficient, the coefficient of determination, and the slope coefficient from an ordinary least-squares regression equation. The measures all assume that the relationship between the independent and the dependent variable is linear. Our attention in this chapter will be limited to the bivariate case, where we have one independent variable ($x$) and one dependent variable ($y$). In Chapter 13, we will examine the multivariate case, where we have more than one independent variable.

# Graphing the Bivariate Distribution Between Two Quantitative Variables: Scatterplots

Throughout this book we have tried to stress the importance and usefulness of displaying data graphically. Let us again remind you that it is no less true in statistics as in real life that "a picture is worth a thousand words." When you are first examining two interval- and ratio-level variables, one of the most instructive things you can do is to draw a picture or graph of what the two variables look like when examined together. In the bivariate case, the graphical display of two interval- and ratio-level variables is called a **scattergram** or **scatterplot**. It is called this because the picture looks like points scattered across your graph. The pattern, or scatter, of data points provides valuable information about the relationship (or lack of a relationship) between the variables. Let's begin this discussion with a simple illustration. In the list that follows, we have data on two variables for 10 observations:

> **Scatterplot:** Graphical display of the linear relationship between two interval/ratio-level variables. Also called a scattergram.

| Observation | x Score | y Score |
| --- | --- | --- |
| 1 | 3 | 3 |
| 2 | 5 | 5 |
| 3 | 2 | 2 |
| 4 | 4 | 4 |
| 5 | 8 | 8 |
| 6 | 10 | 10 |
| 7 | 1 | 1 |
| 8 | 7 | 7 |
| 9 | 6 | 6 |
| 10 | 9 | 9 |

**Get the edge on your studies.**
edge.sagepub.com/bachmansccj4e

- Take a quiz to find out what you've learned.
- Review key terms with eFlashcards.
- Explore additional data sets.

We can construct a scatterplot for these data by first drawing a graph with two axes. The first axis of this graph is the horizontal axis ($x$), or abscissa. The second axis of the graph is formed at a right angle to the first axis and is the vertical axis ($y$), or ordinate. We will label the horizontal axis the $x$ axis and will display the $x$ variable on that axis. To do this, simply place the original measurement scale for the $x$ variable at equal intervals along the axis. We will label the vertical axis the $y$ axis and will display the $y$ variable along that axis. Again, place the measurement scale for the $y$ variable along the vertical axis.

Once you have done this, you can begin to graph your data points. For each observation, find the position of its $x$ score along the horizontal axis. Then follow in a straight line up from that point until you find the corresponding position of its $y$ score along the vertical axis. Place a dot or point here. For example, for the first observation, go along the $x$ axis until you find "3." Then go straight up from that point until you reach "3" on the $y$ axis. Place a point here. This point represents the position on the graph for the $xy$ score of the first observation who had a score of 3 on both the $x$ and the $y$ variable. Continue to do this for each of the 10 observations, placing a point when you have found the intersection of each $x$ and $y$ score. You can see the collection of data points, called the scatterplot, in Figure 12.1.

What does this scatterplot tell us about the $x$ and $y$ scores? Note that all the scores fall on a straight line that ascends from the bottom left of the scatterplot to the top right. This is because in this case, there is a unique relationship between the $x$ and $y$ scores. The $y$ score is always the same as its corresponding $x$ score. That is, if the $y$ score is 4, the corresponding $x$ score is 4, and if $y$ is 6, the $x$ score is 6. Therefore, those observations that have high $x$ scores also have high $y$ scores, and those with low $x$ scores have low $y$ scores. Note also that when the $x$ score increases by one unit, the $y$ score also increases by exactly one unit. For example, when the $x$ score changes from 4 to 5, the corresponding score for the $y$ variable changes from 4 to 5—an increase of one unit. Whenever two variables are related in this manner, when high scores on one variable ($x$) also have high scores on a second variable ($y$) and an increase in one score is associated with an increase in the other score, we have a **positive correlation**, or positive relationship, between $x$ and $y$. As you can clearly see, there is a clear pattern to this data with increasing $x$ scores corresponding to increasing $y$ scores.

**Positive correlation:** As the independent variable increases, the dependent variable also increases.

In the list that follows and in Figure 12.2, we have a different set of $x$ and $y$ scores for 10 observations:

| Observation | x Score | y Score |
|:---:|:---:|:---:|
| 1 | 2 | 9 |
| 2 | 4 | 7 |
| 3 | 9 | 2 |
| 4 | 7 | 4 |
| 5 | 8 | 3 |
| 6 | 1 | 10 |
| 7 | 5 | 6 |
| 8 | 6 | 5 |
| 9 | 10 | 1 |
| 10 | 3 | 8 |

In this case, the data points are still on a straight line, but the pattern is different from that in Figure 12.1. In Figure 12.2, the pattern of the points is one that descends from the top left corner to the bottom right. This is because those observations that have high scores on the $x$ variable have *low* scores on the $y$ variable, and those observations with low scores on the $x$ variable have *high* scores on the $y$ variable. Whenever high scores on

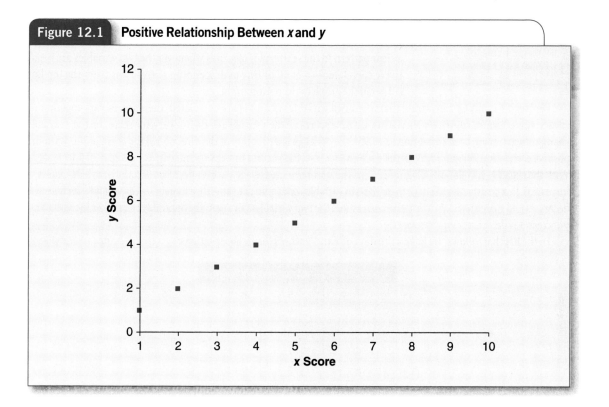

Figure 12.1 Positive Relationship Between *x* and *y*

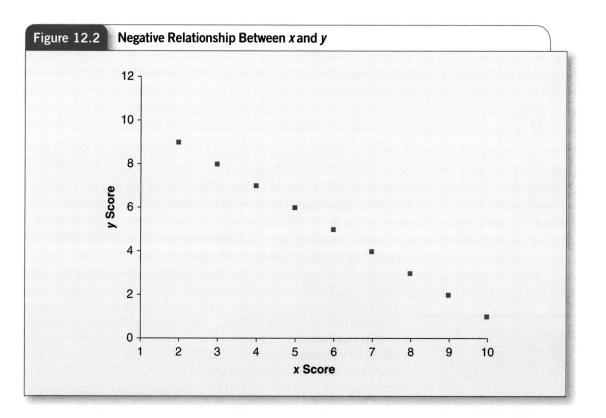

Figure 12.2 Negative Relationship Between *x* and *y*

**Negative correlation:** As the independent variable increases, the dependent variable decreases.

one variable ($x$) correspond to low scores on a second variable ($y$), we have a **negative correlation**, or negative relationship, between $x$ and $y$. There is, then, a clear pattern to the scatterplot of scores whenever the two variables are negatively correlated—a band or line of descending scores runs from the top left corner of the graph to the bottom right.

Figures 12.1 and 12.2 illustrate that when two variables ($x$ and $y$) are correlated, their scores vary together or covary; this is termed *covariation* in statistics. As the scores on the $x$ variable change or vary, the scores on the $y$ variable change or vary. How, or the direction in which, they change is a function of the direction of the correlation. With the positive correlation in Figure 12.1, as the $x$ scores increase, the $y$ scores increase (similarly, as $x$ decreases, $y$ decreases). With the negative correlation in Figure 12.2, as the $x$ scores increase, the $y$ scores decrease (similarly, as $x$ decreases, $y$ increases). In a positive correlation, then, the two variables covary in the same direction ($x$ increases and $y$ increases; $x$ decreases and $y$ decreases). In a negative correlation, the two variables covary in the opposite direction ($x$ increases and $y$ decreases; $x$ decreases and $y$ increases).

In the list that follows, we have a third set of $x$ and $y$ scores for 10 observations:

| Observation | x Score | y Score |
|:---:|:---:|:---:|
| 1 | 6 | 4 |
| 2 | 9 | 4 |
| 3 | 2 | 4 |
| 4 | 7 | 4 |
| 5 | 3 | 4 |
| 6 | 4 | 4 |
| 7 | 1 | 4 |
| 8 | 8 | 4 |
| 9 | 5 | 4 |
| 10 | 10 | 4 |

Figure 12.3 presents the scatterplot of these scores. Note that, unlike the previous two figures, there is no ascending or descending pattern to the scores in this scatterplot. In fact, the scores are perfectly horizontal because for different values of $x$, the $y$ score is always the same ($y = 4$). In other words, the $x$ variable and the $y$ variable do not covary. As $x$ increases or decreases, the value of $y$ stays the same; there is no relationship between $x$ and $y$. To state this one more way, variations in $x$ (increases and decreases) do not result in systematic variations in $y$.

One thing that we can easily learn from a scatterplot, then, is the *direction* of a relationship between two quantitative variables. By the direction of a relationship, we mean whether it is positive or negative. When the scatterplot looks like Figure 12.1, where the pattern of scores resembles an upward slope, we can conclude that the two variables are positively related. In this case, there is positive covariation. When the scatterplot looks like Figure 12.2, where the pattern of scores has a downward slope, we can conclude that the two variables are negatively related. There is negative covariation. And finally, when the scatterplot resembles Figure 12.3, where there is no clear upward or downward slope but a flat line, we can presume that the two variables are not correlated with one another.

In addition to the direction of a relationship, what else can we determine by examining the scatterplot of $x$ and $y$ scores? Let's return to the data illustrated in Figure 12.1. Without being too precise, let's draw a straight line that

**Regression line:** Line depicting the relationship between independent and dependent variables determined by an ordinary least-squares regression equation.

goes through each data point. We have shown this in Figure 12.4. This figure illustrates that if we were to connect the data points, the straight line would go through each data point in its upward slope. In other words, each point would fall exactly on that straight upward-moving line. Later in this chapter we will have more to say about how to fit this straight line to our data points. For now we will simply note that this line is called the linear **regression line**. In the example presented in Figures 12.1 and 12.4, where all the data points fall exactly on a straight upward-sloping line, we say that the two variables have a *perfect positive correlation*: positive because the regression line slopes upward, and perfect because all the points fall exactly on the line. Note that we can also draw a straight line through the data points in Figure 12.2, as shown in Figure 12.5. Here again, all the data points lie precisely on the line, but in this case, the line slopes downward. This figure illustrates a *perfect negative correlation* between two variables.

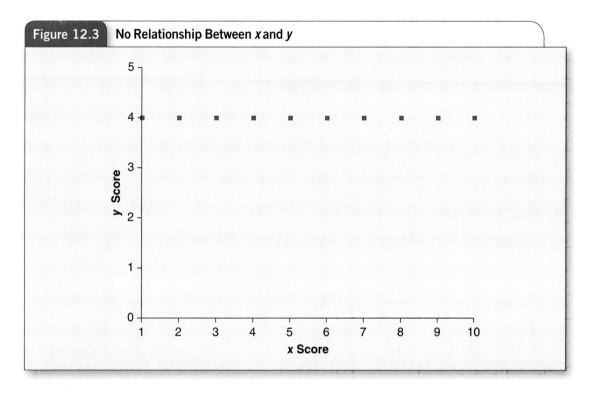

**Figure 12.3**  No Relationship Between *x* and *y*

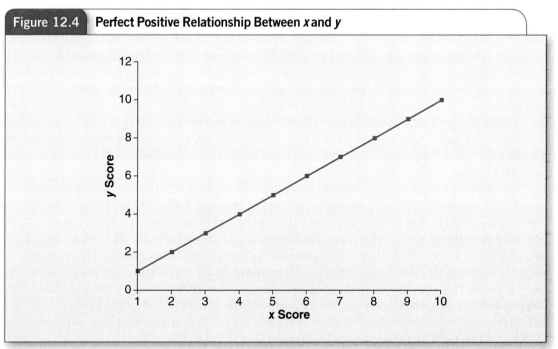

**Figure 12.4**  Perfect Positive Relationship Between *x* and *y*

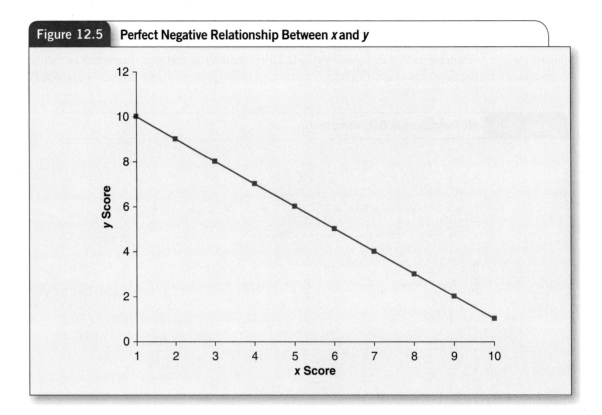

**Figure 12.5** Perfect Negative Relationship Between *x* and *y*

A line through the data points in Figure 12.3 is shown in Figure 12.6. Note that this straight line has neither an upward slope nor a downward slope but is instead a flat line that is horizontal to the *x* axis. This line has no slope. As we suggested earlier, in this example, we have no correlation between *x* and *y*. It might be said that Figure 12.6 presents an example of two variables with absolutely no correlation.

In addition to direction, the second valuable thing we can learn from a scatterplot, then, is an indication of the *strength* or *magnitude* of the relationship. The strength of a relationship can be judged by examining the spread of the data points around a straight line, called the regression line, which passes through them. The closer the data points are to this line, the stronger the relationship or correlation between the two variables. In a perfect positive or perfect negative linear relationship, all of the data points fall exactly on a straight regression line that passes through each data point. The farther the data points are from the line, the weaker the correlation between the two variables. When the two variables are not correlated at all (perfect noncorrelation or no relationship), the points still lie on a straight line, but this line is perfectly horizontal (parallel to the *x* axis). Of course, we never have perfect relationships. We have used these examples of perfect relationships simply to illustrate the concept of the direction and magnitude of a linear relationship.

There is one other very important thing we can learn from a scatterplot, and that is how to predict the score on one variable (the *y* variable) from the score on another variable (the *x* variable). Figures 12.7 and 12.8 show the previous examples of a perfect positive correlation between *x* and *y* and no correlation, respectively. In these figures, the two axes and the straight regression line have been extended to include additional scores. Let's first look at Figure 12.7. In this figure we want to predict what someone's *y* score would be if she or he had an *x* score of 12. To find the *predicted value* of *y* (denoted by the symbol ($\hat{y}$) to distinguish it from its *actual value y*), we first find the value of *x* on the *x* axis (*x* = 12); next we draw a straight line up to the regression line, and then, from that point, we draw another straight line parallel to the *x* axis across to the *y* axis. The predicted value of *y* ($\hat{y}$) is the value of *y* where this line touches the *y* axis. In this case, our predicted value of *y* with *x* = 12 would be 12 ($\hat{y}$ = 12). We could follow the same procedure and determine that for *x* = 13, our predicted *y* score would also be 13.

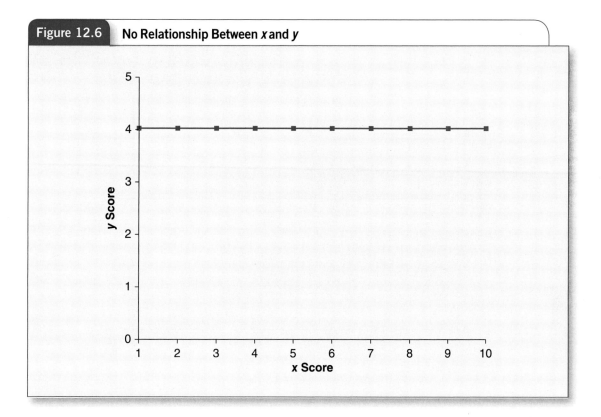

**Figure 12.6** No Relationship Between *x* and *y*

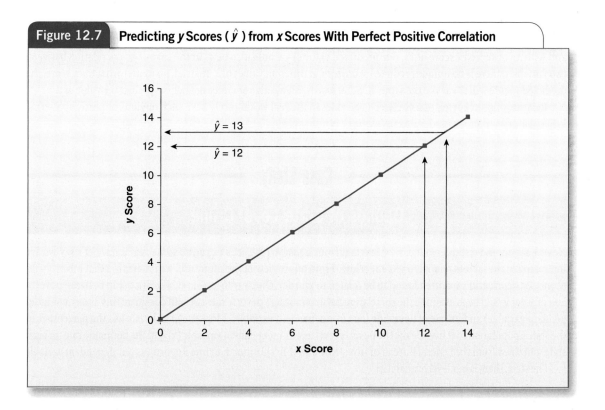

**Figure 12.7** Predicting *y* Scores ($\hat{y}$) from *x* Scores With Perfect Positive Correlation

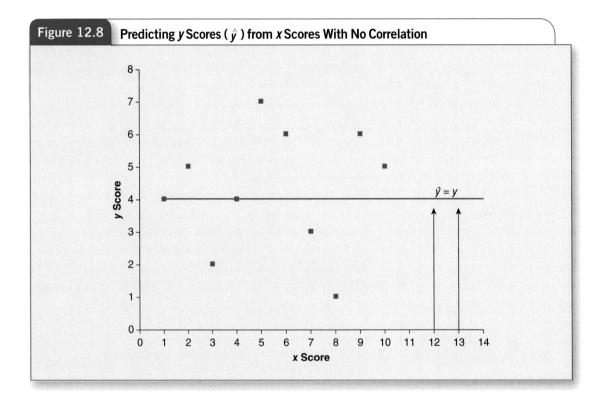

**Figure 12.8** Predicting *y* Scores ($\hat{y}$) from *x* Scores With No Correlation

In Figure 12.8, which shows no strong correlation between *x* and *y*, we could also make predictions about *y* based on information about *x*, but in this case, the predictions would all be the same. That is, no matter what the observed *x* score, if we were to draw a straight line up from the *x* axis to the regression line and then another line over to the *y* axis, we would have the same predicted *y* score ($\hat{y} = 4$). With an observed *x* score of 12 our predicted *y* would be 4, and with an observed *x* score of 13, our predicted value of *y* would also be 4. In the case of no correlation between two variables, there is no unique predicted score for *y* at different values of *x*. Instead, no matter what the *x* score, the predicted *y* score will always be the same. In other words, knowledge of *x* does not help us predict the value of *y*.

Relationships or correlations between variables in the real world rarely have such obvious or perfect patterns. When real crime data are used, patterns become a little less clear.

## Case Study

## Causes of State-Level Crime

Now that you understand what can be learned from a scatterplot, let's examine some real data. Let's say we are interested in the factors related to violent crime. From our review of the literature, we determine that poverty and economic deprivation are often found to be related to murder. One way to look at this relationship between poverty and murder would be to examine the correlation between a state's poverty rate (we will designate this as our *x* or independent variable) and its rate of homicide (our *y* or dependent variable). More specifically, we use the percentage of the state's population that lives below the poverty level as our independent variable (*x*) and the homicide rate for each state, obtained from the Federal Bureau of Investigation's (FBI's) Uniform Crime Reports, as our dependent variable (*y*). The state, then, is our level of analysis.

To examine this issue, we take a random sample of 20 states ($n = 20$) and record the murder rate in each state ($y$), along with the state's rate of poverty for the year 2013 ($x$). These data are shown in Table 12.1. Based on these data, we create the scatterplot displayed in Figure 12.9. This was created the same way the other scatterplots were, by first drawing the $x$ and $y$ axes to accommodate both variables and then simply finding the data point for each case. For example, for the first state, Alaska, we go over to 9.0 on the horizontal or $x$ axis and then up to 3.2 on the vertical or $y$ axis. This point then becomes the point that represents Alaska on our scatterplot.

What kind of relationship do you see in Figure 12.9? By "eyeballing" the data, we can draw a straight line that we think runs though the data points; however, unlike our hypothetical data, these data points do not all fall perfectly on any one line. Instead, we will have to draw our line in such a way that it comes as close to all the data points as possible. A line that appears to fit the data is drawn through the scatterplot and displayed in Figure 12.10. As before, we will use this line to summarize the pattern and strength of the relationship between our two variables, keeping in mind that we know the further the points are away from the line, the weaker the linear relationship, positive or negative.

Based on what we have learned so far in this chapter, we can conclude two things from this scatterplot. First, there does seem to be a positive correlation between poverty and murder rates. The general pattern of the data points, and the line that runs through them, is an upward slope, indicating that as the rate of poverty increases (as $x$ increases), the murder rate also increases ($y$ increases). States that have high poverty rates, then, also tend to have higher rates of murder. Second, the correlation between the two variables is far from perfect. None of the data points falls exactly on the straight line.

| Table 12.1 | Murder Rate per 100,000 and Percentage of Individuals in State Living Below the Poverty Level for 20 States, 2013 | |
|---|---|---|
| State | Murder Rate y | Poverty Rate x |
| Alaska | 3.2 | 9.0 |
| Arizona | 5.5 | 16.5 |
| California | 5.4 | 14.2 |
| Delaware | 4.6 | 10.8 |
| Florida | 5.5 | 14.9 |
| Indiana | 5.3 | 14.4 |
| Louisiana | 12.3 | 17.3 |
| Maine | 2.0 | 12.3 |
| Maryland | 7.7 | 9.1 |
| Massachusetts | 2.7 | 10.3 |
| Michigan | 6.3 | 16.2 |
| Missouri | 6.6 | 14.6 |
| Nebraska | 2.5 | 12.3 |
| New Jersey | 3.7 | 9.4 |
| New Mexico | 10.0 | 18.0 |
| New York | 4.0 | 14.2 |
| Pennsylvania | 5.4 | 12.5 |
| South Carolina | 6.7 | 17.1 |
| Texas | 5.4 | 17.2 |
| Wyoming | 2.0 | 9.8 |

*Source:* Adapted from the Uniform Crime Reports and *Population by Age and Sex 2014* from the FBI and the U.S. Bureau of the Census, respectively.

In fact, many of these points lie fairly far below the line or above it. What we can tell from this scatterplot, then, is that we have a nonperfect positive correlation between a state's murder rate and its poverty rate. These types of relationships are more typical of real crime data than the hypothetical data we examined earlier.

In Table 12.2, we have the same random sample of states but two different variables. In this table, the $x$ variable is the percentage of the population in the state that lives in a nonmetropolitan (rural) area, and the $y$ variable is the rate of robbery. We examine this relationship because we suspect that there is a correlation between how rural or nonmetropolitan a state is and its robbery rate. We think that rural states have lower rates of robbery than urban states because they are likely to be more cohesive, more homogeneous, and less socially disorganized. This is a prediction based on the early "Chicago School" of crime and social disorganization.

Figure 12.11 depicts the scatterplot of the data in Table 12.2. Here we see a downward-sloping pattern of data points. This indicates the existence of a negative correlation between rural population and violent crime. States that are more rural, such as Alaska and Maine, have lower rates of robbery than the less rural states like California. As in the

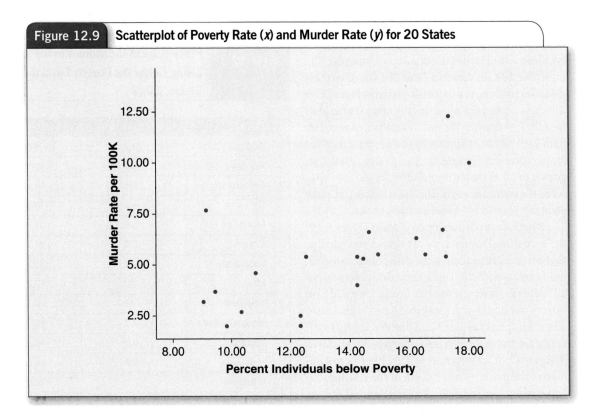

Figure 12.9 | Scatterplot of Poverty Rate (*x*) and Murder Rate (*y*) for 20 States

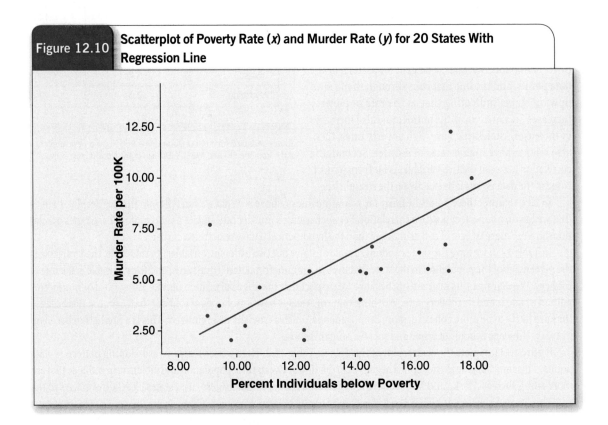

Figure 12.10 | Scatterplot of Poverty Rate (*x*) and Murder Rate (*y*) for 20 States With Regression Line

| Table 12.2 | Robbery Rate per 100,000 and Percentage of Individuals in State Living in Rural Areas for 20 States, 2013 | | | | | |
|---|---|---|---|---|---|---|

| State | Robbery Rate y | % Rural x | State | Robbery Rate y | % Rural x |
|---|---|---|---|---|---|
| Alaska | 94.0 | 30.4 | Michigan | 126.5 | 25.5 |
| Arizona | 123.9 | 9.5 | Missouri | 127.1 | 28.6 |
| California | 173.7 | 5.1 | Nebraska | 74.7 | 28.4 |
| Delaware | 189.7 | 17.4 | New Jersey | 133.7 | 5.4 |
| Florida | 166.8 | 9.1 | New Mexico | 98.7 | 22.1 |
| Indiana | 129.4 | 27.4 | New York | 144.5 | 12.3 |
| Louisiana | 142.3 | 27.0 | Pennsylvania | 142.4 | 22.2 |
| Maine | 30.3 | 57.4 | South Carolina | 126.0 | 34.3 |
| Maryland | 210.7 | 12.8 | Texas | 153.6 | 14.5 |
| Massachusetts | 114.1 | 8.4 | Wyoming | 14.3 | 30.5 |

*Source:* Adapted from the Uniform Crime Reports and *Population by Age and Sex* 2014 from the FBI and the U.S. Bureau of the Census, respectively.

| Figure 12.11 | Scatterplot of Percent Rural (*x*) and Robbery Rate (*y*) for 20 States With Regression Line |
|---|---|

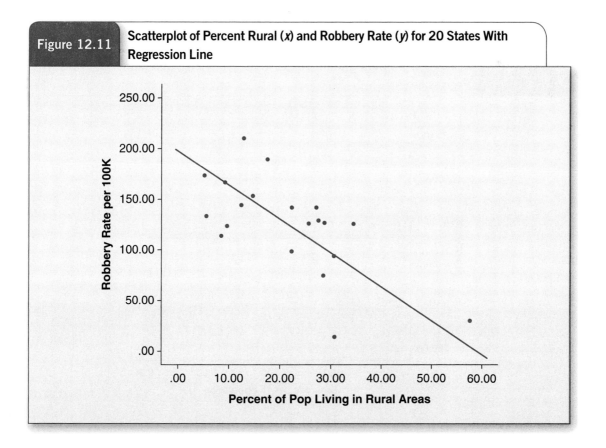

| Table 12.3 | Burglary Rate per 100,000 and Divorce Rate per 1,000 in State Living in Rural Areas for 20 States, 2013 | | | | | |
|---|---|---|---|---|---|---|

| State | Burglary Rate y | Divorce Rate x | State | Burglary Rate y | Divorce Rate x |
|---|---|---|---|---|---|
| Alaska | 514.2 | 7.8 | Michigan | 768.1 | 5.4 |
| Arizona | 817.3 | 5.4 | Missouri | 733.5 | 6.5 |
| California | 622.1 | 5.8 | Nebraska | 499.4 | 6.7 |
| Delaware | 784.0 | 5.4 | New Jersey | 424.2 | 5.1 |
| Florida | 981.2 | 7.5 | New Mexico | 1117.3 | 5.1 |
| Indiana | 815.9 | 7.9 | New York | 321.6 | 6.4 |
| Louisiana | 1036.4 | 7.1 | Pennsylvania | 439.2 | 5.3 |
| Maine | 510.4 | 7.2 | South Carolina | 991.7 | 7.4 |
| Maryland | 647.5 | 5.8 | Texas | 967.4 | 7.1 |
| Massachusetts | 524.1 | 5.5 | Wyoming | 399.8 | 8.2 |

*Source:* Adapted from the Uniform Crime Reports and *Population by Age and Sex* 2014 from the FBI and the U.S. Bureau of the Census, respectively.

| Figure 12.12 | Scatterplot of Divorce (*x*) and Burglary Rate (*y*) for 20 States With Regression Line |
|---|---|

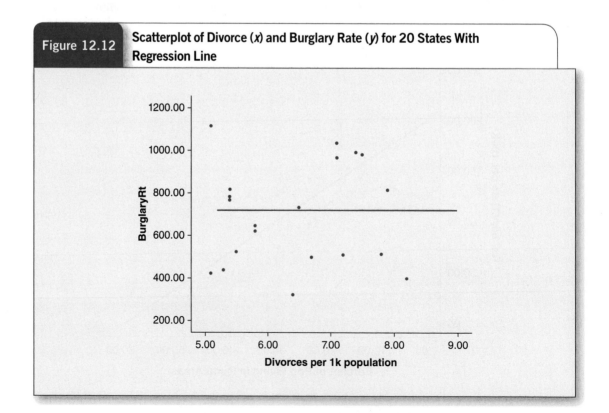

last example, however, the negative correlation between rural population and robbery rates is less than perfect. Not all of the points lie exactly on the regression line.

Let's say we make a third conjecture about our random sample of 20 states. Let's hypothesize that states with high divorce rates also have high rates of burglary. In Table 12.3, we record the number of divorces per 1,000 residents of each state on the $x$ axis and the burglary rate on the $y$ axis. We create a scatterplot for these data in Figure 12.12. Unlike the other two scatterplots using the state-level crime data, however, this one has no clear or discernable pattern. That is, it neither slopes upward nor downward. Also, unlike our hypothetical data, these data points do not lie on a perfectly horizontal line. The line that probably best describes this pattern of data would generally be flat, running through the middle of the data. Moreover, most data points in this scatterplot would be far from the straight line we drew. From this, we would conclude that there probably is very little correlation between these two variables.

In sum, by graphically representing the relationship between two interval- and ratio-level variables in a scatterplot, we can learn about the direction of the relationship or correlation between $x$ and $y$—and a little bit about its strength. If the pattern of the data points and a line drawn through them is an ascending one, we can conclude that the correlation between $x$ and $y$ is positive and linear. If the pattern is a descending one, we can conclude that the correlation is negative and linear. If there is no pattern to the data and the line we draw through the data points is almost horizontal, we may conclude that there is very little correlation between the two variables. We can estimate the strength of the relationship by examining the distance between the actual data points and the straight line. The closer the data points cluster around this line, the stronger the correlation between $x$ and $y$. Correlations that are not strong generally have data points that fall far above and/or below the line. It would be nice if there were a numerical indicator that told us the extent of correlation between two variables, wouldn't it? Fortunately there is, and we discuss it next.

## ▣ The Pearson Correlation Coefficient

The statistic used to measure the linear correlation between two interval- and ratio level variables is called the **Pearson correlation coefficient** or *Pearson product-moment correlation coefficient*. We will refer to this statistic simply as Pearson's *r,* named after its originator, the statistician Karl Pearson. Pearson's *r* measures the strength of the *linear* correlation between two continuous (interval- and ratio-level) variables. The statistic *r* is our sample estimate of the correlation between the two variables in the population. The population correlation coefficient is designated by ρ, the Greek letter rho.

> **Pearson correlation coefficient:**
> Statistic that quantifies the direction and strength of the relationship between two interval/ratio-level variables.

Pearson's correlation coefficient is standardized. By this we mean that the magnitude of *r* does not depend on the natural units of measurement of the *x* and *y* variables (dollars, crimes, IQ points). No matter what the unit of measurement, Pearson's *r* assumes a value of 0 whenever there is no linear correlation between two variables, and it attains a maximum value of ±1.0 when there is a perfect linear correlation between two variables. Figure 12.13 displays a guide to aid you in the interpretation of Pearson's *r.* A correlation of ±1.0 occurs when all points fall exactly on a straight regression line. A Pearson correlation coefficient of +1.00 means that there is a perfect positive correlation between two variables (as in Figure 12.1), an *r* of −1.00 means that there is a perfect negative correlation (as in Figure 12.2), and an *r* of 0.00 means that there is absolutely no linear relationship. The closer the data points cluster around the regression line, the stronger the correlation between the two variables, and the higher the value of *r* will be. If there is no linear pattern in data points, the value of *r* will be closer to zero, indicating very little linear relationship between the two variables.

The calculation of Pearson's *r* is relatively straightforward and involves arithmetic operations you are already very familiar with. As with other statistical formulas, we will provide you with both a definitional formula, which

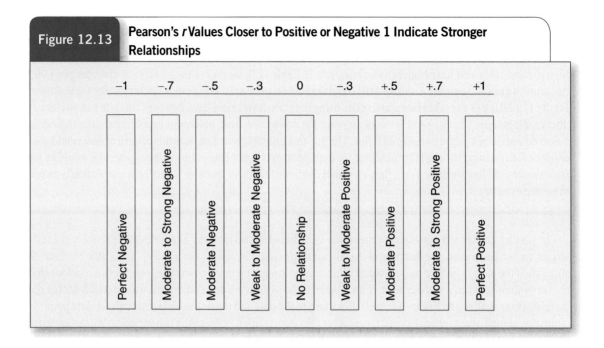

**Figure 12.13** Pearson's *r* Values Closer to Positive or Negative 1 Indicate Stronger Relationships

| −1 | −.7 | −.5 | −.3 | 0 | −.3 | +.5 | +.7 | +1 |

Perfect Negative | Moderate to Strong Negative | Moderate Negative | Weak to Moderate Negative | No Relationship | Weak to Moderate Positive | Moderate Positive | Moderate to Strong Positive | Perfect Positive

more clearly defines the foundation of the statistic, and a computational formula that is easier to use. The definitional formula for Pearson's *r* is:

$$r = \frac{\Sigma(x-\overline{X})(y-\overline{Y})}{\sqrt{\left[\Sigma(x-\overline{X})^2\right]\left[\Sigma(y-\overline{Y})^2\right]}} \tag{12-1}$$

The first term in the numerator of this equation is simply the difference between an *x* score and its mean, whereas the second term is the difference between a *y* score and its mean. In the definitional formula for the correlation coefficient, we multiply these difference scores by each other, we do this for each pair of difference scores, and then we sum over all scores. In other words, we take the difference between the first person's *x* score and the mean of *x*, take the difference between the first person's *y* score and the mean of *y*, and then multiply those two differences. We do this for each observation and sum over observations. Since the mean is defined in statistical terms as the *first moment,* the terms $(x - \overline{X})$ and $(y - \overline{Y})$ are referred to as the first moments about the mean. The correlation coefficient, then, is based on the product of the first moments about the mean of *x* and *y*; hence, it is often referred to as the *product-moment* correlation coefficient.

The product of $(x - \overline{X})$ and $(y - \overline{Y})$ captures the *covariation* between *x* and *y*. That is, it measures the extent to which the *x* and *y* scores vary together, or covary. The stronger the relationship between the two variables, the greater the covariance. A covariation of zero implies that the two variables are not correlated, a positive covariation implies positive correlation, and a negative covariation implies negative correlation. We cannot simply use the size of the covariation as our measure of correlation, however. First of all, the magnitude of the covariation is a function of the measurement units of the variables. For example, other things being equal, we would obtain a much greater covariation if one of our variables were measured in pennies rather than dollars or days rather than months or years. Second, the covariance can often be greater than 1.0, so we have no clear interpretation for it. We can, however, standardize the covariation—that is, make its value independent of the units of measurement. We do this by dividing the covariation in *x* and *y* by a term that includes both the variation in *x* and the variation in *y*. These terms form the denominator of the correlation coefficient in equation 12-1, and it should look very familiar to you. It is simply the product of two terms: the amount of variation in the *x* variable and the amount of variation in the *y* variable. The correlation coefficient, then, expresses the ratio of the covariation in $x$ and $y$ to the product of the variation in $x$ and the variation in $y$. It has a lower limit of $-1.0$ and an upper limit of $+1.0$ and is equal to 0 if there is no linear relationship between two variables.

As you can imagine from going over formula 12-1 in your head, the necessary calculations to estimate $r$ are enough to make you faint. Fortunately, there is a computational formula that involves fewer operations and, therefore, fewer chances of making computational errors. The computing formula for the Pearson correlation coefficient is:

$$r = \frac{n\Sigma xy - (\Sigma x)(\Sigma y)}{\sqrt{\left[ n\Sigma x^2 - (\Sigma x)^2 \right]\left[ n\Sigma y^2 - (\Sigma y)^2 \right]}}$$

(12-2)

Even this formula may appear forbidding to you, but fear not, we can break it down into five simple components that we can then plug into the formula and solve. The computational formula requires the following five sums:

1. $\Sigma xy =$ the sum of each $x$ score times its corresponding $y$ score
2. $\Sigma x =$ the sum of the $x$ scores
3. $\Sigma y =$ the sum of the $y$ scores
4. $\Sigma x^2 =$ the sum of the squared $x$ scores ( $x_1^2 + x_2^2 + \cdots + x_n^2$ )
5. $\Sigma y^2 =$ the sum of the squared $y$ scores ( $y_1^2 + y_2^2 + \cdots + y_n^2$ )

We will use this computational formula to calculate the value of $r$ for the state data in Tables 12.1, 12.2, and 12.3. In calculating the value of $r$, it will be helpful if you first calculate each of the five sums and then insert them into the formula. A listing of the sums in separate columns will make keeping track of the different components of the formula easier. We have provided these calculations in Tables 12.4, 12.5, and 12.6, although you should first try to calculate them yourself.

For the state-level data in Table 12.4, which reports the murder rates and poverty rates for 20 randomly selected states, we calculate the value of $r$ as follows:

$$r = \frac{n\Sigma xy - (\Sigma x)(\Sigma y)}{\sqrt{\left[ n\Sigma x^2 - (\Sigma x)^2 \right]\left[ n\Sigma y^2 - (\Sigma y)^2 \right]}}$$

$$r = \frac{(20)(1,535.1) - (270.1)(106.8)}{\sqrt{\left[ (20)(3,821.8) - (270.1)^2 \right]\left[ (20)(697.8) - (106.8)^2 \right]}}$$

$$r = \frac{30,702 - 28,846.7}{\sqrt{\left[ 76,436 - 72,954 \right]\left[ 13,956 - 11,406.2 \right]}}$$

$$r = \frac{1,855.3}{\sqrt{(3,482)(2,549.8)}}$$

$$r = \frac{1,855.3}{\sqrt{8,878,403.6}}$$

$$r = \frac{1,855.3}{2,979.7}$$

$$r = .62$$

| | Calculation of Pearson Correlation Coefficient, $r$, for Correlation Between |
|---|---|
| **Table 12.4** | **State Murder Rate and Poverty Rate (Table 12.1)** |

| State | Poverty Rate $x$ | Murder Rate $y$ | $x^2$ | $y^2$ | $xy$ |
|---|---|---|---|---|---|
| Alaska | 9.0 | 3.2 | 81.0 | 10.2 | 28.8 |
| Arizona | 16.5 | 5.5 | 272.3 | 30.3 | 90.8 |
| California | 14.2 | 5.4 | 201.6 | 29.2 | 76.7 |
| Delaware | 10.8 | 4.6 | 116.6 | 21.2 | 49.7 |
| Florida | 14.9 | 5.5 | 222.0 | 30.3 | 82.0 |
| Indiana | 14.4 | 5.3 | 207.4 | 28.1 | 76.3 |
| Louisiana | 17.3 | 12.3 | 299.3 | 151.3 | 212.8 |
| Maine | 12.3 | 2.0 | 151.3 | 4.0 | 24.6 |
| Maryland | 9.1 | 7.7 | 82.8 | 59.3 | 70.1 |
| Massachusetts | 10.3 | 2.7 | 106.1 | 7.3 | 27.8 |
| Michigan | 16.2 | 6.3 | 262.4 | 39.7 | 102.1 |
| Missouri | 14.6 | 6.6 | 213.2 | 43.6 | 96.4 |
| Nebraska | 12.3 | 2.5 | 151.3 | 6.3 | 30.8 |
| New Jersey | 9.4 | 3.7 | 88.4 | 13.7 | 34.8 |
| New Mexico | 18.0 | 10.0 | 324.0 | 100.0 | 180.0 |
| New York | 14.2 | 4.0 | 201.6 | 16.0 | 56.8 |
| Pennsylvania | 12.5 | 5.4 | 156.3 | 29.2 | 67.5 |
| South Carolina | 17.1 | 6.7 | 292.4 | 44.9 | 114.6 |
| Texas | 17.2 | 5.4 | 295.8 | 29.2 | 92.9 |
| Wyoming | 9.8 | 2.0 | 96.0 | 4.0 | 19.6 |
| $n = 20$ | $\Sigma x = 270.1$ | $\Sigma y = 106.8$ | $\Sigma x_2 = 3{,}821.8$ | $\Sigma y_2 = 697.8$ | $\Sigma xy = 1{,}535.1$ |

What does this correlation between a state's murder rate and level of poverty of $r = .62$ tell us? Well, the sign of the correlation coefficient informs us that there is a positive linear correlation between a state's murder rate and the percentage of the population that lives below the poverty level. Those states with high murder rates also tend to have high rates of poverty. How do we interpret the magnitude of this correlation? Recall that the value of a Pearson correlation coefficient varies between $-1.0$ (a perfect negative correlation) and $+1.0$ (a perfect positive correlation), with 0 indicating no correlation. One thing we can say about our correlation of .62 is that it is close to .50 and therefore indicates a moderately strong relationship. Unfortunately, there are no clear and agreed-upon rules that tell us what constitutes a "weak," "moderate," or "strong" correlation. It is entirely subjective. We will provide a more exact interpretation of the magnitude of $r$ in the next section of this chapter, but for now, we will use less precise terms such

| Table 12.5 | Calculation of Pearson Correlation Coefficient, *r*, for Correlation Between Percentage of State Population Rural Areas in a State and Rate of Robbery for 20 States (Table 12.2) |

| State | Rural Area (%) $x$ | Robbery Rate $y$ | $x^2$ | $y^2$ | $xy$ |
|---|---|---|---|---|---|
| Alaska | 30.4 | 94.0 | 924.2 | 8836.0 | 2857.6 |
| Arizona | 9.5 | 123.9 | 90.3 | 15351.2 | 1177.1 |
| California | 5.1 | 173.7 | 26.0 | 30171.7 | 885.9 |
| Delaware | 17.4 | 189.7 | 302.8 | 35986.1 | 3300.8 |
| Florida | 9.1 | 166.8 | 82.8 | 27822.2 | 1517.9 |
| Indiana | 27.4 | 129.4 | 750.8 | 16744.4 | 3545.6 |
| Louisiana | 27.0 | 142.3 | 729.0 | 20249.3 | 3842.1 |
| Maine | 57.4 | 30.3 | 3294.8 | 918.1 | 1739.2 |
| Maryland | 12.8 | 210.7 | 163.8 | 44394.5 | 2697.0 |
| Massachusetts | 8.4 | 114.1 | 70.6 | 13018.8 | 958.4 |
| Michigan | 25.5 | 126.5 | 650.3 | 16002.3 | 3225.8 |
| Missouri | 28.6 | 127.1 | 818.0 | 16154.4 | 3635.1 |
| Nebraska | 28.4 | 74.7 | 806.6 | 5580.1 | 2121.5 |
| New Jersey | 5.4 | 133.7 | 29.2 | 17875.7 | 722.0 |
| New Mexico | 22.1 | 98.7 | 488.4 | 9741.7 | 2181.3 |
| New York | 12.3 | 144.5 | 151.3 | 20880.3 | 1777.4 |
| Pennsylvania | 22.2 | 142.4 | 492.8 | 20277.8 | 3161.3 |
| South Carolina | 34.3 | 126.0 | 1176.5 | 15876.0 | 4321.8 |
| Texas | 14.5 | 153.6 | 210.3 | 23593.0 | 2227.2 |
| Wyoming | 30.5 | 14.3 | 930.3 | 204.5 | 436.2 |
| $n = 20$ | $\Sigma x = 428.3$ | $\Sigma y = 2{,}516.4$ | $\Sigma x^2 = 12{,}188.8$ | $\Sigma y^2 = 359{,}678.1$ | $\Sigma xy = 46{,}331.2$ |

as "moderately strong" or "weak." We can conclude from this, then, that there is a moderately strong positive correlation between the poverty rate in a state and its murder rate.

Table 12.5 reports the calculations necessary to estimate the correlation between the percentage of a state's population that lives in a nonmetropolitan area and its rate of robbery. The correlation between these two variables is calculated as follows, but we will refresh your memory of the formula:

$$r = \frac{n\Sigma xy - (\Sigma x)(\Sigma y)}{\sqrt{\left[n\Sigma x^2 - (\Sigma x)^2\right]\left[n\Sigma y^2 - (\Sigma y)^2\right]}}$$

$$r = \frac{(20)(46,331.2) - (428.3)(2,516.4)}{\sqrt{\left[(20)(12,188.8) - (428.3)^2\right]\left[(20)(359,678.1) - (2,516.4)^2\right]}}$$

$$r = \frac{926,624 - 1,077,774.}{\sqrt{[243,776 - 183,440.9][7,193,562 - 6,332,269]}}$$

$$r = \frac{-151,150.1}{\sqrt{(60,335.1)(861,293)}}$$

$$r = \frac{-151,150.1}{\sqrt{51,966,199,284}}$$

$$r = \frac{-151,150.1}{227,961}$$

$$r = -.66$$

This coefficient ($r = -.66$) indicates that there is a moderate negative linear correlation between percentage of rural population and a state's robbery rate. As we predicted, states with a higher percentage of its population living in a rural area have lower rates of robbery than more urban states.

And finally, Table 12.6 reports the calculations to estimate the correlation between the divorce rate in a state and its rate of burglary. The correlation is:

$$r = \frac{(20)(89,736.6) - (128.6)(13,915.3)}{\sqrt{\left[(20)(847.5) - (128.6)^2\right]\left[(20)(10,722,261.6) - (13,915.3)^2\right]}}$$

$$r = \frac{1,794,732 - 1,789,507.6}{\sqrt{[16,950 - 16,538][214,445,232 - 193,635,574.1]}}$$

$$r = \frac{5,222.4}{\sqrt{(412)(20,809,657.9)}}$$

$$r = \frac{5,222.4}{\sqrt{8,573,579,055}}$$

$$r = \frac{5,222.4}{92,593.6}$$

$$r = .056$$

How would you interpret this correlation of .056? It is closer to zero than the other correlation coefficients. In fact, it is almost zero! This indicates that there is a very weak positive linear correlation between the divorce rate in a state and its rate of burglary. Consistent with the appearance of our scatterplot, then, there is not a very strong linear relationship between these two variables. The divorce rate does not appear to influence rates of burglary.

In our examination of the three relationships, we have found a moderately strong positive correlation between a state's murder rate and its poverty rate, a moderately strong negative correlation between a state's percentage of rural population and its rate of robbery, and not much of a linear correlation between a state's divorce rate and its burglary rate.

| Table 12.6 | Calculation of Pearson Correlation Coefficient, *r*, for Correlation Between Divorce Rate and Rate of Burglary for 20 States (Table 12.3) |

| State | Divorce Rate x | Burglary Rate y | $x^2$ | $y^2$ | xy |
|---|---|---|---|---|---|
| Alaska | 7.8 | 514.2 | 60.8 | 264401.6 | 4010.8 |
| Arizona | 5.4 | 817.3 | 29.2 | 667979.3 | 4413.4 |
| California | 5.8 | 622.1 | 33.6 | 387008.4 | 3608.2 |
| Delaware | 5.4 | 784.0 | 29.2 | 614656.0 | 4233.6 |
| Florida | 7.5 | 981.2 | 56.3 | 962753.4 | 7359.0 |
| Indiana | 7.9 | 815.9 | 62.4 | 665692.8 | 6445.6 |
| Louisiana | 7.1 | 1036.4 | 50.4 | 1074125 | 7358.4 |
| Maine | 7.2 | 510.4 | 51.8 | 260508.2 | 3674.9 |
| Maryland | 5.8 | 647.5 | 33.6 | 419256.3 | 3755.5 |
| Massachusetts | 5.5 | 524.1 | 30.3 | 274680.8 | 2882.6 |
| Michigan | 5.4 | 768.1 | 29.2 | 589977.6 | 4147.7 |
| Missouri | 6.5 | 733.5 | 42.3 | 538022.3 | 4767.8 |
| Nebraska | 6.7 | 499.4 | 44.9 | 249400.4 | 3346.0 |
| New Jersey | 5.1 | 424.2 | 26.0 | 179945.6 | 2163.4 |
| New Mexico | 5.1 | 1117.3 | 26.0 | 1248359 | 5698.2 |
| New York | 6.4 | 321.6 | 41.0 | 103426.6 | 2058.2 |
| Pennsylvania | 5.3 | 439.2 | 28.1 | 192896.6 | 2327.8 |
| South Carolina | 7.4 | 991.7 | 54.8 | 983468.9 | 7338.6 |
| Texas | 7.1 | 967.4 | 50.4 | 935862.8 | 6868.5 |
| Wyoming | 8.2 | 399.8 | 67.2 | 159840.0 | 3278.4 |
| n = 20 | Σx = 128.6 | Σy = 13,915.3 | Σx² = 847.5 | Σy² = 10,772,261.6 | Σxy = 89,736.6 |

Although we can interpret a perfect positive correlation as +1.0, a perfect negative correlation as −1.0, and no linear correlation at all as 0.0, what do correlations that fall in between these extremes mean? Although Figure 12.13 provides accepted adjectives to describe correlations that fall between 0 and ±1, there is another statistic that enables us to interpret more precisely the strength of the relationship between two variables. This statistic is called the coefficient of determination, and we turn to it next.

# A More Precise Way to Interpret a Correlation: The Coefficient of Determination

**Coefficient of determination ($r^2$):**
Percentage of the variation in the dependent variable (y) that is explained by the independent variable (x).

The **coefficient of determination**, $r^2$, enables us to interpret more definitively the strength of the association between two interval- and ratio-level variables. It is very easy to obtain once we have already calculated the correlation coefficient. As the symbol $r^2$ suggests, the coefficient of determination is simply the square of the Pearson correlation coefficient. It is interpreted as *the proportion of the variation in the y variable that is explained by the x variable*. Remember, what we are trying to do is to explain variation in the dependent or *y* variable. We want to know why everyone is not the same on *y*, that there is variation in *y*, and that what explains variation in *y* is variation in the independent variable, *x*. So, a good question to ask of our *x* variable is, "how much of the variation in *y* are you explaining?" When the value of $r^2$ is multiplied by 100 to get a percent, it is interpreted as the *percentage of the variation* in the *y* variable that is explained by the *x* variable.

For example, our correlation between the poverty rate and the murder rate for our 20 states was .62. The coefficient of determination is $(.62)^2$, or .38, and can be understood as the amount of variance in murder rates that is explained by the rate of poverty. In this example, 38% of the variation in states' murder rates is explained by state-level rates of poverty. The correlation between percent rural population and the robbery rate was −.66. The coefficient of determination is $(−.66)^2$, or .44, which indicates that 44% of the variation in robbery crime rates for these 20 states is explained by the percentage of the state's population that is living in a rural area. Finally, the correlation between the divorce rate and a state's burglary rate is $(.056)^2$, or .003. This indicates that less than 1% of the variation in burglary rates is explained by the divorce rate in states.

The amount of variation explained varies from 0% to 100%. The more variation explained, the stronger the association or relationship between the two variables. If two variables are perfectly related, the amount of explained variation is 100% ($+1.0^2 = −1.0^2 = 1.0 × 100\%$). If two variables are perfectly unrelated (independent), the amount of variation one variable explains in the other will be 0%. Obviously, the more variation one variable explains in another, the more accurate the predictions of a *y* variable from an *x* variable will be. The magnitude of $r^2$, the coefficient of determination, is, then, the proportion of variation in *y* that is explained by *X*. As the amount of explained variation increases, $r^2$ increases. The greater the proportion of the total variation that is explained by the independent variable, the stronger the linear relationship between *x* and *y*. As you can see, the coefficient of determination ($r^2$) is a very useful measure of association between two continuous variables. Unlike the correlation coefficient ($r$), values of the coefficient of determination between 0 and 1.0 are readily interpretable. Another way to think of this is that values of $r^2$ reflect the amount of improvement in our predictive accuracy. There is an additional way to describe a linear relationship between *x* and *y*, which we turn to next.

# The Least-Squares Regression Line and the Slope Coefficient

**Least-squares regression line:**
Regression line based on the least-squares function to calculate an equation that characterizes the best-fitting line between two interval/ratio variables.

The correlation coefficient ($r$) and the coefficient of determination ($r^2$) are two very helpful statistics in understanding the linear relationship between two interval/ratio variables. One advantage of them both is that you can compare the relative strength of a relationship across different variables and everyone will be able to judge the strength. For example, we know that a relationship that has a correlation of .70 is a stronger relationship than one that has a correlation of .45. Unfortunately, because the values of these statistics are standardized, they don't tell us exactly how a particular independent variable will affect a given dependent variable. The **least-squares regression line** not only provides information about the strength and direction of the relationship between *x* and *y*, but it also enables us to predict values of *y* from values of *x* more precisely. In fact, it tells us exactly what happens to *y* for every one-unit increase in *x*.

# Case Study

## Age and Delinquency

To understand the idea behind the least-squares regression line, we first need to examine how the line is constructed and why it is called the "least-squares" regression line. Let's begin our discussion of the least-squares regression line by looking at the hypothetical data in Table 12.7. This table shows the age of a random sample of 20 youths and the number of self-reported acts of delinquency committed by each youth in the previous year. Age is our designated independent ($x$) variable, and the number of self-reported delinquent acts is our dependent ($y$) variable. Note that both of these variables are measured at the interval/ratio level.

The first thing to note in Table 12.7 is that for any given $x$ value, there are different values for $y$. This means that there are several youths who are the same age but have not committed the same number of delinquent acts. For example, of the four 12-year-old youths in the sample, one committed 0 delinquent acts, one committed 1 delinquent act, one committed 2 delinquent acts, and one committed 3 delinquent acts. The three 13-year-old youths committed different numbers of delinquent acts as well. For each value of $x$, then, there are a number of different $y$ values. Think of these different $y$ values at each value of $x$ as constituting a distribution of $y$ scores. Since there are seven different $x$ scores, there are seven different distributions of $y$ scores. Another way to express this is to say that for every fixed value of $x$, there is a corresponding distribution of $y$ scores. In statistics, these distributions of $y$ scores are often called conditional distributions since the distribution of $y$ scores depends, or is conditional, on the value of $x$. This is similar to a conditional probability, where the probability of one event P($A$) depends on another event ($B$).

Figure 12.14 is the scatterplot illustrating these data. We can tell from "eyeballing" this scatterplot that age and self-reported delinquency are positively related to one another and that this relationship looks reasonably strong and linear. The goal of least-squares regression is to fit a straight line to these data in such a way that the line comes as close to the original data points as possible.

| Table 12.7 | Hypothetical Data for 20 Students | |
| --- | --- | --- |
| Student | Age x | Self-Reported Delinquency y |
| 1 | 12 | 0 |
| 2 | 12 | 2 |
| 3 | 12 | 1 |
| 4 | 12 | 3 |
| 5 | 13 | 4 |
| 6 | 13 | 2 |
| 7 | 13 | 1 |
| 8 | 14 | 2 |
| 9 | 14 | 5 |
| 10 | 14 | 4 |
| 11 | 15 | 3 |
| 12 | 15 | 4 |
| 13 | 15 | 6 |
| 14 | 15 | 8 |
| 15 | 16 | 9 |
| 16 | 16 | 7 |
| 17 | 16 | 6 |
| 18 | 17 | 8 |
| 19 | 17 | 10 |
| 20 | 17 | 7 |

Recall from Chapter 4 that we can determine a central score within a distribution of scores that arithmetically varies the least from all other scores in the distribution. This point of minimum variation, you will remember, is the mean. The mean is that one score around which the variation of the other scores is the smallest or is minimized. In mathematical terms, the mean satisfies the expression:

$$\Sigma(x - \overline{X})^2 = \text{Minimum variance}$$

This expression simply means that the sum of the squared differences (deviations) around any mean is the minimum value that can be defined. Arithmetically, we know that if any value other than the mean were used in the expression, the obtained value would be greater than if the mean was used. In other words, in any distribution of scores, the mean will be that score that is closest to all the other scores.

**Conditional mean of y:** Means of *y* calculated for every value of *x*.

This property of the mean holds true even for a conditional distribution of scores, such as that shown in Table 12.7. If we calculate a mean of *y* at each value of *x* (called the **conditional mean of y**), this mean will be the score that is closest to all other *y* scores at that given value of *x*. We have calculated each of these conditional *y* means for you and report the results in Table 12.8. These conditional means were calculated like any other mean, by summing all values of *y* and then dividing by the total number of these *y* scores. For example, there were four *y* scores (number of self-reported delinquent acts) for those at age 12: 0, 2, 1, and 3. The mean number of self-reported delinquent acts for these four 12-year-old youths is therefore $(0 + 2 + 1 + 3) / 4 = 1.5$. This mean indicates that the 12-year-old youths from this sample reported committing an average of 1.5 delinquent acts. We can similarly calculate conditional means of *y* for each age, as we show in Table 12.8. In Figure 12.15, we show the scatterplot that includes points for both the original scores and each of the conditional means (shown by $\overline{Y}$).

Since the conditional means ($\overline{Y}$) minimize the variance of the *y* scores at each value of *x*, the straight line that comes the closest to going thorough each value of $\overline{Y}$ will be our best-fitting line. By "best fitting" we mean that it is the line that will minimize the variation of the conditional *y* scores about that line. Because the variance is measured by the squared deviations from the mean $(y - \overline{Y})^2$, this regression line is the *least-squares* regression line, and the estimation procedure is referred to as ordinary least-squares (OLS) regression. The least-squares regression line, therefore, is the line where the squared deviations of the conditional means for the *y* scores ($\overline{Y}$) are the least. Figure 12.16 is the scatterplot of the conditional $\overline{Y}$ values from Figure 12.15. We have also included

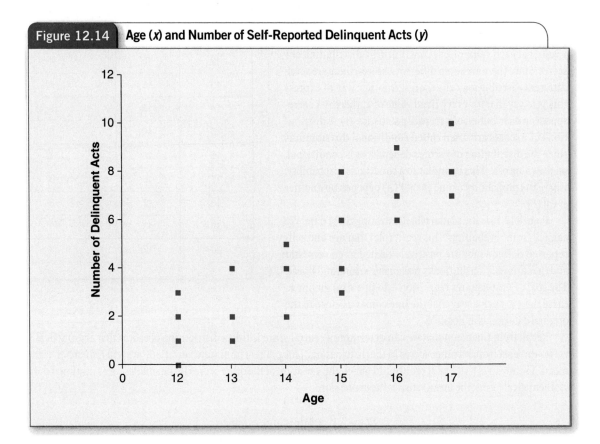

**Figure 12.14** **Age (*x*) and Number of Self-Reported Delinquent Acts (*y*)**

the regression line and the distance (drawn with a vertical line) between each conditional mean and the regression line. This regression line is the best-fitting line in the sense that it is calculated in such a way that this vertical distance is at a minimum. This is simply a beautiful equation!

Mathematically, the equation that defines this least-squares regression line takes the general linear form in the population as:

$$y = \alpha + \beta x \qquad (12\text{-}3)$$

where

$y$ = the score on the y variable

$\alpha$ = the y intercept or constant

$\beta$ = the slope of the regression line

$x$ = the score on the x variable

There are two new terms in this equation, the intercept and the slope, that must be defined and explained. The **y intercept** ($\alpha$) or constant is the point where the regression line crosses the y axis. As you can determine from the equation, it is equal to the value of y whenever $x = 0$. The **slope** of the regression line, $\beta$, called the **beta coefficient** for the population parameter of the slope, or the regression coefficient, measures the amount of change produced in the y variable by a one-unit increase in the x variable, and the sign indicates the direction of that change. For example, a slope of 2 indicates that a one-unit increase in x produces a two-unit increase in y. A slope of –2 indicates that a one-unit increase in x produces a two-unit decrease in y. If the slope in our age and delinquency example were 2, this would indicate that a one-year increase in age (a one-unit change in x) would increase the number of self-reported delinquent acts by 2 (a two-unit change in y).

In equation 12-3, alpha ($\alpha$) is the symbol for the population intercept, and beta ($\beta$) is the slope coefficient in the population. As you should immediately know by now, these two values are virtually always unknown. Thus, we again have to use the sample data to estimate their respective population values. The sample intercept is symbolized by the letter $a$, and the slope of the sample is symbolized by the letter $b$. The sample statistic $a$ is an estimate of the unknown population parameter $\alpha$, and $b$ is an estimate of the unknown population parameter $\beta$. The sample regression equation can thus be rewritten as:

$$y = a + bx \qquad (12\text{-}4)$$

From our sample data, we can estimate our regression equation when we know the values of the intercept and slope. Both values are derived from the original data. We determine the intercept ($a$) by first computing the value of the slope ($b$). The definitional formula for estimating the slope of a regression line is:

$$b = \frac{\Sigma(x - \overline{X})(y - \overline{Y})}{\Sigma(x - \overline{X})^2} \qquad (12\text{-}5)$$

| Table 12.8 | Conditional Means (Means of *y* for fixed values of *x*) for the Data on Age and Self-Reported Delinquency | |
|---|---|---|
| Age | y Scores | Conditional $\overline{Y}$ |
| 12 | 0, 1, 2, 3 | 1.5 |
| 13 | 4, 2, 1 | 2.3 |
| 14 | 2, 5, 4 | 3.7 |
| 15 | 3, 4, 6, 8 | 5.2 |
| 16 | 9, 7, 6 | 7.3 |
| 17 | 8, 10, 7 | 8.3 |

**y intercept:** Value of *y* in an ordinary least-squares (OLS) regression equation when *x* is equal to 0.

**Slope:** Term in an ordinary least-squares (OLS) regression equation that indicates the change in *y* associated with a one-unit change in *x*.

**Beta coefficient:** The name for the population parameter of the slope, but also a name given to the Standardized slope regression coefficient in multiple regression.

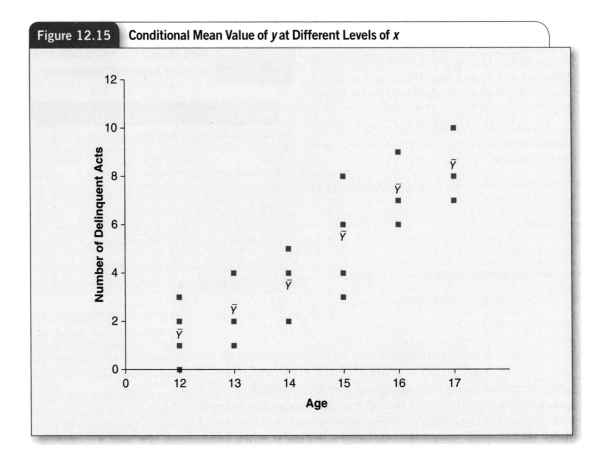

**Figure 12.15** Conditional Mean Value of *y* at Different Levels of *x*

This should look very familiar to you by now. The numerator of the equation is simply the product of each *x* score minus its mean and each *y* score minus its mean, summed over all observations. Remember that the product of these two differences is referred to as the *covariation* between *x* and *y*. It measures the extent to which *x* and *y* vary together, or *covary*. If we divide this sum by *n*, what we get is called the *covariance* between *x* and *y*. The denominator of equation 12-5 is the squared deviation of each *x* score about its mean (the sum of squares for *x*). When divided by *n*, this is the variance. The slope coefficient, then, can be understood as the ratio of the covariance between *x* and *y* to the variance in *x*.

Note that the covariation between *x* and *y*, the numerator in the formula for *b*, can be either positive or negative. Calculating the slope (*b*) from this definitional formula would be a tiresome (and error-prone) task. Fortunately, as with the Pearson correlation coefficient, there is a much easier computational formula for *b*:

$$b = \frac{n\Sigma xy - (\Sigma x)(\Sigma y)}{n\Sigma x^2 - (\Sigma x)^2}$$  **(12-6)**

At first glance this formula looks no easier to use than the definitional formula. But it, too, should be familiar to you by now. We can break this monster up into five component parts that are really quite simple to compute.

1.  $\Sigma xy$ = the sum of the product formed by multiplying each *x* score by each *y* score, and then summing over all scores

2.  $\Sigma x$ = the sum of the *x* scores

3.  $\Sigma y$ = the sum of the *y* scores

4. $\Sigma x^2$ = the sum of the squared $x$ scores $\left( x_1^2 + \cdots + x_2^2 + \cdots + x_n^2 \right)$

5. $(\Sigma x)^2$ = the sum of the $x$ scores squared $\left( x_1 + \cdots + x_2 + \cdots + x_n \right)^2$

6. $n$ = The number of observations, or sample size

We will first illustrate the calculation of $b$ with the hypothetical age and self-reported delinquency data in Table 12.7. We will then return to the example involving our real state-level data.

The calculations necessary to find $b$ for the data in Table 12.7 are shown in Table 12.9. In this table, the component elements of the formula are represented by separate columns. With this information, we can calculate the slope using formula 12.6:

$$b = \frac{n\Sigma xy - (\Sigma x)(\Sigma y)}{n\Sigma x^2 - (\Sigma x)^2}$$

$$b = \frac{(20)(1,409) - (288)(92)}{(20)(4,206) - (288)^2}$$

$$b = \frac{28,180 - 26,496}{84,120 - 82,944}$$

$$b = \frac{1,684}{1,176}$$

$$b = 1.43$$

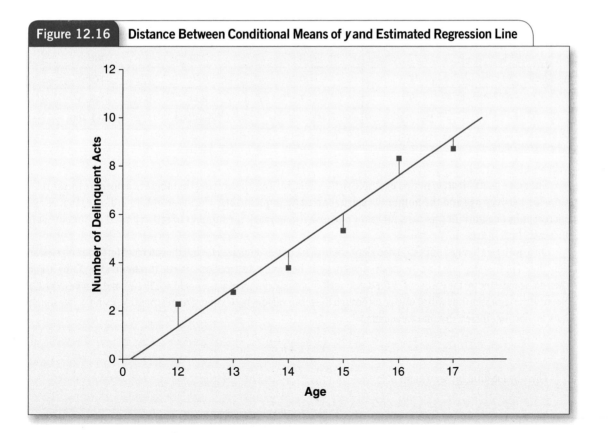

**Figure 12.16**   **Distance Between Conditional Means of *y* and Estimated Regression Line**

| Table 12.9 | Calculations for Determining the Slope (*b*) for the Data on Age and Self-Reported Delinquency | | | |
|---|---|---|---|---|
| ID Number | Age x | Self-Reported Delinquency y | $x^2$ | xy |
| 1 | 12 | 0 | 144 | 0 |
| 2 | 12 | 2 | 144 | 24 |
| 3 | 12 | 1 | 144 | 12 |
| 4 | 12 | 3 | 144 | 36 |
| 5 | 13 | 4 | 169 | 52 |
| 6 | 13 | 2 | 169 | 26 |
| 7 | 13 | 1 | 169 | 13 |
| 8 | 14 | 2 | 196 | 28 |
| 9 | 14 | 5 | 196 | 70 |
| 10 | 14 | 4 | 196 | 56 |
| 11 | 15 | 3 | 225 | 45 |
| 12 | 15 | 4 | 225 | 60 |
| 13 | 15 | 6 | 225 | 90 |
| 14 | 15 | 8 | 225 | 120 |
| 15 | 16 | 9 | 256 | 144 |
| 16 | 16 | 7 | 256 | 112 |
| 17 | 16 | 6 | 256 | 96 |
| 18 | 17 | 8 | 289 | 136 |
| 19 | 17 | 10 | 289 | 170 |
| 20 | 17 | 7 | 289 | 119 |
| n = 20 | Σx = 288 | Σy = 92 | $\Sigma x^2$ = 4,206 | Σxy = 1,409 |

The slope coefficient, *b,* in this example is 1.43. It is positive, indicating that there is a positive linear relationship between age and the number of self-reported delinquent acts. The value of 1.43 indicates that as age increases by one unit (in this case, we know one unit is one year), the number of self-reported delinquent acts increases by 1.43 acts.

Once we have obtained our estimated slope coefficient, it is easy enough to find the intercept (*a*) in our regression equation. The first step is to find the mean values of both the *x* and *y* distributions. We do this by dividing Σ*x* by *n*, and then doing the same for the *y* scores. For the data on self-reported delinquent acts, $\overline{X} = 14.4$ (288 / 20) and $\overline{Y} = 4.6$ (92 / 20). Because the regression line will always pass through the mean value of both *x* and *y*, represented by $\overline{X}$ and $\overline{Y}$, we simply have to substitute these terms into the equation:

$$\overline{Y} = a + b\overline{X}$$

Then, by substitution, we obtain:

$$a = \overline{Y} - b\overline{X}$$

For our example, the solution would be:

$$a = 4.6 - (1.43)(14.4)$$
$$a = 4.6 - 20.59$$
$$a = -15.99$$

Thus, the regression line will cross the $y$ axis at the point where $y = -15.99$ when the value of $x$ equals 0. We can now specify our complete regression equation:

$$y = a + bx$$
$$y = -15.99 + (1.43)x$$

A brief word about the intercept is in order. The intercept is where the regression line crosses the $y$ axis, and it is the expected value of the dependent variable $y$ when the independent variable is equal to zero. We have an intercept of $-15.99$, which would mean that the expected number of delinquent acts when age is equal to zero is a negative 16. That doesn't make much sense, does it? This is because the intercept is substantively meaningful only when an $x$ value of zero has some meaning. It may make sense to speak of 0 dollars, but it makes no real sense to speak of an age equal to 0. In this case, then, when a zero value of the independent variable has no real meaning, neither does the intercept. In other words, sometimes the intercept has a substantive meaning and sometimes it does not. In most cases, we don't spend a great deal of time interpreting the intercept because what we really want to know is the relationship between $x$ and $y$. As such, we focus on interpreting the slope.

## Using the Regression Line for Prediction

After we have computed the regression equation, we can use it to estimate the **predicted value of $y$ ($\hat{y}$)** for any given value of $x$. To find predicted values of $y$, we simply use our regression equation and substitute values for $x$. For example, using the regression equation for age and self-reported delinquent acts, the expected number of delinquent acts for a 17-year-old youth would be:

> **Predicted value of $y(\hat{y})$:** Value of the dependent variable predicted by a regression equation.

$$\hat{y} = -15.99 + (1.43)(17)$$

$$\hat{y} = 8.32$$

This predicted value indicates that we would expect approximately eight self-reported delinquent acts to be reported by a 17-year-old youth. In reality, this predicted $y$ value is simply our "best guess" based on the estimated regression line. It does not mean that every 17-year-old will report eight delinquent acts. Since age and delinquency are linearly related, however, it does mean that our best guess when using the regression equation is better than guessing the number of delinquent acts without it or just using the overall mean number of delinquent acts as our best guess. The stronger the linear relationship between age and self-reported delinquency, the better or more accurate our estimate will be.

We now know two data points that lie exactly on our estimated regression line: the one corresponding to the mean of the $x$ and $y$ values ($\overline{X} = 14.4$, $\overline{Y} = 4.6$) and the one corresponding to the predicted value of $y$ when $x = 17$ ($\overline{Y} = 8.32$) from our prediction equation earlier. Knowing two data points that lie on our regression line enables us to draw the regression line with precision rather than simply "eyeballing" the line. We simply draw a straight line that runs through these two data points, as shown in Figure 12.17. This line represents the "best-fitting" regression line that we could obtain to describe the relationship between age and self-reported delinquency.

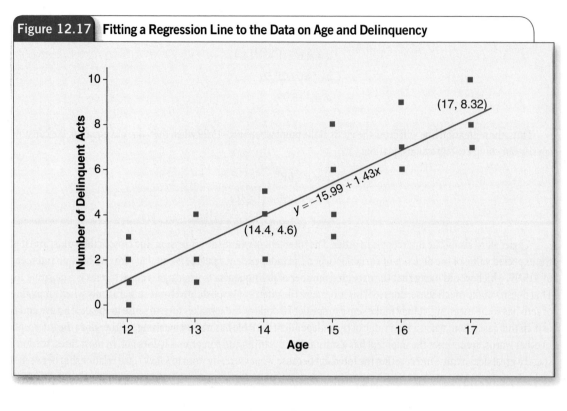

**Figure 12.17** Fitting a Regression Line to the Data on Age and Delinquency

---

## Case Study

## Predicting State Crime Rates

Let's return now to our state-level data and estimate the value of the slope coefficient for each of the three relationships we examined earlier with the correlation coefficient. In Table 12.1, we reported the rate of poverty ($x$) and murder rate ($y$) for each of the randomly selected 20 states. When we plotted these data in a scatterplot (Figure 12.9), we observed a positive relationship between these two variables. This was confirmed by calculation of the correlation coefficient, $r =$ .62, which told us there was a moderate-to-strong positive relationship between poverty and murder in states. We also know that poverty rates explain 38% of the variation in rates of murder ($r^2 = .38$, or 38%).

Now we will fit a regression line to these data by determining first the slope ($b$) and then the intercept ($a$). Because we needed the same information to calculate the correlation coefficient, the calculations necessary to find the slope are already provided for you in Table 12.4. With these calculations and formula 12-6, we can estimate the slope coefficient as:

$$b = \frac{20(1,535.1) - (270.1)(106.8)}{20(3,821.8) - (270.1)^2}$$

$$b = \frac{30,702 - 28,846.7}{76,434 - 72,954}$$

$$b = \frac{1,855.3}{3,482}$$

$$b = .53$$

As with the correlation coefficient, the slope coefficient is positive, indicating that there is a positive linear relationship between a state's murder rate and its poverty rate. The magnitude of the slope is .53, which tells us that a one-unit change in the rate of poverty (a 1% increase in poverty, since the poverty variable is measured as the percentage of the population living below the poverty level), increases the murder rate by .53 units. There is, then, a positive linear relationship between the poverty rate in a state and its murder rate. This slope appears small, but when you examine the murder rates, you can see that the range for this variable is not very large and, hence, the relatively small size of $b$. As we will soon see, it does not indicate that there is a weak relationship between poverty and rates of murder. To increase our understanding, we can add units to $x$ to determine the change in $y$. For example, if a one-unit increase in poverty increases the murder rate by .53 units, we know that a five-unit increase in poverty will increase the rate of murder by 2.65 units ($5 \times .53 = 2.65$). This, then, enables us to demonstrate more meaningfully the effect of $x$ on $y$; increasing the poverty rate by 5%, in this case, will serve to increase the rate of murder by 2.65 murders per 100,000 population.

Let's move on to solve for the entire regression equation. Knowing the value of $b$ and the mean values of $x$ (poverty rate) and $y$ (murder rate), we can now solve for the intercept ($a$). The mean homicide rate for these 20 states is 5.3 (106.8 / 20), and the mean rate of poverty is 13.5 (270.1 / 20). The intercept is, then, equal to:

$$a = \overline{Y} - b\overline{X}$$
$$a = 5.3 - (.53)(13.5)$$
$$a = 5.3 - 7.16$$
$$a = -1.86$$

The point where the regression line crosses the $y$ axis when $x$ is equal to 0 is where $y = -1.86$. We can now write our full regression equation for these data as:

$$y = a + bx$$
$$y = -1.86 + .53(x)$$

With this regression equation, we can now estimate the predicted value of $y$ ($\hat{y}$) at any given value of $x$. For example, the predicted murder rate for a state with a poverty rate of 17 would be:

$$y = a + bx$$
$$y = -1.86 + .53(17)$$
$$y = -1.86 + 9.01$$
$$y = 7.15$$

Exactly what does this predicted value mean? It means that we would predict a state with 17% of its population living below the poverty level would have a murder rate of 7.15 per 100,000. Keep in mind that this is our predicted value of $y$ based on our regression equation estimated from the sample data. It represents our "best guess" of what $y$ will be at a given value of $x$. It does not mean that the $y$ score will be that exact value. Unless all of the sample data points lie exactly on the regression line (which would mean that our two variables were perfectly correlated), our predicted $y$ values ($y$) will usually be different from our observed $y$ value. In regression analysis, this error in predicting the dependent variable is often called the **residual**. In the case of perfect correlation, we can predict one score from another without error and our residuals will be zero. The closer the data points are to the estimated regression line, therefore, the more accurate our predicted $y$ scores and the smaller the residuals. The further the data points are from the line, the less accurate our predicted $y$ scores will be and the greater the residuals. Because we always have error in prediction, we must rewrite the regression equation as:

**Residual:** Difference between the predicted value of $y$ from the regression equation and the observed value at a given $x$ score.

$$y = a + bx + e$$

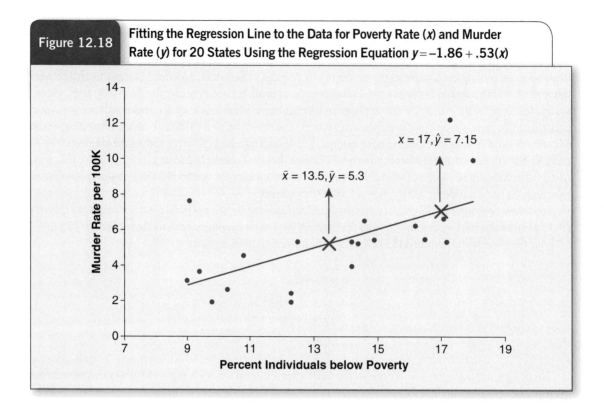

**Figure 12.18** Fitting the Regression Line to the Data for Poverty Rate (*x*) and Murder Rate (*y*) for 20 States Using the Regression Equation $y = -1.86 + .53(x)$

where *e* is the symbol for the error term. The error term reflects the fact that other factors are related to the dependent variable than the one independent variable we have included in our model. This refers to the fact that several factors, not just the one we are looking at, usually help explain a given *y* variable. If we are examining only one of them, we will not be able to predict *y* with perfect precision. In other words, when we look only at *x* and ignore other factors that influence *y*, our predictions will contain some amount of error. The more *y* is determined solely by *x*, the less error we will have. We will have more to say about this in the next chapter, which is about multiple regression. For now, let's return to our problem.

With our predicted value of $\hat{y} = 7.15$ with an *x* score of 17, we now have two data points that fall exactly on our regression line, including the value for the means of *x* and *y* ( $\bar{X} = 13.5$, $\bar{Y} = 5.3$ ). Connecting these two points with a straight line will give us our best-fitting regression line that describes the relationship between the murder rate and the poverty rate. This is shown in Figure 12.18.

Let's go through another example. In Table 12.2, we reported data for 20 states regarding the percentage of each state's population living in a nonmetropolitan area (*x*) and its robbery rate (*y*). In the scatterplot we constructed from these data (Figure 12.11), we observed a negative relationship between these two variables. This was confirmed by the sign of the correlation coefficient ($r = -.66$). The magnitude of the correlation coefficient indicated that the percentage of the population that was rural in a state could explain 44% of the variation in robbery ($r^2 = .44$). Now, we will fit a regression line to these data by determining first the slope (*b*) and then the intercept (*a*). The calculations necessary to calculate the slope were provided in Table 12.5. With these calculations and formula 12-6, we can estimate the slope coefficient to be:

$$b = \frac{n\Sigma xy - (\Sigma x)(\Sigma y)}{n\Sigma x^2 - (\Sigma x)^2}$$

$$b = \frac{(20)(46,331.2) - (428.3)(2,516.4)}{(20)(12,188.8) - (428.3)^2}$$

$$b = \frac{926,624 - 1,077,774.1}{243,776 - 183,440.9}$$

$$b = \frac{-151,150.1}{60,335.1}$$

$$b = -2.51$$

The sign of the slope is negative, indicating a negative linear relationship between percent rural and a state's robbery rate. This means that for every one-unit increase in $x$, there is a $b$ unit *decrease* in $y$. Thus, the magnitude of the slope tells us that for each 1% increase in the state's population that is rural, the robbery rate declines by 2.51 units per 100,000. In other words, the greater the percentage of a state's population that lives in a rural area, the lower the rate of robbery. States with larger percentages of urban residents, therefore, have higher rates of robbery.

We can next calculate the mean for the $x$ variable (percent nonmetropolitan) as $428.3 / 20 = 21.4$ and the mean of $y$ (robbery rate) as $2,516.4 / 20 = 125.8$. With this information, we can determine the intercept:

$$a = 125.8 - (-2.51)(21.4)$$

$$a = 125.8 - (-53.7)$$

$$a = 179.5$$

The point where the regression line crosses the $y$ axis when the value of $x$ is equal to 0 is $y = 179.5$. We can now write our full regression equation as:

$$y = a + bx$$

$$y = 179.5 + -2.51(x)$$

With this regression equation, we can estimate a predicted value of the robbery rate ($\hat{y}$) for a given value of percent rural population. If the percentage of the state that lives in a nonmetropolitan area is 10%, our predicted rate of robbery will be:

$$\hat{y} = 179.5 + -2.51(10)$$

$$\hat{y} = 179.5 + -25.1$$

$$\hat{y} = 154.4$$

Given a state with 10% rural population, then, we would predict a robbery rate of 154.4 robberies per 100,000. We now have two data points that lie exactly on the estimated regression line. One of these points is the mean of the $x$ and $y$ variables $(\bar{X}, \bar{Y})$, which is (21.4, 125.8), and the other is our $x$ value of 10 and the predicted value of $y(\hat{y})$, equal to 154.4. With these two points, we can draw a straight line that runs through them both to establish our regression line; this line represents the best-fitting regression line that describes the linear relationship between these data. We have drawn this line for you on the scatterplot presented in Figure 12.19.

Our final example using the state-level data involved the relationship between the divorce rate in a state and its burglary rate. Recall that the original data for these variables, along with the calculations necessary for determining $b$, were presented in Table 12.6. In our scatterplot from these data (Figure 12.12), we could not discern any clear upward or downward linear pattern in the data points. This suggested to us that the two variables were not very strongly linearly related to one another. The correlation coefficient we obtained of $r = .056$ confirmed this suspicion, indicating that the divorce rate explained less than 1% of the variation in burglary in states. Now, we will more precisely fit a least-squares regression line to the data.

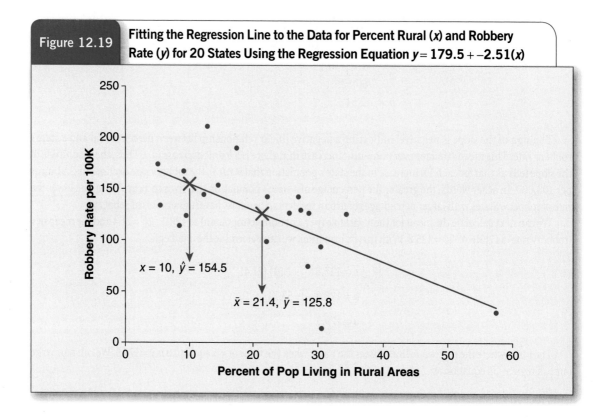

**Figure 12.19** Fitting the Regression Line to the Data for Percent Rural ($x$) and Robbery Rate ($y$) for 20 States Using the Regression Equation $y = 179.5 + -2.51(x)$

As in our other examples, we will begin by estimating the slope of the regression line ($b$) using the calculations provided for us in Table 12.6.

With these calculations we can derive an estimate of $b$ as:

$$b = \frac{n\Sigma xy - (\Sigma x)(\Sigma y)}{n\Sigma x^2 - (\Sigma x)^2}$$

$$b = \frac{(20)(89,736.6) - (128.6)(13,915.3)}{(20)(847.5) - (128.6)^2}$$

$$b = \frac{1,794,732 - 1,789,507.6}{16,950 - 16,538}$$

$$b = \frac{5222.4}{412}$$

$$b = 12.68$$

The sign and magnitude of the slope coefficient indicate that as the divorce rate in a state increases by one unit, the rate of burglary increases by 12.68 units per 100,000. There is, then, a positive linear relationship between the divorce rate in a state and its corresponding rate of burglarly. The mean value of the divorce rate is 6.43 (128.6 / 20), and the mean burglary rate is 695.77 per 100,000 (13,915.3 / 20). With these values, the estimated value of the intercept can be determined as:

$$a = \overline{Y} - b\overline{X}$$

$$a = 695.77 - 12.68(6.43)$$

$$a = 695.77 - 81.53$$

$$a = 614.24$$

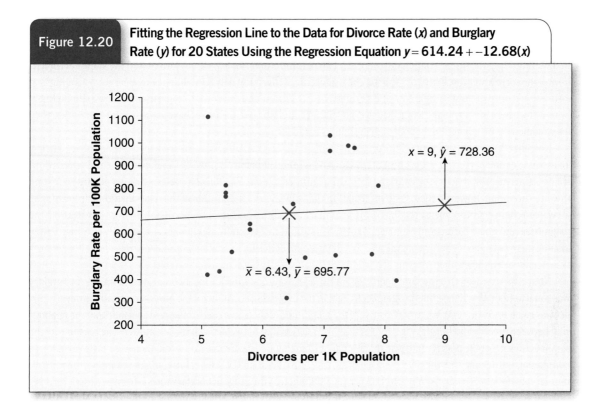

**Figure 12.20** Fitting the Regression Line to the Data for Divorce Rate (*x*) and Burglary Rate (*y*) for 20 States Using the Regression Equation $y = 614.24 + -12.68(x)$

The point where the regression line crosses the *y* axis (the *y* intercept) is where $y = 614.24$. Our complete regression equation for these data can now be defined as:

$$y = a + bx$$
$$y = 614.24 + 12.68(x)$$

For any value of *x*, we can now estimate a predicted value of $y(\hat{y})$. For example, the predicted burglary rate for a state with a divorce rate equal to 9 per 1,000 would be:

$$\hat{y} = 614.24 + 12.68(9)$$

$$\hat{y} = 614.24 + 114.12$$

$$\hat{y} = 728.36$$

Thus, if a state's divorce rate were 9 divorces per 1,000 residents, then based on our estimated regression equation, we would predict that there would be approximately 728 burglaries per 100,000 residents. By knowing this data point along with the mean values of both variables ($\bar{X} = 6.43$, $\bar{Y} = 695.77$), we can now draw our regression line by drawing a straight line that goes through these two points. This is shown in Figure 12.20. Note that this regression line is much more horizontal (flat) than the other two we have drawn using the state-level data, indicating that the divorce rates do not seem to affect burglary rates in states.

## ▣ Comparison of *b* and *r*

In understanding the linear relationship between two continuous variables, we have discussed the slope coefficient (*b*) and the correlation coefficient (*r*). You may be wondering at this point why two statistics are necessary. Couldn't we estimate just one with our sample data and be done with it? The quick answer to your question (and you should know by now that there is *never* really a quick answer) is that although the two measures have some similar properties, they tell us somewhat different things about our continuous variables.

Note that the slope coefficient is interpreted in terms of the original units of measurement of the variables. That is, an increase of one in the *x* variable's unit of measurement (percent below the poverty level, percent rural population) changes (increases/decreases) the *y* variable by *b* units (murder rate per 100,000 and robbery rate per 100,000). Beyond this interpretation, however, there is no information that conveys the magnitude of the relationship. If, for example, we were to change units of measurement, say from dollars to pennies or from rates per 10,000 to rates per 100,000, the magnitude (but not the direction) of our slope coefficient would correspondingly change. That is why we cannot simply assume that a small slope coefficient indicates that the strength of the linear relationship is also small. A small slope coefficient may pack quite a wallop in terms of how strongly related it is to the dependent variable!

Notice, for example, that the slope coefficient in the regression equation for the divorce rate and the rate of burglary was equal to 12.68 (*b* = 12.68), but the slope coefficient in the regression equation for the poverty rate and the rate of murder was equal to .53 (*b* = .53). We cannot compare the magnitude of these two coefficients and conclude that the relationship between divorce and burglary is stronger than the relationship between poverty and murder. The reason why the slope coefficient for the poverty rate is so much smaller than that for the divorce rate is that there is so little variation in our rates of murder and that the rates themselves are much smaller than the rates of burglary. For example, the range of murder rates for our 20 states is from 2 to 12.3 per 100,000, whereas the range of burglary rates is from 321.6 to 1,117.3 per 100,000 population. This range and variation for the burglary rate is much larger than that for murder, and this magnitude of difference in the units of measurement is reflected in the magnitude of the slope (*b*). The correlation coefficient, however, is like a standardized linear measure of association. Its magnitude does not depend on what metric of measurement the variables are measured in. That is why we need the values of both the regression coefficient (*b*) and Pearson's correlation coefficient (*r*). The regression coefficient (*b*) gives us the more precise indicator of the linear change in *y* associated with a change in *x*, whereas the correlation coefficient (*r*) standardizes the magnitude of this relationship so that we can compare the relative strength of relationships across different cases and across different variables. When we examine the correlation coefficients for both cases, we see that the correlation is much stronger for the relationship between murder and poverty (*r* = .62) than for the relationship between divorce and burglary (*r* = .056).

In sum, the slope coefficient measures the *form* of the linear relationship between *x* and *y* but is expressed in terms of the units of measurement of the variables. The correlation coefficient can tell us about the *strength* of the linear relationship between two continuous variables, but it tells us nothing about the precise nature of that relationship. We cannot use the value of *r* to predict *y* values because we do not know how much of an impact *x* has on *y*, nor do we know the original measurement units of the variables. Again, this is because the correlation coefficient is standardized. For this reason, it is important to calculate and report both the slope coefficient (*b*) and the correlation coefficient (*r*). Knowing the values of both *b* and *r*, however, still does not tell us whether there is a significant relationship between *x* and *y*. For this, we need to perform a hypothesis test.

## ▣ Testing for the Significance of *b* and *r*

Because the slope (*b*) and correlation coefficient (*r*) are only sample estimates of their respective population parameters ($\beta$ and $\rho$), we must test for the statistical significance of *b* and *r*. In returning to our state-level data, the question we want to address concerns the relationship between *x* and *y* for the 50 states, not just for our sample of 20. We also include jurisdictions that did not report data to the FBI for the Uniform Crime Reports as our target population. The null hypothesis used for the slope and the correlation coefficient in the population assumes that there is no linear relationship between the $x$ and $y$ variables in the population. Remember that when there is no linear relationship between two variables, both the slope and the correlation coefficient will be equal to zero. Since the numerators for the slope and the correlation coefficient are identical, a hypothesis test about the slope is also a hypothesis test about the correlation coefficient in the bivariate case. The alternative hypothesis assumes that there is a linear relationship between the $x$ and $y$ variables in the population and, thus, that the slope and correlation coefficient are significantly different from zero. As with many other hypothesis tests, the alternative hypothesis can be stated as a one-tailed or two-tailed test. Formally stated, the null and alternative hypotheses for the slope and regression coefficient in the population would be:

$H_0$ : $\beta$ and $\rho = 0$, *or no relationship between x and y*

$H_1$ : $\beta$ and $\rho \neq 0$, *or there is a relationship between x and y*

$H_1$ : $\beta$ and $\rho > 0$, *or there is a positive relationship between x and y*

$H_1$ : $\beta$ and $\rho < 0$, *or there is a negative relationship between x and y*

Remember, we refer to the population parameters in the hypotheses because that is what we are really testing, the relationship between the variables in the population. Before we conduct our hypothesis test, however, we must be sure that our data meet certain assumptions. A few of these assumptions are familiar to you. For example, we must assume that the data were randomly selected. Second, we must assume that both variables are normally distributed. Third, we must assume that the data are continuous—that they are measured at the interval/ratio level. Fourth, we must assume that the nature of the relationship between the two variables is linear. The fifth assumption is really a set of assumptions about the error term. It is assumed that the error component of a regression equation is independent of and therefore uncorrelated with the independent or $x$ variable, that it is normally distributed, that it has an expected value of zero, and that it has constant variance across all levels of $x$. The last assumption is called the assumption of **homoscedasticity**. The assumption of homoscedasticity is simply that the variance of the conditional $y$ scores is the same at each value of $x$.

> **Homoscedasticity:** Assumption in ordinary least-squares (OLS) regression that the error terms are constant across all values of $x$.

---

*Assumptions for Testing Hypotheses about* $\beta$ *and* $\rho$

1. The observations were randomly selected.

2. Both variables have normal distributions.

3. The two variables are measured at the interval/ratio level.

4. The variables are related in a linear form.

5. The error component is independent of and therefore uncorrelated with the independent or $x$ variable, is normally distributed, has an expected value of zero, and has a constant variance across all levels of $x$ (assumption of homoscedasticity).

---

The assumption of homoscedasticity, as well as the assumption of linearity, may be assessed by examining the scatterplots. In Figure 12.21, the relationship between $x$ and $y$ is linear, and the assumption of homoscedasticity is met. At each value of $x$, the variance of $y$ is the same. In other words, the conditional distribution of the $y$ scores at fixed values of $x$ shows the same dispersion. No value of $x$ has a variance in the $y$ scores that is significantly higher or lower compared with the other values of $x$. In Figure 12.22, however, the assumption of homoscedasticity is violated. Although

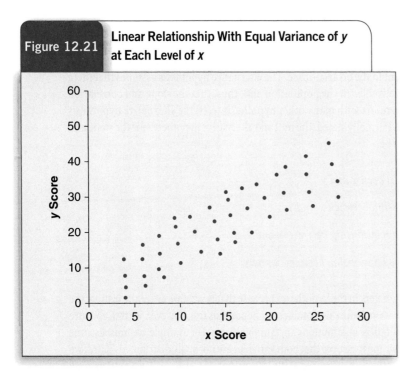

**Figure 12.21** Linear Relationship With Equal Variance of *y* at Each Level of *x*

the relationship is linear, the variance of the *y* scores is much greater at higher values of *x* than at lower values. This can be seen from the fact that there is a "wedge" pattern in the *y* scores as *x* increases. The spread, or dispersion, of *y* scores is greater when *x* is greater than 15. When the assumption of linearity is violated, linear-based statistics such as the Pearson correlation coefficient or the least-squares regression coefficient are not appropriate. When the assumption of homoscedasticity is not supported, you may have to make what are called transformations of your data. That topic, you will be relieved to learn, is beyond the scope of this book. You should be aware, however, that a careful inspection of your scatterplot is always the first order of business because it can warn you of potential problems with your data.

If all assumptions have been met, the significance test for *r* and *b* is relatively straightforward. With the null hypothesis of no linear relationship, the distribution of the sample *r*'s (and *b*'s) is approximated with the *t* distribution, with the degrees of freedom equal to *n* – 2. The *t* statistic for this test has the following formula:

$$t = r\sqrt{\frac{n-2}{1-r^2}} \qquad (12\text{-}7)$$

where

*r* = the estimated sample *r*

*n* = the sample size

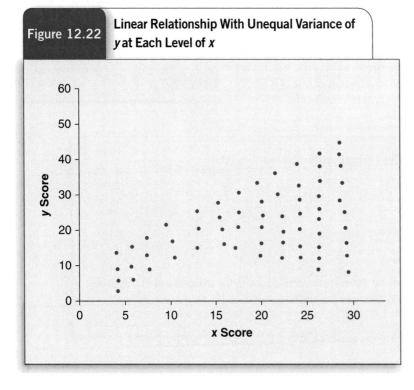

**Figure 12.22** Linear Relationship With Unequal Variance of *y* at Each Level of *x*

For our sample of state data, let's test for the significance of a linear relationship among the three sets of variables. Because we have some idea about the relationship between each independent and dependent variable, we will use one-tailed tests with an alpha level of .05 (one-tailed) and 18 degrees of freedom (20 – 2 = 18). We lose two degrees of freedom because we are estimating two parameters in our regression model, the intercept and the slope. From the *t* table in Table B.3 of Appendix B, we can see that for a one-tailed test with an alpha of .05 and 13 degrees of freedom, the critical *t* value is 1.734. Let's get going.

## Case Study

## Murder and Poverty

**Step 1:** For the relationship between the poverty and the murder rate, we found that $r = .62$ and $b = .53$. Our null hypothesis is that the slope and correlation coefficient are zero—that is, that there is no linear relationship between murder and poverty. Because we believe that there is a positive relationship between the poverty rate and the rate of murder, our research or alternative hypothesis is that both coefficients will be significantly greater than zero, or that as state poverty rates increase, so do rates of murder:

$H_0$: $\beta$ and $\rho$ for murder and poverty rates $= 0$.

$H_1$: $\beta$ and $\rho$ for murder and poverty rates $> 0$.

**Step 2:** To test this null hypothesis, we will use the $t$ statistic and its respective sampling distribution. The question we are really asking is, "If there was no linear relationship between the poverty rate and murder rate in the population, how likely is it that we would obtain a sample $r$ of .62 or greater, or a sample $b$ of .53 or greater?"

**Step 3:** We have already decided to use a one-tailed test with an alpha level of .05 ($\alpha = .05$). The critical value of $t$ from the $t$ table in Appendix B.3 tells us that our obtained value of $t$ for this test must be greater than 1.734 to reject the null hypothesis. So, our decision will be to reject the null hypothesis if $t_{obt} \geq 1.734$.

**Step 4:** Calculate the obtained value of $t$:

$$t = .62\sqrt{\frac{20-2}{1-(.62)^2}}$$

$$t = .62\sqrt{\frac{18}{1-.38}}$$

$$t = .62\sqrt{\frac{18}{.62}}$$

$$t = .62\sqrt{29.03}$$

$$t = .62(5.39)$$

$$t = 3.34$$

**Step 5:** Since our obtained $t$ of 3.34 is greater than the critical $t$ value of 1.734, we can reject the null hypothesis and conclude that there is a statistically significant relationship between poverty rate and murder rate for the 50 U.S. states. States with higher rates of poverty also have higher rates of murder in the population.

## Case Study

## Robbery Rates and Rural Population

Let's move on to our data examining the relationship between percent rural population and robbery. With our sample of 20 states, we found a correlation of $r = -.66$ and a slope of $b = -2.50$. Because we believe that states that have higher rates of rural population will tend to have lower rates of robbery, we will assume that the values of $b$ and $r$ also will be negative. This is reflected in our research hypothesis that follows, which states that the values of $b$ and $r$ in the population will be less than 0. The first step is to formalize our null and research hypotheses:

$H_0$: $\beta$ and $\rho$ for violent crime and rural $= 0$.

$H_1$: $\beta$ and $\rho$ for violent crime and rural $< 0$.

By using an alpha $= .05$ with 18 degrees of freedom for a one-tailed test, we have a critical value of $t$ equal to $-1.734$. We will reject the null hypothesis if $t_{obt}$ is less than or equal to $-1.734$ and will fail to reject the null hypothesis if it is greater than $-1.734$. We can next calculate the obtained value of $t$ from the sample data:

$$t = -.66\sqrt{\frac{20-2}{1-(-.66)^2}}$$

$$t = -.66\sqrt{\frac{18}{1-.44}}$$

$$t = -.66\sqrt{\frac{18}{.56}}$$

$$t = -.66\sqrt{32.14}$$

$$t = -.66(5.67)$$

$$t = -3.74$$

Since the obtained $t$ value of $-3.74$ is less than the critical $t$ value of $-1.734$, we can reject the null hypothesis of no linear relationship. We can conclude that there is a significant negative linear relationship between percent rural and rate of robbery for the 50 states. States with higher percentages of its population in rural areas tend to have significantly lower robbery rates.

# Case Study

## Burglary Rates and Divorce

Finally, let's test the null hypothesis that there is no significant linear relationship between the divorce rate and the rate of burglary. The sample correlation for our data was $r = .056$, and the estimated sample slope coefficient was $b = 12.68$. Our research hypothesis will assume that there is a positive relationship between the divorce rate and the rate of burglary, and along with the null hypothesis, it is formally stated as follows:

$H_0$: $\beta$ and $\rho$ for burglary and divorce $= 0$.

$H_1$: $\beta$ and $\rho$ for burglary and divorce $> 0$.

We are again using a one-tailed hypothesis. With 18 degrees of freedom and $\alpha = .05$, the critical value of $t$ is 1.734. We will reject the null hypothesis if $t_{obt} \geq 1.734$ and fail to reject it if $t_{obt} < 1.734$. The $t$ statistic we would obtain for this relationship is:

$$t = .056\sqrt{\frac{18}{1-(.056)^2}}$$

$$t = .056\sqrt{\frac{18}{1-.0031}}$$

$$t = .056\sqrt{\frac{18}{.9969}}$$

$$t = .056\sqrt{18.06}$$

$$t = .056(4.25)$$

$$t = .24$$

In this case, the obtained $t$ statistic is almost equal to zero. The value of .24 is much less than the critical $t$ value of 1.732. We must therefore fail to reject the null hypothesis. We must conclude that there is not a significant linear relationship between the divorce rate and the burglary rate at the state level. The divorce rate within states does not seem to affect the rate of burglary.

# ▣ The Problems of Limited Variation, Nonlinear Relationships, and Outliers in the Data

Before concluding this chapter on correlation and regression analysis, you need to be aware of some potential pitfalls when examining the linear relationship between two interval- and ratio-level variables. In general, you should always be suspicious of your data, and this suspicion should be overcome only by a careful understanding and inspection of your data at the univariate and bivariate levels—especially with graphical inspections. Exactly what kinds of problems are lurking out there for the unsuspecting correlation and OLS regression user?

One issue is the problem of limited variation in the independent or $x$ variable. Let's say you have an $x$ variable that is distributed in the population over a wide range of scores—say, from 0 to 40. In collecting your sample data, however, you observe $x$ scores range only from 0 to 10. Figure 12.23 shows that it is possible that if this occurs, you may find no correlation between $x$ and some $y$ when there is, in fact, a correlation in the full range of $x$ scores. As you can see in Figure 12.23, the estimated correlation and slope coefficients for the obtained data where the $x$ scores ranged only from 0 to 10 will be close to 0 even though across the total range of $x$

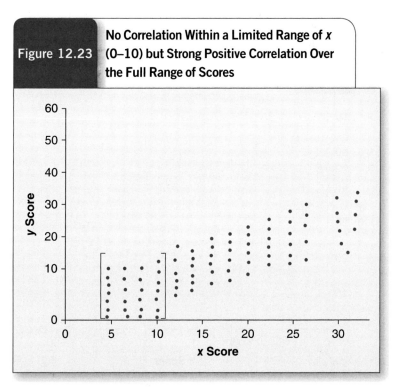

**Figure 12.23** No Correlation Within a Limited Range of $x$ (0–10) but Strong Positive Correlation Over the Full Range of Scores

scores there is a positive correlation. In fact, within any *limited range* of x scores, as Figure 12.23 indicates, there may seem to be no correlation between x and y, and the sample correlation and slope coefficients will be close to 0. You should always be aware of the fact that limited variation in the x variable may lead to sample estimates of no correlation when a correlation may, in fact, exist in the population when a wider range of x scores is taken into account.

A second problem you may see after examining the relationship between two continuous variables is *nonlinearity*. Throughout this chapter we have tried to emphasize the fact that the Pearson correlation coefficient (r) and the slope coefficient (b) both presume that the relationship between the x and y variable is a **linear relationship**. In other words, it is presumed that the data points in a scatterplot fall in an approximately straight line so that the mathematical equation for the straight line ($y = a + bx$) can be used both to describe the relationship and to obtain predicted values of y. The essence of a linearity is that the relationship between x and y is the same at all values of x. In most cases, when r and b = 0, you can assume that there is no relationship between x and y. However, be cautioned that this may not necessarily be the case. The two variables may have a very strong **nonlinear relationship**; in which case, both the correlation coefficient and the slope coefficient would be zero, but the conclusion of no relationship would be false. Take a close look at Figure 12.24 that illustrates this case.

> **Linear relationship:** The effect of x on y is generally the same at all values of x. A linear relationship is positive when x and y increase or decrease in the same direction, or negative, when x and y go in opposite directions.

> **Nonlinear relationship:** Can take several forms but generally indicates a relationship that changes direction as the values of the independent variable increase.

The relationship between the x and y variables in Figure 12.24 is a curvilinear relationship. At low levels of x, there is a moderate negative relationship with y, but at higher x scores, this relationship is positive. In this instance, the estimated correlation coefficient would be near zero as would the slope since the best-fitting straight line would go through the middle of the data, as illustrated in the scatterplot. With such a flat line, neither b nor r would be significantly different from zero. A much better-fitting line would be a curved one, as shown. The curved line shows that there is actually a very strong relationship between x and y, but the relationship happens to be curvilinear rather than linear.

Other examples of nonlinear relationships are shown in Figure 12.25. When the relationship between the variables is nonlinear, as in Figures 12.24 and 12.25, linear-based estimation techniques such as those discussed in this chapter are inappropriate. The least-squares approach of this chapter would underestimate the strength and nature of the true relationship. Unfortunately (or fortunately for you), the estimation of nonlinear relationships is beyond the scope of this book.

Our strong advice is that if you find that $r = b = 0$, do not immediately jump to the conclusion that there is no relationship between your variables. There may be a nonlinear relationship. To avoid this mistake, we again urge you to scrutinize your scatterplots carefully. If there really is no relationship between the two variables, the scatterplot will show a random scatter of data points (no pattern). In this case, the correlation coefficient will correctly be zero. If, however, the scatterplot shows evidence of marked nonlinearity, you should not use the linear statistics of this chapter.

As if these problems were not enough, there is another potential problem out there waiting to fool you. This is the problem posed by outliers. Recall from our discussion of EDA techniques that an **outlier**, as its name suggests, is a data point that is "lying out there," far away from the other scores.

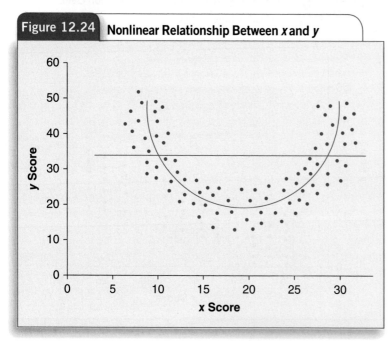

**Figure 12.24** **Nonlinear Relationship Between *x* and *y***

An outlier, then, is either an extremely low score or an extremely high score. The problem that an outlier poses to the unwary data analyst is that it can unduly influence the value of the slope and correlation coefficient. The presence of one or a few extreme scores may lead you to exaggerate the existence of a linear relationship by inflating the magnitudes of $r$ and $b$.

As an example of this, Table 12.10 reports hypothetical data for two variables: the rate of violent crime per 100,000 (the $x$ variable) and the incarceration rate per 100,000 (the $y$ variable). The latter variable is the number of state prisoners with a prison sentence of more than one year, per 100,000 residents of the state. In this example, we are interested in examining whether those states with high rates of serious crime also have high rates of incarceration. We might suspect that the response to high rates of violent crime is to "lock 'em up." You will note from Table 12.10 that the District of Columbia has both an unusually high rate of

| Figure 12.25 | Other Nonlinear Relationships |

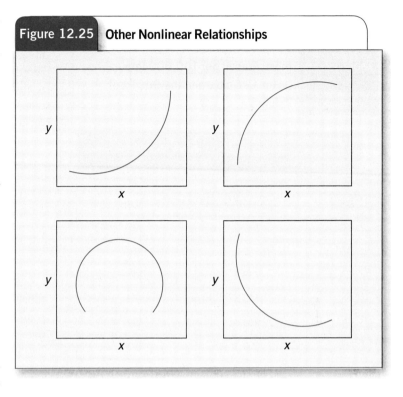

violent crime and an unusually high rate of incarceration. In fact, the violent crime rate for the District of Columbia is more than twice that of the state with the second highest violent crime rate (New York). In addition, its incarceration rate is more than three times higher than the next highest rate (506 per 100,000 for Oklahoma). The District of Columbia, then, represents an extreme case for these two variables; it is an outlier.

You can see just how far out it lies from the other scores in Figure 12.26, which is a scatterplot of the 13 jurisdictions' violent crime and incarceration rate data of Table 12.10. The 12 states lie in a relatively narrow range of values for both the violent crime rate and the incarceration rate. These data points cluster in the bottom left of the scatterplot. The data point representing the District of Columbia lies far away from these other points in the upper right-hand corner of the scatterplot. You can see from this what we mean when we say that for these data, the District of Columbia is an outlier.

The crucial issue, though, is the effect that an outlying score like this has on our analysis and interpretation of the data. We have estimated two regression equations, two slopes, and two correlation coefficients from these data—one from a data set that includes the District of Columbia and one excluding it. Based on the regression equations, we have also drawn two regression lines in Figure 12.26. By looking at these two lines, you can immediately see the effect that an outlier may have. When the District of Columbia is excluded from the analysis, the slope of the regression line is gently ascending, with a slope coefficient of $b = .186$. The correlation coefficient is $r = .403$, with $r^2 = .16$. This would suggest that the relationship between rate of violent crime and rate of incarceration is positive, although not particularly strong. Only 16% of the variation in the incarceration rate is explained by the rate of violent crime.

Note what happens, however, when the District of Columbia is included in the analysis. The regression line that includes the District of Columbia is ascending much more steeply, as reflected in the fact that the magnitude of the slope coefficient is almost three times higher ($b = .533$) than when the District was excluded. The value of the Pearson correlation coefficient increases to .938, and the coefficient of determination ($r^2$) is now .88. With the District of Columbia included in the analysis, then, 88% of the variation in the incarceration rate is explained by the rate of violent crime. We would conclude that there is a very strong positive linear relationship between the two variables.

| Table 12.10 | Hypothetical Rate of Violent Crime per 100,000 Population (*x*) and the Rate of Incarceration per 100,000 Population (*y*) for 12 States and the District of Columbia |
|---|---|

| State | Violent Crime Rate *x* | Incarceration Rate *y* |
|---|---|---|
| AL | 871.1 | 431 |
| CA | 1,119.7 | 368 |
| DE | 621.2 | 397 |
| DC | 2,832.8 | 1,549 |
| GA | 733.2 | 387 |
| IN | 508.5 | 250 |
| LA | 984.6 | 499 |
| MD | 1,000.1 | 383 |
| NY | 1,122.1 | 354 |
| OK | 622.8 | 506 |
| SC | 944.5 | 489 |
| TN | 746.2 | 250 |
| WA | 534.5 | 196 |

Not surprisingly, given the dramatic difference in their magnitude, our test of the statistical significance of *r* and *b* for the two sets of data would lead us to draw very different conclusions about the significance of the relationship between violent crime and incarceration rate. When the District of Columbia is not included in the data, we obtain a *t* value of:

$$t_{obt} = .403\sqrt{\frac{12-2}{1-.162}}$$

$$t_{obt} = .403\sqrt{\frac{10}{.838}}$$

$$t_{obt} = 1.392$$

With 10 (12 − 2) degrees of freedom for a one-tailed hypothesis test, an obtained *t* value of 1.392 would not be greater than the critical value α = .05 ($t_{crit}$ = 1.812). In this situation, we would fail to reject the null hypothesis. Even though a positive correlation exists in the sample, we would conclude from our hypothesis test that there is no significant linear relationship in the population between the violent crime rate and the rate of incarceration.

When we include the District of Columbia in our analysis, however, the obtained *t* value becomes:

$$t_{obt} = .938\sqrt{\frac{13-2}{1-.88}}$$

$$t_{obt} = .938\sqrt{\frac{11}{.12}}$$

$$t_{obt} = 8.981$$

With 11 (13 − 2) degrees of freedom, an obtained *t* value of 8.981 would be significant at α = .05 or α = .01 for a one-tailed test. In this circumstance, we would reject the null hypothesis and conclude that there is a positive linear relationship between the rate of violent crime and the rate of incarceration in the population, all because we included the outlier of the District of Columbia.

The lesson to be learned from this is that extreme scores, or outliers, may have a very pronounced effect on *r* and *b*, as well as on their associated significance tests. In the case of outliers such as the one in our example, we think the most transparent thing to do would be to report the analysis both with and without the outlying score or scores. In detecting outliers and other possible problems, we would once again urge you to examine your scatterplot carefully before rushing into any analysis. If you have not yet grasped a very important theme of this book, let us now unequivocally state it: *There is probably nothing more important than a very slow and careful inspection of your data, complete with descriptive statistics and graphical displays, before proceeding with your statistical analysis!*

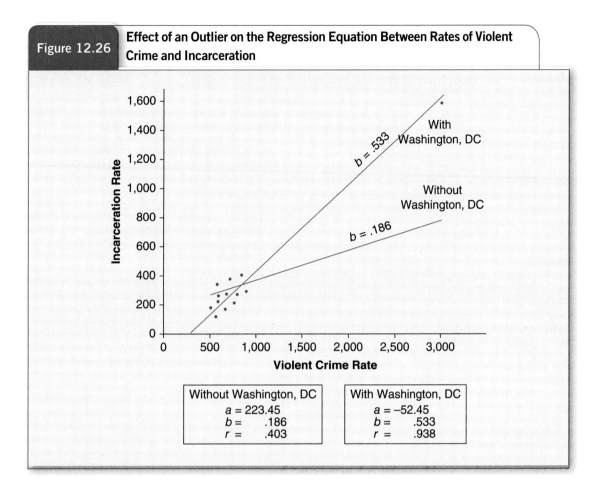

**Figure 12.26** Effect of an Outlier on the Regression Equation Between Rates of Violent Crime and Incarceration

| Without Washington, DC | With Washington, DC |
|---|---|
| a = 223.45 | a = −52.45 |
| b = .186 | b = .533 |
| r = .403 | r = .938 |

## 📖 Summary

in this chapter, we have been concerned with the relationship between two continuous (interval/ratio-level) variables. This relationship is often expressed in terms of the correlation between them. In examining the correlation between two continuous variables ($x$ and $y$), a very important first step is to create a scatterplot or scattergram. The scatterplot is a graphical display of your joint $xy$ data points. From the pattern of these data points, you can discern whether the relationship between your variables is linear (a pattern resembling a straight line), nonlinear (a pattern resembling a curved line), or whether there is no relationship between them (no pattern, but a random scatter of points). If the relationship is linear, you can tell from the scatterplot whether it is positive (the line is ascending) or negative (the line is descending). You can also make a preliminary judgment from your scatterplot about the strength of the linear relationship by roughly sketching a straight line that passes as close to as many data points as possible and examining how close the points fall to the line. The closer the data points cluster to the line, the stronger the linear relationship between the variables.

A more precise way to draw your regression line and calculate predicted values of $y$ $(\hat{y})$, however, would be to use the mathematical equation for a straight line ($y = a + bx$). If your data are linearly related, this regression line is estimated in such a way that it provides the "best linear fit" to your data. Rather than eyeballing the data and drawing a line that seems to come closest to the data points, this equation for the straight line will give us the best fit in terms of minimizing the squared difference between each data point and the mean of $y$ at fixed values of $x$. This is the idea of the "least-squares" regression line. One term in the regression equation is the slope (*b*), which measures the steepness of the line. The magnitude of the slope measures the effect of the *x* variable on the *y* variable with a one-unit change in *x*, and its sign tells us the direction of the relationship. Unfortunately, since the magnitude of the slope coefficient is expressed in terms of the natural units of measurement of the *x* and *y* variable, it is not a very convenient measure of association.

A standardized measure of association for continuous variables is the Pearson correlation coefficient (*r*). The sign of the correlation coefficient is the same as that of its corresponding slope. The value of the correlation coefficient is that it is bounded by ± 1.0, so as the relationship between *x* and *y* gets stronger, the magnitude of *r* gets closer to ±1.0. The drawback to the correlation coefficient as a measure of association is that although an *r* of 0 is indicative of no correlation and an *r* of ± 1.0 indicates a perfect correlation, the magnitudes between these values are not so easy to interpret, beyond subjective assessments such as a "weak" or "moderately strong" correlation.

The squared value of *r* (*r²*), the coefficient of determination, is, however, readily interpretable at all magnitudes. The value of *r²* reflects the amount of variation in the *y* variable that is explained by the *x* variable. Another way to understand this is to view the value of *r²* as an indication of how much we improve our prediction of *y* by knowing the value of *x*.

Once we have estimated the direction and strength of the relationship between two continuous variables with our sample data, we can test for the existence of a significant relationship in the population by using a *t* test.

Finally, in this chapter, we have emphasized the importance of carefully examining a scatterplot of your data before estimating correlation and regression coefficients. The fact that $r = b = 0$ should not uncritically lead you to the conclusion that there is no relationship between *x* and *y*. It may be that even though there is no linear relationship between the two, they have a very strong nonlinear relationship. Furthermore, the value of our correlation and regression coefficients may be dramatically affected by the presence of one or more extreme scores, or outliers, in our data. By examining the scatterplot, we can determine whether we have a nonlinear relationship between *x* and *y* or whether some extreme scores may be trying to lead us astray.

## Key Terms

➤ Review key terms with eFlashcards. $\circledS$SAGE edge™

beta coefficient   365
bivariate correlation   343
coefficient of
    determination (*r²*)   362
conditional mean of *y*   364
homoscedasticity   377
least-squares regression line   362

linear relationship   382
negative correlation   346
nonlinear relationship   382
Pearson's correlation
    coefficient   355
positive
    correlation   344

predicted value of $y(\hat{y})$   369
regression line   346
residual   371
scatterplot   343
slope   365
*y* intercept   365

## Key Formulas

Definitional formula for Pearson's *r* (equation 12-1):

$$r = \frac{\Sigma(x - \bar{X})(y - \bar{Y})}{\sqrt{\left[\Sigma(x - \bar{X})^2\right]\left[\Sigma(y - \bar{Y})^2\right]}}$$

Computational formula for Pearson's correlation coefficient (equation 12-2):

$$r = \frac{n\Sigma xy - (\Sigma x)(\Sigma y)}{\sqrt{\left[n\Sigma x^2 - (\Sigma x)^2\right]\left[n\Sigma y^2 - (\Sigma y)^2\right]}}$$

Ordinary least-squares regression line for the population (equation 12-3):

$$y = \alpha + \beta x$$

Sample regression line (equation 12-4):

$$y = a + bx$$

Definitional formula for the slope coefficient (equation 12-5):

$$b = \frac{\Sigma(x - \bar{X})(y - \bar{Y})}{\Sigma(x - \bar{X})^2}$$

Computational formula for the slope coefficient (equation 12-6):

$$b = \frac{n\Sigma xy - (\Sigma x)(\Sigma y)}{n\Sigma x^2 - (\Sigma x)^2}$$

$t$ statistic for testing null hypothesis about $b$ and $r$ (equation 12-7):

$$t = r\sqrt{\frac{n-2}{1-r^2}}$$

## Practice Problems

➤ Test your understanding of chapter content.
Take the practice quiz. **⑤SAGE edge™**

1. Interpret the following Pearson correlation coefficients.

   a. An $r$ of –.55 between the crime rate in a neighborhood and the median income level per household.

   b. An $r$ of .17 between the number of hours spent working after school and self-reported delinquency.

   c. An $r$ of .74 between number of prior arrests and length of sentence received for most recent conviction.

   d. An $r$ of –.12 between number of jobs held when 15–17 years old and number of arrests as an adult.

   e. An $r$ of –.03 between the divorce rate and a state's rate of violent crime.

2. Square each correlation coefficient in problem 1, and interpret the coefficient of determination.

3. Interpret the following regression slope coefficients:

   a. A $b$ of –.017 between the dollar fines given by a federal court for white-collar crimes and the number of citations for price fixing.

   b. A $b$ of .715 between percent unemployed and property crime rates.

   c. A $b$ of 1,444.53 between a police officer's years of education and his or her salary.

4. In 2014 research, Callie Burt, Gary Sweeten, and Ronald Simons found a moderately strong relationship between scores on a low self-control scale and self-reported acts of crime. Persons with low self-control admitted committing more criminal acts. Let's say you wanted to replicate this study. With the following data for self-control ($x$) (assume that high scores on this scale mean low self-control) and self-reported delinquency ($y$), do the following:

   a. Draw a scatterplot of your data points.

   b. Calculate what the slope of the regression line would be.

   c. Determine what the $y$ intercept is.

   d. What is the predicted number of self-reported offenses ($y$) when the score on the self-control scale is equal to 70?

   e. Calculate the value of $r$, and test for its significance with an alpha level of .01.

   f. How much of the variation in self-reported delinquency is explained by self-control?

   g. What would you conclude about the relationship between self-control and delinquency? Are your findings consistent with those reported by Callie Burt and her colleagues?

| $x$ Self-Control | $y$ Self-Reported Delinquency |
|---|---|
| 45 | 5 |
| 63 | 10 |
| 38 | 2 |
| 77 | 23 |
| 82 | 19 |
| 59 | 7 |
| 61 | 17 |
| 88 | 24 |
| 52 | 14 |
| 67 | 20 |

5. Kyung-Shick Choi, Mitch Librett, and Taylor Collins (2014) found that a gunshot detection system, Shotspotter™, significantly reduced the time it took police to respond to a gun-related crime. You are interested in determining whether this faster

police response time ($x$) will lower the crime rate ($y$) in a given community. You have the following data on the average time it takes the police to respond to a call by a citizen for help in a community, as well as that community's rate of crime. With this data, do the following:

a. Draw a scatterplot of your data points.

b. Calculate what the slope of the regression line would be.

c. Determine what the $y$ intercept is.

d. What is the predicted rate of crime ($\hat{y}$) when the police response time is 11 minutes?

e. Calculate the value of $r$, and determine whether it is significantly different from zero with an alpha level of .05.

f. How much of the variation in the rate of crime is explained by police response time?

g. What would you conclude about the relationship between police response time and crime?

| $x$<br>Police Response Time in Minutes | $y$<br>Community Rate of Crime per 1,000 |
|---|---|
| 14 | 82.9 |
| 3 | 23.6 |
| 5 | 42.5 |
| 6 | 39.7 |
| 5 | 63.2 |
| 8 | 51.3 |
| 7 | 58.7 |
| 4 | 44.5 |
| 10 | 61.2 |
| 12 | 73.5 |

6. A group of citizens has filed a complaint with the police commissioner of a large city. In this complaint, they allege that poor neighborhoods receive significantly less protection than more affluent neighborhoods. The commissioner asks you to examine this issue, and you have the following data on the percentage of the population in the neighborhood that is on welfare ($x$) and the

number of hours of daily police patrols ($y$) in a sample of 12 communities in the city. With these data in mind, do the following:

a. Draw a scatterplot of the data points.

b. Calculate what the slope of the regression line would be.

c. Determine what the $y$ intercept is.

d. What is the predicted number of hours of foot patrol ($\hat{y}$) when the percent unemployed is 30%?

e. Calculate the value of $r$, and test its significance with an alpha of .01.

f. How much of the variation in the number of hours of police patrol is explained by the percentage of the population on welfare?

g. What would you conclude about the relationship between percentage on welfare and number of police patrols?

h. Calculate the value of $b$ and $r$ again, but this time leave out community numbers 11 and 12. What do you conclude now? What do you think causes these very different findings? Draw a scatterplot of these data, and compare it with the one in part (a).

| Community Number | $x$<br>Percentage on Welfare (%) | $y$<br>Hours of Daily Police Patrol |
|---|---|---|
| 1 | 40 | 20 |
| 2 | 37 | 15 |
| 3 | 32 | 20 |
| 4 | 29 | 20 |
| 5 | 25 | 15 |
| 6 | 24 | 20 |
| 7 | 17 | 15 |
| 8 | 15 | 20 |
| 9 | 12 | 10 |
| 10 | 8 | 20 |
| 11 | 4 | 40 |
| 12 | 2 | 50 |

## SPSS Exercises

➤ Explore additional data sets. $SAGE edge™

| Data for Exercise | |
|---|---|
| Data Set | Description |
| 2012 states data.sav | This state-level data set compiles official statistics from various official sources, such as the census, health department records, and police departments. It includes basic demographic data, crime rates, and incidence rates for various illnesses and infant mortality for entire states. |
| Variables for Exercise | |
| Variable Name | Description |
| TobaccoDeathRt | The tobacco-related death rate per 100,000 for a state. |
| PerIndPoverty | The proportion of individuals below the poverty line in a state. |
| BurglarytRt | The burglary rate reported per 100,000 for a state. |
| RobberyRt | The robbery rate reported per 100,000 for a state. |

1. Your advisor, Dr. Smartypants, says: "Let's see how state characteristics end up predicting the robbery rate. Consider the following question: Is there a link between the unhealthy behaviors people engage in and the crime rate? I'm just fishing for results here, but let's see what we find!" He tells you to look into the relationship between the variables TobaccoDeathRt and BurglaryRt to see whether there is a relationship. He wants a graph of the two variables, estimates of the strength of the association, and a regression model to be fitted:

   a. **Constructing a Scatter Plot:** Before running the regression model, we should look at the relationship of the two variables using a scatterplot. This is done by selecting graphs->legacy dialogues-> scatter/dot->simple scatter. Then, put your independent variable on the y axis and the dependent variable on the x axis. Hang on to this graph.

   b. **Estimating Pearson's Correlation Coefficient:** To estimate Pearson's r, select analyze->correlate->bivariate:

      i. This output provides a matrix of correlations. Generally you are only interested in the bottom left half, as the top right half is redundant. Each cell contains several pieces of information: The correlation coefficient, the direction of the association, and the significance of the association presented in each cell. You can tell the level of statistical significance for a particular coefficient at a glance by the asterisks by each correlation coefficient, where $*p < .05$; $**p < .01$; $***p < .001$:

         1. Interpret the correlation coefficient, making special note to address the strength and direction of the association.

   c. **Estimating a regression model:** To do this, select analyze->regression->linear and put the independent and dependent variables in the correct spots:

      i. The output provided gives several pieces of information. The "model summary" box contains R-squared and R (*but not its direction!!!*). Notice that SPSS labels them both with capital letters. The ANOVA box is largely ignorable for your purposes. The "coefficients" box is what we are interested in. "Constant" refers to your intercept. The slope for your regression line is in the row named after your independent variable in the "unstandardized coefficients: B" column. Significance tests for the slope can be found on the far right under the "sig" box:

         1. Write the equation for your regression model in full.

         2. Interpret your regression coefficient. What does it tell us in this case?

         3. Are these results statistically significant? What are the hypotheses you are testing?

         4. Interpret the intercept as well. Is it useful in this scenario?

         5. Note the value for R-squared. What does this coefficient tell us, and why is it important?

   d. Now, put together a few sentences summarizing all your results to Dr. Smartypants. How comfortable are you with these accuracy results. Can you detect any caveats or concerns that must be considered?

2. Dr. Smartypants pulls you aside and confesses that he is more a visual person and would like you to give him a graph with the regression line plotted on it directly:

a. **Adding a regression line to a scatterplot**: First, construct a scatterplot as usual. Then, double click on the image of the graph plot. The Chart Editor will pop up. To add a regression line to the plot, simply select the [📈] button.

3. You turn in your report to Dr. Smartypants, who is clearly very excited. He says, "Holy macaroni! This proves it! The smokers are also robbing everyone; smoking causes criminal impulses! I've got to publish this right away!":

a. What do you think of his conclusion? Do you think it is an accurate interpretation of the data? Write a statement of support of his interpretation, or if you disagree, write a rebuttal and alternative interpretation.

4. You decide that you want to be sure about these results before publishing them by checking for another plausible relationship; perhaps poverty is linked to a high robbery rate:

a. Run all the analyses that you did for part 1 again, this time using the variable PerIndPoverty as your independent variable.

b. Write a summary of your results for Dr. Smartypants that incorporates the results from your scatterplot, correlation, and regression analysis.

5. Based on the analyses you have conducted thus far, what seems to be the most plausible explanation for robbery? If both variables are associated, why might that be the case, and which one do you think is the root cause? Which explanation seems to be more theoretically sound? Are you in a position to make claims of causality?

6. Dr. Smartypants asks you one more favor before you publish your paper together. He wants you to see whether the dependent variable, BurglaryRt, has any problems that might weaken your certainty of your conclusions. In essence, he wants you to check some of your regression assumptions. If you detect any violations of assumptions, consider how they may have influenced your conclusions; are your coefficients biased or just your hypothesis tests, for instance?

a. What level of measurement is this variable?

b. Use SPSS's graphing functions to construct a histogram of BurglaryRt. How would you describe this distribution—skewed left, skewed right, or normally distributed? Is there any evidence of extreme outliers?

c. Return to your scatterplot. Is there any evidence of a nonlinear relationship?

d. **Estimating errors (residuals) in SPSS**: Under the regression dialogue, select "save", and in the top right, you'll find a box for "residuals." Tick off the "unstandardized" box. *Estimate a model with poverty predicting burglary.* A new variable, typically called RES_1, will be created. Create a histogram. Are your errors normally distributed with a mean of roughly 0? Is there any evidence of heteroskedasticity in your errors (e.g., skewness and sudden enormous spikes)?

e. Think carefully about the data you are looking at. It comes from official police records. Can you think of anything that might threaten its accuracy?

7. If you would like additional practice with conducting regression analyses in SPSS, go through exercises 1–6 again with RobberyRt as your dependent variable.

# Part IV: Multitivariate Analysis

*Relationships Between*
*More Than Two Variables*

CHAPTER 13

# Controlling for a Third Variable

## Multiple OLS Regression

> *Not everything that can be counted counts, and not everything that counts can be counted.*
>
> —Albert Einstein

> *Conquest is easy. Control is not.*
>
> —Captain James T. Kirk, Stardate Unknown

---

**LEARNING OBJECTIVES**

1. Explain the importance of controlling for multiple independent variables when predicting a dependent variable.

2. Describe the difference between a bivariate correlation and a partial correlation coefficient.

3. Interpret a multiple coefficient of determination and be able to calculate the change in the multiple $R^2$.

4. Interpret the hypothesis test for a multiple regression model , and understand how it is different from the hypotheses tests for partial slope coefficients.

5. Calculate the multiple regression equation and be able to identify it from SPSS output.

6. Interpret the partial slope coefficient and its corresponding null hypothesis test.

7. Describe how the beta weights are different from unstandardized slope coefficients.

# ▣ Introduction

This chapter represents a very exciting transition in our statistical analyses adventures! Most of our work with inferential statistics has involved bivariate relationships—examining the effects of one independent variable on a dependent variable. However, in our discipline, and in all social sciences more generally, it is virtually never the case that one independent variable alone sufficiently explains the dependent variable. In reality, there are usually several factors that jointly influence the dependent variable. For example, delinquency is not only affected by school grades but also by the delinquency of our friends, our relationships with parents, whether we have jobs during the school year, and a host of other factors. Recidivism is not just influenced by the type of crime someone committed but by many factors including whether he or she received educational training while in prison, or mental health and substance abuse treatment, the support he or she received after release, and so on. We need, therefore, to build on our knowledge of the bivariate regression model by adding more independent variables to that model. When we examine the effect of more than one independent variable on a dependent variable, we employ what is called a **multivariate regression model.** As the name implies, in the *multivariate* model, we have more than one independent variable whose relationships with the dependent variable we wish to estimate. An implicit assumption of the multivariate regression model, therefore, is that there is more than one independent variable that explains the dependent variable and the purpose of the model is to estimate the effect of each of these independent variables simultaneously. In the multivariate model, therefore, we have a correlation coefficient and regression coefficient for each of the independent variables in the model. The corresponding correlation coefficient is called the *partial correlation coefficient,* and the regression coefficient is called the *partial regression coefficient.* In this chapter, we introduce some of the most important features of the multivariate regression model and partial correlation coefficient.

> **Multivariate regression model:** A regression model predicting one dependent variable with two or more independent variables.

# ▣ What Do We Mean by Controlling for Other Important Variables?

Identifying the causes of phenomenon—figuring out why things happen—is the goal of much research. Unfortunately, valid explanations for the causes of things, including crime and the workings of the criminal justice system, are rarely very simple. In Chapter 1, we introduced the term of causal or internal validity. Recall that we can assume causal validity if we find that a change in one variable leads to or produces a change in another variable, *ceteris paribus* (i.e., other things being equal). It is this last clause, "all things being equal," which is the tricky part! Establishing the existence of a causal effect between an independent and a dependent variable is often termed "making a causal inference." The language we use in criminology and criminal justice often implies causality. For example, if a research study finds that arrested men who assault their intimate partners are less likely to assault their partners in the future compared with assaulters who were not arrested, the researcher may conclude that arrest was causally related to this decrease in the likelihood of future violence. When it is found that inmates who participated in a therapeutic community within prison are less likely to recidivate than those who did not participate, we often say that the reduced crime on release was produced or caused by their involvement in a rehabilitation program. But establishing a causal relationship through research is actually very difficult. Specifically, three things need to exist before we can conclude that a causal connection exists between two variables:

> **Get the edge on your studies.**
> edge.sagepub.com/bachmansccj4e
>
> - Take a quiz to find out what you've learned.
> - Review key terms with eFlashcards.
> - Explore additional data sets.
>
> **⑤SAGE edge™**

1. There must be an empirical association between them.

2. The independent variable must precede the dependent variable in time.

3. Other possible causes of the dependent variable must be explicitly considered. That is, the relationship between two variables must be **nonspurious**, which means it is not caused by a third variable.

**Nonspuriousness:** Exists when a relationship between two variables is not explained by a third variable.

The first criterion, demonstrating that there is a statistical association or correlation between the independent and dependent variables, is generally the easiest to satisfy. In fact, we know you have become relatively good at this by now! Establishing the second criterion—that the independent variable occurred prior to the dependent variable—is sometimes very easy and sometimes very difficult. The easy form of the correct temporal order occurs when it is logically impossible for the dependent variable to come first. For example, if we find that males are more likely to drop out of high school than females, the correct temporal order can only be that something about gender causes males to have a higher risk of dropping out since dropping out cannot logically cause gender. The more difficult form of the correct temporal order of our causal variables can frequently be accomplished by a careful research design. For example, if we were trying to determine the effects of watching media violence on adolescents' violent behavior, a researcher would have to set up a study to monitor the violent behavior of participants after he or she observed media violence, thereby establishing the correct time order of the independent and dependent variables. So, for example, the subjects in a study could be randomly assigned to watch two TV programs, one violent and one not, and we could then measure their aggressiveness in a computer game. The watching of the violent TV program was staged first according to the research design. The third criterion, nonspuriousness, is related to the subject matter of this chapter. Nonspuriousness between two variables means that the relationship between them is not caused by a third factor or factors that may be related to them both. When a third variable ($z$), sometimes called an extraneous variable, causes both the independent variable ($x$) and the dependent variable ($y$), there will be a correlation between $x$ and $y$, but this correlation is present because they are both outcomes of the third variable $z$. Thus, $x$ and $y$ are not *causally* related to each other but, rather, are spuriously related; they ($x$ and $y$) are simply two outcomes of a common cause ($z$). They are said to be spuriously related because they both depend on $z$ and not on each other.

Figure 13.1(a) shows a causal relationship among three variables, $x$, $y$, and $z$. The variable $z$ causes $x$, and $x$ in turn causes $y$. In this figure, the relationship between $x$ and $y$ is causal. In Figure 13.1(b), we have the situation where $z$ is the common cause of both $x$ and $y$. Here the dashed line indicates that $x$ and $y$ are correlated not because one causes the other but simply because they both depend on $z$. One of the most vexing problems in making inferences about causality, then, is the possibility that one has not really measured the causal effect of one variable on another because there is some third factor causing them both. To help us make more valid causal inferences, then, we need to measure and consider other variables and control for their effects. One powerful way to control for the effects of other variables is to collect data from a randomized experiment. In a randomized experiment, subjects are randomly placed into "treatment" or "control" groups. Because the assignment into these groups is random, the groups can be considered equivalent. Suppose we wanted to determine whether a prison job training program reduced recidivism after release. If we randomly assigned inmates to either receive the program and not others, the only difference between the two groups after release would be whether they received treatment. As such, if the people who received the job training had lower rates of recidivism compared with those who did not, we can be relatively certain that the program had something to do with this difference.

It is not always possible to conduct true experiments, however. If we are interested in the effect of a good marriage on offenders quitting crime, how can we randomly assign people to get married or not get married, or assign some to a good marriage and some to a bad marriage or no marriage? As you can see, there are many instances where a randomized experimental design cannot or cannot easily be used; in social science, we more frequently than not have observational rather than experimental data. In collecting observational data, we observe but do not manipulate who gets the "treatment" and who does not. For example, we simply observe those who are married or who have good marriages and those who are not or have bad marriages. Since we do not have control with the randomization of subjects, in observational data, we must control for spuriousness statistically. One common technique used statistically to control

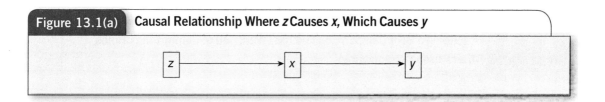

**Figure 13.1(a)**  **Causal Relationship Where *z* Causes *x*, Which Causes *y***

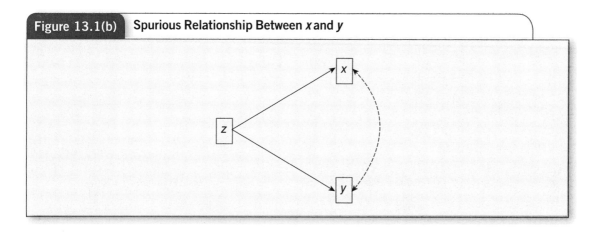

**Figure 13.1(b)**  **Spurious Relationship Between *x* and *y***

for the effects of other variables is multiple regression analysis. But before we discuss this more advanced technique, we want to illustrate the concept of statistical control with an easier-to-understand partial cross-tabulation table.

## Illustrating Statistical Control With Partial Tables

### Case Study

## Boot Camps and Recidivism

The top panel of Figure 13.2 depicts data from a hypothetical study examining the relationship between attending a boot camp prison (a highly regimented, discipline-focused correctional program) and whether people committed a crime after prison (recidivism). As you can see, the 2 × 2 table reveals that prisoners who attended boot camp were slightly less likely to recidivate (47%) than those who did not attend the boot camp (55%). The bottom panel of Figure 13.2, however, depicts this same relationship between attending boot camp and recidivism, while holding constant the offender's gender. In this case, "holding constant" means looking at the relationship between two variables (boot camp attendance and recidivism) within separate levels of a third variable (gender). In this example, notice that in looking at the relationship between attending a boot camp prison and recidivism, we have turned gender into a constant. In the males only table, the relationship between boot camp participation and recidivism cannot be due to gender, and the same holds for the female table.

This bottom table is referred to as a partial cross-tabulation table; it examines the relationship between boot camp attendance and recidivism separately for males and females. When gender is held constant, a much different picture emerges. Within categories of gender, there is no relationship between going to a boot camp and the risk of recidivism. The original relationship between recidivism and boot camp attendance is spurious. It was present primarily because gender is correlated with both going to boot camp and the risk of recidivism. Attending boot camp just appears to reduce recidivism because males were both less likely to attend boot camp and more likely to commit crimes after prison, regardless of whether they attended boot camp or a regular correctional facility.

| Figure 13.2 | Data From a Hypothetical Study Examining the Relationship Between Attending a Boot Camp Prison and the Likelihood of Committing Crimes After Prison (Recidivating) |
| --- | --- |

**All Prisoners, n = 350**

| | Attended Boot Camp | Did Not Attend Boot Camp |
| --- | --- | --- |
| Recidivated | 75 47% | 105 55% |
| Did Not Recidivate | 85 53% | 85 45% |
| | 160 | 190 |

**Female Prisoners, n = 150**

| | Attended Boot Camp | Did Not Attend |
| --- | --- | --- |
| Recidivated | 40 40% | 20 40% |
| Did Not Recidivate | 60 60% | 30 60% |
| | 100 | 50 |

**Male Prisoners, n = 200**

| | Attended Boot Camp | Did Not Attend |
| --- | --- | --- |
| Recidivated | 30 60% | 90 60% |
| Did Not Recidivate | 20 40% | 60 40% |
| | 50 | 150 |

This example illustrates the utility of statistical control. If the original bivariate relationship between an independent variable and a dependent variable still holds even after we have controlled for other variables, we can have more confidence that these variables may actually be causally related. If the original relationship between the two variables disappears, however, then those two original variables may be only spuriously related. As we shall see, the multivariate regression equation gives us the same kind of statistical control that exists in the partial cross-tabulation tables.

# ▣ The Multiple Regression Equation

As we suggested earlier, the **multiple regression equation** (or model) is simply a straightforward extension of the bivariate regression model. The difference between the bivariate and multiple regression models is that the latter has more than one independent variable. In the case of the multiple regression model, we aim to estimate the effect of several independent variables on a dependent variable. Given that there are several independent variables, there will be more than one slope coefficient to estimate. In fact, there will be one slope coefficient for each independent variable that is in the model. Formally, the multiple regression model for the population specifies the dependent variable ($y$) as being a

**Multiple regression equation:**
Equation estimated with two or more independent variables predicting one dependent variable.

linear function of two or more independent variables ($x_1$ $x_2$, and so on) plus an error term that encompasses various omitted factors that are also related to $y$ but we have not included in our model:

$$y = \alpha + \beta_1 x_1 + \beta_2 x_2 + \cdots + \beta_k x_k + \varepsilon \qquad (13\text{--}1)$$

where

$k$ = the number of independent variables

$\varepsilon$ = an error term

There are many similarities between this model and the bivariate regression model of the previous chapter. The $\alpha$ and $\beta$ terms are population parameters that are estimated by sample data. The corresponding sample estimates are $a$ (the intercept) and $b$ (the slope coefficient). As before, the ordinary least-squares (OLS) multivariate regression equation estimates the "best-fitting" regression line to the data. It is best fitting according to the same principle of least squares—it minimizes the sum of the squared deviations between the predicted $y$ values and the observed $y$ values. Similar to the bivariate case, then, the goal of multiple regression is to provide the best-fitting line between a continuous dependent variable and several independent variables.

Despite these similarities, however, the multivariate regression model in equation 13-1 contains some new concepts, as well as different meanings for some old concepts. The multivariate regression model estimated from sample data is represented as:

$$y = a + b_1 x_1 + b_2 x_2 + \cdots b_k x_k + \varepsilon \qquad (13\text{--}2)$$

The intercept ($a$) in this multivariate equation is the predicted value of $y$ when *all* independent variables are equal to 0. The interpretation of the slope coefficient ($b$), which is identified by subscripts, is somewhat different from the bivariate case. Technically, slope coefficients estimated with multiple regression equations are referred to as **partial slope coefficients** or **partial regression coefficients**. The first slope coefficient in equation 13-2, $b_1$, is the partial slope of the linear relationship between the first independent variable and the dependent variable, $y$, *holding all other variables in the model constant*. By holding all other variables constant, we mean after taking their effect on the dependent variable into account. The second slope coefficient, $b_2$, is the partial slope of the linear relationship between the second independent variable and $y$, holding all other variables in the model constant. If you were using five independent variables to predict a dependent variable, there would be five partial slope coefficients, each denoted by its subscript ($b_1$, $b_2$, $b_3$, $b_4$, $b_5$).

> **Partial slope coefficient:** Effect of an independent variable on the dependent variable after controlling for one or more other independent variables.

Each slope coefficient indicates the expected change in the $y$ variable associated with a one-unit change in a given independent variable, when all other independent variables in the model are held constant. This last component of the interpretation, "when all other independent variables are held constant," is important. It is this statistical control that enables us to separate the effect of one independent variable from the effects of other independent variables in the regression model. In other words, the partial slope coefficient measures the effect of one independent variable on the dependent variable when the effects of all the other independent variables in the model on the dependent variable have been considered (e.g., statistically controlled for).

The final term in the multiple regression equation is the error term, $\varepsilon$. As in the bivariate model, the error component in the multiple regression model reflects those explanatory variables that are not included in the model. The practice of good regression analysis consists of including in the model those explanatory variables that are most strongly related to the dependent variable—and unrelated to the other independent variables included in the model. Although the multiple regression equation can be estimated using a large number of independent variables, for ease of presentation, we will concentrate on equations using only two independent variables. The extension to more than two independent variables is relatively straightforward.

---

**Assumptions of the Multivariate Regression Model**

1. The observations are independent.

2. All values of $y$ are normally distributed at each value of $x$.

3. The dependent variable is measured at the interval/ratio level.

4. The relationship between the dependent variable and each of the independent variables is linear.

5. The error term ($\varepsilon$) is independent of, and therefore uncorrelated with, each of the independent variables; is normally distributed; has an expected value of 0; and has constant variance across all levels of $x$.

6. The independent variables are not highly correlated among themselves. That is, there is no multicollinearity.

---

The assumptions of the multiple regression model are identical to those for the case of one independent variable, except for the addition of one new assumption (see the accompanying boxed list). The new assumption in the multivariate regression model is that the independent variables are independent of, or uncorrelated with, one another. Having independent variables that are highly correlated is referred to as the problem of **multicollinearity**. That was the point we were making when we said that the ideal regression analysis is to select independent variables that are strongly related to the dependent variable *and only weakly related or unrelated to each other*. This problem did not arise in the case of one independent variable, but it will be a constant concern as we add to the list of independent variables in our model.

**Multicollinearity:** Occurs whenever the independent variables in your regression equation are too highly correlated with one another.

Why is it so important that the independent variables be uncorrelated with one another? To answer this question, think carefully about what we want to do in multiple regression analysis. We have a dependent variable that we are trying to explain. We have at least two independent variables that may explain this dependent variable. We would like to learn two important things from our multiple regression analysis: (1) How much of the variation in the dependent variable are we explaining by our two independent variables together? (2) How much of this combined explained variation can we say is *uniquely* due to each of the independent variables? The first question asks how much can we explain in the dependent variable. The second asks how much of what we explain is due to the unique contribution of *each* of our independent variables. It is this second question that is difficult to answer when the independent variables are correlated.

Think of two independent variables as lying on a continuum from being completely unique variables with absolutely nothing in common (their correlation is zero), to being identical to one another and having everything in common (their correlation is ±1.0). At one end of this continuum are two variables that are completely unique. These variables are not related to each other, so the correlation between them is near zero or zero. When two variables are correlated, however, it means that they share something in common; they are both measuring some of the same things. The lower the correlation, the more they are unique and the less they have in common; the higher the correlation, however, the less unique they are and the more they have in common. When two independent variables are completely uncorrelated, we are able to separate the combined explained variance of the dependent variable into unique components. For example, we can specify that of the 60% of explained variance in the dependent variable ($y$), two thirds of that is due to $x_1$ and the other one third is due to $x_2$. As two independent variables become correlated, however, some of the explained variance in the dependent variable cannot be uniquely attributed to one or the other variable. That is, some of the explained variance cannot be said to be due to $x_1$ or $x_2$ but can only be said to be due to their shared influence. The stronger the correlation between the two independent variables, the less of the explained variance we can attribute to the unique effect of each variable, and the more we must attribute to the explained variance that they share. When the two variables are very highly correlated, we can attribute no unique explained variance to either of them, and all of the explained variance in the dependent variable is shared between the two.

When the independent variables in a regression equation are highly correlated with one another, they are said to be *collinear*. This means that there is a relationship among the independent variables. The final assumption simply notes that you want to avoid multicollinearity in multiple regression analysis. As we stated earlier, you want your independent variables to be strongly correlated with the dependent variable but not highly correlated with each other.

Fortunately, you can detect problems of multicollinearity in your data. If you have only two independent variables, the easiest way to identify severe multicollinearity is to examine the correlation between them. The higher the correlation between your two independent variables is, the greater the problem of multicollinearity. Although this is not a "hard-and-fast" rule, be suspicious of multicollinearity when the correlation between two independent variables is $r = .70$ or higher. With more than two independent variables, the detection of multicollinearity becomes more of a problem. One simple way to detect it in such cases is to inspect the standard error of your regression coefficients. Multicollinearity will manifest itself in high standard errors for two or more coefficients that are highly correlated. If one variable is dropped from the model, and the standard error of the other is substantially decreased, multicollinearity will frequently be the source. Another way to detect multicollinearity is to regress each independent variable on the other independent variables. In this analysis, each independent variable becomes the dependent variable and the other independent variables serve as independent variables for it. If multicollinearity is not a problem, the amount of explained variance ($r^2$) will be quite low.

We may have gotten a little ahead of ourselves with this detailed discussion of multicollinearity. It is important, however, for you to understand fully this very important assumption of the multiple regression model. Now let's return to the multiple regression model described in equation 13-2 and consider some data to illustrate and give meaning to the concepts we have discussed thus far.

---

# Case Study

## Predicting Delinquency

Table 13.1 presents hypothetical data from a random survey of 23 high-school students who were queried about a number of things, including the number of self-reported delinquent acts in the past year ($y$), their age ($x_1$), and how emotionally close they felt to their family ($x_2$) with a higher score on the close family scale corresponding to a closer connection between the student and family. Two indexes or scales were created that measured students' self-reported delinquency and family closeness. From these data, we are going to estimate the effect that both age and family closeness have on rates of delinquency.

For the sake of this example, let's say that we believe that age will be positively related to delinquency and that family closeness will be negatively related to delinquency. Thus, older students will tend to have higher delinquency scores, and those who are closer to their families will tend to have lower rates of delinquency. In this example, delinquency is our dependent variable ($y$), whereas age ($x_1$) and family closeness ($x_2$) are our two independent variables. Our two-variable regression model, then, looks like this:

$$\text{Delinquency}\,(y) = a + b_1(\text{age}) + b_2(\text{family closeness}) + \varepsilon$$

The mean, standard deviation, and correlation coefficients are presented at the bottom of Table 31.1.

The first step we need to take in computing our multiple regression equation is to calculate each partial slope. The formulas used for calculating partial slope coefficients are:

$$b_1 = \left(\frac{s_y}{s_{x_1}}\right)\left(\frac{r_{yx_1} - \left(r_{yx_2}\right)\left(r_{x_1x_2}\right)}{1 - r_{x_1x_2}^2}\right) \tag{13–3}$$

**Table 13.1** Calculations Necessary to Compute the Partial Slope Coefficient Between Delinquency and Both Age and Family Closeness, $n = 23$

| Delinquency $y$ | Age $x_1$ | Family Closeness $x_2$ | $y^2$ | $x_1^2$ | $x_2^2$ | $x_1 y$ | $x_2 y$ |
|---|---|---|---|---|---|---|---|
| 80 | 17 | 10 | 6,400 | 289 | 100 | 1,360 | 800 |
| 60 | 15 | 20 | 3,600 | 225 | 400 | 900 | 1,200 |
| 50 | 14 | 25 | 2,500 | 196 | 625 | 700 | 1,250 |
| 70 | 17 | 15 | 4,900 | 289 | 225 | 1,190 | 1,050 |
| 10 | 13 | 35 | 100 | 169 | 1,225 | 130 | 350 |
| 15 | 13 | 30 | 225 | 169 | 900 | 195 | 450 |
| 20 | 14 | 28 | 400 | 196 | 784 | 280 | 560 |
| 5 | 13 | 40 | 25 | 169 | 1,600 | 65 | 200 |
| 70 | 13 | 15 | 4,900 | 169 | 225 | 910 | 1,050 |
| 55 | 14 | 20 | 3,025 | 196 | 400 | 770 | 1,100 |
| 40 | 15 | 25 | 1,600 | 225 | 625 | 600 | 1,000 |
| 35 | 16 | 20 | 1,225 | 256 | 400 | 560 | 700 |
| 10 | 17 | 30 | 100 | 289 | 900 | 170 | 300 |
| 15 | 16 | 25 | 225 | 256 | 625 | 240 | 375 |
| 10 | 14 | 20 | 100 | 196 | 400 | 140 | 200 |
| 15 | 16 | 25 | 225 | 256 | 625 | 240 | 375 |
| 0 | 14 | 25 | 0 | 196 | 625 | 0 | 0 |
| 0 | 13 | 35 | 0 | 169 | 1,225 | 0 | 0 |
| 20 | 14 | 20 | 400 | 196 | 400 | 280 | 400 |
| 0 | 13 | 20 | 0 | 169 | 400 | 0 | 0 |
| 20 | 14 | 30 | 400 | 196 | 900 | 280 | 600 |
| 45 | 16 | 30 | 2,025 | 256 | 900 | 720 | 1,350 |
| 50 | 17 | 25 | 2,500 | 289 | 625 | 850 | 1,250 |
| $\Sigma = 695$ | $\Sigma = 338$ | $\Sigma = 568$ | $\Sigma = 34,875$ | $\Sigma = 5,016$ | $\Sigma = 15,134$ | $\Sigma = 10,580$ | $\Sigma = 14,560$ |

$\bar{Y} = 30.22$    $\bar{X}_{x_1} = 14.70$    $\bar{X}_{x_2} = 24.70$

$s_y = 25.11$    $s_{x_1} = 1.49$    $s_{x_2} = 7.09$

$r_{yx_1} = .445$

$r_{yx_2} = -.664$

$r_{x_1 x_2} = -.366$

$$b_2 = \left( \frac{s_y}{s_{x_2}} \right) \left( \frac{r_{yx_2} - \left( r_{yx_1} \right)\left( r_{x_1x_2} \right)}{1 - r_{x_1x_2}^2} \right) \qquad (13\text{--}4)$$

where

$b_1$ = the partial slope of $x_1$ on $y$

$b_2$ = the partial slope of $x_2$ on $y$

$s_y$ = the standard deviation of $y$

$s_{x_1}$ = the standard deviation of the first independent variable ($x_1$)

$s_{x_2}$ = the standard deviation of the second independent variable ($x_2$)

$r_{yx_1}$ = the bivariate correlation between $y$ and $x_1$

$r_{yx_2}$ = the bivariate correlation between $y$ and $x_2$

$r_{x_1x_2}$ = the bivariate correlation between $x_1$ and $x_2$

Note that you need not only the bivariate correlation coefficient between each of the two independent variables and the dependent variable ($r_{yx_1}$, $r_{yx_2}$) but also the bivariate correlation between the two independent variables ($r_{x_1x_2}$). In our examples of the multiple regression model, we will go through the calculations of each component of the partial slope coefficient, but we will provide you with each bivariate correlation coefficient.

As shown in the tables, the bivariate correlation coefficients indicate that the relationship between age and delinquency is positive ($r = .445$) and the relationship between family closeness and delinquency is negative ($r = -.664$). These correlation coefficients suggest that older students tend to have higher levels of delinquency but that students with stronger family closeness tend to have lower levels of delinquency. In addition, age and family closeness are negatively related to each other ($r_{x_1x_2} = -.366$); older youth are less close to their family than younger youth. The correlation between our two independent variables ($r = -.366$) is not very high, so we do not have to worry about the problem of multicollinearity.

With these correlation coefficients, together with the standard deviation of each of the variables and formulas 13-3 and 13-4, we can calculate the partial slope coefficient for each independent variable. From these partial slope coefficients, we will be able to ascertain the effect of each independent variable on the dependent variable, while holding the other independent variable constant. These calculations are shown for you as follows.

Partial slope coefficient for the effect of age on delinquency:

$$b_1 = \left( \frac{25.11}{1.49} \right)\left( \frac{.445 - (-.664)(-.366)}{1 - (-.366)^2} \right)$$

$$b_1 = (16.85)\left( \frac{.445 - .243}{1 - .134} \right)$$

$$b_1 = (16.85)\left( \frac{.202}{.866} \right)$$

$$b_1 = (16.85)(.233)$$

$$b_1 = 3.93$$

Partial slope coefficient for the effect of family closeness on delinquency:

$$b_2 = \left(\frac{25.11}{7.09}\right)\left(\frac{-.664-(.445)(-.366)}{1-(-.366)^2}\right)$$

$$b_2 = (3.54)\left(\frac{-.664-(-.163)}{1-.134}\right)$$

$$b_2 = (3.54)\left(\frac{-.501}{.866}\right)$$

$$b_2 = (3.54)(-.58)$$

$$b_2 = -2.05$$

The partial slope coefficient for the effect of age on delinquency is $b_1 = 3.93$. This indicates that, on average, with every one-year increase in age (since age is measured in years), the delinquency score increases by 3.93 offenses, while holding constant an individual's closeness to family. Similarly, the partial slope coefficient for the effect of family closeness on the delinquency score is $b_2 = -2.05$. This indicates that, on average, for every one-unit increase in an individual's family closeness, there is a 2.05-unit decrease in delinquency, while holding constant an individual's age.

Now that we have obtained the partial slope coefficients for the independent variables of age $(b_1)$ and family closeness $(b_2)$, we can compute the final unknown element in the least-squares regression equation, the intercept $(a)$. This is done in the same way we obtained the intercept in the bivariate regression equation—by substituting the mean of the dependent variable $(\bar{Y})$ and the means of the two independent variables $(\bar{X}_{x_1}$ and $\bar{X}_{x_2})$ into the equation below and solving for $a$:

$$a = \bar{Y} - b_1\bar{X}_1 - b_2\bar{X}_2$$
$$a = 30.22 - 3.93(14.70) - (-2.05)(24.70)$$
$$a = 30.22 - (57.77) - (-50.64)$$
$$a = 23.09$$

The intercept value in these equations indicates that when both independent variables are equal to zero, the average value of $y$ will be equal to 23.09. Now that we have solved for the intercept $(a)$ and both partial regression slopes, our multiple regression equation for delinquency can be expressed as:

$$\hat{y} = a + b_1x_1 + b_2x_2$$
$$\hat{y} = 23.09 + (3.93)(x_1) + (-2.05)(x_2)$$
$$\hat{y} = 23.09 + (3.93)(\text{age}) + (-2.05)(\text{family closeness})$$

Just like the bivariate regression equation we examined in the last chapter, this least-squares multiple regression equation provides us with the best-fitting line to our data. However, we can no longer represent the equation graphically with a simple straight line fitted to a two-dimensional $(x,y)$ scattergram. With two independent variables in our regression, we have to use our imagination to visualize the fitting of a regression plane to a three-dimensional scatter of points that is defined by each of the coefficients $(a, b_1, b_2)$. As you can imagine, this exercise in imagery becomes even more complex as more independent variables are brought into the equation. With $k$ independent variables, the regression equation is represented by a plane in $k$-dimensional space. However, we can still use this multivariate equation to predict scores on our dependent variable, number of delinquent acts committed, from scores on the independent variables of age and family closeness. For example, our best prediction of a delinquency score $(\hat{y})$ for an 18-year-old and a score on the family closeness index of 15 would be obtained by substituting these two $x$ values into the least-squares regression formula as shown:

$$\hat{y} = a + b_1 x_1 + b_2 x_2$$
$$\hat{y} = 23.09 + 3.93(18) + (-2.05)15$$
$$\hat{y} = 23.09 + 70.74 + (-30.75)$$
$$\hat{y} = 63.08$$

Our multiple regression equation predicts that an 18-year-old adolescent with a score on the family closeness index of 15 (relatively low, meaning poor family closeness) would have a predicted delinquency score of 63.08. It is always informative to compare predicted values of $y$ for two different scores on the same independent variable while holding the other independent variables constant. So let's predict what the delinquency score would be for that same 18-year-old (18) but, this time, with a relatively strong closeness to family (30 rather than 15). By using our regression equation, the predicted delinquency score would be:

$$\hat{y} = 23.09 + 3.93(18) + (-2.05)30$$
$$\hat{y} = 23.09 + 70.74 + (-61.50)$$
$$\hat{y} = 32.33$$

As you can see here, by doubling the family closeness score for an 18-year-old, the predicted delinquency score is almost reduced by half from 63.08 to 32.33.

We want to emphasize a note of caution in comparing partial slope coefficients. Remember that you cannot compare the relative strength of a relationship between $x$ and $y$ based on the magnitude of $b$ the partial slope coefficient. Specifically, just because the partial slope for age on delinquency scores was 3.93 while holding family closeness constant, and that slope coefficient for family closeness on delinquency scores was –2.05 while holding age constant, we cannot conclude that the effect of age on delinquency is stronger than the effect of family closeness. Similar to the bivariate model in the last chapter, *in a multiple regression analysis, you cannot determine which independent variable has the strongest effect on the dependent variable by comparing unstandardized partial slope coefficients*. Remember from our discussion in the last chapter that the slope coefficient is measured in terms of the unit of measurement of the $x$ variable—that is, a one-unit change in $x$ produces a $b$-unit change in the $y$ variable. The size of the partial slope coefficient, then, reflects the underlying units of measurement. In the bivariate model we solved this problem by calculating a standardized coefficient that was not dependent on the independent variable's unit of measurement: the correlation coefficient. A similar standardized coefficient in multiple regression is called the *standardized partial slope* or *beta weight*. (This is not to be confused with beta, the population parameter for the slope coefficient). We will examine beta weights next.

## 🖽 Comparing the Strength of a Relationship Using Beta Weights

To compare the effects of two independent variables on a dependent variable, it is necessary to remove differences in the units of measurement (e.g., dollars compared to cents, years compared to months, etc.). One way of doing this is to convert all of the variables in the regression equation to a common measurement scale. This can be achieved by computing a *standardized partial slope coefficient*, called a beta weight, from the obtained partial slope coefficient. If we do this, we will have two partial slope coefficients for each independent variable, one standardized (the beta weight) and one in the original measurement scale.

**Beta weight:** Standardized slope coefficient in an ordinary least-squares (OLS) regression model.

The formulas used to obtain **standardized partial slopes** or **beta weights**, symbolized $b^*$, from a multiple regression equation with two independent variables are:

$$b^*_{x_1} = b_{x_1}\left(\frac{s_{x_1}}{s_y}\right)$$

(13–5)

$$b^*_{x_2} = b_{x_2}\left(\frac{s_{x_2}}{s_y}\right)$$

(13–6)

As the formulas indicate, computation of the beta weight involves multiplying the partial slope coefficient $(b_1)$ obtained for an independent variable by the ratio of the standard deviation of that variable $(s_{x_1})$ to the standard deviation of the dependent variable $(s_y)$. The interpretation of a beta weight is relatively straightforward. Like a partial slope coefficient, beta coefficients can be either positive or negative. A positive beta coefficient indicates a positive linear relationship between the independent and the dependent variable, whereas a negative beta weight indicates a negative linear relationship. The standardized partial slope will always have the same sign as the unstandardized partial slope. Similar to the interpretation of a correlation coefficient, the larger the beta weight, the stronger the relationship between the independent and dependent variables. More specifically, the beta weights show the expected change in a standardized score on the dependent variable for a one-unit change in a standardized score of the independent variable, while holding constant the other independent variable. If we want to know the *relative importance* of two variables, then, we can compare the absolute value of the magnitudes of their respective beta weights. The variable with the larger beta weight has the stronger effect on the dependent variable.

Let's go through an example using the delinquency data. Recall that the partial slope coefficient for age $(b_1)$ was equal to 3.93 and the partial slope coefficient for family closeness $(b_2)$ was equal to –2.05. The standard deviations for age and family closeness are 1.49 and 7.09, respectively (Table 13.1). To determine the beta weight for each independent variable, we simply plug these values into equations 13-5 and 13-6:

$$b^*_{x_1} = (3.93)\left(\frac{1.49}{25.11}\right)$$

$$b^*_{x_1} = .233$$

$$b^*_{x_2} = (-2.05)\left(\frac{7.09}{25.11}\right)$$

$$b^*_{x_2} = .579$$

By using the absolute value of these beta weights, we can compare the effect of one independent variable on the dependent variable with the effect of the other, without our comparison being distorted by a variable's unit of measurement. From the beta weights displayed earlier, we can immediately ascertain that family closeness has a much stronger relationship with delinquency $\left(b^{*}_{x_2} = |-.579|\right)$ than does age $\left(b^{*}_{x_1} = |.233|\right)$.

There are two other ways of assessing the relative importance of independent variables in a multiple regression analysis. One method, with which you are already familiar from our treatment of bivariate regression, is to calculate correlation coefficients and coefficients of determination. The second way is to compare the absolute value of the magnitude of the obtained $t$ value for each independent variable from a hypothesis test that the slope coefficient is equal to zero. We will explore the multivariate equivalent of correlation coefficients and coefficients of determination in the next section, and then we will examine hypothesis tests for the significance of partial slope coefficients in the section after that.

## 🔲 Partial Correlation Coefficients

Another way of addressing the relative effects of our independent variables is to compute something called the **partial correlation coefficient**. We can also compute the **multiple coefficient of determination ($R^2$)**. Both of these coefficients enable us to investigate the question of the relative importance of independent variables, although they do so in somewhat different ways. Interpreting the partial correlation coefficient and multiple coefficient of determination, however, is analogous to interpreting their bivariate equivalents, so you should have no problem with this section. We will begin our discussion with the partial correlation coefficient.

> **Partial correlation coefficient:** Correlation between two variables after controlling for a third variable.

> **Multiple coefficient of determination ($R^2$):** Value of $R^2$ when there are two or more independent variables predicting a dependent variable.

The magnitude of a partial correlation coefficient indicates the correlation or strength of the linear relationship between a given independent variable and a dependent variable when the effect of another independent variable is held constant or removed. The partial correlation coefficient is, therefore, like the Pearson correlation coefficient you learned about in the last chapter, only now we are controlling for another variable. In the example we are currently using, the partial correlation between age and delinquency would measure the relationship between these two variables when the effect of closeness to the family has been removed or controlled. Similarly, the partial correlation between family closeness and delinquency would measure the relationship between these variables when the effect of the person's age has been controlled.

In referring to the partial correlation coefficient, we will continue with the same subscripts we have used throughout this chapter, with one additional twist. We will use the partial correlation symbol $r_{yx_1 \cdot x_2}$ to show the correlation between the dependent variable ($y$) and the first independent variable ($x_1$), while controlling for the second independent variable ($x_2$). Similarly, we will use the partial correlation symbol $r_{yx_2 \cdot x_1}$ to show the correlation between the dependent variable ($y$) and the second independent variable ($x_2$), while controlling for the first independent variable ($x_1$). The subscript to the right of the dot indicates the variable whose effect is being controlled. The formulas used to obtain partial correlation coefficients for two independent variables with a dependent variable are:

$$r_{yx_1 \cdot x_2} = \frac{r_{yx_1} - \left(r_{yx_2}\right)\left(r_{x_1 x_2}\right)}{\sqrt{1 - r_{yx_2}^2}\sqrt{1 - r_{x_1 x_2}^2}} \tag{13–7}$$

$$r_{yx_2 \cdot x_1} = \frac{r_{yx_1} - \left(r_{yx_1}\right)\left(r_{x_1 x_2}\right)}{\sqrt{1 - r_{yx_1}^2}\sqrt{1 - r_{x_1 x_2}^2}} \tag{13–8}$$

In Table 13.1, we have all the values we need to calculate these coefficients for our delinquency data. Recall that the bivariate correlation between age and delinquency was $r_{yx_1} = .445$, the correlation between family closeness and delinquency was $r_{yx_2} = -.664$, and the correlation between age and family closeness was $r_{x_1x_2} = -.366$. With this information, we can now compute the partial correlation coefficients for both independent variables as shown in the following equations.

Partial correlation coefficient for age and delinquency, controlling for family closeness:

$$r_{yx_1.x_2} = \frac{.445 - (-.664)(-.366)}{\sqrt{1-(-.664)^2}\sqrt{1-(-.366)^2}}$$

$$r_{yx_1.x_2} = .29$$

Partial correlation coefficient for family closeness and delinquency, controlling for age:

$$r_{yx_1.x_2} = \frac{-.664 - (.445)(-3.66)}{\sqrt{1-(.445)^2}\sqrt{1-(-.366)^2}}$$

$$r_{yx_1.x_2} = -.60$$

The partial correlation between age and delinquency is .29, while controlling for family closeness. The partial correlation between family closeness and delinquency is –.60, while controlling for age. Since the partial correlation for family closeness (–.60) is greater than the partial correlation for age (.29) in absolute value, family closeness has the stronger effect on a student's involvement in delinquent behavior. This is consistent with our conclusion when we used beta weights (standardized partial slopes). In general, the relative explanatory power of two independent variables can be determined by comparing their partial correlation coefficients. The variable with the largest partial correlation coefficient (absolute value) has the strongest relationship with the dependent variable.

We should note here that the reason why the partial correlation coefficients for both independent variables is less than their respective bivariate correlation coefficients is that since the two independent variables are themselves correlated ( $r_{x_1x_2} = -.366$), they share a certain amount of the total explanatory power or explained variance. In other words, in this particular regression model, there are four sources that explain delinquency:

1. That which is due uniquely to the effect of age

2. That which is due uniquely to the effect of family closeness

3. That which is due to the *joint effect* of age and family closeness

4. That which is due to all other factors not explicitly included in the model but whose effect is manifested through the error term ($\varepsilon$)

What the partial correlation (and partial slope) coefficients reflect is the unique effect of each independent variable on the dependent variable. That is, they reveal the effect of each independent variable that is not shared with the other independent variable. The greater the correlation between the two independent variables ( $r_{x_1x_2}$ ), the weaker the first two sources and the stronger the joint effect.

We illustrate this point in Figure 13.3, which shows a Venn diagram. Think of the entire area of the Venn diagram as the variance explained in the dependent variable. Some of this variance is explained uniquely by $x_1$, the first independent variable, and some of this variance is uniquely explained by $x_2$, the second independent variable. The intersection of the two circles is the variation in the dependent variable that is jointly explained by $x_1$ and $x_2$. The intersection shows that the two independent variables are correlated with each other. The stronger the correlation between the two independent variables, the larger the size of the intersection and the more difficult it is to untangle their unique effects from their joint effects. In one extreme case, where the two variables are not correlated at all, there is no intersection and all the variance in the dependent variable is uniquely explained by the two independent variables. In the other extreme case, where the correlation between $x_1$ and $x_2$ is 1.0, all of the area is covered by the intersection and all variance in the dependent variable is jointly explained. In this instance, you could use one of the independent variables to explain variation in the dependent variable, but you can't use both because it would violate the multicollinearity assumption. More practically, however, why would you need to include both since would be identical and provide perfectly redundant information?

## Multiple Coefficient of Determination, $R^2$

Another way to disentangle the separate effects of the independent variables on the dependent variable is to compute the increase in the amount of explained variance when each independent variable is separately added to the regression model. With two independent variables, this requires taking the amount of variation in the dependent variable explained by both independent variables (called the $R^2$ for the full model) and subtracting the amount of variance explained by each independent variable when it is alone in the model (called the $R^2$ for the reduced model). This gives you the amount of variance that is explained uniquely by each independent variable $\left( R^2_{full} - R^2_{reduced} \right)$.

To do this, of course, requires knowing how much of the variance in the dependent variable is explained by both independent variables together. We obtain this value by computing what is termed the multiple coefficient of determination, which is symbolized by a capital $R^2$ to differentiate it from the bivariate coefficient of determination $r^2$. The multiple coefficient of determination indicates the proportion of variance in the dependent variable that is explained by all the independent variables combined. You might think of the multiple coefficient of determination as an indicator of how well your model fits the data, in terms of the combined ability of the independent variables to explain the dependent variable. The range of $R^2$ is from 0%, which indicates that the independent variables explain no variance in the dependent variable, to a maximum of 100%, which indicates that the independent variables explain all of the variance. As the independent variables explain a larger amount of the variance (i.e., as $R^2$ approaches 100%), the estimated regression model provides a better fit to the data.

Calculating the $R^2$ in a multivariate model should be easy right? If the $r^2$ for the effect of age on delinquency is .20 [$(.445)^2$] and the $r^2$ for the effect of family closeness on delinquency is .44 [$(-.664)^2$], we can simply add these two together and conclude that when both variables are in the model, our $R^2$ should be .64. Unfortunately, to obtain the multiple coefficient of determination, we cannot simply add together the separate bivariate coefficients of determination. Why

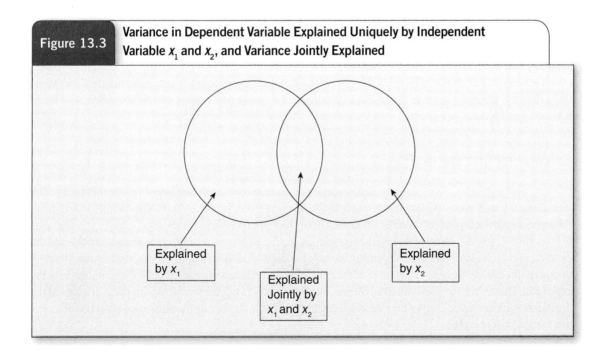

| Figure 13.3 | Variance in Dependent Variable Explained Uniquely by Independent Variable $x_1$ and $x_2$, and Variance Jointly Explained |

Explained by $x_1$

Explained Jointly by $x_1$ and $x_2$

Explained by $x_2$

not? Remember that the independent variables are also virtually always correlated with each other (see Figure 13.3). If the independent variables in a multiple regression equation are correlated, the estimated value of $R^2$ reflects both the amount of variance that each variable uniquely explains and that which they share through their joint correlation. As a result, there will be a joint effect on the dependent variable that cannot be attributed to one variable alone. Again, the amount of this joint effect is a function of the extent to which the two independent variables are correlated themselves. The more highly correlated our independent variables are, the more explained variance they share, the less likely that the separate $r^2$ values will sum to the $R^2$. What we need, therefore, is a way to calculate the real $R^2$ value.

For a two-independent variable regression equation, the multiple coefficient of determination is found with the following formula:

$$R^2 = r_{yx_1}^2 + (r_{yx_2 . x_1}^2)(1 - r_{yx_1}^2) \qquad \textbf{(13–9)}$$

where

$R^2$ = the multiple coefficient of determination

$r_{yx_1}^2$ = the bivariate correlation between $x_1$ and $y$, squared

$r_{yx_2 . x_1}^2$ = the partial correlation of $x_2$ and $y$ while controlling for $x_1$, squared

$r_{yx_1}^2$ = the bivariate correlation between $x_1$ and $y$, squared

Before we explain the different components of this formula, let's compute the multiple coefficient of determination with our delinquency data. We have already calculated all of the values we need, so we can simply plug them into formula 13-8:

$$R^2 = (.445)^2 + (-.602)^2 \left[ 1 - (.445)^2 \right]$$
$$R^2 = (.198) + (.362)(.802)$$
$$R^2 = (.198) + .290$$
$$R^2 = .488$$

This $R^2$ indicates the proportion of variance explained in the dependent variable by both independent variables in the regression equation. The obtained $R^2$ of .488 indicates that combined, age and family closeness score together explain almost one half (49%) of the variation in delinquency scores. Notice right away that this value of $R^2$ is not the same as the sum of the individual $r^2$ values, and now you know why: shared variance between $x_1$ and $x_2$.

## Calculating Change in $R^2$

How can we disentangle the contribution of each independent variable to this total explained variance? What does the formula for the multiple coefficient of determination (formula 13-9) do? It first lets one independent variable do all the explaining in the dependent variable that it can. That is the first expression after the equals sign ($r_{yx_1}^2$). The value of this term is simply the square of the bivariate correlation coefficient between the first independent variable and the dependent variable. After the first independent variable has done all of the explaining it can, the second variable is then given the chance to explain what *it* can of the remaining unexplained variation. That is the second term in the expression. This term is the squared partial correlation coefficient between the second independent variable and the dependent variable (controlling for the first independent variable), multiplied by the proportion of variance that the first variable cannot explain:

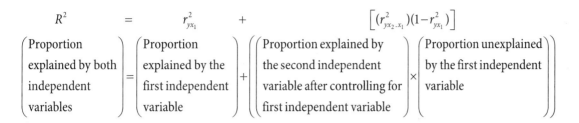

The magnitude of $R^2$ will be the same no matter which of the two independent variables appears first. The following two formulas, then, will produce identical results:

$$R^2 = r_{yx_1}^2 + (r_{yx_2.x_1}^2)(1 - r_{yx_1}^2)$$

and

$$R^2 = r_{yx_2}^2 + (r_{yx_1.x_2}^2)(1 - r_{yx_2}^2)$$

In the first formula, we let $x_1$ explain all the variance it can in the dependent variable, and then we let $x_2$ explain what it can of the remaining variance. In the second formula, we let $x_2$ first do all the explaining *it* can in the dependent variable, and then we let $x_1$ explain what remains. The combined explanatory power of the two variables will always be the same. However, although the value of $R^2$ will be the same no matter which variable is considered first, the amount of explained variance that is attributed to a given variable will differ, depending on the order that it appears in the formula. The first variable considered will explain more variance unless the two independent variables are not correlated at all. If there is a substantial correlation between the two independent variables, the first variable considered will be "given credit" for the explained variance that they share. In this circumstance, the variance explained by the second variable that is not already explained by the first will be small. It is therefore a good idea to estimate $R^2$ with each variable appearing first to see how much additional variance the second-considered variable can explain above that explained by the first-considered variable.

As you can now perhaps see, the expression for the multiple coefficient of determination can give us some idea of the contribution to the total explained variance made by each variable. To see this more clearly, we can rewrite our two expressions for the multiple coefficient of determination as follows:

$$R_{yx_1x_2}^2 - r_{yx_1}^2 = \left(r_{yx_2.x_1}^2\right)\left(1 - r_{yx_1}\right)^2$$
$$R_{yx_1x_2}^2 - r_{yx_2}^2 = \left(r_{yx_1.x_2}^2\right)\left(1 - r_{yx_2}\right)^2$$

In the first formula, the expression on the left-hand side of the equals sign is the difference between the total amount of explained variance in the two-variable regression model and that which would be explained by the first variable if it alone appeared in the regression equation. You can see that the latter is just the squared bivariate correlation between the first independent variable and the dependent variable. The expression to the right of the equals sign reflects the amount of variance explained by the second variable that is left unexplained by the first. This latter component of the total explained variance is often referred to as the **$R^2$ change** because it reflects the change in the amount of variance explained when the second variable is entered into the regression model. If the change in variance explained is substantial, it tells us that the second variable can give us information about the dependent variable that we do not get from the first independent variable.

The second formula is a corollary formula for $R^2$ change. The expression on the left-hand side of the equals sign is the difference between the total amount of

**Adjusted $R^2$:** Value of $R^2$ adjusted to take into account the number of independent variables in the model predicting the dependent variable.

explained variance in the two-variable regression model and that which would be explained by the second variable if it alone appeared in the regression equation. The $r_{yx_2}^2$ term is just the squared bivariate correlation between the second independent variable and the dependent variable in the one-variable regression model. The expression to the right of the equals sign reflects the amount of variance explained by the first independent variable that is left unexplained by the second. This formula measures the change in explained variance that we can uniquely attribute to the first independent variable because it reflects the amount of variance it explains over and above that explained by the second independent variable. We will illustrate the $R^2$ change term with our delinquency data.

First, let's let age explain all the variance in the dependent variable that it can:

$$R^2 = (.445)^2 + (-.602)^2 \left[1 - (.445)^2\right]$$
$$R^2 = .198 + (.362)(.802)$$
$$R^2 = .198 + .290$$
$$R^2 = .488$$

In this calculation of the multiple coefficient of determination for delinquency scores, age is the independent variable considered first. It explains 19.8% of the total 48.8% of the explained variance in delinquency scores. After age explains all it can, family closeness is considered, and it explains the remaining 29%. The change in the value of $R^2$ when family closeness is added to the regression model, then, is 29%.

In the calculations that follows, family closeness scores appear first. Family closeness is given the opportunity to explain all the variance in delinquency that it can, and then age is entered to explain the remaining variance left unexplained:

$$R^2 = (-.664)^2 + (.290)^2 \left[1 - (-.664)^2\right]$$
$$R^2 = .441 + (.084)(.559)$$
$$R^2 = .441 + .047$$
$$R^2 = .488$$

The combined variance explained is still 48.8%, so no matter which variable is considered first, the total amount of explained variance remains the same. We find here that family closeness explains 44.1% of the variance when considered first, and age explains an additional 4.7% of the variance, above and beyond that explained by the family closeness variable. Thus, the change in the value of $R^2$ when family closeness is added to the regression model is only 4.7%. Since the change in $R^2$ when family closeness is added to the model is 29% and the change in $R^2$ when age is added to the model is not quite 5%, we would conclude that family closeness is a more important variable in explaining delinquency than age.

You should also note here that about one half of the variance in delinquency remains unexplained by age and family closeness ($1 - R^2 = .512$, or 51%). This gives us a clue that there are factors other than age and family closeness that help explain why some kids are more likely than others to engage in delinquent activity. This would lead us on a search for other suitable independent variables to add to our regression model. We would then add a third or a fourth or more additional independent variables to our model. To make a good explanatory model, then, we should also include other factors theorized or empirically found to be associated with the dependent variable but not strongly correlated with the other independent variables. We should seek advice from the empirical literature predicting delinquency or delinquency theory to determine what other factors should be included in our model!

The next questions we need to address are as follows: (1) "Is there a statistically significant relationship between the independent variables in our multiple regression equation and the dependent variable?" (2) "Is there a significant relationship between each of the independent variables singly and the dependent variable?" We will discuss issues of hypothesis testing with multiple regression models in the next section.

# ▣ Hypothesis Testing in Multiple Regression

So far in this chapter, we have focused on calculating and interpreting the various coefficients associated with multiple regression analysis. However, since we are really interested in knowing whether the total amount of variance explained is significantly different from zero, and in estimating the value of the *population* partial slope coefficients ($\beta_1$, $\beta_2$) from the sample coefficients ($b_1$ and $b_2$), we must now examine issues of hypothesis testing. In multiple regression analysis, we are interested in testing hypotheses about the multiple coefficient of determination and the partial slope coefficients. Calculating the standard error of these coefficients for these hypothesis tests, however, gets a bit labor-intensive and tricky. For this reason, we are going to rely on statistical output from the computer software package SPSS (Statistical Package for the Social Sciences) to conduct the hypotheses tests. In the remainder of this chapter, therefore, we will simply report the results of the calculations and work through the interpretation with you. With the data we use, you can use any other statistical software package and you will get the identical information we provide.

Figure 13.4 presents the SPSS computer output for the multiple regression equation predicting delinquency that we have been examining. As a reminder, SPSS displays only three decimal places; however, if you are in SPSS and you click on the coefficient, you will see that there are actually six decimal places being used for the calculations. That is why the number we calculate by hand with only three places may not be exactly like those calculated by SPSS. Despite this difference in accuracy, if you use the output displayed in the last coefficient box, you can see that the regression equation is virtually identical to the one we calculated by hand:

$$y = 23.10 + 3.92(\text{age}) + -2.05(\text{family attachments})$$

The first null hypothesis of interest states that all slope coefficients in the regression equation are equal to zero. This is the same as saying that the multiple coefficient of determination $R^2$ is equal to zero in the population. The alternative hypothesis states that the slopes for all independent variables when used together are not equal to zero. This can be expressed as shown:

$H_0: \beta_1, \beta_2, \beta_3, \ldots \beta_k = 0$    or    $R^2 = 0$

$H_1: \beta_1, \beta_2, \beta_3, \ldots \beta_k \neq 0$    or    $R^2 \neq 0$

For us to reject the null hypothesis, only one of the partial slope coefficients needs to be significantly different from zero. To determine the results of this hypothesis test, we need to examine the boxes labeled "Model Summary" and "ANOVA." The former displays the results of the sample $R^2$, which we have already calculated by hand to be .488.

An *F* test is used to test the null hypothesis that the population $R^2$ is equal to zero. This *F* test is comparable with the *F* test we conducted with the analysis of variance. It is based on two sources of variability in our data: explained and unexplained variability. These correspond to two estimates of the population variance: explained/regression variance and unexplained/residual variance. You should be familiar with these terms from the previous chapter on bivariate regression models. The regression variance is the variance in the data we can explain from our regression equation. Hence, it is often referred to as explained variance. It is estimated as the ratio of the regression sum of squares to its degrees of freedom. The regression sum of squares is the sum of the squared differences between the predicted value of $y$ ($\hat{y}$), based on the regression equation, and the mean of $y$ ($\overline{Y}$). The number of degrees of freedom for the regression sum of squares is equal to $p$, where $p$ is the number of predictors or independent variables in the regression model. This ratio of regression sum of squares to degrees of freedom is one estimate of the population variance. In Figure 13.4, this estimate of the variance is labeled the Regression "Mean Square." The residual variance is the variance in our data unexplained by the regression equation. It is estimated as the ratio of the residual sum of squares to its degrees of freedom. The residual sum of squares is the sum of the squared differences between the observed value of $y$ and its predicted

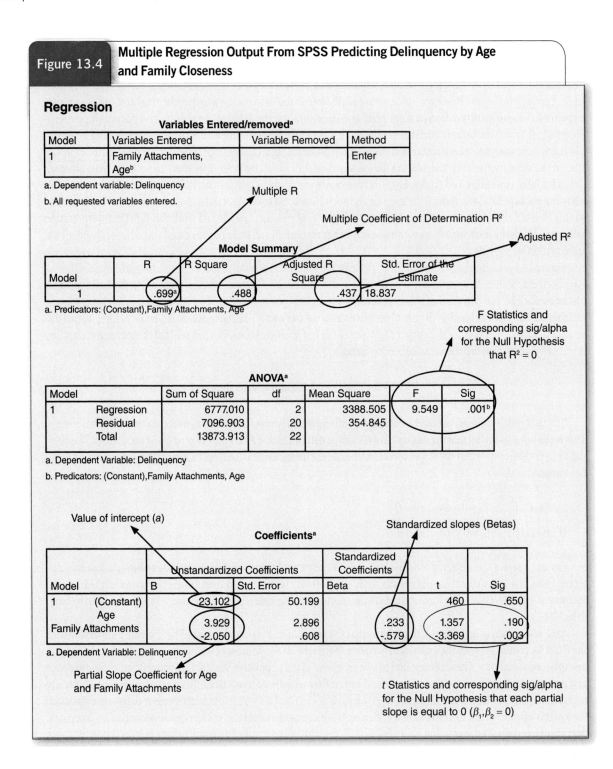

**Figure 13.4** Multiple Regression Output From SPSS Predicting Delinquency by Age and Family Closeness

value $(\hat{y})$. The number of degrees of freedom for the residual sum of squares is equal to $n - (p + 1)$ (the extra 1 is for the intercept). This ratio of residual sum of squares to degrees of freedom is the second estimate of the population variance, and in Figure 13.4, it is labeled the Residual "Mean Square."

The $F$ test for the significance of $R^2$ is based on the ratio of these two estimates of variance or mean squares:

$$F = \frac{\text{Regression variance}}{\text{Residual variance}}$$

which is the same as:

$$F = \frac{\text{Mean Square for the regression}}{\text{Mean Square for the residual}}$$

The obtained value of $F$ can be directly compared with a critical $F$ at a chosen alpha level with $p$ and $n - (p + 1)$ degrees of freedom. If $F_{obt} > F_{crit}$, your decision is to reject the null hypothesis. Luckily for you, most software programs including SPSS give you the exact probability of getting this sample statistic, $F$, if the null hypothesis is true. In this case, we can see under the "Sig." (abbreviation for significance) column after the $F$ value that the exact significance or alpha in this case is equal to .001. This tells us that we would be wrong in rejecting the null hypothesis less than one time in a thousand! If this exact significance is lower than our chosen alpha, we can reject the null hypothesis. If the reported significance is greater than your alpha level, you fail to reject the null hypothesis. For example, if we chose an alpha of .05, and the significance we obtained was .07, that would be telling us that we would be wrong 7% of the time, which is more than the 5% we are willing to be wrong. In that case, we must fail to reject the null hypothesis.

Let's continue with our example more formally. Our formal null and alternative hypotheses for this test state:

$$H_0 : \beta_{age}, \beta_{attachment} = 0 \quad \text{or} \quad R^2_{age,\,attachment} = 0$$
$$H_1 : \beta_{age}, \beta_{attachment} \neq 0 \quad \text{or} \quad R^2_{age,\,attachment} \neq 0$$

Let's use an alpha of .05 for our hypothesis test, so our decision rule will be to reject the null hypothesis if the estimated probability of our obtained $F$ statistic is .05 or less. Figure 13.4 tells us that the probability of obtaining an $F$ value of 9.549 if the null hypothesis is true is equal to .001. This significance is less than alpha = .05, so we can safely reject the null hypothesis that both of the slope coefficients when used together to predict the dependent variable are equal to zero. We can instead conclude that there is a significant linear relationship between at least one of the independent variables (age and family closeness) and delinquency scores for high-school students.

If we want to know which specific partial slopes are significantly different from zero, we must perform hypothesis tests on our individual slope coefficients. The hypothesis tests associated with partial slopes are very similar to the tests we conducted in the last chapter for bivariate slope coefficients. Specifically, we want to determine whether each partial slope coefficient is significantly different from zero. The null hypothesis in this case would state that the true population parameter for each independent variable $\beta$ is equal to zero. Just as we did with the bivariate slope hypothesis tests in the last chapter, we use the $t$ statistic and sampling distribution to test this hypothesis. The calculations for the $t$ statistic in the multiple regression case are, however, much more complicated. The $t$ statistic we use for our partial slope coefficient hypothesis test is simply the ratio of the partial slope to the standard error of the slope:

$$t = \frac{b_i}{s_{bi}}$$

The sampling distribution used for this $t$ statistic is the Student's $t$ with $(n - p - 1)$ degrees of freedom, where $p$ is the number of independent variables in the regression equation.

This formula may look simple, but the complicated part is in estimating the denominator—the standard error of the partial slope. For a two-variable multiple regression problem $(x_1, x_2)$, the estimate for the standard error of the slope can be derived from the following formulas:

$$S_{byx_1 \cdot x_2} = \sqrt{\frac{\text{Residual mean square}}{\Sigma x_1^2 (1 - r_{x_1 x_2}^2)}}$$

$$S_{byx_2 \cdot x_1} = \sqrt{\frac{\text{Residual mean square}}{\Sigma x_2^2 (1 - r_{x_1 x_2}^2)}}$$

where

$\Sigma x_1^2 =$ the sum of the squared $x_1$ scores

$\Sigma x_2^2 =$ the sum of squared $x_2$ scores

$r_{x_1 x_2}^2 =$ the squared correlation coefficient between $x_1$ and $x_2$

If we were going to make a decision by calculating this $t$ value by hand, the next step in our hypothesis test is to select an alpha level with the appropriate degrees of freedom and determine what the critical value of $t$ is. You can now select an alpha level (let's use an alpha of .05) and go to the $t$ table (Table B.3) in Appendix B with $n - p - 1$ degrees of freedom and find the critical value of $t$. For this example, with $n = 23$ and $p = 2$ (we have two independent variables), we have $23 - 2 - 1$, or 20, degrees of freedom. The critical value of $t$ with $\alpha = .05$ for a two-tailed hypothesis test and 20 degrees of freedom is $\pm 2.086$. If our obtained $t$ is greater than or equal to 2.086 or less than or equal to -2.086, we will reject the null hypothesis.

Again, however, we will rely on the computer output to do our calculations for us. The necessary information to conduct a hypothesis test is shown in Figure 13.4, displayed in the box labeled "Coefficients" where we found the regression equation coefficients. In this box, you will find the partial slopes ($\beta$), the standard error of each slope, the beta coefficients (beta weights or the standardized partial slopes), the resulting $t$ values obtained for each slope, and the *exact* significance level (two-tailed) that corresponds to each $t$ value. We are interested in testing the null hypothesis associated with each partial slope coefficient, which states that there is no relationship in the population between age and delinquency when holding family closeness constant and that there is no linear relationship in the population between family closeness and delinquency when holding age constant. That is, we are testing the null hypothesis that the population parameters, $\beta_{x_1}$ and $\beta_{x_2}$, are each equal to zero. The alternative hypotheses state that the slope coefficients in the population are not equal to zero, which means this will be a two-tailed hypothesis test. These null and alternative hypotheses for each partial slope can be expressed as follows:

$H_0 : \beta_{\text{age}} = 0$

$H_1 : \beta_{\text{age}} \neq 0$

$H_0 : \beta_{\text{family attachment}} = 0$

$H_1 : \beta_{\text{family attachment}} \neq 0$

Like the $F$ test, the output provided by most computer software packages gives the *exact probability* of each $t$ statistic (two-tailed) under the assumption that the null hypothesis is true. This exact probability is displayed in Figure 13.4 under the column labeled "Sig." (for the significance of $t$) for each slope. Note that we do not care about the significance of the intercept. Your decision to reject the null hypothesis about the partial slope coefficients is the same as before. If this reported significance is less than or equal to your chosen alpha level, your decision is to reject the null hypothesis. If the reported probability is greater than your selected alpha level, your decision is to fail to reject the null hypothesis. Remember that if you are conducting a one-tailed hypothesis test, you need to cut this reported exact probability in half. To conduct our hypothesis test, all we need now is the obtained $t$ statistic for each partial slope coefficient and its corresponding level of significance. You can find the obtained $t$ values under the heading "t" in Figure 13.4 and its significance (Sig.) in the final column.

We can see from Figure 13.4 that the partial slope coefficient for the effect of age on delinquency is 3.929 and the obtained $t$ value for that partial slope coefficient is 1.357. The exact probability or significance (alpha) of a sample slope coefficient this large if the population coefficient were actually zero is .190 (sig. = .190). This means that if we reject the null hypothesis, we will be wrong about 19% of the time. We are willing to be wrong only 5% of the time ($\alpha$ = .05). Thus, we must fail to reject the null hypothesis. We would conclude, therefore, that there is no significant relationship between age and delinquency in the population once students' closeness to their families is controlled.

The partial slope coefficient for family closeness is –2.05, and the obtained $t$ value is –3.369. If we look at the exact probability, we can see that the probability of getting a $t$ that large if the null hypothesis is true is only .003. Since the exact probability is less than .05 (.003 < .05), we will reject this null hypothesis. Let us put this another way. If the partial slope coefficient in the population were actually zero, we would obtain a sample value of –2.05 by chance alone less than 3 times out of 1,000, less than 1% of the time. This is much less than our alpha of .05. As such, we will reject the null hypothesis that the slope coefficient in the population is equal to zero and conclude that there is a significant negative linear effect of family closeness on delinquency even after controlling for age. In the population, then, we can conclude that youth with stronger closeness to their families will have lower level of delinquency.

We suggested to you earlier that in addition to its use in conducting hypothesis tests, the obtained $t$ statistic can also be used to compare the relative effects of two independent variables on the dependent variable. If you want to know which independent variable has the stronger effect, simply compare the absolute value of each variable's obtained $t$ statistic. For a given regression equation, the greater the $t_{obt}$, the stronger the effect the variable has on the dependent variable. In our example, the obtained $t$ for the partial slope for age was 1.357, and the $t_{obt}$ for family closeness was –3.369. Since the absolute value of 3.369 is greater than 1.357, we would conclude that family closeness has a stronger effect on delinquency than on age. This conclusion is consistent with our earlier findings using the standardized slope coefficients.

Before we move onto another example, let's discuss one more piece of information that most regression statistical software packages provide—the adjusted $R^2$ statistic. You can see from the information provided in Figure 13.4 that although the value of $R^2$ is .488, the adjusted $R^2$ is less than that, at .437. What the adjusted $R^2$ does is take into account how many independent variables you have in the model and how well they are explaining the dependent variable. If you want to have a larger value of $R^2$ for your model, you might just keep including independent variables—if you do, the $R^2$ will not decrease but will increase (unless the model "blows up" and you get a negative $R^2$, a sure sign you did something wrong). Of course, you might just be adding variables that increase your $R^2$ by a tiny amount but do not do much explaining. The "adjustment," which the adjusted $R^2$ does is actually a penalty for including independent variables in your model that are not doing any explaining—it penalizes you for adding independent variables that do not explain much of the dependent variable. The value of the adjusted $R^2$ tells you the percent of variance explained by the independent variables that are actually affecting the dependent variable. If you add an independent variable to your model that is actually doing its job and explaining the dependent variable, adjusted $R^2$ will be greater than your unadjusted $R^2$. If, however, you are adding variables that are not very good at explaining $y$, then your adjusted $R^2$ will be lower than your unadjusted $R^2$. In our earlier case, this is what we see so we suspect that many one of our independent variables is not really pulling its explanatory weight, and given the $t$ values, it is probably age. The formula for the adjusted $R^2$ statistic is:

$$R^2_{adjusted} = R^2 - \frac{k(1-R^2)}{n-k-1} \qquad \textbf{(13–10)}$$

Let's move on to another example from the criminal justice literature. For the remainder of the chapter, we will emphasize the interpretation of multiple regression analysis rather than the calculation of these coefficients.

# 🔳 Another Example: Prison Density, Mean Age, and Rate of Inmate Violence

Research that has examined the factors related to inmate misconduct in prison settings, which includes both minor offenses and serious violence, has found many relevant explanatory variables including those at the institutional level (i.e., security level of prison and cleanliness of housing) and those measuring individual attributes of prisoners (i.e., mean age and the criminal history of inmates). One institutional aspect that has received a great deal of attention is prison overcrowding. Results of this research have remained inconsistent. A recent study by Bierie (2012) took a novel approach to study this issue by surveying staff in 114 federal prisons across the United States. By using U.S. Bureau of Prison data to measure the dependent variable of inmate violence within each prison, David Bierie (2012) included a measure of prison overcrowding as one of the independent variables along with a measure of prison conditions obtained from survey questions asking staff members about the presence of things like insects and rodents, inadequate sanitation, and noise in the prison.

Let's set up a hypothetical study investigating the extent to which prison overcrowding is related to the rate of inmate-to-inmate assault. To do this, we select a sample of prisons and collect data for three variables: inmate-to-inmate assault rates (dependent variable), prison population density (which we will use as our measure of overcrowding), and the mean age of inmates in the facility, with density and mean age as our independent variables. The unit of analysis here is the prison, not individual inmates. We operationalize the "prison density index" by dividing a prison's inmate population by the prison's official rated inmate capacity. For example, if a prison had a population of 500 and a rated capacity of 400, it would yield a density index of 1.25, indicating that the facility was 25% over capacity or overcrowded by 25%. We suspect that the rate of inmate assault is positively related to the extent to which the prison is overcrowded. We collect information on age because previous research has found that compared with facilities with older populations, prisons with younger inmates tend to have higher rates of inmate-to-inmate assault.

The hypothetical data we obtain from a random sample of 30 correctional facilities is presented in Table 13.2. Also reported in Table 13.2 are all of the component values necessary to calculate the bivariate correlation coefficients between each of the variables, in addition to the correlation coefficients themselves. We will not go through the labor of computing these correlation coefficients by hand here, but it would be a good exercise for you to do so on your own before moving on.

The bivariate correlation coefficients shown in Table 13.2 indicate that both independent variables have moderately strong relationships with the dependent variable. The relationship between overcrowding (prison density) and inmate-to-inmate assault rates is moderate and positive ($r = .61$), indicating that overcrowding within prisons tends to increase the number of assaults between inmates. The correlation between the age of inmates and inmate-to-inmate assault rates is negative and moderately strong (r = –.76), indicating that prisons with a younger inmate population tend to have higher assault rates than prisons with older inmate populations. The correlation between our two independent variables is –.55. Although not small, the $R^2$ value is only .30, indicating that 30% of the variance in one independent variable is explained by the other. The correlation is not large enough to create a problem of multicollinearity.

With these bivariate correlation coefficients and the respective standard deviations of each variable, we can calculate the partial slope coefficients from equations 13-3 and 13-4. The partial slope coefficient for prison overcrowding regressed on inmate assault rates is:

$$b_1 = \left(\frac{3.78}{.27}\right)\left(\frac{.61-(-.76)(-.55)}{1-(-.55)^2}\right)$$

$$b_1 = (14)\left(\frac{.61-.42}{1-.30}\right)$$

$$b_1 = (14)\left(\frac{.19}{.70}\right)$$

$$b_1 = 3.8$$

| Table 13.2 | Hypothetical Inmate-to-Inmate Assault Rates per 100 Inmate Population, Prison Density Index (Overcrowding), and Mean Age of Inmates for a Random Sample of 30 Prisons | | |
|---|---|---|---|

| Case | Prison | Assault Rate $y$ | Density Index $x_1$ | Mean Age $x_2$ |
|---|---|---|---|---|
| 1 | Prison A | 10.2 | 1.5 | 25.8 |
| 2 | Prison B | 8.2 | 1.0 | 32.1 |
| 3 | Prison C | 11.3 | 1.6 | 26.2 |
| 4 | Prison D | 9.2 | 1.2 | 29.6 |
| 5 | Prison E | 5.3 | 1.0 | 34.5 |
| 6 | Prison F | 8.5 | 1.1 | 27.5 |
| 7 | Prison G | 8.6 | 1.3 | 30.2 |
| 8 | Prison H | 7.5 | .9 | 33.2 |
| 9 | Prison I | 15.3 | 1.9 | 27.2 |
| 10 | Prison J | 10.5 | 1.5 | 26.3 |
| 11 | Prison K | 12.5 | 1.5 | 28.3 |
| 12 | Prison L | 5.4 | 1.1 | 32.3 |
| 13 | Prison M | 10.5 | 1.4 | 23.5 |
| 14 | Prison N | 15.4 | 1.4 | 24.5 |
| 15 | Prison O | 12.8 | 1.2 | 24.5 |
| 16 | Prison P | 13.5 | 1.3 | 27.5 |
| 17 | Prison Q | 17.5 | 1.8 | 25.8 |
| 18 | Prison R | 11.5 | 1.6 | 32.6 |
| 19 | Prison S | 19.0 | 1.4 | 21.2 |
| 20 | Prison T | 14.2 | 1.2 | 26.5 |
| 21 | Prison U | 11.4 | 1.6 | 32.0 |
| 22 | Prison V | 9.8 | 1.1 | 29.9 |
| 23 | Prison W | 6.6 | .9 | 36.2 |
| 24 | Prison X | 8.9 | 1.0 | 35.0 |
| 25 | Prison Y | 10.6 | 1.1 | 29.8 |
| 26 | Prison Z | 12.5 | 1.2 | 25.6 |
| 27 | Prison AA | 7.4 | 1.1 | 33.5 |
| 28 | Prison BB | 3.3 | 1.2 | 38.2 |
| 29 | Prison CC | 17.5 | 1.7 | 25.2 |
| 30 | Prison DD | 13.2 | .9 | 33.1 |
| | | $\Sigma_y = 328.10$ | $\Sigma x_1 = 38.7$ | $\Sigma x_2 = 877.80$ |
| | | $\bar{Y} = 10.94$ | $\bar{X}_{x_1} = 1.29$ | $\bar{X}_{x_2} = 29.26$ |
| | | $s_y = 3.78$ | $s_{x_1} = .27$ | $s_{x_2} = 4.19$ |
| | | $\Sigma y^2 = 4002.07$ | $\Sigma x_1^2 = 52.11$ | $\Sigma x_2^2 = 26{,}193.2$ |
| | $\Sigma yx_1 = 441.7$ | $\Sigma yx_2 = 9{,}251.0$ | $\Sigma x_1 x_2 = 1{,}114.2$ | |
| | $r_{yx_1} = .61$ | $r_{yx_2} = -.76$ | $r_{x_1 x_2} = -.55$ | |

The partial slope coefficient for mean age of prison inmate population regressed on inmate assault rates is:

$$b_2 = \left(\frac{3.78}{4.19}\right)\left(\frac{-.76-(.61)(-.55)}{1-(-.55)^2}\right)$$

$$b_2 = (.9)\left(\frac{-.76-(-.34)}{1-.30}\right)$$

$$b_2 = (.9)\left(\frac{-.42}{.70}\right)$$

$$b_2 = -.54$$

The partial slope coefficient for overcrowding, $b_1$, indicates that, on average, inmate-to-inmate assault rates increase by a value of 3.8 with every 1% increase in prison overcrowding, while holding constant the mean age of the inmate population. The partial slope coefficient for mean inmate age, $b_2$, indicates that, on average, assault rates between inmates decrease by $-.54$ with every one-year increase in mean age, while holding constant prison density.

These partial slopes help us determine the form of the linear effect for a given independent variable. However, since their magnitude is affected by the underlying units of measurement, they are not very useful in comparing relative effects across independent variables. This is why it is necessary to calculate other statistics, such as the standardized partial slope coefficient or beta weight ($b^*$). Before we do this, however, we will solve the multiple regression equation for this model:

$$y = a + b_1x_1 + b_2x_2$$
$$y = a + (3.8)x_1 + (-.54)x_2$$

Now that we have obtained the partial slopes for overcrowding ($b_1$) and age ($b_2$), we can compute the intercept value by substituting the mean of the dependent variable and the means of the two independent variables (Table 13.2) into the equation:

$$a = \bar{y} - b_1\bar{x}_1 - b_2\bar{x}_2$$
$$a = 10.94 - (3.8)(1.29) - (-.54)(29.26)$$
$$a = 10.94 - 4.90 - (-15.8)$$
$$a = 21.84$$

The intercept value we obtained from these equations indicates that when both independent variables are equal to zero, the average value of $y$, our inmate assault rate, will be equal to 21.84. This gives us the full multiple regression equation as follows:

$$y = 21.84 + 3.8(\text{overcrowding}) - .54(\text{mean age})$$

Now that we have solved for the intercept and both partial slope coefficients, we can obtain predicted values of $y$ based on given values of our two independent variables. For example, the predicted rate of inmate assaults in a prison with a density index of 1.6 and a mean inmate age of 24 would be:

$$\hat{y} = 21.84 + (3.8)(1.6) + (-.54)(24)$$
$$\hat{y} = 21.84 + 6.08 + (-12.96)$$
$$\hat{y} = 14.96$$

Our least-squares multiple regression equation predicts that a prison with an overcrowding index of 1.6 and a mean inmate age of 24 would have an inmate-to-inmate assault rate of about 15. Remember that the predictions we make using this regression equation will not be perfect, and we will continue to have error in our regression equation and our predictions from that equation.

Now let's return to the issue of comparing the relative magnitude of the effects for our two independent variables. Recall that standardized partial slope coefficients, called beta weights ($b^*$), are one way to achieve this end.

By using formulas 13-5 and 13-6, let's compute the beta weights for overcrowding and mean age:

$$b^*_{\text{density}} = (3.8)\left(\frac{.27}{3.78}\right)$$
$$b^*_{\text{density}} = (3.8)(.071)$$
$$b^*_{\text{density}} = .270$$

$$b^*_{\text{age}} = (-.54)\left(\frac{4.19}{3.78}\right)$$
$$b^*_{\text{age}} = (-.54)(1.108)$$
$$b^*_{\text{age}} = -.598$$

The absolute value of the beta weight obtained for age is more than double that of the beta weight obtained for prison overcrowding (–.598 vs. .270). This indicates that mean inmate age in prison settings has a much stronger effect on inmate-to-inmate assaults than the extent to which the prison is overcrowded.

Another way of assessing the relative importance of the independent variables in predicting the dependent variable is through the partial correlation coefficients and a partitioning of the multiple coefficient of determination. By using formulas 13-7 and 13-8, respectively, let's first compute the partial correlation coefficients $r_{yx_1.x_2}$ and $r_{yx_1.x_2}$ .

Partial correlation coefficient for overcrowding and assault controlling for age:

$$r_{yx_1.x_2} = \frac{.61 - (-.76)(-.55)}{\sqrt{1 - (-.76)^2}\sqrt{1 - (-.55)^2}}$$

$$r_{yx_1.x_2} = \frac{.61 - .42}{\sqrt{1 - .58}\sqrt{1 - .30}}$$

$$r_{yx_1.x_2} = \frac{.19}{(.648)(.837)}$$

$$r_{yx_1.x_2} = \frac{.19}{.542}$$

$$r_{yx_1.x_2} = .351$$

Partial correlation coefficient for age and assaults controlling for overcrowding:

$$r_{yx_2 \cdot x_1} = \frac{-.76 - (.61)(-.55)}{\sqrt{1 - (.61)^2} \sqrt{1 - (-.55)^2}}$$

$$r_{yx_2 \cdot x_1} = \frac{-.76 - (-.34)}{\sqrt{1 - .37} \sqrt{1 - .30}}$$

$$r_{yx_2 \cdot x_1} = \frac{-.42}{(.794)(.837)}$$

$$r_{yx_2 \cdot x_1} = \frac{-.42}{.66}$$

$$r_{yx_2 \cdot x_1} = -.636$$

The partial correlation coefficient between age and assault when controlling for prison overcrowding is equal to $-.636$. Its absolute value is greater than the partial correlation between overcrowding and assault when controlling for inmate age (.351). This would lead us to conclude that age is more important than overcrowding in explaining inmate assault rates.

With these partial correlation coefficients, we can calculate the multiple coefficient of determination. By using formula 13-9, we obtain the multiple coefficient of determination for overcrowding and age on assault as follows:

$$R^2_{yx_2 x_1} = (.61)^2 + (-.636)^2 \left[ 1 - (.61)^2 \right]$$

$$R^2_{yx_2 x_1} = (.37) + (.41)(1 - .37)$$

$$R^2_{yx_2 x_1} = .63$$

The obtained $R^2_{yx_1 x_2} = .63$ indicates that both overcrowding and mean age, when used together, explain 63% of the variance in inmate-to-inmate assault rates within prisons.

With the multiple coefficient of determination calculated, we can now determine the relative contribution in explained variance made by each independent variable. Recall that we do this by subtracting the bivariate coefficient of determination for each variable from the multiple coefficient of determination. For example, to determine the relative contribution of age in explaining assault rates, we simply subtract the bivariate coefficient of determination for overcrowding on inmate assaults $(r_{yx_1})^2$ by the multiple coefficient of determination. This will give us the proportion of explained variance added to the total when mean age is added to the model explaining inmate assault rates.

In the calculated multiple coefficient of determination, we found that prison density by itself explains 37% of the variance in inmate assault rates. When age is considered, it contributes an additional 26% to the total explained variance over and above that explained by prison density. The $R^2$ change value for age is, then, 26% (63% – 37%). This indicates that age contributes unique information about the dependent variable of assault rates that is not available through knowledge of overcrowding.

When age is the first variable considered, we find that:

$$R^2_{yx_1 x_2} = (-.76)^2 + (.351)^2 \left[ 1 - (-.76)^2 \right]$$

$$R^2_{yx_1 x_2} = (.58) + (.12)(.42)$$

$$R^2_{yx_1 x_2} = .58 + .05$$

$$R^2_{yx_1 x_2} = .63$$

By itself, age explains 58% of the total variance, whereas prison overcrowding explains only 5% additional variance beyond that explained by age. It would seem, then, that although both variables contribute to the total explained variance, the age of the inmates gives us more information about assault rates than does the extent of overcrowding.

Even though the adjusted value of $R^2$ is already displayed for you in Table 13.5, you can see that if we plugged the appropriate values into the equation, we would obtain the same result:

$$R^2_{adjusted} = .63 - \frac{(2)(1-.63)}{30-2-1}$$

$$R^2_{adjusted} = .63 - \frac{(2)(.37)}{27}$$

$$R^2_{adjusted} = .60$$

In this example, the unadjusted $R^2$ value is .63 and its adjusted value is .60, so the shrinkage in the amount of explained variance in this particular regression model is slight, but when using multiple regression, we recommend that you should examine both the unadjusted and the adjusted $R^2$ values.

Let's move on to testing the significance of our partial slope coefficients and the significance of the entire multiple regression equation. We first want to address the extent to which there is a significant linear relationship among the dependent variable, the number of inmate assaults, and our two independent variables, prison overcrowding and inmate age, considered in combination. The null and research hypotheses for this test can be expressed as follows:

$$H_0 = \beta_{overcrowding}, \beta_{age} = 0, \text{ or } \quad R^2_{overcrowding,age} = 0$$

$$H_1 = \beta_{overcrowding}, \beta_{age} \neq 0, \text{ or } \quad R^2_{overcrowding,age} \neq 0$$

As we stated earlier, this hypothesis test really determines whether the $R^2$ value is significantly different from zero. If we reject this null hypothesis, we can conclude that at least one of the partial slope coefficients is significantly different from zero. Our next set of hypothesis tests will then determine which specific slopes are significantly different from zero.

We will use the $F$ statistic and sampling distribution to test the null hypothesis about $R^2$. For this example, we are going to rely on both the SPSS output and finding the critical value of $F$ to make our decision. We will adopt an alpha level of .01 for this test and will find $F_{crit}$ with the appropriate degrees of freedom. With a sample size of 30 and two independent variables, our $F$ test has 2 and 27 degrees of freedom. For an alpha level of .01 with 2 and 27 degrees of freedom, our critical value of $F$ is 5.49. Our decision rule, then, is to reject the null hypothesis if $F_{obt} \geq 5.49$ and fail to reject if $F_{obt} < 5.49$.

All of the information necessary to make a decision about the null hypothesis is provided in the top portion of Figure 13.5. The obtained value of $F$ for the entire equation is equal to 23.201. Since an $F_{obt}$ of 23.201 is greater than the critical $F$ of 5.49, our decision is to reject the null hypothesis. We can see that the exact significance level is really much less than .01—it is .000. You may be thinking, "Does this mean that we risk 0% error?" Remember that there are actually six decimal places for this number, but you can't see them all because SPSS displays only three decimals. As such, rest assured that there is a one somewhere in this significance level because when working with probability theory, you can never be 100% certain or risk 0% error! Still, we can safely reject the null hypothesis (at least at the .001 level) in this case and conclude that there is a significant linear relationship between prison overcrowding and the mean age of the inmate population when they are used together to predict rates of inmate-to-inmate assault.

We will next determine exactly which independent variable(s) is (are) significant in predicting the dependent variable. The null hypotheses we are testing is that the population parameters, $\beta_1$ and $\beta_2$, are each equal to zero. The alternative hypotheses state that the slope coefficients for the effect of inmate age and prison overcrowding on inmate assaults in the population are not equal to zero. These hypothesis tests can be formally expressed as follows:

$$H_0 : \beta_{overcrowding} = 0$$

$$H_1 : \beta_{overcrowding} \neq 0$$

$$H_0 : \beta_{age} = 0$$

$$H_1 : \beta_{age} \neq 0$$

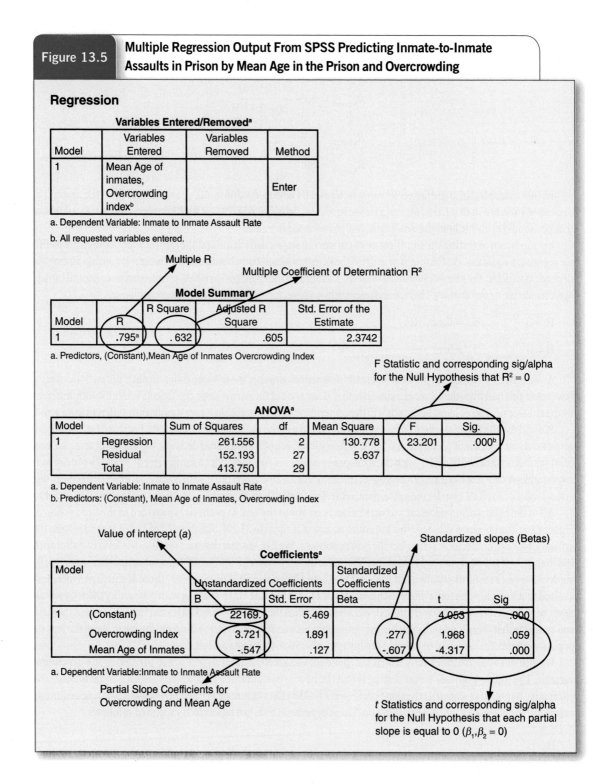

| Figure 13.5 | **Multiple Regression Output From SPSS Predicting Inmate-to-Inmate Assaults in Prison by Mean Age in the Prison and Overcrowding** |

## Regression

**Variables Entered/Removed[a]**

| Model | Variables Entered | Variables Removed | Method |
|---|---|---|---|
| 1 | Mean Age of inmates, Overcrowding index[b] | | Enter |

a. Dependent Variable: Inmate to Inmate Assault Rate

b. All requested variables entered.

Multiple R

Multiple Coefficient of Determination R²

**Model Summary**

| Model | R | R Square | Adjusted R Square | Std. Error of the Estimate |
|---|---|---|---|---|
| 1 | .795[a] | .632 | .605 | 2.3742 |

a. Predictors, (Constant),Mean Age of Inmates Overcrowding Index

F Statistic and corresponding sig/alpha for the Null Hypothesis that R² = 0

**ANOVA[a]**

| Model | | Sum of Squares | df | Mean Square | F | Sig. |
|---|---|---|---|---|---|---|
| 1 | Regression | 261.556 | 2 | 130.778 | 23.201 | .000[b] |
| | Residual | 152.193 | 27 | 5.637 | | |
| | Total | 413.750 | 29 | | | |

a. Dependent Variable: Inmate to Inmate Assault Rate

b. Predictors: (Constant), Mean Age of Inmates, Overcrowding Index

Value of intercept (a)

Standardized slopes (Betas)

**Coefficients[a]**

| Model | | Unstandardized Coefficients | | Standardized Coefficients | | |
|---|---|---|---|---|---|---|
| | | B | Std. Error | Beta | t | Sig |
| 1 | (Constant) | 22169. | 5.469 | | 4.053 | .000 |
| | Overcrowding Index | 3.721 | 1.891 | .277 | 1.968 | .059 |
| | Mean Age of Inmates | -.547 | .127 | -.607 | -4.317 | .000 |

a. Dependent Variable:Inmate to Inmate Assault Rate

Partial Slope Coefficients for Overcrowding and Mean Age

t Statistics and corresponding sig/alpha for the Null Hypothesis that each partial slope is equal to 0 ($\beta_1, \beta_2 = 0$)

The next step in our hypothesis test is to select an alpha level, determine our degrees of freedom, and identify the critical value of our test statistic. Let's continue with the alpha of .01. The statistic we will use to test our null hypothesis is Student's $t$, and the sampling distribution we will use is the $t$ distribution with $n - p$ degrees of freedom (where $p$ is equal to the number of independent variables in our regression model). We will conduct this hypothesis test with the exact probability of $t_{obt}$.

From Figure 13.5, you can see that the partial slope coefficient for the effect of age on inmate assaults is –.547 (because of rounding errors, our hand calculation of this $b$ was –.54), and the $t$ statistic is -4.317, with an exact two-tailed probability of this $t_{obt}$ being equal to .000. Since this probability is less than our critical alpha of .01, we are led to reject the null hypothesis. Our conclusion will be that the age of the inmate population is significantly related to the rate of inmate-to-inmate assaults even after controlling for the overcrowding index. As the mean age of the inmate population increases, rates of assault between inmates decrease. In other words, our sample data indicate that prisons with younger inmate populations tend to have significantly higher rates of assault between inmates than prisons with older inmate populations even after controlling for the effects of overcrowding.

The slope coefficient for the effect of prison density on inmate assaults is 3.721, with a $t$ value of 1.968. This corresponds to an exact two-tailed probability level of .059. Since this is greater than our alpha level of .01, we must fail to reject the null hypothesis that the slope coefficient in the population for prison overcrowding is equal to zero. We conclude that there is no significant linear relationship between overcrowding and rate of inmate-to-inmate assault within prisons. Finally, note that the absolute value of $t_{obt}$ for age (4.317) is greater than that for prison density (1.968). This would also lead us to believe that inmate age has more of an effect than prison density on the rate of inmate assaults. As such, despite the fact that both independent variables were related to inmate-to-inmate assaults at the bivariate level, when they were used to predict the assault rate controlling for each other, only the mean age retained its significance.

Before we conclude, we want to provide one more multiple regression example, which includes a dichotomous independent variable. No worries, however, as we are going to rely exclusively on SPSS output for this example with our focus on interpretation!

## Case Study

### Using a Dichotomous Independent Variable: Predicting Murder Rates in States

The data for this case study come from the state-level data we introduced in the last chapter. The dependent variable we are going to examine is state rates of murder, and the independent variables will be the percentage of individuals in states who live below the poverty line and a dichotomous variable indicating whether the state resides in the southern region of the United States (coded 1) or not (coded 0). We are examining this southern indicator to test the southern culture of honor thesis documented by a classic experiment by Richard Nisbett and Dov Cohen (1996). After their experiment, they contended that Southerners were more likely to approve of violence as a form of social control in response to perceived insults and in defense of self or their homes (Nisbett & Cohen, 2013). It is this tolerance of violence in the defense of honor, some contend, that is responsible for higher rates of murder in the South. Recent research, however, has failed to find a relationship between an individual's defensive gun use and whether he or she lived or was born in the South (Copes, Kovandizic, Miller, & Williamson, 2014). Viviana Andreescu, John Shutt, and Gennaro Vito (2011) found that homicide rates did not significantly differ in Appalachian counties in the South versus non-South after controlling for other cultural and structural variables like family stability. In our case study here, we will use this regional indicator to illustrate how to interpret the slope of a dichotomous variable. We want to state at the outset that dichotomies must be coded "0" and "1" to be easily interpreted in OLS regression analyses. Although we are relying on SPSS, we have provided the data and all coefficients necessary for hand calculations in Table 13.3 if you want to have some extra practice!

Figure 13.6 provides the SPSS output for our regression model predicting the murder rates with state poverty and regional location. We have not placed circles around the coefficients in this example to help you learn how to read output. We will start with the model summary statistics of the multiple $R$ and $R^2$. The multiple $R$ indicates a moderate-to-strong relationship between the murder rate in states and independent variables of poverty and regional location.

Together, these independent variables explain 49% (.49) of the variance in murder rates according to the $R^2$ statistic. The null and research hypotheses for this is:

$$H_0 = \beta_{poverty}, \beta_{region} = 0, \text{ or } R^2_{poverty,region} = 0$$

$$H_1 = \beta_{poverty}, \beta_{region} \neq 0, \text{ or } R^2_{poverty,region} \neq 0$$

Let's adopt an alpha/significance level for this test of .05. We can see in the ANOVA summary statistics that the value of $F$ for this test is equal to 8.17, which corresponds to a significance level of .003. This tells us that we will be wrong in rejecting the null hypothesis less than 1% of the time. Since we are willing to be wrong 5% of time in this case ($\alpha = .05$), we can reject the null hypothesis and conclude that at least one of the independent variables has a significant linear relationship with murder rates in states.

Moving on to the regression model in the Coefficients box in Figure 13.6, we see the value of the intercept ($a$), which is provided in the row labeled "constant," is equal to –1.617. Along with the unstandardized slope coefficients for the independent variables, this tells us that the linear regression equation is:

$$y = -1.617 + .475_{poverty} + 1.812_{region}$$

The slope for poverty indicates that for a one-unit increase in poverty in states, the murder rate increases by .475 units even after holding constant regional location. The null hypothesis test for this slope is:

$$H_0 = \beta_{poverty} = 0$$
$$H_1 = \beta_{poverty} \neq 0$$

Figure 13.6 indicates that the $t$ statistic for this test is equal to 3.145 and corresponds to a significance level of 006. This tells us that we will be wrong in rejecting the null hypothesis less than 1% of the time, which is lower than our alpha of .05. As such, we can safely reject this null hypothesis and conclude that there is a significant linear relationship between poverty and murder at the state level net of regional location. States that have higher rates of poverty also have higher rates of murder.

Now let's move on to the slope coefficient for regional location in the South. This is not a continuous independent variable, but it has only two values: 0 for those states not in the South and 1 for those states in the South. So how do we interpret this? The "one-unit increase" is $x$ is actually what happens to $y$ when $x$ changes from 0 to 1, which in this case is non-South to South. The unstandardized slope here tells us that when states reside in the South, the murder rate increases by 1.812 units after controlling for poverty. You can perhaps more easily see this if we predict the value of murder for states in the South versus non-South, holding constant poverty at its mean ($\bar{X}_{poverty} = 13.5$). Let's first predict the murder rate for a state with an average poverty rate (13.5) that resides in the non-South (coded 0):

$$\hat{y} = -1.617 + .475(13.5) + 1.812(0)$$
$$\hat{y} = -1.617 + 6.413 + 0$$
$$\hat{y} = 4.796$$

Now let's predict the murder rate with the same average poverty rate but this time residing in the South (coded 1):

$$\hat{y} = -1.617 + .475(13.5) + 1.812(1)$$
$$\hat{y} = -1.617 + 6.413 + 1.812$$
$$\hat{y} = 6.608$$

| Table 13.3 | Data and Calculations Necessary to Compute the Partial Slope Coefficient Among Murder Rates, Poverty Rate, and South Region (0 = Non-South, 1 = South), $n = 20$ States |
|---|---|

| Case | State | Murder Rate $y$ | Percent Poor $x_1$ | Southern Region $x_2$ |
|---|---|---|---|---|
| 1 | Alaska | 3.2 | 9.0 | 0 |
| 2 | Arizona | 5.5 | 16.5 | 0 |
| 3 | California | 5.4 | 14.2 | 0 |
| 4 | Delaware | 4.6 | 10.8 | 1 |
| 5 | Florida | 5.5 | 14.9 | 1 |
| 6 | Indiana | 5.3 | 14.4 | 0 |
| 7 | Louisiana | 12.3 | 17.3 | 1 |
| 8 | Maine | 2.0 | 12.3 | 0 |
| 9 | Maryland | 7.7 | 9.1 | 1 |
| 10 | Massachusetts | 2.7 | 10.3 | 0 |
| 11 | Michigan | 6.3 | 16.2 | 0 |
| 12 | Missouri | 6.6 | 14.6 | 0 |
| 13 | Nebraska | 2.5 | 12.3 | 0 |
| 14 | New Jersey | 3.7 | 9.4 | 0 |
| 15 | New Mexico | 10.0 | 18.0 | 0 |
| 16 | New York | 4.0 | 14.2 | 0 |
| 17 | Pennsylvania | 5.4 | 12.5 | 0 |
| 18 | South Carolina | 6.7 | 17.1 | 1 |
| 19 | Texas | 5.4 | 17.2 | 1 |
| 20 | Wyoming | 2.0 | 9.8 | 0 |
| | | $\Sigma_y = 106.8$ | $\Sigma x_1 = 270.1$ | $\Sigma x_2 = 6$ |
| | | $\bar{Y} = 5.34$ | $\bar{X}_{x_1} = 13.5$ | $\bar{X}_{x_2} = .30$ |
| | | $s_y = 2.59$ | $s_{x_1} = 3.03$ | $s_{x_2} = .47$ |
| | | $\Sigma y^2 = 697.4$ | $\Sigma x_1^2 = 3821.8$ | $\Sigma x_2^2 = 6$ |
| | $\Sigma yx_1 = 1534.8$ | $\Sigma yx_2 = 42.2$ | $\Sigma x_1 x_2 = 86.4$ | |
| | $r_{yx_1} = .62$ | $r_{yx_2} = .44$ | $r_{y_1 x_2} = .56$ $r_{x_1 x_2} = .20$ | |

As you can see, the difference between these predicted values of murder is about 1.812, which is the value of the partial slope coefficient for the variable "State in South" in the model. Now let's test the null hypothesis that there is no relationship between regional location and rates of murder:

$H_0 = \beta_{regoin} = 0$

$H_1 = \beta_{regoin} \neq 0$

**Figure 13.6** Multiple Regression Output From SPSS Predicting Murder Rates With Percent Poor and Southern Region (0 = Non-South, 1 = South) for n = 20 States

**Variables Entered/Removed[a]**

| Model | Variables Entered | Variables Removed | Method |
|---|---|---|---|
| 1 | State in South, Percent Individuals below poverty[b] | | Enter |

a. Dependent Variable: Murder Rate per 100K

b. All requested variables entered.

**Model Summary**

| Model | R | Square | Adjusted R Square | Std. Error of the Estimate |
|---|---|---|---|---|
| 1 | .700[a] | .490 | .430 | 1.9525 |

a. Predictors: (Constant), State in South, Percent Individuals below poverty

**ANOVA[a]**

| Model | | Sum of Squares | df | Mean Square | F | Sig. |
|---|---|---|---|---|---|---|
| 1 | Regression | 62.298 | 2 | 31.149 | 8.170 | .003[b] |
| | Residual | 64.810 | 17 | 3.812 | | |
| | Total | 127.108 | 19 | | | |

a. Dependent Variable: Murder Rate per 100K

b. Predictors: (Constant), State in South, Percent Individuals below poverty

**Coefficients[a]**

| Model | | Unstandardized Coefficients | | Standardized Coefficients | | t | Sig. |
|---|---|---|---|---|---|---|---|
| | | B | Std.Error | Beta | | | |
| 1 | (Constant) | −1.617 | 2.049 | | −.789 | | .441 |
| | Percent Individuals below poverty | .475 | .151 | .556 | 3.145 | | .006 |
| | State in South | 1.812 | .972 | .329 | 1.864 | | .080 |

a. Dependent Variable: Murder Rate per 100K

As shown in Figure 13.6, the $t$ value for southern location is equal to 1.864 and corresponds to a significance level of .080. That tells us that instead of the 5% error we are willing to make, we would be wrong in this case 8% of the time. As such, we must fail to reject the null hypothesis in this case and generalize that there is no relationship between murder rates in the South and non-South after controlling for poverty. We could have gotten a hint from this also by comparing the unadjusted value of $R^2$ (.49) with the adjusted value (.43). The value diminishes when we add a second independent variable that is not explaining very much of the dependent variable—in this case, the variable, "State in the South." The penalty we incur for including variables that are not explaining the dependent variable, then, is a drop in the $R^2$ value.

## ▣ Summary

In this chapter, we have examined techniques of multiple regression analysis. The multiple regression model is really a straightforward extension of the bivariate, or one-independent-variable, model. The slope coefficient in the multiple regression model, the partial slope coefficient, reflects the change in the dependent variable for a one-unit change in one independent variable while all other independent variables are held constant. The relative explanatory power of independent variables can be assessed by partial correlation coefficients, beta weights, standardized regression coefficients, the value of the $R^2$ change, and the absolute value of the $t$ ratios. In deciding which explanatory variables to include in a multiple regression model, the optimal strategy is to include those variables that are strongly correlated with the dependent variable but uncorrelated with other independent variables. We have also illustrated how to examine the relationship between a dichotomous independent variable coded 0 and 1 within an OLS regression model.

## Key Terms

> ➤ Review key terms with eFlashcards. **⑤SAGE** edge™

adjusted $R^2$ 409
beta weight 404
multicollinearity 398
multiple coefficient of
 determination ($R^2$) 405

multiple regression
 equation 396
multivariate regression model 393
nonspuriousness 394
partial correlation coefficient 405

partial regression
 coefficient 397
partial slope coefficient 397
$R^2$ change 409

## Key Formulas

Multiple regression model for population (equation 13-1):

$$y = \alpha + \beta_1 x_1 + \beta_2 x_2 + \cdots + \beta_k x_k + \varepsilon$$

Multivariate regression equation (equation 13-2):

$$y = a + b_1 x_1 + b_2 x_2 + \cdots b_k x_k + \varepsilon$$

Partial slope coefficients (equations 13-3 and 13-4):

$$b_1 = \left(\frac{s_y}{s_{x_1}}\right)\left(\frac{r_{yx_1} - \left(r_{yx_2}\right)\left(r_{x_1 x_2}\right)}{1 - r_{x_1 x_2}^2}\right)$$

$$b_2 = \left(\frac{s_y}{s_{x_2}}\right)\left(\frac{r_{yx_2} - \left(r_{yx_1}\right)\left(r_{x_1 x_2}\right)}{1 - r_{x_1 x_2}^2}\right)$$

Beta weights (equations 13-5 and 13-6):

$$b*_{x_1} = b_{x_1}\left(\frac{s_{x_1}}{s_y}\right)$$

$$b*_{x_2} = b_{x_2}\left(\frac{s_{x_2}}{s_y}\right)$$

Partial correlation coefficients (equations 13-7 and 13-8):

$$r_{yx_1 . x_2} = \frac{r_{yx_1} - \left(r_{yx_2}\right)\left(r_{x_1 x_2}\right)}{\sqrt{1 - r_{yx_2}^2}\sqrt{1 - r_{x_1 x_2}^2}}$$

$$r_{yx_2 . x_1} = \frac{r_{yx_1} - \left(r_{yx_1}\right)\left(r_{x_1 x_2}\right)}{\sqrt{1 - r_{yx_1}^2}\sqrt{1 - r_{x_1 x_2}^2}}$$

Multiple coefficient of determination, $R^2$ (equation 13-9):

$$R^2 = r_{yx_1}^2 + (r_{yx_2 . x_1}^2)(1 - r_{yx_1}^2)$$

Adjusted $R^2$ (equation 13-10):

$$R_{adjusted}^2 = R^2 - \frac{k(1 - R^2)}{n - k - 1}$$

## Practice Problems

> Test your understanding of chapter content.
> Take the practice quiz. **$SAGE edge**

1. Suppose we were interested in the extent to which rates of divorce and mean age of the population within states affected state-level rates of violent crime. To examine these relationships, we took a random sample of 35 states and obtained the divorce rate per 100,000 population for each, the mean age in each state, and rates of violent crime per 100,000.

    Assume that we obtained the multiple regression output shown in Figure 13.7. With this output, answer the following questions:

    a. Specify the exact least-squares multiple regression equation.

    b. Interpret both partial slope coefficients and the intercept value.

    c. By using this output, how would you examine the relative importance of each independent variable?

    d. What is the total variance explained?

    e. Conduct a hypothesis test using the obtained output for both the entire regression model and the independent slope coefficients. Use a two-tailed alpha level of .01 for both tests. What are your formal hypothesis statements? What do you conclude based on the $F$ test and the two $t$ tests?

2. Suppose we are interested in the reasons why escapes occur in local jails. To investigate this issue, we take a random sample of 30 jails. We ask the jail managers how many escapes they had from their facilities in the past year. This is our dependent variable. Based on

| Figure 13.7 | Multiple Regression Output for Problem 1 Predicting the Violent Crime Rate for States |
|---|---|

**Variables Entered/Removed[a]**

| Model | Variables Entered | Variables Removed | Method |
|---|---|---|---|
| 1 | Divorce Mean Age | | Enter |

**Model Summary**

| Model | R | R Square | Adjusted R Square | Std. Error of the Estimate |
|---|---|---|---|---|
| 1 | .795[a] | .632 | .609 | 1.9525 |

a. Predictors: (Constant), Divorce, Mean Age

**ANOVA[a]**

| Model | | Sum of Squares | df | Mean Square | F | Sig. |
|---|---|---|---|---|---|---|
| 1 | Regression | 324.538 | 2 | 162.26 | 27.531 | .000[b] |
| | Residual | 188.604 | 20 | 5.893 | | |

a. Dependent Variable: Violent Crime Rate per 100K
b. Predictors: (Constant), Divorce, Mean Age

**Coefficients[a]**

| Model | | Unstandardized Coefficients B | Unstandardized Coefficients std. Error | Standardized Coefficients Beta | t | Sig. |
|---|---|---|---|---|---|---|
| 1 | (Constant) | 19.642 | 2.736 | | .600 | .552 |
| | Divorce | .871 | .204 | .594 | 4.268 | .000 |
| | Mean Age | −.146 | .047 | −.133 | −3.110 | .001 |

our knowledge of the literature, we also know that work-related morale and the extent to which facilities are understaffed affect things like supervision and motivation to identify and solve problems. To measure the level of morale, we ask jail employees to respond to a number of questions regarding their morale (e.g., I think my supervisors appreciate my work, I feel secure in my job, I like the people I work with, etc.). With their responses, we compute a morale index with high scores indicating high morale and low scores indicating low morale. To determine the extent to which an institution is understaffed, we construct a jail-staff-to-inmate ratio. Again, high scores indicate a large number of staff relative to inmates and low scores indicate a small number of jail staff relative to inmates. The data we obtain are listed as follows:

a. What would the values of $b_1$ and $b_2$ be from these sample statistics? Interpret these coefficients.

b. From your calculated partial slope coefficients and sample means, solve for the value of the intercept ($a$). What is the complete multiple regression equation?

c. By using the earlier multiple regression equation, predict the value of $y$ (number of escapes) from a morale score of 8 and a staff ratio score of .3.

d. Calculate the beta weights for each of the partial slope coefficients. What do they tell you about the relative importance of each independent variable?

e. Calculate the multiple coefficient of determination from these sample statistics. What does this coefficient indicate?

| Jail | # of Escapes | Morale Score | Staff-to-Inmate Ratio |
|------|------|------|------|
| 1 | 12.00 | 3.00 | .22 |
| 2 | 10.00 | 7.00 | .41 |
| 3 | 3.00 | 14.00 | .66 |
| 4 | 7.00 | 8.00 | .45 |
| 5 | 9.00 | 9.00 | .32 |
| 6 | 13.00 | 5.00 | .33 |
| 7 | 17.00 | 2.00 | .10 |
| 8 | 12.00 | 5.00 | .30 |
| 9 | 15.00 | 4.00 | .20 |
| 10 | 9.00 | 5.00 | .50 |
| 11 | 3.00 | 7.00 | .60 |
| 12 | 5.00 | 3.00 | .40 |
| 13 | 11.00 | 2.00 | .20 |
| 14 | 14.00 | 5.00 | .50 |
| 15 | 7.00 | 8.00 | .40 |
| 16 | 10.00 | 5.00 | .20 |
| 17 | 14.00 | 3.00 | .30 |
| 18 | 15.00 | 2.00 | .40 |
| 19 | 17.00 | 2.00 | .10 |
| 20 | 6.00 | 8.00 | .20 |
| 21 | 9.00 | 4.00 | .20 |
| 22 | 3.00 | 10.00 | .50 |
| 23 | 2.00 | 11.00 | .60 |
| 24 | 4.00 | 7.00 | .30 |
| 25 | 13.00 | 2.00 | .30 |
| 26 | 11.00 | 8.00 | .50 |
| 27 | 14.00 | 4.00 | .30 |
| 28 | 9.00 | 4.00 | .30 |
| 29 | 5.00 | 11.00 | .40 |
| 30 | 4.00 | 14.00 | .50 |

The statistics necessary to calculate the slope coefficients are as follows:

| | | |
|------|------|------|
| $\Sigma_y = 283$ | $\Sigma_{x_1} = 182$ | $\Sigma_{x_2} = 10.7$ |
| $s_y = 4.49$ | $s_{x_1} = 3.47$ | $s_{x_2} = .15$ |
| $\bar{y} = 9.43$ | $\bar{x}_1 = 6.07$ | $\bar{x}_2 = .36$ |
| $\Sigma y^2 = 3255$ | $\Sigma x_{x_1}^2 = 1454$ | $\Sigma x_{x_1}^2 = 4.44$ |
| | $r_{yx_1} = -.77$ | |
| | $r_{yx_2} = -.63$ | |
| | $r_{x_1x_2} = .67$ | |
| $r_{yx_1.x_2} = -.59$ | $r_{yx_2.x_1} = -.245$ | |

3. In a 2014 article, Monica Miller, Jonathan Maskaly, Clayton Peoples, and Alexandra Sigillo conducted a study on jurors'

religious characteristics and their verdicts and sentencing decisions. They found that those people who were high on religious fundamentalism saw the character of the offender rather than environmental factors as a cause of crime and, therefore, were more punitive in their response to crime. You wanted to conduct a similar study. You first developed three attitude scales: one that measured punitiveness toward the criminal (PUN), one that measured religious fundamentalism (REL), and one that measured a person's belief that environmental factors are responsible for crime (ENV). Those who score high on the punitiveness scale want to punish convicted criminals severely, those who score high on the religious fundamentalism scale take a strict interpretation of the Bible, and those who score high on the environmental factors scale think that social factors are to blame for crime rather than the evil character of the offender. Based on the Miller and colleagues (2014) study, you expect that religious fundamentalism will be positively related to punitiveness and that a belief in environmental causes of crime will be negatively related to punitiveness. You take a random sample of 15 persons who respond to a questionnaire that contains your attitude scales. You conduct a multiple regression analysis on your data and present the results in Figure 13.8. With this output, answer the following questions.

a. Specify the exact least-squares multiple regression equation.

b. Interpret both partial slope coefficients and the intercept value.

c. By using this output, how would you examine the relative importance of each independent variable?

d. What is the total variance explained?

e. Conduct a hypothesis test using the obtained output for both the entire regression model and for the independent slope coefficients. Use an alpha level of .01 for both tests. What are your formal hypothesis statements? What do you conclude based on the $F$ test and the two $t$ tests?

f. By using the multiple regression equation, predict the punitiveness score for a person who has a religious fundamentalism score of 8 and an environmental factor score of 2.

---

**Figure 13.8** **Multiple Regression Output for Problem 3**

**Variables Entered/Removed[a]**

| Model | Variables Entered | Variables Removed | Method |
|-------|-------------------|-------------------|--------|
| 1 | ENV, REL | | Enter |

**Model Summary**

| Model | R | R Square | Adjusted R Square |
|-------|---|----------|-------------------|
| 1 | .811[a] | .659 | .602 |

a. Predictors: (Constant), ENV,REL

**ANOVA[a]**

| Model | | Sum of Squares | df | Mean Square | F | Sig. |
|-------|---|----------------|-----|-------------|---|------|
| 1 | Regression | 481.341 | 2 | 240.670 | 11.565 | .001[b] |
| | Residual | 249.058 | 12 | 20.754 | | |

**Coefficients[a]**

| Model | | Unstandardized Coefficients | | Standardized Coefficients | t | Sig. |
|-------|---|---|---|---|---|---|
| | | B | std. Error | Beta | | |
| 1 | (Constant) | 16.245 | 5.514 | | 2.946 | .012 |
| | ENV | −1.467 | .443 | −.608 | − 3.312 | .006 |
| | REL | 1.075 | .980 | .346 | 1.184 | .084 |

## SPSS Exercises

➤ Explore additional data sets. $SAGE edge™

| Data for Exercise | |
|---|---|
| **Data Set** | **Description** |
| 2013 YRBS.sav | The 2013 YRBS, short for Youth Risk Behavior Survey, is a national study of high-school students. It focuses on gauging various behaviors and experiences of the adolescent population, including substance use and some victimization. |
| **Variables for Exercise** | |
| **Variable Name** | **Description** |
| WeaponCarrying | A scale based on three questions asking how often the student carries a weapon in and outside of school. High values indicate carrying weapons more frequently. |
| Qn24 | A binary indicator for if the respondent had been bullied in the past year, where 1 = yes and 0 = no. |
| Qn25 | A binary indicator for if the respondent had been bullied online in the past year, where 1 = yes and 0 = no. |
| Age | A respondent's age in years, ranging from 12 to 18+. |
| Sex | A binary variable where 1 = female and 2 = male. |
| White | A binary variable where 0 = non-white and 1 = white. |
| Grade | The grade that the respondent was in, ranging from 9th grade to 12th grade. |
| HostileEnvironment | An index assessing a student's experience of hostility in his or her school. This includes feeling unsafe in school and getting in any fights or being threatened. Higher values indicate higher levels of hostility experienced. |

1. Why do some students carry weapons inside and outside of school? Who are those students? Dr. Smartypants is at it again: He is wondering if perhaps students who are bullied are the ones who are most prone to carrying weapons. To study this, he asks to you run a regression model with two indicators of if the student had been bullied on or offline. He hypothesizes that offline bullying is more likely to cause weapon carrying since it is in person. In his theory, offline bullying is unlikely to have an effect:

   a. What are your null and research hypotheses? Be sure to include hypotheses for both independent variables and your regression model F test.

   b. **Multiple Regression in SPSS:** As with single-variable regression, begin by selecting analyze->regression->linear. Place the variable Weaponcarrying in the dependent variable spot and both qn24 and qn25 in the independent variable slot. That's it! Select ok. You'll notice that the output is all but identical to the output provided within this chapter's text!

   c. Use this output to answer the following:

   i. What does the model's ANOVA table tell you in this case?

   ii. What proportion of the variance in the weapon carrying scale is explained by these two variables?

   iii. What do the slope coefficients for each tell us? Recall that these are binary indicators, so a one-unit change in this case reflects the difference between not bullied and bullied students. The hypothesis tests?

   iv. How do you interpret the Intercept in this case?

   v. Is Dr. Smartypants's theory supported by these results?

2. Dr. Smartypants says he'd like to control for some additional variables to minimize the risk of confounding. In particular, he wants to control for student age, being male, year in school, and if the student is White versus non-White. To do this, include the variables age, sex, White, and grade in the model:

   a. Does this change your results or conclusions?

   b. How has your model $R$-squared changed?

   c. Do you find any interesting or new effects in the independent variables you have added?

d. Take a look at the column called "standardized coefficients." These are your beta weights. What coefficients have the strongest effect on the dependent variable?

e. Briefly summarize your results for Dr. Smartypants. Are there any confounders or concerns that need to be considered?

3. You decide to check if multicollinearity may be an issue for your analysis. One simple way to look at this is to see if your independent variables are strongly correlated with one another. Consider a correlation coefficient of .5 to be evidence of multicollinearity in this case:

a. Do you find any evidence of multicollinearity? If so, explain why those two variables might be collinear.

b. If multicollinearity was found, reestimate your multiple regression model with one of the problem variables removed. Have your substantive conclusions changed?

4. You realize there is a potential confounder at play here. Maybe instead of bullying being the "cause" of weapon use, it's actually a sense of fear and hostility in the school? If a person gets bullied, they might get in fights or just feel unsafe. Perhaps it is students who are exposed to a great deal of conflict and hostility that are carrying weapons? Let's make sure the bullying effects are still present after controlling for that confounder!

a. Estimate your multiple regression model with the bullying variables, age, sex, and White. This time also add the variable HostileEnvironment.

b. Have your results (not) changed? Does this model fit better than earlier models? What is your strongest effect in the model, based on your standardized coefficients and *t* statistics?

c. Write a memo to Dr. Smartypants that uses the results of this model to either support or critique his theory presented in question 1. Be sure to include your model *R*-squared and how it has/hasn't changed, what happens when you control for the confounder, and the "why" that explains why the variables are related to the dependent variable.

d. If you were tasked with developing an intervention to prevent weapon carrying in school, what would you recommend? What should be prioritized?

e. Have you met the criteria for causality in this final model? If no, what more must be done?

# CHAPTER 14

# Regression Analysis With a Dichotomous Dependent Variable

## *Logit Models*

> *At its most fundamental, information is a binary choice. In other words, a single bit of information is one yes-or-no choice.*
>
> —James Gleick
>
> *There are only 10 types of people in the world; those who understand binary and those who don't.*
>
> —Anonymous

**LEARNING OBJECTIVES**

1. List the problems that can occur when using ordinary least-squares (OLS) regression to predict the values of a dichotomous dependent variable.

2. Describe the estimation procedures used to predict a dichotomous dependent variable with the logistic regression model.

3. Identify the logistic regression equation from Statistical Package for the Social Sciences (SPSS) output.

4. Interpret both the slope coefficients and the exponential of the slope coefficients from a logistic regression equation.

5. Transform the slope coefficients in a logistic regression model into predicted probabilities of a dependent variable.

6. Conduct a hypothesis test for the slope coefficient in a logistic regression model.

7. Explain how to interpret slope coefficients from multivariate logistic regression models.

8. Describe how to assess model fit for logistic regression models.

# ▣ **Introduction**

**Dichotomous variable:** Two-category variable.

**Logistic regression model:** Used to predict a dependent variable with two categories (0, 1), called a binary or dichotomous variable. It is used to estimate the probability of a binary response based on one or more independent variables.

As you have already learned in this book, many variables that we want to learn about in criminology and criminal justice are dichotomous. A dichotomous dependent variable has only two outcomes; when these outcomes are coded "0" and "1," they are called binary dependent variables. Examples of dichotomous or binary dependent variables in criminology and criminal justice include whether someone has committed a crime, whether he or she appears for trial after posting bail or "skips out," whether he or she tests positive or negative for drugs after an arrest, and whether he or she is sentenced to prison or some nonpenal punishment. Each of these is an example of a **dichotomous variable**. Just as with variables measured at other levels, we are still interested in explaining these dichotomous variables using explanatory or independent variables.

In Chapters 12 and 13, we learned about ordinary least-squares (OLS) regression. In this model, one or more independent variables measured at any level were presumed to be linearly related to a dependent variable measured at the interval/ratio level. We learned that the OLS regression model is a very good and general tool for analyzing the relationship between independent variables and a continuous dependent variable. However, even though the OLS model is a very general tool, it is not so flexible that it is the only one we need to learn. In this chapter, you will learn the problems inherent when using the OLS regression model to predict dichotomous dependent variables. We will then introduce you to another type of regression-based model called the **logistic regression model**, which is appropriate to use when the dependent variable is binary or dichotomous. Similar to the OLS model, we can predict the values of a dichotomous dependent variable using one or more independent variables, and we can determine whether a logistic regression coefficient is significantly different from zero. To build a foundation for this logistic regression, we will introduce an OLS model for binary (0,1) dependent variables called the linear probability model. We will then discuss the possible problems with the linear probability model and move to a discussion of the logistic regression model.

## Estimating an OLS Regression Model With a Dichotomous Dependent Variable—The Linear Probability Model

### Case Study

### Age at First Delinquent Offense and Adult Criminality

For our first example, let's look at the relationship between the age at which someone begins offending (often referred to in the criminology literature as "age of onset") and whether he or she commits a criminal offense as an adult (at 18 years of age or older). For a random sample of 40 adults, all of whom have admitted committing a delinquent offense before age 18, we asked them at what age they committed their first offense and whether they have committed an offense after age 18. In this example, the age at which one commits his or her first delinquent offense is our independent variable, and it is continuous. Whether this person has committed a crime as an adult is our dichotomous dependent variable, where a value of 0 is given to an adult who has not committed an offense as an adult and a value of 1 is given if he or she has. These data are shown in Table 14.1.

By looking at Table 14.1, you can see that there might be a relationship between age at onset of delinquency and adult offending. You notice that more of those with younger onset ages have committed an offense as an adult, compared with those who commit their first delinquent offense at a later age. We learned in Chapters 12 and 13 that you can get a good initial sense of the possible relationship between your variables by doing a scatterplot. Figure 14.1 presents the scatterplot for the data in Table 14.1. Note that unlike the case with a continuous dependent variable, there are only two points on the y axis, indicating either that there was an adult offense committed (0) or that there was not (1). All of the data points in the scatterplot fall on one of two lines parallel to the x axis; each of these lines corresponds to one of the two possible values of the dependent variable. It appears from this scatterplot that most of the "1" values (committed an adult offense) cluster at the younger onset ages, whereas most of the "0" values (did not commit an adult offense) cluster at the older onset ages. It seems, therefore, that age at onset of delinquency and adult offending do covary and that the relationship between the two variables is likely to be negative (i.e., a greater risk of adult offending as age of onset decreases).

If we wanted to, we could now presume that the relationship between onset age of delinquency and adult offending is a linear one and fit an ordinary least-squares regression line (a straight line) to our observed data points. This regression equation would take the form:

$$y = a + bx + \varepsilon \tag{14–1}$$

where

$a$ = the $y$ intercept or constant

$b$ = the OLS regression coefficient reflecting the linear relationship between age at onset of delinquency and adult offending

$x$ = age at onset of delinquency

$y$ = 0 if an adult criminal offense was not committed, 1 if there was an adult offense

$\varepsilon$ = an error term

| Table 14.1 | Data on Age of Onset of Delinquency (Age at First Delinquent Offense) and the Commission of a Crime as an Adult (18 Years of Age and Older) |
|---|---|

| Age at First Delinquent Offense | Adult Offense | Age at First Delinquent Offense | Adult Offense |
|---|---|---|---|
| 10 | 1 | 14 | 1 |
| 10 | 1 | 14 | 1 |
| 10 | 1 | 14 | 0 |
| 10 | 1 | 14 | 0 |
| 10 | 0 | 14 | 0 |
| 11 | 1 | 15 | 1 |
| 11 | 1 | 15 | 0 |
| 11 | 1 | 15 | 0 |
| 11 | 1 | 15 | 0 |
| 11 | 0 | 15 | 0 |
| 12 | 1 | 16 | 1 |
| 12 | 1 | 16 | 0 |
| 12 | 1 | 16 | 0 |
| 12 | 0 | 16 | 0 |
| 12 | 0 | 16 | 0 |
| 13 | 1 | 17 | 0 |
| 13 | 1 | 17 | 0 |
| 13 | 0 | 17 | 0 |
| 13 | 0 | 17 | 0 |
| 13 | 0 | 17 | 0 |

| Figure 14.1 | Scatterplot of Age at Delinquency Onset and Adult Offending |
|---|---|

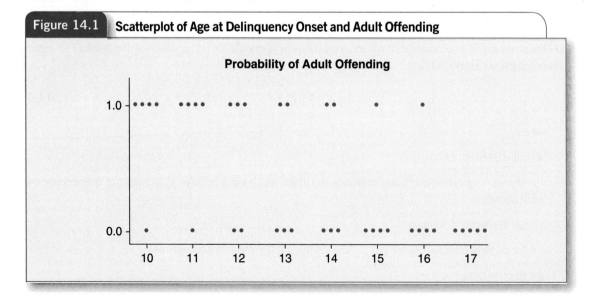

In this OLS regression equation, observed values of the dependent variable $y$ (whether someone committed a criminal offense as an adult) are restricted to be either 0 or 1. Since the expected value of $y$ is limited to 0 or 1, the regression equation models the relationship between the independent variable and the probability of the dependent variable. OLS models such as these, which assume a linear relationship between an independent variable and the probability of a dependent variable, are often referred to as linear probability models. Our regression equation in equation 14-1, then, describes the probability that someone will commit an adult offense given the age at which that person first committed a delinquent offense. The regression coefficient, $b$, measures the linear change in the probability of committing an adult offense with each one-year increase in delinquency onset age. Like any linear model, the slope coefficient is the effect on $y$ of a one-unit increase in $x$ at any place on the $x$ continuum.

By using the data in Table 14.1, we will estimate an ordinary least-squares regression equation for the probability of an adult arrest. When we do so, we observe the following regression equation:

$$\hat{y} = 2.00 - .117x$$

The $y$ intercept is 2.00, so when $x = 0$ the predicted probability of $y$ is 2 adult offenses. In this case, the constant has no meaningful interpretation since it is the predicted number of adult offenses when the age of onset is 0. The slope coefficient ($b$) is -.117. The sign of this linear probability coefficient tells us that the relationship between onset age and the probability of adult offending is negative—those who commit their first delinquent act at an earlier age are more likely than those who do so at a later age to commit an offense as an adult. The magnitude of the coefficient tells us that a one-year increase in delinquency onset age reduces the probability of an adult offense by .117. Again, since the relationship is presumed to be linear, the reduction of .117 in the probability of adult offending for each one-year decline in age of onset is the same at every point on the $x$ range. With this regression equation, we can determine the predicted probability of an adult offense for individuals who commit their first delinquent act at 12 years of age:

$$\hat{y} = 2.00 - (.117)12$$
$$= .596$$

The predicted probability of an adult offense for individuals who committed their first delinquent act at 13 years of age is:

$$\hat{y} = 2.00 - (.117)13$$
$$= .479$$

Note that increasing the age of one's first delinquent offense from 12 years old to 13 years old results in a decrease in the probability of an adult offense by .117 ($.479 - .596 = -.117$). This corresponds to the fact that the sign of the regression coefficient is negative, indicating that higher onset ages are related to a reduced probability of adult offending. In addition, the size of the decrease in the probability of an adult offense between one with an onset age of 12 compared with age 13 is .117, which is the magnitude of the OLS regression coefficient.

Let's now use the linear probability equation to estimate the probability of adult offending for someone who committed his first delinquent offense at 8 years of age:

$$\hat{y} = 2.00 - (.117)8$$
$$= 1.064$$

Although it is always hazardous to estimate the probability of an event that is beyond one's data (note that we do not have anyone in the observed data whose delinquency onset age was 8), it is especially problematic here. We have a predicted probability of 1.064 of committing an adult offense for someone who commits his or her first delinquent act at age 8. This is impossible because, as we learned in Chapter 6, probabilities have an upper bound of 1.0. One problem with using an OLS regression model on binary dependent variables, then, is that it may lead to predicted probabilities of the dependent variable that lie outside the limiting values of 0 and 1.0.

The reason why predicted values of *y* for the dependent variable may be less than 0 or greater than 1 is that the OLS model assumes that the line that best fits the data is a straight line (that is what a linear relationship means). As we have said, an implication of this is that a one-unit increase in the independent variable, *x*, produces the same change in the expected probability of the dependent variable, *y, at all values of x*. In other words, the linear probability model assumes that the relationship between the independent variable and the probability of the dependent variable is linear across all possible values of the independent variable. In our example, this means that the probability that someone will commit an adult offense is a linear function of onset age (*x*) and that a one-unit change in onset age produces a –.117 decrease in the probability of adult offending at all values of onset age. This prediction of probabilities less than 0.0 or greater than 1.0 can also occur when you have large outliers in your data.

Another issue with using a linear probability model (indeed, any linear model) is that the relationship between your independent and dependent variable may not be linear. *How* an independent variable is related to the dependent variable, linear or nonlinear, is referred to as the *functional form* of the model. Let us illustrate. We will use the data in Table 14.1 to draw a scatterplot of the relationship between age at onset of delinquency and whether someone commits an offense as an adult. We will also include in that scatterplot the linear regression line that we would get by using equation 14-1 and a curved line rather than a straight one. Looking at Figure 14.2 reveals several things that indicate that onset age and adult offending might not best be characterized as a linear or a straight-line relationship. First, it clearly appears that the straight regression line from the linear probability model does not provide a very good fit through these data points. The curved line does, however, appear to provide a better fit than the straight line. This would lead us to believe that the relationship between onset age and adult offending is nonlinear rather than linear. This nonlinear relationship means that the expected change in the dependent variable for a one-unit change in the independent variable is not constant for each value of the independent variable (as the linear model assumes). It would appear instead that the effect of a one-unit change in the independent variable is greater for the values in the middle of the observed distribution and that the effect of onset age becomes smaller as the probability of adult offending approaches either 0 or 1.

If this were not enough, there is another problem with the linear probability model. One assumption of the ordinary least-squares model is that the error term is normally distributed and independent of the *x* (independent) variable. To examine this assumption with our current problem, we will calculate a predicted value of *y* ( $\hat{y}$, the predicted probability of an adult offense, the dependent variable) at each value of *x* (age at onset of delinquency, the independent variable) and then determine the error term by subtracting the observed value of *y* from this predicted value ( $\hat{y}$ ). We have calculated each of these predicted *y* values and the error term for each value of *x*, and they are reported in Table 14.2. Note that for each observed value of the

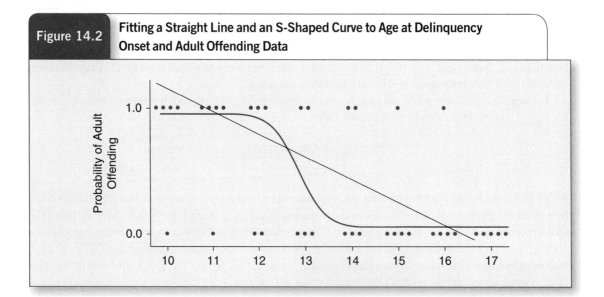

**Figure 14.2** **Fitting a Straight Line and an S-Shaped Curve to Age at Delinquency Onset and Adult Offending Data**

independent variable, there are only two possible values for the error term. For example, among those who committed their first delinquent offense at 10 years of age, the predicted probability of committing an offense as an adult is .830. For those who committed an adult offense ($y = 1$), the error is .171, whereas for those who did not commit an adult offense ($y = 0$), the error is −.830. As you can see from Table 14.2, because the dependent variable takes on only two values (0 or 1), the error term in our regression equation (equation 14-1) can assume only two values for any given value of $x$. This means that the error term is not normally distributed but is distributed as a binomial variable. You may remember from our earlier discussion of binomial variables that the variance

is estimated as $\sqrt{\dfrac{pq}{n}}$ , where $q = 1 - p$. The variance of a

binomial variable does not have constant variance but is greatest when $p = .50$ and declines as $p$ approaches 0 and 1. The variance of a binomially distributed error term in a linear probability model, therefore, is not constant but depends on the predicted value of $y$. Observations where the predicted value of $y$ are closer to 0 and 1 will have small variances, and observations where the predicted value of $y$ is closer to .50 will have greater variances. Because the error terms in a linear probability model do not have constant variance, the errors are said to be heteroscedastic, in violation of the OLS assumption of homoscedasticity. As a consequence of **heteroscedasticity**, hypothesis tests about estimated parameters such as the regression coefficient $b$ may be incorrect.

**Table 14.2** Predicted Probability of $y$ ($\hat{y}$) and the Value of the Error Term ($y - \hat{y}$) for Each Value of Age at Onset of Delinquency (Data in Table 14.1)

| Age at Onset | $\hat{y}$ | $(y - \hat{y})$ for: $y = 0$ | $y = 1$ |
|---|---|---|---|
| 10 | .84 | −.84 | .16 |
| 11 | .74 | −.74 | .26 |
| 12 | .61 | −.61 | .39 |
| 13 | .47 | −.47 | .53 |
| 14 | .32 | −.32 | .68 |
| 15 | .21 | −.21 | .79 |
| 16 | .13 | −.13 | .87 |
| 17 | .07 | −.07 | .93 |

**Heteroscedasticity:** Occurs when the assumption of **homoscedasticity** is violated and indicates that the error terms are not constant across all values of $x$.

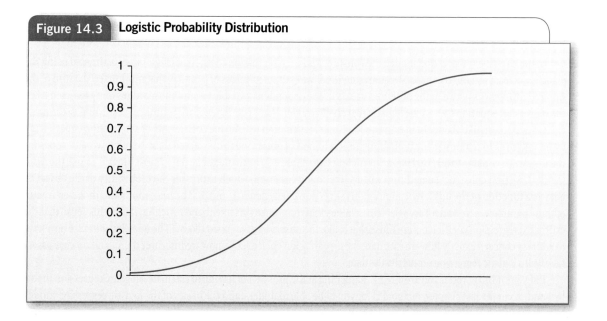

**Figure 14.3** Logistic Probability Distribution

An advantage of *carefully* using a linear probability model is that unlike logistic regression coefficients (which we study next), the regression coefficients are easy to interpret. As we showed you earlier, the slope coefficient reflects the expected change in the probability of the dependent variable for a one-unit increase in the independent variable.

Another regression model to use when the dependent variable is binary is the logistic regression model. The logistic probability distribution is an S-shaped probability distribution that would seem to fit the case of a dichotomous variable quite well. An example of the cumulative logistic distribution is shown in Figure 14.3. What we will do now is use the cumulative logistic probability distribution to develop a regression strategy similar to the OLS method we currently have in our toolbox. The difference between the logit model and OLS is that the former is a nonlinear model and does not require the assumption of constant variance. The OLS and logistic regression models do, however, share some assumptions, such as the assumption that the dependent variable is an additive function of one or more independent variables, that the observations are random and independent, and that no two independent variables are highly correlated.

## ▣ The Logit Regression Model With One Independent Variable

As mentioned, the **logistic regression model** is based on something called the cumulative logistic probability distribution, which was illustrated in Figure 14.3. In the logistic regression model, we can also estimate the probability of a binary event occurring (or something called the log of the odds of the dependent variable occurring). In the case of one independent variable, one way (there are others) to write the logistic regression model is:

$$\text{Prob(Event)} = \frac{1}{1 + e^{-(\beta_0 + \beta_1 x)}} \tag{14-2}$$

where

$\beta_0$ = the constant ($y$ intercept) for the model estimated from the data

$\beta_1$ = the regression coefficient estimated from the data

$x$ = the independent variable

$e$ = the base of the natural logarithms, which is approximately equal to 2.718

In the OLS linear regression model, the constant and each regression coefficient (slope) were estimated using the principle of least squares. In the least-squares method, we estimated values of $\beta_0$ and $\beta_1$ that minimized the sum of the squared differences between the observed values of the dependent variable ($y$) and those values of $y$ predicted from the regression equation ($\hat{y}$). In the logistic regression model, these coefficients are estimated according to the principle of maximum likelihood. In maximum likelihood estimation (MLE), the coefficients of a regression equation are estimated so as to maximize the probability or likelihood of obtaining the observed data. In other words, values for the unknown constant and regression coefficients are chosen so as to make the data "most likely." To use the MLE method, we first construct something called a likelihood function, which expresses the probability of the observed data as a function of the unknown population regression coefficients $\beta_0$ and $\beta_1$. The maximum likelihood estimates of these parameters ($b_0$ and $b_1$) are selected as values that maximize this likelihood function. It is in this sense that the estimated regression coefficients are those that make the observed data "most likely." The questions that we now have to address concern exactly how we estimate these regression coefficients, how we interpret them, and how we assess how well a logistic regression model fits the data.

Put your mind at rest if you are already panicking at the prospect of having to calculate a logistic regression model by hand. As in the last chapter, our goal is for you to be able to understand the basics of the logistic regression model.

To achieve this, we use models estimated with computer programs and concentrate on interpretation rather than on calculation. In fact, nobody does logistic regression by hand; we all use computer software. Although the specific computer output you get from a logistic regression procedure varies with the software program you use, most give you at a minimum the following information: (a) the constant and estimated logistic regression coefficient for each independent variable in the model, (b) the estimated standard error of each coefficient, (c) a Wald or $t$ test for the statistical significance of the estimated regression coefficient (whether it is significantly different from zero), and (d) various indicators of how well the model fits the data.

With such computer software, we estimated a logistic regression model for the data in Table 14.1 on the onset age of delinquency and whether someone commits an offense as an adult. We show you the results of this logistic regression in Table 14.3. Before we begin interpreting these results, let's reintroduce the logistic regression model with one independent variable (equation 14-2):

$$\text{Prob(Event)} = \frac{1}{1 + e^{-(\beta_0 + \beta_1 x)}}$$

The logistic regression equation 14-2 does not look anything like the OLS equation we learned in the last two chapters or even the linear probability model. We can, however, write the logistic regression equation a little differently so that it looks more familiar. We will let $P$ be the probability of the dependent variable occurring. In our example this will be the probability that someone commits a criminal offense as an adult. Let's begin by multiplying both sides of the equation above by $1 + e^{-(\beta_0 + \beta_1 x_1)}$ to get:

$$1 + e^{-(\beta_0 + \beta_1 x_1)} P = 1$$

We then divide both sides by $P$ and subtract 1 to get:

$$e^{-(\beta_0 + \beta_1 x_1)} = \frac{1}{P} - 1$$

or

$$e^{-(\beta_0 + \beta_1 x_1)} = \frac{1 - P}{P}$$

| Table 14.3 | **Results of Logistic Regression Analysis for Age at Onset of Delinquency and Adult Offending (Data in Table 14.1)** | | | | | |
|---|---|---|---|---|---|---|
| Variable | Beta | Standard Error | Wald Statistic | df | Sig. | Odds Multiplier or (Exp)B |
| Constant | 7.640 | 2.064 | 8.068 | 1 | | |
| Onset age | -.598 | .197 | 9.214 | 1 | .001 | .550 |
| -2 Log likelihood for baseline model (constant only): 54.548 | | | | | | |
| -2 Log likelihood for model with age at onset: 41.553 | | | | | | |

Since by definition $e^{-(\beta_0 + \beta_1 x_1)} = \dfrac{1}{e^{(\beta_0 + \beta_1 x_1)}}$ , we can rewrite this expression as:

$$e^{(\beta_0 + \beta_1 x_1)} = \frac{P}{1-P}$$

Next, by taking the natural logarithm of both sides, we obtain the following regression equation:

$$\beta_0 + \beta_1 x_1 = \ln\left(\frac{1-P}{P}\right)$$

And then moving expressions from one side of the equals sign to the other, we have:

$$\ln\left(\frac{P}{1-P}\right) = \beta_0 + \beta_1 x_1 \qquad\qquad \textbf{(14-3)}$$

This now looks a little bit more like our familiar regression model, with a dependent or $y$ variable on the left-hand side and a constant and regression coefficient for the independent or $x$ variable on the right-hand side. The dependent variable, however, looks a little unusual, and deserves some comment.

The expression $\left(\dfrac{P}{1-P}\right)$ is the probability of an event ($P$) over its complement ($1-P$), where the latter term is the probability that the event does not occur. The ratio of a probability to its complement is the odds of an event occurring. If, for instance, the probability of an event is .80, then the odds of it occurring are 4 to 1 (.80 / .20 = 4), whereas an event with a .50 probability has an odds of 1.00 (.50 / .50 = 1), or even odds. The term "ln" in front of the odds stands for the natural logarithm. The dependent variable in the logistic regression equation 14-3, therefore, is not the probability of an event but the natural log of the odds of the event occurring. In the example we have been working with in this chapter, the dependent variable is the natural log of the odds that someone will commit an adult offense. The effect of transforming equation 14-2 into equation 14-3 is that we have made linear the relationship between the $x$ variable and the log of the odds of the dependent variable. In other words, although the $x$ variable is nonlinearly related to the probability of $y$, it is related in a linear way to the log of the odds of $y$. In the linear form of the model in equation 14-3, the effect of the independent variable on the log of the odds of the dependent variable is the same at each value of $x$.

Because the dependent variable in a logistic regression analysis is the natural log of the odds of the dependent variable, the regression coefficient is interpreted as the change in the natural log of the odds that is associated with a one-unit change in the independent variable. For example, in our delinquency onset and adult offending example, the logistic regression coefficient is equal to –.598 (Table 14.3). This tells us that a one-unit (one-year) increase in the age at which someone commits his or her first delinquent offense decreases the log of the odds (from now on, "the log of the odds" will refer to the natural log of the odds) of an adult offense by .598. We say that the log-odds version of the model is additive because this effect of –.598 on the log of the odds of $y$ is the same at each value of $x$. For example, using equation 14-3, the predicted values of the dependent variable for four different onset ages are shown as follows:

| Age | Predicted Log Odds of y |
|---|---|
| 10 | 1.660 |
| 11 | 1.062 |
| 12 | .4640 |
| 13 | −.1340 |

Note that the difference in the predicted log of the odds of the dependent variable decreases by .598 for each one year increase in age. This decrease of .598 in the log of the odds of the dependent variable corresponds to the value of the logistic regression coefficient for age of onset ($b = -.598$).

Sometimes it is easier to think of the odds of an event rather than the log of the odds, so we can take the antilog of the estimated regression coefficient, thereby "getting rid of" the log part. This antilog of the logistic regression coefficient is generally referred to as the "odds multiplier" and can be obtained with most hand calculators (taking the antilog of a number is the same as exponentiating it). SPSS places these coefficients in a column labeled "Exp(B)" indicating that they are the exponents of the logistic regression coefficients. If the logistic regression coefficient is positive, the value of its antilog or odds multiplier will be greater than 1, indicating an increase in the odds of the dependent variable occurring. If the logistic regression coefficient is negative, the value of its antilog or odds multiplier will be less than 1, indicating a reduction in the odds of the dependent variable. When the coefficient is zero, the antilog or odds multiplier will be equal to 1.0, indicating that when the independent variable increases by one unit, the odds of the dependent variable are not changed. In our logistic regression example shown in Table 14.3, the antilog or odds multiplier of $-.598$ is .550 ($e^{-.598} = .550$). The first thing this tells us is that since the odds multiplier is less than 1, the effect of increasing the age at onset of delinquency is to lower the odds of committing an offense as an adult (i.e., lessening the risk of an adult offense). In addition, the magnitude tells us that when the age at which someone commits his or her first delinquent act increases by one year, the odds of that person committing an offense as an adult decreases by a factor of .550.

Thus, if an exponentiated logistic regression coefficient or odds multiplier is 1.0, the independent variable is not related to or associated with the dependent variable. Note that the further the exponentiated coefficient is from 1.0, the stronger the relationship between the independent and dependent variables. We can, then, take the distance of the exponentiated logistic regression coefficient from 1.0 as a rough indicator of the size of the effect of the independent variable. As an additional way to interpret our logistic regression coefficient, we can take this distance of the odds multiplier from 1.0 and then multiply it by 100 to get the *percent change in the odds of the dependent variable* for a one-unit change in the independent variable:

$$\text{\% change in odds of dependent variable} = (e^b - 1) \times 100$$

In our example with the onset age data, we estimated a logistic regression coefficient of $-.598$, which when exponentiated, yields the odds multiplier .550 ($e^{-.598} = .550$). When we subtract 1 from this, we get $-.450$. By multiplying this value by 100, we get $-45\%$, which tells us that there is a 45% decline in the odds of the dependent variable with a one-unit increase in the age at which offending begins. If you find that talking about the odds or the percent change in the odds of an event is not much easier than talking about the log of the odds of an event occurring, we would readily agree. We would now like to show you how you can take the information from a logistic regression analysis and determine the probability of an event.

## Predicted Probabilities in Logit Models

Although the logistic regression coefficient is not directly interpreted as a probability, we can use the results from our regression analysis to obtain an estimate of the probability of an event occurring. From equation 14-2 and the logistic regression results in Table 14.3, the estimated probability ($\hat{p}$) of committing an offense as an adult can be found for any given value of the independent variable $x$ with the following formula:

$$\hat{p} = \frac{1}{1 + e^{-(b_0 + b_1 x_1)}}$$

Following Dennis Roncek (1991), we can multiply the right-hand side of this equation by 1 in the form of:

$$\frac{e^{(b_0 + b_1 x_1)}}{e^{(b_0 + b_1 x_1)}}$$

so that we have a formula for the probability (*P*) that does not have a negative sign for *e* in the denominator:

$$\hat{p} = \frac{e^{(b_0 + b_1 x_1)}}{1 + e^{(b_0 + b_1 x_1)}} \tag{14-4}$$

To find the predicted probability of a given value of x, the independent variable, this formula instructs you to choose a particular value of the independent variable (*x*), multiply it by the obtained logistic regression coefficient (*b*), add the value of the constant, and then exponentiate this sum. The result is the numerator of the estimated probability, and the denominator is 1 plus the numerator. Let's go through some examples with the logistic regression equation estimated from our data on age of onset and adult offending.

From the results of our logistic regression model reported in Table 14.3, we can determine that the log of the odds that one who commits his or her first delinquent offense at 10 years of age will commit an adult offense is:

$$\ln \frac{\hat{p}}{1 - \hat{p}} = 7.640 - .598(10)$$

$$\ln \frac{\hat{p}}{1 - \hat{p}} = 1.660$$

We can then use this log of the odds to plug into our estimated probability equation:

$$\hat{p} = \frac{e^{1.66}}{1 + e^{1.66}}$$

$$\hat{p} = \frac{5.26}{6.26}$$

$$\hat{p} = .84$$

The predicted probability of committing an offense as an adult for someone who committed his or her first delinquent act at age 10, then, is .84. The corresponding probability that this person would *not* commit an adult offense is 1 − .84 = .16. The predicted odds of committing an adult offense for someone who first commits a delinquent act at age 10, then, is equal to:

$$\left( \frac{.84}{.16} \right) = 5.25$$

Now, let's increase the age of delinquency onset by one year and ask what the probability of committing an adult offense is for one who commits his or her first delinquent offense at 11 years of age. The log odds would be:

$$\ln \frac{\hat{p}}{1 - \hat{p}} = 7.640 - .598(11)$$

$$\ln \frac{\hat{p}}{1 - \hat{p}} = 1.062$$

We can then use this log of the odds to plug into our estimated probability equation:

$$\hat{p} = \frac{e^{1.062}}{1 + e^{1.062}}$$

$$\hat{p} = \frac{2.89}{3.89}$$

$$\hat{p} = .74$$

The predicted probability of committing an offense as an adult for someone who committed his or her first delinquent act at age 11, then, is .74. The corresponding probability that he or she would *not* commit an adult offense is $1 - .74 = .26$. The odds of committing an adult offense for someone who first commits a delinquent offense at age 11, then, is equal to:

$$\left(\frac{.74}{.26}\right) = 2.85$$

Note that by increasing the age of the first delinquent offense by one year (from age 10 to age 11), we have decreased the log odds of an adult offense by .598 ($1.062 - 1.660 = -.598$). This value of $-.598$ by which we have reduced the log odds of committing an adult offense is precisely the value of the logistic regression coefficient for age of onset of delinquency ($b = -.598$; see Table 14.3). You can now see more clearly that the logistic regression coefficient reflects the change in the natural logarithm of the odds of the dependent variable for a one-unit (in this case, one-year) change in the independent variable. Second, note that the odds of an adult offense are 5.25 for one who first commits a delinquent act at age 10 and are reduced to 2.85 for one who commits his or her first delinquent act one year later, at age 11. This is a 45% reduction in the odds of the dependent variable occurring:

$$\left(\frac{2.85 - 5.25}{5.25}\right) \times 100 = -\ 45 \text{ percent.}$$

This is what we obtained earlier when we subtracted 1 from the odds multiplier for our logistic regression coefficient:

$$\% \text{ reduction in odds of dependent variable} = (e^b - 1) \times 100$$

Note also that by increasing the age at onset of delinquency, we have reduced the probability of an adult offense by .10 ($.84 - .74$). The probability that someone who committed his or her first delinquent offense at age 10 is .10 higher than the probability for someone whose onset age of delinquency is one year later, at age 11. Please note that the difference in the probabilities of adult offending (.10) *is not* the value of the logistic regression coefficient ($b_{\text{onset age}} = -.598$). The logistic regression coefficient, therefore, does not tell us the change in the probability of the dependent variable for a one-unit change in the independent variable but the change in the log of the odds of the dependent variable occurring. Finally, since the odds of committing an adult offense for someone who was 11 years old at the time of his or her first delinquent act are 2.85 ($.74 / .26$), and the odds of an adult offense for someone whose first delinquent act was at age 10 are 5.25 ($.84 / .16$), the ratio of these two odds is equal to .543, which within rounding error is the value of the "odds multiplier" in our logistic regression analysis in Table 14.3. The "odds multiplier," then, is actually the ratio of two ratios (odds multiplier = $.543 = 2.85 / 5.25$).

We have stressed that the logistic regression coefficient cannot be interpreted directly in probability terms, but we can use it to estimate the predicted probability of the dependent variable at different values of the independent variable. By using equation 14-4, in the second column of Table 14.4, we have calculated for you (you should do your own calculations for practice) the predicted probability of an adult offense for each age at the onset of delinquency from 10 years to 17 years ($\hat{p}$). We have also provided some other important information. In the third column, we have reported the probability that there will be no adult offense committed $(1 - \hat{p})$; and in the fourth column, we have shown the change in predicted probability with each increase of one year in the onset age. In the fifth column, we have reported the predicted odds of committing an adult offense for each delinquency onset age:

$$\left( \frac{\hat{p}}{1 - \hat{p}} \right)$$

Finally, in the last column, we have reported the natural log of the odds that an adult offense was committed:

$$\ln \left( \frac{\hat{p}}{1 - \hat{p}} \right) = 7.640 - (.598)(\text{onset age})$$

There are several important things to learn about logistic regression analysis from Table 14.4. First, note that the probability that an offense is committed as an adult decreases as the age at onset of delinquency increases. The predicted probability of an adult offense is .84 when delinquency first occurs at age 10, and then it decreases to .74 at age 11, to .61 at age 12, to .47 at age 13, to .32 at age 14, to .21 at age 15, to .13 at age 16, and to .07 at age 17. The fact that the probability of an adult offense decreases as the age at the onset of delinquency increases is consistent with the negative sign we obtained for our logistic regression coefficient for onset age. Second, note that the change in the probability of an adult offense with a one-year increase in the onset age is not the same at each one-year increase in age. The change in probability is greater when the predicted probability is near .50 than when it is higher or lower than that. For example, increasing the onset age of delinquency from 10 years to 11 years decreases the probability of an adult offense by .10, and increasing the onset age from 16 to 17 years decreases the probability of an adult offense by .06, but increasing the onset age from 13 to 14 years decreases the probability of an adult offense by .15. In other words, unlike the case of ordinary least-squares regression, the change in the probability of the dependent variable with a one-unit change in

| Table 14.4 | Predicted Probabilities, Change in Probability by Increasing Age by One Year, and Natural Log of the Odds (Log Odds) for Relationship Between Age at Onset of Delinquency and Adult Crime (Data in Table 14.3) | | | | |
|---|---|---|---|---|---|
| Age at Onset of Delinquency | $\hat{p}$ Predicted Probability | $1 - \hat{p}$ | Change in Predicted Probability | Odds | Log Odds |
| 10 | .84 | .16 | — | 5.250 | 1.660 |
| 11 | .74 | .26 | −.10 | 2.846 | 1.062 |
| 12 | .61 | .39 | −.13 | 1.564 | .464 |
| 13 | .47 | .53 | −.14 | .887 | −.134 |
| 14 | .32 | .68 | −.15 | .471 | −.732 |
| 15 | .21 | .79 | −.11 | .266 | −1.330 |
| 16 | .13 | .87 | −.08 | .149 | −1.928 |
| 17 | .07 | .93 | −.06 | .075 | −2.526 |

the independent variable is not the same at different values of the independent variable in a logistic regression. That is because in logistic regression, we are fitting to the data not a straight line but an S-shaped curve, and as you can see from Figure 14.3, the slope (measuring the effect of $x$, or the independent variable) is greater in the middle of the probability distribution (when the predicted probability is near .50) than at either of the two ends. The effect of the independent variable on the probability of the dependent variable is nonlinear in a logistic regression. The effect of a given explanatory variable $x$ on the probability of the dependent variable $y$ depends on the specific value of $x$.

By looking at the odds column, we can clearly see that, as is consistent with the predicted probability results and the sign of the logistic regression coefficient, the odds of an adult offense decrease as the age at onset of delinquency increases. The odds that an adult offense is committed are 2.846 if the first delinquent act is committed at age 11, but the odds decrease to 1.564 if delinquency onset does not occur until age 12. Recall that the odds of these events are ratios: the ratio of the probability that an adult offense is committed to the probability that an adult offense is not committed:

$$\left( \frac{\hat{p}}{1-\hat{p}} \right)$$

Now take the ratio of the odds that an adult offense is committed for an onset age of 12 (1.564) to the odds that an adult offense is committed for an onset age of 11 (2.846). This ratio of two odds, or **odds ratio**, is equal to .550:

> **Odds ratio:** Exponential of a logistic regression slope coefficient.

$$\left( \frac{1.564}{2.846} = .550 \right)$$

so by increasing the age at onset of delinquency from 11 to 12 years we are reducing the odds of an adult offense by a factor of .550 (i.e., we are cutting the odds by slightly more than one half). This value of .550, you will recall, is the value of the "odds multiplier" we found in our logistic regression analysis (see Table 14.3). This odds multiplier reflects the change in the odds of the dependent variable occurring when the dependent variable increases by one unit (one year in this case). At any value of age of delinquency onset, if you take the ratio of the odds of an adult offense to the odds of an adult offense for one year younger, you will find a value of .550 (within rounding error). The change in the odds of the dependent variable at different values of the independent variable, then, is constant at different values of $x$. In our example, increasing the age at onset of delinquency by one year reduces the odds of an adult offense by slightly more than one half.

Finally, look at the last column in Table 14.4, which reports the natural log of the odds (the log odds) of an adult offense. The log odds of an adult offense for one whose first delinquent act was at age 10 are 1.660: 7.640 − (.598)10 = 1.660. Increasing the age at onset of delinquency to age 11 decreases the log odds of an adult offense to 1.062. In other words, increasing the independent variable by one year (from 10 years to 11 years) results in a decline in the odds of the dependent variable by .598 (1.660 −1.062 = .598). This is precisely the value of the logistic regression coefficient we obtained (−.598; see Table 14.3). The difference in the log of the odds of the dependent variable between any two adjacent ages will be .598. Thus, increasing the age at onset of delinquency by one year decreases the log of the odds of an adult offense by .598.

We would like to end this section by emphasizing two important points. First, with a continuous independent variable, the logistic regression coefficient cannot be directly interpreted in probability terms. The obtained logistic regression coefficient of −.598 *is not the decrease in the probability* of an adult offense that occurs by increasing the age at the onset of delinquency by one year; rather, it is *the change in the natural log of the odds* of an adult offense. Second, because the relationship between the independent and dependent variables in a logistic regression analysis is nonlinear (the effect of $x$ on the probability of $y$ depends on the value of $x$), the logistic regression coefficient cannot be interpreted in the same manner as an ordinary least-squares regression coefficient. When the relationship between $x$ and $y$ is nonlinear, the change in the probability of $y$ with a one-unit change in the independent variable is not constant.

## Significance Testing for Logistic Regression Coefficients

The regression coefficient from our logistic model ($b$) is a sample estimate of an unknown population parameter ($\beta$) that reflects the relationship between age at onset of delinquency and the probability of adult offending in the population. As we did with the slope coefficient in an ordinary least-squares regression, we can conduct a statistical test to determine whether a given logistic regression coefficient is significantly different from zero in the population. The null hypothesis of this test is that the population coefficient is equal to zero ($H_0$: $\beta = 0$), implying that there is no relationship between the independent and dependent variables. The research or alternative hypothesis would be either the nondirectional alternative that the logistic regression coefficient is different from zero ($H_1$: $\beta \neq 0$) or one of the directional alternatives ($H_1$: $\beta > 0$ or $\beta < 0$).

Depending on which statistical software package you use to run your logistic regression, the hypothesis test will be done with either a *t statistic* or a *Wald statistic*. Most of these statistical software programs routinely report the standard error of the regression coefficient along with the estimated logistic regression coefficient. The standard error for our logistic coefficient is reported in Table 14.3. If you have the standard error of the regression coefficient, you can conduct your own *t test*. The obtained *t* statistic is simply the ratio of the estimated regression coefficient to its standard error:

$$t_{\text{obtained}} = \frac{\text{Estimated regression coefficient}}{\text{Standard error of the regression coefficient}}$$

The *t* statistic is distributed as a Student's *t* distribution with $n - k$ degrees of freedom. In this case, $k$ refers to the number of parameters that are estimated in the model (the constant counts as an estimated parameter). Thus, in the example we have here, there are two estimated parameters—the constant ($b_0$) and the coefficient for the effect of delinquency onset age ($b_1$)—so there are $n - 2$ or 38 degrees of freedom. With our knowledge of 38 degrees of freedom, and knowledge of our chosen alpha level and of whether we are conducting a one-tailed or a two-tailed hypothesis test, we could get a critical value of *t* from our *t* table (Table B.3 in Appendix B), and compare the obtained *t* with the critical *t*, and make a decision about the null hypothesis.

A comparable hypothesis test of whether $\beta = 0$ can be conducted with the Wald statistic, which is used in SPSS output. The Wald statistic has a chi-square distribution, so observed values of the Wald are compared with critical values from a chi-square table. The critical value is based on the alpha level selected and on the number of degrees of freedom. The degrees of freedom for the Wald statistic depend on the level of measurement for each independent variable. With continuous independent variables, there is 1 degree of freedom. In this case, the Wald statistic is simply the square of the *t* statistic: Wald $= t^2 = (b / \text{standard error})^2$. With nominal or ordinal variables, there are $k - 1$ degrees of freedom, where $k$ is the number of categories or levels of the variable. For example, an ordinal-level measure of social class with three categories (lower, middle, and upper class) would have 2 degrees of freedom ($3 - 1 = 2$).

Let's test the null hypothesis that the logistic regression coefficient for the relationship between the age at onset of delinquency and adult offending is equal to zero against the alternative that it is less than zero (since we can appeal to a great deal of theory and prior research that suggests that the earlier the onset of delinquency, the greater the risk of future crime):

$$H_0 : \beta_{\text{onset age}} = 0$$
$$H_1 : \beta_{\text{onset age}} < 0$$

Our research or alternative hypothesis, therefore, is that delinquency onset age and adult offending are negatively related. We will use an alpha of .05 for our hypothesis test. We will first test this hypothesis with the *t* statistic. The *t* distribution appears in Table B.3 of Appendix B. There is no row for 38 degrees of freedom, so we will use 40 degrees of freedom. We find that with a one-tailed alternative hypothesis and an alpha of .05, the critical value of $t$ is $-1.684$. The critical region is any obtained value of $t$ less than or equal to $-1.684$, and our decision rule is to reject the null hypothesis if $t_{obt} \leq -1.684$. We can calculate our obtained $t$ statistic from the information provided in Table 14.3. With an estimated logistic regression coefficient of $-.598$ and a standard error of .197:

$$t_{obt} = \frac{b}{\text{standard error of } b}$$

$$t_{obt} = \frac{-.598}{.197}$$

$$t_{obt} = -3.04$$

Since $t_{obt} < -1.684$, our decision is to reject the null hypothesis and presume that the logistic regression coefficient in the population is significantly less than zero. We would conclude that age at onset of delinquency and the probability of adult offending are negatively related in the population; youth who commit their first delinquent offense at an earlier age are at greater risk of committing a criminal offense as an adult than those who commit their first delinquent offense later.

Now, let's conduct the identical hypothesis test with the Wald statistic. Using the chi-square table in Table B.4 of Appendix B, we can see that the critical value of Wald with an alpha of .05 and 1 degree of freedom is 3.841. Our critical region is any obtained Wald statistic that is greater than or equal to 3.841, and our decision rule is to reject the null hypothesis if our obtained Wald statistic is greater than or equal to 3.841. From Table 14.3, we can see that the obtained Wald is 9.214. Since this is greater than our critical value of 3.841, our decision is to reject the null hypothesis that $\beta = 0$ and conclude that the age at onset of delinquency and the risk of offending as an adult are significantly related in the population. If you did not want to use the Wald statistic but wanted a $t$ test, you could simply take the square root of the Wald. The square root of 9.246 is 3.04, which is exactly the same as the value of the $t$ statistic in the preceding paragraph. We would reject the null hypothesis. Usually, statistical software programs report the exact two-tailed probability of your obtained test statistic. If you are conducting a one-tailed hypothesis test (as we are doing in this example), you need to divide this reported two-tailed probability by 2 to get the correct one-tailed probability.

## Model Goodness-of-Fit Measures

When we did an OLS regression analysis, we had a measure of how good the variable or variables were at explaining the variance in the dependent variable. This was the $R^2$ coefficient or the coefficient of determination. Although statisticians have developed a few "pseudo-$R^2$" measures for logistic regression models that are comparable with the OLS $R^2$ coefficient, none is exactly like it and not many have gained wide acceptance. In addition, some software packages with logistic regression capability report one or more of these "pseudo-$R^2$" measures, whereas others do not. For these reasons, we will not discuss these measures in this chapter but suggest that you review the statistical literature. Nevertheless, there is a way in which we can ascertain how well our logistic regression model fits the data.

A crude test of the model's fit is to test the null hypothesis that all the independent variables in the model are equal to zero. This is comparable with what we did with the $F$ test in the OLS regression model. In the case of a logistic regression, we determine the *likelihood* of a given model, which is the probability of obtaining the observed results given the sign and magnitude of the estimated regression parameters. Because the likelihood is a number less than 1, it has become conventional to use $-2$ times the natural logarithm of the likelihood (often referred to as $-2LL$ or the likelihood ratio statistic) as an indicator of how well a given model fits the data. A good model, one wherein the probability of the observed results is high, is one with a *small value of* $-2LL$, so small values of $-2LL$ are better than larger values. If the model had a perfect fit to the data, the likelihood would equal 1.0, and $-2LL$ would equal zero.

To determine how well a statistical model (say the logistic regression model about age of onset that we have been examining in this example) fits the data, the first step is to estimate a "baseline" model that includes no independent variables, only the constant. From this model, we determine the value of $-2LL$, which measures how likely the observed results are with no independent variables considered. We then estimate a model that includes the constant and the independent variable or variables we are considering, and we determine the –2LL for this model. If the independent variable (or variables) is useful in explaining the dependent variable, the fit of the model that includes these variables will be better than the baseline or constant-only model, and how useful the independent variable is will be observed in a lower –2LL value. The difference between –2LL for the baseline model and –2LL for the model with the independent variable (variables) in it is a chi-square statistic. The number of degrees of freedom for this chi-square statistic is equal to the difference in the degrees of freedom between the two respective models (baseline and the one that includes the independent variable). We can, therefore, conduct a chi-square test that all of the logistic regression coefficients in the independent variable model are equal to zero. This is comparable with the OLS *F* test.

In Table 14.3, we report the value of –2LL for two models. The first is the baseline model that includes only the constant. The value of this initial log likelihood function is 51.548. The number of degrees of freedom in this logistic regression model is $n - k$, where $k$ is the number of parameters being estimated. In this baseline model, only the constant is being estimated, so there are 40 – 1 or 39 degrees of freedom. The next model contains age at onset of delinquency as an additional parameter to be estimated. The value of the log likelihood function for this model is 41.553. Since we estimate one more parameter in addition to the constant (the logistic regression coefficient for delinquency onset age), there are 38 degrees of freedom for this model.

The statistical test that all independent variables in the model are equal to zero is a chi-square test. Our obtained value of chi-square is the difference in the –2LL between the model that includes the independent variable and the baseline model with only the constant. The degrees of freedom for the chi-square test is equal to the difference between the degrees of freedom for the two models. We will use an alpha level of .05 for our hypothesis test. With 1 degree of freedom and an alpha of .05, the critical value of chi-square is 3.841 (from Table B.4 of Appendix B). Therefore, our critical region is any obtained value of chi-square greater than or equal to 3.841, and our decision rule is to reject the null hypothesis if our obtained value of chi-square is greater than or equal to 3.841. The obtained chi-square from the difference between the model with independent variables and the baseline model will always be positive because the model fit will not get worse (we will not have a higher value of –2LL) when we estimate additional parameters. In our problem, the difference between the –2LL values is 12.995. Our obtained value of chi-square of 12.995 is greater than the critical value of 3.841, so we would reject the null hypothesis that all independent variables in the model are equal to zero. Of course, we knew this because we have only one independent variable in our model at the moment (age at onset of delinquency), and we knew that this was significantly different from zero based on our *t* test and Wald test. This chi-square test for model fitness will become more useful when we discuss models with more than one independent variable.

## Case Study

## Race and Capital Punishment

Before we complicate things by introducing another independent variable into our model, let's go through another example of a logistic regression model with one independent variable. In this second example, we will have a binary (dichotomous) independent variable as well as a binary dependent variable. The independent variable in this example is the race of the victim in a homicide, where the value of 0 means the victim was African American and 1 means the victim was White. The dependent variable is the decision of the local prosecutor to charge the defendant with a capital crime (a charge that could bring a sentence of death), where the value 0 is given if the prosecutor charges a noncapital crime and 1 is given if the prosecutor charges the homicide as a capital murder. In the state where we have collected our data, the local prosecutor has a great deal of discretion in whether to charge a murder as a capital crime, and we think that one factor that might affect this decision is the race of the victim. We took a sample of 29 murder cases in this state and recorded the race of the victim and what the prosecutor's charging decision was. The data for this example are shown in Table 14.5, and from these data, we created a contingency table, or cross-tabulation, showing the joint distribution of the independent and dependent variables in Table 14.6.

From Table 14.6, you can see that there were 18 cases where the victim was African American and 11 cases where the victim was White. In 14 of the 18 cases with an African American victim, the prosecutor charged a noncapital crime, and in the other 4 cases, the prosecutor charged a capital murder. In 3 of the 11 cases with a White victim, the prosecutor charged a noncapital crime, and in the other 8 cases, the prosecutor charged the suspect with capital murder. One of the first things we can do with these data is calculate the probability or relative risk that a prosecutor will charge a capital offense in African American and White victim cases. By doing this, we can determine that the risk of a capital murder charge was .22 (4 / 18) for suspects who killed African Americans and .73 (8 / 11) for those who killed Whites. The odds of a capital murder charge, then, are .28 (.22 / .78) for cases with an African American victim and 2.70 (.73 / .27) for cases with a White victim. There is a much greater risk of being charged with a capital crime for those who murdered Whites compared with those who murdered African Americans. This difference in the relative risk of a capital murder charge would lead us to suspect that there is a relationship between the race of the victim in a murder case and the probability of a capital murder charge.

To examine this relationship further, we decide to do a logistic regression analysis with the prosecutor's charging decision as the dependent variable and the race of the victim as the independent variable. The results for this logistic regression analysis are shown in Table 14.7. The estimated regression model is:

$$\ln\left(\frac{\text{Probability of capital charge}}{\text{Probability of noncapital charge}}\right) = -1.253 + 2.234x_1$$

The logistic regression coefficient for the relationship between the race of the victim and the log odds of a capital murder charge is 2.234. Since the independent variable is coded 0 for African American victims and 1 for White victims, the sign of this coefficient tells us that the log odds of a capital murder charge are higher for those who kill Whites compared with those who kill African Americans. The magnitude of the regression coefficient tells us that a one-unit change in the independent variable (that is, going from an African American victim to a White victim) increases the log odds of a capital murder charge by 2.234.

To examine the logistic regression coefficient further, we would like to show you that we could have estimated this logistic regression model by hand calculations directly from the observed joint frequency distribution of the variables in Table 14.6. We have already discovered that the odds of a capital murder charge in cases with an African American victim are .28 and that the corresponding odds for a White homicide victim are 2.70. By keeping in mind that a logistic regression coefficient is the natural log of the odds of the dependent variable occurring in cases with White victims to the odds of the dependent variable occurring in cases with African American victims, we can express this relationship in the following equation:

**Table 14.5** Race of Victim and the Decision of the Prosecutor to File a Capital Charge for 29 Hypothetical Cases

| Case Number | Victim's Race* | Prosecutor's Charging Decision** |
|:---:|:---:|:---:|
| 1 | 0 | 0 |
| 2 | 0 | 0 |
| 3 | 0 | 0 |
| 4 | 0 | 0 |
| 5 | 0 | 0 |
| 6 | 0 | 0 |
| 7 | 0 | 0 |
| 8 | 0 | 0 |
| 9 | 0 | 0 |
| 10 | 0 | 0 |
| 11 | 1 | 0 |
| 12 | 1 | 0 |
| 13 | 0 | 1 |
| 14 | 0 | 1 |
| 15 | 0 | 1 |
| 16 | 1 | 1 |
| 17 | 1 | 1 |
| 18 | 1 | 1 |
| 19 | 1 | 1 |
| 20 | 1 | 1 |
| 21 | 1 | 1 |
| 22 | 1 | 1 |
| 23 | 0 | 0 |
| 24 | 0 | 0 |
| 25 | 0 | 0 |
| 26 | 1 | 1 |
| 27 | 0 | 1 |
| 28 | 1 | 0 |
| 29 | 0 | 0 |

*Coded 0 for African American victim and 1 for White victim.

**Coded 0 for charge of noncapital crime and 1 for charge of capital crime.

$$b_{\text{victim's race}} = \ln\left(\frac{\text{Odds of capital charge for White victim cases}}{\text{Odds of capital charge for African American victim cases}}\right)$$

The logistic regression coefficient, then, is the natural log of two odds, or an odds ratio. From this equation and our knowledge of the odds of a capital charge for the two kinds of murder cases, we can find (within rounding error because the probabilities for both odds are rounded) the value of the logistic regression coefficient:

$$b_{\text{victim's race}} = \ln\left(\frac{2.70}{.28}\right)$$

$$b_{\text{victim's race}} = \ln(9.64)$$

$$b_{\text{victim's race}} = 2.266$$

As you can see from this solution, the logistic regression coefficient for the victim's race is simply the natural log of the two ratios: the odds that the prosecutor will charge a capital offense when the victim is White $(.73 / .27 = 2.70)$ and the odds of a capital charge when the victim is African American $(.22 / .78 = .28)$. The regression coefficient tells us that when a White victim is slain, the log of the odds of a capital charge is higher by a factor of approximately 2.2.

Now, if we exponentiate or take the antilog of the logistic regression coefficient for the victim's race $(e^{2.234} = 9.34)$, we get what we have called the odds ratio or odds multiplier. Note that the odds ratio is simply the ratio of two odds. One of these odds is the odds of a capital charge in a White victim case (2.70), and the other is the odds of a capital charge in an African American victim case (.28). The ratio of these two odds (2.70 / .28) is approximately equal to our odds multiplier of 9.3 (2.70 / .28 is actually equal to 9.64, but we mentioned that there is rounding error in the probabilities that make up both of these ratios). This tells us that the odds of a capital charge are over nine times higher in killings of Whites than in killings of African Americans. We remind you that this does not mean that the probability of a capital charge in cases with a White victim is more than nine times higher than in cases with an African American victim—*only that the odds are.* By using our percent formula, we can say that there is an 834% increase in the odds of a capital charge comparing White victim cases with African American victim cases $[(9.34 - 1) \times 100 = 834\%]$.

If we wanted to test the significance of the regression coefficient for victim's race, we could use the *t* test and take the ratio of the regression coefficient to its estimated standard error. We would then compare this obtained *t* with a critical *t* at some alpha level and with the appropriate degrees of freedom. The degrees of freedom are equal to $n - k$, where $n$ is our sample size and $k$ is the number of unknown population parameters we are estimating in our model (the constant counts as 1,

| Table 14.6 | Joint Frequency Distribution of Race of Homicide Victim and the Charging Decision of the Prosecutor |

| Prosecutor's Decision | African-American | White | Total |
|---|---|---|---|
| Non-capital charge | 14 | 3 | 17 |
| Capital charge | 4 | 8 | 12 |
| Total | 18 | 11 | 29 |

| Table 14.7 | Results of Logistic Regression Analysis for Race of Homicide Victim and Prosecutor's Charging Decision (Data in Table 14.5) |

| Variable | Beta | Standard Error | Wald Statistic | df | Sig. | Exp(B) |
|---|---|---|---|---|---|---|
| Constant | −1.253 | .567 | 4.88 | 11 | | |
| Victim's race | 2.234 | .883 | 6.40 | 11 | .011 | 9.34 |
| −2 Log likelihood for baseline model (constant only): 39.336 | | | | | | |
| −2 Log likelihood with victim's race in model: 31.960 | | | | | | |

and each independent variable counts as 1). The null hypothesis would be that the regression coefficient in the population is equal to zero ($\beta_{\text{victim's race}} = 0$), against either a one-tailed ($\beta_{\text{victim's race}} < 0$ or ($\beta_{\text{victim's race}} > 0$) or a two-tailed alternative ($\beta_{\text{victim's race}} \neq 0$).

Let's conduct a hypothesis test for the regression coefficient involving victim's race, and let's test the two-tailed non-directional alternative, with an alpha of .05. To find our critical value of $t$, we go to the $t$ table (Table B.3 in Appendix B), with $n - 2$ or 27 degrees of freedom and our two-tailed alpha of .05. From the table, we can find that our critical value of $t$ is ±2.052. The critical region comprises all obtained $t$ coefficients that are either less than or equal to –2.052 or greater than or equal to 2.052. Our decision rule will be to reject the null hypothesis if $t_{\text{obt}} \leq -2.052$ or if $t_{\text{obt}} \geq 2.052$. Our obtained value of $t$ is equal to 2.53 (2.234 / .883 = 2.53). Since this obtained $t$ falls in the critical region (2.53 > 2.052), our decision is to reject the null hypothesis. We would conclude that there is a relationship in the population between the race of the victim killed in a homicide and the prosecutor's decision to charge the murder as a capital crime.

We can assess the fit of this logistic regression model by examining the improvement in the likelihood function when we compare the baseline (constant-only) model with one that includes the victim's race. From Table 14.7, we can see that with no independent variables in the model, the value of –2LL is 39.336. With the race of the victim as an independent variable in the model, the value of –2LL is 31.960. The difference between these two values (the improvement in the fit of the model) is 7.376. We know that this difference is distributed as a chi-square statistic with 1 degree of freedom, so we can test the null hypothesis that all independent variables in the model are equal to zero by comparing this obtained chi-square with a critical value. With an alpha of .05 and 1 degree of freedom (the difference in the degrees of freedom between the two models), the critical value of chi-square is 3.841. Our obtained value is greater than this, so our decision is to reject the null hypothesis that all independent variables in the model are equal to zero.

---

# Logistic Regression Models With Two Independent Variables

## Case Study

## Age at Which Delinquency First Occurs and Gender

In the logistic regression models discussed thus far, we considered the effect of only one independent variable. Although looking at only one variable when first learning about a new statistical technique is useful because it keeps things simple, one-variable models are not very accurate depictions of the real world. This is because events are rarely well explained by considering only one factor or variable. To explain and understand our dependent variable better, whatever it is, we will have to make our initial regression equation more complicated and consider other possible explanatory factors. In this section, we discuss the two-variable logistic regression model. We will learn the basics of this two-variable model with the understanding that generalizations to models with more than two variables will be straightforward.

One of the first decisions you have to make in moving from a one-variable to a two-variable regression model is which variable should you add. The answer to this question is not strictly a statistical matter but is based on your substantive understanding of the issue. Your selection of each new independent variable should be based either on a sound theoretical expectation or on the results of previous research. Whatever the source, you should be confident that the variable you add is capable of explaining or helping you understand the dependent variable. As we explained in Chapter 13, if you think a potential explanatory or independent variable is not related to the dependent variable and is strongly related to another independent variable, you should not include it in your model. In other words, the independent variables should not be strongly related to each other, but each should be strongly related to the dependent variable. Ideally, then, the independent variable you add should have a strong correlation with the dependent variable but a weak correlation with the other independent variable. As we learned in the previous chapter, when independent variables are too strongly correlated, they are said to be multicollinear, and multicollinearity will create problems in our regression analysis.

As our first example, let's use the data on age at onset of delinquency and adult offending. What we are trying to explain here is why some people offend as adults and others do not, and we discovered with our one-variable model is that the earlier the age that one commits a delinquent offense, the greater risk he or she is of committing a crime as an adult. In addition to the age at which somebody first commits a delinquent offense, another variable that may explain the probability of adult criminal offending is the individual's gender. The research literature in criminology consistently finds that males are more likely to offend, both as adolescents and as adults, than females. Based on this, we find it reasonable to expect that males would begin their offending at an earlier age than females and that males are more likely to commit adult crimes than females. Our new data, which now include the gender of each person, are displayed in Table 14.8. Age of onset is still coded as the age at which the person first committed a delinquent offense. Gender is coded 0 for females and 1 for males. The dependent variable remains despite whether an adult offense was committed; "no" is coded as 0 and "at least one offense" as 1. In our data, gender is a very good candidate as a second independent variable. Gender is strongly related to adult offending (Pearson's $r = .65$) and is only weakly related to the age at the time of one's first delinquent offense ($r = .33$). In this new example, then, we have two independent variables: the age at which delinquency is first committed and the person's gender.

Our two-variable logistic regression model looks like this:

$$\ln\frac{p}{1-p} = \beta_0 + \beta_1 x_1 + \beta_2 x_2$$

$$\ln\frac{p}{1-p} = b_0 + b_{1(\text{onset of delinquency})} + b_{2(\text{gender})}$$

The equation tells us that the dependent variable, the log of the odds of an adult crime, is related to both the age at which delinquency first occurs and one's gender. As in the one-independent-variable model, the three unknown parameters of this two-variable model ($\beta_0$, $\beta_1$, and $\beta_2$) are all estimated according to the maximum likelihood principle. By using our computer software, the results of this two-variable logistic regression model are shown in Table 14.9. Our equation for adult offending is:

$$\ln\frac{p}{1-p} = 6.582 - .643(\text{delinquency onset age}) + 3.244(\text{gender})$$

In words, this means that the log of the odds of committing an adult offense is negatively related to the age at which delinquency first occurs and positively related to gender. We know that in a multivariate model (a regression model with more than one independent variable), we measure the effect of one independent variable while "holding constant" the effect of the others. Holding the gender of the person constant, then, a one-unit (one-year) increase in the age at which delinquency is first committed lowers the log of the odds of the dependent variable by .643. We can also interpret this coefficient by using our percent change formula:

$$\text{Percent change in odds of dependent variable} = (e^{-.643} - 1) \times 100$$
$$\text{Percent change in odds of dependent variable} = (.526 - 1) \times 100$$
$$\text{Percent change in odds of dependent variable} = -47\%$$

So we can say that a one-year increase in the age at which delinquency first is committed reduces the odds of an offense in adulthood by 47%, while holding gender constant. While holding the age at onset of delinquency constant, a one-unit increase in gender (being male rather than female) increases the log of the odds of adult offending by 3.244. In other words, those who commit delinquent offenses at an earlier age and males (since "male" is coded 1 and "female"

| Table 14.8 | Data on Age at Onset of Delinquency (Age at First Delinquent Offense), Gender, and the Commission of a Crime as an Adult (18 Years of Age and Older) | | | | |

| Age at First Delinquent Offense | Gender | Adult Offense | Age at First Delinquent Offense | Gender | Adult Offense |
|---|---|---|---|---|---|
| 10 | 1 | 1 | 14 | 0 | 1 |
| 10 | 1 | 1 | 14 | 1 | 1 |
| 10 | 1 | 1 | 14 | 1 | 0 |
| 10 | 0 | 1 | 14 | 0 | 0 |
| 10 | 0 | 0 | 14 | 0 | 0 |
| 11 | 1 | 1 | 15 | 1 | 1 |
| 11 | 1 | 1 | 15 | 0 | 0 |
| 11 | 1 | 1 | 15 | 0 | 0 |
| 11 | 1 | 1 | 15 | 0 | 0 |
| 11 | 0 | 0 | 15 | 1 | 0 |
| 12 | 1 | 1 | 16 | 1 | 1 |
| 12 | 1 | 1 | 16 | 0 | 0 |
| 12 | 0 | 1 | 16 | 0 | 0 |
| 12 | 0 | 0 | 16 | 0 | 0 |
| 12 | 0 | 0 | 16 | 0 | 0 |
| 13 | 1 | 1 | 17 | 1 | 0 |
| 13 | 1 | 1 | 17 | 0 | 0 |
| 13 | 1 | 0 | 17 | 0 | 0 |
| 13 | 0 | 0 | 17 | 0 | 0 |
| 13 | 0 | 0 | Í7 | 0 | 0 |

| Table 14.9 | Results of Two-Variable Logistic Regression Analysis for Age at Onset of Delinquency, Gender, and Adult Offending (Data in Table 14.8) | | | | |

| Variable | Beta | Standard Error | Wald Statistic | df | Sig. | Exp(B) |
|---|---|---|---|---|---|---|
| Constant | 6.582 | 3.237 | 4.134 | 1 | | |
| Onset Age | -.643 | .258 | -6.211 | 1 | .006 | .526 |
| Gender | 3.244 | 1.048 | 9.582 | 1 | .001 | 25.648 |
| -2 Log likelihood for baseline model (constant only): 54.548 | | | | | | |
| -2 Log likelihood for model with two independent variables: 27.922 | | | | | | |

is coded 0) are more likely to commit an offense as an adult. The odds multiplier tells us that the odds of an adult crime being committed are approximately cut in half for each year increase in the age at which delinquency first occurs, and they are nearly 26 times higher for males than for females.

Since the log of the odds of a dependent variable is no more easily understood in a two-variable logistic regression model than in a one-variable model, we can estimate the predicted probability of the dependent variable occurring at different values of the independent variables. For example, the predicted probability of an adult offense for a male ($x_2 = 1$) who committed his first delinquent act at age 10 ($x_1 = 10$) would be:

$$\hat{p} = \frac{e^{b_0 + b_1(\text{onset age}) + b_2(\text{gender})}}{1 + e^{b_0 + b_1(\text{onset age}) + b_2(\text{gender})}}$$

$$\hat{p} = \frac{e^{6.582 - .643(10) + 3.244(1)}}{1 + e^{6.582 - .643(10) + 3.244(1)}}$$

$$\hat{p} = \frac{e^{3.396}}{1 + e^{3.396}}$$

$$\hat{p} = \frac{29.844}{30.844}$$

$$\hat{p} = .97$$

Let's now change this case to a female who commits her first delinquent offense at age 10:

$$\hat{p} = \frac{e^{b_0 + b_1(\text{onset age}) + b_2(\text{gender})}}{1 + e^{b_0 + b_1(\text{onset age}) + b_2(\text{gender})}}$$

$$\hat{p} = \frac{e^{6.582 - .643(10) + 3.244(0)}}{1 + e^{6.582 - .643(10) + 3.244(0)}}$$

$$\hat{p} = \frac{e^{.152}}{1 + e^{.152}}$$

$$\hat{p} = \frac{1.164}{2.164}$$

$$\hat{p} = .54$$

The probability of an adult offense decreases almost in half between a male who first commits a delinquent offense at age 10 and a female. Now, let's take a male whose delinquency begins at age 11 rather than at age 10:

$$\hat{p} = \frac{e^{b_0 + b_1(\text{onset age}) + b_2(\text{gender})}}{1 + e^{b_0 + b_1(\text{onset age}) + b_2(\text{gender})}}$$

$$\hat{p} = \frac{e^{6.582 - .643(11) + 3.244(1)}}{1 + e^{6.582 - .643(11) + 3.244(1)}}$$

$$\hat{p} = \frac{e^{2.753}}{1 + e^{2.753}}$$

$$\hat{p} = \frac{15.690}{16.690}$$

$$\hat{p} = .94$$

When the age at onset of delinquency is increased by one year for a 10-year-old male, the probability of adult offending barely diminishes, from .97 to .94, but the difference between a male and a female who committed their first delinquent act at age 10 was dramatic. This clearly tells us that the probability of adult offending is affected more by gender than by the age at which delinquent conduct first occurs.

Just as we did in our one-variable logistic regression model, we can test the null hypothesis that each of the two regression coefficients is equal to zero in the population against some alternative hypothesis. This test, you will recall, is based on either the Wald statistic or the $t$ statistic, where:

$$t = \frac{b}{\text{standard error of } b}$$

and Wald $= t^2$. The null hypothesis we would test is that each regression slope $b$ is equal to zero, controlling for all other independent variables in the model. The null and alternative hypotheses regarding the relationship between age at onset of delinquency and adult offending are:

$$H_0 : \beta_{\text{onset age}} = 0, \text{ controlling for gender}$$
$$H_1 : \beta_{\text{onset age}} < 0, \text{ controlling for gender}$$

We are testing the directional alternative hypothesis that there is an inverse relationship between the age at onset of delinquency and adult offending because a substantial amount of empirical literature suggests that the earlier one gets involved in delinquency, the higher the risk of offending in the future.

The null and alternative hypotheses regarding the relationship between gender and adult offending are:

$$H_0 : \beta_{\text{gender}} = 0, \text{ controlling for onset age}$$
$$H_1 : \beta_{\text{gender}} > 0, \text{ controlling for onset age}$$

We are testing the directional alternative hypothesis that there is a positive relationship between gender and adult offending. Recall that the variable gender is coded 1 for males and 0 for females and that the research in our field consistently shows that males are more likely to commit criminal offenses at every age than females. Given this, the expected sign of the regression coefficient should be positive. Both hypothesis tests will be conducted with an alpha of .05, and we will do a Wald test. Recall that the Wald statistic is simply the square of the ratio of the regression coefficient to its standard error and that it has a chi-square distribution with 1 degree of freedom. With an alpha of .05 and a one-tailed hypothesis test, the critical value of chi-square that will lead us to reject the null hypothesis is 3.841. By looking at the obtained Wald statistic for the coefficients in Table 14.9, we can see that both are greater than 3.841, and we would reject both null hypotheses. We would conclude that in the population, the age at which one first commits a delinquent offense is significantly related to the probability of adult offending, when we have controlled for gender, and that a person's gender is significantly related to the probability of adult offending, when we have controlled for the age at the onset of delinquency.

Because both independent variables are significantly related to the dependent variable, we may want to know about the *relative importance* of each. The next question we may want the answer to, then, is which independent variable is more important in explaining the dependent variable. There are a number of ways we can quickly assess the relative importance of explanatory variables in a multivariable logistic regression analysis. We've already discussed one way. We can calculate the probability of the dependent variable for different values of one of the independent variables, keeping the value of the second independent variable the same or constant, and then repeat the process for the second independent variable. For example, we looked at the change in the probability of an adult offense for both a male and a female who committed their first delinquent act at age 10, and we found that the male was substantially more likely to commit an adult offense than the female (.97 vs. .54). We then compared a male who committed his first delinquent act at age 10 with another who committed his first such act at age 11, and we found that the predicted probability of an adult offense was lower, although not as different as was the case for gender (.97 vs. .94). This suggests that gender has more of an impact on the probability of adult offending than does the age at which delinquency begins. Another very simple way to examine the relative strength of our independent variables is to compare the magnitude of the $t$ or Wald coefficients. Of two coefficients, the one with the larger (absolute value) $t$ or Wald statistic has the greater explanatory "punch." For example, in the two-variable regression model for adult offending that we have just examined, the absolute value of the Wald statistic for the age at onset of delinquency was 6.211, and for gender it was 9.582. It would seem, then, that gender is more strongly related to the probability of adult offending, when we have controlled for onset age, than is onset age when we have controlled for gender.

Yet another way to determine the relative strength of our independent variables is to compare the likelihood ratio statistic (-2LL) for two models: (1) a model that includes all independent variables and the constant, and (2) a model that includes all independent variables except one. The difference between the likelihood ratio statistics for the two models can then be compared with different independent variables dropped from the model. The variable whose removal from the model results in a more substantial deterioration of the fit of the model has the stronger effect.

For example, our two-variable logistic regression model has a likelihood ratio statistic of 27.922 (see Table 14.9). When gender is not included in the model, the likelihood ratio statistic is 41.553 (see Table 14.3). The model that does not include gender, then, shows a worse fit to the data, and the difference between the model with and without gender is 13.56. When age is not included in the model and gender is in the model alone, the likelihood ratio statistic is 36.595. The difference between this model and the two-variable model is 8.60. Because the drop in the likelihood ratio statistic is greater when gender is removed (13.56) than when age is removed (8.60), gender is more strongly related to the probability of adult offending than is age at the onset of delinquency. (Keep in mind that a lower value of the likelihood ratio statistic indicates a better-fitting model.)

Just as we did with our one-variable logistic regression model, we can test the overall fit of our model with the likelihood ratio statistic. We will compare the likelihood ratio statistic for the model that includes only the constant (the baseline model) with the model that includes both independent variables. The difference between these two likelihood ratio statistics is a chi-square statistic with degrees of freedom equal to the difference between the degrees of freedom for the two respective models. This tests the hypothesis that the regression coefficients for all independent variables in the model are equal to zero. You will again remember that this hypothesis test is equivalent to the $F$ test in an ordinary least-squares regression analysis.

In Table 14.9, you can see that the likelihood ratio statistic for the baseline (constant-only) model is 54.548. This model has only one parameter to estimate, so there are $n - k = 40 - 1$ or 39 degrees of freedom. When age at onset of delinquency and gender are added to the model, the likelihood ratio statistic drops to 27.922. This model has three parameters to estimate, so there are 37 degrees of freedom ($40 - 3 = 37$). The difference in the likelihood ratio statistic between the two models, therefore, is 26.626 (54.548 − 27.922) with 2 degrees of freedom (39 $df$ − 37 $df$). Let's test the null hypothesis that all independent variables in the model are equal to zero against the alternative that they are not equal to zero:

$$H_0 : \beta_{\text{onset age}} = 0, \beta_{\text{gender}} = 0$$
$$H_1 : \beta_{\text{onset age}} \neq 0, \beta_{\text{gender}} \neq 0$$

We will test the null hypothesis that all regression coefficients are equal to zero with an alpha of .01. From the table of chi-square values (Table B.4), you can see that the critical value of chi-square with an alpha of .01 and 2 degrees of freedom is 9.210. Since our obtained value of chi-square (26.626) is greater than the obtained value of 9.210, our decision is to reject the null hypothesis.

# Case Study

## Race of Victim, the Brutality of a Homicide, and Capital Punishment

Let's return to our example of the logistic regression equation involving the race of the victim and the prosecutor's decision to charge the suspect with capital or noncapital murder. In our one-variable logistic regression model, we found that prosecutors were more likely to charge a case as a capital crime if the homicide involved the killing of a White victim as opposed to an African American victim. More specifically, the odds of a capital charge were about nine times greater for those cases that involved the killing of a White victim.

Although this finding may suggest that the prosecutor's decision to seek a death sentence is based at least in part on the race of the victim, we cannot yet be confident of this conclusion. It may be that prosecutors are more likely to charge a homicide as a capital offense in White victim cases because, on average, killings of Whites are conducted in a more brutal and aggravated manner than those killings of African American victims. Therefore, the brutality of the offense, rather than race, may be most important. If in fact it is the brutality of the offense that governs the prosecutor's charging decision, then once we have controlled for the brutality of the homicide, the previously observed relationship between the victim's race and the charging decision should diminish and may even vanish.

Let's say that in addition to the race of the victim, we had other detailed information about each of the 29 homicide cases we sampled, including such information as the number of victims killed, the type of weapon used, whether the victim pleaded for her or his life, and other indicators of how brutal the homicide was. With this information we were able to classify each of the 29 homicides as either not especially brutal (coded 0) or brutally committed (coded 1). Keep in mind that the victim's race is coded 0 for African American victims and 1 for White victims, and the dependent variable is coded 0 for a noncapital charge and 1 for a capital charge. These data are shown in Table 14.10.

With the information in Table 14.10, we estimated a two-independent-variable logistic regression model, and the results appear in Table 14.11.

The regression equation is:

$$\ln\left(\frac{P}{1-P}\right) = -2.684 + 2.797(\text{victim's race}) + 3.233(\text{brutality})$$

Both logistic regression equations are positive. Having controlled for the brutality of the offense, we find that the log of the odds of a capital charge has increased by 2.797 in a White victim case compared with a case with an African American victim. When we control for the race of the victim, the log of the odds of a capital charge is 3.233 higher for homicides that have at least one brutality factor than for those where brutality is absent. The odds multiplier tells us that the odds of a capital charge are 16 times higher in White victim than in Black victim cases, when we have controlled for brutality, and are greater than 25 times higher in brutal than in nonbrutal homicide cases, controlling for the race of the victim. The decision of the prosecutor to charge a homicide as a capital offense, then, is related both to the race of the victim and to the presence of brutality in the case. These findings also indicate that the race of the victim effect does not exist simply because killings of White victims are more brutal than the killings of African American victims; something else must be at work here.

Since it is hard to get a sense of what these effects mean for the victim's race and for the presence of brutality, let's calculate the probability of a capital charge in four kinds of offenses involving:

1. A White victim and no brutality

2. A White victim and brutality

| Table 14.10 | Race of Victim, Presence of Brutality, and the Decision of the Prosecutor to File a Capital Charge for 29 Hypothetical Cases | | |
|:---:|:---:|:---:|:---:|

| Case Number | Victim's Race* | Brutality** | Prosecutor's Charging Decision*** |
|:---:|:---:|:---:|:---:|
| 1 | 0 | 0 | 0 |
| 2 | 0 | 0 | 0 |
| 3 | 0 | 0 | 0 |
| 4 | 0 | 0 | 0 |
| 5 | 0 | 0 | 0 |
| 6 | 0 | 0 | 0 |
| 7 | 0 | 0 | 0 |
| 8 | 0 | 0 | 0 |
| 9 | 0 | 1 | 0 |
| 10 | 0 | 0 | 0 |
| 11 | 1 | 0 | 0 |
| 12 | 1 | 0 | 0 |
| 13 | 0 | 0 | 1 |
| 14 | 0 | 1 | 1 |

| Case Number | Victim's Race* | Brutality** | Prosecutor's Charging Decision*** |
|:---:|:---:|:---:|:---:|
| 15 | 0 | 1 | 1 |
| 16 | 1 | 0 | 1 |
| 17 | 1 | 1 | 1 |
| 18 | 1 | 1 | 1 |
| 19 | 1 | 1 | 1 |
| 20 | 1 | 1 | 1 |
| 21 | 1 | 0 | 1 |
| 22 | 1 | 0 | 1 |
| 23 | 0 | 1 | 0 |
| 24 | 0 | 0 | 0 |
| 25 | 0 | 0 | 0 |
| 26 | 1 | 1 | 1 |
| 27 | 0 | 1 | 1 |
| 28 | 1 | 0 | 0 |
| 29 | 0 | 0 | 0 |

*Coded 0 for African American and 1 for White.

**Coded 0 for no brutality present and 1 for brutality present.

***Coded 0 for a noncapital crime and 1 for a capital crime.

3. An African American victim and no brutality

4. An African American victim and brutality

The probability of a capital charge for a homicide with a White victim and no brutality is:

$$\hat{p} = \frac{e^{b_0 + b_1 \text{(victim's race)} + b_2 \text{(brutality)}}}{1 + e^{b_0 + b_1 \text{(victim's race)} + b_2 \text{(brutality)}}}$$

$$\hat{p} = \frac{e^{-2.684 + 2.797(1) + 3.233(0)}}{1 + e^{-2.684 + 2.797(1) + 3.233(0)}}$$

$$\hat{p} = \frac{e^{.113}}{1 + e^{.113}}$$

$$\hat{p} = \frac{1.12}{2.12}$$

$$\hat{p} = .53$$

| Table 14.11 | Results of Two-Variable Logistic Regression Analysis for Race of Victim, Homicide Brutality, and Prosecutor's Charging Decision (Data From Table 14.10) | | | | | |
|---|---|---|---|---|---|---|

| Variable | Beta | Standard Error | Wald Statistic | df# | Sig. | Exp (B) |
|---|---|---|---|---|---|---|
| Constant | −2.684 | 1.049 | 6.546 | 1 | | |
| Victim's Race | 2.797 | 1.235 | 5.129 | 1 | .012 | 16.403 |
| Brutality | 3.233 | 1.277 | 6.410 | 1 | .010 | 25.365 |
| −2 Log likelihood for baseline model (constant only): 39.336 | | | | | | |
| −2 Log likelihood for model with two independent variables: 22.523 | | | | | | |

The probability of a capital charge for a homicide with a White victim and brutality is:

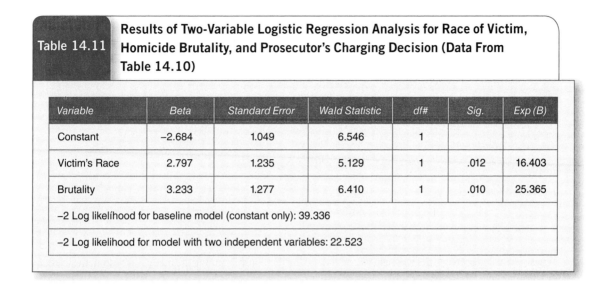

$$\hat{p} = \frac{e^{b_0 + b_1(\text{victim's race}) + b_2(\text{brutality})}}{1 + e^{b_0 + b_1(\text{victim's race}) + b_2(\text{brutality})}}$$

$$\hat{p} = \frac{e^{-2.684 + 2.797(1) + 3.233(1)}}{1 + e^{-2.684 + 2.797(1) + 3.233(1)}}$$

$$\hat{p} = \frac{e^{3.346}}{1 + e^{3.346}}$$

$$\hat{p} = \frac{28.39}{29.39}$$

$$\hat{p} = .96$$

The probability of a capital charge for a homicide with an African American victim and no brutality is:

$$\hat{p} = \frac{e^{b_0 + b_1(\text{victim's race}) + b_2(\text{brutality})}}{1 + e^{b_0 + b_1(\text{victim's race}) + b_2(\text{brutality})}}$$

$$\hat{p} = \frac{e^{-2.684 + 2.797(0) + 3.233(0)}}{1 + e^{-2.684 + 2.797(0) + 3.233(0)}}$$

$$\hat{p} = \frac{e^{-2.684}}{1 + e^{-2.684}}$$

$$\hat{p} = \frac{.07}{1.07}$$

$$\hat{p} = .06$$

And the probability of a capital charge for a homicide with an African American victim and brutality is:

$$\hat{p} = \frac{e^{b_0 + b_1(\text{victim's race}) + b_2(\text{brutality})}}{1 + e^{b_0 + b_1(\text{victim's race}) + b_2(\text{brutality})}}$$

$$\hat{p} = \frac{e^{-2.684 + 2.797(0) + 3.233(1)}}{1 + e^{-2.684 + 2.797(0) + 3.233(1)}}$$

$$\hat{p} = \frac{e^{.549}}{1 + e^{.549}}$$

$$\hat{p} = \frac{1.73}{2.73}$$

$$\hat{p} = .63$$

These estimated probabilities will help us understand the relationship among the race of the victim, the brutality of the homicide, and the prosecutor's charging decision.

Note that in cases where there is no brutality, the probability that the prosecutor will charge a capital murder is substantially higher in White victim than in Black victim cases ($\hat{p}$ = .53 vs. .06, respectively). This difference in predicted probabilities between homicides involving victims of different races is less pronounced but also exists in cases where brutality is present ($\hat{p}$ = .96 vs. .63). By holding constant the brutality of the crime, therefore, the race of the victim still matters for the prosecutor's charging decision: killers of Whites are substantially more likely to be charged with a capital crime than are defendants who kill African Americans. It is *not* true, then, that our earlier finding that prosecutors are more likely to seek a capital charge in White victim cases is due to the fact that these crimes are more brutally done than Black victim homicides.

Note also that when the race of the victim is held constant, there is a strong effect for the brutality of the crime, and this is particularly true in cases with an African American victim. When the victim was White, the probability that the defendant will be charged with a capital crime is much higher if the homicide was done in a brutal manner ($\hat{p}$ = .96 vs. .53). This effect is even stronger when the victim is African American, where the probability of a capital charge is more than 10 times higher when there is brutality in the homicide than when it is absent ($\hat{p}$ = .63 vs. .06). What these predicted probabilities clearly tell us is that both the race of the victim and the presence of brutality in a homicide make a difference to the prosecutor when she or he decides whether to charge a crime as a capital or a noncapital offense.

We can test the null hypothesis that each of the two estimated logistic regression coefficients are not significantly different from zero in the population with either the Wald test or the *t* statistic. The null and alternative hypotheses are:

$$H_0 : \beta_{\text{race of victim}} = 0, \text{ controlling for brutality}$$
$$H_1 : \beta_{\text{race of victim}} > 0, \text{ controlling for brutality}$$

$$H_0 : \beta_{\text{brutality}} = 0, \text{ controlling for victim's race}$$
$$H_1 : \beta_{\text{brutality}} > 0, \text{ controlling for victim's race}$$

In both cases, the alternative or research hypothesis is the directional one that the coefficient in the population is significantly greater than zero. This is because homicides involving White victims and those where there is brutality are both coded as 1, and we expect these cases to have a greater probability of a capital charge.

We will test the null hypothesis with an alpha level of .05, and we have 1 degree of freedom for each hypothesis test. From our chi-square table (Table B.4 in Appendix B), we can see that the critical value of chi-square is 3.841. We will reject the null hypothesis if the absolute value of our obtained Wald statistic (remember that the Wald statistic follows a chi-square distribution) is greater than or equal to 3.841. In looking at Table 14.11, we can see that the Wald statistic for both race of victim and the presence of brutality is greater than 3.841. We would therefore reject the null hypothesis that the coefficients in the population are equal to zero. We would conclude that both the race of the victim and the presence of brutality in the case are significantly related to the prosecutor's charging decision even after controlling for the other of these variables. Remember, the "Sig." column also provides the exact level of alpha, so there is really no need to do this using the critical value.

If we wanted to examine the relative explanatory power of our two variables, we could do a couple of things. One would be to compare the absolute value of their respective Wald statistics. The Wald statistic for the race of the victim from Table 14.11 is 5.129, whereas for the presence of brutality, it is 6.410. We would conclude from this that the presence of brutality has a more pronounced impact on the prosecutor's charging decision than does the race of the victim. We can also compare the likelihood ratio statistic for our two-variable model with another model where each of the independent variables is removed. When both race of victim and brutality are in the regression model, the value of –2LL is 22.523. When the victim's race is dropped from the model, the resulting model's fit is less satisfactory, with a –2LL value of 29.565. The difference between this and the two-variable model is 7.042. When brutality is dropped from the models, this model's fit is even less satisfactory, with a –2LL value of 31.960. The difference between this and the two-variable model is 9.437. Since the fit of the model deteriorates more when brutality is dropped than when the race of the victim is dropped, brutality has the stronger effect.

Finally, we can examine the overall fit of the model by comparing the likelihood ratio statistic for a baseline model that includes only the constant with that for the two-variable model. The difference between these two likelihood ratio statistics is a chi-square statistic with 2 degrees of freedom. This test is analogous to the $F$ test in an ordinary least-squares regression in that all independent variables in the model are equal to zero. We will use an alpha of .05 for our hypothesis test. With an alpha of .05 and 2 degrees of freedom, the critical value of chi-square is 5.991. Our decision, then, will be to reject the null hypothesis that all independent variables in the model are equal to zero if our obtained chi-square is greater than or equal to 5.991. Our null hypothesis and the alternative hypothesis are:

$$H_0 : \beta_{\text{race of victim}} = 0, \beta_{\text{brutality}} = 0$$
$$H_1 : \beta_{\text{race of victim}} \neq 0, \beta_{\text{brutality}} \neq 0$$

Table 14.11 indicates that the likelihood ratio statistic for the baseline model (constant only) is 39.336 and that for the model with two independent variables is 22.523. The difference is 16.813. This obtained chi-square statistic is greater than the critical value of 5.991, so our decision is to reject the null hypothesis that all logistic regression coefficients in the model are equal to zero.

# ▣ Summary

In this chapter, we have examined both bivariate and multivariate regression models when we have a dichotomous or a binary dependent variable. We could estimate an ordinary least-squares regression model with a dichotomous dependent variable that is coded "0" and "1". This is called a linear probability model. One problem with the linear probability model is that it may violate key assumptions of the OLS model—that the error terms are normally distributed and homoscedastic. In addition, if we make probability predictions outside of the range of our observed $x$ values (for example, our independent variable is age and ranges from 11 years to 22 years and we try to predict the probability of one who is 35 years old), the predicted $y$ may not be confined between 0 and 1, which would violate the bounding rule of probabilities. An alternative to the linear probability model is the logistic regression model.

The logistic regression model is based on the cumulative logistic distribution. The dependent variable in this regression model is the natural logarithm of the odds of the dependent variable occurring. The logistic regression model enables us to estimate regression coefficients that show the relationship between any independent variable and our dichotomous dependent variable. Because translating these coefficients is a bit clumsy, we learned how to convert our logistic regression information into estimated probabilities, how to test hypotheses if our logistic regression coefficient is significantly different from zero in the population, and how to compare the relative magnitude of more than one independent variable.

## Key Terms

➤ Review key terms with eFlashcards. **⑤SAGE** edge™

dichotomous variable    434

heteroscedasticity    439

likelihood ratio statistic    449

logistic regression model    434

odds ratio    447

## Key Formulas

Linear probability model (equation 14-1):

$$y = a + bx + \varepsilon$$

Logistic regression model (equation 14-3):

$$\ln\left(\frac{P}{1-P}\right) = \beta_0 + \beta_1 x_1$$

Predicted probabilities from logit model (equation 14-4):

$$\hat{p} = \frac{e^{(b_0 + b_1 x_1)}}{1 + e^{(b_0 + b_1 x_1)}}$$

## Practice Problems

➤ Test your understanding of chapter content. Take the practice quiz. **⑤SAGE** edge™

1. Out of a group of 700 criminal defendants:

   a. If 250 test positive for drugs, what is the probability that any one defendant randomly chosen will have tested positively? What are the odds?

   b. If 500 have at least one prior arrest, what is the probability that any one defendant chosen randomly will have a prior arrest? What are the odds?

   c. If 630 have a juvenile record, what is the probability that any one defendant chosen randomly will have a juvenile record? What are the odds?

   d. If 180 are eventually sentenced to prison, what is the probability that any one defendant chosen randomly will be sent to prison? What are the odds?

2. The results from a hypothetical logit regression analysis are presented as follows using gender of the defendant (female = 0, male = 1) as the independent variable to predict guilty verdicts (not guilty = 0, guilty = 1) in 52 randomly selected cases involving homicides committed by one spouse against another:

| Variable | Beta | Standard Error | Wald Statistic | df | Sig. |
|---|---|---|---|---|---|
| Gender | .3278 | .1369 | 5.736 | 1 | .016 |
| Constant | .0561 | .1105 | .257 | 1 | .611 |

a. Interpret the regression coefficient.

b. Test the null hypothesis that the logistic regression coefficient for gender in the population is zero against the alternative hypothesis that it is different from zero. Use an alpha of .05.

c. Compute the probabilities of a guilty verdict for both male and female defendants from the earlier equation. What are their respective odds of a guilty verdict?

3. The following table reports the results of a two-independent-variable logistic regression model. The dependent variable is the decision of the police to arrest a suspect (0 = no, 1 = yes). One independent variable is the expressed desire of the victim that the suspect be arrested (0 = no, 1 = yes), and the second is the age of the victim. The sample size is 63:

| Variable | Beta | Standard Error | df | Wald |
|---|---|---|---|---|
| Desire | .8147 | .9385 | 1 | .753 |
| Age | .1593 | .0410 | 1 | 15.124 |
| Constant | − 7.246 | | | |
| | Initial log likelihood function (constant-only model)<br>−2 log likelihood: 66.406<br>With Desire and Age in the model<br>−2 log likelihood: 34.586 | | | |
| | Chi-Square | | | Df |
| Model chi-square | 31.821 | | | 1 |

With this table, answer the following questions:

a. What is the equation for the two-independent-variable logistic regression model?

b. Interpret the two regression coefficients.

c. What is the predicted probability of arrest for a victim who expresses that an arrest should be made and who is 50 years old?

d. By using an alpha level of .05, test the null hypothesis that the logistic regression coefficient for the variable "victim's desire for an arrest" is equal to zero against the alternative that it is greater than zero. By using an alpha level of .05, test the null hypothesis that the logistic regression coefficient for the variable "victim's age" is equal to zero against the alternative that it is greater than zero.

e. Which variable is more important in understanding the police decision to make an arrest? What are your conclusions from this model?

## SPSS Exercises

➤ Explore additional data sets. ⑤SAGE edge™

| Data for Exercise | |
|---|---|
| Data Set | Description |
| GSS 2014.sav | The General Social Survey (GSS) is a nationally representative survey that is conducted every two years. It covers a wide range of "core" topics such as political and religious views while rotating in new topics. It is a split ballot omnibus survey. |
| Variables for Exercise | |
| Variable Name | Description |
| Cappun | A binary variable asking whether a respondent supported or opposed the death penalty, where 1 = support and 0 = oppose. |

*(Continued)*

(Continued)

| Variables for Exercise | |
|---|---|
| Variable Name | Description |
| Grass | A binary asking if respondents think marijuana should be made legal or not, where 1 = yes and 2 = no. |
| Polhitbin | A measure based on three questions about whether it was ok for police to hit a citizen. A 1 indicates that the respondent always felt it was ok, where a 0 indicates disagreement on at least one question. |
| Sex | The sex of the respondent where 1 = male and 2 = female. |
| LowIncome | A binary indicator of the respondent's family income, where 1 = less than 19,999 a year and 0 = 20,000 or more a year. |
| HighEduc | A binary indicator of the respondent's education, where 0 = high-school education or less and 1 = some college or more. |
| White | A binary indicator of race, where 1 = White and 0 = non-White. |
| Age | A respondent's age in years. |
| Liberal | A binary indicator of whether a respondent identifies as liberal (1) or not (0). |
| Conservative | A binary indicator of whether a respondent identifies as conservative (1) or not (0). |
| TooHarsh | A binary indicator of whether a respondent feels courts are too harsh on criminals (1) or not (0). |
| NotEnough | A binary indicator of whether a respondent feels courts are not harsh enough on criminals (1) or not (0). |

1. Who is for or against marijuana legalization? This is a question that is becoming increasingly pressing for both criminologists and politicians in light of successful decriminalization in many states. We'll begin with a single variable and then move toward a more elaborate analysis:

   a. Check the frequencies for the variable Grass first. What proportion of Americans are in favor of capital punishment?

   b. To begin with, we'll look to see whether certain age groups are more or less likely to favor marijuana legalization. We'll fit a logistic regression model to examine this:

      i. **Fitting a Logistic Regression model in SPSS:** Select analyze->regression->binary logistic. Then, simply plug in your independent variables in the appropriate slots, just as you would with the OLS interface.

      ii. **Logistic regression output:** That's a lot of output! For your purposes, only worry about the "omnibus tests of model coefficients", "model summary", and the "variables in the equation" box.

      iii. First, look at the omnibus test box. The significance test here is for your model chi-square, which is based in part on the –2 log likelihood statistic directly beneath it. What does this model chi-square test tell us?

      iv. Take a look at the results in the "variables in equation" box. Like the OLS output, it provides a value for B, but in this case, it isn't easy to interpret. You want the value for "EXP(B)", which stands for exponentiated B. This is more commonly known as an odds ratio or odds multiplier. How do you interpret the odds ratio for age?

      v. What are your null and research hypotheses? How do you interpret them?

   c. Now run a model that also accounts for being low income, well educated, White, and female:

      i. How has your model –2 log likelihood statistic changed? Is this an improvement in fit, or is it worse?

      ii. Interpret all the odds ratios and hypothesis tests for your coefficients.

      iii. Write a few sentences describing who is most likely to be in favor of marijuana legislation based on your data. Be sure to note some of your results, but do so in a way that a layperson could follow.

   d. Let's add a variable that might answer the "why" people are in favor or opposed more directly: a person's political views. At bare minimum, we should be distinguishing among liberals, moderates, and conservatives if possible. But this is a categorical variable with three categories, we've only handled binaries. How do we handle this kind of variable?

      i. **Regression with independent variables with multiple categories:** All you must do is include *all but one* category in the model. That omitted category becomes a reference group. In this case, we're going to omit moderates, so our odds ratios would show that liberals have X% greater odds of being pro marijuana legalization than moderates.

      ii. Estimate a regression model with the binary variables "liberal" and "conservative" in the model. Remember that we're leaving moderates out, so they are the reference group.

iii. Interpret these new results and their hypothesis tests. What do you conclude about the role of political affiliation and marijuana legalization? Have any of the other effects in the model changed?

2. Another major issue of recent years is the legality (and the usefulness) of capital punishment. What does the American population think about capital punishment overall, and are some groups more or less likely to be in favor?

   a. Construct a frequency table for the variable cappun. What proportion of Americans are in favor of capital punishment?

   b. Estimate a logistic regression model with the variable cappun as dependent variable and age, higheduc, lowincome, sex, and White as independent variables.

      i. What do your results suggest? Interpret all statistically significant odds ratios fully.

      ii. What coefficients have the strongest effect. Note the Wald statistics.

      iii. Write a few sentences explaining the significance of these results. Take a moment also to speculate *why* the significant variables might affect attitudes toward capital punishment.

   c. If people think the courts aren't sentencing harshly enough, are they also more likely to be in favor of the death penalty? To do this, we'll include a pair of dummy variables indicating whether the respondent thinks the courts are too harsh (variable tooharsh) or not harsh enough (notenough). The omitted reference category in this case is that the courts give appropriate sentences. For more information on this dummy variable method, see part 1d:

      i. What are your conclusions from this analysis? Have any of your coefficients substantially changed?

3. In light of recent events, one hot issue is police violence against citizens. A binary variable, polhitbin, indicates whether a respondent feels it is ok to hit a citizen across a variety of scenarios that were presented to the respondent. Let's see whether there are any demographic differences in who is/isn't in favor of police hitting citizens:

   a. Run a frequency of polhitbn. Are the majority of Americans in favor or sometimes opposed to police hitting citizens?

   b. Estimate a logistic regression model with polhitbin as a dependent variable and sex, White, lowincome, higheduc, and age as predictors:

      i. What does your model chi-square tell you in this case?

      ii. What are the substantive results of your model. Interpret all statistically significant odds ratios fully.

      iii. Why, theoretically, do you think you've found what you've found? Why would these relationships exist?

# Appendix A

## Review of Basic Mathematical Operations

## ▣ Introduction

Many of you undoubtedly have avoided taking a statistics class because you believed that the mathematics involved would be too difficult for your meager skills. After many years of teaching undergraduate statistics courses, we have probably heard all the stories.

Some students protest, "I'm not very good at math, so how can I ever hope to pass a statistics course? Statistics is nothing but math!" Others are more pessimistic, "I've *never* been good at math. I did lousy in junior high, high school, and college. I just have a mental block against doing math!" Others are only slightly more optimistic, claiming that they are simply rusty: "I haven't had a math course since high school. I've forgotten everything since then!"

This anxiety you brought with you to the course was probably only made worse when you thumbed through the chapters of this book, seeing all the equations, formulas, and strange symbols. Even letters in a different alphabet! "Boy," you thought, "I am sunk. Maybe I should change my major or start planning for summer school!" Put your mind at rest; you need do none of those things. The study of statistics does require some mathematical skills, but they are no more than the ability to add, subtract, multiply, and divide. Let us assure you that if you can do these simple mathematical operations, you can do statistics.

In this statistics text, we have emphasized the conceptual and logical dimension of statistical analyses of crime data. Most complex statistical analyses are now performed by computer programs. You will undoubtedly learn one of these programs in this or some other course. The study site for this text introduces you to one such statistical software program called SPSS. This stands for the Statistical Package for the Social Sciences. This is only one such statistical package that will do the calculations for you for the statistics described in this book. There are many others available, and all of them perform high-speed and accurate calculations of simple and complex statistics.

Although computer software programs can perform the calculations for us much quicker than we could by hand and with far greater accuracy, we need to know some basics about statistics so that we know which statistical analyses to perform in which situations. We also need to know how to interpret and diagnose the mass of statistical information most computer programs spit out for us. In other words, no matter how fast, accurate, or sophisticated the statistical computer package you use, *you still need to know what you are doing*. Therefore, in this statistics course, you need to learn how to hand-calculate the various statistical procedures.

The hand calculation of statistics is not that daunting a task. Again, all you need to know how to do mathematically is to add, subtract, multiply, and divide. The task will be made simpler by two things we have provided in each chapter of the text:

1. Clear and simplified examples.

2. A step-by-step approach in which even the most difficult statistical procedures are broken down into simple steps.

In addition, you will probably find it necessary to use a hand calculator to do the numerical operations for you. There are a great many kinds of calculators on the market now. Some of these calculators seem as complex as personal computers with graphic screens and everything! Others, in addition to basic mathematical operations, actually calculate some of the statistics in this book for you, such as standard deviations and correlation coefficients.

We would recommend that you use a calculator for your calculations. You do not, however, need a very fancy or expensive one. All you really need is a calculator that, in addition to mathematical operations such as adding and subtracting, has a square root key ($\sqrt{}$) and a square key ($x^2$). The square key will enable you to square (multiply by itself) any number. A simple calculator that does these things is all you really need to work the problems described in this text.

Before we describe some simple mathematical operations, we would like to show you some common symbols used in statistics. Mathematical operations involve many symbols in their own right; as if this were not difficult enough, many statistics are symbolized by a Greek letter. To help you through the symbolism, the following are some common math symbols and Greek letters you will find in this text:

# Common Mathematical Symbols

| | | | |
|---|---|---|---|
| + | Addition | > | Is greater than |
| − | Subtraction | ≥ | Is greater than or equal to |
| × | Multiplication | ≈ | Is approximately equal to |
| / or ÷ | Division | $x^2$ | The number $x$ squared |
| = | Equals | $\sqrt{x}$ | The square root of the number $x$ |
| ≠ | Is not equal to | ln $x$ | The natural log of the number $x$ |
| ± | Plus or minus | log $x$ | The common log of the number $x$ |
| < | Is less than | $|x|$ | The absolute value of the number $x$ |
| ≤ | Is less than or equal to | | |

# Common Greek Letters Used In Statistics

| Uppercase | Lowercase | |
|---|---|---|
| A | α | alpha |
| B | β | beta |
| Γ | γ | gamma |
| Δ | δ | delta |
| E | ε | epsilon |
| Λ | λ | lambda |
| M | μ | mu |
| P | ρ | rho |
| Σ | σ | sigma |
| T | τ | tau |
| Φ | φ | phi |
| X | χ | chi |

# Mathematical Operations

Most of you are familiar with the four basic mathematical operations: addition, subtraction, multiplication, and division. In this text, the operations of addition and subtraction are shown with their common symbols, + and −. In the text, the operations of multiplication and division are shown with several different symbols. For example, the operation of multiplying $x$ by $y$ may be shown as $xy$, $x \times y$, or $(x)(y)$. The operation of dividing $x$ by $y$ may be shown as $x \div y$ or $x / y$.

In addition to the standard operations of addition, subtraction, multiplication, and division, there are three other very frequent mathematical operations in statistics. One of these is the squaring of a number. A number squared is symbolized by the number being squared shown with a superscript of 2. For example, 4 squared is shown as $4^2$, and 7 squared is shown as $7^2$. When you square a number, you multiply that number by itself, so 4 squared is equal to $4 \times 4 = 16$, and 7 squared is equal to $7 \times 7 = 49$. These expressions tell us that 4 squared is equal to 16 and that 7 squared is equal to 49. One squared is equal to 1 because $1^2 = 1 \times 1 = 1$. When calculating the square of fractions, it is probably easier first to convert the fraction to a decimal and then square. For example, the square of one half $(\frac{1}{2})^2$ would be equal to $.50^2$ or $(.50)(.50) = .25$. The square of one-third $(\frac{1}{3})^2$ would be equal to $.33^2$ or $(.33)(.33) = .1089$.

A second frequent mathematical operation in statistics is taking the square root of a number. This is symbolized by placing the number we want the square root of within something called a radical sign ($\sqrt{\ }$). For example, the square root of 2 is shown as $\sqrt{2}$, and the square root of 9 is shown as $\sqrt{9}$. The square root of a number is the value that, when squared, results in the original number. For example, the square root of 9 is 3 ($\sqrt{9} = 3$) because when 3 is squared, we obtain 9 ($3^2 = 3 \times 3 = 9$). The square root of 25 is 5 ($\sqrt{25} = 5$) because when 5 is squared, we obtain 25 ($5^2 = (5)(5) = 25$). As with the squaring of fractions, it will probably be easier to convert a fraction into a decimal before taking the square root. For example, the square root of one half ($\sqrt{1/2}$) is equal to $\sqrt{5}$, which is equal to .707 because $.707^2 = .5$. The square root of a negative number, $\sqrt{-x}$, is not defined because there is no number $x$ that, when squared (multiplied by itself), results in a negative number. This is because the multiplication of two negative numbers always results in a positive product.

The third other operation that you will frequently see in this text is the summation operation. This is actually an addition operation, but because it appears with its own symbol, we need to call special attention to it. The operation of summation is symbolized by the uppercase Greek letter sigma ($\Sigma$). The summation sign stands for "the sum of," and the operation requires you to add a series of scores for a given variable. For example, presuming that there are five scores for the variable Age (itself symbolized as $x$), the ages of five persons might be as follows:

$$x_1 = 13 \qquad x_4 = 20$$
$$x_2 = 18 \qquad x_5 = 17$$
$$x_3 = 25$$

The operation $\Sigma x$ instructs you to sum or add each of these $x$ scores or ages. That is, instead of stating that you should take the first person's age and add it to the second person's age, and then add this sum to the third person's age, and so on, a formula will simply state the sum of all the $x$ scores or $\Sigma x$. In this example, then, $\Sigma x = 13 + 18 + 25 + 20 + 17 = 93$. Think of the symbol $\Sigma$, then, as a mathematical operation that says "add all of the $x$ scores up and determine the sum."

# Order of Operations

Many statistical formulas require you to perform several mathematical operations at once. At times these formulas may seem very complex, requiring addition, division, squaring, square roots, and summation. Your task of comprehending statistical formulas would not be so difficult if it did not matter how all the calculations were performed, so long as they were all completed. Unfortunately, however, statistical formulas require not only that all mathematical operations be conducted but also that they be conducted in the right order because you will get different results depending on the order in which the operations are performed!

For example, take the following very simple equation that requires you to add and divide a few numbers:

$$15 + 10 \div 5$$

Note that you will get completely different results depending on whether you complete the addition before dividing or do the dividing first:

$$(15 + 10) \div 5 \qquad 15 + (10 \div 5)$$
$$25 \div 5 = 5 \qquad 15 + 2 = 17$$

As you can see, the order in which you perform your mathematical operations does make a substantial difference and must, therefore, be correctly followed. Fortunately, there are some standard rules that tell you the order in which operations should be performed. Furthermore, we would like to emphasize that even the most complex formula or mathematical expression can be simplified by solving it in sequential steps. We now illustrate these rules of operation and our recommended step-by-step approach for solving mathematical expressions.

The first rule is that any operation that is included in parentheses should be performed before operations not included in parentheses. For example, for the expression:

$$15 + (10 \div 5) \times (7 \times 2)$$

the order of operations would be first to divide 10 by 5 and multiply 7 by 2. We now have simplified the expression to:

$$15 + 2 \times 14$$

How do we solve the remainder of this? Do we first add 15 + 2 and then multiply by 14 to get 238? Or do we first multiply 2 by 14 and then add 15 to get 43?

The second rule of the order of operations is that you should first obtain all squares and square roots, then perform multiplication and division, and last complete any addition and subtraction. Because in the expression just listed we have no squares or square roots to calculate, we know that we should first multiply the 2 and 14 to get 28:

$$15 + 28$$

After this, we should add 28 to 15 to get the final sum of 43.

To summarize, the rules of operation for solving mathematical expressions are, in order:

- Solve all expressions in parentheses.
- Determine the value of all squares and square roots.
- Perform all division and multiplication operations.
- Perform all addition and subtraction operations.

We will practice these rules with some exercises momentarily, but first we need to illustrate the parentheses rule in combination with the rule of squares.

The rules are to perform all operations within parentheses first, then squares and square roots, next multiplication and division, and then addition and subtraction. As an example, assume that we have the following six scores: 46, 29, 61, 14, 33, and 25. With these scores, examine the two expressions, $\Sigma x^2$ and $(\Sigma x)^2$. These two expressions look virtually identical because they both require a summation of scores and that a number be squared. Note, however, that in the first expression, there are no parentheses. We know that the summation sign tells us that we have to add the six scores. Before we do this, however, following the correct order of operations, we must first square each $x$ score and then sum them:

$$\begin{aligned} \Sigma x^2 &= 46^2 + 29^2 + 61^2 + 14^2 + 33^2 + 25^2 \\ &= 2,116 + 841 + 3,721 + 196 + 1,089 + 625 \\ &= 8,588 \end{aligned}$$

In this first expression, then, we have followed the order of operations by first squaring each $x$ score and then taking the sum (squaring before addition).

Note that in the second expression, we have parentheses $(\Sigma x)^2$. As the order of operations is to conduct all calculations within parentheses first, this expression tells us first to sum the six scores and then square the sum:

$$\begin{aligned} (\Sigma x^2) &= (46 + 29 + 61 + 14 + 33 + 25)^2 \\ &= 208^2 \\ &= 43,264 \end{aligned}$$

To reiterate the point made earlier, $\Sigma x^2$, called the sum of the $x$ squares, is obtained by first squaring each $x$ score and then adding all squared numbers. This is different from the expression, $(\Sigma x)^2$, called the sum of the $x$s, squared, which is obtained by first adding up all the $x$ scores and then squaring the sum.

# Operations With Negative Numbers and Fractions in Denominators

In many statistical calculations you have both positive and negative scores. Positive scores are shown with no sign at all, so that a positive 10 appears as 10. Negative numbers are shown with a minus sign in front of them, so that a negative 10 appears as −10. Negative numbers are less than zero, and positive numbers are greater than zero. It is important to keep track of the signs of numbers because it makes a substantial difference for the final result of a mathematical operation.

For example, when a positive number is added to a positive number, nothing special happens, and the sum of the two numbers can be obtained directly: $10 + 14 = 24$. When a negative number is added to a positive number, however, it has the same effect as subtraction. For example, adding a negative 14 to 10 is the same thing as subtracting 14 from 10: $10 + (−14) = 10 − 14 = (−4)$. When a positive number is subtracted from another positive number, nothing special happens, and the difference between the two numbers can be obtained directly: $25 − 10 = 15$. When a negative number is subtracted from either a positive or a negative number, its sign changes to that of a positive number, so that $25 − (−10) = 25 + 10 = 35$, $(−10) − (−7) = (−10) + 7 = (−3)$. Remember, then, that the subtraction of a negative number changes the sign of the number from negative to positive.

When two positive numbers are multiplied, nothing special happens, and the product of the two numbers can be obtained directly: $6 \times 3 = 18$. When two numbers are multiplied and one is positive and the other negative, the resulting product is negative. For example: $25 \times (−3) = −75$; $(−14) \times 5 = −70$. When two negative numbers are multiplied, the resulting product is always positive: $(−23) \times (−14) = 322$. So the rule is that the multiplication of either two positive or two negative numbers results in a positive product, whereas the multiplication of one positive and one negative number results in a negative product.

The same pattern occurs when the operation is division rather than multiplication. When two positive numbers are divided, nothing special happens, and the result (the *quotient*) is positive: $125 \div 5 = 25$; $10 \div 20 = .5$. When two numbers are divided and one is positive and the other negative, the quotient is negative: $250 \div (-25) = (-10)$; $(-33) \div 11 = -3$. When two negative numbers are divided, the quotient always is positive: $(-16) \div (-4) = 4$. So the rule is that the division of either two positive or two negative numbers results in a positive quotient, whereas the division of one positive and one negative number results in a negative quotient.

## 🔲 Rounding Numbers Off

Whenever you are working with statistical formulas, you need to decide how precise you want your answer to be. For example, should your answer be correct to the tenth decimal place? The fifth? The third? It is also important to decide when to round up and when to round down. For example, having decided that we want to be accurate only to the second decimal place, should the number 28.355 be rounded up to 28.36 or rounded down to 28.35? It is important to make these decisions explicit because two people may get different answers to the same statistical problem simply because they employed different rounding rules.

Unfortunately, no rule about when to round off can always be hard and fast. When we are dealing with large numbers, we can frequently do our calculations with whole numbers (integers). In this case, we would not gain much precision by carrying out our calculations to one or two decimal places. When we are dealing with much smaller numbers, however, it may be necessary, to be as precise as possible, to take a number out to three or four decimal places in our calculations. With smaller numbers, there is a substantial gain in precision by including more decimal places in our calculations. Whenever possible, however, we have tried to limit our precision to two decimal places. This means that most of the time, numbers will include only two decimal places. We warn you, however, that this will not always be the case.

The question about how to round can be answered a little more definitively. When rounding, the following convention should be applied. When deciding how to round, look at the digit to the right of the last digit you want to keep. If you are rounding to the second decimal place, then, look at the third digit to the right of the decimal point. If this digit is larger than 5, you should round up. For example, 123.148 becomes 123.15, and 34.737 becomes 34.74. If this digit is less than 5, you should round down. For example, 8.923 becomes 8.92, and 53.904 becomes 53.90.

What do you do in the case where the third digit is a 5, as in 34.675, for example? Do you round up or round down? You cannot simply say that you should always round up or always round down because there will be systematic bias to your rounding decision. Your decision rule will be consistent to be sure, but it will be biased because numbers are always being overestimated (if rounded up) or underestimated (if rounded down). You would like your decision rule to be consistent but consistently fair—that is, never in the same direction. This way, sometimes the 5 will be rounded up and sometimes it will be rounded down, and the number of times it is rounded up and down will be approximately the same. One way to ensure this is to adopt the following rounding rule: If the third digit is a 5, then look at the digit immediately *before* the 5; if that digit (the second decimal place) is an even number, then round up; if it is an odd number, then round down. For example, the number 34.675 should be rounded down to 34.67 because the number immediately before the 5 is an odd number. The number 164.965 should be rounded up to 164.97 because the number before the 5 is an even number. Note that the number of occasions you will decide to round up (if the immediately preceding digit is an even number 0, 2, 4, 6, or 8) is the same as the number of occasions when you will decide to round down (if the immediately preceding digit is an odd number 1, 3, 5, 7, 9). Because even numbers should appear in our calculations as frequently as odd numbers, there is no bias to our rounding decision rule.

## 🔲 Examples

Let's go through a few examples step by step to make sure that we understand all the rules and procedures. We will begin by solving the following problem:

$$25 + 192 - (3 + 5)^2$$

Following the rules of operation, we first solve within the parentheses:

$$25 + 192 - (8)^2$$

Then we square the 8:

$$25 + 192 - 64$$

Now we can solve for the final answer either by adding 25 to 192 and then subtracting 64 or by subtracting 64 from 192 and then adding 25. Either way, we get the same result:

$$217 - 64 = 153$$

$$25 + 128 = 153$$

Now let's solve a more complicated-looking problem. Please note that this problem is only more *complicated-looking*. When we solve it step by step, you will see that it is very manageable and that all you really need to know is addition, subtraction, multiplication, and division:

$$[(32 + 17)^2 / 10] + [\sqrt{16} / (10 - 6)^2]$$

First, we solve within parentheses:

$$[(49)^2 / 10] + [\sqrt{16} / (4)^2]$$

Then we calculate all squares and square roots:

$$(2,401 / 10) + (4 / 16)$$

Next we do the division:

$$240.1 + .25$$

Finally, we do the addition:

$$240.35$$

Here is one more problem, and it's probably as difficult as any you will encounter in this book:

$$\sqrt{\frac{(116 - 27)^2 + 21}{\sqrt{15 + 1}}} - \frac{(212 - 188)}{2}$$

Following the rules of operations, we first want to solve within all the parentheses:

$$\sqrt{\frac{(89)^2 + 21}{\sqrt{15 + 1}}} - \frac{24}{2}$$

Then we calculate all squares and square roots. Note, however, that in the denominator of the first term, we first have to use addition (15 + 1) before taking the square root of the sum. Note also that we cannot take the square root

of the entire first term until we solve for all that is under the square root sign:

$$\sqrt{\frac{7,921 + 21}{4}} - 12$$

Now we continue to solve that part of the problem within the square root by first completing the numerator (by addition) and then dividing:

$$\sqrt{\frac{7,942}{4}} - 12$$

$$\sqrt{1,985.5} - 12$$

Finally, now that we have completed all the operations within the square root sign, we can complete that:

$$44.56 - 12$$

Note that the result for the first expression was 44.558. Because the third decimal place is greater than 5, we round the second digit up, so that 44.558 becomes 44.56. Then we complete the problem by subtracting 12:

$$32.56$$

We hope that you now feel greater confidence in solving math equations. As long as things are performed in a step-by-step manner, in accordance with the rules of operations, everything in any equation can be solved relatively easily. To make sure that you comprehend these rules, as well as to brush up on your math skills, complete the following exercises.

We have provided answers for you at the end of the section. If you can do these problems, you are ready to tackle any of the statistics problems in this text. If some of the problems in the exercises give you difficulty, simply review that section of this appendix or consult a mathematics book for some help.

## ▣ Practice Problems

1. Calculate each of the following:

   a. $5^2 + 3$

   b. $(35 / 7) - 4$

   c. $\sqrt{64} + 7 - (4/2)$

   d. $[(35)(.3)] / 10 + 15$

2. Calculate each of the following:

a. $45 + \sqrt{\dfrac{125}{15 - (3)^2}}$

b. $18 + (12 \times 10) - \sqrt{150} - 50$

c. $(18 + 12) \times 10 - \sqrt{150} - 50$

d. $[(23 + 17) - (5 \times 4)] / (8 + 2)^2$

e. $(-5) \times 13$

f. $(-5) \times (-13)$

g. $[18 + (-7)] \times [(-4) - (-10)]$

h. $125 / -5$

i. $450 - [(-125 / -10) / 2]$

3. With these 10 scores, 7, 18, 42, 11, 34, 65, 30, 27, 6, 29, perform the following operations:

a. $\Sigma x$

b. $(\Sigma x)^2$

c. $\Sigma x^2$

4. Round the following numbers off to two places to the right of the decimal point:

a. 118.954

b. 65.186

c. 156.145

d. 87.915

e. 3.212

f. 48.565

g. 48.535

## Solutions to Problems

1. a. 28

b. 1 (Remember to do the division before the subtraction.)

c. 13

d. 16.05

2. a. 49.56

b. 128

c. 290

d. .20 (Remember to do all operations within parentheses first, starting with the innermost parentheses.)

e. −65

f. 65

g. 66

h. −25

i. 443.75 (Following the rules of operation, you should have divided the two negative numbers (−125 and −10) first, then divided by 2, and finally subtracted that quotient from 450.)

3. a. This expression says to sum all $x$ scores: $7 + 18 + 42 + 11 + 34 + 65 + 30 + 27 + 6 + 29 = 269$.

b. Note the parentheses in this expression. It tells you to first sum all the $x$ scores and then square the sum: $(7 + 18 + 42 + 11 + 34 + 65 + 30 + 27 + 6 + 29)^2 = (269)^2 = 72,361$.

c. Following the order of operations, first square each $x$ score, and then sum these squared scores: $7^2 + 18^2 + 42^2 + 11^2 + 34^2 + 65^2 + 30^2 + 27^2 + 6^2 + 29^2 = 49 + 324 + 1,764 + 121 + 1,156 + 4,225 + 900 + 729 + 36 + 841 = 10,145$.

4. a. 118.95

b. 65.19

c. 156.15 (Round up because the number to the left of the 5 is an even number.)

d. 87.91 (Round down because the number to the left of the 5 is an odd number.)

e. 3.21

f. 48.57

g. 48.53

# Appendix B

*Statistical Tables*

## Table B.1  Table of Random Numbers

| | | | | | | | | | | | | |
|---|---|---|---|---|---|---|---|---|---|---|---|---|
| 16408 | 81899 | 04153 | 53381 | 79401 | 21438 | 83035 | 92350 | 36693 | 31238 | 59649 | 91754 | 72772 |
| 18629 | 81953 | 05520 | 91962 | 04739 | 13092 | 97662 | 24822 | 94730 | 06496 | 35090 | 04822 | 86774 |
| 73115 | 35101 | 47498 | 87637 | 99016 | 71060 | 88824 | 71013 | 18735 | 20286 | 23153 | 72924 | 35165 |
| 57491 | 16703 | 23792 | 49323 | 45021 | 33132 | 12544 | 41035 | 80780 | 45393 | 44812 | 12515 | 98931 |
| 30405 | 83946 | 23632 | 14422 | 15059 | 45799 | 22716 | 19792 | 09983 | 74353 | 68668 | 30429 | 70735 |
| 16631 | 35006 | 85900 | 98275 | 32388 | 52390 | 16815 | 69298 | 82732 | 38480 | 73817 | 32523 | 41961 |
| 96773 | 20206 | 42559 | 78985 | 05300 | 22164 | 24369 | 54224 | 35083 | 19687 | 11052 | 91491 | 60383 |
| 38935 | 64202 | 14349 | 82674 | 66523 | 44133 | 00697 | 35552 | 35970 | 19124 | 63318 | 29686 | 03387 |
| 31624 | 76384 | 17403 | 53363 | 44167 | 64486 | 64758 | 75366 | 76554 | 31601 | 12614 | 33072 | 60332 |
| 78919 | 19474 | 23632 | 27889 | 47914 | 02584 | 37680 | 20801 | 72152 | 39339 | 34806 | 08930 | 85001 |
| 03931 | 33309 | 57047 | 74211 | 63445 | 17361 | 62825 | 39908 | 05607 | 91284 | 68833 | 25570 | 38818 |
| 74426 | 33278 | 43972 | 10119 | 89917 | 15665 | 52872 | 73823 | 73144 | 88662 | 88970 | 74492 | 51805 |
| 09066 | 00903 | 20795 | 95452 | 92648 | 45454 | 09552 | 88815 | 16553 | 51125 | 79375 | 97596 | 16296 |
| 42238 | 12426 | 87025 | 14267 | 20979 | 04508 | 64535 | 31355 | 86064 | 29472 | 47689 | 05974 | 52468 |
| 16153 | 08002 | 26504 | 41744 | 81959 | 65642 | 74240 | 56302 | 00033 | 67107 | 77510 | 70625 | 28725 |
| 21457 | 40742 | 29820 | 96783 | 29400 | 21840 | 15035 | 34537 | 33310 | 06116 | 95240 | 15957 | 16572 |
| 21581 | 57802 | 02050 | 89728 | 17937 | 37621 | 47075 | 42080 | 97403 | 48626 | 68995 | 43805 | 33386 |
| 55612 | 78095 | 83197 | 33732 | 05810 | 24813 | 86902 | 60397 | 16489 | 03264 | 88525 | 42786 | 05269 |
| 44657 | 66999 | 99324 | 51281 | 84463 | 60563 | 79312 | 93454 | 68876 | 25471 | 93911 | 25650 | 12682 |
| 91340 | 84979 | 46949 | 81973 | 37949 | 61023 | 43997 | 15263 | 80644 | 43942 | 89203 | 71795 | 99533 |
| 91227 | 21199 | 31935 | 27022 | 84067 | 05462 | 35216 | 14486 | 29891 | 68607 | 41867 | 14951 | 91696 |
| 50001 | 38140 | 66321 | 19924 | 72163 | 09538 | 12151 | 06878 | 91903 | 18749 | 34405 | 56087 | 82790 |
| 65390 | 05224 | 72958 | 28609 | 81406 | 39147 | 25549 | 48542 | 42627 | 45233 | 57202 | 94617 | 23772 |
| 27504 | 96131 | 83944 | 41575 | 10573 | 08619 | 64482 | 73923 | 36152 | 05184 | 94142 | 25299 | 84387 |
| 37169 | 94851 | 39117 | 89632 | 00959 | 16487 | 65536 | 19071 | 39782 | 17095 | 02330 | 74301 | 00275 |
| 11508 | 70225 | 51111 | 38351 | 19444 | 66499 | 71945 | 05422 | 13442 | 78675 | 84081 | 66938 | 93654 |
| 37449 | 30362 | 06694 | 54690 | 04052 | 53115 | 62757 | 95348 | 78662 | 11163 | 81651 | 50245 | 34971 |
| 46515 | 70331 | 85922 | 38329 | 57015 | 15765 | 97161 | 17869 | 45349 | 61796 | 66345 | 81073 | 49106 |
| 30986 | 81223 | 42416 | 58353 | 21532 | 30502 | 32305 | 86482 | 06174 | 07901 | 54339 | 58861 | 74818 |
| 63798 | 64995 | 46583 | 09785 | 44160 | 78128 | 83991 | 42865 | 92520 | 83531 | 80377 | 35909 | 81250 |

| | | | | | | | | | | | | |
|---|---|---|---|---|---|---|---|---|---|---|---|---|
| 82486 | 84846 | 99254 | 67632 | 43218 | 50076 | 21361 | 64816 | 51202 | 88124 | 41870 | 52689 | 51275 |
| 21885 | 32906 | 92431 | 09060 | 64297 | 51674 | 64126 | 62570 | 26123 | 05155 | 59194 | 52799 | 28225 |
| 60336 | 98782 | 07408 | 53458 | 13564 | 59089 | 26445 | 29789 | 85205 | 41001 | 12535 | 12133 | 14645 |
| 43937 | 46891 | 24010 | 25560 | 86355 | 33941 | 25786 | 54990 | 71899 | 15475 | 95434 | 98227 | 21824 |
| 97656 | 63175 | 89303 | 16275 | 07100 | 92063 | 21942 | 18611 | 47348 | 20203 | 18534 | 03862 | 78095 |
| 03299 | 01221 | 05418 | 38982 | 55758 | 92237 | 26759 | 86367 | 21216 | 98442 | 08303 | 56613 | 91511 |
| 79626 | 06486 | 03574 | 17668 | 07785 | 76020 | 79924 | 25651 | 83325 | 88428 | 85076 | 72811 | 22717 |
| 85636 | 68335 | 47539 | 03129 | 65651 | 11977 | 02510 | 26113 | 99447 | 68645 | 34327 | 15152 | 55230 |
| 18039 | 14367 | 61337 | 06177 | 12143 | 46609 | 32989 | 74014 | 64708 | 00533 | 35398 | 58408 | 13261 |
| 08362 | 15656 | 60627 | 36478 | 65648 | 16764 | 53412 | 09013 | 07832 | 41574 | 17639 | 82163 | 60859 |
| 79556 | 29068 | 04142 | 16268 | 15387 | 12856 | 66227 | 38358 | 22478 | 73373 | 88732 | 09443 | 82558 |
| 92608 | 82674 | 27072 | 32534 | 17075 | 27698 | 98204 | 63863 | 11951 | 34648 | 88022 | 56148 | 34925 |
| 23982 | 25835 | 40055 | 67006 | 12293 | 02753 | 14827 | 23235 | 35071 | 99704 | 37543 | 11601 | 35503 |
| 09915 | 96306 | 05908 | 97901 | 28395 | 14186 | 00821 | 80703 | 70426 | 75647 | 76310 | 88717 | 37890 |
| 59037 | 33300 | 26695 | 62247 | 69927 | 76123 | 50842 | 43834 | 86654 | 70959 | 79725 | 93872 | 28117 |
| 42488 | 78077 | 69882 | 61657 | 34136 | 79180 | 97526 | 43092 | 04098 | 73571 | 80799 | 76536 | 71255 |
| 46764 | 86273 | 63003 | 93017 | 31204 | 36692 | 40202 | 35275 | 57306 | 55543 | 53203 | 18098 | 47625 |
| 03237 | 45430 | 55417 | 63282 | 90816 | 17349 | 88298 | 90183 | 36600 | 78406 | 06216 | 95787 | 42579 |
| 86591 | 81482 | 52667 | 61582 | 14972 | 90053 | 89534 | 76036 | 49199 | 43716 | 97548 | 04379 | 46370 |
| 38534 | 01715 | 94964 | 87288 | 65680 | 43772 | 39560 | 12918 | 86537 | 62738 | 19636 | 51132 | 25739 |

*Source:* Adapted with permission from Byer. W. H. (Ed.). 1991. *CRC Standard Probability and Statistics: Tables and Formulae, XII.3.* Boca Raton, Florida: CRC Press.

## Table B.2 — Area Under the Standard Normal Curve (z Distribution)*

| z | .00 | .01 | .02 | .03 | .04 | .05 | .06 | .07 | .08 | .09 |
|-----|-------|-------|-------|-------|-------|-------|-------|-------|-------|-------|
| 0.0 | .0000 | .0040 | .0080 | .0120 | .0160 | .0199 | .0239 | .0279 | .0319 | .0359 |
| 0.1 | .0398 | .0438 | .0478 | .0517 | .0557 | .0596 | .0636 | .0675 | .0714 | .0753 |
| 0.2 | .0793 | .0832 | .0871 | .0910 | .0948 | .0987 | .1026 | .1064 | .1103 | .1141 |
| 0.3 | .1179 | .1217 | .1255 | .1293 | .1331 | .1368 | .1406 | .1443 | .1480 | .1517 |
| 0.4 | .1554 | .1591 | .1628 | .1664 | .1700 | .1736 | .1772 | .1808 | .1844 | .1879 |
| 0.5 | .1915 | .1950 | .1985 | .2019 | .2054 | .2088 | .2123 | .2157 | .2190 | .2224 |
| 0.6 | .2257 | .2291 | .2324 | .2357 | .2389 | .2422 | .2454 | .2486 | .2517 | .2549 |
| 0.7 | .2580 | .2611 | .2642 | .2673 | .2704 | .2734 | .2764 | .2794 | .2823 | .2852 |
| 0.8 | .2881 | .2910 | .2939 | .2967 | .2995 | .3023 | .3051 | .3078 | .3106 | .3133 |
| 0.9 | .3159 | .3186 | .3212 | .3238 | .3264 | .3289 | .3315 | .3340 | .3365 | .3389 |
| 1.0 | .3413 | .3438 | .3461 | .3485 | .3508 | .3531 | .3554 | .3577 | .3599 | .3621 |
| 1.1 | .3643 | .3665 | .3686 | .3708 | .3729 | .3749 | .3770 | .3790 | .3810 | .3830 |
| 1.2 | .3849 | .3869 | .3888 | .3907 | .3925 | .3944 | .3962 | .3980 | .3997 | .4015 |
| 1.3 | .4032 | .4049 | .4066 | .4082 | .4099 | .4115 | .4131 | .4147 | .4162 | .4177 |
| 1.4 | .4192 | .4207 | .4222 | .4236 | .4251 | .4265 | .4279 | .4292 | .4306 | .4319 |
| 1.5 | .4332 | .4345 | .4357 | .4370 | .4382 | .4394 | .4406 | .4418 | .4429 | .4441 |
| 1.6 | .4452 | .4463 | .4474 | .4484 | .4495 | .4505 | .4515 | .4525 | .4535 | .4545 |
| 1.7 | .4554 | .4564 | .4573 | .4582 | .4591 | .4599 | .4608 | .4616 | .4625 | .4633 |
| 1.8 | .4641 | .4649 | .4656 | .4664 | .4671 | .4678 | .4686 | .4693 | .4699 | .4706 |
| 1.9 | .4713 | .4719 | .4726 | .4732 | .4738 | .4744 | .4750 | .4756 | .4761 | .4767 |
| 2.0 | .4772 | .4778 | .4783 | .4788 | .4793 | .4798 | .4803 | .4808 | .4812 | .4817 |
| 2.1 | .4821 | .4826 | .4830 | .4834 | .4838 | .4842 | .4846 | .4850 | .4854 | .4857 |
| 2.2 | .4861 | .4864 | .4868 | .4871 | .4875 | .4878 | .4881 | .4884 | .4887 | .4890 |
| 2.3 | .4893 | .4896 | .4898 | .4901 | .4904 | .4906 | .4909 | .4911 | .4913 | .4916 |
| 2.4 | .4918 | .4920 | .4922 | .4925 | .4927 | .4929 | .4931 | .4932 | .4934 | .4936 |
| 2.5 | .4938 | .4940 | .4941 | .4943 | .4945 | .4946 | .4948 | .4949 | .4951 | .4952 |
| 2.6 | .4953 | .4955 | .4956 | .4957 | .4959 | .4960 | .4961 | .4962 | .4963 | .4964 |
| 2.7 | .4965 | .4966 | .4967 | .4968 | .4969 | .4970 | .4971 | .4972 | .4973 | .4974 |
| 2.8 | .4974 | .4975 | .4976 | .4977 | .4977 | .4978 | .4979 | .4979 | .4980 | .4981 |
| 2.9 | .4981 | .4982 | .4982 | .4983 | .4984 | .4984 | .4985 | .4985 | .4986 | .4986 |
| 3.0 | .4987 | .4987 | .4987 | .4988 | .4988 | .4989 | .4989 | .4989 | .4990 | .4990 |

*Source:* Adapted with permission from Frederick Mosteller and Robert E. K. Rourke, 1973. *Sturdy Statistics.* Table A = 1. Reading, MA: Addison-Weskey.

* Proportion of the area under the normal curve corresponding to the distance between the mean (0) and a point that is $z$ standard deviation units away from the mean.

## Table B.3 | The *t* Distribution

| | Level of Significance for a One-Tailed Test | | | | | |
|---|---|---|---|---|---|---|
| | .10 | .05 | .025 | .01 | .005 | .0005 |
| | Level of Significance for a Two-Tailed Test | | | | | |
| | .20 | .10 | .05 | .02 | .01 | .001 |
| 1 | 3.078 | 6.314 | 12.706 | 31.821 | 63.657 | 636.619 |
| 2 | 1.886 | 2.920 | 4.303 | 6.965 | 9.925 | 31.598 |
| 3 | 1.638 | 2.353 | 3.182 | 4.541 | 5.841 | 12.941 |
| 4 | 1.533 | 2.132 | 2.776 | 3.747 | 4.604 | 8.610 |
| 5 | 1.476 | 2.015 | 2.571 | 3.365 | 4.032 | 6.859 |
| 6 | 1.440 | 1.943 | 2.447 | 3.143 | 3.707 | 5.959 |
| 7 | 1.415 | 1.895 | 2.365 | 2.998 | 3.499 | 5.405 |
| 8 | 1.397 | 1.860 | 2.306 | 2.896 | 3.355 | 5.041 |
| 9 | 1.383 | 1.833 | 2.262 | 2.821 | 3.250 | 4.781 |
| 10 | 1.372 | 1.812 | 2.228 | 2.764 | 3.169 | 4.587 |
| 11 | 1.363 | 1.796 | 2.201 | 2.718 | 3.106 | 4.437 |
| 12 | 1.356 | 1.782 | 2.179 | 2.681 | 3.055 | 4.318 |
| 13 | 1.350 | 1.771 | 2.160 | 2.650 | 3.012 | 4.221 |
| 14 | 1.345 | 1.761 | 2.145 | 2.624 | 2.977 | 4.140 |
| 15 | 1.341 | 1.753 | 2.131 | 2.602 | 2.947 | 4.073 |
| 16 | 1.337 | 1.746 | 2.120 | 2.583 | 2.921 | 4.015 |
| 17 | 1.333 | 1.740 | 2.110 | 2.567 | 2.898 | 3.965 |
| 18 | 1.330 | 1.734 | 2.101 | 2.552 | 2.878 | 3.922 |
| 19 | 1.328 | 1.729 | 2.093 | 2.539 | 2.861 | 3.883 |
| 20 | 1.325 | 1.725 | 2.086 | 2.528 | 2.845 | 3.850 |
| 21 | 1.323 | 1.721 | 2.080 | 2.518 | 2.831 | 3.819 |
| 22 | 1.321 | 1.717 | 2.074 | 2.508 | 2.819 | 3.792 |
| 23 | 1.319 | 1.714 | 2.069 | 2.500 | 2.807 | 3.767 |
| 24 | 1.318 | 1.711 | 2.064 | 2.492 | 2.797 | 3.745 |
| 25 | 1.316 | 1.708 | 2.060 | 2.485 | 2.787 | 3.725 |
| 26 | 1.315 | 1.706 | 2.056 | 2.479 | 2.779 | 3.707 |
| 27 | 1.314 | 1.703 | 2.052 | 2.473 | 2.771 | 3.690 |
| 28 | 1.313 | 1.701 | 2.048 | 2.467 | 2.763 | 3.674 |
| 29 | 1.311 | 1.699 | 2.045 | 2.462 | 2.756 | 3.659 |
| 30 | 1.310 | 1.697 | 2.042 | 2.457 | 2.750 | 3.646 |
| 40 | 1.303 | 1.684 | 2.021 | 2.423 | 2.704 | 3.551 |
| 60 | 1.206 | 1.671 | 2.000 | 2.390 | 2.660 | 3.460 |
| 120 | 1.289 | 1.658 | 1.980 | 2.358 | 2.617 | 3.373 |
| ∞ | 1.282 | 1.645 | 1.960 | 2.326 | 2.576 | 3.291 |

*Source:* TABLE B-3 is adapted with permission from Table III of Fisher and Yates, *Statistical Tables for Biological, Agriculltural and Medical Research* (6th ed.). Published by Longman Group UK Ltd., 1974.

| Table B.4 | Critical Values of the Chi-Square Statistic at the .05 and.01 Significance Level |

| Area to the Right of the Critical Value | | |
| --- | --- | --- |
| | Level of significance | |
| df | .05 | .01 |
| 1 | 3.841 | 6.635 |
| 2 | 5.991 | 9.210 |
| 3 | 7.815 | 11.345 |
| 4 | 9.488 | 13.277 |
| 5 | 11.070 | 15.086 |
| 6 | 12.592 | 16.812 |
| 7 | 14.067 | 18.475 |
| 8 | 15.507 | 20.090 |
| 9 | 16.919 | 21.666 |
| 10 | 18.307 | 23.209 |
| 11 | 19.675 | 24.725 |
| 12 | 21.026 | 26.217 |
| 13 | 22.362 | 27.688 |
| 14 | 23.685 | 29.141 |
| 15 | 24.996 | 30.578 |
| 16 | 26.296 | 32.000 |
| 17 | 27.587 | 33.409 |
| 18 | 28.869 | 34.805 |
| 19 | 30.144 | 36.191 |
| 20 | 31.410 | 37.566 |

| Area to the Right of the Critical Value | | |
| --- | --- | --- |
| | Level of significance | |
| df | .05 | .01 |
| 21 | 32.671 | 38.932 |
| 22 | 33.924 | 40.289 |
| 23 | 33.924 | 40.289 |
| 24 | 36.415 | 42.980 |
| 25 | 37.652 | 44.314 |
| 26 | 38.885 | 45.642 |
| 27 | 40.113 | 46.963 |
| 28 | 41.337 | 48.278 |
| 29 | 42.557 | 49.588 |
| 30 | 43.773 | 50.892 |
| 40 | 55.758 | 63.691 |
| 50 | 67.505 | 76.154 |
| 60 | 79.082 | 88.379 |
| 70 | 90.531 | 100.425 |
| 80 | 101.879 | 112.329 |
| 90 | 113.145 | 124.116 |
| 100 | 124.342 | 135.807 |

Source: Adapted from Donald Owen, *Handbook of Statistical Tables,* © 1962 by Addison-Wesley Publishing Company. Inc. Reprinted by permission of Addison-Wesley Publishing Company, Inc.

## Table B.5a  The *F* Distribution ($\alpha = 0.01$ in the Right Tail)

| df (within) | \ df (between) | | Numerator Degrees of freedom | | | | | | | |
|---|---|---|---|---|---|---|---|---|---|---|
| | | 1 | 2 | 3 | 4 | 5 | 6 | 7 | 8 | 9 |
| | 1 | 4052.2 | 4999.5 | 5403.4 | 5624.6 | 5763.6 | 5859.0 | 5928.4 | 5981.1 | 6022.5 |
| | 2 | 98.503 | 99.000 | 99.166 | 99.249 | 99.299 | 99.333 | 99.356 | 99.374 | 99.388 |
| | 3 | 34.116 | 30.817 | 29.457 | 28.710 | 28.237 | 27.911 | 27.672 | 27.489 | 27.345 |
| | 4 | 21.198 | 18.000 | 16.694 | 15.977 | 15.522 | 15.207 | 14.976 | 14.799 | 14.659 |
| | 5 | 16.258 | 13.274 | 12.060 | 11.392 | 10.967 | 10.672 | 10.456 | 10.289 | 10.158 |
| | 6 | 13.745 | 10.925 | 9.7795 | 9.1483 | 8.7459 | 8.4661 | 8.2600 | 8.1017 | 7.9761 |
| | 7 | 12.246 | 9.5466 | 8.4513 | 7.8466 | 7.4604 | 7.1914 | 6.9928 | 6.8400 | 6.7188 |
| | 8 | 11.259 | 8.6491 | 7.5910 | 7.0061 | 6.6318 | 6.3707 | 6.1776 | 6.0289 | 5.9106 |
| | 9 | 10.561 | 8.0215 | 6.9919 | 6.4221 | 6.0569 | 5.8018 | 5.6129 | 5.4671 | 5.3511 |
| | 10 | 10.044 | 7.5594 | 6.5523 | 5.9943 | 5.6363 | 5.3858 | 5.2001 | 5.0567 | 4.9424 |
| | 11 | 9.6460 | 7.2057 | 6.2167 | 5.6683 | 5.3160 | 5.0692 | 4.8861 | 4.7445 | 4.6315 |
| | 12 | 9.3302 | 6.9266 | 5.9525 | 5.4120 | 5.0643 | 4.8206 | 4.6395 | 4.4994 | 4.3875 |
| | 13 | 9.0738 | 6.7010 | 5.7394 | 5.2053 | 4.8616 | 4.6204 | 4.4410 | 4.3021 | 4.1911 |
| | 14 | 8.8616 | 6.5149 | 5.5639 | 5.0354 | 4.6950 | 4.4558 | 4.2779 | 4.1399 | 4.0297 |
| | 15 | 8.6831 | 6.3589 | 5.4170 | 4.8932 | 4.5556 | 4.3183 | 4.1415 | 4.0045 | 3.8948 |
| | 16 | 8.5310 | 6.2262 | 5.2922 | 4.7726 | 4.4374 | 4.2016 | 4.0259 | 3.8896 | 3.7804 |
| | 17 | 8.3997 | 6.1121 | 5.1850 | 4.6690 | 43359 | 4.1015 | 3.9267 | 3.7910 | 3.6822 |
| | 18 | 8.2854 | 6.0129 | 5.0919 | 4.5790 | 4.2479 | 4.0146 | 3.8406 | 3.7054 | 3.5971 |
| | 19 | 8.1849 | 5.9259 | 5.0103 | 4.5003 | 4.1708 | 3.9386 | 3.7653 | 3.6305 | 3.5225 |
| | 20 | 8.0960 | 5.8489 | 4.9382 | 4.4307 | 4.1027 | 3.8714 | 3.6987 | 3.5644 | 3.4567 |
| | 21 | 8.0166 | 5.7804 | 4.8740 | 4.3688 | 4.0421 | 3.8117 | 3.6396 | 3.5056 | 3.3981 |
| | 22 | 7.9454 | 5.7190 | 4.8166 | 4.3134 | 3.9880 | 3.7583 | 3.5867 | 3.4530 | 3.3458 |
| | 23 | 7.8811 | 5.6637 | 4.7649 | 4.2636 | 3.9392 | 3.7102 | 3.5390 | 3.4057 | 3.2986 |
| | 24 | 7.8229 | 5.6136 | 4.7181 | 4.2184 | 3.8951 | 3.6667 | 3.4959 | 3.3629 | 3.2560 |
| | 25 | 7.7698 | 5.5680 | 4.6755 | 4.1774 | 3.8550 | 3.6272 | 3.4568 | 3.3239 | 3.2172 |
| | 26 | 7.7213 | 5.5263 | 4.6366 | 4.1400 | 3.8183 | 3.5911 | 3.4210 | 3.2884 | 3.1818 |
| | 27 | 7.6767 | 5.4881 | 4.6009 | 4.1056 | 3.7848 | 3.5580 | 3.3882 | 3.2558 | 3.1494 |
| | 28 | 7.6356 | 5.4529 | 4.5681 | 4.0740 | 3.7539 | 3.5276 | 3.3581 | 3.2259 | 3.1195 |
| | 29 | 7.5977 | 5.4204 | 4.5378 | 4.0449 | 3.7254 | 3.4995 | 3.3303 | 3.1982 | 3.0920 |
| | 30 | 7.5625 | 5.3903 | 4.5097 | 4.0179 | 3.6990 | 3.4735 | 3.3045 | 3.1726 | 3.0665 |
| | 40 | 7.3141 | 5.1785 | 4.3126 | 3.8283 | 3.5138 | 3.2910 | 3.1238 | 2.9930 | 2.8876 |
| | 60 | 7.0771 | 4.9774 | 4.1259 | 3.6490 | 3.3389 | 3.1187 | 2.9530 | 2.8233 | 2.7185 |
| | 120 | 6.8509 | 4.7865 | 3.9491 | 3.4795 | 3.1735 | 2.9559 | 2.7918 | 2.6629 | 2.5586 |
| | ∞ | 6.6349 | 4.6052 | 3.7816 | 3.3192 | 30173 | 2.8020 | 2.6393 | 2.5113 | 2.4073 |

Denominator Degrees of Freedom

## Table B.5b  The *F* Distribution ($\alpha = 0.05$ in the Right Tail)

| df (within) \ df (between) | Numerator Degrees of Freedom | | | | | | | | | |
|---|---|---|---|---|---|---|---|---|---|---|
| | 10 | 12 | 15 | 20 | 24 | 30 | 40 | 60 | 120 | ∞ |
| 1 | 241.88 | 243.91 | 245.95 | 248.01 | 249.05 | 250.10 | 251.14 | 252.20 | 253.25 | 254.31 |
| 2 | 19.396 | 19.413 | 19.429 | 19.446 | 19.454 | 19.462 | 19.471 | 19.479 | 19.487 | 19.496 |
| 3 | 8.7855 | 8.7446 | 8.7029 | 8.6602 | 8.6385 | 8.6166 | 8.5944 | 8.5720 | 8.5494 | 8.5264 |
| 4 | 5.9644 | 5.9117 | 5.8578 | 5.8025 | 5.7744 | 5.7459 | 5.7170 | 5.6877 | 5.6581 | 5.6281 |
| 5 | 4.7351 | 4.6777 | 4.6188 | 4.5581 | 4.5272 | 4.4957 | 4.4638 | 4.4314 | 4.3985 | 4.3650 |
| 6 | 4.0600 | 3.9999 | 3.9381 | 3.8742 | 3.8415 | 3.8082 | 3.7743 | 3.7398 | 3.7047 | 3.6689 |
| 7 | 3.6365 | 3.5747 | 3.5107 | 3.4445 | 3.4105 | 3.1758 | 3.3404 | 3.3043 | 3.2674 | 3.2298 |
| 8 | 3.3472 | 3.2839 | 3.2184 | 3.1503 | 3.1152 | 3.0794 | 3.0428 | 3.0053 | 2.9669 | 2.9276 |
| 9 | 3.1373 | 3.0729 | 3.0061 | 2.9365 | 2.9005 | 2.8617 | 2.8259 | 2.7872 | 2.7475 | 2.7067 |
| 10 | 2.9782 | 2.9110 | 2.8450 | 2.7740 | 2.7372 | 2.6996 | 2.6609 | 2.6211 | 2.5801 | 2.5379 |
| 11 | 2.8536 | 2.7876 | 2.7186 | 2.6464 | 2.6090 | 2.5705 | 2.5309 | 2.4901 | 2.4480 | 2.4045 |
| 12 | 2.7534 | 2.6866 | 2.6169 | 2.5436 | 2.5055 | 2.4663 | 2.4259 | 2.3842 | 2.3410 | 2.2962 |
| 13 | 2.6710 | 2.6037 | 2.5331 | 2.4589 | 2.4202 | 2.1801 | 2.3392 | 2.2966 | 2.2524 | 2.2064 |
| 14 | 2.6022 | 2.5342 | 2.4630 | 2.3879 | 2.3487 | 2.1082 | 2.2664 | 2.2229 | 2.1778 | 2.1307 |
| 15 | 2.5437 | 2.4753 | 2.4034 | 2.3275 | 2.2878 | 2.2468 | 2.2043 | 2.1601 | 2.1141 | 2.0658 |
| 16 | 2.4935 | 2.4247 | 2.3522 | 2.2756 | 2.2354 | 2.1938 | 2.1507 | 2.1058 | 2.0589 | 2.0096 |
| 17 | 2.4499 | 2.3807 | 2.3077 | 2.2304 | 2.1898 | 2.1477 | 2.1040 | 2.0584 | 2.0107 | 1.9604 |
| 18 | 2.4117 | 2.3421 | 2.2686 | 2.1906 | 2.1497 | 2.1071 | 2.0629 | 2.0166 | 1.9681 | 1.9168 |
| 19 | 2.3779 | 2.3080 | 2.2341 | 2.1555 | 2.1141 | 2.0712 | 2.0264 | 1.9795 | 1.9302 | 1.8780 |
| 20 | 2.3479 | 2.2776 | 2.2033 | 2.1242 | 2.0825 | 2.0391 | 1.9938 | 1.9464 | 1.8963 | 1.8432 |
| 21 | 2.3210 | 2.2504 | 2.1757 | 2.0960 | 2.0540 | 2.0102 | 1.9645 | 1.9165 | 1.8657 | 1.8117 |
| 22 | 2.2967 | 2.2258 | 2.1508 | 2.0707 | 2.0283 | 1.9842 | 1.9380 | 1.8894 | 1.8380 | 1.7831 |
| 23 | 2.2747 | 2.2036 | 2.1282 | 2.0476 | 2.0050 | 1.9605 | 1.9139 | 1.8648 | 1.8128 | 1.7570 |
| 24 | 2.2547 | 2.1834 | 2.1077 | 2.0267 | 1.9838 | 1.9390 | 1.8920 | 1.8424 | 1.7896 | 1.7330 |
| 25 | 2.2365 | 2.1649 | 2.0889 | 2.0075 | 1.9643 | 1.9192 | 1.8718 | 1.8217 | 1.7684 | 1.7110 |
| 26 | 2.2197 | 2.1479 | 2.0716 | 1.9898 | 1.9464 | 1.9010 | 1.8533 | 1.8027 | 1.7488 | 1.6906 |
| 27 | 2.2043 | 2.1323 | 20558 | 1.9736 | 1.9299 | 1.8842 | 1.8361 | 1.7851 | 1.7306 | 1.6717 |
| 28 | 2.1900 | 2.1179 | 2.0411 | 1.9586 | 1.9147 | 1.8687 | 1.8203 | 1.7689 | 1.7138 | 1.6541 |
| 29 | 2.1768 | 2.1045 | 2.0275 | 1.9446 | 1.9005 | 1.8543 | 1.8055 | 1.7537 | 1.6981 | 1.6376 |
| 30 | 2.1646 | 2.0921 | 2.0148 | 1.9317 | 1.8874 | 1.8409 | 1.7918 | 1.7396 | 1.6835 | 1.6223 |
| 40 | 2.0772 | 2.0035 | 1.9245 | 1.8389 | 1.7929 | 1.7444 | 1.6928 | 1.6373 | 1.5766 | 1.5089 |
| 60 | 1.9926 | 1.9174 | 1.8364 | 1.7480 | 1.7001 | 1.6491 | 1.5943 | 1.5343 | 1.4673 | 1.3893 |
| 120 | 1.9105 | 1.8337 | 1.7505 | 1.6587 | I.6084 | 1.5543 | 1.4952 | 1.4290 | 1.3519 | 1.2539 |
| ∞ | 1.8307 | 1.7522 | 1.6664 | 1.5705 | 1.5173 | 1.4591 | 1.3940 | 1.3180 | 1.2214 | 1.0000 |

## Table B.6  The Studentized Range Statistic, $q$

q Value When Alpha = .05

| df (within) | k = 2 | 3 | 4 | 5 | 6 | 7 | 8 | 9 | 10 | 11 | 12 | 13 | 14 | 15 | 16 | 17 | 18 | 19 | 20 |
|---|---|---|---|---|---|---|---|---|---|---|---|---|---|---|---|---|---|---|---|
| 1 | 18.0 | 27.0 | 32.8 | 37.1 | 40.4 | 43.1 | 45.4 | 47.4 | 49.1 | 50.6 | 52.0 | 53.2 | 54.3 | 55.4 | 56.3 | 57.2 | 58.0 | 58.8 | 59.6 |
| 2 | 6.09 | 8.3 | 9.8 | 10.9 | 11.7 | 12.4 | 13.0 | 13.5 | 14.0 | 14.4 | 14.7 | 15.1 | 15.4 | 15.7 | 15.9 | 16.1 | 16.4 | 16.6 | 16.8 |
| 3 | 4.50 | 5.91 | 6.82 | 7.50 | 8.04 | 8.48 | 8.85 | 9.18 | 9.46 | 9.72 | 9.95 | 10.15 | 10.35 | 10.52 | 10.69 | 10.84 | 10.98 | 11.11 | 11.24 |
| 4 | 3.93 | 5.04 | 5.76 | 6.29 | 6.71 | 7.05 | 7.35 | 7.60 | 7.83 | 8.03 | 8.21 | 8.37 | 8.52 | 8.66 | 8.79 | 8.91 | 9.03 | 9.13 | 9.23 |
| 5 | 3.64 | 4.60 | 5.22 | 5.67 | 6.03 | 6.33 | 6.58 | 6.80 | 6.99 | 7.17 | 7.32 | 7.47 | 7.60 | 7.72 | 7.83 | 7.93 | 8.03 | 8.12 | 8.21 |
| 6 | 3.46 | 4.34 | 4.90 | 5.31 | 5.63 | 5.89 | 6.12 | 6.32 | 6.49 | 6.65 | 6.79 | 6.92 | 7.03 | 7.14 | 7.24 | 7.34 | 7.43 | 7.51 | 7.59 |
| 7 | 3.34 | 4.16 | 4.68 | 5.06 | 5.36 | 5.61 | 5.82 | 6.00 | 6.16 | 6.30 | 6.43 | 6.55 | 6.66 | 6.76 | 6.85 | 6.94 | 7.02 | 7.09 | 7.17 |
| 8 | 3.26 | 4.04 | 4.53 | 4.89 | 5.17 | 5.40 | 5.60 | 5.77 | 5.92 | 6.05 | 6.18 | 6.29 | 6.39 | 6.48 | 6.57 | 6.65 | 6.73 | 6.80 | 6.87 |
| 9 | 3.20 | 3.95 | 4.42 | 4.76 | 5.02 | 5.24 | 5.43 | 5.60 | 5.74 | 5.87 | 5.98 | 6.09 | 6.19 | 6.28 | 6.36 | 6.44 | 6.51 | 6.58 | 6.64 |
| 10 | 3.15 | 3.88 | 4.33 | 4.65 | 4.91 | 5.12 | 5.30 | 5.46 | 5.60 | 5.72 | 5.83 | 5.93 | 6.03 | 6.11 | 6.20 | 6.27 | 6.34 | 6.40 | 6.47 |
| 11 | 3.11 | 3.82 | 4.26 | 4.57 | 4.82 | 5.03 | 5.20 | 5.35 | 5.49 | 5.61 | 5.71 | 5.81 | 5.90 | 5.99 | 6.06 | 6.14 | 6.20 | 6.26 | 6.33 |
| 12 | 3.08 | 3.77 | 4.20 | 4.51 | 4.75 | 4.95 | 5.12 | 5.27 | 5.40 | 5.51 | 5.62 | 5.71 | 5.80 | 5.88 | 5.95 | 6.03 | 6.09 | 6.15 | 6.21 |
| 13 | 3.06 | 3.73 | 4.15 | 4.45 | 4.69 | 4.88 | 5.05 | 5.19 | 5.32 | 5.43 | 5.53 | 5.63 | 5.71 | 5.79 | 5.86 | 5.93 | 6.00 | 6.05 | 6.11 |
| 14 | 3.03 | 3.70 | 4.11 | 4.41 | 4.64 | 4.83 | 4.99 | 5.13 | 5.25 | 5.36 | 5.46 | 5.55 | 5.64 | 5.72 | 5.79 | 5.85 | 5.92 | 5.97 | 6.03 |
| 15 | 3.01 | 3.67 | 4.08 | 4.37 | 4.60 | 4.78 | 4.94 | 5.08 | 5.20 | 5.31 | 5.40 | 5.49 | 5.58 | 5.65 | 5.72 | 5.79 | 5.85 | 5.90 | 5.96 |
| 16 | 3.00 | 3.65 | 4.05 | 4.33 | 4.56 | 4.74 | 4.90 | 5.03 | 5.15 | 5.26 | 5.35 | 5.44 | 5.52 | 5.59 | 5.66 | 5.72 | 5.79 | 5.84 | 5.90 |
| 17 | 2.98 | 3.63 | 4.02 | 4.30 | 4.52 | 4.71 | 4.86 | 4.99 | 5.11 | 5.21 | 5.31 | 5.39 | 5.47 | 5.55 | 5.61 | 5.68 | 5.74 | 5.79 | 5.84 |
| 18 | 2.97 | 3.61 | 4.00 | 4.28 | 4.49 | 4.67 | 4.82 | 4.96 | 5.07 | 5.17 | 5.27 | 5.35 | 5.43 | 5.50 | 5.57 | 5.63 | 5.69 | 5.74 | 5.79 |
| 19 | 2.96 | 3.59 | 3.98 | 4.25 | 4.47 | 4.65 | 4.79 | 4.92 | 5.04 | 5.14 | 5.23 | 5.32 | 5.39 | 5.46 | 5.53 | 5.59 | 5.65 | 5.70 | 5.75 |
| 20 | 2.95 | 3.58 | 3.96 | 4.23 | 4.45 | 4.62 | 4.77 | 4.90 | 5.01 | 5.11 | 5.20 | 5.28 | 5.36 | 5.43 | 5.49 | 5.55 | 5.61 | 5.66 | 5.71 |
| 24 | 2.92 | 3.53 | 3.90 | 4.17 | 4.37 | 4.54 | 4.68 | 4.81 | 4.92 | 5.01 | 5.10 | 5.18 | 5.25 | 5.32 | 5.38 | 5.44 | 5.50 | 5.54 | 5.59 |
| 30 | 2.89 | 3.49 | 3.84 | 4.10 | 4.30 | 4.46 | 4.60 | 4.72 | 4.83 | 4.92 | 5.00 | 5.08 | 5.15 | 5.21 | 5.27 | 5.33 | 5.38 | 5.43 | 5.48 |
| 40 | 2.86 | 3.44 | 3.79 | 4.04 | 4.23 | 4.39 | 4.52 | 4.63 | 4.74 | 4.82 | 4.91 | 4.98 | 5.05 | 5.11 | 5.16 | 5.22 | 5.27 | 5.31 | 5.36 |
| 60 | 2.83 | 3.40 | 3.74 | 3.98 | 4.16 | 4.31 | 4.44 | 4.55 | 4.65 | 4.73 | 4.81 | 4.88 | 4.94 | 5.00 | 5.06 | 5.11 | 5.16 | 5.20 | 5.24 |
| 120 | 2.80 | 3.36 | 3.69 | 3.92 | 4.10 | 4.24 | 4.36 | 4.48 | 4.56 | 4.64 | 4.72 | 4.78 | 4.84 | 4.90 | 4.95 | 5.00 | 5.05 | 5.09 | 5.13 |
| ∞ | 2.77 | 3.31 | 3.63 | 3.86 | 4.03 | 4.17 | 4.29 | 4.39 | 4.47 | 4.55 | 4.62 | 4.68 | 4.74 | 4.80 | 4.85 | 4.89 | 4.93 | 4.97 | 5.01 |

(Continued)

**Table B.6** (Continued)

q Value When Alpha = .01

| df (within) | k=2 | 3 | 4 | 5 | 6 | 7 | 8 | 9 | 10 | 11 | 12 | 13 | 14 | 15 | 16 | 17 | 18 | 19 | 20 |
|---|---|---|---|---|---|---|---|---|---|---|---|---|---|---|---|---|---|---|---|
| 1 | 90.0 | 135 | 164 | 186 | 202 | 216 | 227 | 237 | 246 | 253 | 260 | 266 | 272 | 277 | 282 | 286 | 290 | 294 | 298 |
| 2 | 14.0 | 19.0 | 22.3 | 24.7 | 26.6 | 28.2 | 29.5 | 30.7 | 31.7 | 32.6 | 33.4 | 34.1 | 34.8 | 35.4 | 36.0 | 36.5 | 37.0 | 37.5 | 37.9 |
| 3 | 8.26 | 10.6 | 12.2 | 13.3 | 14.2 | 15.0 | 15.6 | 16.2 | 16.7 | 17.1 | 17.5 | 17.9 | 18.2 | 18.5 | 18.8 | 19.1 | 19.3 | 19.5 | 19.8 |
| 4 | 6.51 | 8.12 | 9.17 | 9.96 | 10.6 | 11.1 | 11.5 | 11.9 | 12.3 | 12.6 | 12.8 | 13.1 | 13.3 | 13.5 | 13.7 | 13.9 | 14.1 | 14.2 | 14.4 |
| 5 | 5.70 | 6.97 | 7.80 | 8.42 | 8.91 | 9.32 | 9.67 | 9.97 | 10.24 | 10.48 | 10.70 | 10.89 | 11.08 | 11.24 | 11.40 | 11.55 | 11.68 | 11.81 | 11.93 |
| 6 | 5.24 | 6.33 | 7.03 | 7.56 | 7.97 | 8.32 | 8.61 | 8.87 | 9.10 | 9.30 | 9.49 | 9.65 | 9.81 | 9.95 | 10.08 | 10.21 | 10.32 | 10.43 | 10.54 |
| 7 | 4.95 | 5.92 | 6.54 | 7.01 | 7.37 | 7.68 | 7.94 | 8.17 | 8.37 | 8.55 | 8.71 | 8.86 | 9.00 | 9.12 | 9.24 | 9.35 | 9.46 | 9.55 | 9.65 |
| 8 | 4.74 | 5.63 | 6.20 | 6.63 | 6.96 | 7.24 | 7.47 | 7.68 | 7.87 | 8.03 | 8.18 | 8.31 | 8.44 | 8.55 | 8.66 | 8.76 | 8.85 | 8.94 | 9.03 |
| 9 | 4.60 | 5.43 | 5.96 | 6.35 | 6.66 | 6.91 | 7.13 | 7.32 | 7.49 | 7.65 | 7.78 | 7.91 | 8.03 | 8.13 | 8.23 | 8.32 | 8.41 | 8.49 | 8.57 |
| 10 | 4.48 | 5.27 | 5.77 | 6.14 | 6.43 | 6.67 | 6.87 | 7.05 | 7.21 | 7.36 | 7.48 | 7.60 | 7.71 | 7.81 | 7.91 | 7.99 | 8.07 | 8.15 | 8.22 |
| 11 | 4.39 | 5.14 | 5.62 | 5.97 | 6.25 | 6.48 | 6.67 | 6.84 | 6.99 | 7.13 | 7.25 | 7.36 | 7.46 | 7.56 | 7.65 | 7.73 | 7.81 | 7.88 | 7.95 |
| 12 | 4.32 | 5.04 | 5.50 | 5.84 | 6.10 | 6.32 | 6.51 | 6.67 | 6.81 | 6.94 | 7.06 | 7.17 | 7.26 | 7.36 | 7.44 | 7.52 | 7.59 | 7.66 | 7.73 |
| 13 | 4.26 | 4.96 | 5.40 | 5.73 | 5.98 | 6.19 | 6.37 | 6.53 | 6.67 | 6.79 | 6.90 | 7.01 | 7.10 | 7.19 | 7.27 | 7.34 | 7.42 | 7.48 | 7.55 |
| 14 | 4.21 | 4.89 | 5.32 | 5.63 | 5.88 | 6.08 | 6.26 | 6.41 | 6.54 | 6.66 | 6.77 | 6.87 | 6.96 | 7.05 | 7.12 | 7.20 | 7.27 | 7.33 | 7.39 |
| 15 | 4.17 | 4.83 | 5.25 | 5.56 | 5.80 | 5.99 | 6.16 | 6.31 | 6.44 | 6.55 | 6.66 | 6.76 | 6.84 | 6.93 | 7.00 | 7.07 | 7.14 | 7.20 | 7.26 |
| 16 | 4.13 | 4.78 | 5.19 | 5.49 | 5.72 | 5.92 | 6.08 | 6.22 | 6.35 | 6.46 | 6.56 | 6.66 | 6.74 | 6.82 | 6.90 | 6.97 | 7.03 | 7.09 | 7.15 |
| 17 | 4.10 | 4.74 | 5.14 | 5.43 | 5.66 | 5.85 | 6.01 | 6.15 | 6.27 | 6.38 | 6.48 | 6.57 | 6.66 | 6.73 | 6.80 | 6.87 | 6.94 | 7.00 | 7.05 |
| 18 | 4.07 | 4.70 | 5.09 | 5.38 | 5.60 | 5.79 | 5.94 | 6.08 | 6.20 | 6.31 | 6.41 | 6.50 | 6.58 | 6.65 | 6.72 | 6.79 | 6.85 | 6.91 | 6.96 |
| 19 | 4.05 | 4.67 | 5.05 | 5.33 | 5.55 | 5.73 | 5.89 | 6.02 | 6.14 | 6.25 | 6.34 | 6.43 | 6.51 | 6.58 | 6.65 | 6.72 | 6.78 | 6.84 | 6.89 |
| 24 | 3.96 | 4.54 | 4.91 | 5.17 | 5.37 | 5.54 | 5.69 | 5.81 | 5.92 | 6.02 | 6.11 | 6.19 | 6.26 | 6.33 | 6.39 | 6.45 | 6.51 | 6.56 | 6.61 |
| 30 | 3.89 | 4.45 | 4.80 | 5.05 | 5.24 | 5.40 | 5.54 | 5.65 | 5.76 | 5.85 | 5.93 | 6.01 | 6.08 | 6.14 | 6.20 | 6.26 | 6.31 | 6.36 | 6.41 |
| 40 | 3.82 | 4.37 | 4.70 | 4.93 | 5.11 | 5.27 | 5.39 | 5.50 | 5.60 | 5.69 | 5.77 | 5.84 | 5.90 | 5.96 | 6.02 | 6.07 | 6.12 | 6.17 | 6.21 |
| 60 | 3.76 | 4.28 | 4.60 | 4.82 | 4.99 | 5.13 | 5.25 | 5.36 | 5.45 | 5.53 | 5.60 | 5.67 | 5.73 | 5.79 | 5.84 | 5.89 | 5.93 | 5.98 | 6.02 |
| 120 | 3.70 | 4.20 | 4.50 | 4.71 | 4.87 | 5.01 | 5.12 | 5.21 | 5.30 | 5.38 | 5.44 | 5.51 | 5.56 | 5.61 | 5.66 | 5.71 | 5.75 | 5.79 | 5.83 |
| ∞ | 3.64 | 4.12 | 4.40 | 4.60 | 4.76 | 4.88 | 4.99 | 5.08 | 5.16 | 5.23 | 5.29 | 5.35 | 5.40 | 5.45 | 5.49 | 5.54 | 5.57 | 5.61 | 5.65 |

*Source:* H. L. Hartner "Table of Range and Studentized Range." *The Annuals of Mathematical Statistics.* Vol. 31. 31. No. 4. 1960. Reprinted with permission from the Institute of Mathematical Statistics.

# Appendix C

## Solutions for Odd-Numbered Practice Problems

### ▣ Chapter 1

1. If a systematic random sample is selected using a list that is not ordered in any way, the results should be similar to a sample selected using a simple random sample.

3. The goal in obtaining or selecting a sample is to select it in a way that increases the chances of this sample being representative of the entire population. Using probability sampling techniques not only serves to minimize any potential bias we may have when selecting a sample, thereby making our sample more representative of the population, but also it allows us to gain access to probability theory in our data analysis. This body of mathematical theory allows us to estimate more accurately the degree of error we have when generalizing results obtained from known sample statistics to unknown population parameters.

5. We could use the probability sampling technique of selecting a weighted sample or the nonprobability sampling technique of quota sampling.

7. Nonprobability samples are appropriate when we want to sample a unique population, such as gang members or other deviant individuals, who are not available from some population list. Purposive/judgment samples and snowball samples are often used in these cases. In addition, if your research is exploratory in nature, it is appropriate to use a nonprobability sample.

### ▣ Chapter 2

1. a. Quantitative; Interval/Ratio; b. Quantitative; interval/ratio; c. Quantitative; interval/ratio; d. Qualitative; nominal; e. Qualitative; nominal; f. Quantitative; interval/ratio.

3. Arrest is the independent variable, and future drunk-driving behavior is the dependent variable.

5. The numerator would be the number of victimizations against people 14–18 years old, and the denominator would be the total population of people 14–18 years old.

7.

|  | f | Proportion | % |
|---|---|---|---|
| Less than $10 | 16 | 0.029 | 2.9 |
| $10–$49 | 39 | 0.072 | 7.2 |
| $50–$99 | 48 | 0.088 | 8.8 |
| $100–$249 | 86 | 0.159 | 15.9 |
| $250–$999 | 102 | 0.188 | 18.8 |
| $1,000 or more | 251 | 0.463 | 46.3 |
|  | n = 542 |  |  |

9. The units of analysis are states. The independent variable would likely be unemployment, and the dependent variable would be crime.

## Chapter 3

1. The first grouped frequency distribution is not a very good one for a number of reasons. First, the interval widths are not all the same size. Second, the class intervals are not mutually exclusive. A score of 10 could go into either the second or the third class interval. Third, the first class interval is empty; it has a frequency of zero. Fourth, there are too few class intervals; the data are "bunched up" into only three intervals, and you do not get a very good sense of the distribution of these scores. The second grouped frequency distribution avoids all of these four problems.

3. a. "Self-reported drug use" is measured at the ordinal level because our values consist of rank-ordered categories. We do not have interval/ratio-level measurement because although we can state that someone who reported using drugs "a lot" used drugs more frequently than someone who reported "never" using drugs, we do not know exactly how much more frequently.

   b. Since there were 30 students who reported "never" using, 150 – 30, or 120, must have been using drugs at some level of frequency. The ratio of users to nonusers, then, is 120 / 30, or 4 to 1.

   c. 35 / 10, or 3.5 to 1.

   d. The first thing we would want to do is arrange the data in some order. Since we have ordinal-level data, we can order the categories in ascending or descending order.

| Value | f | P | % |
|---|---|---|---|
| Never | 30 | .2000 | 20.00 |
| A few times | 75 | .5000 | 50.00 |
| More than a few times | 35 | .2333 | 23.33 |
| A lot | 10 | .0667 | 6.67 |

   e. Since the proportion of nonusers ("never") was .20, the proportion of respondents who reported using drugs must be 1 – .20, or .80. Another way to determine this is to determine the relative frequency of users (75 + 35 + 10) / 150 = 120 / 150 = .80.

   f. .0667 of the respondents reported using drugs "a lot."

5. a.

| Value | f | cf | P | cP | % | c% |
|---|---|---|---|---|---|---|
| 10 | 5 | 5 | .20 | .20 | 20 | 20 |
| 11 | 3 | 8 | .12 | .32 | 12 | 32 |
| 12 | 0 | 8 | .00 | .32 | 0 | 32 |
| 13 | 2 | 10 | .08 | .40 | 8 | 40 |
| 14 | 2 | 12 | .08 | .48 | 8 | 48 |
| 15 | 7 | 19 | .28 | .76 | 28 | 76 |
| 16 | 3 | 22 | .12 | .88 | 12 | 88 |
| 17 | 0 | 22 | .00 | .88 | 0 | 88 |
| 18 | 0 | 22 | .00 | .88 | 0 | 88 |
| 19 | 1 | 23 | .04 | .92 | 4 | 92 |
| 20 | 2 | 25 | .08 | 1.00 | 8 | 100 |

   b.

| Value | f | P | % |
|---|---|---|---|
| Male | 16 | .64 | 64 |
| Female | 9 | .36 | 36 |

   c. By using the cumulative frequency column, we can determine that 10 recruits scored 13 or lower on the exam. That means that 25 – 10, or 15, recruits must have scored 14 or higher, so 15 recruits passed the exam. Since 15 / 25 = .60, we can calculate that 60% of the recruits passed the test. We could also have used the cumulative percentage column to find this answer. By using the cumulative percentage column, we can determine that 40% of the recruits scored 13 or lower on the exam. This means that 100% – 40%, or 60%, of the recruits must have scored 14 or higher and passed the exam.

   d. Three of the 25 recruits, or .12 of the total (3 / 25), received a score of 18 or higher on the exam and "passed with honors."

e. By using the cumulative frequency column, we can easily see that 10 recruits received a score of 13 or lower on the exam.

f. In this class of recruits, .64 were male and .36 were female.

g. The test scores would have to be graphed with a histogram since the data are quantitative and would look as follows:

**Distribution of Test Scores for Recruit Class**

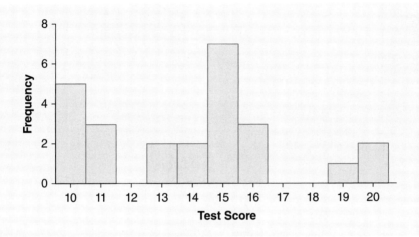

A pie chart of the percentages for the gender data would look as follows:

**Gender Distribution of Recruit Class**

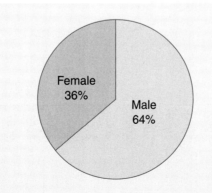

h. A cumulative frequency distribution for the test scores would look as follows:

**Cumulative Frequency Line Graph for Test Score Data**

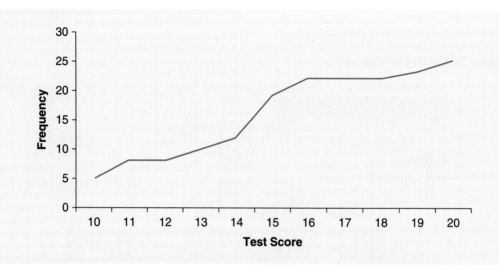

7. A time plot of the property crime victimization data from the NCVS over the time period 1973–2013 would look as follows:

**Time Plot of NCVS Property Crime Victimization Rates per 1,000 Households**

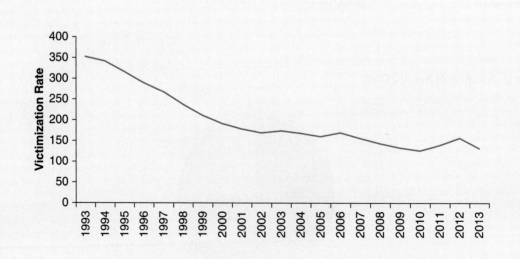

The time plot shows a fairly consistent downward trend in the property crime victimization rate for the duration of the period. The sharpest decline is during the 1990s. Beginning in 2001, there was a leveling off of the rate of property victimizations until 2006. After which, there was another consistent decline in the property victimization rate until 2010 when there was a short increase before a final drop resulted in a property victimization rate in 2013 that was approximately 37% of what it was in 1993.

| Year | Original Number of Arrests | Smoothed Number |
| --- | --- | --- |
| 1994 | 117,300 | 117,300 |
| 1995 | 116,200 | 113,300 |
| 1996 | 106,400 | 104,967 |
| 1997 | 92,300 | 95,200 |
| 1998 | 86,900 | 86,133 |
| 1999 | 79,200 | 81,567 |

| Year | Original Number of Arrests | Smoothed Number |
| --- | --- | --- |
| 2000 | 78,600 | 79,900 |
| 2001 | 81,900 | 80,567 |
| 2002 | 81,200 | 81,800 |
| 2003 | 82,300 | 82,400 |
| 2004 | 83,700 | 83,867 |
| 2005 | 85,600 | 86,700 |
| 2006 | 90,800 | 89,600 |
| 2007 | 92,400 | 92,467 |
| 2008 | 94,200 | 93,867 |
| 2009 | 95,000 | 91,433 |
| 2010 | 85,100 | 87,667 |
| 2011 | 82,900 | 83,400 |
| 2012 | 82,200 | 82,200 |

**Estimated Number of Arrests of Adults for Robberies**

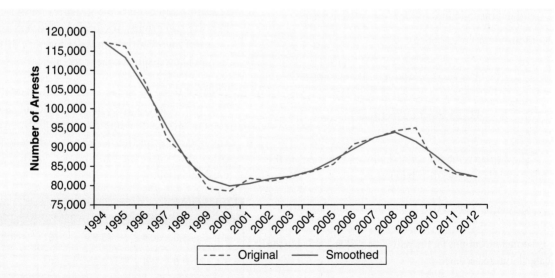

# Chapter 4

1. The mode for these data is "some friends" because this value appears more often than any other value ($f = 85$). The mode tells us that in our sample, more youths reported having "some" delinquent friends than any other possible response. We could not calculate a mean with these data because this variable is measured at the ordinal level, and the mean requires data measured at the interval/ratio level. For example, although we can say that a person with "some" delinquent friends has more delinquent friends than a person with "none," we do not know exactly how many more (1? 2? 10?). Without this knowledge, we cannot calculate the mean as a measure of central tendency.

3. The best measure of central tendency for these data is probably the median. The mean would not be the best in this case because it would be inflated by the presence of a positive outlier. New Orleans, Louisiana, with a homicide rate of 43.3 per 100,000, has a homicide rate substantially higher than the other cities. When New Orleans is included in the data, the mean is equal to 10.62 homicides per 100,000, and the median is 7.25.

5. The most appropriate measure of central tendency for these data is the mode because the data are measured at the nominal level. The modal, or most frequent, reason for requesting the police when the subject was without mental illness is for a "potential offense."

7. Mean number of executions:

$$\bar{X} = \frac{42 + 37 + 52 + 46 + 43 + 43 + 39 + 35}{8}$$

$$\bar{X} = 42.125 \text{ exeutions per year}$$

The median is the average of the 4th and 5th years in the rank-ordered frequency distribution:

$$\text{Median} = (42 + 43)/2 = 42.5 \text{ executions per year}$$

When executions for the year 2006 (53) are added to the data, the mean becomes:

$$\bar{X} = \frac{390}{9} = 43.33 \text{ exeutions per year}$$

The median remains the same, and the mean is increased slightly. Since they are both relatively similar, both would be appropriate measures of center.

9. The mean is equal to:

$$\bar{X} = \frac{1200}{20}$$

$$\bar{X} = 60 \text{ beats per minunte}$$

The median is equal to 60.5 beats per minute.

The mean and the median are very comparable with one another. This suggests that there are no or few extreme (outlying) scores in the data and that the data are not skewed.

# Chapter 5

1. Measures of central tendency capture the most "typical" score in a distribution of scores (the most common, the score in the middle of the ranked distribution, or the average), whereas measures of dispersion capture the variability in our scores, or how they are different from each other or different from the central tendency. It is important to report both central tendency and dispersion measures for our variables because two groups of scores may be very similar in terms of their central tendency but very different in terms of how dispersed the scores are.

3. The first thing we need to do is to calculate the mean. This problem will give you experience in calculating a mean for grouped data. You should find the mean equal to 8.6 prior thefts. We are now ready to do the calculations necessary to find the variance and standard deviation.

| $m_i$ | $m_i - \bar{X}$ | $(m_i - \bar{X})^2$ | $f$ | $f(m_i - \bar{X})^2$ |
|---|---|---|---|---|
| 2 | $2 - 8.6 = -6.6$ | 43.56 | 76 | 3,310.56 |
| 7 | $7 - 8.6 = -1.6$ | 2.56 | 52 | 133.12 |
| 12 | $12 - 8.6 = -3.4$ | 11.56 | 38 | 439.28 |
| 17 | $17 - 8.6 = 8.4$ | 70.56 | 21 | 1,481.76 |

| $m_i$ | $m_i - \bar{X}$ | $(m_i - \bar{X})^2$ | $f$ | $f(m_i - \bar{X})^2$ |
|---|---|---|---|---|
| 22 | $22 - 8.6 = 13.4$ | 179.56 | 10 | 1,795.60 |
| 27 | $27 - 8.6 = 18.4$ | 338.56 | 8 | 2,708.48 |
| | | | | $\Sigma = 9,868.80$ |

$$s^2 = \frac{9,868.80}{204}$$
$$s^2 = 48.38$$

The variance is equal to 48.38.

$$s = \sqrt{\frac{9,868.80}{204}}$$
$$s = 6.96$$

The standard deviation is equal to 6.95.

5. Let's calculate the variation ratio for each of the three years:

$$VR_{1980} = 1 - \frac{852}{1,723}$$
$$VR_{1980} = .50$$

$$VR_{1990} = 1 - \frac{979}{2,161}$$
$$VR_{1990} = .55$$

$$VR_{2000} = 1 - \frac{1,211}{3,202}$$
$$VR_{2000} = .62$$

$$VR_{2010} = 1 - \frac{1,300}{3,612}$$
$$VR_{2010} = .64$$

The variation ratio is consistently increasing from 1980 to 2010, which tells us that the dispersion in the nominal-level data is increasing. Practically, this says that the racial heterogeneity of the penitentiary is increasing over time.

7. Here are the summary statistics necessary to construct boxplots for the murder rates for states by region.

| South | |
|---|---|
| $N = 17$ | Higher outer fence = 13.9 |
| Mdn = 5.9 | High inner fence = 10.45 |
| $Q_1 = 4.7$ | Low inner fence = 1.25 |
| $Q_3 = 7$ | Lower outer fence = −2.2 |
| IQR = 2.3 | High adjacent value = 7.4 |
| | Low adjacent value = 3.8 |
| | mild outliers = 10.8 and 13.9 |

| West | |
|---|---|
| $N = 13$ | Higher outer fence = 10.8 |
| Mdn = 3 | High inner fence = 7.65 |
| $Q_1 = 2.4$ | Low inner fence = −.75 |
| $Q_3 = 4.5$ | Lower outer fence = −3.9 |
| IQR = 2.1 | High adjacent value = 5.6 |
| | Low adjacent value = 1.8 |

| Midwest | |
|---|---|
| $N = 12$ | Higher outer fence = 12.3 |
| Mdn = 3.5 | High inner fence = 8.775 |
| $Q_1 = 2.9$ | Low inner fence = −.625 |
| $Q_3 = 5.25$ | Lower outer fence = −4.15 |
| IQR = 2.35 | High adjacent value = 7 |
| | Low adjacent value = 1.5 |

| Northeast | |
|---|---|
| $N = 9$ | Higher outer fence = 11 |
| Mdn = 3.2 | High inner fence = 7.55 |
| $Q_1 = 1.8$ | Low inner fence = −1.65 |
| $Q_3 = 4.1$ | Lower outer fence = −5.1 |
| IQR = 2.3 | High adjacent value = 5.4 |
| | Low adjacent value = 1.1 |

Here are the boxplots by region:

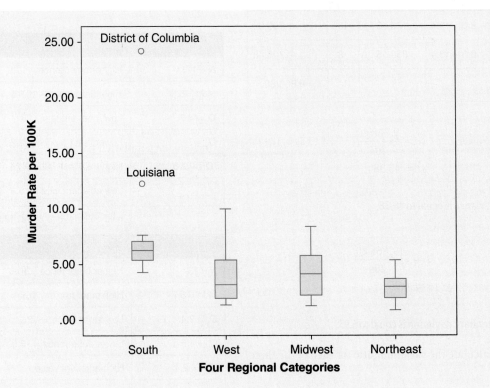

# 回 Chapter 6

1.  a.  $P(x = \$30,000) = 16 / 110 = .145$

    b.  $P(x = \$35,000) = 7 / 110 = .064$

    c.  Yes, they are mutually exclusive events because a person cannot simultaneously have a starting salary of both $30,000 and $35,000. There is no joint probability of these two events.

    d.  $P(x \geq \$31,000) = (19 / 110) + (12 / 110) + (15 / 110) + (8 / 110) + (7 / 110) = (61 / 110) = .555$

    e.  There are two ways to calculate this probability. First: $P(x \leq \$30,000) = (16 / 110) + (10 / 110) + (9 / 110) + (8 / 110) + (6 / 110) = (49 / 110) = .445$. Or you can recognize that this event is the complement of the event in problem d and calculate the probability as $1 - .555 = .445$.

    f.  $P(x = \$28,000$ or $\$30,000$ or $\$31,500$ or $\$32,000$ or $\$32,500) = (10 / 110) + (16 / 110) + (19 / 110) + (12 / 110) + (15 / 110) = (72 / 110) = .655$

    g.  $P(x < \$25,000) = 0$

    h.  $P(x = \$28,000$ or $\$32,000$ or $\$35,000) = (10 / 110) + (12 / 110) + (7 / 110) = (29 / 110) = .264$

3.  a.  $z = 1.5$

    b.  $z = -1.7$

    c.  $z = -3.0$

    d.  .0668, or slightly more than 6% of the cases, have an IQ score greater than 115.

    e.  .6832

    f.  A raw score of 70 corresponds to a $z$ score of $-3.0$. The probability of a $z$ score less than or equal to $-3.0$ is .001.

    g.  A raw score of 125 corresponds to a $z$ score of 2.5. The probability of a $z$ score greater than or equal to 2.5 is .006.

5.  a.  A raw score of 95 is better than .9332, or 93%, of the scores. It is not in the top 5%, however, so this candidate would not be accepted.

b. A raw score of 110 is better than .9987, or 99%, of the scores. It is in the top 5%, and this candidate would be accepted.

c. A z score of 1.65 or higher is better than 95% of the scores. The z score of 1.65 corresponds to a raw score of 96.5, and that is the minimum score you need to get accepted.

7. a. The area to the right of a z score of 1.65 is equal to .0495.

b. The area to the left of a z score of −1.65 is equal to .0495.

c. The area either to the left of a z score of −1.96 or to the right of a z score of 1.96 is equal to .025.

d. The area to the right of a z score of 2.33 is .0099.

9. a. To see how unusual 9 prior arrests are in this population, let's transform the raw score into a z score:

$$z = \frac{9-6}{2} = 1.50$$

Taking a z score of 1.50 to the z table, we can see that the area to the right of this score comprises approximately 7% of the area of the normal curve. Those who have 9 prior arrests, then, are in the top 7% of this population. Since they are not in the top 5%, we would not consider them unusual.

b. A raw score of 11 prior arrests corresponds to a z score of:

$$z = \frac{11-6}{2} = 2.50$$

A z score of 2.50 is way at the right or upper end of the distribution. z scores of 2.50 or greater are greater than approximately 99% of all the other scores. This person does have an unusually large number of prior arrests since he or she is in the top 5%.

c. A raw score of 2 prior arrests corresponds to a z score of:

$$z = \frac{2-6}{2} = -2.0$$

A z score of −2.0 falls lower than almost 98% of all the other scores. The person with only two prior arrests, then, does have an unusually low number for this population since he or she is in the bottom 5%.

# Chapter 7

1. The purpose of confidence intervals is to give us a range of values for our estimated population parameter, rather than a single value or a point estimate. The estimated confidence interval gives us a range of values within which we believe, with varying degrees of confidence, that the true population value falls. The advantage of providing a range of values for our estimate is that we will be more likely to include the population parameter. Think of trying to estimate your final exam score in this class. You are more likely to be accurate if you are able to estimate an interval within which your actual score will fall, such as "somewhere between 85 and 95," than if you have to give a single value as your estimate, such as "it will be an 89." Note that the wider you make your interval (consider "somewhere between 40 and 95"), the more accurate you are likely to be in that your exam score will probably fall within that very large interval. However, the price of this accuracy is precision; you are not being very precise in estimating that your final exam score will be between 40 and 95. In this case, you will be very confident but not very precise. Note also that the more narrow or precise your interval is, the less confident you may be about it. If you predicted that your final exam score would be between 90 and 95, you would be very precise. You would probably also be far less confident of this prediction than of the one where you stated your score would fall between 40 and 95. Other things (such as sample size) being equal, there is a trade-off between precision and confidence.

3.

$$95\% \text{ c.i.} = 4.5 \pm 1.96\left(\frac{3.2}{\sqrt{110}}\right)$$

$$95\% \text{ c.i.} = 4.5 \pm 1.96\left(\frac{3.2}{10.49}\right)$$

$$95\% \text{ c.i.} = 4.5 \pm 1.96(.31)$$

$$95\% \text{ c.i.} = 4.5 \pm .61$$

$$3.89 \leq \mu \leq 5.11$$

We are 95% confident that the mean level of marijuana use in our population of teenagers is between 3.89 times and 5.11 times a year. This means that if we were to take an infinite number of samples of size 110 from this population and estimate a confidence interval around the mean for each sample, 95% of those confidence intervals would contain the true population mean.

5. The standard deviation of the sampling distribution is the standard deviation of an infinite number of sample estimates [means $(\overline{X})$ or proportions $(p)$], each drawn from a sample with sample size equal to $n$. It is also called the standard error. The sample size affects the value of the standard error (see problems 3 and 4). At a fixed confidence level, increasing the sample size will reduce the size of the standard error and, consequently, the width of the confidence interval.

7. To find a 95% confidence interval around a sample mean of 560 with a standard deviation of 45 and a sample size of 15, you would have to go to the $t$ table. With $n = 15$, there are 14 degrees of freedom. Since confidence intervals are two-tailed problems, the value of $t$ you should obtain is 2.145. Now you can construct the confidence interval:

$$95\% \text{ c.i.} = 560 \pm 2.145\left(\frac{45}{\sqrt{15}}\right)$$

$$95\% \text{ c.i.} = 560 \pm 2.145\left(\frac{45}{3.87}\right)$$

$$95\% \text{ c.i.} = 560 \pm 2.145(11.63)$$

$$95\% \text{ c.i.} = 560 \pm 24.94$$

$$5365.06 \leq \mu \leq 584.94$$

You can say that you are 95% confident that the true police response time is between 535 seconds (almost 9 minutes) and 587 seconds (almost 10 minutes).

9. We would see that when we increased the confidence interval from a 95% to a 99% confidence interval, the width of the confidence interval would also increase. This is because being more confident that our estimated interval contains the true population parameter (99% confident as opposed to 95% confident) comes at the price of a wider interval (all other things being equal). You should remember, from the discussion in the chapter, that you can increase the level of your confidence without expanding the width of the interval by increasing your sample size.

## 📖 Chapter 8

1. The $z$ test and $z$ distribution may be used for making one-sample hypothesis tests involving a population mean under two conditions: (1) if the population standard deviation ($\sigma$) is known, and (2) if the sample size is large enough ($n \geq 30$) so that the sample standard deviation (s) can be used as an

unbiased estimate of the population standard deviation. If either of these two conditions is not met, hypothesis tests about one population mean must be conducted with the $t$ test and $t$ distribution.

3. The null and alternative hypotheses are:

$$H_0: \mu = 4.6$$
$$H_1: \mu < 4.6$$

Since our sample size is large ($n > 30$), we should use the $z$ test and $z$ distribution. With an alpha of .01 and a one-tailed test, our critical value of $z$ is 2.33. Our decision rule is to reject the null hypothesis if our obtained value of $z$ is 2.33 or greater (reject $H_0$ if $z_{obt} > 2.33$). The value of $z_{obt}$ is:

$$z_{obt} = \frac{6.3 - 4.6}{1.9/\sqrt{61}}$$
$$z_{obt} = \frac{1.7}{.243}$$
$$z_{obt} = 6.99$$

Because 6.99 is greater than the critical value of 2.33 and falls in the critical region, we will reject the null hypothesis that the population mean is equal to 4.6 times. Based on our sample data, we can conclude that the actual average number of times the average U.S. citizen cheated on taxes in the past 10 years is greater than 4.6 times.

5. The null and alternative hypotheses are:

$$H_0: \mu = 25.9$$
$$H_1: \mu \neq 25.9$$

The critical value of $z$ is $\pm 2.58$. The value of $z_{obt}$ is:

$$z_{obt} = \frac{27.3 - 25.9}{6.5/\sqrt{175}}$$
$$z_{obt} = \frac{1.40}{6.5/13.23}$$
$$z_{obt} = \frac{1.40}{.49}$$
$$= 2.86$$

Because this value is greater than the critical value of 2.58 and falls in the critical region, we reject the null hypothesis that the population mean is equal to 25.9 months.

7. The null and alternative hypotheses are:

$$H_0: \mu = 4$$

$$H_1: \mu > 4$$

With 11 degrees of freedom, an alpha of .01, and a one-tailed test, our critical value of $t$ is 2.718. Our decision rule is to reject the null hypothesis if our obtained value of $t > 2.718$. The value of $t_{obt}$ is:

$$t_{obt} = \frac{6.3 - 4}{1.5 / \sqrt{12}}$$

$$t_{obt} = \frac{2.30}{1.5 / 3.46}$$

$$t_{obt} = \frac{2.30}{.43}$$

$$= 5.35$$

Because this is greater than the critical value of 2.718 and falls in the critical region, we decide to reject the null hypothesis that the population mean is equal to four arrests. Based on our sample data, we will conclude that the number of arrests is higher in the population.

9. The null and alternative hypotheses are:

$$H_0: p = .45$$

$$H_1: p < .45$$

Because this is a problem involving a population proportion with a large sample size $(n = 200)$, we can use the $z$ test and the $z$ distribution. Our decision rule is to reject the null hypothesis if our obtained value of $z$ is −2.33 or less. The value of $z_{obt}$ is:

$$z_{obt} = \frac{.23 - .45}{\sqrt{\frac{.45(.55)}{200}}} = -6.25$$

Because our obtained value of $z$ is less than the critical value of −2.33 and falls in the critical region, we will reject the null hypothesis that the population proportion is equal to .45 or 45%. Based on our sample data, we can conclude that the percentage is lower.

11. The null and alternative hypotheses are:

$$H_0: p = .31$$

$$H_1: p > .31$$

Because this is a problem involving a population proportion with a large sample size $(n = 110)$, we can use the $z$ test

and the $z$ distribution. Our decision rule is to reject the null hypothesis if our obtained value of $z$ is 1.65 or greater. The value of $z_{obt}$ is:

$$z_{obt} = \frac{.46 - .31}{\sqrt{\frac{.31(.69)}{110}}} = 3.40$$

Because this is greater than the critical value of 1.65 and falls in the critical region, we will reject the null hypothesis that the population proportion is equal to .31 or 31%, and conclude, based on our sample data, that it is higher.

## ▣ Chapter 9

1. a. The type of institution is the independent variable, and satisfaction with one's job is the dependent variable.

   b. There are a total of 185 observations.

   c. There are 115 persons who were not satisfied with their job and 70 persons who reported that they were satisfied with their job.

   d. There were 45 people working in medium security institutions and 140 employed in maximum security institutions.

   e. This is a 2 × 2 contingency table.

   f. 30 correctional officers are in medium-security institutions and like their jobs.

   g. 100 correctional officers are in maximum-security institutions and do not like their jobs.

   h. There is $(2 - 1)(2 - 1)$ or 1 degree of freedom.

   i. The risk of not being satisfied with your job is:

$$.33\left(\frac{15}{45}\right)$$

in medium-security institutions and:

$$.71\left(\frac{100}{140}\right)$$

in maximum-security institutions.

It looks as if the type of institution one works in is related to one's job satisfaction. Officers are far more likely to be dissatisfied with their job if they work in a maximum-security facility than if they work in a medium-security facility.

j. **Step 1:**

$H_0$: Type of institution and level of job satisfaction are independent.

$H_1$: Type of institution and level of job satisfaction are not independent.

**Step 2:** Our test statistic is a chi-square test of independence, which has a chi-square distribution.

**Step 3:** With 1 degree of freedom and an alpha of .05, our $\chi^2_{crit} = 3.841$. The critical region is any obtained chi-square to the right of this. Our decision rule is to reject the null hypothesis when $\chi^2_{obt} \geq 3.841$.

**Step 4:** When we calculate our obtained chi-square, we find that it is $\chi^2_{obt} = 21.11$.

**Step 5:** With a critical value of 3.841 and an obtained chi-square statistic of 21.11, our decision is to reject the null hypothesis. Our conclusion is that type of institution employed at and job satisfaction for a correctional officer are not independent; there is a relationship between these two variables in the population. Those who work in medium-security prisons are more satisfied compared with those who work in maximum-security prisons.

We could use several different measures of association for a $2 \times 2$ contingency table. Our estimated value of Yule's Q would be $-.67$, which would tell us that there is a strong negative relationship between type of institution and job satisfaction. More specifically, we would conclude that those who work in maximum-security facilities have less job satisfaction. Since we have a $2 \times 2$ table, we could also have used the phi-coefficient as our measure of association. Our estimated value of phi is .34. Phi indicates that there is a moderate association or correlation between type of institution and job satisfaction (remember that the phi-coefficient is always positive).

3. a. The independent variable is the jurisdiction where a defendant was tried, and the dependent variable is the type of sentence the defendant receives.

b. There are a total of 425 observations.

c. There are 80 defendants from rural jurisdictions, 125 from suburban courts, and 220 who were tried in urban courts.

d. There are 142 defendants who received jail time only, 95 who were fined and sent to jail, 112 who were sentenced to less than 60 days of jail time, and 76 who were sentenced to 60 or more days of jail.

e. This is a $4 \times 3$ contingency table.

f. There are 38 defendants from suburban courts who received less than 60 days of jail time as their sentence.

g. There are 22 defendants tried in rural courts who received a sentence of a fine and jail.

h. There are $(4 - 1) \times (3 - 1)$ or 6 degrees of freedom.

i. You would use the column marginal to calculate cell percentages because jurisdiction is the independent variable. You should find that 20% of those in rural courts are sentenced to 60 or more days of jail compared with 16% of those in suburban courts and with 18% of those in urban courts. There seems to be a slight relationship here, with those tried in rural courts more likely to be sentenced to more than 60 days of jail time.

j. **Step 1:**

$H_0$: Place where tried and type of sentence are independent.

$H_1$: Place where tried and type of sentence are not independent.

**Step 2:** Our test statistic is a chi-square test of independence, which has a chi-square distribution.

**Step 3:** With 6 degrees of freedom and an alpha of .01, our $\chi^2_{crit} = 16.812$. The critical region is any obtained chi-square to the right of this. Our decision rule is to reject the null hypothesis when $\chi^2_{obt} \geq 16.812$.

**Step 4:** When we calculate our obtained chi-square, we find that it is $\chi^2_{obt} = 21.85$.

**Step 5:** With a critical value of 16.812 and an obtained chi-square statistic of 21.85, our decision is to reject the null hypothesis. Our conclusion is there is a relationship between where in the state a defendant was tried and the type of sentence the defendant received. Location of the trial and type of sentence are both nominal-level variables. It seems that rural courts are more likely to give long jail sentences compared with either suburban or urban courts. We will use lambda as our measure of association. The value of lambda is:

$$\lambda = \frac{283 - 269}{283}$$
$$\lambda = .05$$

Out lambda coefficient tells us that there is only a very weak relationship between the location of the trial and the type of sentence.

5.  a. Employment is the independent variable, and the number of arrests within three years after release is the dependent variable.

    b. There are 115 observations or cases.

    c. There are 45 persons who reported having stable employment, 30 who reported sporadic employment, and 40 who reported being unemployed.

    d. There are 54 persons who had no arrests within three years and 61 who had one or more arrests.

    e. This is a $2 \times 3$ contingency table.

    f. 16 persons who were sporadically employed had one or more arrests.

    g. 10 unemployed persons had no arrests.

    h. There are $(2-1) \times (3-1) = 2$ degrees of freedom.

    i. For those with stable employment, the risk of having one or more arrests is .33, for those with sporadic employment it is .53, and for the unemployed it is .75. The relative risk of at least one arrest increases as the individual's employment situation becomes worse.

    j. **Step 1:**

    $H_0$: Employment status and the number of arrests within three years are independent.

    $H_1$: Employment status and the number of arrests within three years are not independent.

    **Step 2:** Our test statistic is a chi-square test of independence, which has a chi-square distribution.

**Step 3:** With 2 degrees of freedom and an alpha of .05, our $\chi^2_{\text{crit}} = 5.991$. The critical region is any obtained chi-square to the right of this. Our decision rule is to reject the null hypothesis when $\chi^2_{\text{obt}} \geq 5.991$.

**Step 4:** When we calculate our obtained chi-square, we find that it is $\chi^2_{\text{obt}} = 15.36$.

**Step 5:** With a critical value of 5.991 and an obtained chi-square statistic of 15.36, our decision is to reject the null hypothesis. Our conclusion is that employment status and the number of crimes upon release are not independent. There is a relationship between the two variables in the population.

Since both employment status and the number of arrests within three years are ordinal-level variables, we will use gamma as our measure of association. The value of gamma is:

$$\gamma = \frac{1,800 - 520}{1,800 + 520}$$
$$\gamma = .55$$

There is a moderately strong positive association between employment status and the number of arrests. More specifically, as one moves from stable to sporadic to unemployed, the risk of having one or more arrests increases.

## Chapter 10

1. An independent variable is the variable that affects influences the dependent variable. In causal terms, the independent variable is the cause, and the dependent variable is the effect. Low self-control is taken to affect one's involvement in crime, so self-control is the independent variable and involvement in crime is the dependent variable.

3. The null and alternative hypotheses are:

$$H_0 : \mu = \mu_2$$
$$H_1 : \mu_1 < \mu_2$$

The correct test is the pooled variance independent samples $t$ test, and our sampling distribution is Student's $t$

distribution. We reject the null hypothesis if $t_{obt} \leq -2.390$. The obtained value of $t$ is:

$$t_{obt} = \frac{2.1 - 8.2}{\sqrt{\frac{[(40-1)(1.8)^2] + [(25-1)(1.9)^2]}{40+25-2}} \sqrt{\frac{40+25}{(40)(25)}}}$$

$$t_{obt} = -13.01$$

Because our obtained value of $t$ is less than the critical value and falls into the critical region, we decide to reject the null hypothesis of equal means. We conclude that those whose peers would disapprove of their driving drunk actually drive drunk less frequently than those whose coworkers are more tolerant of driving drunk in the population.

5. The null and alternative hypotheses are:

$$H_0: \mu_1 = \mu_2$$

$$H_1: \mu_1 < \mu_2$$

The problem instructs you not to presume that the population standard deviations are equal ($\sigma_1 \neq \sigma_2$), so the correct statistical test is the separate variance $t$ test, and the sampling distribution is Student's $t$ distribution. With approximately 60 $df$ and an alpha of .05 for a one-tailed test, the critical value of $t$ is 1.671. The value for $t_{obt}$ is:

$$t_{obt} = \frac{18.8 - 21.3}{\sqrt{\frac{(4.5)^2}{50-1} + \frac{(3.0)^2}{25-1}}}$$

$$t_{obt} = -2.82$$

Because $t_{obt} \leq t_{crit}$, we reject the null hypothesis of equal population means. Our conclusion is that the mean score on the domestic disturbance scale is significantly lower for males than for females. In other words, we can conclude that in the population, male police officers are less likely to see the fair handling of domestic disturbances as an important part of police work.

7. The null and alternative hypotheses are:

$$H_0: p_1 = p_2$$

$$H_1: p_1 > p_2$$

Because this is a difference of proportions problem, the correct test statistic is the $z$ test, and our sampling distribution is the $z$ or standard normal distribution. Our decision rule is to reject the null hypothesis if $z_{obt} \geq 2.33$.

The value of $z_{obt}$ is:

$$z_{obt} = \frac{.43 - .17}{\sqrt{(.32)(.68)} \sqrt{\frac{100+75}{(100)(75)}}}$$

$$z_{obt} = 3.65$$

Because our obtained $z$ is greater than the critical value of $z$ (2.33) and $z_{obt}$ falls into the critical region, we reject the null hypothesis. Delinquent children have a significantly greater proportion of criminal parents than do nondelinquent children.

## 📖 Chapter 11

1. An analysis of variance can be performed whenever we have a continuous (interval- or ratio-level) dependent variable and a categorical variable with three or more levels or categories, and we are interested in testing hypotheses about the equality of our population means.

3. It is called the analysis of variance because we make inferences about the differences among population means based on a comparison of the *variance* that exists within each sample, relative to the variance that exists between the samples. More specifically, we examine the ratio of variance between the samples to the variance within the samples. The greater this ratio, the more between-samples variance there is relative to within-sample variance. Therefore, as this ratio becomes greater than 1, we are more inclined to believe that the samples were drawn from different populations with different population means.

5. The formulas for the three degrees of freedom are:

$$df_{total} = n-1$$
$$df_{between} = k-1$$
$$df_{within} = n-k$$

To check your arithmetic, make sure that $df_{total} = df_{between} + df_{within}$.

7.

a. The independent variable is the state's general policy with respect to drunk driving ("get tough," make a "moral appeal," or not do much), and the dependent variable is the drunk driving rate in the state.

b. The correct degrees of freedom for this table are:

$$df_{between} = k - 1 = 3 - 1 = 2$$

$$df_{within} = n - k = 45 - 3 = 42$$

$$df_{total} = n - 1 = 45 - 1 = 44$$

You can see that $df_{between} + df_{within} = df_{total}$

The ratio of sum of squares to degrees of freedom can now be determined:

$$SS_{between} / df_{between} = 475.3 / 2 = 237.65$$

$$SS_{within} / df_{within} = 204.5 / 42 = 4.87$$

The $F$ ratio is $F_{obt} = 237.65 / 4.87 = 48.80$.

c.

$$H_0: \mu_{get\,tough} = \mu_{moral\,appeal} = \mu_{control}$$

$$H_1: \mu_{get\,tough} \neq \mu_{moral\,appeal} \neq \mu_{control}$$

Our decision rule will be to reject the null hypothesis if $F_{obt} \geq 5.18$.

$F_{obt} = 48.80$. Since our obtained value of $F$ is greater than the critical value, our decision is to reject the null hypothesis. We conclude that the population means are not equal.

d. Going to the studentized table, you find the value of $q$ to be equal to 4.37. To find the critical difference, you plug these values into your formula:

$$CD = 4.37 \sqrt{\frac{4.87}{15}}$$

$$= 2.49$$

The critical difference for the mean comparisons, then, is 2.49. Find the absolute value of the difference between each pair of sample means and test each null hypothesis.

$$H_0: \mu_{get\,tough} = \mu_{moral\,appeal}$$

$$H_1: \mu_{get\,tough} \neq \mu_{moral\,appeal}$$

| "Get Tough" | 125.2 |
|---|---|
| "Moral Appeal" | $-119.7$ |
| | $|5.5|$ |

Since the absolute value of the difference in sample means is greater than the critical difference score of 2.49, we would reject the null hypothesis. States that make a "moral appeal" have significantly lower levels of drunk driving on average than do states that "get tough."

$$H_0: \mu_{get\,tough} = \mu_{control}$$

$$H_1: \mu_{get\,tough} \neq \mu_{control}$$

| "Get Tough" | 125.2 |
|---|---|
| "Control" | $-145.3$ |
| | $|20.1|$ |

Since the absolute value of the difference in sample means is greater than the critical difference score of 2.49, we would reject the null hypothesis. States that "get tough" with drunk driving by increasing the penalties have significantly lower levels of drunk driving on average than do states that do nothing.

$$H_0: \mu_{moral\,appeal} = \mu_{control}$$

$$H_1: \mu_{moral\,appeal} \neq \mu_{control}$$

| "Moral Appeal" | 119.7 |
|---|---|
| "Conrol" | $-145.3$ |
| | $|25.6|$ |

The "moral appeal" states have significantly lower levels of drunk driving than the control states. It appears, then, that doing *something* about drunk driving is better than doing little or nothing.

e. Eta squared is:

$$\eta^2 = \frac{475.3}{679.8}$$

$$\eta^2 = .70$$

This tells us that there is a moderately strong relationship between the state's response to drunk driving and the rate of drunk driving in that state. Specifically, about 70% of the variability in levels of drunk driving is explained by the state's public policy.

9. a. The independent variable is the number of friends each girl has, and the dependent variable is the number of delinquent acts each girl is encouraged to commit.

b.  The total sum of squares = 154.

The between-groups sum of squares = 98.

within-group sum of square = 56.

c.

$$df_{between} = k - 1 = 3 - 1 = 2$$

$$df_{within} = n - k = 21 - 3 = 18$$

$$df_{total} = n - 1 = 21 - 1 = 20$$

You can see that $df_{between} + df_{within} = df_{total}$

The ratio of sum of squares to degrees of freedom can now be determined:

$$SS_{between} / df_{between} = 98 / 2 = 49$$

$$SS_{within} / df_{within} = 56 / 18 = 3.11$$

The $F$ ratio is:

$$F_{obt} = \frac{49}{3.11} = 15.75$$

d.

$$H_0: \mu_{A\,lot} = \mu_{some} = \mu_{few}$$

$$H_1: \mu_{A\,lot} \neq \mu_{some} \neq \mu_{few}$$

With an alpha of .05 and 2 between-groups and 18 within-group degrees of freedom, our critical value of F is 3.55. Our decision rule is to reject the null hypothesis when Fobtained ≥ 3.55. The obtained F is 15.75; Fobtained > Fcritical, so our decision is to reject the null hypothesis and conclude that some of the population means are different from each other.

e.  The value of the critical difference score is:

$$CD = 3.61 \sqrt{\frac{3.11}{7}}$$

$$CD = 2.41$$

A sample mean difference equal to or greater than an absolute value of 2.41 will lead us to reject the null hypothesis. We will now conduct a hypothesis test for each pair of population means.

$$H_0: \mu_{A\,lot} = \mu_{some}$$

$$H_1: \mu_{A\,lot} \neq \mu_{some}$$

| "A lot" | 7 |
|---|---|
| "some" | −6 |
| | \|1\| |

Since this difference is less than the critical difference score of 2.41, we will fail to reject the null hypothesis. Girls who have a lot of friends are no different in the number of delinquent acts they are encouraged to commit than girls who have some friends.

$$H_0: \mu_{A\,lot} = \mu_{few}$$

$$H_1: \mu_{A\,lot} \neq \mu_{few}$$

| "A lot" | 7 |
|---|---|
| "few" | −2 |
| | \|5\| |

Since this difference is greater than the critical difference score of 2.41, we will reject the null hypothesis. Girls who have a lot of friends are encouraged to commit significantly more delinquent acts than girls who have a few friends.

$$H_0: \mu_{some} = \mu_{few}$$

$$H_1: \mu_{some} \neq \mu_{few}$$

| "some" | 6 |
|---|---|
| "few" | −2 |
| | \|4\| |

Since this difference is greater than the critical difference score of 2.41, we will reject the null hypothesis. Girls who have some friends are encouraged to commit significantly more delinquent acts than girls who have a few friends.

It would appear that Chapple and colleagues' (2014) hypothesis is correct. The presence of more friends in a friendship network puts females at higher risk of being encouraged to commit delinquent behavior.

f.

$$\eta^2 = \frac{98}{154}$$

$$\eta^2 = .64$$

There is a moderately strong relationship between the number of friends in a girl's friendship group and the number of delinquent acts she is encouraged to commit.

## 📖 Chapter 12

1. a. There is a moderate negative linear relationship between the median income level in a neighborhood and its rate of crime. As the median income level in a community increases, its rate of crime decreases.

   b. There is a weak positive linear relationship between the number of hours spent working after school and self-reported delinquency. As the number of hours spent working after school increases, the number of self-reported delinquent acts increases.

   c. There is a strong positive linear relationship between the number of prior arrests and the length of current sentence. As the number of prior arrests increases, the length of the sentence received for the last offense increases.

   d. There is a weak negative linear relationship between the number of jobs held between the ages of 15 and 17 and the number of arrests as an adult.

   e. There is virtually no linear relationship between the divorce rate and a state's rate of violent crime.

3. a. A $1 increase in the fine imposed decreases the number of price-fixing citations by .017 units.

   b. A 1% increase in unemployment increases the rate of property crime by .715 units.

   c. An increase of one year in education increases a police officer's salary by $1,444.53.

5. a.

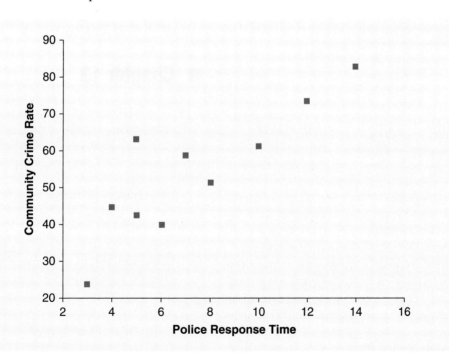

   b. The value of the regression coefficient is:

   $$b = \frac{10(4,491.4) - 74(541.1)}{10(664) - (74)^2}$$

   $$b = \frac{4,872.6}{1,164}$$

   $$b = 4.19$$

The value of the slope coefficient is 4.19. This tells us that a one-minute increase in police response time increases the crime rate by 4.19 per 1,000. The longer the response time is, the higher the crime rate. Stated conversely, the shorter the response time is, the lower the crime rate.

c. The value of the $y$ intercept is:

$$54.11 = a + 4.19(7.4)$$

$$54.11 = a + 31.01$$

$$54.11 - 31.01 = a$$

$$a = 23.1$$

Thus, the value of the $y$ intercept, or $a$, is equal to 23.1.

d. The predicted community rate of crime when the police response time is 11 minutes can now be determined from our regression prediction equation:

$$\hat{y} = 23.1 + 4.19(11)$$

$$\hat{y} = 23.1 + 46.09$$

$$\hat{y} = 69.19$$

The predicted crime rate, therefore, is 69.19 crimes per 1,000 population.

e. The value of $r$ is:

$$r = \frac{10(4,491.4) - 74(541.1)}{\sqrt{\left[10(664) - (74)^2\right]\left[10(32,011.3) - (541.1)^2\right]}}$$

$$r = \frac{4,872.6}{5,639.6}$$

$$r = .86$$

There is a strong positive correlation between low self-control and the number of self-reported criminal offenses.

We now want to conduct a hypothesis test about $r$. Our null hypothesis is that $r = 0$, and our alternative hypothesis is that $r > 0$. We predict direction because we have reason to believe that there is a positive correlation between the number of minutes it takes the police to respond and the community's rate of crime (the longer the response time, the higher the crime rate). To determine whether this estimated $r$ value is significantly different from zero with an alpha level of .05, we calculate a $t$ statistic, with $n - 2$ degrees of freedom. We go to the $t$ table to find our critical value of $t$ with $10 - 2 = 8$ degrees of freedom, an alpha level of .05, and a one-tailed test. The critical value of $t$ is 1.86. Our decision rule is to reject the null hypothesis if $t_{obt} \geq 1.86$. Now we calculate our $t_{obt}$:

$$t = .86\sqrt{\frac{10 - 2}{1 - (.86)^2}}$$

$$t = .86(5.54)$$

$$t = 4.76$$

We have a $t_{obt}$ of 4.76. Since $4.76 > 1.86$, we decide to reject the null hypothesis. There is a significant positive correlation between the length of police response time and the community crime rate. In the population, communities with high police response times tend to have high rates of crime.

f. Our $r$ was .86, $(.86)^2 = .74$, so 74% of the variation in community crime rates is explained by police response time.

g. Based on our results, we would conclude that there is a significant positive linear relationship between police response time and community crime rate. In the population, communities with high police response times tend to have high rates of crime.

## 🔲 Chapter 13

1. a. The least-squares regression equation for this problem is:

$$y = a + b_1 x_1 + b_2 x_2$$

$$y = 19.642 + (.871)(\text{divorce rate}) + (-.146)(\text{age})$$

b. The partial slope coefficient for the variable divorce indicates that as the divorce rate per 100,000 population increases by 1, the rate of violent crime per 100,000 increases by .871 units, controlling for the mean age of the state's population. The partial slope coefficient for the variable age indicates that as the mean age of the state's population increases by one year, the rate of violent crime per 100,000 decreases by .146 units, controlling for the divorce rate. The intercept is equal to 19.642. This tells us that when both the divorce rate and the mean age are equal to zero, the rate of violent crime is 19.642 per 100,000.

c. The standardized regression coefficient for divorce is .594, and that for age is −.133. Based on this, we would conclude that the divorce rate is more influential in explaining state violent crime rates than is the mean age of the population. A second way to look at the relative strength of the independent variables is to compare the absolute value of their respective $t$ ratios. The $t$ ratio for divorce is 4.268, and that for age is −3.110. Based on this, we would conclude that the divorce rate is more influential in explaining rates of violence than is the mean age of a state's population.

d. The divorce rate and mean age together explain approximately 63% of the variance in rates of violent crime. The adjusted $R^2$ value is .61, indicating that 61% of the variance is explained.

e. The null and alternative hypotheses are:

$$H_0 : \beta_1, \beta_2 = 0; \text{ or } R^2 = 0$$

$$H_1 : \beta_1, \beta_2 \neq 0; \text{ or } R^2 \neq 0$$

$F_{obt} = 27.531$. The probability of obtaining an $F$ of 27.531 if the null hypothesis were true is .00001. Since this probability is less than our alpha of .01, our decision is to reject the null hypothesis that all the slope coefficients are equal to zero and conclude that at least one of the independent variables is significant when explaining the violent crime rate.

$$H_0 : \beta_{divorce} = 0$$

$$H_1 : \beta_{divorce} \neq 0$$

$t_{obt} = 4.268$. The probability of obtaining a $t$ this size if the null hypothesis were true is equal to .0001. Since this probability is less than our alpha level of .01, we decide to reject the null hypothesis. We conclude that the population partial slope coefficient for the effect of the divorce rate on the rate of violent crime is significantly different from 0. States with higher divorce rates also have higher rates of violent crime.

$$H_0 : \beta_{age} = 0$$

$$H_1 : \beta_{age} \neq 0$$

$t_{obt} = -3.110$. The probability of obtaining a $t$ statistic this low if the null hypothesis is true is equal to .0011. Since this is less than .01, we will reject the null hypothesis that there is no relationship in the population between the mean age of a state and its rate of violent crime. States with younger populations tend to have higher rates of violence.

3. a. The least-squares regression equation from the supplied output would be:

$$\hat{y} = 16.245 + (-1.467)(\text{ENV}) + (1.076)(\text{REL})$$

b. The partial slope coefficient for the environmental factors variable is −1.467. This tells us that as a person's score on the environmental causes of crime scale increases by 1, his or her score on the punitiveness scale decreases by 1.467, controlling for religious fundamentalism. The partial slope coefficient for the religious fundamentalism scale is 1.076. As a person's score on religious fundamentalism increases by one unit, his or her score on the punitiveness scale increases by 1.076, controlling for score on the environmental scale. The value of the intercept is 16.245. When both independent variables are zero, a person's score on the punitiveness scale is 16.245.

c. The beta weight for ENV is −.608. The beta weight for REL is .346. A one-unit change in the ENV variable produces almost twice as much change in the dependent variable as the REL variable. Comparing these beta weights would lead us to conclude that the environmental factors scale is more important in explaining punitiveness scores than the religious fundamentalism variable.

The $t$ ratio for ENV is −3.312, whereas that for REL is only 1.884. We would again conclude that ENV has the greater influence on the dependent variable.

d. The adjusted $R^2$ coefficient indicates that together, the environmental factors and religious fundamentalism scales explain approximately 60% of the variance in the punitiveness measure.

e.

$$H_0 : \beta_{ENV}, \beta_{REL} = 0; \text{ or } R^2 = 0$$

$$H_1 : \beta_{ENV}, \text{ or } \beta_{REL} \neq 0; \text{ or } R^2 \neq 0$$

The probability of an $F$ of 11.565 if the null hypothesis were true is .001. Since this probability is less than our chosen alpha of .01, our decision is to reject the null hypothesis that all the slope coefficients are equal to zero and conclude that at least one of the independent variables is significantly related to punitive attitudes.

$$H_0 : \beta_{ENV} = 0$$

$$H_1 : \beta_{ENV} \neq 0$$

The output gives you a $t_{obt}$ of $-3.312$, and the probability of obtaining a $t$ this size if the null hypothesis were true is equal to .0062. Since this probability is less than our chosen alpha level of .01, we decide to reject the null hypothesis. We conclude that the population partial slope coefficient is less than 0. People who are more likely to believe that environmental factors are responsible for crime are less likely to have punitive attitudes toward criminal offenders.

$$H_0 : \beta_{REL} = 0$$

$$H_1 : \beta_{REL} \neq 0$$

The $t$ ratio for the variable ENV is $t_{obt} = 1.884$. The probability of obtaining a $t$ statistic of this magnitude if the null hypothesis were true is equal to .0840. Since this probability is greater than .01, our decision is to fail to reject the null hypothesis. The partial slope coefficient between religious fundamentalism and punitiveness toward criminal offenders is not significantly different from zero in the population, once we control for a belief in environmental causes of crime:

$$\hat{y} = 16.245 + (-1.467)(\text{ENV}) + (1.076)(\text{REL})$$

$$\hat{y} = 16.245 + (-1.467)(2) + (1.076)(8)$$

$$\hat{y} = 16.245 + (-2.934) + 8.608$$

$$\hat{y} = 21.919$$

## 🔲 Chapter 14

1. a. Probability $= 250 / 700 = .36$ Odds $= .36 / .64 = .56$

   b. Probability $= 500 / 700 = .71$ Odds $= .71 / .29 = 2.45$

   c. Probability $= 630 / 700 = .90$ Odds $= .90 / .10 = 9.00$

   d. Probability $= 180 / 700 = .26$ Odds $= .26 / .74 = .35$

3. a. The equation for the model is:

$$\ln\left(\frac{P}{1-P}\right) = -7.246 + (.8147)(\text{desire}) + (.1593)(\text{age})$$

b. A one-unit increase in the desire of the victim to have an arrest made increases the log of the odds of an arrest by .8147, when the age of the victim is held constant. The log of the odds of an arrest increases by .1593 when the victim's age increases by one year, the expressed desire of the victim for an arrest being held constant.

c. The expected log of the odds that an arrest will be made is:

$$\ln\frac{\hat{p}}{1-\hat{p}} = -7.246 + .8147 + .1593(50)$$

$$\ln\frac{\hat{p}}{1-\hat{p}} = -7.246 + 8.7797$$

$$\ln\frac{\hat{p}}{1-\hat{p}} = 1.5337$$

so the predicted probability that an arrest will be made is:

$$\hat{p} = \frac{e^{1.5337}}{1+e^{1.5337}}$$

$$\hat{p} = \frac{4.635}{5.635}$$

$$\hat{p} = .82$$

The odds of an arrest in this case are $.82 / .18 = 4.56$.

d. The two null and alternative hypotheses are:

$$H_0 : b_{\text{desire}} = 0$$

$$H_1 : b_{\text{desire}} > 0$$

$$H_0 : b_{\text{age}} = 0$$

$$H_1 : b_{\text{age}} > 0$$

The Wald statistic is distributed as a chi-square statistic. With 1 degree of freedom and an alpha of .05, the critical value of chi-square is 3.841. We will reject the null hypothesis if our Wald statistic for a given logistic regression coefficient is greater than or equal to 3.841. The Wald statistic for the variable "victim's desire" is .753. This is not greater than or equal to 3.841 so we will fail to reject the null hypothesis. The Wald statistic for the variable "age" is 15.124 which is greater than our critical value of 3.841, so we would reject the null hypothesis and conclude that there is a positive relationship in the population between the age of the victim and the decision of the police to arrest the suspect. The older the victim is, the more likely it is that a suspect will be arrested.

e. The coefficient for desire is not significant once age is controlled. The coefficient for age is significant even with desire controlled. On the basis of this, we would conclude that the age of the victim has more of an effect on the odds of an arrest than does the desire of the victim that an arrest be made.

# Glossary

**Adjusted $R^2$:** Value of $R^2$ adjusted to take into account the number of independent variables in the model predicting the dependent variable.

**Alphanumeric data:** Values of a variable that are represented by letters rather than by numbers.

**Alternative hypothesis (research hypothesis):** Alternative state of affairs that is presumed to exist if the null hypothesis is rejected. Sometimes referred to as the research hypothesis.

**Analysis of variance (ANOVA):** Statistical model used to test the differences between three or more group means.

**Availability sampling:** Sampling in which elements are selected on the basis of convenience.

**Beta coefficient:** The name for the population parameter of the slope, but also a name given to the standardized slope regression coefficient in multiple regression.

**Beta weight:** Standardized slope coefficient in an ordinary least-squares (OLS) regression model.

**Between-groups sum of squares:** Measures the variability between groups for an ANOVA.

**Bimodal distribution:** Distribution that contains two distinct modes with the greatest frequency, even if the frequencies are not exactly equal.

**Binary variable:** Dichotomous variable that has been coded 0 or 1.

**Binary variable:** Two-category variable coded 1 and 0; also called a dichotomous variable.

**Binomial coefficient $\binom{n}{k}$:** Number of ways of picking $k$ unordered outcomes from $n$ possibilities. It is also known as a combination.

**Binomial distribution:** Probability distribution for which there are just two possible outcomes with fixed probabilities that sum to 1.0.

**Bivariate correlation:** Measures the linear relationship between two variables.

**Bounding rule of probabilities:** Probability of any event can never be less than zero nor greater than $0 \leq -1: 0: \leq P(A) \leq 1.0$.

**Boxplot:** Graphical technique to display the distribution of a variable that is part of the exploratory data analysis (EDA) family.

**Causal relationship:** When you can determine that an independent variable causes a dependent variable by establishing an empirical relationship, correct time order, and nonspuriousness.

**Causal validity (internal validity):** When we can assume that our independent variable did cause the dependent variable.

**Central limit theorem:** Statistical theorem that states that the sampling distribution of any statistic will approximate normality as the sample size increases.

**Chi-square test of independence:** Tests the null hypothesis that two nominal- or ordinal-level variables are independent.

**Class interval:** In creating a grouped frequency distribution, the class interval defines the range of values that are included in each interval.

**Coefficient of determination ($r^2$):** Percentage of the variation in the dependent variable ($y$) that is explained by the independent variable ($x$).

**Column marginal, or column frequency:** Total frequencies for the variable displayed on the column of a cross-tabulation table.

**Complement of an event:** Complement of event $A$ is the set of all outcomes of a sample space that are not $A$. It is calculated as $1 - P(A)$.

**Conditional mean of y:** Means of $y$ calculated for every value of $x$.

**Conditional probability:** Probability of one event occurring ($A$) given that another event has occurred ($B$), written as $P(A|B)$.

**Confidence interval:** Statistical interval around a point estimate (e.g., mean) that we can provide a level of confidence to for capturing the true population parameter.

**Confidence level:** Level of confidence (e.g., 95% or 99%) that is set for a statistical inference from the sample to the population.

**Confidence limits:** Numerical lower and upper values that correspond to any given confidence interval around a point estimate from the sample.

**Constant:** Characteristic or property that does not vary but takes on only one value.

**Contingency coefficient ($C$):** Statistical measure of association that quantifies the strength or magnitude of a relationship between two nominal-level variables.

**Contingency table:** Shows the joint distribution of two categorical variables. A contingency table is defined by the number of rows and the number of columns it has. A contingency table with 3 rows and

2 columns is a "3 by 2" contingency table. Also called a cross-tabulation table.

**Continuous measure:** Measure with numbers indicating the values of variables as points on a continuum.

**Count or frequency:** Number of units in the sample that has a particular value in a variable distribution.

**Cramer's *V*:** Statistical measure of association that quantifies the strength or magnitude of a relationship between two nominal-level variables.

**Critical difference (CD) score:** Calculated by Tukey's Honest Significant Difference (HSD) test to determine the significant difference between a series of group mean combinations after the null hypothesis from an ANOVA has been rejected.

**Critical region of a probability distribution:** Defines the entire class of outcomes that will lead us to reject the null hypothesis. If the event we observe falls into the critical region, our decision will be to reject the null hypothesis.

**Critical region:** Region set by the alpha level to determine the rejection region for a null hypothesis test.

**Critical value:** Value of a particular test statistic that corresponds with an alpha level for any particular null hypothesis test or confidence interval.

**Cumulative frequency distribution:** Frequency distribution reserved for ordinal or interval/ratio-level data made by starting with the lowest value of the variable (or the highest value) and cumulating (keeping a running tally or sum) the frequencies in each adjacent value until the highest value is reached (or the lowest value is reached). The sum of a cumulative frequency distribution should be equal to the total number of cases (*n*).

**Cumulative percentages:** Identical to a cumulative frequency distribution

except that what is cumulated is the percentage at each value. The cumulative summing of percentages can go either from the lowest to the highest score or from the highest to the lowest score. The sum of a cumulative percentage distribution should be 100%.

**Cumulative proportions:** Identical to a cumulative frequency distribution except that what is cumulated is the proportion at each value. The cumulative summing of proportions can go either from the lowest to the highest score or from the highest to the lowest score. The sum of a cumulative percentage distribution should be 1.0.

**Degrees of freedom (*df*):** Value necessary along with a given alpha value to determine the critical value and region for a null hypothesis test or for a confidence interval.

**Dependent variable:** Variable that is expected to change or vary depending on the variation in the independent variable.

**Descriptive research:** Research in which phenomena are defined and described.

**Descriptive statistics:** Statistics used to describe the distribution of a sample or population.

**Dichotomous variable:** Two-category variable.

**Dichotomy:** Variable having only two values.

**Directional alternative hypothesis:** Alternative hypothesis that specifies that the parameter of interest is larger or smaller than the value specified in the null hypothesis.

**Directional hypothesis test:** When a research/alternative hypothesis states the directional difference expected.

**Element:** Units of a population that are sampled.

**Eta squared:** Describes the ratio of variance explained in the dependent variable by an independent variable.

**Evaluation research:** Research about social programs or interventions.

**Exhaustive intervals:** Class intervals must provide a place to count all original values of the variable distribution.

**Expected frequencies of a contingency table:** Joint frequency distribution we would expect to see if the two categorical variables were independent of each other. The expected frequencies, therefore, are calculated under the assumption of the null hypothesis—or no relationship between the two variables.

**Explanatory research:** Research that seeks to identify causes and/or effects of social phenomena.

**Exploratory data analysis (EDA):** Class of techniques to display variable distributions, which were originally developed by John Tukey.

***F* test:** Used for several null hypothesis tests, including determining the significance of $R^2$ in a multiple regression model and the significance of an ANOVA model.

**Frequency or empirical distribution:** Distribution of values that make up a variable distribution.

**General addition rule of probabilities (Rule 2b):** If two events are not mutually exclusive, the probability of event *A* occurring or event *B* occurring is equal to the sum of their separate probabilities minus their joint probability: $P(A \text{ or } B) = P(A) + P(B) - P(A \text{ and } B)$.

**General multiplication rule of probabilities (Rule 3b):** If two events are not independent of each other, the probability of event *A* occurring and event *B* occurring is equal to the product of the unconditional probability of event *A* and the conditional probability of event *B* given *A*: $P(A \text{ and } B) = P(A) \times P(B \mid A)$.

**Generalizability:** Extent to which information from a sample can be used to inform us about persons, places, or events that were not studied in the entire population from which the sample was taken.

**Grouped frequency distribution:** Reports the values of a quantitative continuous variable in intervals or a range of values, rather than reporting every distinct value.

**Heteroscedasticity:** Occurs when the assumption of **homoscedasticity** is violated and indicates that the error terms are not constant across all values of $x$.

**Histogram:** Method of graphing the distribution of an interval/ratio-level variable. It consists of a series of bars at each value of a variable where the height of the bar reflects the frequency of a value, its proportion, or its percentage.

**Homoscedasticity:** Assumption in ordinary least-squares (OLS) regression that the error terms are constant across all values of $x$.

**Hypothesis:** Tentative statement about empirical reality, involving the relationship between two or more variables.

**Independent events:** Two events, $A$ and $B$, are independent when the unconditional probability of $A$ is equal to the conditional probability of $A$ given $B$: $P(A) = P(A|B)$. When two events are independent, knowledge of one event does not help predict the probability of the other event occurring.

**Independent random samples:** Samples that are randomly and independently selected.

**Independent variable:** Variable that is expected to cause or lead to variation or change in the dependent variable.

**Inferences:** Specific statements (see *Generalizability*) about a population that are inferred (generalized) from a sample to a population.

**Inferential statistics:** Statistical tools for estimating how likely it is that a statistical result based on data from a random sample is representative of the population from which the sample has been selected.

**Interquartile range:** Measure of dispersion appropriate for interval/ ratio-level data. It measures the range of scores in the middle 50% of a distribution of continuous scores and is calculated as the difference between the score at the third quartile (the 75th percentile) and the score at the first quartile (the 25th percentile).

**Interval width:** Number of different values that are contained within the class interval. For example, for the given interval 0–5 arrests, the width is 6 because the interval contains the values 0, 1, 2, 3, 4, 5, or 6 arrests.

**Interval-ratio level of measurement:** Variables that we assume can be added and subtracted as well as multiplied and divided regardless of whether they have true-zero points.

**Interval-level variable:** In addition to an inherent rank order, a value's relationship to other values is known. There is an equal and constant distance between adjacent values. Therefore, the values can be added and subtracted.

**Joint frequency distribution:** For two categorical variables, the intersection of two values or categories.

**Joint probability:** Probability of two events $A$ and $B$ occurring simultaneously.

**Lambda ($\lambda$):** Statistical measure of association that quantifies the strength or magnitude of a relationship between two nominal-level variables.

**Least-squares regression line:** Regression line based on the least-squares function to calculate an equation that characterizes the best-fitting line between two interval/ratio variables.

**Level of measurement:** Mathematical nature of the values for a variable.

**Line graph (polygon):** Method of graphing interval/ratio-level data.

**Linear relationship:** The effect of $x$ on $y$ is generally the same at all values of $x$. A linear relationship is positive when $x$ and $y$ increase or decrease in the same direction, or negative, when $x$ and $y$ go in opposite directions.

**Logistic regression model:** Used to predict a dependent variable with two categories (0, 1), called a binary or dichotomous variable. It is used to estimate the probability of a binary response based on one or more independent variables.

**Matched or dependent samples:** Samples in which individuals are either dependent or matched on several characteristics (i.e., age, race, gender, etc.) or before-and-after samples of the same people.

**Matched-groups $t$ test:** Statistical test to determine the difference between two dependent or matched group means.

**Mean:** Arithmetic average of a group of scores calculated as the sum of the scores divided by the total number of scores. The mean is an appropriate measure of central tendency for interval/ratio-level data.

**Mean deviation score:** Distance between a score and the mean of the group of scores $(x_i - \overline{X})$.

**Measurement validity:** When we have actually measured what we intended to measure.

**Measures of association:** Statistics that inform us about the strength, or magnitude, as well as the direction of the relationship between two variables.

**Measures of central tendency:** Summary statistics that capture the "typical," "average," or "most likely" score or value in a variable distribution.

**Measures of dispersion:** Capture how different the values of a variable are. The more dispersion there is in a variable, the more different the values are from each other or from some central tendency and the more heterogeneity in the data.

**Median:** Score at the 50th percentile in a rank-ordered distribution of scores. Thus, one half of a variable's values are less than the median and one half are greater than the median.

**Midpoints:** Exact middle value in an interval of a grouped distribution. The midpoint is found by summing the lower and upper limits (stated or real) and dividing by 2.

**Mode:** Value of a variable that occurs more often than any other value.

**Moving average:** Taking an average over two or more data points to smooth out fluctuations in the data.

**Multicollinearity:** Occurs whenever the independent variables in your regression equation are too highly correlated with one another.

**Multivariate regression model:** A regression model predicting one dependent variable with two or more independent variables.

**Multiple regression equation:** Equation estimated with two or more independent variables predicting one dependent variable.

**Multiplication rule of probabilities:** "Or" rule of probabilities; it defines the probability of two or more events occurring simultaneously or their joint probability.

**Multistage cluster sampling:** Sampling in which elements are selected in two or more stages, with the first stage being the random selection of naturally occurring clusters and the last stage being the random selection of multilevel elements within clusters.

**Mutually exclusive events:** Events that cannot occur at the same time. In other words, there is no intersection of mutually exclusive events so their joint probability is equal to zero.

**Mutually exclusive intervals:** Class intervals must not overlap.

**National Incident-Based Reporting System (NIBRS):** Official reports about crime incidents that are reported to police departments across the United States and then voluntarily reported to the Federal Bureau of Investigation (FBI), which compiles them for statistics purposes. This system is slowly replacing the older UCR program.

**Negative correlation:** As the independent variable increases, the dependent variable decreases.

**Negative relationship between two variables:** An increase in one variable is related to a decrease in the other.

**Negatively skewed distribution:** Long "tail" is found on the left side of the distribution (toward the negative numbers).

**Nominal-level variables:** Values that represent categories or qualities of a case only.

**Nondirectional alternative hypothesis:** Alternative hypothesis that simply states that the null hypothesis is incorrect; it does not state whether the parameter of interest is larger or smaller than the value specified in the null hypothesis.

**Nondirectional hypothesis test:** When a research/alternative hypothesis does not state the direction of difference; it only states that there is a relationship between the independent and dependent variables.

**Nonlinear relationship:** Can take several forms but generally indicates a relationship that changes direction as the values of the independent variable increase.

**Non–mutually-exclusive events:** Events that can occur simultaneously. The joint probability of non–mutually-exclusive events is, therefore, greater than zero.

**Nonprobability sampling methods:** These methods are not based on random selection and do not allow us to know in advance the likelihood of any element of a population being selected for the sample.

**Nonspuriousness:** Exists when a relationship between two variables is not explained by a third variable.

**Normal distribution:** Continuous probability distribution that is unimodal and symmetric about its mean, where a known area of the curve falls within given standard deviation units from the mean.

**Normal distribution:** Symmetrical distribution that has the greatest frequency of its cases in the middle of the distribution with fewer cases at each end or "tail" of the distribution. A normal distribution looks like a bell when drawn and it is often referred to as a "bell-shaped" distribution.

**Null hypothesis:** Hypothesis that is tested; it always assumes there is no relationship between the independent and dependent variables.

**Null hypothesis:** In a hypothesis test, the null hypothesis is the hypothesis that is initially assumed to be true. It is called the null hypothesis because it presumes that there is no relationship (null) between the variables being tested.

**Numeric data:** Values of a variable that represent numerical qualities.

**Observed frequencies of a contingency table:** Joint distribution of two categorical variables that we actually observed in our sample data.

**Odds ratio:** Exponential of a logistic regression slope coefficient.

**One-tailed hypothesis test:** When a research/alternative hypothesis states the directional difference expected. Also called directional hypothesis test.

**Ordinal-level variables:** Values that not only represent categories but also have a logical order.

**Outlier:** Unusually high or low value or score for a variable.

**Partial correlation coefficient:** Correlation between two variables after controlling for a third variable.

**Partial slope coefficient:** Effect of an independent variable on the dependent variable after controlling for one or more other independent variables.

**Pearson correlation coefficient:** Statistic that quantifies the direction and strength of the relationship between two interval/ratio-level variables.

**Percent change score:** Score that quantifies the percent change of a score between two different time periods or other units.

**Percentage differences:** One way to examine the bivariate relationship in a contingency table. The rule is to calculate the percentages based on the marginals of the independent variable and compare different levels of the independent variable at the same level or category of the dependent variable.

**Percentages:** Number of some value in a variable distribution that is divided by total possible scores and then is multiplied by 100.

**Pie chart/bar chart:** Graphical ways to display nominal- or ordinal-level variables. These charts can include frequencies, proportions, or percentages. Pie charts represent quantities as slices and bar charts represent quantities as bars.

**Point estimates:** Sample statistics such as the mean and proportion that are sample estimates of the same values in the population.

**Police reports:** Data used to measure crime based on incidents that become known to police departments.

**Pooled variance estimate of the standard error of the difference:** Estimate of the standard error for an independent samples $t$ test when it can be assumed that the standard deviations of both groups are not significantly different.

**Population:** Larger set of cases or aggregate number of people that a researcher is actually interested in or wishes to know something about.

**Population parameter:** Statistic (i.e., mean, proportion, etc.) obtained from a population. Since we rarely have entire population data, we typically estimate population parameters using sample statistics.

**Population parameter:** Statistic obtained from the population.

**Positive correlation:** As the independent variable increases, the dependent variable also increases.

**Positive relationship between two variables:** An increase in one variable is related to an increase in the other.

**Positively skewed distribution:** Long "tail" is found on the right side of the distribution (toward the positive numbers).

**Predicted value of $y$ ($\hat{y}$):** Value of the dependent variable predicted by a regression equation.

**Probability distribution:** Distribution of all possible outcomes of a trial and the associated probability of each outcome.

**Probability of an event (event A):** Number of times $A$ can occur over the total number of events or trials. The formula for the probability of an event is:

$$P(A) = \frac{\text{Number of times event } A \text{ can occur}}{\text{Total number of possible events or trials}}$$

**Probability sampling methods:** These methods rely on random selection or chance and allow us to know in advance how likely it is that any element of a population is selected for the sample.

**Proportion differences:** If we do the percentage difference comparison with proportions (probabilities) rather than percentages, we are looking at the **relative risk** of the dependent variable at a given level of the independent variable.

**Proportionate reduction in error (PRE) measure:** Statistics that tell us how much we can reduce prediction errors by knowing the value of an independent variable.

**Proportions:** Number of some value in a variable distribution that is divided by total possible scores.

**Purposive or judgment sampling:** Nonprobability sampling method in which elements are selected for a purpose usually because of their unique position.

$Q_1$: First quartile or 25th percentile in a distribution of scores.

$Q_2$: Second quartile or the 50th percentile, also called the median, in a distribution of scores.

$Q_3$: Third quartile or 75th percentile in a distribution of scores.

**Qualitative or categorical variables:** Values that refer to qualities or categories. They tell us what kind, what group, or what type a value is referring to.

**Quantitative or continuous variables:** Values that refer to quantities or different measurements. They tell us how much or how many a variable has.

**Quota sampling:** Nonprobability sampling method in which elements are selected to ensure that the sample represents certain characteristics in proportion to their prevalence in the population or to oversampled segments of the population.

**Random digit dialing (RDD):** Random dialing by a machine of numbers within designated phone prefixes, which creates a random sample for phone surveys.

**Random selection:** The fundamental aspect of probability sampling. The essential characteristic of random selection is that every element of the population has a known and independent chance of being selected for the sample.

**Range:** Measure of dispersion appropriate for interval/ratio-level data. It is calculated as the difference between the highest value or score and the lowest: Range = Highest value - Lowest value.

**Rate:** Number of a phenomenon divided by the total possible, which is then multiplied by a constant such as 1,000, 10,000, or 100,000.

**Ratio:** Expresses the relationship between two numbers and indicates their relative size

**Ratio-level variables:** Variables that we assume can be added and subtracted as well as multiplied and divided and that have true zero points.

**Real class limits:** Real limits in a grouped distribution take into account the space between the adjacent intervals. For example, for an interval with stated limits of 0–5 and 6 –11 prior arrests, the real limits are .5–5.5 and 5.5–11.5.

**Regression line:** Line depicting the relationship between independent and dependent variables determined by an ordinary least-squares regression equation.

**Relative frequency:** See **Proportions**.

**Reliability:** Measure that is reliable when it yields consistent scores or observations of a given phenomenon on different occasions. Reliability is a prerequisite for measurement validity.

**Residual:** Difference between the predicted value of $y$ from the regression equation and the observed value at a given $x$ score.

**Restricted addition rule of probabilities ("Or" Rule 2a):** If two events are mutually exclusive, the probability of event $A$ occurring *or* event $B$ occurring is equal to the sum of their separate probabilities: $P(A \text{ or } B) = P(A) + P(B)$.

**Restricted multiplication rule of probabilities (Rule 3a):** If two events are independent of each other, the probability of event $A$ occurring and event $B$ occurring is equal to the product of their separate probabilities: $P(A \text{ and } B) = P(A) \times P(B)$.

**Row marginal:** Total frequencies for the categories of a variable displayed in the rows of a cross-tabulation table.

**Sample:** Subset of the population that a researcher must often use to make generalizations about the larger population.

**Sample statistic:** Statistic (i.e., mean, proportion, etc.) obtained from a sample of the population.

**Sample statistic:** Statistic obtained from a sample.

**Sampling distribution of sample mean differences:** Theoretical distribution of the difference between an infinite number of sample means.

**Sampling distribution of the mean:** Theoretical sampling distribution we would obtain if we drew an infinite number of same-sized samples and calculated the mean.

**Sampling distribution:** Probability distribution of a sample statistic (e.g., mean or proportion) drawn from a very large number of samples from some given population.

**Sampling error:** The difference between a sample estimate (called a sample statistic) and the population value it is estimating (called a population parameter).

**Sampling variation:** Differences between the sample and the population that are due to chance or sample variation.

**Scatterplot:** Graphical display of the linear relationship between two interval/ratio-level variables. Also called a scattergram.

**Science:** Set of logical, systematic, documented methods with which to investigate nature and natural processes; the knowledge produced by these investigations.

**Separate variance estimate of the standard error of the difference:** Estimate of the standard error for an independent samples $t$ test when it cannot be assumed that the standard deviations of both groups are not significantly different.

**Significance or alpha level (α):** Risk we are willing to take in rejecting a true null hypothesis. For example, if we select an alpha level of .05, we are willing to be incorrect .05 or 5% of the time.

**Simple random sample:** Method of sampling in which every sample element is selected only on the basis of chance through a random process.

**Skewed distribution:** Non-normal (nonsymmetrical) distribution.

**Slope:** Term in an ordinary least-squares (OLS) regression equation that indicates the change in $y$ associated with a one-unit change in $x$.

**Smoothing:** Creating new data points for trend data to smooth out the short-term fluctuations to identify long-term trends.

**Snowball sample:** Type of purposive sample that identities one member of a population and then asks him or her to identify others in the population. The sample size increases as a snowball would rolling down a slope.

**Standard deviation:** Square root of the squared deviations about the mean.

**Standard error (standard error of the mean; standard error of the proportion):** Standard deviation of the statistic (e.g., mean or proportion) from the sampling distribution of a large number of sample values. When the sampling distribution is of sample means, the standard deviation of the sampling distribution is called the standard error of the mean. When the sampling distribution is of sample proportions, the standard deviation of the sampling distribution is called the standard error of the proportion.

**Standard error of the mean:** Standard deviation of the sampling distribution of the mean.

**Standard error of the proportion:** Standard deviation of the sampling distribution of the proportion.

**Standard normal probability distribution:** Special case of the normal distribution. It is the distribution of a normal random variable that has a mean of zero and a standard deviation of one.

**Standard score ($z$ score):** Score from the standard normal probability distribution that indicates how many standard deviation units a score is from the mean of zero.

**Stated class limits:** Lowest value that is included in an interval and the highest value that is included in an interval.

**Stratified or weighted sampling:** Method of sampling in which sample elements are selected separately from population strata or are weighted differently for selection in advance by the researcher.

**Surveys:** Research method used to measure the prevalence of behavior, attitudes, or any other phenomenon by asking a sample of people to fill out a questionnaire either in person, through the mail or Internet, or on the telephone.

**Systematic random sampling:** Method of sampling in which sample elements are selected from a list or from sequential files, with every $k$th element being selected after the first element is selected randomly within the first interval.

**$t$ distribution (Student's $t$ distribution):** Statistical sampling distribution used in many statistical tests including for the construction of confidence intervals and the difference between two means.

**$t$ test:** Statistical test used to test several null hypotheses including the difference between two means.

**Theory:** Logically interrelated set of propositions about empirical reality that can be tested.

**Time plot:** Plot showing the distribution of data points over some period of time. An example would be a count of the annual number of executions in the United States from 1977 to 2015.

**Total sum of squares:** Measures the total variability in the sample for an ANOVA.

**True experimental design:** When two groups are randomly assigned with one group receiving the treatment or program (experimental group) while the other group (control group) does not. After the program or treatment, a post-test determines whether there is a change in the experimental group.

**Tukey's Honest Significant Difference (HSD) test:** Tests the difference between a series of group mean combinations after the null hypothesis from an ANOVA has been rejected.

**Two-tailed hypothesis test:** Research/alternative hypothesis that does not state the direction of difference; it only states that there is a relationship between the independent and dependent variables. Also called a nondirectional test.

**Type I error:** Probability of rejecting a null hypothesis that is in fact true. It is equal to the alpha probability level.

**Type II error:** Probability of retaining a null hypothesis that is in fact false.

**Ungrouped frequency distribution:** Every value of a variable is displayed in contract to a grouped frequency distribution that displays intervals that correspond to the data values.

**Uniform Crime Reports (UCR):** Official reports about crime incidents that are reported to police departments across the United States and then voluntarily reported to the Federal Bureau of Investigation (FBI), which compiles them for statistics purposes.

**Units of analysis:** Particular units or aggregations (e.g., people and cities) that constitute an observation in a data set.

**Univariate analysis:** Examining the distribution of one variable.

**Variable:** Characteristic or property that can vary or take on different values or attributes.

**Variance:** Measures the average squared deviations from the mean for an interval/ratio variable.

**Variation ratio:** Appropriate measure of dispersion to use when variables are measured at the nominal or purely ordinal level. It measures the proportion of cases of a variable that are not in the modal value. The greater the magnitude of the variation ratio, the more dispersion or variability there is in the nominal or ordinal variable.

**Within-group sum of squares:** Measures the variability within a group for an ANOVA.

**$y$ intercept:** Value of $y$ in an ordinary least-squares (OLS) regression equation when $x$ is equal to 0.

**Goodman and Kruskal's gamma:** Statistical measure of association that quantifies the strength or magnitude of a relationship between two ordinal-level variables. **Also called Yule's Q with a** $2 \times 2$ table.

**$z$ distribution:** Statistical sampling distribution used in many statistical tests including for the construction of confidence intervals, for determining the difference between two means, and for calculating the number of standard deviations an observation is above or below the mean.

**$z$ test:** Statistical test used to test several null hypotheses including the difference between two means.

# References

Agnew, R. (1992). Foundation for a general strain theory of crime and delinquency. *Criminology, 30*, 47–87.

Andreescu, V., Shutt, J. E., & Vito, G. F. (2011). The violent South: Culture of honor, social disorganization, and murder in Appalachia. *Criminal Justice Review, 36*(1), 76–103.

Bachman, R., & Schutt, R. (2017). *The practice of research in criminology and criminal justice* (6th ed.). Thousand Oaks, CA: Sage.

Bierie, D. M. (2012). Is tougher better? The impact of physical prison conditions on inmate violence. *International Journal of Offender Therapy and Comparative Criminology, 56*, 338–355.

Blalock, H. (1979). *Social Statistics* (2nd ed.). New York, NY: McGraw-Hill.

Braga, A. A., Weisburd, D. L., Waring, E. J., Mazerolle, L. G., Spelman, W., & Gajewski, F. (1999). Problem-oriented policing in violent crime places: A randomized controlled experiment. *Criminology, 37*, 541–580.

Bureau of Justice Statistics. (1993–2013). *National Crime Victimization Survey Property Crime Trends, 1993-2013.* Accessed from http://www.ojp.usdoj.gov/bjs/

Burt, C. H., Sweeten, G., & Simons, R. L. (2014). Self-control through emerging adulthood: Instability, multidimensionality, and criminological significance. *Criminology, 52*, 450–487.

Buss, A. H., & Warren, W. L. (2000). *The aggression questionnaire.* Los Angeles, CA: Wester Psychological Services.

Cameron, M. O. (1964). *The booster and the snitch: Department store shoplifting.* New York, NY: Free Press.

Caplan, J. M., Kennedy, L. W., & Piza, E. L. (2013). Joint utility of event-dependent and environmental crime analysis techniques for violent crime forecasting. *Crime & Delinquency, 59*(2), 243–270.

Chapple, C., Vaske, J., & Worthen, M. G. F. (2014). Gender differences in associations with deviant peer groups: Examining individual, interactional, and compositional factors. *Deviant Behavior, 35*, 394–411.

Charette, Y., Crocker, A. G., & Billette, I. (2014). Police encounters involving citizens with mental illness: Use of resources and outcomes. *Psychiatric Services, 65*(4), 511–516.

Choi, K.-S., Librett, M., & Collins, T. J. (2014). An empirical evaluation: Gunshot detection system and its effectiveness on police practices. *Police Practice and Research, 15*, 48–61.

Cohn, D., Taylor, P., Lopez, M. H., Gallagher, C. A., Parker, K., & Maass, K. T. (2013). *Gun homicide rate down 49% since 1993 peak: Public unaware.* Washington, D.C.: Pew Research Center.

Copes, H., Kovandzic, T. V., Miller, J. M., & Williamson, L. (2014). The lost cause? Examining the Southern culture of honor through defensive gun use. *Crime & Delinquency, 60*(3), 356–378.

Core Institute. (2015). *Core Alcohol and Drug Survey: Long form.* Carbondale, IL: FIPSE Core Analysis Grantee Group, Core Institute, Student Health Programs, Southern Illinois University.

Daly, K. (1987). Discrimination in the criminal courts: Family, gender, and the problem of equal treatment. *Social Forces, 66*, 152–175.

Daly, K. (1994). *Gender, crime and punishment.* New Haven, CT: Yale University Press.

Death Penalty Information Center. (2015). Website. Accessed http://www.deathpenaltyinfo.org

DeCoster, S., & Zito, R. C. (2010). Gender and general strain theory: The gendering of emotional experiences and expressions. *Journal of Contemporary Criminal Justice, 26*(2), 224–245.

Durose, M. R., Cooper, A. D., & Snyder, H. N. (2014). *Recidivism of prisoners released in 30 states in 2005: Patterns from 2005 to 2010* (Special Report). Washington, D.C.: U.S. Department of Justice, Office of Justice Programs, Bureau of Justice Statistics.

Duxbury, L., Higgins, C., & Halinski, M. (2015). Identifying the antecedents of work-role overload in police organizations. *Criminal Justice and Behavior, 42*, 361–381.

Elliott, D., & Ageton, S. (1980). Reconciling race and class differences in self-reported and official estimates of delinquency. *American Sociological Review, 45*, 95–110.

Engen, R. L., Gainey, R. R., Crutchfield, R. D., & Weis, J. G. (2003). Discretion and disparity under sentencing guidelines: The role of departures and structured sentencing alternatives. *Criminology, 41*, 99–130.

Esbensen, F. A., Osgood, D. W., Peterson, D., Taylor, T. J., & Carson, D. C. (2013). Short- and long-term outcome results from a multisite evaluation of the G.R.E.A.T. program. *Criminology & Public Policy, 12*(3), 375–411.

Federal Bureau of Investigation. (2000). *Hate Crime Statistics—2000.* Washington, D.C.: Author.

Federal Bureau of Investigation. (2013a). *Crime in the United States.* Washington, D.C.: Author.

Federal Bureau of Investigation. (2013b). *Hate Crime Statistics—2013.* Washington, D.C.: Author.

Federal Bureau of Investigation. (various dates). *Uniform Crime Reports: Crime in the United States: 1990, 1995, 2000, 2005-2014.* Washington, D.C.: Author.

Francis, K. A. (2014). General strain theory, gender, and the conditioning influence of negative internalizing emotions on youth risk behaviors. *Youth Violence and Juvenile Justice, 12*, 58–76.

Gallup. (2014a). *Hacking tops list of crimes Americans worry about most.* October 27. Retrieved from http://www.gallup.com/poll/178856/hacking-tops-list-crimes-americans-worry.aspx

Gallup. (2014b). *Less than half of Americans support stricter gun laws.* October 31. Retrieved from http://www.gallup.com/poll/179045/less-half-americans-support-stricter-gun-laws.aspx?g_source=gun%20laws&g_medium=search&g_campaign=tiles

Glueck, S., & Glueck, E. (1950). *Unraveling juvenile delinquency.* Cambridge, MA: Harvard University Press.

Gottfredson, M. R., & Hirschi, T. (1990). *A general theory of crime.* Stanford, CA: Stanford University Press.

Grasmick, H. G., Tittle, C. R., Bursik, R. J. Jr., & Arneklev, B. J. (1993). Testing the core implications of Gottfredson and Hirschi's general theory of crime. *Journal of Research in Crime and Delinquency, 30,* 5–29.

Harlan, C., Brown, D. L., & Fisher, M. (2015). Night of S.C. killings started with prayers and a plot against humanity. *The Washington Post,* June 19.

Hays, W. L. (1994). *Statistics.* Belmont, CA: Wadsworth.

Hirschi, T. (1969). *Causes of delinquency.* Berkeley: University of California Press.

Holtfreter, K. (2013). Gender and "other people's money": An analysis of white-collar offender sentencing. *Women & Criminal Justice, 23*(4), 326–344.

Ingram, J. R., & Terrill, W. (2014). Relational demography and officer occupational attitudes: The influence of workgroup context. *Journal of Criminal Justice, 42,* 309–320.

Jennings, W. G., Hahn Fox, B., & Farrington, D. P. (2014). Inked into crime? An examination of the causal relationship between tattoos and life-course offending among males from the Cambridge Study in Delinquent Development. *Journal of Criminal Justice, 42,* 77–84.

Jennings, W. G., Piquero, N. L., Gover, A. R., & Perez, D. M. (2009). Gender and general strain theory: A replication and exploration of Broidy and Agnew's gender/strain hypothesis among a sample of Southwestern Mexican American adolescents. *Journal of Criminal Justice, 37*(4), 404–417.

Kennedy, L., Caplan, J., & Piza, E. (2013). Risk clusters, hotspots, and spatial intelligence: Risk terrain modeling as an algorithm for police allocation strategies. *Journal of Quantitative Criminology, 27*(3), 339–362.

Kim, R. H., & Clark, D. (2013). The effect of prison-based college education programs on recidivism: Propensity score matching approach. *Journal of Criminal Justice, 41*(3), 196–204.

Lane, J., & Fox, K. A. (2013). Fear of property, violent, and gang crime: Examining the shadow of sexual assault thesis among male and female offenders. *Criminal Justice and Behavior, 40,* 472–496.

Loughran, T. A., Pogarsky, G., Piquero, A. R., & Paternoster, R. (2012). Re-examining the functional form of the certainty effect in deterrence theory. *Justice Quarterly, 29,* 712–741.

MacDonald, J. M., Piquero, A. R., Valois, R. F., & Zullig, K. J. (2005). The relationship between life satisfaction, risk-taking behaviors, and youth violence. *Journal of Interpersonal Violence, 20,* 1495–1518.

MacKenzie, D. L. (2013). First do no harm: A look at correctional policies and programs today. *Journal of Experimental Criminology, 9*(1), 1–17.

McCarthy, T., & Gambino, L. (2015). Charleston shootings: NRA blames victims as reactions echo Newtown. *The Guardian,* June 20.

McCuish, E. C., Corrado, R., Lussier, P., & Hart, S. D. (2014). Psychopathic traits and offending trajectories from early adolescence to adulthood. *Journal of Criminal Justice, 42,* 66–76.

Mears, D. P., Wang, X., & Bales, W. D. (2014). Does a rising tide lift all boats? Labor market changes and their effects on the recidivism of released prisoners. *Justice Quarterly, 31,* 822–851.

Megargee, E. I. (1972). Standardized reports of work performance and inmate adjustment for use in correctional settings. *Correctional Psychologist, 5,* 48–58.

Meldrum, R., Barnes, J. C., & Hay, C. (2015). Sleep deprivation, low self-control, and delinquency: A test of the strength model of self-control. *Journal of Youth Adolescence, 44,* 465–477.

Miller, J. (2015). Contemporary modes of probation officer supervision: The triumph of the "synthetic" officer. *Justice Quarterly, 32,* 314–336.

Miller, M. K., Maskaly, J., Peoples, C. D., & Sigillo, A. E. (2014). The relationship between mock jurors' religious characteristics and their verdicts and sentencing decisions. *Psychology of Religion and Spirituality, 6,* 188–197.

Motavalli, J. (2012). *Flying vs. driving: It's complicated.* Cartalk.com, May 16 (Archives).

National Law Enforcement Officers Memorial Fund. (2015). *Officer deaths by year.* Retrieved June 27, 2015, from http://www.nleomf.org/facts/officer-fatalities-data/year.html

Nisbett, R. E., & Cohen, D. (1996). *The culture of honor.* Boulder, CO: Westview Press.

Nisbett, R. E., & Cohen, D. (2014). The lost cause? Examining the southern subculture of violence through defensive gun use. *Crime and Delinquency, 60,* 356–380.

Pew Research Center. (2015). *A public opinion trend that matters: Priorities for gun policy.* January 9.

Piquero, N. L., Fox, K., Piquero, A., Capowich, G., & Mazerolle, P. (2010). Gender, general strain theory, negative emotions, and disordered eating. *Journal of Youth and Adolescence, 39*(4), 380–382.

Puzzanchera, C., & Kang, W. (2014). *Easy access to FBI arrest statistics 1994-2012.* Retrieved from http://www.ojjdp.gov/ojstatbb/ezaucr/

Raine, A. (1994). *The psychopathology of crime: Criminal behavior as a clinical disorder.* New York, NY: Academic Press.

Raine, A., Fung, A. L. C., Portnoy, J., Choy, O., & Spring, V. L. (2014). Low heart rate as a risk factor for child and adolescent proactive aggressive and impulsive psychopathic behavior. *Aggressive Behavior, 40,* 290–299.

Rapaport, E. (1991). The death penalty and gender discrimination. *Law and Society Review, 25,* 367–383.

Regoli, R. M., & Hewitt, J. D. (1994). *Delinquency in society: A child-centered approach.* New York, NY: McGraw-Hill.

Riedel, M. (2012). *Research strategies for secondary data.* Thousand Oaks, CA: Sage.

Roncek, D. W. (1991). Using logit coefficients to obtain the effects of independent variables on changes in probabilities. *Social Forces, 70*(2), 509–518.

Rydberg, J., & Pizarro, J. M. (2014). Victim lifestyle as a correlate of homicide clearance. *Homicide Studies, 18,* 342–362.

Schnapp, P. (2015). Identifying the effect of immigration on homicide rates in U.S. cities: An instrumental variables approach. *Homicide Studies, 19*(2), 103–122.

Sherman, L. W., & Berk, R. A. (1984a). The specific deterrent effects of arrest for domestic assault. *American Sociological Review, 49,* 261–272.

Sherman, L. W., & Berk, R. A. (1984b). *The Minneapolis domestic violence experiment.* Washington, D.C.: The Police Foundation.

Sherman, L. W., Gartin, P., & Buerger, M. (1989). Hot spots of predatory crime: Routine activities and the criminology of place. *Criminology, 27,* 27–56.

Sherman, L. W., & Harris, H. M. (2015). Increased death rates of domestic violence victims from arresting vs. warning suspects in the Milwaukee Domestic Violence Experiment (MilDVE). *Journal of Experimental Criminology, 11,* 1–20.

Short, J. F. Jr., & Nye, I. (1958). Reported behavior as a criterion of deviant behavior. *Social Problems, 5,* 207–213.

Skilling, T. A., & Sorge, G. B. (2014). Measuring antisocial values and attitudes in justice-involved male youth. *Criminal Justice and Behavior, 41*(8), 992–1007.

Spohn, C. C., & Spears, J. W. (1997). Gender and case processing decisions: A comparison of case outcomes for male and female defendants charged with violent felonies. *Women & Criminal Justice, 8*, 29–45.

Starr, S. (2015). Estimating gender disparities in federal criminal cases. *American Law and Economics Review, 17*, 127–159.

Steffensmeier, D., Kramer, J., & Streifel, C. (1993). Gender and punishment. *Criminology, 31*, 411–446.

Steinmetz, N. M., & Austin, D. M. (2014). Fear of criminal victimization on a college campus: A visual and survey analysis of location and demographic factors. *American Journal of Criminal Justice, 39*, 511–537.

St. Jean, P. K. B. (2007). *Pockets of crime: Broken windows, collective efficacy, and the criminal point of view*. Chicago, IL: University of Chicago Press.

Sutherland, E. H. (1949). *White collar crime*. New York, NY: Dryden Press.

Sutherland, R., Sindicich, N., Barrett, E., Whittaker, E., Peacock, A., Hickey, S., & Burns, L. (2015). Motivations, substance use and other correlates amongst property and violent offenders who regularly inject drugs. *Addictive Behaviors, 45*, 207–213.

Thornberry, T. P., Krohn, M., Lizotte, A., & Bushway, S. (2008). *The Rochester Youth Development Survey*. Hindelang Criminal Justice Research Center, University of Albany. Retrieved from http://www.albany.edu/hindelang/youth_study.html

Truman, J. L., & Langton, L. (2014). *Criminal victimization, 2013*. Washington, D.C.: Bureau of Justice Statistics, U.S. Department of Justice.

Tucker, M. C., & Rodriguez, C. M. (2014). Family dysfunction and social isolation as moderators between stress and child physical abuse risk. *Journal of Family Violence, 29*, 175–186.

U.S. Bureau of the Census. (2014). *Population by age and sex*. Retrieved from http://www.census.gov/population/age/

Vera Institute of Justice. (2012). *The cost of prisons: What incarceration costs taxpayers*. New York, NY: Author.

Wallerstein, J. S., & Wyle, C. J. (1947). Our law-abiding law breakers. *Probation, 25*, 107–112.

Welsh, W. N., Zajac, G., & Bucklen, K. (2014). For whom does prison based drug treatment work? Results from a randomized experiment. *Journal of Experimental Criminology, 10*(2), 151–177.

Worrall, J., Els, N., Piquero, A., & TenEyck, M. (2014). The moderating effects of informal social control in the sanctions-compliance nexus. *American Journal of Criminal Justice, 39*(2), 341–357.

Zajac, G., Lattimore, P. K., Dawes, D., & Winger, L. (2015). An implementation is local: Initial findings from the process evaluation of the Honest Opportunity Probation and Enforcement (HOPE) Demonstration Field Experiment. *Federal Probation, 79*(1), 31–36.

Zhao, J., & Ren, L. (2015). Exploring the dimensions of public attitudes toward the police. *Police Quarterly, 18*, 3–26.

# Index

Addition rule of probabilities, 150–152, 155

Adjacent values, boxplots and, 135, 138

Adjusted multiple coefficient of determination, 409, 415, 421

Adolescent employment, 263–264

Adult criminality, delinquency and, 435–440

Age and delinquency case study, 363–369, 453–458

Aggression questionnaires (AQs), 31

Alcohol, estimating consumption of, 192–194

Alcohol abuse, adolescent employment *versus,* 263–264

Alpha level in analysis of variance, 321

   critical region and, 217–218

   for difference between two proportions, 305

   for estimated regression coefficient, 452–453, 458

   as hypothesis testing step, 217

   in nondirectional research hypothesis, 220

   for partial slope coefficient, 421–422

   in pooled variance estimate, 281

   in risk of convicting the innocent, 215

   in separate variance estimate, 290

   for significance, 163

   small samples and, 227, 229

   for Tukey's HSD test, 325

Alphanumeric data, 26

Alternative hypothesis, 286

   in analysis of variance, 321

   directional, 284

     for car theft probability case, 162, 165

     for estimated regression coefficient, 457

     testing with, 221–226, 231

   in literacy program case study, 217

   nondirectional, 162

   in sentence length case study, 220

   for slope and correlation coefficient, 377

Analysis. *See also* Exploratory data analysis (EDA)

   trend, 68–74

   units of, 38–39

Analysis of variance (ANOVA), 312–341

   definition of, 314

   hypothesis testing with, 321–324

   introduction to, 313

   logic of, 313–315

   measure of association with, 326–327

   in multiple regression, 411

   probation success case study with, 328–329

   regional homicide rates case study with, 329–335

   total, between-groups, and within groups, 316–321

   Tukey's HSD test for, 324–326

Andreescu, Viviana, 423

"And rule" of probabilities, 152

ANOVA. *See* Analysis of variance (ANOVA)

Antilog, 443, 452

Association. *See* Measures of association

Association of Certified Fraud Examiners (ACFE), 209

ATF (Federal Bureau of Alcohol, Tobacco, and Firearms), 228–229

Availability samples, 14

Average score. *See* Mean

Bar charts, 46–50

Before-after research design, 294

Bell-shaped curve, distributions in, 66

Berk, Richard, 289

Bernoulli event, 164

Bernoulli process, 157

Best fitting lines, 364–365

Beta coefficient, 365

Beta weights, 404–405, 414, 418–419

Between groups sum of squares, 319, 322

Between groups variability, 316–323

Bias, 45, 190, 472

Bimodal distribution, 84–85

Binary variable, 33, 434. *See also* Regression analysis with dichotomous dependent variable

Binomial distribution

   hypothesis testing with, 160–167

   as probability distribution, 157–160

Binomial theorem, 159

Bivariate correlation, 342–390. *See also* Multiple regression

   bivariate distribution graphs for, 343–355

     linear regression line from, 346–347

     negative relationship shown by, 344–347

     no relationship shown by, 346–348

     positive relationship shown by, 343–345, 347–348

     state-level crime case study with, 350–355

   coefficient of determination and, 362

   least squares regression line and, 362–375

     age and delinquency case study in, 363–369

     for prediction, 369

     state crime rate prediction case study in, 370–375

   limited variation in, 381–382

   nonlinear relationships in, 382

   outliers in, 382–385

   Pearson correlation coefficient and, 355–361

   significance tests for b and r in, 376–381

   slope coefficient *versus* correlation coefficient in, 376

*Booster and the Snitch: Department Store Shoplifting, The* (Cameron), 15
Boot camps case study, 286–288, 395–396
Bounding rule of probabilities, 149, 155
"Box and whisker plot," 91
Boxplots. *See* Exploratory data analysis (EDA)
Bureau of Justice Statistics (BJS) National Crime Victimization
    Survey (NCVS), 4, 6, 13
    multistage cluster sampling for, 12
    samples for, 9
    variables presented by, 34, 37–38
Burglary and divorce case study, 380–381

California Psychological Inventory, Socialization (SO)
    scale of, 225
Cameron, Mary, 15
Capital punishment
    race and, 450–453
    race and homicide brutality case study on, 459–463
Car theft, probability of, 160–167
Caseload size and probation success case study,
    328–329
Case studies
    ATF seizures, 228–229
    burglary and divorce, 380–381
    car theft probability, 160–167
    caseload size and probation success, 328–329
    clearing homicides, 203–204
    counsel and sentences, 259–262
    descriptive research, 5–6
    drug and alcohol use vs. adolescent employment,
        263–264
    evaluation research, 8–9
    executions in the United States, 71–74
    explanatory research, 7
    gender and police officer work, 258–259
    gun control, 232–234
    intimate partner assault, 289–291
    literacy programs, 210–219
    mean sentence length, 219–221
    mean socialization levels of offenders, 225–226
    murder and poverty, 379
    on delinquency
        age and, 363–369
        age and adult criminality and, 435–440
        age and gender and, 453–458
        liking school and, 247–248
        onset and future offending and, 264–266
        predicting delinquency, 399–403
        siblings and, 300–302
    on estimating alcohol consumption, 192–194
        community policing effects, 202–203
    on gender
        emotions and, 244–247
        sentencing and, 291–293
    on police
        problem-oriented policing and, 296–299
        response time and neighborhood status and, 253–257
        response time of, 50–53
    on predicting murder rates in states, 423–426
    on prisons
        density and inmate assault in, 416–423
        expenditures for, 281–283
    on race
        brutality and capital punishment and, 459–463
        capital punishment and, 450–453
    on recidivism, 56–66
        boot camps and, 286–288, 395–396
        education and, 305–306
    probation officer behavior, 194–196
    probation success, 328–329
    random drug testing of inmates, 234–236
    rates, importance of, 35–36
    regional homicide rates, 329–335
    social disorganization, 284–286
    state crime rate prediction, 370–375
    state-level crime, 350–355
    work-role overload in policing, 198–201
Categorical data, 26. *See also* Hypothesis testing
    with categorical data
Categorical variables, 25
Causal inference, 393
Causal validity, 19, 393
Causation. *See* Multiple regression; Partial correlation
    coefficients
Cell frequencies, 248–251
Central Limit Theorem
    in difference between two proportions hypothesis testing, 303
    large samples and, 231
    in literacy program case study, 215
    probability and, 174–179
    sampling distribution of mean differences and, 278
    small samples and, 196–197, 227
Central tendency, measures of, 81–104
    definition of, 82
    introduction to, 81–82
    mean as, 93–99
        advantage and disadvantages of, 98–99
        calculation of, 93–96
        for grouped data, 96–98
    median as, 87–92
    mode as, 82–87
Charts, 46–50
Chi-square test
    computational formula for, 252–257
    critical values and, 480
    of independence, 248–252
    likelihood ratio statistic as, 450
    two-variable, 243–248
    for Wald statistic, 448, 457–458

Clark, David, 305
Class intervals, 58–65, 97, 125
Clearing homicides case study, 203–204
Coding of data, 27
Coefficients. *See also* Correlation coefficients
   of determination, 362
      exponentiated logistic regression, 443, 452
      logistic regression, 448–449
      multiple, 405, 407–408, 419–420
Cohen, Dov, 423
Columbine High School (Colorado), 5
Column marginals, in contingency tables, 245, 250–251
Combined explained variance, 409–410
Community-oriented policing, 202–203
Complement of an event, 149
Concordant pairs (CP), 265–266
Conditional distribution, 363
Conditional mean of $y$, 364, 366–367
Conditional probabilities, 152–155
Confidence intervals
   definition of, 187
   examples of, 193, 198–201
   interpretation of, 188
   for population means, 191–192
   for proportions and percentages, 201–204
   small sample estimation of, 196–201
Confidence level, 191
Confidence limits, 193
Constants, 25
Contingency coefficient measure of association, 259–260
Contingency tables, 244–253
   degrees of freedom from, 250–251
   description of, 244–245
   example of, 247–248
   of observed and expected frequencies, 249–250
   percentage differences in, 246–247
Continuous measures, 33
Continuous probability distribution, 167–174
   area under curve of, 169–170
   description of, 167–168
   standard scores and, 171–174
Continuous variables, 25
Control group, treatment group *versus*, 293–294
Correlation coefficients. *See also* Bivariate correlation;
     Partial correlation coefficients
   Pearson, 355–361
   significance tests for, 376–381
   slope coefficient *(b) versus,* 376
   state crime rates predictions using, 370
Correlation ratio, 327
Counsel and sentences, 259–262
Counting rule, 158
Counts, variables presented as, 34–36
Covariance, 254, 346, 356

Covariation, 346, 366
Cramer's $V$ measure of association, 260, 262
Critical difference (CD) score, 324–326, 331, 334–335
Critical region, 165–166, 217–219, 449
Critical values
   of chi-square statistic, 480
   in confidence intervals, 202
   of $F$, 321
   in pooled variance estimate, 281
   in separate variance estimate, 290–291
   of test statistic, 217, 227
Cumulative frequency distribution, 51, 54
Cumulative logistic probability distribution, 440
Cumulative percentages, 53–56
Cumulative proportions, 52, 54
Curvilinear relationships, 382

Data coding, 27
Data set, 25
Decision rules, 213, 229
Degrees of freedom (*df*)
   in analysis of variance, 322–323, 329
   contingency tables and, 250–251
   for estimated regression coefficient, 452–453, 462
   for likelihood ratio statistic, 450
   outliers and, 384
   in pooled variance estimate, 280–281
   for sampling distribution of $t$, 197
   in separate variance estimate, 288, 290
   for separate variance $t$ test, 292
   for small sample hypothesis testing, 227
   total, within groups, and between groups, 320–321
   for Tukey's HSD test, 325
Delinquency
   adult criminality and, 435–440
   age, gender and, 453–458
   age and, 363–369
   case study on, 7. *See also* Case studies, on delinquency
   future offending and, 264–266
   gender and, 274
   IQ score related to, 93
   liking school and, 247–248
   measurement validity of, 17–18
   National Opinion Survey of Crime and
      Justice on, 4
   siblings and, 300–302
   surveys on, 6
Dependent samples, 293–302
   hypothesis testing of, 293–295
   problem-oriented policing case study in, 296–299
   siblings and delinquency case study in, 300–302
Dependent variables. *See* Independent and dependent
     variables; Regression analysis with dichotomous
     dependent variable

Descriptive research, 5–6
Descriptive statistics, 16, 147
Determination
    coefficient of, 362, 419–420
    multiple coefficient of, 405, 407–408, 419–420
Deviation. *See* Mean deviation; Standard deviation;
        Variance
Dichotomies, 33
Dichotomous dependent variable. *See* Regression analysis with
        dichotomous dependent variable
Dichotomous independent variable, 423–426
Digit dialing, random, 11
Directional alternative hypothesis, 284
    for car theft probability case, 162, 165
    for estimated regression coefficient, 457
    testing with, 221–226, 231
Discordant pairs (DP), 265–266
Discrete probability distributions, 157–160
Dispersion, measures of, 105–144
    computational formulas for, 127–131
    exploratory data analysis in, 131–139
        of felony conviction data, 131–137
    for grouped data, 125–127
    for interval and ratio-level variables, 111–116
        interquartile range as, 113–116
        range as, 111–113
    introduction to, 106–107
    for nominal and ordinal-level variables, 107–111
    standard deviation as, 116–120
    for ungrouped data, 120–124
    variance as, 119–120
Distributions, 42–80. *See also* Bivariate correlation
    bimodal, 84–85
    binomial, 157–160
    conditional, 363
    cumulative logistic, 440
    cumulative logistic probability, 440
    definition of, 25
    $F$, 321, 481–482
    introduction to, 43–44
    joint, 153–154
    joint frequency, 244
    probability, 156–157, 166
    qualitative data in, 44–50
        pie charts and bar charts for, 46–50
        tables for, 45–46
    quantitative data in, 50–66
        grouped, 56–66
        grouped frequency, 63–66
        histograms for, 53–54
        line graphs and polygons for, 54–56
        ungrouped, 50–53
    rank-ordered, 87, 114
    sampling, 174–179, 212, 215–216, 421
    shape of, 66–67

skewed, 99, 136–137
standard normal
    area under curve of, 169–170
    description of, 167–168
    standard scores and, 171–174
standard normal probability, 170–171
Student's $t$, 197, 227, 479
    in time plots, 67–74
    for Wald statistic, 448
    $z$, 170, 191, 196–197, 478
Divorce and burglary case study, 380–381
Domestic violence, 289–291
Double bar charts, 49
Drug abuse, 263–264
Drug testing of inmates, random, 234–236
Duxbury, Linda, 198

Education and recidivism case study, 305–306
Efficiency, of estimates, 190
Elliot, Delbert, 4
Emotions, gender and, 244–247
Empirical association, 394
Empirical distributions, 25
Employment
    adolescent, 263–264
Epsilon, for error term, 372
Error
    in hypothesis testing, 163
    prediction, 260–261
    proportionate reduction, 260
    residual as, 371
    rounding, 53
    sampling, 9, 16
    standard
        accuracy of estimates and, 196
        confidence level and, 192, 194
        of the difference, 279–280, 288
        of difference between two means, 277–278
        of difference between two proportions, 306
        of mean, 175, 212
        of proportion, 202, 232
        of regression coefficients, 441
        of slope, 414
    Type I, 213, 215, 250, 314
    Type II, 213, 215, 250
Estimation, 185–207. *See also* Hypothesis testing; Linear
        probability model
    of confidence intervals
        from small samples, 196–201
        for proportions and percentages, 201–204
    of delinquency, 399
    introduction to, 186–187
    maximum likelihood (MLE), 440
    of pooled population proportion, 303–305
    of pooled standard deviation, 304

of pooled variance, 279–281
of population means, 190–196
of population variance, 411
properties of, 190
of separate variance, 288
of variability between and within groups, 322–323
Eta squared, 327
Evaluation research, 8–9
Events
    odds of, 442–443, 451–452, 454, 456
    probability and, 148–155
Executions in the United States case study, 71–74
Exhaustive intervals, 59
Expected frequencies, 249–250
Explanatory power, 406
Explanatory research, 6–7
Exploratory data analysis (EDA)
    boxplot construction, 137–139
    of felony conviction data, 131–137
    outliers and, 382–383
Exponentiated logistic regression coefficient, 443, 452
Extreme outliers, in scores, 135, 137

Factorial, 158
FBI (Federal Bureau of Investigation), Uniform Crime Reporting
    (UCR) Program of, 3, 17, 45, 83, 111, 350
    definition of, 5–6
F distribution, 321, 481–482
Federal Bureau of Alcohol, Tobacco, and Firearms (ATF), 228–229
Fence, in boxplots, 134–135, 138
Fractions, operations with, 471–472
Frequency
    bar charts for, 47–48
    cell, 248–251
    of hate crime incidents, 45–46
    marginal, 246
    observed, 252
    pie charts for, 46–47
    polygons for, 54
    relative, 37
    variables presented as, 34, 36
Frequency distribution
    bimodal, 84–85
    cumulative, 51, 54
    definition of, 25
    grouped, 57–59, 61
    joint, 244
    probability distributions *versus,* 156–157, 159
    ungrouped, 51, 53, 56–57, 96
F test, 279, 316, 320–322, 329, 411, 421. *See also* Analysis of
    variance (ANOVA)
Functional form of the model, 438

Gallup polls, 187–188, 232
Gang Resistance Education Training (G.R.E.A.T.), 8, 19

Gender
    delinquency and, 453–458
    emotions an, 244–247
    sentencing and, 291–293
Gender and police officer work case study,
        258–259
General addition rule of probabilities, 150–152
Generalizability of studies, 9–10, 13
General multiplication rule of probabilities, 152
General rule of probabilities, 155
General strain theory, 7, 151
Gilmore, Gary, 71
Glueck, Eleanor, 300
Glueck, Sheldon, 300
Goodman and Kruskal's gamma measure of association,
        262, 265–266
Goodness-of-fit, logit regression models for, 449–450
Gosset, W. E., 197
Gottfredson, Michael, 7, 123
Graphs
    of dispersion, 131–139
    line, 54–56
Greek letters, as statistical symbols, 469
Grouped frequency distribution, 57–59, 61
Grouped quantitative data
    case study with, 56–66
    dispersion measure of, 125–127
    frequency in, 63–66
    mean for, 96–98
    median for, 89–91
    standard deviation of, 130–131
    variance of, 130–131
Guinness Brewing Co., 197
Gun control attitudes, 232–234

Halinski, Michael, 198
Harris, Eric, 5
Harris, Heather, 289
*Hate Crimes Statistics,* 45
*Hate Crimes Statistics Act of 1990,* 45
Heterogeneity, 106, 109–110, 122–123
Heteroscedasticity, 439
Higgins, Chris, 198
High adjacent values, boxplots and, 135, 138
Hirschi, Travis, 7, 123
Histograms
    description of, 53, 62–63
    mode and, 82, 84–86
    of probability distributions, 159–160
Homicides
    clearing, case study of, 203–204
    regional rates of, 329–335
Homogeneity, 106
Homoscedasticity, 377–378, 439
Hot spots, for crime, 296

Hypothesis testing, 208–240. *See also* Analysis of variance (ANOVA); Estimation
  binomial distribution for, 160–167
  case study of, 160–167
  definition of, 7
  directional and nondirectional, 221–226
  for estimated regression coefficient, 453
  introduction to, 209–210
  of large sample population proportions and percentages, 231–236
  of logistic regression coefficients, 448–449
  in multiple regression, 411–415
  of single population mean, 210–221
    literacy program case study of, 210–219
    mean sentence length case study of, 219–221
  for slope and correlation coefficient, 376–377
  of small sample population means, 227–231
  standard normal distribution for, 174
Hypothesis testing of two population means or proportions, 274–311
  of independent samples, 279–293
    gender and sentencing case study in, 291–293
    intimate partner assault case study in, 289–291
    pooled variance estimate model for, 279–281
    prison expenditures case study in, 281–283
    separate variance estimate model for, 288
    social disorganization case study in, 284–286
  of large samples, 303–306
  of matched-groups or dependent samples, 293–302
    problem-oriented policing case study in, 296–299
    siblings and delinquency case study in, 300–302
  sample mean differences in, 274–276
  sampling distribution of mean differences in, 276–279
Hypothesis testing with categorical data, 242–272
  chi-square test for
    computational formula for, 252–257
    of independence, 248–252
    two-variable, 243–248
  introduction to, 243
  measures of association for
    for nominal-level variables, 258–262
    for ordinal-level variables, 262–266

Impulse control, 7
Independence. *See* Chi-square test
Independent and dependent variables, 7, 423–426. *See also* Logit regression models
Independent events, probability and, 153–155
Independent random samples
  education and recidivism case study in, 305–306
  gender and sentencing case study in, 291–293
  intimate partner assault case study in, 289–291
  pooled variance estimate model for, 279–281
  prison expenditures case study in, 281–283

  separate variance estimate model for, 288
  social disorganization case study in, 284–286
Inferential statistics, 16, 147–148, 174. *See also* Estimation
Inmate assault, prison density and, 416–423
Interquartile range (IQR), 112–116, 132–134
Inter-University Consortium for Political and Social Research (ICPSR), 4
Interval(s)
  class, 58–65, 97, 125
  midpoints of, 65–66, 97
  width of, 59–60
Interval-level measurement, 31, 33, 63–64
  interquartile range for, 113–116
  mode for, 82
  range for, 111–113
  variance for, 119
Interval-level variable, 31
Interval validity, 19
Interval variables. *See* Bivariate correlation
Intimate partner assault case study, 289–291
IQ scores, 93

Joint distribution, 153–154
Joint frequency distribution, 244
Joint probabilities, 150–151
Judgment samples, 15–16

Kim, Ryang, 305
Klebold, Dylan, 5

Lambda (λ) measure of association, 260–262
Least squares regression line. *See* Regression analysis
Levels of measurement, 26–33
  comparing of, 33
  interval, 31, 33
  nominal, 28
  ordinal, 28–31
  ratio, 32–33
Likelihood ratio statistic, 449, 458
Likert, Rensis, 31
Likert-type scales, 31
Linear correlation, 355
Linear probability model, 435–440
Linear relationships, 382
Line graphs, 54–56
Literacy program, hypothesis testing in, 210–219
Logistic regression model, 434
Logit regression models
  with one independent variable, 440–453
    goodness-of-fit measures for, 449–450
    overview of, 440–443
    predicted probabilities in, 443–447
    race and capital punishment case study of, 450–453
    significance testing for, 448–449

with two independent variables, 453–463
   delinquency, age, and gender case study with, 453–458
   race, brutality, and capital punishment case study in, 459–463
Log odds, 447
Log-odds version of model, 442–443
Low adjacent values, boxplots and, 135, 138

MacKenzie, Doris, 286, 288
"Making a causal inference," 393
Marginals, in contingency tables, 245–246, 250–251
Matched-groups or dependent samples, 293–302
   hypothesis testing of, 293–295
   problem-oriented policing case study in, 296–299
   siblings and delinquency case study in, 300–302
Mathematical operations, 468–474
   examples of, 472–474
   negative numbers and fractions in, 471–472
   order of, 470–471
   overview of, 469–470
   rounding in, 472
   symbols in, 469
Maximum likelihood estimation (MLE), 440
Mean, 93–99. See also Analysis of variance (ANOVA); Hypothesis testing of two population means or proportions; Standard deviation; Variance
   advantage and disadvantages of, 98–99
   as average score, 82
   calculation of, 93–96
   conditional mean of $y$, 364, 366–367
   differences in samples of, 274–276
   estimation of population, 190–196
   for grouped data, 96–98
   as minimum variance, 363–364
   of normal distributions, 168–170, 172–173
   outliers and, 99
   population, 175, 190
      hypothesis testing case studies on, 210–221
      hypothesis testing of, 227–231
      null hypothesis formal statement and, 231
   of probability distributions, 159
   sampling distribution of, 212, 215–216
   sampling distribution of differences in, 276–279
   standard error of, 175, 190, 212
Mean deviation, 95
Mean deviation score, 116
Mean socialization levels of offenders, 225–226
Measurement, 24–41
   introduction to, 25–26
   levels of, 26–33
      comparing of, 33
      interval, 31, 33
      nominal, 28
      ordinal, 28–31
      ratio, 32–33

units of analysis in, 38–39
   variables in, 33–37
Measurement validity, 17–18
Measures of association. See also Chi-square test
   analysis of variance (ANOVA) and, 326–327
   for nominal-level variables, 258–262
   for ordinal-level variables, 262–266
Median, 82
   advantages and disadvantages of, 91–92
   boxplots and, 132, 136
   calculation of, 87–92
   mean versus, 94
   outliers and, 99
Megargee, Edwin, 225
Midpoints, of intervals, 65–66, 97
Mild outliers, in scores, 135
Miller, Joel, 194
Minimum absolute value, critical difference as, 325–326
Minneapolis Domestic Violence Experiment, 289
Modal response, 261
Mode
   calculation of, 82–87
   for nominal and ordinal measurements, 82
Moving average, of data, 70
Multicollinearity, 398–399
Multiple coefficient of determination, 405, 407–408, 419–420
Multiple regression, 392–432. See also Partial correlation coefficients
   beta weights for, 404–405
   causation determination by, 393–395
   equation for, 396–403
      delinquency prediction by, 399–403
      overview of, 396–399
   hypothesis testing in, 411–415
   prison density and assault case study with, 416–423
Multiplication rule of probabilities, 152–155
Multistage cluster sampling, 12
Multivariate equation, 403
Multivariate regression model, 393, 398
Murder and poverty case study, 379
Mutually exclusive events, 150–151
Mutually exclusive intervals, 58

National Crime Victimization Survey (NCVS). See Bureau of Justice Statistics (BJS) National Crime Victimization Survey (NCVS)
National Incident-Based Reporting System (NIBRS), 5–6
National Institute of Justice, 289
National Intimate Partner Violence and Sexual Victimization Surveys, 11
National Opinion Survey of Crime and Justice, 4
National Survey on Drug Use and Health, 234
National Youth Survey (NYS), 4, 6, 17
Natural logarithm (ln), 442
Negative correlation, 344, 346, 351, 355, 372–373

Negatively skewed distributions, 67
Negative numbers, 471–472
Negative relationship, in Yule's $Q$ measure of association, 263–264
Neighborhood socioeconomic status, 253–257
Nisbett, Richard, 423
Nominal-level measurement, 44–45
    description of, 28, 33
    dispersion measure of, 107–111
    mode for, 82–84
Nondirectional hypothesis testing
    for boot camp efficacy case study, 287
    for car theft probability case study, 162
    definition of, 217
    directional hypothesis testing *versus*, 221–226
    formal statement of, 231
    for matched groups, 296
    *z* score example from, 220
Nonlinear relationships, 382
Non-mutually exclusive events, 150–151
Nonprobability sampling techniques, 10, 13–16
Nonspuriousness, 394
Normal distributions, 66, 167–170
Null hypothesis. *See also* Chi-square test
    in analysis of variance, 321, 326, 329
    for car theft probability case, 161–166
    for difference between two proportions, 305
    for directional and nondirectional hypothesis testing, 231
    for estimated regression coefficient, 457–458
    in gun control case study, 233–234
    of independence, 249, 251, 256
    in literacy program case study, 213–217
    for logistic regression coefficients, 448–449
    for matched groups, 294–296, 301
    in multiple regression, 411, 413
    for partial slope coefficient, 421–422
    in sentence length case study, 220–221
    for slope and correlation coefficient, 377–378
Numeric data, 26
Nye, F. Ivan, 17

Observed frequencies, 249, 252
Odds multiplier, 443, 452, 459
Odds of event, 442–443, 451–452, 454, 456
Odds ratio, 447, 452
Offenders
    delinquency onset and, 264–266
    mean socialization levels of, 225–226
One-tailed hypothesis testing, 221, 227, 284, 380. *See also* Directional alternative hypothesis; Nondirectional hypothesis testing
Ordinal-level measurement, 63–64
    description of, 28–31, 33
    dispersion measure of, 107–111
    mode for, 82

Ordinary least-squares (OLS) regression, 364, 397, 419. *See also* Linear probability model
"or" rule, 150
Outcome variables. *See* Independent and dependent variables
Outliers, scores as, 67
    in bivariate correlation, 382–385
    boxplots and, 131–132, 135
    definition of, 91
    in mean calculation, 98–99
Overlapping bar charts, 49

Parameters, 174
Partial correlation coefficients, 405–410
    multiple coefficient of determination and, 407–410
    overview of, 405–407
    in prison density case study, 419–420
Partial cross-tabulation tables, 395–396
Partial regression coefficients, 397
Partial slope coefficients
    definition of, 397
    equation for, 401–402
    population, 411
    in prison overcrowding case study, 416, 418–419
    significance of, 421
    unstandardized, 403
Pearson, Karl, 355
Pearson correlation coefficient, 355–361, 366, 376, 383
Pearson's *r*, 356
Percent(s)
    change as, 69–70
    in measurement, 36–37
Percentage differences
    in contingency tables, 246
    description of, 261
Percentages
    confidence intervals for, 201–204
    cumulative, 53–56
    hypothesis testing of, 231–236
Percent change score, 69
Percentiles, 114
Perfect negative correlation, 347
Perfect positive correlation, 347
Phi-coefficient measure of association, 258–259
Pie charts, 46–50
Point estimates, 187, 191. *See also* Estimation
Police
    problem-oriented policing and, 296–299
    response time of, 50–53, 95–96, 253–257
Police reports, 5
Polygons, 54–56
Pooled estimate of the population proportion, 303–305
Pooled standard deviation, estimated, 304
Pooled variance estimate model, 279–281

Population means, 175, 190. *See also* Analysis of variance (ANOVA); Hypothesis testing of two population means or proportions
  hypothesis testing of, 210–221
    large samples for, 227–231
    literacy program case study of, 210–219
    mean sentence length case study of, 219–221
  null hypothesis formal statement and, 231
Population parameters, 16, 187
Populations
  Central Limit Theorem and, 174–179
  estimation of means of, 190–196
  hypothesis testing of, 231–236
  overview of, 9–11
  partial slope coefficients for, 403
  rural, 379–380
Population standard deviation, 174
Positive correlation, 344, 351, 355, 374
Positively skewed distributions, 67
Positive relationship, in Yule's Q measure of association, 263–264
Poverty and murder case study, 379
Precision, 127, 194
Prediction, 260–261, 369
Pre-post research design, 294
Primary Sampling Units (PSUs), 12
Prisons
  density and inmate assault case study on, 416–423
  expenditures case study on, 281–283
  literacy program case study in, 210–219
Probability, 146–184
  of adult offenses, delinquency and, 456–458
  binomial distribution of, 157–160
  of capital charge, 451–453
  Central Limit Theorem and, 174–179
  conditional, 363
  distribution of, 156–157, 166, 281
  hypothesis testing and, 160–167
  introduction to, 147–149
  linear probability model and, 435–440
  in literacy program case study, 214–216
  logit regression models to predict, 443–447
  mode and, 82–84, 86
  as odds of event, 442–443
  rules of, 149–155
    on events, 149–153
  of sample mean differences, 276
  sampling techniques for, 10–13, 188–189
  standard normal distribution of, 167–174
    area under curve of, 169–170
    description of, 167–168
    standard scores and, 171–174
Probation officer behavior case study, 194–196
Probation success case studies, 328–329
Problem-oriented policing case study, 296–299

Product-moment correlation coefficient, 355–356. *See also* Pearson correlation coefficient
Proportionate reduction error (PRE) measure of association, 260
Proportions. *See also* Hypothesis testing of two population means or proportions
  confidence intervals for, 201–204
  cumulative, 52, 54
  hypothesis testing of, 231–236
  in measurement, 36–37
  standard error of, 232
"Pseudo-$R^2$" measures, in logistic regression models, 449
Purposive samples, 15–16

Qualitative data
  pie charts and bar charts for, 46–50
  tables for, 45–46
  variables in, 26
Quantitative data
  grouped, 56–66
  grouped frequency, 63–66
  histograms for, 53–54
  line graphs and polygons for, 54–56
  ungrouped, 50–53
  variables in, 26
Quartiles, 132–133. *See also* Interquartile range (IQR)
Quota samples, 14

$R^2$. *See* Multiple coefficient of determination
Race
  capital punishment and, 450–453
  homicide brutality, capital punishment and, 459–463
Random numbers, table of, 476–477
Random samples, 11–12, 174–175, 219, 278–279
Random selection, 10
Range
  of data, 59–60
  as dispersion measurement, 111–113
  interquartile, 113–116, 132–134
Rank-ordered distribution, 87, 114
Rates, variables presented as, 34–36
Ratio, 36
Ratio-level measurement, 63–64
  description of, 32–33
  interquartile range of, 113–116
  mode for, 82
  range for, 111–113
  variance for, 119
Ratio-level variables. *See* Bivariate correlation
Reading levels, mean, 210–219
Real class limits, 64–65
Rearrest, mean time to, 93–95
Recidivism
  boot camps and, 286–288, 395–396
  education and, 305–306
  grouped distributions on, 56–66

Regional homicide rates case study, 329–335
Regression analysis. *See also* Multiple regression
    least squares, 362–375
        age and delinquency case study in, 363–369
        for prediction, 369
        state crime rate prediction case study in, 370–375
    linear, 346–347
    outliers and, 383
    regression coefficient in, 365, 376
Regression analysis with dichotomous dependent variable, 433–467
    introduction to, 434–435
    linear probability model for, 435–440
    logit regression model with one independent variable for, 440–453
        goodness-of-fit measures for, 449–450
        overview of, 440–443
        predicted probabilities in, 443–447
        race and capital punishment case study of, 450–453
        significance testing for, 448–449
    logit regression model with two independent variables for, 453–463
        delinquency, age, and gender case study with, 453–458
        race, brutality, and capital punishment case study in, 459–463
Relative frequency, 37
Relative risk, 36, 247
Reliability, 18
Ren, Ling, 202
Replication, 289
Research hypothesis, 161. *See also* Alternative hypothesis
Residual, error as, 371, 411
Response time, police, 50–53, 95–96
Restricted addition rule of probabilities, 150
Restricted multiplication rule of probabilities, 152
Risk, relative, 36, 247
Rochester Youth Development Study (RYDS), 6
Roncek, Dennis, 443
Rounding numbers, 53, 472
Row marginals, in contingency tables, 245, 250–251
Rural populations and robbery rates case study, 379–380

Sample(s). *See also* Hypothesis testing of two population means or proportions; Random samples
    confidence intervals and, 196–201
    overview of, 9–11
    snowball, 15
    standard deviation of, 120, 122–123, 126
    stratified or weighted, 13
    variance of, 119–121, 126
Sample regression equation, 365
Sample statistic, 16, 174, 187
    difference between sample means as, 279
    in difference between two proportions hypothesis testing, 303
    separate variance *t* test as, 292

*t* as, 380–381
    for two-sample mean problem, 303
    *z* test as, 306
Sampling distribution of mean differences, 276–279
Sampling distributions
    Central Limit Theorem and, 174–179
    *F* statistic, 421
    of the mean, 212, 215–216
    Student's *t*, 197
Sampling error, 10, 16
Sampling notion of probability, 149
Sampling techniques, 10–16
    nonprobability, 13–16
    probability, 10–13, 188–189
Sampling variation, 212–213
Scatterplots, 343–355
    of curvilinear relationships, 382–383
    least squares regression line from, 363, 370–371, 373–374
    of negative relationship, 344–346
    of no relationship, 346–348
    of perfect negative correlation, 347
    of perfect positive correlation, 347
    of positive relationship, 343–345
    predictions from, 348–350
    regression line from, 346–348
    state-level crime case study and, 350–355
    three-dimensional, 403
Schools, liking, delinquency and, 247–248
School violence, 4–5
Science, definition of, 4
S-curves, 447
Secondary data analysis, 3, 26
Self-control, 7
Self-reporting surveys, 6, 17
Sentences
    counsel and, 259–262
    gender and, 291–293
    mean length of, 219–221
Separate variance estimate model, 288
Seung-Hui, Cho, 4–5
Sherman, Lawrence, 289
Short, James, 17
Shutt, John, 423
Siblings and delinquency case study, 300–302
Significance
    level of, 163–166, 210, 217, 220, 250
    of logit regression coefficients, 448–449, 452
    of partial slope coefficient, 421
    of slope coefficient and correlation coefficient, 376–381
    statistical, 275
Simple random sampling, 11
Single-bias hate crime, 45
Skewed distributions, 66–67, 99, 136–137

Skilling, Tracey, 31
Slope coefficient *(b)*, 397, 399–402
    in age and delinquency case study, 367–368
    correlation coefficient *(r) versus*, 376
    definition of, 365
    in linear probability model, 437
    in logit regression model, 447
    significance tests for, 376–381
Smoothing, of data, 70, 74
Snowball sample, 15
Social disorganization, 284–286
Socialization levels of offenders, mean, 225–226
Socioeconomic status, neighborhood, 253–257
Software programs for statistics, 3
Sorge, Geoff, 31
Spouse Assault Replication Program (SARP), 289
SPSS (Statistical Package for Social Sciences), 411, 468
Standard deviation
    computational formulas for, 127–131
    definition of, 120
    for difference between two proportions, 303–304
    of distribution of sample means, 175
    of grouped data sample, 125–127
    for matched groups, 297, 299, 301
    of mean sentence length, 293
    of normal distributions, 169–170
    overview of, 116–120
    for partial slope coefficients, 401
    population, 174, 192
    of probability distributions, 159
    sample, 120
    of sampling distribution, 278
    of ungrouped data sample, 120–124
Standard error, 192, 194
    of the difference, 279–280, 288
    of difference between two means, 277–278
    for difference between two proportions, 306
    of the mean, 175, 190, 212
    of the proportion, 202, 232
    for regression coefficients, 441
    of slope, 414
Standardized partial slope coefficients, 403–404
Standard normal distribution, 167–174, 215–216
    area under curve of, 169–170
    description of, 167–168
    standard scores and, 171–174
Standard normal probability distribution, 170–171
Standard scores, 171–174
State crime rate prediction case study, 370–375
Stated class limits, 60
State-level crime case study, 350–355
Statistical significance, 275
Statistical tables
    of critical value of chi-square statistic, 480
    of *F* distribution, 481–482
    of qualitative data, 45–46
    of random numbers, 476–477
    of studentized range statistic, 483–484
    of *t* distribution, 479
    of *z* distribution, 478
Statistics, overview of, 1–22
    descriptive and inferential, 16
    introduction to, 2–4
    nonprobability, 13–16
    populations and samples in, 9–11
    probability, 10–13
    role of, 4–9
    sampling techniques in, 10–16
    validity of, 16–19
Strain theory, general, 151
Stratified or weighted sampling, 13
Studentized range statistic, 324–325, 331, 483–484
Student's *t* distribution, 197, 227, 479
Summation symbol (λ), 470–471
Sum of squares
    between groups, 319, 322
    residual, 411–412
    total, 319
    variance estimate from, 323
    within groups, 319, 322
Supplementary Homicide Reports (SHR), 4
Surveys, self-reporting, 6, 17
Sutherland, Edwin, 209
Symbols, mathematical, 469
Symmetrical distributions, 167, 173
Systematic random sampling, 11–12

Tables. *See* Statistical tables
Tails of distributions, 66–67
*t* distribution. *See* Student's *t* distribution; *t* test
Theory, definition of, 7
Tied pairs, 265
Time plots, 67–74
"Time until failure" variable, 56
Total explained variance, 408–409
Total sum of squares, 319
Total variability, 316–321
Treatment effect, 294, 315
Trend analysis, 68–74
True experimental design, 8
Truncated median position (TMP), 113, 132
*t* test, 227–231, 384
    for difference between two sample means, 278–279
    for estimated regression coefficient, 441, 448, 452, 462
    matched group, 294–295
    separate variance, 292–293
    with three or more means, 313–314
Tukey, John W., 131, 134
Tukey's HSD (Honest Significant Difference) test,
    313, 324–326, 331

Two-tailed hypothesis testing, 197, 217, 221. *See also* Directional alternative hypothesis; Nondirectional hypothesis testing
Type I error, 163, 213, 215, 250, 314
Type II error, 163, 213, 215, 250

Unbiased estimate of population mean, 190
Unconditional probabilities, 152–155
Ungrouped frequency distribution, 51, 53, 56–57, 96
Ungrouped quantitative data, 50–53
    dispersion measure of, 120–124
    standard deviation of, 129
    variance of, 129
Uniform Crime Reports (UCR). *See* FBI (Federal Bureau of Investigation), Uniform Crime Reporting (UCR) Program of
Unimodal distributions, 167
Unit normal distribution, 171
Units of analysis, 26, 38–39
Univariate analysis, 43
University of Colorado, 4
University of Michigan, 4
Unstandardized partial slope coefficients, 403
U.S. Congress, Hate Crimes Statistics Act of 1990, 45
U.S. Department of Justice, 4

Validity, 16–19
Variables. *See also* Chi-square test; Logit regression models
    binary, 33, 434
    categorical, 25
    continuous, 25
    covariance of, 254
    definition of, 25
    interval and ratio-level, 111–116
    level of measurement, 28
    nominal and ordinal-level, 107–111
    presenting, 33–37
    qualitative, 26
    quantitative, 26
    ratio-level, 32–33
    "time until failure," 56
Variance. *See also* Analysis of variance (ANOVA)
    combined explained, 409–410
    computational formulas for, 127–131

estimate of pooled, 279–281
estimate of separate, 288
explained/regression, 411
of grouped data sample, 125–127
minimum, 363–364
of normal distributions, 168
overview of, 119–120
total explained, 408–409
of ungrouped data sample, 120–124
Venn diagrams to show, 406–407
Variation
    limited, 381–382
    ratio of, 107–111
    sampling, 212–213
Venn diagrams, 406–407
Vertical bar charts, 48
Violence
    domestic, 289–291
    youth, 5–7
Virginia Tech University, 5
Vito, Gennaro, 423

Wald test, 441, 448, 457–458, 462–463
Wallerstein, James, 17
"War on Drugs," 17
Weighted samples, 12–13
Within groups sum of squares, 319, 322
Within groups variability, 316–322
Work-role overload in policing case study, 198–201
Wyle, Clement, 17

$y$, conditional mean of, 364, 366–367
$y$-intercept, of regression line, 365, 369, 375
Youth Risk Behavior Survey (YRBS), 6–7
Youth violence, 5–7
Yule's $Q$ measure of association, 262–264, 266

$z$ distribution, 170, 196–197, 478
Zhao, Jihong, 202
$z$ scores, 171–174, 191–192, 216
$z$ test, 303, 306

# MKSAP® 16

## Medical Knowledge Self-Assessment Program®

# Neurology

# Welcome to the Neurology section of MKSAP 16!

Inside, look for new insights on headache and facial pain, head injury, epilepsy, stroke, dementia, movement disorders, multiple sclerosis and other demyelinating diseases. In addition, you will find advice on disorders of the spinal cord, neuromuscular disorders, neuro-oncology, and brain death. All of these topics are uniquely focused on the needs of generalists and subspecialists *outside* of neurology.

The publication of the 16th edition of Medical Knowledge Self-Assessment Program heralds a significant event, culminating 2 years of effort by dozens of leading subspecialists across the United States. Our authoring committees have strived to help internists succeed in Maintenance of Certification, right up to preparing for the MOC examination, and to get residents ready for the certifying examination. MKSAP 16 also helps you update your medical knowledge and elevates standards of self-learning by allowing you to assess your knowledge with 1,200 all-new multiple-choice questions, including 96 in Neurology.

MKSAP began more than 40 years ago. The American Board of Internal Medicine's examination blueprint and gaps between actual and preferred practices inform creation of the content. The questions, refined through rigorous face-to-face meetings, are among the best in medicine. A psychometric analysis of the items sharpens our educational focus on weaknesses in practice. To meet diverse learning styles, we offer MKSAP 16 online and in downloadable apps for tablets, laptops, and phones. We are also introducing the following:

*High-Value Care Recommendations:* The Neurology section starts with several recommendations based on the important concept of health care value (balancing clinical benefit with costs and harms) to address the needs of trainees, practicing physicians, and patients. These recommendations are part of a major initiative that has been undertaken by the American College of Physicians, in collaboration with other organizations.

*Content for Hospitalists:* This material, highlighted in blue and labeled with the familiar hospital icon (🏥), directly addresses the learning needs of the increasing number of physicians who work in the hospital setting. MKSAP 16 Digital will allow you to customize quizzes based on hospitalist-only questions to help you prepare for the Hospital Medicine Maintenance of Certification Examination.

We hope you enjoy and benefit from MKSAP 16. Please feel free to send us any comments to mksap_editors@acponline.org or visit us at the MKSAP Resource Site (mksap.acponline.org) to find out how we can help you study, earn CME, accumulate MOC points, and stay up to date. I know I speak on behalf of ACP staff members and our authoring committees when I say we are honored to have attracted your interest and participation.

Sincerely,

*Patrick Alguire*

Patrick Alguire, MD, FACP
Editor-in-Chief
Senior Vice President
Medical Education Division
American College of Physicians

# Neurology

## Committee

**Blair Ford, MD, Editor**[2]
Professor of Clinical Neurology
Department of Neurology, Neurological Institute
Columbia University Medical Center
New York, New York

**Jack Ende, MD, MACP, Associate Editor**[1]
Professor of Medicine
University of Pennsylvania
Chief, Department of Medicine
Penn Presbyterian Medical Center
Philadelphia, Pennsylvania

**Elizabeth E. Gerard, MD**[1]
Assistant Professor of Neurology
Director, Women's Epilepsy Program
Northwestern Comprehensive Epilepsy Center
Department of Neurology
Feinberg School of Medicine
Northwestern University
Chicago, Illinois

**Daniel M. Harrison, MD**[2]
Assistant Professor of Neurology
Department of Neurology
Johns Hopkins University School of Medicine
Baltimore, Maryland

**Robert G. Kaniecki, MD**[2]
Director, The Headache Center
Chief, Headache Division
Assistant Professor of Neurology
University of Pittsburgh
Pittsburgh, Pennsylvania

**Erik P. Pioro, MD, PhD**[2]
Staff Neurologist
Barry Winovich ALS Research Chair
Director, Section of ALS and Related Disorders
Department of Neurology, Neurological Institute
Cleveland Clinic
Cleveland, Ohio

**Joshua Z. Willey, MD, MS**[2]
Assistant Professor of Neurology
Department of Neurology, Neurological Institute
Columbia University Medical Center
New York, New York

## SPECIAL REVIEWER

**Mark W. Green, MD**[2]
Professor of Neurology
Director of Headache and Pain Medicine
Mount Sinai School of Medicine
New York, New York

## Editor-in-Chief

**Patrick C. Alguire, MD, FACP**[1]
Senior Vice President, Medical Education
American College of Physicians
Philadelphia, Pennsylvania

## Deputy Editor-in-Chief

**Philip A. Masters, MD, FACP**[1]
Senior Medical Associate for Content Development
American College of Physicians
Philadelphia, Pennsylvania

## Senior Medical Associate for Content Development

**Cynthia D. Smith, MD, FACP**[2]
American College of Physicians
Philadelphia, Pennsylvania

## Neurology Clinical Editor

Richard S. Eisenstaedt, MD, FACP[1]

## Neurology Reviewers

John K. Chamberlain, MD, MACP[1]
Thomas E. Finucane, MD, FACP[1]
Gloria Fioravanti, DO, FACP[1]
Faith T. Fitzgerald, MD, MACP[1]
Steven L. Lewis, MD[1]
Peter Wiernik, MD, FACP[2]

## Neurology Reviewers Representing the American Society for Clinical Pharmacology & Therapeutics

Carol J. Collins, MD[1]
Linda A. Hershey, MD[1]
Kevin J. Leary, MD, FACP[1]

## Neurology ACP Editorial Staff

**Ellen McDonald, PhD**[1], Senior Staff Editor
**Sean McKinney**[1], Director, Self-Assessment Programs
**Margaret Wells**[1], Managing Editor
**Linnea Donnarumma**[1], Assistant Editor

## ACP Principal Staff

**Patrick C. Alguire, MD, FACP**[1]
*Senior Vice President, Medical Education*

**D. Theresa Kanya, MBA**[1]
*Vice President, Medical Education*

**Sean McKinney**[1]
*Director, Self-Assessment Programs*

**Margaret Wells**[1]
*Managing Editor*

**Valerie Dangovetsky**[1]
*Program Administrator*

**Becky Krumm**[1]
*Senior Staff Editor*

**Ellen McDonald, PhD**[1]
*Senior Staff Editor*

**Katie Idell**[1]
*Senior Staff Editor*

**Randy Hendrickson**[1]
*Production Administrator/Editor*

**Megan Zborowski**[1]
*Staff Editor*

**Linnea Donnarumma**[1]
*Assistant Editor*

**John Haefele**[1]
*Assistant Editor*

**Developed by the American College of Physicians**

---

1. Has no relationships with any entity producing, marketing, re-selling, or distributing health care goods or services consumed by, or used on, patients.

2. Has disclosed relationships with entities producing, marketing, re-selling, or distributing health care goods or services consumed by, or used on, patients. See below.

## Conflicts of Interest

The following committee members, reviewers, and ACP staff members have disclosed relationships with commercial companies:

**Blair Ford, MD**
*Consultantship*
Medtronic, Inc.

**Mark W. Green, MD**
*Honoraria*
GlaxoSmithKline
*Speakers Bureau*
GlaxoSmithKline

**Daniel M. Harrison, MD**
*Honoraria*
Direct One Communications
*Research Grants/Contracts*
Bayer Schering Pharma

**Robert G. Kaniecki, MD**
*Speakers Bureau*
GlaxoSmithKline, Merck, OrthoMcNeil

**Erik P. Pioro, MD, PhD**
*Consultantship*
Avanir Pharmaceuticals, Inc.
*Honoraria*
Avanir Pharmaceuticals, Inc.
*Speakers Bureau*
Avanir Pharmaceuticals, Inc.

**Cynthia D. Smith, MD, FACP**
*Stock Options/Holdings*
Merck and Company

**Joshua Z. Willey, MD, MS**
*Honoraria*
Cardionet

**Peter Wiernik, MD, FACP**
*Royalties*
Churchill-Livingstone
*Honoraria*
Celgene, Millenium
*Consultantship*
Celgene
*Speakers Bureau*
Celgene

## Acknowledgments

The American College of Physicians (ACP) gratefully acknowledges the special contributions to the development and production of the 16th edition of the Medical Knowledge Self-Assessment Program® (MKSAP® 16) made by the following people:

*Graphic Services:* Michael Ripca (Technical Administrator/Graphic Designer) and Willie-Fetchko Graphic Design (Graphic Designer).

*Production/Systems:* Dan Hoffmann (Director, Web Services & Systems Development), Neil Kohl (Senior Architect), and Scott Hurd (Senior Systems Analyst/Developer).

*MKSAP 16 Digital:* Under the direction of Steven Spadt, Vice President, ACP Digital Products & Services, the digital version of MKSAP 16 was developed within the ACP's Digital Product Development Department, led by Brian Sweigard (Director). Other members of the team included Sean O'Donnell (Senior Architect), Dan Barron (Senior Systems Analyst/Developer), Chris Forrest (Senior Software Developer/Design Lead), Jon Laing (Senior Web Application Developer), Brad Lord (Senior Web Developer), John McKnight (Senior Web Developer), and Nate Pershall (Senior Web Developer).

The College also wishes to acknowledge that many other persons, too numerous to mention, have contributed to the production of this program. Without their dedicated efforts, this program would not have been possible.

## Introducing the MKSAP Resource Site (mksap.acponline.org)

The MKSAP Resource Site (mksap.acponline.org) is a continually updated site that provides links to MKSAP 16 online answer sheets for print subscribers; access to MKSAP 16 Digital, Board Basics® 3, and MKSAP 16 Updates; the latest details on Continuing Medical Education (CME) and Maintenance of Certification (MOC) in the United States, Canada, and Australia; errata; and other new information.

## ABIM Maintenance of Certification

Check the MKSAP Resource Site (mksap.acponline.org) for the latest information on how MKSAP tests can be used to apply to the American Board of Internal Medicine for Maintenance of Certification (MOC) points.

## RCPSC Maintenance of Certification

In Canada, MKSAP 16 is an Accredited Self-Assessment Program (Section 3) as defined by the Maintenance of Certification Program of The Royal College of Physicians and Surgeons of Canada (RCPSC) and approved by the Canadian Society of Internal Medicine on December 9, 2011. Approval of this and other Part A sections of MKSAP 16 extends from July 31, 2012, until July 31, 2015. Approval of Part B sections of MKSAP 16 extends from December 31, 2012, to December 31, 2015. Fellows of the Royal College may earn three credits per hour for participating in MKSAP 16 under Section 3. MKSAP 16 will enable Fellows to earn up to 75% of their required 400 credits during the 5-year MOC cycle. A Fellow can achieve this 75% level by earning 100 of the maximum of 174 *AMA PRA Category 1 Credits*™ available in MKSAP 16. MKSAP 16 also meets multiple CanMEDS Roles for RCPSC MOC, including that of Medical Expert, Communicator, Collaborator, Manager, Health Advocate, Scholar, and Professional. For information on how to apply MKSAP 16 CME credits to RCPSC MOC, visit the MKSAP Resource Site at mksap.acponline.org.

## The Royal Australasian College of Physicians CPD Program

In Australia, MKSAP 16 is a Category 3 program that may be used by Fellows of The Royal Australasian College of Physicians (RACP) to meet mandatory CPD points. Two CPD credits are awarded for each of the 174 *AMA PRA Category 1 Credits*™ available in MKSAP 16. More information about using MKSAP 16 for this purpose is available at the MKSAP Resource Site at mksap.acponline.org and at www.racp.edu.au. CPD credits earned through MKSAP 16 should be reported at the MyCPD site at www.racp.edu.au/mycpd.

## Continuing Medical Education

The American College of Physicians is accredited by the Accreditation Council for Continuing Medical Education (ACCME) to provide continuing medical education for physicians.

The American College of Physicians designates this enduring material, MKSAP 16, for a maximum of 174 *AMA PRA Category 1 Credits*™. Physicians should claim only the credit commensurate with the extent of their participation in the activity.

Up to 14 *AMA PRA Category 1 Credits*™ are available from July 31, 2012, to July 31, 2015, for the MKSAP 16 Neurology section.

## Learning Objectives

The learning objectives of MKSAP 16 are to:
- Close gaps between actual care in your practice and preferred standards of care, based on best evidence
- Diagnose disease states that are less common and sometimes overlooked and confusing
- Improve management of comorbid conditions that can complicate patient care
- Determine when to refer patients for surgery or care by subspecialists
- Pass the ABIM Certification Examination
- Pass the ABIM Maintenance of Certification Examination

## Target Audience

- General internists and primary care physicians
- Subspecialists who need to remain up-to-date in internal medicine
- Residents preparing for the certifying examination in internal medicine
- Physicians preparing for maintenance of certification in internal medicine (recertification)

## Earn "Same-Day" CME Credits Online

For the first time, print subscribers can enter their answers online to earn CME credits in 24 hours or less. You can submit your answers using online answer sheets that are provided at mksap.acponline.org, where a record of your MKSAP 16 credits will be available. To earn CME credits, you need to answer all of the questions in a test and earn a score of at least 50% correct (number of correct answers divided by the total number of questions). Take any of the following approaches:

1. Use the printed answer sheet at the back of this book to record your answers. Go to mksap.acponline.org, access the appropriate online answer sheet, transcribe your answers, and submit your test for same-day CME credits. There is no additional fee for this service.

2. Go to mksap.acponline.org, access the appropriate online answer sheet, directly enter your answers, and submit your test for same-day CME credits. There is no additional fee for this service.

3. Pay a $10 processing fee per answer sheet and submit the printed answer sheet at the back of this book by mail or fax, as instructed on the answer sheet. Make sure you calculate your score and fax the answer sheet to 215-351-2799 or mail the answer sheet to Member and Customer Service, American College of Physicians, 190 N. Independence Mall West, Philadelphia, PA 19106-1572, using the courtesy envelope provided in your MKSAP 16 slipcase. You will need your 10-digit order number and 8-digit ACP ID number, which are printed on your packing slip. Please allow 4 to 6 weeks for your score report to be emailed back to you. Be sure to include your email address for a response.

If you do not have a 10-digit order number and 8-digit ACP ID number or if you need help creating a username and password to access the MKSAP 16 online answer sheets, go to mksap.acponline.org or email custserv@acponline.org.

## Permission/Consent for Use of Figures Shown in MKSAP 16 Neurology Multiple-Choice Questions

The figure shown in Self-Assessment Test item 8 is adapted with permission from Laforest C, Selva D, Crompton J, Leibovitch I. Clinical observations: Entopic phenomenon as initial presentation of acute myelogenous leukemia. Ann Intern Med. 2005;143(11):847. [PMID: 16330805] The figure shown in Self-Assessment Test item 90 is adapted with permission from Virtual Dx, Physical Examination Findings, item 23. Copyright 2010 American College of Physicians. All Rights Reserved. Available (to program subscribers) at:

http://virtualdx.acponline.org/self-assessment/questions/pef_q023. Accessed March 19, 2012.

## Disclosure Policy

It is the policy of the American College of Physicians (ACP) to ensure balance, independence, objectivity, and scientific rigor in all of its educational activities. To this end, and consistent with the policies of the ACP and the Accreditation Council for Continuing Medical Education (ACCME), contributors to all ACP continuing medical education activities are required to disclose all relevant financial relationships with any entity producing, marketing, re-selling, or distributing health care goods or services consumed by, or used on, patients. Contributors are required to use generic names in the discussion of therapeutic options and are required to identify any unapproved, off-label, or investigative use of commercial products or devices. Where a trade name is used, all available trade names for the same product type are also included. If trade-name products manufactured by companies with whom contributors have relationships are discussed, contributors are asked to provide evidence-based citations in support of the discussion. The information is reviewed by the committee responsible for producing this text. If necessary, adjustments to topics or contributors' roles in content development are made to balance the discussion. Further, all readers of this text are asked to evaluate the content for evidence of commercial bias and send any relevant comments to mksap_editors@acponline.org so that future decisions about content and contributors can be made in light of this information.

## Resolution of Conflicts

To resolve all conflicts of interest and influences of vested interests, the ACP precluded members of the content-creation committee from deciding on any content issues that involved generic or trade-name products associated with proprietary entities with which these committee members had relationships. In addition, content was based on best evidence and updated clinical care guidelines, when such evidence and guidelines were available. Contributors' disclosure information can be found with the list of contributors' names and those of ACP principal staff listed in the beginning of this book.

## Hospital-Based Medicine

For the convenience of subscribers who provide care in hospital settings, content that is specific to the hospital setting has been highlighted in blue. Hospital icons (🏥) highlight where the hospital-only content begins, continues over more than one page, and ends.

## Educational Disclaimer

The editors and publisher of MKSAP 16 recognize that the development of new material offers many opportunities for error. Despite our best efforts, some errors may persist in print. Drug dosage schedules are, we believe, accurate and in accordance with current standards. Readers are advised, however, to ensure that the recommended dosages in MKSAP 16 concur with the information provided in the product information material. This is especially important in cases of new, infrequently used, or highly toxic drugs. Application of the information in MKSAP 16 remains the professional responsibility of the practitioner.

The primary purpose of MKSAP 16 is educational. Information presented, as well as publications, technologies, products, and/or services discussed, is intended to inform subscribers about the knowledge, techniques, and experiences of the contributors. A diversity of professional opinion exists, and the views of the contributors are their own and not those of the ACP. Inclusion of any material in the program does not constitute endorsement or recommendation by the ACP. The ACP does not warrant the safety, reliability, accuracy, completeness, or usefulness of and disclaims any and all liability for damages and claims that may result from the use of information, publications, technologies, products, and/or services discussed in this program.

## Publisher's Information

## Unauthorized Use of This Book Is Against the Law

MKSAP 16 ISBN: 978-1-938245-00-8
(Neurology) ISBN: 978-1-938245-05-3

Printed in the United States of America.

For order information in the U.S. or Canada call 800-523-1546, extension 2600. All other countries call 215-351-2600. Fax inquiries to 215-351-2799 or email to custserv@acponline.org.

## Errata and Norm Tables

Errata for MKSAP 16 will be available through the MKSAP Resource Site at mksap.acponline.org as new information becomes known to the editors.

MKSAP 16 Performance Interpretation Guidelines with Norm Tables, available July 31, 2013, will reflect the knowledge of physicians who have completed the self-assessment tests before the program was published. These physicians took the tests without being able to refer to the syllabus, answers, and critiques. For your convenience, the tables are available in a printable PDF file through the MKSAP Resource Site at mksap.acponline.org.

# Table of Contents

**Headache and Facial Pain**

Approach to the Patient with Headache . . . . . . . . . . . 1
Secondary Headaches . . . . . . . . . . . . . . . . . . . . . . . . 1
  Common Features and Evaluation . . . . . . . . . . . 1
  Thunderclap Headache . . . . . . . . . . . . . . . . . . . . 3
  Idiopathic Intracranial Hypertension
  (Pseudotumor Cerebri) . . . . . . . . . . . . . . . . . . . 4
  Trigeminal Neuralgia (Tic Douloureux) . . . . . . . 4
Primary Headaches . . . . . . . . . . . . . . . . . . . . . . . . . 5
  Migraine . . . . . . . . . . . . . . . . . . . . . . . . . . . . . . 5
  Tension-Type Headache . . . . . . . . . . . . . . . . . . 9
  Cluster Headache . . . . . . . . . . . . . . . . . . . . . . 10
  Related Primary Headache Syndromes . . . . . . . 10

**Head Injury**

Traumatic Brain Injury . . . . . . . . . . . . . . . . . . . . . 10
Concussive Head Injury . . . . . . . . . . . . . . . . . . . . 11
Postconcussion Syndrome . . . . . . . . . . . . . . . . . . . 11
Epidural and Subdural Hematoma . . . . . . . . . . . . . 12
Head Injury in a Military Population . . . . . . . . . . . 12

**Epilepsy**

Features and Epidemiology of Epilepsy . . . . . . . . . . 12
Initial Approach to the Patient with a First Seizure . . . 13
Clinical Presentations of Seizures . . . . . . . . . . . . . . 14
  Partial Seizures . . . . . . . . . . . . . . . . . . . . . . . . 14
  Generalized Seizures . . . . . . . . . . . . . . . . . . . . 14
Epilepsy Syndromes . . . . . . . . . . . . . . . . . . . . . . . 15
  Partial (Focal) Epilepsy . . . . . . . . . . . . . . . . . . 15
  Idiopathic Generalized Epilepsy . . . . . . . . . . . . 15
Comorbidities and Complications of Epilepsy . . . . . 16
  Mood Disorders . . . . . . . . . . . . . . . . . . . . . . . . 16
  Cognitive Problems . . . . . . . . . . . . . . . . . . . . . 16
  Osteoporosis . . . . . . . . . . . . . . . . . . . . . . . . . . 16
  Sudden Unexplained Death in Epilepsy . . . . . . . 16
Diagnostic Evaluation of Seizures and Epilepsy . . . . 16
  Imaging Studies . . . . . . . . . . . . . . . . . . . . . . . . 16
  Electroencephalography . . . . . . . . . . . . . . . . . . 17
  Clinical Evaluation and Video
  Electroencephalographic Monitoring . . . . . . . . 17
Treatment of Epilepsy . . . . . . . . . . . . . . . . . . . . . . 18
  Antiepileptic Drug Therapy . . . . . . . . . . . . . . . 18
  Nonpharmacologic Therapy . . . . . . . . . . . . . . . 21

Status Epilepticus . . . . . . . . . . . . . . . . . . . . . . . . . 22
  Generalized Convulsive Status Epilepticus . . . . . 22
  Nonconvulsive Status Epilepticus . . . . . . . . . . . 22

**Stroke**

Epidemiology and Definition of Stroke . . . . . . . . . . 24
Diagnosis of Stroke . . . . . . . . . . . . . . . . . . . . . . . . 24
Stroke Subtypes . . . . . . . . . . . . . . . . . . . . . . . . . . 24
  Transient Ischemic Attack . . . . . . . . . . . . . . . . 24
  Ischemic Stroke . . . . . . . . . . . . . . . . . . . . . . . . 26
  Hemorrhagic Stroke . . . . . . . . . . . . . . . . . . . . 27
Acute Ischemic Stroke . . . . . . . . . . . . . . . . . . . . . 28
  Clinical Diagnosis . . . . . . . . . . . . . . . . . . . . . . 28
  Imaging Techniques . . . . . . . . . . . . . . . . . . . . . 29
  Treatment . . . . . . . . . . . . . . . . . . . . . . . . . . . . 29
Acute Hemorrhagic Stroke . . . . . . . . . . . . . . . . . . 32
  Intracerebral Hemorrhage . . . . . . . . . . . . . . . . 32
  Subarachnoid Hemorrhage . . . . . . . . . . . . . . . . 33
Other Types of Stroke . . . . . . . . . . . . . . . . . . . . . 33
  Dural Sinus Venous Thrombosis . . . . . . . . . . . . 33
  Carotid and Vertebral Artery Dissection . . . . . . 36
  Asymptomatic Aneurysm . . . . . . . . . . . . . . . . . 36
Admission to Stroke Units and Stroke Centers . . . . . 36
Secondary Stroke Prevention . . . . . . . . . . . . . . . . . 36
  Hypertension . . . . . . . . . . . . . . . . . . . . . . . . . . 36
  Dyslipidemia . . . . . . . . . . . . . . . . . . . . . . . . . . 36
  Antithrombotic Treatment . . . . . . . . . . . . . . . . 37
  Surgery for Secondary Stroke . . . . . . . . . . . . . . 38
Prevention of Stroke Complications . . . . . . . . . . . . 38
  Neurologic Worsening . . . . . . . . . . . . . . . . . . . 38
  Medical Complications . . . . . . . . . . . . . . . . . . . 39
  Perioperative Stroke . . . . . . . . . . . . . . . . . . . . 39
Primary Prevention of Stroke . . . . . . . . . . . . . . . . . 40
  Asymptomatic Carotid Stenosis . . . . . . . . . . . . 40
Stroke Recovery and Long-Term Prognosis . . . . . . . 40

**Dementia**

General Overview . . . . . . . . . . . . . . . . . . . . . . . . . 40
  Definition and Description . . . . . . . . . . . . . . . . 40
  Evaluation of the Patient with Suspected
  Dementia . . . . . . . . . . . . . . . . . . . . . . . . . . . . 41
  Differential Diagnosis of Dementia . . . . . . . . . . 42
  Diagnosis of Alzheimer Diseaseand Other
  Dementias . . . . . . . . . . . . . . . . . . . . . . . . . . . . 42

Alzheimer Disease. . . . . . . . . . . . . . . . . . . . . . . . . . 43
    Prevalence . . . . . . . . . . . . . . . . . . . . . . . . . 43
    Pathogenesis . . . . . . . . . . . . . . . . . . . . . . . 43
    Clinical Features . . . . . . . . . . . . . . . . . . . . 43
    Pathologic Features . . . . . . . . . . . . . . . . . . 44
    Treatment . . . . . . . . . . . . . . . . . . . . . . . . . 44
Non-Alzheimer Dementias . . . . . . . . . . . . . . . . . 45
    Dementia with Lewy Bodies . . . . . . . . . . . . 45
    Frontotemporal Dementia . . . . . . . . . . . . . . 46
    Vascular Dementia . . . . . . . . . . . . . . . . . . . . 46
    Normal Pressure Hydrocephalus . . . . . . . . . . 46
    Dementia and Driving . . . . . . . . . . . . . . . . . 47

## Movement Disorders

Overview of Movement Disorders . . . . . . . . . . . . . 47
Parkinson Disease . . . . . . . . . . . . . . . . . . . . . . . . . 47
    Clinical Features of Parkinson Disease . . . . . . . . 48
    Diagnosis of Parkinson Disease . . . . . . . . . . . . 49
    Treatment of Parkinson Disease . . . . . . . . . . . 49
Parkinson-Plus Syndromes . . . . . . . . . . . . . . . . . . 51
Gait Disturbance. . . . . . . . . . . . . . . . . . . . . . . . . . 51
    Ataxia . . . . . . . . . . . . . . . . . . . . . . . . . . . . . 52
Essential Tremor. . . . . . . . . . . . . . . . . . . . . . . . . . 52
Dystonia. . . . . . . . . . . . . . . . . . . . . . . . . . . . . . . . 53
Chorea . . . . . . . . . . . . . . . . . . . . . . . . . . . . . . . . . 53
Tardive Dyskinesia . . . . . . . . . . . . . . . . . . . . . . . . 54
Myoclonus . . . . . . . . . . . . . . . . . . . . . . . . . . . . . . 54
Tic Disorders and Tourette Syndrome . . . . . . . . . . . 55
Wilson Disease . . . . . . . . . . . . . . . . . . . . . . . . . . . 55
Neuroleptic Malignant Syndrome . . . . . . . . . . . . . . 56
Restless Legs Syndrome . . . . . . . . . . . . . . . . . . . . . 56

## Multiple Sclerosis and Other Demyelinating Diseases

Spectrum, Pathophysiology, and Epidemiology. . . . . . 57
Presenting Signs and Symptoms of Multiple Sclerosis . . 57
Diagnosis of Multiple Sclerosis . . . . . . . . . . . . . . . . 58
    Diagnostic Criteria and Testing . . . . . . . . . . . . 58
    Differential Diagnosis of Multiple Sclerosis . . . . . 59
Clinical Course of Multiple Sclerosis . . . . . . . . . . . . 59
Treatment of Multiple Sclerosis. . . . . . . . . . . . . . . . 61
    Lifestyle Modifications and General Health Care . . 61
    Treatment of Acute Exacerbations . . . . . . . . . . . 61
    Disease-Modifying Therapies . . . . . . . . . . . . . . 62
    Symptomatic Management . . . . . . . . . . . . . . . . 63

## Disorders of the Spinal Cord

Presenting Symptoms and Signs of Myelopathies . . . . 64
Compressive Myelopathies . . . . . . . . . . . . . . . . . . . 65
    Clinical Presentation . . . . . . . . . . . . . . . . . . . 65
    Diagnosis. . . . . . . . . . . . . . . . . . . . . . . . . . . . 65
    Treatment . . . . . . . . . . . . . . . . . . . . . . . . . . . 65
Noncompressive Myelopathies . . . . . . . . . . . . . . . . 66
    Clinical Presentation, Diagnosis, and
    Management . . . . . . . . . . . . . . . . . . . . . . . . . 66

## Neuromuscular Disorders

Peripheral Neuropathies . . . . . . . . . . . . . . . . . . . . 68
    Overview. . . . . . . . . . . . . . . . . . . . . . . . . . . . 68
    Classification, Findings, and Diagnosis. . . . . . . . 68
    Mononeuropathies . . . . . . . . . . . . . . . . . . . . . 70
    Polyneuropathies . . . . . . . . . . . . . . . . . . . . . . 70
Treatment of Neuropathic Pain. . . . . . . . . . . . . . . . 73
Amyotrophic Lateral Sclerosis . . . . . . . . . . . . . . . . . 73
Neuromuscular Junction Disorders . . . . . . . . . . . . . 74
    Myasthenia Gravis . . . . . . . . . . . . . . . . . . . . . 74
    Lambert-Eaton Myasthenic Syndrome. . . . . . . . 74
Myopathies. . . . . . . . . . . . . . . . . . . . . . . . . . . . . . 75
    Overview. . . . . . . . . . . . . . . . . . . . . . . . . . . . 75
    Inflammatory Myopathy . . . . . . . . . . . . . . . . . 76
    Endocrine-Related Myopathies . . . . . . . . . . . . . 76

## Neuro-oncology

Intracranial Tumors . . . . . . . . . . . . . . . . . . . . . . . 77
Primary Central Nervous System Tumors . . . . . . . . . 78
Management of Intracranial Tumors. . . . . . . . . . . . . 79
Paraneoplastic Syndromes . . . . . . . . . . . . . . . . . . . 79

## Brain Death

Description and Findings . . . . . . . . . . . . . . . . . . . . 80
Apnea Test . . . . . . . . . . . . . . . . . . . . . . . . . . . . . . 81

## Bibliography . . . . . . . . . . . . . . . . . . . . . . . . . . . 81

## Self-Assessment Test . . . . . . . . . . . . . . . . . . . . . 85

## Index . . . . . . . . . . . . . . . . . . . . . . . . . . . . . . . . 153

# Neurology High-Value Care Recommendations

The American College of Physicians, in collaboration with multiple other organizations, is embarking on a national initiative to promote awareness about the importance of stewardship of health care resources. The goals are to improve health care outcomes by providing care of proven benefit and reducing costs by avoiding unnecessary and even harmful interventions. The initiative comprises several programs that integrate the important concept of health care value (balancing clinical benefit with costs and harms) for a given intervention into various educational materials to address the needs of trainees, practicing physicians, and patients.

To integrate discussion of high-value, cost-conscious care into MKSAP 16, we have created recommendations based on the medical knowledge content that we feel meet the below definition of high-value care and bring us closer to our goal of improving patient outcomes while conserving finite resources.

**High-Value Care Recommendation**: A recommendation to choose diagnostic and management strategies for patients in specific clinical situations that balance clinical benefit with cost and harms with the goal of improving patient outcomes.

Below are the High-Value Care Recommendations for the Neurology section of MKSAP 16.

- Do not routinely order neuroimaging or other diagnostic tests (electroencephalography, lumbar puncture, or blood testing) in patients with primary headaches; the diagnostic yield of a brain MRI or a head CT scan in patients with a chronic headache and no other concerning signs or symptoms is less than 1% (see Item 58).
- Do not use the combination of aspirin and clopidogrel for secondary prevention of stroke because this combination has no additional benefit over a single antiplatelet agent alone and has a higher risk of bleeding (see Item 34).
- Order CT of the head rather than MRI of the brain to rule out an intracerebral hemorrhage, subarachnoid bleeding, or hydrocephalus in a patient with an acute stroke because CT is more cost-effective, less time consuming, and more readily available than MRI (see Item 8).
- Treat neuropathic pain with generic tricyclic antidepressants (amitriptyline and nortriptyline) because they are generally better tolerated and much less expensive than pregabalin, although their use may be limited by the development of anticholinergic adverse effects.
- After brain death has been established with apnea testing, do not perform confirmatory testing with electroencephalography or transcranial Doppler ultrasonography because it is unnecessary (see Item 7).

# Neurology

## Headache and Facial Pain

### Approach to the Patient with Headache

Headache is a nearly universal phenomenon, with a lifetime prevalence greater than 90% in the general population. A headache is most often symptomatic of a benign recurrent disorder but, at times, may reflect an isolated catastrophic condition. The second edition of the International Classification of Headache Disorders (ICHD-2) divides headache into primary (defined by symptoms) and secondary (defined by cause) disorders (**Table 1**). Less than 5% of headache presentations to emergency departments result from secondary headache. Once serious underlying causes of headache are excluded, the possibility of migraine must be considered because greater than 90% of patients who have recurrent headache on presentation to an emergency department or physician's office will have migraine. An algorithmic approach to a patient with headache is presented in **Figure 1**. ◩

## Secondary Headaches

### Common Features and Evaluation

Because primary headaches are defined by symptom complex and secondary headaches by cause, extensive symptom overlap is possible. The presence of a secondary headache syndrome may be signaled by the presence of one of the following red flags in the history or examination:

- First or worst headache
- Abrupt-onset or thunderclap attack
- Progression or fundamental change in headache pattern
- Abnormal physical examination findings
- Neurologic symptoms lasting longer than 1 hour

| TABLE 1. International Classification of Headache Disorders |
| --- |
| **Primary Headaches** |
| Migraine |
| Tension-type headache |
| Cluster headache and other trigeminal autonomic cephalalgias |
| Other primary headaches<br>  Primary stabbing, cough, exertional, and sexual headaches<br>  Primary thunderclap headache<br>  Hemicrania continua<br>  Hypnic headache<br>  New daily persistent headache |
| **Secondary Headaches** |
| Headache attributed to head and neck trauma (postconcussion syndrome, subdural hematoma) |
| Headache attributed to a cranial or cervical vascular disorder (stroke, hemorrhage, dissection) |
| Headache attributed to a nonvascular intracranial disorder (brain neoplasm, arachnoid cyst) |
| Headache attributed to a substance or its withdrawal (nitrates, alcohol, caffeine) |
| Headache attributed to infection (meningitis, cerebral abscess) |
| Headache attributed to a disorder of homeostasis (hypercapnia, dialysis, hypertension) |
| Headache or facial pain attributed to a disorder of extracranial head and neck structures (eye, sinus) |
| Headache attributed to a psychiatric disorder (depression, anxiety disorders) |
| Cranial neuralgias, central and primary facial pain, and other headaches (trigeminal neuralgia) |
| Headache, neuralgia, and facial pain disorders not already mentioned |

Source: Headache Classification Subcommittee of the International Headache Society. The International Classification of Headache Disorders: 2nd edition. Cephalalgia. 2004;24(suppl 1):16-22. [PMID: 14979299].

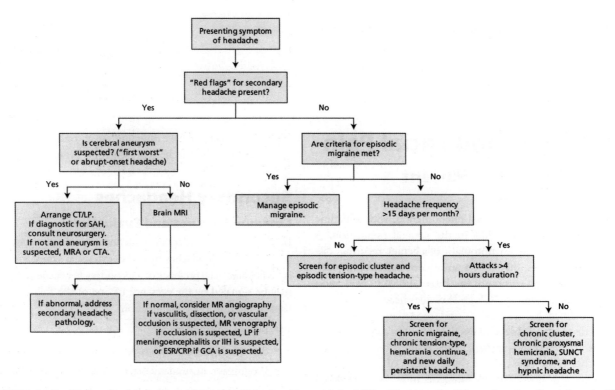

**FIGURE 1.** Algorithmic approach to a patient with headache. CRP = C-reactive protein level; CTA = CT angiography; ESR = erythrocyte sedimentation rate; GCA = temporal (giant cell) arteritis; IIH = idiopathic intracranial hypertension; LP = lumbar puncture; MRA = magnetic resonance angiography; SAH = subarachnoid hemorrhage; SUNCT = short-lasting unilateral neuralgiform headache with conjunctival injection and tearing syndrome.

- New headache in persons younger than 5 years or older than 50 years
- New headache in patients with cancer, immunosuppression, or pregnancy
- Headache associated with alteration in or loss of consciousness
- Headache triggered by exertion, sexual activity, or Valsalva maneuvers

Although most of these warning signs are found in the history, a focused neurologic examination is essential in the complete evaluation of a patient with headache. In addition to cognitive, sensorimotor, and reflex testing, a thorough cranial nerve assessment is essential, with examination of the optic discs, visual fields, and eye movements. Further information may be gained by evaluating the cranium, cervical spine, carotid and temporal arteries, temporomandibular joint, and the ears and sinuses.

Further diagnostic evaluation is required when a red flag of secondary headache is identified. Neuroimaging is the most sensitive diagnostic tool in the assessment of this type of headache. CT of the head is the preferred imaging modality in the settings of skull fracture, acute subarachnoid or intracerebral hemorrhage, and paranasal sinus disease. Although CT may be more widely available and less expensive than MRI, an MRI of the brain is more sensitive in identifying intracranial pathology and, therefore, is the study of choice in most other clinical settings of acute or chronic headache. Contrast administration may be helpful in settings of malignant or inflammatory disease. The addition of CT or MR angiographic or venographic studies may be useful when vascular pathology, such as vascular occlusion, aneurysm, or malformation, is considered. Cerebrospinal fluid (CSF) examination may be warranted in patients with subarachnoid hemorrhage (SAH) with a normal CT or when meningoencephalitis, meningeal carcinomatosis, and disorders of intracranial hypertension or hypotension are suspected. Electroencephalography, evoked potentials, or plain radiographs play no role in the routine evaluation of the patient with headache. On occasion, serologic studies may be of value. Measurement of the erythrocyte sedimentation rate and C-reactive protein level are necessary to evaluate potential temporal (giant cell) arteritis, which often presents as a global nondescript headache in an older person reporting a new headache associated with malaise and fatigue. Temporal artery biopsy may be required to confirm the diagnosis. (For a further discussion of giant cell arteritis, see MKSAP 16 Rheumatology.) Serum toxicology, carboxyhemoglobin determination, and thyroid function tests also may help identify specific secondary explanations for a headache presentation.

## Thunderclap Headache

Thunderclap headache is defined as a severe headache that reaches maximum intensity within 60 seconds of onset. Although classically associated with SAH, thunderclap headache also may be caused by other conditions, ranging from benign to life-threatening ones (**Table 2**). Because approximately 25% of thunderclap headache presentations result from an SAH, this type of headache should be approached as a neurologic emergency, and CT of the head without contrast should be performed without delay. CT sensitivity within the first 24 hours of the hemorrhage is approximately 90% to 95% but decreases markedly with each successive day. When results of CT are negative for SAH, lumbar puncture must be performed. CSF analysis should include determination of opening pressure, protein and glucose levels, erythrocyte and leukocyte counts (with leukocyte differential), and the presence of spectroscopic xanthochromia; this last finding is reported to be 98% sensitive in documenting hemorrhage within 12 hours of the event.

Vascular causes other than SAH also must be considered with the initial presentation of thunderclap headache. Ischemic stroke, intracerebral hemorrhage, and acute venous thrombosis all may manifest as a thunderclap headache, typically with

signs of cortical or brainstem dysfunction. Dissection of the internal carotid or vertebral arteries additionally may present with acute headache or neck pain, which is sometimes complicated by ipsilateral Horner syndrome or findings indicative of subsequent embolic stroke. Arterial dissections are rarely spontaneous and often associated with cervical trauma, sometimes of a relatively minor nature.

The term reversible cerebral vasoconstriction syndrome, previously known as Call-Fleming syndrome, was applied in 2007 to a group of disorders characterized by recurrent thunderclap headache associated with transient segmental cerebral vasoconstriction. The diagnostic criteria proposed for this syndrome consist of recurrent thunderclap headache with possible focal neurologic signs, normal or near-normal CSF, and angiographic documentation of multifocal segmental cerebral vasoconstriction that completely resolves within 12 weeks. Reversible cerebral vasoconstriction syndrome can occur without an identifiable cause or may be associated with preeclampsia or eclampsia, exposure to certain medications (sympathomimetic agents, ergots) or blood products (transfused erythrocytes, immune globulin), or catecholamine-secreting tumors. This condition must be distinguished from primary cerebral angiitis and secondary vasculitis affecting the central nervous system (CNS), both of which have different therapeutic recommendations and prognoses. No clinical trial data are available on which to base therapeutic recommendations. Given the moderate risk of acute infarction during the period of vasoconstriction (up to 54% in one clinical series), administration of a calcium channel blocker (nimodipine or verapamil) is recommended. Alternatively, short-term high-dose corticosteroids have been reported to be effective, and intravenous magnesium has had a reported benefit in patients with eclampsia- or preeclampsia-induced reversible cerebral vasoconstriction syndrome.

Several primary headache disorders also may be associated with recurrent thunderclap headache (see Table 2). Although the location of pain may vary, the headache is characterized by abrupt-onset headache that is sharp or explosive in quality, often lasting seconds to minutes, and occasionally followed by a lingering dull or throbbing pain of more modest intensity. The headache attacks may be spontaneous or provoked by certain physical maneuvers, such as coughing, exercising, or participating in sexual activity. Persons with a history of migraine may be more prone to these disorders. The prognosis is benign. Indomethacin is uniquely effective among the NSAIDs for many with such presentations, whereas β-adrenergic blockers may help those with exertional triggers.

| TABLE 2. Conditions Associated with Thunderclap Headache |
| --- |
| **Secondary Headache Disorders** |
| Subarachnoid hemorrhage |
| Sentinel bleeding from an unruptured cerebral aneurysm |
| Intraparenchymal hematoma |
| Dissection of a carotid or vertebral artery |
| Cerebral arterial, venous, or sinus thrombosis |
| Pituitary apoplexy |
| Spontaneous intracranial hypotension |
| Reversible cerebral vasoconstriction syndromes |
| Posterior reversible encephalopathy syndrome |
| Colloid cyst occlusion of the third ventricle |
| **Primary Headache Disorders** |
| Primary stabbing headache ("ice-pick" headache) |
| Primary cough headache |
| Primary exertional headache |
| Primary headache associated with sexual activity |
| Primary thunderclap headache |

- Calcium channel blockers, such as verapamil and nimodipine, are considered first-line therapies for thunderclap headache associated with reversible cerebral vasoconstriction syndrome.

## Idiopathic Intracranial Hypertension (Pseudotumor Cerebri)

CSF pressure elevation in the absence of obstruction or an intracranial space-occupying lesion signifies the presence of benign or idiopathic intracranial hypertension (IIH). Both names are misnomers because the clinical course is not always benign and the condition frequently is related to an identifiable cause. Greater than 90% of affected persons are female, and most are overweight and of child-bearing age. Headache (90%), visual symptoms (72%), and tinnitus (60%) are the most common presenting symptoms. Visual disturbances may include intermittent or persistent blurring, diplopia, or brief episodes of darkening or dimming of vision termed visual obscurations. Papilledema is almost always present on examination, and patients may present with cranial nerve VI palsy. Diagnosis requires documentation of elevated pressure (>250 mm $H_2O$ in adults) in the CSF obtained by lumbar puncture with the patient in the lateral decubitus position. CSF composition is typically normal, although occasionally a low protein content is noted. Results of neuroimaging studies are either normal or show slit-like ventricles. Although only 25% of patients with IIH may report visual impairment at presentation, 90% exhibit some form of visual loss on perimetry, most commonly enlargement of the physiologic blind spot or generalized visual field constriction. The loss of visual field may become progressive and lead to blindness.

Treatment begins with identification and management of identifiable causes of intracranial hypertension (**Table 3**). Lumbar puncture may be palliative, at least temporarily, and serial punctures are the treatment of choice for IIH during pregnancy. Acetazolamide, 250 to 500 mg twice daily, may [*carbonic anhydrase inhibitor/diuretic*] help reduce CSF production, and dosages as high as 4 g/d can be used, if tolerated. Paresthesias, dizziness or drowsiness, taste distortion (particularly with carbonated substances), and kidney stones may complicate acetazolamide use. Additionally, both retrospective and prospective series have documented the clinical benefit of weight reduction in patients with IIH. If these conservative therapies are unsuccessful, as determined by assessment of symptoms or visual perimetry, surgical shunting or decompressive procedures should be considered. Optic nerve fenestration, an ophthalmologic procedure involving incisions in the optic nerve sheath behind the eye, may be helpful in two thirds of patients with threatened loss of vision in medically refractory IIH. Lumboperitoneal and ventriculoperitoneal shunts also may be required for IIH that is unresponsive to medical therapy.

| TABLE 3. Possible Causes of Intracranial Hypertension |
| --- |
| **Obstruction to CSF flow** |
| Scarring from trauma or meningitis |
| **Obstruction to venous drainage** |
| Venous sinus thrombosis |
| Superior vena cava syndrome or elevated right-sided heart pressures |
| Dural arteriovenous malformation with shunt |
| **Exogenous agents** |
| Hypervitaminosis A (secondary to excess vitamin A intake) |
| Isotretinoin |
| Anabolic steroids and growth hormone |
| Corticosteroid withdrawal |
| Tetracycline, doxycycline, minocycline |
| **Endocrine disorders and other conditions** |
| Addison disease |
| Hypoparathyroidism |
| Polycystic ovary syndrome |
| Obesity |
| Pregnancy |
| CSF = cerebrospinal fluid. |

## Trigeminal Neuralgia (Tic Douloureux)

Classically a disorder of older adults, trigeminal neuralgia is characterized by recurrent episodes of brief electrical shooting pain limited to the face or forehead. It is the most frequently diagnosed form of facial pain, with a population prevalence of 4 per 100,000. This condition usually affects the second (cheek) or third (jaw/chin) divisions of the trigeminal nerve. Only 5% of patients with trigeminal neuralgia have pain involving the first division, in contrast to patients with herpes zoster reactivation affecting the trigeminal nerve, which commonly begins in the ophthalmic branch and leads to clinical symptoms in the forehead, cornea, and nose. Typical trigeminal neuralgia has a bilateral distribution in less than 5% of patients and is never synchronous when bilateral. Although by definition the pain lasts only a fraction of a second to 2 minutes, it can recur in repeated trains or paroxysms. Nearly all patients report triggering factors, such as talking, chewing, touching specific trigger points on the face (either incidentally or while shaving), eating, applying cosmetics, or brushing the teeth. Occasionally, exposure to a breeze, bright light, or loud noise also can be provocative. The pain can recur daily for weeks to months and then spontaneously remit for months or years, or it may display a more chronic progressive course.

Onset of trigeminal neuralgia is after age 40 years in 90% of affected patients. Evidence suggests that the likely cause is vascular compression of the trigeminal root entry zone at the level of the pons, which leads to focal demyelination and aberrant neural discharge. In younger persons, the most common cause is multiple sclerosis. Although fewer than 10% of patients with trigeminal neuralgia will have a causative intracranial lesion, an MRI of the brain with contrast must be obtained.

Carbamazepine remains the first-line drug for medical management, with oxcarbazepine being a reasonable alternative. Carbamazepine should be initiated at a low dose, generally 100 mg twice daily; the dosage is then gradually increased, with monitoring of serum drug levels and sodium values. Evidence is weaker for second-line agents, such as baclofen, gabapentin, clonazepam, or lamotrigine. In patients with partial response to carbamazepine or oxcarbazepine, adding a second-line agent is reasonable. Patients should receive an adequate trial of at least three drugs or drug combinations before interventional or surgical treatment is considered.

Medical management is unsuccessful in approximately 30% of patients with trigeminal neuralgia. Other options include selective nerve fiber destruction (rhizotomy), which may require balloon compression, radiofrequency thermal lesioning, glycerol injection, or focused stereotactic (gamma knife) radiation. Microvascular decompression, which can manually separate the compressing vessel from the trigeminal nerve, may be appropriate for younger patients in relatively good health. Compared with noninvasive procedures, which have success rates of 50% to 85%, microvascular decompression has long-term success rates of 90%, with lower risks of postoperative numbness in the face or cornea.

**KEY POINT**

- Carbamazepine is a first-line drug for medical management of trigeminal neuralgia, and patients should receive an adequate trial of at least three drugs or drug combinations before interventional or surgical treatment is considered.

# Primary Headaches

Most primary headaches can be diagnosed on the basis of a comprehensive history and physical examination and do not require neuroimaging or other diagnostic tests (such as electroencephalography, lumbar puncture, and blood testing). The diagnostic yield of a brain MRI or a head CT scan in patients with a chronic headache and no concerning signs or symptoms is less than 1%.

## Migraine

### Epidemiology and Clinical Features

More than 90% of patients who have recurrent headache on presentation to primary care offices or emergency departments have migraine. This extraordinarily high figure results from the high prevalence of migraine, which affects approximately 13% of adults in the United States, and the disabling nature of the condition. Migraine usually begins in late childhood or early adolescence and follows various courses: the headache may go into remission after a few years, recur in

cycles of variable headache activity for many years or decades, or evolve into a chronic and more refractory state (in a minority of patients). Migraine is more common in preadolescent boys than girls but becomes three times more common in adult women than men. Prevalence peaks in the fifth decade of life, drops significantly in the sixth and seventh decades, and is exceedingly uncommon in later decades. Although a typical migraine episode consists of a unilateral, throbbing headache accompanied by photophobia, phonophobia, and nausea, extensive variability exists in the clinical expressions of migraine, often leading to misdiagnoses of tension headache in the presence of bilateral steady pain or sinus headache when the discomfort is a frontal or facial pressure (**Table 4**).

Migraine is preceded or accompanied by focal neurologic symptoms termed aura in up to 30% of patients. The most common aura is a visual experience consisting of a flashing light or an enlarging blind spot rimmed with a shimmering edge or jagged lines in the peripheral vision. Common nonvisual auras include spreading unilateral numbness or tingling affecting the face and upper extremities, disturbed thinking or speech, and dizziness. An aura is defined as typical if it involves any combination of visual, hemisensory, or language abnormalities, with each symptom developing over a minimum of 5 minutes and lasting a maximum of 60 minutes. The associated migraine usually occurs within 1 hour, but some auras do not progress to head pain. Auras should be investigated further if they extend beyond 60 minutes, involve any focal motor weakness (hemiplegic migraine), or display brainstem symptoms, such as diplopia, dysphagia, ataxia, vertigo, dysarthria, or synchronous bilateral sensory dysfunction (basilar migraine).

Migraine is subclassified according to not only the presence or absence of aura, but also the monthly frequency of headache occurrences. Most episodes occur fewer than 15 days per month and are classified as episodic migraine. Chronic (previously "transformed") migraine occurs at least 15 days per month for more than 3 months, with the individual headache episodes meeting the criteria for migraine on at least 8 of those days. Chronic migraine affects 2% of the world population and results in substantial individual disability and enormous societal costs. Transformation of episodic into chronic migraine has been shown to occur at a rate of 3% per year in the general population and 14% per year in headache clinic populations. Risk factors for such transformation, as suggested by available evidence, are listed below:

- Older age
- Major life changes or significant stressors
- Female sex
- Low education/socioeconomic status
- Head/neck trauma
- Obesity

**TABLE 4.** International Headache Society Criteria for Migraine Diagnosis

**Without Aura**

A. At least five attacks fulfilling criteria B-D

B. Headache attacks lasting 4-72 hours (untreated or unsuccessfully treated)

C. Headache with at least two of the following four characteristics:
  1. Unilateral location
  2. Pulsating quality
  3. Moderate or severe pain intensity that inhibits or prohibits daily activities
  4. Aggravation by walking on stairs or similar routine physical activity

D. During headache, occurrence of at least one of following symptoms:
  1. Nausea/vomiting
  2. Photophobia/phonophobia

E. Exclusion of secondary headaches

**With Aura**

A. At least two attacks fulfilling criteria B and C

B. Headache with at least three of the following four characteristics:
  1. One or more fully reversible aura symptoms indicating focal cerebral cortical and/or brainstem dysfunction
  2. At least one aura symptom that develops gradually over more than 4 minutes, or two or more symptoms that occur in succession
  3. Duration <60 minutes for an aura symptom, with duration proportionally increased if more than one aura symptom is present
  4. Headache after aura with an intervening free interval <60 minutes; headache may also begin before or simultaneously with the aura

C. Exclusion of secondary headaches

Adapted with permission from Headache Classification Subcommittee of the International Headache Society. The International Classification of Headache Disorders: 2nd edition. Cephalalgia. 2004;24(suppl 1):24-27. [PMID: 14979299] Copyright 2004 International Headache Society. Reprinted by Permission of SAGE.

- Presence of comorbid pain and sleep or psychiatric disorders
- High caffeine or nicotine intake
- Overtreatment with acute headache medications

The final risk factor listed for migraine transformation, overtreatment with acute medication, results in what is now termed medication overuse headache (rather than rebound headache). Medication overuse headache is present in up to 80% of persons with chronic migraine seeking medical attention, and thus it is critical to question all these patients about the use of both prescription and nonprescription products while taking a headache history. Several studies assessing the relationship between migraine transformation and acute medication use have drawn the same conclusions, namely, that opiates (critical exposure 8 days per month) and barbiturates (critical exposure 5 days per month) are associated with high rates of migraine progression, but NSAIDs and triptans induce progression only in those with frequent episodic migraine (10-14 days per month).

### Acute Migraine Treatment

Evidence from well-designed placebo-controlled trials supports the efficacy of NSAIDs, dihydroergotamine, and triptans in the treatment of acute migraine (**Table 5**). No evidence supports the efficacy of butalbital compounds and little evidence supports the efficacy of isometheptene compounds in the treatment of acute migraine, despite their widespread use. Opioids are recommended only in rare circumstances when migraine-specific agents and NSAIDs are contraindicated or have been ineffective. Antiemetics are helpful as adjunctive therapies when used with NSAIDs or triptans.

NSAIDs can be effective for patients with milder forms of migraine. Triptans are first-line therapies for acute migraine in patients whose attacks do not reliably respond to simple or combination analgesics. Extensive evidence documents the benefit of seven different commercially available triptan agents in oral, nasal, and parenteral formulations. Oral formulations are appropriate when nausea is mild to moderate and vomiting is absent at the time of treatment. Because comparative studies do not clearly establish superiority of one oral triptan over another, the choice of a specific agent may be made on the basis of formulary availability and previous therapeutic trials. Subcutaneous sumatriptan, the only injectable version, is the fastest and most efficacious of the triptan agents and is indicated for migraine accompanied by severe nausea or vomiting, for migraines already established by the time of awakening, or in patients who do not respond consistently to oral or nasal preparations. Triptans are contraindicated in patients with known or suspected vasospastic or ischemic

**TABLE 5.** Acute Migraine Therapies

| Drug | Recommended Dose |
|---|---|
| **NSAIDs[a]** | |
| Aspirin | 325-900 mg |
| Ibuprofen | 400-800 mg |
| Naproxen sodium | 250-1000 mg |
| Combination of acetaminophen/aspirin/caffeine | 2 tablets |
| **Migraine-Specific Oral Agents[a]** | |
| Almotriptan | 6.25-12.5 mg |
| Eletriptan | 20-40 mg |
| Frovatriptan | 2.5 mg |
| Naratriptan | 1-2.5 mg |
| Rizatriptan | 5-10 mg |
| Sumatriptan | 25-100 mg |
| Sumatriptan-naproxen | 85-500 mg |
| Zolmitriptan | 2.5-5 mg |
| **Nonoral Therapies[a]** | |
| Dihydroergotamine | 1 mg nasally |
| Dihydroergotamine | 1 mg subcutaneously |
| Prochlorperazine | 10 mg intravenously |
| Sumatriptan | 5-20 mg nasally |
| Sumatriptan | 4-6 mg subcutaneously |
| Zolmitriptan | 5 mg nasally |

[a]Doses listed may be administered twice daily.

vascular disorders, uncontrolled hypertension, and hemiplegic or basilar migraine subtypes. Adverse effects include limb heaviness, flushing, paresthesias, and tightness in the chest, neck, or throat; they are almost always benign and can be mitigated by lowering the triptan dose, switching to an alternative triptan, or treating earlier in the attack. Although severe cardiovascular reactions have been reported, the incidence is estimated at less than one event per 4 million treatments. Drug interactions are rare, and recent evidence suggests that combining triptans with antidepressants does not significantly increase the risk of the serotonin syndrome.

The goal of acute migraine treatment is complete resolution of the migraine within 1 to 2 hours and return to normal function, without significant adverse effects or recurrence of headache, within 24 hours. This optimal outcome is maximized by using NSAIDs or migraine-specific agents early in the attack, specifically when the pain is still mild. This strategy of early intervention has been shown to enhance the efficacy of migraine-specific therapies in several prospective trials. The use of acute migraine medications should be strictly limited to fewer than 10 days per month to avoid the potential development of medication overuse headache.

Patients with migraine in urgent or emergent care settings may have either a particularly severe acute attack or status migrainosus, which by definition is a single migraine attack extending beyond 72 hours. For most of these patients, prescribed NSAID or triptan therapies have not worked. Intravenous dopamine antagonists, often in combination with intravenous diphenhydramine (to limit or eliminate possible dystonic reactions) and hydration, may be helpful. Intravenous preparations of ketorolac and sodium valproic acid also are quite useful, and the addition of a single dose of dexamethasone appears to lower the rate of recurrence. Parenteral dihydroergotamine is an extremely effective option for patients who have not taken triptans or ergots within 24 hours and represents the cornerstone of inpatient management of refractory migraine. **H**

**Migraine Prevention**

Migraine prevention begins with identification and reduction or elimination of triggers and risk factors. Regular sleep and eating patterns, adequate hydration, daily exercise, and a reduced intake of dietary caffeine, artificial sweeteners, and additives (such as monosodium glutamate) can help prevent migraine attacks. Regular school or work attendance should be strongly encouraged in patients with migraine. Behavioral therapies of value include relaxation training, electromyographic and thermal biofeedback, and cognitive behavioral therapy. Evidence is currently insufficient to recommend acupuncture, chiropractic manipulation, oxygen therapy, occlusion adjustment, hypnosis, and transcutaneous electrical nerve stimulation for the prevention of migraine. The herbs feverfew and butterbur root, the mineral magnesium, the vitamin riboflavin, and the antioxidants coenzyme $Q_{10}$ and α-lipoic acid all have some evidence of efficacy in migraine prevention. Pharmacologic prophylaxis of migraine is indicated in the six situations listed below.

1. Headache frequency greater than 2 days per week (or 8 days per month)

2. Use of acute medications, successfully or unsuccessfully, more than 2 days per week

3. Headache attacks that remain disabling despite aggressive acute intervention, as documented by impaired lifestyle, unimproved disability status, or use of rescue medications more frequently than monthly

4. Presence of prolonged aura (>1 hour), complex aura (basilar or hemiplegic), or migraine-induced stroke

5. Contraindications to, failure or overuse of, or adverse events with acute therapies

6. Patient preference

The major classes of agents available for migraine prevention are β-adrenergic blockers, antidepressants, anticonvulsants, calcium channel antagonists, nonsteroidal agents, and serotonin receptor antagonists. The selection of a drug should be based first on efficacy, with consideration given to coexisting psychiatric or medical disease, patient preference, and patient adherence. Evidence for episodic migraine prevention is strongest for propranolol (60-240 mg/d), timolol (5-30 mg/d), amitriptyline (30-150 mg/d), divalproex sodium (500-2000 mg/d), and topiramate (100-200 mg/d). Recent trials have documented the efficacy of only two agents for chronic migraine: oral topiramate and injectable onabotulinumtoxinA. Topiramate is contraindicated in patients with a history of kidney stones. Patients taking oral topiramate who have no history of kidney stone formation should be advised to keep well hydrated because of the increased risk of kidney stone formation associated with the drug.

Patient education about the goals, use, and expectations of migraine preventive therapies is crucial in maximizing the chances of therapeutic success. The patient must understand that although these therapies may reduce the frequency or severity of attacks, improve the efficacy of acute medications, and assist in the management of comorbidities, they rarely result in complete headache eradication. Prophylactic agents are generally titrated upward over a few weeks and then sustained for 4 to 8 weeks before benefit is realized. Adherence can be enhanced with the use of daily or twice-daily dosing. Most clinicians recommend a 6- to 12-month maintenance phase after a response (often defined as a 50% reduction in headache frequency) has been achieved, followed by a tapering phase. Avoiding the use of acute headache medications, analgesics, decongestants, and stimulants for more than 10 days per month is critical in ensuring optimal benefit from the prophylactic drug. In those patients overusing acute medications, such as butalbital and opiate compounds, a gradual taper over several weeks may be necessary, and full response to preventive therapies may be delayed by several months.

## Migraine in Women

### Migraine and Menstruation

The influence of estrogen on migraine is shown by the threefold greater prevalence of migraine in women than men and by the significant changes in migraine incidence associated with changes in female reproductive status. Menstrually related migraine is defined as migraine that occurs both during (days 2 through 3) and outside menses, whereas pure menstrual migraine occurs exclusively during the menstrual period. Recent data confirm that menstrual attacks exhibit greater intensity and duration compared with nonmenstrual episodes. Evidence supports acute treatment with sumatriptan, rizatriptan, mefenamic acid, and combination sumatriptan-naproxen sodium. For predictable attacks offering the possibility of perimenstrual prophylaxis (5-7 days), transcutaneous estradiol, oral frovatriptan, and naratriptan have established efficacy. Because multiple studies have linked menstrual migraine attacks with estrogen withdrawal, some

have advocated continuous hormonal therapy with monophasic oral contraceptives as a means of prevention.

Controversy exists regarding the use of estrogen-containing oral contraceptives in women with migraine with aura. The literature suggests that women with any migraine type who use combined oral contraceptives have a twofold to fourfold increased risk of stroke compared with women without a history of migraine. The relationship between use of combined oral contraceptives and stroke appears to be dose dependent, with pills containing more than 50 micrograms of estrogen carrying the greatest risk. However, many women without other risk factors for stroke or a history of smoking have been managed safely and successfully with lower-dose combined preparations. In one study of young women (age 25-29 years) with a baseline 10-year ischemic stroke rate of 2.7 per 10,000, the rate climbed to 11 for those with migraine with aura and 23 for those with migraine with aura who used oral contraceptives. The World Health Organization recommends that women with aura avoid oral contraceptive use, and the American College of Obstetrics and Gynecology recommends using alternative forms of contraception for most women with migraine with aura.

Progestin-only contraceptives and copper and progesterone–containing intrauterine devices can be safely used in women with migraine.

### Migraine and Pregnancy

Although migraine can initially develop or worsen during pregnancy, approximately two thirds of women with migraine experience improvement or remission of attacks during the last 6 months of pregnancy because of the sustained estrogen levels of the second and third trimesters. Nonpharmacologic therapies, including magnesium supplementation and natural remedies (such as rest and local application of ice), are strongly preferred for migraine prevention during pregnancy and for attacks persisting throughout pregnancy. All acute and preventive migraine therapies have FDA and Teratogen Information System (TERIS) pregnancy ratings for safety of use during pregnancy, and the American Academy of Pediatrics provides additional safety information for lactating mothers. A pregnant woman with migraine can use conventional acute therapies, such as acetaminophen and metoclopramide, certain opiates, and NSAIDs (until week 32), all of which are classified as Pregnancy Category B (no evidence of risk in humans but no controlled human studies). NSAIDs have been linked with fetal patent ductus arteriosus when used later in pregnancy, and therefore they should be discontinued prior to week 32. Prednisone carries a Category B rating and may be useful in truncating stretches of active migraine. Triptans are rated Pregnancy Category C (risk to humans not ruled out) and can be used when the benefits outweigh the risks; a prospective sumatriptan pregnancy registry has produced no evidence of significant teratogenicity to date. Because potential risk exists for most drugs used in migraine prevention, their use should be limited to women with particularly frequent or disabling migraine attacks. β-Blockers, such as metoprolol and propranolol, are rated Category C but have demonstrated relative safety during pregnancy; they should be tapered during the last weeks of pregnancy to avoid maternal or fetal bradycardia during labor.

Recent population-based studies have documented increased risk of adverse pregnancy outcomes for women with migraine, including low-birth-weight neonates, preterm deliveries, eclampsia, and placental abruption.

*Migraine and Perimenopause*

The hormonal fluctuations accompanying perimenopause may activate migraine and necessitate more aggressive treatment measures. The agents and strategies are no different from those used to manage active migraine at other times of life. However, hormonal replacement therapy can be added for hormonal stability.

---

**KEY POINTS**

- The headache of migraine with aura occurs within 1 hour of onset of transient focal neurologic symptoms, such as visual, sensory, or language abnormalities, that develop over a minimum of 5 minutes and last a maximum of 60 minutes.

- NSAIDs, dihydroergotamine, and triptans are effective in the management of acute migraine.

- The pharmacologic agents with the strongest evidence of effectiveness in the prevention of episodic migraine are propranolol, timolol, amitriptyline, divalproex sodium, and topiramate.

- Women with any migraine type who use combined oral contraceptives have a twofold to fourfold increased risk of stroke compared with women without a history of migraine who use these contraceptives.

- Because potential risk to the fetus exists for most drugs used in migraine prevention, their use during pregnancy should be limited to women with particularly frequent or disabling migraine attacks.

---

## Tension-Type Headache

Tension-type headache is the most common, but least distinct, of the primary headache disorders. Although the most prevalent headache type in the general population, tension-type headache typically does not have the severity or impact of migraine and thus infrequently provokes a visit to a physician. This category of headache is divided into episodic and chronic subtypes, with the episodic subtype including attacks that occur fewer than 15 days per month or 180 days per year and the chronic subtype including more frequent attacks. Population-based studies suggest 1-year prevalence rates of 40% for the episodic subtype and 2.5% for the

chronic subtype; the lifetime prevalence of tension-type headache approaches 90%. Diagnosis of tension-type headache by ICHD-2 criteria is based on negative characteristics (that rule out migraine or secondary headaches). Whereas migraine is characterized primarily by the positive features of photophobia and/or phonophobia, nausea and/or vomiting, and pain worsening with activity, tension-type headache is characterized by the absence of these features. By definition, a single tension-type headache episode can last from 30 minutes to 7 days.

Unlike the unilateral, throbbing, moderate-to-severe pain of migraine, tension-type headache is characterized by bilateral, steady, mild-to-moderate discomfort. Prodrome, aura, and residual symptoms after the headache (postdrome) are not present, and headaches rarely develop nocturnally. Many persons report gradual escalation of discomfort throughout the day. Stress and sleep disruption are the two most commonly reported triggers. Disability is typically minimal or nonexistent, and physical activity often decreases headache intensity. Some patients with tension-type headache report scalp tenderness or muscular tension or soreness in the cervical region. Because the clinical features of tension-type headache are somewhat vague and nonspecific, the label has been mistakenly applied to both secondary headache and migraine. The latter two diagnoses must be excluded before a headache can be considered to be tension type. The episodic subtype generally requires no diagnostic procedures, but the chronic subtype warrants brain MRI.

Aspirin and acetaminophen have been shown to be equally effective and superior to placebo for treating tension-type headache in controlled clinical trials, whereas comparative studies of these agents versus others suggest superior benefits from ibuprofen and naproxen sodium. The addition of caffeine significantly increases the efficacy of aspirin and acetaminophen. Muscle relaxants and benzodiazepines have no role in the management of this disorder.

The evidence supporting preventive treatments for tension-type headache is much less robust. For example, scientific support for relaxation and biofeedback therapies for tension-type headache is strong, and stress management programs using cognitive behavioral techniques have proved useful. However, no evidence supports the use of cervical manipulation and physical therapy. Although tricyclic antidepressants are frequently used for prevention of tension-type headache, a recent meta-analysis found antidepressants no more effective than placebo in reducing headache frequency or intensity.

---

**KEY POINTS**

- The diagnosis of tension-type headache relies on negative characteristics that rule out migraine or secondary headaches.

- Stress and sleep disruption are the two most commonly reported triggers of tension-type headache, and disability is typically minimal or nonexistent.

## Cluster Headache

Cluster headache is a rare and exquisitely painful primary headache disorder that occurs in either episodic or chronic patterns. Male sex and tobacco use are risk factors for development of this type of headache, and alcohol may trigger attacks during a cluster cycle. Headache clusters generally last several weeks or months, with attacks of pain potentially recurring one to eight times daily and lasting 15 to 180 minutes each. The pain is typically periorbital or temporal, intense, boring, and associated with restlessness and ipsilateral autonomic features, such as ptosis, lacrimation, conjunctival injection, and nasal congestion and rhinorrhea. The attacks often exhibit circadian rhythm and most commonly occur within a few hours of falling asleep. To exclude structural mimics, patients with symptoms suggestive of cluster headache should undergo brain MRI.

The medical treatment of cluster headache includes acute, transitional, and maintenance prophylaxis. The acute treatment of choice is inhaled oxygen delivered by face mask at 6 to 12 L/min for 10 minutes, which is effective in greater than 75% of patients. A recent meta-analysis of existing trials of acute pharmacotherapy documented the best evidence for oxygen, subcutaneous sumatriptan, and nasal zolmitriptan. No evidence supports the use of opioids in the treatment of cluster headache. Transitional prophylaxis, which refers to the short-term use of fast-acting agents, typically involves either corticosteroids or an occipital nerve block. The mainstay of prophylactic therapy is verapamil, often at high doses. Serial electrocardiograms also may be necessary to monitor potential cardiac conduction defects in patients on verapamil. Some evidence supports the use of lithium and melatonin. For medically refractory cluster headache, surgical intervention and occipital nerve or deep brain stimulators are being studied.

### KEY POINT

- Cluster headache episodes, which generally last several weeks or months with headache recurring one to eight times daily for 15 to 180 minutes each time, are associated with exquisite pain that is typically periorbital or temporal, intense, boring, and associated with restlessness and ipsilateral ocular or nasal autonomic features.

## Related Primary Headache Syndromes

The related syndromes of chronic paroxysmal hemicrania and short-lasting unilateral neuralgiform headache with conjunctival injection and tearing (SUNCT) also present with episodes of piercing trigeminal pain associated with cranial autonomic features but differ from cluster headache in frequency and duration. Chronic paroxysmal hemicrania attacks have a mean duration of 15 minutes and can recur 8 to 40 times daily. This headache type responds dramatically and specifically to indomethacin. SUNCT is defined by episodes lasting a mean of 60 seconds and recurring 1 to 30 times per hour. Although SUNCT has no reliable treatment, some case reports document improvement with use of lamotrigine.

# Head Injury

## Traumatic Brain Injury

Traumatic brain injury (TBI) results from the exposure of the brain to physical forces that cause either temporary dysfunction or permanent damage to brain tissue.

Patients with moderate to severe brain injuries at presentation should be staged according to the Glasgow Coma Scale (**Table 6**). Those with mild TBI (90%) typically have a benign clinical course without the need of diagnostic or therapeutic intervention. Patients with moderate to severe TBI and those with mild TBI accompanied by prolonged symptoms should undergo a neuroimaging study. Head CT with bone windows will help exclude acute skull fracture or hematoma and is the procedure of choice in acute settings. For persons with chronic posttraumatic symptoms, MRI of

**TABLE 6.** Glasgow Coma Scale[a]

| Head Injury Characteristic | Points |
|---|---|
| **Eye-Opening Response** | |
| Spontaneous (eyes open with blinking at baseline) | 4 |
| To verbal stimuli, command, speech | 3 |
| To pain only (not applied to face) | 2 |
| No response | 1 |
| **Verbal Response** | |
| Oriented | 5 |
| Confused conversation but able to answer questions | 4 |
| Inappropriate words | 3 |
| Incomprehensible speech | 2 |
| No response | 1 |
| **Motor Response** | |
| Obeys commands for movement | 6 |
| Purposeful movement to painful stimulus | 5 |
| Withdraws in response to pain | 4 |
| Flexion in response to pain (decorticate posturing) | 3 |
| Extension in response to pain (decerebrate posturing) | 2 |
| No response | 1 |

[a]Coma classification (total points): ≤8 points, severe; 9-12 points, moderate; 13-15 points, mild.

the brain may be more sensitive in detecting abnormalities of underlying brain parenchyma.

**KEY POINTS**

- Patients with moderate to severe brain injuries on presentation should be staged according to the Glasgow Coma Scale.
- The neuroimaging procedure of choice for traumatic brain injury in acute settings is CT of the head.

## Concussive Head Injury

Concussion is defined as a trauma-induced alteration in mental status that may or may not involve a loss of consciousness. Grade 1 concussion is characterized by transient confusion without amnesia or loss of consciousness that resolves completely within 15 minutes. Grade 2 concussion also involves transient confusion without loss of consciousness but is associated with a period of amnesia and mental status abnormalities lasting longer than 15 minutes. Grade 3 concussion is defined as a brief (seconds) or prolonged (minutes) loss of consciousness. A focused neurologic examination is necessary in the acute setting, with investigation of cognition (orientation, language, and memory), vision (acuity, visual fields, and extraocular movements), and coordination (gait and extremities) being of greatest importance. Head CT or brain MRI is recommended for persons with grade 2 and 3 concussions who have persistent abnormalities on examination or symptoms lasting longer than 1 week because shear injury may result in intracranial hematomas or parenchymal edema, both of which evolve over time.

Athletes with grade 1 concussions should be removed from the contest and examined immediately and then at 5-minute intervals. If all mental status and postconcussive symptoms (at rest and with exertion) clear within 15 minutes, they may return to the contest. A second grade 1 concussion on the same day should eliminate the athlete from competition until he or she is asymptomatic for 1 week at rest and with exercise.

Athletes with grade 2 concussion should be removed from the contest and prohibited from returning to competition that day; they should be examined frequently on site and reexamined the next day. If asymptomatic for 1 week at rest and with exertion and if neurologic examination findings are normal, they may return to competition. After a second grade 2 concussion, return to play should be deferred until the athlete is free of symptoms at rest and with exertion for a minimum of 2 weeks.

Athletes with a grade 3 concussion should be transported to the nearest emergency department if unconsciousness is prolonged or if any worrisome signs, such as confusion, ataxia, slurred speech, or visual anomalies, are detected on examination. The management of grade 3 concussions in athletes is outlined in **Table 7.**

**TABLE 7.** Management of Grade 3 Concussions in Athletes

| **Brief Grade 3 Concussion, First Occurrence** |
| --- |
| Removal from competition |
| If examination findings normal, home with family observation |
| If examination findings abnormal, emergency department evaluation with neuroimaging |
| Withhold from competition until asymptomatic for 1 week |
| **Prolonged Grade 3 Concussion, First Occurrence** |
| Removal from competition |
| Emergency department evaluation with neuroimaging |
| Withhold from competition until asymptomatic for 2 weeks |
| **Grade 3 Concussion, Second Occurrence** |
| Removal from competition |
| Emergency department evaluation and neuroimaging as outlined above |
| Withhold from competition until asymptomatic for 4 weeks |

The immediate postconcussion assessment and cognitive testing (ImPACT) test is a validated instrument now applied to most athletes competing at the high school, collegiate, or professional level. The ImPACT test provides computerized neurocognitive assessment tools and services used by physicians, athletic trainers, and other licensed health care professionals to help determine an athlete's ability to return to play after a concussion. Return to competition is often based on resolution of symptoms and return to baseline on the ImPACT test.

**KEY POINT**

- Brain MRI is recommended for persons with grade 2 and 3 concussions who have persistent abnormalities on examination or symptoms lasting longer than 1 week.

## Postconcussion Syndrome

Postconcussion syndrome (PCS) can occur after a closed head injury or after a cervical spine extension-flexion injury, also known as whiplash. This syndrome is characterized by a complex of somatic and neuropsychological symptoms that by definition develops within 2 weeks of the injury (**Table 8**). Pathophysiology may vary considerably between patients and is usually multifactorial. Pain in the head and neck may arise from injury to nervous system (brain, cervical roots) or cervical spine musculoskeletal elements; vertigo or imbalance from damage to the brain or vestibular system; and cognitive, psychological, and sleep disturbances from trauma to brain structures. Brain dysfunction may result from destruction that

**TABLE 8. Symptoms of Postconcussion Syndrome**

| Headache and Neck Pain |
| --- |
| Tension-type headache |
| Migraine |
| Cervicogenic headache |
| Intracranial hypotension |
| **Neurologic Symptoms** |
| Dizziness or vertigo |
| Tinnitus or hearing loss |
| Visual blurring or diplopia |
| Light and noise hypersensitivities |
| Diminished taste and smell |
| Poor memory or concentration |
| Tremors (rare) |
| Seizures (rare) |
| **Psychological and Somatic Symptoms** |
| Irritability |
| Anxiety |
| Depression |
| Fatigue |
| Insomnia or hypersomnia |
| Decreased libido |
| Decreased appetite |

is obvious on neuroimaging or may arise from less apparent diffuse axonal injury, impaired cerebrovascular autoregulation, neurochemical perturbations, or psychological decompensation. Women are twice as likely as men to be affected, and older age is associated with less rapid and less complete recovery. Neither the intensity nor the persistence of the syndrome easily correlates with the severity of injury or the duration of unconsciousness.

Management of PCS is largely supportive and rehabilitative, with medical treatments directed at specific symptoms. Headache, mood or anxiety disorders, and vestibular dysfunction are all often treated with a combination of pharmacologic and nonpharmacologic approaches. Cognitive symptoms are more difficult to address directly but may necessitate retraining of attention and executive functioning skills.

## Epidural and Subdural Hematoma

Epidural hematomas nearly always result from a direct head injury causing fracture of the temporal bone and laceration of the middle meningeal artery. Headache, mental status abnormalities, and rapid neurologic decline with ipsilateral pupillary dilatation may occur. Without immediate surgical

evacuation, patients with epidural hematomas can die within a matter of hours.

Subdural hematomas arise from injury to the small bridging veins between the cortex and the dura, and the clinical course often is more indolent. Acute subdural hematomas may develop over hours, and chronic subdural hematomas may develop over weeks to months. Abnormalities of the clinical examination and neuroimaging studies that indicate pressure on adjacent brain tissue are evaluated by a neurosurgeon to determine the need for surgical evacuation.

Intracerebral and subarachnoid hemorrhages may occasionally arise from trauma, but the former is much more common as a complication of hypertension or stroke, and the latter as a complication of ruptured cerebral aneurysms.

**KEY POINT**

- Without immediate surgical evacuation, patients with epidural hematomas can die within a matter of hours.

## Head Injury in a Military Population

Even in peacetime, military personnel have a higher rate of TBI than civilians. The use of unconventional weaponry has increased the risk of TBI for military personnel who were engaged in combat operations in Iraq and Afghanistan. Reported rates of concussion for military personnel returning from deployment are between 10% and 20%, with 5% of returning service members remaining symptomatic from PCS. To ensure the identification and prompt treatment of affected military personnel, the U.S. Congress has mandated that all military personnel returning from combat be screened for the effects of TBI. Chronicity of PCS among returning military personnel may result from numerous factors, including concurrent musculoskeletal pain or injury, posttraumatic stress disorder or other affective illness, ongoing cognitive impairment, social stressors within the family or military unit, and insomnia. A multidisciplinary approach involving pharmacologic agents, psychotherapy, and physical therapies and modalities (local injections, stretching) may be necessary.

**KEY POINT**

- All military personnel should be screened for the effects of traumatic brain injury when they return from combat.

# Epilepsy

## Features and Epidemiology of Epilepsy

Seizures result from abnormal, excessive, or synchronous neuronal activity in the cerebral cortex. Most seizures occur in children or adults older than 65 years, and most are provoked by a distinct inciting event. Seizure precipitants include fever, infection, intoxication, drug withdrawal or initiation, metabolic derangements, sleep deprivation, or an acute neurologic insult. A diagnosis of epilepsy is made only when a patient has had two or more unprovoked seizures. The cumulative lifetime incidence of epilepsy in the general U.S. population is 3%. There are more than 30 different epilepsy syndromes, which are sometimes confined to a specific age range and are markedly divergent in clinical expression, treatability, and prognosis.

## Initial Approach to the Patient with a First Seizure

The immediate assessment of an acute seizure is focused on stabilizing the patient, evaluating the airway and vital signs, and rapidly identifying and correcting reversible causes. If the plasma glucose level cannot be immediately evaluated, thiamine followed by glucose should be given. Laboratory studies should include basic metabolic and liver chemistry studies, urine toxicology, and measurement of serum alcohol levels, as indicated. Urgent head CT also may be indicated.

The clinical history of a first seizure should include a careful description of the event by a reliable witness. Several common events can mimic seizures in adults (**Table 9**). Syncope, for example, can be followed by tonic stiffening or generalized myoclonic jerks that are easily confused with a generalized tonic-clonic seizure. Convulsive syncope occurs in 5% to 15% of patients with cardiogenic or vasovagal syncope. The distinction between seizures and other events relies heavily on the clinical presentation. Further assessment should probe for a history of more subtle seizures that may not have been previously recognized by the patient or family and should include questions about epilepsy risk factors:

- Family history of epilepsy
- Childhood febrile convulsions
- History of trauma with loss of consciousness
- History of central nervous system infection
- Central nervous system lesion (brain tumor, vascular malformation, stroke)
- Prenatal or birth injury

Precipitating factors, such as sleep deprivation and toxic exposures, should also be ascertained.

If a first seizure results from a toxic or metabolic cause, further diagnostic evaluation may not be necessary, and management should focus on correcting the underlying cause. Neuroimaging is recommended in any patient with a first seizure and is essential in all patients with an abnormal neurologic examination or a history suggestive of a partial seizure. Lumbar puncture should be considered in a patient with a seizure in the setting of fever, headache, stiff neck, or altered mental status. Seizures are a common presentation of viral encephalitis, in which only subtle clinical signs of infection, such as low-grade fever and personality change, may be present. All immunocompromised patients with a first seizure should have a brain MRI and a lumbar puncture.

**TABLE 9. Characteristics of Seizures and Common Mimics in Adults**

| Characteristic | Seizure | Nonepileptic Seizure | Syncope | TIA | Migraine | Vertigo |
|---|---|---|---|---|---|---|
| Warning/aura | Variable (<1 min) | Variable | Lightheaded feeling; sweating | None | Variable (15-30 min) | None |
| Duration | 1-2 min | 5-15 min | Seconds to minutes | Minutes to hours | Hours | Minutes to days |
| Effect of posture | None | Variable | Variable | None | None | Variable |
| Symptoms during episode | Tonic-clonic movement, paresthesias, aphasia | Pelvic thrusting, jerking that waxes and wanes, forced eye closure | Loss of tone, brief clonic jerks | Hemiparesis, hemisensory loss, visual loss, aphasia | Visual disturbance, vertigo, paresthesias | Nausea, ataxia |
| Altered consciousness | Common | Common | Sometimes | Rare | Rare | None |
| Incontinence | Variable | Variable | Variable | None | None | None |
| Heart rate | Increased | Variable | Irregular/ decreased | Variable | No effect | Variable |
| Symptoms after episode | Confusion, fatigue | Variable | Alert | Alert | Fatigue | Alert |
| EEG during event | Epileptiform pattern | No effect | Diffuse slowing | Focal slowing | Rare slowing | No effect |

EEG = electroencephalogram; TIA = transient ischemic attack.

**H**
**CONT.**

Electroencephalography (EEG) typically is not indicated on an emergent basis, unless there is a prolonged postictal state.

Because seizures are unpredictable, all patients who have experienced a seizure should be counseled to avoid situations in which a loss of consciousness would be dangerous, including unsupervised swimming or bathing and climbing to a height. Driving privileges are restricted in patients who have had a seizure in the United States, but the laws differ from state to state. State laws typically do not distinguish between a patient who has had a single seizure and a patient with epilepsy. Some states mandate that a physician report a seizure occurrence to the Department of Motor Vehicles. **H**

### KEY POINT

- Neuroimaging is recommended in any patient with an unprovoked seizure and is essential in all patients with an abnormal neurologic examination, a history suggestive of a partial seizure, or impaired immune function.

## Clinical Presentations of Seizures

Seizures are basically of two types: partial (focal) and generalized. A partial seizure has its onset in a limited region of the cerebral cortex, and a generalized seizure involves the cortex diffusely. The presentation of a seizure depends on the anatomic localization of the involved cortical neurons that are excited and hypersynchronized during the seizure. The aura, if present, is a clue to the cortical origin of the seizure discharge. Most acute symptomatic seizures are generalized, whereas most epilepsy syndromes presenting in adulthood involve partial seizures.

### Partial Seizures

In a partial seizure, the abnormal electrical discharge may remain localized to a small population of neurons or spread to involve larger regions of the cortex. Partial seizures are subclassified as simple, complex, or secondarily generalized seizures. A simple partial seizure is a focal seizure that does not impair awareness, whereas a complex partial seizure involves an alteration of consciousness that typically occurs when the seizure spreads to involve one or both temporal lobes. When a partial seizure spreads to involve both hemispheres diffusely, the result is a generalized convulsion that is known as a secondarily generalized seizure.

The classic jacksonian march is a simple partial motor seizure characterized by rhythmic contraction of a group of muscles, typically the fingers, followed by a spread of motor activity to the arm and then to the ipsilateral face; this pattern reflects the spread of electrical discharge across the motor homunculus of the primary motor cortex. If a seizure begins in the sensory cortex of the parietal lobe, the patient may experience paresthesias that spread in a similar pattern but have no outward clinical manifestations. These types of simple partial seizures, which cause purely subjective symptoms, are known as epileptic auras.

The most common epileptic auras originate in the temporal lobe. These sensations are often difficult for a patient to describe but are highly stereotyped; a patient may only be able to indicate that he or she "knows the feeling." Common auras of temporal lobe seizures include vague, rising epigastric sensations; experiential phenomena, such as déjà vu or intense fear; or autonomic disturbances, such as palpitations or temperature changes. Temporal lobe auras can be misdiagnosed as panic attacks. Because only a small part of the cortex is involved, EEG during simple partial seizures often does not demonstrate epileptiform patterns, which makes the diagnosis more difficult.

Simple partial seizures can progress to complex partial seizures or secondarily generalized seizures. Complex partial seizures are defined as an alteration of consciousness that typically lasts 1 to 2 minutes, but patients may remain confused for as long as 5 to 10 minutes after the seizure has ended. During complex partial seizures, patients often appear to have a blank stare and exhibit stereotyped automatisms, such as lip smacking, repetitive swallowing, or fumbling movements of the hands. Many patients with this type of seizure only remember the aura and do not report any change in consciousness; other patients have no aura or have no memory of their seizures. For these reasons, it is essential to obtain a history of the seizure from a reliable observer.

Secondarily generalized tonic-clonic seizures are convulsions that begin as partial seizures and are characterized by impaired awareness, diffuse muscle contraction (tonic phase), and rhythmic jerking of all limbs (clonic phase). These seizures, which are often accompanied by urinary incontinence or tongue biting, usually resolve within 1 to 2 minutes and may be followed by postictal confusion or agitation for 10 to 15 minutes. Secondarily generalized convulsions are sometimes clinically indistinguishable from convulsions that begin as generalized seizures. Focal features, such as unilateral twitching or the patient's report of an epileptic aura before the onset of the convulsion, can help make the diagnosis of a secondarily generalized seizure. Sometimes a patient will have a focal deficit (such as limb weakness) contralateral to the site of seizure onset, a phenomenon known as Todd paralysis.

### Generalized Seizures

Generalized seizures involve both hemispheres at the onset of the ictus. Primary generalized tonic-clonic seizures are convulsions that occur with little or no warning. Absence seizures are another type of generalized seizure characterized by a momentary lapse of consciousness (typically less than 5 seconds). The term "absence seizure" is often misused to describe a complex partial seizure. Absence seizures are most characteristic of childhood absence epilepsy, which typically resolves by puberty but can also occur in adults with idiopathic generalized epilepsy syndromes.

Myoclonic seizures are brief shocklike muscular contractions that can occur in rapid succession and usually are not associated with an impairment of consciousness. These seizures are characteristic of juvenile myoclonic epilepsy and also can occur in toxic-metabolic states and after anoxic brain injury.

**KEY POINTS**

- A simple partial seizure does not impair awareness, whereas a complex partial seizure involves an alteration of consciousness that typically occurs when the seizure spreads to involve one or both temporal lobes.
- Absence seizures, which are uncommon in adult patients, are a type of generalized seizure characterized by a momentary lapse of consciousness.

## Epilepsy Syndromes

Patients with epilepsy often experience more than one seizure type. An epilepsy syndrome is defined by the constellation of seizure types in a given patient and by his or her EEG and MRI findings. As with individual seizures, epilepsy syndromes are classified as partial (focal) or generalized. Most epilepsy syndromes presenting in adulthood are focal epilepsies.

### Partial (Focal) Epilepsy

Temporal lobe epilepsy is the most common focal epilepsy, accounting for 30% to 50% of all epilepsy syndromes. Complex partial seizures with epigastric or psychic auras are the most common manifestation of temporal lobe epilepsy, but patients may also experience simple partial and secondarily generalized seizures. Some patients with this temporal lobe epilepsy have evidence of hippocampal atrophy on brain MRI (mesial temporal sclerosis) (**Figure 2**).

Other causes of focal epilepsies include brain tumors, strokes, vascular malformations (**Figure 3**), and abnormalities of cortical development (**Figure 4**). Often, however, a symptomatic lesion cannot be found.

### Idiopathic Generalized Epilepsy

Idiopathic generalized epilepsy accounts for approximately one third of all epilepsy syndromes. Idiopathic generalized epilepsy is diagnosed in most affected patients before age 20 years, but up to one third of patients with the disorder have their first seizure as an adult. These late-onset seizures are often precipitated by alcohol or sleep deprivation. Patients may experience only generalized tonic-clonic seizures, only absence seizures, or any combination of myoclonic, absence, and generalized tonic-clonic seizures. The EEG characteristically demonstrates bursts of generalized spike-wave activity, and neuroimaging findings are normal.

Juvenile myoclonic epilepsy is one of the most common forms of idiopathic generalized epilepsy in adult patients.

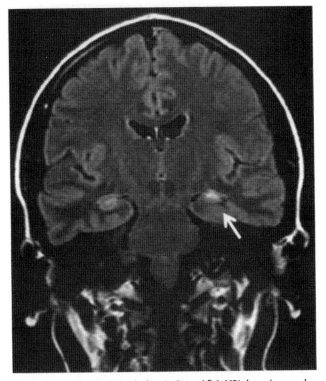

**FIGURE 2.** Mesial temporal sclerosis. Coronal flair MRI shows increased signal intensity and atrophy of the left mesial temporal lobe (*arrow*).

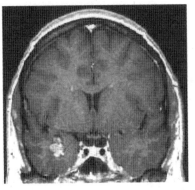

**FIGURE 3.** Cavernous malformation. Coronal T1-weighted MRI shows an intra-axial mass (cavernous hemangioma) in the right temporal lobe with a surrounding hemosiderin ring.

Affected patients often experience morning myoclonus that can manifest as "jitteriness" and cause them to drop things. A family history of convulsive seizures or myoclonic jerks is common. Generalized tonic-clonic seizures may be infrequent, but patients typically require life-long antiepileptic treatment to prevent future convulsions. Some patients with juvenile myoclonic epilepsy also experience absence seizures.

**KEY POINTS**

- Temporal lobe epilepsy, the most common form of epilepsy in adults, typically presents with complex partial seizures.

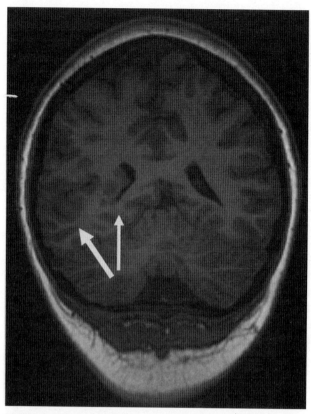

**FIGURE 4.** Focal cortical dysplasia with periventricular nodular heterotopia. Coronal MRI showing a focal area of thickened cortex in the right temporal region (*thick arrow*) and nodules of abnormal neuronal tissue along the ventricular surface (*thin arrow*).

- Juvenile myoclonic epilepsy, one of the most common forms of idiopathic generalized epilepsy in adult patients, requires life-long antiepileptic therapy to prevent future convulsions.

# Comorbidities and Complications of Epilepsy

## Mood Disorders

Both major depressive disorder and bipolar disorder are more common in persons with epilepsy (20% to 60% of patients) than in those with other chronic diseases. All antiepileptic drugs (AEDs) carry a black box warning indicating a potentially increased risk of suicide, which is based on a pooled analysis of clinical trials. Although somewhat controversial, these studies emphasize the need to routinely screen patients with epilepsy for depressive symptoms and suicidal ideation.

## Cognitive Problems

Cognitive problems are common in patients with epilepsy. Although this symptom may be a manifestation of depression or an adverse effect of AEDs, many patients experience independent cognitive decline as a manifestation of their epilepsy.

In particular, patients with temporal lobe epilepsy exhibit deficits in visual or verbal memory. Attention problems are common in patients with frontal lobe epilepsy and generalized epilepsy syndromes. Neuropsychological testing may be useful in differentiating between the global effects of antiseizure medications and specific neurocognitive deficits. At times, video EEG monitoring also is indicated to determine whether subclinical or unrecognized seizures are contributing to a patient's cognitive difficulty.

## Osteoporosis

The risk of skeletal fractures in patients with epilepsy is two to six times greater than in the general population. Subclinical osteoporosis is also more common in patients with epilepsy who take AEDs. Baseline and interval bone mineral density screening is recommended for all patients with epilepsy, particularly those who have been taking enzyme-inducing antiepileptic medications for over 5 years. Calcium and vitamin D supplementation also is recommended.

## Sudden Unexplained Death in Epilepsy

The mortality rate of patients with epilepsy is two to three times higher than the rate in the general population. Many deaths in patients with epilepsy are direct complications of seizures or their underlying disorder, but approximately 17% occur in otherwise healthy persons, without a precipitating seizure. Sudden unexplained death in epilepsy is poorly understood but likely related to a disturbance in cardiac or respiratory autoregulation; death often occurs during sleep. Risk factors include refractory epilepsy, cognitive impairment, generalized tonic-clonic seizures, and poor medication adherence.

**KEY POINTS**

- Major depressive disorder, bipolar disorder, and cognitive problems are common in patients with epilepsy.
- The risks of skeletal fracture and sudden unexplained death are higher in persons with epilepsy than in the general population.

# Diagnostic Evaluation of Seizures and Epilepsy

## Imaging Studies

In the acute setting, a head CT is the imaging study of choice for most patients with a new-onset seizure. A CT scan will identify an acute symptomatic cause of the seizure, such as hemorrhage. Eventually, patients with an unprovoked seizure also should undergo brain MRI, which is more sensitive for detecting the structural lesions associated with epilepsy. Additional imaging tests often used to evaluate patients for epilepsy surgery include magnetoencephalography, single-photon emission CT, PET, and functional MRI.

## Electroencephalography

A routine EEG is a 30- to 60-minute scalp recording of electric potentials from the brain, optimally in both the awake and the sleep state. Seizures are rarely recorded on a routine EEG, but the presence of interictal epileptiform discharges is highly correlated with an increased risk of recurrent seizures. The likelihood that a single 30-minute EEG will record interictal epileptiform discharges in a patient with epilepsy is approximately 25% to 50%, varying by the type of epilepsy. An EEG can help confirm the presence of epilepsy but cannot be used to exclude the diagnosis. EEG also can be useful to discriminate between a focal and generalized epilepsy syndrome (**Figures 5 and 6**).

## Clinical Evaluation and Video Electroencephalographic Monitoring

Although both brain MRI and routine EEG are useful in the clinical evaluation of epilepsy, both have limitations. The specific diagnostic tests a clinician orders should reflect his or her clinical suspicion of whether a patient's events represent seizures. For example, in a patient with a history of recurrent episodes of déjà vu, one of which was followed by a tonic-clonic seizure, an EEG and MRI are indicated to verify the diagnosis of temporal lobe epilepsy and evaluate for a symptomatic lesion. However, both of these studies may be negative, and the diagnosis and treatment of epilepsy will rest on the clinical history. In contrast, a patient with a clear history of vasovagal syncope should not be treated for seizures on the basis of an isolated EEG or MRI finding. A careful clinical history, therefore, is the most important part of the diagnostic evaluation of seizures and epilepsy. In those patients in whom discriminating between seizures and other paroxysmal disorders on the basis of history alone is impossible, inpatient monitoring with video EEG is often necessary to clarify the diagnosis.

Epilepsy monitoring units are inpatient units designed for continuous, simultaneous video and EEG monitoring. Patients are admitted electively to the hospital for 2 to 7 days, during which time their AEDs may be withdrawn. Recording several seizures is usually necessary to completely characterize an epilepsy syndrome and is recommended for any patient whose seizures have not responded to two or more AEDs to determine candidacy for epilepsy surgery.

Another major function of inpatient video EEG monitoring is to discriminate between epileptic and nonepileptic seizures. Nonepileptic seizures, also known as psychogenic nonepileptic seizures or "pseudoseizures," are common. Up to 20% of patients seen at epilepsy referral centers have psychogenic nonepileptic seizures. The diagnosis is more common among women (70%) and is often associated with a history of childhood abuse.

A high index of suspicion is critical for making a diagnosis of nonepileptic events, particularly in patients who do not respond to AED therapy. Early diagnosis by video EEG

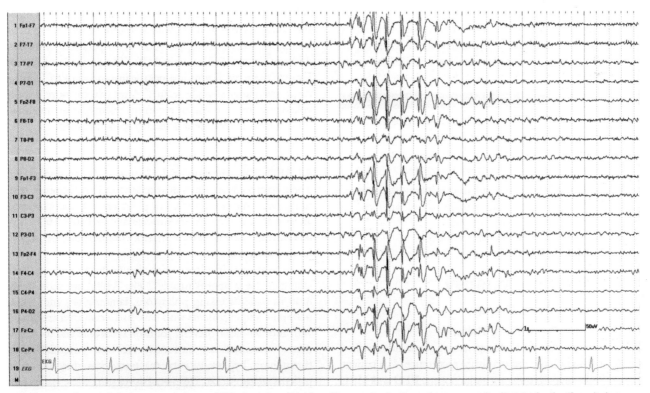

**FIGURE 5.** Characteristic electroencephalogram (EEG) of a patient with idiopathic generalized epilepsy shows a generalized interictal epileptiform discharge during drowsiness. A concurrent electrocardiogram is shown below the EEG.

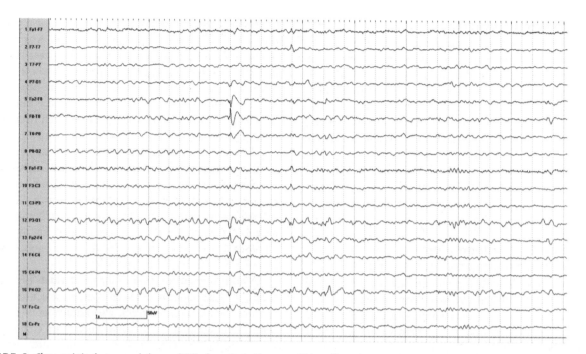

**FIGURE 6.** Characteristic electroencephalogram (EEG) of a patient with temporal lobe epilepsy demonstrating an interictal right temporal epileptiform discharge during sleep. Unlike the epileptiform discharge in Figure 5, the spike-wave discharge in this EEG is focal and is maximal in the F8 and T8 electrodes, which are over the right temporal region. Even numbers to the left of the EEG represent electrodes over the right side of the head, and odd numbers represent electrodes over the left side of the head.

and referral to appropriate psychological resources provide the best chance of a good outcome. Limiting or eliminating unnecessary AEDs is critical, particularly in women of childbearing age. Approximately 10% to 30% of patients with psychogenic nonepileptic seizures also have epileptic seizures, which underscores the need for a careful and complete assessment.

> **KEY POINTS**
>
> - Because negative results on MRI and electroencephalography do not exclude the diagnosis of epilepsy, a careful clinical history is critical in the diagnostic evaluation of a patient with seizures.
> - Inpatient video electroencephalographic monitoring should be considered in any patient whose seizures have not responded to two or more antiepileptic drugs or require further characterization.

# Treatment of Epilepsy

## Antiepileptic Drug Therapy

### Starting Antiepileptic Drug Therapy

The decision to start AED therapy after a single unprovoked seizure is based on the risk of seizure recurrence. In a patient with a single idiopathic seizure and a normal EEG and MRI, the 2-year recurrence risk is 30% to 40%. Because seizure medications will only reduce this risk by approximately 50%, AED therapy is not typically initiated in these circumstances.

The risk of seizure recurrence is higher in patients older than 65 years and in those with a history of significant head trauma or focal seizure, postictal Todd paralysis, and focal findings on an EEG or brain MRI. The presence of one or more of these risk factors justifies the institution of AED treatment, even after a single seizure. After two or more unprovoked seizures, the risk of recurrent seizures is greater than 60%, and AED treatment is usually recommended.

### Adverse Effects of Antiepileptic Drugs

All AEDs have the potential to cause sedation and ataxia. These symptoms are often dose related and may improve over time; they can be exacerbated by polytherapy. Other common adverse effects of AEDs are summarized in **Table 10**. Severe idiosyncratic adverse effects are not common but are important to recognize.

The average incidence of an allergic drug rash in patients taking AEDs is approximately 2.8%. Rashes are most common in patients taking phenytoin, lamotrigine, and carbamazepine and in patients who have had a rash after treatment with another AED. Stevens-Johnson syndrome and toxic epidermal necrolysis are extremely rare but potentially life-threatening hypersensitivity reactions that may occur in patients taking AEDs. The risk of developing these syndromes is substantially increased with rapid titration of lamotrigine

**TABLE 10.** Adverse Effects of Antiepileptic Drugs

| Drug | Common Side Effects | Serious Adverse Reactions |
|------|---------------------|---------------------------|
| Carbamazepine | Sedation, dizziness, ataxia, mild leukopenia, hyponatremia | Aplastic anemia, agranulocytosis, hepatic failure, rash, Stevens-Johnson syndrome, severe hyponatremia |
| Felbamate | Insomnia, weight loss, nausea, headache | Aplastic anemia, hepatic failure |
| Gabapentin | Sedation, lower extremity edema, weight gain | — |
| Lacosamide | Sedation, dizziness, ataxia, diplopia, nausea, shortened PR interval on ECG | Cardiac conduction abnormalities, hypersensitivity syndrome |
| Lamotrigine | Insomnia, headache, acne, dizziness, double vision | Rash, Stevens-Johnson syndrome, hepatic failure, blood dyscrasias |
| Levetiracetam | Irritability, sedation | Depression, psychosis, blood dyscrasias |
| Oxcarbazepine | Sedation, dizziness, ataxia, mild leukopenia, hyponatremia | Rash, Stevens-Johnson syndrome, hypersensitivity syndrome, severe hyponatremia |
| Phenobarbital | Sedation, nausea, ataxia | Rash, Stevens-Johnsons syndrome, hepatic failure, blood dyscrasias, barbiturate withdrawal syndrome |
| Phenytoin | Sedation, dizziness, ataxia | Rash, Stevens-Johnson syndrome, blood dyscrasias, gingival hyperplasia, hepatic failure, hypersensitivity syndrome, lupus-like syndrome, cardiac conduction abnormalities |
| Pregabalin | Sedation, weight gain, lower extremity edema | — |
| Topiramate | Word-finding difficulty, anorexia | Kidney stones, acute angle closure glaucoma, heatstroke, metabolic acidosis |
| Valproic acid | Weight gain, tremor, hirsutism, hair loss, hyperammonemia, menstrual irregularity | Hepatic failure, pancreatitis, aplastic anemia, thrombocytopenia, platelet dysfunction |
| Vigabatrin | Sedation, headache, dizziness | Peripheral vision loss (irreversible), peripheral neuropathy, rash |
| Zonisamide | Sedation, anorexia | Kidney stones, rash |

ECG = electrocardiogram.

and combination lamotrigine and valproic acid. Because Asian patients with the HLA-B*1502 allele have an increased risk of Stevens-Johnson syndrome, clinicians should consider pharmacogenomic testing before starting therapy with phenytoin, carbamazepine, oxcarbazepine, or lamotrigine; levetiracetam is a reasonable alternative.

## Selection of Antiepileptic Drugs
In general, there is no evidence of greater efficacy for newer versus older AEDs. Because most newer AEDs have been studied as adjunctive therapy, only a few of them have FDA indications for monotherapy. In practice, however, many of the newer generation AEDs are used as first-line monotherapy because of their favorable side-effect profile and fewer drug-drug interactions. Whereas nearly all AEDs can be used to treat partial (focal) epilepsies, some agents (such as carbamazepine, gabapentin, phenytoin, and pregabalin) can exacerbate generalized epilepsy syndromes. For patients with generalized epilepsy, broad-spectrum AEDs, such as lamotrigine, levetiracetam, topiramate, zonisamide, and valproic acid, are good first-line options.

Because data suggesting the superiority of one AED over another are sparse, the choice of a specific agent is often based on the side-effect profile most tolerable for an individual patient (**Table 11**).

## Antiepileptic Drugs in Women
Women with epilepsy require special treatment consideration. Valproic acid should be avoided in women of childbearing age because of its much higher risk than other AEDs of teratogenesis and exacerbation of symptoms of polycystic ovary syndrome (such as hirsutism and weight gain). Several AEDs have complex interactions with hormonal contraceptives that must be reviewed with the patient, and planning pregnancy in advance is especially important in women with epilepsy.

### Antiepileptic Drugs and Pregnancy
In utero exposure to AEDs is associated with a 4% to 6% risk of major congenital malformations, which is approximately two to three times the risk in the general population. Valproic acid has been consistently associated with an increased risk of fetal malformations (6%-17%) and also has been shown to have an adverse effect on fetal cognitive development at higher dosages. In contrast, carbamazepine and lamotrigine have been associated with relatively lower rates of major congenital malformations (2%-4%) in large studies.

| TABLE 11. Commonly Used Antiepileptic Drugs | | | | |
|---|---|---|---|---|
| **Drug** | **Partial (Focal) Epilepsy** | **Generalized Epilepsy** | **Metabolism** | **Added Considerations** |
| Carbamazepine | X | — | Hepatic | May decrease levels of other drugs, including hormonal contraceptives |
| | | | | Less well tolerated in older patients |
| Gabapentin | X | — | Renal | Well tolerated in older patients |
| | | | | Few drug-drug interactions |
| | | | | May cause weight gain |
| Lacosamide | X | — | Hepatic/Renal | May cause PR prolongation or syncope |
| | | | | May cause dizziness, especially with other sodium channel–blocking agents (phenytoin, carbamazepine, lamotrigine, oxcarbazepine) |
| Lamotrigine | X | X | Hepatic/Renal | May help treat comorbid mood disorder |
| | | | | Well tolerated in older patients[a] |
| | | | | Has complex interactions with hormonal contraceptives |
| | | | | Initiation is slow due to increased risk of Stevens-Johnson syndrome |
| Levetiracetam | X | X | Renal | Well tolerated in older patients |
| | | | | Few drug-drug interactions |
| | | | | May be associated with depression/psychosis/irritability |
| Oxcarbazepine | X | — | Hepatic/Renal | May decrease levels of other drugs and efficacy of hormonal contraceptives |
| | | | | Less well tolerated in older patients |
| Phenytoin | X | X | Hepatic | May decrease levels of other drugs and efficacy of hormonal contraceptives |
| | | | | Less well tolerated in older patients |
| Pregabalin | X | — | Renal | Few drug-drug interactions |
| | | | | May cause weight gain |
| Topiramate | X | X | Renal | May cause weight loss |
| | | | | May help treat comorbid headache disorder |
| | | | | Increased risk of kidney stones and glaucoma |
| | | | | Decreases efficacy of hormonal contraceptives |
| Valproic acid | X | X | Hepatic | Significantly increased risk of teratogenesis |
| | | | | Unfavorable side effects for women (hirsutism) |
| | | | | May cause weight gain |
| | | | | May increase levels of other drugs |
| Vigabatrin | X | — | Hepatic/Renal | Restricted prescribing in US due to risk of irreversible peripheral vision loss |
| | | | | Indicated for infantile spasms; used in adults with highly refractory partial seizures or Lennox-Gastaut syndrome |
| Zonisamide | X | X | Renal | May cause weight loss |
| | | | | Increased risk of kidney stones |
| | | | | May be associated with depression/ psychosis |

X = used for this condition.

[a]Highest rate of retention and best efficacy in this population.

Only limited data are available on the effects of other AEDs in pregnancy. Early studies of levetiracetam and oxcarbazepine also have demonstrated low rates of fetal malformations. Phenytoin and phenobarbital have been associated with relatively higher fetal malformation rates (3%-7% and 6.5%-14%, respectively); both of these drugs are considered pregnancy category D medications (evidence of human fetal risk, but potential benefits may warrant use of these drugs in pregnant women, despite potential risks). Additionally, recent data showing an increased risk of cleft palate with fetal exposure to topiramate (1.4% versus 0.07% for unexposed fetuses) has elevated this AED to a category D drug.

In general, the most appropriate AED for a pregnant woman is the drug that has best controlled her seizures at the lowest possible dosage. Switching AEDs during pregnancy is not typically recommended because polytherapy further increases the risk of malformations. Furthermore, most fetal malformations occur in the first 4 to 6 weeks of pregnancy, typically before a woman knows she is pregnant. Because most pregnancies are not planned, prepregnancy optimization of a patient's AED regimen should occur well before a woman with epilepsy plans to start a family. Additionally, all women with epilepsy should take folic acid, 0.4 to 5 mg/d, which may decrease the likelihood of neural tube defects.

AED levels must be followed closely during pregnancy. Lamotrigine and oxcarbazepine are particularly sensitive to the effect of estrogen on glucuronidation, which leads to an increase in hepatic metabolism. The levels of these AEDs can drop precipitously during pregnancy and result in increased seizure frequency.

### Antiepileptic Drugs and Breastfeeding

Breastfeeding is considered generally safe with most AEDs. Excretion into the breast milk varies by drug. Although data are limited, the known benefits of breastfeeding are felt by many to outweigh any theoretical risk of infant exposure via breast milk.

### Antiepileptic Drugs and Contraception

Contraception can be a particular challenge in women with epilepsy because AEDs have complex interactions with oral contraceptives and other hormonal methods. Some of the older enzyme-inducing AEDs, including carbamazepine, phenytoin, and phenobarbital, decrease both estrogen and progestin levels and thus inactivate many forms of hormonal contraception. Topiramate, oxcarbazepine, and felbamate can have a similar effect. Lamotrigine is metabolized by glucuronidation, a process induced by estrogens; estrogen-containing contraceptive agents can reduce lamotrigine levels and lead to more seizures if a patient's dosage is not increased. Lamotrigine also can decrease progestin levels, thereby making certain forms of contraception less effective.

## Dosing and Monitoring of Antiepileptic Drug Levels

AEDs are best tolerated when started at a low dosage and slowly titrated upward. The target dosage for a patient is the one that best controls seizures with the fewest adverse effects. AED serum levels are most useful when a patient has reached this optimal seizure control to establish the corresponding therapeutic level for that patient. In general, published therapeutic serum ranges should not be used to determine appropriate drug dosing if a patient is doing well clinically. Because of the metabolic and hematologic effects of some AEDs, basic metabolic tests, liver chemistry studies, and a complete blood count are typically recommended on an annual or semiannual basis.

## Discontinuing Antiepileptic Drugs

If a patient has been seizure free for 2 to 4 years, an attempt to wean him or her from AEDs is reasonable. Seizure recurrence after AED withdrawal in such a patient is 30% to 40%. Patients with normal findings on MRI, EEG, and neurologic examination are more likely to remain in remission. The risks and benefits of recurrent seizures must be discussed with the patient, including the implications for driving.

## Nonpharmacologic Therapy

### Intractable Epilepsy and Epilepsy Surgery

Approximately 50% of patients with epilepsy will become seizure free with their first AED, and an additional 13% will respond to a trial of a second drug. Patients who do not respond to either their first or second drug, however, have a less than 10% chance of experiencing seizure remission with pharmacotherapy. Any patient with seizures that do not respond to a second drug is considered to have refractory epilepsy and should be referred for subspecialty evaluation at a comprehensive epilepsy center to confirm the diagnosis of epilepsy and determine if the patient is a candidate for epilepsy surgery.

Epilepsy surgery is a good option for many patients with refractory focal epilepsy. The goal of epilepsy surgery is to remove the area of the cortex that is the epileptogenic focus. The highest rates of surgical cure (seizure remission) are seen in patients with known lesions, such as a low-grade tumor or vascular malformation, or with temporal lobe epilepsy associated with mesial temporal sclerosis.

## Other Alternative Therapies

In recent years, several invasive, nonpharmacologic techniques have been developed for patients with medically refractory epilepsy. These approaches include the vagus nerve stimulator, deep brain stimulation of the anterior nucleus of the thalamus, and the responsive neurostimulator. These invasive procedures are palliative and may reduce seizure frequency or severity in some patients with refractory epilepsy.

A ketogenic diet, rich in fat and low in carbohydrates, can be very effective in children with refractory epilepsy but is a very difficult regimen to follow as an adult. Some patients report improved seizure control with a modified low-carbohydrate diet when used in combination with AEDs.

---

**KEY POINTS**

- After two or more unprovoked seizures, the risk of recurrent seizures is greater than 60%, and antiepileptic drug therapy is usually recommended.
- Valproic acid should be avoided in women of childbearing age because of its high risk of teratogenesis.
- Epilepsy surgery to remove the area of the cortex that is the epileptogenic focus is often used in patients with refractory focal epilepsy.

---

# Status Epilepticus

## Generalized Convulsive Status Epilepticus

Generalized convulsive status epilepticus is a medical emergency with significant morbidity and mortality. Its incidence in the United States is 20 to 40 per 100,000 persons per year, and its most common causes in adult patients are subtherapeutic levels of AEDs, cerebrovascular disease, hypoxic injury, alcohol or drug intoxication or withdrawal, and metabolic derangements. More than 50% of patients presenting with generalized convulsive status epilepticus do not have a history of epilepsy. The overall 30-day mortality rate is 20% but varies greatly by cause. For example, when status epilepticus is secondary to anoxic brain injury, the mortality rate is greater than 70%, but when secondary to subtherapeutic AED levels, the condition is rarely fatal.

Traditionally, generalized convulsive status epilepticus has been defined as continuous or repetitive seizure activity lasting longer than 30 minutes. Practically, the management of this type of status epilepticus should begin as soon as a seizure has lasted longer than 5 minutes (**Figure 7**). Prompt treatment of generalized convulsive status epilepticus is essential given the morbidity associated with ongoing convulsions and because continuing seizures become more refractory to treatment over time. Acute complications include rhabdomyolysis, hypoxia, and metabolic acidosis; chronic complications include cognitive deficits and future seizures.

Intravenous lorazepam followed by phenytoin is the first-line management of this condition. When available, the prodrug fosphenytoin is preferable to phenytoin for the initial infusion. Both drugs carry a risk of cardiac conduction abnormalities and hypotension, but fosphenytoin can be administered faster and does not carry the risk of thrombophlebitis or skin necrosis that is associated with phenytoin extravasation. Fosphenytoin can also be administered intramuscularly. To avoid confusion, fosphenytoin is dosed in phenytoin equivalents. For example, intravenous fosphenytoin, 100 equivalents, has the same pharmacologic effect as intravenous phenytoin, 100 mg.

If a patient requires a third drug for ongoing convulsions or if he or she is medically unstable, intubation and intravenous anesthesia are typically required. There is no consensus on which anesthetic agent should be used or the ideal depth or duration of anesthesia, but it is known that prolonged infusions of high-dose propofol can lead to a syndrome characterized by rhabdomyolysis and multiorgan failure. The anesthetic infusion should be titrated upward, at least until convulsive activity has ceased, and then the patient should be monitored with continuous EEG to exclude nonconvulsive status epilepticus or ongoing electrographic seizures.

## Nonconvulsive Status Epilepticus

Nonconvulsive status epilepticus is defined as frequent or continuous EEG seizures without generalized motor manifestations. Approximately 20% of patients successfully treated for generalized convulsive status epilepticus will continue to manifest EEG seizures. For this reason, all patients who do not demonstrate a resolving mental status within 20 minutes after convulsions have stopped should be monitored with continuous EEG monitoring, including patients receiving anesthesia.

As with generalized convulsive status epilepticus, prognosis after the nonconvulsive type depends on the underlying cause. There is little agreement on the treatment implications of this diagnosis, and the management plan must be tailored to the individual patient.

### Nonconvulsive Status Epilepticus and Nonconvulsive Seizures in Critically Ill Patients

Nonconvulsive status epilepticus and nonconvulsive seizures in critically ill patients is an increasingly recognized entity that has been reported in 30% of selected patients on EEG monitoring in the neurologic intensive care unit and in 10% of patients in the medical intensive care unit. These patients are often comatose without other manifestations of seizure. In a comatose patient, only 50% of seizures will be detected on a 1-hour EEG. The sensitivity increases to 80% with 12 to 24 hours of continuous EEG monitoring and approaches 96% after 48 hours of monitoring. The presence of nonconvulsive status epilepticus and nonconvulsive seizures is associated with worse outcomes in patients with acute brain injury.

### Nonconvulsive Status Epilepticus in Noncritically Ill Patients

Nonconvulsive status epilepticus also can occur without a preceding history of tonic-clonic seizures, coma, or neurologic injury and most commonly manifests as absence status epilepticus and complex partial status epilepticus outside the intensive care unit. These two subtypes typically present with fluctuating mental status that can mimic delirium and persist for days before diagnosis. Patients may maintain some degree of interaction with their environment but typically are confused and may exhibit frequent blinking or automatisms. Absence

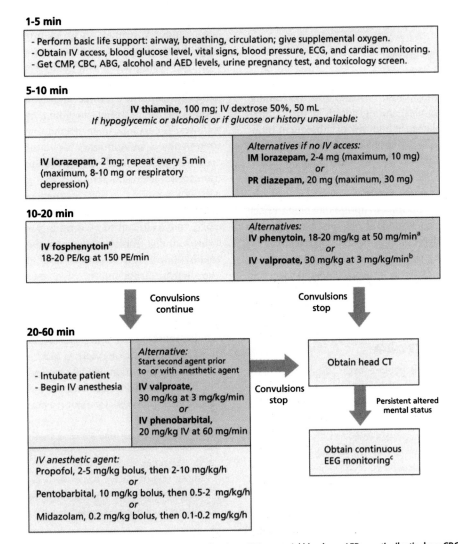

**1-5 min**

- Perform basic life support: airway, breathing, circulation; give supplemental oxygen.
- Obtain IV access, blood glucose level, vital signs, blood pressure, ECG, and cardiac monitoring.
- Get CMP, CBC, ABG, alcohol and AED levels, urine pregnancy test, and toxicology screen.

**5-10 min**

IV thiamine, 100 mg; IV dextrose 50%, 50 mL
*If hypoglycemic or alcoholic or if glucose or history unavailable:*

| | |
|---|---|
| **IV lorazepam,** 2 mg; repeat every 5 min (maximum, 8-10 mg or respiratory depression) | *Alternatives if no IV access:* **IM lorazepam,** 2-4 mg (maximum, 10 mg) *or* **PR diazepam,** 20 mg (maximum, 30 mg) |

**10-20 min**

| | |
|---|---|
| **IV fosphenytoin**[a] 18-20 PE/kg at 150 PE/min | *Alternatives:* **IV phenytoin,** 18-20 mg/kg at 50 mg/min[a] *or* **IV valproate,** 30 mg/kg at 3 mg/kg/min[b] |

Convulsions continue       Convulsions stop

**20-60 min**

| | |
|---|---|
| - Intubate patient<br>- Begin IV anesthesia | *Alternative:* Start second agent prior to or with anesthetic agent **IV valproate,** 30 mg/kg at 3 mg/kg/min *or* **IV phenobarbital,** 20 mg/kg IV at 60 mg/min |

Convulsions stop → Obtain head CT

*IV anesthetic agent:*
Propofol, 2-5 mg/kg bolus, then 2-10 mg/kg/h
*or*
Pentobarbital, 10 mg/kg bolus, then 0.5-2 mg/kg/h
*or*
Midazolam, 0.2 mg/kg bolus, then 0.1-0.2 mg/kg/h

Persistent altered mental status → Obtain continuous EEG monitoring[c]

**FIGURE 7.** Algorithm for treatment of generalized convulsive status epilepticus. ABG = arterial blood gas; AED = antiepileptic drug; CBC = complete blood count; CMP = comprehensive metabolic panel; ECG = electrocardiogram; EEG = electroencephalographic; IM = intramuscular; IV = intravenous; PE = phenytoin equivalent; PR = per rectum.

[a]Monitor ECG and blood pressure with fosphenytoin and phenytoin; monitor for drug extravasation with phenytoin.

[b]Consider valproic acid (valproate) as first-line therapy in those with known idiopathic generalized epilepsy; avoid when possible in women of childbearing age.

[c]Should be obtained for all patients not recovering mental status, including those receiving IV anesthesia.

status epilepticus and complex partial status epilepticus typically occur in patients with a history of generalized and focal epilepsy, respectively, but de novo absence status epilepticus ("spike-wave stupor") can also occur in older patients without a history of epilepsy, particularly in the setting of benzodiazepine withdrawal.

The diagnosis of nonconvulsive status epilepticus can be confirmed by video EEG monitoring or by a paradoxical improvement in mental status in response to a low-dose benzodiazepine. Although prompt control of seizures is considered important in patients with this disorder, the management approach is typically different from that in other forms of status epilepticus. Patients are treated with benzodiazepines and other AEDs, but intravenous anesthesia and intubation are sometimes deferred, if possible, because these interventions may cause a greater morbidity than nonconvulsive status epilepticus itself, particularly in older patients. **H**

**KEY POINTS**

- The management of generalized convulsive status epilepticus, which has an overall 30-day mortality rate of 20%, should begin as soon as a seizure has lasted longer than 5 minutes.

- The diagnosis of nonconvulsive status epilepticus can be confirmed by video electroencephalographic monitoring or by a paradoxical improvement in mental status in response to a low-dose benzodiazepine.

# Stroke

## Epidemiology and Definition of Stroke

Stroke is the third leading cause of death and the leading cause of long-term disability among adults in the United States. Survivors of stroke are at high risk of subsequent morbidity and mortality. Men are more commonly affected by stroke than women except in persons older than 85 years, among whom stroke incidence is highest.

Generally of sudden onset, stroke causes focal neurologic impairment because of occlusion or rupture of a blood vessel supplying a particular brain region. Stroke can be classified as ischemic (or cerebral infarction) due to an occluded artery or as hemorrhagic due to a ruptured artery. The term hemorrhagic stroke does not include all intracranial hemorrhage; the latter term is more heterogeneous and also includes bleeding in the skull vault due to trauma or a tumor.

## Diagnosis of Stroke

The initial evaluation of a patient with suspected stroke includes careful consideration of the sequence and timing of neurologic events, an appraisal of all risk factors and medical contributors to stroke, and a detailed neurologic examination. The initial assessment can identify candidates for acute treatment and provide an early prognosis of mortality or recovery. The focused and highly structured National Institutes of Health Stroke Scale (**Table 12**) is used by qualified practitioners as the initial examination. This scale is well validated and correlates with short- and long-term outcomes and objective measures, such as the size of the cerebral infarction. Performing the scale on all stroke patients is a common requirement for stroke center certification.

Hemorrhagic stroke cannot be reliably distinguished from ischemic stroke on clinical grounds alone. The presence of coma, meningismus, seizures at onset, vomiting, headache, and a diastolic blood pressure greater than 110 mm Hg makes the diagnosis of hemorrhagic stroke more likely, but hemorrhagic stroke can present without any of these findings. Modern neuroimaging is necessary to identify the brain territory involved in a stroke and understand the pathophysiology involved. In the acute setting, head CT without contrast is the initial test of choice to confirm or exclude hemorrhagic stroke (**Figure 8**). MRI is the subsequent test of choice and can identify acute and subacute ischemia, hemorrhage, nonvascular lesions, or another underlying cause. Diffusion-weighted MRI (**Figure 9**) can reveal hyperintensity within minutes of acute cerebral infarction, whereas other sequences are helpful in identifying vasogenic edema or cerebral microhemorrhages.

The gold standard for evaluating the cerebral vasculature remains catheter-based angiography, but its invasiveness and unavailability in most hospitals make it impractical. Magnetic resonance angiography without contrast is widely available and commonly included in stroke-protocol MRI. The presence of arterial stenoses and aneurysms can be readily shown with this technique, although it is prone to artifact and tends to overestimate the degree of stenosis. CT angiography is generally less prone to artifact and can reveal significant details about vascular anatomy, including the presence of arterial stenoses, aneurysms, or malformations. Doppler-flow ultrasonography is an additional tool available for evaluation of cerebral arteries and allows the visualization of blood flow in the carotid arterial system and the intracranial vasculature. MRI is not required before treatment of acute ischemic stroke with thrombolytic agents, may not be available around the clock, and is difficult to perform in patients with agitation or claustrophobia. Vascular imaging in the acute setting with CT angiography is now commonly used to identify patients who may benefit from endovascular treatment or to identify potential sources of hemorrhage. The choice of vascular imaging is frequently driven by other clinical considerations, such as the presence of kidney failure (which precludes iodinated contrast), the unavailability of or contraindications (such as cardiac pacemakers) to MRI, or the unavailability of a certified ultrasonography laboratory.

Examples of different vascular imaging techniques for a patient with symptomatic carotid artery stenosis are shown in **Figure 10.**

> **KEY POINT**
> - In the acute setting, head CT without contrast is the initial test of choice to confirm or exclude hemorrhagic stroke; subsequent MRI can identify acute ischemia or a nonvascular cause.

## Stroke Subtypes

### Transient Ischemic Attack

The former definition of a transient ischemic attack (TIA) included any focal neurologic deficit caused by impaired cerebral blood flow that lasted less than 24 hours. With the use of MRI and diffusion-weighted imaging as sensitive markers of acute infarction, it became apparent that many patients previously classified as having TIAs actually had evidence of cerebral infarction. A more recent definition adopted by the American Heart Association/American Stroke Association describes TIA as a transient neurologic deficit resulting from focal brain, spinal cord, or retinal ischemia without acute infarction.

TIA is a neurologic emergency with a high short-term risk of subsequent stroke; approximately 40% of patients with ischemic stroke experience a TIA beforehand. The risk of subsequent stroke at 90 days approaches 10% in patients who have a TIA, and up to 25% may have a new vascular event (stroke, new TIA, cardiovascular event, or death). Most of the stroke risk is in the first 48 hours, during which 5.3% of patients are at risk. The risk of subsequent stroke is lower in patients with an ischemic stroke than in patients with a TIA, and the 5-year risk of mortality or cardiovascular disease is equivalent between stroke and TIA.

The goal of admitting a patient with a TIA to the hospital is to avoid these negative outcomes, but because the incidence of TIA is substantial, admitting all such patients is impractical. Therefore, identifying those patients at highest

| TABLE 12. National Institutes of Health Stroke Scale[a] | |
|---|---|
| **Parameter (Testing Method)** | **Scores** |
| 1a. LOC | 0 = normal<br>1 = not alert but arousable by minor stimulation<br>2 = not alert and requires constant verbal or painful stimuli to remain interactive<br>3 = unresponsive or responds with only reflexive movements |
| 1b. LOC, questions (state month and age) | 0 = answers both correctly<br>1 = answers one correctly<br>2 = answers neither correctly |
| 1c. LOC, commands (close and open eyes; make fist or close one hand) | 0 = performs both tasks correctly<br>1 = performs one task correctly<br>2 = performs neither task correctly |
| 2. Gaze (track a finger in a horizontal plane) | 0 = normal<br>1 = partial gaze palsy or isolated cranial nerve paresis<br>2 = forced gaze deviation or total gaze paresis |
| 3. Visual fields (each eye tested individually) | 0 = no visual loss<br>1 = partial hemianopia<br>2 = complete hemianopia<br>3 = bilateral hemianopia |
| 4. Facial strength (show teeth, raise eyebrows, close eyes) | 0 = normal<br>1 = minor paralysis (flattening of the nasolabial fold or asymmetry on smiling)<br>2 = partial paralysis (paralysis of the lower face only)<br>3 = complete paralysis (upper and lower face) |
| 5. Arm strength (hold arm with palms down or lift arm for 10 s) | 0 = no drift<br>1 = some drift but does not hit bed<br>2 = drifts down to bed<br>3 = no effort against gravity<br>4 = no movement |
| 6. Leg strength (hold leg at 30 degrees for 5 s) | 0 = no drift<br>1 = some drift but does not hit bed<br>2 = drifts down to bed<br>3 = no effort against gravity<br>4 = no movement |
| 7. Limb ataxia (finger-nose-finger test, heel-knee-shin slide) | 0 = absent<br>1 = present in one limb<br>2 = present in two limbs |
| 8. Sensation (pinch/pinprick tested in face, arm, and leg) | 0 = normal<br>1 = mild to moderate sensory loss or loss of sensation in only one limb<br>2 = complete sensory loss |
| 9. Language (describe a picture, name six objects, and read five sentences) | 0 = no aphasia<br>1 = mild to moderate aphasia (difficulty with fluency and comprehension; meaning can be identified)<br>2 = severe aphasia (fragmentary language, meaning cannot be clearly identified)<br>3 = global aphasia or mute |
| 10. Dysarthria (repeat or read words) | 0 = normal<br>1 = mild to moderate<br>2 = severe (speech not understandable) |
| 11. Extinction/inattention (visual and tactile stimuli applied on right and left sides) | 0 = normal<br>1 = visual or tactile extinction or mild hemispatial neglect<br>2 = profound hemi-inattention or extinction to more than one modality |

LOC = level of consciousness.

[a]Maximum score = 42.

Adapted from www.ninds.nih.gov/doctors/NIH_Stroke_Scale.pdf. Certification available at http://learn.heart.org/ihtml/application/student/interface.heart2/nihss.html.

risk of stroke becomes central. The well-validated ABCD$^2$ score (Age, Blood pressure, Clinical presentation, Duration of symptoms, and the presence of Diabetes mellitus) stratification tool can help clinicians identify patients with TIA who are at highest risk of subsequent stroke (**Table 13**). Hospital admission is recommended for all patients seen within 72 hours of initial symptoms whose ABCD$^2$ score is at least 3. In patients who also have transient monocular blindness, a score less than 3 may be sufficient for hospital admission because the prompt identification of extracranial internal carotid artery (ICA) stenosis requiring revascularization is essential, given the high risk of recurrent ischemic stroke. **H**

## Ischemic Stroke

Ischemic stroke is now defined by the presence of cerebral infarction on imaging, although the absence of a lesion on a CT scan or diffusion-weighted image (which can occur if the infarct is small or located in the brainstem) does not exclude ischemic stroke as a diagnosis. In the United States, 20% of ischemic strokes are cardioembolic, 20% result from large artery atherosclerosis, 25% are small subcortical infarcts, and 30% are cryptogenic strokes, for which no cause is identified. The remaining 5% have rare causes, such as cerebral artery dissection or vasculitis.

## Cardioembolic Stroke

The most clearly documented cause of cardioembolic stroke is atrial fibrillation, although other conditions also predispose to this type of stroke, including a low ejection fraction, an intracardiac thrombus, a cardiac tumor, and valvular vegetations. Atrial fibrillation is the most likely cause of ischemic stroke in patients older than 85 years, a population also most at risk of mechanical falls, which are a relative contraindication to anticoagulation. Cardioembolic stroke is more likely in patients with multiple infarcts on neuroimaging or infarcts involving the surface of the brain.

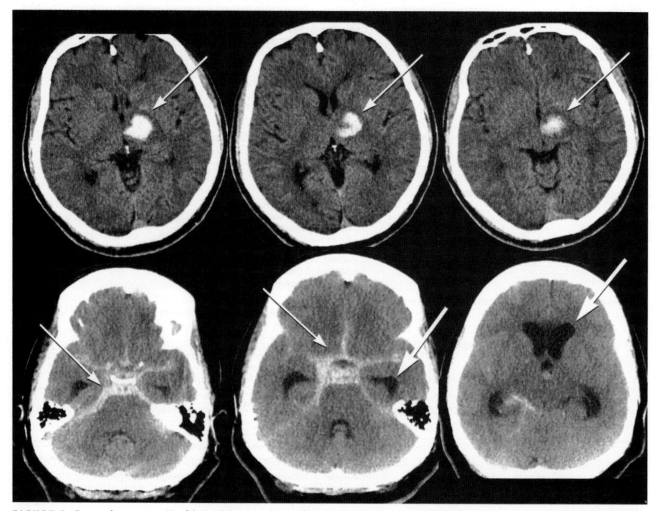

**FIGURE 8.** *Top panel,* noncontrast CTs of the head showing an acute left thalamic intracerebral hemorrhage (*arrows*) without hydrocephalus or intraventricular extension. *Bottom panel,* noncontrast CTs of the head showing an acute subarachnoid hemorrhage that involves the basal cisterns (*thinner arrows*) with associated hydrocephalus (*thicker arrows*).

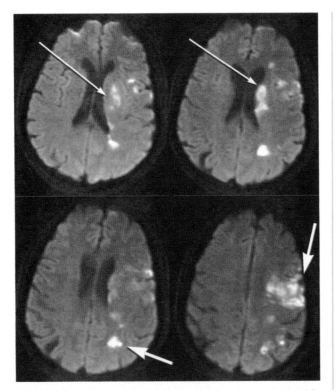

**FIGURE 9.** Diffusion-weighted MRIs from a patient with symptomatic left middle cerebral artery atherosclerosis reveal an acute infarction in deep (*thinner arrows*) and superficial (*thicker arrows*) structures in the left cerebral hemisphere.

### Large Artery Atherosclerosis

Atherosclerosis of the large cerebral arteries may cause stroke by the formation of artery-to-artery emboli or, less commonly, by locally depressed cerebral blood flow. Large artery atherosclerosis may involve the extracranial ICA or the principal intracranial arteries, most commonly the ICA, middle cerebral artery, or vertebrobasilar system. The risk of recurrent stroke in all large cerebral vessel locations is similar, approximately 13% per year, and is greatest when the degree of stenosis is greater than 70%. In a patient with cerebral ischemia due to symptomatic ICA stenosis, the highest risk of subsequent stroke occurs in the first 2 weeks after the initial event. ICA disease is most common in persons of European ancestry, and intracranial atherosclerosis is most common in persons of Asian and African ancestry. Among patients with intracranial atherosclerosis, recurrent stroke is most common in those with a greater than 70% stenosis and in those whose blood pressure remains greater than 140/80 mm Hg. Whether patients with intracranial atherosclerosis should undergo stenting in addition to the best medical treatment is unknown.

### Small Subcortical Infarcts

Small subcortical infarcts, also known as lacunae, result from lipohyalinosis of the small penetrating arteries that feed off the middle cerebral, anterior cerebral, posterior cerebral, and vertebrobasilar arteries. Lacunar infarcts, which commonly occur in the setting of hypertension, cause discrete clinical syndromes resulting from ischemia in subcortical gray and white matter structures, such as a pure motor hemiparesis or pure sensory stroke, without the cortical signs of aphasia or hemianopia. Common lacunar syndromes are described in **Table 14**.

### Cryptogenic Stroke

Cryptogenic stroke is the most prevalent ischemic stroke subtype and is characterized by imaging findings that suggest an embolic event without any evidence on evaluation of a cardioembolic source or large artery atherosclerosis. The recurrent stroke rate of this type of ischemic stroke is relatively low. A proportion of patients (close to 25% in recent studies) with this stroke subtype may have paroxysmal atrial fibrillation, which can be identified by prolonged cardiac rhythm monitoring.

## Hemorrhagic Stroke

Hemorrhagic stroke comprises 17% of all strokes in the United States, with an equal proportion of intracerebral hemorrhage (ICH) and subarachnoid hemorrhage (SAH).

### Intracerebral Hemorrhage

ICH is more common in Asian countries, which perhaps reflects the greater impact of hypertension in those countries. Two distinct pathologies of ICH exist. A deep-location hemorrhage is most likely due to hypertension and typically originates in the basal ganglia or cerebellum. A lobar hemorrhage located near the surface of the brain can also be caused by hypertension, although cerebral amyloid angiopathy is a more likely cause. The differential diagnosis of ICH includes vascular malformation, infection, and brain tumor with hemorrhage. Because a cerebral hemorrhage may obscure an underlying tumor, a repeat imaging study must be obtained 4 to 6 weeks after the initial event. ICH has a much higher mortality than ischemic stroke.

### Subarachnoid Hemorrhage

SAH is typically caused by a ruptured cerebral saccular aneurysm, although other rare causes, such as an arteriovenous malformation and mycotic aneurysms, do exist. A chief symptom of sudden-onset severe headache, especially if associated with impaired consciousness, should prompt consideration of SAH. If a CT scan of the head is negative for subarachnoid blood but the clinical suspicion remains high, a lumbar puncture to look for erythrocytes and xanthochromia is required. The mortality associated with SAH is higher than with other brain hemorrhages because most affected patients die before reaching the hospital. SAH is graded by a clinical and radiographic scale, both of which have a good association with medical and neurologic complications and with long-term outcome.

- The ABCD² score (based on Age, Blood pressure, Clinical presentation, Duration of symptoms, and the presence of Diabetes mellitus) can help clinicians identify patients with transient ischemic attacks who are at highest risk of subsequent stroke and would benefit from hospital admission.
- Ischemic stroke connotes the presence of cerebral infarction, although the lesion is not always evident on CT scans or diffusion-weighted MRIs.

- The differential diagnosis of intracerebral hemorrhage, which has a much higher mortality than ischemic stroke, includes vascular malformation, infection, and brain tumor with hemorrhage.

# Acute Ischemic Stroke

## Clinical Diagnosis

An algorithm for the evaluation of acute ischemic stroke is provided in **Figure 11**. The initial goal of the diagnostic

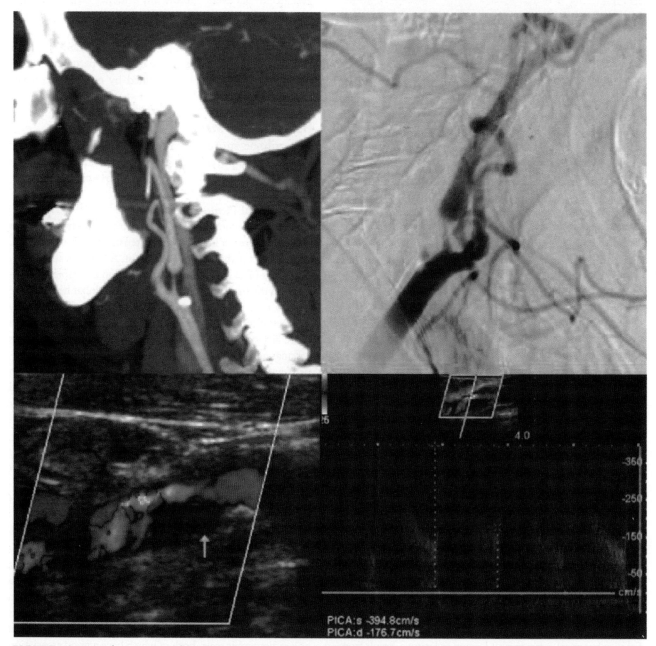

**FIGURE 10.** Images from a patient with symptomatic internal carotid artery stenosis. *Top left*, CT angiogram of the extracranial internal carotid artery showing high-grade stenosis at its origin. *Top right*, digital subtraction angiography from the same patient. *Bottom*, Duplex ultrasonograms from the same patient; *arrow on left* indicates the plaque and associated stenosis. PICA = proximal internal carotid artery.

evaluation is to achieve medical and cardiorespiratory stabilization. The primary focus of the subsequent evaluation is to determine whether the patient is a candidate for thrombolytic treatment. Determining the time of onset is key to this process. For patients whose strokes are not witnessed, the time of onset is when they were last witnessed to be without symptoms, which often is when they went to bed. Patients outside the treatment window should not receive thrombolysis.

Determination of the blood glucose level is a critical component of the acute stroke evaluation to exclude other conditions that may mimic stroke and to identify hyperglycemia, which is associated with poor outcome after stroke. Other laboratory studies required acutely include a complete blood count, basic metabolic panel, measurement of the serum troponin level, and a coagulation profile. An electrocardiogram is needed to rule out acute myocardial infarction

and evaluate for atrial fibrillation, and a chest radiograph is commonly obtained to rule out aortic dissection, although this step is not required.

## Imaging Techniques

A CT of the head without contrast will easily rule out ICH, the principal initial criterion for excluding thrombolysis (see Figure 8). Subtle signs of early infarction can sometimes be seen on a head CT scan (**Figure 12**), but many patients with acute ischemic stroke have normal results on head CT. Other imaging modalities have been proposed for the acute setting, although none is required before beginning thrombolysis; waiting for results of these studies should never delay the initiation of treatment.

## Treatment

### Thrombolysis

The effectiveness of thrombolysis with recombinant tissue plasminogen activator (rtPA) administered within 3 hours of acute ischemic stroke was examined in the National Institute of Neurological Diseases and Stroke trial. Compared with a placebo infusion, rtPA was associated with improved functional outcomes at 3 months but not with earlier neurologic improvement or lower mortality. National guidelines recommend that treatment be initiated within 1 hour of arrival at the emergency department. rtPA is a fibrinolytic agent that converts plasminogen to plasmin in the presence of fibrin to initiate fibrinolysis at the site of thrombus formation, which improves blood flow to areas of the brain that are ischemic but not yet infarcted (ischemic penumbra). A small number of patients with acute ischemic stroke will be eligible for reperfusion therapy, and an even smaller number will actually receive it. **Figure 13** presents a proposed algorithm for the treatment of acute ischemic stroke. More recent evidence has shown a benefit of rtPA up to 4.5 hours after stroke onset, although

| TABLE 13. ABCD² Scoring System[a] | |
|---|---|
| **Patient Characteristics** | **Score[b]** |
| Age ≥60 y | 1 |
| Blood pressure ≥140/90 mm Hg | 1 |
| Clinical symptoms | |
| Focal weakness with the TIA | 2 |
| Speech impairment without weakness | 1 |
| Duration of TIA | |
| ≥60 min | 2 |
| 10-59 min | 1 |
| Diabetes mellitus present | 1 |

TIA = transient ischemic attack.

[a]Based on Age, Blood pressure, Clinical presentation, Duration of symptoms, and the presence of Diabetes mellitus.

[b]Score and 2-day stroke risk based on score: 0-1 = 0%; 2-3 = 1.3%; 4-5 = 4.1%; 6-7 = 8.1%.

| TABLE 14. Classic Lacunar Syndromes | | |
|---|---|---|
| **Syndrome** | **Structure(s) Involved** | **Artery(ies) Involved** |
| Pure motor hemiparesis | Internal capsule, corona radiata | Lenticulostriate artery from the middle cerebral artery |
| | Pons, medullary pyramids | Basilar artery penetrator |
| Pure sensory | Thalamus | Inferolateral artery from the posterior cerebral artery |
| Sensorimotor | Thalamus, internal capsule, caudate, putamen | Middle cerebral and posterior cerebral penetrators |
| Ataxic hemiparesis | Pons | Basilar artery penetrator |
| | Internal capsule | Lenticulostriate artery from the middle cerebral artery |
| Dysarthria-clumsy hand syndrome | Internal capsule (anterior limb) | Lenticulostriate artery from the middle cerebral artery |
| Hemiballism, dystonia, and other movement disorders | Basal ganglia | Lenticulostriate artery from the middle cerebral artery |
| Eye movement disturbances with variable additional focal neurologic deficits | Brainstem | Basilar artery penetrator |

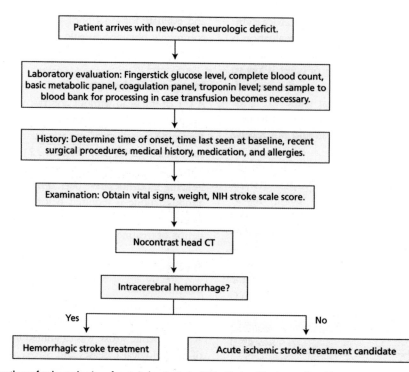

**FIGURE 11.** Clinical pathway for the evaluation of acute ischemic stroke. NIH = National Institutes of Health.

exclusion criteria (age greater than 80 years, severe stroke, diabetes mellitus with a previous infarct, and any anticoagulant use) are more restrictive than for treatment 3 hours or less from onset. Despite the extended window for rtPA administration, patients derive the greatest benefit the sooner they are treated. The exclusion criteria for rtPA are provided in **Table 15**; some of these criteria are relative rather than absolute.

The most feared complication of rtPA treatment is symptomatic intracranial hemorrhage, which occurs in 6.4% of treated patients and has a mortality rate approaching 50%. The principal risk factors for hemorrhage after rtPA administration include a large infarct size, poor blood pressure control, hyperglycemia, and treatment after the appropriate time window. The presence of nausea, headache, or worsening findings on neurologic examination should prompt immediate discontinuation of rtPA infusion and repeat head CT. All patients who receive intravenous rtPA should be monitored for 24 hours in an intensive care unit or stroke unit, where blood pressure and neurologic status can be monitored closely. Surgical procedures and antithrombotic treatment should be avoided for 24 hours after rtPA administration, but arterial puncture is permitted at a compressible site, if necessary.

In recent years, catheter-based approaches to treat acute ischemic stroke have been developed. These techniques include local delivery of the thrombolytic agent at the site of a vascular occlusion or mechanical thrombectomy by means of an intra-arterial catheter. Intra-arterial thrombolysis has been shown to improve recanalization rates and clinical outcomes and is recommended for middle cerebral artery infarctions up to 6 hours after stroke onset. Prospective phase III clinical trials have not yet been completed to support the use of endovascular clot removal, although endovascular approaches within 8 hours from stroke onset are a reasonable alternative for patients who cannot receive intravenous rtPA because they have absolute exclusion criteria or are beyond the 4.5-hour time window. Patients with a large cerebral artery occlusion are less likely to benefit from intravenous rtPA than those with other stroke subtypes, and endovascular treatment after intravenous rtPA is commonly performed. However, the clinical benefit of this approach has yet to be proved by phase III clinical trials.

**Blood Pressure Treatment in Acute Ischemic Stroke**
The treatment of blood pressure in the acute setting depends on whether the patient will be treated with intravenous rtPA. In patients who are candidates for this agent, blood pressure should be less than 185/110 mm Hg, which can be achieved by the continuous infusion of labetalol or nicardipine. Nitroglycerin and nitroprusside should be avoided because they may lower blood pressure excessively or raise intracranial pressure. After rtPA infusion, blood pressure should be targeted to less than 180/105 mm Hg; labetalol or nicardipine is again appropriate for patients whose blood pressure exceeds these limits. In patients ineligible for intravenous rtPA, blood pressure parameters are liberalized. In these patients, blood pressures up to 220/120 mm Hg are permitted with the intention of improving cerebral perfusion, which is frequently

accomplished by withholding home antihypertensive medications. This blood pressure target is maintained until the patient is discharged home or transferred to a rehabilitation facility. Antihypertensive agents should not be withheld in patients who have active myocardial ischemia or are at risk for an exacerbation of heart failure.

## Acute Antithrombotic Agents

Antithrombotic agents remain the most commonly used drugs for acute stroke prevention. Two large clinical trials showed a benefit of treatment with aspirin over placebo in short-term mortality and recurrent stroke risk when administered within 48 hours of ischemic stroke onset. Heparin and

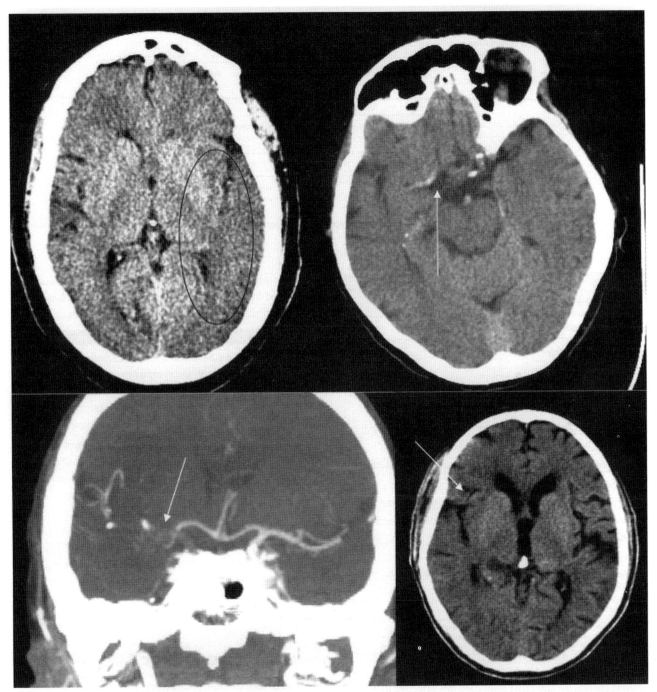

**FIGURE 12.** Head CT findings in acute ischemic stroke. *Top left,* sulcal effacement and loss of the gray-white differentiation *(oval circle)* in a patient 1.5 hours after the witnessed onset of global aphasia. *Top right,* hyperdensity *(arrow)* in the proximal right middle cerebral artery in a patient with left hemiparesis and left hemi-inattention 60 minutes after last being seen well. *Bottom left,* CT angiogram of the patient from panel B that shows absent contrast in the right internal carotid and proximal middle cerebral arteries *(arrow)*, consistent with a thrombus in the artery. *Bottom right,* loss of the insular ribbon on the right *(arrow)* compared with the left where the gray-white differentiation is clearly seen in a patient 2 hours after onset of left hemiparesis.

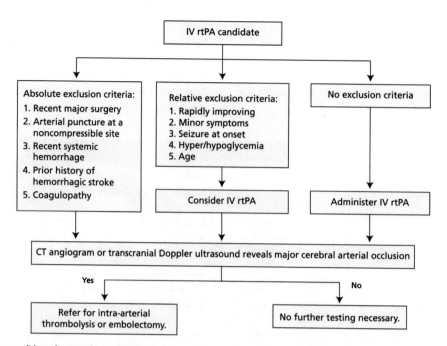

**FIGURE 13.** Selecting candidates for recombinant tissue plasminogen activator therapy 3 hours or less after an ischemic stroke. IV = intravenous; rtPA = recombinant tissue plasminogen activator.

---

**TABLE 15.** Exclusion Criteria for Administering Intravenous Tissue Plasminogen Activator 3 Hours or Less After an Ischemic Stroke

| Contraindications to rtPA |
|---|
| Minor or rapidly improving symptoms |
| Seizure at stroke onset |
| Other stroke or trauma within 3 months |
| Major surgery within the last 14 days |
| History of intracerebral hemorrhage |
| Sustained blood pressure ≥185/110 mm Hg |
| Aggressive drug therapy needed to control blood pressure |
| Suspicion of subarachnoid hemorrhage |
| Arterial puncture at a noncompressible site within 7 days |
| Heparin received within the last 48 hours and PTT elevated |
| INR >1.7 |
| Platelet count <100,000/μL (100 × 10⁹/L) |
| Plasma glucose level <50 mg/dL (2.8 mmol/L) or >400 mg/dL (22.2 mmol/L) |

PTT = partial thromboplastin time; rtPA = recombinant tissue plasminogen activator.

Source: Tissue plasminogen activator for acute ischemic stroke. The National Institute of Neurological Disorders and Stroke rt-PA Stroke Study Group. N Engl J Med. 1995;333(24):1581-1587. [PubMed 7477192]

in those with cervicocephalic arterial dissections. Caution is warranted in patients with large cerebral infarcts because of the risk of hemorrhagic conversion of the ischemic stroke.

**KEY POINTS**

- Algorithms based on the nature and duration (usually <3 hours) of neurologic symptoms can identify patients with acute stroke for whom the emergent administration of recombinant tissue plasminogen activator can reduce subsequent functional impairment.

- The most serious complication of administering recombinant tissue plasminogen activator is symptomatic intracranial hemorrhage, which occurs in 6.4% of treated patients and has a mortality rate approaching 50%.

- In patients who are candidates for thrombolytic therapy, blood pressure should be less than 185/110 mm Hg, which can be achieved by the continuous infusion of labetalol or nicardipine; for those who are not candidates for such therapy, blood pressure should be less than 220/120 mm Hg until hospital discharge.

# Acute Hemorrhagic Stroke

## Intracerebral Hemorrhage

Patients who sustain an ICH are at high risk of immediate neurologic and cardiac complications and should be admitted to an intensive care unit with staff experienced in treating neurologic diseases. The immediate neurologic complications

related agents, on the other hand, are not effective in reducing mortality or recurrent stroke in patients with cardioembolic or noncardioembolic stroke. Heparin may be considered in the acute setting for stroke caused by atrial fibrillation after cardiac surgery, in patients with a mechanical heart valve, or

of ICH include expansion of the hematoma and elevated intracranial pressure.

Strategies aimed at preventing hematoma expansion have been disappointing, although lowering blood pressure is safe and effective. In patients with a systolic blood pressure greater than 200 mm Hg or a mean arterial pressure greater than 150 mm Hg, aggressive blood pressure lowering by means of an intravenous infusion of medication (such as labetalol or nicardipine) with frequent monitoring of vital signs (at least every 5 minutes) should be considered. If the systolic blood pressure is greater than 180 mm Hg or the mean arterial pressure is greater than 130 mm Hg, intravenous medications should still be considered. A blood pressure target of 160/90 mm Hg or mean arterial pressure of 110 mm Hg is recommended, although in patients with ICH whose systolic blood pressure is 150 to 220 mm Hg, lowering it to 140 mm Hg seems safe. Blood pressure in patients with elevated intracranial pressure may need to be managed with the help of an intracranial pressure monitor. Elevated intracranial pressure can occur because of mass effect from the hematoma and associated edema or from extension of blood into the ventricular system with subsequent hydrocephalus. The latter occurrence is a neurosurgical emergency and requires emergent ventricular shunting. Attempting to reduce hematoma expansion with recombinant factor VII does not yield an overall improved prognosis and is associated with a greater incidence of thrombotic events.

In patients with oral anticoagulant–associated ICH, treatment should include reversing the hemorrhagic diathesis as quickly as possible by stopping the anticoagulant and administering an appropriate reversal agent, such as intravenous vitamin K, fresh frozen plasma, or prothrombin complex concentrates. The efficacy and safety of platelet transfusions in the setting of antiplatelet-associated ICH have not been established. For patients with ICH who experience elevated intracranial pressure, the mainstay of treatment is medical stabilization followed by surgical evacuation of the hematoma. Intubation and short-term hyperventilation are the initial steps in treatment followed by osmotherapy with either mannitol or hypertonic saline.

Whether clot removal should be performed in all patients with ICH remains uncertain. In selected patients, such as those with a cerebellar ICH greater than 3 cm in size or with neurologic deterioration, surgical removal is recommended. In patients with a superficial hemorrhage greater than 30 mL, this approach can also be considered.

### Subarachnoid Hemorrhage

SAH is associated with neurologic decline and early mortality. The main risk factors for aneurysmal SAH are tobacco use and hypertension. In the acute setting, patients with SAH have sudden-onset severe headache ("worst headache ever") with associated coma or other impairments in alertness and consciousness. The presence of a large dilated pupil is an additional localizing feature and occurs because of cerebral herniation or mass effect from a posterior communicating artery aneurysm. Funduscopic examination may reveal subhyaloid hemorrhages. These signs and symptoms should prompt an immediate investigation with head CT to confirm or exclude hydrocephalus or global cerebral edema. The initial clinical grade (Hunt-Hess scale) has a high predictive value for mortality and medical complications: grade 1 patients have isolated headaches and have excellent outcomes, whereas grade V patients who present with coma have a greater than 60% mortality rate and a high risk for medical complications. CT angiography may help identify the source of the SAH, which is most commonly a saccular aneurysm at major arterial bifurcations (**Figure 14**). Angiography is essential to delineate the anatomy of a ruptured cerebral aneurysm and to rule out other causes of SAH, such as intracranial arterial dissection or mycotic aneurysms.

Early complications of SAH include rebleeding, elevated intracranial pressure, global cerebral edema, and hydrocephalus from the presence of blood in the ventricular system. External shunting of the cerebrospinal fluid is often required with SAHs and has the additional benefit of enabling monitoring of intracranial pressure. By the fifth day after initial aneurysmal bleeding, secondary cerebral injury can result from seizures, worsening hydrocephalus, or delayed cerebral ischemia because of arterial vasospasm. Nimodipine is administered to prevent vasospasm, and cerebral ischemia is sometimes prevented by elevating mean arterial pressures with the use of systemic vasopressors.

### KEY POINTS

- For patients with elevated intracranial pressure resulting from an intracerebral hemorrhage, the mainstay of therapy is medical stabilization and emergent neurosurgical evaluation to determine if the hematoma should be surgically evacuated.

- Angiography is essential to delineate the anatomy of a ruptured cerebral aneurysm and to rule out other causes of subarachnoid hemorrhage, such as intracranial arterial dissection or mycotic aneurysms.

- The chief causes of a decline in neurologic status after subarachnoid hemorrhage are rebleeding and elevated intracranial pressure in the acute setting and arterial vasospasm 5 days or more after the hemorrhage.

## Other Types of Stroke

### Dural Sinus Venous Thrombosis

Venous thrombosis should be considered in the differential diagnosis of focal neurologic symptoms and is often accompanied by severe headache, a depressed level of consciousness, and seizures. Funduscopic examination should be performed in all patients with these symptoms because papilledema may be present in at least 50% of patients with dural sinus thrombosis. The

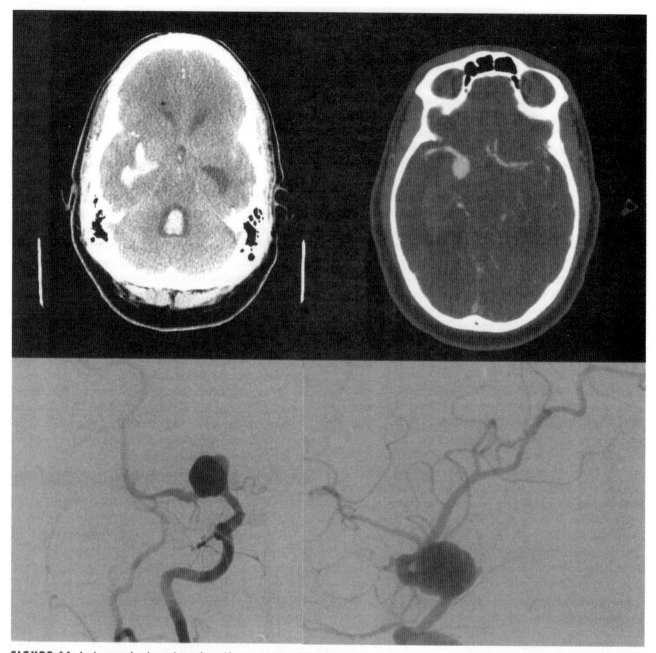

**FIGURE 14.** Angiograms showing an internal carotid artery aneurysm in a patient with a subarachnoid hemorrhage. *Top left,* CT angiogram showing an extensive subarachnoid hemorrhage with intraventricular extension. *Top right,* CT angiogram showing a large right internal carotid artery aneurysm. *Bottom left,* anterior-posterior view of a digital subtraction angiogram of the right intracranial internal carotid artery showing the same large aneurysm. *Bottom right,* lateral view of the digital subtraction angiogram showing the same large aneurysm.

occlusion of a central vein or sinus quickly results in an elevated intracranial pressure that causes the headache. The most common location is the superior sagittal sinus, but the lateral and deep sinuses also may be involved. Thrombosis of the cavernous sinus results in a characteristic neurologic syndrome that includes lesions of cranial nerves III, IV, V (V1 and V2), and occasionally VI, sometimes with ocular engorgement and dilated periocular veins. Involvement of the cortical veins can lead to venous infarction and ICH.

Risk factors for dural sinus venous thrombosis include venous hypercoagulable disorders, systemic malignancy, trauma, systemic inflammatory disorders (such as ulcerative colitis), severe dehydration or infection, or pregnancy. A head CT scan with contrast may show filling defects in the dural sinuses and the so-called "empty delta sign," which can be observed in the confluence of sinuses. Magnetic resonance venography is now the diagnostic examination of choice for dural sinus venous thrombosis and can be performed safely in pregnancy (**Figure 15**). The definitive treatment for venous thrombosis has not been established, but most experts recommend anticoagulation with heparin and related agents followed by warfarin for 6 months, even in the setting of ICH. Anticoagulation can be started after the diagnosis is confirmed unless surgical intervention is planned or there is evidence of an expanding cerebral hematoma. The overall prognosis and mortality is dependent on the underlying cause. Patients with a hypercoagulable disorder generally have excellent outcomes, but those with an infectious cause have a high risk of mortality, which reflects the underlying natural history of central nervous system infections.

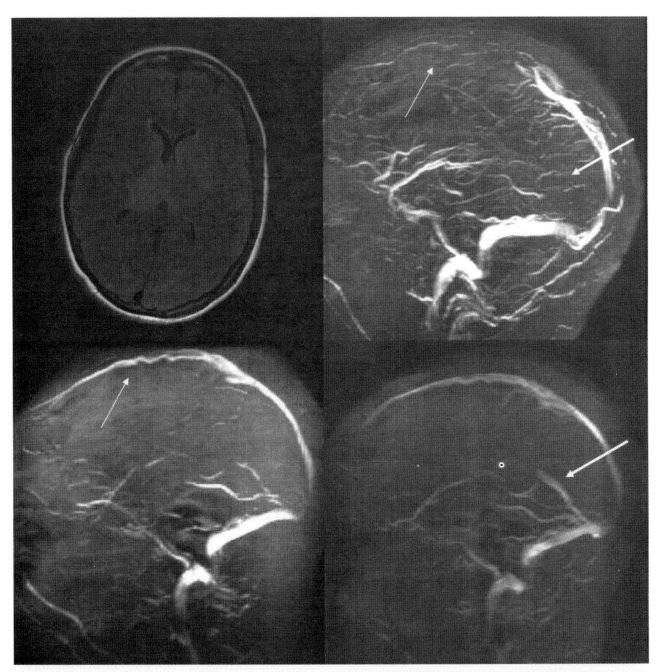

**FIGURE 15.** Imaging studies of a patient with dural sinus venous thrombosis. *Top left*, fluid-attenuated inversion recovery (FLAIR) MRI showing extensive vasogenic edema in the basal ganglia. *Top right*, magnetic resonance venogram (MRV) of the brain at presentation showing absent deep cerebral venous structures (*thicker arrow*) and absence of the anterior half of the superior sagittal sinus (*thinner arrow*). *Bottom left*, MRV 1 week after initiating intravenous heparin showing improved flow in the superior sagittal sinus (*arrow*). *Bottom right*, MRV 6 months after initiation of warfarin showing reconstitution of the deep cerebral venous structures and superior sagittal sinus (*arrow*).

### Carotid and Vertebral Artery Dissection

Cervicocephalic dissection is an uncommon but important cause of stroke, especially in persons younger than 50 years. ICA dissections present with focal cerebral ischemia or TIA, but symptoms due to local mass effect are also possible. Headache or neck pain is a prominent feature of ICA dissection, which may have no identified preceding trauma. The presence of a partial Horner syndrome (ptosis and miosis without anhidrosis) with head or neck pain should prompt investigation for ICA dissection. Doppler ultrasonography, CT angiography, or MR angiography may visualize narrowing of the ICA but not confirm dissection. The cause of the associated stroke is primarily thrombus formation at the site of dissection with subsequent artery-to-artery embolism, and pathologic examination reveals a hematoma within layers of the tunica media. The imaging modality of choice is an MRI of the soft tissues in the neck, which will demonstrate a crescent-shaped hematoma within the ICA wall on T1-weighted images (**Figure 16**). Heparin followed by a course of warfarin for 3 to 6 months is commonly used in treating arterial dissection, although the superiority of this approach over antiplatelet agents has not been established.

Extracranial vertebral artery dissection is similar in pathophysiology and treatment to ICA dissection, but the risk of recurrence may be higher, and symptoms are primarily due to posterior circulation ischemia. Intracranial arterial dissections are less common but can present with SAH or ischemic symptoms. **H**

### Asymptomatic Aneurysm

Advances in modern neuroimaging have led to the identification of frequent, often incidental, unruptured cerebral aneurysms in otherwise healthy persons. Aneurysm size and location are the most important predictors of subsequent rupture. In the anterior cerebral circulation, the risk of rupture over 5 years is negligible until an aneurysm reaches 12 mm in diameter; in the posterior circulation, the risk of rupture increases as aneurysms become greater than 7 mm. The risk of endovascular or open neurosurgical procedures to occlude or clip aneurysms is significant, and thus the most prudent approach is watchful waiting with repeated neuroimaging to monitor increasing aneurysmal size. Modifiable risk factors for aneurysmal rupture, such as hypertension and tobacco use, should be treated.

#### KEY POINTS

- Magnetic resonance venography is now the diagnostic examination of choice for dural sinus venous thrombosis and can be performed safely in pregnancy.
- The primary cause of the stroke associated with carotid and vertebral artery dissection is thrombus formation at the site of dissection with subsequent artery-to-artery embolism.

- Size and location are the major predictors of subsequent rupture for incidentally discovered cerebral aneurysms; the most prudent management is watchful waiting with repeated neuroimaging to monitor increasing aneurysmal size, particularly for anterior cerebral aneurysms less than 12 mm in diameter and posterior circulation aneurysms less than 7 mm in diameter.

## Admission to Stroke Units and Stroke Centers

Admission to a specialized stroke unit improves clinical outcomes after stroke, including the 1-year mortality rate. A stroke unit brings together a multidisciplinary team of specialists familiar with the assessment and management of stroke; the physical, medical, and emotional needs of affected patients; and appropriate rehabilitation procedures, deep venous thrombosis prophylaxis, and dysphagia management. For patients with any stroke subtype, admission to a stroke unit is the only nonsurgical intervention known to reduce mortality at 1 year, with a benefit that can extend up to 10 years after stroke. The use of formalized protocols for preventing medical and neurologic complications and an emphasis on early mobilization with physical and occupational therapy appear to drive these long-lasting benefits.

## Secondary Stroke Prevention

Stroke survival entails ongoing medical vigilance. Patients who are discharged from the hospital after a stroke have a substantial risk of recurrent stroke, myocardial infarction, and death. Because few patients receive acute treatment for stroke, prevention of future events is the cornerstone of stroke management.

### Hypertension

The presence of hypertension has the greatest effect on the risk of stroke, regardless of the cause. Therefore, hypertension should be treated after a stroke, even in the absence of a history of hypertension. Clinical trial data indicate that the risk of recurrent stroke increases in those patients whose blood pressure is allowed to remain above 140/80 mm Hg. For more information on hypertension and stroke risk, see MKSAP 16 Nephrology.

### Dyslipidemia

Hyperlipidemia is a key and modifiable risk factor in stroke recurrence. In all patients with a serum LDL cholesterol level greater than 100 mg/dL (2.59 mmol/L) who have stroke, recent clinical trial data support the use of a high-dose statin for the prevention of recurrent ischemic stroke and myocardial infarction, despite the mild increase in the risk of ICH.

## Antithrombotic Treatment

The pathophysiology of ischemic stroke will frequently dictate the choice of an antithrombotic agent. Only in atrial fibrillation and intracardiac thrombus have warfarin and direct thrombin inhibitors been established as the treatment of choice for stroke prevention. All patients with atrial fibrillation who have a TIA or stroke should receive anticoagulation unless a clear contraindication exists. In aortic arch atheroma,

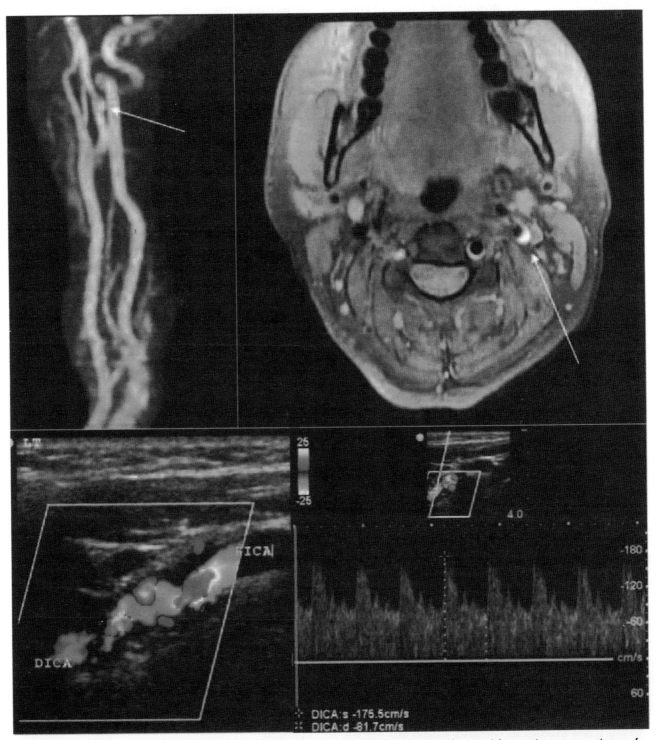

**FIGURE 16.** Left internal carotid artery (ICA) dissection in a 32-year-old woman with a left frontal cerebral infarct. *Top left,* magnetic resonance angiogram of the neck showing mild irregularity in the distal extracranial internal carotid artery with a possible pseudoaneurysm (*arrow*). *Top right,* T1-weighted MRI of the soft tissues in the neck showing a crescent-shaped hematoma (*arrow*) within the ICA wall. *Bottom,* carotid Duplex ultrasonograms from the same patient showing turbulent flow in the mid- to distal internal carotid artery with associated accelerated systolic and diastolic velocities. DICA = distal ICA; LT = left; PICA = proximal ICA.

the optimal antithrombotic treatment remains controversial, with no evidence supporting warfarin over antiplatelet agents. If full anticoagulation with warfarin or dabigatran is not possible, as in patients with recurrent falls or a previous ICH due to amyloid angiopathy, other effective strategies for stroke prevention in patients with atrial fibrillation exist, including aspirin, 325 mg/d, or aspirin combined with clopidogrel.

Antiplatelet agents are recommended over anticoagulation in patients with stroke who have intracranial atherosclerosis because warfarin was associated in one clinical trial with an increase in mortality compared with high-dose aspirin. For patients with cryptogenic and small-vessel stroke, warfarin and aspirin are equivalent in reducing the risk of recurrent ischemic stroke, although antiplatelet agents are sometimes favored because of their ease of use. For stroke prevention in patients without atrial fibrillation, the most commonly used aspirin dosage is 81 mg/d. Several studies have shown modest differences between aspirin, clopidogrel, and dipyridamole in preventing recurrent stroke and adverse cardiovascular outcomes in patients with stroke. In one trial, clopidogrel showed an overall modest benefit in the primary outcome of composite vascular events (recurrent ischemic stroke, myocardial infarction, or vascular death), particularly in patients with peripheral arterial disease. However, clopidogrel versus the combination of aspirin and dipyridamole was equivalent in a recent clinical trial. Clopidogrel is prescribed for stroke prevention in patients who have peripheral arterial disease, and clopidogrel or aspirin and dipyridamole are reasonable options for those who have had a recurrent ischemic stroke despite optimal risk factor management while treated with aspirin. Adherence to an aspirin and dipyridamole regimen can be difficult because of the high incidence of headache, and the cost of the combination agent or clopidogrel can be problematic for many patients. At this time, the combination of aspirin and clopidogrel is not commonly used in patients without cardioembolic stroke unless dictated by the presence of vascular stents or a previous myocardial infarction. See MKSAP 16 Cardiovascular Medicine for more information.

## Surgery for Secondary Stroke

### Carotid Revascularization Procedures for Internal Carotid Artery Atherosclerosis

Symptomatic extracranial ICA stenosis of greater than 70% is a well-established risk factor for recurrent stroke, with a 26% risk within 2 years of initial stroke. Carotid revascularization significantly reduces the risk of minor and major ipsilateral stroke and is of greatest benefit when performed early. Internal carotid endarterectomy has been the gold standard procedure for the past 20 years and is beneficial as long as the surgeon has a complication rate of less than 5%. Angioplasty combined with stenting is now an additional option for patients with symptomatic carotid stenosis, and recent clinical trial results have indicated that the outcome of stroke, myocardial infarction, or death is equivalent for this procedure and endarterectomy.

Compared with angioplasty and stenting, carotid endarterectomy has a higher risk of perioperative myocardial infarction, but angioplasty and stenting has a higher risk of perioperative stroke, especially in those older than 70 years.

### Hemicraniectomy

Infarctions of the middle cerebral artery involving more than 50% of the arterial territory that are accompanied by severe brain swelling have a mortality rate of 80%. According to data from three pooled European studies, hemicraniectomy significantly reduces mortality and severe disability (from 76% to 25%) in patients with malignant middle cerebral artery infarction. This benefit is greatest if hemicraniectomy is performed within 48 hours of stroke onset, before clinical herniation has occurred. The procedure opens the bony encasement of the skull and decompresses the brain.

### Patent Foramen Ovale Closure

Patent foramen ovale, with or without an atrial septal aneurysm, may be a cause of ischemic stroke, particularly in young persons. Although the optimal treatment of this condition remains unknown, a recently completed multicenter trial showed no benefit of percutaneous closure of patent foramen ovale for stroke prevention. Aspirin and warfarin appear equivalent treatments. For a further discussion, see MKSAP 16 Cardiovascular Medicine.

### KEY POINTS

- All patients with atrial fibrillation who have a transient ischemic attack or stroke should receive anticoagulation unless a clear contraindication exists.

- Clopidogrel is indicated for patients with ischemic stroke and peripheral arterial disease to prevent recurrent stroke; the combination of aspirin and clopidogrel has no additional benefit over a single antiplatelet agent alone in stroke prevention.

- Symptomatic extracranial internal carotid artery stenosis of greater than 70% is a well-established risk factor for recurrent stroke, with a 26% risk within 2 years of initial stroke.

- The optimal treatment of patients with stroke and a patent foramen ovale, with or without an atrial septal aneurysm, remains unclear; however, aspirin and warfarin appear to be equivalent treatments, and no clear benefit to stroke prevention has been shown for percutaneous closure.

# Prevention of Stroke Complications

## Neurologic Worsening

Patients with an ischemic stroke or a TIA may have a recurrent stroke while still hospitalized, although the risk appears higher with TIAs and can be determined by the ABCD$^2$ score. In patients with stroke recurrence, two major mechanisms have been noted: (1) extension of the previous infarct due to expansion of the area of the ischemic territory and (2) a separate, distinct stroke due to either ongoing stroke pathophysiology or a complication of stroke therapy. Preventing expansion of the ischemic territory can be achieved by not treating hypertension while using antithrombotic medication. The hemorrhagic conversion of an ischemic stroke typically occurs in the first 24 hours but can occur up to 2 weeks after the initial infarction. Hemorrhagic conversion is most likely to occur with large infarcts and cardiac embolism and is also associated with vessel recanalization during thrombolytic treatment. Neurologic decline after stroke may also result from seizure, urinary tract infection, pneumonia, hypoglycemia, or sedative medication use.

## Medical Complications

Medical complications after stroke are common, particularly in older patients with medical comorbidities and in patients with more severe stroke syndromes, and result in increased length of hospital stay, poor functional outcome, and mortality. During the first week after a stroke, medical complications include cardiac disease, deep venous thrombosis, urinary tract infection, and pneumonia. Many of these complications stem from immobility, and thus early physical and occupational therapy with an emphasis on ambulation and moving out of bed has a critical role. After 1 week, the same complications pertain but additional complications also arise, including falls and fractures, depression, and skin breakdown because of immobility.

Cardiac complications after stroke also occur, which is not surprising because heart disease and stroke share common risk factors. Heart failure after stroke has been attributed to new myocardial infarction or arrhythmia, hypertension due to withholding antihypertensive agents, and a cerebral stress–related cardiomyopathy that is associated with mild elevations in serum troponin levels, nonspecific ischemic changes in the anterolateral leads on electrocardiography, and a reversible global decline in left ventricular systolic function. The latter is most likely to occur in patients with ICH, high-grade SAH, and large ischemic strokes.

Infectious complications after stroke are primarily due to pneumonia and urinary tract infections. Most pneumonia is attributed to aspiration of food and drink taken orally, a more likely occurrence in older patients and those with dysphagia and early speech impairment. Implementation of dysphagia screening protocols early in the hospital admission can reduce the incidence of pneumonia in patients with stroke and are recommended by the Joint Commission National Quality Core Measures. Feeding through a nasogastric tube or percutaneous endoscopic gastrostomy tube can achieve nutritional goals in patients unable to swallow safely, although aspiration may still occur from regurgitation of gastric contents if the head of the bed is not kept higher than 30 degrees. The timing of when to place a percutaneous endoscopic gastrostomy tube remains unclear. Urinary tract infections also are common after stroke because of urinary retention after cerebral injury or the unnecessary use of urine catheters; these catheters can be safely removed in many patients with stroke.

The presence of hemiparesis makes the incidence of deep venous thrombosis particularly common in patients with stroke, especially within the first week after onset. Deep venous thrombosis and the subsequent development of a pulmonary embolism can be prevented with early implementation of prophylaxis strategies. In patients with ischemic stroke, unfractionated heparin (5000 units every 8 hours) or low-molecular-weight heparin is effective in reducing the risk of deep venous thrombosis and should be started by the first hospital day. In hemorrhagic stroke, either agent should be started by hospital day 1 to 4 as long as the source of the bleeding, such as an aneurysm, has been identified and treated or there is no evidence of active intracranial bleeding; in the interim, mechanical (pneumatic) compression devices should be used for prophylaxis. Graded compression stockings do not appear to be effective in reducing the risk of deep venous thrombosis. In patients with stroke who have acute-onset hypoxemia, pulmonary embolism should be considered as a cause, although pneumonia, sleep apnea, and diaphragmatic dysfunction are other possibilities.

Infectious complications and poststroke depression can have a significant effect on long-term recovery after stroke. Other complications that may emerge in the more chronic setting are sleep-disordered breathing, fatigue, pain, falls and fractures, diabetes mellitus, and cognitive dysfunction.

## Perioperative Stroke

With increasing numbers of surgical procedures has come an increase in the incidence of perioperative stroke. Most of these strokes are ischemic and occur as a complication of cardiothoracic surgery. The most common cause of perioperative stroke after cardiothoracic surgery is postoperative atrial fibrillation rather than hypotension. Preexisting symptomatic carotid artery disease and coronary artery bypass grafting with valve replacement increase the likelihood of perioperative stroke in cardiac surgery. Spinal cord infarcts also can occur in the perioperative period as a complication of aortic dissection or subsequent aortic grafting.

**KEY POINT**

- Deep venous thrombosis and the subsequent development of a pulmonary embolism after stroke can be prevented with early implementation of prophylaxis strategies, such as early mobilization, administration of low-molecular-weight or unfractionated heparin, and mechanical compression devices.

# Primary Prevention of Stroke

Table 16 lists common risk factors for ischemic and hemorrhagic stroke. Primary prevention of these stroke risk factors is discussed in MKSAP 16 Cardiovascular Medicine, Endocrinology and Metabolism, General Internal Medicine, and Nephrology.

## Asymptomatic Carotid Stenosis

Asymptomatic patients with ICA stenosis of greater than 70% have a lower risk of ischemic stroke than symptomatic patients have. On the basis of older clinical trial data, the risk of stroke in asymptomatic carotid stenosis approximates 2% per year with medical treatment, which is reduced to 1% per year with endarterectomy; the greater benefit of surgery pertains only if the complication rate for the surgeon is less than 3%. More recent data indicate that the risk of stroke in asymptomatic carotid stenosis is likely to be less than 1%, especially among patients treated with statins. In many centers, carotid revascularization is not performed in patients with asymptomatic carotid stenoses unless ancillary studies suggest a higher risk, such as the presence of microembolic signals or the failure to vasodilate with a carbon dioxide challenge on transcranial Doppler ultrasonography.

## Stroke Recovery and Long-Term Prognosis

Most stroke survivors have some form of residual disability. Between 15% and 30% of stroke survivors are permanently disabled and require assistance with most of their activities of daily living. Three months after stroke, 20% of survivors will require institutional care. Six months after stroke, 50% of survivors have a hemiparesis, 30% to 50% are unable to walk without assistance, 30% have bladder incontinence, and almost 20% have aphasia. Nevertheless, 50% to 70% of stroke survivors are able to regain functional independence, which highlights the critical importance of intensive rehabilitation strategies to improve stroke recovery. Whereas the severity of the initial neurologic deficit is the strongest predictor of long-term disability, even patients with initial complete paralysis can make significant gains in motor function. Factors that can influence recovery after stroke include recurrent stroke, major depression, age, premorbid physical fitness and level of independence, and pain. Early, aggressive interventions aimed at improving neurologic impairment, poststroke depression, and pain can have significant beneficial effects on stroke recovery and highlight the importance of multidisciplinary inpatient and outpatient care for stroke survivors.

**KEY POINT**

- The severity of the initial neurologic deficit after stroke is the strongest predictor of long-term disability.

# Dementia

## General Overview

### Definition and Description

Dementia is a progressive deterioration of cognitive function severe enough to impair occupational or social functioning.

| TABLE 16. | Common Risk Factors for Ischemic and Hemorrhagic Stroke | |
|---|---|---|
| **Ischemic Stroke/TIA** | **Intracerebral Hemorrhage** | **Subarachnoid Hemorrhage** |
| **Shared Risk Factors** | | |
| Hypertension | Hypertension | Hypertension |
| Cocaine abuse | Cocaine abuse | Cocaine abuse |
| Tobacco use | Tobacco use | Tobacco use |
| | Arteriovenous malformation | Arteriovenous malformation |
| **Other Risk Factors** | | |
| Diabetes mellitus | Amyloid angiopathy | Intracranial artery dissection |
| Atrial fibrillation | Decreased LDL cholesterol level | Polycystic kidney disease |
| Low ejection fraction and intracardiac thrombus | Elevated HDL cholesterol level | |
| Cervicocephalic arterial dissection | Anticoagulant agent use | |
| Aortic arch atheromatous disease | Antiplatelet agent use | |
| Cardiac valve vegetations | | |
| Patent foramen ovale | | |

TIA = transient ischemic attack.

The major risk factor for dementia is aging, and in the aging population of the United States, the already epidemic prevalence of dementia continues to grow. Dementia causes enormous hardship for patients and families and places a vast social and economic burden on society. Advanced stage dementia is a state of total dependence in which individuals are unable to communicate, recognize family members, remain continent of urine or feces, or ambulate. It is a terminal illness with a 6-month mortality rate of 25% and a median survival of 1.3 years, similar to more commonly recognized end-of-life conditions, such as metastatic cancer or end-stage heart failure.

The evaluation of a person with suspected dementia has three parts: (1) a formal assessment of cognitive domains using standardized tests; (2) an appraisal of the patient's capacity for social interaction and activities of daily living; and (3) an evaluation of the cause of the dementia, especially the possibility that the cause may be treatable and the dementia reversible. Dementia should be distinguished from other derangements of intellect and behavior, such as age-related memory loss, an acute confusional state, a chronic vegetative state, or psychiatric conditions, including depression and psychosis (**Table 17**).

Age-related cognitive decline is universal and chiefly affects memory, learning, and problem solving. Virtually every person older than 40 years reports occasional forgetfulness for details or interruptions in retrieving names or numbers previously committed to memory. These changes are attributed to a gradual loss of mental processing capacity and speed due to alterations in synaptic connections. Morphologic changes common to normal aging underlie age-related memory loss, including cerebral atrophy, cell loss in the cortex (especially the medial temporal lobes), neuronal shrinkage, and a gradual development of amyloid-containing neuritic plaques.

Mild cognitive impairment (MCI) describes a loss of cognitive ability that exceeds the expected age-related memory loss but does not interfere significantly with daily activities. This condition is thought to represent a transitional stage between normal aging and dementia, with affected persons progressing toward probable Alzheimer disease at a rate of approximately 10% to 15% per year. Not all persons with MCI develop dementia, but it is currently not possible to identify those who will progress to Alzheimer disease or to prevent the conversion from MCI to dementia using medication. Risk factors for the progression of MCI to dementia include a family history of Alzheimer disease, a memory deficit greater than 1.5 standard deviations below normal, the apolipoprotein E4 allele, and reduced hippocampal volumes on neuroimaging.

## Evaluation of the Patient with Suspected Dementia

The evaluation of dementia presumes a normal level of consciousness and ability to focus. Patients with delirium, psychosis, or a level of consciousness that is depressed or fluctuating cannot be properly evaluated. A patient's ability to undergo a battery of cognitive tests can be ascertained by giving the patient a long task that requires sustained attention, such as counting backward from 20 or reciting the months of the year backward.

Several convenient screening test batteries are available for the bedside or office evaluation of cognitive function. The most widely used is the Folstein Mini–Mental State Examination, a useful 30-point tool that contains items for memory, language, calculation, and executive function. The Montreal Cognitive Assessment (www.mocatest.org) is another convenient 30-point battery that includes a brief trail-making task, in which a sequence of letters and numbers must be connected; a clock-drawing task; and a word-finding task. This assessment thus tests the cognitive domains of executive function, visuospatial processing, and verbal fluency more effectively than the Folstein Mini–Mental State Examination. On both screening tests, a score less than 22 indicates dementia. The speed of responses to a cognitive battery, and not simply the answers themselves, also must be observed because a slow response time, or bradyphrenia, is an aspect of dementia. Some patients with MCI and mild Alzheimer disease perform in the normal range on screening tests, and only a complete neuropsychological evaluation, which is a lengthy

| TABLE 17. | Definitions of Impaired Attention and Cognition |
|---|---|
| Mild cognitive impairment | Deterioration in memory, learning, and problem solving that is greater than expected for age and educational level but does not interfere with occupational or social function |
| Dementia | Progressive deterioration of cognitive function measureable by standardized tests and sufficient to impair social or occupational function |
| Delirium | A state of fluctuating attention, impaired concentration, incoherence, disorientation (usually of acute onset), and agitated confusion in which excitement, hyperarousal, and disturbances of perception may be present |
| Persistent vegetative or minimally conscious state | A state of wakefulness lacking awareness of one's environment or purposeful activity, usually caused by severe injury to the cerebral hemispheres, with sufficient sparing of the diencephalon and brainstem to allow persistent autonomic and motor reflexes and sleep-wake cycles; complex reflexes noted in some patients, including eye movements, yawning, and motor responses to noxious stimuli, but no awareness of self or environment |

battery of many standardized tests, will fully reveal a patient's cognitive deficits and abilities.

The evaluation of dementia also considers a patient's educational level; a patient who never learned to read or write cannot be expected to produce a sentence and is, therefore, illiterate but does not necessarily have dementia. Because the diagnosis of dementia depends on establishing a decline from a prior level of occupational or social function, the testimony of family members or other witnesses may be required.

Dementia is often accompanied by a number of behavioral and motor signs. Passivity is frequently reported by family members of patients with dementia and manifests during the evaluation when the patient sits quietly as the spouse or caretaker provides the historical details. Primitive neurologic reflexes also may appear in patients with dementia, such as grasp and rooting reflexes, a snout reflex, a palmomental sign, a glabellar sign, and a tendency to retropulse (move backward) on standing. Depression should be excluded as the apparent cause of the cognitive decline because the psychomotor retardation of depression can mimic dementia but does not correlate with brain pathology and is reversible with effective treatment.

The clinical manifestations of dementia depend more on the location of pathologic changes than on the disease process itself. Most neurodegenerative diseases are not site specific but, rather, involve overlapping brain regions. The overall clinical pattern of dementia often can be divided into cortical and subcortical types. The prototypic cortical dementia is Alzheimer disease, which produces characteristic memory deficits, language impairment, and other features attributable to disease of the associative parietotemporal cortices. By contrast, subcortical dementias, of which the prototype is Parkinson disease–associated dementia, include features of parkinsonism, apathy, bradyphrenia, and depression.

## Differential Diagnosis of Dementia

The differential diagnosis of cognitive impairment is best considered in terms of its time course. An acute confusional state caused by a metabolic derangement or an overdose of sedatives, anticholinergic medication, or alcohol is not dementia and will resolve when the inciting factor is corrected. A course marked by sudden acute deficits, vascular events, and radiologic evidence of cerebrovascular disease is compatible with vascular dementia. A rapidly progressive (over weeks to several months) dementia suggests a paraneoplastic disorder, such as limbic encephalitis, or a prion disease, such as Creutzfeldt-Jakob disease. A gradual loss of memory coupled with impairments in other cognitive domains, such as language or executive function, is most likely Alzheimer disease, the most common cause of dementia. If the memory impairment is part of a neurobehavioral syndrome with depression, apathy, abulia, or disinhibition, a frontotemporal dementia is more likely.

## Diagnosis of Alzheimer Disease and Other Dementias

From a clinical standpoint, a dementia can usually be categorized as a degenerative, infectious, vascular, inflammatory, metabolic, traumatic, toxic, or neoplastic/paraneoplastic process. The largest category by far is neurodegenerative dementia, although in routine clinical practice, this categorization is generally not confirmed pathologically. The patient with progressive cognitive deterioration presents several practical diagnostic challenges: (1) confirming the diagnosis of dementia; (2) excluding diseases that may resemble dementia, such as depression; and (3) searching for treatable or reversible causes of dementia (**Table 18**).

The diagnosis of dementia is based primarily on the clinical pattern of the cognitive change, the rate of progression, and the association with neurologic and other medical illness, such as parkinsonism or cerebrovascular disease or infection. The clinical impression is supplemented by the judicious use and interpretation of nonspecific laboratory testing, with the primary aim of identifying reversible causes of dementia. Thyroid function tests, a serum vitamin $B_{12}$ level, a complete blood count, an erythrocyte sedimentation rate, a VDRL test, and head CT or brain MRI are indicated in the evaluation of a patient with dementia. Cerebrospinal

| TABLE 18. Treatable or Reversible Causes of Dementia | |
|---|---|
| Nutritional | Vitamin $B_{12}$ deficiency, thiamine deficiency |
| Inflammatory and autoimmune | Systemic lupus erythematosus, CNS vasculitis, sarcoidosis, granulomatosis with polyangiitis (also known as Wegener granulomatosis), paraneoplastic disease |
| Infectious | Brain abscess, chronic meningitis (TB, fungal infection, cryptococcosis, toxoplasmosis), HIV, CNS Whipple disease, syphilis, viral encephalitis |
| Endocrine | Hypothyroidism, hyperthyroidism, hypoparathyroidism |
| Structural | Hydrocephalus, brain tumor, subdural hematoma, postconcussive syndrome |
| Toxic/metabolic | Drug intoxication, alcoholism, withdrawal states, heavy metal exposure |
| Psychiatric | Depression, catatonia, schizophrenia |

CNS = central nervous system; TB = tuberculosis.

fluid (CSF) examination is not indicated in the routine evaluation of dementia but is an important diagnostic test in special clinical circumstances:

- Rapidly progressive dementia
- Age of onset less than 60 years
- Systemic cancer, infection, or inflammatory autoimmune disease
- Immunosuppressed or immunodeficiency state
- Positive syphilis serology

Brain biopsy is the most definitive diagnostic test, but its routine use cannot be justified because of its risks and costs.

---

**KEY POINTS**

- Persons with mild cognitive impairment develop Alzheimer disease at an approximate rate of 10% to 15% per year.
- A score less than 22 on either the Folstein Mini–Mental State Examination or the Montreal Cognitive Assessment indicates dementia.

---

# Alzheimer Disease

## Prevalence

Alzheimer disease is the leading cause of dementia in developed countries, accounting for enormous suffering, loss of productivity, and caregiver burden. Over 4 million people in the United States have Alzheimer disease, which is the leading cause of institutionalization in chronic care facilities. Although Alzheimer disease is not an inevitable consequence of getting older, the prevalence of the disease doubles every 5 years after age 65 years. It is estimated that 20% to 40% of individuals older than 85 years have Alzheimer disease. Alzheimer disease usually occurs sporadically, but a small number (<1%) of affected persons have a familial form inherited in an autosomal dominant mode with early onset. Mutations in the genes for tau protein metabolism, such as presenilin, account for a fraction of cases and reveal clues about the biologic events leading to the pathologic changes.

## Pathogenesis

The pathogenesis of Alzheimer disease remains incompletely understood. Converging evidence from genetic and immunohistochemical studies implicates β-amyloid protein as a key pathologic agent. β-Amyloid is derived from the amyloid precursor protein, which is normally bound to neuronal membranes. The pathologic cleavage of this protein results in elevated levels of β-amyloid.

The normal sequence of proteolysis of the amyloid precursor protein by a series of secretases does not result in neuronal toxicity, but in Alzheimer disease, the resulting 42–amino acid product leads to amyloid and neuronal damage. Apolipoprotein E interacts with the β-amyloid protein, and the E4 isoform of apolipoprotein E is a genetic marker that increases the accuracy of diagnosis by approximately 4%. Notably, the gene encoding the amyloid precursor protein resides on chromosome 21, where the gene for familial Alzheimer disease is located.

## Clinical Features

The onset of dementia is usually so insidious that the diagnosis can be made only in retrospect after cognitive decline or disengagement from routine activities or behavioral pattern becomes obvious. Persistent forgetfulness is the hallmark of Alzheimer disease, beginning with objects, appointments, names, and other apparently trivial items. As the disease progresses past the point of normal age-related forgetfulness, memories are lost and problems with word-finding ability become apparent. Sometimes, a confusional episode is triggered by an environmental stress, such as a surgery, a head injury, or a medication. The ability to perform complex mental operations, such as reading or calculating, or to execute multistep tasks, such as planning a meal or shopping, declines. Visuospatial impairment and apraxia develop, with patients losing the ability to dress themselves, perform complex motor actions, or use tools, such as a television remote control or a telephone.

Patients may be anxious or confused and may report chronic vague cephalic sensations, such as dizziness or "not feeling right." In the absence of gait or motor impairment, they may wander and become lost. Patients lose their ability to empathize with others and become absorbed in their immediate needs, regressing to the psychological dependence of a child. They may become demanding, belligerent, paranoid, agitated, or anxious. Some patients develop a misidentification delusion, or Capgras syndrome, in which they believe their family members or caretakers are imposters. Agitation, psychosis, aggression, and disinhibited behavior are common, may overwhelm the level of supervision and resources available in the home environment, and may lead to institutionalization. The sleep cycle is disturbed, with prolonged daytime somnolence and nocturnal agitation. Impairments in bladder and bowel control leading to incontinence are typical. Balance is eventually impaired, and patients may develop aspects of parkinsonism. With time, patients who survive deteriorate to a flexion posture and a persistent vegetative state, becoming bedridden and prone to the complications of prolonged immobility. The disease course may take 5 to 15 years, depending on the length of the prodrome, rate of progression, and development of complications.

To date, no reliable or convenient disease-specific biologic markers for Alzheimer disease exist, and the diagnosis essentially depends on the exclusion of other causes of dementia by using the diagnostic approach detailed earlier. A number of CSF biologic markers—β-amyloid protein 1-42 and tau proteins—are under investigation as ways of diagnosing Alzheimer disease but are not standard tests. The role of single-photon emission CT or PET scans, which provide markers of regional brain metabolic activity and blood flow and generally reflect cerebral atrophy, is not established. Amyloid imaging is a promising diagnostic modality that is currently under development.

## Pathologic Features

The gross pathologic features of Alzheimer disease include diffuse brain atrophy, with corresponding widening of the sulci and enlargement of the ventricles appreciable on CT scans and MRIs. The degree of the widening and enlargement correlates with the impairment in cognition. The histologic features of Alzheimer disease include neurofibrillary tangles (composed of knotted loops, strands of silver-stained material within the cell bodies of neurons, and helices of hyperphosphorylated tau microtubular protein), amyloid-containing neuritic plaques, and granulovacuolar degeneration of neurons (**Figure 17**). The most severely affected brain

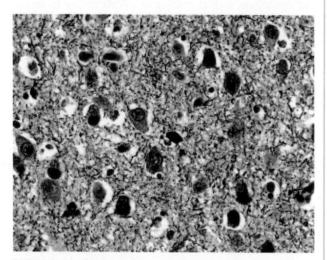

**FIGURE 17.** Photomicrograph showing Alzheimer disease. Neuritic plaques and neurofibrillary tangles are evident in this photomicrograph of an immunohistologic slide of an autopsy specimen from the amygdala of a 71-year-old man (Bielschowsky, original magnification ×200).

Photomicrograph courtesy of Dr. Jean-Paul Vonsattel.

regions are the hippocampus, temporal lobe, and the acetylcholine-containing basal nucleus of Meynert.

## Treatment

Alzheimer disease is not curable, and no approach is effective in slowing the disease progression. The pharmacologic approach is aimed at improving the brain cholinergic deficit in Alzheimer disease by using cholinesterase inhibitors (donepezil, rivastigmine, tacrine, and galantamine). In randomized, multicenter, double-blind trials, these agents have been shown to improve the cognitive function of persons with mild, moderate, or severe dementia due to Alzheimer disease and to improve caregivers' ratings of patients' capacity for daily living activities. Memantine, a drug that blocks the glutamatergic $N$-methyl-D-aspartate receptor, has also shown clinical benefit in patients with moderate to severe Alzheimer disease and as an adjunctive agent for patients on a cholinesterase inhibitor. The antioxidants vitamin E and selegiline may reduce the rates of institutionalization for patients with Alzheimer disease, although the effect is modest. New approaches targeting the overproduction of β-amyloid are the focus of research. **Table 19** summarizes the pharmacologic approach to Alzheimer disease.

In addition to improving cognitive performance of patients with Alzheimer disease, the therapeutic approach has several other goals: (1) managing the behavioral complications of agitation, psychosis, confusion, aggression, insomnia, depression, and anxiety; (2) identifying and eliminating medications that may cause cognitive impairment or excessive sedation, such as anticholinergic agents (to which older patients with dementia are especially susceptible) or benzodiazepines; (3) identifying and treating intercurrent medical illness that may cause acute changes in cognition, such as infection or dehydration; (4) providing comfort and safety to patients; (5) providing support to caregivers and preventing caregiver burnout; and (6) preventing the late-stage neurologic and medical complications of motor impairment and immobility, such as falls, dysphagia, aspiration, infections, and skin breakdown.

| **TABLE 19.** Medications for Treating Alzheimer Disease | | | | |
|---|---|---|---|---|
| **Drug** | **Class** | **Target Dosage** | **Titration Schedule** | **Adverse Effects** |
| Donepezil | Acetylcholinesterase inhibitor | 10 mg/d | 4-6 wk | Nausea, vomiting, diarrhea, vivid dreams |
| Rivastigmine | Acetylcholinesterase inhibitor | 6 mg twice daily | 2-4 wk | Nausea, vomiting, diarrhea, dizziness |
| Tacrine | Acetylcholinesterase inhibitor | 20-40 mg four times daily | 8-12 wk | Hepatic toxicity requiring liver enzyme monitoring |
| Galantamine | Acetylcholinesterase inhibitor; nicotinic receptor agonist | 12 mg twice daily | 4 wk | Nausea, vomiting, diarrhea, dizziness; possible cardiac effects |
| Memantine | $N$-methyl-D-aspartate inhibitor | 10 mg twice daily | 4 wk | Agitation and confusion |

A clinician's first reaction to a new behavioral disturbance may be to prescribe a new medication, but it is important to explore, if possible, nonpharmacologic strategies to modify patient behavior, such as reassurance or distraction. Depression is common in Alzheimer disease and can be treated with serotonin reuptake inhibitors; drugs with anticholinergic effects, such as tricyclic antidepressants, should be avoided because they can potentiate cognitive impairment. Psychosis, paranoia, agitation, and violent behavior can be treated with sedatives and tranquilizers, including neuroleptic agents and benzodiazepines. In general, agents with less of a dopamine receptor–blocking effect are preferred because dopamine antagonists can cause parkinsonism and gait impairment. Agents for anxiety and insomnia are often needed but carry a risk of inducing confusion. Additional treatment guidelines are provided in **Table 20**.

End-stage dementia is complicated by feeding impairment, the loss of bladder and bowel control, and the inability to transfer, ambulate, or perform any activity. Patients with advanced dementia may be subjected to burdensome interventions of questionable benefit (hospitalization, emergency department visits, parenteral therapy, and tube feeding). Palliative care is currently underutilized in this population.

### KEY POINTS

- The gross pathologic features of Alzheimer disease include diffuse brain atrophy, with corresponding widening of the sulci and enlargement of the ventricles appreciable on CT scans and MRIs.

- Although no effective strategies exist for reversing or slowing the progression of Alzheimer disease, donepezil, rivastigmine, tacrine, galantamine, and memantine may provide short-lived improvements in cognition.

## Non-Alzheimer Dementias

### Dementia with Lewy Bodies

The second most common cause of dementia, according to published studies, is dementia with Lewy bodies, which accounts for 15% to 25% of all patients with dementia. The progressive dementia that eventually affects up to 80% of all patients with Parkinson disease is attributed to the development of cortical Lewy bodies.

Patients with dementia with Lewy bodies may demonstrate a pattern of cognitive impairment with psychiatric features of personality change, apathy, depression, and psychosis. These patients may be especially susceptible to the hallucinatory effects of dopamine agonists and levodopa. Abnormal dream enactment behavior during rapid-eye movement (REM) sleep in which patients fight or call out in their sleep (REM sleep behavior disorder) may precede the onset of cognitive decline or motor symptoms by years. The fully developed syndrome of dementia with Lewy bodies includes motor signs of parkinsonism, which is often axial in distribution and poorly responsive to levodopa.

The pathologic hallmark of dementia with Lewy bodies is the widespread presence of Lewy bodies, which are eosinophilic intracytoplasmic accumulations of α-synuclein revealed by ubiquitin and α-synuclein immunohistochemical staining techniques (**Figure 18**). Although transitional forms between Alzheimer disease and dementia with Lewy bodies exist, including a Lewy body variant of Alzheimer disease, dementia with Lewy bodies in its pure form is characterized by the presence of cortical Lewy bodies and the absence of neurofibrillary tangles and Alzheimer neuritic plaque pathology. The therapeutic approach to dementia with Lewy bodies is the same as that for Alzheimer disease. For example, cholinesterase inhibitors, such as rivastigmine, have been

| **TABLE 20.** Guidelines for Treating Alzheimer Disease and Other Dementias |
|---|
| Ensure a safe, familiar, nonthreatening, well-lighted environment with simple routines, vigilance, and reassurance. |
| Address causes of frustration and irritability, such as pain, infection, and hunger. |
| Treat depression and anxiety. |
| Treat agitation and psychosis with low-dose atypical neuroleptics. |
| Encourage frequent engagement and socialization. |
| Encourage exercise. |
| Encourage cognitive tasks. |
| Optimize hearing, vision, and orientation. |
| Avoid dehydration, falls, infections, and aspiration. |

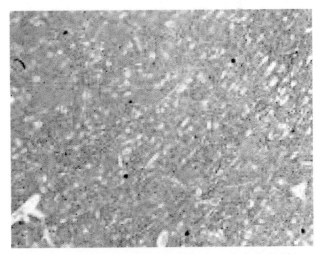

**FIGURE 18.** Photomicrograph showing diffuse Lewy body disease, neocortical type. This image is from the fifth cortical layer of the cingulate gyrus subjected to antibodies directed against α-synuclein aggregates and shows at least six Lewy body–containing neurons (discrete black dots). The normal neuropil has a golden finely granular appearance (α-synuclein, original magnification ×100).

Photomicrograph courtesy of Dr. Jean-Paul Vonsattel.

shown to improve the cognitive performance of patients with this type of dementia. Because persons with dementia with Lewy bodies often develop parkinsonism, levodopa is used to treat motor symptoms of the disease, and general measures are required for fall prevention. Hallucinations and psychosis are treated by antipsychotic agents that do not block dopamine receptors, such as clozapine.

**KEY POINT**

- The pathologic hallmark of dementia with Lewy bodies is the widespread presence of eosinophilic intracytoplasmic accumulations of α-synuclein (Lewy bodies).

## Frontotemporal Dementia

Frontotemporal dementia is a heterogeneous clinical syndrome of behavioral and cognitive deterioration combined with parkinsonism and motoneuron disease. The cognitive and behavioral features include disinhibition, poor judgment, impulsivity, perseveration, obsessionality, apathy, depression, memory loss, executive dysfunction, and loss of verbal fluency. Originally described as a syndrome of circumscribed cerebral atrophy confined to the frontal and temporal lobes (Pick disease), frontotemporal dementia is now considered a family of disorders defined by the abnormal accumulations of tau protein. Pathologically, the tau protein appears to become hyperphosphorylated and then to aggregate in neurons or glia (**Figure 19**). Several frontotemporal dementias are familial with autosomal dominant inheritance and are caused by mutations in the tau protein, located on chromosome 17.

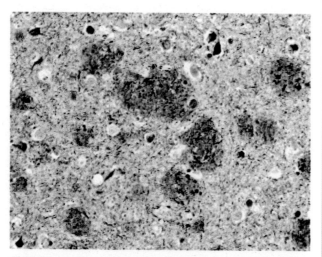

**FIGURE 19.** Photomicrograph from the amygdala of a 71-year-old man with a clinical diagnosis of frontotemporal dementia whose pathologic findings suggest Alzheimer disease. Shown are neuritic plaques (large, round, or oval darker areas, including argyrophilic threads or dystrophic neurites) and intermingled argyrophilic neuronal tangles (comma-shaped or round dotlike black corpuscles) (Bielschowsky, original magnification ×100).

Photomicrograph courtesy of Dr. Jean-Paul Vonsattel.

**KEY POINT**

- The clinical features of frontotemporal dementia include disinhibition, poor judgment, impulsivity, perseveration, obsessionality, apathy, depression, memory loss, executive dysfunction, and loss of verbal fluency.

## Vascular Dementia

Vascular dementia, at one time considered the second most common progressive dementia after Alzheimer disease, is much less common than formerly believed. In many cases, brain tissue formerly thought to show arteriosclerotic dementia later revealed Alzheimer changes when modern histochemical techniques were applied.

Vascular dementia is a consequence of progressive ischemic brain injury and comprises two main patterns of disease: (1) a series of obvious stepwise deteriorations in cognition corresponding to clinical strokes affecting the territories of large cerebral vessels and (2) a more gradual accumulation of cognitive deficits that reflects a spreading confluence of cerebral ischemia. The category of vascular dementia includes the autosomal dominant syndrome of cerebral arteriopathy with subcortical infarcts and leukoencephalopathy. The radiologic hallmark of vascular dementia is the demonstration of cerebral ischemia, whether in the form of multiple strokes or confluent ischemia. The differential diagnosis includes conditions that cause multiple discrete infarcts, such as endocarditis or vasculitis, and conditions that cause progressive leukoencephalopathy, such as progressive multifocal leukoencephalopathy or advanced multiple sclerosis.

**KEY POINT**

- The radiologic hallmark of vascular dementia is the presence of cerebral ischemia in the form of multiple strokes or confluent ischemia.

## Normal Pressure Hydrocephalus

Normal pressure hydrocephalus (NPH) comprises the distinctive triad of cognitive decline, gait impairment, and urinary urgency and incontinence in the setting of normal CSF pressure, usually less than 150 mm $H_2O$. Unlike other causes of gait impairment and dementia, NPH is potentially reversible if diagnosed and treated in a timely fashion. NPH usually is considered to be idiopathic but sometimes results from previous meningitis, a subarachnoid hemorrhage, or an inflammatory condition affecting the absorption of CSF. The associated cognitive deficits include memory impairments and nonverbal cognitive deficits, such as difficulty with executive processing. The gait disturbance is characterized by short shuffling steps, a wide base, a tendency to retropulse, an abnormal pull test, and a characteristic hesitation or freezing at the moment of step initiation and on turns. In contrast to other disorders that cause lower-body parkinsonism, including Parkinson disease and vascular parkinsonism, the patient with NPH tends to have near-normal leg function in supine and sitting positions. The urinary urgency and incontinence, which reflects loss of frontal control over micturition, completes the triad.

The first diagnostic step in a patient with suspected NPH is a brain imaging study, such as MRI. The diagnosis is suggested by an expansion of the entire ventricular system in the absence of sulcal atrophy or an obstruction (such as aqueductal stenosis). Radionuclide studies and a single removal of a large volume of CSF are not accurate in the diagnosis of this disorder. The best predictor of shunt-responsive hydrocephalus is clinical improvement in gait after a continuous lumbar drainage procedure over 2 or 3 days at a rate of 10 mL/h, which approximates the change in CSF dynamics that will occur with a shunt. This test, however, is prone to false-negative results and to a potent placebo effect. The treatment is shunt placement using an externally controlled programmable valve that allows the careful regulation of CSF pressure.

> **KEY POINT**
> • The best treatment of normal pressure hydrocephalus is shunt placement using an externally controlled programmable valve that allows the careful regulation of cerebrospinal fluid pressure.

### Dementia and Driving

As the population ages and the prevalence of dementia increases, more persons with dementia are driving, which has led to widespread concerns about safety. Although few guidelines exist regarding dementia and driving, clinicians frequently are asked by family members or patients themselves to determine whether someone with dementia should no longer drive. A Folstein Mini–Mental State Examination score less than 22 provides a useful clue about the presence of dementia but does not discriminate between those who can and cannot drive safely. A patient's self-assessment of safe driving ability is not a reliable indicator of competence on the roads. Dementia specialists typically also consider other factors, such as a patient's memory, spatial processing, and executive functioning, in the assessment of that patient's ability to drive safely. A recent American Academy of Neurology practice parameter guideline recommends considering additional factors, including a caregiver's rating of a patient's driving ability as marginal or unsafe, a history of crashes or traffic citations, reduced driving mileage, self-reported avoidance of certain traffic situations, and aggressive or impulsive personality characteristics. A rating scale that assesses orientation, judgment, participation in community affairs, self-directed participation in home activities, and personal care has been shown to be helpful in assessing driving risk. State laws regarding driving and reporting vary, but at the very least a physician can recommend a driver's test for persons with cognitive impairment who may be unsafe behind the wheel.

> **KEY POINT**
> • A rating scale that assesses orientation, judgment, participation in community affairs, self-directed participation in home activities, and personal care has been shown to be helpful in assessing driving risk in persons with dementia.

# Movement Disorders

## Overview of Movement Disorders

Movement disorders are conditions marked by inadequate or excessive movement (**Table 21**). Neurologic disorders that result in a paucity or slowness of movement are termed hypokinetic disorders, a category exemplified by Parkinson disease. Hyperkinetic disorders are characterized by excessive and involuntary movements. Hyperkinetic disorders usually are assigned to one or more of five main categories of abnormal movement: (1) tremor, (2) tic, (3) dystonia, (4) chorea, and (5) myoclonus. Many, but not all, movement disorders result from disordered function of the basal ganglia, a group of interconnected subcortical nuclei. The basal ganglia comprise the substantia nigra, putamen, caudate, globus pallidus, thalamus, and subthalamic nucleus, all of which form an extrapyramidal motor control system with extensive reciprocal connections to the cortex, brainstem, and cerebellum.

## Parkinson Disease

Parkinson disease is the only neurodegenerative disease linked to the loss of a specific neurotransmitter, namely, dopamine. The prevalence of Parkinson disease is estimated to be between 0.1% and 0.5% in the United States, with approximately 1 million persons affected by the disorder. Parkinson disease has a median onset of approximately 56 years and is rare before age 30 years. Approximately 13% of patients with Parkinson disease have an affected first-degree relative. As with all neurodegenerative diseases, the major risk factor for Parkinson disease is aging. Epidemiologic studies also have established an association between the disorder and the use of well water, herbicide and pesticide exposure, and manganese toxicity. Trauma is also a risk factor for Parkinson disease, on the basis of evidence in retrospective case-control studies, and cigarette smoking appears to have an inverse correlation with the subsequent development of the disorder.

Sporadic Parkinson disease is common, accounting for 90% of affected patients, but in a small number of families, the disorder is clearly inherited as a genetic disorder. Within the past 10 years, the identification of several Parkinson disease–causing gene mutations has contributed to the hypothesis that defective ubiquitin proteolysis may lead to a cascade

| TABLE 21. General Classification of Abnormal Movements | | |
|---|---|---|
| **Type of Movement** | **Clinical Features** | **Selected Causes** |
| **Hypokinetic** | | |
| Parkinsonism | Akinesia/bradykinesia, rigidity, tremor at rest, postural instability, gait freezing, and flexion posture | Parkinson disease, diffuse Lewy body disease, atypical neurodegenerative Parkinson-plus syndromes, hydrocephalus, vascular parkinsonism, neuroleptic-induced parkinsonism, and Wilson disease |
| **Hyperkinetic** | | |
| Tremor | Repetitive oscillation of a body part that occurs at rest and with postural holding or action (An intention tremor is an action tremor that increases toward the end of the action.) | At rest: Parkinson disease<br><br>With action or postural holding: physiologic tremor, essential tremor, midbrain and cerebellar tremor, dystonic tremor<br><br>Intention tremor: cerebellar outflow tremor caused by disorders of the cerebellum (degenerative disorders, toxic disorders, or multiple sclerosis) |
| Tic | Stereotyped, automatic, purposeless movements and vocalizations | Tourette syndrome, cerebral palsy and other developmental delay syndromes, autism, and Huntington disease |
| Dystonia | Torsional movements that are partially sustained and produce twisting postures | Idiopathic or primary dystonia, dopa-responsive dystonia, anoxic/hypoxic injury, trauma, postencephalitic dystonia, acute drug-induced and tardive dystonia |
| Chorea | Random, quick, unsustained, purposeless movements that have an unpredictable flowing pattern | Huntington disease, neuroacanthocytosis, post-infectious chorea, drug-induced chorea, vascular chorea, autoimmune chorea, and chorea gravidarum |
| Myoclonus | Sudden, shocklike movements of an isolated body part | Physiologic myoclonus, essential myoclonus, metabolic encephalopathy, postanoxic myoclonus, and progressive myoclonic epilepsy |
| Akathisia | Inner restlessness coupled with repetitive movements | Parkinsonism, drug-induced acute or tardive akathisia, and restless legs syndrome |

of events that results in the formation of α-synuclein–containing Lewy bodies and the death of dopaminergic cells. An *LRRK2* gene mutation is the most common cause of monogenic Parkinson disease.

## Clinical Features of Parkinson Disease

Parkinsonism is a syndrome characterized by any combination of five cardinal features: (1) tremor in a limb at rest, (2) rigidity, (3) bradykinesia, (4) loss of postural reflexes, and (5) gait freezing. The manifestations of Parkinson disease vary from a barely perceptible tremor to severe, generalized akinetic-rigid parkinsonism. Bradykinesia, the most characteristic clinical sign of Parkinson disease, correlates well with the striatonigral deficit of the disease and produces slowness of movement with a characteristic decrement in the amplitude of all repetitive actions. This sign is also manifested by paucity of spontaneous or adventitious movements; affected patients sit unnaturally still, like a statue, and demonstrate a lack of facial expressiveness ("facial masking"). In addition to whole-body slowness and impairment in fine motor movements, other consequences of bradykinesia include drooling of saliva due to a lack of spontaneous swallowing, soft monotonous speech, micrographia, a reduced arm swing when walking, and a short, shuffling gait.

A tremor at rest is perhaps the most obvious feature of Parkinson disease and is also the clinical sign that most closely correlates with classic, idiopathic Parkinson disease on postmortem analyses. The tremor at rest readily disappears when holding a posture or during manual activities, in contrast to an essential tremor, which is an action tremor. Approximately 75% of patients with idiopathic Parkinson disease have a tremor at rest, and this sign can disappear during the course of the illness. Rigidity is demonstrated by passively flexing, extending, and rotating body parts and has a cogwheeling aspect, especially in the presence of a tremor. At times, rigidity can cause discomfort and pain, especially around the shoulder. Parkinson disease typically begins asymmetrically and involves the arm or hand. The classic presentation of the disease is the gradual development of an intermittent tremor at rest in one hand, or even one digit, accompanied by slight bradykinesia and rigidity.

One of the most disabling symptoms of Parkinson disease is gait freezing, also referred to as gait ignition failure or a magnetic gait. At times, freezing can be so disabling that affected persons are unable to walk. The most dangerous motor impairment in Parkinson disease is the loss of postural reflexes (or postural instability), which can be tested by an abrupt pull backward. When combined with axial rigidity and bradykinesia, the loss of postural reflexes places a person at extreme risk of falling, which often results in fractures and is the cause of severe morbidity and mortality in this disorder.

In recent years, focus has intensified on the many symptoms of Parkinson disease that do not involve the motor system and may not relate directly to a simple defect of dopamine. Parkinson disease is a true multisystem disorder that may affect all of the body's physiologic systems, including the musculoskeletal system, swallowing, respiration, the gastrointestinal system, and the genitourinary system. Olfactory function typically is impaired in Parkinson disease, even in the very early stages. Drooling (sialorrhea) is one of the most socially disabling symptoms of Parkinson disease. Parkinson-related dementia is the second most common cause of dementia after Alzheimer disease. A list of nonmotor complications of Parkinson disease is provided in **Table 22**.

### Diagnosis of Parkinson Disease

Parkinsonism is a constellation of symptoms and signs that can occur in various medical contexts and at various ages. Identifying the cardinal features of rigidity, bradykinesia, tremor, and postural instability is essential. In adults, the most common form of parkinsonism is Parkinson disease itself, but many other causes exist, including other neurodegenerative forms of parkinsonism (known as "Parkinson-plus" syndromes), drug-induced parkinsonism, posttraumatic vascular hydrocephalus, and Wilson disease. Disorders associated with prominent and early-onset freezing include progressive supranuclear palsy, multiple system atrophy, and vascular parkinsonism. Parkinsonism in a child or young adult can result from juvenile Parkinson disease, hydrocephalus, trauma, carbon monoxide toxicity, exposure to dopamine type 2 ($D_2$) receptor–blocking drugs, and metabolic disorders that affect the basal ganglia, such as dopa-responsive dystonia and Wilson disease. A brain MRI is indicated in the evaluation of parkinsonism to evaluate the basal ganglia and rule out hydrocephalus or vascular lesions. The differential diagnosis of parkinsonism also includes depression, which can cause psychomotor slowing that can mimic parkinsonism of neurologic origin.

No biologic marker conveniently confirms the diagnosis of Parkinson disease, but advanced neuroimaging techniques may help establish a dopaminergic deficit in selected patients. For example, 18-fluorodopa–labeled PET scans typically show a reduction in fluorodopa uptake, particularly in the putamen, in the brains of patients with Parkinson disease, even in its early stages. Scans from single-photon emission CT show decreased striatal binding of iodobenzamide, a $D_2$ receptor ligand, and decreased presynaptic dopamine reuptake of $[^{123}I]$-2β-carbomethoxy-3β-(4-iodophenyl)tropane, a dopamine transporter ligand. Currently, these studies are not part of routine clinical practice but are sometimes used in clinical studies as objective disease markers. These tests, although expensive, can be helpful in selected patients when the clinical presentation is unclear.

In the absence of readily available biologic markers, the diagnosis of Parkinson disease can be made with certainty only at autopsy. Parkinson disease is defined pathologically as a neurodegenerative disorder with the following two features: (1) depigmentation of the substantia nigra associated with degeneration of melanin and dopamine-containing neurons, especially in the zona compacta; and (2) the presence of Lewy bodies in the zona compacta of the substantia nigra and other brain regions.

### Treatment of Parkinson Disease

Regardless of the stage of Parkinson disease, the primary goals of therapy are to optimize the patient's level of motor, social, and intellectual function; to prevent falls; and to minimize any complications of treatment. Suppressing all visible signs of Parkinson disease by using increasing dosages of medication is not a reasonable treatment goal and will increase the likelihood of adverse effects.

| **TABLE 22.** Nonmotor Complications of Parkinson Disease | |
| --- | --- |
| **Type of Complication** | **Symptoms** |
| Cognitive | Bradyphrenia, confusion, dementia |
| Behavioral | Depression, anxiety, hallucinations/delusions, psychosis, compulsive/addictive behaviors, hypersexuality, passivity, apathy |
| Sleep related | Sleep fragmentation, restless legs syndrome, rapid eye movement behavior disorder, excessive daytime sleepiness, sleep-wake reversal, drug-induced sleep attacks |
| Autonomic | Postural hypotension, bladder and sexual dysfunction, constipation, sialorrhea, seborrhea, excessive sweating |
| Musculoskeletal | Truncal and neck flexion, falls and fractures, arthritis and other mechanical complications of Parkinson disease |
| Pain related | Painful dystonia, pain due to mechanical factors, visceral ("off") painful sensations, primary central pain |

In recent decades, several agents have been proposed to slow the progression of Parkinson disease, including vitamin E, selegiline, rasagiline, glutathione, and coenzyme $Q_{10}$. No agent has yet been shown to be effective in this regard, and no evidence-based recommendation exists for any putative neuroprotective agent in the disorder. Some agents, such as selegiline, can delay the need for levodopa, but this effect results from the drug's slight symptomatic benefit and is not a neuroprotective action.

The most effective drugs for suppressing the cardinal motor signs of Parkinson disease (tremor, bradykinesia, and rigidity) are dopamine agonists and levodopa, but many other medications are available, including combination agents and extended-release agents with long-lasting effects (**Table 23**). Nearly 50 years after its introduction, levodopa combined with the decarboxylase inhibitor carbidopa (or benserazide in Europe) to prevent the peripheral metabolism of levodopa remains the gold standard drug. Because Parkinson disease is a chronic progressive disorder, patients require lifelong treatment. Medications and their dosages should change over time as adverse effects and new symptoms are encountered. The treatment regimen for Parkinson disease should always include recommendations for physical activity and/or physical therapy, a balanced diet, and optimal sleep quality.

Early mild Parkinson disease often requires no specific drug treatment. With time, however, symptoms begin to interfere with occupational or social function, and symptomatic relief is eventually indicated. The scientific literature has not resolved the essential question of when to initiate levodopa in patients with Parkinson disease, and many physicians delay its use as long as possible. The general, but not unanimous, consensus is that dopamine agonists should be used as first-line symptomatic treatment. However, these drugs dysregulate the brain's dopamine-dependent reward systems and result in a higher incidence of sedation and compulsive behaviors than levodopa. Patients taking dopamine agonist medication to control Parkinson disease should be warned about the potential for developing abnormal, compulsive behaviors, such as excessive gambling, excessive shopping, hypersexuality, and other uncontrollable urges. In older patients, their use also is associated with confusion and hallucinations. Many clinicians, therefore, recommend levodopa as an initial treatment for patients older than 70 years. Most specialists in Parkinson disease consider balance impairment, gait freezing, and falling to be absolute indications for levodopa treatment.

In late-stage Parkinson disease, the focus of treatment is on avoiding falls or injury, preventing the complications of immobility, treating dysphagia, preventing aspiration, maintaining nutrition, and addressing the cognitive and psychiatric complications of the disorder, such as depression, sleep disturbances, and psychosis.

Patients with advanced Parkinson disease who undergo surgery are at increased risk of confusion, aspiration, autonomic dysfunction (hypotension, constipation, urinary retention), and a slow recovery from immobility. Surgery that requires patients to stop taking oral medication places special demands on those who are dependent on dopamine drugs for mobility and function. Patients with Parkinson disease may have difficulty being weaned from mechanical ventilation because of dysphagia, aspiration, and poor chest wall mobility.

Within 5 years of treatment with a dopamine agonist or levodopa, 50% of patients notice two major complications, namely, motor fluctuations and dyskinesias. Wearing-off motor fluctuations involve a return of parkinsonian symptoms and signs, such as bradykinesia, tremor, rigidity, immobility, and gait freezing, within 3 hours of the patient's taking the medication. Sometimes, the motor fluctuations are accompanied by anxiety, depressive feelings, painful symptoms, dystonia, and autonomic disturbances. The wearing-off episodes tend to be mild at first but become more severe, prolonged, and disabling over time.

Dyskinesias are choreic twisting, writhing movements caused by dopaminergic medications. In a few patients, dyskinesias can be violent and ballistic. The presence of wearing-off motor fluctuations and dyskinesias heralds a phase of complex medical management in which many patients with Parkinson disease should be under the care of a specialist. Attempts to limit dyskinesias by reducing the medication

| TABLE 23. Drugs for Parkinson Disease |
| --- |
| **Dopamine precursor** |
| Levodopa |
| **Decarboxylase inhibitors** |
| Carbidopa |
| Benserazide[a] |
| **Dopamine agonists** |
| Bromocriptine |
| Pergolide |
| Pramipexole |
| Ropinirole |
| Apomorphine |
| Cabergoline[a] |
| Lisuride[a] |
| Piribedil[a] |
| **Catechol-*O*-methyltransferase inhibitors** |
| Entacapone |
| Tolcapone |
| **Dopaminergic/anticholinergic/glutamine antagonist** |
| Amantadine |
| **Monoamine oxidase type B inhibitors** |
| Selegiline |
| Lazabemide |
| Rasagiline |
| [a]Available in Europe. |

dosage tend to cause more parkinsonism, and treating the prolonged wearing-off states with more medication exacerbates the dyskinesias. Amantadine can help suppress dyskinesias in some patients.

Deep brain stimulation of the globus pallidus interna or subthalamic nucleus was approved by the FDA approximately a decade ago as an effective means of controlling wearing-off motor fluctuations and dyskinesias and should be considered in selected patients with advanced Parkinson disease (**Table 24**). Additionally, deep brain stimulation of the ventral intermediate thalamus suppresses medication-refractory parkinsonian tremor. The largest series available provides 5-year follow-up data documenting long-term reductions of tremor, bradykinesia, and rigidity with concomitant long-term improvements in quality of life. However, Parkinson disease involves progressive neurodegeneration, and many patients develop the long-term complications of speech impairment, postural instability, gait freezing, truncal flexion, and dementia, symptoms that do not respond to deep brain stimulation.

**TABLE 24.** Patient Selection for Deep Brain Stimulation in Parkinson Disease

| **Characteristics of Good Candidates** |
| --- |
| Typical Parkinson disease with tremor |
| Good response to individual doses of levodopa |
| Dyskinesias |
| Wearing-off motor fluctuations |
| Good general health |
| Strong family and social support network |
| **Characteristics of Poor Candidates** |
| Atypical parkinsonism |
| Poor response to levodopa |
| Dementia or apathy |
| Depression or anxiety |
| Severe medical illness |
| Poor social support |

**KEY POINTS**

- The classic presentation of Parkinson disease is the gradual development of an intermittent tremor at rest in one hand, or even one digit, accompanied by slight bradykinesia and rigidity.

- Regardless of the stage of Parkinson disease, the primary goals of therapy are to optimize the patient's level of motor, social, and intellectual function; to prevent falls; and to minimize any treatment complications.

- Within 5 years of treatment with a dopamine agonist or levodopa, the most effective drugs for suppressing the motor signs of Parkinson disease, 50% of patients develop motor fluctuations and dyskinesias.

# Parkinson-Plus Syndromes

Approximately 10% of patients with generalized bradykinesia and rigidity have an atypical form of parkinsonism marked by a more rapid disease progression, a poor response to levodopa replacement, and defining clinical features, including ocular palsy, dystonia, cerebellar signs, myoclonus, autonomic failure, and apraxia (inability to perform familiar, purposeful movements in the absence of any motor or sensory impairment). Although tremor is absent in up to 25% of patients with classic idiopathic Parkinson disease, the absence of a tremor should raise the suspicion of atypical parkinsonism. When falling is an early symptom, the diagnosis is almost never Parkinson disease but instead a Parkinson-plus syndrome.

The three main types of Parkinson-plus syndromes, which account for approximately 10% to 15% of patients with parkinsonism, are progressive supranuclear palsy, corticobasal ganglionic degeneration, and multiple system atrophy. In general, these syndromes are characterized by atremulous symmetric parkinsonism that is more aggressive than Parkinson disease and leads to early falling and dysphagia. These syndromes are unresponsive to levodopa replacement, advance rapidly, and lead to death within 8 to 12 years, on average.

The clinical hallmarks of progressive supranuclear palsy are distinctive eye findings (including impairment of vertical eye movements [square wave jerks, slow saccades, and a supranuclear gaze paresis]), facial dystonia, and axial rigidity. Corticobasal ganglionic degeneration presents as an asymmetric dystonic syndrome with apraxia, cortical sensory loss, tremor, myoclonus, and dementia. The multiple system atrophy category includes a variant with autonomic failure, sometimes termed Shy-Drager syndrome; a variant characterized by a progressive cerebellar syndrome; and a form dominated by dystonia, termed striatonigral degeneration.

**KEY POINT**

- Parkinson-plus syndromes are unresponsive to levodopa replacement, advance rapidly, and lead to death within 8 to 12 years, on average.

# Gait Disturbance

The neurologic examination of a patient who falls should focus primarily on detecting weakness, whether of corticospinal tract or peripheral origin; proprioceptive deficits due to neuropathy or dorsal column degeneration; parkinsonism; or ataxia. The gait is observed for speed, stability, symmetry, stride length, floor clearance, posture, arm swing, base width, and turning.

The hallmark of an ataxic gait is a widened stance with a tendency to lurch and veer. The tandem stepping test, in which the patient is asked to walk a straight line, can reveal ataxia, as can having the patient attempt to stand on one foot. In contrast, the parkinsonian gait is a narrow-based and shuffling gait, with a stooped or tilted posture, short steps, hesitation, and en bloc turning due to axial core rigidity. The characteristic hemiparetic gait is accompanied by upper motoneuron signs of weakness, spasticity, and hyperreflexia. The choreic gait is characterized by twitching and lurching, and the dystonic gait by twisting and posturing of the foot or leg. The antalgic gait, which results from mechanical factors and pain in the foot, leg, knee, or hip, is accompanied by pain on weight bearing that is compensated for by a quick weight transfer to the unaffected side. This maneuver produces a shortened stepping phase on the affected side and allows patients to spend less time on the painful side. A psychogenic gait is typically inconsistent, incongruous, and elaborate, often with expressions of great effort, unconvincing displays of weakness or impairment, sudden genuflections, and extreme lurching without falling.

The Romberg test for ataxia is performed by having the patient stand with feet together and eyes closed. Excessive sway requiring a corrective step is abnormal. The Romberg test supports the diagnosis of ataxia but does not specifically localize its source, whether myelopathic, cerebellar, vestibular, or peripheral, because all types of ataxia worsen in the absence of visual cues.

The pull test, which is often omitted from a routine neurologic examination, is the prime determinant of falling risk from parkinsonism. In this test, the examiner stands behind the patient and, after giving a warning, pulls backward sharply enough to draw the patient off his or her base. The normal response is a quick corrective backward step. More than one step backward, a series of ineffective backward steps, or frank toppling into the examiner's arms are abnormal responses and indicate a substantial future risk of backward falls.

Normative performance standards for gait testing in an older population are not established, but a good starting point for the clinician is that falling is always pathologic. For more information on falls in older patients, see MKSAP 16 General Internal Medicine.

### Ataxia

Ataxia is a syndrome of gait and stance impairment. The differential diagnosis depends on whether the symptoms are acute, subacute, or chronic. Acute ataxia is caused by an intoxicant (such as alcohol), a benzodiazepine, phenytoin, or a vascular event (such as a cerebellar or brainstem hemorrhage or ischemic stroke). Subacute ataxia, in which a severe cerebellar syndrome develops over several weeks, is typical of a paraneoplastic syndrome (such as paraneoplastic cerebellar degeneration) or prion disease. Most adult-onset chronic ataxia syndromes involve cerebellar degeneration, with cerebellar

and brainstem atrophy visible on MRI. Further evaluation includes measurement of serum vitamin $B_{12}$ and vitamin E levels and, in familial cases of chronic ataxia, genetic tests for spinocerebellar ataxia. Some persons with sporadic ataxia have antigliadin antibodies, without celiac disease.

The most common adult-onset progressive ataxia syndromes are multiple system atrophy, cerebellar type (formerly called olivopontocerebellar atrophy), and the spinocerebellar atrophy disorders, including Machado-Joseph disease (spinocerebellar ataxia type 3). There is essentially no effective medical treatment of cerebellar ataxia. The mainstay of treatment is physical therapy, the use of assistive devices, and vigilance to prevent falls.

KEY POINT

- Most adult-onset chronic ataxia syndromes involve cerebellar degeneration, with cerebellar and brainstem atrophy visible on MRI.

## Essential Tremor

One of the most prevalent movement disorders, essential tremor is a syndrome that causes tremors of the hands. The onset has a bimodal distribution, with peaks in adolescence and middle age. The condition is familial in approximately 50% of affected patients. Epidemiologic studies have linked essential tremor with anxiety disorder and alcohol dependence in some families.

Essential tremor presents clinically as a fine tremor of the hands that impairs manual tasks, such as pouring, using eating utensils or tools, placing a key in a lock, holding objects, and writing. The tremor may involve the neck, which produces a horizontal or vertical head tremor. Essential tremor also may cause a vocal tremor. In contrast to the tremor at rest of Parkinson disease, which typically vanishes with action, essential tremor is present with action and, therefore, more disabling. Whereas the handwriting of a patient with Parkinson disease is typically cramped but usually free from tremor, the handwriting of a patient with essential tremor is large and tremulous. Moreover, a unilateral tremor is characteristic of Parkinson disease; essential tremor can affect both hands and be even slightly more pronounced in the nondominant hand.

All healthy persons manifest a fine action tremor that is virtually invisible under ordinary circumstances but may become evident under conditions of fatigue, muscular exertion, anxiety, stimulant use, sleep deprivation, alcohol use, caffeine or benzodiazepine withdrawal, or strong emotion, such as fear, anger, or anxiety (including stage fright). On the basis of appearance alone, it is difficult to distinguish mild essential tremor from physiologic tremor, but the latter occurs in relation to readily identifiable inciting factors. The list of drugs that can cause or exacerbate tremor is long and includes β-agonists (theophylline, terbutaline, and epinephrine), stimulants (amphetamines, methylphenidate, cocaine, and caffeine), cyclosporine, interferon, valproic acid, lithium, corticosteroids, and serotonin reuptake inhibitors. In the evaluation of patients with action tremors, the possibility of drug-induced tremor should always be considered. Identifying and removing the offending agent, if possible, will lead to resolution of the tremor. Propranolol is effective for situational physiologic tremor. Unlike essential tremor, physiologic tremors are generally confined to the hands and voice and do not progress over time.

The term "benign" essential tremor is misleading. Although not fatal, essential tremor is a progressive and disabling disorder, and affected patients do not experience their increasing disability as trivial. Patients with advanced chronic essential tremor may develop ataxia with balance impairment and cerebellar signs of dysarthria and dysmetria that cannot be explained purely by the tremor. Autopsies of persons with essential tremor have revealed pathologic changes in the cerebellum.

A small percentage of persons with essential tremor of many years' duration will develop a unilateral tremor at rest. These persons typically exhibit ipsilateral signs of mild parkinsonism, including decreasing speed of repetitive finger tapping, a decreased arm swing, mild rigidity, and an asymmetric gait. The development of Parkinson disease is not considered part of the natural history of essential tremor, but there are rare families in which both disorders occur together. Additionally, autopsy studies have detected Lewy body pathology in a small subset of patients with essential tremor.

The treatment of essential tremor is distinct from that of Parkinson disease. The oldest and most effective medications are propranolol and primidone. Secondary, less effective medications include gabapentin, methazolamide, and topiramate. Alcohol can temporarily abolish essential tremor but is obviously not recommended as a treatment because of its effects on cognition and behavior, the risk of addiction, and the rebound in tremor that occurs when the alcohol wears off. Deep brain stimulation of the ventral intermediate thalamic nucleus is effective at controlling even medication-refractory essential tremor.

Fragile X tremor ataxia syndrome causes a tremor resembling essential tremor as well as causing ataxia, dysarthria, parkinsonism, and dementia. In the evaluation of an adult with tremor and dementia—an association that does not occur in essential tremor—testing for the fragile X premutation should be considered, especially if there is a family history of mental retardation.

**KEY POINTS**

- Essential tremor is familial in approximately 50% of affected patients.

- The oldest and most effective medications to treat essential tremors are propranolol and primidone.

# Dystonia

The pathology of dystonia, whether infectious, ischemic, hypoxic, drug-induced, metabolic, genetic, or degenerative, always involves the basal ganglia. Dystonia describes a torsional, twisting movement that is slightly sustained at the peak of contraction and may cause twisted postures. Dystonia that is confined to a body part is known as focal or generalized dystonia. As with hemicerebral symptoms of any type (hemiparesis, hemisensory loss, hemineglect, hemiparkinsonism), hemidystonia implies a structural lesion of the brain, such as a stroke, hemorrhage, tumor, or focal infection.

The most common types of focal dystonia involve the neck (spasmodic torticollis), face and jaw (craniofacial dystonia), eyelids (blepharospasm), or hands. Examples of occupational overuse or task-induced manual dystonia include writer's cramp and musician's dystonia. The differential diagnosis of dystonia includes Parkinson disease (which can cause dystonia in addition to the cardinal symptoms of bradykinesia, tremor, and rigidity), tardive dystonia (induced by certain drugs), and postanoxic or posthypoxic dystonia (most likely caused by a cardiac arrest or delayed cardiopulmonary resuscitation). Major causes of dystonia include birth injury, Wilson disease, and various metabolic and genetic abnormalities.

Dopamine-responsive dystonia is caused by a defect in bioamine synthesis. All persons with generalized dystonia should receive an early trial of levodopa to detect this rare but treatment-responsive condition.

Focal dystonia can be dramatically relieved by injections of botulinum toxin A or B. Overall, the treatment of generalized dystonia is limited and unsatisfactory. Except for the dopamine-responsive type, generalized dystonia typically does not respond to medication. High-dose anticholinergic agents and baclofen are considered first-line drugs. Tardive dystonia may respond to the dopamine-depleting agents reserpine and tetrabenazine. Patients with refractory disease may be considered for bilateral continuous electric stimulation of the globus pallidus internal nuclei.

**KEY POINT**

- Although focal dystonia can be dramatically relieved by injections of botulinum toxin A or B, the treatment of generalized dystonia is generally limited and unsatisfactory.

# Chorea

Like dystonia, chorea is linked pathologically to the basal ganglia. The hallmark of chorea is its pattern of discrete, randomly occurring jerks or twitches that may be generalized or confined to a single body part. The chewing and grimacing movements of classic orobuccolingual tardive dyskinesia have a choreic appearance but also a pattern that is not strictly random; these movements are sometimes termed choreiform.

The most common type of chorea encountered in clinical practice is the dyskinesia produced by dopamine drugs in patients with Parkinson disease. The most common neurodegenerative choreic disorder is Huntington disease, a progressive fatal degeneration of the caudate nucleus that causes generalized chorea, dysarthria, parkinsonism, psychiatric disease, personality deterioration, dementia, and death. The differential diagnosis of chorea includes systemic lupus erythematosus and other autoimmune diseases, use of estrogen-containing drugs, thyrotoxicosis, and pregnancy (chorea gravidarum, a self-limited chorea that resolves after delivery). Acute severe chorea can result from hyperglycemic nonketotic acidosis. Ballism, the large-amplitude twitching and flinging of one or more limbs on one (hemiballism) or both (biballism) sides of the body is actually a proximal chorea. The acute development of hemiballism suggests an infarct of the contralateral subthalamic nucleus. All types of chorea can be reduced in severity by dopamine-depleting or $D_2$ receptor–blocking agents, although these agents carry the risk of inducing tardive dyskinesia. Most cases of chorea resolve over weeks to months.

## Tardive Dyskinesia

The term neuroleptic was coined in reference to tranquilizers that block central $D_2$ receptors, such as haloperidol. Neuroleptic-induced movement disorders are sometimes referred to as extrapyramidal symptoms, a phrase that oversimplifies a complex group of disorders, each with its own distinct clinical features, treatment, and prognosis (Table 25).

All $D_2$ receptor–blocking agents have the potential to cause persistent acute, subacute, and chronic movement disorders. Classic tardive dyskinesia is a choreiform movement of the face that, once developed, may persist permanently, even if the offending agent is withdrawn. Newer agents marketed as atypical or second generation neuroleptics may also induce tardive syndromes through their $D_2$ receptor–blocking action, but these agents are less potent and appear to have a lower propensity to cause tardive dyskinesia and drug-induced parkinsonism.

Most $D_2$–blocking agents are neuroleptics used for the treatment of psychosis. In addition, many other agents used for depression (amoxapine), gastrointestinal illness (metoclopramide), and cardiac disease (flunarizine) are dopamine antagonists with the potential to cause tardive dyskinesia syndromes. All physicians who prescribe these agents must warn their patients of the possibility of developing a permanent movement disorder.

## Myoclonus

Myoclonus is a single, rapid, shocklike muscle jerk. This disorder can be distinguished from a tremor, which is a repetitive

**TABLE 25.** Movement Disorders and Symptoms Caused by Dopamine Receptor Antagonists

| Type of Movement Disorder | Symptoms |
| --- | --- |
| **Acute Reaction** | |
| Acute dystonia | Immediate dystonic spasm, often involving the neck, face, larynx, or eye (oculogyric crisis); rapidly reversed with intravenous diphenhydramine |
| Acute akathisia | Acute sensation of restlessness coupled with an urge to move or pace |
| **Tardive (Late-Appearing, Persistent) Syndromes** | |
| Classic tardive dyskinesia | Repetitive choreiform oral-facial-lingual movements |
| Tardive dystonia | Sustained dystonic muscle spasms, often affecting the face, neck, arms, and trunk |
| Tardive akathisia | Chronic sensation of restlessness, coupled with an urge to move or pace |
| **Subacute or Chronic Syndrome, Reversible** | |
| Drug-induced parkinsonism | Dose-dependent parkinsonism caused by dopamine-blocking agents; sometimes clinically indistinguishable from Parkinson disease; gradually resolves if the offending agent is removed |

oscillation, or a tic, which is stereotyped purposeless movement that is partly suppressible and preceded by an uncomfortable inner prodrome or urge. Myoclonus may be the dominant symptom of a neurologic illness, such as posthypoxic (postanoxic) myoclonus or essential myoclonus, or part of a large constellation of neurologic symptoms, such as Creutzfeldt-Jakob disease. Furthermore, myoclonus may arise from any level of the neuraxis, including the cortex, subcortex, spinal cord, or peripheral nerves. Some forms of myoclonus, such as a hiccup, which is a myoclonic spasm of the diaphragm, are physiologic. Focal myoclonus, which is restricted to a body part, may result from a focal lesion in the cerebral cortex, such as a tumor or stroke. A hemifacial spasm is a focal myoclonus confined to the muscles of the facial nerve and is usually caused by focal neurovascular compression or demyelination. Palatal myoclonus results from a focal brainstem lesion, such as a tumor or one caused by trauma. Multifocal or generalized myoclonus is caused by a disease involving the cerebral cortex diffusely, such as prolonged cerebral hypoxia (or anoxia) or encephalitis. Spinal myoclonus involves a spinal segment and is caused by a focal lesion, such as a stroke or tumor. The treatment of myoclonus consists of anticonvulsant agents with antimyoclonic activity, such as valproic acid, clonazepam, and levetiracetam. The differential diagnosis of myoclonus is provided in **Table 26**.

**TABLE 26.** Differential Diagnosis of Myoclonus

| | |
|---|---|
| Physiologic symptoms | Sleep states (hypnic jerks, nocturnal myoclonus), hiccup (singultus) |
| Epileptic symptoms | Childhood myoclonic epilepsy, epilepsia partialis continua, progressive myoclonic epilepsy syndrome (includes mitochondrial encephalopathies) |
| Symptoms associated with static or progressive encephalopathy | Alzheimer disease, Creutzfeldt-Jakob disease, viral encephalitis, paraneoplastic disorders (opsoclonus-myoclonus), metabolic disorders (uremia, hepatic encephalopathy), toxic serotonin syndrome, postanoxic syndromes, posttraumatic syndromes |

# Tic Disorders and Tourette Syndrome

Tic disorders are conditions that cause repetitive, stereotyped, purposeless brief actions, gestures, sounds, and words that emerge suddenly from a background of normal motor activity. These disorders can exist in pure form but are often associated with comorbid psychiatric symptoms. Tic disorders usually begin in childhood, but a substantial number of adults have tics. The common belief is that one third of patients with childhood tics experience complete remission by the end of adolescence, with the remainder continuing to have symptoms. Most adults with tics are seen only when their tics cause embarrassment or a disturbance in occupational or social function.

Most simple motor tics, such as blinking, ocular deviations, facial grimacing, neck movements, and shoulder shrugging, are generally quick and short-lived, although others, such as limb muscle tensing and abdominal tightening, are slower and sustained movements. In contrast, complex tics are sequenced, stereotyped acts, such as repetitive tapping or touching or pantomiming an obscene gesture (copropraxia), that may have the appearance of compulsive acts. The distinction between simple and complex tics is not always clear. Simple vocal or phonic tics include throat-clearing noises, grunting, clicking, sniffing, barking, squeaking, and other purposeless sounds. Complex verbal tics consist of repetitive, purposeless words and phrases, including obscenities (coprolalia). Patients with tics often report a premonitory sensation or urge coincident with a build-up of inner tension that is relieved temporarily when the tic is expressed.

The prototypic tic disorder is Tourette syndrome, which usually begins during childhood and has a hereditary nature, a 3:1 male predominance, and an association with psychiatric disease. Tourette syndrome is worldwide in distribution, with estimates of the incidence ranging from 0.45% to almost 20%, depending on the methodology used. Approximately half of patients with Tourette syndrome exhibit symptoms of obsessive-compulsive disorder (such as compulsive checking and counting, perfectionism, and obsessive fears or worries) or evidence of either attention-deficit/hyperactivity disorder (inattention, distractibility, impulsivity, and hyperactivity) or pure attention-deficit disorder without hyperactivity. In addition to these disorders, the behavioral spectrum of Tourette syndrome includes generalized anxiety disorder, panic attacks, phobias, and mood disorders.

The first step in the management of all tic disorders is determining whether treatment is needed. The goal of treatment is not to achieve complete tic suppression but to allow a patient to function and live normally. Centrally acting α-agonists, such as clonidine or guanfacine, are considered first-line drugs because of their favorable adverse-effect profile; clonazepam also may be helpful. Medications that reduce or blunt dopaminergic transmission predictably suppress tics, but they carry a higher risk of adverse effects. The catecholamine-depleting agents tetrabenazine and reserpine are effective in tic suppression but may cause hypotension, sedation, reversible parkinsonism, and depression. Neuroleptic drugs (such as haloperidol, risperidone, olanzapine, ziprasidone, and pimozide), which act as dopamine receptor antagonists, are the most predictably effective tic-suppressing medications but represent a treatment of last resort because of the small but grave risk of tardive dyskinesia. Patients with focal tics restricted to a small part of the body, such as blinking, may be treated successfully by using injections of botulinum toxin.

**KEY POINTS**

- Tourette syndrome, the prototypic tic disorder, has a hereditary nature, a 3:1 male predominance, and an association with psychiatric disease.

- Although neuroleptic drugs are the most predictably effective tic-suppressing medications, centrally acting α-agonists, such as clonidine, should be used first because neuroleptic drugs carry the small but grave risk of tardive dyskinesia.

# Wilson Disease

Despite its rarity, Wilson disease should be part of the differential diagnosis of any movement disorder in a young adult because it is the only curable metabolic disease affecting the basal ganglia. The consequence of overlooking the diagnosis is permanent neurologic impairment due to irreversible copper deposition in the basal ganglia and cerebellum. Wilson disease results from an autosomal recessive inborn error of metabolism caused by a mutation of the copper P-type adenosine triphosphatase encoded on chromosome 13q14.3. This mutation leads to a failure of copper excretion in bile, which results in copper accumulation in the liver and brain.

Wilson disease presents clinically in three patterns: hepatic, psychiatric, and neurologic. The most common neurologic presentation in a young adult is parkinsonism, although dystonia, ataxia, and a cerebellar outflow tremor that is marked by large-amplitude proximal tremors and dysmetria ("wing-beating" tremor) also can occur. Copper deposition in the Descemet membrane of the cornea produces the characteristic brown Kayser-Fleischer ring, which is present in virtually all persons with neurologic involvement but is sometimes difficult to discern in brown-eyed persons. The diagnosis can be confirmed by a low serum ceruloplasmin level (present in 95% of affected patients) or an elevated 24-hour urine copper excretion, but the gold standard is an elevated level of copper in the liver. Unfortunately, no simple genetic test for Wilson disease exists because of the number of mutations, but the diagnosis, once considered, is readily made.

The treatment consists of the chelating agents D-penicillamine, trientine, tetrathiomolybdate, zinc sulfate or acetate, and a copper-restricted diet. Liver transplantation is curative.

### KEY POINT

- Wilson disease should be considered in the differential diagnosis of any movement disorder in a young patient because of the availability of curative treatment through copper chelation or liver transplantation.

# Neuroleptic Malignant Syndrome

Neuroleptic malignant syndrome is an idiosyncratic, potentially life-threatening disorder characterized by three main features: (1) hyperthermia usually accompanied by other autonomic dysfunctions, such as tachycardia, diaphoresis, and labile blood pressure; (2) extrapyramidal signs, typically muscle rigidity or dystonia and elevated muscle enzyme levels; and (3) delirium. The pathophysiologic mechanism of and individual susceptibility to neuroleptic malignant syndrome are not well understood.

The syndrome usually begins abruptly while the patient is taking therapeutic, not toxic, dosages of medication. All agents that block $D_2$ receptors can induce the syndrome, including risperidone and other atypical neuroleptic agents. The syndrome may have a variable onset but in most patients reaches a maximum severity within 72 hours. Prolonged hyperthermia and generalized muscle contractions can cause rhabdomyolysis with kidney injury.

Treatment of neuroleptic malignant syndrome involves discontinuing the causative drug(s) and providing supportive measures. Administration of the dopamine agonist bromocriptine can reverse the syndrome, and the muscle relaxant dantrolene can inhibit the excessive muscle contractions that generate myoglobinemia. Reexposure to dopamine receptor antagonists does not necessarily lead to recurrence of the syndrome. Residual catatonia lasting weeks to months has been reported after recovery from the acute syndrome, with some patients responding to electroconvulsive therapy. Neuroleptic malignant syndrome must be differentiated from serotonin syndrome, which is characterized by confusion, myoclonus, shivering, and diaphoresis triggered by an overdose of serotoninergic medication or by the concurrent use of a serotonin reuptake inhibitor and a monoamine oxidase inhibitor.

### KEY POINT

- The prolonged hyperthermia and generalized muscle contractions that can occur in neuroleptic malignant syndrome may cause rhabdomyolysis with kidney injury.

# Restless Legs Syndrome

Restless legs syndrome is a common chronic condition that usually begins during middle age and worsens with time. The disorder affects 3% to 10% of persons worldwide and often is familial and inherited in an autosomal dominant fashion. The cause is unknown, but the response to dopaminergic medication implies a role of central dopamine pathways in the pathophysiology of the disorder. Several medical conditions are associated with an increased prevalence of restless legs syndrome, including iron deficiency, uremia, peripheral neuropathy, diabetes mellitus, rheumatoid arthritis, pregnancy, and fibromyalgia.

The key diagnostic features of this disorder are ill-defined discomfort and unusual sensations ("dysesthesias") in the legs, which are sometimes described as intolerable tingling, crawling, creeping, stretching, pulling, or prickling sensations. The symptoms of restless legs syndrome typically occur during rest or sleep or when patients are drowsy and attempting to fall asleep. The discomfort is associated with an urge to move the legs or walk about, which immediately relieves the unpleasant sensations.

Restless legs syndrome has long been linked to periodic limb movements, a movement disorder that occurs during early-stage sleep. The full cycle of these limb movements consists of brief jerks of either leg, dorsiflexion of the foot and great toe, and a briefly sustained tonic flexion spasm of the entire leg that has the appearance of an exaggerated flexor withdrawal reflex. The limb movements tend to recur approximately every 20 seconds in sequences that may last for hours.

Several classes of medication are effective in restless legs syndrome, including dopaminergic agents, opioids, benzodiazepines, and anticonvulsant agents, and are usually taken as a single dose before bed. The dopamine agonists bromocriptine and pramipexole are considered first-line drugs. Codeine and stronger opiates can help relieve the symptoms of restless legs syndrome but carry a risk of dependence. Clonazepam, carbamazepine, baclofen, and clonidine also have been reported as successful treatments. Some patients, especially those treated with levodopa, develop dependence and rebound symptoms. In patients with restless legs syndrome who also have iron deficiency with a serum ferritin level less than 45 to 50 ng/mL (45-50 micrograms/L), iron replacement is indicated and may be curative. Any treatment approach must also include optimization of sleeping habits, including avoidance of caffeine and nicotine in the evening.

**KEY POINT**

- The dopamine agonists bromocriptine and pramipexole are considered first-line drugs for treating restless legs syndrome.

# Multiple Sclerosis and Other Demyelinating Diseases

## Spectrum, Pathophysiology, and Epidemiology

Multiple sclerosis (MS), the most common cause of central nervous system (CNS) demyelination, is a chronic condition caused by immune-mediated injury to the brain, spinal cord, and optic nerves. The condition is characterized pathologically by focal demyelinating white matter plaques that are usually associated with inflammation and occasionally with axonal transection. Autopsy studies also have shown both focal and diffuse gray matter abnormalities that are worse with disease duration and severity. Neurologic symptoms and disability may arise acutely from disruption of white matter pathways and chronically from subsequent degenerative changes occurring in both white and gray matter.

MS affects approximately 400,000 people in the United States, with a female to male ratio of approximately 3:1. Age at onset follows a unimodal distribution, with most patients having their first symptoms between age 20 and 40 years. MS is the most common cause of nontraumatic neurologic disability in this age group. Although rare, pediatric cases are known to occur, as are new diagnoses in those older than 50 years.

A genetic predisposition to MS exists, with the disorder having an increased prevalence among those of northern European descent. Although recent genome-wide assays have identified risk alleles for MS in genes for the major histocompatibility complex, interleukin-2 receptor, and interleukin-7 receptor, genetics does not explain all MS risk; twin studies have shown a concordance of only 25% in monozygotic twins and 2.4% in dizygotic twins. Therefore, genetic risk may be modulated by multiple environmental factors.

MS risk increases with increasing latitude, a fact that may provide clues about the potential environmental triggers of

the disease. Because the risk of MS depends on geographic location before adolescence and is not affected by changes in location after adolescence, any environmental trigger must act early in life. Reduced sunlight exposure during childhood at higher latitudes also may explain the geographic phenomenon because vitamin D deficiency has been found to significantly increase the risk of developing MS. Exposure to endemic infectious agents during childhood has been proposed as an explanation, with Epstein-Barr virus being the strongest candidate. Although serologic evidence of Epstein-Barr virus exposure typically is greater in those with MS, this phenomenon is not universal. Also, it is unclear whether this exposure acts as a primary trigger of the disease or is merely an underlying characteristic of the immune system of persons with MS.

Although MS is the most common and well-known of the CNS demyelinating diseases, others exist, such as neuromyelitis optica, acute disseminated encephalomyelitis, and idiopathic transverse myelitis. Neuromyelitis optica, also known as Devic disease, causes demyelination in the optic nerves and spinal cord but, unlike MS, tends to spare the brain. The disorder appears more common in nonwhite populations and has a greater female to male ratio (9:1) than MS.

The multifocal symptoms associated with acute disseminated encephalomyelitis, which typically occurs during childhood but can occur in adults, usually present subacutely and result from profound, simultaneous demyelination in multiple regions of the CNS. This disorder often follows an infection. An initial episode of acute disseminated encephalomyelitis may be difficult to distinguish from a first attack of MS, but patients with acute disseminated encephalomyelitis typically have associated encephalopathy and fevers. Moreover, they typically have a greater extent of brain involvement on MRI and a more significant cerebrospinal fluid (CSF) lymphocytosis than do patients with a typical flare of MS.

For a discussion of transverse myelitis, see Disorders of the Spinal Cord.

**KEY POINT**

- Neurologic symptoms and disability in multiple sclerosis most likely arise acutely from disruption of white matter pathways and chronically from subsequent degenerative changes occurring in both white and gray matter.

## Presenting Signs and Symptoms of Multiple Sclerosis

Because MS can affect all parts of the CNS, nearly any neurologic symptom can occur. Symptoms often can be traced to functional disruption of white matter tracts, which pathologically correlates with focal demyelinating plaques. Such plaques can develop acutely because of focal inflammation, which results in a clinical exacerbation, often termed a relapse or a flare. Symptoms of this type typically evolve over a few days and can last, if untreated, for weeks to months before improving.

Optic neuritis, which causes an acute loss of vision and pain with eye movement, is a common presenting syndrome. Funduscopic examination sometimes reveals inflammation of the optic nerve in the affected eye and an afferent pupillary defect, such as dilation of the affected pupil when light is moved from the unaffected eye.

Myelitis, or inflammation of the spinal cord, is another common clinical syndrome of MS and typically causes sensory or motor symptoms below the involved spinal level. Unlike many other spinal cord processes, MS tends to cause a partial myelitis, and thus symptoms of complete spinal cord transection are exceedingly rare. Paralysis is typically flaccid in the early stage and progresses to become spastic at a later stage. Spinal cord involvement also can trigger the Lhermitte sign, which typically is described as electric shock sensations provoked by head and neck movement, and disrupt the somatic and autonomic pathways that regulate bladder and bowel function.

Brainstem involvement often results in eye movement abnormalities that result in diplopia or sensations of oscillopsia (the appearance of objects moving in a jerking motion). Disconjugate eye movements, nystagmus, or an internuclear ophthalmoplegia (inability to adduct one eye and nystagmus in the abducting eye) can be seen on examination. Disruption of vestibular or cerebellar pathways can also lead to vertigo and ataxia.

In contrast to cerebrovascular disease, cortical syndromes, such as aphasia and neglect, do not often occur in MS. Cortical involvement in MS tends to cause more subtle, chronic symptoms, such as cognitive dysfunction and fatigue.

Uhthoff phenomenon is a temporary worsening of any MS symptom in the presence of elevations in body temperature. This symptom is a common feature of the disorder that reflects reduced neuronal conductance at higher temperatures and does not signify a heat-induced MS relapse. **H**

**KEY POINTS**

- Optic neuritis, which causes an acute loss of vision and pain with eye movement, and myelitis, which is associated with sensory or motor symptoms below the involved spinal level, are common symptoms of multiple sclerosis.

- In contrast to cerebrovascular disease, multiple sclerosis (MS) is not associated with cortical syndromes, such as aphasia and neglect; cortical involvement in MS tends to cause more subtle, chronic symptoms, such as cognitive dysfunction and fatigue

# Diagnosis of Multiple Sclerosis

## Diagnostic Criteria and Testing

The diagnostic criteria for MS require evidence of dissemination of disease activity in space and time. A combination of clinical evidence and neuroimaging and ancillary test results is necessary to make the diagnosis. In persons with few clinical episodes and few findings on neurologic examination, the diagnosis depends on ancillary testing to reveal the dissemination of white matter plaques.

MRI is the major diagnostic tool in MS. Scans from this imaging technique can reveal the disorder's characteristic white matter lesions (**Figure 20**), which are typically ovoid in

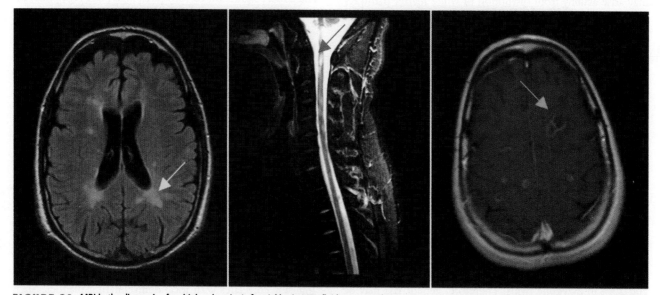

**FIGURE 20.** MRI in the diagnosis of multiple sclerosis. *Left*, axial brain MRI, fluid-attenuated inversion recovery sequence, showing typical ovoid periventricular lesions (*yellow arrow*). *Center*, MRI of the sagittal cervical spine, T2 sequence, showing multiple spinal cord lesions (*red arrow*). *Right*, axial brain MRI, postgadolinium T1 sequence, showing multiple contrast-enhancing lesions that indicate active inflammation. Note the open ring appearance of some of the lesions (*green arrow*), which helps to differentiate demyelinating lesions from contrast-enhancing, infectious, or neoplastic lesions, which usually are closed rings.

shape and located in a periventricular distribution. Many MS lesions cluster around the corpus callosum and are oriented in a distribution perpendicular to the corpus callosum, which is a distinguishing feature not present in vascular lesions. Other lesions also can be positioned in an intracortical, juxtacortical, or infratentorial (brainstem, cerebellum, spinal cord) distribution. Lesions in which active inflammation is occurring enhance with the infusion of gadolinium contrast. These characteristics are part of the diagnostic criteria of MS and can be used to differentiate the disorder from other causes of white matter lesions, such as migraine, microvascular ischemic disease, and the sequelae of head trauma. The latter lesions tend to be subcortical, do not enhance with contrast, and are infrequently located in the brainstem, cerebellum, or spinal cord. These are important distinctions because the finding of white matter lesions on MRI can lead to unnecessary neurologic testing and misdiagnosis.

When neuroimaging study findings suggest MS but are inconclusive, an analysis of the CSF can support the diagnosis. The CSF of approximately 85% of persons with MS contains oligoclonal bands that are not present in their serum and also has an elevated IgG index and synthesis rate. Mild elevations in the leukocyte count or protein level are sometimes present in the CSF.

Electrophysiologic studies also are sometimes helpful in the diagnosis of MS. Abnormalities on electrophysiologic tests that measure the speed of conduction along central white matter tracts, such as visual evoked potentials, somatosensory evoked potentials, or brainstem auditory evoked responses, can provide indirect evidence of white matter lesions not evident on imaging.

Optical coherence tomography, which uses near-infrared light to quantify the thickness of the nerve fiber layer in the retina, also can be used as an ancillary testing technique. Reduced thickness often is seen in patients with MS as a long-term sequela of previous optic neuritis but also can be present in those without a distinct history of optic neuritis.

## Differential Diagnosis of Multiple Sclerosis

Whenever the diagnosis of MS is being considered, conditions that mimic the disorder should be part of the differential diagnosis (**Table 27**). Various rheumatologic, inflammatory, infectious, and metabolic disorders can cause neurologic symptoms and MRI changes that are sometimes incorrectly diagnosed as MS. The previously mentioned syndromes of acute disseminated encephalomyelitis and transverse myelitis are part of the differential diagnosis of MS; many persons with these initial diagnoses later develop other symptoms that lead to a diagnosis of MS. In persons with recurrent optic neuritis and myelitis but little brain involvement, neuromyelitis optica should be considered. Because of the common nature of non-specific MRI findings, neurologic symptoms that are due to psychiatrically based somatization in the setting of depression,

anxiety, or somatoform disorders can sometimes mistakenly lead to a diagnosis of MS.

**KEY POINTS**

- The diagnostic criteria for multiple sclerosis require evidence of dissemination of disease activity in space and time.
- MRIs of patients with multiple sclerosis show characteristic white matter lesions, which are typically ovoid in shape and located in a periventricular distribution.
- The cerebrospinal fluid of many patients with multiple sclerosis contains oligoclonal bands not present in their serum, has an elevated IgG index and synthesis rate, and sometimes shows mild elevations in leukocyte count or protein level.

# Clinical Course of Multiple Sclerosis

The clinical course of MS follows one of three distinct patterns, namely, relapsing-remitting, secondary progressive, or primary progressive disease (**Figure 21**). Early in the course of MS, many patients (approximately 85%) experience symptoms in a relapsing manner. Those with a first relapsing demyelinating event that lacks enough evidence for a diagnosis of MS to be made are said to have a clinically isolated syndrome. The development of clinically definite MS in these patients depends on the presence or absence of brain lesions on MRI at the time of initial presentation because the 10-year risk of MS is approximately 90% in those with brain lesions and less than 20% in those without these lesions. Further attacks in those with a clinically isolated syndrome suggest a conversion to relapsing-remitting MS.

The frequency and severity of relapsing-remitting attacks are quite heterogeneous, with substantial variation not only between patients but also over time within the same patient. Symptoms occurring in the setting of relapse tend to peak after a few days to weeks and are followed by a period of recovery. Recovery can be full early in the disease course, but over time, recovery becomes less complete, and residual disability accrues.

Approximately two thirds of patients with a relapsing-remitting course eventually convert to secondary progressive MS, at which point relapses become infrequent or cease completely, but progressive neurologic symptoms and disability continue. The median time to conversion from relapsing-remitting MS to the secondary progressive form is between 10 and 15 years.

Approximately 15% of patients with MS will never experience a clear relapse but will have a progressive course from the time of disease onset. Known as primary progressive MS, this disease course generally presents later in life (fifth or sixth decade) and, despite its greater propensity for neurologic disability, typically is associated with fewer lesions on MRI than the relapsing-remitting type. The rate and degree of disability progression are highly variable, with approximately 25% of affected patients having rapid progression (requiring gait-assist devices within 7 years) and another 25% having very slow progression (not requiring gait-assist devices even after 25 years). Although early studies of the natural history of this disease type had implicated gender and age at onset as predictors of more rapid progression, more recent studies have supported only early disability accrual as a predictor of long-term progression rates.

With the increased availability of MRI and more liberal diagnostic criteria, the diagnosis of MS also has been associated with a very mild form of the disease. Benign MS is the term used to describe the disease in those persons who experience few relapses and minimal disability. The existence of this entity is still under debate, and some long-term studies of patients with this form have shown eventual secondary progression. Radiologically isolated syndrome, in which patients with no demyelinating symptoms have incidental MRI changes that meet the diagnostic criteria for MS, is an even

| TABLE 27. Differential Diagnosis of Multiple Sclerosis | |
|---|---|
| **Disorder** | **Notes** |
| **Neoplastic** | |
| Primary CNS neoplasm (glioma or lymphoma), metastatic disease | Neoplasms have progressively worsening symptoms and neuroimaging findings. When imaging cannot differentiate neoplasms from demyelinating disease, brain biopsy is indicated. |
| Paraneoplastic syndromes | Paraneoplastic syndromes may cause progressive cerebellar ataxia or myeloneuropathy (neuropathy affecting the spinal cord and peripheral nerves). Additionally, paraneoplastic limbic encephalitis can cause personality and mental status changes in addition to seizures and movement disorders. Metastatic evaluation and antibody testing may lead to diagnosis. |
| **Metabolic disorders** | |
| Vitamin $B_{12}$ deficiency | Vitamin $B_{12}$ deficiency can cause optic neuropathy, cognitive changes, and subacute combined degeneration of the spinal cord (spasticity, weakness, and vibratory and proprioceptive sensory loss) |
| Copper deficiency | Copper deficiency can cause a myelopathy identical to that in vitamin $B_{12}$ deficiency. |
| Zinc toxicity | Zinc toxicity can cause an acquired copper deficiency. |
| Vitamin E deficiency | Vitamin E deficiency can cause cerebellar ataxia. |
| **Vascular disorders** | |
| Sporadic and genetic stroke syndromes (hypercoagulability disorders) | Microvascular ischemic disease can cause nonspecific white matter changes on MRI and is often confused with MS; age, other vascular risk factors, and findings on neurologic examination should help to distinguish it from MS. |
| CNS vasculitis | Primary CNS vasculitis, which can be diagnosed by catheter angiography or tissue biopsy, can presen with both stroke-like changes on MRI and meningeal contrast enhancement. |
| Susac syndrome | Susac syndrome causes a small-vessel arteriopathy, which causes dysfunction of the retina and cochlea and lesions of the corpus callosum on MRI. |
| Dural arteriovenous fistula | Dural arteriovenous fistulas can result in spinal cord infarction or vascular congestion with cord lesions that can be confused with MS lesions. These fistulas have a subacute clinical progression, without remission or relapse. |
| **Systemic inflammatory disease** | Differentiated from MS by the presence of symptoms and findings unique to the underlying systemic disorder, in addition to neurologic symptoms. |
| SLE | SLE can present with white matter changes on MRI and encephalopathy. |
| Sjögren syndrome | Sjögren syndrome can cause an NMO-like disorder with optic neuritis and myelitis. |
| Sarcoidosis | Sarcoidosis can affect the parenchyma and meninges of the brain and spinal cord. |
| Behçet syndrome | Behçet syndrome can cause brainstem abnormalities and encephalopathy and occasionally is associated with myelopathy. |
| Infections (HIV, Lyme disease, HTLV, syphilis) | These disorders (except HTLV) can cause encephalopathy and myelopathy and can be diagnosed with appropriate serology and CSF analysis. |
| Migraine | Subcortical white matter lesions can occur in patients with migraine and often be confused with MS lesions. CADASIL should be considered a possible diagnosis in patients with a familial syndrome of migraine, subcortical strokes, mood disorders, and early dementia. |
| Somatoform disorders | Psychiatric disorders can sometimes present with neurologic-like symptoms that are due to somatization, conversion, and similar conditions. Neurologic evaluation findings will be normal. |

CADASIL = cerebral autosomal dominant arteriopathy with subcortical infarcts and leukoencephalopathy; CNS = central nervous system; CSF = cerebrospinal fluid; HTLV = human T-lymphotropic virus; MS = multiple sclerosis; NMO = neuromyelitis optica; SLE = systemic lupus erythematosus.

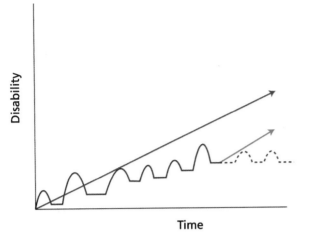

**FIGURE 21.** Schematic representation of the varying clinical courses of multiple sclerosis (MS). Neurologic disability severity is shown on the *y* axis, with time shown on the *x* axis. Relapsing-remitting MS (*blue line*) is characterized by intermittent exacerbations (*humps in line*). Early in the disease course, residual disability from each exacerbation is minimal, whereas later in the disease course, residual disability can be significant. After 10 to 15 years, most patients with relapsing-remitting disease convert to secondary progressive MS (*green line*), although some patients do not (*dotted blue line*). During the secondary progressive phase, disability accrues at a steady pace without clear exacerbations. Some patients have a primary progressive form of MS from disease onset (*red line*) and experience progressive disability accrual with no exacerbations.

more controversial entity, and the long-term prognosis of patients with this condition is still being studied.

> **KEY POINT**
>
> - Early in the course of MS, many patients (approximately 85%) experience symptoms in a relapsing manner; approximately two thirds of patients with a relapsing-remitting course eventually convert to secondary progressive MS, with a median time to conversion of between 10 and 15 years.

# Treatment of Multiple Sclerosis

## Lifestyle Modifications and General Health Care

Maintenance of a healthy active lifestyle is necessary for all patients with MS. Although some patients tend to avoid physical activity because of disability and fatigue, strengthening, stretching, and aerobic exercise is recommended. Maintenance of musculature in affected areas helps minimize disability and preserves appropriate muscle tone. Physical therapy and home exercise programs are useful in this regard, especially in the time after a clinical relapse. Although symptoms may appear worse with exertion-related body temperature increases (Uhthoff phenomenon), patients should be told that this exertion does not cause neurologic injury.

Avoidance of heat, such as hot showers or outdoor exposure on hot days, and body-cooling strategies should be advised as a means of overcoming these symptoms.

An active lifestyle also can help preserve bone health, which is especially important because the risk of osteoporosis is increased in those with MS because of reductions in physical activity, increased rates of vitamin D deficiency, and the effects of repeated corticosteroid use. Vitamin D and calcium supplementation are suggested.

Despite the beliefs of some patients and providers, strong evidence suggests that influenza immunization does not increase the risk of MS attacks, and no evidence supports the notion that other standard immunizations have any effect on the risk of relapse. Additionally, strong evidence suggests that the risk of MS relapse is significantly increased in the setting of common infections, and thus current guidelines recommend strategies, including immunizations, designed to reduce the risk of infections. Because of the increased risk of urinary tract infections in patients whose MS symptoms include bladder involvement, strategies designed to reduce the risk of these infections, such as intermittent catheterization or prophylactic administration of antibiotics, also are recommended, if necessary.

Pregnancy can have a substantial effect on disease activity in MS, with a significantly reduced risk of relapse in the third trimester but an increased risk of relapse in the first 3 months after delivery. The impact of breast feeding on the relapse rate remains controversial, with various studies presenting conflicting evidence.

Smoking cessation is advised for those with MS because of the threefold increase in the risk of secondary progression associated with cigarette smoking.

## Treatment of Acute Exacerbations

Patients with new symptoms suggestive of an MS relapse should be evaluated to determine if acute therapy is warranted. Before initiating treatment, the possibility of a pseudorelapse, which is a transient worsening of underlying neurologic symptoms in the setting of infection or another systemic illness, should be considered. If a pseudorelapse is suspected, tests to determine the presence of an occult infection or metabolic disturbance should be performed. Resolution of the underlying trigger for the pseudorelapse improves symptoms.

For confirmed clinical relapses, intravenous methylprednisolone, 1 g/d for 3 to 5 days, is often administered, followed by an optional 10- to 14-day oral prednisone taper. Although this treatment has not been shown to reduce the amount of long-term disability sustained in a relapse, it substantially hastens the rate of recovery. Because of the unclear long-term benefit and the potential for adverse effects, acute high-dose corticosteroid therapy is usually reserved for attacks resulting in sustained impairment in functional systems that interferes substantially with activities of daily living. The typical adverse effects of short-term high-dose corticosteroids are insomnia, hyperglycemia, a metallic taste, gastrointestinal distress, fluid retention, irritability, and, on rare occasions, psychosis. Frequent corticosteroid treatment also predisposes patients to the long-term adverse effects of these drugs, such as bone density loss and early cataracts. Relapses that are refractory to corticosteroid treatment may respond to rescue therapy with plasmapheresis.

### Disease-Modifying Therapies

In addition to treatment for individual relapses, most patients with relapsing-remitting MS receive chronic maintenance therapy with immunomodulatory or immunosuppressive medications. These disease-modifying therapies have been shown to reduce the relapse rate, slow disability progression, and reduce the accumulation of new demyelinating lesions on MRI. Additionally, the first-line therapies of interferon and glatiramer acetate have been shown to delay conversion to clinically definite MS in patients with a clinically isolated syndrome and suspicious brain lesions; early treatment initiation is recommended for these patients. Eight disease-modifying therapies (**Table 28**) that differ in their route of administration, mechanism of action, and potential adverse effects have been approved by the FDA. Choosing an appropriate therapy from these options depends on patient tolerability and disease activity.

The interferon-beta preparations (beta-1a and beta-1b) use an immunomodulatory cytokine that may direct the immune response away from autoimmunity and protect the blood-brain barrier. Interferon beta-1a is administered either once weekly by intramuscular injection or three times weekly by subcutaneous injection, whereas interferon beta-1b is administered every other day by subcutaneous injection. The interferons have been shown to reduce the relapse rate by approximately one third compared with placebo and to have positive effects on disability progression and MRI findings. Head-to-head studies have shown general equivalence for most of the interferons, although more frequent administration resulted in slightly increased efficacy in some studies.

Glatiramer acetate is administered by daily subcutaneous injection. This medication is a copolymer of four amino acids that, among other mechanisms of action, may bind major histocompatibility complex molecules and induce a shift in the immune response away from autoimmunity. Glatiramer acetate also has been shown to reduce the relapse rate by approximately one third compared with placebo and appears equivalent to the interferons in head-to-head studies.

Natalizumab is a monoclonal antibody that binds $\alpha_4$ integrin cellular adhesion molecules on activated T cells and thereby inhibits their ability to bind to vascular endothelium and prevents transmigration into the CNS. The drug is administered by once-monthly intravenous infusions. Natalizumab is highly effective, reducing the relapse rate by two thirds and slowing disability progression by approximately 40%. However, this drug is not used as a first-line therapy because of its increased risk of progressive multifocal leukoencephalopathy, a progressive and potentially lethal

**TABLE 28.** Disease-Modifying Therapies for Multiple Sclerosis

| Medication | Potential Adverse Effects | Recommended Monitoring | Pregnancy Category[a] |
|---|---|---|---|
| Interferon beta-1a (two formulations) and interferon beta-1b (two formulations) | Flulike symptoms, fatigue, depression, increased spasticity, elevated aminotransferase levels, and injection site reactions | CBC and liver chemistry studies every 6 months | C |
| Glatiramer acetate | Injection site reactions, lipoatrophy of skin at injection sites, and rare systemic panic-attack-like syndrome | None | B |
| Natalizumab | Black box warning of increased risk of PML. Common adverse effects of headache and chest discomfort. Rare hepatotoxicity, infusion reactions, and anaphylactoid reactions. | Rigorous, regimented, industry-sponsored monitoring (TOUCH® program) | C |
| Fingolimod | Elevated aminotransferase levels, lymphopenia, increased risk of serious herpesvirus infection, hypertension, bradycardia (usually only with the first dose), and macular edema. | Cardiac monitoring for administration of first dose; ophthalmologic screening; liver chemistry studies and CBC. | C |
| Mitoxantrone | Black box warnings for cardiotoxicity and acute myeloid leukemia. Other adverse effects of infection, nausea, oral sores, alopecia, menstrual irregularities, and blue discoloration of urine. | Required monitoring of cardiac function by echocardiography or multigated radionuclide angiography before each infusion and regular CBC | D |

CBC = complete blood count; PML = progressive multifocal leukoencephalopathy.

[a]Pregnancy category definitions: B, fetal risk in animal studies but no adequate human studies *or* fetal risk in animal studies but adequate human studies with no risk; C, fetal risk in animal studies and no adequate human studies, but potential benefit to pregnant women may outweigh risk; D, fetal risk in human studies, but potential benefit to pregnant women may outweigh risk.

CNS demyelinating disease that is caused by reactivation of the JC virus. Although the risk is quite small (approximately 1:1000), the medication is only available under a strict monitoring program designed to detect any evidence of this reaction as early as possible. Because of these precautions, natalizumab is only indicated as a second-line agent for patients unable to tolerate first-line therapies because of disease breakthrough or adverse effects.

Fingolimod is the only oral disease-modifying agent. This medication is a sphingosine-1-phosphate modulator that restricts activated lymphocytes to lymph nodes and may also have direct neuroprotective effects. Fingolimod significantly reduces the relapse rate, risk of disability progression, and accumulation of new lesions on MRI. Fingolimod has been associated with rare but potentially harmful side effects, including increased rates of serious herpesvirus infection, hypertension, bradycardia, lymphopenia, liver function abnormalities, and macular edema.

Mitoxantrone is an anthracenedione chemotherapeutic agent that reduces lymphocyte proliferation and decreases the relapse rate and disability progression in MS. This drug is the only disease-modifying therapy that has shown benefit for secondary progressive MS. Despite mitoxantrone's efficacy, cardiac toxicity and the risk of secondary leukemia have significantly limited its use.

No disease-modifying therapy has been shown to benefit primary progressive MS. This lack of efficacy may be due to differences in pathology between MS stages. Relapsing-remitting MS may represent a stage of the disease with a greater degree of inflammation, whereas neurodegenerative pathology may predominate in progressive forms of MS. Research is currently ongoing for agents that may have neuroprotective or remyelinating mechanisms of action, which may benefit those with progressive MS in the future.

## Symptomatic Management

Although the disease-modifying therapies may help prevent further relapses and subsequent disability, these medications do not address the neurologic symptoms that persist as long-term sequelae of prior disease activity. Proper care of patients with MS involves attention to each of these symptoms, with proper symptomatic therapy and nonpharmacologic support to increase quality of life (**Table 29**).

Spasticity due to corticospinal tract involvement in MS can result in painful muscle cramps, spasms, or even contractures. Muscle relaxants, such as baclofen, tizanidine, or cyclobenzaprine, can be taken to reduce spasticity and prevent painful cramps. Physical therapists also can suggest stretching exercises to help reduce spasticity and prevent contractures. If symptoms are severe, botulinum toxin can be strategically injected to reduce spasticity in a manner that may increase functional use of a limb. Intrathecal baclofen pumps also may be implanted to reduce disabling or painful spasticity.

Neuropathic pain, a common symptom in MS, can be treated with tricyclic antidepressants, gabapentin, pregabalin, duloxetine, tramadol, or similar agents; generic tricyclic antidepressants (amitriptyline and nortriptyline) are generally better tolerated and much less expensive than pregabalin, although their use may be limited by the development of anticholinergic adverse effects. Treatment of trigeminal neuralgia with carbamazepine and other modalities is discussed in Headache and Facial Pain.

Many patients with MS experience disabling fatigue that is typically worse in the afternoons and early evening

---

**TABLE 29.** Symptomatic Management in Multiple Sclerosis

| Symptom | Nonpharmacologic Management | Pharmacologic Management |
|---|---|---|
| Spasticity | Physical therapy, stretching, massage therapy | Baclofen (oral or intrathecal pump), tizanidine, cyclobenzaprine, benzodiazepines, carisoprodol, botulinum toxin |
| Neuropathic pain | N/A | Gabapentin, pregabalin, duloxetine, tricyclic antidepressants, tramadol, carbamazepine, topiramate, capsaicin patch |
| Fatigue | Proper sleep hygiene, regular exercise | Modafinil, amantadine |
| Depression | Individual or group counseling | Antidepressants (such as SSRIs, SNRIs, tricyclic antidepressants), antipsychotics |
| Cognitive dysfunction | Cognitive rehabilitation and accommodation strategies | No proven therapy |
| Mobility | Physical and occupational therapy, use of braces, canes, rolling walkers, electrostimulatory walk-assist devices | Dalfampridine |
| Urinary urgency/frequency | Timed voids, avoidance of caffeine | Oxybutynin, tolterodine |
| Urinary retention | Manual pelvic pressure, intermittent catheterization | None |

N/A = not applicable; SNRIs = serotonin norepinephrine reuptake inhibitors; SSRIs = selective serotonin reuptake inhibitors.

and of variable intensity. Before initiating pharmacologic therapy, clinicians must ensure that the fatigue is not due to sleep apnea, restless legs syndrome, insomnia, anemia, hypothyroidism, depression, or other medical conditions. Adjustment of sleep hygiene, regular exercise, and treatment of underlying depression can often improve MS-related fatigue. If fatigue persists despite such approaches, pharmacologic therapy with stimulants can be useful. Modafinil, which is also used to treat narcolepsy, can be given at a dosage of 200 mg/d to treat MS-related fatigue. Amantadine, which also has antiviral and antiparkinsonian properties, can be used at 100 mg twice daily to reduce fatigue symptoms.

Many patients with MS experience symptoms of depression. Whether the depression stems directly from the demyelinating process, occurs as an adverse effect of therapy (for example, with an interferon-beta preparation), or arises as an emotional response to dealing with a disabling chronic disease, the risk of suicide is increased among patients with MS. Clinicians should be vigilant for signs of depression and have a low threshold for initiating pharmacologic antidepressant therapy, scheduling prompt follow-up evaluation, and offering referrals for individual or group therapy.

Cognitive dysfunction is present in at least 50% of patients with MS. An often misunderstood and underdiagnosed component of the disease, this symptom can preclude employment and impair patients' ability to perform activities of daily living. Data supporting any pharmacologic therapies for this symptom are poor. Formal neuropsychological testing and consultation with a neuropsychological specialist for cognitive rehabilitation and accommodative strategies sometimes can be of benefit.

Maintenance of mobility in patients with MS is important. Physical and occupational therapy consultations can provide therapeutic exercise to improve the efficacy and safety of gait. Braces, canes, and rolling walkers also can be of use, as can electrostimulatory walk-assist devices. The drug dalfampridine, a voltage-gated potassium channel antagonist, recently was approved by the FDA for patients with gait impairment due to any form of MS. This medication may increase conductance through demyelinated axons and has been shown in clinical trials to improve walking speed and leg strength.

Bladder function is often impaired in patients with MS. Urinary frequency and urgency can be managed by abstaining from caffeine, timed voiding, and anticholinergic agents, such as oxybutynin and tolterodine. In patients with the additional symptoms of urinary hesitancy and retention, however, anticholinergic agents should be avoided because they can cause increased urinary retention. These mixed bladder symptoms should be evaluated by a urologist, and intermittent catheterization should be considered.

**KEY POINTS**

- In patients with multiple sclerosis, maintenance of the musculature of affected areas through exercise may minimize disability.

- Strong evidence suggests that the risk of relapse in multiple sclerosis is significantly increased in the setting of common infections, and thus current guidelines recommend strategies (including immunizations) designed to reduce the risk of infection.

- In patients with relapsing-remitting multiple sclerosis, chronic maintenance therapy with one of the eight FDA-approved disease-modifying therapies can reduce the relapse rate, slow disability progression, and reduce the accumulation of new demyelinating lesions on MRI.

- Muscle relaxants, such as baclofen, tizanidine, or cyclobenzaprine, and stretching exercises help reduce spasticity and prevent painful muscle cramps in patients with multiple sclerosis.

# Disorders of the Spinal Cord

## Presenting Symptoms and Signs of Myelopathies

Accurate and timely recognition of spinal cord disorders (or myelopathies) is critical because of the vulnerable and compartmentalized design of the spinal cord. Many critical pathways pass through this delicate structure of small diameter, and even a small lesion or injury can result in significant disability. Spinal cord disorders can be intrinsic (intramedullary), which means they result from primary disease within the spinal cord, or extrinsic (extramedullary), which means they result from external compression.

The presenting symptoms and signs of a spinal cord syndrome often occur at or below the site of a lesion. For example, neck or back pain often occurs at the site of a lesion, whereas spastic paresis or paralysis (usually accompanied by hyperreflexia and extensor plantar responses) occurs below the level of the lesion (quadriparesis for cervical lesions and paraparesis for thoracic lesions) when the corticospinal tracts are involved. Cauda equina lesions also can result in paresis because the cauda equina comprises spinal roots, but the weakness is of a lower motoneuron type, with flaccidity and areflexia. Involvement of spinal sensory pathways results in numbness and sensory loss that, on examination, is often present only distinctly below the level of the lesion. The spinal sensory level is best determined with an ascending pinprick examination, including the trunk. Some patients experience a neuropathic squeezing or band-like sensation around the

**H CONT.** chest or abdomen at the level of the lesion, which sometimes leads to an unnecessary cardiac, pulmonary, or gastrointestinal evaluation, if misdiagnosed. Bowel and bladder function can often be involved, with incontinence occurring in more severe disease. Gait is often abnormal in those with myelopathies, ranging from subtle spastic gait or ataxia to complete paralysis and wheelchair or bedbound status. **H**

---

**KEY POINTS**

- Accurate and timely recognition of spinal cord disorders (or myelopathies) is critical because of the vulnerable and compartmentalized design of the spinal cord, in which even a small lesion or injury can result in significant disability

- The presenting symptoms and signs of a spinal cord syndrome often occur at or below the site of a lesion.

- In patients with myelopathy, the spinal sensory level is best determined with an ascending pinprick examination, including the trunk; bowel and bladder function are often involved, with incontinence occurring in more severe disease.

---

# Compressive Myelopathies

## Clinical Presentation

**H** When a spinal cord syndrome is recognized clinically, prompt neuroimaging is the most useful tool to differentiate between (and sometimes diagnose) intrinsic and extrinsic disorders. Spinal cord compression, which should be treated as a neurologic emergency to prevent severe and irreversible disability, can occur in various settings, such as a metastatic neoplasm, a vertebral fracture (pathologic or traumatic), an epidural abscess, or an epidural hematoma. Neck or back pain is often the initial symptom, followed rapidly by weakness, sensory changes, and bowel or bladder dysfunction. However, many patients with compressive cervical myelopathy may not experience these symptoms, and thus compressive cervical myelopathy should be part of the differential diagnosis of leg weakness, especially in an older patient with arthritis, probable osteoporosis, or frequent falls. Affected patients also may have focal tenderness on examination. Fever can be a significant early finding in spinal epidural abscess. However, at least half the patients with this condition lack fever or other signs suggestive of infection. Recent neurosurgical intervention should suggest the possibility of an epidural abscess, whereas a history of recent anticoagulation should suggest an epidural hematoma.

## Diagnosis

MRI of the spinal cord is the best tool to establish the diagnosis of spinal cord compression. Although CT myelography can also establish the diagnosis and may be needed in patients with implantable devices that preclude the use of MRI, the technique is difficult to perform on an emergent basis and does not produce images of the cord parenchyma.

## Treatment

Therapeutic strategies for compressive myelopathies are determined by the underlying cause. Epidural hematoma and abscess both require immediate surgical decompression, with resolution of the underlying bleeding diathesis for a hematoma and antibiotic treatment for an abscess. Despite conflicting evidence from clinical trials, most institutions give an immediate bolus of high-dose corticosteroids to patients seen within 8 hours of a traumatic compressive spinal cord injury; patients with this injury also may require spinal stabilization surgery.

Emergent administration of high-dose corticosteroids, most often dexamethasone, is also indicated acutely for suspected epidural metastases (**Figure 22**). High-level evidence supports the additional use of decompressive surgery followed by radiotherapy, as opposed to radiotherapy alone, for most metastatic tumors that compress the spinal cord. Clinical trials have shown that decompressive surgery provides the best chance for future ambulation. Tumor types that are exceptionally sensitive to radiation (such as leukemia, lymphoma, myeloma, and germ-cell tumors) may not require surgical decompression. Surgery is sometimes deferred in patients with a poor overall prognosis or functional status, or if there is no clear neurologic deficit. **H**

Chronic spinal degenerative changes also can cause a compressive myelopathy. These changes have a similar but more protracted presentation than any acute spinal cord compression, with progressive leg weakness, spasticity, distal numbness, and bladder impairment. Neuroimaging can reveal cervical spondylosis and canal stenosis caused by hypertrophic changes of vertebral bodies and facet joints, usually in tandem with multiple disk herniations. In severe cases, myelomalacia (scarring) may be seen as increased signal intensity within the cord parenchyma. Examination often reveals upper motoneuron signs (weakness, spasticity, hyperreflexia, and an extensor plantar response), but lower motoneuron signs (atrophy, hyporeflexia) may be found at the level of stenosis because of anterior horn and root compression; the combination of cervical spine stenosis and root impingement is termed myeloradiculopathy. Spinal stenosis and disk herniation are uncommon in the thoracic spine but quite common in the lumbar spine. Lumbar spinal stenosis can elicit symptoms of groin, thigh, leg, or buttock pain and possibly neuroclaudication (pain, weakness, and numbness that may increase with activity and improve with rest). Physical therapy and symptomatic management of spasticity and pain can help some patients, but surgical decompression is sometimes required.

---

**KEY POINT**

- MRI of the spinal cord is the best tool to diagnose spinal cord compression.

---

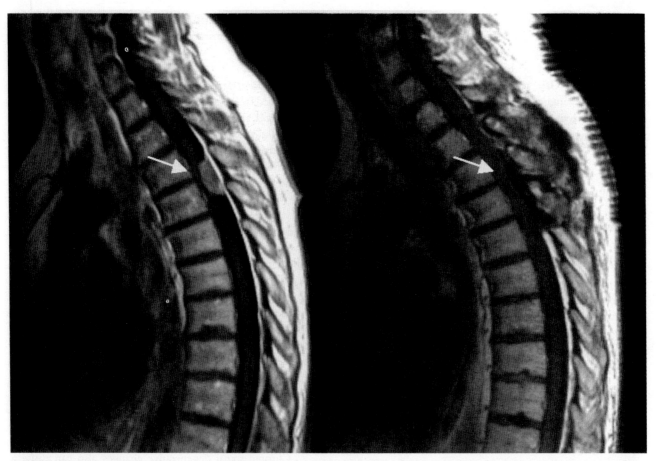

**FIGURE 22.** Spinal cord compression due to tumor. MRI of the thoracic spine of a 60-year-old woman with progressive lower extremity weakness. A postcontrast T1 image (*left*) shows spinal cord compression by a mass lesion (*arrow*). *Right*, compression was relieved (*arrow*) after surgical resection. Pathologic analysis of the lesion suggested meningioma.

## Noncompressive Myelopathies

### Clinical Presentation, Diagnosis, and Management

Noncompressive myelopathy may be idiopathic or caused by various inflammatory, infectious, metabolic, vascular, or genetic disorders. Multiple sclerosis, neuromyelitis optica, sarcoidosis, and rheumatologic disease can cause inflammatory demyelinating myelopathies (see Multiple Sclerosis and Other Demyelinating Diseases for further discussion).

Idiopathic transverse myelitis is a monophasic demyelinating myelopathy characterized by inflammation of a segment of the spinal cord (**Figure 23**). This disorder typically occurs as a postinfectious syndrome (usually after viral gastroenteritis or an upper respiratory tract infection) with a subacute onset of weakness, sensory changes, and bowel or bladder dysfunction and is sometimes preceded by back pain or a thoracic banding sensation. Transverse myelitis usually presents clinically as a partial myelopathy and not a complete transverse lesion, and thus sensory findings can occur without motor findings, and motor findings without sensory findings.

Diagnostic criteria for the idiopathic type require clinical features of the syndrome, evidence of inflammation (such as contrast enhancement of the lesion on MRI or leukocytosis in the cerebrospinal fluid), and exclusion of other potential causes. Intravenous methylprednisolone (1 g) should be given acutely and then daily for 3 to 5 days. Transverse myelitis that is refractory to corticosteroid therapy may require treatment with plasmapheresis or cyclophosphamide (or both). Because this syndrome is monophasic, recurrence of symptoms beyond 30 days of initial onset suggests the presence of other diseases, such as multiple sclerosis. ◨

The differential diagnosis of transverse myelitis includes several infections, such as herpes simplex virus, varicella zoster, West Nile virus, human T-lymphotropic virus, Lyme disease, and neurosyphilis, all of which can cause an inflammatory myelopathy. HIV also can cause a transverse myelitis–like syndrome at the time of seroconversion or a chronic, degenerative vacuolar myelopathy. *Mycobacterium tuberculosis* can infect the meninges and spinal cord and cause myelopathic symptoms.

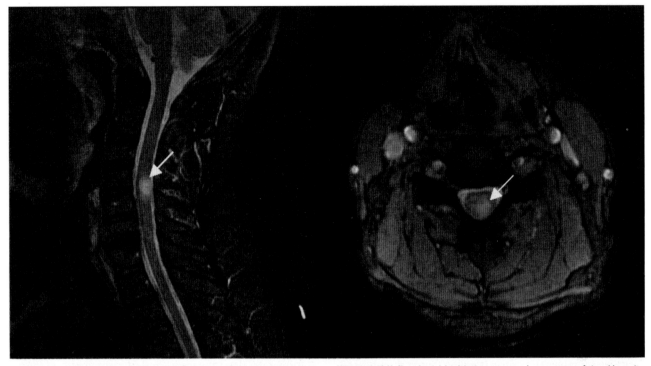

**FIGURE 23.** Transverse myelitis. MRIs of a 53-year-old man with transverse myelitis. Sagittal (*left*) and axial (*right*) T2 sequences show an area of signal hyperintensity in the cervical cord (*arrows*), mostly posterior with lateral extension to the left hemicord. This pattern could be consistent with disorders that have a predilection for the posterior columns, such as vitamin $B_{12}$ and copper deficiencies and neurosyphilis, although inflammatory transverse myelitis and multiple sclerosis can also affect this region.

Metabolic changes likewise can cause chronic noncompressive myelopathies. Severe vitamin $B_{12}$ deficiency may result in a subacute combined degeneration of corticospinal tracts and the dorsal columns, which results in a spastic paresis and reduction in vibration and position sense. An MRI may show increased signal in the affected white matter pathways, with results of laboratory studies showing a low serum vitamin $B_{12}$ level, an elevated serum methylmalonic acid level, and macrocytic anemia. Replacement therapy will usually halt progression of but may not improve symptoms. Similarly, copper deficiency, whether due to nutritional deficiency, malabsorption, or zinc toxicity, can also cause subacute combined degeneration of the spinal cord and may be clinically indistinguishable from vitamin $B_{12}$ deficiency.

Vascular disorders also can cause noncompressive myelopathy. Spinal cord infarction, often in the distribution of the anterior spinal artery, typically presents with acute onset of bilateral weakness. Some loss of pain and temperature sensation also may occur, but vibration and position sense are often spared because of the redundant vascular supply to the posterior aspect of the cord. The underlying mechanism is usually cardioembolic or due to local thrombosis but may result from prolonged hypotension during cardiovascular surgery or surgery involving the aorta. Dural arteriovenous fistulas of the spinal vascular supply can result in chronic myelopathy because of venous congestion; this disorder is most common in men older than 50 years and in those who have had previous spinal surgical procedures. Although MRI can occasionally show vascular flow voids, the gold standard of diagnosis is catheter-based angiography. These malformations can be treated by endovascular procedures or surgical ligation.

Several genetic disorders cause noncompressive myelopathy. Hereditary spastic paraplegia comprises a group of disorders that cause chronic, progressive, ascending weakness and spasticity, often beginning in childhood or adolescence. Genetic screening is available for the more commonly known mutations. Female carriers of X-linked adrenoleukodystrophy can develop a chronic progressive myelopathy called adrenomyeloneuropathy. The diagnosis is confirmed by elevated blood levels of very-long-chain fatty acids.

**KEY POINT**

- Diagnostic criteria for idiopathic transverse myelitis require clinical features of the syndrome, evidence of inflammation (such as contrast enhancement of a lesion on MRI or leukocytosis in the cerebrospinal fluid), and exclusion of other potential causes.

# Neuromuscular Disorders

## Peripheral Neuropathies

### Overview

Peripheral nerve disease or neuropathy is categorized by distribution into focal disease (mononeuropathy or multiple mononeuropathies) or widespread disease (polyneuropathy) and by underlying pathology into axonal (sparing the myelin sheath), demyelinating (sparing the axon), or mixed types. Peripheral neuropathies may affect motor, sensory, or autonomic nerves or a combination of these nerves. Peripheral neuropathies are differentiated from central nervous system dysfunction by history and examination findings, although the distinctions are not always clear (Table 30).

### KEY POINT

- Peripheral neuropathies may affect motor, sensory, or autonomic nerves or a combination of these nerves.

### Classification, Findings, and Diagnosis

Peripheral neuropathy sensory symptoms can be classified as negative (numbness), positive (tingling, burning, and dysesthesia), or both together. The distribution of sensory symptoms reflects the peripheral nerve territory involved, with mononeuropathies having a discrete distribution and polyneuropathies showing a symmetric distal-to-proximal gradient. Motor symptoms (such as weakness and gait imbalance) can follow or coexist with sensory abnormalities. Dysfunction of autonomic nerves results in orthostatic hypotension, cardiac arrhythmias, and changes in sweating patterns. Diabetes mellitus is the most common cause of peripheral neuropathy, but the extensive differential diagnosis includes vasculitis, inflammatory diseases, infections, connective tissue diseases, infiltrative diseases, and paraneoplastic syndromes.

The evaluation of a patient with a suspected neuromuscular disorder is based on history, with emphasis on symptom chronology, anatomic distribution, presence of autonomic symptoms, medical comorbidities, family history, and medications. Physical findings include weakness, sensory loss or hyperesthesia, and decreased or absent deep tendon reflexes (Table 31).

Small-fiber neuropathy, affecting pain and temperature transmitting fibers, can be particularly challenging to diagnose because sensory and autonomic symptoms occur in the absence of clinical weakness. Burning dysesthesia of the feet or hands is a characteristic feature of small-fiber neuropathy and frequently occurs in patients with poorly controlled diabetes mellitus.

Appropriate laboratory tests include serum protein electrophoresis, a complete blood count, erythrocyte sedimentation rate determination, and measurement of fasting plasma glucose, hemoglobin $A_{1c}$, and vitamin $B_{12}$ levels. Cerebrospinal fluid (CSF) analysis may be required in patients with rapidly progressive neuropathy (such as Guillain-Barré syndrome) or in patients with demyelinating neuropathy or mononeuritis multiplex.

Electromyography (EMG), for the purpose of this discussion, includes nerve conduction studies and needle

| TABLE 30. | Features Distinguishing PNS from CNS Causes of Dysfunction | |
|---|---|---|
| Features | PNS Origin | CNS Origin |
| **History** | | |
| Onset | Subacute or insidious | Often sudden (stroke) or gradual (space-occupying lesion) |
| Motor symptoms/distribution | Yes/focal, unilateral, or generalized | Yes/usually focal or unilateral |
| Sensory symptoms/distribution | Possible/focal, unilateral, or generalized | Possible/usually focal or unilateral |
| Cramps and fasciculations | Possible | No |
| Other CNS-related symptoms | No | Yes (such as headache, visual loss, or seizure) |
| **Neurologic Examination Findings** | | |
| Atrophy | Yes (sometimes prominent) | No (or mild if related to disuse) |
| Fasciculations | Possible | No |
| Stretch reflexes | Normal or diminished | Hyperreflexia, pathologic (such as extensor plantar response) |
| Sensory abnormalities | In nerve territory, dermatome, or stocking-glove distribution | In an entire limb |
| EMG | Positive results | Negative results |

CNS = central nervous system; EMG = electromyography; PNS = peripheral nervous system.

**TABLE 31.** Common Symptoms and Signs of Neuromuscular Disorders

| Symptoms and Signs | Differential Diagnosis |
|---|---|
| **Weakness** | |
| Distal muscles | Dying-back polyneuropathy (as in diabetes mellitus) |
| Ascending | Guillain-Barré syndrome |
| Proximal muscles | Lambert-Eaton myasthenic syndrome, myopathy, polyradiculopathy |
| Fluctuating | Myasthenia gravis |
| Focal asymmetric | ALS, inclusion body myositis, radiculopathy |
| Extraocular muscles | Myasthenia gravis, mitochondrial myopathy |
| Bulbar (lips, palate, tongue) | ALS, inclusion body myositis, myasthenia gravis |
| With atrophy | ALS and other conditions with axonal loss |
| Without atrophy | Myasthenia gravis and other conditions without axonal loss |
| **Cramps** | |
| Fasciculations | ALS, Guillain-Barré syndrome, radiculopathy |
| **Numbness, Paresthesias, Burning** | |
| Hypoesthesia to pinprick and temperature | Dying-back polyneuropathy (diabetes), Guillain-Barré syndrome |
| Symmetric gradient (stocking-glove) distribution | Generalized polyneuropathy |
| Hyperpathia | Small-fiber neuropathy |
| Dermatomal pattern | Radiculopathy, peripheral nerve lesion |
| With hyporeflexia | Polyneuropathy affecting large fibers |
| Without hyporeflexia | Small-fiber neuropathy |
| **Autonomic Dysfunction** | |
| Decreased sweat output, abnormal results on QSART | Amyloid neuropathy, diabetic polyneuropathy, Guillain-Barré syndrome, small-fiber neuropathy |
| Early satiety and constipation from delayed gastric emptying | |
| Erectile dysfunction, impotence | |
| Resting tachycardia from cardiac dysrhythmias | |
| Syncope from orthostatic hypotension | |

ALS = amyotrophic lateral sclerosis; QSART = quantitative sudomotor axon reflex testing.

electrode examination, which are separate but complementary techniques that help confirm and quantify peripheral neuropathy. Nerve conduction studies evaluate only larger myelinated sensory nerve fibers and thus cannot detect small-fiber neuropathies. Needle electrode examination can detect active denervation of muscles only after at least 3 weeks have elapsed since nerve injury. **H**

Small-fiber neuropathies are best evaluated by quantitative sensory testing for pressure and thermal function, a quantitative sudomotor axon reflex test for sweating, and determination of intraepidermal nerve fiber density on skin biopsy (**Figure 24**). Sural nerve biopsy can be useful in suspected vasculitis or amyloidosis. Despite extensive testing, however, no cause is found in up to one third of patients with peripheral neuropathy.

**KEY POINTS**

- Appropriate laboratory tests in the diagnosis of peripheral neuropathy include serum protein electrophoresis, a complete blood count, erythrocyte sedimentation rate determination, and measurement of fasting plasma glucose, hemoglobin $A_{1c}$, and vitamin $B_{12}$ levels; cerebrospinal fluid analysis may be required in patients with rapidly progressive neuropathy.

- Despite extensive testing, no cause is found in up to one third of patients with peripheral neuropathy.

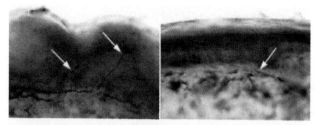

**FIGURE 24.** Photomicrographs of skin biopsy samples. Samples were immunostained for protein gene product 9.5 to reveal intraepidermal nerve fibers. *Left,* normal fibers in a healthy person (*arrows*). *Right,* depleted fibers in a patient with small-fiber neuropathy (*arrow*).

## Mononeuropathies

Mononeuropathies typically involve a single nerve (as in carpal tunnel syndrome) or two or more nerves at different sites (as in mononeuropathy multiplex with wrist and foot drop).

### Carpal Tunnel Syndrome

In median nerve mononeuropathy at the wrist, also known as carpal tunnel syndrome, compression of the median nerve results in sensory symptoms of numbness and tingling in the thumb, index finger, and/or middle fingers. Sensory symptoms may occasionally involve the entire hand and even radiate proximally to the wrist. With increasing severity, weakness of thumb opposition and abduction develops. Symptoms are exacerbated by prolonged wrist flexion (for example, during sleep) or extension (for example, while holding a steering wheel or book) and by improper hand positioning (for example, when typing on a keyboard). Reproduction of symptoms by prolonged wrist flexion (Phalen maneuver) or percussion over the carpal ligament and median nerve (Tinel sign) supports the diagnosis; EMG can confirm the diagnosis, quantify the severity of compression, and exclude other conditions causing similar symptoms (such as cervical radiculopathy).

Treatment includes wrist splints, occupational therapy, local corticosteroid injections or short-term oral corticosteroids, and improved control of underlying metabolic contributors, such as diabetes mellitus. NSAIDs have not been shown to be effective in randomized studies, and gabapentin has only demonstrated efficacy in an open label trial of patients with carpal tunnel syndrome. Nonsurgical treatment can be effective in the short term, but surgery is indicated in patients with progressive symptoms.

### Bell Palsy

Bell palsy refers to paralysis of the facial nerve resulting in weakness of ipsilateral facial muscles. This peripheral nerve compression can be differentiated from central causes (such as stroke) by evaluating forehead and periorbital muscles. With a lesion of the central nervous system, lower facial muscles are primarily affected, and the forehead and orbicularis oculi muscles are relatively spared. Peripheral nerve compression, as seen in Bell palsy, causes more widespread facial paralysis, including the upper and lower face, with an inability to close both eyes tightly or raise both eyebrows. Patients may also report hyperacusis, dry mouth, and impaired taste. Abrupt onset of symptoms building over 1 to 2 days is typical.

Patching the eye and lubricating the cornea are essential to prevent abrasions. Spontaneous recovery of function is good to excellent in approximately 70% of patients, although some patients are left with substantial weakness and evidence of aberrant reinnervation causing synkinesis (such as voluntary smiling causing involuntary eyelid closure). Use of prednisone in the first 72 hours has been shown in clinical trials to hasten the time to recovery and increase the percentage of patients with complete recovery. However, the use of antiherpesvirus agents as monotherapy has not shown benefit, and studies evaluating combined corticosteroid and antiherpesvirus therapy have reported inconsistent results.

### Brachial and Lumbosacral Plexopathies

The brachial plexus and lumbosacral plexus control sensory and motor innervation of the upper and lower limbs, respectively. Dysfunction of the brachial plexus can result from trauma, carcinomatous infiltration, radiation, and neuralgic amyotrophy, which is an idiopathic inflammatory disorder manifesting as severe shoulder or arm pain followed by sensory loss and weakness. Lumbosacral plexopathy can be structural (caused by compression by a tumor or hematoma, especially in the iliopsoas muscle, and best revealed by a CT scan) or nonstructural (caused by radiation, diabetes [diabetic amyotrophy], or vasculitis).

### KEY POINTS

- In carpal tunnel syndrome, compression of the median nerve results in sensory symptoms of numbness and tingling in the thumb, index finger, and/or middle fingers

- Treatment of carpal tunnel syndrome includes wrist splints, occupational therapy, local corticosteroid injections, and improved control of metabolic contributors, such as diabetes mellitus.

- Corticosteroids improve clinical outcomes in patients with Bell palsy if administered within the first 72 hours of symptom onset.

## Polyneuropathies

Polyneuropathy, the dysfunction of multiple nerves at multiple sites, may be acquired or hereditary. The pathophysiology involves damage to nerve axons (axonal neuropathies), the myelin sheath (demyelinating neuropathies), or small to medium blood vessels supplying the nerves (vasculitic neuropathies). Acquired polyneuropathies are most common with diabetes mellitus and alcoholism and predominate in developed countries.

In generalized polyneuropathy, the longest nerves are affected most severely. Symptoms usually begin in the feet, ascend up the limbs, and then affect the hands in a stocking-glove distribution; progression along the limbs is distal to proximal. Symptoms of pain are common, especially at night, because of small unmyelinated fiber involvement. Asymmetric involvement in polyneuropathy should prompt consideration of other causes, such as radiculopathy, plexopathy, mononeuritis multiplex, motoneuron disease, or compressive mononeuropathy.

## Neuropathies of Diabetes Mellitus and Impaired Glucose Tolerance

Diabetes mellitus can cause almost any kind of neuropathy, and often different types of neuropathy coexist in the same patient (**Table 32**). Diabetes predisposes to multifactorial nerve injury due to nerve compression, ischemia, inflammation, and metabolic changes. Distal sensorimotor peripheral neuropathy is the most common disorder and presents with numbness, tingling, and burning pain in a stocking-glove distribution. Single mononeuropathies (such as median, ulnar, and isolated cranial neuropathy) are common complications of diabetes. In patients with long-standing diabetes, autonomic dysfunction becomes increasingly prevalent. Tight glucose control and reduction of cardiovascular risk factors have been shown to improve symptoms of diabetic neuropathy and slow disease progression.

Diabetic amyotrophy (also known as diabetic lumbosacral radiculoneuropathy) is a painful proximal neuropathy affecting patients with even mild or previously undiagnosed diabetes. Onset of severe unilateral leg pain with occasional numbness is acute or subacute and is followed by proximal weakness and subsequent atrophy. Significant weight loss often precedes its onset. Progression occurs over weeks to months, sometimes with spread to the contralateral lower extremity or upper extremities. EMG reveals characteristic findings of L2 to L4 radiculopathies, with or without evidence of a distal sensorimotor polyneuropathy. Aggressive diabetic control, analgesia, and physical therapy are the mainstays of treatment. The use of immunomodulators is controversial.

Small-fiber neuropathy occurs in patients with mild to severe diabetes and even in patients with only impaired glucose tolerance. Patients typically report burning, lancinating extremity pain without weakness. Careful screening for diabetes is essential in all patients with new small-fiber neuropathy.

## Hereditary Neuropathies

Hereditary neuropathies should be suspected in patients with few paresthesias and chronic distal weakness progressing slowly over many years. The prototypic hereditary motor and sensory neuropathy is Charcot-Marie-Tooth (CMT) disease, a spectrum of disorders arising from mutations in several genes encoding for myelin formation, structure, and function. The two most common forms are demyelinating (CMT1) and axonal (CMT2). Both share the clinical features of numbness, distal extremity weakness, unsteady gait, areflexia, high arches, hammer toes, and atrophy of distal extremity muscles and foreleg muscles ("stork leg" deformity). In CMT1, which begins in the first or early second decade of life, peripheral nerves become palpable as demyelination and remyelination proceed. CMT2 is the axonal form that begins in the second or third decade with prominent sensory loss that can result in trophic foot ulcers. In contrast to small-fiber neuropathies, dysesthetic pain is not present in CMT disease. EMG helps differentiate between the demyelinating and axonal forms and thus guides genetic testing. Treatment is supportive with physical therapy and appropriate orthotics.

## Inflammatory Polyradiculoneuropathies

Guillain-Barré syndrome (GBS) and chronic inflammatory demyelinating polyneuropathy (CIDP) are inflammatory polyneuropathies caused by acquired immune-mediated inflammation of nerve roots and peripheral nerves. The disorders are best distinguished by symptom duration.

### Guillain-Barré Syndrome

The most common cause of acute diffuse neuromuscular paralysis, GBS results from immune-mediated attacks on peripheral nerve myelin or axonal components because of shared epitopes. Affected patients initially experience rapid onset of symmetric weakness of the upper and lower limbs over days to weeks, generally in the setting of a recent infection (particularly with *Campylobacter jejuni*), trauma, or

| **TABLE 32.** Peripheral Nerve Dysfunction in Diabetes Mellitus | |
|---|---|
| **Classification** | **Signs and Symptoms** |
| Autonomic neuropathy | Constipation, early satiety, erectile dysfunction, hyperhidrosis or hypohidrosis, and orthostatic hypotension |
| Diabetic lumbosacral radiculoneuropathy (diabetic amyotrophy) | Pain in proximal leg (severe) followed by weakness, with or without sensory loss (proximal), and with or without weight loss |
| Mononeuropathy | Sensory loss with or without pain at onset, weakness in distribution of single nerve (such as the median or a cranial nerve) |
| Radiculopathy | Sensory loss or pain, thoracic levels often affected, weakness in distribution of nerve root(s) |
| Sensorimotor peripheral neuropathy | Asymptomatic (sometimes), distal sensory loss and weakness (length dependent), pain (often) |
| Small-fiber neuropathy | Burning extremity pain without weakness, usually distal or lower, may be non–length dependent |

surgery. The disorder generally progresses over 2 weeks, with most patients (~90%) at their worst by 4 weeks. Facial, oropharyngeal, oculomotor, and diaphragmatic muscles may be involved. Although many patients describe paresthesias or neuropathic pain in the hands and feet, objective sensory loss is usually mild or absent. Low back pain, presumably due to inflammatory demyelination at the spinal nerve root level and often mistaken for compressive lumbosacral radiculopathy, can herald the onset of GBS. In patients with severe weakness and respiratory failure, dysautonomia (for example, labile blood pressure, severe constipation, and cardiac arrhythmias) may develop. All patients with suspected GBS should be monitored carefully, and hospitalization should be considered because of the risk of rapid progression to respiratory failure or autonomic instability. **H**

The diagnosis of GBS rests on historical, physical examination, and lumbar puncture findings. Neurologic examination typically reveals weakness and decreased or absent deep tendon reflexes. CSF analysis usually reveals a normal cell count and an increased protein level (albuminocytologic dissociation) in 80% to 90% of affected patients; glucose levels are normal. Findings of CSF pleocytosis should prompt evaluation for other conditions that can mimic GBS, including infections (such as Lyme disease or West Nile virus), vasculitis, or leptomeningeal disease from sarcoidosis or carcinomatosis. EMG results typically show a predominantly demyelinating process unless a rare axonal variant is present (5%-10% of GBS presentations). Pulmonary function testing, including measurement of FVC and negative inspiratory force, can help establish a baseline and monitor respiratory status during disease progression, particularly because 15% to 30% of affected patients require ventilatory support.

GBS is usually monophasic and self-limited but may require aggressive supportive treatment. Intravenous immune globulin and plasma exchange are equally effective in treating the disorder, especially when started within 7 to 14 days of symptom onset. If deterioration is rapid and the clinical index of suspicion for GBS is high, therapy should not be delayed while awaiting results of confirmatory studies (such as nerve conduction studies). Either treatment results in shortening of time to recovery by approximately 40% to 50%. Intravenous immune globulin is usually given at a dosage of 0.4 g/kg/d for 3 to 6 days, although patients with more severe disease may need therapy of longer duration. Plasma exchange is usually performed four to six times over 8 to 10 days for a total of 200 to 250 mL/kg. Combination therapy does not provide additional benefit. Corticosteroids are of no benefit in the treatment of GBS and may even slow recovery.

Up to 10% of treated patients will relapse with increased weakness requiring repeated courses of treatment. Markers of poor prognosis include older age, diarrheal illness as a prodrome, rapidly progressive weakness, substantial axonal loss on early EMG, and the need for ventilatory support. Supportive treatment is critical, including pain management,

nutritional support, bowel care, cardiorespiratory monitoring, treatment of dysautonomia, infection surveillance, venous thrombosis prophylaxis, and physical and occupational therapy. Despite disease severity, prognosis is good in 80% of patients, with only mild to no residual disability.

### Chronic Inflammatory Demyelinating Polyradiculoneuropathy

Patients with CIDP may first have signs and symptoms resembling GBS that progress or relapse more than 8 weeks after onset. Alternatively, they may begin with more slowly evolving symmetric motor, and to a lesser extent sensory, dysfunction in both proximal and distal muscles over 3 to 6 months. Symptoms may be progressive (especially in older patients) or relapsing-remitting (more often in younger patients). Sensory signs and symptoms (such as pain) often are more prominent in CIDP than GBS and primarily reflect larger myelinated fiber dysfunction. Examination reveals weakness, sensory loss, and absent or decreased deep tendon reflexes. Screening should be performed for diabetes, monoclonal paraproteinemia, and connective tissue disease. Findings of demyelination and denervation on EMG confirm the diagnosis of CIDP. CSF analysis reveals a sometimes dramatic increase in protein level with a normal leukocyte count. The role of nerve (often sural) biopsy in the evaluation of CIDP is controversial because evidence of demyelination may be missed or the sampled nerve may be too degenerated to provide useful information. Nevertheless, biopsy may be useful when EMG changes are nondiagnostic and may reveal another cause mimicking CIDP (such as vasculitis or amyloidosis).

Treatment of CIDP involves ongoing immunosuppression, typically with prednisone, intravenous immune globulin, or plasma exchange, all of which have shown equal efficacy in controlled trials.

### Critical Illness Polyneuropathy

Many patients (up to 50%-70%) with sepsis and multiorgan failure in intensive care settings longer than 7 to 14 days develop critical illness polyneuropathy. This polyneuropathy of uncertain pathogenesis usually is identified during weaning from mechanical ventilation when a patient is unable to progress to unassisted breathing despite adequate cardiopulmonary function. It can also present as generalized or distal flaccid paralysis and atrophy of primarily lower extremity muscles during or after recovery from critical illness. Typical findings include distal sensory loss, decreased or absent deep tendon reflexes, and relative sparing of cranial nerves. A careful history, physical examination, and EMG evaluation are required in these severely ill patients to exclude similar disorders, although this is more difficult in patients who are uncooperative or have encephalopathies. EMG findings that are relatively specific for critical illness polyneuropathy include axonal sensory and motor polyneuropathy without evidence of conduction block and decremental response on repetitive nerve stimulation. Unless there is some coexistent critical illness myopathy, the needle electrode examination reveals evidence of only motor axon loss. The serum creatine kinase (CK) level is normal, as are CSF protein levels; the latter finding differentiates this condition from GBS.

Treatment is primarily supportive and includes aggressive management of underlying medical conditions (including sepsis) and prevention of additional complications (such as deep venous thrombosis). Aggressive physical and occupational therapy are essential. Neuromuscular junction blocking agents should be avoided, if possible. Whether tight control of plasma glucose levels with intensive insulin therapy (target level of 80-110 mg/dL) improves the outcome of critical illness polyneuropathy remains undetermined. In addition to length of stay in the intensive care unit, other contributors to a poor prognosis include increased plasma glucose and decreased serum albumin levels. Long-term data are limited, but approximately 30% of patients with the disorder have significant residual weakness, including quadriplegia.

**KEY POINTS**

- In generalized polyneuropathy, the longest nerves are affected most severely, with symptoms usually beginning in the feet, ascending up the limbs, and then affecting the hands in a stocking-glove distribution.

- Diabetes mellitus can cause almost any kind of neuropathy, and often different types of neuropathy coexist in the same patient.

- Guillain-Barré syndrome (GBS) is usually self-limited but may require aggressive supportive treatment with intravenous immune globulin or plasma exchange therapy; if deterioration is rapid and the clinical suspicion of GBS is high, therapy should not be delayed while awaiting results of confirmatory studies.

## Treatment of Neuropathic Pain

Neuropathic pain is typically described as tingling, burning, electrical, or dysesthetic; usually involves the distal extremities; and is worse at night. This pain is a common feature of polyneuropathies affecting small fibers, as frequently occurs in diabetes mellitus. A recent evidence-based guideline for treatment of painful diabetic neuropathy by the American Academy of Neurology recommends pregabalin as being effective for relief of painful diabetic neuropathy (Level A evidence); this drug, however, is expensive, and many patients are unable to tolerate it because of adverse effects. Drugs listed as probably effective (Level B evidence) are venlafaxine, duloxetine, amitriptyline, nortriptyline, gabapentin, valproic acid, opioids (morphine sulfate, tramadol, and oxycodone controlled-release), and capsaicin. Tricyclic antidepressants, such as amitriptyline and nortriptyline, are much less expensive; these drugs, however, may be associated with the

anticholinergic adverse effects of dry eyes, orthostatic hypotension, constipation, urinary retention, drowsiness, and weight gain. Duloxetine and gabapentin are generally well tolerated but are more expensive and can be associated with weight gain and drowsiness. Opioids generally should be avoided but may be considered for acute, severe pain or when other treatments have been unsuccessful. Tramadol, a non-narcotic centrally acting agent, can be used as an adjunct to control pain. Medications should be started at low dosages, slowly increased as tolerated, and continued for at least 4 weeks to determine effectiveness. Combined use of several medications with different mechanisms of action often is more successful than use of a single agent.

**KEY POINT**

- Neuropathic pain—typically described as a tingling, burning, electrical, or dysesthetic sensation—usually involves the distal extremities, is worse at night, and is typical of polyneuropathies affecting small fibers, as frequently occurs in diabetes mellitus.

## Amyotrophic Lateral Sclerosis

Amyotrophic lateral sclerosis (ALS) is an incurable progressive neurodegenerative disease of unknown cause that results in muscle paralysis and death from respiratory failure, usually within 3 to 5 years of symptom onset. ALS is diagnosed when clinical evidence shows progressive dysfunction of both upper motoneuron and lower motoneuron pathways in one or more areas of the body without other explanation. Common upper motoneuron features are spasticity, hyperreflexia, and pathologic reflexes, including extensor plantar responses. Typical lower motoneuron features are muscle weakness, atrophy, fasciculations, and cramps. Approximately two thirds of patients with ALS first develop focal limb weakness and one third initially have bulbar dysfunction. Cognitive abnormalities (typically, behavioral and language dysfunction) caused by coexisting frontotemporal dysfunction (see Dementia) can be identified in up to 50% of all affected patients. ALS is increasingly viewed as a complex neurodegenerative syndrome with diverse mechanisms.

Because no single test can confirm an ALS diagnosis, a combination of laboratory, neuroimaging, and electrodiagnostic procedures are necessary to rule out treatable mimics. MRI can identify brain and spinal cord pathology (such as strokes and demyelination) resulting in limb or bulbar dysfunction. EMG can demonstrate the extent of lower motoneuron involvement and exclude other conditions (such as multifocal motor neuropathy with conduction block or inclusion body myositis) that may be treatable.

Management of ALS, which is best coordinated by an experienced neurologist, is largely supportive and directed toward relieving symptoms, prolonging independence, and improving quality of life. Percutaneous endoscopic gastrostomy tube placement improves quality of life by assuring adequate caloric intake, hydration, and an alternative means of administering medications in patients with significant dysphagia or weight loss. Symptomatic dyspnea, orthopnea, and hypercarbia are indicators to initiate noninvasive bilevel positive pressure ventilation. Presently, riluzole is the only FDA-approved drug to slow disease progression, although it extends survival by only approximately 3 months in clinical trials.

**KEY POINTS**

- Amyotrophic lateral sclerosis is an incurable progressive neurodegenerative disease of unknown cause that results in muscle paralysis and death from respiratory failure, usually within 3 to 5 years of symptom onset.

- Management of amyotrophic lateral sclerosis is largely supportive and directed toward symptomatic relief, prolonging independence, and improving quality of life.

# Neuromuscular Junction Disorders

## Myasthenia Gravis

Myasthenia gravis results from an autoantibody that blocks postsynaptic neuromuscular junctions. A generalized form and a less common ocular/oculobulbar form exist. The classic clinical feature of this disorder is fluctuating, fatigable muscle weakness that worsens with activity and improves with rest. Symptoms also are aggravated by increased body temperature, stress, and infection. All voluntary muscles can be affected, especially the ocular and bulbar muscles. Approximately half of affected patients initially have diplopia or ptosis, and half of these develop generalized disease within 2 years. Bulbar symptoms, including slurred speech, dysphagia, nasal regurgitation of liquids, and fatigue while chewing, are presenting features in approximately 15% of these patients.

Neurologic examination may reveal bilateral asymmetric ptosis worsened by prolonged upward gaze, an expressionless or sagging appearance of facial muscles, a "snarling" smile, nasal speech worsened by prolonged speaking, and limb weakness that increases with exercise. Pupillary responses, deep tendon reflexes, and sensory examination findings are normal. Myasthenia gravis has a bimodal age predominance, affecting younger women (age 20-30 years) and older men (age ≥50 years). Most affected patients have identifiable autoantibodies directed against the postsynaptic acetylcholine receptor or against muscle-specific tyrosine kinase (MuSK) receptors.

Thyroid-stimulating hormone levels should be checked because 30% of affected patients have thyroid disease. Edrophonium testing may be insensitive but has a high positive predictive value when unequivocal improvement in an objectively weak muscle can be shown. EMG testing, including single-fiber EMG, has a 97% to 99% sensitivity but lacks specificity. Thymic abnormalities, such as hyperplasia and thymoma, are present in 75% of affected patients, although less often in those with autoantibodies against MuSK receptors. CT of the chest should be performed. Other cancers occasionally associated with myasthenia gravis include small cell lung cancer, breast cancer, and Hodgkin lymphoma.

Pyridostigmine, an acetylcholinesterase inhibitor, is first-line therapy and may be sufficient in very mild disease, although MuSK receptor antibody–positive disease is less responsive. In more severe or generalized disease, immune suppression with prednisone, mycophenolate mofetil, azathioprine, cyclosporine, or rituximab may result in disease remission. When first used, however, corticosteroids may transiently worsen weakness. In refractory myasthenia gravis with severe limb weakness or respiratory or bulbar dysfunction possibly requiring intubation or nasogastric feeding, intravenous immune globulin or plasma exchange can be considered. Affected patients with antibodies against MuSK receptors tend to respond well to plasma exchange and immunosuppression. Thymectomy may be recommended when a CT scan shows evidence of thymoma. Aminoglycosides, β-blockers, calcium channel blockers, neuromuscular blocking agents, many antiarrhythmic agents, morphine, and barbiturates all interfere with neuromuscular junction transmission in various ways and are relatively contraindicated in patients with myasthenia gravis.

**KEY POINT**

- Pyridostigmine, an acetylcholinesterase inhibitor, is first-line therapy for myasthenia gravis and may be sufficient in very mild disease; in more severe or generalized disease, immune suppression with prednisone, mycophenolate mofetil, azathioprine, cyclosporine, or rituximab may result in disease remission.

## Lambert-Eaton Myasthenic Syndrome

Lambert-Eaton myasthenic syndrome is a rare disorder caused by autoantibody attack against voltage-gated P/Q-type calcium channels at the presynaptic neuromuscular junction. This disorder has a paraneoplastic manifestation in approximately 50% of affected patients and should prompt a search for an underlying malignancy, particularly small cell lung cancer. Conversely, approximately 5% of patients with small cell lung cancer develop Lambert-Eaton myasthenic syndrome. Affected patients have progressive proximal limb weakness, usually beginning in the lower limbs, and decreased or absent deep tendon reflexes. Oculobulbar weakness can occur, although less severely than in myasthenia gravis. Autonomic nerve dysfunction can be prominent and cause orthostatic hypotension, constipation, erectile dysfunction, and cardiac arrhythmias. The cardinal feature of Lambert-Eaton myasthenic syndrome is facilitation or improvement in deep tendon reflexes and muscle strength after isometric exercise.

The diagnosis is confirmed by elevated titers of P/Q-type calcium channel antibodies or by facilitation of motor response on EMG (nerve conduction study) after briefly exercising or rapidly and repetitively stimulating the muscle. Thorough evaluation for occult malignancy should include age-appropriate screening and CT scans of the chest, abdomen, and pelvis, with consideration of whole-body PET if clinically warranted. Effective treatment of the underlying malignancy usually results in neuromuscular improvement. Symptomatic therapies, which increase available postsynaptic acetylcholine, include anticholinesterase inhibitors, such as pyridostigmine.

> **KEY POINT**
>
> - Lambert-Eaton myasthenic syndrome has a paraneoplastic manifestation in approximately 50% of affected patients and should prompt a search for underlying malignancy, especially small cell lung cancer.

# Myopathies

## Overview

Myopathies are inherited or acquired disorders primarily affecting skeletal and cardiac muscles, although facial, bulbar, and respiratory muscles also may be involved. Reflexes and sensation are generally intact. Myopathies typically present as painless progressive weakness without sensory deficit. The most common weakness is in the limbs and follows a symmetric proximal to distal pattern. Some myopathies (such as inclusion body myositis and hereditary myopathies) may present with focal or distal weakness. Asymmetric onset of weakness, although common in inclusion body myositis, should prompt consideration of motoneuron disease. Weakness of facial and ocular muscles suggests a neuromuscular junction disorder or a hereditary myopathy.

Medical history taking should focus on age at onset, anatomic distribution, rate of progression, medical comorbidities, medications, and family history. Minimal or very slow evolution over years suggests congenital myopathies, muscular dystrophy, or inclusion body myositis; subacute development over months to years suggests endocrine dysfunction; and rapid progression over weeks to months suggests inflammatory and toxic myopathies. Episodic weakness with normal interictal strength (signs of periodic paralysis) suggests certain metabolic myopathies. Pain, although absent in most myopathies, can suggest myotonic dystrophy and infectious, toxic, metabolic, and infiltrative myopathies (sarcoidosis, amyloidosis). Myoglobinuria, although a rare finding, can suggest a metabolic myopathy. Frontal balding, cataracts, and mental retardation are features associated with myotonic dystrophy. The finding of a characteristic rash strongly suggests an inflammatory myopathy, such as dermatomyositis.

The serum CK level is elevated in most patients with myopathy and is useful in monitoring disease activity and response to treatment. However, patients with slowly progressive myopathies (such as inclusion body myositis) may have a normal CK level, and elevated levels also are associated with other disorders and medications (**Table 33**). Aldolase is a less specific marker than CK in myopathy because the level can increase in hepatic and hematologic disease.

EMG is useful in the evaluation of patients with suspected myopathy because it can show myopathic features (short duration, low-amplitude, polyphasic motor unit potentials) in those with normal or borderline CK levels, outline the extent and distribution of disease, and identify muscle biopsy sites. CK levels should be determined before EMG because needle insertion into muscle will itself cause enzymatic elevations. Biopsy should be performed in moderately but not severely affected muscles to avoid nonspecific end-stage changes. Molecular genetic testing is an essential adjunct to muscle biopsy in patients with suspected hereditary myopathies and may even obviate the need for biopsy, if results are positive.

> **KEY POINTS**
>
> - Myopathies typically present as painless progressive weakness, usually of the limbs, without sensory deficit.
> - The serum creatine kinase level is elevated in most patients with myopathy and is useful in monitoring disease activity and response to treatment; patients with slowly progressive myopathies may have normal CK levels.

| TABLE 33. Elevated Serum Creatine Kinase Levels and Associated Conditions | |
| --- | --- |
| **CK Level** | **Condition** |
| Normal or <5 times the upper limit of normal | ALS, CIDP, endocrinopathies, exercise (strenuous), GBS, hyperCKemia (no weakness or underlying disease), inclusion body myositis, muscle trauma (mild to moderate), post–needle electrode examination (EMG), seizure, stroke, toxic myopathy (mild; for example, from statins), and viral infection |
| >5 to 10 times the upper limit of normal | Dystrophies (such as Duchenne muscular dystrophy), inflammatory myopathies (such as polymyositis and dermatomyositis), muscle trauma (severe), rhabdomyolysis, and toxic myopathy (severe; for example, from statins) |

ALS = amyotrophic lateral sclerosis; CIDP = chronic inflammatory demyelinating polyneuropathy; CK = creatine kinase; EMG = electromyography, GBS = Guillain-Barré syndrome.

## Inflammatory Myopathy

For information on inflammatory myopathy, see MKSAP 16 Rheumatology.

## Endocrine-Related Myopathies

### Corticosteroid-Induced Myopathy

Corticosteroid-induced myopathy classically is associated with proximal limb weakness, mostly of the legs, in patients taking chronic corticosteroids. A definitive diagnosis is difficult to establish. Women reportedly are affected twice as often as men, with additional risk conferred by the use of high-dose (≥30 mg/d) prednisone. Patients typically have a cushingoid body habitus and may have other stigmata of chronic corticosteroid use. Neurologic examination reveals intact ocular, facial, and distal extremity strength; normal sensory examination findings; and normal deep tendon reflexes. Serum CK levels and results of EMG testing are normal; an elevated CK level or abnormal EMG result suggests the presence of another myopathy or recurrence of a partly treated myositis. In patients treated with corticosteroids for an inflammatory myopathy, concern for corticosteroid-induced myopathy should be prompted by continued or worsening proximal muscle weakness after a decrease in or normalization of CK levels. Muscle biopsy is nondiagnostic in corticosteroid-induced myopathy and reveals only atrophy of type IIb muscle fibers. Slow tapering of corticosteroid therapy with the goal of discontinuation is the only effective treatment, although physical therapy also should be emphasized.

### Thyrotoxic Myopathy

Patients with classic hyperthyroidism or hypothyroidism may have symmetric proximal muscle weakness. Patients with hyperthyroidism may have muscle atrophy and fasciculations, whereas patients with hypothyroidism may have muscle hypertrophy. Serum CK levels and EMG findings are usually normal. Correction of the endocrine disorder is associated with resolution of the myopathy.

### Myopathy Associated with Vitamin D Deficiency

Vitamin D deficiency, whether alone or in the context of osteomalacia, can be associated with myalgia, bone pain, and diffuse fatigue. Proximal limb weakness has been described in osteomalacia but also in severe vitamin D deficiency alone. For a detailed discussion of vitamin D deficiency, see MKSAP 16 Endocrinology and Metabolism.

### Inherited Myopathies

The inherited myopathies are a heterogeneous group of disorders with a wide range of presentations, including slowly progressive undiagnosed disease in adulthood. Diagnosis is based on family history, overall clinical picture, muscle biopsy results, and genetic testing (when available). Molecular and genetic abnormalities have been identified in some, but not all, inherited myopathies. In muscular dystrophies, proximal muscle weakness is the usual presenting symptom, with variable involvement of other muscles. Weakness can be asymmetric and involve axial (shoulder and hip girdle) and facial musculature. Cardiomyopathy and conduction defects at times may be more prominent than skeletal muscle weakness. X-linked inheritance patterns are seen in Duchenne and Emery-Dreifuss muscular dystrophy. Myotonia (inability to relax a muscle after isometric contraction, as when releasing a grip after a handshake) is an important finding in myotonic dystrophy. A positive family history and recognition of specific patterns of weakness aid in diagnosis. The serum CK level is generally elevated. EMG and muscle biopsy can assist in the diagnosis but are not pathognomonic unless specific markers of disease are identified by immunohistochemistry (such as absent dystrophin immunostaining of a biopsy specimen from a patient with suspected Duchenne muscular dystrophy).

Congenital myopathies often are associated with dysmorphic facial and skeletal features, neuropathy, and cardiomyopathy. Muscle channelopathies (such as malignant hyperthermia and periodic paralyses) may only manifest in adulthood under specific stressors, including high carbohydrate meals, severe exertion, and anesthesia. In metabolic myopathies, glycogen and lipid metabolism disorders result in cramping, stiffness, and pain shortly after exertion. Mitochondrial myopathies present in various ways, including exercise intolerance (for example, fatigue), myalgia, and occasionally ptosis or extraocular movement abnormalities (ophthalmoplegia), which can mimic myasthenia gravis (**Figure 25**).

### Critical Illness Myopathy

Critical illness myopathy is usually identified during weaning from mechanical ventilation when a patient is unable to progress to unassisted breathing and is more common than

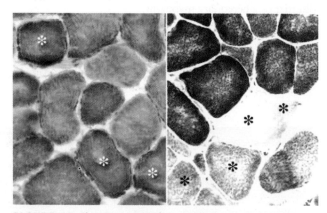

**FIGURE 25.** Photomicrographs of mitochondrial myopathy biopsy samples. Histochemically stained muscle biopsy specimens reveal features of mitochondrial myopathy. *Left,* abnormal accumulations of mitochondria at myofiber periphery produce trichrome-positive "ragged red fibers" (*asterisks*). *Right,* several myofibers are variably deficient in cytochrome oxidase staining (*asterisks*).

Photomicrographs courtesy of Richard Prayson, MD.

critical illness polyneuropathy. Use of intravenous corticosteroids is the strongest risk factor for its development, although neuromuscular blocking agents also increase the risk. Patients have generalized flaccid weakness, usually of the proximal upper and lower extremities, neck, diaphragm, and (sometimes) facial muscles. Sensation, if testable, is unaffected.

Serum CK levels often are elevated and tend to peak within a few days of corticosteroid infusion. Muscle biopsy is nonspecific. Treatment is primarily supportive and aimed at decreasing the corticosteroid dosage. No convincing evidence supports using tight control of plasma glucose levels with intensive insulin therapy to improve outcomes in critical illness myopathy. 🄷

### Toxic Myopathies

Exposure to toxins should be considered in all patients with presenting symptoms of myopathy. The clinical presentation of proximal muscle weakness, myalgia, and cramps should prompt a careful review of current and recent medications, particularly statins. A recent increase in statin dosage, a change from one statin to another, or the addition of another drug (such as a fibric acid derivative) that increases myopathy risk can be accompanied by new muscle symptoms and progression. The concomitant use of drugs that inhibit cytochrome P3A4, including macrolides, cyclosporine, itraconazole, and protease inhibitors, will increase myopathy risk in patients taking lovastatin, simvastatin, and atorvastatin because these drug are metabolized by the same pathway. In these patients, other statin options (such as pravastatin, rosuvastatin, or fluvastatin) that are not similarly metabolized may be preferable. Serum CK levels can range from barely increased to the high values associated with rhabdomyolysis. Other medications also are known to cause toxic myopathy (**Table 34**). Acute or chronic alcohol abuse also can cause a dose-dependent myopathy. Discontinuation of the responsible medication or substance generally results in gradual recovery.

### KEY POINT

- The clinical presentation of proximal muscle weakness, myalgia, and cramps should prompt a careful review of current and recent medications, particularly statins, to detect toxic myopathy.

# Neuro-oncology

## Intracranial Tumors

The signs and symptoms of an intracranial tumor depend on its location and rate of growth. Intracranial tumors most commonly involve the cerebral hemispheres and typically present

**TABLE 34.** Drugs Potentially Causing Myopathy

| | |
|---|---|
| Anti-HIV therapy | Zidovudine, HAART |
| Antiviral therapy | Interferon, clevudine[a] |
| Cholesterol-lowering therapy | Statins (especially simvastatin, atorvastatin, lovastatin; increased risk when combined with fibrates and fenofibrates), ezetimibe, neutraceuticals (for example, red yeast rice) |
| Emetics | Emetine, ipecac |
| Immunosuppressants | Corticosteroids, leflunomide, TNF-$\alpha$ inhibitors (for example, adalimumab) |
| Microtubule inhibitors (acute gout, antineoplastic therapies) | Colchicine, vincristine |
| Rheumatologic therapy (antimalarial class) | Chloroquine, hydroxychloroquine |

HAART = highly active antiretroviral therapy; TNF = tumor necrosis factor.

[a]Investigational drug, not FDA approved.

with seizures. More rapidly growing hemispheric tumors often present with focal neurologic deficits, such as hemiparesis, hemineglect, or visual field cuts. The first sign of frontal lobe tumors may be subtle personality changes only recognized after the diagnosis is made. Nonspecific symptoms of a brain tumor include headache, nausea, vomiting, visual changes, and gait disorders.

The differential diagnosis of an intracranial tumor includes abscess, demyelinating disease, vascular malformation, toxoplasmosis, tuberculosis, sarcoidosis, and radiation necrosis. Diagnostic evaluation of a patient with a suspected brain tumor should include MRI with intravenous contrast. In many instances, specific signal characteristics on an MRI can distinguish a tumor from other intracranial lesions and will often suggest the tumor pathology (**Table 35**). CT can be useful in detecting calcifications and tumor invasion into bone. Magnetic resonance spectroscopy, PET, and single-photon emission CT also can help clarify the diagnosis.

Brain metastases are the most common type of intracranial tumor. The tumors most likely to metastasize to the brain are lung cancer, breast cancer, and melanoma. Although identifying and obtaining a tissue diagnosis from the primary lesion is best, brain biopsy may be necessary if the primary lesion cannot be identified or is inaccessible. 🄷

### KEY POINTS

- Intracranial tumors most commonly involve the cerebral hemispheres and typically present with seizures; brain metastases, typically from lung or breast cancer or melanoma, are the most common type.

- The diagnostic evaluation of a patient with a suspected brain tumor should include MRI with intravenous contrast.

**TABLE 35.** Clinical and Radiographic Features of Intracranial Tumors

| Tumor Type | Typical Age at Onset | Imaging Findings | Treatment | Median Survival |
|---|---|---|---|---|
| Metastatic tumor | 60+ y | Multifocal lesions at gray-white matter junction; ring enhancement with contrast | Radiation, with or without surgery | 10-16 mo |
| Glioma | | | | |
| Astrocytoma | | Infiltrating white matter lesion | Surgery | |
| Low-grade (fibrillary) | 30-50 y | No enhancement | Surgery, with or without radiation | 7-8 y |
| Anaplastic | 35-55 y | Contrast enhancement | Surgery and radiation, with or without chemotherapy (temozolomide) | 3-4 y |
| Glioblastoma multiforme | 45-65 y | Possible hemorrhage, possible multifocal or "butterfly" lesions (bihemispheric) | Surgery and radiation, with or without chemotherapy (temozolomide or bevacizumab) | 12-15 mo |
| Oligodendroglioma | 30-50 y | Infiltrating white matter lesion; vague contrast enhancement with a "honeycomb" pattern and calcifications that are best seen on CT scan | Surgery and chemotherapy (carmustine or temozolomide), with or without radiation | (see below) |
| Low-grade | | | | 6-10 y |
| Anaplastic | | | | 3-4 years |
| Ependymoma | 30-40 y[a] | Posterior fossa or spinal cord lesion; contrast enhancement and calcifications, with or without hydrocephalus | Possible surgery, possible radiation | 15-20 y |
| Meningioma | 50-65 y | Extradural (outside of the brain); calcified, with diffusely enhancing "lightbulb" sign | Possible surgery, possible artery embolization, possible radiation (rare) | (see below) |
| Benign | | | | Rarely limits life expectancy |
| Atypical | | | | 13 y |
| Anaplastic | | | | 3-4 y |
| Schwannoma | 40-50 y | Cerebropontine angle; contrast enhancement | Possible surgery | Rarely limits life expectancy |
| Medulloblastoma | 20-30 y[a] | Posterior fossa (cerebellum); contrast enhancement and hydrocephalus | Surgery and radiation, with or without chemotherapy | 17-18 y |
| Primary central nervous system lymphoma | | Homogeneous white matter lesion; diffusely enhancing, periventricular, and often multifocal | Corticosteroids and chemotherapy (methotrexate), with or without radiation | 2-4 y |
| Immunocompetent | 60-70 y | | | |
| AIDS-related | 30-40 y | | HAART therapy | 1-2 y |

HAART = highly active antiretroviral therapy.

[a]Age range given is for adult presentation; tumor is most common in children.

# Primary Central Nervous System Tumors

Glioblastoma multiforme (**Figure 26**) is the most aggressive primary brain tumor and also the most common, accounting for 20% of all primary central nervous system (CNS) tumors and 50% of gliomas in the adult population. Other glial tumors include low-grade (fibrillary) astrocytomas, anaplastic astrocytomas, oligodendrogliomas, and ependymomas. Compared with gliomas, other primary CNS tumors, such as meningiomas (**Figure 27**), schwannomas, and medulloblastomas, have a much better prognosis. Biopsy and pathologic examination of tissue usually is required to make a definitive diagnosis and determine the course of treatment. If the MRI

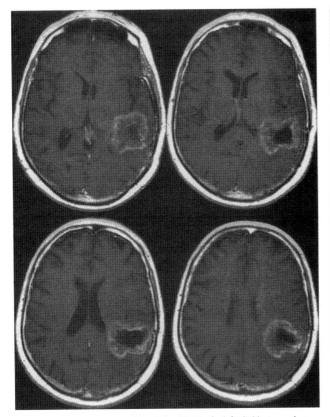

**FIGURE 26.** Postcontrast T1-weighted MRIs of a left glioblastoma that show an extensive mass with a ring contrast enhancement surrounding a necrotic center.

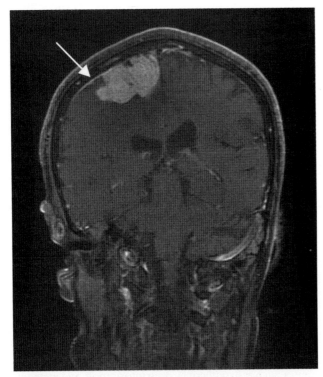

**FIGURE 27.** Coronal postcontrast T1-weighted MRI showing a right parafalcine meningioma with associated edema and mass effect. Note the "dural tail" (*arrow*).

and clinical course suggest a low-grade or benign lesion, however, biopsy may not be necessary, and the tumor may be followed over time with serial imaging.

Primary CNS lymphoma (PCNSL) is a non-Hodgkin lymphoma confined to the CNS. PCNSL can involve the cerebral hemispheres, brainstem, leptomeninges, or eyes. Largely confined to the white matter, PCNSL is less likely than other tumors to present with seizures and more typically manifests with subacute progressive cognitive or behavioral changes. Biopsy is usually necessary for diagnosis. In rare instances, the diagnosis can be confirmed by finding lymphomatous cells on slit-lamp examination of the eye or cytologic examination of the cerebrospinal fluid (CSF). Three separate large-volume CSF samples are recommended when looking for cytology consistent with PCNSL.

## Management of Intracranial Tumors

Prophylactic antiepileptic drug treatment of brain tumors is not recommended if the patient has not had a seizure. Corticosteroids may be used to minimize tumor-associated vasogenic edema, which can exacerbate symptoms of intracranial pressure. If, however, PCNSL is suspected by clinical and radiographic presentation, corticosteroids should be deferred, if possible. Because PCNSL is so exquisitely sensitive to corticosteroids, the administration of these drugs can significantly decrease the yield of a diagnostic biopsy. With the exception of PCNSL, surgical maximal resection is the first step in treatment of most brain tumors. Adjunctive treatment with chemotherapy or radiation therapy depends on the tumor type.

Lower extremity deep venous thromboses and pulmonary emboli are common complications of CNS tumors. Therefore, thromboembolism prophylaxis should be used.

Delayed cerebral radiation necrosis is a rare complication of brain tumor treatment and can occur 6 to 12 months after radiation therapy. Radiation-induced changes to normal brain tissue in the area of the tumor can mimic brain tumor recurrence, both clinically and radiographically. Differentiation often requires open biopsy.

> **KEY POINT**
>
> - Corticosteroids may be used as treatment of intracranial tumors to minimize tumor-associated vasogenic edema (which can exacerbate symptoms of intracranial pressure) except when primary central nervous system lymphoma is suspected.

## Paraneoplastic Syndromes

The central and peripheral nervous systems are susceptible to tumor-associated immune-mediated injury, which results in various paraneoplastic syndromes (**Table 36**). An immune

**TABLE 36.** Selected Paraneoplastic Syndromes and Neuronal Paraneoplastic Antibodies

| Paraneoplastic Syndrome | Symptoms | Tumor | Antibody |
|---|---|---|---|
| Cerebellar degeneration | Ataxia, dysarthria, dizziness, vertigo | Breast cancer | ANNA-1 (anti-Hu), ANNA-3, MA, PCA-1 (anti-Yo) |
| | | Hodgkin lymphoma | Tr |
| | | SCLC | ANNA-1 (anti-Hu), ANNA-3, CRMP-5, MA, PCA-2, VGCC |
| | | Ovarian cancer | ANNA-1 (anti-Hu), ANNA-3, PCA-1 (anti-Yo) |
| | | Testicular cancer | ANNA-1 (anti-Hu), ANNA-3, CRMP-5, MA |
| | | Thymoma | CRMP-5 |
| Limbic encephalitis | Personality change, psychosis, seizures, oral dyskinesias[a] | Ovarian or testicular teratoma | NMDA |
| | | Lung cancer, thymoma | VGKC |
| Neuropathy | Painful sensory neuropathy, sensory ataxia, autonomic dysfunction | SCLC | ANNA-1 (anti-Hu), VGCC |
| Opsoclonus-myoclonus | Involuntary eye movements and muscle jerks, ataxia | Breast cancer, SCLC | ANNA-2 (anti-Ri) |
| Stiff-person syndrome | Muscle stiffness and spasms | Breast cancer, lung cancer | Amphiphysin, CRMP-5 |
| | | Thymoma | CRMP-5 |

SCLC = small-cell lung cancer.

[a]Limbic encephalitis also (but less commonly) can produce a rapidly progressive or subacute dementia.

reaction to the primary tumor is thought to be responsible for the generation of autoantibodies that cross-react with epitopes on specific nervous system structures. The presence of a paraneoplastic syndrome should be suspected in a patient with an unexplained subacute progressive neurologic disorder. The diagnosis can be confirmed by identifying one of the antibodies known to be responsible for these clinical entities in serum or CSF. The absence of a known paraneoplastic antibody does not exclude the diagnosis of a paraneoplastic syndrome, however, because new antibodies are still being discovered. For example, an anti-NMDA antibody has recently been identified and is associated with limbic encephalitis, a syndrome of subacute psychosis, personality change, seizures, and oral dyskinesias (involuntary mouth movements).

The suspicion of a paraneoplastic syndrome should prompt a thorough evaluation for cancer, including PET and CT of the chest, abdomen, and pelvis. Some syndromes have been associated with nonmalignant tumors. For example, the anti-NMDA encephalitis described previously is most commonly associated with ovarian teratomas. An ultrasound or MRI of the pelvis is recommended if this syndrome is suspected. The definitive treatment of a paraneoplastic syndrome is removal of the primary neoplasm. Unfortunately, the neurologic symptoms may precede the oncologic diagnosis by several years, and the tumor often is not identifiable. Symptomatic treatment of paraneoplastic syndromes includes intravenous immune globulin, plasmapheresis, and corticosteroid administration.

**KEY POINTS**

- The presence of a paraneoplastic syndrome should be suspected in a patient with an unexplained subacute progressive neurologic disorder.
- The diagnosis of a paraneoplastic syndrome can be confirmed by identifying one of the causative antibodies in serum or cerebrospinal fluid.

# Brain Death

## Description and Findings

Brain death indicates an irreversible and total absence of cerebral and brainstem function. Brain death must be distinguished from the locked-in state, in which a patient is fully conscious and alert but paralyzed and unable to speak or breathe because of a destructive lesion of the brainstem. The determination of brain death requires knowing the cause of the catastrophic brain damage and excluding reversible causes, such as hypothermia, drug intoxication, and metabolic encephalopathy. A total lack of spontaneous movement, respiration, or cerebral responses to all visual, auditory, and cutaneous stimuli characterizes brain death, although spinal reflexes may persist in some instances. The pupils typically are midposition, fixed, and dilated, with no spontaneous eye movements. Additionally, corneal reflexes are absent, which indicates pontine and midbrain damage; response to oculocephalic or caloric (oculovestibular) maneuvers is lacking, which indicates pontine damage; and the gag reflex, cough, and respiration are absent, which indicates damage to the medulla. **H**

### KEY POINT

- The determination of brain death requires knowing the cause of the catastrophic brain damage and excluding reversible causes, such as a reversible brainstem lesion (locked-in syndrome), hypothermia, drug intoxication, and metabolic encephalopathy.

## Apnea Test

The apnea test, which is often required by institutions for brain death determination in patients on artificial life support, evaluates the medullary respiratory center and its response to hypercarbia. The patient is removed from the ventilator and given 100% oxygen by cannula. A baseline arterial blood gas value is obtained, with a required starting $PCO_2$ of 40 to 60 mm Hg. At 1 and 5 minutes later, repeat arterial blood gas levels are obtained while the patient is observed for spontaneous respirations. If the $PCO_2$ increases by more than 20 mm Hg and spontaneous respirations are lacking, the test is considered to be positive. Two positive tests performed at least 6 hours apart are diagnostic of brain death, as long as no mitigating factors, such as sedatives or hypothermia, are present. An electrically silent electroencephalogram or the demonstration of absent cerebral blood flow provides physiologic confirmation of brain death.

### KEY POINT

- Two positive apnea tests performed at least 6 hours apart are diagnostic of brain death, as long as mitigating factors, such as sedatives or hypothermia, are absent.

## Bibliography

### Headache and Facial Pain

Bigal ME, Kurth T, Santanello N, et al. Migraine and cardiovascular disease: a population-based study. Neurology. 2010;74(8):628-635. [PMID: 20147658]

Cohen AS, Burns B, Goadsby PJ. High-flow oxygen for treatment of cluster headache: a randomized trial. JAMA. 2009;302(22):2451-2457. [PMID: 19996400]

Francis GJ, Becker WJ, Pringsheim TM. Acute and preventive pharmacologic treatment of cluster headache. Neurology. 2010;75(5):463-473. [PMID: 20679639]

Gillman PK. Triptans, serotonin agonists, and serotonin syndrome (serotonin toxicity): a review. Headache. 2010;50(2):264-272. [PMID: 19925619]

Holland S, Silberstein SD, Freitag F, Dodick DW, Argoff C, Ashman E. Evidence-based guideline update: NSAIDs and other complementary treatments for episodic migraine prevention in adults: Report of the Quality Standards Subcommittee of the American Academy of Neurology and the American Headache Society. Neurology. 2012;78(17):1346-1353. [PMID: 22529203]

Kruit MC, van Buchem MA, Launer LJ, Terwindt GM, Ferrari MD. Migraine is associated with an increased risk of deep white matter lesions, subclinical posterior circulation infarcts and brain iron accumulation: the population-based MRI CAMERA study. Cephalalgia. 2010;30(2):129-136. [PMID: 19515125]

Loder E. Triptan therapy in migraine. N Engl J Med. 2010;363(1):63-70. [PMID: 20592298]

Schwedt TJ, Demaerschalk BM, Dodick DW. Patent foramen ovale and migraine: a quantitative systematic review. Cephalalgia. 2008;28(5):531-540. [PMID: 18355348]

Silberstein SD, Holland S, Freitag F, Dodick DW, Argoff C, Ashman E. Evidence-based guideline update: Pharmacologic treatment for episodic migraine prevention in adults: Report of the Quality Standards Subcommittee of the American Academy of Neurology and the American Headache Society. Neurology. 2012;78(17):1337-1345. [PMID: 22529202]

Torelli P, Allais G, Manzoni GC. Clinical review of headache in pregnancy. Neurol Sci. 2010;31 (suppl 1):S55-S58. [PMID: 20464584]

Verhagen AP, Damen L, Berger MY, Passchier J, Koes BW. Lack of benefit for prophylactic drugs of tension-type headache in adults: a systematic review. Fam Pract. 2010;27(2):151-165. [PMID: 20028727]

### Head Injury

Afari N, Harder LH, Madra NJ, et al. PTSD, combat injury, and headache in veterans returning from Iraq/Afghanistan. Headache. 2009;49(9):1267-1276. [PMID: 19788469]

DeKosky ST, Ikonomovic MD, Gandy S. Traumatic brain injury—football, warfare, and long-term effects. N Engl J Med. 2010;363(14):1293-1296. [PMID: 20879875]

Mansell JL, Tierney RT, Higgins M, McDevitt J, Toone N, Glutting J. Concussive signs and symptoms following head impacts in collegiate athletes. Brain Inj. 2010;24(9):1070-1074. [PMID: 20597635]

Theeler BJ, Erickson JC. Mild head trauma and chronic headaches in returning US soldiers. Headache. 2009;49(4):529-534. [PMID: 19220499]

Wilk JE, Thomas JL, McGurk DM, Riviere LA, Castro CA, Hoge CW. Mild traumatic brain injury (concussion) during combat: lack of association of blast mechanism with persistent postconcussive symptoms. J Head Trama Rehabil. 2010;25(1):9-14. [PMID: 20051900]

### Epilepsy

Arif H, Buchsbaum R, Pierro J, et al. Comparative effectiveness of 10 antiepileptic drugs in older adults with epilepsy. Arch Neurol. 2010;67(4):408-415. [PMID: 20385905]

Arif H, Buchsbaum R, Weintraub D, et al. Comparison and predictors of rash associated with 15 antiepileptic drugs. Neurology. 2007;68(20):1701-1709. [PMID: 17502552]

Epilepsy Foundation. Driver's licensing overview. Available at: www.epilepsyfoundation.org/resources/drivingandtravel.cfm. Accessed February 6, 2012.

French JA, Pedley TA. Clinical practice. Initial management of epilepsy. N Engl J Med. 2008;359(2):166-176. [PMID: 18614784]

Harden CL, Meador KJ, Pennell PB, et al; American Academy of Neurology; American Epilepsy Society. Practice parameter update: management issues for women with epilepsy—focus on pregnancy (an evidence-based review): teratogenesis and perinatal outcomes: report of the Quality Standards Subcommittee and Therapeutics and Technology Assessment Subcommittee of the American Academy of Neurology and American Epilepsy Society. Neurology. 2009;73(2):133-141. [PMID: 19398681]

Krumholz A, Wiebe S, Gronseth G, et al; Quality Standards Subcommittee of the American Academy of Neurology; American Epilepsy Society. Practice parameter: evaluating an apparent unprovoked first seizure in adults (an evidence-based review): report of the Quality Standards Subcommittee of the American Academy of Neurology and the American Epilepsy Society. Neurology. 2007;69(21):1996-2007. [PMID: 18025394]

Kwan P, Brodie MJ. Early identification of refractory epilepsy. N Engl J Med. 2000;342(5):314-319. [PMID: 10660394]

Nei M, Hays R. Sudden unexpected death in epilepsy. Curr Neurol Neurosci Rep. 2010;10(4):319-326. [PMID: 20446062]

Treiman DM, Meyers PD, Walton NY, et al. A comparison of four treatments for generalized convulsive status epilepticus. Veterans Affairs Status Epilepticus Cooperative Study Group. N Engl J Med. 1998;339(12):792-798. [PMID: 9738086]

Wiebe S, Blume WT, Girvin JP, Eliasziw M; Effectiveness and Efficiency of Surgery for Temporal Lobe Epilepsy Study Group. A randomized, controlled trial of surgery for temporal-lobe epilepsy. N Engl J Med. 2001;345(5):311-318. [PMID: 11484687]

### Stroke

Adams HP Jr, del Zoppo G, Alberts MJ, et al; American Heart Association; American Stroke Association Stroke Council; Clinical Cardiology Council; Cardiovascular Radiology and Intervention Council; Atherosclerotic Peripheral Vascular Disease and Quality of Care Outcomes in Research Interdisciplinary Working Groups. Guidelines for the early management of adults with ischemic stroke: a guideline from the American Heart Association/American Stroke Association Stroke Council, Clinical Cardiology Council, Cardiovascular Radiology and Intervention Council, and the Atherosclerotic Peripheral Vascular Disease and Quality of Care Outcomes in Research Interdisciplinary Working Groups: the American Academy of Neurology affirms the value of this guideline as an educational tool for neurologists [errata in Stroke. 2007;38(6):e38 and Stroke. 2007;38(9):e96]. Stroke. 2007;38(5):1655-1711. [PMID: 17431204]

del Zoppo GJ, Saver JL, Jauch EC, Adams HP Jr; American Heart Association Stroke Council. Expansion of the time window for treatment of acute ischemic stroke with intravenous tissue plasminogen activator: a science advisory from the American Heart Association/American Stroke Association [erratum in Stroke. 2010;41(9):e562]. Stroke. 2009;40(8):2945-2948. [PMID: 19478221]

Easton JD, Saver JL, Albers GW, et al; American Heart Association; American Stroke Association Stroke Council; Council on Cardiovascular Surgery and Anesthesia; Council on Cardiovascular Radiology and Intervention; Council on Cardiovascular Nursing; Interdisciplinary Council on Peripheral Vascular Disease. Definition and evaluation of transient ischemic attack: a scientific statement for healthcare professionals from the American Heart Association/American Stroke Association Stroke Council; Council on Cardiovascular Surgery and Anesthesia; Council on Cardiovascular Radiology and Intervention; Council on Cardiovascular Nursing; and the Interdisciplinary Council on Peripheral Vascular Disease. The American Academy of Neurology affirms the value of this statement as an educational tool for neurologists. Stroke. 2009;40(6):2276-2293. [PMID: 19423857]

Furie KL, Kasner SE, Adams RJ, et al; American Heart Association Stroke Council, Council on Cardiovascular Nursing, Council on Clinical Cardiology, and Interdisciplinary Council on Quality of Care and Outcomes Research. Guidelines for the prevention of stroke in patients with stroke or transient ischemic attack: a guideline for healthcare professionals from the American Heart Association/American Stroke Association. Stroke. 2011;42(1):227-276. [PMID: 20966421]

Huttner HB, Schwab S. Malignant middle cerebral artery infarction: clinical characteristics, treatment strategies, and future perspectives. Lancet Neurol. 2009;8(10):949-958. [PMID: 19747656]

Kumar S, Selim MH, Caplan LR. Medical complications after stroke. Lancet Neurol. 2010; 9(1):105-118. [PMID: 20083041]

Marquardt L, Geraghty OC, Mehta Z, Rothwell PM. Low risk of ipsilateral stroke in patients with asymptomatic carotid stenosis on best medical treatment: a prospective, population-based study. Stroke. 2010;41(1):e11-e17. [PMID: 19926843]

Morgenstern LB, Hemphill JC III, Anderson C, et al; American Heart Association Stroke Council and Council on Cardiovascular Nursing. Guidelines for the management of spontaneous intracerebral hemorrhage: a guideline for healthcare professionals from the American Heart Association/American Stroke Association. Stroke. 2010;41(9):2108-2129. [PMID: 20651276]

Sandercock PA, Gibson LM, Liu M. Anticoagulants for preventing recurrence following presumed non-cardioembolic ischaemic stroke or transient ischaemic attack. Cochrane Database Syst Rev. 2009;(2):CD000248. [PMID: 19370555]

Stam J. Thrombosis of the cerebral veins and sinuses. N Eng J Med. 2005;352(17):1791-1798. [PMID: 15858188]

Stroke Unit Trialists' Collaboration. Organised inpatient (stroke unit) care for stroke. Cochrane Database Syst Rev. 2007;(4):CD000197. [PMID: 17943737]

van Gijn J, Kerr RS, Rinkel GJ. Subarachnoid haemorrhage. Lancet. 2007;369(9558):306-318. [PMID: 17258671]

Wiebers DO, Whisnant JP, Huston J III, et al; International Study of Unruptured Intracranial Aneurysms Investigators. Unruptured intracranial aneurysms: natural history, clinical outcome, and risks of surgical and endovascular treatment. Lancet. 2003;362(9378):103-110. [PMID: 12867109]

### Dementia

Iverson DJ, Gronseth GS, Reger MA, et al; Quality Standards Subcommittee of the American Academy of Neurology. Practice parameter update: evaluation and management of driving risk in dementia: report of the Quality Standards Subcommittee of the American Academy of Neurology. Neurology. 2010;74(16):1316-1324. [PMID: 20385882]

Mangialasche F, Solomon A, Winblad B, Mecocci P, Kivipelto M. Alzheimer's disease: clinical trials and drug development. Lancet Neurol. 2010;9(7):702-716. [PMID: 20610346]

McKeith IG, Dickson DW, Lowe J, et al; Consortium on DLB. Diagnosis and management of dementia with Lewy bodies: third report of the DLB consortium [erratum in Neurology. 2005;65(12):1992]. Neurology. 2005;65(12):1863-1872. [PMID: 16237129]

Mitchell SL, Teno JM, Kiely DK, et al. The clinical course of advanced dementia. N Engl J Med. 2009;361(16):1529-1538. [PMID: 19828530]

Nasreddine ZS, Phillips NA, Bédirian V, et al. The Montreal Cognitive Assessment, MoCA: a brief screening tool for mild cognitive impairment. J Am Geriatr Soc. 2005;53(4):695-699. [PMID: 15817019]

### Movement Disorders

Allen RP, Picchietti D, Hening WA, Trenkwalder C, Walters AS, Montplaisi J; Restless Legs Syndrome Diagnosis and Epidemiology workshop at the National Institutes of Health; International Restless Legs Syndrome Study Group. Restless legs syndrome: diagnostic criteria, special considerations, and epidemiology. A report from the Restless Legs Syndrome Diagnosis and Epidemiology Workshop at the National Institutes of Health. Sleep Med. 2003;4(2):101-119. [PMID: 14592341]

Chesson AL Jr, Wise M, Davila D, et al. Practice parameters for the treatment of restless legs syndrome and periodic limb movement disorder. An American Academy of Sleep Medicine Report. Standards of Practice Committee of the American Academy of Sleep Medicine. Sleep. 1999;22(7):961-968. [PMID: 10566915]

Follett KA, Weaver FM, Stern M, et al; CSP 468 Study Group. Pallidal versus subthalamic deep-brain stimulation for Parkinson's disease. N Engl J Med. 2010;362(22):2077-2091. [PMID: 20519680]

Jeste DV. Tardive dyskinesia rates with atypical antipsychotics in older adults. J Clin Psychiatry. 2004;65(Suppl 9):21-24. [PMID: 15189108]

Pahwa R, Factor SA, Lyons KE, et al; Quality Standards Subcommittee of the American Academy of Neurology. Practice Parameter: treatment of Parkinson disease with motor fluctuations and dyskinesia (an evidence-based review): report of the Quality Standards Subcommittee of the American Academy of Neurology. Neurology. 2006;66(7):983-995. [PMID: 16606909]

Zesiewicz TA, Elbe R, Louis ED, et al; Quality Standards Subcommittee of the American Academy of Neurology. Practice parameter: therapies for essential tremor: report of the Quality Standard Subcommittee of the American Academy of Neurology. Neurology. 2005;64(12):2008-2020. [PMID: 15972843]

Zesiewicz TA, Sullivan KL, Arnulf I, et al; Quality Standards Subcommittee of the American Academy of Neurology. Practice parameter: treatment of nonmotor symptoms of Parkinson disease: report of the Quality Standards Subcommittee of the American Academy of Neurology. Neurology. 2010;74(11):924-931. [PMID: 20231670]

### Multiple Sclerosis and Other Demyelinating Diseases

Frohman EM, Goodin DS, Calabresi PA, et al; Therapeutics and Technology Assessment Subcommittee of the American Academy of Neurology. The utility of MRI in suspected MS: report of the Therapeutics and Technology Assessment Subcommittee of the American Academy of Neurology. Neurology. 2003;61(5):602-611. [PMID: 12963748]

Frohman EM, Racke MK, Raine CS. Multiple sclerosis—the plaque and its pathogenesis. N Engl J Med. 2006;354(9):942-955. [PMID: 16510748]

Goodin DS, Cohen BA, O'Connor P, Kappos L, Stevens JC; Therapeutics and Technology Assessment Subcommittee of the American Academy of Neurology. Assessment: the use of natalizumab (Tysabri) for the treatment of multiple sclerosis (an evidence-based review): report of the Therapeutics and Technology Assessment Subcommittee of the American Academy of Neurology. Neurology. 2008;71(10):766-773. [PMID: 18765653]

Goodin DS, Frohman EM, Garmany GP Jr, et al; Therapeutics and Technology Assessment Subcommittee of the American Academy of Neurology and the MS Council for Clinical Practice Guidelines. Disease modifying therapies in multiple sclerosis: report of the Therapeutics and Technology Assessment Subcommittee of the American Academy of Neurology and the MS Council for Clinical Practice Guidelines. Neurology. 2002;58(2):169-178. [PMID: 11805241]

Hiremath GS, Cettomai D, Baynes M, et al. Vitamin D status and effect of low-dose cholecalciferol and high-dose ergocalciferol supplementation in multiple sclerosis. Mult Scler. 2009;15(6):735-740. [PMID: 19383644]

Kappos L, Radue EW, O'Connor P, et al; FREEDOMS Study Group. A placebo-controlled trial of oral fingolimod in relapsing multiple sclerosis. N Engl J Med. 2010;362(5):387-401. [PMID: 20089952]

Marriott JJ, Miyasaki JM, Gronseth G, O'Connor PW; Therapeutics and Technology Assessment Subcommittee of the American Academy of Neurology. Evidence report: The efficacy and safety of mitoxantrone (Novantrone) in the treatment of multiple sclerosis: Report of the Therapeutics and Technology Assessment Subcommittee of the American Academy of Neurology. Neurology. 2010;74(18):1463-1470. [PMID: 20439849]

Polman CH, Reingold SC, Edan G, et al. Diagnostic criteria for multiple sclerosis: 2005 revisions to the "McDonald Criteria". Ann Neurol. 2005;58(6):840-846. [PMID: 16283615]

Rutschmann OT, McCrory DC, Matchar DB; Immunization Panel of the Multiple Sclerosis Council for Clinical Practice Guidelines. Immunization and MS: a summary of published evidence and recommendations. Neurology. 2002;59(12):1837-1843. [PMID: 12499473]

Wingerchuk DM. Diagnosis and treatment of neuromyelitis optica. Neurologist. 2007;13(1):2-11. [PMID: 17215722]

### Disorders of the Spinal Cord

Bracken MB. Steroids for acute spinal cord injury. Cochrane Database Syst Rev. 2002;(3):CD001046. [PMID: 12137616]

Greenberg BM, Thomas KP, Krishnan C, Kaplin AI, Calabresi PA, Kerr DA. Idiopathic transverse myelitis: corticosteroids, plasma exchange, or cyclophosphamide. Neurology. 2007;68(19):1614-1617. [PMID: 17485649]

Jung HH, Wimplinger I, Jung S, Landau K, Gal A, Heppner FL. Phenotypes of female adrenoleukodystrophy. Neurology. 2007;68(12):960-961. [PMID: 17372139]

Narvid J, Hetts SW, Larsen D, et al. Spinal dural arteriovenous fistulae: clinical features and long-term results. Neurosurgery. 2008;62(1):159-166. [PMID: 18300903]

Patchell RA, Tibbs PA, Regine WF, et al. Direct decompressive surgical resection in the treatment of spinal cord compression caused by metastatic cancer: a randomised trial. Lancet. 2005;366(9486):643-648. [PMID: 16112300]

Transverse Myelitis Consortium Working Group. Proposed diagnostic criteria and nosology of acute transverse myelitis. Neurology. 2002;59(4):499-505. [PMID: 12236201]

### Neuromuscular Disorders

Brannagan TH 3rd. Current treatments of chronic immune-mediated demyelinating polyneuropathies. Muscle Nerve. 2009;39(5):563-578. [PMID: 19301378]

Bril V, England J, Franklin GM, et al; American Academy of Neurology; American Association of Neuromuscular and Electrodiagnostic Medicine; American Academy of Physical Medicine and Rehabilitation. Evidence-based guideline: Treatment of painful diabetic neuropathy: report of the American Academy of Neurology, the American Association of Neuromuscular and Electrodiagnostic Medicine, and the American Academy of Physical Medicine and Rehabilitation. Neurology. 2011;76(20):1758-1765. [PMID: 21482920].

Camdessanché JP, Jousserand G, Ferraud K, et al. The pattern and diagnostic criteria of sensory neuronopathy: a case-control study. Brain. 2009;132(pt 7):1723-1733. [PMID: 19506068]

England JD, Gronseth GS, Franklin G, et al; American Academy of Neurology. Practice parameter: evaluation of distal symmetric polyneuropathy: role of autonomic testing, nerve biopsy, and skin biopsy (an evidence-based review). Report of the American Academy of Neurology, American Association of Neuromuscular and Electrodiagnostic Medicine, and American Academy of Physical Medicine and Rehabilitation. Neurology. 2009;72(2):177-184. [PMID: 19056667]

Hermans G, De Jonghe B, Bruyninckx F, Van den Berghe G. Interventions for preventing critical illness polyneuropathy and critical illness myopathy. Cochrane Database Syst Rev. 2009;(1):CD006832. [PMID: 19160304]

Hughes RA, Swan AV, Raphaël JC, Annane D, van Koningsveld R, van Doorn PA. Immunotherapy for Guillain-Barré syndrome: a systematic review. Brain. 2007;130(pt 9):2245-2257. [PMID: 17337484]

Huisstede BM, Hoogvliet P, Randsdorp MS, Glerum S, van Middelkoop M, Koes BW. Carpal tunnel syndrome. Part I: effectiveness of non-surgical treatments—a systematic review. Arch Phys Med Rehabil. 2010;91(7):981-1004. [PMID: 20599038]

Huisstede BM, Randsdorp MS, Coert JH, Glerum S, van Middelkoop M, Koes BW. Carpal tunnel syndrome. Part II: effectiveness of surgical treatments—a systematic review. Arch Phys Med Rehabil. 2010;91(7):1005-1024. [PMID: 20599039]

Joy TR, Hegele RA. Narrative review: statin-related myopathy. Ann Intern Med. 2009;150(12):858-868. [PMID: 19528564]

Miller RG, Jackson CE, Kasarskis EJ, et al; Quality Standards Subcommittee of the American Academy of Neurology. Practice parameter update: the care of the patient with amyotrophic lateral sclerosis: multidisciplinary care, symptom management, and cognitive/behavioral impairment (an evidence-based review): report of the Quality

Standards Subcommittee of the American Academy of Neurology. Neurology. 2009;73(15):1227-1233. [PMID: 19822873]

Tesfaye S, Selvarajah D. The Eurodiab study: what has this taught us about diabetic peripheral neuropathy? Curr Diab Rep. 2009;9(6):432-434. [PMID: 19954687]

Thaera GM, Wellik KE, Barrs DM, Dunckley ED, Wingerchuk DM, Demaerschalk BM. Are corticosteroid and antiviral treatments effective for Bell palsy? A critically appraised topic. Neurologist. 2010;16(2):138-140. [PMID: 20220455]

Wieske L, Harmsen RE, Schultz MJ, Horn J. Is critical illness neuromyopathy and duration of mechanical ventilation decreased by strict glucose control? Neurocrit Care. 2011;14(3):475-481. [PMID: 21267673]

## Neuro-oncology

Buckner JC, Brown PD, O'Neill BP, Meyer FB, Wetmore CJ, Uhm JH. Central nervous system tumors. Mayo Clin Proc. 2007;82(10):1271-1286. [PMID: 17908533]

Dalmau J, Gleichman AJ, Hughes EJ, et al. Anti-NMDA-receptor encephalitis: case series and analysis of the effects of antibodies. Lancet Neurol. 2008;7(12):1091-1098. [PMID: 18851928]

Darnell RB, Posner JB. Paraneoplastic syndromes involving the nervous system. N Engl J Med. 2003;349(16):1543-1554. [PMID: 14561798]

Hoffman S, Propp JM, McCarthy BJ. Temporal trends in incidence of primary brain tumors in the United States, 1985-1999. Neuro Oncol. 2006;8(1):27-37. [PMID: 16443945]

Glantz MJ, Cole BF, Forsyth PA, et al. Practice parameter: anticonvulsant prophylaxis in patients with newly diagnosed brain tumors. Report of the Quality Standards Subcommittee of the American Academy of Neurology. Neurology. 2000;54(10):1886-1893. [PMID: 10822423]

Smith JS, Chang EF, Lamborn KR, et al. Role of extent of resection in the long-term outcome of low-grade hemispheric gliomas. J Clin Oncol. 2008;26(8):1338-1345. [PMID: 18323558]

Stupp R, Hegi ME, Mason WP, et al; European Organisation for Research and Treatment of Cancer Brain Tumour and Radiation Oncology Groups; National Cancer Institute of Canada Clinical Trials Group. Effects of radiotherapy with concomitant and adjuvant temozolamide versus radiotherapy alone on survival in glioblastoma in a randomised phase III study: 5-year analysis of the EORTC-NCIC trial. Lancet Oncol. 2009;10(5):459-466. [PMID: 19269895]

Surma-aho O, Niemelä M, Vilkki J, et al. Adverse long-term effects of brain radiotherapy in adult low-grade glioma patients. Neurology. 2001;56(10):1285-1290. [PMID: 11376174]

Whittle IR, Smith C, Navoo P, Collie D. Meningiomas. Lancet. 2004;363(9420):1535-1543. [PMID: 15135603]

## Brain Death

Wijdicks EF, Varelas PN, Gronseth GS, Greer DM; American Academy of Neurology. Evidence-based guideline update: determining brain death in adults: report of the Quality Standards Subcommittee of the American Academy of Neurology. Neurology. 2010;74(23):1911-1918. [PMID: 20530327]

# Neurology
# Self-Assessment Test

This self-assessment test contains one-best-answer multiple-choice questions. Please read these directions carefully before answering the questions. Answers, critiques, and bibliographies immediately follow these multiple-choice questions. The American College of Physicians is accredited by the Accreditation Council for Continuing Medical Education (ACCME) to provide continuing medical education for physicians.

The American College of Physicians designates MKSAP 16 Neurology for a maximum of 14 *AMA PRA Category 1 Credits*™. Physicians should claim only the credit commensurate with the extent of their participation in the activity.

## *Earn "Same-Day" CME Credits Online*

For the first time, print subscribers can enter their answers online to earn CME credits in 24 hours or less. You can submit your answers using online answer sheets that are provided at mksap.acponline.org, where a record of your MKSAP 16 credits will be available. To earn CME credits, you need to answer all of the questions in a test and earn a score of at least 50% correct (number of correct answers divided by the total number of questions). Take any of the following approaches:

> ➢ Use the printed answer sheet at the back of this book to record your answers. Go to mksap.acponline.org, access the appropriate online answer sheet, transcribe your answers, and submit your test for same-day CME credits. There is no additional fee for this service.

> ➢ Go to mksap.acponline.org, access the appropriate online answer sheet, directly enter your answers, and submit your test for same-day CME credits. There is no additional fee for this service.

> ➢ Pay a $10 processing fee per answer sheet and submit the printed answer sheet at the back of this book by mail or fax, as instructed on the answer sheet. Make sure you calculate your score and fax the answer sheet to 215-351-2799 or mail the answer sheet to Member and Customer Service, American College of Physicians, 190 N. Independence Mall West, Philadelphia, PA 19106-1572, using the courtesy envelope provided in your MKSAP 16 slipcase. You will need your 10-digit order number and 8-digit ACP ID number, which are printed on your packing slip. Please allow 4 to 6 weeks for your score report to be emailed back to you. Be sure to include your email address for a response.

If you do not have a 10-digit order number and 8-digit ACP ID number or if you need help creating a username and password to access the MKSAP 16 online answer sheets, go to mksap.acponline.org or email custserv@ acponline.org.

CME credit is available from the publication date of July 31, 2012, until July 31, 2015. You may submit your answer sheets at any time during this period.

**Directions**

*Each of the numbered items is followed by lettered answers. Select the **ONE** lettered answer that is **BEST** in each case.*

Self-Assessment Test

## Item 1

A 37-year-old woman is evaluated for a 1-week history of headache. She describes the headache as constant, worse when she first awakens, and characterized by a feeling of increased pressure. She reports no other focal neurologic symptoms. The patient has a 10-pack-year history of tobacco use. Her only medication is a low-dose estrogen oral contraceptive.

On physical examination, temperature is normal, blood pressure is 112/78 mm Hg, pulse rate is 62/min and regular, and respiration rate is 16/min; BMI is 37. Bilateral papilledema is noted. The Valsalva maneuver increases the headache pain. All other general and neurologic examination findings are unremarkable.

Results of laboratory studies show a normal leukocyte count, a platelet count of 322,000/μL ($322 \times 10^9$/L), an INR of 1.1, and an activated partial thromboplastin time of 36 s.

An MRI of the brain without contrast is normal.

**Which of the following is the most appropriate next diagnostic test?**

(A) Cerebral angiography
(B) Lumbar puncture
(C) Magnetic resonance venography
(D) Measurement of serum lupus anticoagulant level

## Item 2

A 71-year-old man is evaluated in the intensive care unit 11 days after undergoing surgery to relieve a bowel obstruction. His postoperative course has been complicated by septic shock and multiorgan failure, for which he has received intravenous fluids, broad-spectrum antibiotics, vasopressors, corticosteroids, and insulin. He has been on mechanical ventilation for 10 days. For the past 72 hours, he has been hemodynamically stable, but attempts at weaning him from the ventilator have been unsuccessful. The patient previously was given muscle relaxants and neuromuscular junction–blocking agents, but these have been withheld for the past 4 days.

On physical examination, the patient is alert, follows commands, and cooperates with the examiner. Vital signs are stable. Cranial nerves are intact. Flaccid quadriparesis of the upper and lower extremities is noted that is greater proximally than distally. Areflexia is present.

Results of laboratory studies show a serum creatine kinase level of 850 units/L and a plasma glucose level of 200 mg/dL (11.1 mmol/L).

Results of electromyography show absent sensory responses in the legs and low amplitudes in the hands. Short duration, low-amplitude motor units consistent with myopathy are noted.

**Which of the following is the most likely diagnosis?**

(A) Corticosteroid myopathy
(B) Critical illness myopathy
(C) Guillain-Barré syndrome
(D) Myasthenia gravis

## Item 3

A 50-year-old man is seen for a new-patient evaluation. He reports a recent diagnosis of Parkinson disease made after a 2-year history of stiffness in his right arm, a tendency to posture when walking, an awkward and stiffly inverted step when using the right leg, but no tremor. During this period, his voice became softer and slightly high pitched. The patient lost his sense of smell 10 years ago and has a 2-year history of diplopia when reading, a 9-month history of urinary urgency and impotence, and no history of dementia, depression, or psychosis. He has been taking high-dose levodopa replacement therapy since diagnosis without improvement in symptoms.

**Which of the following features in the patient's history is most suggestive of an atypical parkinsonism syndrome?**

(A) Absence of a tremor
(B) Diplopia
(C) Impotence
(D) Loss of olfaction
(E) Poor response to levodopa

## Item 4

A 50-year-old man is evaluated in the emergency department for recent onset of vomiting and a 2-week history of headache that has become progressively worse. His wife reports that for the past 2 months, he has been much clumsier than usual and has otherwise "not seemed himself." The patient has no personal or family medical history of note and takes no medication.

On physical examination, temperature is 37.2 °C (99.0 °F), blood pressure is 150/90 mm Hg, pulse rate is 110/min, and respiration rate is 13/min. Signs of left neglect are noted. Fingers in the left visual field are also not recognized. Subtle left facial weakness, a left pronator drift, and decreased sensation on the left are present. Reflexes are 1+ on the right and 3+ on the left. The left toe is upgoing.

An MRI shows a 4- × 3- × 3-cm intraparenchymal ring-enhancing lesion in the right parietal lobe with surrounding edema and areas of central necrosis and hemorrhage. A chest radiograph shows no lesion.

**Which of the following is the most likely diagnosis?**

(A) Glioblastoma multiforme
(B) Meningioma
(C) Oligodendroglioma
(D) Schwannoma

## Item 5

A 56-year-old man is evaluated in the emergency department 6 hours after onset of left hemiplegia, right gaze deviation, and dense hemineglect. The patient is fully awake. He has a history of hypertension for which he takes lisinopril.

Findings on physical examination, including vital signs, are unremarkable.

Results of laboratory studies are normal.

An electrocardiogram shows no ischemic changes. A CT scan of the head shows early infarct changes in the entire right hemisphere, and a transcranial Doppler ultrasound shows absence of flow in the right intracranial circulation.

Twelve hours later, he becomes more somnolent. On repeat examination, he does not respond to voice and withdraws weakly from pain on the right. The right pupil is large, irregular, and unresponsive. A repeat CT scan of the head shows a 9-mm midline shift and a well-demarcated right middle cerebral artery infarction.

**Which of the following is the most appropriate next step in management?**

(A) Aspirin, rectally
(B) Decompressive hemicraniectomy
(C) Dexamethasone, intravenously
(D) Intracranial pressure monitoring
(E) Lumbar puncture

## Item 6

A 78-year-old woman is evaluated in the emergency department for an 8-week history of a progressively worsening and constant daily global headache. The patient also reports fatigue and malaise but has had no fevers, nausea, photophobia, visual changes, focal weakness or numbness, or history of headaches. She has osteoarthritis for which she takes occasional acetaminophen.

On physical examination, temperature is normal, blood pressure is 130/84 mm Hg, pulse rate is 80/min, and respiration rate is 14/min. Scalp tenderness in the bilateral temporal-parietal areas is noted, but no papilledema, nuchal rigidity, or focal neurologic findings are found.

**Laboratory studies:**

| | |
|---|---|
| Erythrocyte sedimentation rate | 76 mm/h |
| Hemoglobin | 11 g/dL (110 g/L) |
| Leukocyte count | Normal, with a normal differential |
| C-reactive protein | 3 mg/dL (30 mg/L) |

**Which of the following is the most appropriate next step in management?**

(A) Cerebral angiography
(B) CT of the head
(C) Lumbar puncture
(D) Prednisone therapy

## Item 7

A 45-year-old woman is evaluated in the emergency department for headache and impaired consciousness 60 minutes after onset of symptoms. She has a history of hypertension

treated with lifestyle modification. The patient has a 20-pack-year smoking history.

On physical examination, blood pressure is 158/68 mm Hg, pulse rate is 68/min and regular, and respiration rate is 16/min. Nuchal rigidity is noted. The pupils are reactive and symmetric in size and shape. On neurologic examination, the patient requires constant painful stimuli to follow commands and answer questions and moves the left side of the body less than the right. Results of funduscopic examination are shown.

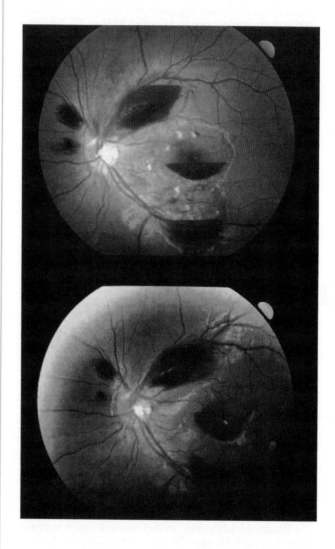

Results of laboratory studies show a platelet count of 320,000/μL (320 × 10⁹/L), an INR of 1.1, and a serum creatinine level of 1.1 mg/dL (97.2 μmol/L).

**Which of the following is the most appropriate diagnostic test?**

(A) Cerebral angiography
(B) CT of the head without contrast
(C) Lumbar puncture
(D) MRI of the brain without contrast

## Item 8

A 57-year-old man is evaluated in the emergency department 20 minutes after being found comatose in his bed. The patient has a history of hypertension, smoking, and cocaine abuse. He was intubated at the scene and is admitted to the intensive care unit.

On physical examination, the patient is unresponsive. Temperature is 35.6 °C (96.0 °F), blood pressure is 150/98 mm Hg, and pulse rate is 78/min. Neurologic examination shows unreactive dilated pupils; absent corneal, oculocephalic, and oculovestibular responses; no response to painful stimuli; no gag reflex; and no response to tracheal aspiration. Results of a repeat neurologic examination 24 hours later are unchanged.

Urine toxicology is negative for any drugs. Results of blood gas studies show an arterial $P_{CO_2}$ of 44 mm Hg (5.9 kPa) and $P_{O_2}$ of 250 mm Hg (33.3 kPa).

**Which of the following is the most appropriate next test to diagnose brain death?**

(A) Apnea test
(B) CT angiography
(C) Electroencephalography
(D) Transcranial Doppler ultrasonography

## Item 9

A 19-year-old woman is admitted to the hospital because of a 2-week history of bilateral leg weakness and numbness accompanied by urinary incontinence that began after a viral gastrointestinal illness of 3 days' duration. She has no personal or family medical history of note and takes no medication.

On physical examination, temperature is 36.7 °C (98.1 °F), blood pressure is 96/55 mm Hg, and pulse rate is 66/min. Bilateral leg weakness, loss of sensation below the umbilicus, and hyperreflexia in the lower extremities are noted.

**Laboratory studies:**

| | |
|---|---|
| Vitamin B$_{12}$ | 455 pg/mL (336 pmol/L) |
| HIV antibodies | Negative |
| Human T-lymphotropic virus antibodies | Negative |
| Cerebrospinal fluid (CSF) | |
| Leukocyte count | 45/µL (45 × 10$^6$/L) |
| Glucose | 57 mg/dL (3.2 mmol/L) |
| Protein | 65 mg/dL (650 mg/L) |
| Polymerase chain reaction | No evidence of herpes simplex virus or varicella zoster virus |

A T2-weighted MRI of the thoracic spine reveals hyperintensity in the thoracic cord at the T9 level, which enhances with administration of gadolinium. Cultures for acid-fast bacilli and CSF bacteria are negative.

High-dose intravenous methylprednisolone is administered. After 5 days, symptoms have not improved.

**Which of the following is the most appropriate next step in treatment?**

(A) Glatiramer acetate
(B) Increased dosage of methylprednisolone
(C) Methotrexate
(D) Plasmapheresis

## Item 10

A 62-year-old woman is evaluated after a recent stroke. She had an ischemic stroke 4 months ago due to 90% stenosis of the basilar artery that resulted in residual left visual field loss. The patient has hypertension, type 2 diabetes mellitus, dyslipidemia, and a 40-pack-year history of smoking. Medications are chlorthalidone, glyburide, clopidogrel, and atorvastatin.

On physical examination, blood pressure is 150/92 mm Hg sitting and standing, pulse rate is 62/min and regular sitting and standing, and respiration rate is 16/min. No carotid bruits are detected. Neurologic examination shows a left visual field cut.

Results of laboratory studies show a hemoglobin A$_{1c}$ value of 6.8%, a serum creatinine level of 1.1 mg/dL (97.2 µmol/L), and an LDL cholesterol level of 68 mg/dL (1.76 mmol/L).

An electrocardiogram shows occasional premature ventricular complexes but no atrial fibrillation.

**In addition to counseling the patient about smoking cessation, which of the following is the most appropriate treatment?**

(A) Ezetimibe
(B) Intracranial stenting
(C) Lisinopril
(D) Warfarin

## Item 11

An 18-year-old man is evaluated on the sidelines 30 minutes after sustaining a helmet-to-helmet blow to the head in a high school football game. He briefly lost consciousness on the field but was able to walk to the sidelines without assistance. Findings of a brief examination on the field were normal. The patient has no medical history of note. He asks to return to the game.

Physical examination findings, including vital signs and findings from a neurologic examination, are normal. Results of repeat sideline testing performed 30 minutes later are also normal.

**Which of the following is the most appropriate next step in management?**

(A) CT of the head
(B) Exclusion from competition for 1 week
(C) Overnight hospitalization
(D) Return to competition

## Item 12

A 24-year-old woman comes for a routine evaluation 2 weeks after having a second complex partial (focal) seizure and receiving a diagnosis of temporal lobe epilepsy. The patient was recently married and wants to have children. She takes no medication.

Physical examination findings are normal.

Results of laboratory studies, including a complete blood count and comprehensive metabolic panel, are normal.

**Which of the following drugs is most appropriate for this patient?**

(A) Carbamazepine
(B) Phenobarbital
(C) Phenytoin
(D) Valproic acid

## Item 13

A 68-year-old man is brought to the office by his wife, who expresses concern about her husband's ability to drive safely. The patient has a 6-year history of Parkinson disease. He is independent in all activities of daily living and does not have impaired mobility. He has not had any motor vehicle accidents and insists that his driving skills are good, but his wife notes that he has stopped driving in the city and seems to have trouble judging turns and parking.

On physical examination, vital signs are normal. Neurologic examination shows mild bradyphrenia (slowness of thought), good short-term recall, slight reduction in word fluency, and impaired ability to draw a cube or a clock face. He scores 27/30 on the Mini–Mental State Examination.

**Which of the following is the most appropriate recommendation regarding driving for this patient?**

(A) Continue driving if supervised
(B) Drive only during the daytime
(C) Relinquish driver's license
(D) Undergo a driving evaluation

## Item 14

A 60-year-old man is evaluated for a 4-month history of slowly progressive right hand weakness. The patient says that his recent symptoms have made it difficult to manipulate wires and grip tools when working as an electrician. He says he has no hand numbness or pain.

On physical examination, vital signs are normal. Fasciculations in the right arm and atrophy of right thenar eminence and first web space are noted. Muscle strength testing reveals decreased right grip strength, moderate weakness (4/5) of the finger abductors, and significant weakness (3/5) of right first dorsal interosseous and thumb abductor muscles. Tendon reflexes are 3+ in the right arm with brisk finger flexors and 1+ in the left arm and lower limbs. Results of a sensory examination are normal.

**Which of the following is the most likely diagnosis?**

(A) Amyotrophic lateral sclerosis
(B) Carpal tunnel syndrome
(C) Cervical radiculopathy
(D) Neuralgic amyotrophy

## Item 15

A 71-year-old woman is evaluated in the emergency department 90 minutes after onset of left-sided weakness and slurred speech. She has a history of type 2 diabetes mellitus. Medications are glyburide and metformin.

On physical examination, blood pressure is 178/80 mm Hg, pulse rate is 60/min and regular, and respiration rate is 16/min. No carotid bruits are heard. On neurologic examination, left facial weakness and left arm and leg weakness are noted; weakness is more pronounced in the left arm than left leg.

Laboratory studies:

| | |
|---|---|
| Activated partial thromboplastin time | 36 s |
| Platelet count | 410,000/µL ($410 \times 10^9$/L) |
| INR | 0.9 |
| Creatinine | 1.1 mg/dL (97.2 µmol/L) |

A CT scan of the head without contrast is normal.

Six hours after infusion of intravenous recombinant tissue plasminogen activator, her blood pressure is 190/90 mm Hg and pulse rate is 68/min; the neurologic examination findings are unchanged except for increasing anxiousness.

**Which of the following is the most appropriate next step in treatment?**

(A) Aspirin
(B) Cryoprecipitate
(C) Diazepam
(D) Nicardipine
(E) Nitroprusside

## Item 16

A 56-year-old man is evaluated for a 6-month history of generalized fatigue, slowly progressive weakness in the legs, difficulty climbing stairs and raising his arms above his head, and a 2-month history of dry mouth and impotence. He reports that on two occasions in the past month he almost lost consciousness when rising quickly from a sitting position. The patient has a 38-pack-year smoking history.

On physical examination, blood pressure in the right arm is 130/80 sitting and 100/60 standing and pulse rate is 80/min and regular sitting and 84/min and regular standing. Muscle strength testing reveals moderate weakness in the arms and proximal legs, especially when the patient rises from a low chair. Repeated testing slightly improves strength. Stretch reflexes are diffusely reduced or absent but increase to normal after brief exercise. Results of cranial nerve testing, cerebellar function testing, and sensory testing are normal.

Results of laboratory studies show an erythrocyte sedimentation rate of 75 mm/h and a serum creatine kinase level of 120 units/L.

A chest radiograph is suspicious for left hilar lymphadenopathy.

**Which of the following diagnostic tests should be performed next?**

(A) Acetylcholine receptor antibody assay
(B) Lumbar puncture
(C) Muscle biopsy
(D) Nerve conduction studies

## Item 17

A 76-year-old man is evaluated in the emergency department for a 36-hour history of right-sided weakness and difficulty speaking. The patient has hypertension and atrial fibrillation. He also has a 45-pack-year history of smoking. His usual medications are metoprolol, hydrochlorothiazide, amlodipine, and warfarin.

On physical examination, blood pressure is 118/62 mm Hg, pulse rate is 86/min and irregular, and respiration rate is 16/min. Bilateral carotid bruits are noted. Cardiac auscultation reveals an irregularly irregular rhythm with variable intensity of $S_1$. All other general physical examination findings are normal. On neurologic examination, aphasia, a right visual field cut, and right arm weakness are noted.

**Laboratory studies:**

| | |
|---|---|
| INR | 1.5 |
| Platelet count | 190,000/µL (190 × 10⁹/L) |
| Creatinine | 0.9 mg/dL (79.6 µmol/L) |
| LDL cholesterol | 50 mg/dL (1.30 mmol/L) |

A CT scan of the head shows an acute infarct in the left frontal lobe involving one third of the middle cerebral artery distribution.

**Which of the following is the most appropriate treatment?**

(A) Aspirin
(B) Intravenous heparin
(C) Simvastatin
(D) Subcutaneous low-molecular-weight heparin

## Item 18

A 78-year-old woman is evaluated in the emergency department for a 1-week history of progressive agitation and confusion. She has no history of fever or falling episodes. The patient lives in a nursing home, has advanced dementia, and is dependent on others for all activities of daily living. She can indicate when she needs to void and generally is not incontinent. She can ambulate with a cane but must be accompanied because of a tendency to wander. Although she enjoys being around others and can make simple conversation with family members and nursing home personnel, she does not recognize anyone by name or remember what was said. She has a history of osteoarthritis, hypertension, atrial fibrillation, anxiety, and depression. There have been no recent additions or changes to her medications, which are hydrochlorothiazide, warfarin, amitriptyline, alprazolam, and oxybutynin.

Physical examination is noncontributory.

Results of a complete blood count, comprehensive metabolic profile, and urinalysis are normal. A chest radiograph reveals no evidence of infection or heart failure.

**Which of the following is most appropriate as an initial step in management?**

(A) Add donepezil
(B) Add risperidone
(C) Discontinue anticholinergic and sedative medications
(D) Obtain an electroencephalogram

## Item 19

A 45-year-old man is evaluated for a 2-week history of recurring headaches characterized by severe unilateral pain in the orbitotemporal region that last from 30 to 45 minutes and are associated with ipsilateral tearing and a clear nasal discharge. The pain seems to intensify when he is supine and causes him to rock or pace throughout the room. He had similar headaches 3 years ago, but a head CT at that time showed normal findings. He has a 4-year history of hypertension treated with amlodipine and a 20-pack-year smoking history. His mother has a history of migraine.

On physical examination, temperature is 37.2 °C (99.0 °F), blood pressure is 140/90 mm Hg, pulse rate is 84/min, and respiration rate is 14/min. General and neurologic examination findings are normal.

**Which of the following is the most appropriate acute headache treatment?**

(A) Amoxicillin
(B) Hydrocodone
(C) Oral sumatriptan
(D) Oxygen
(E) Verapamil

## Item 20

A 32-year-old woman is evaluated in the emergency department for an episode of loss of consciousness that occurred 20 minutes ago after a routine blood draw. Witnesses saw her fall to the ground and then shake all four extremities violently for 15 seconds; she regained consciousness quickly. The patient recalls feeling sweaty and light-headed for approximately 2 minutes before losing consciousness. She has had a diarrheal illness for the past 2 days. She has had similar feelings when having her blood drawn but has never lost consciousness before. The patient has no other significant medical history and takes no medication.

On physical examination, vital signs are normal, with no evidence of orthostatic hypotension. General physical and neurologic examination findings are normal.

Results of laboratory studies, including a complete blood count, a basic metabolic panel, liver chemistry studies, plasma glucose level, and urine toxicology, are normal. Measurement of human chorionic gonadotropin level is negative for pregnancy.

A CT scan of the head is normal.

**Which of the following is the most appropriate initial management?**

(A) Initiation of levetiracetam and outpatient electroencephalography (EEG)

**CONT.**

(B) Initiation of valproic acid and outpatient EEG
(C) Measurement of serum prolactin level
(D) Outpatient EEG and MRI of the brain
(E) Reassurance

## Item 21

A 30-year-old woman is evaluated for a 4-week history of generalized twitching and hand clumsiness. For the past month, she has been dropping objects, although she reports no weakness in her hands. She is in the second trimester of her second pregnancy. Personal and family medical history is unremarkable, with no history of movement disorders. The patient takes no medication.

On physical examination, vital signs are normal. Generalized random, flowing, twitching movements of her fingers, limbs, and toes are noted. Her gait is narrow based with frequent jerks.

Urinalysis results are normal.

**Which of the following is the most likely diagnosis?**

(A) Chorea gravidarum
(B) Huntington disease
(C) Systemic lupus erythematosus
(D) Tardive dyskinesia

## Item 22

A 32-year-old woman is evaluated in the hospital for a series of explosive holocranial headaches occurring 1 day after the uncomplicated delivery of her third child. The first headache occurred while she was nursing the newborn, lasted 90 minutes, and resolved without sequelae. She was aroused from a nap by a similar episode the next morning and had a third attack that evening. She has a history of migraine but describes these recent headaches as being different in quality. Her only medications have been prenatal vitamins with iron and vitamin D.

On physical examination, temperature is 37.5 °C (99.5 °F), blood pressure is 112/62 mm Hg, pulse rate is 70/min, and respiration rate is 14/min. All other findings from the general physical and neurologic examinations are normal.

A CT scan of the head with contrast is normal. Results of a lumbar puncture are shown.

**Cerebrospinal fluid:**

| | |
|---|---|
| Erythrocytes | 12/µL (12 × 10⁶/L) |
| Leukocytes | 2/µL (2 × 10⁶/L) |
| Glucose | 60 mg/dL (3.3 mmol/L) |
| Protein | 40 mg/dL (400 mg/L) |
| Pressure (opening) | Normal |

**Which of the following is the most appropriate next step in management?**

(A) Brain MRI
(B) Cerebrovascular imaging
(C) Indomethacin
(D) Sumatriptan

## Item 23

A 27-year-old woman is evaluated 4 hours after she awoke with drooping of the left face, inability to close the left eye, mild numbness and tingling of the left cheek, dizziness, nausea, a mild headache, a dry mouth, and increased sensitivity to noise. Two weeks ago, she had a flulike illness with rhinorrhea, a sore throat, and a cough that resolved spontaneously. She has a history of uncomplicated migraine for which she takes acetaminophen as needed.

On physical examination, vital signs are normal. No lesions of the skin or mucous membranes are noted. Neurologic examination reveals severe weakness of the left upper and lower facial muscles and an inability to close the left eye completely. Sensory examination shows that facial sensation is normal bilaterally. The remainder of the neurologic examination is unremarkable.

**Which of the following is the most appropriate treatment?**

(A) Acyclovir
(B) Intravenous methylprednisolone
(C) Prednisone
(D) Sumatriptan

## Item 24

A 56-year-old woman is evaluated in the emergency department for sudden onset of a severe generalized headache that began 36 hours ago and has not responded to over-the-counter medications. The patient has a history of hypertension treated with lifestyle modifications. She has a 30-pack-year smoking history.

On physical examination, blood pressure is 148/68 mm Hg, pulse rate is 96/min and regular, and respiration rate is 16/min. Nuchal rigidity is noted. Other general examination findings are normal.

Results of laboratory studies are notable for a platelet count of 190,000/µL (190 × 10⁹/L), an INR of 0.9, and a serum creatinine level of 0.9 mg/dL (79.6 µmol/L).

A CT scan of the head without contrast is normal.

**Which of the following is the most appropriate next diagnostic test?**

(A) CT of the head with contrast
(B) Lumbar puncture
(C) Magnetic resonance angiography of the head and neck
(D) MRI of the brain without contrast

## Item 25

A 76-year-old woman is evaluated in the emergency department for a 2-week history of difficulty walking and four episodes of falling backward. The patient was previously mobile and independent with the use of a walker. She has an 8-year history of Parkinson disease characterized by bilateral tremors at rest, generalized bradykinesia and rigidity, start hesitation and freezing, postural instability, and a tendency to retropulse. She also has osteoarthritis of the knees and spine but no dementia. Medications are levodopa-carbidopa and acetaminophen.

Physical examination reveals a thin, alert patient with a kyphotic posture. Vital signs are normal. Bilateral mild hand tremors at rest, neck flexion, and a markedly increased neck tone are noted. The legs are stiff, with three beats of clonus elicited by ankle dorsiflexion, and the toes are upgoing. The arms and hands have normal strength. Sensory examination shows decreased vibration perception to the mid-shins. Her deep tendon reflexes are brisk, with spread, and the plantar responses are extensor. She has difficulty lifting her legs off the gurney and is unable to stand because of leg weakness. On tests of repetitive actions, such as finger tapping, the patient exhibits slowness and decrementing. Gait and balance cannot be tested because of her inability to stand.

**Which of the following is the most appropriate next step in management?**

(A) CT myelography
(B) Head CT
(C) Increased dosage of levodopa-carbidopa
(D) Lumbar puncture
(E) MRI of the cervical spine

## Item 26

A 30-year-old man is examined during a new-patient evaluation. He has a 16-year history of seizures characterized by an uncomfortable feeling in his stomach followed by smacking movements of his lips and impaired awareness for 1 to 2 minutes. The patient had a febrile convulsion at age 2 years but has had no convulsions since that time. He has taken valproic acid, gabapentin, and levetiracetam for his seizures but continues to have at least four seizures annually. He currently takes levetiracetam.

Physical examination findings are noncontributory.

An electroencephalogram shows right temporal epileptiform sharp waves. An MRI is shown.

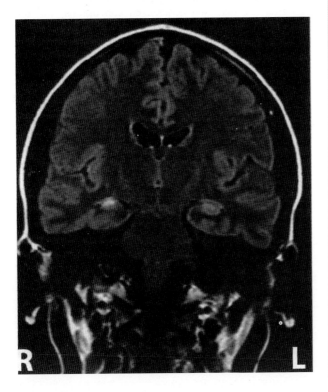

**Which of the following treatments is most likely to lead to seizure remission?**

(A) Addition of carbamazepine to the levetiracetam
(B) Corpus callosotomy
(C) Right temporal lobectomy
(D) Substitution of carbamazepine for levetiracetam
(E) Vagal nerve stimulation

## Item 27

A 16-year-old girl is evaluated in the emergency department for a 3-day history of fever and a 2-day history of headache, visual loss in the right eye, stumbling gait, and confusion. She was previously healthy and takes no medication.

On physical examination, temperature is 38.7 °C (101.7 °F), blood pressure is 95/50 mm Hg, pulse rate is 105/min, and respiration rate is 18/min. Neurologic examination shows impaired mental status with poor attentiveness, orientation to name only, and 0/3 recall of listed objects at 3 minutes. Visual acuity is 20/200 in the right eye with a right afferent pupillary defect. Examination of the extremities shows hyperreflexia and 4/5 left arm and leg muscle strength.

An analysis of cerebrospinal fluid (CSF) from a lumbar puncture shows a leukocyte count of 93/μL ($93 \times 10^6$/L), with 90% lymphocytes; a glucose level of 56 mg/dL (3.1 mmol/L); and a protein level of 82 mg/dL (820 mg/L). Bacterial cultures are negative for any organisms, and a polymerase chain reaction performed on the CSF is negative for herpes simplex virus.

T2-weighted and fluid-attenuated inversion recovery (FLAIR) MRIs of the brain and orbits show multiple large hyperintense lesions throughout the bilateral periventricular and subcortical areas. Contrast administration shows gadolinium uptake in the right optic nerve and in many of the periventricular and subcortical lesions.

**Which of the following is the most likely diagnosis?**

(A) Acute disseminated encephalomyelitis
(B) Bacterial meningitis
(C) Herpes encephalitis
(D) Multiple sclerosis
(E) Neuromyelitis optica

## Item 28

A 56-year-old man is evaluated for increasing frequency and intensity of headaches. He has a 20-year history of sporadic headaches that for the past 6 months have escalated in frequency to several times per month, without significant change in quality. The headaches frequently develop in the afternoon, worsen in the evening, and typically resolve during sleep. Discomfort is moderate in intensity, is described as tightness in the occipital and temporal regions, and is not disabling. Phonophobia is minimal and nausea and photophobia are absent. The patient also reports neck stiffness. Acetaminophen was previously effective but no longer relieves his symptoms.

On physical examination, vital signs are normal. Tenderness is noted in the paraspinal cervical muscles with normal cervical range of motion. Neurologic examination findings are normal.

Head CT scans, with and without contrast, are normal.

**Which of the following is the most appropriate next step in management?**

(A) Amitriptyline, daily
(B) Cyclobenzaprine
(C) Ibuprofen
(D) MRI of the cervical spine
(E) Physical therapy

## Item 29

A 34-year-old woman is evaluated for a 3-day history of partial vision loss in the left eye and pain on movement of that eye. She has a history of migraine. Her only medication is ibuprofen as needed for headache.

On physical examination, temperature is 37.2 °C (99.0 °F), blood pressure is 105/60 mm Hg, pulse rate is 60/min, and respiration rate is 12/min; BMI is 28. Visual acuity is 20/200 in the left eye and 20/30 in the right eye. A left afferent pupillary defect is noted. Funduscopic examination shows no papilledema.

An MRI of the left orbit shows contrast enhancement of the left optic nerve. An MRI of the brain shows three white matter lesions, each measuring approximately 3 mm; two of these lesions are periventricular.

**After acute management with intravenous methylprednisolone, which of the following is the most appropriate long-term management?**

(A) Daily acetazolamide
(B) Initiation of glatiramer acetate
(C) Intranasal sumatriptan, as needed
(D) Repeat MRI of the brain every 6 months

## Item 30

A 68-year-old man is evaluated for memory loss. He still teaches history at the local university, supervises graduate students, and writes chapters of textbooks. He reports having difficulty remembering the names of his students and colleagues, forgetting telephone numbers, and often misplacing his glasses. The patient has not experienced confusion and has no history of depression, hallucinations, or head trauma. He drives, manages his own financial affairs, and is fully independent.

Physical examination shows an anxious-appearing man. Vital signs are normal, as are other findings from the general physical examination. He scores 29/30 on the Mini–Mental State Examination.

**Which of the following is the most appropriate next step in management?**

(A) Brain MRI
(B) Determination of apolipoprotein E4 status

(C) Formal neuropsychological testing
(D) Trial of donepezil
(E) Reassurance

## Item 31

An 86-year-old woman is evaluated in the emergency department 60 minutes after onset of difficulty speaking and right arm weakness. The patient has a 5-year history of atrial fibrillation for which she takes warfarin. She has no history of previous stroke or gastrointestinal or genitourinary bleeding.

On physical examination, blood pressure is 170/100 mm Hg and pulse rate is 86/min and irregular. Neurologic examination shows global aphasia, right hemiparesis, left gaze preference, and a right visual field cut.

Laboratory studies show an INR of 1.1, a platelet count of 180,000/μL ($180 \times 10^9$/L), and a fasting plasma glucose level of 120 mg/dL (6.7 mmol/L).

A CT scan of the head shows no acute infarct or hemorrhage.

**Which of the following is the most appropriate next step in treatment?**

(A) High-dose aspirin
(B) Intravenous heparin
(C) Intravenous recombinant tissue plasminogen activator
(D) Labetalol

## Item 32

A 25-year-old woman is examined during a routine evaluation. Idiopathic generalized epilepsy was diagnosed 2 years ago after she had two generalized convulsions, and the patient began taking lamotrigine. She had two more seizures the following year but has been seizure free since her lamotrigine dosage was increased last year to 150 mg twice daily.

Physical examination findings, including vital signs, are normal.

She wishes to begin a combined oral contraceptive.

**Which of the following is the best management of her antiepileptic drug regimen?**

(A) Increase the dosage of lamotrigine
(B) Switch to carbamazepine
(C) Switch to phenytoin
(D) Switch to topiramate
(E) Make no change in her antiepileptic drug therapy

## Item 33

A 72-year-old man is evaluated for a 2-month history of hallucinations. He describes frequently seeing small imaginary animals resembling badgers in the house, a situation he finds annoying rather than threatening. His wife notes that he often points out strangers in the backyard, but no one is ever there. These visions may occur at any time of the day but are especially prevalent in the evening. Additionally, the patient often has disturbed sleep, screaming out as if engaged in a chase or combat; these episodes frighten his wife, but he has no recollection of nightmares the next morning. He has a history of parkinsonism characterized by slowness, stiffness, a stooped posture, and a tendency to shuffle when he is tired. History is otherwise unremarkable. He has not taken any medication, including levodopa, for the parkinsonism but goes to physical therapy twice a week.

Results of physical examination are unremarkable.

**Which of the following is the most likely diagnosis?**

(A) Alzheimer disease
(B) Dementia with Lewy bodies
(C) Frontotemporal dementia
(D) Neurosyphilis

## Item 34

A 57-year-old man has a follow-up evaluation 3 months after discharge from the hospital, where he was treated for an ischemic stroke. He has a history of hypertension, dyslipidemia, and peripheral arterial disease for which he has required no revascularization procedures. Medications are enalapril, hydrochlorothiazide, rosuvastatin, and aspirin.

On physical examination, blood pressure is 138/68 mm Hg, pulse rate is 68/min and regular, and respiration rate is 16/min. Cardiac examination reveals no carotid bruits. Neurologic examination shows only a right pronator drift.

Results of laboratory studies show a platelet count of 340,000/μL (340 × 10⁹/L), a serum creatinine level of 1.1 mg/dL (97.2 μmol/L), and an LDL cholesterol level of 68 mg/dL (1.76 mmol/L).

A head CT scan and a brain MRI show a left pontine infarct. An electrocardiogram shows normal sinus rhythm with no ischemic changes. A transthoracic echocardiogram and a magnetic resonance angiogram of the head and neck are normal.

**Which of the following is the most appropriate treatment?**

(A) Add clopidogrel
(B) Add ticlopidine
(C) Add warfarin
(D) Substitute clopidogrel for aspirin
(E) Substitute warfarin for aspirin

## Item 35

A 56-year-old woman is evaluated in the emergency department for a 3-week history of progressively frequent headaches. The episodes now recur once or twice per hour and have an average duration of 10 to 15 minutes. She describes the headache pain as intense, searing, localized to the right periorbital region, and associated with drooping of the right eyelid, swelling and redness of the right eye, tearing, and nausea. NSAIDs and opiate analgesic agents have not relieved her symptoms.

On physical examination, blood pressure is 136/92 mm Hg and pulse rate is 76/min. Examination of the eyes reveals subtle right ptosis and miosis. All other physical examination findings are normal.

Laboratory studies show a normal erythrocyte sedimentation rate.

An MRI of the brain with contrast is normal.

**Which of the following is the most appropriate treatment?**

(A) Carbamazepine
(B) Indomethacin
(C) Prednisone
(D) Topiramate
(E) Verapamil

## Item 36

A 34-year-old woman is evaluated in the emergency department for acute onset of a severe headache. She has hypertension treated with lisinopril.

On physical examination, blood pressure is 160/100 mm Hg, pulse rate is 78/min, and respiration rate is 12/min. General medical examination findings are normal. Neurologic examination shows that she is somnolent but readily arousable, with symmetric and briskly reactive pupils and a left arm drift.

Results of routine laboratory studies are normal.

A CT scan of the head shows a subarachnoid hemorrhage, with a thick clot in the right sylvian fissure, but no hydrocephalus or cerebral edema. Angiography shows a 10-mm right middle cerebral artery aneurysm.

The patient undergoes urgent aneurysmal clipping with no complications and is started on nimodipine. She is transferred to the intensive care unit and has no further symptoms until 6 days after initial evaluation, when she is less responsive and has new left arm paralysis on neurologic examination.

**Which of the following is the most appropriate next diagnostic step?**

(A) CT angiography of the head
(B) Electroencephalography
(C) Lumbar puncture
(D) MRI of the brain

## Item 37

A 42-year-old woman is evaluated for a 3-month history of increasingly frequent headaches and a 1-month history of daily bilateral frontotemporal discomfort. The patient began having headache attacks 9 years ago after the birth of her second child. Episodes originally occurred once or twice monthly and were initially characterized by unilateral severe throbbing pain, nausea with vomiting, and photophobia. Occasionally, a visual aura of "spinning tops" preceded the headache pain by 45 minutes, with the headache extending for 36 to 48 hours, but she has experienced no auras in the past 6 months. Visual blurring now accompanies her headaches intermittently but daily. Although previously helpful, oral triptans have not provided any relief over the past 3 months. Medications are oral zolmitriptan, a monophasic oral contraceptive, and a daily aspirin-aceta-minophen-caffeine combination.

Physical examination results, including vital signs and findings from a neurologic examination, are unremarkable.

A CT of the head obtained 9 years ago when the headaches began was normal.

**Which of the following is the most appropriate next step in management?**

(A) Analgesic discontinuation
(B) Erythrocyte sedimentation rate determination
(C) Lumbar puncture
(D) MRI of the brain

## Item 38

A 53-year-old woman is evaluated in the emergency department for a 2-day history of low back pain, generalized weakness, gait imbalance, and dizziness on standing. Three weeks ago, she had an acute gastrointestinal illness with diarrhea, nausea, vomiting, and abdominal bloating that resolved after 1 week. She says she now has no abdominal symptoms.

On physical examination, temperature is normal, blood pressure is 125/80 mm Hg supine and 100/60 mm Hg standing, pulse rate is 90/min supine and 95/min standing, and respiration rate is 18/min. Muscle strength testing reveals diffuse weakness, especially of the distal lower limbs (ankle dorsiflexor strength, 4/5). Stretch reflexes are absent. Sensory examination findings are normal.

**Laboratory studies:**

| | |
|---|---|
| Erythrocyte sedimentation rate | 12 mm/h |
| Hemoglobin | 12.8 g/dL (128 g/L) |
| Leukocyte count | 8400/µL (8.4 × 10⁹/L) |
| Platelet count | 300,000/µL (300 × 10⁹/L) |
| Protein | 4 g/dL (40 g/L) |
| Antinuclear antibody titer | 1:40 |
| Urinalysis | Normal |
| Cerebrospinal fluid analysis | |
|   Erythrocyte count | 1/µL (1 × 10⁶/L) |
|   Leukocyte count | 0 |
|   Glucose | 30 mg/dL (1.7 mmol/L) |
|   Protein | 15 mg/dL (150 mg/L) |
|   Gram stain | Negative for organisms |

A chest radiograph is normal.

**Which of the following is the most likely diagnosis?**

(A) Acute transverse myelitis
(B) Guillain-Barré syndrome
(C) Leptomeningeal sarcoidosis
(D) Polyarteritis nodosa

## Item 39

A 58-year-old woman is seen for a follow-up evaluation of Parkinson disease, which she has had for 12 years. She was initially treated with ropinirole to which levodopa-carbidopa was added as the disease progressed. After 5 years of good control on medication, she began to experience involuntary

generalized twisting and writhing movements after taking each dose of levodopa-carbidopa and noticed that the medication's effect waned after several hours.

Over the past 2 years, she has tried to manage her disease by taking higher and more frequent doses of levodopa-carbidopa, a long-acting preparation of levodopa-carbidopa, entacapone to prolong the levodopa effect, and amantadine for choreic movements. She now requires medication treatment every 2 hours and has twisting and writhing with each dose. Her symptoms vary between good mobility, accompanied by generalized and at times ballistic movements, and wearing-off motor fluctuations, with generalized tremors, slowness, and gait impairment.

**Which of the following is the best treatment for this patient?**

(A) Deep brain stimulation
(B) Gene therapy
(C) Physical therapy and use of a walker or wheelchair
(D) Supervised discontinuation of all medications followed by gradual reintroduction

## Item 40

A 59-year-old woman is evaluated in the emergency department for a 4-day history of low back pain, leg weakness, and urinary incontinence. She was discharged from the hospital 1 week ago after undergoing a lumbar diskectomy as treatment for lumbosacral radiculopathy. Additional history includes nonvalvular atrial fibrillation with good systolic function and hypertension. Medications are warfarin, metoprolol, and acetaminophen as needed.

On physical examination, temperature is 36.6 °C (97.9 °F), blood pressure is 145/65 mm Hg, and pulse rate is 68/min. Strength testing reveals 3/5 weakness in the right leg and 4/5 weakness in the left leg. Reflexes are 2+ in the arms, 1+ in the left patellar region, and 0 in the right patellar region and bilateral Achilles tendons. Laxity of the anal sphincter is noted.

Laboratory studies show an erythrocyte sedimentation rate of 3 mm/h, a leukocyte count of 5800/µL (5.8 × 10⁹/L), and an INR of 3.0.

MRIs of the lumbosacral spine show a compressive epidural lesion at L2 through L5, which is isointense with slight contrast enhancement on a T1-weighted scan and hyperintense on a T2-weighted scan.

**Which of the following is the most appropriate management?**

(A) Add high-dose intravenous methylprednisolone
(B) Add intravenous vancomycin and ceftazidime
(C) Discontinue warfarin and reverse the anticoagulation
(D) Perform a lumbar puncture

## Item 41

A 78-year-old woman is evaluated in the emergency department 12 hours after onset of left-sided weakness and slurred speech. She reports being unable to swallow water at home. She has a history of hypertension and type 2 diabetes mellitus, both of which she tries to control with lifestyle modifications.

On physical examination, blood pressure is 190/90 mm Hg, pulse rate is 68/min and regular, and respiration rate is 16/min. Cardiac examination reveals no carotid bruits. Neurologic examination reveals facial weakness on the left side, severe dysarthria, left-sided hemiplegia, left-sided sensory loss, and normal mental status.

Results of laboratory studies show a serum creatinine level of 1.1 mg/dL (97.2 μmol/L) and no serum troponins; urinalysis findings are normal.

A CT scan of the head shows a faint hypodensity in the right posterior limb of the internal capsule. An electrocardiogram shows normal sinus rhythm with no ischemic changes. A chest radiograph is normal.

**Which of the following is the most appropriate treatment of this patient's elevated blood pressure?**

(A) Intravenous hydralazine
(B) Oral candesartan
(C) Oral labetalol
(D) Oral nitroglycerin
(E) No treatment is required

## Item 42

A 62-year-old man is evaluated for worsening cognition. He has a history of mild dementia. His daughter, who brought him to the office, says that he does not recognize her anymore but believes instead that she is an imposter who looks and sounds like his daughter but is actually a stranger trying to deceive him. She further states that her father does not believe his house is the same one he has lived in for the past 40 years. When she points to family portraits and other personal items, he states that someone put them there to trick him. The situation is very distressing to both father and daughter.

**Which of the following is the most likely diagnosis?**

(A) Anosognosia
(B) Capgras syndrome
(C) Confabulation
(D) Reduplicative paramnesia

## Item 43

A 50-year-old man is examined in the hospital for sudden onset of tonic-clonic movements of all four extremities that have continued for more than 5 minutes. He had a biopsy of a tumor on the right temporal lobe 2 days ago. The patient has a history of hypertension treated with lisinopril. His only other medication in the hospital is hydrocodone.

On physical examination, the patient is diaphoretic and intermittently exhibiting leftward head and eye deviation associated with asynchronous clonic jerking of the extremities. Blood pressure is 150/90 mm Hg, pulse rate is 120/min, and respiration rate is 22/min.

Blood glucose level by fingerstick measurement is 70 mg/dL (3.9 mmol/L). Results of other laboratory tests are pending.

**Which of the following is the most appropriate first-line treatment?**

(A) Levetiracetam
(B) Lorazepam
(C) Phenytoin
(D) Valproic acid

## Item 44

A 30-year-old woman is evaluated for a 1-year history of fatigue, headaches, poor sleep, depression, intermittently blurred vision, and weakness when climbing stairs. She takes no medication.

On physical examination, vital signs are normal. Bilateral ptosis and diplopia are noted, but funduscopy findings are normal. Strength testing reveals mild weakness of the hip flexors. Tendon stretch reflexes are normal, as are results of a sensory examination.

Results of laboratory studies are positive for autoantibodies directed against muscle-specific tyrosine kinase receptors but are negative for antibodies against the acetylcholine receptor.

**Which of the following diagnostic tests should be performed next?**

(A) CT of the chest
(B) Edrophonium test
(C) Lumbar puncture
(D) MRI of the brain

## Item 45

A 32-year-old woman is evaluated in the emergency department for a 3-day history of a shooting, electrical sensation radiating down her back with neck movements, a 1-week history of progressively worsening numbness and weakness of the right arm and leg, and a 3-month history of significant daytime fatigue. Twelve years ago, she had ocular pain and blurry vision in the right eye for 1 week but never sought medical attention. Family history is significant for two strokes in her father and type 2 diabetes mellitus and hypertension in her mother. She takes no medication.

On physical examination, blood pressure is 105/50 mm Hg, pulse rate is 80/min, and respiration rate is 14/min. Weakness of the right arm and leg is observed. Testing of reflexes shows hyperreflexia on the right side with an upgoing toe. Sensory testing reveals a loss of pinprick sensation on the right side below the C5 dermatome. No visual field or language deficits are noted.

**On the basis of her history and clinical findings, which of the following is the most likely diagnosis?**

(A) Cardioembolic stroke
(B) Cervical disk herniation
(C) Complex migraine
(D) Multiple sclerosis

## Item 46

A 19-year-old woman is evaluated in the emergency department for a 6-month history of occasional headache that became daily 3 months ago. She describes the headache pain as a band of tightness extending around her skull that is moderately intense in the morning but fluctuates in intensity throughout the day. She has noted occasional visual blurring during the day and a rhythmic "whooshing" sound in her ears at night. Neck stiffness has increased over the past few weeks. Her only medication is acetaminophen, which she takes 1 to 2 days per week.

On physical examination, temperature is 37.5 °C (99.5 °F), blood pressure is 126/80 mm Hg, pulse rate is 66/min, and respiration rate is 12/min; BMI is 34. Neurologic examination reveals papilledema and partial left cranial nerve VI palsy. No other cranial nerve findings are present, and there is no nuchal rigidity.

Laboratory studies show a normal leukocyte count with a normal differential.

An MRI and a magnetic resonance venogram of the brain are normal.

**Which of the following is the most appropriate diagnostic test to perform next?**

(A) Carotid ultrasonography
(B) CT of the sinuses
(C) Lumbar puncture
(D) MRI of the cervical spine

## Item 47

A 22-year-old woman is evaluated in the emergency department after having a new-onset convulsion. Three weeks ago, she had a flulike illness with muscle aches. Since that time, her family and friends have noticed that she has been behaving oddly, accusing her boyfriend of stealing from her and saying she thought she heard a radio announcer in her head who was "playing tricks" with her memory. Medical history is significant for a benign ovarian teratoma.

On physical examination, temperature is 36.7 °C (98.0 °F), blood pressure is 110/60 mm Hg, pulse rate is 90/min, and respiration rate is 14/min. Intermittent involuntary chewing movements of the mouth are noted.

A lumbar puncture is performed.

**Cerebrospinal fluid analysis:**

| | |
|---|---|
| Erythrocytes | 0 |
| Leukocytes | 11/µL (11 × 10⁶/L), with 100% lymphocytes |
| Glucose | 70 mg/dL (3.9 mmol/L) |
| Protein | 55 mg/dL (550 mg/L) |

A fluid-attenuated inversion recovery MRI shows increased signals in both mesial temporal lobes.

**Which of the following is the most likely diagnosis?**

(A) Anti-Hu paraneoplastic encephalitis
(B) Anti–NMDA receptor encephalitis
(C) Herpes encephalitis
(D) Viral meningitis

## Item 48

A 65-year-old man is reevaluated 4 days after being hospitalized for an intracerebral hemorrhage of the right putamen diagnosed on a CT scan. He has a history of poorly controlled hypertension, for which he currently takes enalapril and hydrochlorothiazide, and chronic kidney disease. On admission, the dosages of his antihypertensive medications were increased, and labetalol was added.

On physical examination, blood pressure is 118/62 mm Hg, pulse rate is 86/min and regular, and respiration rate is 16/min; his blood pressure has been less than 130/80 mm Hg for the past 36 hours. No lower extremity edema is noted. On neurologic examination, dysarthria and complete paralysis of the left face, arm, and leg are noted.

**Laboratory studies:**

| | |
|---|---|
| Activated partial thromboplastin time | 36 s |
| INR | 0.9 |
| Platelet count | 410,000/µL (410 × 10⁹/L) |
| Creatinine | 3.2 mg/dL (283 µmol/L) |

Two subsequent head CT scans obtained 1 and 3 days after admission showed no expansion of the hematoma. A magnetic resonance angiogram shows no evidence of an aneurysm or a vascular malformation.

**Which of the following is the most appropriate prophylaxis for the prevention of venous thromboembolism?**

(A) Graded elastic pressure stockings
(B) Low-dose warfarin
(C) Placement of an inferior vena cava filter
(D) Subcutaneous unfractionated heparin

## Item 49

A 47-year-old woman is evaluated for a 6-month history of severe fatigue in the afternoon that is often disabling. The patient has a 15-year history of multiple sclerosis. She states that her mood is good and that she is not feeling depressed or sad. She describes no problems with her sleep, and her partner reports no unusual movements or apnea spells. In the morning, she feels well rested. Medications are glatiramer acetate, low-dose baclofen, and a daily multivitamin.

Physical and neurologic examination findings, including vital signs, are normal.

Results of laboratory studies show a hemoglobin level of 12.9 g/dL (129 g/L), a normal mean corpuscular volume, and a serum thyroid-stimulating hormone level of 1.3 µU/mL (1.3 mU/L).

**Which of the following is the most appropriate treatment of her fatigue?**

(A) Amantadine
(B) Iron supplementation
(C) Levothyroxine
(D) Memantine
(E) Substitution of an interferon beta for glatiramer acetate

## Item 50

A 65-year-old man is evaluated for a 4-month history of numbness in the right hand and arm, a tremor in the right hand, and general difficulty using the right hand. The patient, who is right handed, first became aware of awkwardness when attempting to write. He gradually developed difficulty eating with utensils, cutting with scissors, and brushing his teeth. He is otherwise healthy, has no toxic habits, and takes no medication.

On physical examination, vital signs are normal. The right hand is curled into a flexed posture in the patient's lap. Occasional myoclonic jerks are noted in the right arm. Hand grasp is firm, and hand muscles appear strong. The patient can slowly elevate the hand and hold the fingers outstretched but is unable to use the hand in any task. When asked to pantomime how to cut a loaf of bread, he makes rough chopping motions that do not convey the idea of cutting. Although he can detect pinprick, light touch, and proprioception in his right hand, he cannot guess the shape of an object placed in his palm or identify a letter sketched into his palm. Findings from an examination of the left hand are normal, as is the rest of the neurologic examination.

**Which of the following is the most likely diagnosis?**

(A) Alien hand syndrome
(B) Apraxia
(C) Asomatognosia
(D) Hemiparkinsonism

## Item 51

A 45-year-old man is evaluated for a 12-month history of increasingly severe, frequent migraine. The patient has a 25-year history of migraine characterized by a dull throbbing over one side of his head, nausea, and sensitivity to noise and light. These headaches previously occurred a few times each year and typically resolved after a nap or with ibuprofen but, over the past year, have been occurring one to two times per week. Medical history is significant for kidney stones that have been treated twice with lithotripsy.

Physical examination findings and results of laboratory studies are normal.

**Which of the following drugs given for migraine prophylaxis is contraindicated in this patient?**

(A) Amitriptyline
(B) Propranolol
(C) Topiramate
(D) Valproic acid

## Item 52

An 80-year-old woman is evaluated for slowly progressive gait impairment. Over the past year, she has developed a slow shuffling gait and occasional hesitation or freezing when initiating steps that is more pronounced with turning in a tight space or moving through a doorway. She also has developed urinary urgency and frequency, with two episodes of incontinence in the past 9 months. The patient

reports that her friends have told her she seems less outgoing and much quieter in conversation than before. She believes that her cognition is normal, and she manages all her own affairs. She has no other neurologic symptoms.

Physical examination shows a slightly stooped older woman. Vital signs are normal, as are speech and mental status. Gait assessment reveals a narrow-based gait with a tendency to hesitate on initiating the first step. On the pull test, she takes too many steps backward but recovers.

**Which of the following is the most appropriate first step in management?**

(A) MRI of the brain
(B) Serial lumbar punctures
(C) Single-photon emission CT
(D) Trial of levodopa

## Item 53

A 30-year-old woman is evaluated for episodic migraine without aura that first presented in high school and has persisted into the third trimester of her current pregnancy. The headache attacks occur two to four times monthly and last 12 to 24 hours. She experiences moderately severe pain, significant nausea, no vomiting, and pronounced photophobia with most of the attacks. Her only medication is prenatal vitamins.

Physical examination findings, including vital signs, are normal.

**Which of the following is the most appropriate treatment?**

(A) Acetaminophen
(B) Amitriptyline
(C) Naproxen
(D) Oxygen
(E) Rizatriptan

## Item 54

A 17-year-old boy is evaluated for a 3-month history of involuntary sounds and movements and repetitive coughing. His parents report several other repetitive behaviors, including frequent eye blinking, facial grimacing, rocking back and forth, and tapping of his knuckles on tables in an exact rhythmic pattern. These behaviors are most prevalent in the afternoon after school and sometimes last for 20 minutes. When asked why he performs these movements, the patient says that he "can't resist an urge to let them come out," that he feels better after he releases them, and that he can temporarily suppress them at any time. In school, he has always been a good student who is attentive and has never been disruptive; his teachers have observed no abnormal movements in class. He is sociable and has many friends. He had pharyngitis 2 months ago but currently takes no medication. His father had a transient tic during childhood.

On physical examination, vital signs are normal. The patient exhibits no abnormal movements or behaviors, except when asked to demonstrate them.

**Which of the following is the most appropriate treatment?**

(A) Clonidine
(B) Haloperidol
(C) Tetrabenazine
(D) Reassurance

## Item 55

A 76-year-old man is evaluated for an episode of left-handed weakness involving all five digits that occurred yesterday and gradually subsided over 3 hours. He has had two similar episodes in the past 2 weeks. He reports no other problems and has no pertinent personal or family medical history. An exercise stress test performed 1 year ago had normal results. His only medication is aspirin, 81 mg/d.

On physical examination, blood pressure is 156/78 mm Hg and pulse rate is 76/min and regular. Cardiac examination reveals a right carotid bruit. Other physical examination findings are normal.

Results of laboratory studies show a serum LDL cholesterol level of 156 mg/dL (4.04 mmol/L).

An electrocardiogram shows normal sinus rhythm with no evidence of ischemia. A carotid duplex ultrasound shows 80% to 99% stenosis of the right internal carotid artery, which is confirmed by CT angiography. An MRI of the brain shows a 5-mm infarct in the right middle cerebral artery distribution.

**Which of the following will have the greatest impact in reducing the risk of recurrent stroke in this patient?**

(A) Carotid endarterectomy
(B) Carotid stenting
(C) Clopidogrel
(D) Simvastatin

## Item 56

A 28-year-old man is evaluated for a constant, global, bandlike headache of mild intensity and for slight photophobia without phonophobia or nausea. He recently completed 10 years of military service with recent tours of duty in a combat zone. During combat, he received minor injuries when exposed to enemy fire and experienced transient hearing loss after a tank he was riding in struck an explosive device. Since that event, he has had intermittent vertigo, tinnitus, minor difficulties with concentration, and increased irritability. He has had no nightmares, his sleep has been normal, and he has no ongoing concerns about the trauma or any "reliving" of the event.

Physical and neurologic examination findings are normal, as are results of laboratory studies.

**Which of the following is the most likely diagnosis?**

(A) Meniere disease
(B) Migraine headache
(C) Postconcussion syndrome
(D) Posttraumatic stress disorder
(E) Tension-type headache

## Item 57

A 62-year-old woman is evaluated in the stroke unit for a 2-day history of difficulty speaking and right arm weakness. She has a history of hypertension and dyslipidemia and a 35-pack-year smoking history. Medications are lisinopril, atenolol, simvastatin, and aspirin.

On physical examination, blood pressure is 148/78 mm Hg, pulse rate is 84/min and regular, and respiration rate is 12/min. Other general medical examination findings are normal. Neurologic examination shows mild sensory aphasia and right arm drift.

An MRI of the brain shows an acute infarct in the left middle cerebral artery distribution that appears embolic. A magnetic resonance angiogram of the head and neck is normal. An electrocardiogram shows sinus rhythm and is normal. Telemetry performed over the next 3 days shows occasional premature ventricular complexes. A transesophageal echocardiogram shows no intracardiac thrombus, normal left atrial appendage velocities, and a patent foramen ovale with an atrial septal aneurysm. No evidence of deep venous thrombosis is found.

**Which of the following is the most appropriate next step in management?**

(A) Percutaneous patent foramen ovale closure
(B) Prolonged cardiac rhythm monitoring
(C) Surgical closure of the patent foramen ovale
(D) Warfarin

## Item 58

A 28-year-old man is evaluated for a 5-year history of recurrent headache that occurs several times per month and lasts 12 to 24 hours. He describes the headache as a bilateral frontal pressure associated with nasal congestion and sensitivity to light, sound, and smell. The pain is generally moderate in intensity but worsens when he bends forward or exercises and has caused him to miss 3 days of work recently. He has no nausea or visual or neurologic symptoms. The patient has a history of nonseasonal allergic rhinitis treated with pseudoephedrine and loratadine and a family history of headaches in his paternal grandmother. His only other medication is naproxen, which he takes as needed for the headache pain but has become less effective over time.

Physical examination findings, including vital signs and results of neurologic examination, are normal.

**Which of the following is the most appropriate management of this patient's disorder?**

(A) CT scan of the sinuses
(B) MRI of the brain
(C) Nasal corticosteroids
(D) Oxycodone
(E) Sumatriptan

## Item 59

A 35-year-old woman is evaluated for a 2-year history of insomnia. She reports experiencing unpleasant crawling sensations in her legs that prevent her from falling asleep. Although she has had similar symptoms since her late 20s, they were initially infrequent and mild. In recent years, the sensations have become more distressing and prevalent, occurring almost every night and sometimes on airplane trips and long car rides. The only medication that has brought any relief is codeine. Her grandmother experienced similar sensations.

Results of physical examination, including vital signs, are normal. Her neurologic examination findings are also normal, with no evidence of parkinsonism, peripheral neuropathy, or systemic illness.

**Which of the following is the most likely diagnosis?**

(A) Akathisia
(B) Nocturnal leg cramps
(C) Nocturnal myoclonus
(D) Restless legs syndrome

## Item 60

A 68-year-old woman is assessed for falling risk. She has fallen backward three times in the past 6 months. The patient additionally reports general unsteadiness, which causes her to hold onto railings tightly. She otherwise feels well and takes no medication.

On physical examination, vital signs are normal. A cautious narrow-based gait, stooped posture, and decreased arm swing are noted.

**Which of the following physical examination evaluations will most accurately predict her future falling risk?**

(A) Dix-Hallpike maneuver
(B) Proprioception
(C) Pull test
(D) Romberg test

## Item 61

A 20-year-old man is evaluated in the emergency department for a witnessed convulsive seizure while eating breakfast. He says he was out late drinking with friends the night before. The patient never previously has had convulsions but reports often dropping things in the morning because of sudden uncontrollable jerks of his hand and arm. He also has been told that he occasionally "zones out" for approximately 10 seconds at a time. His mother has a history of two tonic-clonic seizures and similar symptoms in the morning.

On physical examination, temperature is 37.2 °C (99.0 °F), blood pressure is 130/80 mm Hg, pulse rate is 95/min, and respiration rate is 16/min. General and neurologic physical examination findings are normal.

Results of laboratory studies show a blood ethanol level of 20 mg/dL (4.3 mmol/L) and normal complete blood count, basic metabolic panel, and liver chemistry studies. A fingerstick blood glucose measurement is 92 mg/dL (5.1 mmol/L).

A CT scan of the head is normal.

**Which of the following is the most likely diagnosis?**

(A) Childhood absence epilepsy
(B) Juvenile myoclonic epilepsy
(C) Seizure related to alcohol
(D) Temporal lobe epilepsy

## Item 62

An 82-year-old woman is evaluated during a routine examination. She reports no symptoms in the past 6 months and says she feels well. She has hypertension, New York Heart Association functional class II heart failure, type 2 diabetes mellitus, dyslipidemia, and COPD. Medications are aspirin, losartan, carvedilol, furosemide, metformin, and albuterol, as needed. She was taking simvastatin but stopped 2 months ago because of joint pains. At that time, her serum creatine kinase level was 86 units/L.

On physical examination, vital signs are normal. Cardiopulmonary examination reveals a left carotid bruit and end-expiratory wheezes. On neurologic examination, her Mini–Mental State Examination score is 25/30; all other findings are normal.

Results of laboratory studies show a serum total cholesterol level of 242 mg/dL (6.27 mmol/L), an LDL cholesterol level of 142 mg/dL (3.68 mmol/L), and an HDL cholesterol level of 36 mg/dL (0.93 mmol/L).

A magnetic resonance angiogram of the neck shows 60% stenosis of the left internal carotid artery, and an MRI of the brain shows moderate cerebral atrophy.

**Which of the following is the most appropriate next step in treatment?**

(A) Add pravastatin
(B) Change aspirin to clopidogrel
(C) Perform carotid artery stenting
(D) Perform carotid endarterectomy

## Item 63

A 39-year-old man is evaluated for a 5-month history of stiffness when walking and leg pain that is worse in the evening. He has a 7-year history of multiple sclerosis. Medications are interferon beta-1a and vitamin D.

On physical examination, temperature is 37.1 °C (98.8 °F), blood pressure is 125/60 mm Hg, and pulse rate is 66/min. Stiffness and tightening of the muscles in the lower extremities that are more pronounced with passive movement are noted. Reflexes are 3+ in the lower extremities with upgoing toes bilaterally. Gait examination shows a stiff-legged appearance when the patient walks.

Laboratory studies show a serum creatine kinase level of 35 units/L.

**Which of the following is the most appropriate management?**

(A) Electromyography (nerve conduction study)
(B) MRI of the lumbosacral spine
(C) Oxybutynin administration
(D) Tizanidine administration

## Item 64

A 32-year-old man is evaluated in the emergency department for a 12-hour history of severe agitation and tremors. The patient has a history of developmental delay and chronic schizoaffective disorder and resides in a group home. Medications are lithium, valproic acid, and fluphenazine.

Physical examination shows an agitated overweight man in three-point restraints. Temperature is 39.4 °C (103.0 °F), blood pressure is 110/65 mm Hg, and pulse rate is 110/min. Generalized tremors, rigidity, agitation, and diaphoresis are noted.

Results of laboratory studies show a serum creatine kinase level of 1480 units/L.

**Which of the following is the most likely diagnosis?**

(A) Lithium intoxication
(B) Malignant hyperthermia
(C) Neuroleptic malignant syndrome
(D) Serotonin syndrome

## Item 65

A 46-year-old woman is admitted to the stroke unit for new-onset left hemiparesis and left-sided neglect.

On physical examination, temperature is normal, blood pressure is 140/78 mm Hg, pulse rate is 68/min, and respiration rate is 12/min. Cardiopulmonary examination is normal. Other notable findings are a right carotid bruit, right Horner syndrome, left visual and tactile extinction, left facial weakness, dysarthria, and left arm and leg weakness (strength, approximately 3/5). On bedside dysphagia screening, she is unable to safely swallow water and has a mild cough.

Results of laboratory studies show an INR of 1.1, a serum creatinine level of 0.9 mg/dL (79.6 µmol/L), and an LDL cholesterol level of 68 mg/dL (1.76 mmol/L).

A CT scan of the head shows a right middle cerebral artery infarction. An MRI of the neck shows an intraluminal thrombus consistent with internal carotid artery dissection.

Low-molecular-weight heparin is started.

**Which of the following is the most appropriate next step in management?**

(A) Amoxicillin-clavulanate
(B) Early rehabilitation
(C) Modafinil
(D) Stenting of the internal carotid artery

## Item 66

A 25-year-old man is evaluated for a 4-month history of gait impairment. He began having difficulty walking after a marble countertop slipped off a packing crate onto his right leg at work. The patient sustained a large bruise and swelling but no fracture. Over the next 3 days, he limped on his right foot. Gradually, he developed a tendency for the right leg to jerk and "give out" with weight-bearing. Despite trials of physical therapy, exercise, and muscle relaxants, his leg jerks and gait steadily worsened.

Physical examination shows an articulate, pleasant man who can sit comfortably in a chair. Vital signs are normal. Leg tenderness, joint swelling, muscle atrophy, and musculoskeletal deformity are absent, and leg strength, deep tendon reflexes, plantar responses, and sensory examination findings are normal. The patient performs the heel-to-shin test and toe tapping test without difficulty. When he tries to stand, he reports discomfort on weight bearing and lurches from side to side when he walks; both knees have a tendency to buckle as he walks. He can perform tandem walking but sways markedly and almost falls, recovering by grasping the walls. On the pull test, his legs nearly collapse but he recovers.

**Which of the following is the most likely diagnosis?**

(A) Peripheral injury dystonia
(B) Posttraumatic stress syndrome with dystonia
(C) Psychogenic gait
(D) Reflex sympathetic dystrophy

## Item 67

A 65-year-old man is examined during a new-patient evaluation. He has a history of a left parietal stroke and has had two complex partial seizures characterized by a burning sensation in his right arm followed by impaired attention and automatisms. The patient is right-handed. His only medication is aspirin.

On physical examination, vital signs are normal. Right inferior quadrantanopia and decreased sensation in the right face and arm are noted.

Results of laboratory studies, including a complete blood count and comprehensive metabolic panel, are normal.

A CT scan shows a chronic infarct in the left parietal lobe.

**Which of the following is the most appropriate drug for this patient?**

(A) Carbamazepine
(B) Lamotrigine
(C) Oxcarbazepine
(D) Phenytoin

## Item 68

A 76-year-old man is evaluated in the emergency department for a 3-day history of severe pain and spasms in his neck and lower back, mild dizziness when standing or walking, and some mental cloudiness. He attributes these symptoms to a low-velocity automobile collision he was involved in 4 days ago. He has no focal weakness or numbness and no alterations in his vision or speech. The patient has a history of atrial fibrillation treated with digoxin, warfarin, and metoprolol.

On physical examination, blood pressure is 142/80 mm Hg and pulse rate is 74/min and irregular. Paraspinal muscle spasms in the cervical and lumbosacral areas are present. Examination of the extremities shows normal reflexes and sensory and motor findings. A mildly ataxic gait is noted.

Which of the following is the most appropriate initial step in management?

(A) CT of the head
(B) Cyclobenzaprine
(C) Meclizine
(D) Physical therapy

## Item 69

A 22-year-old man is evaluated for muscle jerks. Three months ago, he was hospitalized with primary respiratory arrest after a drug overdose; resuscitation had been started 2 minutes after his collapse. He was in a coma on a ventilator for 3 weeks and developed diffuse jerking of all limbs, especially the legs, as he emerged from the coma. He gradually returned to a normal level of cognition but cannot walk or use his hands because of muscle jerks.

Physical examination shows a thin, pleasant man sitting quietly in a wheelchair. No muscle jerks or tremors at rest are noted. When the patient lifts his arms, he exhibits shock-like proximal jerks. The finger-to-nose test is disrupted by superimposed muscle jerks. On standing, he experiences leg and trunk jerks and sudden lapses in muscle tone.

**Which of the following is the most likely diagnosis?**

(A) Cerebellar (spinocerebellar) degeneration
(B) Myoclonic epilepsy
(C) Posthypoxic myoclonus
(D) Wernicke encephalopathy

## Item 70

A 44-year-old woman is evaluated for a 30-year history of severe headache that occurs once or twice per month and lasts 1 to 2 days. The headache pain affects the left side of her head, is pulsating in nature, and is associated with nausea and photophobia. Once or twice each year, the attacks are preceded by 30 minutes of unilateral flashing lights followed by partial visual loss. Several different NSAIDs have been ineffective; she currently takes ibuprofen as needed.

On physical examination, vital signs are normal. Findings from the general physical examination, including a neurologic examination, also are normal.

An MRI of the brain performed 1 year ago after a 1-hour episode of partial visual loss showed several punctate white matter hyperintensities. A transthoracic echocardiogram also obtained at that time showed a small patent foramen ovale.

**Which of the following is the most appropriate treatment?**

(A) Butalbital with acetaminophen and caffeine
(B) Daily aspirin
(C) Foramen ovale closure
(D) Propranolol
(E) Sumatriptan

## Item 71

A 32-year-old woman is evaluated for a 5-year history of seizures characterized by violent shaking of all limbs and sometimes by incontinence and impaired consciousness. The seizures typically last 5 to 15 minutes and occur several times per month. Multiple trials of antiepileptic drugs, including valproic acid, pregabalin, and levetiracetam, have been ineffective in controlling the seizures.

On physical examination, vital signs are normal; BMI is 25. All other general physical and neurologic examination findings are normal.

A brain MRI and an electroencephalogram (EEG) obtained 2 years ago were normal.

**Which of the following tests is most likely to provide a definitive diagnosis?**

(A) Ambulatory EEG monitoring over 24 hours
(B) Inpatient video EEG monitoring
(C) Repeat brain MRI
(D) Repeat outpatient EEG

## Item 72

A 21-year-old woman is evaluated during her spring break from college. Her only symptom is a recent change in her handwriting, which has become smaller and harder to read. The patient states that she enjoys her classes, but her parents, who accompanied her, are concerned that she is becoming depressed and overwhelmed by her workload and that she seems to be "slowing down." She has no history of toxic exposures, weight loss, infection, headache, or trauma.

Physical examination shows a pleasant, serious young woman in no distress. Vital signs are normal. No cognitive deficits are noted. Facial expressivity is diminished, and the blink rate is reduced. Her voice is soft, and she has excess saliva. A glabellar sign is present. Motor examination shows increased tone in the arms. Finger tapping movements are slow and decremental, and arm swing is reduced when she walks.

**Which of the following is the most appropriate next step in management?**

(A) Genetic test for the *LRRK2* mutation
(B) Psychiatric evaluation
(C) Serum carboxyhemoglobin measurement
(D) Serum ceruloplasmin measurement

## Item 73

A 46-year-old man is evaluated in the emergency department 4 hours after onset of right-sided weakness and slurred speech. He has a history of hypertension, type 2 diabetes mellitus, and an ischemic stroke 2 years ago with excellent recovery. He stopped his medications 6 months ago.

On physical examination, the patient is awake and interactive. Blood pressure is 170/100 mm Hg, pulse rate is 102/min and regular, and respiration rate is 16/min. No carotid bruits are heard. On neurologic examination, he has slurred speech and makes occasional paraphasic errors. A right visual field cut and right arm and leg drift are noted. The patient has normal results of a bedside dysphagia evaluation.

Laboratory studies:

| | |
|---|---|
| Activated partial thromboplastin time | 36 s |
| INR | 0.9 |
| Platelet count | 410,000/μL (410 × 10⁹/L) |
| Creatinine | 2.1 mg/dL (186 μmol/L) |
| LDL cholesterol | 190 mg/dL (4.92 mmol/L) |
| Troponins | Normal |

A CT scan of the head without contrast shows a loss of the left insular ribbon. A magnetic resonance angiogram confirms severe extracranial carotid artery stenosis. An electrocardiogram is normal.

**Which of the following is the most appropriate next step in treatment?**

(A) Atorvastatin
(B) Intravenous recombinant tissue plasminogen activator
(C) Nicardipine
(D) Warfarin

## Item 74

A 56-year-old man is evaluated for a 2-week history of diffuse myalgia and gradually increasing weakness. The myalgia is significant and interferes with his daily activities. The patient has a history of hypothyroidism and hyperlipidemia. Four weeks ago, he started taking itraconazole for a confirmed diagnosis of fungal onychomycosis. Other medications are levothyroxine and simvastatin.

On physical examination, vital signs are normal. Muscle strength testing reveals mild proximal limb weakness. Hyporeflexia of the stretch reflexes is noted. Changes consistent with onychomycosis are present in the third and fourth toenails, bilaterally.

Results of laboratory studies show a hemoglobin level of 13.2 g/dL (132 g/L), a thyroid-stimulating hormone level of 3.0 μU/mL (3.0 mU/L), and a creatine kinase level of 934 units/L; 6 months ago, the creatine kinase level was 120 units/L.

**Which of the following is the most appropriate management of this patient's disorder?**

(A) Decrease levothyroxine dosage
(B) Discontinue simvastatin and itraconazole
(C) Measure serum 1,25-dihydroxyvitamin D level
(D) Obtain a muscle biopsy

## Item 75

A 32-year-old woman is evaluated for worsening headache. She has a 19-year history of migraine with aura that started with menarche. The patient describes recurrent attacks of pulsatile pain on the left side of her head that last 1 or 2 days and are often accompanied by nausea, vomiting, and disability.

The episodes are occasionally preceded by 50 minutes of partial visual loss surrounded by colorful lights and occasionally complicated by ipsilateral facial or upper extremity numbness lasting 60 to 90 minutes. Her attacks have become more frequent and now occur two to three times per week. She also has a severe headache for 4 days during menses. The episodes are responsive to oral sumatriptan. Her mother had a stroke at age 50 years. Her only medication is sumatriptan.

Physical examination findings, including vital signs, are normal.

An MRI of the brain is normal.

**Which of the following is the most appropriate next step in the management of this patient's migraine?**

(A) Butalbital with acetaminophen and caffeine
(B) Lumbar puncture
(C) Naproxen sodium daily
(D) Oral contraceptives
(E) Topiramate

## Item 76

A 67-year-old man is evaluated for a 2-year history of increasing forgetfulness and withdrawal from social activities that started when he retired. According to his wife, he seldom leaves the house since retirement and seems confused, at times repeating questions or having difficulty retrieving words. His gait has become slow and shuffling, and he has toppled backward on two occasions; he also often drops food from his plate into his lap. She further reports that his conversation has become sparse and that he sometimes says no when he means yes. The patient does not read anymore because he loses track of the lines of print.

On physical examination, vital signs are normal. Generalized slowness, marked rigidity of the neck, and a wide-eyed staring facial expression are noted. When he looks straight ahead, inappropriate saccades cause his eyes temporarily to jerk off target (square wave jerks). He has difficulty looking up or down fully. Speech is soft, hoarse, and dysarthric. No tremor is detected. He has a narrow-based gait with decreased arm swing, en bloc turning, and hesitation on turning. A pull test shows a tendency to retropulse. On mental status examination, the patient's responses are slow but usually accurate. Errors in short-term memory, word fluency, and tests of spatial processing, such as copying a cube, are noted.

Results of laboratory studies and neuroimaging are pending.

**Which of the following is the most likely diagnosis?**

(A) Alzheimer disease
(B) Dementia with Lewy bodies
(C) Parkinson disease
(D) Progressive supranuclear palsy

## Item 77

A 63-year-old man is evaluated in the emergency department for a 2-day history of mid-back pain, leg weakness, and urinary incontinence. He was treated with surgical

**CONT.**

resection for prostate cancer 1 year ago. He has no other medical history of note.

On physical examination, temperature is 36.8 °C (98.2 °F), blood pressure is 138/60 mm Hg, and pulse rate is 94/min. Bilateral leg weakness, decreased sensation to pinprick below the T9 level, and mild laxity of the anal sphincter are noted.

Laboratory studies show a serum prostate-specific antigen level of 34 ng/mL (34 µg/L) and a normal complete blood count.

An MRI of the thoracic spine shows a contrast-enhancing epidural lesion causing spinal cord compression.

**In addition to starting intravenous corticosteroids, which of the following interventions is likely to provide the best chance for future ambulation in this patient?**

(A) Androgen-deprivation therapy
(B) Chemotherapy
(C) Decompressive surgery
(D) Radiation therapy

## Item 78

A 58-year-old man is evaluated in the emergency department for a change in mental status. His family members report that over the past 5 weeks, he has become progressively withdrawn and irritable, sometimes erupting in violent outbursts, and occasionally has exhibited jerking movements. He no longer has any desire to groom himself or eat and soils himself rather than using the bathroom. The patient has stopped participating in conversation and rarely indicates his own thoughts or needs. He becomes belligerent when approached by anyone, including family members. He was previously healthy and held a highly demanding job. He has a 33-pack-year smoking history and used to drink a martini every evening but stopped smoking and drinking alcohol 5 weeks ago. He takes no medication.

Physical examination shows a disheveled and cachectic man lying in a fetal position who refuses to participate in the examination. Vital signs are normal. He tracks the examiner with his eyes and blinks when he senses a threat in all quadrants. He has a glabellar sign, snout reflex, palmomental reflexes, and bilateral grasp reflexes. He is thin but exhibits normal strength. On sensory testing, he withdraws briskly to pinprick stimulation. He grasps the examiner's hands tightly in an attempt to stand but retropulses.

An MRI of the brain is normal.

**Which of the following is the most likely diagnosis?**

(A) Alzheimer disease
(B) Creutzfeldt-Jakob disease
(C) Frontotemporal dementia
(D) Herpes simplex encephalitis

## Item 79

A 73-year-old woman is evaluated in the emergency department for left-sided weakness that began 36 hours ago. She reports no changes in her vision or speech. The patient has

a history of hypertension and coronary artery disease. Medications are aspirin, losartan, metoprolol, and atorvastatin.

On physical examination, blood pressure is 160/78 mm Hg, pulse rate is 78/min and regular, and respiration rate is 16/min. Other findings from the general medical examination are normal. Neurologic examination shows severe paralysis of the left face, arm, and leg.

Results of laboratory studies are normal.

A CT scan of the head shows an infarct in the right posterior limb of the internal capsule. An electrocardiogram is normal.

**Which of the following is the most appropriate immediate next step in management?**

(A) Admit to a stroke unit
(B) Admit to rehabilitation
(C) Admit to the general medical ward
(D) Admit to the medical intensive care unit

## Item 80

A 37-year-old woman is evaluated for worsening multiple sclerosis (MS). She has had three relapses in the past year that were treated with corticosteroids. A recent MRI showed additional ovoid lesions since diagnosis. The patient also has a history of major depression treated with paroxetine. She has taken glatiramer acetate since MS was diagnosed 1 year ago. The decision is made to change the patient's MS medication from glatiramer acetate to natalizumab.

Physical examination findings, including vital signs, are normal.

Results of laboratory studies are normal.

**Which of the following is a potential complication of her new therapy?**

(A) Dose-dependent cardiotoxicity
(B) Flulike symptoms
(C) Progressive multifocal leukoencephalopathy
(D) Skin lipoatrophy
(E) Worsening of her underlying depression

## Item 81

A 56-year-old man is evaluated in the emergency department 7 hours after onset of right-sided weakness. He has a history of hypertension and osteoarthritis. Medications are hydrochlorothiazide and daily aspirin.

On physical examination, the patient is fully awake and interactive. Blood pressure is 220/110 mm Hg, pulse rate is 86/min and regular, and respiration rate is 16/min. No papilledema is detected. Neurologic examination findings include slurred speech, a lack of movement in the right arm, trace antigravity movement in the right leg, and profound sensory loss to all modalities on the right side.

Results of laboratory studies show an INR of 1.2, a platelet count of 375,000/µL (375 × 10⁹/L), and a serum creatinine level of 1.4 mg/dL (124 µmol/L). Urine toxicology results are positive for cocaine.

**CONT.** A CT scan of the head without contrast shows a right thalamic intracerebral hemorrhage with intraventricular extension and mild enlargement of the ventricles.

**Which of the following is the most appropriate treatment?**

(A) External ventricular drain placement
(B) Labetalol infusion
(C) Metoprolol intravenously
(D) Platelet transfusion

## Item 82

A 24-year-old woman is evaluated for a 3-week history of painful muscle spasms and twisting movements in the neck and trunk. She says that her neck feels as if it is being pulled backward. She also reports general restlessness and an inability to keep still. Her medical history is notable for asthma, type 1 diabetes mellitus, and gastroparesis with reflux. The patient has no family history of neuropsychiatric disorders or liver disease. Medications are albuterol, insulin, omeprazole, and metoclopramide.

On physical examination, vital signs are normal. When the patient is seated, her neck pulls backward and her chin elevates; mild grimacing movements also are noted. On standing and walking, her trunk arches backward, sometimes with her arms pulling forward.

**Which of the following is the most likely diagnosis?**

(A) Huntington disease
(B) Juvenile Parkinson disease
(C) Tardive dystonia
(D) Wilson disease

## Item 83

A 27-year-old man is evaluated for a 16-year history of gradually worsening headache. He describes attacks of severe periorbital throbbing pain that occurs exclusively on the left, lasts 6 to 8 hours, and is accompanied by slight nausea, bilateral tearing, and moderate sensitivity to light and sound. The frequency of these attacks has increased to 15 days per month. High-dose ibuprofen and naproxen have become less effective in relieving the pain over the past year. The patient also has asthma treated with albuterol and salmeterol-fluticasone. He has no symptoms of depression.

Findings on physical examination, including vital signs, and neurologic examination are normal.

Results of laboratory studies also are normal.

**Which of the following is the most appropriate treatment?**

(A) Amitriptyline
(B) Fluoxetine
(C) Propranolol
(D) Verapamil
(E) Vitamin D

## Item 84

A 65-year-old man is evaluated for a 2-month history of odd behavior. He is a retired high school principal and has a 5-year history of Parkinson disease. According to his wife, his lifelong interest in repairing household items has lately escalated out of control. Increasingly, the patient starts new tasks he never completes, staying up all night taking apart appliances and furniture but never fixing or reassembling them, and leaves parts strewn throughout the house. The patient insists that he is making necessary repairs and will soon put everything back together. His Parkinson symptoms remain well controlled with ropinirole and levodopa-carbidopa. His motor function is generally good, and he is able to function independently.

On physical examination, temperature is 36.7 °C (98.1 °F), blood pressure is 126/80 mm Hg sitting and standing, pulse rate is 72/min, and respiration rate is 16/min; BMI is 27.

**Which of the following is the most likely cause of this patient's symptoms?**

(A) Dementia with Lewy bodies
(B) Dopamine agonist medication
(C) Frontotemporal dementia
(D) Progression of Parkinson disease

## Item 85

A 35-year-old man is evaluated in the emergency department after having a seizure. His wife, who witnessed the event, reports that he had involuntary movements of his left arm followed by a tonic-clonic seizure. His medical history is otherwise unremarkable. He emigrated from China 18 years ago.

On physical examination, vital signs are normal. Other findings include a left pronator drift and an upgoing toe on the left.

Results of laboratory studies, including a complete blood count, comprehensive metabolic panel, blood ethanol level, and urine toxicology screen, are normal.

A CT scan of the head shows a small right frontal meningioma.

**Which of the following drugs should be started in the emergency department?**

(A) Carbamazepine
(B) Lamotrigine
(C) Levetiracetam
(D) Oxcarbazepine
(E) Phenytoin

## Item 86

A 75-year-old woman is evaluated for a 60-minute episode of right arm weakness and dysarthria. The symptoms have not recurred. She has hypertension and type 2 diabetes mellitus. Medications are aspirin, metoprolol, enalapril, and metformin.

On physical examination, blood pressure is 156/94 mm Hg, pulse rate is 62/min and regular, and respiration rate is 16/min. No carotid bruits are noted. Neurologic examination findings are normal.

Results of laboratory studies obtained 3 weeks ago show a hemoglobin $A_{1c}$ value of 7.1% and a serum LDL cholesterol level of 68 mg/dL (1.76 mmol/L).

**Which of the following is the most appropriate next step in management?**

(A) Addition of clopidogrel
(B) Immediate hospital admission
(C) Outpatient MRI of the brain
(D) 24-Hour electrocardiographic monitoring

## Item 87

A 63-year-old man is evaluated for a 2-week history of low back pain, occasional numbness and intense pain of the left anterior thigh, buckling of the left knee, chronic paresthesias of the feet, and difficulty walking. The thigh pain keeps him up at night. His gait has worsened over the past 2 days because of intermittent pain in the right leg. Six weeks ago, he developed a severe flulike illness with symptoms of nausea, vomiting, diarrhea, and a 6.8-kg (15.0-lb) weight loss. He has a 2-year history of diet-controlled type 2 diabetes mellitus. His only medication is codeine.

On physical examination, vital signs are normal; BMI is 31. The patient uses a cane when walking and has an antalgic gait. Atrophy of the left anterior thigh muscles is noted. Muscle strength testing reveals marked weakness of hip flexors (3/5 on the left and 4/5 on the right) and of knee extensors (3/5 on the left and 4/5 on the right). Muscle strength in the ankle dorsiflexors is 5/5, bilaterally. The patellar stretch reflex is absent on the left and normal on the right. Achilles reflexes are diminished bilaterally. Sensory examination reveals decreased sensation to light touch and pinprick over the left anteromedial thigh but normal findings in the bilateral legs and feet.

Results of laboratory studies show a hemoglobin $A_{1c}$ value of 7.5%

**Which of the following is the most likely diagnosis?**

(A) Diabetic amyotrophy
(B) Diabetic polyneuropathy
(C) Guillain-Barré syndrome
(D) Meralgia paresthetica

## Item 88

A 45-year-old woman is reevaluated for a long-standing history of headaches that started in her teenage years and are associated with her menses. She says that the headaches changed in quality 6 weeks ago and are now present once weekly. Her menses have become more irregular. She has a history of hypertension and a 20-pack-year history of smoking. Family history is notable only for migraines. Medications are hydrochlorothiazide, propranolol, and NSAIDs for symptomatic headache relief.

On physical examination, blood pressure is 138/78 mm Hg, pulse rate is 62/min and regular, and respiration rate is 16/min. All other general and neurologic examination findings are normal.

An MRI and magnetic resonance angiogram of the brain reveal a 4-mm right middle cerebral artery aneurysm but are otherwise normal.

**Which of the following is the most appropriate management?**

(A) Aneurysmal clipping
(B) Endovascular coiling
(C) Repeat neuroimaging in 5 years
(D) Tobacco cessation counseling

## Item 89

A 42-year-old man is evaluated for a 4-day history of progressively worsening imbalance and vertigo accompanied by repeated falls. He has a 6-year history of multiple sclerosis. Medications are interferon beta-1a and gabapentin for occasional neuropathic pain.

On physical examination, temperature is 37.7 °C (99.9 °F), blood pressure is 124/66 mm Hg, and pulse rate is 80/min. Internuclear ophthalmoplegia is noted on the left. Gait testing shows imbalance when he walks. The patient is unable to perform tandem stepping or to maintain balance during the Romberg test, even with the eyes open.

**Which of the following is the most appropriate first step in treatment?**

(A) Increased gabapentin dosage
(B) Intravenous methylprednisolone administration
(C) Oral prednisone administration
(D) Substitution of interferon beta-1b for interferon beta-1a

## Item 90

A 35-year-old woman is evaluated for a 1-day history of sharp right-sided neck pain and a throbbing right hemicranial headache centered near the orbit. The patient describes a 5-year history of chronic intermittent neck pain involving the cervical and upper thoracic regions. She has chiropractic manipulation when the pain lasts more than 1 week. During chiropractic manipulation yesterday, however, the pain abruptly became worse, consisting of intense left-sided neck discomfort. She further reports photophobia, nausea, and mild neck stiffness.

On physical examination, vital signs are normal; BMI is 35. Right ptosis and miosis are noted; a clinical photograph is shown.

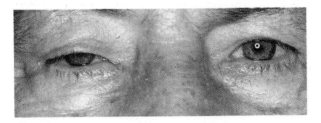

Moderate spasm of the cervical paraspinal muscles bilaterally is seen. The optic discs, visual acuity and fields, and extraocular movements are normal. Gait and results of sensory, motor, and reflex examinations also are normal.

**Which of the following is the most likely diagnosis?**

(A) Acute migraine
(B) Acute stroke
(C) Carotid artery dissection
(D) Cervical disk herniation

## Item 91

A 42-year-old woman is evaluated in the emergency department for a 3-day history of worsening leg spasms and pain and urinary frequency and urgency. She has a 10-year history of multiple sclerosis characterized by mild leg spasms and pain and started using a cane 4 years ago. Medications are interferon beta-1a, baclofen, pregabalin, and extended-release oxybutynin.

On physical examination, temperature is 38.4 °C (101.1 °F), blood pressure is 105/65 mm Hg, and pulse rate is 108/min. Muscle spasticity and hyperreflexia are noted bilaterally in the lower extremities. The patient walks with a slow, stiff-legged gait and needs the assistance of a cane.

A urine dipstick test is positive for leukocytes, leukocyte esterase, and nitrite.

An ultrasound of the bladder shows a postvoid residual volume of 200 mL.

**Which of the following is the most appropriate treatment?**

(A) Administer a 3-day course of methylprednisolone
(B) Administer a 7-day course of ciprofloxacin
(C) Decrease the baclofen dosage
(D) Increase the oxybutynin dosage

## Item 92

A 52-year-old man is evaluated in the emergency department for a 5-day history of occasionally severe right low back and flank pain that radiates to the right thigh and anterior foreleg and is accompanied by numbness and tingling. The pain started shortly after he fell on his back while moving heavy furniture. He experienced no head trauma and has no bowel or bladder dysfunction. He has a history of atrial fibrillation. His only medication is warfarin.

On physical examination, temperature is normal, blood pressure is 135/80 mm Hg, pulse rate is 95/min and regular, and respiration rate is 16/min. The patient is lying with his right hip in flexion. Ecchymosis of the right lateral thigh to the right lateral knee with no edema is noted. Muscle strength testing shows pain and weakness in the right hip with flexion and adduction and in the right ankle dorsiflexors. The right patellar and adductor stretch reflexes are trace positive, compared with the left, and other reflexes are normal. Pinprick sensation is diminished over the right thigh and medial foreleg.

Results of laboratory studies show a hemoglobin level of 7 g/dL (70 g/L) and an INR of 3.2.

**Which of the following diagnostic tests should be performed next?**

(A) CT of the abdomen
(B) Electromyography
(C) MRI of the lumbar spine
(D) Plain radiograph of the lumbar spine

## Item 93

A 29-year-old woman comes to discuss treatment options for relapsing-remitting multiple sclerosis, which was recently diagnosed after she had two episodes of optic neuritis. She takes no medication.

On physical examination, blood pressure is 120/55 mm Hg and pulse rate is 80/min; BMI is 31. Other general physical and neurologic examination findings are unremarkable. After a discussion of the multiple treatment options, the patient elects to begin interferon beta-1b as a chronic disease-modifying therapy for multiple sclerosis.

**Which of the following is the most appropriate regular testing this patient should have to detect adverse effects of treatment?**

(A) Annual brain MRI
(B) Annual ophthalmologic examination
(C) Biannual liver chemistry tests
(D) Biannual measurement of blood urea nitrogen and serum creatinine levels

## Item 94

A 43-year-old woman is evaluated for a 6-month history of gradually worsening neck pain. The patient has worked as a hairdresser for the past 18 years and has developed an uncomfortable pulling sensation in her neck that makes it difficult for her to keep her head straight when working. She has no medical history of note and takes no medication.

On physical examination, vital signs are normal. The right sternocleidomastoid muscle is hypertrophic, and the region of the left trapezius muscle is tender. The head has a tendency to rotate to the left and tilt to the right.

**Which of the following is the most appropriate next step in treatment?**

(A) Baclofen
(B) Botulinum toxin injections
(C) Chiropractic manipulation
(D) Orthopedic consultation
(E) Trihexyphenidyl

## Item 95

An 85-year-old woman is evaluated for a 2-week history of unilateral pain in the right cheek and jaw that lasts for 5 to 60 seconds and occurs multiple times each hour. The pain may be triggered by chewing, face washing, or tooth brushing and interferes with her ability to eat. The patient has no fever, conjunctival injection, lacrimation, rhinorrhea, nasal congestion, or facial rash. She has a family history of migraine in her mother and stroke in her father. She takes no medication.

On physical examination, temperature is 37.3 °C (99.1 °F), blood pressure is 108/70 mm Hg, pulse rate is 88/min, and respiration rate is 16/min. Right-sided facial hypersensitivity to touch is noted, but no facial rash, ptosis, miosis, or conjunctival injection is present.

Results of laboratory studies, including an erythrocyte sedimentation rate and C-reactive protein level, are normal.

An MRI of the brain with contrast is normal.

**Which of the following is the most appropriate treatment?**

(A) Acyclovir
(B) Carbamazepine
(C) Gabapentin
(D) Microvascular decompression
(E) Prednisone

## Item 96

A 54-year-old man is evaluated for a 9-month history of progressively worsening paresthesia in the legs that has recently spread to the hands and a 6-month history of an ataxic gait. The patient developed a malabsorption syn-

drome 3 years ago after gastric bypass surgery. He takes a daily multivitamin, iron, ascorbic acid, calcium, and vitamins D, $B_6$, and $B_{12}$.

On physical examination, temperature is 37.2 °C (99.0 °F), blood pressure is 110/60 mm Hg, and pulse rate is 70/min; BMI is 31. Neurologic examination shows decreased vibratory sensation in the hands and feet and decreased position sense in the feet. Hip flexion strength is 4/5 bilaterally, and reflexes are 3+ throughout with upgoing toes.

**Laboratory studies:**

| | |
|---|---|
| Hemoglobin | 12.9 g/dL (129 g/L) |
| Mean corpuscular volume | 102 fL |
| Vitamin $B_{12}$ | 590 pg/mL (435 pmol/L) |
| Rapid plasma reagin | Nonreactive |

T2-weighted MRIs of the cervical and thoracic spines show slight hyperintensity in the posterior columns from approximately C4 through T9 with no contrast enhancement.

**Which of the following serum levels should be measured next?**

(A) Copper
(B) Folate
(C) 25-Hydroxyvitamin D
(D) Thiamine
(E) Vitamin A

# Answers and Critiques

## Item 1     Answer: C

**Educational Objective:** Evaluate suspected dural sinus venous thrombosis with magnetic resonance venography.

This patient should next undergo magnetic resonance venography. Her headache, which is worse in the morning and with performing the Valsalva maneuver, is consistent with one caused by elevated intracranial pressure. Given the headache characteristics, her history of tobacco and oral contraceptive use, and the presence of papilledema, she most likely has dural sinus venous thrombosis. Dural sinus venous thrombosis may present with signs and symptoms of intracranial hypertension, such as headache, papilledema, and visual problems; focal neurologic findings or seizures; and mental status changes, including stupor and coma. Major risk factors for cerebral sinus venous thrombosis in adults include conditions that predispose to spontaneous thromboses, such as inherited or acquired thrombophilia, pregnancy, oral contraceptive use, malignancy, sepsis, and head trauma. Other diagnostic possibilities include pseudotumor cerebri and viral or bacterial meningitis.

Of all the possible imaging modalities, magnetic resonance venography is the most sensitive test for detecting the thrombus and the occluded dural sinus or vein and thus is the test of choice for diagnosing dural sinus venous thrombosis. After the diagnosis is established, the recommended treatment is smoking cessation, discontinuation of oral contraceptives, and systemic anticoagulation to prevent sequelae related to elevated intracranial pressure for 6 months if no hypercoagulable disorder is found.

Cerebral angiography may demonstrate absence of the dural sinuses but is an expensive and invasive test and is not routinely indicated for diagnosing dural sinus venous thrombosis.

Lumbar puncture may ultimately be required in this patient to confirm elevated intracranial pressure, which is already suggested by the presence of papilledema, or to diagnose pseudotumor cerebri. This diagnosis, however, requires exclusion of a dural sinus venous thrombosis. The lack of fever or elevated leukocyte count makes meningitis unlikely as a diagnosis and a lumbar puncture unnecessary.

Measurement of the serum lupus anticoagulant level in this patient is inappropriate. Hypercoagulable testing would be indicated to determine the duration of anticoagulation needed in this patient only after a dural sinus venous thrombosis was diagnosed. The lupus anticoagulant is unlikely to be present if the coagulation profile is normal.

### KEY POINT

- The diagnostic test of choice for diagnosing dural sinus venous thrombosis is magnetic resonance venography.

**Bibliography**

Stam J. Thrombosis of the cerebral veins and sinuses. N Eng J Med. 2005;352(17):1791-1798. [PMID: 15858188]

## Item 2     Answer: B

**Educational Objective:** Diagnose critical illness myopathy.

This patient has critical illness myopathy, which is seen in severely ill patients after a prolonged (>7 days) stay in the intensive care unit (ICU). Inability to extubate and predominantly proximal flaccid limb weakness are classic findings. Critical illness myopathy is characterized by an elevated serum creatine kinase (CK) level. Predisposing factors include the patient's prolonged ICU stay, use of corticosteroids and neuromuscular junction–blocking agents, and hyperglycemia.

Corticosteroid myopathy presents with predominantly proximal weakness, preserved reflexes, a normal serum CK level, and normal or only mildly myopathic findings on electromyography (EMG).

Guillain-Barré syndrome can share the clinical presentation of critical illness myopathy. The serum CK level, however, would be normal.

Patients with generalized myasthenia gravis typically have limb weakness, diplopia, slurred speech, dysphagia, and dyspnea. Findings on neurologic examination include ptosis, impaired ocular motility, and limb weakness that increases with repeated testing (fatigable weakness). Deep tendon reflexes and sensory examination findings are normal. Results of EMG in myasthenia gravis would show characteristic decremental motor responses on repetitive stimulation. The patient's findings are not consistent with myasthenia gravis.

### KEY POINT

- Critical illness myopathy can occur in severely ill patients after a prolonged stay in the intensive care unit and is characterized by an inability to extubate, flaccid limb weakness, and an elevated serum creatine kinase level.

**Bibliography**

Griffiths RD, Hall JB. Intensive care unit-acquired weakness. Crit Care Med. 2010;38(3):779-787. [PMID: 20048676]

## Item 3    Answer:  E

**Educational Objective:** Distinguish between atypical parkinsonism and Parkinson disease on clinical grounds.

The sign most suggestive of an atypical parkinsonism syndrome in this patient is the absence of response to high-dose levodopa replacement. Parkinson disease remains a clinical diagnosis that is based on a cardinal set of clinical features, including resting tremor, bradykinesia, rigidity, and postural instability; the tremor, bradykinesia, and rigidity are asymmetric. Sustained levodopa responsiveness is expected in Parkinson disease and helps confirm the clinical diagnosis. All patients with suspected parkinsonism should have an adequate trial of levodopa. A lack of response indicates that the neurodegenerative process extends substantially beyond the nigrostriatal pathway and involves other basal ganglion structures. In the absence of a standard, convenient, readily affordable diagnostic test for Parkinson disease, the diagnosis depends on the response to levodopa.

The absence of a tremor should raise the suspicion of atypical parkinsonism, although tremor is absent in up to 30% of patients with classic idiopathic Parkinson disease, as confirmed by autopsy. Therefore, the absence of a tremor is less suggestive of an atypical parkinsonism syndrome than is the lack of response to levodopa replacement.

Convergence insufficiency is a common finding in patients with Parkinson disease, causing diplopia while reading, and is not suggestive of atypical parkinsonism.

Many patients with Parkinson disease have autonomic dysfunction, including constipation, urinary urgency and incontinence, impotence, orthostasis, and temperature instability. Therefore, the presence of impotence in this patient does not exclude Parkinson disease as a diagnosis. When autonomic symptoms are especially severe and overshadow the motor signs of the disorder, further autonomic testing may be indicated, and a diagnosis of the atypical parkinsonism syndrome of multiple system atrophy, autonomic type, may be made.

The absence of olfaction is a frequent finding in Parkinson disease, sometimes preceding the onset of motor signs by many years, and has not been associated with atypical parkinsonism syndromes.

### KEY POINT

- Absence of a response to levodopa is most suggestive of an atypical parkinsonism syndrome.

### Bibliography

Rao G, Fisch L, Srinivasan S, et al. Does this patient have Parkinson disease? JAMA. 2003;289(3):347-353. [PMID: 12525236]

## Item 4    Answer:  A

**Educational Objective:** Diagnose glioblastoma multiforme.

The most likely diagnosis in this patient is glioblastoma multiforme. Glioblastoma multiforme is the most common and most aggressive intraparenchymal tumor in adults, accounting for 20% of all primary central nervous system (CNS) tumors and 50% of gliomas in the adult population. MRIs typically demonstrate a ring-enhancing lesion with areas of central necrosis and hemorrhage.

Meningiomas are the most common primary brain tumors in adults but are extraparenchymal and extradural. On imaging, they typically enhance diffusely and may have a dural tail. They are typically slow growing, have a more insidious presentation, and have a much better prognosis than gliomas.

Oligodendrogliomas account for only 3.7% of primary CNS brain tumors. On MRIs, they are intraparenchymal lesions that usually do not enhance with contrast or have necrosis. Although more aggressive subtypes of oligodendrogliomas, such as oligoastrocytoma and anaplastic oligodendroglioma, may have the same radiologic features as glioblastoma multiforme, they are very rare and not the most likely diagnosis in this patient.

Schwannomas are benign tumors of the nerve sheath that make up 8% of primary CNS tumors. They are extraparenchymal lesions that typically affect cranial nerve VIII and manifest as hearing loss or tinnitus. On MRI, they sometimes appear as enhancing lesions at the cerebellopontine angle. Schwannomas also have a much better prognosis than gliomas.

### KEY POINT

- On MRIs, glioblastoma multiforme typically has a ring-enhancing lesion with areas of central necrosis and hemorrhage.

### Bibliography

Buckner JC, Brown PD, O'Neill BP, Meyer FB, Wetmore CJ, Uhm JH. Central nervous system tumors. Mayo Clin Proc. 2007;82(10):1271-1286. [PMID: 17908533]

## Item 5    Answer:  B

**Educational Objective:** Manage a space-occupying cerebral infarction.

The patient should undergo decompressive hemicraniectomy. He had a malignant hemispheric infarction and now has developed cerebral herniation. Osmotherapy, such as administration of mannitol, can be a useful first step that will cause an increase in serum osmolality and a temporary reduction in cerebral water content and intracranial volume. However, this is only a temporizing measure until surgical intervention with hemicraniectomy can be performed. According to data from three pooled European studies, hemicraniectomy significantly reduces mortality and severe disability (from 76% to 25%) in patients with malignant middle cerebral artery infarction. This benefit is greatest if hemicraniectomy is performed within 48 hours of stroke onset, before clinical herniation has occurred.

**CONT.**

Although aspirin will help reduce his risk of recurrent stroke, it cannot change the natural history of cerebral herniation and thus is an inappropriate choice for this patient.

Dexamethasone and other corticosteroids may be useful in treating the mass effect caused by tumors or infection but are not effective in reducing the edema caused by hemorrhage or stroke.

The patient has clinical evidence of elevated intracranial pressure and should be taken to the operating room. An intracranial pressure monitor may be indicated after the operative intervention, particularly if the examination findings require further evaluation (such as a Glasgow Coma Scale score of less than 8).

A lumbar puncture may be indicated in some patients to measure intracranial pressure but should not be performed in patients with evidence of a mass effect in the brain because of the possibility of worsening cerebral herniation.

**KEY POINT**

- **Decompressive hemicraniectomy has been shown to significantly reduce mortality and severe disability in patients with a malignant middle cerebral artery infarction.**

**Bibliography**

Huttner HB, Schwab S. Malignant middle cerebral artery infarction: clinical characteristics, treatment strategies, and future perspectives. Lancet Neurol. 2009;8(10):949-958. [PMID: 19747656]

**Item 6    Answer: D**
**Educational Objective:** Evaluate a patient with a secondary headache.

This patient should undergo immediate treatment with prednisone followed by a temporal artery biopsy. She has a form of secondary headache, which is a chief diagnostic consideration in a patient older than 50 years who develops new headaches with progression over several weeks. The clinical picture of progressive global nondescript headache in an elderly person reporting malaise, fatigue, and tenderness over the temporal artery is characteristic of temporal arteritis. The incidence of this condition, which is more common among women and white persons, peaks in the eighth decade. Elevations in the erythrocyte sedimentation rate (ESR) and C-reactive protein (CRP) level strongly suggest the diagnosis. In patients with a strong suspicion of temporal arteritis, high-dose corticosteroid therapy is indicated before biopsy to decrease the risk for visual loss. Available data suggest that when the biopsy is performed within 4 weeks of initiating corticosteroid therapy, the results will be unaffected.

The clinical picture does not suggest a stroke, intracranial mass, cerebral aneurysm, or cerebrovascular occlusion. Therefore, cerebral angiography or CT of the head is unnecessary.

Given the duration of the headache, the absence of fever and nuchal rigidity, and the normal leukocyte count and findings on neurologic examination, meningitis or other conditions detected by analysis of cerebrospinal fluid from a lumbar puncture are unlikely.

Besides the mandatory testing of the ESR and CRP levels in patients older than 50 years with new headache, serologic studies are generally of little utility in the evaluation of headache.

**KEY POINT**

- **Secondary headache is a chief diagnostic consideration in a patient older than 50 years who develops new headaches with progression over several weeks.**

**Bibliography**

Salvarani C, Cantini F, Boiardi L, Hunder GG. Polymyalgia rheumatica and giant-cell arteritis. N Engl J Med. 2002;347(4):261-271. [PMID: 12140303]

**Item 7    Answer: B**
**Educational Objective:** Diagnose acute stroke by using rapid neuroimaging.

This patient should undergo CT of the head without contrast. At presentation, she has headache, impaired consciousness, and focal neurologic symptoms, all of which suggest a cerebral mass lesion with elevated intracranial pressure. The presence of subhyaloid hemorrhages on funduscopic examination suggests an aneurysmal subarachnoid hemorrhage. Because the examination findings are neither sensitive nor specific enough for this diagnosis to be made, prompt neuroimaging is required. CT is readily available, can be quickly performed, and is the test of choice to rule out intracerebral hemorrhage, subarachnoid bleeding, and hydrocephalus, which may require rapid neurosurgical intervention.

Cerebral angiography is inappropriate because the immediate source of impaired consciousness should be evaluated with parenchymal imaging. Angiography may ultimately be required to identify the cause of the hemorrhage, such as cerebral aneurysm or vascular malformations, but CT is first necessary to confirm bleeding and to detect possible hydrocephalus or a mass effect that may require immediate surgical intervention.

Lumbar puncture should not be performed as the initial diagnostic test in the setting of headache, impaired consciousness, and focal neurologic symptoms until a mass lesion has been ruled out because of the risk of precipitating cerebral herniation.

Besides being more time consuming, not readily available, and less cost-effective, MRI of the brain leaves the patient in a less-monitored setting during the scanning than does CT. In the acute setting, mass effect and herniation should be diagnosed as quickly as possible to enable rapid neurosurgical intervention.

**H** CONT.

### KEY POINT

- **CT of the head without contrast is the test of choice to rule out intracerebral hemorrhage, subarachnoid bleeding, and hydrocephalus.**

**Bibliography**

Runchey S, McGee S. Does this patient have a hemorrhagic stroke? Clinical findings distinguishing hemorrhagic stroke from ischemic stroke. JAMA. 2010;303(22):2280-2286. [PMID: 20530782]

**H** **Item 8** **Answer: A**

**Educational Objective:** Diagnose brain death.

This patient should next undergo an apnea test. He sustained a catastrophic cerebral hemorrhage with follow-up examination findings consistent with brain death, including coma and absence of motor responses, pupillary responses, corneal reflexes, oculovestibular reflexes, jaw jerk, gag reflex, reaction to craniofacial pain, cough with tracheal suctioning, and sucking or rooting reflexes. An apnea test is the only additional test after the clinical examination required for determination of brain death. In this test, which is initiated when the arterial $P_{CO_2}$ is between 40 and 60 mm Hg (5.3-8.0 kPa) and the patient is normothermic and has received no sedative medications, the patient is disconnected from the ventilator to obtain a baseline $P_{CO_2}$ value. During this time, the patient can receive supplemental oxygen by various techniques described in various protocols. Arterial blood gas measurements are repeated at 1 minute, 5 minutes, and (up to) 8 minutes while spontaneous respirations are observed. The apnea test is considered positive for brain death if the increase in arterial $P_{CO_2}$ is greater than 20 mm Hg (2.7 kPa) without observed respirations. The above procedure is based on American Academy of Neurology practice parameters, but local hospital and state policies may differ in exact specifics regarding pre-apnea test requirements about $P_{CO_2}$ levels and timing of blood draws, vital sign and temperature cut-offs, number of clinical examinations, or medical specialty of the examiner(s).

CT angiography is inappropriate in a patient with examination findings consistent with brain death. Although an underlying vascular malformation or evidence of hematoma expansion ("spot sign") may be present, further treatment is not indicated, given the severity of neurologic injury.

Further confirmatory testing with electroencephalography or transcranial Doppler ultrasonography also is not required for determining brain death unless the patient is unable to tolerate the apnea test because of hemodynamic instability or the presence of other confounding factors, such as benzodiazepine use.

### KEY POINT

- **An apnea test is the only confirmatory test required in a patient with examination findings consistent with brain death.**

**Bibliography**

Wijdicks EF, Varelas PN, Gronseth GS, Greer DM; American Academy of Neurology. Evidence-based guideline update: determining brain death in adults: report of the Quality Standards Subcommittee of the American Academy of Neurology. Neurology. 2010;74(23):1911-1918. [PMID: 20530327]

**H**

**Item 9** **Answer: D**

**Educational Objective:** Treat corticosteroid-refractory idiopathic transverse myelitis.

This patient should undergo plasmapheresis. She has had an episode of postinfectious idiopathic transverse myelitis, as suggested by her examination findings of bilateral leg weakness, loss of sensation below the umbilicus, and hyperreflexia in the lower extremities; her laboratory results showing leukocytosis in the cerebrospinal fluid; and the evidence of inflammation indicated by the contrast enhancement on her MRI. The presence of a sensory spinal cord level and hyperreflexia on examination localize her disorder to the spinal cord, which rules out Guillain-Barré syndrome. Transverse myelitis presumably results from an autoimmune process. First-line treatment for this disorder is high-dose corticosteroids, such as methylprednisolone, to which this patient did not respond. For corticosteroid-refractory transverse myelitis, the best available evidence supports the use of plasmapheresis and/or cyclophosphamide as rescue treatment.

Glatiramer acetate is a disease-modifying agent used in the treatment of multiple sclerosis (MS). Thought to modulate immune responses relevant to MS pathophysiology, glatiramer acetate is well tolerated and reduces the relapse rate by approximately one third. It has no role in the treatment of acute transverse myelitis.

The patient is already receiving a high-dose corticosteroid, and no medical evidence suggests that increasing the dosage would be beneficial.

Although methotrexate has anti-inflammatory effects, it also is not an established treatment for corticosteroid-refractory transverse myelitis.

### KEY POINT

- **The best available evidence supports the use of plasmapheresis and/or cyclophosphamide as rescue treatment for corticosteroid-refractory transverse myelitis.**

**Bibliography**

Greenberg BM, Thomas KP, Krishnan C, Kaplin AI, Calabresi PA, Kerr DA. Idiopathic transverse myelitis: corticosteroids, plasma exchange, or cyclophosphamide. Neurology. 2007;68(19):1614-1617. [PMID: 17485649]

**Item 10** **Answer: C**

**Educational Objective:** Manage intracranial atherosclerosis.

The patient should be given lisinopril to lower her blood pressure. She had an ischemic stroke due to atherosclerotic stenosis of the basilar artery and remains at high risk of recurrent stroke. A blood pressure greater than 140/80 mm Hg and stenosis greater than 70% have been shown to be associated with a higher risk of recurrent stroke. Scant evidence supports maintaining higher blood pressures in the chronic setting for prevention of hemodynamic infarcts. Her history of diabetes mellitus also makes lisinopril a good option because the drug is used to help prevent and delay the progression of diabetic nephropathy.

Ezetimibe has not been shown to be beneficial in reducing atherosclerosis-related outcomes when combined with a statin, which this patient takes. She is already at an appropriate target for LDL cholesterol.

Intracranial stenting for secondary stroke prevention remains an experimental procedure at this time. Additionally, the patient has not yet received best medical treatment, which includes reducing her blood pressure to less than 130/80 mm Hg, achieving glycemic control, and stopping smoking. Again, her LDL cholesterol level is already at an appropriate level.

Clinical trials have shown warfarin to be superior to antiplatelet agents only in patients with atrial fibrillation. The Warfarin and Aspirin for Symptomatic Intracranial Arterial Stenosis trial was stopped prematurely by its data safety monitoring board because of excess mortality in the warfarin arm compared with the aspirin arm.

### KEY POINT

- Blood pressures greater than 140/80 mm Hg have been associated with an increased risk of recurrent stroke and thus should be treated.

### Bibliography
Turan TN, Cotsonis G, Lynn MJ, Chaturvedi S, Chimowitz M; Warfarin-Aspirin Symptomatic Intracranial Disease (WASID) Trial Investigators. Relationship between blood pressure and stroke recurrence in patients with intracranial arterial stenosis. Circulation. 2007;115(23):2969-2975. [PMID: 17515467]

## Item 11    Answer:  B
**Educational Objective:**  Manage concussion.

This patient should be prohibited from returning to competition for a minimum of 1 week. Concussion is defined as a trauma-induced alteration in mental status that may be associated with transient loss of consciousness. Neither a grade 1 nor a grade 2 concussion involves a loss of consciousness. They are distinguished by the duration of amnesia and mental status abnormalities, with symptoms of grade 1 concussion resolving within 15 minutes and those of grade 2 lasting longer than 15 minutes. A grade 3 concussion, such as this patient sustained, is defined as a brief (seconds) or prolonged (minutes) loss of consciousness. Although athletes who sustain grade 1 concussions are permitted to return to the contest on the same day as their injury, those with grade 2 or 3 concussions must be removed and prohibited from returning that day. Grade 3 concussions further eliminate return to competition until the athlete is asymptomatic for 1 week.

In persons with a grade 2 or 3 concussion, CT (or other neuroimaging modality) is indicated on the day of injury if they have persistently abnormal findings on neurologic examination or after 1 week if their symptoms persist throughout that time.

Hospitalization is indicated in the presence of traumatic findings on neuroimaging studies or with persistent abnormalities on physical examination.

Return to competition before 1 week has passed is prohibited in the setting of grade 3 concussions.

### KEY POINT

- Athletes with a grade 3 concussion, which is defined as a brief (seconds) or prolonged (minutes) loss of consciousness, should be prohibited from returning to competition until they are asymptomatic for 1 week.

### Bibliography
Practice parameter: the management of concussion in sports (summary statement). Report of the Quality Standards Subcommittee. Neurology. 1997;48(3):581-585. [PMID: 9065530]

## Item 12    Answer:  A
**Educational Objective:**  Treat a woman of reproductive age with the appropriate antiepileptic drug.

Of the choices provided, carbamazepine is the most appropriate antiepileptic drug (AED) for this woman of reproductive age, especially one who is actively pursuing pregnancy. The greatest risk from AED exposure most likely occurs during the first several weeks of gestation when major organogenesis occurs, typically before a woman even realizes she is pregnant. It is not advisable to adjust AED therapy when a woman is actively trying to conceive. For this reason, the first drug used in women of reproductive age should be an agent that poses a low risk of fetal malformations. A class I study showed no increased risk of fetal malformations in pregnant women exposed to carbamazepine compared with the general population. Other studies have shown a major congenital malformation rate of 2% to 4% in pregnant women exposed to carbamazepine, which is one to two times the risk of the general population. Lamotrigine, levetiracetam, and oxcarbazepine are other AEDs commonly used in this population. To date, the reported rates of fetal malformations with these AEDs also have been low.

Valproic acid has been consistently associated with the highest rate of major congenital malformations (6%-17%) and also has been shown to have an adverse effect on fetal cognitive development at higher dosages. Consequently, this drug should be avoided when possible in women of reproductive age.

Only limited data are available on the effects of other AEDs on pregnancy, but early pregnancy registry studies suggest that phenobarbital and phenytoin are associated with relatively higher fetal malformation rates (3%-7% and 6.5%-14%, respectively).

**KEY POINT**

- Carbamazepine is an appropriate antiepileptic drug for women of reproductive age, especially those who are actively pursuing pregnancy.

**Bibliography**

Harden CL, Meador KJ, Pennell PB, et al; American Academy of Neurology; American Epilepsy Society. Practice parameter update: management issues for women with epilepsy—focus on pregnancy (an evidence-based review): teratogenesis and perinatal outcomes: report of the Quality Standards Subcommittee and Therapeutics and Technology Assessment Subcommittee of the American Academy of Neurology and American Epilepsy Society. Neurology. 2009;73(2):133-141. [PMID: 19398681]

## Item 13     Answer:  D

**Educational Objective:**  Assess driving safety in a patient with cognitive impairment and Parkinson disease.

The most prudent recommendation in this situation is for the patient to take a driving evaluation, often available through a rehabilitation center. There are no strict rules about driving for patients with any level of cognitive impairment, with or without Parkinson disease, and driving performance cannot be adequately simulated or evaluated during an office visit. In Parkinson disease, cognitive impairment, not the motor deficits, is the primary threat to driving safely. This patient's difficulty with visuospatial tasks, such as cube and clock drawing, is directly relevant to driving because drivers must accurately gauge spatial relationships while performing multiple simultaneous tasks when operating a vehicle. A patient's insistence that his or her driving ability is not impaired is not considered a reliable indicator of competence behind the wheel.

Although keeping the roads safe is critical for society, restricting the freedom of persons with cognitive impairment, some of whom can drive safely, by requiring that they drive only under supervision or relinquish their licenses is considered excessive. Although performing a formal assessment of driving safety is not the mandate of physicians, clinical clues suggesting potential driving impairment are often revealed in the office through the report of family members, a history of accidents, aggressive or impulsive personality characteristics, poor judgment, impaired spatial processing and executive function, and a reduction in ability to manage one's affairs. When such clues exist, a firm recommendation for a formal driving assessment is warranted.

Recommending that the patient drive during only daylight hours is inappropriate because the problem is not one of impaired vision but of visual processing.

**KEY POINT**

- A firm recommendation of formal driving assessment is warranted for patients with cognitive impairment.

**Bibliography**

Iverson DJ, Gronseth GS, Reger MA, Classen S, Dubinsky RM, Rizzo M; Quality Standards Subcommittee of the American Academy of Neurology. Practice parameter update: evaluation and management of driving risk in dementia: report of the Quality Standards Subcommittee of the American Academy of Neurology. Neurology. 2010;74(16):1316-1324. [PMID: 20385882]

## Item 14     Answer:  A

**Educational Objective:**  Diagnose amyotrophic lateral sclerosis.

This patient's presentation is most suggestive of early amyotrophic lateral sclerosis (ALS), which can be difficult to diagnose when symptoms and signs are limited. The key diagnostic feature of ALS is the combined presence of upper motoneuron (UMN) and lower motoneuron (LMN) findings in the absence of any other pathology. UMN signs include spasticity, increased tone, hyperreflexia, and pathologic reflexes (such as extensor plantar responses). LMN signs include fasciculations, atrophy, decreased tone, and hyporeflexia. Weakness occurs in both UMN and LMN lesions, although more profoundly in LMN ones. Atrophy occurs most characteristically in LMN lesions but also can result from disuse after longstanding UMN disorders, such as stroke or spinal cord injury. This patient has brisk reflexes of the entire right upper limb, which is consistent with a UMN lesion of the brain or spinal cord, especially if asymmetric. This finding, in the setting of LMN signs, such as muscle atrophy and fasciculations, is suspicious for ALS.

Carpal tunnel syndrome is a compressive median neuropathy (LMN lesion) that typically causes sensory symptoms and signs and weakness of the thenar muscles but does not cause any UMN abnormalities.

Likewise, cervical radiculopathy would cause only LMN lesions and would not be expected to result in hyperreflexia, unless an associated compressive myelopathy were present.

Neuralgic amyotrophy is thought to result from inflammation of the brachial plexus. The cause is unknown but thought to be autoimmune. The most typical cases are heralded by severe pain, sometimes awakening the patient at night, followed by weakness in the distribution of the brachial plexus, often with winging of the scapula. The pain may last weeks before subsiding. The absence of pain or sensory symptoms in this patient excludes this diagnosis.

**KEY POINT**

- The key diagnostic feature of amyotrophic lateral sclerosis is the combined presence of upper motoneuron and lower motoneuron findings in the absence of any other pathologic findings.

**Bibliography**

Bedlack RS. Amyotrophic lateral sclerosis: current practice and future treatments. Curr Opin Neurol. 2010;23(5):524-529. [PMID: 20613515]

**H** **Item 15** **Answer: D**

**Educational Objective:** Manage elevated blood pressure after administration of recombinant tissue plasminogen activator.

The patient should next receive nicardipine. She had onset of an acute ischemic stroke 90 minutes before her initial evaluation and a blood pressure lower than 185/110 mm Hg on physical examination. Therefore, she was appropriately treated with intravenous recombinant tissue plasminogen activator (rtPA). After treatment with rtPA, intracerebral hemorrhage is the most serious potential complication, and an elevated blood pressure is a major risk factor for hemorrhage. Treatment guidelines indicate that after rtPA infusion, blood pressure should be less than 180/105 mm Hg. This patient's posttreatment systolic blood pressure exceeds the guideline limits and should be reduced. Nicardipine and labetalol are options to reduce the blood pressure in this circumstance.

Aspirin is inappropriate treatment at this time because antithrombotic medications must be withheld for at least 24 hours after rtPA administration.

Intracerebral hemorrhage due to thrombolytic therapy presents with headache, nausea, vomiting, and a worsening of the neurologic examination findings. If a hemorrhage is clinically suspected in the setting of intravenous thrombolytic therapy, the rtPA infusion should be stopped and a repeat CT scan of the head obtained to document intracerebral bleeding. In patients who experience documented intracerebral bleeding secondary to thrombolytic therapy, reversal of the thrombolytic state with cryoprecipitate and platelet infusion should be considered. However, in the absence of documented intracerebral bleeding, the administration of these agents is not indicated.

Diazepam also should not be administered. Although the patient's hypertension may be anxiety induced, treatment of the hypertension to prevent intracerebral hemorrhage is the priority. Additionally, benzodiazepines in the setting of acute stroke may impair recovery from neuronal injury and thus should be avoided.

Nitroprusside also is inappropriate to begin at this time. Nitroprusside is relatively contraindicated in patients with acute ischemic stroke or hemorrhage because of the possibility of increasing intracranial pressure.

**KEY POINT**

- Nicardipine can be used to reduce blood pressures of 180/105 mm Hg or greater in patients treated with intravenous recombinant tissue plasminogen activator for acute ischemic stroke.

**Bibliography**

Cumbler E, Glasheen J. Management of blood pressure after acute ischemic stroke: an evidence-based guide for the hospitalist. J Hosp Med. 2007;2(4):261-267. [PMID: 17705177]

**Item 16** **Answer: D**

**Educational Objective:** Diagnose Lambert-Eaton myasthenic syndrome.

Pre- and postexercise nerve conduction studies should be performed in this patient. He has typical features of Lambert-Eaton myasthenic syndrome (LEMS), including progressive proximal limb weakness and depressed tendon reflexes that often improve with repeated exercise (facilitation) and autonomic nerve dysfunction (dry mouth, orthostatic hypotension, erectile dysfunction). Malignancy is found in approximately 50% of patients with LEMS and usually is due to small cell lung cancer. Production of P/Q-type (voltage-gated) calcium channel antibodies, which is detectable in most affected patients, results in impaired calcium influx into the nerve terminal and reduced acetylcholine release. Diagnosis is confirmed when motor nerve stimulation during nerve conduction studies results in a greater than 100% increase (facilitation) of muscle potential amplitude after a brief (approximately 10 second) period of exercise.

Acetylcholine receptor antibodies are not present in LEMS but usually are present in myasthenia gravis. Muscle use in myasthenia gravis worsens rather than improves strength, and motor responses decrease with slow, repetitive nerve stimulation rather than increase after brief exercise. Patients with myasthenia gravis do not have autonomic symptoms and have normal tendon reflexes.

Analysis of cerebrospinal fluid obtained from a lumbar puncture shows normal results in LEMS, but the protein level often is elevated in chronic inflammatory demyelinating polyneuropathy (CIDP), which can also present with progressive proximal muscle weakness and hyporeflexia. Autonomic dysfunction is unusual in CIDP, and nerve conduction study findings are different from those of LEMS.

Muscle biopsy is helpful when evaluating a suspected myopathy but is unnecessary in this patient, given the clinical findings and normal serum creatine kinase level.

**KEY POINT**

- A diagnosis of Lambert-Eaton myasthenic syndrome is confirmed when motor nerve stimulation during nerve conduction studies results in a greater than 100% increase of muscle potential amplitude after a brief period of exercise.

**Bibliography**

Petty R. Lambert Eaton myasthenic syndrome. Pract Neurol. 2007;7(4):265-267. [PMID: 17636143]

## Item 17    Answer:  A

**Educational Objective:** Treat acute ischemic stroke with antithrombotic therapy.

This patient should receive aspirin. He has an acute ischemic stroke at presentation, most likely because his INR level was subtherapeutic. Both the International Stroke Trial (IST) and Chinese Acute Stroke Trial (CAST) have shown a statistically significant reduction in the risk of recurrent stroke and mortality at 14 days for aspirin, 160 mg/d, versus placebo in patients with ischemic stroke. Therefore, all patients with ischemic stroke should be treated with aspirin, at a minimum dosage of 160 mg/d, unless there is an absolute contraindication. Depending on the size of the infarct, the patient should be transitioned to warfarin for secondary stroke prevention 1 to 4 weeks after the initial infarct.

Intravenous heparin and subcutaneous low-molecular-weight heparin are inappropriate for this patient because clinical trials have shown no benefit of acute anticoagulation for acute stroke prevention, even in patients with presumed embolic stroke. In the Trial of Org 10172 in Acute Stroke Treatment (TOAST) and the IST, heparinoids did not show an overall benefit in preventing stroke; any beneficial effect on ischemic stroke was offset by the risk of hemorrhagic stroke. In the Heparin in Acute Embolic Stroke Trial (HAEST), heparin showed no greater benefit than aspirin in preventing recurrent stroke at 14 days in patients admitted with acute ischemic stroke. Acute anticoagulation for acute ischemic stroke is thus used in patients who (1) have mechanical valves; (2) have atrial fibrillation with small infarcts after cardiac surgery; or (3) have cervicocephalic dissection.

Simvastatin is inappropriate for this patient, whose LDL cholesterol level is within the normal range. The Stroke Prevention by Aggressive Reduction in Cholesterol Levels (SPARCL) trial showed a benefit of high-dose statins in reducing recurrent stroke risk in patients with a serum LDL cholesterol level greater than 100 mg/dL (2.59 mmol/L). Additionally, this trial was limited to patients 1 month after an incident stroke.

### KEY POINT

- All patients who have an ischemic stroke or transient ischemic attack should be treated with aspirin, at a minimum dosage of 160 mg/d, unless an absolute contraindication exists.

**Bibliography**

Sandercock PA, Counsell C, Gubitz GJ, Tseng MC. Antiplatelet therapy for acute ischaemic stroke. Cochrane Database Syst Rev. 2008;(3):CD000029. [PMID: 18646056]

## Item 18    Answer:  C

**Educational Objective:** Manage agitation and confusion in a patient with Alzheimer disease.

Older patients with cognitive impairment are especially susceptible to the effects of anticholinergic and sedative medications, such as those this patient is taking, and these drugs should be discontinued immediately, if possible. Confusion and agitation in an elderly patient with dementia are usually due to a superimposed medical condition, such as an occult infection, head trauma, stroke, metabolic derangement, or drug toxicity. Older patients may not develop a fever or systemic signs in the presence of pneumonia or a urinary tract infection, and thus infection should always be considered. Confusion also can be triggered by an environmental stress, such as a surgery, a head injury, or a medication, in older persons with dementia. Although this patient's history and physical examination revealed no signs of trauma, an acute change in mental status could indicate a fall with subsequent subdural hematoma. Therefore, a CT scan of the head also should be considered. Results of the already obtained metabolic profile should detect any metabolic derangement.

Donepezil, galantamine, and rivastigmine are acetylcholinesterase inhibitors currently approved for the treatment of mild to moderate Alzheimer disease. For the most part, treatment goals focus on delaying the worsening of Alzheimer disease symptoms, although some patients can actually show temporary partial improvement. Donepezil is not an appropriate treatment for delirium and will not be helpful in treating this patient's advanced dementia.

No FDA-approved therapies for delirium exist. However, evidence does exist demonstrating that low-dose antipsychotic agents, such as risperidone, are effective in its treatment. Both typical and atypical antipsychotic drugs carry a black box warning because of their approximately 1.6-fold increased risk of mortality and may exacerbate any coexisting signs of parkinsonism, including postural instability. A far better and safer strategy would be to discontinue unnecessary medications known to increase confusion.

Electroencephalography is not appropriate in this patient whose agitation is unlikely to represent seizure activity or postictal confusion.

### KEY POINT

- Acute confusion in a patient with dementia requires a complete medical assessment, including evaluation for occult infection.

**Bibliography**

Blass DM, Rabins PV. In the clinic. Dementia. Ann Intern Med. 2008;148(7):ITC4-1-ITC4-16. [PMID: 18378944]

## Item 19    Answer:  D

**Educational Objective:** Treat episodic cluster headaches.

This patient should be treated with oxygen. He has a history of recurrent headaches that meet the criteria for episodic cluster headache. His attacks involve episodes of severe unilateral pain in the orbitotemporal region that last between 15 and 180 minutes and are associated with the ipsilateral autonomic features of tearing and rhinorrhea and with motor restlessness. He is male and a tobacco user, both risk factors for the development of cluster headache. Cluster episodes usually last 6 to 8 weeks and remission periods usually last 2 to 6 months, but the duration of episodes and remission varies greatly among patients. Although no comparative studies with subcutaneous sumatriptan are available, superior safety and tolerability profiles favor oxygen as the acute treatment of choice. When delivered by face mask at 10 L/min for 10 minutes, oxygen is effective in greater than 75% of affected patients.

Amoxicillin has no role in the treatment of cluster headache or in most patients with acute sinusitis. A recent review concluded that after 10 days of rhinosinusitis symptoms, antibiotic therapy and watchful waiting are equally acceptable. In this patient, the absence of purulent nasal discharge and fever argue against the diagnosis of sinusitis.

Opioid agents, such as hydrocodone, may be effective analgesics but have no role as first-line therapy for any primary headache syndrome. No evidence supports their use in acute cluster headache.

Although subcutaneous and intranasal sumatriptan have been shown to be effective in the treatment of acute cluster headache, oral sumatriptan has not. Zolmitriptan in both intranasal and subcutaneous forms also is an effective treatment of acute cluster headache. However, the presence of cardiovascular risk factors, such as uncontrolled hypertension and long-standing tobacco use, warrants attention before initiation of any triptan therapy.

Verapamil and oral corticosteroids are effective therapies for the prevention of cluster headache but are not indicated for acute headache treatment.

> **KEY POINT**
> - Oxygen therapy is an effective treatment for acute cluster headache.

**Bibliography**

Cohen AS, Burns B, Goadsby PJ. High-flow oxygen for treatment of cluster headache: a randomized trial. JAMA. 2009;302(22):2451-2457. [PMID: 19996400]

### Item 20     Answer:  E
**Educational Objective:** Manage convulsive syncope.

This patient should be offered reassurance. She had an episode of convulsive syncope, which can occur in 5% to 15% of patients with cardiogenic or vasovagal syncope. This patient's episode was provoked, and the prodrome she experienced is similar to near-syncopal episodes she has had in the past, which makes convulsive syncope the most likely cause. Reassurance alone is the appropriate management at this time.

Antiepileptic drugs, such as levetiracetam and valproic acid, are not indicated for convulsive syncope. They also are

not typically recommended for a first seizure unless the patient has risk factors or focal findings on an electroencephalogram (EEG) or MRI.

Serum prolactin levels may increase after a seizure, but this finding is nonspecific and does not distinguish between seizure and syncope.

Focal findings on an EEG or MRI may make a diagnosis of seizure more likely when the history is uncertain, but neither EEG nor neuroimaging should be the initial step in management.

> **KEY POINT**
> - In a young patient with convulsive syncope, further testing with electroencephalography or MRI is typically unnecessary.

**Bibliography**

Lusic' I, Pintaric' I, Hozo I, Boic' L, Capkun V. Serum prolactin levels after seizure and syncopal attacks. Seizure. 1999;8(4):218-222. [PMID: 10452919]

### Item 21     Answer:  A
**Educational Objective:** Diagnose chorea gravidarum.

This patient most likely has chorea gravidarum, a self-limited chorea that occurs during pregnancy. Chorea is a movement disorder characterized by quick muscle jerks in a random, flowing pattern. The best-known common cause of adult-onset chorea is Huntington disease, but the differential diagnosis of chorea is large and includes infectious diseases, encephalitides, systemic lupus erythematosus, porphyria, antiphospholipid antibody syndrome, and HIV infection. Chorea also can result from alcohol intoxication or withdrawal, hyperglycemia, thyroid and parathyroid disease, uremia, cardiac surgery, and certain drugs, including levodopa, amantadine, opiates, valproic acid, carbamazepine, phenytoin, digoxin, isoniazid, and estrogen-containing oral contraceptives. This patient's chorea gravidarum most likely results from the elevated estrogen levels of pregnancy and will spontaneously resolve after delivery. Some women experience recurrent chorea with successive pregnancies.

Huntington disease is a hereditary, progressive, neurodegenerative disorder characterized by increasingly severe motor impairment, cognitive decline, and psychiatric symptoms. In addition to chorea, other motor symptoms include ataxia, dystonia, slurred speech, swallowing impairment, and myoclonus. Various psychiatric symptoms, such as dysphoria, agitation, irritability, anxiety, apathy, disinhibition, delusions, and hallucinations, are commonly seen. The absent family history and acute onset during pregnancy make Huntington disease unlikely in this patient.

This patient has none of the musculoskeletal, mucocutaneous, or kidney manifestations of systemic lupus erythematosus, which makes this diagnosis unlikely.

Tardive dyskinesia is also an unlikely diagnosis. All medications that block dopamine type 2 ($D_2$) receptors can cause acute dystonic reactions. Dystonic movements are due to sustained contraction of agonist and antagonist muscles, which results in twisting and repetitive movements or sustained abnormal postures. These movements most frequently affect the ocular muscles (oculogyric crisis) and the face, jaw, tongue, neck, and trunk. The limbs are rarely affected. This patient lacks the choreiform movement of the face typical of classic tardive dyskinesia and is taking no $D_2$ receptor–blocking agent, the cause of the disorder.

**KEY POINT**

- Chorea gravidarum is a self-limited chorea that occurs during pregnancy.

**Bibliography**

Bordelon YM, Smith M. Movement disorders in pregnancy. Semin Neurol. 2007;27(5):467-475. [PMID: 17940926]

### Item 22      Answer:  B

**Educational Objective:**  Manage reversible cerebral vasoconstriction syndrome.

Cerebrovascular imaging should be performed in this patient with a thunderclap headache. CT angiography and MR angiography are less invasive than conventional angiography and may be effective screening tools for cerebrovascular pathology. A thunderclap headache is a severe and explosive headache that is maximal in intensity at or within 60 seconds of onset. Every thunderclap headache must be immediately evaluated to detect potentially catastrophic conditions, especially subarachnoid hemorrhage. An underlying disorder, most commonly vascular, is detected in 30% to 80% of patients. Recurrent thunderclap headaches such as the ones this patient is having may arise from both primary and secondary headache disorders. Reversible cerebral vasoconstriction syndrome, which comprises a group of disorders characterized by recurrent thunderclap headache associated with transient segmental cerebral vasoconstriction, is characterized by severe headaches of the thunderclap variety occurring over a few days or weeks, often without abnormalities on clinical examination. Neuroimaging studies and cerebrospinal fluid analysis show no evidence of subarachnoid hemorrhage. Segmental cerebral artery vasoconstriction is documented by angiographic studies. This condition may present during pregnancy or the puerperium.

Recurrent thunderclap headaches occurring over several days warrant specific imaging of the intracranial vasculature, as provided by angiography, rather than of the parenchyma, which is provided by MRI.

Indomethacin is appropriate in the management of primary versions of thunderclap headache, such as those associated with cough, exertion, and sexual activity. Secondary sources of thunderclap headache must first be excluded

before primary headache can be diagnosed definitively, which necessitates a cerebrovascular imaging study.

Sumatriptan can treat an attack of acute migraine but is not indicated for acute thunderclap headache of unknown origin.

**KEY POINT**

- Cerebrovascular imaging is used to document reversible cerebral vasoconstriction syndrome, which comprises a group of disorders characterized by recurrent thunderclap headache occurring over a few days or weeks and is associated with transient segmental cerebral vasoconstriction.

**Bibliography**

Ducros A, Bousser MG. Reversible cerebral vasoconstriction syndrome. Pract Neurol. 2009;9(5):256-267. [PMID: 19762885]

### Item 23      Answer:  C

**Educational Objective:**  Treat acute Bell palsy.

This patient has acute onset of Bell palsy and should receive prednisone. Mounting evidence implicates an inflammatory/infectious cause of Bell palsy that is most likely due to human herpesvirus 1. Peripheral nerve compression, as seen in Bell palsy, causes more widespread facial paralysis, including paralysis of the upper and lower face and an inability to close the eyes tightly or raise the eyebrows. Patients also report dry mouth, hyperacusis, impaired taste, and pain and numbness near the ear. Abrupt onset of symptoms building over 1 to 2 days is typical. The most appropriate treatment is prednisone, 40 mg/d, preferably administered within the first 72 hours.

The use of antiherpesvirus agents, such as acyclovir, as monotherapy for Bell palsy has not been shown to be helpful. A prodromal viral illness can sometimes precede Bell palsy, as it did in this patient.

High-dose intravenous corticosteroids, such as methylprednisolone, can be used in the treatment of acute exacerbations of multiple sclerosis but are not indicated in the treatment of Bell palsy. This patient is less likely to have multiple sclerosis than isolated Bell palsy because this is her first episode of a neurologic deficit, and most of the neurologic examination is unremarkable.

This patient's headache is relatively mild and, therefore, sumatriptan is not indicated. Migraine headaches, when complicated, can result in facial weakness but not in a Bell palsy distribution. In Bell palsy, both the upper and lower facial muscles are affected (lower motoneuron cranial nerve VII weakness). In migraine-associated weakness (upper motoneuron cranial nerve VII weakness), the lower facial muscles are weak, but the upper facial muscles are spared.

**KEY POINT**

- The most appropriate treatment of Bell palsy is prednisone, preferably administered within the first 72 hours

## Bibliography

Thaera GM, Wellik KE, Barrs DM, Dunckley ED, Wingerchuk DM, Demaerschalk BM. Are corticosteroid and antiviral treatments effective for Bell palsy? A critically appraised topic. Neurologist. 2010;16(2):138-140. [PMID: 20220455]

## Item 24    Answer:    B

**Educational Objective:**  Evaluate suspected subarachnoid hemorrhage.

This patient should have a lumbar puncture. At presentation, she has sudden onset of a severe headache, which is most concerning for subarachnoid hemorrhage. In a minority of patients with a small amount of blood in the subarachnoid space, a head CT may initially be normal. When this occurs, a lumbar puncture is required to detect erythrocytes or xanthochromia (a yellowish discoloration caused by the breakdown of erythrocytes) in the cerebrospinal fluid (CSF). Because xanthochromia may not develop for 6 hours or longer after the initial event, the presence of erythrocytes in the CSF should prompt consideration of a subarachnoid hemorrhage. A lumbar puncture is also helpful for excluding other diagnoses, such as meningitis, and for measuring the opening pressure.

Because the initial CT of the head without contrast was normal, a CT with contrast is unlikely to show a mass lesion sufficient in size to cause headache. CT angiography or venography may eventually be used to rule out aneurysms or dural sinus thrombosis, but subarachnoid hemorrhage first needs to be ruled out in the acute setting.

Although magnetic resonance angiography (MRA) eventually may be necessary to exclude dissection or aneurysms as the cause of this patient's symptoms, it is inappropriate at this time. Unless the presence of a subarachnoid hemorrhage is first established, an aneurysm detected on MRA or other vascular imaging may be an incidental finding that does not require surgical intervention.

The effectiveness of MRI for diagnosing subarachnoid hemorrhage remains under investigation. Additionally, MRI is time consuming and may not differentiate subarachnoid hemorrhage from other diagnoses well enough. Unlike CSF analysis, MRI does not afford the additional benefit of measuring the CSF opening pressure.

Of note, clinical examination findings, including those from funduscopy, have insufficient sensitivity and specificity to establish the diagnosis of subarachnoid hemorrhage.

### KEY POINT

- **In a patient with a suspected subarachnoid hemorrhage and normal results on a head CT scan, a lumbar puncture is the most appropriate next step in evaluation.**

## Bibliography

Perry JJ, Spacek A, Forbes M, et al. Is the combination of negative computed tomography result and negative lumbar puncture result sufficient to rule out subarachnoid hemorrhage? Ann Emerg Med. 2008;51(6):707-713. [PMID: 18191293]

## Item 25    Answer:    E

**Educational Objective:**  Manage suspected spinal cord compression in a patient with Parkinson disease.

An MRI of the cervical spine should be obtained next. In this previously ambulatory patient, the acute onset of leg weakness and an inability to walk suggest a cause other than Parkinson disease. Her physical examination findings are notable for increased tone with ankle clonus, hyperreflexia, extensor plantar responses, and profound leg weakness. Her arm strength and reflexes are normal, which suggests the possibility of spinal cord compression—most likely traumatic—from a combination of cervical arthritis, stenosis, and trauma. Many patients with cervical myelopathy may not experience neck pain or exhibit the full triad of upper motoneuron weakness, a sensory level, and bowel or bladder impairment. As such, the possibility of cervical myelopathy must be considered in the differential diagnosis of leg weakness, especially in an older patient with arthritis, likely osteoporosis, and frequent falls. An MRI of the spine is the best tool to establish the diagnosis of spinal cord compression.

Although CT myelography can also establish the diagnosis of cervical myelopathy and may be needed in patients in whom MRI is precluded, this technique is difficult to perform on an emergent basis and does not produce images of the spinal cord parenchyma.

A CT of the head will not show compression of the cervical spine.

This patient's symptoms are not consistent with a worsening of her Parkinson disease, and thus increasing her dosage of levodopa-carbidopa is unlikely to be helpful.

A lumbar puncture and subsequent examination of the cerebrospinal fluid would help establish a diagnosis of Guillain-Barré syndrome, which can cause a rapidly progressive subacute paraplegia. However, the clinical scenario and examination findings make this diagnosis unlikely.

### KEY POINT

- **Compressive cervical myelopathy can cause acute leg weakness, especially in an older patient, and is best diagnosed with MRI.**

## Bibliography

Tracy JA, Bartleson JD. Cervical spondylotic myelopathy. Neurologist. 2010;16(3):176-187. [PMID: 20445427]

## Item 26    Answer:    C

**Educational Objective:**  Treat selected patients with refractory temporal lobe epilepsy with surgery.

This patient should undergo a right temporal lobectomy. He has medication-refractory right temporal lobe epilepsy associated with mesial temporal sclerosis. The goal of epilepsy surgery is to remove the area of the cortex that is the epileptogenic focus. The highest rates of surgical cure are seen in patients with known lesions, such as a low-grade tumor or vascular malformation, or with temporal lobe epilepsy associated with mesial temporal sclerosis. A right temporal lobectomy would offer a greater than 60% chance of seizure freedom (up to 80%, depending on results of further evaluation).

This patient's seizures have been refractory to more than two medications. The likelihood that adding (or substituting) a new medication (such as carbamazepine) to his regimen would lead to seizure remission is less than 10%.

Corpus callosotomy is a palliative surgery typically performed in children with symptomatic generalized epilepsy with tonic or atonic seizures. It is not appropriate for this patient with focal epilepsy.

Although vagal nerve stimulation reduces seizure frequency by 50% in 50% of patients, seizure remission is not common after placement of a vagal nerve stimulator.

> **KEY POINT**
>
> - Patients with epilepsy who have temporal lobe epilepsy associated with mesial temporal sclerosis or known lesions, such as a low-grade tumor or vascular malformation, experience the highest rates of seizure remission after surgery.

**Bibliography**

Kwan P, Sperling MR. Refractory seizures: try additional antiepileptic drugs (after two have failed) or go directly to early surgery evaluation? Epilepsia. 2009;50(Suppl 8):57-62. [PMID: 19702735]

### Item 27      Answer: A
**Educational Objective:** Diagnose acute disseminated encephalomyelitis.

This patient's history, clinical and laboratory findings, and MRIs are most consistent with acute disseminated encephalomyelitis. This inflammatory demyelinating disorder typically occurs in children and young adults and is often considered to be a postinfectious phenomenon, although a direct link to infection has never been proved. The multifocal symptoms associated with this disorder typically present subacutely and result from profound, simultaneous demyelination in multiple regions of the central nervous system. Other associated symptoms are headache, fever, and encephalopathy, all of which this patient has and none of which is consistent with multiple sclerosis. Laboratory studies usually reveal significant lymphocytic pleocytosis in the cerebrospinal fluid (CSF) and large, multifocal areas of demyelination on MRI. Acute disseminated encephalomyelitis typically is a one-time, self-limited phenomenon and is not recurrent in nature.

This patient's clinical syndrome, CSF findings, and negative bacterial culture are not consistent with bacterial meningitis.

Although herpes encephalitis can present with fevers, headaches, and encephalopathy, this virus does not affect the optic nerve and usually only affects the medial temporal lobes on MRI. Additionally, the polymerase chain reaction performed on this patient's CSF was negative for viruses.

Although multiple sclerosis also causes central nervous system demyelination, acute flares are not associated with fevers, encephalopathy, or profound lymphocytosis in the CSF. Distinguishing between the two disorders can present a diagnostic challenge.

Neuromyelitis optica typically presents with optic nerve or spinal cord involvement but is not associated with the profound supratentorial brain demyelination seen in this patient or with fevers and encephalopathy.

> **KEY POINT**
>
> - Acute disseminated encephalomyelitis is a subacute inflammatory demyelinating disorder in children and young adults characterized by simultaneous demyelination in multiple regions of the central nervous system.

**Bibliography**

Dale RC, de Sousa C, Chong WK, Cox TC, Harding B, Neville BG. Acute disseminated encephalomyelitis, multiphasic disseminated encephalomyelitis and multiple sclerosis in children. Brain. 2000;123(Pt 12):2407-2422. [PMID: 11099444]

### Item 28      Answer: C
**Educational Objective:** Manage a tension-type headache.

This patient should begin taking ibuprofen for his tension-type headache. Episodic tension-type headache is defined as episodes of recurrent nondisabling headache lasting 30 minutes to 7 days. Often recognized as a featureless headache, it is characterized by bilateral, steady, mild-to-moderate intensity discomfort that is unaffected by physical activity. Whereas migraine is characterized primarily by the positive features of photophobia and/or phonophobia, nausea and/or vomiting, and pain worsening with activity, tension-type headache is characterized by the absence of these features. Aspirin and acetaminophen are more effective than placebo in treating these headaches, but comparative studies suggest superior benefit from the NSAIDs ibuprofen and naproxen.

Although tricyclic antidepressants, such as amitriptyline, have been commonly prescribed for tension-type headache, data from recent clinical trials suggest they may be no more effective than placebo. Additionally, the relatively low headache frequency in this patient does not justify daily pharmacotherapy.

Muscle relaxants, such as cyclobenzaprine, have no role in the management of tension-type headache. Similarly, benzodiazepines, which depress the central nervous system, have not been shown to be effective.

Given the change in headache pattern over the previous 6 months, the brain neuroimaging already performed was warranted. However, in the absence of any cervical root or spinal cord findings on examination, a cervical MRI is unnecessary.

No evidence supports recommending physical therapy for patients with tension-type headache.

**KEY POINT**

- Comparative studies have shown a superior benefit of the NSAIDs ibuprofen and naproxen compared with tricyclic antidepressants in treating tension-type headache.

**Bibliography**

Fumal A, Schoenen J. Tension-type headache: current research and clinical management. Lancet Neurol. 2008;7(1):70-83. [PMID: 18093564]

## Item 29    Answer:  B

**Educational Objective:** Initiate long-term treatment for a patient with a clinically isolated syndrome.

Glatiramer acetate should be initiated in this patient. She is experiencing acute optic neuritis, as evidenced by the unilateral ocular symptoms, afferent pupillary defect, and contrast enhancement of the optic nerve on MRI. Acute management with intravenous methylprednisolone is the standard-of-care treatment for acute optic neuritis. Following this, the patient's long-term management strategy needs to be decided. Although this patient's MRI does not meet the full diagnostic criteria for multiple sclerosis (MS), the presence of three lesions suspicious for demyelination raises her risk of developing MS to approximately 90% in the next 10 to 15 years. In such patients, use of glatiramer acetate reduces the risk of MS development in the first 3 years after an initial demyelinating event by 45%. Similar data exist for the interferon-beta medications.

Acetazolamide is used as treatment for benign idiopathic intracranial hypertension. Although this disorder can cause visual changes, they are usually bilateral and associated with headache, and papilledema is seen on examination. Additionally, this disorder will not cause contrast enhancement on an orbital MRI.

Sumatriptan is used as abortive therapy for acute migraine. Although migraine can occasionally cause visual symptoms and can be associated with some white matter hyperintensities on MRI, it does not cause an afferent pupillary defect or contrast enhancement of the optic nerve.

A "watch and wait" approach with repeat imaging for long-term clinical monitoring is insufficient because of the presence of periventricular white matter lesions on her brain MRI. If her MRI had revealed no white matter lesions, the risk of conversion to multiple sclerosis would have been low and long-term monitoring indicated.

**KEY POINT**

- In a patient with acute optic neuritis and MRI lesions suggestive of demyelination, treatment with intravenous methylprednisolone and disease-modifying agents, such as glatiramer acetate or interferon-beta agents, decreases the short-term risk of multiple sclerosis.

**Bibliography**

Comi G, Martinelli V, Rodegher M, et al; PreCISe study group. Effect of glatiramer acetate on conversion to clinically definite multiple sclerosis in patients with clinically isolated syndrome (PreCISe study): a randomised, double-blind, placebo-controlled trial. Lancet. 2009;374(9700):1503-1511. [PMID: 19815268]

## Item 30    Answer:  E

**Educational Objective:** Manage age-related memory loss.

This patient should be reassured that his degree of memory loss is a normal part of aging. His symptoms of memory impairment are primarily related to short-term memory (recall of names, numbers, faces, and the location of placed objects). In other cognitive domains, he continues to function at a high level, with no evidence of deterioration from his previous performance and no impairment in social or occupational function. Nothing suggests that his perceived memory loss is progressive. His score on the Mini–Mental State Examination does not meet clinical criteria for dementia. Memory loss that does not interfere significantly with a patient's social or occupational function does not indicate dementia and requires no evaluation or treatment.

Mild cognitive impairment (MCI) describes a loss of cognitive ability that exceeds the expected age-related memory loss but does not interfere significantly with daily activities. The boundary between MCI and dementia is unclear, although 10% to 15% of patients with MCI will meet the criteria for dementia within 1 year. Currently, no method exists by which to identify persons with predementia MCI, and no neuroprotective agent has been shown to prevent this progression.

If this patient had evidence of dementia or a history of head trauma, MRI of the brain (or CT of the head) would be appropriate. However, it serves no purpose in age-related memory loss or MCI.

Determination of this patient's apolipoprotein E4 status could help define his risk of developing Alzheimer disease but would not indicate if he had the disorder; his symptoms do not support that diagnosis.

Although formal neuropsychological testing can more fully reveal a patient's cognitive deficits and abilities, this intervention is unnecessary in this patient who is functioning normally.

Donepezil is a cholinesterase inhibitor shown to improve the cognitive function of persons with mild, moderate, and even severe dementia due to Alzheimer disease. The drug has no role in preventing or treating age-related memory loss or in preventing the progression from MCI to dementia.

**KEY POINT**

- Memory loss that does not interfere significantly with a patient's social or occupational function does not indicate dementia and requires no evaluation or treatment.

**Bibliography**

Petersen RC. Clinical practice. Mild cognitive impairment. N Engl J Med. 2011;364(23):2227-2234. [PMID: 21651394]

## Item 31     Answer: C

**Educational Objective:** Treat acute ischemic stroke with thrombolysis.

This patient should receive intravenous recombinant tissue plasminogen activator (rtPA). She is evaluated only 60 minutes after onset of acute ischemic stroke, which is well within the window for administration of the drug, and has a measurable deficit on neurologic examination. She does not meet any of the exclusion criteria that would prevent administration: her INR and platelet count are within the guideline limits, her blood pressure is less than 185/110 mm Hg, and imaging shows no hemorrhage. The National Institute of Neurological Diseases and Stroke (NINDS) rtPA trial showed that patients who received intravenous rtPA within 3 hours of stroke onset had a greater likelihood of clinical improvement at 3 months than did those who received placebo. The trial had no upper limit of neurologic deficit or age.

High-dose (325-mg) aspirin is appropriate for patients who are not eligible for intravenous rtPA. However, in those who have received intravenous rtPA, antiplatelet agents must be withheld for at least 24 hours.

Intravenous heparin does not reduce the risk of recurrent embolic stroke or mortality in patients with stroke who have atrial fibrillation and thus is the wrong therapeutic choice for this patient.

Administering labetalol to lower this patient's blood pressure is also inappropriate. For an uncomplicated ischemic stroke in patients without concurrent acute coronary artery disease or heart failure, antihypertensive medications should be withheld unless the systolic blood pressure is greater than 220 mm Hg or the diastolic blood pressure is greater than 120 mm Hg. If the patient is eligible for thrombolysis, blood pressure must be lowered and stabilized below 185 mm Hg systolic and 110 mm Hg diastolic before thrombolytic therapy is started. Because this patient's blood pressure (170/100 mm Hg) is less than those limits, an antihypertensive medication, such as labetalol, is not required. After thrombolysis, the target blood pressure is less than 180 mm Hg systolic and 105 mm Hg diastolic for at least 24 hours.

**KEY POINT**

- Intravenous recombinant tissue plasminogen activator should be administered to a patient with ischemic stroke if it can be given within 3 hours of stroke onset and the patient meets the guideline criteria.

**Bibliography**

Wardlaw JM, Murray V, Berge E, del Zoppo GJ. Thrombolysis for acute ischaemic stroke. Cochrane Database Syst Rev. 2009;(4):CD000213. [PMID: 19821269]

## Item 32     Answer: A

**Educational Objective:** Recognize the interaction between oral contraceptives and antiepileptic drugs.

If this patient begins using combined oral contraceptives, her lamotrigine dosage will need to be increased. Lamotrigine is metabolized by glucuronidation, a process induced by estrogens. Estrogen-containing combined oral contraceptives can reduce the levels of lamotrigine by as much as 40% to 60% and lead to more seizures if a patient's dosage is not increased. This increase is typically managed by establishing a baseline therapeutic level for the patient before starting combined oral contraceptives, increasing the dosage of lamotrigine after they are started, and then rechecking drug levels in 7 to 10 days. Lamotrigine levels also can increase during the placebo week of combined oral contraceptives, which occasionally leads to adverse effects. Contraceptive alternatives for women taking lamotrigine include medroxyprogesterone acetate and an intrauterine device; because lamotrigine decreases progesterone levels by 20%, the medroxyprogesterone acetate dosage may have to be adjusted. Low-dose combined oral contraceptives also are not recommended for this reason.

The World Health Organization recommends that combined hormonal contraception should be avoided in women taking carbamazepine, phenytoin, barbiturates, primidone, topiramate, or oxcarbazepine because these drugs increase the metabolism of oral contraceptives and decrease their effectiveness. Therefore, switching the patient to carbamazepine, phenytoin, or topiramate would risk an unplanned pregnancy. In addition, carbamazepine and phenytoin may exacerbate seizures in patients with idiopathic generalized epilepsies and thus would not be good alternatives for this patient. Furthermore, it is best to continue giving the patient lamotrigine, which has been controlling her seizures well.

Making no change to the patient's antiepileptic drug therapy is inappropriate because of the previously discussed drug interaction between lamotrigine and oral contraceptives.

**KEY POINT**

- Estrogen-containing combined oral contraceptives in patients with epilepsy can reduce lamotrigine (and some other antiepileptic drug [AED]) levels and lead to more seizures if the AED dosage is not increased.

**Bibliography**

Gaffield ME, Culwell KR, Lee CR. The use of hormonal contraception among women taking anticonvulsant therapy. Contraception. 2011;83(1):16-29. [PMID: 21134499]

## Item 33    Answer:  B

**Educational Objective:**  Diagnose dementia with Lewy bodies associated with psychotic features.

The combination of visual hallucinations, dream enactment behavior (rapid eye movement [REM] sleep behavior disorder), and atremulous parkinsonism suggests a diagnosis of dementia with Lewy bodies (diffuse Lewy body disease). Even when a patient recognizes the hallucinations as imaginary, their continued presence is usually disturbing to the patient and family and may necessitate treatment. His motor symptoms of parkinsonism remain mild and do not require symptomatic treatment. In the future, as his disease progresses, he will eventually require dopaminergic agents, which will likely exacerbate his hallucinations. Dopamine agonists are contraindicated in patients with Lewy body disease, and the drug of choice is levodopa when symptomatic therapy is required.

Alzheimer disease is a common comorbidity in patients with dementia with Lewy bodies. However, this diagnosis does not in itself sufficiently account for the additional features of parkinsonism, dream enactment behavior, and visual hallucinations.

Because the hallmark features of frontotemporal dementia, such as apathy, perseveration, hoarding, disinhibition, and other personality changes, are lacking in this patient, that diagnosis is unlikely.

Neurosyphilis is not a cause of rapid eye movement behavior disorder, although it can cause dementia.

**KEY POINT**

- The combination of mild parkinsonism and prominent visual hallucinations suggests a diagnosis of dementia with Lewy bodies (diffuse Lewy body disease).

**Bibliography**

Weisman D, McKeith I. Dementia with Lewy bodies. Semin Neurol. 2007;27(1):42-47. [PMID: 17226740]

## Item 34    Answer:  D

**Educational Objective:**  Manage antiplatelet agents for secondary stroke prevention in a patient with a previous ischemic stroke.

This patient should receive clopidogrel instead of aspirin. He has a small subcortical infarction and a history of peripheral arterial disease. The Clopidogrel versus Aspirin in Patients at Risk of Ischemic Events (CAPRIE) study randomized patients with ischemic stroke, myocardial infarction, or peripheral arterial disease to aspirin versus clopidogrel, with a primary outcome of stroke, myocardial infarction, or death. Overall, clopidogrel was superior to aspirin in preventing the primary outcome, with the benefit being greatest among participants with peripheral arterial disease. The absolute risk reduction in clopidogrel versus aspirin for the primary outcome was 0.5% per year. The combination of aspirin and dipyridamole could be another appropriate option for secondary stroke prevention.

In the Management of Atherothrombosis with Clopidogrel in High-Risk Patients with Recent Transient Ischemic Attacks or Ischemic Stroke (MATCH) trial, the combination of aspirin and clopidogrel for ischemic stroke prevention was associated with a slight reduction in risk of ischemic stroke, but this was offset by hemorrhagic complications. Combining aspirin and clopidogrel thus has limited utility in the secondary prevention of stroke unless there are cardiac comorbidities.

Although ticlopidine has been shown to be superior to aspirin in preventing recurrent stroke, it can cause agranulocytosis and thrombotic thrombocytopenic purpura. This safety profile makes ticlopidine a second-line agent. Therefore, adding ticlopidine to this patient's regimen or substituting it for aspirin is inappropriate.

In small subcortical strokes, lacunar strokes, and other noncardioembolic ischemic strokes, aspirin and warfarin were shown to be equivalent in the Warfarin-Aspirin Recurrent Stroke Study (WARSS). This patient has no evidence of atrial fibrillation or other high-risk cardioembolic symptoms that necessitate treatment with warfarin or direct thrombin inhibitors.

The combination of aspirin and warfarin does not provide any additional protection against recurrent ischemic stroke and is associated with greater rates of hemorrhagic complications.

**KEY POINT**

- Clopidogrel has been shown to be superior to aspirin for secondary stroke prevention, and combining the agents has limited utility because of hemorrhagic complications.

**Bibliography**

Paciaroni M, Bogousslavsky J. Primary and secondary prevention of ischemic stroke. Eur Neurol. 2010;63(5):267-278. [PMID: 20357456]

Answers and Critiques

## Item 35    Answer:  B

**Educational Objective:**  Treat chronic paroxysmal hemicrania.

This patient should begin taking indomethacin. Chronic paroxysmal hemicrania is a syndrome related to cluster headache that differs in frequency and duration. Both conditions are contained in the group of headaches known as trigeminal autonomic cephalalgias, which are characterized by trigeminal nerve–mediated pain and ipsilateral autonomic features, such as lacrimation, ptosis, conjunctival injection, nasal congestion, or rhinorrhea. The discomfort in these conditions is typically severe, sharp, and of a boring, searing, or penetrating quality, generally contained within the first or ophthalmic distribution of the trigeminal nerve. The trigeminal autonomic cephalalgias differ in the duration and frequency of episodes and in their response to therapy. Whereas cluster headache attacks last 15 to 180 minutes and occur 1 to 8 times daily, chronic paroxysmal hemicrania has a mean duration of 15 minutes and may recur 8 to 40 times daily. This type of primary headache responds dramatically and specifically to indomethacin. A third and much less prevalent type of trigeminal autonomic cephalalgia is short-lasting unilateral neuralgiform headache with conjunctival injection and tearing (SUNCT syndrome). This type recurs dozens or hundreds of times daily, lasts seconds to minutes, and lacks any reliable therapy.

The anticonvulsant agent carbamazepine is the first-line drug in the medical management of trigeminal neuralgia, which also is characterized by severe pain along the distribution of the trigeminal nerve. The pain of trigeminal neuralgia is paroxysmal, usually lasts 2 to 3 seconds, and may occur in volleys of jabs or stabs of pain. The paroxysms are often punctuated by pain-free periods lasting seconds to hours. Characteristically, the painful episodes are associated with trigger zones, particularly around the mouth and nostrils. Trigeminal neuralgia differs from the trigeminal autonomic cephalalgias (such as chronic paroxysmal hemicrania) in its predominant pain location in the second and third branches of the trigeminal nerve and the absence of any autonomic features.

Given the temporal pattern of this patient's headache and her normal erythrocyte sedimentation rate, temporal (giant cell) arteritis is an unlikely diagnosis, and high-dose prednisone is not indicated.

Although excellent evidence supports the use of topiramate for prevention of migraine, limited evidence supports its use for prevention of cluster headache, and no evidence supports its use for prevention of chronic paroxysmal hemicrania.

Similarly, although verapamil may be the preventive agent of choice for cluster headache, this drug is not effective in preventing chronic paroxysmal hemicrania.

### KEY POINT

- **Chronic paroxysmal hemicrania responds dramatically and specifically to indomethacin.**

**Bibliography**

Goadsby PJ, Cittadini E, Cohen AS. Trigeminal autonomic cephalalgias: paroxysmal hemicrania, SUNCT/SUNA, and hemicrania continua. Semin Neurol. 2010;30(2):186-191. [PMID: 20352588]

## Item 36    Answer:  A

**Educational Objective:**  Diagnose complications after subarachnoid hemorrhage.

The patient with subarachnoid hemorrhage should undergo CT angiography of the head. The complications after subarachnoid hemorrhage are classified as early versus late. In the first 48 hours after hemorrhage, aneurysm rerupture and hydrocephalus are the principal causes of neurologic deterioration. Starting at day 5, the risk of cerebral arterial vasospasm emerges. This complication typically presents with a decline on neurologic examination and may lead to cerebral infarction, which may worsen already existing brain injury. CT angiography can accurately diagnose cerebral vasospasm requiring medical therapy, the cornerstone of which is induced hypertension. In patients with cerebral vasospasm, intra-arterial therapy with calcium channel blockers or angioplasty of the artery in spasm may be performed. CT angiography has the additional benefit of imaging the ventricles, which enables a diagnosis of hydrocephalus to be made, and when combined with perfusion imaging can demonstrate impaired cerebral blood flow due to vasospasm.

Convulsive and nonconvulsive status epilepticus, which is associated with poor neurologic outcome, is common and underdiagnosed after hemorrhagic stroke. If neuroimaging does not find a cause of neurologic decline that is readily addressed with medical or surgical treatment, electroencephalography may be an appropriate next step.

Lumbar puncture may be useful to measure intracranial pressure and diagnose postoperative meningitis. Repeat imaging, however, is first required to ensure that no mass effect is present that could precipitate cerebral herniation after a lumbar puncture.

MRI may provide information on cerebral infarction but is less accurate than other means for determining vasospasm. Additionally, MRI takes longer to complete than other tests, which would delay treatment of a vasospasm or hydrocephalus.

### KEY POINT

- **In patients with a subarachnoid hemorrhage, CT angiography is appropriate for accurately diagnosing cerebral vasospasm, which emerges as a potential complication 5 days after the initial hemorrhage.**

**Bibliography**

van Gijn J, Kerr RS, Rinkel GJ. Subarachnoid hemorrhage. Lancet. 2007;369(9558):306-318. [PMID: 17258671]

## Item 37    Answer:  D

**Educational Objective:**  Diagnose a secondary headache.

This patient may have a secondary headache syndrome and should undergo an MRI of the brain. Secondary headache disorders are characterized by unstable or progressive temporal patterns and usually raise a "red flag" of concern during the history or examination. This patient has a long-standing history of migraine with aura, but the headache pattern has become more frequent over the past 3 months, and the new neurologic symptom of visual blurring has developed. Although this change may represent a premenopausal worsening of migraine or the superimposition of medication overuse headache syndrome, the presence of an intracranial mass lesion must be excluded with neuroimaging. Brain MRI is preferable to head CT in the evaluation of subacute or chronic headache because of improved sensitivity resulting from superior anatomic resolution.

Medication overuse headache, previously known as "rebound" headache, may be a contributing factor in the transformation of episodic migraine into a pattern of chronic daily headache. Because the presence of daily visual blurring would not be explained by analgesic overuse, however, the analgesic does not have to be discontinued, and the neuroimaging study remains the management step of first choice.

Although obtaining an erythrocyte sedimentation rate is necessary in patients with suspected temporal (giant cell) arteritis, this disorder is extremely uncommon in patients younger than 50 years without significant rheumatologic symptoms.

This patient has no indications of meningitis, such as acute onset, fever, and neck stiffness, which would warrant a lumbar puncture as the initial diagnostic test. Additionally, before a lumbar puncture can be safely performed, an intracranial mass lesion must be excluded with brain neuroimaging.

**KEY POINT**

- In a patient with a headache of an unstable or progressive temporal pattern that raises a "red flag" of concern during the history or examination, an MRI is appropriate to exclude an intracranial mass lesion.

**Bibliography**

DeLuca GC, Bartleson JD. When and how to investigate the patient with headache. Semin Neurol. 2010;30(2):131-144. [PMID: 20352583]

 ## Item 38    Answer:  B

**Educational Objective:** Diagnose Guillain-Barré syndrome.

This patient's history, symptoms, and clinical and laboratory findings are most consistent with Guillain-Barré syndrome (GBS), which often occurs in the setting of a recent infection, trauma, or surgery. Low back pain, presumably due to inflammatory demyelination at the spinal nerve root level and often mistaken for compressive lumbosacral radiculopathy, can herald the onset of GBS. The key finding in this patient is the presence of albuminocytologic (protein-cell) dissociation in the cerebrospinal fluid (CSF) (elevated CSF protein level but no leukocytes). The absence of CSF pleocytosis is typical of GBS.

Acute transverse myelitis often follows a viral infection and presents with subacute ascending weakness and often with bladder involvement. Transverse myelitis can occur in the setting of systemic lupus erythematosus. However, this diagnosis is unlikely in this previously healthy patient with a low antinuclear antibody titer and normal findings on a complete blood count, erythrocyte sedimentation rate measurement, and urinalysis.

Any part of the central and peripheral nervous system can be affected by sarcoidosis. The diagnosis should be considered in patients with established sarcoidosis who develop neurologic symptoms or in patients with neurologic symptoms who have other findings consistent with sarcoidosis. In a previously healthy patient without constitutional or pulmonary symptoms and with a normal chest radiograph, leptomeningeal disease from sarcoidosis is unlikely.

Patients with polyarteritis nodosa typically present with fever, abdominal pain, arthralgia, and weight loss that develop over days to months. Two thirds of these patients have mononeuritis multiplex. Central nervous system involvement is uncommon but does occur. Patients with polyarteritis nodosa usually have anemia, leukocytosis, and an elevated erythrocyte sedimentation rate, which are absent in this patient.

**KEY POINT**

- The presence of albuminocytologic (protein-cell) dissociation in cerebrospinal fluid is characteristic of Guillain-Barré syndrome.

**Bibliography**

Pritchard J. Guillain-Barré syndrome. Clin Med. 2010;10(4):399-401. [PMID: 20849020]

## Item 39    Answer:  A

**Educational Objective:** Treat the wearing-off motor fluctuations and dyskinesia of advanced Parkinson disease with deep brain stimulation.

The best management option for this patient is deep brain stimulation surgery. She developed Parkinson disease at age 46 years and, after many years of treatment, has now developed wearing-off motor fluctuations and drug-induced dyskinesia, two of the most serious complications of chronic treatment of Parkinson disease. Her condition is difficult to correct because efforts to reduce the dyskinesia by lowering the medication dosage lead to more pronounced wearing-off episodes, and attempts to improve the wearing-off motor fluctuations by increasing the medication exacerbate the dyskinesia. It is unlikely that further medical treatment or medication adjustments will substantially improve her quality of life.

Deep brain stimulation of the subthalamic nucleus or globus pallidus bilaterally can dramatically improve dyskinesia and wearing-off motor fluctuations and should be considered for this patient. She is an ideal candidate for this surgery because her idiopathic Parkinson disease is still responsive to individual doses of levodopa and she has no contraindications to surgery, including severe medical illness, dementia, or depression. Deep brain stimulation, although effective for wearing-off fluctuations and dyskinesia, has limitations in that it does not slow or reverse disease progression and is an elective procedure that carries operative risks.

Although under investigation, gene therapy currently is not a standard treatment option for treating Parkinson disease.

Physical therapy and the use of devices to increase mobility and prevent falls can be helpful adjuncts in the treatment of advanced Parkinson disease but do not specifically address the pharmacologic issues of wearing-off motor fluctuations and dyskinesia and thus are not the best treatment option.

A drug holiday (discontinuation and then reintroduction of her medications) is most likely to trigger acute parkinsonian symptoms in this patient and thus is inappropriate treatment.

KEY POINT

- Incapacitating wearing-off motor fluctuations and dyskinesia are primary indications for deep brain stimulation in patients with Parkinson disease.

**Bibliography**
Morley JF, Hurtig HI. Current understanding and management of Parkinson disease: five new things. Neurology. 2010;75(18 Suppl 1):S9-S15. [PMID: 21041778]

## Item 40     Answer:  C
**Educational Objective:** Manage external spinal cord compression by an epidural hematoma.

The most appropriate management for this patient is discontinuation of warfarin and reversal of the anticoagulation. She most likely has cauda equina syndrome secondary to external compression of the spinal cord by a spinal epidural hematoma. Her recent surgery is a risk factor for this disorder, which was likely exacerbated by early reinitiation of warfarin after the procedure. Stopping the warfarin and reversing the anticoagulation should be performed in preparation for subsequent surgical decompression.

Adding high-dose methylprednisolone to her treatment regimen is inappropriate because none of the clinical, laboratory, or imaging findings suggests the presence of an inflammatory disorder. In addition, no evidence suggests that an acute compressive lesion would respond to corticosteroids.

Although an epidural abscess is part of the differential diagnosis in this patient, the lack of fever, elevated leukocyte count, or elevated erythrocyte sedimentation rate makes the diagnosis highly unlikely and intravenous administration of antibiotics, such as vancomycin and ceftazidime, inappropriate.

The presence of a solid lesion in the lumbar region precludes the use of lumbar puncture in this patient in her current state of anticoagulation because the procedure is likely to exacerbate the underlying epidural hematoma.

KEY POINT

- In a patient being treated with warfarin for atrial fibrillation who develops cauda equina syndrome secondary to external compression of the spinal cord by a spinal epidural hematoma, discontinuing warfarin therapy and reversing the anticoagulation will help in preparation for a subsequent surgical decompression.

**Bibliography**
Glotzbecker MP, Bono CM, Wood KB, Harris MB. Postoperative spinal epidural hematoma: a systematic review. Spine. 2010;35(10):E413-E420. [PMID: 20431474]

## Item 41     Answer:  E
**Educational Objective:** Manage hypertension in the acute setting of ischemic stroke.

This patient does not require treatment of her elevated blood pressure (190/90 mm Hg) at this time. Because her initial evaluation occurred 12 hours after her acute ischemic stroke, she is not a candidate for intravenous recombinant tissue plasminogen activator (rtPA). The American Heart Association guidelines support allowing blood pressures of up to 220/120 mm Hg in patients with ischemic stroke who are ineligible for rtPA treatment, unless evidence of end-organ damage (active ischemic coronary disease, heart failure, aortic dissection, hypertensive encephalopathy, acute kidney failure, or preeclampsia/eclampsia) exists. Treatment with antihypertensive agents in the acute setting may lead to neurologic worsening due to a decline in cerebral perfusion in the area of the tissue at risk (penumbra). In the recently completed Scandinavian Candesartan Acute Stroke Trial (SCAST), treatment with candesartan was associated with a trend toward worse outcomes, primarily because of worsening neurologic status. The blood pressure target of less than 220/120 mm Hg is maintained until hospital discharge to home or a rehabilitation facility, at which time patients can begin or resume taking antihypertensive medication.

Intravenous hydralazine is inappropriate because the patient does not require immediate treatment for hypertension. Candesartan, labetalol, and nitroglycerin are inappropriate for the same reason. Additionally, because this patient is at high risk for aspiration, oral medications should not be administered until a formal dysphagia screen is performed.

**KEY POINT**

- Patients with ischemic stroke who are ineligible to receive recombinant tissue plasminogen activator and have no evidence of end-organ damage should not be treated for elevated blood pressure of up to 220/120 mm Hg.

**Bibliography**

Sandset EC, Bath PM, Boysen G, et al; SCAST Study Group. The angiotensin-receptor blocker candesartan for treatment of acute stroke (SCAST): a randomised, placebo-controlled, double-blind trial. Lancet. 2011;377(9767):741-750. [PMID: 21316752]

**Item 42     Answer:  B**

**Educational Objective:** Recognize delusional thinking as a primary symptom of dementia.

This patient has Capgras syndrome. He has the delusion that his daughter is an imposter, believing that his real daughter has been replaced by a fraudulent double. Delusions are fixed, unshakable, false ideas, often with a paranoid aspect, that are symptoms of several psychiatric and neurologic disorders. In the context of a neurodegenerative disease, a delusional misidentification is a sign of the underlying disorder, and not a primary psychiatric illness, such as paranoid schizophrenia. Capgras syndrome also can involve places, as with this patient who believes that his own home is only a replica of the real one. At the core of the delusion is the loss of emotional connection to a meaningful person or place. The pathologic substrate involves the right hemisphere, which plays an essential role in recognition and emotional familiarity. Capgras syndrome can occur with focal lesions of the right hemisphere or in neurodegenerative disorders with diffuse involvement, such as Alzheimer disease. Reassurance and attempts to reason with the patient are likely to fail, and treatment with antipsychotic agents is often indicated for this condition.

Anosognosia is unawareness of a neurologic deficit and often involves hemiplegia or vision (Anton syndrome). Confabulation consists of distorted or invented statements without a conscious desire to deceive and occurs in the context of retrograde amnesia and impaired anterograde learning due to lesions of the medial temporal lobes; it is a well-recognized feature of the alcohol-induced Korsakoff amnestic syndrome. Reduplicative paramnesia, in many ways the opposite of Capgras syndrome, is a delusion of familiarity in which a patient in a hospital bed insists that he or she is at home. None of these other delusional states are exhibited by this patient.

**KEY POINT**

- Patients with Capgras syndrome, a delusional misidentification syndrome associated with lesions of the right hemisphere, have the delusion of imposters, believing that important and familiar persons in their lives have been replaced by fraudulent doubles.

**Bibliography**

Devinsky O. Delusional misidentifications and duplications: right brain lesions, left brain delusions. Neurology. 2009;72(1):80-87. [PMID: 19122035]

**Item 43     Answer:  B**

**Educational Objective:** Treat a patient with generalized convulsive status epilepticus with the appropriate first-line drug.

This patient is exhibiting symptoms of generalized convulsive status epilepticus and should be treated with lorazepam as soon as possible. In the past, status epilepticus was defined as a seizure persisting or recurring without recovery for 30 minutes. Generally, however, most seizures do not last longer than 1 to 3 minutes, and seizures lasting more than 5 minutes should be managed as status epilepticus. Prompt treatment of generalized convulsive status epilepticus is essential given the morbidity associated with ongoing convulsions and because continuing seizures become more refractory to treatment over time. Acute complications include rhabdomyolysis, hypoxia, and metabolic acidosis; chronic complications include cognitive deficits and future seizures. Airway, breathing, and circulatory status should be assessed at presentation and monitored continuously. Initial laboratory studies should include a complete blood count, measurement of serum electrolyte (including sodium) and plasma glucose levels, toxicology screen, and measurement of serum antiepileptic drug levels, when appropriate. CT of the head also is indicated in any patient with status epilepticus, especially if the patient has had a recent neurosurgical intervention.

Benzodiazepines are considered first-line agents for treatment of status epilepticus, and intravenous lorazepam (0.1 mg/kg) is the preferred agent. Lorazepam is typically followed by the administration of phenytoin or, if available, fosphenytoin, which is, the prodrug of phenytoin. Diazepam also has been shown to be effective for status epilepticus, and rectal diazepam can be used when intravenous access is not available. Whereas diazepam's effect on seizure activity is more rapid, lorazepam has a much longer duration of action against seizures than does diazepam.

No data exist on levetiracetam used as a first-line agent for generalized convulsive status epilepticus. Therefore, this drug is inappropriate as treatment.

Phenytoin (or fosphenytoin) and valproic acid are accepted second-line agents for status epilepticus but

CONT.

should be given in combination with or immediately after a benzodiazepine.

> **KEY POINT**
>
> - Prompt treatment of generalized convulsive status epilepticus with lorazepam, usually followed by phenytoin or fosphenytoin, is essential given the morbidity associated with ongoing convulsions and because continuing seizures become more refractory to treatment over time.

**Bibliography**

Arif H, Hirsch LJ. Treatment of status epilepticus. Semin Neurol. 2008;28(3):342-354. [PMID: 18777481]

## Item 44    Answer:  A

**Educational Objective:**  Diagnose myasthenia gravis.

This patient should next have a CT of the chest. Her symptoms and clinical findings are most consistent with myasthenia gravis. Myasthenia gravis is caused by an immune-mediated attack on postsynaptic neuromuscular junctions. Approximately 85% of affected patients have antibodies directed against the acetylcholine receptor. Among patients without acetylcholine receptor antibodies, approximately 50% have antibodies directed against muscle-specific tyrosine kinase (MuSK) receptors. Although thymic hyperplasia and thymoma, which are present in 75% of patients with myasthenia gravis, are less likely in MuSK autoantibody receptor–positive disease, these disorders should first be ruled out with a chest CT scan because surgical resection would generally be warranted if either were present.

Pyridostigmine, an acetylcholinesterase inhibitor, is often sufficient to treat mild forms of myasthenia gravis, but MuSK autoantibody receptor–positive forms are less responsive to the drug. Treatment with immunosuppression or plasma exchange has been shown to have a good response in myasthenia gravis with MuSK autoantibody receptor–positive disease and thus is more appropriate for this patient.

An edrophonium test is helpful in diagnosing myasthenia gravis if clear-cut improvement in muscle strength or function can be demonstrated after edrophonium injection. This test would be relatively insensitive for diagnosing myasthenia gravis in this patient because the ocular findings are fluctuating and the limb weakness is only mild, which makes improvement difficult to assess. Determining readiness for resuscitation is advised before performing this test because it may result in bradycardia or cardiac dysrhythmias (such as atrial fibrillation) in sensitive persons.

Lumbar puncture with subsequent analysis of the cerebrospinal fluid provides no useful information for the diagnosis of myasthenia gravis.

An MRI of the brain would be useful to exclude intracranial lesions causing headache or diplopia but is normal in patients with myasthenia gravis, which this patient's clinical and laboratory findings most strongly suggest.

> **KEY POINT**
>
> - Patients with myasthenia gravis should have a chest CT to evaluate the presence of thymic hyperplasia or thymoma.

**Bibliography**

Scherer K, Bedlack RS, Simel DL. Does this patient have myasthenia gravis? JAMA. 2005;293(15):1906-1914. [PMID: 15840866]

## Item 45    Answer:  D

**Educational Objective:**  Diagnose multiple sclerosis on the basis of clinical evidence.

Given her history and clinical findings, this patient most likely has multiple sclerosis (MS) that has resulted in a partial demyelinating myelitis. The time course of symptoms is consistent with a demyelinating event, and the examination localizes best to the cervical cord, especially in light of the C5 sensory level. Her history also suggests demyelination in the setting of MS, given the electrical sensation with neck movement (Lhermitte sign), the prior episode of visual loss (optic neuritis), and the concurrent daytime fatigue. MRI of the brain should be performed to look for the ovoid white matter lesions typical of MS.

A cardioembolic stroke is not a likely diagnosis in the setting of the progressive onset of symptoms, the lack of any language deficits despite significant right-sided motor and sensory changes, and the examination findings that localize to the spinal cord.

A cervical disk herniation would not explain all of the patient's symptoms, especially her fatigue and ocular symptoms.

A complex migraine is unlikely because the patient was not experiencing headache. Although migraine can sometimes result in subtle focal neurologic symptoms, it would not result in the profound fixed deficits seen in this patient.

> **KEY POINT**
>
> - Multiple sclerosis can result in a partial demyelinating myelitis.

**Bibliography**

Frohman EM, Wingerchuk DM. Clinical practice. Transverse myelitis. N Engl J Med. 2010;363(6):564-572. [PMID: 20818891]

## Item 46    Answer:  C

**Educational Objective:**  Diagnose idiopathic intracranial hypertension.

This patient should have a lumbar puncture with subsequent analysis of the cerebrospinal fluid (CSF). In this

**CONT.**

young woman with obesity, progressive headache, papilledema, and normal findings on brain neuroimaging, the most likely diagnosis is idiopathic intracranial hypertension, also known as pseudotumor cerebri. This condition is most commonly found among young obese women and frequently presents with headache, visual disturbances, and tinnitus. Cranial nerve VI palsy is a false-localizing sign associated with elevated intracranial pressure. Diagnosis of idiopathic intracranial hypertension requires CSF from a lumbar puncture that documents elevated intracranial pressure with otherwise normal findings.

Carotid lesions typically do not cause isolated cranial nerve VI palsy. They also do not raise intracranial pressure. Therefore, carotid ultrasonography is not needed in this patient.

The presence of papilledema and cranial nerve palsy localizes the pathology to the intracranial cavity. Secondary headache disorders involving the paranasal sinuses would not be expected to result in such findings without some extension into the cranial vault, which would have been visualized by the brain MRI and magnetic resonance venogram. CT of the sinuses is thus unnecessary.

Although neck stiffness is present and the headaches exhibit some qualities of tension-type headache, the pathology is clearly intracranial, given the physical examination findings. MRI of the cervical spine is unlikely to contribute to the diagnosis.

---

**KEY POINT**

- **Diagnosis of idiopathic intracranial hypertension requires cerebrospinal fluid from a lumbar puncture that documents elevated intracranial pressure with otherwise normal findings.**

**Bibliography**
Wall M. Idiopathic intracranial hypertension. Neurol Clin. 2010;28(3):593-617. [PMID: 20637991]

---

**Item 47      Answer:  B**

**Educational Objective:** Diagnose anti–NMDA receptor encephalitis.

The most likely diagnosis in this patient is anti–NMDA receptor encephalitis, which classically presents with limbic encephalitis characterized by subacute memory disturbance, personality change, psychosis, encephalopathy, and seizures. Oral dyskinesia (involuntary mouth movements) are also a common presentation of this paraneoplastic syndrome, which is most commonly associated with unilateral or bilateral ovarian teratomas. The onset of the syndrome may be heralded by a flulike prodrome. A fluid-attenuated inversion recovery (FLAIR) MRI may show an increased signal in one or both temporal lobes. Results of cerebrospinal fluid (CSF) analysis can be normal but typically demonstrate a mild lymphocytic pleocytosis and normal or mildly elevated protein level. A definitive diagnosis is made

by finding anti–NMDA receptor antibodies in the CSF or serum. Finding a teratoma on a pelvic ultrasound or MRI makes anti–NMDA receptor encephalitis highly likely as a diagnosis, but this finding is not necessary, given that the syndrome has been documented in men and in women without teratomas. The best outcomes in women with anti–NMDA receptor encephalitis have been seen with early oophorectomy (of at least one and sometimes both ovaries) coupled with plasmapheresis, intravenous immune globulin, or corticosteroids.

The anti-Hu (anti-ANNA-1) autoantibody is associated with a paraneoplastic syndrome that typically involves motor or sensory symptoms. Limbic encephalitis is the presenting symptom in 10% to 20% of affected patients. Anti-Hu autoantibodies are typically found in older patients, however, and are most commonly associated with small-cell lung cancer, not ovarian teratomas.

Herpesviruses can also cause a limbic encephalitis, and the presentation may also include memory disturbance, psychosis, and seizures. In an immunocompetent patient, however, the disease course is usually more acute than occurred in this patient, with fulminant symptoms evolving over days instead of weeks. Fever is usually present. Oral dyskinesia is not a typical finding in herpes encephalitis. The CSF in herpes encephalitis classically shows a lymphocytic pleocytosis (100-200/µL), with or without an elevated protein level, but results of CSF analysis also can be normal. Erythrocytes are also often present in CSF after nontraumatic lumbar punctures in patients with herpes encephalitis, but this finding is not sensitive or specific enough to make the diagnosis. The MRI also may show increased FLAIR signals in one or both temporal lobes. Although herpes encephalitis is not the most likely diagnosis, polymerase chain reaction of the CSF for herpesvirus is still appropriate (present in 94%-97% of such patients), and the patient should be treated empirically with intravenous acyclovir until the diagnosis is clarified, given the significant morbidity and mortality associated with herpes encephalitis if left untreated.

Meningitis, or inflammation/infection of the meninges or outer covering of the brain, is distinct from encephalitis, which describes inflammation/infection of the brain parenchyma. Meningitis does not cause memory disturbances, psychosis, or seizures. The CSF usually demonstrates a lymphocytic pleocytosis (100-200/µL). MRI may demonstrate enhancement of the meningeal membranes but not inflammation of the brain.

---

**KEY POINT**

- **A definitive diagnosis of anti–NMDA receptor encephalitis is made by finding anti–NMDA receptor antibodies in the cerebrospinal fluid or serum.**

**Bibliography**
Dalmau J, Gleichman AJ, Hughes EG, et al. Anti-NMDA-receptor encephalitis: case series and analysis of the effects of antibodies. Lancet Neurol. 2008;7(12):1091-1098. [PMID: 18851928]

H **Item 48      Answer:  D**

**Educational Objective:**  Prevent venous thromboembolism after stroke.

This patient should receive subcutaneous unfractionated heparin. He is at high risk for venous thromboembolism (deep venous thrombosis and pulmonary embolism) because of his recent stroke and subsequent hemiparesis and immobility. He had an intracerebral hemorrhage, but CT scans of the head have remained stable, and no active source of bleeding in the brain has been identified. Thromboembolism prophylaxis is safe in this setting and should be administered by hospital day 4. Although low-molecular-weight heparin may be slightly superior to unfractionated heparin in preventing deep venous thrombosis, this patient's chronic kidney disease is a relative contraindication to using low-molecular-weight heparin.

Graded elastic pressure stockings without pneumatic compression have been shown to be ineffective in reducing the risk of deep venous thrombosis in patients with stroke.

Although commonly used to prevent deep venous thrombosis in patients who have orthopedic surgery, low-dose warfarin has not been shown to have this effect in patients with stroke.

An inferior vena cava filter is inappropriate for this patient with hemorrhagic stroke because no ongoing bleeding has been identified and because heparinoids are safe and effective in preventing deep venous thrombosis. Inferior vena cava filters for prevention of venous thromboemboli are reserved for patients with an active source of uncontrolled intracranial bleeding and for patients with severe traumatic brain injury to whom anticoagulants cannot be administered.

**KEY POINT**

- **Low-dose low-molecular-weight or unfractionated heparin is recommended in patients at high risk for venous thromboembolism after an intracerebral hemorrhage by hospital day 4.**

**Bibliography**

Kumar S, Selim MH, Caplan LR. Medical complications after stroke. Lancet Neurol. 2010;9(1):105-118. [PMID: 20083041]

**Item 49      Answer:  A**

**Educational Objective:**  Treat multiple sclerosis–related fatigue.

This patient should be treated with amantadine. She is experiencing multiple sclerosis (MS)–related fatigue, a common but often overlooked symptom of the disorder. Fatigue is described as exhaustion that is unrelated to physical activity and may be exacerbated by hot weather. Exclusion of anemia, sleep disorders, depression, hypothyroidism, and other medical conditions is required to make a diagnosis of MS-related fatigue. Adequate rest, regular physical exercise, and treatment with stimulant drugs can be helpful. Currently, the most frequently prescribed treatments for this symptom are amantadine and modafinil. Amantadine also has antiviral and antiparkinsonian properties.

Although iron deficiency anemia should be part of the differential diagnosis when a patient with MS has fatigue, this patient does not show any evidence of anemia on laboratory testing.

Hypothyroidism is a reasonable consideration in a patient with MS who has fatigue, but this patient's serum thyroid-stimulating hormone level is in the normal range, which makes levothyroxine therapy unnecessary.

Memantine has been evaluated and found ineffective for improving MS-related cognitive deficits, which this patient does not have, and has no reported benefit in diminishing symptoms of fatigue in patients with the disorder.

Changing this patient's medication from glatiramer acetate to one of the interferon beta options is inappropriate because her fatigue is not an adverse effect of the glatiramer acetate. Her fatigue also does not constitute an MS relapse, which might necessitate a therapeutic switch.

**KEY POINT**

- **Amantadine and modafinil are used as symptomatic treatments of multiple sclerosis–related fatigue.**

**Bibliography**

Braley TJ, Chervin RD. Fatigue in multiple sclerosis: mechanisms, evaluation, and treatment. Sleep. 2010;33(8):1061-1067. [PMID: 20815187]

**Item 50      Answer:  B**

**Educational Objective:**  Diagnose apraxia.

This patient most likely has apraxia, which is the inability to perform a previously learned skilled motor task despite intact motor and sensory systems, clear comprehension, and full cooperation. The major subtype of apraxia present in this patient is ideomotor apraxia, in which a patient has a clear concept of the proposed action but cannot execute it. Apraxia is identified clinically by asking the patient to demonstrate a common motor task, such as saluting, cutting a loaf of bread, hammering a nail, lighting a match, or using scissors. The diagnosis depends on excluding other causes of motor impairment as the main impediment to performing the task, such as severe weakness, parkinsonism, dysmetria, or tremor. Apraxia involves a lesion of the dominant parietal lobe and is a defining clinical feature of Parkinson-plus syndromes; it may also be a presenting feature of a neurodegenerative disease, such as Alzheimer disease or corticobasal degeneration.

Corticobasal degeneration is a rare, sporadic, degenerative condition. Clinical manifestations include gait impairment, dystonia, myoclonus, tremor, and slurred speech. Neurologic examination shows asymmetric rigidity, bradykinesia, and dystonia in most patients (hemiparkinsonism). The presence of alien hand syndrome, in which an upper extremity moves independently of conscious voluntary control, combined with these other signs suggests corticobasal degeneration. This patient does not exhibit signs of alien hand syndrome, and his right-sided symptoms are not typical of hemiparkinsonism.

Asomatognosia is a neurologic disorder in which patients do not recognize a part of their body as their own and is typically associated with lesions of the right parietal cortex. The patient's symptoms are not consistent with asomatognosia.

> **KEY POINT**
> - Apraxia is the inability to perform a previously learned skilled motor task despite intact motor and sensory systems, clear comprehension, and full cooperation.

**Bibliography**

Messina D, Cerasa A, Condino F, et al. Patterns of brain atrophy in Parkinson's disease, progressive supranuclear palsy and multiple system atrophy. Parkinsonism Relat Disord. 2011;17(3):172-176. [PMID: 21236720]

## Item 51    Answer:   C

**Educational Objective:**  Recognize the adverse-effect profile of topiramate.

Topiramate is contraindicated in this patient. Both topiramate and zonisamide are antiepileptic drugs used for migraine prophylaxis that carry an increased risk of kidney stone formation. Both have weak carbonic anhydrase inhibitory activity and inhibit proximal tubule reabsorption of bicarbonate, which results in a clinical syndrome similar to proximal renal tubular acidosis. Patients taking these drugs are at increased risk of forming calcium phosphate and, more rarely, calcium oxalate stones. Additionally, studies have documented a reduction in urine citrate excretion in such patients, which is an additional risk for calcium stone formation. Therefore, topiramate should not be taken by this patient who has a significant history of kidney stones. Patients without a history of kidney stones should be counseled on the increased risk and advised to stay well hydrated when they begin taking topiramate or zonisamide for migraine prophylaxis.

An increased risk of kidney stones has not been associated with propranolol, amitriptyline, or valproic acid, all of which are reasonable medications for migraine prophylaxis in this patient.

> **KEY POINT**
> - Both topiramate and zonisamide are associated with an increased risk of calcium-containing kidney stones and thus should be avoided in patients with a history of such stones.

**Bibliography**

Welch BJ, Graybeal D, Moe OW, Maalouf NM, Sakhaee K. Biochemical and stone-risk profiles with topiramate treatment. Am J Kidney Dis. 2006;48(4):555-563. [PMID: 16997051]

## Item 52    Answer:   A

**Educational Objective:**  Diagnose the cause of lower body parkinsonism.

This patient should undergo an MRI of the brain. She has gait freezing, a shuffling walk, and mild postural instability (evidenced by the results of a pull test), all signs of parkinsonism involving the lower body. In addition, she has developed urinary urgency and a possible change in her mentation, manifesting as mild social withdrawal. Taken together, these symptoms could represent an early stage in the development of the normal pressure hydrocephalus (NPH) triad of gait impairment, urinary incontinence, and cognitive change. Identifying NPH, especially in its earliest stages, is essential because it may be reversible. The first diagnostic step in a patient with suspected NPH should be a brain imaging study, such as MRI, which can identify hydrocephalus (if present) by showing evidence of ventriculomegaly. Vascular disease causing periventricular ischemia can mimic the gait impairment of NPH and also can be readily identified on a brain MRI.

If imaging reveals expanded lateral and third ventricles in the absence of obstruction, removal of a large volume of cerebrospinal fluid (CSF) by either serial lumbar punctures or continuous drainage can approximate the change in CSF dynamics that will occur with a shunt. However, a trial of CSF drainage should not be attempted in the absence of enlarged ventricles on brain MRI.

Single-photon emission CT scans are abnormal in patients with NPH, but these studies do not clearly predict shunt responsiveness, and their role in managing suspected NPH is not established.

Levodopa is effective in treating Parkinson disease, especially in patients older than 70 years, but has no benefit in the management of NPH.

> **KEY POINT**
> - The diagnosis of normal pressure hydrocephalus, which is characterized by the triad of gait impairment, urinary incontinence, and cognitive change, can be suggested by findings on a brain MRI.

**Bibliography**

Lee WJ, Wang SJ, Hsu LC, Lirng JF, Wu CH, Fuh JL. Brain MRI as a predictor of CSF tap test response in patients with idiopathic normal pressure hydrocephalus. J Neurol. 2010;257(10):1675-1681. [PMID: 20512347]

## Item 53    Answer:   A

**Educational Objective:**  Treat migraine during pregnancy.

This patient should be treated with acetaminophen. Although migraine often improves during pregnancy, many women continue to experience episodes throughout all three trimesters. Nonpharmacologic therapies are emphasized, with hydration, rest, and local application of ice all effective means of treating an acute attack. For pregnant women who require medical management, only medications with appropriate FDA and Teratogen Information System (TERIS) ratings for safety of use should be selected as treatment during pregnancy. The drug of choice for this patient is acetaminophen, one of the few acute migraine agents rated pregnancy category B (no evidence of risk in humans but no controlled human studies) by the FDA. This is often combined with metoclopramide or ondansetron, also both category B drugs, if nausea or vomiting is a significant migraine-related symptom during pregnancy.

Recent population-based studies have documented an increased risk of adverse pregnancy outcomes for women with migraine, including low-birth-weight, preterm deliveries, eclampsia, and placental abruption.

Amitriptyline is rated category C (risk to humans not ruled out) by the FDA. Although it is effective in migraine prevention, the low monthly migraine frequency in this patient does not warrant preventive pharmacotherapy.

Naproxen is rated category B by the FDA in the first two trimesters of pregnancy, but concerns of fetal patent ductus arteriosus and maternal bleeding at delivery render this option unsuitable for third trimester management of migraine.

Oxygen may be effective in the management of acute cluster headache, but no significant data support its use in acute migraine.

Rizatriptan carries an FDA pregnancy rating of category C and should be used in pregnant patients only after category B options have been exhausted.

**KEY POINT**

- **Acetaminophen, combined with metoclopramide or ondansetron for relief of the nausea and vomiting that can accompany migraine, is appropriate for use in pregnant women with migraine because these agents are unlikely to have a negative effect on the fetus.**

**Bibliography**

Brandes JL. Headache related to pregnancy: management of migraine and migraine headache in pregnancy. Curr Treat Options Neurol. 2008;10(1):12-19. [PMID: 18325295]

## Item 54     Answer: D
**Educational Objective:** Treat a tic disorder.

No intervention is necessary for this patient except for reassurance. This patient has a tic disorder consisting of several motor tics involving the face, a phonic tic (coughing), and a more elaborate tapping behavior that could represent a complex tic or a compulsion. His tics are preceded by an uncomfortable inner prodromal sensation, and a release of internal tension occurs after movements are discharged. The family history is positive for a tic disorder. Although

this patient meets the criteria for Tourette syndrome, his tics are mild, are nondisruptive to others, and do not cause self-consciousness. He does not exhibit the psychiatric comorbidities that often accompany tic disorders, such as attention-deficit/hyperactivity disorder and obsessive-compulsive disorder or anxiety. The primary goal of treating a tic disorder is to improve the affected person's level of social, occupational, or scholastic function, none of which are impaired in this patient. Therefore, no intervention is required other than reassurance.

Disabling and disruptive tics are treated with drugs that block dopamine receptors, such as clonidine, pimozide, and haloperidol, but such treatment is inappropriate for this patient whose tic disorder does not impair his ability to function normally in his social life or school environment. Tetrabenazine, an orphan drug used to treat hyperkinetic movement disorders and the chorea associated with Huntington disease, is also inappropriate for this patient.

**KEY POINT**

- **Treatment of tic disorders is indicated only when the disorder impairs a patient's social, academic, or occupational function or causes psychiatric comorbidities.**

**Bibliography**

Jankovic J. Differential diagnosis and etiology of tics. Adv Neurol. 2001;85:15-29. [PMID: 11530424]

## Item 55     Answer: A
**Educational Objective:** Manage symptomatic internal carotid artery disease.

This patient should be referred for immediate carotid endarterectomy of the right internal carotid artery. He has had an acute ischemic stroke caused by symptomatic high-grade carotid stenosis. His risk for recurrent stroke is approximately 26% over the next 2 years. Carotid endarterectomy has been shown to be highly effective in reducing the risk of recurrent stroke (number needed to treat, 17) in the immediate poststroke period. With symptomatic carotid stenosis, the risk of recurrent stroke is 1% per day for the first 2 weeks after a stroke or transient ischemic attack, which indicates that the greatest benefit is gained when the procedure is performed early.

Carotid stenting would be inappropriate for this patient. The Carotid Revascularization Endarterectomy Versus Stenting Trial (CREST) showed that for the primary outcomes of stroke, myocardial infarction, and death, stenting and endarterectomy were not statistically significantly different. For the outcomes of recurrent stroke and death, endarterectomy was superior to stenting because stenting poses a greater risk of perioperative stroke than does endarterectomy. Older patients benefited the most from endarterectomy, which also was associated with a lower risk of perioperative stroke.

No evidence supports the use of clopidogrel in the acute poststroke period in patients with symptomatic high-grade carotid stenosis. Antiplatelet agents generally provide only a marginal benefit in reducing the risk of stroke compared with surgery.

Statins have yet to be established as safe or efficacious in the immediate poststroke setting. Although the Stroke Prevention by Aggressive Reduction in Cholesterol Levels (SPARCL) study showed that statins significantly reduced the risk of recurrent stroke in patients with a serum LDL cholesterol level greater than 100 mg/dL (2.59 mmol/L), the trial did not start enrolling participants until 30 days after stroke onset.

**KEY POINT**

- Early carotid endarterectomy is indicated in patients with symptomatic high-grade carotid stenosis and is associated with a lower risk of perioperative stroke than stenting.

**Bibliography**

Brott TG, Hobson RW 2nd, Howard G, et al; CREST Investigators. Stenting versus endarterectomy for treatment of carotid-artery stenosis. N Engl J Med. 2010;363(1):11-23. [PMID: 20505173]

## Item 56     Answer:   C

**Educational Objective:** Diagnose postconcussion syndrome in a patient returning from military service.

This patient most likely has postconcussion syndrome, which is characterized by a complex of somatic, neurologic, and psychiatric symptoms after a concussive head injury. Common symptoms include headache, fatigue, sleep disturbances, difficulties with concentration and memory, and emotional lability with an increased tendency for depression, anxiety, and irritability. Dizziness and tinnitus also are frequently reported. Approximately 10% to 20% of military personnel returning from combat deployment have had a reported concussion, and 5% of them have some evidence of postconcussion syndrome. Studies have shown that patients with this disorder score lower than control patients on neuropsychological tests that measure attention, verbal learning, reasoning, and information processing. Additionally, abnormalities on functional neuroimaging, such as PET or single-photon emission CT, have been reported. The precise pathophysiologic basis for the constellation of complaints remains unknown.

Meniere disease does cause vertigo, tinnitus, and sensorineural hearing loss in affected patients but does not explain the neuropsychiatric symptoms reported by this patient.

Despite the presence of photophobia, this patient's headache does not meet criteria for migraine in that it is bilateral, bandlike, and mild in intensity.

Posttraumatic stress disorder can cause cognitive and emotional symptoms, such as memory loss and irritability, and may provoke headaches, but the absence of persistent memories, dreams, or flashbacks of the traumatic event favors an alternative explanation for this patient's presentation.

Although the pain described is typical of chronic tension-type headache, the other neuropsychiatric symptoms reported are not and suggest that another diagnosis is more likely.

**KEY POINT**

- Common symptoms of postconcussion syndrome include headache, fatigue, sleep disturbances, difficulties with concentration and memory, and emotional lability with an increased tendency for depression, anxiety, and irritability.

**Bibliography**

Evans RW. Persistent post-traumatic headache, postconcussion syndrome, and whiplash injuries: the evidence for a non-traumatic basis with an historical review. Headache. 2010;50(4):716-724. [PMID: 20456159]

## Item 57     Answer:   B

**Educational Objective:** Manage cryptogenic ischemic stroke.

This patient's condition should be managed with prolonged cardiac rhythm monitoring. She has infarcts that appear embolic on an MRI and no evidence of proximal arterial disease. As such, her stroke is classified as a cryptogenic ischemic stroke. According to data from recent studies, up to 25% of patients with cryptogenic ischemic stroke have paroxysmal atrial fibrillation on prolonged cardiac monitoring. A diagnosis of atrial fibrillation would be the only reason for this patient to start warfarin for stroke prevention. The risk of recurrent stroke in patients with an otherwise isolated patent foramen ovale, with or without an atrial septal aneurysm, is low in most clinical trials.

Percutaneous or surgical closure of a patent foramen ovale has not been shown to reduce the risk of ischemic stroke in patients with an otherwise cryptogenic stroke. Patent foramen ovale, especially in combination with an atrial septal aneurysm, is associated with an increased risk of ischemic stroke in epidemiologic studies, but the optimal medical treatment remains unknown. Preliminary results from the CLOSURE I trial showed no significant difference in the risk of stroke recurrence in patients with cryptogenic stroke randomized to either the percutaneous patent foramen ovale closure arm or the best medical treatment arm.

Warfarin is an inappropriate treatment for this patient at this time, pending results of cardiac rhythm monitoring. No clinical trials, including a substudy of the Warfarin-Aspirin Recurrent Stroke Study (WARSS), have shown the superiority of warfarin compared with aspirin in the prevention of recurrent cryptogenic stroke, even in the presence of a patent foramen ovale.

> **KEY POINT**
>
> • Up to 25% of patients with cryptogenic ischemic stroke have paroxysmal atrial fibrillation on prolonged cardiac monitoring.

**Bibliography**

Tayal AH, Tian M, Kelly KM, et al. Atrial fibrillation detected by mobile cardiac outpatient telemetry in cryptogenic TIA or stroke. Neurology. 2008;71(21):1696-1701. [PMID: 18815386]

## Item 58     Answer: E

**Educational Objective:** Manage migraine without aura.

This patient should be treated with sumatriptan. He reports episodes of moderate to severe headache that meet the diagnostic criteria for migraine. Migraine without aura can be diagnosed if the following diagnostic criteria are fulfilled:

• Headache lasting 4 to 72 hours
• Headache with at least two of the following characteristics:
  ○ Is unilateral
  ○ Is pulsatile
  ○ Is of moderate or severe intensity
  ○ Is aggravated by routine physical activity
• Headache accompanied by at least one of the following associated symptoms:
  ○ Nausea and/or vomiting
  ○ Photophobia and/or phonophobia
• At least five headache attacks that fulfill these criteria
• History and findings from physical and neurologic examinations not suggestive of any underlying organic disease

This patient's attacks have recurred for 5 years, fit the 4- to 72-hour duration of migraine, and possess two of the four pain-feature requirements (moderate intensity and aggravation by routine activity) and one of the two associated feature requirements (photophobia and phonophobia). In the absence of contraindications, the use of triptans, such as sumatriptan, is an appropriate treatment for a migraine that does not respond to NSAIDs.

Given that the patient's headache meets the criteria for migraine and that no findings suggest an alternative diagnosis, neither CT of the patient's sinuses nor treatment with nasal corticosteroids is indicated.

An MRI of the brain or any other neuroimaging study is unnecessary in this patient in the presence of a stable 5-year pattern of episodic headaches that meet criteria for migraine, normal findings on neurologic examination, and the absence of any red flags of secondary headache.

Evidence-based guidelines do not support the use of oxycodone or other opioids in the treatment of acute migraine except when NSAIDs or triptans fail or are contraindicated.

> **KEY POINT**
>
> • In the absence of contraindications, the use of triptans, such as sumatriptan, is an appropriate treatment for a migraine that does not respond to NSAIDs.

**Bibliography**

Loder E. Triptan therapy in migraine. N Engl J Med. 2010;363(1):63-70. [PMID: 20592298]

## Item 59     Answer: D

**Educational Objective:** Diagnose restless legs syndrome.

The patient has restless legs syndrome, a common movement disorder characterized by a deep, ill-defined discomfort or dysesthesia usually involving the legs that occurs when a person is trying to fall asleep. The leg discomfort is coupled with an urge to move, and movement reduces or eliminates the uncomfortable sensations. This disorder typically occurs during middle age but may start in one's 20s. Often familial, restless legs syndrome may worsen over time. Treatment with dopamine agonists or opiates can alleviate symptoms.

Most patients with restless legs syndrome also experience periodic limb movements of sleep, which involve recurrent, patterned leg jerks and tonic spasms that sometimes resemble a flexion reflex, usually occur every 20 seconds during early-stage sleep, and generally resolve deeper in the sleep cycle. Periodic limb movements of sleep may disturb the sleeping partner and also awaken the patient, which leads to inadequate or fragmented sleep and subsequent daytime drowsiness. The diagnosis can be confirmed by polysomnography. Some cases are associated with iron deficiency, and thus it is advisable to check the serum ferritin level. Both restless legs syndrome and periodic limb movements of sleep result from dopaminergic deficiency and can be treated with dopamine agonists, such as pramipexole or ropinirole.

Akathisia is a form of restlessness coupled with an urge to move but is not accompanied by the dysesthesia of restless legs syndrome or periodic limb movements of sleep. Akathisia is more often experienced as a generalized sensation and not one confined to the legs.

Nocturnal leg cramps are painful, sustained muscle contractions usually involving the calves. The uncomfortable sensations reported by this patient do not match this description.

This patient's symptoms do not resemble the hypnic jerks or the "sleep starts" associated with physiologic myoclonus, in which a limb or the trunk may suddenly jerk as a person is falling asleep.

**KEY POINT**

- Restless legs syndrome is a common movement disorder characterized by a deep, ill-defined discomfort or dysesthesia usually involving the legs that occurs when a person is trying to fall asleep; the discomfort is coupled with an urge to move, which reduces or eliminates the uncomfortable sensations.

**Bibliography**

Bayard M, Avonda T, Wadzinski J. Restless legs syndrome. Am Fam Physician. 2008;78(2):235-240. [PMID: 18697508]

## Item 60      Answer:  C

**Educational Objective:**   Predict future falling risk.

The pull test is the best means to predict the risk of future falls in a patient with a history of backward falls. This test consists of asking the patient to stand in front of the examiner and prepare for a quick tug backward that will be forceful enough to displace his or her center of gravity off base. The correct response to the tug is a quick compensatory backward step. A patient with postural instability, a cardinal feature of parkinsonism, does not take an adequate backward step and may tumble into the arms of the examiner, who can stop him or her from falling. Alternatively, a patient may take a series of ineffectual short steps. In either case, the pull test establishes a falling risk. The most likely cause of an abnormal pull test is Parkinson disease or a related parkinsonism disorder.

Nystagmus elicited by a Dix-Hallpike maneuver may be helpful in differentiating peripheral vestibular from central nervous system causes of vertigo. While seated on the examination table, the patient is asked to lie down quickly, first with one ear turned toward the table and then with the other ear turned toward the table. When this maneuver results in nystagmus lasting for 10 or 20 seconds and is possibly accompanied by vertigo, a disorder of the vestibular system is suggested. This patient has no symptoms of dizziness or vertigo and thus this test will have limited usefulness in predicting future falling risk.

Proximal muscle weakness is often associated with myopathic disorders. Patients may have difficulty rising from a chair, climbing stairs, or holding their arms above shoulder level, but patients with proximal muscle weakness do not typically fall backward. Proprioception allows for the appreciation of joint position and movement. Loss of proprioception most commonly occurs in patients with peripheral neuropathy, spinal cord disease, and severe hemicranial cerebral cortex disease. Patients with abnormal proprioception may have an abnormal gait (high-stepping, feet slapping) but do not fall backward.

The Romberg test is a test for ataxia and proprioceptive loss in which the patient stands with his or her feet together and eyes closed. If the patient sways or loses balance, the test is considered positive. A positive Romberg test supports the diagnosis of ataxia but does not specifically localize its origin

in the nervous system because all types of ataxia worsen in the absence of visual cues. However, a positive Romberg test in a patient unable to perform a tandem stepping test does suggest a disease of the cerebellum, cerebellar pathways, or vestibular system. This patient does not have a tendency to lurch and veer, as would be expected with an ataxic gait.

**KEY POINT**

- The pull test is the best means to predict the risk of future falls in a patient with a history of backward falls.

**Bibliography**

Munhoz RP, Li JY, Kurtinecz M, et al. Evaluation of the pull test technique in assessing postural instability in Parkinson's disease. Neurology. 2004;62(1):125-127. [PMID: 14718714]

## Item 61      Answer:  B

**Educational Objective:**  Diagnose juvenile myoclonic epilepsy.

This patient has juvenile myoclonic epilepsy. Most patients with this disorder have infrequent convulsive seizures that are often provoked by alcohol or sleep deprivation. They often also have myoclonic seizures (often experienced as "shakiness") that are worse in the morning. They may or may not additionally have absence seizures. A family history of convulsive seizures or myoclonic jerks is common.

Convulsions may occur in childhood absence epilepsy, but myoclonus is not typical of this syndrome. Furthermore, most patients with childhood absence epilepsy have complete remission of seizures by puberty.

The history of morning jerks and absence seizures indicates that this patient's seizure was epileptic and not a single provoked seizure from alcohol intoxication.

A convulsive seizure with or without an aura can be the initial presentation of temporal lobe epilepsy, but patients with this disorder typically do not experience early morning myoclonus.

**KEY POINT**

- Patients with juvenile myoclonic epilepsy have infrequent convulsive seizures often provoked by alcohol or sleep deprivation and can also experience absence seizures and myoclonic seizures that are worse in the morning.

**Bibliography**

Genton P, Gelisse P. Juvenile myoclonic epilepsy. Arch Neurol. 2001;58(9):1487-1490. [PMID: 11559326]

## Item 62      Answer:  A

**Educational Objective:** Treat asymptomatic extracranial carotid artery stenosis.

This patient should begin taking pravastatin. She has asymptomatic internal carotid artery stenosis with a low risk of ischemic stroke or transient ischemic attack but a higher risk with operative intervention. Carotid revascularization for asymptomatic patients is not indicated when the stenosis is less than 70%. She has no additional risk factors for stroke, such as stenosis greater than 80%, rapidly progressive stenosis, or asymptomatic infarcts on imaging, and thus should be treated with optimal medical management. Her lipid profile shows significant atherogenic dyslipidemia, and a statin (other than simvastatin) is indicated to lower her serum LDL cholesterol level to less than 100 mg/dL (2.59 mmol/L) for stroke prevention.

Myalgia is common in patients taking statins and, given her joint pain when taking simvastatin, pravastatin is the next best choice. Creatine kinase levels should be obtained in patients with myalgia to detect myopathy because progression to rhabdomyolysis, myoglobinuria, and acute kidney injury is possible if myopathy is present. Myopathy is more likely to occur with higher doses of statins and when statins are used in combination with other drugs, including fibrates, nicotinic acid (niacin), macrolide antibiotics, some antifungal agents, and cyclosporine. With improvements in best medical therapy, particularly statins, the risk of stroke has been declining in patients with asymptomatic carotid stenosis. Recent data indicate that the annual risk of stroke in asymptomatic carotid stenosis may be less than 1%, especially among patients treated with statins.

No clear evidence shows that clopidogrel is superior to aspirin for the primary prevention of stroke in the setting of asymptomatic internal carotid artery stenosis.

This patient's age (>80 years) and multiple medical comorbidities all make her a poor candidate for endovascular or surgical interventions. The benefit of carotid revascularization is more modest in patients with asymptomatic than with symptomatic stenosis. Furthermore, the benefit of revascularization in patients with 50% to 70% stenosis is less well established in women with symptomatic disease.

> **KEY POINT**
>
> - In patients with dyslipidemia, statin therapy is indicated for primary prevention of stroke.

**Bibliography**

Marquardt L, Geraghty OC, Mehta Z, Rothwell PM. Low risk of ipsilateral stroke in patients with asymptomatic carotid stenosis on best medical treatment: a prospective, population-based study. Stroke. 2010; 41(1):e11-e17. [PMID: 19926843]

## Item 63     Answer: D
**Educational Objective:** Manage multiple sclerosis–related spasticity.

This patient should receive tizanidine. The patient has multiple sclerosis (MS) and is experiencing upper motoneuron spasticity with associated muscle spasms and cramping pain. Examination findings supporting this diagnosis include movement-dependent spasticity and hyperreflexia. Patients with this type of spasticity can experience significant pain due to muscle overactivity and may also have impaired gait due to stiffness. Spasticity, spasms, and cramping usually respond to a combination of physical therapy (stretching) and oral antispasticity drugs. Tizanidine, a centrally acting $\alpha_2$-adrenergic agonist, exerts muscle relaxant properties by helping modulate interneuron activity and polysynaptic reflex activity. Other possible treatment options are baclofen and cyclobenzaprine. Of these three drugs, none is the clear first-line choice. Patients with severe and refractory symptoms may require trials of botulinum toxin injections or an intrathecal baclofen pump.

This patient has a normal serum creatine kinase level, upper motoneuron signs on examination, and no signs of an inflammatory myopathy (such as polymyositis) or neuromuscular disorder (such as amyotrophic lateral sclerosis) for which electromyography would be appropriate.

MRI of the lumbosacral spine only images the lower conus medullaris, cauda equina, and lumbar spinal roots. MS does not affect the lumbar spinal roots, and the clinical examination is consistent with upper motoneuron dysfunction, which would localize higher on the spinal cord or brain. Therefore, this test is inappropriate for this patient.

Oxybutynin is used to treat an overactive bladder, which can occur in patients with MS but does not significantly alter muscle tone and thus is unlikely to help in this patient.

> **KEY POINT**
>
> - Tizanidine, baclofen, and cyclobenzaprine are appropriate treatments for multiple sclerosis–related spasticity.

**Bibliography**

Chou R, Peterson K, Helfand M. Comparative efficacy and safety of skeletal muscle relaxants for spasticity and musculoskeletal conditions: a systematic review. J Pain Symptom Manage. 2004;28(2):140-175. [PMID: 15276195]

## Item 64     Answer: C
**Educational Objective:** Diagnose neuroleptic malignant syndrome.

This patient with fever, tremors, agitation, and parkinsonism on examination is most likely to have neuroleptic malignant syndrome (NMS). This potentially life-threatening disorder is characterized by hyperthermia that is usually accompanied by autonomic dysfunction, such as tachycardia, diaphoresis, or labile blood pressure; extrapyramidal signs, typically muscle rigidity or dystonia and elevated muscle enzyme levels; and altered mental status. The syndrome represents an idiosyncratic reaction to exposure to antipsychotic neuroleptic medications, and the most common offending agents are haloperidol and fluphenazine.

**CONT.** NMS usually develops over 24 hours and peaks within 72 hours. The syndrome can occur with all drugs that cause central dopamine type 2 receptor blockade and usually occurs soon after starting a new drug or with dose escalation. NMS also has been reported in patients with Parkinson disease who abruptly discontinue their dopamine drugs. Most patients with NMS develop muscle rigidity, hyperthermia, cognitive changes, autonomic instability, diaphoresis, sialorrhea, seizures, cardiac arrhythmias, and rhabdomyolysis within 2 weeks after initiating the drug. Symptoms can occur any time during drug therapy and may persist for up to 1 month, or longer if parenteral medications were given.

Acute lithium toxicity can produce neurologic findings, including ataxia, agitation, tremors, fasciculations, or myoclonic jerks. Lithium toxicity, however, does not produce hyperthermia.

Malignant hyperthermia is an inherited skeletal muscle disorder characterized by a hypermetabolic state precipitated by exposure to volatile inhalational anesthetics (halothane, isoflurane, enflurane, desflurane, and sevoflurane) and the depolarizing muscle relaxants succinylcholine and decamethonium. Increased intracellular calcium leads to sustained muscle contractions with skeletal muscle rigidity, tachycardia, hypercarbia, hypertension, hyperthermia, tachypnea, and cardiac arrhythmias. Rhabdomyolysis and acute kidney injury can develop. The patient has not been exposed to the requisite drugs that account for this diagnosis.

Like NMS, the serotonin syndrome presents with high fever, muscle rigidity, and cognitive changes. Findings unique to the serotonin syndrome are shivering, hyperreflexia, myoclonus, and ataxia. The serotonin syndrome is caused by the use of serotonin reuptake inhibitors, a category of drug to which this patient has not been exposed.

**KEY POINT**

- **Neuroleptic malignant syndrome is a potentially lethal condition that develops after exposure to dopamine receptor antagonists and is characterized by muscle rigidity, hyperthermia, cognitive changes, autonomic instability, diaphoresis, sialorrhea, seizures, cardiac arrhythmias, and rhabdomyolysis.**

**Bibliography**
Gillman PK. Neuroleptic malignant syndrome: mechanisms, interactions, and causality. Mov Disord. 2010;25(12):1780-1790. [PMID: 20623765]

**Item 65        Answer:  B**
**Educational Objective:**  Institute early rehabilitation after a stroke.

Early rehabilitation should be initiated in this patient as soon as she is medically stable. She has had an acute ischemic stroke with an identified cause that resulted in significant motor dysfunction. Without early mobility, she is at high risk for deep venous thrombosis, atelectasis, contractures, and skin breakdown. Patients with motor or cognitive dysfunction from stroke should be further evaluated in an expedited manner by physical and occupational therapists and by speech and swallow therapists for the ability to swallow liquids safely. Early rehabilitation can have significant beneficial effects on stroke recovery. Other steps to improve stroke recovery include screening for and treating poststroke depression and minimizing the occurrence of poststroke medical complications, such as pneumonia and urinary tract infections.

Amoxicillin-clavulanate is inappropriate because the patient has no clinical evidence of pneumonia. She is afebrile and has normal results on pulmonary examination, despite being at risk for aspiration. Prophylactic antibiotics in patients with stroke who are at risk for aspiration have not been shown to be effective in reducing the incidence of pneumonia.

The central nervous system stimulant modafinil is unlikely to help this patient. In general, pharmacologic agents, including amphetamines, have yet to be shown to improve stroke recovery.

Stenting of the internal carotid artery is inappropriate in this patient who has not experienced recurrent symptoms and has no evidence of continuing ischemia. Stenting in the setting of carotid artery dissection, in fact, remains a risky and unproved procedure.

**KEY POINT**

- **Aggressive rehabilitation as soon as patients are medically stable can have significant beneficial effects on stroke recovery.**

**Bibliography**
Stroke Unit Trialists' Collaboration. Organised inpatient (stroke unit) care for stroke [update of Cochrane Database Syst Rev. 2002;(1):CD000197]. Cochrane Database Syst Rev. 2007;(4):CD000197. [PMID: 17943737]

**Item 66        Answer:  C**
**Educational Objective:**  Diagnose a psychogenic gait.

This patient is exhibiting a psychogenic gait. An excessive, elaborate gait that varies in appearance from moment to moment is inconsistent with a lesion of the nervous system. Pathologic gaits of neurologic origin are consistent in pattern and tend to involve minimal or inadequate movement. A psychogenic gait is typically inconsistent, incongruous, and elaborate, often with expressions of great effort, unconvincing displays of weakness or impairment, sudden genuflections, and extreme lurching without falling. The genuflecting gait in particular is not consistent with a neurologic disorder. In this instance, the work-related injury may be contributing to the persistence of symptoms.

Diagnosing an unusual gait that is compromised by chorea, dystonia, tremor, or myoclonus can be difficult. Prolonged observation, however, will reveal that such hyperkinetic gaits are extremely consistent in pattern throughout the period of observation and do not vary in findings from visit to visit, as expected for a fixed condition of the nervous system.

Peripheral injury dystonia, posttraumatic stress syndrome with dystonia, and reflex sympathetic dystrophy may cause a fixed dystonic posture, coupled with pain, sensory changes, and autonomic instability of the limb. These syndromes are not consistent with this patient's presentation and the findings of his clinical examination.

### KEY POINT

- A variable, elaborate, inconsistent gait suggests a nonneurologic cause, such as a psychogenic movement disorder.

#### Bibliography

Baik JS, Lang AE. Gait abnormalities in psychogenic movement disorders. Mov Disord. 2007;22(3):395-399. [PMID: 17216648]

## Item 67    Answer:  B

**Educational Objective:**  Treat a patient older than 60 years with the appropriate antiepileptic drug.

This older patient should be treated with lamotrigine. The seizure description, physical findings, and CT scan confirm that he has had complex partial (focal) seizures. Antiepileptic drugs (AEDs) are just as likely to be unsuitable in particular patients because of adverse effects as from lack of efficacy. Approximately 5% of patients will discontinue the first AED prescribed because of a serious idiosyncratic reaction. Another 15% will discontinue because of non–life-threatening adverse effects, such as sedation, mood disorder, or weight gain. Lamotrigine is a first-line drug for treating partial and generalized epilepsy that is well tolerated in older patients. It has been shown to have the highest rate of retention and best efficacy in this population.

Carbamazepine, oxcarbazepine, and phenytoin are all first-line drugs used to treat partial epilepsy but are less well tolerated in older patients. Common adverse effects include dizziness, lethargy, and gait instability. All three drugs are hepatic enzyme inducers and thus may reduce the efficacy of concomitant medications that these patients may be taking. Carbamazepine and oxcarbazepine are often both associated with hyponatremia, particularly in older patients.

### KEY POINT

- Lamotrigine is a first-line drug for treating partial and generalized epilepsy that is well tolerated, has the highest rate of retention, and has the best efficacy among older patients.

#### Bibliography

Arif H, Buchsbaum R, Pierro J, et al. Comparative effectiveness of 10 antiepileptic drugs in older adults with epilepsy. Arch Neurol. 2010;67(4):408-415. [PMID: 20385905]

## Item 68    Answer:  A

**Educational Objective:**  Manage a subdural hematoma.

This patient should have a CT scan of the head. Subdural hematoma is a key consideration in a patient with recent head or neck trauma and cognitive symptoms. Whereas epidural hematoma development generally requires direct trauma to the skull, a subdural hematoma may occur after relatively minor injuries to the cervical spine or head that create concussive forces within the cranium. Unlike epidural hematoma, which presents rapidly because of laceration of the middle meningeal artery, a subdural hematoma involves disruption of bridging veins between the brain parenchyma and dura and may develop slowly over days to weeks. Older populations are particularly prone to subdural hematomas, and the use of anticoagulant therapy, which is also common in this group, is another risk factor for intracranial hemorrhage. A CT scan of the head without contrast is generally diagnostic for acute subdural hematomas and is the imaging modality of choice for acute head trauma.

After a diagnosis of subdural hematoma is confirmed, a neurosurgical consultation is indicated. Patient presentation, examination abnormalities, and CT findings are all considerations weighed by the neurosurgeon in determining the necessity and timing of surgical evacuation.

This patient reports mental cloudiness and has ataxia on examination. These intracranial concerns override the back and neck pain and spasms he is experiencing. The muscle relaxant cyclobenzaprine would address only the symptom of paraspinal spasm and may worsen the cognitive and gait dysfunction in this older patient.

Similarly, meclizine may be effective in the management of the dizziness of vestibular origin that sometimes follows whiplash injuries, but the physical examination findings in this patient should provoke a search for alternative explanations for his dizziness and ataxia.

Physical therapy rehabilitation is premature before neuroimaging has been completed in a patient with this history and these examination findings.

### KEY POINT

- A CT scan of the head without contrast is generally diagnostic for acute subdural hematomas and is the imaging modality of choice for acute head trauma.

#### Bibliography

Panczykowski DM, Okonkwo DO. Premorbid oral antithrombotic therapy and risk for reaccumulation, reoperation, and mortality in acute subdural hematomas. J Neurosurg. 2011;114(1):47-52. [PMID: 20722610]

## Item 69     Answer: C

**Educational Objective:** Diagnose posthypoxic myoclonus.

This patient most likely has posthypoxic myoclonus. Prolonged cerebral hypoxia or anoxia, such as this patient experienced, can result in a syndrome of generalized myoclonus, originally known as Lance-Adams syndrome. The clinical features of posthypoxic (or postanoxic) myoclonus include powerful, shocklike muscle jerks; activation of symptoms with action or stimulation; and negative myoclonus (the sudden lapse of a sustained posture [asterixis]). Because negative myoclonus interrupts sustained muscular postural support, it can represent a severe barrier to upright stance and walking. The origin of posthypoxic myoclonus is the cortex, which is hyperexcitable after a hypoxic or an anoxic injury. The most likely cause of posthypoxic myoclonus is a cardiac arrest or delayed cardiopulmonary resuscitation. The syndrome is extremely difficult to treat and has a poor prognosis. The treatment of choice is anticonvulsant therapy with agents that are active in myoclonic epilepsy, such as valproic acid, levetiracetam, and clonazepam.

Cerebellar degeneration does not explain this patient's presentation. The spinocerebellar ataxia syndromes have an autosomal dominant pattern of inheritance and are associated with chronic, progressive cerebellar ataxia, with a mean age of onset in the fourth and fifth decades. This type of ataxia typically presents as gait unsteadiness and extremity incoordination but not myoclonic jerks with muscle activation, as seen in this patient.

Myoclonic epilepsy is an idiopathic generalized epilepsy syndrome characterized by both myoclonic seizures on awakening and generalized tonic-clonic seizures. These seizure types occur independently, but a flurry of myoclonic seizures may presage a generalized tonic-clonic seizure. Onset is usually in adolescence.

Wernicke encephalopathy characteristically results in ataxia but is also associated with ophthalmoplegia (paresis of eye muscles), confusion, peripheral neuropathy, and even seizures. Caused by thiamine (vitamin $B_1$) deficiency, Wernicke encephalopathy most commonly occurs in persons with alcoholism but has also been reported in patients who have undergone bariatric surgery, have had a prolonged period of fasting, have had repeated episodes of vomiting, or have been on prolonged parenteral nutrition without adequate vitamin supplementation.

### KEY POINT

- The most likely cause of posthypoxic myoclonus is a cardiac arrest or delayed cardiopulmonary resuscitation.

### Bibliography
Venkatesan A, Frucht S. Movement disorders after resuscitation from cardiac arrest. Neurol Clin. 2006;24(1):123-132. [PMID: 16443134]

## Item 70     Answer: E

**Educational Objective:** Treat migraine with aura in a patient with cardiovascular comorbidities.

This patient should next receive sumatriptan. Her headache is characteristic of migraine with aura and meets the diagnostic criteria of exhibiting at least two of four pain features (unilateral location, pulsatile nature, moderate to severe intensity, and aggravation by routine activity) and at least one of two associated features (nausea or photophobia/phonophobia). The once or twice yearly visual symptoms meet symptomatic and duration criteria for typical aura and do not possess any characteristics suggestive of transient ischemic attack. NSAIDs have been unsuccessful for this patient, and evidence-based guidelines suggest advancing to triptan use.

No evidence supports the use of butalbital with acetaminophen and caffeine as acute migraine therapy. In addition, butalbital poses a drug-dependency risk. Therefore, this drug regimen should not be considered a first- or second-line therapy for this patient.

Brain MRIs of patients with migraine often show white matter hyperintensities. Nothing suggests that those on this patient's MRI are ischemic in nature, and thus daily aspirin therapy is unnecessary.

Given the absence of good, prospective, controlled evidence that patent foramen ovale closure is beneficial in the treatment of migraine, patients with this structural abnormality should not undergo the procedure to treat migraine.

Although propranolol is an effective agent for preventing migraine, daily prophylactic medication is not needed in this patient who has only one to two headache attacks per month, for a maximum of 4 days per month. The use of an acute migraine medication is appropriate when strictly limited to fewer than 10 days per month to avoid the potential development of medication overuse headache.

### KEY POINT

- Sumatriptan is appropriate to treat acute exacerbations of migraine with aura.

### Bibliography
Schwedt TJ, Demaerschalk BM, Dodick DW. Patent foramen ovale and migraine: a quantitative systematic review. Cephalalgia. 2008;28(5):531-540. [PMID: 18355348]

## Item 71     Answer: B

**Educational Objective:** Diagnose psychogenic nonepileptic seizures with video electroencephalographic monitoring.

In this patient with intractable seizures, inpatient video electroencephalographic (EEG) monitoring is indicated to capture and characterize the patient's typical events. With this procedure, patients are admitted electively to the hospital for 2 to 7 days, during which time EEG results and videos of the patient are continuously recorded. The patient's antiepileptic drugs (AEDs) may be withdrawn during this admission. Recording several seizures is usually necessary to completely characterize an epilepsy syndrome. Patients with epileptic seizures that have not responded to more than two medications should be monitored to define their epilepsy syndrome and determine their candidacy for epilepsy surgery.

The clinician also should maintain a high index of suspicion for psychogenic nonepileptic seizures in patients whose epilepsy has been refractory to multiple medications. Up to 20% of patients seen at epilepsy referral centers have psychogenic nonepileptic seizures. Making a diagnosis of nonepileptic events is critical to avoid the morbidity of unnecessary medical treatment (AEDs, intubation). Although the duration of this patient's seizures raises the suspicion of nonepileptic events because most epileptic seizures last less than 5 minutes, the distinction between epileptic and nonepileptic seizures can be very difficult to make on the basis of history alone. Evidence of urinary incontinence, self injury, or loss of consciousness does not help distinguish between epileptic and nonepileptic events.

Although ambulatory EEG monitoring may be able to identify epileptic seizures, it is not the best way to distinguish between epileptic and nonepileptic events because it is usually performed without video recording. In both frontal lobe seizures and psychogenic nonepileptic seizures, the EEGs are often normal or obscured by artifact. Frontal lobe seizures also are more likely to be clinically stereotyped, and the definitive diagnosis can be made only after reviewing the videos of several events. Furthermore, a patient's medications may need to be withdrawn for diagnosis, which can only occur in a supervised inpatient setting.

A brain MRI was appropriately obtained 2 years ago to exclude an intracranial pathologic lesion that might be the basis of epilepsy or a psychiatric disease. A repeat brain MRI at this time, however, is unlikely to be helpful and would not yield a definitive diagnosis.

The duration of outpatient EEG is typically 30 minutes, which is often too short a period to capture an event. A normal EEG thus does not rule out a diagnosis of epilepsy. In addition, the presence of interictal epileptiform discharges on a routine EEG may make a diagnosis of epilepsy more likely but does not exclude nonepileptic seizures, which can occur in patients with a history of epilepsy. The key to diagnosis in this patient is to witness the clinical features of a typical event in a video recording.

**KEY POINT**

- Inpatient video electroencephalographic monitoring is indicated in patients whose epileptic seizures have not responded to multiple medications to capture and characterize the patient's typical events.

**Bibliography**
Reuber, M. Psychogenic nonepileptic seizures: answers and questions. Epilepsy Behav. 2008;12(4):622-635. [PMID: 18164250]

## Item 72  Answer:  D

**Educational Objective:**  Diagnose Wilson disease in a young patient.

This patient's serum ceruloplasmin level should be measured. She has two cardinal signs of parkinsonism, rigidity and bradykinesia, and several secondary signs, including a glabellar sign, increased saliva, facial masking, cramped handwriting, and decreased arm swing. Parkinsonism can result from the psychomotor retardation of a major depressive disorder, but affected patients usually also manifest other signs of depression, including depressed mood, feelings of worthlessness, suicidal ideation, abnormal sleep patterns, and poor appetite.

The differential diagnosis of a young person with parkinsonism must include Wilson disease (hepatolenticular degeneration), which is reversible if diagnosed early. Wilson disease results from an autosomal recessive inborn error of metabolism caused by a mutation of the copper P-type adenosine triphosphatase encoded on chromosome 13q14.3. This mutation leads to a failure of copper excretion in bile, which results in copper accumulation in the liver and brain. The most common neurologic presentation of Wilson disease is parkinsonism, although dystonia, ataxia, tremor, psychiatric symptoms, and hepatic disease are also presentations. A slit-lamp examination to detect a Kayser-Fleischer ring and measurement of the serum ceruloplasmin level are the screening tests for Wilson disease. More sensitive tests that can be performed if the level of clinical suspicion is high enough include a 24-hour urine copper collection and liver biopsy for quantitative copper content.

Other causes of parkinsonism in young persons include juvenile Parkinson disease, including *LRRK2*-associated Parkinson disease; juvenile Huntington disease; carbon monoxide poisoning; trauma; brain tumor; hydrocephalus; and rare metabolic diseases, such as mitochondrial encephalopathy, late-onset pantothenate kinase deficiency, or rapid-onset dystonia-parkinsonism. None of these possibilities seems likely in this patient, but an appropriate neuroimaging study should be performed.

This patient exhibits no symptoms of depression and does not require a psychiatric evaluation.

**KEY POINT**

- The most common neurologic presentation of Wilson disease is parkinsonism.

**Bibliography**
Lorincz MT. Neurologic Wilson's disease. Ann N Y Acad Sci. 2010;1184:173-187. [PMID: 20146697]

## Item 73  Answer:  A

**Educational Objective:**  Treat a patient with an ischemic stroke with a statin.

This patient should now receive atorvastatin. He had an ischemic stroke in the distribution of the internal carotid artery. Given his severe stenosis and other risk factors, the stroke was most likely atherosclerotic. In all patients with stroke and an LDL cholesterol level greater than 100 mg/dL (2.59 mmol/L), clinical trial data support the use of a high-dose statin to prevent recurrent ischemic stroke and myocardial infarction.

Although this patient is still within the expanded 4.5-hour treatment window for a recombinant tissue plasminogen activator (rtPA), he is not a candidate for treatment because of his history of ischemic stroke and diabetes mellitus.

In patients with stroke who are not candidates for intravenous rtPA, a blood pressure of less than 220/120 mm Hg is recommended in the acute setting unless evidence of end-organ damage (such as myocardial infarction or kidney injury) exists. Therefore, using an antihypertensive agent, such as nicardipine, in this patient is inappropriate at this time.

Warfarin also is inappropriate for this patient, who does not have a history of atrial fibrillation. In large artery atherosclerosis, warfarin was not shown to be superior to antiplatelet agents in the Warfarin-Aspirin Recurrent Stroke Study (WARSS).

> **KEY POINT**
> - In patients with stroke and a serum LDL cholesterol level greater than 100 mg/dL (2.59 mmol/L), clinical trial data support the use of a statin to prevent recurrent ischemic stroke and myocardial infarction.

**Bibliography**
Furie KL, Kasner SE, Adams RJ, et al; American Heart Association Stroke Council, Council on Cardiovascular Nursing, Council on Clinical Cardiology, and Interdisciplinary Council on Quality of Care and Outcomes Research. Guidelines for the prevention of stroke in patients with stroke or transient ischemic attack: a guideline for healthcare professionals from the American Heart Association/American Stroke Association. Stroke. 2011;42(1):227-276. [PMID: 20966421]

## Item 74     Answer:  B

**Educational Objective:**  Manage suspected drug-induced myopathy.

This patient should stop taking simvastatin and itraconazole. Statin medications may cause an acute or subacute painful proximal myopathy with rhabdomyolysis. Myalgia, with or without a slight increase in the serum creatine kinase level, is more commonly reported. A recent increase in statin dosage or the addition of another drug that inhibits cytochrome P3A4, which is the pathway by which most statins are metabolized, substantially increases the risk of myopathy. Inhibitors include macrolides, fibrates, and protease inhibitors (such as itraconazole). Discontinuing the responsible medications generally results in gradual recovery from drug-induced myopathy.

This patient's thyroid-stimulating hormone level is within the target range for persons receiving thyroid replacement therapy. Therefore, decreasing the levothyroxine dosage is not indicated. Although most patients with hyperthyroidism do not report limb weakness as a presenting symptom, symmetric proximal limb weakness is typically found on examination. Other signs and symptoms of hyperthyroidism include anxiety, tremor, heat intolerance, insomnia, and weight loss. Myalgia and fatigue are also commonly reported. Serum creatine kinase measurement and findings on electromyography (EMG) are typically normal. After treatment of the thyrotoxic state, the myopathy usually resolves over several months.

Strong evidence suggests that vitamin D deficiency, even in the absence of osteomalacia, is associated with myalgia and proximal limb weakness. A low serum 1,25-dihydroxyvitamin D level can suggest the diagnosis. The serum creatine kinase level, however, is usually normal, as are EMG findings.

A muscle biopsy is not indicated. Polymyositis manifests as a symmetric muscle weakness that usually affects the proximal muscles. Affected patients may have difficulty with activities that involve raising their hands above their head and have difficulty rising from a chair and climbing stairs. Muscle pain in patients with an inflammatory myopathy is atypical and, if present, is generally mild. A diagnosis of an inflammatory myopathy is established in patients with a compatible clinical presentation accompanied by elevated serum muscle enzyme levels and characteristic pathologic findings on muscle biopsy. The distribution of this patient's weakness and prominent pain make inflammatory myositis unlikely and a muscle biopsy unnecessary.

> **KEY POINT**
> - In a patient already taking a statin, the introduction of a drug that inhibits its breakdown can substantially increase the risk of myopathy.

**Bibliography**
Joy TR, Hegele RA. Narrative review: statin-related myopathy. Ann Intern Med. 2009;150(12):858-868. [PMID: 19528564]

## Item 75     Answer:  E

**Educational Objective:**  Manage a menstrually related migraine with prophylaxis.

This woman should receive topiramate as migraine prophylaxis. She has a history of migraine with aura that is becoming more frequent. She describes recurrent attacks of disabling unilateral pulsatile headache preceded by visual and sensory auras and accompanied by nausea and vomiting. The attacks are responsive to aggressive acute management, but the number of headache days per month continues to climb. The clinical presentation of migraine seen in this patient, including headache frequency, use of acute headache medications on 2 or more days per week, and the presence of a prolonged (>1 hour) aura, warrants the introduction of a pharmacologic preventive agent to promote a reduction in attack frequency. Evidence-based guidelines suggest that topiramate, propranolol, timolol, amitriptyline, and divalproex sodium should be considered first-line preventive medications for episodic migraine, and recent clinical trials have documented the efficacy of topiramate and injectable onabotulinumtoxinA for chronic migraine prophylaxis.

No evidence (or indication) suggests that butalbital compounds should be used in the management of migraine. Because sumatriptan has been effective for this patient, no acute migraine drug substitution is warranted.

In the absence of papilledema and in the presence of a typical migraine history, lumbar puncture has no role in this headache assessment.

The use of daily NSAIDs, such as naproxen, in migraine prophylaxis is unsupported by evidence, although evidence does exist that frequent analgesic use may contribute to a medication overuse or "rebound" headache syndrome.

Oral contraceptives may be helpful in the management of menstrually related migraine, particularly when given continuously in an attempt to suppress menses. They should be avoided in women (such as this patient) who have a history of migraine with atypical or prolonged aura (>60 minutes) or other stroke risk factors, such as a maternal history of early stroke.

**KEY POINT**

- Topiramate is an effective agent for migraine prophylaxis.

**Bibliography**
Brandes JL, Saper JR, Diamond M, et al; MIGR-002 Study Group. Topiramate for migraine prevention: a randomized controlled trial. JAMA. 2004;291(8):965-973. [PMID: 14982912]

## Item 76    Answer: D

**Educational Objective:** Diagnose progressive supranuclear palsy.

This patient most likely has progressive supranuclear palsy. He has developed a syndrome of dementia, atremulous parkinsonism, and eye movement abnormalities over 2 years. The dementia is marked by cognitive slowing, passivity, and apathy, which suggest a subcortical localization. His inability to read and his messy eating habits can be ascribed to convergence insufficiency and vertical gait impairment His parkinsonism is characterized by a dystonic facial appearance, axial rigidity, gait hesitation, and postural instability. Taken together, these symptoms suggest a Parkinson-plus syndrome, specifically progressive supranuclear palsy. The hallmark findings of progressive supranuclear palsy are impairment of vertical eye movements, square wave jerks (couplets of inappropriate horizontal saccades), a supranuclear gaze paresis, facial dystonia, and axial rigidity. An aggressive

Parkinson-plus syndrome, this disorder is characterized by rapid disease progression and early falling, with a time to a first falling episode of 1.5 years, compared with 8 years for Parkinson disease.

On neuroimaging studies, patients with Parkinson-plus syndromes exhibit marked atrophy of the brainstem and midbrain. The pathology includes widespread neurofibrillary tangle deposition throughout the basal ganglia, midbrain, brainstem, and cerebellum, corresponding to the clinical localization. The condition is relentlessly progressive, leading to death (usually by aspiration) within 8 to 12 years.

This patient's increasing forgetfulness, word-finding difficulties, and slowed gait are typical of Alzheimer disease, but his eye findings, postural instability and absence of tremor are not.

Although this patient has dementia and parkinsonism, he has not had visual hallucinations or symptoms of rapid eye movement sleep behavior disorder, which makes a diagnosis of Lewy body dementia less likely.

The rapid progression of symptoms, the absence of a tremor, and the visual findings make Parkinson disease an unlikely diagnosis in this patient.

**KEY POINT**

- The hallmark findings of progressive supranuclear palsy are impairment of vertical eye movements, square wave jerks (couplets of inappropriate horizontal saccades), a supranuclear gaze paresis, facial dystonia, and axial rigidity.

**Bibliography**
Wenning GK, Colosimo C. Diagnostic criteria for multiple system atrophy and progressive supranuclear palsy. Rev Neurol. 2010;166(10):829-833. [PMID: 20813385]

## Item 77    Answer: C

**Educational Objective:** Treat epidural spinal cord metastases.

This patient should next undergo decompressive surgery followed by radiation therapy. The most common cause of spinal cord compression is tumor metastasis to a vertebral body, which results in direct extension into the epidural space or a pathologic fracture. Pain is the most common initial presenting symptom in patients with spinal cord compression, with neurologic symptoms typically evolving later. The diagnosis must be established before the patient develops motor weakness or other neurologic deficits because a significant number of patients with spinal cord compression do not recover neurologic function. Corticosteroids should be administered immediately in patients with suspected spinal cord compression for improved pain management and prevention of further neurologic impairment; dexamethasone is the most commonly used therapeutic regimen. When feasible, decompressive surgery should be performed next, followed by radiation therapy. This treatment regimen is more effective than radiation alone in treating selected patients

**CONT.**

with spinal cord compression caused by metastatic cancer and provides the best chance for future ambulation.

Androgen-deprivation therapy (with a gonadotropin-releasing hormone agonist or surgical castration) is used as adjuvant therapy in patients with high-risk disease and as first-line treatment in patients with an increasing serum prostate-specific antigen level after initial definitive therapy for prostate cancer or in those with metastatic disease. It is not an effective treatment for spinal cord compression.

Chemotherapy is not an effective treatment for metastatic cancer causing spinal cord compression unless the tumor is highly sensitive to chemotherapy, such as lymphoma.

Although radiation therapy does provide benefit for most tumor types, evidence from clinical trials shows that the addition of surgical decompression before radiation therapy is superior to radiation therapy alone, and direct head-to-head comparisons show more long-term benefit from surgery than radiation therapy.

> **KEY POINT**
> - Clinical trials have shown that decompressive surgery provides the best chance for future ambulation in patients with epidural spinal cord metastases.

**Bibliography**
George R, Jeba J, Ramkumar G, Chacko AG, Leng M, Tharyan P. Interventions for the treatment of metastatic extradural spinal cord compression in adults. Cochrane Database Syst Rev. 2008(4):CD006716. [PMID: 18843728]

**Item 78    Answer:  B**

**Educational Objective:** Diagnose the rapidly progressive dementia of Creutzfeldt-Jakob disease.

This patient most likely has Creutzfeldt-Jakob disease, a rapidly progressive dementia associated with myoclonus. The most striking feature of this patient's history is the rapid deterioration in mental status and personality. Over 5 weeks, he has declined from a high level of function to a state of inanition. In the absence of trauma, intoxication, infection, fever, or other systemic signs of disease, only two neurologic conditions can produce such a rapid deterioration in cognition and behavior, namely, a prion disorder (such as Creutzfeldt-Jakob disease) and a paraneoplastic syndrome (such as limbic encephalitis). Creutzfeldt-Jakob disease causes a spongiform encephalopathy devoid of inflammatory signs; neuroimaging shows no abnormal enhancement.

Because of the patient's age and the rapid progression of his cognitive decline, Alzheimer disease is an unlikely diagnosis.

Frontotemporal dementia may produce a constellation of symptoms similar to those of this patient, but its time course is much longer.

Clinical features of herpes simplex encephalitis include fever, hemicranial headache, language and behavioral abnormalities, memory impairment, cranial nerve deficits, and seizures. On T1-weighted MRIs, edema and hemorrhage in the temporal lobes, hypodense areas, and nonhomogeneous contrast enhancement may be identified. Bilateral temporal lobe involvement is nearly always pathognomonic for herpes simplex encephalitis but is a late development. The patient's features are not consistent with herpes simplex encephalitis.

> **KEY POINT**
> - In a rapidly progressive dementia, prion diseases, such as Creutzfeldt-Jakob disease, and paraneoplastic syndrome are diagnostic possibilities.

**Bibliography**
Rosenbloom MH, Atri A. The evaluation of rapidly progressive dementia. Neurologist. 2011;17(2):67-74. [PMID: 21364356]

**Item 79    Answer:  A**

**Educational Objective:** Treat an older woman with a cerebral infarction in a stroke unit.

This patient should be admitted to the nearest stroke unit. Several studies have shown that admission to an organized inpatient stroke unit compared with a general medical ward is associated with a reduction in mortality at 1 year and that benefits persist up to 10 years after stroke onset. Stroke units are likely to be beneficial because of the multidisciplinary nature of care, with an emphasis on specialized nursing and early rehabilitation.

Admission to rehabilitation may ultimately be indicated, but at this time hemodynamic stability needs to be established, and evaluation for stroke cause, including cardiac testing and vascular imaging, is required.

No clear indication exists that this patient requires admission to the intensive care unit, particularly given that her blood pressure should not be lowered acutely.

> **KEY POINT**
> - Admission of patients with stroke to an inpatient stroke unit compared with a general medical ward is associated with a reduction in mortality at 1 year, and that benefit persists for up to 10 years after stroke onset.

**Bibliography**
Stroke Unit Trialists' Collaboration. Organised inpatient (stroke unit) care for stroke [update of Cochrane Database Syst Rev. 2002;(1):CD000197]. Cochrane Database Syst Rev. 2007;(4):CD000197. [PMID: 17943737]

**Item 80    Answer:  C**

**Educational Objective:** Anticipate the adverse effects of natalizumab therapy.

Natalizumab has been associated with an approximately 1:1000 risk of central nervous system infection with the JC virus, resulting in progressive multifocal leukoencephalopathy (PML). Patients taking natalizumab for multiple sclerosis (MS) should be advised to inform their physicians of any new or progressively worsening neurologic symptoms, which might signify the onset of PML. MRI should be repeated in this setting, and if any lesions suspicious for PML are seen, cerebrospinal fluid testing for the JC virus with polymerase chain reaction can be performed. The current recommendations are to immediately stop natalizumab if PML is diagnosed and then to use plasmapheresis to remove unbound circulating antibody.

Dose-dependent cardiotoxicity occurs with mitoxantrone treatment of MS but has not been reported for natalizumab. Flulike symptoms are a common adverse effect of interferon treatment but have not been observed with natalizumab. Skin lipoatrophy is commonly seen at frequent injection sites with glatiramer acetate treatment but not with natalizumab administration. Worsening of underlying depression is a reported adverse effect of the interferon betas but not of natalizumab.

**KEY POINT**

- Natalizumab is a disease-modifying therapy for multiple sclerosis that has been associated with an approximately 1:1000 risk of central nervous system infection with the JC virus, resulting in progressive multifocal leukoencephalopathy.

**Bibliography**

Clifford DB, De Luca A, Simpson DM, Arendt G, Giovannoni G, Nath A. Natalizumab-associated progressive multifocal leukoencephalopathy in patients with multiple sclerosis: lessons from 28 cases [erratum in Lancet Neurol. 2010;9(5):463]. Lancet Neurol. 2010;9(4):438-446. [PMID: 20298967]

**Item 81    Answer:  B**

**Educational Objective:**  Treat elevated blood pressure after an intracerebral hemorrhage.

The patient should receive an infusion of labetalol. He has an intracerebral hemorrhage likely due to hypertension, cocaine abuse, and (possibly) aspirin. Hematoma expansion is an important predictor of a poor outcome in intracerebral hemorrhage, and hypertension is one of the principal risk factors for expansion. Blood pressure levels above 140/80 mm Hg after intracerebral hemorrhage are also associated with poor outcome. In this patient, systolic blood pressure should be lowered by means of an intravenous infusion of antihypertensive medication, with monitoring of vital signs every 5 minutes, particularly because the systolic blood pressure is greater than 200 mm Hg. In patients whose systolic blood pressure is greater than 180 mm Hg, a target blood pressure of 160/90 mm Hg is reasonable as long as there are no signs of elevated intracranial pressure; if intracranial pressure is elevated, a target systolic blood pressure of 140 mm Hg appears to be safe, according to recently published guidelines. Because labetalol is

unlikely to interact with cocaine and cause an increase in blood pressure, it is the appropriate option.

Placement of an external ventricular drain is inappropriate in this awake and interactive patient, despite the hydrocephalus seen on imaging. If the patient were to develop impaired consciousness, then cerebrospinal fluid shunting may be necessary to reduce elevated intracranial pressure.

Although metoprolol may lower this patient's blood pressure, it is contraindicated in patients with cocaine intoxication because of unopposed α-activity potentially leading to coronary, and potentially cerebrovascular, vasoconstriction.

Whether platelet transfusions improve outcomes in patients with intracerebral hemorrhage or prevent hematoma expansion in patients taking antiplatelet agents remains unknown. Additionally, platelet transfusion may be associated with potential risks to the patient, including transfusion syndrome and volume overload.

**KEY POINT**

- Labetalol is appropriate for patients with hypertensive intracerebral hemorrhages associated with cocaine abuse to decrease blood pressure and prevent hematoma expansion.

**Bibliography**

Morgenstern LB, Hemphill JC 3rd, Anderson C, et al; American Heart Association Stroke Council and Council on Cardiovascular Nursing. Guidelines for the management of spontaneous intracerebral hemorrhage: a guideline for healthcare professionals from the American Heart Association/American Stroke Association. Stroke. 2010;41(9):2108-2129. [PMID: 20651276]

**Item 82    Answer:  C**

**Educational Objective:**  Diagnose tardive dystonia.

This patient has developed tardive dystonia involving her neck and trunk that is most likely caused by the metoclopramide she is taking. The associated facial grimacing (a classic finding in tardive dyskinesia) and restlessness (akathisia) make the diagnosis of tardive dystonia certain because this constellation of symptoms does not occur in any other context. Tardive dystonia is a forceful, sometimes painful sustained contraction of muscles leading to twisted postures that must be distinguished from tardive dyskinesia, which consists of flowing, patterned choreic movements of the face. Both are caused by exposure to dopamine type 2 ($D_2$) receptor antagonists, but the difference in the appearance of the movements has an important bearing on the treatment and prognosis. Tardive dystonia is more disabling than tardive dyskinesia and also harder to treat. The therapeutic approach includes a gradual discontinuation of the offending agent, treatment with anticholinergic or dopamine receptor–depleting agents, and the judicious use of botulinum toxin injections.

Huntington disease is a familial disorder causing generalized chorea, dementia, and behavioral changes. This patient does not exhibit these symptoms.

Juvenile Parkinson disease can cause parkinsonism in a child or young adult. This patient does not exhibit symptoms of parkinsonism.

Wilson disease causes copper accumulation in the basal ganglia and liver and may present as progressive parkinsonism or dystonia. Symptom onset is usually in childhood or teenage years. This patient does not have parkinsonism, Kayser-Fleischer rings, or a family history of neuropsychiatric or hepatic disease, which renders the diagnosis of Wilson disease unlikely.

**KEY POINT**

- Tardive dystonia, a disorder whose classic findings include facial grimacing and akathisia, can be induced by dopamine receptor antagonists, such as metoclopramide and antipsychotic drugs.

**Bibliography**
Fernandez HH, Friedman JH. Classification and treatment of tardive syndromes. Neurologist. 2003;9(1):16-27. [PMID: 12801428]

## Item 83    Answer:  A
**Educational Objective:**  Treat migraine without aura.

This patient should receive amitriptyline as a preventive medication for his increasingly frequent headache attacks. Given his history of headaches dating back to childhood and the absence of any red flags indicating a secondary headache, a primary headache syndrome is clearly present. These attacks meet criteria for migraine without aura (unilateral, pulsating headache lasting 4-72 hours that is accompanied by photophobia, phonophobia, and nausea) and may be quickly distinguished from cluster headache by episode duration (>3 hours) and from tension-type headache by their severe intensity and association with nausea, photophobia, and phonophobia. Approximately 38% of patients with migraine need preventive treatment, but preventive medications are prescribed to only 3% to 13% of these patients. The major class of agents available for migraine prevention is the tricyclic antidepressants, to which amitriptyline belongs. This drug, propranolol, timolol, divalproex sodium, and topiramate have the strongest available evidence of effectiveness.

No significant evidence supports the use of fluoxetine or other selective serotonin reuptake inhibitors in the prevention of migraine.

Propranolol, a nonselective β-blocker, is an effective drug for migraine prevention, but its use is contraindicated in the presence of asthma.

Verapamil is an effective agent for preventing cluster headache. Evidence of its effectiveness in preventing migraine, however, is quite limited.

Although data support the use of several nutritional supplements, such as magnesium and riboflavin, in migraine prevention, no evidence supports the use of vitamin D in this context.

**KEY POINT**

- Strong evidence supports the use of amitriptyline, propranolol, timolol, divalproex sodium, and topiramate for migraine prevention.

**Bibliography**
Silberstein SD. Preventive migraine treatment. Neurol Clin. 2009;27(2):429-443. [PMID: 19289224]

## Item 84    Answer:  B
**Educational Objective:**  Diagnose dopamine agonist–caused compulsive behavior.

This patient is most likely exhibiting medication-related compulsive behavior caused by the ropinirole he is taking. Ropinirole is a dopamine agonist, and dopamine agonists are generally used as first-line treatment of symptomatic Parkinson disease in patients younger than 70 years. He is exhibiting the compulsive behavioral syndrome of punding, which is characterized by excessive, compulsive, repetitive complex activity that serves no essential purpose. Punding, like other compulsive or addictive behaviors (such as excessive gambling, shopping, Internet use, or hypersexual behavior), results from dysregulation of the brain's dopamine-dependent reward systems and can be caused by dopaminergic medication. The first step in treatment is usually a reduction of dopaminergic medication.

Dementia with Lewy bodies is a progressive dementia that eventually affects up to 80% of all patients with Parkinson disease. Its hallmark features are dream-enactment behavior, cognitive decline, parkinsonism, and visual hallucinations. Compulsive behavior is not a typical symptom of this disorder.

Because many of the hallmark features of frontotemporal dementia, such as apathy, impulsivity, perseveration, hoarding, obsessionality, and disinhibition, are lacking in this patient, that diagnosis also is unlikely.

This patient's Parkinson disease is controlled well by the medications he is taking. He has good motor function and no physical impediments to performing activities of daily living. Increasing compulsivity does not indicate worsening Parkinson disease but is an adverse effect of his dopaminergic medication.

**KEY POINT**

- Patients with Parkinson disease who take dopamine agonist medication can exhibit compulsive behavior, such as punding, a tendency to repetitively perform unnecessary tasks.

**Bibliography**
O'Sullivan SS, Evans AH, Lees AJ. Punding in Parkinson's disease. Pract Neurol. 2007;7(6):397-399. [PMID: 18024780]

## Item 85      Answer:  C

**Educational Objective:**  Identify patients with the HLA-B*1502 allele at increased genetic risk for Stevens-Johnson syndrome.

This patient should receive levetiracetam. Although not all first seizures require initiation of an antiepileptic drug, this patient has several indications that his likelihood for seizure recurrence is high. He had a partial (focal) seizure and a focal lesion on a CT scan. He also has focal findings on clinical examination after the seizure that suggest Todd paralysis. Because this patient has a focal lesion, he also may be a candidate for epilepsy surgery if his paralysis is refractory to medication, but medication trials should be attempted first. Carbamazepine, lamotrigine, levetiracetam, oxcarbazepine, and phenytoin are all reasonable first-line options for partial epilepsy, but levetiracetam is the only medication that can be started immediately in this patient because of his Asian heritage. In an Asian patient with the HLA-B*1502 allele, the risk of Stevens-Johnson syndrome is increased with exposure to carbamazepine, lamotrigine, oxcarbazepine, and phenytoin. Therefore, genetic testing is recommended before starting these medications in Asian patients.

> **KEY POINT**
> - In an Asian patient with the HLA-B*1502 allele, the risk of Stevens-Johnson syndrome is increased with exposure to carbamazepine, lamotrigine, oxcarbazepine, and phenytoin but not with exposure to levetiracetam.

**Bibliography**
Hung SI, Chung WH, Liu ZS; et al. Common risk allele in aromatic antiepileptic-drug induced Stevens-Johnson syndrome and toxic epidermal necrolysis in Han Chinese. Pharmacogenomics. 2010;11(3):349-356. [PMID: 20235791]

## Item 86      Answer:  B

**Educational Objective:**  Manage a transient ischemic attack.

This patient most likely has had a transient ischemic attack (TIA) and should be admitted to the hospital immediately. Her ABCD$^2$ score is 7 (one point for an Age of 60 years or greater, one point for a Blood pressure of 140/90 mm Hg or greater, two points for the Clinical symptom of hemiparesis, two points for Duration of 60 minutes or greater, and one point for the presence of Diabetes mellitus), which indicates a 2-day stroke risk of 8.1%. The American Heart Association guidelines recommend hospital admission for all patients with probable TIAs whose ABCD$^2$ scores are 3

or greater. A noninvasive stroke evaluation can be completed more quickly in the hospital, with a particular focus on excluding cerebral infarction as a cause of symptoms and diagnosing the presence of intracardiac thrombi and extracranial internal carotid artery stenosis.

No evidence supports the combination of aspirin and clopidogrel for stroke prevention, and the use of the two agents in TIA remains investigational. The combination of aspirin and clopidogrel was associated with a reduction in the risk of recurrent stroke or myocardial infarction in a major study, but the benefit was offset by a significant increase in the risk of intracerebral hemorrhage.

MRI may be ultimately indicated in this patient to rule out ischemic stroke and, in combination with magnetic resonance angiography, to evaluate the cause of the patient's transient ischemic attack. However, MRI is often not readily available and, in any case, would not influence the decision to admit the patient.

Although 24-hour electrocardiographic monitoring may be indicated for the evaluation of paroxysmal atrial fibrillation, the immediate next step is to admit this patient to the hospital for observation and to complete a stroke evaluation and monitor for recurrence.

> **KEY POINT**
> - All patients with probable transient ischemic attacks whose ABCD$^2$ scores (based on Age, Blood pressure, Clinical symptoms, Duration, and presence of Diabetes mellitus) are 3 or greater should be admitted to the hospital for evaluation.

**Bibliography**
Giles MF, Rothwell PM. Transient ischaemic attack: clinical relevance, risk prediction and urgency of secondary prevention. Curr Opin Neurol. 2009;22(1):46-53. [PMID: 19155761]

## Item 87      Answer:  A

**Educational Objective:**  Diagnose diabetic amyotrophy.

This patient's symptoms and clinical findings are typical of diabetic amyotrophy, a lumbar polyradiculopathy affecting primarily muscles of the thigh (L2 through L4 spinal levels). Diabetic amyotrophy, which can follow a period of significant weight loss in persons with diabetes mellitus, classically presents with severe pain at onset followed by development of weakness and numbness. Progression occurs over weeks to months, sometimes with spread to the contralateral lower extremity or upper extremities. The disorder can occur in severe, mild, and even undiagnosed diabetes.

Diabetic polyneuropathy is a length-dependent dying-back axonopathy presenting with distal to proximal sensory loss, paresthesias, pain, and distal lower extremity weakness. Clinical examination typically reveals absent or significantly decreased Achilles reflexes, a gradient stocking distribution of sensory loss, and weakness of the distal lower extremity muscles. This patient's anterior thigh pain and normal distal extremity sensation argue against this diagnosis.

Although Guillain-Barré syndrome (GBS) can present with significant low back pain, this patient's severe thigh pain would be very unusual in GBS. Numbness and, frequently, weakness in GBS are typically symmetric and radiate proximally to distally. Tendon reflexes would be diffusely hypoactive or absent in both legs.

Meralgia paresthetica causes only sensory loss with mild to moderate dysesthesia over the lateral thigh without any associated lower extremity weakness.

Electromyography after at least 3 weeks of symptoms is useful in differentiating between these four conditions.

> **KEY POINT**
> - Diabetic amyotrophy is a lumbar polyradiculopathy affecting primarily muscles of the thigh (L2 through L4 spinal levels) that classically presents with severe pain at onset followed by development of weakness and numbness over weeks to months.

**Bibliography**

Younger DS. Diabetic lumbosacral radiculoplexus neuropathy: a postmortem studied patient and review of the literature. J Neurol. 2011;258(7):1364-1367. [PMID: 21327851]

**Item 88      Answer:  D**

**Educational Objective:** Manage an unruptured cerebral aneurysm.

Tobacco cessation counseling is indicated for this patient to help prevent further aneurysmal expansion and rupture. The cerebral aneurysm is an incidental finding because aneurysms of this size are unlikely to cause headaches. Her symptoms are most likely due to a transformed migraine, which may occur as women transition through menopause. In a case-control analysis of patients with aneurysmal rupture, cigarette smokers were at increased risk (relative risk for women, 4.7) for subarachnoid hemorrhage compared with nonsmokers, and the risk increased with the number of cigarettes smoked. In this study, patients who smoked and were hypertensive had a 15 times increased risk of subarachnoid hemorrhage compared with controls.

Natural history data from prospective cohort studies allow valid site- and size-specific rupture rates to be calculated, which can be very useful in routine clinical practice. For patients without a previous subarachnoid hemorrhage, the lowest-risk aneurysms (annual rupture risk of approximately 0.5%) were those in the anterior circulation and were less than 7 mm in diameter.

Neither aneurysmal clipping nor endovascular coiling is appropriate in this patient because the aneurysm is 4 mm in size and located in the anterior circulation. The risk of subsequent rupture is small enough (0.05% annually) to be offset by the risk of surgical or endovascular intervention.

Repeat neuroimaging on an annual basis is recommended for tracking any change in the size of the cerebral aneurysm. If the aneurysm remains stable and the patient is asymptomatic, the neuroimaging interval can be lengthened to every 2 or 3 years, but 5 years is always too long to wait.

> **KEY POINT**
> - The main risk factors for rupture of cerebral aneurysms are hypertension and tobacco use.

**Bibliography**

Wiebers DO, Whisnant JP, Huston J 3rd, et al; International Study of Unruptured Intracranial Aneurysms Investigators. Unruptured intracranial aneurysms: natural history, clinical outcome, and risks of surgical and endovascular treatment. Lancet. 2003;362(9378):103-110. [PMID: 12867109]

**Item 89      Answer:  B**

**Educational Objective:** Treat an acute exacerbation of multiple sclerosis.

Intravenous methylprednisolone, 1g/d for 3 to 5 days, is the most appropriate treatment of this patient's worsening multiple sclerosis (MS) symptoms. He is experiencing an acute exacerbation, or relapse, of his underlying MS. The data supporting the use of high-dose intravenous corticosteroids in MS relapses come from the Optic Neuritis Treatment Trial and have been supported by numerous subsequent studies. Although this treatment regimen clearly helps speed recovery from an MS attack, controversy remains as to whether this approach has a significant effect on long-term disability outcomes. Severe corticosteroid-refractory relapses may respond to rescue therapy with plasmapheresis. Physical, occupational, or speech therapy may be necessary to enhance adaptation during the recovery period, depending on the type, severity, and therapeutic responsiveness of the relapse.

Gabapentin is used in MS to help control neuropathic pain, which is not among the patient's current symptoms. Increasing the dosage would not benefit his gait and balance problems.

A course of oral prednisone is also inappropriate. The aforementioned Optic Neuritis Treatment Trial showed that oral prednisone was not only inferior to high-dose intravenous corticosteroids but actually led to a worse outcome than placebo.

Although a change in this patient's chronic disease-modifying therapy may be worth considering, switching from interferon beta-1a to interferon beta-1b is not the appropriate first step in the acute treatment of his current relapse.

> **KEY POINT**
> - Intravenous methylprednisolone is an appropriate treatment of an acute exacerbation of multiple sclerosis.

**Bibliography**

Beck RW, Cleary PA, Anderson MM Jr, et al. A randomized, controlled trial of corticosteroids in the treatment of acute optic neuritis. The Optic Neuritis Study Group. N Engl J Med. 1992;326(9):581-588. [PMID: 1734247]

## Item 90     Answer:  C

**Educational Objective:**  Diagnose carotid artery dissection.

The combination of abrupt-onset cervical pain and examination findings consistent with Horner syndrome are classic signs of dissection of the carotid artery. Pain in the head/neck region is the most common symptom of cervical artery dissection, described by 70% of those with vertebral and up to 95% of those with carotid artery lesions. The headaches often arise abruptly and are of thunderclap onset in 20% of patients. The pain is generally located in the ipsilateral neck, face, orbit, or frontotemporal cranial areas. Most patients will eventually develop additional neurologic symptoms or signs, often hours to days after the onset of pain. Such developments may include Horner syndrome, amaurosis fugax, retinal infarction, pulsatile tinnitus, diplopia, or other stroke manifestations. Although dissection may occur spontaneously, it usually has a traumatic cause, such as cervical manipulation. Imaging of the brain and cerebral vasculature (the latter with magnetic resonance angiography, CT angiography, or conventional angiography) is indicated.

Although the patient's headache description is similar to a migraine, the formal definition of migraine requires at least five attacks that are not better explained by secondary headache possibilities. This patient has exhibited no pattern of recurrent migraine headache.

Both transient ischemic attacks and acute strokes can present with headache or neck pain as part of the symptom complex. However, an isolated Horner syndrome would be unlikely to arise from cerebral or brainstem infarction, and no evidence suggests cerebral ischemia on neurologic examination.

Cervical disk herniation may present with neck pain and headache, with the headache being more posterior in location. Compression of cervical roots might cause signs of cervical radiculopathy and, thus, focal weakness or sensory changes in the upper extremity, but not isolated Horner syndrome.

**KEY POINT**

- **The combination of abrupt-onset cervical pain and examination findings consistent with Horner syndrome are classic signs of dissection of the carotid artery.**

**Bibliography**

Caplan L. Dissections of brain-supplying arteries. Nat Clin Pract Neurol. 2008;4(1):34-42. [PMID: 18199995]

## Item 91     Answer:  B

**Educational Objective:**  Differentiate between a pseudorelapse and a multiple sclerosis flare.

This patient should be given a 7-day course of ciprofloxacin. She has worsening of preexisting multiple sclerosis (MS) symptoms of spasticity and pain in her legs and also has urinary symptoms. In this setting, an MS exacerbation and a pseudorelapse of MS are both possibilities, and distinguishing between them is necessary to make a proper treatment decision.

This patient most likely is having a pseudorelapse or worsening of her underlying neurologic deficits in the presence of an occult infection or metabolic disturbance. A urinary tract infection is suggested by her urinary symptoms, fever, and urine dipstick results. The urinary retention shown by her bladder ultrasound may predispose this patient to these infections. Proper treatment of MS pseudorelapses involves resolving the underlying trigger, in this case the urinary tract infection, which can be treated with ciprofloxacin. Successful treatment of the infection or supportive care, such as antipyretic agents for a viral upper respiratory tract infection, will be followed by neurologic improvement.

A 3-day course of methylprednisolone is an appropriate choice for patients with a distinct MS relapse. In this patient, however, administering the drug without treating the urinary tract infection could potentially lead to worsening of the infection because of the medication's immunosuppressive effects.

Decreasing the baclofen dosage is likely to worsen her spasticity and does not address her urinary symptoms.

Increasing the oxybutynin dosage is likely to worsen her urinary retention and potentially cause future complications without improving her current symptoms.

**KEY POINT**

- **Proper treatment of pseudorelapses of multiple sclerosis involves resolving the causative infection or metabolic derangement.**

**Bibliography**

Hufschmidt A, Shabarin V, Rauer S, Zimmer T. Neurological symptoms accompanying urinary tract infections. Eur Neurol. 2010;63(3):180-183. [PMID: 20197663]

## Item 92     Answer:  A

**Educational Objective:**  Diagnose acute lumbar plexopathy in a patient who has experienced back trauma.

This patient should have a CT of the abdomen. The most immediate concern is to rule out an iliopsoas hematoma causing lumbar plexus compression. CT of the abdomen is the most appropriate test with which to visualize acute hemorrhage. The clinical picture described is that of an acute L2-L4 lumbar plexopathy in addition to a "psoas sign," which is pain brought on by extension of the hip and painful limitation of hip movement.

Electromyography is the next most helpful test after CT of the abdomen but would not reveal active denervation until at least 3 weeks after the injury.

An MRI of the lumbar spine would be useful if an acute disk herniation was suspected but not with a plexopathy due to hemorrhage, as suggested by this patient's extensive bruising, pain, and psoas sign.

A plain radiograph of the lumbar spine could show a vertebral fracture, but a simple compression fracture is unlikely to be associated with neurologic impairment and will not cause the psoas sign.

**KEY POINT**

- In a patient with symptoms suggesting an acute L2-L4 lumbar plexopathy and painful hip extension (psoas sign), an abdominal CT scan is the most appropriate diagnostic test to rule out an iliopsoas hematoma.

**Bibliography**

Lenchik L, Dovgan DJ, Kier R. CT of the iliopsoas compartment: value in differentiating tumor, abscess, and hematoma. AJR Am J Roentgenol. 1994;162(1):83-86. [PMID: 8273696]

## Item 93      Answer:  C
**Educational Objective:** Evaluate for adverse effects of multiple sclerosis treatment.

This patient should have biannual liver chemistry tests performed. She has elected to begin interferon beta therapy. The interferon betas are associated with many potential adverse effects, including flulike symptoms after injections, elevated serum aminotransferase levels, lymphopenia, and worsening of underlying spasticity, depression, or migraines. Therefore, checking her liver chemistry test results every 6 months while she receives interferon therapy is appropriate so that suitable treatment changes can be made, if needed. Although transient elevations of liver enzyme levels are common, persistent elevations typically necessitate a temporary reduction (by half) in dosing or a temporary discontinuation of the drug with a later rechallenge.

Although MRI at set intervals might be an appropriate step in monitoring the efficacy of interferon therapy, it would not be an appropriate screening tool to monitor for any of the potential adverse effects of this medication class.

Obtaining ophthalmologic examinations at regular intervals may be a generally good practice for patient with MS, but this step does not monitor for any of the known adverse effects of the interferon betas. Frequent ophthalmologic examinations or optical coherence tomography scans would be useful screening tools for patients taking fingolimod, another disease-modifying therapy for multiple

sclerosis, because this medication can be associated with rare cases of macular edema.

Biannual monitoring of the blood urea nitrogen and serum creatinine levels is unnecessary in this patient because interferon medications are not associated with kidney dysfunction.

**KEY POINT**

- Increased serum aminotransferase levels are a potential adverse effect of interferon-beta therapy.

**Bibliography**

Goodin DS, Frohman EM, Garmany GP Jr, et al; Therapeutics and Technology Assessment Subcommittee of the American Academy of Neurology and the MS Council for Clinical Practice Guidelines. Disease modifying therapies in multiple sclerosis: report of the Therapeutics and Technology Assessment Subcommittee of the American Academy of Neurology and the MS Council for Clinical Practice Guidelines. Neurology. 2002;58(2):169-178. [PMID: 11805241]

## Item 94      Answer:  B
**Educational Objective:** Treat spasmodic torticollis.

This patient has spasmodic torticollis, a focal dystonia of the neck, and should be treated with botulinum toxin injections. Some forms of focal dystonia may represent an occupational overuse syndrome, such as writer's cramp, musician's dystonia, or task-specific focal dystonia of the hand. Spasmodic torticollis is a common disabling focal dystonia of unknown cause that develops sporadically in adults, typically in middle age, and affects women more often than men. Torticollis can be characterized by its directionality. This patient has a rotational torticollis, the most common phenotype, but others experience backward pulling (retrocollis) or forward pulling and neck flexion (anterocollis). The pathophysiology of torticollis is unknown, and evaluation for secondary causes is typically unrevealing. Torticollis rarely goes into spontaneous remission, and the illness is lifelong.

The treatment of choice for dystonia is injections of botulinum toxin, directed to selected muscles of the neck involved in the abnormal pulling and twisting. Botulinum toxin is especially effective at reducing the pain associated with torticollis, is safe, and has no systemic adverse effects. Local adverse effects may include muscle aching, dry mouth, and dysphagia. The main limitation of this approach is that the treatment benefit wears off within 3 months, which necessitates repeat injections.

The medical treatment of spasmodic dystonia, which consists of anticholinergic agents (baclofen, trihexyphenidyl) and other muscle relaxants, is generally unsatisfactory.

Chiropractic manipulation and orthopedic intervention have not been shown to relieve the symptoms of dystonia and thus are inappropriate.

- **The treatment of choice for spasmodic torticollis and other dystonias is injections of botulinum toxin.**

**Bibliography**
Comella CL, Pullman SL. Botulinum toxins in neurological disease. Muscle Nerve. 2004;29(5):628-644. [PMID: 15116366]

## Item 95     Answer: B

**Educational Objective:** Treat trigeminal neuralgia.

This patient has trigeminal neuralgia for which the first-line initial treatment is carbamazepine, with oxcarbazepine a reasonable alternative. Classically presenting in an older population, trigeminal neuralgia is characterized by paroxysms of pain generally localized to the face and forehead and affects the second and third branches of the trigeminal nerve. Pain episodes last seconds to minutes, and nearly all patients report trigger points in the oral or facial regions. Neurologic examination findings and brain MRIs with contrast are typically normal in patients with trigeminal neuralgia, although an MRI of the brain with contrast must be obtained because a small percentage of patients will have a causative intracranial lesion. Medical management is unsuccessful in approximately 30% of patients.

The antiviral agents acyclovir, valacyclovir, and famciclovir are appropriate to treat herpes zoster infection, but when this infection involves the trigeminal nerve, patients usually have pain, cutaneous vesicular eruptions, and/or keratitis. This patient exhibits no symptoms of herpes zoster infection.

Gabapentin is a second-line treatment for trigeminal neuralgia with limited evidence supporting its efficacy.

Although craniotomy with microvascular decompression is sometimes used to treat trigeminal neuralgia, the invasive nature of this procedure relegates its use to patients with medically refractory disease, especially younger patients in good health.

Prednisone may be useful as treatment of certain conditions that present with unilateral head or face pain, such as cluster headache, temporal (giant cell) arteritis, or Tolosa-Hunt syndrome, a rare condition characterized by painful ophthalmoplegia secondary to an idiopathic granulomatous inflammation of the cavernous sinus. However, the absence of orbital symptoms or signs, the lower facial location of pain with trigger zones, the normal erythrocyte sedimentation rate and C-reactive protein level, and the normal MRI with contrast exclude these diagnoses.

- **Trigeminal neuralgia is characterized by paroxysms of pain generally localized to the face and forehead and affects the second and third branches of the trigeminal nerve.**

**Bibliography**
Chole R, Patil R, Degwekar SS, Bhowate RR. Drug treatment of trigeminal neuralgia: a systematic review of the literature. J Oral Maxillofac Surg. 2007;65(1):40-45. [PMID: 17174762]

## Item 96     Answer: A

**Educational Objective:** Diagnose noncompressive myelopathy caused by copper deficiency.

This patient's serum copper level should be measured next to detect copper deficiency. The Roux-en-Y gastric bypass is a dual-mechanism bariatric surgery combining a small gastric reservoir, which restricts oral intake, with a small-bowel bypass, which induces mild malabsorption. Nutritional deficiencies of vitamin $B_{12}$, iron, calcium, folate, and 25-hydroxyvitamin D are common in patients after gastric bypass. Less frequently, deficiencies of magnesium, copper, zinc, vitamin A, other B-complex vitamins, and vitamin C may occur. This patient has a myelopathy (as evidenced by the hyperreflexia and upgoing toes) localizing to the posterior columns and bilateral corticospinal tracts. Common entities that cause dysfunction in this pattern are vitamin $B_{12}$ deficiency, neurosyphilis, and copper deficiency. Copper deficiency causes a chronic syndrome similar to subacute combined degeneration and is also associated with macrocytic anemia. Therefore, this deficiency can be difficult to differentiate from vitamin $B_{12}$ deficiency. Common causes are zinc toxicity, nutritional deficiency, or malabsorption syndrome, which is the likely cause in this patient.

Folate deficiency is not associated with myelopathy, and thus measuring the serum folate level in this patient would not be diagnostic.

Although low vitamin D levels have been associated with several conditions, including elevated risks for autoimmune disease, vitamin D deficiency itself is not causative of myelopathy.

Thiamine deficiency is associated with Wernicke-Korsakoff syndrome and not myelopathy. Therefore, obtaining the serum thiamine level would not help diagnose myelopathy.

Vitamin A deficiency can cause blindness, and hypervitaminosis A has been associated with benign idiopathic intracranial hypertension. However, alterations in the serum vitamin A level are not associated with myelopathy.

- **Copper deficiency, which can be caused by zinc toxicity, nutritional deficiency, or malabsorption syndrome, can result in a myelopathy localizing to the posterior columns and bilateral corticospinal tracts.**

**Bibliography**
Juhasz-Pocsine K, Rudnicki SA, Archer RL, Harik SI. Neurologic complications of gastric bypass surgery for morbid obesity. Neurology. 2007;68(21):1843-1850. [PMID: 17515548]

# Index

Note: Page numbers followed by f and t denote figures and tables, respectively. Test questions are indicated by Q.

ABCD² score, in stroke, 26, 28, 29t, 38–39, Q86
Abscesses, epidural, 65
Absence seizures, 14
Acetaminophen
    in pregnancy, 8, Q53
    for tension-type headaches, 9
Acquired immunodeficiency syndrome (AIDS). See HIV/AIDS
Acute disseminated encephalomyelitis, 59
African Americans, intracranial atherosclerosis in, 27
Aggression, in Alzheimer disease, 43, 44
Aging. See also Elderly
    as dementia risk factor, 41
    as memory loss risk factor, 41, Q30
Agitation, in Alzheimer disease, 43, 44, 45, Q18
Akathisia, 48t
Alcohol use/abuse
    as myopathy cause, 77
    as neuropathy cause, 70–71
Almotriptan, for migraine, 7t
Alzheimer disease
    agitation in, 43, 44, 45, Q18
    amyloid plaques in, 43, 44
    behavioral changes in, 43, 44, 45
    Capgras syndrome in, 43
    caregivers for, 43, 44
    clinical features of, 43–44
    cognitive impairment in, 41, 43, 44
    confusion in, 43, Q18
    course of, 43
    diagnosis of, 42–43
    early-onset familial, 43
    end-stage, 45
    epidemiology of, 43
    evaluation of, 41–42
    genetic factors in, 43
    genetic marker for, 43
    Lewy body variant of, 45
    living arrangements for, 43
    memory loss in, 42
    mild cognitive impairment and, 41
    palliative care for, 45
    pathology of, 43, 44, 45, 46f
    prevalence of, 43
    progression toward, 41
    safety precautions in, 43, 45t
    sleep disorders in, 43
    treatment of, 44–45, 44t, 45t
    urinary incontinence in, 43, 45
Amantadine
    for multiple sclerosis-related fatigue, 63t, Q49
    for Parkinson disease, 50t, 51
Amitriptyline
    for migraine, 8, 9, Q83
    for neuropathic pain, 73
Amyloid-β, in Alzheimer disease, 43, 44
Amyloid imaging, in Alzheimer disease, 44
Amyotrophic lateral sclerosis, 73–74, Q14
Amyotrophy, diabetic, 71, 71t, Q87
Aneurysms, intracranial
    asymptomatic, 36
    in stroke, 33, 34f, 36
    treatment of, 36, Q86
Angiitis, primary cerebral, 3
Angiography, computed tomography. See Computed tomography angiography
Angioplasty, for carotid artery stenosis, 38
Anticoagulants. See also Warfarin
    for dural sinus venous thrombosis, 35

    as intracerebral hemorrhage cause, 33
    for stroke, 26, 37–38, Q17
Anticonvulsants, 18–21, 20t
    adverse effects of, 16, 18–19, 19t, 20t, 21
    in breastfeeding, 21
    dosages of, 21
    drug interactions of, 19, 20t, 21, Q32
    in the elderly, Q67
    for epilepsy, 18–21, 20t
    metabolism of, 20t
    monitoring of, 21
    for myoclonus, 54
    for nonepileptic seizures, 17–18
    in pregnancy, 19, 21, Q12
    selection of, 19
    teratogenicity of, 19, 21, 22, Q12
Antidepressants
    for Alzheimer disease, 45
    for multiple sclerosis, 64
    for neuropathic pain, 63, 63t, 73
    as tardive dyskinesia cause, 54
Antiemetics, for migraine, 6, Q53
Antiepileptics. See Anticonvulsants
Antiplatelet agents, for stroke, 33, 38, Q34
Antipsychotics
    for Alzheimer disease, 45
    for Lewy body dementia, 46
Antithrombotic therapy, 30, 31–32, 33, 37–38, Q17
Anxiety
    in Alzheimer disease, 43, 44, 45
    in Parkinson disease, 49t
Aortic arch, atheroma of, 37–38, 40t
Aphasia, in stroke, 40
Apnea test, 81, Q8
Apolipoprotein E, in Alzheimer disease, 43
Apraxia, Q50
    in Alzheimer disease, 43
    in Parkinson-plus syndromes, 51
Areflexia, in myelopathy, 64
Arteriosclerosis. See Atherosclerosis
Ascending pinprick examination, 64
Asians
    intracerebral hemorrhage in, 27
    intracranial atherosclerosis in, 27
    Stevens-Johnson syndrome in, 18, 19, 19t, 20t, Q85
Aspirin
    for migraine, 7t
    for stroke, 31, 38, Q17
    for tension-type headache, 9
Astrocytomas, 78, 78t
Ataxia
    adult-onset chronic, 52
    anticonvulsant-related, 19t
    evaluation of, 52
    subacute, 52
    tremor and, 53
Atheroma, of the aortic arch, 37–38, 40t
Atherosclerosis, intracranial, stroke and, 27, 38, Q10
Athletes, concussions in, 11, 11t, Q11
Atrial fibrillation
    anticoagulation therapy for, 37, 38, Q40
    stroke and, 26, 27, 32, Q57
    stroke prevention in, 37, 38
Attention deficits
    in dementia, 40t
    in Tourette syndrome, 55
Aura
    in epilepsy, 14, 15
    in migraine, 5, 6t, 7, 13t, Q70
    in seizures, 13t

Autonomic dysfunction, in peripheral neuropathy, 69t
Autonomic neuropathy, 71, 71t

Back pain
    in compressive myelopathy, 65
    in spinal cord disorders, 64
Baclofen
    for multiple sclerosis, 63, 64, Q63
    for restless legs syndrome, 56–57
    for spasticity, 63, 63t
Ballism, 54
Basal ganglia
    in movement disorders, 47
    in Wilson disease, 55
Bell palsy, 70
Benserazide, for Parkinson disease, 50, 50t
Benzodiazepines
    for Alzheimer disease, 45
    withdrawal, in status epilepticus, 23
β-Blockers
    for migraine prevention, 7
    in pregnancy, 9
Biballism, 54
Biofeedback, for migraine, 7
Biopsy
    brain
        in brain tumors, 78
        in dementia, 43
    muscle, in mitochondrial myopathy, 76f
    sural nerve, 69
    temporal artery, 2
Bipolar disorder, epilepsy and, 16
Blepharospasm, 53
Botulinum toxin
    for focal dystonia, 53
    for spasmodic torticollis, Q94
    for spasticity, 63
    for tics, 55
Brachial plexopathy, 70
Bradykinesia
    in atypical parkinsonism, 51
    in Parkinson disease, 48, 49, 50
Brain death, 80–81, Q8
Brain injury. *See also* Head injury
    ischemic, as frontotemporal dementia cause, 46
Brain tumors, 77–80, 78t
    epilepsy and, 15
    intracerebral hemorrhage and, 27
    management of, 79
    metastatic, 78t
    *vs.* multiple sclerosis, 60t
    radiographic features of, 78t
Breast cancer
    metastases in, 77
    myasthenia gravis and, 74
Breast feeding
    anticonvulsant use in, 21
    in multiple sclerosis, 61
Bromocriptine
    for neuroleptic malignant syndrome, 56
    for restless legs syndrome, 57
Burning dysesthesia, in peripheral neuropathies, 68, 69t

Caffeine
    for migraine, 7t
    as migraine cause, 6, 7
Calcium channel blockers
    for migraine, 7
    for reversible cerebral vasoconstriction syndrome, 3, 4
Call-Fleming syndrome, 3
Cancer. *See also specific sites and types*
    headache in, 2
    Lambert-Eaton myasthenic syndrome and, 74, 75, Q16
    paraneoplastic syndromes of, 79–80, 80t
Capgras syndrome, 43, Q42
Capsaicin, for neuropathic pain, 73
Carbamazepine, 18, 19, 20t, Q85
    adverse effects of, 18, 19, 19t
    for epilepsy, 20t
    interaction with hormonal contraceptives, 21
    in pregnancy, 19, Q12
    for restless legs syndrome, 56–57

    for trigeminal neuralgia, 5
Carbidopa, for Parkinson disease, 50, 50t
Cardiovascular disease, stroke and, 39
Carotid artery. *See also* Internal carotid artery
    dissection of, 36, Q90
    stenosis of, Q62
Carotid endarterectomy, 38, Q55
Carotid revascularization, 38
Carpal tunnel syndrome, 70
Catechol-*O*-methyltransferase inhibitors, for Parkinson disease, 50t
Cauda equina syndrome, 64, Q40
Cavernous malformations, 15f, 15t
Cavernous sinus, thrombosis of, 34
Central nervous system demyelination, 57. *See also* Demyelinating diseases
Cerebellar degeneration, 80t
Cerebellar-type atrophy, 52
Cerebral angiography. *See* Computed tomography angiography
Cerebral artery
    aneurysm of, 33, 34f
    dissection of, stroke and, 26
    occlusion of, stroke and, 30, 31f
Cerebral edema, in stroke, 24. *See also* Increased intracranial pressure, in stroke
Cerebral infarction, 24, 26, 28, Q29. *See* Stroke, ischemic
    space-occupying, Q5
Cerebral ischemia, in vascular dementia, 46
Cerebral perfusion, management of, in stroke, 30–31
Cerebral vasospasm, 35, Q36
Cerebrospinal fluid
    in anti-NMDA receptor encephalitis, 80, Q47
    in chronic inflammatory demyelinating polyradiculoneuropathy, 72
    in dementia, 42–43
    in Guillain-Barré syndrome, 72, Q38
    in headache, 2
    in idiopathic intracranial hypertension, 4, 4t, Q46
    in multiple sclerosis, 59
    in normal pressure hydrocephalus, 46
    in paraneoplastic syndromes, 80
    in peripheral neuropathy, 68
    in primary central nervous system lymphoma, 79
    shunts for
        in idiopathic intracranial hypertension, 4
        in normal pressure hydrocephalus, 47
Cervicocephalic arterial dissection, stroke and, 36, 40t
Charcot-Marie-Tooth disease, 71
Chelating agents, for Wilson disease, 56
Children
    absence seizures in, 14
    Parkinson disease in, 49
    refractory epilepsy in, 21–22
    tic disorders in, 55
Cholinesterase inhibitors
    for Alzheimer disease, 44, 44t, 45
    for Lewy body dementia, 45–46
Chorea, 48t, 53–54
Chorea gravidarum, 54, Q21
Chronic inflammatory demyelinating polyneuropathy, 71, 72
Clonazepam, for restless legs syndrome, 56–57
Clonidine
    for restless legs syndrome, 56–57
    for tics, 55
Clopidogrel, for stroke, 38, Q34
Cluster headaches, 10, Q19
Cocaine abuse, as intracranial hemorrhage cause, Q81
Coenzyme Q$_{10}$, for Parkinson disease, 50
Cognitive impairment
    aging-related, 41
    in Alzheimer disease, 43, 44, 45
    in amyotrophic lateral sclerosis, 73
    in dementia, 40, 42
    differential diagnosis of, 42
    driving in, 47, Q13
    in epilepsy, 16
    in Lewy body dementia, 45
    in multiple sclerosis, 63t, 64
    in normal pressure hydrocephalus, 46
    in Parkinson disease, 49t
Compression devices, for deep venous thrombosis prevention, 39
Computed tomography
    in Alzheimer disease, 44, 45
    in concussion, 11
    in dementia, 42
    in dural sinus venous thrombosis, 34

in epilepsy, 16
in headache, 2
in myasthenia gravis, 74, Q44
in Parkinson disease, 49
in stroke, 24, 24f, 26f, 29, 30, 31f, Q7
in subarachnoid hemorrhage, 26f, 27, Q36
in subdural hematoma, 10, 33, Q68
in traumatic brain injury, 10, 11
Computed tomography angiography
in internal carotid artery dissection, 36
in subarachnoid hemorrhage, 33, Q36
Computed tomography myelography, in spinal cord disorders, 65
Concussion. *See also* Head injury
in athletes, 11, 11t, Q11
postconcussion syndrome of, 11–12, 12t, Q56
Confusion, in Alzheimer disease, 43, Q18
Copper accumulation, in Wilson disease, 55–56
Copper deficiency
*vs.* multiple sclerosis, 60t
as noncompressive myelopathy cause, Q96
Cortical development abnormalities, as epilepsy cause, 15, 16f
Corticobasal ganglionic degeneration, 51
Corticosteroids. *See also* Prednisone
adverse effects of, 52–53, 61–62
for brain tumors, 79
for multiple sclerosis, 61–62
resistance to, in transverse myelitis, 66, Q9
for reversible cerebral vasoconstriction syndrome, 3
as tremor cause, 52–53
C-reactive protein, in headache, 2, 2f
Creatine kinase, in myopathies, 75, 75t, Q2
Creutzfeldt-Jakob disease, 54, Q78
Critical illness myopathy, 76–77, Q2
Critical illness polyneuropathy, 72–73
Critically ill patients, status epilepticus in, 22–23
Cyclobenzaprine, for multiple sclerosis, 63, 64, Q63
Cyclophosphamide, for transverse myelitis, 66, Q9

Dabigatran, for stroke, 38
Dalfampridine, for multiple sclerosis, 64
Decarboxylase inhibitors, for Parkinson disease, 50, 50t
Deep brain stimulation
for epilepsy, 21
for essential tremor, 53
for Parkinson disease, 51, 51t, Q39
Déjà vu, 17
Delirium
definition of, 41t
in neuroleptic malignant syndrome, 56
Delusions, in dementia, 43, Q42
Dementia, 40-47. *See also* Alzheimer disease
Capgras syndrome in, 43, Q42
cortical *vs.* subcortical, 42
in corticobasal ganglionic degeneration, 51
definition of, 40–41, 41t
delusions in, 43, Q42
diagnosis of, 41–42, 42–43
differential diagnosis of, 42
driving with, 47, Q13
evaluation of, 41–42, 41t
frontotemporal, 42, 46, 46f, 73
Lewy body, 45–46, 45f, Q33
mild cognitive impairment and, 41
mortality rate in, 41
neurodegenerative, 42
in Parkinson disease, 42, 49
in Pick disease, 46
rapidly progressive, Q78
reversible, 42, 42t
treatment of, 45t
tremor and, 53
vascular, 42, 46
Demyelinating diseases, 57-64, Q27. *See also* Multiple sclerosis
Depression
in Alzheimer disease, 44, 45
*vs.* dementia, 42
as dementia cause, 42t
in Lewy body dementia, 45
in multiple sclerosis, 63t, 64
in Parkinson disease, 42, 49t, 50
poststroke, 39, 40

Devic disease, 57
Diabetes mellitus
neuropathies and, 68, 70–71, 71t, 73
stroke and, 26, 29–30, 39, 40t
Diabetic amyotrophy, 71, 71t, Q87
Diabetic lumbosacral radiculoneuropathy. *See* Diabetic amyotrophy
Diet, for epilepsy control, 21–22
Dihydroergotamine, for migraine, 6, 7t, 9
Dipyridamole, for stroke prevention, 38
Disability, in stroke, 40
Disease-modifying therapies
for multiple sclerosis, 62–63, 62t, 64
for optic neuritis, Q29
Divalproex sodium, for migraine, 8, 9, Q83
Donepezil, for Alzheimer disease, 44, 44t, 45
Dopamine agonists
adverse effects of, 50–51, Q84
for Parkinson disease, 50, 50t, Q84
for restless legs syndrome, 56
Dopamine deficiency, in Parkinson disease, 47
Dopamine precursors, for Parkinson disease, 50t
Dopamine receptor-blocking agents
as movement disorders cause, 54t
as neuroleptic malignant syndrome cause, Q64
as tardive dyskinesia cause, 54, Q82
for tics, 55
Dopamine-responsive dystonia, 53
Driving
with dementia, 47, Q13
with epilepsy, 14
with Parkinson disease, Q13
with seizures, 14
Drooling. *See* Sialorrhea
Drug therapy. *See also specific drugs and disorders*
as myopathy cause, 77, 77t
as tremor cause, 52–53
Duchenne muscular dystrophy, 76
Duloxetine, for neuropathic pain, 73
Dural arteriovenous fistulas, *vs.* multiple sclerosis, 60t
Dysarthria-clumsy hand syndrome, 29t
Dysesthesias, 56
in small-fiber neuropathy, 68
Dyskinesias, drug-induced, 50–51
in Parkinson disease, 54, Q39
Dyslipidemia. *See* Hyperlipidemia
Dysphagia
in Parkinson disease, 50
in stroke, 39
Dysplasia, cortical, 16f
Dystonia, 48t, 53
in neuroleptic malignant syndrome, 56
in Parkinson disease, 49t
tardive, 53, Q82

Edema, tumor-associated vasogenic, 79
Elderly
compressive cervical myelopathy in, Q25
epilepsy treatment in, Q67
ischemic stroke in, 26
trigeminal neuralgia in, 4–5
Electroencephalography. *See also* Video electroencephalography monitoring
in epilepsy, 17, 17f, 18f
in seizures, 14
in status epilepticus, 22, 23
Electromyography, in peripheral neuropathy, 68–69
Electrophysiologic studies, in multiple sclerosis, 59
Eletriptan, for migraine, 7t
Embolism, pulmonary, stroke and, 39
Emery-Dreifuss muscular dystrophy, 76
Empty delta sign, of dural sinus venous thrombosis, 34
Encephalitis
anti-NMDA receptor, Q47
limbic, 80, 80t
viral, 13
Encephalomyelitis, acute disseminated, 57, Q27
Ependymomas, 78, 78t
Epidural hematoma, 12, 65, Q40
Epidural spinal cord metastases, Q77
Epilepsy, 12–23
clinical features of, 12–13, 13t
comorbidities of, 16

Epilepsy (*Continued*)
    complications of, 16
    diagnosis of, 13, 16–18
    electroencephalography in, 17, 17f, 18f
    epidemiology of, 12–13
    generalized, 15
    idiopathic generalized, 15, 17f
    imaging studies in, 16
    juvenile myoclonic, 15, 16, Q61
    *vs.* myoclonus, 55t
    partial (focal), 15
    refractory, 21–22, Q26
    temporal lobe, 15, 15f, 18f
        refractory, Q26
    treatment of, 18–22
        discontinuation of, 21
        nonpharmacologic, 21–22
        pharmacologic, 18–21, 20t
Epilepsy monitoring units, 17–18
Epilepsy surgery, 21, 22, Q26
Epilepsy syndromes, 15–16
Epstein-Barr virus infection, multiple sclerosis and, 57
Extrapyramidal symptoms, 54
Eye disorders
    in multiple sclerosis, 58
    in myopathy, 76
    in progressive supranuclear palsy, 51, Q76
    in stroke, 29t
Eye protection, in Bell palsy, 70

Facial masking, in Parkinson disease, 48
Facial nerve palsy, 70
Facial pain, in trigeminal neuralgia, 4
Falls
    gait evaluation in, 51
    in Parkinson disease, 49
    in parkinsonism, 51, 52
    risk prediction of, 52, Q60
Fatigue, in multiple sclerosis, 58, 63–64, 63t, Q49
Felbamate
    adverse effects of, 19t
    interaction with hormonal contraceptives, 21
Fibrinolytics. *See also* Thrombolytics
    for stroke, 29–30
Fingolimod, for multiple sclerosis, 62t, 63
Fistulas, dural arteriovenous, *vs.* multiple sclerosis, 60t
Folic acid, supplemental, in pregnancy, 21
Folstein Mini-Mental State Examination, 41, 43, 47
Fosphenytoin, for status epilepticus, 22, Q43
Fractures
    epilepsy and, 16
    stroke and, 39
Fragile X tremor ataxia syndrome, 53
Frovatriptan, for migraine, 7t
Funduscopy, in dural sinus venous thromboembolism, 33–34

Gabapentin
    adverse effects of, 19, 19t, 20t
    for epilepsy, 20t
    for neuropathic pain, 63t
Gait, 51–52
    antalgic, 52
    ataxic, 51, 52
    choreic, 52
    evaluation of, 51–52
    in multiple sclerosis, 64
    in normal pressure hydrocephalus, 46–47
    in Parkinson disease, 48–49, 50
    in parkinsonism, 46–47, 52
    psychogenic, 52, Q66
    in spinal cord disorders, 65
Galantamine, for Alzheimer disease, 44, 44t, 45
Glasgow Coma Scale, 10, 10t, 11
Glatiramer acetate
    for multiple sclerosis, 62, 62t, Q29
    for optic neuritis, Q29
Glioblastoma multiforme, 78, 78t, 79f, Q4
Gliomas, 78t
Glucose intolerance, polyneuropathy in, 71
Glutathione, for Parkinson disease, 50
Guillain-Barré syndrome, 71–72, 73, Q38

Hallucinations
    in Lewy body dementia, 45, 46, Q33
    in Parkinson disease, 49t
Haloperidol, for tic disorders, 55
Headache, 1-10. *See also* Migraine
    algorithmic approach to, 2f
    cervicogenic, 12t
    cluster, 10, Q19
    in dural sinus venous thromboembolism, 33
    first or worst, 1, 33
    in idiopathic intracranial hypertension, 4
    imaging studies in, 2
    in internal carotid artery dissection, 36
    medication overuse, 6
    pain patterns in, 1
    in paroxysmal hemicrania, 10
    in postconcussion syndrome, 12t
    primary, 1, 1t, 3t, 5–10
    secondary, 1–5, 1t, Q6, Q37
    in subarachnoid hemorrhage, 2, 2f, 27, 33
    in SUNCT syndrome, 2f, 10
    tension-type, 9–10, Q28
        in postconcussion syndrome, 12t
    thunderclap, 1, 3, 3t
        in reversible cerebral vasoconstriction syndrome, 3, 3t, Q22
    in trigeminal neuralgia, 4–5
Head injury, 10–11
    concussion in, 11, 11t
    in military personnel, 12
    traumatic brain injury, 10–11, 12
Hematoma
    epidural, 12, 65, Q40
    iliopsoas, 70, Q92
    subdural, 12, Q68
Hemiballism, 54
Hemicrania, chronic paroxysmal, 10, Q35
Hemicraniectomy, 38, Q5
Hemiparesis, in stroke, 29t, 31f, 39, 40
Hemorrhage
    intracerebral, 12, Q7, Q48
        in cocaine abuse, Q81
        stroke and, 26f, 27, 32–33
    intracranial
        complications of, 39
        *vs.* hemorrhagic stroke, 24
        recombinant tissue plasminogen activator-related, 30, 32
        statin-related, 36
        risk factors for, 40t
    subarachnoid, 12, 33, Q7, Q24
        complications of, 39, Q36
        headache and, 2, 2f
        internal carotid artery aneurysm and, 34f
        normal pressure hydrocephalus and, 46
        stroke and, 26f, 27
        thunderclap headache and, 3, 3t
Heparin
    for dural sinus venous thrombosis, 35
    for stroke, 31–32, 39
    for venous thromboembolism, Q48
Hereditary neuropathies, 71
Hereditary spastic paraplegia, 67
Heterotopia, periventricular nodular, 16f
HIV/AIDS
    brain tumors in, 78t
    transverse myelitis-like syndrome of, 66
Horner syndrome, Q90
Human immunodeficiency virus infection . *See* HIV/AIDS
Huntington disease, 54
Hydrocephalus, Q7
    normal pressure, 46–47, Q52
    posttraumatic vascular, 49
Hypercoagulable disorders, dural sinus venous thrombosis and, 34, 35
Hyperkinetic disorders, 47, 48t. *See also* Parkinson disease
Hyperlipidemia, stroke risk factor, 36, Q62
Hyperreflexia, in myelopathy, 64
Hypertension
    intracranial idiopathic, 4, 4t, Q46
    management of, in stroke, 30–31, 33
    stroke and, 36, 40t, Q10, Q41
Hyperthermia, in neuroleptic malignant syndrome, 56, Q64
Hypokinetic disorders, 48t

Ibuprofen
for migraine, 7t
for tension-type headache, 9, Q28
Immediate postconcussion assessment and cognitive testing (ImPACT) test, 11
Immunization, in multiple sclerosis, 61, 64
Immunocompromised patients. *See also* HIV/AIDS
dementia in, 43
headache in, 2
seizures in, 13–14
Immunoglobulin G, in multiple sclerosis, 59
IMPACT test (immediate postconcussion assessment and cognitive testing) test, 11
Incontinence
in Alzheimer disease, 43, 45
in normal pressure hydrocephalus, Q52
in spinal cord disorders, 65
Increased intracranial pressure, in stroke, 33
Indomethacin
for chronic progressive hemicrania, 10, Q35
for thunderclap headaches, 3
Infarcts, subcortical (lacunar), 27, 29t
Infections
dementia and, 42t
multiple sclerosis and, 64
stroke and, 39
Inflammatory myopathies, 76
Inflammatory polyradiculoneuropathies, 71–72
Interferon beta
for multiple sclerosis, 62, 62t, Q29, Q93
for optic neuritis, Q29
Internal carotid artery
aneurysm of, 34f
dissection of, in stroke, 36, 37f
stenosis of, Q55
asymptomatic, 40
revascularization procedures for, 38
in stroke, 27, 28f
Intracranial tumors. *See* Brain tumors
Intravenous immune globulin
for Guillain-Barré syndrome, 72
for myasthenia gravis, 74
Ischemia, cerebral, in vascular dementia, 46
Ischemic penumbra, 29
Ischemic stroke. *See* Stroke

Jacksonian seizures, 14
Juvenile myoclonic epilepsy, 15, 16, Q61

Kayser-Fleischer rings, 56

Labetalol, for hypertension
in cocaine abuse, Q81
in stroke, 32, 33
Lacosamide
adverse effects of, 19t, 20t
for epilepsy, 20t
Lacunae, 27
Lacunar syndromes, 27, 29t
Lambert-Eaton myasthenic syndrome, 74–75
Lamotrigine
adverse effects of, 18–19, 19t, 20t, 21, Q85
in the elderly, Q67
for epilepsy, 20t
interaction with hormonal contraceptives, 21, Q32
Levetiracetam
adverse effects of, 19t, 20t
teratogenicity of, 21
Levodopa
adverse effects of, 50–51
nonresponse to, in atypical parkinsonism, Q3
for Parkinson disease, 50, 50t
Lewy bodies
in Alzheimer disease, 45
in essential tremor, 53
in Parkinson disease, 47–48, 49
Lewy body dementia, 45–46, 45f, Q33
Lhermitte sign, in multiple sclerosis, 58
Lipid-lowering agents. *See also* Statins
for stroke patients, 36
Lipohyalinosis, arterial, 27
Lisinopril, in stroke, Q10
Liver transplantation, for Wilson disease, 56

Lorazepam, for status epilepticus, 22, Q43
Lumbar puncture
in idiopathic intracranial hypertension, 4, Q46
in seizure patients, 13–14
in subarachnoid hemorrhage, Q24
Lumbar spinal stenosis, 65
Lumbosacral plexopathy, 70, Q92
Lung cancer
brain tumors and, 77
small-cell
Lambert-Eaton myasthenic syndrome and, 74, 75
myasthenia gravis and, 74
Lymphoma
Hodgkin, myasthenia gravis and, 74
primary central nervous system, 78t, 79

Magnetic resonance angiography, in internal carotid artery dissection, 36, 37f
Magnetic resonance imaging
in Alzheimer disease, 44, 45
of brain tumors, 77, 78–79
in compressive cervical myelopathy, Q25
in concussion, 11
in dementia, 42
in epilepsy, 16, 17
in headache, 2, Q37
in idiopathic transverse myelitis, 67
in multiple sclerosis, 58–59, 58f, 60
in normal pressure hydrocephalus, 47, Q52
in parkinsonism, 49
in seizures, 13–14
in spinal cord compression, 65, Q25
in stroke, 24, 24f
in traumatic brain injury, 10–11
Magnetic resonance venography
in dural sinus venous thrombosis, 34–35, 35f, Q1
in pregnancy, 34–35
Major depressive disorder, epilepsy and, 16
Medication overuse headache, 6
Medulloblastomas, 78, 78t
Melanoma, brain metastasis in, 77
Memantine, for Alzheimer disease, 44, 44t
Memory loss
aging-related, 41, Q30
in Alzheimer disease, 42, 43
in frontotemporal dementia, 46
Meningiomas, 78, 78t, 79f
Meningitis, normal pressure hydrocephalus and, 46
Menstrual migraine, 8, Q75
Mesial temporal sclerosis, 15, 15f, 15t, Q26
Metastases
to the brain, 77
to the spinal cord, Q77
Methylprednisolone
for multiple sclerosis, 61–62, Q89
for optic neuritis, Q29
for transverse myelitis, 66
Metoclopramide, for migraine, in pregnancy, Q53
Metoprolol, for migraine, in pregnancy, 9
Migraine, 1t, 5–9
with aura, 5, 6t, 7, 13t, Q70
without aura, 5, 6t, Q58, Q83
characteristics of, 13t
chronic, 5–6
clinical features of, 5–6, 6t
diagnosis of, 5–6, 6t
epidemiology of, 5–6
frequency of, 5
medication overuse headache and, 6
menstrual, 8, Q75
*vs.* multiple sclerosis, 60t
perimenopausal, 9
in postconcussion syndrome, 12t
in pregnancy, 8–9
prevention of, 7–8
*vs.* tension-type headache, 5
treatment of
acute, 6–7, 7t
in pregnancy, 8–9, Q53
in women, 8–9
Mild cognitive impairment, 41, 43. *See also* Dementia
Military personnel, head injuries in, 12, Q56

Mini-Mental State Examination, 41, 43, 47
Mitochondrial myopathies, 76, 76f
Mitoxantrone, for multiple sclerosis, 62t, 63
Modafinil, for multiple sclerosis-related fatigue, 63t, 64, Q49
Monoamine oxidase type B inhibitors, for Parkinson disease, 50, 50t
Monoclonal antibodies
    for multiple sclerosis, 62–63, 62t
    for myasthenia gravis, 74
Mononeuropathies, 68, 70, 71, 71t
Montreal Cognitive Assessment, 41
Mood disorders, epilepsy and, 16
Movement disorders, 47–57
    chorea, 53–54
    dystonia, 53
    hyperkinetic, 47
    hypokinetic, 47
    myoclonus, 54, 55t
    neuroleptic-induced, 54, 56
    restless legs syndrome, 56–57
    in stroke, 29t
    tardive dyskinesia, 54
    tic disorders, 55
    Tourette syndrome, 55
    Wilson disease, 55–56
Multiple mononeuropathies, 68
Multiple sclerosis, 57–64, 66
    acute exacerbations of, 61–62, Q89
    benign, 60–61
    course of, 59–61
    diagnosis of, 58–59, Q45
    differential diagnosis of, 59, 60t
    epidemiology of, 57
    fatigue in, 58, 63–64, 63t, Q49
    general health care in, 61
    genetic factors in, 57
    lifestyle modifications for, 61
    mobility maintenance in, 61, 64
    pathophysiology of, 57
    pregnancy in, 61
    primary progressive, 59–60, 61f, 63
    pseudorelapse in, 61, Q91
    relapse or flare of, 57–58
    relapsing-remitting, 59–60, 61, 61f, 63
    secondary progressive, 59, 61, 61f
    signs and symptoms of, 57–58
    spasticity in, 58, 63, 63t, Q63
    spectrum of, 57
    treatment of, 61–64, Q29, Q80, Q89
        adverse effects of, 61–62, 63, Q93
        symptomatic management, 63–64, 63t
    trigeminal neuralgia and, 4
Multiple system atrophy, 49, 51, 52
Muscle disorders. See Myopathies
Muscle relaxants, for multiple sclerosis, 63, 64
Muscle strength, impaired. See Weakness
Muscular dystrophy, 76
Musician's dystonia, 53
Myasthenia gravis, 74, Q44
Mycobacterium tuberculosis, 66
Myelitis
    idiopathic transverse, 57, 59, 66, 67f
        corticosteroid-resistant, 66, Q9
    in multiple sclerosis, 58, Q45
Myeloneuropathies. See Myelopathies
Myelopathies, 64–67
    compressive, 65, 66t
    noncompressive, 66–67, Q96
Myoclonic seizures, 15
Myoclonus, 48t, 54
    in atypical parkinsonism, 51
    differential diagnosis of, 55t
    posthypoxic, 54, Q69
Myopathies, 75–77
    inflammatory, 76
    inherited, 76
    thyrotoxic, 76
    toxic, 77, Q74
    vitamin D deficiency-associated, 76

Naproxen sodium, for migraine, 7t
Naratriptan, for migraine, 7t

Natalizumab, for multiple sclerosis, 62, 63, 62t, Q80
National Institutes of Health Stroke Scale, 24, 25t
Neck pain
    in compressive myelopathy, 65
    in internal carotid artery dissection, 36
    in postconcussion syndrome, 12t
    in spinal cord disorders, 64
Nerve ablation, for trigeminal neuralgia, 5
Neuralgia, trigeminal, 4–5, Q95
    in multiple sclerosis, 63
Neuritis, optic, 58, 59, Q29
Neurofibrillary tangles, in Alzheimer disease, 44, 44f
Neuroleptic malignant syndrome, 56, Q64
Neuroleptics
    for Alzheimer disease, 45
    as movement disorder cause, 54
    for tics, 55
Neurologic reflexes, primitive, in dementia, 42
Neuromuscular disorders, 68–77
    amyotrophic lateral sclerosis, 73–74
    differential diagnosis of, 69t
    myopathies, 75–77
    neuromuscular junction disorders, 74–75
    peripheral neuropathies, 67–73
    signs and symptoms of, 69t
Neuromuscular junction disorders, 74–74
Neuromyelitis optica, 57, 66
Neuro-oncology. See Brain tumors
Neuropathic pain
    in multiple sclerosis, 63, 63t
    in spinal cord disorders, 64–65
    treatment of, 73
Neuropathies. See Peripheral neuropathies
Neuropsychological evaluations, of dementia, 41–42
Neurostimulation, for epilepsy, 21
Nicardipine, for hypertension, in stroke, 32, 33
Nimodipine, for reversible cerebral vasoconstriction syndrome, 3, 4
Nitroglycerin, contraindication in ischemic stroke, 30
Nitroprusside, contraindication in ischemic stroke, 30
Nonsteroidal anti-inflammatory drugs (NSAIDs)
    for migraine, 6, 7, 7t
        in pregnancy, 8
    overuse of, as migraine cause, 6
Nortriptyline, for neuropathic pain, 73
Numbness, in neuromuscular disorders, 69t

Obesity, idiopathic intracranial hypertension in, 4
Obsessive-compulsive disorder, 55
Oligodendrogliomas, 78, 78t
Olivopontocerebellar atrophy, 52
Opioids
    for migraine, 6
    for neuropathic pain, 73
Opsoclonus-myoclonus, 80t
Optic nerve fenestration, for idiopathic intracranial hypertension, 4
Optic neuritis, 58, Q29
Oral contraceptives
    interaction with anticonvulsants, 21, Q32
    migraine and, 8, 9
    as stroke risk factor, 8
Osteoporosis, anticonvulsant-related, 16
Oxcarbazepine
    adverse effects of, 19t, 20t, 21, Q85
    interaction with hormonal contraceptives, 21
    teratogenicity of, 21
Oxygen therapy, for cluster headache, 10, Q19

Pain
    in headache, 1
    neuropathic
        in multiple sclerosis, 63, 63t
        in spinal cord disorders, 64–65
        treatment of, 73
Palsy, progressive supranuclear, 49, 51, Q76
Panic attacks, vs. temporal lobe auras, 14
Paralysis
    in multiple sclerosis, 58
    in spinal cord disorders, 65
Paraneoplastic syndromes, 79–80, 80t, Q78
    vs. multiple sclerosis, 60t
Paresthesias, in peripheral neuropathy, 68, 69t

Parkinson disease, 47–51
    *vs.* atypical parkinsonism, 50, Q3
    compressive cervical myelopathy in, Q25
    compulsive behavior in, 50, Q84
    dementia in, 42
    diagnosis of, 49
    dystonia in, 53
    early-stage, 50
    gait in, 48–49, 50
    genetic factors in, 47–48, 53
    idiopathic, 48
    juvenile, 49
    late-stage, 50
    nonmotor complications of, 49, 49t
    prevalence of, 47
    sporadic, 47
    treatment of, 49–51, 50t
        adverse effects of, 50–51, Q84
        deep brain stimulation, 51, 52t, Q39
        pharmacologic, 49–51, 50t
    tremor in, 48, 48t, 50, 52, 53
Parkinsonism
    atypical, 51
        *vs.* Parkinson disease, 50, Q3
    causes of, 48t
    clinical features of, 48t
    drug-induced, 49
    gait in, 46–47, 52
    Lewy body dementia and, 46
    non-Parkinson disease–related, 49
    vascular, 49
    in Wilson disease, 56, Q72
Parkinson-plus syndromes, 49, 51
Paroxysmal hemicrania, 10, Q35
Passivity, in dementia, 42
Patent foramen ovale, stroke and, 38, 40t
Perimenopause, migraine in, 9
Peripheral neuropathies, 68–73
    *vs.* central nervous system dysfunction, 68, 68t
    classification of, 68–69
    diabetic, 68, 70–71, 71t, 73
    diagnosis of, 68–69
    differential diagnosis of, 68, 69t
    hereditary, 71
    mononeuropathies, 70, 71, 71t
    paraneoplastic, 80t
    polyneuropathies, 68, 70–73, 71t
Persistent vegetative state
    in Alzheimer disease, 43
    definition of, 41t
Phenobarbital
    adverse effects of, 19t, 21
    interaction with hormonal contraceptives, 21
    teratogenicity of, 21
Phenytoin
    adverse effects of, 18, 19, 19t, 20t, 21, Q85
    interaction with hormonal contraceptives, 21
    for status epilepticus, 22, Q43
    teratogenicity of, 21
Phonic tics, 55
Pick disease, 46
Plaques, amyloid, in Alzheimer disease, 43, 44
Plasma exchange, for Guillain-Barré syndrome, 72
Polycystic ovarian syndrome, 19
Polyneuropathies, 68, 70–73
    acquired, 70–71
    critical illness, 72–73
    hereditary, 70, 71–72
Polyradiculoneuropathies, inflammatory, 71–72
Postconcussion syndrome, 11–12, 12t, Q56
Pramipexole, for restless legs syndrome, 57
Prednisone
    for Bell palsy, Q23
    for chronic inflammatory demyelinating polyradiculoneuropathy, 72
    for migraine, in pregnancy, 8
    for multiple sclerosis, 61
Pregabalin
    adverse effects of, 19t, 20t, 73
    for neuropathic pain, 63, 73
Pregnancy
    anticonvulsants in, 19, 21, Q12
    antimalarial drugs in, 8–9
    headache in, 2
    magnetic resonance venography in, 34–35, 36
    migraine in, 8–9
    in multiple sclerosis, 61
Presenilin, in Alzheimer disease, 43
Primary central nervous systems tumors, 78–79, 78t
Primidone, for essential tremor, 53
Primitive neurologic reflexes, in dementia, 42
Prochlorperazine, for migraine, 7t
Progressive multifocal leukoencephaly, 46, 62, 62t, Q80
Progressive supranuclear palsy, 49, 51, Q76
Propofol, for status epilepticus, 22
Propranolol
    for essential tremor, 53
    for migraine, 8, 9, Q83
        in pregnancy, 9
Pseudoseizures, 17–18
Pseudotumor cerebri, 4, 4t
Psychogenic nonepileptic seizures, 17–18, Q71
Psychosis
    in Alzheimer disease, 44, 45
    in Lewy body dementia, 45, 46, Q33
    in Parkinson disease, 50
Pull test, 52, Q60
Pulmonary embolism, stroke and, 39
Punding, Q84
Pyridostigmine, for myasthenia gravis, 74

Radiation therapy, for brain tumors, 79
Radiculopathy, in diabetes mellitus, 71t
Ragged red fibers, 76f
Rasagiline, for Parkinson disease, 50, 50t
Rashes, anticonvulsant-related, 18, 19t
REM sleep behavior disorder. *See also* Sleep disorders
    in Lewy body dementia, 45
Reperfusion therapy, for stroke, 29
Restless legs syndrome, 56–57, 64, Q59
Revascularization, carotid, 38
Reversible cerebral vasoconstriction syndrome, 3, 3t, Q22
Rigidity
    in neuroleptic malignant syndrome, 56, Q64
    in Parkinson disease, 48, 49, 50
    in progressive supranuclear palsy, 51
Riluzole, for amyotrophic lateral sclerosis, 74
Risperidone, as neuroleptic malignant syndrome cause, 56
Rivastigmine
    for Alzheimer disease, 44, 44t, 45
    for Lewy body dementia, 45–46
Rizatriptan, for migraine, 7t
Romberg test, 52, Q60

Sarcoidosis, 66
Schwannomas, 78, 78t
Sedation, anticonvulsant-related, 18
Sedatives, for Alzheimer disease, 45
Seizures. *See also* Epilepsy
    absence, 14
    assessment of, 13–14
    characteristics of, 13t
    clinical presentations of, 14–15
    complex partial, 14, 15
    convulsive, 15
    in dural sinus venous thromboembolism, 33
    epidemiology of, 12–13
    generalized, 14–15
    imaging studies in, 16
    Jacksonian, 14
    mimics, 13t
    myoclonic, 15
    nonepileptic, 13t, 17–18
    partial (focal), 14, 15
    psychogenic nonepileptic, 17–18, Q71
    recurrence of, 18
    secondarily generalized, 14
    simple partial, 14
    in status epilepticus, 22
    tonic-clonic, 14, 15
Selective serotonin reuptake inhibitors. *See also* Antidepressants
    for Alzheimer disease, 45
    for migraine, 7
    as tremor cause, 52–53

Selegiline
  for Alzheimer disease, 44
  for Parkinson disease, 50, 50t
Sensorimotor peripheral neuropathy, 71t
Shunts, cerebrospinal fluid
  in idiopathic intracranial hypertension, 4
  in normal pressure hydrocephalus, 47
Shy-Drager syndrome, 51
Sialorrhea
  in neuroleptic malignant syndrome, Q64
  in Parkinson disease, 49
Skin biopsy, in small-fiber neuropathy, 70f
Sleep disorders
  in Alzheimer disease, 43, 44
  in Lewy body dementia, 45
  in Parkinson disease, 49t, 50
  in stroke, 39
Small-fiber neuropathies, 68, 69, 70f
  in diabetes mellitus, 71, 71t
Smoking cessation
  in cerebral aneurysm, Q88
  in multiple sclerosis, 61
Soldiers, head injuries in, 12, Q56
Somatoform disorders, *vs.* multiple sclerosis, 60t
Spasticity
  in compressive myelopathies, 65
  in multiple sclerosis, 58, 63, 63t, Q63
Spinal cord compression, 64, 65, 66f, Q25, Q40
Spinal cord disorders, 64-65, Q77. *See also* Myelopathies
  in multiple sclerosis, 58f
Spinocerebellar atrophy disorders, 52
Statins
  as myopathy cause, 77, 77t, Q74
  for stroke, 36, Q62, Q73
Status epilepticus, 22-23
  generalized convulsive, 22, 23, 23f, Q43
  nonconvulsive, 22-23
Stevens-Johnson syndrome, anticonvulsant-related, 18-19, 19t, Q85
Stiff-person syndrome, 80t
Stork leg deformity, 71
Strength, impaired. *See* Weakness
Striatonigral degeneration, 51
Stroke, 24-40
  acute, 28-33
    neuroimaging in, 29, 31, Q7
  cardiogenic, 32
  complications of, prevention of, 38-39
  diagnosis of, 24, 25t, Q7
  disability in, 40
  dural sinus venous thrombosis and, 33-35
  dysphagia in, 39
  as epilepsy cause, 15
  hemorrhagic, 24, 27
    acute, 32-33
    differentiated from ischemic stroke, 24
    increased intracranial pressure in, 33
    risk factors for, 40t
  hypertension management in, 30-31, Q10
  ischemic, 24
    acute, 28-32, 30f, 32f, Q17, Q31
    in asymptomatic carotid stenosis, 40
    cardioembolic, 26-27, 27f
    classification of, 26
    cryptogenic, 26, 27, Q57
    diagnosis of, 28-29, 30f
    differentiated from hemorrhagic stroke, 24
    hemorrhagic conversion of, 39
    hypertension in, Q41
    imaging studies in, 31f, 29
    prevention of, 31-32, 36
    recurrent, 36, 38-39
    risk factors for, 40t
    time of onset of, 29
    treatment of, 29-32, 32f, Q73
  morbidity and mortality in, 24, 25, Q79
  neurologic deficits in, 38-39, 40
  perioperative, 39
  prevention of
    primary, 40
    secondary, 36-38, Q34
  recovery in, 40, Q65

  recurrent, 36, 38-39
  rehabilitation in, 40, Q65
  risk factors for, 36
  stroke unit admission for, 36
  subtypes of, 24-28
  transient ischemic attacks and, 24-26
Stroke centers and units, 36, Q79
Subarachnoid hemorrhage. *See* Hemorrhage, subarachnoid
Subdural hematoma, 12, Q68
Sudden death, in epilepsy, 16
Suicide, antiepileptic drug-related, 16
Sumatriptan
  for cluster headache, 10
  for migraine, 6, 7t, Q58, Q70
    in pregnancy, 8
SUNCT syndrome, 2f, 10
Supranuclear palsy, progressive, 49, 51, Q76
Sural nerve, biopsy of, 69
Surgery, as stroke cause, 39
Susac syndrome, *vs.* multiple sclerosis, 60t
Syncope
  characteristics of, 13t
  convulsive, 17, Q20
  vasovagal, 17
Systemic inflammatory disease, *vs.* multiple sclerosis, 60t

Tacrine, for Alzheimer disease, 44, 44t, 45
Tandem stepping test, 52
Tardive akathisia, 54t
Tardive dyskinesia, 54, 55
Tardive dystonia, 53, Q82
Tau proteins
  in Alzheimer disease, 43
  in frontotemporal dementia, 46, 46f
Temporal artery, biopsy of, 2
Temporal lobe epilepsy, 15, 15f, 17, 18f
  refractory, Q26
Temporal lobe seizures, 14
Teratogens
  anticonvulsants, 19, 21, 22, Q12
  antimigraine drugs, 8-9
Thiamine deficiency, as dementia cause, 42t
Thrombolysis, intra-arterial, for stroke, 30
Thrombolytics, for stroke, 29-30, Q31
Thrombosis
  deep venous, stroke and, 39
  dural sinus venous, 33-35, Q1
  intracardiac, stroke and, 37, 40t
Thyroid disease
  myasthenia gravis in, 74
  myopathy in, 76
Thyrotoxic myopathies, 76
Tic disorders, 48t, 55, Q54
Tic douloureux. *See* Neuralgia, trigeminal
Timolol, for migraine, 8, 9, Q83
Tissue plasminogen activator, recombinant, for stroke, 29-30, 32f, Q15, Q31
  contraindications to, 32t
Tizanidine, for multiple sclerosis, 63, 64, Q63
Todd paralysis, 14
Topiramate
  adverse effects of, 19, 19t, 20t, 21
  interaction with hormonal contraceptives, 21
  for migraine, 8, 9, Q75, Q83
  teratogenicity of, 21
Torticollis, spasmodic, 53, Q94
Tourette syndrome, 55
Toxic epidermal necrolysis, drug-related, 18-19
Toxins, as myopathy cause, 77, 77t
Tramadol, for neuropathic pain, 73
Tranquilizers, for Alzheimer disease, 45
Transient ischemic attacks, 24-26, Q86
  anticoagulation therapy for, 37, 38, Q17
  characteristics of, 13t
  definition of, 24
  recurrent, 38-39
Trauma, as Parkinson disease risk factor, 47
Traumatic brain injury, 10-11
  in military personnel, 12
Tremor, 48t
  drug-induced, 52-53
  essential, 52-53

fragile X, 53
*vs.* myoclonus, 54
in Parkinson disease, 48, 48t, 50, 52, 53
in Wilson disease, 56
Tricyclic antidepressants. *See* Antidepressants
Trigeminal neuralgia. *See* Neuralgia, trigeminal
Triptans
contraindications to, 6–7
for migraine, 6–7, 7t, Q58
overuse of, as migraine cause, 6
Tube feeding
in Alzheimer disease, 73–74
in stroke, 39

Uhthoff phenomenon, 58, 61
Urinary frequency, in multiple sclerosis, 63t, 64
Urinary incontinence
in Alzheimer disease, 43, 45
in normal pressure hydrocephalus, Q52
in spinal cord disorders, 65
Urinary tract infections, in multiple sclerosis, 61
Urinary urgency, in multiple sclerosis, 63t, 64

Vagus nerve stimulation, for epilepsy, 21
Valproic acid
adverse effects of, 18–19, 19t, 20t, 22
for neuropathic pain, 73
teratogenicity of, 19, 22
Valsalva maneuver, as headache cause, 2
Vascular disorders
*vs.* multiple sclerosis, 60t
noncompressive myelopathy and, 67
Vasculitis, stroke and, 26
Vasospasm, cerebral, 33, Q36
Venlafaxine, for neuropathic pain, 73
Verapamil, for reversible cerebral vasoconstriction syndrome, 3, 4
Verbal tics, 55
Vertebral artery dissection, stroke and, 36
Vertigo, characteristics of, 13t

Video electroencephalography monitoring
in epilepsy, 17–18
in psychogenic nonepileptic seizures, Q71
in status epilepticus, 23
Vigabatrin, adverse effects of, 19t, 20t
Viral disease, *vs.* transverse myelitis, 66
Vitamin B$_{12}$ deficiency
dementia and, 42t
*vs.* multiple sclerosis, 60t
noncompressive myelopathy and, 67
Vitamin D deficiency
multiple sclerosis and, 61
myopathy and, 76
Vitamin E
for Alzheimer disease, 44
for Parkinson disease, 50
Vitamin E deficiency, *vs.* multiple sclerosis, 60t
Vocal tics, 55

Warfarin
for dural sinus venous thrombosis, 35, 35f
for stroke, 37, 38
Weakness
in Guillain-Barré syndrome, 72
in myasthenia gravis, 74
in myopathy, 76, 77
in peripheral neuropathy, 68, 69t
White matter lesions, in multiple sclerosis, 57, 59
Wilson disease, 49, 53, 55–56
parkinsonism in, 56, Q72
tremor in, 56
Writer's cramp, 53

X-linked adrenoleukodystrophy, 67

Zolmitriptan
for cluster headache, 10
for migraine, 7t
Zonisamide, adverse effects of, 19, 19t, 20t, Q51

**A** | **NAME AND ADDRESS (Please complete.)**

Last Name _____ First Name _____ Middle Initial

Address _____

Address cont. _____

City _____ State _____ ZIP Code

Country _____

Email address _____

**ACP**
AMERICAN COLLEGE OF PHYSICIANS
INTERNAL MEDICINE | Doctors for Adults

**Medical Knowledge
Self-Assessment
Program® 16**

**TO EARN *AMA PRA CATEGORY 1 CREDITS*™
YOU MUST:**

1. Answer all questions.
2. Score a minimum of 50% correct.

====================================

**TO EARN *FREE* SAME-DAY
*AMA PRA CATEGORY 1 CREDITS*™ ONLINE:**

1. Answer all of your questions.
2. Go to **mksap.acponline.org** and access the appropriate answer sheet.
3. Transcribe your answers and submit for CME credits.
4. You can also enter your answers directly at **mksap.acponline.org** without first using this answer sheet.

**To Submit Your Answer Sheet by Mail or FAX for a $10 Administrative Fee per Answer Sheet:**

1. Answer all of your questions and calculate your score.
2. Complete boxes A–F.
3. Complete payment information.
4. Send the answer sheet and payment information to ACP, using the FAX number/address listed below.

**B** | **Order Number**

(Use the Order Number on your MKSAP materials packing slip.)

**C** | **ACP ID Number**

(Refer to packing slip in your MKSAP materials for your ACP ID Number.)

**COMPLETE FORM BELOW ONLY IF YOU SUBMIT BY MAIL OR FAX**

Last Name | First Name | MI

**Payment Information. Must remit in US funds, drawn on a US bank.**

**The processing fee for each paper answer sheet is $10.**

☐ Check, made payable to ACP, enclosed

Charge to   ☐ **VISA**   ☐ **MasterCard**   ☐ **AMERICAN EXPRESS**   ☐ **DISCOVER**

Card Number _____

Expiration Date _____ / _____
          MM     YY

Security code (3 or 4 digit #s) _____

Signature _____

**Fax to:** 215-351-2799

Questions?
Go to **mskap.acponline.org** or email **custserv@acponline.org**

**Mail to:**
Member and Customer Service
American College of Physicians
190 N. Independence Mall West
Philadelphia, PA 19106-1572

## D TEST TYPE

| TEST TYPE | Maximum Number of CME Credits |
|---|---|
| ○ Cardiovascular Medicine | 18 |
| ○ Dermatology | 10 |
| ○ Gastroenterology and Hepatology | 14 |
| ○ Hematology and Oncology | 20 |
| ○ Neurology | 14 |
| ○ Rheumatology | 14 |
| ○ Endocrinology and Metabolism | 12 |
| ○ General Internal Medicine | 24 |
| ○ Infectious Disease | 16 |
| ○ Nephrology | 16 |
| ○ Pulmonary and Critical Care Medicine | 16 |

## E CREDITS CLAIMED ON SECTION
### (1 hour = 1 credit)

Enter the number of credits earned on the test to the nearest quarter hour. Physicians should claim only the credit commensurate with the extent of their participation in the activity.

## F

**Enter your score here.**

Instructions for calculating your own score are found in front of the self-assessment test in each book.

You must receive a minimum score of 50% correct.

_____ %

Credit Submission Date: _____

1 Ⓐ Ⓑ Ⓒ Ⓓ Ⓔ
2 Ⓐ Ⓑ Ⓒ Ⓓ Ⓔ
3 Ⓐ Ⓑ Ⓒ Ⓓ Ⓔ
4 Ⓐ Ⓑ Ⓒ Ⓓ Ⓔ
5 Ⓐ Ⓑ Ⓒ Ⓓ Ⓔ

6 Ⓐ Ⓑ Ⓒ Ⓓ Ⓔ
7 Ⓐ Ⓑ Ⓒ Ⓓ Ⓔ
8 Ⓐ Ⓑ Ⓒ Ⓓ Ⓔ
9 Ⓐ Ⓑ Ⓒ Ⓓ Ⓔ
10 Ⓐ Ⓑ Ⓒ Ⓓ Ⓔ

11 Ⓐ Ⓑ Ⓒ Ⓓ Ⓔ
12 Ⓐ Ⓑ Ⓒ Ⓓ Ⓔ
13 Ⓐ Ⓑ Ⓒ Ⓓ Ⓔ
14 Ⓐ Ⓑ Ⓒ Ⓓ Ⓔ
15 Ⓐ Ⓑ Ⓒ Ⓓ Ⓔ

16 Ⓐ Ⓑ Ⓒ Ⓓ Ⓔ
17 Ⓐ Ⓑ Ⓒ Ⓓ Ⓔ
18 Ⓐ Ⓑ Ⓒ Ⓓ Ⓔ
19 Ⓐ Ⓑ Ⓒ Ⓓ Ⓔ
20 Ⓐ Ⓑ Ⓒ Ⓓ Ⓔ

21 Ⓐ Ⓑ Ⓒ Ⓓ Ⓔ
22 Ⓐ Ⓑ Ⓒ Ⓓ Ⓔ
23 Ⓐ Ⓑ Ⓒ Ⓓ Ⓔ
24 Ⓐ Ⓑ Ⓒ Ⓓ Ⓔ
25 Ⓐ Ⓑ Ⓒ Ⓓ Ⓔ

26 Ⓐ Ⓑ Ⓒ Ⓓ Ⓔ
27 Ⓐ Ⓑ Ⓒ Ⓓ Ⓔ
28 Ⓐ Ⓑ Ⓒ Ⓓ Ⓔ
29 Ⓐ Ⓑ Ⓒ Ⓓ Ⓔ
30 Ⓐ Ⓑ Ⓒ Ⓓ Ⓔ

31 Ⓐ Ⓑ Ⓒ Ⓓ Ⓔ
32 Ⓐ Ⓑ Ⓒ Ⓓ Ⓔ
33 Ⓐ Ⓑ Ⓒ Ⓓ Ⓔ
34 Ⓐ Ⓑ Ⓒ Ⓓ Ⓔ
35 Ⓐ Ⓑ Ⓒ Ⓓ Ⓔ

36 Ⓐ Ⓑ Ⓒ Ⓓ Ⓔ
37 Ⓐ Ⓑ Ⓒ Ⓓ Ⓔ
38 Ⓐ Ⓑ Ⓒ Ⓓ Ⓔ
39 Ⓐ Ⓑ Ⓒ Ⓓ Ⓔ
40 Ⓐ Ⓑ Ⓒ Ⓓ Ⓔ

41 Ⓐ Ⓑ Ⓒ Ⓓ Ⓔ
42 Ⓐ Ⓑ Ⓒ Ⓓ Ⓔ
43 Ⓐ Ⓑ Ⓒ Ⓓ Ⓔ
44 Ⓐ Ⓑ Ⓒ Ⓓ Ⓔ
45 Ⓐ Ⓑ Ⓒ Ⓓ Ⓔ

46 Ⓐ Ⓑ Ⓒ Ⓓ Ⓔ
47 Ⓐ Ⓑ Ⓒ Ⓓ Ⓔ
48 Ⓐ Ⓑ Ⓒ Ⓓ Ⓔ
49 Ⓐ Ⓑ Ⓒ Ⓓ Ⓔ
50 Ⓐ Ⓑ Ⓒ Ⓓ Ⓔ

51 Ⓐ Ⓑ Ⓒ Ⓓ Ⓔ
52 Ⓐ Ⓑ Ⓒ Ⓓ Ⓔ
53 Ⓐ Ⓑ Ⓒ Ⓓ Ⓔ
54 Ⓐ Ⓑ Ⓒ Ⓓ Ⓔ
55 Ⓐ Ⓑ Ⓒ Ⓓ Ⓔ

56 Ⓐ Ⓑ Ⓒ Ⓓ Ⓔ
57 Ⓐ Ⓑ Ⓒ Ⓓ Ⓔ
58 Ⓐ Ⓑ Ⓒ Ⓓ Ⓔ
59 Ⓐ Ⓑ Ⓒ Ⓓ Ⓔ
60 Ⓐ Ⓑ Ⓒ Ⓓ Ⓔ

61 Ⓐ Ⓑ Ⓒ Ⓓ Ⓔ
62 Ⓐ Ⓑ Ⓒ Ⓓ Ⓔ
63 Ⓐ Ⓑ Ⓒ Ⓓ Ⓔ
64 Ⓐ Ⓑ Ⓒ Ⓓ Ⓔ
65 Ⓐ Ⓑ Ⓒ Ⓓ Ⓔ

66 Ⓐ Ⓑ Ⓒ Ⓓ Ⓔ
67 Ⓐ Ⓑ Ⓒ Ⓓ Ⓔ
68 Ⓐ Ⓑ Ⓒ Ⓓ Ⓔ
69 Ⓐ Ⓑ Ⓒ Ⓓ Ⓔ
70 Ⓐ Ⓑ Ⓒ Ⓓ Ⓔ

71 Ⓐ Ⓑ Ⓒ Ⓓ Ⓔ
72 Ⓐ Ⓑ Ⓒ Ⓓ Ⓔ
73 Ⓐ Ⓑ Ⓒ Ⓓ Ⓔ
74 Ⓐ Ⓑ Ⓒ Ⓓ Ⓔ
75 Ⓐ Ⓑ Ⓒ Ⓓ Ⓔ

76 Ⓐ Ⓑ Ⓒ Ⓓ Ⓔ
77 Ⓐ Ⓑ Ⓒ Ⓓ Ⓔ
78 Ⓐ Ⓑ Ⓒ Ⓓ Ⓔ
79 Ⓐ Ⓑ Ⓒ Ⓓ Ⓔ
80 Ⓐ Ⓑ Ⓒ Ⓓ Ⓔ

81 Ⓐ Ⓑ Ⓒ Ⓓ Ⓔ
82 Ⓐ Ⓑ Ⓒ Ⓓ Ⓔ
83 Ⓐ Ⓑ Ⓒ Ⓓ Ⓔ
84 Ⓐ Ⓑ Ⓒ Ⓓ Ⓔ
85 Ⓐ Ⓑ Ⓒ Ⓓ Ⓔ

86 Ⓐ Ⓑ Ⓒ Ⓓ Ⓔ
87 Ⓐ Ⓑ Ⓒ Ⓓ Ⓔ
88 Ⓐ Ⓑ Ⓒ Ⓓ Ⓔ
89 Ⓐ Ⓑ Ⓒ Ⓓ Ⓔ
90 Ⓐ Ⓑ Ⓒ Ⓓ Ⓔ

91 Ⓐ Ⓑ Ⓒ Ⓓ Ⓔ
92 Ⓐ Ⓑ Ⓒ Ⓓ Ⓔ
93 Ⓐ Ⓑ Ⓒ Ⓓ Ⓔ
94 Ⓐ Ⓑ Ⓒ Ⓓ Ⓔ
95 Ⓐ Ⓑ Ⓒ Ⓓ Ⓔ

96 Ⓐ Ⓑ Ⓒ Ⓓ Ⓔ
97 Ⓐ Ⓑ Ⓒ Ⓓ Ⓔ
98 Ⓐ Ⓑ Ⓒ Ⓓ Ⓔ
99 Ⓐ Ⓑ Ⓒ Ⓓ Ⓔ
100 Ⓐ Ⓑ Ⓒ Ⓓ Ⓔ

101 Ⓐ Ⓑ Ⓒ Ⓓ Ⓔ
102 Ⓐ Ⓑ Ⓒ Ⓓ Ⓔ
103 Ⓐ Ⓑ Ⓒ Ⓓ Ⓔ
104 Ⓐ Ⓑ Ⓒ Ⓓ Ⓔ
105 Ⓐ Ⓑ Ⓒ Ⓓ Ⓔ

106 Ⓐ Ⓑ Ⓒ Ⓓ Ⓔ
107 Ⓐ Ⓑ Ⓒ Ⓓ Ⓔ
108 Ⓐ Ⓑ Ⓒ Ⓓ Ⓔ
109 Ⓐ Ⓑ Ⓒ Ⓓ Ⓔ
110 Ⓐ Ⓑ Ⓒ Ⓓ Ⓔ

111 Ⓐ Ⓑ Ⓒ Ⓓ Ⓔ
112 Ⓐ Ⓑ Ⓒ Ⓓ Ⓔ
113 Ⓐ Ⓑ Ⓒ Ⓓ Ⓔ
114 Ⓐ Ⓑ Ⓒ Ⓓ Ⓔ
115 Ⓐ Ⓑ Ⓒ Ⓓ Ⓔ

116 Ⓐ Ⓑ Ⓒ Ⓓ Ⓔ
117 Ⓐ Ⓑ Ⓒ Ⓓ Ⓔ
118 Ⓐ Ⓑ Ⓒ Ⓓ Ⓔ
119 Ⓐ Ⓑ Ⓒ Ⓓ Ⓔ
120 Ⓐ Ⓑ Ⓒ Ⓓ Ⓔ

121 Ⓐ Ⓑ Ⓒ Ⓓ Ⓔ
122 Ⓐ Ⓑ Ⓒ Ⓓ Ⓔ
123 Ⓐ Ⓑ Ⓒ Ⓓ Ⓔ
124 Ⓐ Ⓑ Ⓒ Ⓓ Ⓔ
125 Ⓐ Ⓑ Ⓒ Ⓓ Ⓔ

126 Ⓐ Ⓑ Ⓒ Ⓓ Ⓔ
127 Ⓐ Ⓑ Ⓒ Ⓓ Ⓔ
128 Ⓐ Ⓑ Ⓒ Ⓓ Ⓔ
129 Ⓐ Ⓑ Ⓒ Ⓓ Ⓔ
130 Ⓐ Ⓑ Ⓒ Ⓓ Ⓔ

131 Ⓐ Ⓑ Ⓒ Ⓓ Ⓔ
132 Ⓐ Ⓑ Ⓒ Ⓓ Ⓔ
133 Ⓐ Ⓑ Ⓒ Ⓓ Ⓔ
134 Ⓐ Ⓑ Ⓒ Ⓓ Ⓔ
135 Ⓐ Ⓑ Ⓒ Ⓓ Ⓔ

136 Ⓐ Ⓑ Ⓒ Ⓓ Ⓔ
137 Ⓐ Ⓑ Ⓒ Ⓓ Ⓔ
138 Ⓐ Ⓑ Ⓒ Ⓓ Ⓔ
139 Ⓐ Ⓑ Ⓒ Ⓓ Ⓔ
140 Ⓐ Ⓑ Ⓒ Ⓓ Ⓔ

141 Ⓐ Ⓑ Ⓒ Ⓓ Ⓔ
142 Ⓐ Ⓑ Ⓒ Ⓓ Ⓔ
143 Ⓐ Ⓑ Ⓒ Ⓓ Ⓔ
144 Ⓐ Ⓑ Ⓒ Ⓓ Ⓔ
145 Ⓐ Ⓑ Ⓒ Ⓓ Ⓔ

146 Ⓐ Ⓑ Ⓒ Ⓓ Ⓔ
147 Ⓐ Ⓑ Ⓒ Ⓓ Ⓔ
148 Ⓐ Ⓑ Ⓒ Ⓓ Ⓔ
149 Ⓐ Ⓑ Ⓒ Ⓓ Ⓔ
150 Ⓐ Ⓑ Ⓒ Ⓓ Ⓔ

151 Ⓐ Ⓑ Ⓒ Ⓓ Ⓔ
152 Ⓐ Ⓑ Ⓒ Ⓓ Ⓔ
153 Ⓐ Ⓑ Ⓒ Ⓓ Ⓔ
154 Ⓐ Ⓑ Ⓒ Ⓓ Ⓔ
155 Ⓐ Ⓑ Ⓒ Ⓓ Ⓔ

156 Ⓐ Ⓑ Ⓒ Ⓓ Ⓔ
157 Ⓐ Ⓑ Ⓒ Ⓓ Ⓔ
158 Ⓐ Ⓑ Ⓒ Ⓓ Ⓔ
159 Ⓐ Ⓑ Ⓒ Ⓓ Ⓔ
160 Ⓐ Ⓑ Ⓒ Ⓓ Ⓔ

161 Ⓐ Ⓑ Ⓒ Ⓓ Ⓔ
162 Ⓐ Ⓑ Ⓒ Ⓓ Ⓔ
163 Ⓐ Ⓑ Ⓒ Ⓓ Ⓔ
164 Ⓐ Ⓑ Ⓒ Ⓓ Ⓔ
165 Ⓐ Ⓑ Ⓒ Ⓓ Ⓔ

166 Ⓐ Ⓑ Ⓒ Ⓓ Ⓔ
167 Ⓐ Ⓑ Ⓒ Ⓓ Ⓔ
168 Ⓐ Ⓑ Ⓒ Ⓓ Ⓔ
169 Ⓐ Ⓑ Ⓒ Ⓓ Ⓔ
170 Ⓐ Ⓑ Ⓒ Ⓓ Ⓔ

171 Ⓐ Ⓑ Ⓒ Ⓓ Ⓔ
172 Ⓐ Ⓑ Ⓒ Ⓓ Ⓔ
173 Ⓐ Ⓑ Ⓒ Ⓓ Ⓔ
174 Ⓐ Ⓑ Ⓒ Ⓓ Ⓔ
175 Ⓐ Ⓑ Ⓒ Ⓓ Ⓔ

176 Ⓐ Ⓑ Ⓒ Ⓓ Ⓔ
177 Ⓐ Ⓑ Ⓒ Ⓓ Ⓔ
178 Ⓐ Ⓑ Ⓒ Ⓓ Ⓔ
179 Ⓐ Ⓑ Ⓒ Ⓓ Ⓔ
180 Ⓐ Ⓑ Ⓒ Ⓓ Ⓔ

MK1019

# Composition:
# From
# Snapshots to
# Great Shots

**Laurie Excell**

with

John Batdorff
David Brommer
Rick Rickman
Steve Simon

Peachpit
Press

**Composition: From Snapshots to Great Shots**
Laurie Excell, with John Batdorff, David Brommer, Rick Rickman, and Steve Simon

Peachpit Press
1249 Eighth Street
Berkeley, CA 94710
510/524-2178
510/524-2221 (fax)

Find us on the Web at www.peachpit.com
To report errors, please send a note to errata@peachpit.com
Peachpit Press is a division of Pearson Education

Acquisitions Editor: Ted Waitt
Project Editor: Susan Rimerman
Production Editor: Lisa Brazieal
Developmental/Copy Editor: Anne Marie Walker
Proofreader: Elaine Merrill
Composition: WolfsonDesign
Indexer: James Minkin
Cover Design: Mimi Heft
Cover Image: Laurie Excell

ISBN-13  978-0-321-74132-5
ISBN-10      0-321-74132-3

9 8 7 6 5 4

Printed and bound in the United States of America

# ABOUT THE AUTHORS

**Laurie Excell** is a professional wildlife and nature photographer. Her images have been published in *Outdoor Photographer, Outdoor Photography* (UK), *Photoshop User, Elements Techniques,* and *Layers* magazines. She leads popular wildlife photography adventures in North America and is an instructor at Photoshop World. Prior to working as a professional photographer, Laurie spent more than two decades in photographic sales, helping pros and hobbyists decide which equipment suited their particular needs. See her work at laurieexcell.com.

**John Batdorff** is an award-winning landscape and travel photographer who splits his time between Chicago and Montana. He is the author of *Nikon D7000: From Snapshots to Great Shots* (Peachpit), and his work has been featured in the National Museum of Wildlife Art in Jackson Hole. He loves the outdoors and traveling, and sharing his images with others. See his work and read his popular photography blog at www.batdorffphotography.com.

**David Brommer** is a New York City-based photographer who currently works as the B&H Photo Event Space Manager. Well versed in photography from pixels to platinum, David has built up a body of work centering on portraits of fringe society. David operated the gallery Suspect Photography in Seattle during the 90s and continues to explore new technology and old techniques. See his work at seattlesuspects.com.

**Rick Rickman** is a Pulitzer Prize-winning Southern California photographer with 30 years', experience. His work has been featured on many covers of *Time* and *Newsweek* magazines. His project and documentary work has appeared in publications such as *National Geographic, Life, Sports Illustrated,* and *Smithsonian.* Rick has traveled the world covering Olympic competitions, wars, and political upheavals as well as innumerable social interests and events. His abilities cross over every photographic discipline, and his greatest motivator is the challenge presented by each opportunity. See his work at rickrickman.com.

**Steve Simon** has been passionate about documenting the beauty and drama of the human condition for his entire photographic life. The author of four photography books, with works in major museum collections around the world, he has had solo shows in New York, Buenos Aires, Toronto, and Montreal. His work has been featured at the Visa Pour L'Image Photojournalism Festival, in Perpignan, France. He is on the Apple Aperture Advisory Board and faculty of International Center of Photography (ICP) and School of Visual Arts (SVA) in New York. He has led workshops all over the world, including Mentor Series, Macworld, PhotoPlus Expo, and Gulf Photo Plus in Dubai. His forthcoming books include: *Steve Simon's Nikon Dream System* (Lark) and *The Passionate Photographer* (New Riders). See his work at stevesimonphoto.com.

# DEDICATION

To my mom and dad, Ramona and Harold Excell, and to my loving husband, Frank Lohr, for all your love and support in this crazy adventure that I have embarked upon.

# ACKNOWLEDGMENTS

This book would not be possible if not for the perseverance of Nikki McDonald and Ted Waitt, and their unwavering desire to have me as an author for Peachpit. Thanks.

Thanks to Anne Marie Walker and Susan Rimerman for their patience and guidance in getting my first book to print.

My knowledge of photography is the sum of all the photographers I have known and who inspire me, as well as the students I meet at various workshops to the pros I am fortunate to call my friends. I thank each and every one of you for sharing your passion for photography. I am a better person for each experience.

I want to thank the four other photographers whose names are also on this book. I appreciate your contribution and words of wisdom in your fields of expertise:

John Batdorff—Chapter 7, "Black and White"

Rick Rickman—Chapter 8, "Sports and Composition"

David Brommer—Chapter 9, "Beyond the Rule of Thirds"

Steve Simon—Chapter 10, "The Compositional Dance"

I would be remiss not to mention at least a couple of photographers who have influenced me with their wisdom and passion for photography: Moose Peterson, my mentor, my friend, my big brother. You recognized that spark of interest in me and mentored me along the way to a full-blown passion for photographing the natural world. You held me to a high standard, but none higher than the standard to which you hold yourself. For this I thank you. Joe McNally for your friendship and guidance, and for telling me to say yes to the things that scare me the most. The rewards of that simple word far exceed the fear of the unknown. Thank you!

And most of all I want to thank my father for giving me the gift of photography when I was a child; my mother for her unwavering belief in me and the certainty that I can do anything I set my mind to while maintaining an objective view of my work; and my loving husband, Frank—I could not sustain the crazy pace without your love and support. You encourage me to go, go when I know that you really want me to stay, stay. I love you, honey.

—Laurie Excell

# Contents

**INTRODUCTION**                                                           viii

**CHAPTER 1: EQUIPMENT**                                                      1

The Equipment You Use Directly Affects Your Photographic Style

Poring Over the Equipment                                                     2

Poring Over the Equipment                                                     4

What's In My Bag                                                              6

My Top Ten Basic Camera Settings                                            23

Chapter 1 Assignments                                                       29

**CHAPTER 2: EXPOSURE TRIANGLE**                                            33

ISO, Aperture and Shutter Speed, and Their Relationship to
     Each Other and to Light                                                33

Poring Over the Picture                                                     36

Understanding the Exposure Triangle                                         38

Chapter 2 Assignments                                                       53

**CHAPTER 3: LIGHT**                                                        57

Light Is the Key Element in Image Making!                                   57

Poring Over the Picture                                                     58

Poring Over the Picture                                                     60

The Quality and Quantity of Light                                           62

Direction of Light                                                          70

Exposure Compensation                                                       74

Chapter 3 Assignments                                                       78

**CHAPTER 4: LINES, SHAPES, AND PATTERNS**                                  81

Lines, Shapes, and Patterns Make Up the Visual Path that Leads
     Your Eye Through the Frame to the Point of Interest

Poring Over the Picture                                                     82

Poring Over the Picture                                                     84

Curves                                                                      86

Lines                                                                       88

Patterns                                                                    93

Framing                                                                     95

Vertical or Horizontal Shots?                                              97

Layers                                                                    100

Chapter 4 Assignments                                                     102

## CHAPTER 5: COLOR                                                       **105**

Understanding Color and Its Role in Making Dynamic Images

Poring Over the Picture                                                    106

Poring Over the Picture                                                    108

Color Wheel                                                               110

Complementary Colors                                                       112

Emotion of Color                                                          113

Black and White Colors                                                    116

Colors as Patterns                                                        118

Colors and White Balance                                                  119

Significance of Color                                                      122

Chapter 5 Assignments                                                     124

## CHAPTER 6: SPATIAL RELATIONSHIPS                                       **127**

The What, Where, When, Why, and How That Go Into the
    Making of a Good Composition

Poring Over the Picture                                                    128

Poring Over the Picture                                                    130

Point of View                                                            132

Visual Depth                                                             133

Scale                                                                    136

Perspective                                                              136

In Your Face, or, Environmental Composition                              140

Horizon Line                                                             144

Rule of Thirds                                                           146

Chapter 6 Assignments                                                     148

## CHAPTER 7: BLACK AND WHITE                                            **151**

Learning to See in Black and White

Poring Over the Picture                                                    152

Poring Over the Picture                                                    154

When to Go Black and White                                               156

Learning to Live and See in a Black-and-White World                      156

Approaching the Shot                                                      163

Once I'm Committed: My Thought Process                                   164

My Standard Camera Settings                                              167

Postprocessing for Black and White 171

My Kit 173

Break the Rules and Have Fun 174

Chapter 7 Assignments 175

## CHAPTER 8: SPORTS AND COMPOSITION 177

### A Totally Different Animal

Poring Over the Picture 178

Poring Over the Picture 180

Learning to Handle the Complexities of Sports Photography 182

Dealing with Speed 183

The Two Most Important Questions 187

Learning Lessons from Your Mistakes 196

Chapter 8 Assignments 201

## CHAPTER 9: BEYOND THE RULE OF THIRDS 203

### A Brief History, Some Psychology, and Positive and Negative Space

Poring Over the Picture 204

Poring Over the Picture 206

Where Did Composition Originate? 208

Good Composition Is in Our DNA! 210

Deconstruction and Psychology of a Composition 214

Positive and Negative Space 218

Thoughts on Cropping and Printing 225

Chapter 9 Assignments 227

## CHAPTER 10: THE COMPOSITIONAL DANCE 229

Poring Over the Picture 230

Poring Over the Picture 232

The Dance 234

Work the Scene 236

Change Your Vantage Point 238

Be in the Moment 240

Choices and Limitations 242

Have Patience 245

Review Your Work 247

Follow the Magic 247

Experience Leads to Intuition 250

Chapter 10 Assignments 251

## INDEX 252

# Introduction

Taking your photography from snapshots to great shots begins with having a solid understanding of your camera and lenses so that you can intuitively move from one camera setting to another, capturing the moment as it unfolds. Although this is a book on composition, I start at the beginning, with the camera, and provide you with the building blocks to establish a strong foundation for making photographs rather than simply taking them. I cover the basic camera settings I use that enable me to capture peak of action or to chase the light as it dances across the landscape. The lens you use directly impacts your photographic style. Having a lens that complements your vision of the world is part of the process of making great shots, so I spend some time discussing lenses, to give you a better grasp of what lenses do and why you may need one type of lens over another. And, finally, I cover some essential accessories and filters that I carry in my bag to further enable me to make the images you see in this book.

Understanding light and exposure is probably one of the biggest roadblocks to making great images. In Chapter 2, I explain the exposure triangle and how aperture, shutter speed, and ISO relate to each other. Knowing which exposure combination to select gives you the creative control needed to bring your vision to life—from capturing great depth of field with everything within the frame in great detail, to isolating your subject and making it pop, to capturing peak of action or implying motion through the use of creative blur. For more in-depth coverage of exposure, check out Jeff Revell's book *Exposure: From Snapshots to Great Shots.*

Light is what gives your subject shape, form, and texture; it has quality and quantity. Light is what gives your images mood, drama, and emotion. Without light, there would be no photographs. Knowing how to capture that light can be the difference between a simple snapshot and a great shot. Shadow and light lead your viewer's eye through your image and to your subject. One of the first things I look at when bringing the camera to my eye is the play of light on the scene before me and how I can use the light to make a dramatic image.

After you have read the first three chapters and have gone through the settings on your camera and worked through the assignments, you then need to take a look at the way you arrange the elements within your photographs—in other words, explore your composition. You have probably heard many of the "rules" about what makes a good composition. I like to think of the rules more as suggestions to making better images that capture your viewer's attention, giving them a sense of what you saw and felt the moment you clicked the shutter. Chapter 4 discusses the use of lines, shapes, and patterns to direct the path your viewers take through your images to get to the subject. I cover leading lines, straight lines, S-curves, and the way they come together to create graphic elements of shapes and patterns.

Continuing down the composition path, Chapter 5 discusses color, the use of complementary and contrasting colors, and the emotional impact that the variety of colors have on your viewers.

I wrap up my part of the book in Chapter 6, with discussions and illustrations of spatial relationships and subject placement—from frame-filling to environmental compositions, placement of horizon lines, vertical versus horizontal orientation, camera angle, perspective, and much more.

After completing the first six chapters, you will have a much better grasp of what makes a compelling image and how to take your photography from snapshots to great shots. But wait—there's more. The additional chapters in this book are written by four outstanding photographers, who have expertise in various photographic fields. They have graciously contributed their perception of composition and how it relates to their subjects, using their outstanding images to illustrate the points they make. In Chapter 7, John Batdorff covers black-and-white composition; in Chapter 8, Rick Rickman discusses sports and action photography; in Chapter 9, David Brommer takes you beyond the rule of thirds; and in Chapter 10, Steve Simon discusses the compositional dance.

So what are you waiting for! It's time to get started on your journey from taking snapshots to making great shots.

*Don't forget to share your results with the book's Flickr group!*

*Join the group here: flickr.com/groups/composition_fromsnapshotstogreatshots*

# Equipment

## THE EQUIPMENT YOU USE DIRECTLY AFFECTS YOUR PHOTOGRAPHIC STYLE

With the technology of today's digital cameras, anyone can take good pictures. However, it takes the right equipment and skill behind the camera as well as in the digital darkroom to make great photographs. Does your camera offer the features that best suit your needs? Does it have a full frame or cropped sensor? Can you get fast enough frames per second to capture peak of action? If you're shooting in low light, does your camera offer low enough noise to produce acceptable results? Does your equipment complement your photographic style, or is your photographic style determined by the equipment you own? Answering these questions, and others, helps to determine which camera is right for you. Many manufacturers offer a variety of cameras, lenses, and accessories to customize your system to best suit your style.

The lenses you own dictate what you will include within your frame as well as what you will leave out. The aperture you select controls what is in sharp focus and what is blurred (depth of field).

Your camera settings can help you capture the image you see in your mind's eye. How you adjust the exposure settings, the focus points, the color space, and so on makes a photograph uniquely yours.

# PORING OVER THE EQUIPMENT

Cameras are available in a variety of formats, from full frame (24X36) to 1.5/1.6X cropped sensors and 4/3 format. The sensor size plays a role in the number of pixels your camera has as well as how it handles low light. Your camera's sensor size affects the focal length of your lenses by the rated magnification (crop) factor of the camera. For example, for those of you with most Nikons (entry level to mid-range), you'll need to multiply your lenses' focal length by 1.5X; for Canons in the same category, multiply your lenses' focal length by 1.6X; and for 4/3 sensors, multiply your lenses' focal length by 2X to get the equivalent focal length of the lenses on your camera. The cropped sensor gives a sense of greater magnification by cropping the image on a smaller sensor. Many people like the extra "magnification" of the cropped sensor for moving in tighter on the subject. On the other hand, full-frame sensors make it possible to go to ultra-wide angles, with lenses being their actual, designated focal length with no multipliers, to increase the magnification. Full size sensors generally have lower noise (which means more room for the pixels to spread out). The 4/3 camera systems relinquish sensor size in favor of compact physical size.

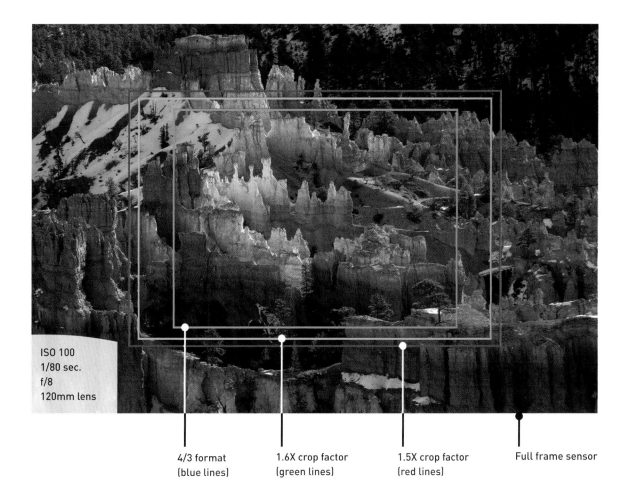

ISO 100
1/80 sec.
f/8
120mm lens

4/3 format
(blue lines)

1.6X crop factor
(green lines)

1.5X crop factor
(red lines)

Full frame sensor

# PORING OVER THE EQUIPMENT

Selecting the lens that best matches your vision is the next step in defining your style. You'll need to consider more than just focal length and angle of view. There is maximum aperture to think about, Vibration Reduction/Image Stabilization, AF-S/USM (silent wave focus motors), and minimum focus distance, not to mention size, weight, and cost. The decisions you make about which lens to choose will play an important role in the outcome of your image. Take control of your photography by using a lens for its features, not just because it came with the camera.

These images were all made from the same location; the camera was set at ISO 200 using aperture priority at f/16.

14–24mm 2.8 @ 14mm

24–70mm 2.8 @ 24mm

24–70mm 2.8 @ 70mm

70–200mm 2.8 @ 200mm

200–400mm 4.0 @ 400mm

600mm 4.0

# WHAT'S IN MY BAG

I am fortunate enough to have the privilege of photographing the natural wonders of our world. These marvels range from grandiose landscapes to intimate wildlife encounters. It's not uncommon for me to go from bundling up in layer upon layer of arctic wear to brave the below-zero temperatures of winter in Yellowstone National Park directly to the hot and humid shores of Tampa Bay. With water lapping at my legs, you'll find me scooting along on my belly inch by forward inch, camera attached to my 600mm f/4 lens sliding smoothly along in its custom ground pod and on a Frisbee from the local pet store, as I stalk small shorebirds at their eye level. Lightning? No problem, I have the tools to capture lightning in my bag. If I need more reach, I have a teleconverter or two handy at all times. If I need to make adjustments to my camera in the predawn darkness, there's a flashlight in my pocket. If I need a little more light on the subject? I reach for my flash along with the off-camera cord. Having the right tools in my bag (**Figure 1.1**) and the proficiency to use them at a moment's notice is what allows me to make the images I do.

FIGURE 1.1
My Moose MP-1 bag and all my essential accessories.

| | |
|---|---|
| Nikon D3X/D3X or 2-D3S bodies | Nikon SB-900 w/ SC-29 TTL cord |
| Nikon AF 16mm 2.8 Fisheye | Lexar Pro 32 GB 600X, 16 GB 600X CF cards |
| Nikon AF-S 14–24mm 2.8 | EN-EL4 spare battery (one per camera) |
| Nikon AF-S 24–70mm 2.8 | Nikon MC-36 remote release |
| Nikon AF-S 70–200mm 2.8 VR II | Flashlight |
| Nikon AF-S 200–400mm F4 VR II | Circular polarizer, graduated ND, Vari-ND |
| Nikon AF-S 600mm F4 VR | Raincoat for camera |
| Nikon TC-14E II, TC 17E II, TC 20E III | Microfiber cloth |

## CAMERAS

As a nature photographer, I am exposed to some pretty harsh environments, from minus temperatures and sulphuric steam in Yellowstone to sand and salt on the beaches of Florida. Loving weather the way I do, it's not uncommon for me to get caught in a downpour. I chose my camera bodies based on the fact that they are rugged enough to withstand whatever conditions I put them through. In addition, I need a high-performance camera to enable me to capture peak of action when a bird flies past or a bear takes off running through a stream in hot pursuit of a fish. Here are the cameras I use and some key features that were influential in my decision making:

Nikon D3X:

- Ultra high-resolution sensor (24 megapixels) for fine detail and large output
- 100 percent "what you see is what you get" viewfinder
- Full frame (FX) sensor

Nikon D3S (X2):

- High performance (speed = nine frames per second) for capturing peak of action
- Low noise in low-light situations or at high ISO settings
- 100 percent "what you see is what you get" viewfinder
- Full frame (FX) format
- High resolution (12 megapixels)

## LENSES

With the huge selection of lenses available, it's hard to decide which lens is best suited for your unique style. Is the convenience of a zoom lens preferable to the speed of a prime lens? Variable and fixed-aperture zoom lenses are also available to choose from, but which best suits your needs and budget? What about VR (Vibration Reduction) or IS (Image Stabilization) for hand-holding in low light? I always recommend buying the best lenses you can afford. A wider aperture may be the difference between a sharp image and one that isn't quite sharp enough.

I buy the fastest, sharpest lenses Nikon has to offer to assist me in making the best images I can (**Figure 1.2**). I utilize the speed of Nikon's fast lenses as well as Vibration Reduction and my ability to hand hold at much slower shutter speeds than I could otherwise. Silent Wave motors in most of my lenses ensure that I have the quickest and quietest focus possible; they also give me the ability to instantly reach up and take control of the focus ring without having to fumble for the AF switch.

### FIGURE 1.2
Here are the Nikon lenses I use.

(From left to right: AF 16mm 2.8D, AF-S 14–24mm 2.8G, AF-S 24–70mm 2.8G, AF-S 70–200mm 2.8G VR II, AF-S 200–400mm 4.0G VR II, AF-S 600mm 4.0 VR)

The angle of view chart you see in **Figure 1.3** depicts the range of coverage of different lenses, from the 180-degree angle of view of a fisheye to the very narrow, isolating angle of view of a super telephoto. The angle of view determines just how much of a given scene will be included as well as what will be excluded in your images.

An AF 16mm f/2.8 Fisheye lens with its 180-degree, all-encompassing angle of view allows me to capture everything in sight within the frame (**Figure 1.4**). The fisheye is known and loved for its distortion.

FIGURE 1.3
Angle of view chart
for various lenses.

400mm 6°

200mm 12°

100mm 19°

50mm 46°

24mm 84°

14mm 114°

16mm 180°

Angle of View

FX Format

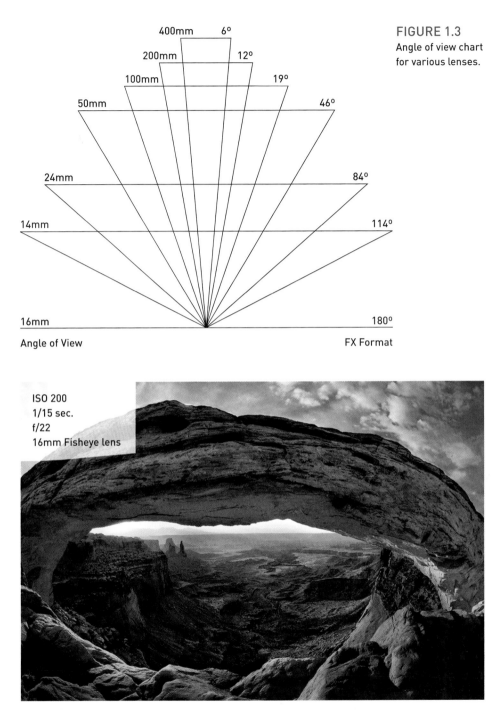

ISO 200
1/15 sec.
f/22
16mm Fisheye lens

FIGURE 1.4
With nearly 40
people crowding
around Mesa Arch,
the Fisheye lens
was called into
service, enabling
me to move in close
to eliminate the
people and still
frame the arch from
side to side.

I use an AF-S 14-24mm f/2.8 ultra-wide, rectilinear (corrected against distortion) lens that covers 114–84 degrees for sweeping landscapes with dramatic foregrounds (**Figure 1.5**).

**FIGURE 1.5**
Moving in tight on the foreground, closing the aperture down to a small opening (more on apertures in Chapter 2), and tilting the camera to include the distant horizon gives images great visual depth and invites the viewer to enter your world through the portal of your photographs.

ISO 100
1/125 sec.
f/13
14–24mm
2.8 lens @ 14mm

The AF-S 24–70mm f/2.8 is a great all-around, mid-range zoom (**Figure 1.6**). This is my "carry-everywhere lens," with its 84–34 degree angle of view.

The AF-S 70–200mm f/2.8 VR II, with its tack-sharp optics, is a great mid-range telephoto zoom lens for portraits as well as for pulling details out of a scene (**Figure 1.7**). The VR II allows me to hand hold the camera at up to four stops slower than normal. Both the speed (2.8) and the focal length of the 70-200mm allow me to focus on my subject and have the background disappear into a soft blur of diffused colors.

An AF-S 200–400mm f/4 VR II is my main "big game" and intimate landscape lens (**Figure 1.8**). This is my lens of choice for hand-holding from a boat to capture birds in flight or breaching whales.

ISO 200
1/350 sec.
f/16
24–70mm
2.8 lens @ 45mm

ISO 200
1/250 sec.
f/11
70–200mm lens
@ 125mm

**FIGURE 1.6**
With coverage from wide to slightly telephoto, the mid-range zoom is ideal for both environmental as well as head-and-shoulder portraits.

**FIGURE 1.7**
I truly appreciate the versatility of a telephoto zoom when I have a frame-filling subject moving towards me. I simply reach out and turn the zoom ring to a wider focal length and keep shooting.

**FIGURE 1.8**
A zoom lens in the telephoto range can be invaluable when you can't move enough to get closer to your subject. Simply let your lens do the walking by zooming in on your subject for a tighter composition.

ISO 400
1/125 sec.
f/5.6
200–400mm lens
@ 240mm

An AF-S 600mm f/4 VR is the "big gun" for wildlife photography (**Figure 1.9**). I'm an in-your-face kind of photographer. I want to be up close and personal with my subjects.

**FIGURE 1.9**
The 600mm helps me isolate my subjects from the background, which makes them pop.

## TELECONVERTERS

Teleconverters are designed to increase the magnification of telephoto lenses. When your 600mm still doesn't get you that frame-filling composition, simply attach a teleconverter between the body and lens, and increase the focal length of your lens by the teleconverter's multiplication factor. **Figure 1.10** shows the teleconverters I use.

A TC-14E II increases the magnification of my telephoto lenses by 1.4 times, with a one-stop loss of light (example: 200–400mm f/4 with 1.4X= 280–560mm f/5.6).

The TC-17E II increases the magnification of my telephoto lenses by 1.7 times, with a one-and-a-half stop loss of light (example: 200–400mm f/4 with 1.7X= 340–680mm f/6.7). At a maximum aperture of f/6.7, the speed of focus slows down noticeably; the center AF is the strongest sensor.

**FIGURE 1.10**
TC-14E II, 1.4X (left); TC-17E II, 1.7X (center); TC-20E III, 2X (right). Autofocus works best at apertures of 5.6 or wider. Adding a teleconverter to your lens reduces the maximum aperture, possibly slowing down the focus speed or disabling it all together.

A TC-20E III increases the magnification of my telephoto lenses by two times, with a two-stop loss of light (**Figure 1.11**). With the 2X on, AF is slowed down significantly, and I will usually resort to manual focus (example: 600mm f/4 with 2X= 1200mm f/8.0).

**FIGURE 1.11**
Adding the 2X teleconverter to my 600mm lens and lowering the tripod to the ground gave me the best angle of view when this hooded warbler caught a crane fly.

ISO 400
1/2000 sec.
f/8
600mm f/4 lens
with TC-20E III

## LENS SHADES

All I can say is, "use them!" Lens shades block extraneous light from entering the front element and bouncing around within the lens, degrading the clarity of the image. They are also great protection for the front element because they protrude in front of the optics, protecting them from bumps and bangs.

**Without lens shade**
**With lens shade**

## FILTERS

Filters expand your ability to create an image with the visual impact that you felt when you clicked the shutter. Your eyes adjust to the extreme shadows and high-lights of a bright day. You see colors for their values, whereas your cameras see colors in temperatures. In my bag, I carry a few filters to help me capture the colors and compact the exposure as desired.

### POLARIZER

A circular polarizer removes the reflection of a blue sky from the landscape, the glare of water off rocks, the sheen of light glancing off a smooth surface, and more. And here you thought it was just to make the sky bluer and the clouds puffier. But it does all of the above and that too. Simply thread it onto your lens and turn the front ring until the reflection disappears and the colors turn richer and warmer. **Figures 1.12** and **1.13** show an image shot without and with a polarizer.

FIGURE 1.12
Without a polarizer.

ISO 100
1/20 sec.
f/16
24–70mm lens
@ 44mm

FIGURE 1.13
With a polarizer.
A polarizing filter
removes the reflec-
tion of the blue
sky, bringing out
the colors of Grand
Prismatic Springs.

## POLARIZER

A polarizer is a great stand-in when you need to drop the shutter speed in very bright light. Simply thread the polarizer onto your lens and turn it until the shutter speed is at its slowest (one-and-one-half to two stops reduction in light).

## GRADUATED NEUTRAL DENSITY

The exposure range in the image of Mount Hood was greater than my camera could capture in one click (**Figure 1.14**). If I exposed for the sky, I lost detail in the reflection (too dark). If I exposed for the reflection, I lost detail in the sky and mountain (too bright). With a straight line along the horizon separating the brighter area from the dark, I simply held my graduated neutral density filter (**Figure 1.15**) in front of the lens and was able to compact the exposure another three stops, which gave me good values in both the mountain and the reflection (**Figure 1.16**).

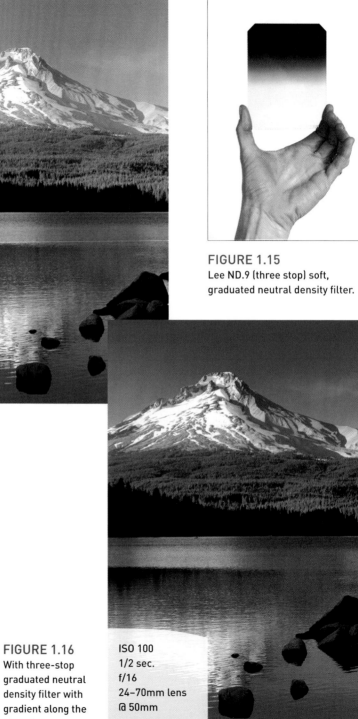

**FIGURE 1.14**
Without graduated
neutral density
filter.

**FIGURE 1.15**
Lee ND.9 (three stop) soft,
graduated neutral density filter.

**FIGURE 1.16**
With three-stop
graduated neutral
density filter with
gradient along the
shoreline.

ISO 100
1/2 sec.
f/16
24–70mm lens
@ 50mm

## VARIABLE-NEUTRAL DENSITY

When the light is too bright to allow for a slow shutter speed, I pull out my Singh Ray Vari-ND filter (**Figure 1.17**). It has a range of two to eight stops of light reduction. Simply thread it on the front of the lens and turn it until you get the desired shutter speed.

Figures 1.18 and 1.19 show an image shot without and with my Singh Ray Vari-ND filter.

**FIGURE 1.17**
Singh Ray Vari-ND filter.

ISO 100
1/40 sec.
f/8
70–200mm 2.8 lens with
TC-14E II @ 240mm

**FIGURE 1.18**
Without the Vari-ND filter.

ISO 100
1/2 sec.
f/8
70–200mm 2.8 lens with
TC -14E II @ 240mm

**FIGURE 1.19**
With the Vari-ND filter.

## ACCESSORIES

Several additional accessories can come in handy when you're on a shoot. Here are the accessories that are always in my bag.

An SB-900 TTL (through-the-lens) fill flash removes color cast on overcast days or in shade and adds fill light to shadows. Having a flash in my bag gives me added control over light (**Figure 1.20**).

FIGURE 1.20
Using fill flash on an overcast day is an excellent way to remove color cast from your subject and add some extra punch. Fill flash will add catchlights to your subject's eyes.

ISO 200
1/30 sec.
f/8
600mm f4 lens
with TC-17E II

Lexar Professional 16 and 32 GB 600X CompactFlash cards store my images. Media is cheap, I shoot a lot, and I don't ever want to run out of cards when on an important shoot, so I carry a wallet full of high-speed, high-capacity cards. The high-speed cards surpass the camera's write speed and download onto my computer quickly.

I carry a spare EN-EL4 battery for each camera to ensure that I can keep shooting no matter how long the day and how heavy the action. The same battery fits all of my cameras, which is a huge convenience for compatibility and also lightens the load of having to carry extra chargers when I travel.

A Nikon MC-36 Remote Release has an interval timer that I use for photographing star trails or group shots, and a lock for shooting extended periods of time in Bulb mode.

A flashlight/headlamp is essential because nature photographers are out before dawn and often well past sunset, so we need a good light to see our cameras and make adjustments. A headlamp provides hands-free light.

A Shutter Hat raincoat protects my camera and lenses up to 200mm from adverse weather. I use a Hydrophobia for my camera with either the 200–400mm or the 600mm lens attached.

Microfiber cloth keeps my lenses clean and shiny.

My MP-1 bag was designed by wildlife photographer Moose Peterson. The MP-1 will hold up to a 600mm with a body attached. Every bag in the MP series (MP-1, MP-3, MP-5, and MP-7) is designed to fit in the overhead of the smallest commuter plane, giving me the confidence that I won't have to relinquish my camera equipment to a gate check.

The tripod/head combinations (**Figure 1.21**) I use are Gitzo GT5541LS Wimberley Head II (Gimbal head: **Figure 1.22**) to support my long lenses, and the Gitzo GT3541LS with the Really Right Stuff BH-55 for everything else. I rely on the lightweight strength and durability of the Gitzo tripods in the field. In addition to their light weight and stability, the positive locking and release of the 6X twist adjustments make setting up and dismantling a quick job. The lack of a center column allows me to get down to eye level with many of my subjects.

When lightning strikes, I am ready with my trusty Lightning Trigger (**Figure 1.23**). I simply plug it into the camera and sit back while the Lightning Trigger fires the camera for me (**Figure 1.24**).

FIGURE 1.21
My tripod/head combination.

**FIGURE 1.22**
The Wimberley Head II.

**FIGURE 1.23**
With the Lightning Trigger plugged in to my camera, I am able to photograph lightning without having to set my camera in Bulb mode and hold the shutter open while hoping for a strike within the area of sky I am aiming at. I just set up my camera, plug in the Lightning Trigger, and enjoy the show.

**FIGURE 1.24**
Capturing this awesome lightning bolt while storm chasing would not have been possible without my Lightning Trigger.

ISO 100
1/15 sec.
f/11
24–70mm
2.8 @ 24mm

# MY TOP TEN BASIC CAMERA SETTINGS

To take full advantage of my camera, I've customized it's menus to suit my shooting style. As a nature photographer, I need to be ready at a moment's notice to capture the action as it unfolds before me. The highest resolution possible is critical, as is the high performance of a fast camera. I am no stranger to shooting in low light and at high ISO settings when required to capture the moment, so low noise is important. Here are my basic camera settings on a D3; refer to your manual for your settings.

## 1. APERTURE PRIORITY

My camera's exposure mode is set to aperture priority (A/ AV) nearly all the time for the control it gives me over all aspects of making an image. By changing the aperture, I can control just how much of the image will be in focus and what will be out of focus (depth of field: **Figure 1.25**), which enables me to direct where the viewer's eye goes within the frame. The aperture I select in turn controls the shutter speed based on the light and ISO (**Figure 1.26**). I'll go into greater detail about aperture priority in Chapter 2, "Exposure Triangle."

ISO 200
1/125 sec.
f/22
24–70mm 2.8
lens @ 32mm

FIGURE 1.25
A small aperture gives me great depth from foreground to background.

FIGURE 1.26
Opening up the lens
to a wider aperture
results in a faster
shutter speed to
stop action.

ISO 1280
1/350 sec.
f/8
70–200mm
2.8 lens @ 116mm

## 2. CONTINUOUS FOCUS DYNAMIC

I have my camera set to Continuous AF Dynamic. I focus on the subject using a single focus point, and the camera uses the information from the selected focus point plus the surrounding 20 points to track a moving subject, keeping it in sharp focus, which allows me to concentrate on composition. As long as the subject stays within the target area, focus will remain locked on it.

## 3. CONTINUOUS HIGH ADVANCE

With my camera set at Continuous High Advance (nine frames per second), I can fire off a blistering sequence of frames (**Figure 1.27**), capturing peak of action.

**FIGURE 1.27**
As I tracked the yellow-crowned night heron stalking its breakfast, I saw it take off after a crab and simply depressed the shutter while panning the bird. As a result, I captured a sequence of images from the chase to the catch.

ISO 200
1/1500 sec.
f/5.6
600mm lens

## 4. 3D MATRIX METERING

I rely on my camera's metering system to provide me with the technically correct exposure. The 1005 pixel 3D Matrix Metering (Evaluative Metering on Canon cameras) evaluates the scene, determines how much dark versus light area there is, compares the scene to a database of tens of thousands of images, and produces the best overall exposure for the given light values (**Figure 1.28**).

FIGURE 1.28
A five-stop range of light shows detail between the brightest area (clouds) and the darkest area (shadows on the Mittens).

ISO 100
1/50 sec.
f/16
24–70mm 2.8
lens @ 38mm

## 5. RAW VS. JPEG FORMAT

For the most information, resolution, and versatility, I have my cameras set to RAW + JPEG. RAW format gives me the greatest amount of tonal range and detail possible. I have the ability to make adjustments to exposure, white balance, and many other settings before processing the file, maintaining the highest quality and flexibility. RAW has tens of thousands of tonal values as opposed to JPEG's hundreds of tonal values. In addition, a RAW file has trillions of colors compared to a JPEG's mere millions. Is more always better? It depends on your final output needs. If I'm shooting an image strictly for the Web or to send via email, I may shoot in JPEG format because the file is processed instantly and is basically ready to send with little to no postprocessing necessary. When I want to squeeze every last drop of color, tone, and detail from the image, I'll use the RAW file format so I can tweak the file and do additional creative processing in the digital darkroom. Once I have that finished file, I can convert it to JPEG for the Web or email, or I can output to large prints.

## 6. COLOR SPACE

Adobe RGB provides me with the largest color palette possible to work with (**Figure 1.29**). I have the ability to capture subtle gradations in colors with smooth transitions. Shooting in Adobe RGB gives me all the colors I need for print, and if I want to go to the Web, email, or an online lab, I simply convert to the appropriate profile after the fact. My finished images provide all the detail possible to go any which way I need.

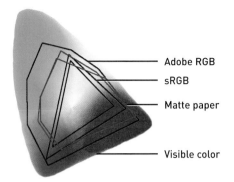

Adobe RGB

sRGB

Matte paper

Visible color

**FIGURE 1.29**
The Adobe RGB color space offers the greatest range of color for even transitions between colors and shades of light to dark.

## 7. HIGHLIGHT WARNING

Highlight warning (affectionately called "blinkies") gives me exposure information that helps me decide if any exposure corrections are needed at the point of capture (**Figure 1.30**). I set the blinkies to be active in the Playback menu. When I review my images, if there are areas that are blown out with no detail, the problem areas blink black>white>black>white repeatedly. With this information, I can determine whether or not I need to make any exposure adjustments.

**FIGURE 1.30**
I use blinkies to determine whether I have exposure issues to deal with.

## 8. FILE NUMBER SEQUENCE

On a good day I can easily shoot several cards. Later, in the digital darkroom while I am downloading images, if there are files with the same name, the computer will ask whether I want to overwrite the files. After a long tiring day, I may very well click the wrong button. With File number sequence turned On (**Figure 1.31**), the camera continues to consecutively number the images on the new card, avoiding any duplicate numbers from the previous card, and keeps me and my images in order.

FIGURE 1.31
Avoid overwriting images by turning the File number sequence to On!

## 9. AF-ON (AEL/AFL)

I use AF-ON to lock focus and exposure, leaving my camera set to Continuous mode to capture action at a moment's notice. But there are times when I don't have a focus point to select from based on my composition. Rather than reaching down and switching the camera to Manual (and possibly missing some action), I simply focus on the subject, hold down the AF-ON button, compose the frame to my liking, and fire away. As long as I hold the AF-ON (AEL/AFL) button, the focus will be locked. When the subject moves, I simply release the AF-ON button and go back to my normal continuous focus with tracking. Be sure to check your instruction manual to set this function.

## 10. ISO

I begin with my ISO at its lowest setting for greatest detail and lowest noise. I'll raise the ISO as needed to achieve the desired aperture/shutter speed combination.

As discussed earlier in the chapter, the ISO you set directly affects the aperture/shutter speed combination that you can select. Higher ISO allows you to shoot at faster shutter speeds in lower light or at smaller apertures, with noise being the trade-off. By selecting the lowest ISO you can get away with, you have the lowest noise possible in a given light situation. Even with the low-noise capabilities of today's cameras, I shoot at the lowest ISO I can for the highest resolution and clarity in my images.

If a higher ISO is required to achieve the effect you desire, by all means raise your ISO; a sharp, noisy photograph is better than a blurry image. It's a compromise that allows you to capture the image in low-light situations.

# Chapter 1 Assignments

The following assignments are designed to give you a better understanding of your equipment and how to set it up to suit your style of photography. Each subsequent chapter builds on the previous one, so be sure to stop at the end of each chapter and do the assignments, to build a strong foundation for making great shots.

### Equipment Inventory

Take a moment to look over your equipment. Does your camera offer you the performance you need for your photography style? Do your lenses cover the full range of focal lengths that you need to capture the image you see in your mind's eye? Do you have a spare battery, or two? Do you have enough memory to shoot for a day, a week, and so forth? Is your tripod stable enough to support your equipment? Make a list of the equipment you currently own, the gaps that need filling, and the equipment that will fill those gaps. This list will provide direction the next time you are in the market for a new camera, lens, accessory, and so on.

While you're examining your equipment, record all the serial numbers, purchase dates, and purchase costs. Then file away your inventory in the event you ever need it for insurance. You do have insurance, don't you?

## Basic Camera Settings

Dust off that instruction manual, grab your camera, and get comfortable so you can review all of your camera's buttons, dials, and menus. I know, I know, this is boring. But, believe me, you will thank me later. Familiarize yourself with the locations of important buttons and dials. Learn what the menus contain and file away that information in your memory for later in case you need to make changes. Set your camera's menus to suit your photographic style.

## Focal Length Exercise

**Part 1** This exercise will give you a good sense of the lenses you have and their ability to frame your subject. Set up your tripod at a location that has an interesting subject. Attach your widest lens, compose the photograph, and click. Repeat the process with each lens you have, shooting at the widest to the longest focal length of your zoom lenses from the same spot. Then compare the images to see how wide a shot your lens will capture compared to how tight it will frame up your subject.

**Compare** Compare the differences in focal lengths from a specific distance to see the coverage your lenses give you.

**Part 2** Using your tripod and the same lenses you used in Part 1, this time attach your longest lens first and compose a scene with a subject that fills the frame. Next, zooming out or changing lenses to the next longest, move forward until the subject fills the frame the same amount it did with the previous lens. Continue changing lenses and moving in closer with each change to fill the frame with the subject until you have used all your lenses.

**Compare** Compare the backgrounds in each image. The subject should be the same size in each frame, but the background will change based on the angle of view of the lens in use.

*Share your results with the book's Flickr group!*

*Join the group here: flickr.com/groups/composition_fromsnapshotstogreatshots*

2

ISO 100
1/13 sec
f/8
95mm lens

# Exposure Triangle

## ISO, APERTURE AND SHUTTER SPEED, AND THEIR RELATIONSHIP TO EACH OTHER AND TO LIGHT

Each and every image you make is influenced by light. Your camera meters the quality, quantity, and direction of the light, and provides you with exposure information that you can use to make images that represent your vision. Once you have the exposure information, it is up to you to decide what the best ISO, aperture, and shutter speed combination will best capture the mood of the scene you are photographing. I'll take each element of the exposure triangle, illustrate the effect of selecting the best aperture, shutter speed, and ISO for each image, and explain why.

For more on exposure, check out Jeff Revell's awesome book *Exposure: From Snapshots to Great Shots* (Peachpit, 2011).

# PORING OVER THE PICTURE

Setting my camera on a tripod allowed me to set my aperture to a small opening, yielding both great depth of field, from the frost-covered tree in the foreground to the falls beyond. It also resulted in a slow shutter speed to blur the water, giving it that silky look.

Keeping my ISO set to 100 was also instrumental in the slowness of the shutter speed. Understanding each element and its relationship to the others enabled me to control the final outcome of my image. With a gray, overcast sky and the monochromatic light, I planned on converting the image to black and white when I finished it.

A slow shutter speed blurred the water, emphasizing the feeling of motion.

A small aperture enabled me to capture sharp focus from foreground to background.

ISO 100
1/6 sec
f/22
70mm lens

# PORING OVER THE PICTURE

I made several subconscious decisions in a matter of seconds as I turned my lens on the backlit grizzly. With my ISO already dialed to its lowest setting, I opened up the aperture to f/5.6 to render the bear in sharp focus and throw the background out of focus, into a soft blur. The resulting high shutter speed had no effect one way or the other because neither I nor the bear was moving.

The distance from the bear to the background mountains was so great that it was easy to blur them with a wide aperture.

Dialing in -1 exposure compensation darkened the bear, saturated the colors, and emphasized this rim-lit fur.

# UNDERSTANDING THE EXPOSURE TRIANGLE

For every exposure, there are at least six different combinations available that will give you the same exposure value. But in many cases, each combination produces radically different effects, from a sharp subject and soft background (shallow depth of field) to everything from near to infinity in sharp focus (great depth of field). Your shutter speed controls stop-action or blur-motion, and the ISO controls the camera meter's sensitivity to light with high ISO settings for low light and low ISO for higher resolution and low noise.

If any one element in the exposure triangle changes, the other settings will be affected. Using the Exposure Triangle in **Figure 2.1** as a starting point, let's look at the results of changing our settings:

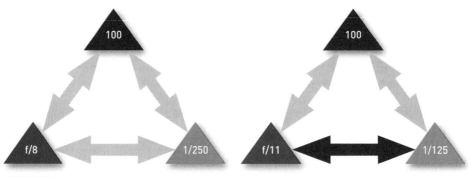

**FIGURE 2.1**
The Exposure Triangle with a basic exposure on a partly sunny day: ISO is set to 100, aperture is set to f/8, and the resulting shutter speed is 1/250 sec.

ET 100 ISO, f/11 at 1/125 sec. Changing my aperture from f/8 to f/11 causes my shutter speed to slow from 1/250 sec to 1/125 sec.

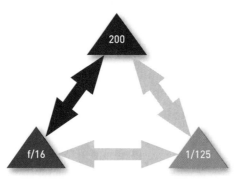

ET 200 ISO, f/16 at 1/125 sec. If I need a faster shutter speed, I increase the ISO to 200 to keep 1/125 sec.

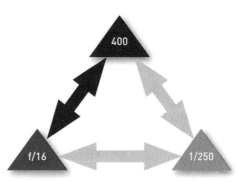

ET 400 ISO, f/16 at 1/250 sec. If I find that I need an even faster shutter speed, increasing my ISO to 400 gives me 1/250 sec at f/16.

## ISO

ISO is the camera sensor's sensitivity to light. The lower the number (100, 200, etc.), the brighter the light you need to make a correct exposure. If there is bright light and you can keep your ISO at its lowest setting, the result will be ultrafine detail, high resolution, and low noise. You have the capabilities to change from one ISO to another from frame to frame. With today's low-noise cameras, you may wonder why it's important to control the ISO rather than simply dialing it up to a higher setting and shooting away. Although it's true that cameras have lower noise, I still want the least noise possible, and I want the creative control changing my ISO affords me. Selecting the ISO is the first step I take when making an exposure decision (**Figure 2.2**).

ISO 100
3 sec.
f/38
105mm macro lens

**FIGURE 2.2**
With my camera mounted on a tripod, and a stationary subject, I was able to dial my ISO to its lowest setting and the aperture to its smallest opening. This gave me the highest resolution, lowest-noise image, with the greatest depth of field possible.

High ISO (800, 1600, etc.), on the other hand, allows me to shoot in lower light. I can shoot at higher shutter speeds or smaller apertures when I adjust my ISO to a higher setting. A result of a higher ISO setting is noise (noise is that rainbow of colorful specks that appear on your image when you shoot at high ISO or long exposures), but if raising the ISO enables me to get a shot I wouldn't be able to capture otherwise (**Figure 2.3**), I'll take the added noise and deal with it by using noise-reduction software when I process my image. This is one of the many compromises you will be faced with when deciding the best exposure settings for a given image.

**FIGURE 2.3**
With the light nearly gone, I had to raise my ISO to 3200 to capture the bobcat preening on a log. Without the ability to raise my ISO, I would not have been able to make this image.

ISO 3200
1/60 sec
f/4
600mm lens

In each of the preceding scenarios, the exposure value (the light falling on the sensor) is exactly the same, but the end result can be very dramatic depending on the combination you choose.

ISO

- Low ISO has higher resolution, requires more light or a wider aperture, or a slower shutter speed.
- High ISO has more noise, requires less light or a smaller aperture, or a faster shutter speed.

## APERTURE

The aperture value is the size of the lens opening (called the f-stop). The aperture is the opening in the lens that allows light to pass through to the sensor (**Figure 2.4**).

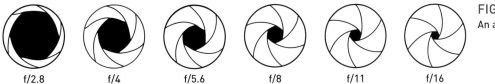

| f/2.8 | f/4 | f/5.6 | f/8 | f/11 | f/16 |

FIGURE 2.4
An aperture chart.

Aperture is a big factor in controlling depth of field and is the setting that confuses people the most. The smaller the number (1.4, 2.8), the wider the opening (**Figure 2.5**); the wider the opening, the more light the lens allows through the diaphragm. Wider apertures give less depth of field and result in faster shutter speeds (**Figure 2.6**).

With overcast skies and the possibility of some action, I diaied up my ISO to 800 and set the lens to a fairly wide aperture to be able to stop the action when this coyote leapt into the air to pounce on a mouse (**Figure 2.7**).

**FIGURE 2.5**
A wide aperture has less depth of field; think small number equals shallow depth of field.

ISO 200
1/1500 sec
f/5.6
600mm lens

FIGURE 2.6
Wide apertures also allow in more light, enabling you to shoot at a faster shutter speed (more on that coming right up) and stop the action.

ISO 200
1/1500 sec
f/8
600mm lens

FIGURE 2.7
It took a fast ISO and shutter speed to capture this action. The resulting wide aperture blurred any detail in the background.

ISO 800
1/500 sec
f/6.7
600mm lens

## DEPTH OF FIELD

Depth of field is the area within the frame that appears in acceptably sharp focus. Increased depth of field is achieved by using a small aperture (a big number, for example, f/11, f/16, etc.). Less depth of field happens when the lens is opened to a wider aperture (a small number, for example, f/1.4, f/2.8, etc.).

In contrast, the larger the number, the smaller the lens opening. The smaller the opening, the less light the lens allows through the diaphragm, with a slow shutter speed as a result (**Figures 2.8** and **2.9**).

### FIGURE 2.8
A small aperture (big number) provides more depth of field; think big equals more.

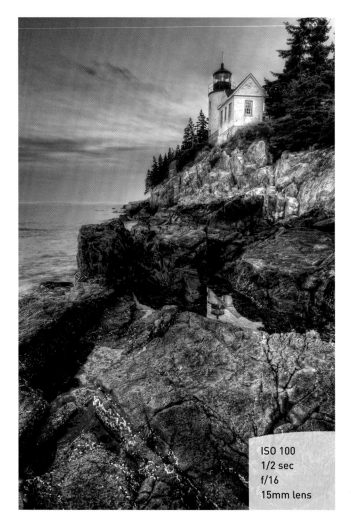

ISO 100
1/2 sec
f/16
15mm lens

ISO 100
1.5 sec
f/22
110mm lens

FIGURE 2.9
A small aperture
(big number) with
its small opening
results in a slower
shutter speed. (It
takes light longer
to pass through a
small hole.)

A small aperture requires either a slower shutter speed or a faster ISO. To achieve the blurred motion look of the water in **Figure 2.10**, I closed down the aperture and left the ISO at a low setting.

**FIGURE 2.10**
Here I achieved the blurred motion of the water and depth of field from the near foreground to infinity.

ISO 100
1/2 sec
f/22
19mm lens

- The larger the opening, the smaller the number; the smaller the number, the shallower the depth of field and the faster the shutter speed (**Figure 2.11**).

- The smaller the opening, the larger the number; the larger the number, the greater depth of field and the slower the shutter speed (**Figure 2.12**).

ISO 100
1/20 sec
f/2.8
95mm lens

### FIGURE 2.11

A wide aperture allowed me to focus on the leaf, throwing the background into a colorful blur.

ISO 100
1/100 sec
f/22
95mm lens

### FIGURE 2.12

Closing down the aperture to f/22 made the background busy and distracting without bringing it into sharp focus.

## SHUTTER SPEED

The shutter speed is the length of time the shutter is open to allow the light to pass through the aperture to the sensor (**Figure 2.13**). Shutter speeds control stop action and blur-motion (**Figure 2.14**). I usually set the ISO and aperture, and let the camera select the shutter speed, knowing that I have the ability to override the shutter speed by changing the aperture.

**FIGURE 2.13**
A Shutter Speed chart.

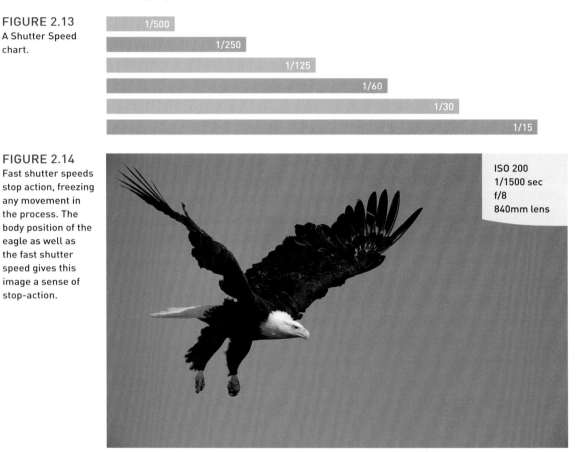

1/500
1/250
1/125
1/60
1/30
1/15

**FIGURE 2.14**
Fast shutter speeds stop action, freezing any movement in the process. The body position of the eagle as well as the fast shutter speed gives this image a sense of stop-action.

ISO 200
1/1500 sec
f/8
840mm lens

### FAST SHUTTER SPEEDS

Fast shutter speeds require a lot of light, a wide aperture, a high ISO, or a combination thereof.

Slow shutter speeds blur movement, giving a sense of slow motion. The blurred wingtips of a bird in flight and the soft cotton candy of moving water are both effects of slow shutter speeds (**Figure 2.15**).

ISO 400
1/60 sec
f/8
600mm lens

**FIGURE 2.15**
To capture the sharp eye and blurred wings of the sandhill crane in flight required good panning skills because I had to shoot at a slow shutter speed to blur the wings, and pan (follow) at the same rate as the bird was moving to keep the eye sharp.

## SLOW SHUTTER SPEEDS

Slow shutter speeds are achieved in low light, at a closed-down aperture, a low ISO, or with a combination thereof.

## APERTURE/SHUTTER SPEED RELATIONSHIP

The aperture I select directly affects the shutter speed the camera selects (**Figure 2.16**) I shoot in aperture priority mode most of the time. If I want a fast shutter speed, I simply turn the aperture to a wider opening to produce a faster shutter speed with a resulting shallower depth of field. If I want to blur motion, I turn the aperture dial to a smaller opening; the resulting slow shutter speeds create a blurred effect.

**FIGURE 2.16**
The Aperture/
Shutter Speed
chart illustrates the
relationship of the
size of the aperture
to the duration of
the shutter speed.

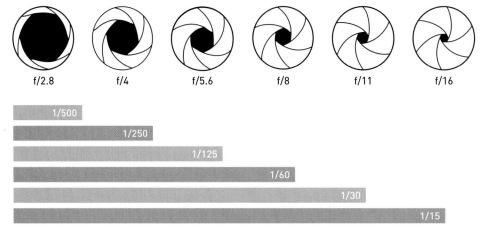

f/2.8    f/4    f/5.6    f/8    f/11    f/16

1/500
1/250
1/125
1/60
1/30
1/15

Figure 2.17 shows an image with a slightly overcast sky. The light was flat, eliminating any shadows, with soft diffused light. The subject was not moving so I was able to keep the ISO down without concern for shutter speed and with an aperture of f/5.6 (wide open on a 600mm with a TC-14E 1.4X teleconverter).

**FIGURE 2.17**
Here I was able to
make the back-
ground a soft
blur, directing the
viewer's attention
to the American
oystercatcher.
A high ISO plus a
wide aperture equal
a shallow depth
of field.

ISO 400
1/500 sec
f/5.6
840mm lens

In **Figure 2.18**, closing down the aperture to f/22 resulted in the shutter speed slowing down to 1/30 sec, which didn't really matter. With a proper long lens technique and a relatively still subject, I could shoot at the slower shutter speed.

ISO 400
1/30 sec
f/22
840mm lens

FIGURE 2.18
With a slower shutter speed, I increased the depth of field, giving the background a textured look to it.

With my camera in aperture-priority mode, I photographed a waterfall, beginning with my ISO at 100, an aperture of f/8, and a shutter speed of 1/180 sec (**Figure 2.19A**). Closing down the aperture to f/11 slowed the shutter speed to 1/90 sec (**Figure 2.19B**). An aperture of f/16 gave me a shutter speed of 1/45 sec (**Figure 2.19C**). And at f/22 the shutter speed was 1/20 sec (**Figure 2.19D**), which was the slowest shutter speed I could get; my aperture was closed down as far as it would go, and my ISO was at its slowest. A shutter speed of 1/20 sec still wasn't giving me the look I wanted, so I reached into my bag and pulled out my Vari-ND (see the "Accessories" section in Chapter 1). Threading it onto my lens, I rotated the front ring until I was able to shoot at one second, giving me the blurred motion and silky look that I was after (**Figure 2.20**).

## FIGURE 2.19

All four images are the same exposure but use a different combination of aperture and shutter speeds to get a different effect with the moving water.

**A.** 100 ISO, f/8 at 1/180 sec

**B.** 100 ISO, f/11 at 1/90 sec

**C.** 100 ISO, f/16 at 1/45 sec

**D.** 100 ISO, f/22 at 1/20 sec

## FIGURE 2.20

Variable neutral density allows me to shoot at slow shutter speeds in bright light (a two- to eight-stop reduction in exposure).

Part of composition is telling your story in a way that the viewer will understand without your being there to explain it. Composition includes depth of field, which is mainly controlled by aperture; motion, which is controlled by shutter speed; light; and how you handle exposure to control the path your viewer's eyes take through your image. By combining the information you learned in Chapter 1 and in this chapter, you now have the basic the foundation that will start you on your journey toward better storytelling through lens selection, camera settings (aperture/shutter speed/ISO), and exposure, and their roles in the outcome of your images. Take some time to complete a few assignments before moving on, to make sure you have a good grasp of this very important element in your photography.

# Chapter 2 Assignments

After finishing the first two chapters and completing the following assignments, you should have a basic understanding of the equipment in your bag and of how to navigate your camera's buttons and dials, as well a better understanding of the exposure triangle and how to use ISO, aperture, and shutter speed to make your images "speak" to their viewers.

### ISO Test

Find a subject to photograph indoors without a flash and set your camera on a tripod so each image will be composed identically. Set your lens to about f/5.6 or f/8 (aperture priority) and then cycle through the different ISO settings, from your lowest 100/200 to your highest 1600/3200+. Review the images on your computer and compare the noise levels at different ISO settings. This will give you a comfort zone as to how high you feel you can set your ISO to get the shot.

### Aperture Test

Try to find a scene with a foreground, middle-ground, and background element (preferably a stationary subject). Set your camera on your tripod and compose the image to your liking. Focus about a third to halfway into the scene, set your ISO relatively low (you're using a tripod), set your camera to aperture priority, and cycle through the aperture settings, letting the shutter speed fall where it will. Review the images on your computer screen to see the difference the aperture makes in depth of field.

Try the same assignment again two more times, first cycling through your aperture settings with your subject close to the background and then with your subject farther from the background, to compare the role of distance of subject to background and depth of field.

Using the same lens and same aperture setting, shoot the same subject from different distances to see how distance to subject affects depth of field.

Using all the lenses you have, starting with the longest lens, compose a recognizable image within the frame and click, zoom back, or change lenses to your next longest and move forward until your subject fills the same amount of the frame that it did with the longer lens. Leaving the aperture the same in each shot, continue changing lenses to wider angles and moving in closer to your subject to get the same image size.

Compare all four situations, and review the EXIF data to see the effect the different situations have on depth of field.

### Shutter-Speed Test

Find a few moving subjects—moving water in a stream or a waterfall, moving cars (be careful), birds in flight, or anything that you can repeatedly photograph at different shutter speeds. You'll be comparing the effect of different shutter speeds on the feeling of stop-action or blur-motion. Mount your camera on a tripod and compose the image. Leaving the ISO the same, begin at your lens's widest aperture and keep clicking at each stop. As you begin to close down the aperture to a smaller opening, notice the effect of the small aperture on your shutter speed. This is one test for which you need the tripod for support as much as for accuracy of the test.

*Share your results with the book's Flickr group!*

*Join the group here: flickr.com/groups/composition_fromsnapshotstogreatshots*

3

ISO 100
1/90 sec.
f/11
55mm lens

# Light

## LIGHT IS THE KEY ELEMENT IN IMAGE MAKING!

Without light, there would be no photographs. In fact, the word photography means "drawing with light." Light has quality, quantity, color, and direction, which provide shape, texture, and character to your images. There is a reason that I get up at 0'dark thirty while most people in the world are still tucked snugly in their warm beds. I drive in the predawn hours to arrive at a location that is cloaked in darkness. I set up my camera in the dark, using a flashlight to make sure my ISO and aperture are adjusted to my liking as I prepare to make my first image of the day. It's up to me to choose the best settings to enhance the quality of light.

# PORING OVER THE PICTURE

Crashing waves on the Oregon coast had me heading up the dunes in hopes the morning fog would lift. As the sun burned through the fog and washed over the sandstone cliffs, there was plenty of light. So, I was able to keep my ISO at a low setting and still have enough depth of field and a fast enough shutter speed to render the image that I saw in my mind's eye.

With the sun burning through the morning fog, the rich, warm colors of the sandstone cliffs are accentuated.

ISO 200
1/200 sec.
f/16
75mm lens

Fog has a diffusion effect, softening shadows and isolating the subject from the background.

Sunlight reflects off the crashing waves, creating a translucent quality in the water.

Late afternoon light skims across the wheat fields in Palouse, Washington, creating a painterly effect of shadow and light in lovely shades of green. Sidelight adds contrast and texture to the undulating hills, adding visual depth to the scene. Within a few short minutes of setting up my camera, the sun dropped below the horizon, leaving the fields in shadow. Knowing my camera and settings as well as I do enabled me to capture the moment before it was gone.

An aperture setting of f/8 was enough to render the scene in focus due to the fact that everything was at infinity.

With my camera mounted on a tripod, while photographing a stationary subject, I was able to select an aperture that gave me the depth of field necessary without worrying about the resulting slow shutter speed.

ISO 200
1/6 sec.
f/8
160mm lens

# THE QUALITY AND QUANTITY OF LIGHT

Photography is all about chasing the light. The light you chase has quality and quantity. It's the quality and quantity of light that I look for in my photographs. The rich, warm tones of sunrise or sunset, the deep blue of twilight, the diffused colors of an overcast day, or the harsh shadows of midday all play a big part in the end result of my images. Understanding light will make you a better photographer.

## SUNRISE AND SUNSET: THE GOLDEN HOURS

It's anticipation of the quality of light a beautiful sunrise bestows upon the landscape that pulls me from my warm bed, or the quality of light at sunset that keeps me out shooting during the dinner hour. While the sun is low on the horizon, bathing the world in its warm glow, the exposure is well within the five-stop range that my sensor needs to capture detail in both the shadows and highlights (**Figure 3.1**). If I turn 180 degrees, I can photograph into the sun using the bright, colorful light as a background for an interesting silhouette (**Figure 3.2**). During the first hours of daylight, the light is low, necessitating the need for a tripod for stability or to increase the ISO enough to achieve a shutter speed fast enough to hand hold the camera. The choice is yours—greater detail versus greater noise.

FIGURE 3.1
Sunrise at Highland Lighthouse, Cape Cod. Mounting my camera on a tripod allowed me to select an aperture that would yield enough depth of field to render the lighthouse in sharp focus without my worrying about the resulting slow shutter speed.

ISO 100
1/5 sec.
f/8
40mm lens

ISO 100
1 sec.
f/8
55mm lens

Quality of light is fleeting. Every February in Yosemite National Park, there is a phenomenon that lasts for about two weeks. The conditions have to be just right, with no clouds to block the sun and enough water flowing over Horsetail Falls. As the sun begins to set, the angle of light throws the canyon wall into darkness and light hits the falls, lighting them as if they were on fire (**Figure 3.3**). Talk about quality of light!

## MIDDAY

As the sun rises higher in the sky, the *quantity* of light increases, the warmth of first light fades away, and the contrast between shadow and light becomes greater. The brighter light, as the sun moves higher in the sky, means that I can shoot at a faster shutter speed or a smaller aperture without the need to increase my ISO (see "Understanding the Exposure Triangle," in Chapter 2). As the light gets brighter and the contrast between shadow and light increases, rather than putting away my camera, I look to the shadows as backdrops for graphic elements (**Figure 3.4**).

**FIGURE 3.3**
The setting sun casts its light towards Horsetail Falls, illuminating it as if it were on fire. Shooting wide open to keep a faster shutter speed was necessary because I was hand-holding my camera. A –1 stop of light darkened the rock wall, enhancing the light on the falls.

ISO 100
1/180 sec.
f/ 2.8
200mm lens

ISO 200
1/500 sec.
f/8
195mm lens

FIGURE 3.4
Midday light, with its hard shadows, turns objects into graphic elements. The sun acts like a point source of light on sunny days, throwing shadows into the mix for added drama. I tend to dial in minus exposure compensation to darken the shadows, making them a deep black that makes a nice contrast against a lit subject. Minus exposure compensation darkened the shadows, making the column stand out.

Slot canyons are best photographed at midday, when the sun is high in the sky. The light works its way into the canyon through a slim opening, bouncing from one red wall to the other, bringing out the colors of the sandstone (**Figure 3.5**).

**FIGURE 3.5**
Midday light, Upper Antelope Canyon, Arizona. With the sun directly overhead, light penetrates into the deep canyon, bouncing off the walls and turning them to a rich, warm color. Dust falls from above into the slot canyons, and the light bounces off the dust creating God beams. Minus exposure compensation increased the visibility of the shaft of light against the saturated colors of the canyon walls.

ISO 100
2.2 sec.
f/22
35mm lens

## DIFFUSED, OVERCAST LIGHT

Overcast days light the landscape as if there was a giant softbox in the sky. Without shadows and contrast, the light is flat, with more detail visible. I like overcast days when photographing mammals, birds, people, flowers, and water (**Figure 3.6**).

ISO 200
1/125 sec.
f/6.7
850mm lens

**FIGURE 3.6**
Diffused light brings out the details in mammals' fur. Adding a 1.4X teleconverter to my 600mm lens enabled me to fill the frame with the pronghorn's head. A tripod allowed me to shoot wide open at 1/125 of a second, with my ISO set to 200 to avoid noise.

As the day wears on, the sun begins its descent and the shadows grow long once again; it's the light that keeps me out shooting until the last rays of sun are gone. And if I'm lucky and the photo gods cooperate, I'll keep shooting, capturing the blue cast of twilight (**Figure 3.7**).

**FIGURE 3.7**
Twilight at Heceta Head Lighthouse, Oregon. Long after the sun has set, the sea fog begins to roll in, making the light more prominent in the dark.

ISO 200
1.5 sec.
f/2.8
195mm lens

## CHANGING LIGHT

Light is constantly changing. Different times of the day reveal different elements in a subject. The late afternoon light shines on the Golden Gate Bridge, bringing attention to the famous red structure (**Figure 3.8**).

As the sun drops below the horizon, the light disappears from the bridge. The image takes on the cool colors of evening (**Figure 3.9**).

ISO 200
1/125 sec.
f/ 8
29mm lens

**FIGURE 3.8**
Late afternoon light illuminates the Golden Gate Bridge. With the camera mounted on a tripod, I was able to photograph the same subject at different times of the day, into the evening, illustrating the difference in light over a few hours time.

ISO 200
3 sec.
f/ 8
29mm lens

**FIGURE 3.9**
The sun drops below the horizon, plunging the Golden Gate Bridge into darkness.

In the evening, artificial lights illuminate the Golden Gate once again, brightening the red of the bridge. A long exposure with moving cars on the bridge added light streaks, which produced the feeling of motion (**Figure 3.10**).

**FIGURE 3.10**
Evening approaches and the bridge is lit once again, causing the bright red to stand out against the dark blue sky.

ISO 200
30 sec.
f/ 8
29mm lens

# DIRECTION OF LIGHT

Light has three directions in relationship to the camera. The way light falls on my subject determines how I will set my exposure. Front-lit subjects are easy to expose. With no contrast or shadows to deal with, the exposure is well within the range the sensor can handle, so I simply compose and click. Backlight is the opposite of front light, with the light coming from behind the subject, casting it into silhouette. Sidelight adds drama, texture, and shape to an image.

## FRONT LIGHT

Front light lacks shadows. Consequently, it lacks the texture, shape, or dimension of sidelight or backlight. It is, however, a very easy exposure to make. Simply meter your scene, and choose the best exposure combination to suit your subject. With a simple click, you have a nice image. Using a fisheye to photograph Emerald Pool in Yellowstone National Park with front light reveals a glimpse into the depth of the pool (**Figure 3.11**). The lack of shadows reveals the detail in the feathers of a tricolored heron pausing to preen (**Figure 3.12**). Selecting a wide aperture renders the heron in sharp focus and softens the background, making the subject pop.

ISO 100
1/500 sec.
f/8
16mm lens

ISO 100
1/1000 sec.
f/4
600mm lens

FIGURE 3.11
Emerald Pool, Yellowstone National Park.

FIGURE 3.12
Tricolored heron preening, with front light showing the details in its feathers.

## BACKLIGHT

Backlighting (shooting towards the light source) turns your subject into a silhouette. Images that have an interesting shape and form make great subjects when I'm photographing into the sun. The mood of a backlit scene varies depending on how I handle the exposure. Because my camera can't handle the exposure range between shadow and light in a backlit scene, I use the shadows to accentuate the shape of a familiar landmark, the Mittens in Monument Valley. By positioning myself so the sun was partially blocked by the formation, and closing down my aperture to its smallest setting of f/22, I was able to add a creative starburst to the pinpoint of sunlight (**Figure 3.13**). With the knowledge that I would get a starburst effect from shooting into the sun with a small aperture, I took creative license with my fisheye lens to capture a person for scale (more on scale in Chapter 6), backlit against the North Window in Arches National Park (**Figure 3.14**). The scatter of light added creative lens flare (which normally is something I try to avoid).

FIGURE 3.13
The rising sun backlights the Mittens, in Monument Valley, Arizona.

ISO 100
1/10 sec.
f/22
24mm lens

FIGURE 3.14
Backlit photographer with creative lens flare.

ISO 100
1/500 sec.
f/22
16mm fisheye lens

## SIDELIGHT

Sidelight occurs when you are positioned at a right angle to the light source, working the shadows to define shape, form, and texture. The contrast of shadow and light adds a three-dimensional feeling to a two-dimensional image. The simplicity and lack of color in the image of a lighthouse window made for a very high-contrast, graphic look (**Figure 3.15**).

ISO 100
1/2000 sec.
f/5.6
200mm lens

FIGURE 3.15
Sidelight adds shape, form, and texture to the light-house window.

Using sidelight for dramatic effect, I turned my lens on an alligator as it lifted its head out of the water. With only a moment to capture this image before the alligator dropped back into the depths of the lake, I had to act quickly. Knowing how my camera would react to the light, I was able to make a split-second exposure decision and capture the fleeting moment. The water acted as a reflector, bouncing light up into the alligator's face (**Figure 3.16**). The exposure range was too great to capture detail in the shadows, emphasizing the alligator's teeth and eye, which is where I want the viewer's eye to travel within the frame. Just like the lens you select decides what you include as much as what you exclude in your frame, shadow and light further enhance this effect. By excluding part of the alligator's face, the sense of drama and mystery is increased.

FIGURE 3.16

Water acts as a
natural reflector,
bouncing light
up into the
alligator's face.

ISO 100
1/400 sec.
f/8
390mm lens

# EXPOSURE COMPENSATION

Exposure compensation gives me creative control of my exposure. I rely on my camera's meter to give me the best overall exposure for a given scene. Once I have my base exposure, I need to decide on the mood I am trying to capture. I choose among several aperture, shutter speed, and ISO settings. I also have the ability to take control of my exposure and override the camera for dramatic effect.

Window light is a wonderful source of light. In **Figure 3.17** I asked Donald to stand at an angle to the window, controlling the direction the light traveled across his face. Shadow and light gave Donald's face shape and form that front light would have eliminated. By dialing in −1½ exposure compensation, I increased the shadows, which in turn accentuated the character in Donald's face. Donald, a seasoned model, was able to hold very still, which gave me the ability to keep my ISO low to avoid noise and still shoot hand-held at 1/30 sec. with my lens wide open. With a very shallow depth of field, it was essential that Donald's eye remain in sharp focus. Using my 200mm lens, I composed a tight head-and-shoulders portrait of Donald.

Donald's face lent itself to the dramatic lighting, whereas the same effect would not flatter a lovely woman. Knowing light and what works best with different subjects enabled me to capture two distinctly different looks. In **Figure 3.18** I used the window light again. But this time the window was a wall of glass, which increased the size of the light source and created a much softer, brighter, more airy feeling to the portrait of my friend Leila. In this case I dialed in +½ exposure compensation to add to the bright feel. Wanting to show Leila in her home environment, I used a 90mm focal length to include more of her surroundings.

ISO 100
1/30 sec.
f/2.8
200mm lens

ISO 100
1/20 sec.
f/2.8
90mm lens

FIGURE 3.17
Using window light and having Donald turn at an angle to the window enhanced the character of his wonderful face.

FIGURE 3.18
Using a larger source of light added to the bright airy feeling.

Knowing how my meter will react to a given light situation, I dialed in +1 exposure compensation on this kittiwake against a white sky to achieve a high-key look (**Figure 3.19**). Had I gone with the reading my camera gave me, I would have ended up with an image that was darker and moodier, with less detail on the bird. Using my camera's Highlight Warning (see "My Top Ten Basic Camera Settings," in Chapter 1), I could see that the sky was blown out without detail. In this case I chose to accept the blown-out sky to create the effect I was after.

FIGURE 3.19
Dialing in plus exposure compensation gave this kittiwake image a high key look.

ISO 200
1/1000 sec.
f/5.6
380mm lens

Photographing roseate spoonbills in Tampa Bay with front light against the darker mangrove trees caused my Highlight Warnings to blink, warning me of overexposure with no detail on the bird. I dialed in –1 exposure compensation to capture the detail in the spoonbill, which in turn darkened the background to nearly black, causing the spoonbill to stand out dramatically (**Figure 3.20**).

ISO 100
1/20 sec.
f/2.8
90mm lens

**FIGURE 3.20**
Dialing in minus exposure compensation gave me a proper exposure of the roseate spoonbill.

# Chapter 3 Assignments

With a greater understanding of light, you will have much more control over the outcome of your images. Remember that light is the single most important element in your photographs. How you work with the light and your exposures directly relates to whether your images will look the way you visualize them.

## Quality and Quantity of Light

Find a subject close to your home that you can revisit over the course of several days at different times. Photograph the subject under different light conditions to see the effects light has on the mood and character of your subject. Shoot at sunrise, sunset, midday, twilight, and on an overcast day. Then compare the images to see the effects the light has on the subject. Review your exposures and study the EXIF data to see how your settings changed at different times of day based on the quantity of light.

## Direction of Light

Once again, you will need to stretch this assignment over a few days to be able to see the change in the direction of light. Select a few subjects that you can photograph from several angles so you can compare the direction of light and how it affects your subject. Begin with front lighting. Move around so the light is behind your subject and take another photograph. Then shoot your subject with the light coming from the side. Compare the results to see what effect the direction of light has on your subject.

## Exposure Compensation

If you have a bracket setting on your camera, you can use it for this assignment. With your camera mounted on a tripod, shoot a sequence of at least five photographs beginning with the metered value followed by a shot at –1 exposure compensation and then –2 exposure compensation. Then dial in +1 and +2, and shoot at each exposure setting. Compare the results to see the effect of darkening the image and adding drama or lightening the subject to make it feel brighter.

*Share your results with the book's Flickr group!*

*Join the group here: flickr.com/groups/composition_fromsnapshotstogreatshots*

4

ISO 100
30 sec.
f/22
42mm lens

# Lines, Shapes, and Patterns

## LINES, SHAPES, AND PATTERNS MAKE UP THE VISUAL PATH THAT LEADS YOUR EYE THROUGH THE FRAME TO THE POINT OF INTEREST

Composition is the art of arranging the elements within your frame into a pleasing image. It's up to you to determine what your subject is and to arrange the elements within the frame accordingly. Lines and shapes are important elements in composition. Lines draw your viewer into (or out of) the frame. They give direction. An S-curve (a curve that is shaped like an S) gently meanders through the frame, leading the viewer deeper into the frame, whereas a straight line is more direct. Curved lines are soft; straight lines have a more rigid feel.

Do you use a straight line or a diagonal line to reach the subject? Both will take the viewer there, but each has a different impact. Merging lines create a sense of distance, or vanishing point. Shapes are the result of a series of lines that come together to form a circle, square, triangle, and so on. Just like lines, the shape of your subject creates its own dynamic whether it's round, square, triangular, free-form, and so forth. Lines often lead to shapes, giving your images form. Patterns are repeating lines and shapes that make up an image.

# PORING OVER THE PICTURE

Lines and shapes come together to create graphic elements in a photograph. The Conservatory of Flowers in San Francisco's Golden Gate Park is a perfect subject to illustrate lines (both straight and diagonal), shapes, and form all in one image.

The soft shape of the clouds contrasts nicely with the hard lines and shapes of the building.

The many converging lines within the image create a multitude of shapes—square, rectangle, triangle, curves.

I found that converting the image to black and white made an even stronger graphic photograph.

A series of lines draws the viewer's eye through the photograph beginning in the lower left (1) and leading diagonally to a vertical line moving upwards (2) towards the next horizontal line moving to the left (3) and continuing on throughout the frame.

ISO 100
1/200 sec.
f/8
32mm lens

1

2

3

# PORING OVER THE PICTURE

Moving in close on the foreground trees in a quaking-aspen forest increases the feel of visual depth by creating a vanishing point of trees getting smaller and smaller as they recede into the distance. A simple composition of straight lines becomes a compelling image that invites the viewer to take a walk through the forest just as I did when I made the image.

Diffused light (Chapter 3) brings out the detail, color, and texture of the trees.

Vertical lines signify strength and power. Photographing them in a horizontal composition adds a feeling of expanse to the composition.

Using a mid-range zoom to move in tighter on the forest gives an intimate feel to the image.

ISO 200
1/45 sec.
f/8
42mm lens

# CURVES

Curves create a gentle, meandering path that leads the viewer through your image to the subject (**Figure 4.1**). Curves are lines but with a softer feel to them. With an S-curve, the path to your subject is not as direct as a line, so it gives a sense of peace and calm. S-curves are great leading lines to a subject (**Figure 4.2**), and they are such strong elements that they can stand alone as the subject itself (**Figure 4.3**). Whenever I see an S-curve, my eye follows it to see where it leads and to see whether it will make a good photograph.

**FIGURE 4.1**
Centering myself in the middle of the path and using a fairly small aperture (Chapter 2) for increased depth of field creates a composition that invites the viewer to step into the frame and wander down the path and through the forest. I find S-curves to be friendly lead-in lines in composition.

ISO 200
1/45 sec.
f/8
62mm lens

ISO 200
1/350 sec.
f/11
550mm lens

### FIGURE 4.2

The curve of a great blue heron's neck leads from the left side of the frame to the fish he has clamped in his beak, creating a very natural pose.

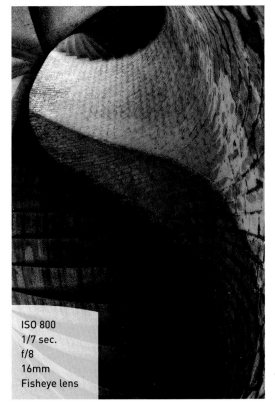

ISO 800
1/7 sec.
f/8
16mm
Fisheye lens

### FIGURE 4.3

An S-curve is such a strong element in composition that the curve itself can be the subject, as in this image of a curved staircase at Fort Point in San Francisco. Using a Fisheye lens emphasized the curvature of the staircase. Hand-holding the camera at 1/7 sec. required a faster ISO to gain enough depth and sharpness.

# LINES

All images are made up of a series of lines, shapes, and forms (**Figure 4.4**). Lines are what lead viewers into the frame and to the subject (also known as leading lines). When artfully composed, an image will have leading lines that direct the viewer's eye where you want it to go. They may be bold and noticeable, creating a direct path to the subject, or they can be subtle and less obvious. Straight lines convey a sense of strength and power and often have a static feel to them. Diagonal lines also signify power, but rather than being static, they convey a sense of motion within a still photograph.

**FIGURE 4.4**
Lines, circles, and shapes make up this graphic image of an old church. Black and white emphasizes the graphic quality.

ISO 200
1/500 sec.
f/5.6
70mm lens

## STRAIGHT LINES

Straight lines can pass through an image horizontally or vertically. A horizontal line going through a photograph can create a sense of calm, giving a static feel to an image (**Figure 4.5**). I find straight, horizontal lines in a photograph to be dividing lines or barricades, keeping the viewer on the outside looking in. Depending on what you are trying to accomplish, a horizontal line can either make or break an image. On the other hand, a vertical line can give a sense of strength and height, leading me directly into the frame with no question as to where I am trying to direct the viewer's eye (**Figure 4.6**). When making a bold composition with a straight line leading towards the subject, I like to center myself on the leading line to give the image symmetry and power. Vertical lines can be leading lines, or they can be the subject itself, as in the case of the tree trunks covered in snow, in **Figure 4.7**.

ISO 200
1/400 sec.
f/4
35mm lens

**FIGURE 4.5**
The spider-web-covered fence blocks me from entering the cemetery, which creates a strong message. Using a wider aperture to blur the background further emphasizes the fence, with just a hint of the cemetery beyond.

ISO 100
1/320 sec.
f/8
10.5mm
Fisheye lens

**FIGURE 4.6**

The dock leading to the beautiful lake scene beyond is as much a part of the picture as the subject it leads your eye towards. I used a 180-degree Fisheye lens to include as much in the frame as possible.

ISO 100
1/180 sec.
f/8
95mm lens

**FIGURE 4.7**

Rather than being leading lines, the tall, straight tree trunks with their branches covered in snow are the subject in this image. The contrast of white against the reddish trunks makes this a very simple yet strong composition.

# DIAGONAL LINES

I like to use diagonal lines moving through the frame to convey a sense of motion that is hard to capture in a still photograph. I often use diagonal lines to lead the viewer's eye to the subject, as in **Figure 4.8**. The fence leads through the fields to Jenne Farm in the distance.

Diagonal lines can create a graphic element when they converge, as in the close-up of a dew-covered spiderweb in **Figure 4.9**. The nature of a spiderweb creates a sense of vanishing point as the drops start big and become smaller as they move towards the center of the web.

ISO 100
1/320 sec.
f/8
10.5mm
Fisheye lens

ISO 400
1/350 sec.
f/8
105mm
micro lens

**FIGURE 4.8**
Diagonal lines have a feel of movement that is hard to convey with straight lines. This image of Jenne Farm, with the fence line leading to the buildings, incorporates a diagonal line that becomes curved with the rolling hills.

**FIGURE 4.9**
Shooting on a parallel plane with the spider web allowed me to use a mid-range aperture of f/8 and still have depth of field throughout. The slight breeze forced me to increase my ISO to reach a faster shutter speed. Hand-holding the camera gave me more versatility in my composition.

Diagonal lines can also be the subject, as in the image of a sand fence as it zigzags along the beach towards the ocean (**Figure 4.10**).

FIGURE 4.10
Moving in close with a wide-angle lens emphasizes the entry point into the frame, with the diagonal lines moving back and forth and leading the viewer to the beach beyond. The ocean and sky in the background are supporting elements in the image, to give it a sense of place (Chapter 6).

ISO 200
1/125 sec.
f/22
32mm lens

# PATTERNS

Patterns are graphic images that have the same subject duplicated over and over within the frame. Repeating lines and shapes make up these patterns. Nature, in all her beauty, provides us with endless patterns to photograph.

The intricate design of a dahlia provides great patterns as petal after petal unfolds to reveal the flower's beauty (**Figure 4.11**).

ISO 200
1/250 sec.
f/8
125mm lens

**FIGURE 4.11**
Using a telephoto zoom, I focused at minimum-focus distance to fill the frame with the flower.

The wake from a boat created a pattern of waves that caught the light and my attention (**Figure 4.12**). I used a telephoto to fill the frame with the repeating pattern, excluding everything else.

Sometimes even the simplest subjects become compelling when another element is added, such as the icicles hanging from the rock wall in **Figure 4.13**. The vertical lines of the icicles contrast with the round rocks.

**FIGURE 4.12**

I increased my ISO to 400mm to be able to achieve a fast shutter speed because I was photographing the wake from a moving boat.

ISO 400
1/250 sec.
f/22
280mm lens

**FIGURE 4.13**

Icicles on a rock wall created a pattern of vertical lines. I like the warmth of the rocks and the way they contrast with the cooler, blue colors of the icicles. Blue conveys coldness in an image (more on color in Chapter 5).

ISO 100
1/90 sec.
f/5.6
155mm lens

# FRAMING

When I think of framing, I think of my image hanging on the wall with a nice mat and frame to show it off. However, there are other methods of framing an image: in the viewfinder, using foreground elements to "frame" the subject. While photographing in Central Park in New York, my attention was drawn to two arches. I liked the way they repeated each other, giving vanishing-point feel with the foreground arch being much larger than the background arch. I patiently waited for the people to move through, when another photographer with a similar idea stepped into the frame (**Figure 4.14**). Liking the sense of scale (Chapter 6) that the photographer added to the image, I quickly clicked off a few shots. Framing can be a very effective use of elements to highlight the subject. Be careful not to use it too heavily, or it becomes the focus of the photograph.

ISO 200
1/45 sec.
f/8
112mm lens

## FIGURE 4.14

The photographer changed the effect of the image I was composing from a simple graphic to a framed composition. The giant arches framed the smaller photographer and added a sense of scale to the image that would not have happened without him in the frame.

Using the foliage to frame the trees in Muir Woods in California creates a sense of looking through a peephole (**Figure 4.15**).

Teardrop Arch is an iconic subject that has been photographed over and over (**Figure 4.16**). Many people use a vertical composition to fill the frame with the rock wall, using the arch to reveal Monument Valley in the distance through the arch. Looking for a slightly different composition, I turned my camera to a horizontal composition and zoomed back to include the edge of the arch. I like the effect of part of the image framed and part of it wide open. I think it adds to the sense of place.

**FIGURE 4.15**
I mounted my camera on a tripod to enable me to shoot at a smaller aperture to render sharp focus on both the foliage and the trees beyond and still keep my ISO low, which resulted in a slow shutter speed.

**FIGURE 4.16**
With no place to set up a tripod and needing a fairly small aperture for increased depth of field, I braced myself using proper hand-holding techniques to shoot at a slow shutter speed.

ISO 200
1.5 sec.
f/16
100mm lens

ISO 100
1/15 sec.
f/16
35mm lens

# VERTICAL OR HORIZONTAL SHOTS?

Vertically or horizontally—which way do you turn the camera? Most cameras are set up with grips that lend themselves to being held comfortably in a horizontal, or landscape, orientation. The higher-end cameras and mid-range cameras with external grips allow the use of vertical, or portrait, composition with the same comfortable grip and shutter release. Which direction do you turn when you're composing an image? It depends on what you want to include and what you want to exclude. There is no right or wrong. Many times, it's simply a matter of preference and what you are trying to communicate in your images.

On a snowy winter morning at Bryce Canyon National Park, I was heading for my car when a lone picnic table covered in snow caught my attention (**Figure 4.17**). My first reaction was to photograph the scene in a vertical format to lend height to the tall trees. On a whim, I turned the camera back to a horizontal position and clicked a few frames. Upon reviewing the images, I decided I liked the spacious feel that I was able to capture in the horizontal orientation (**Figure 4.18**). Both images work; I simply like

ISO 100
1/10 sec.
f/11
35mm lens

**FIGURE 4.17**
My first reaction to the snowy scene was to turn the camera to a vertical composition to emphasize the tall trees.

ISO 100
1/10 sec.
f/11
30mm lens

**FIGURE 4.18**
Here I turned the camera to a horizontal composition, zoomed out a bit more, and found I liked the more spacious feel that I was able to achieve.

the horizontal image better. Had I not turned the camera, I would have been perfectly happy with the vertical image. It was an overcast morning, and I knew when I clicked the shutter that the images would be flat, but I had black and white in mind when I was making these images. Using NIK B&W Infrared software added drama and impact to these otherwise flat-light images.

While photographing the wheat fields in the Palouse region in eastern Washington, I stopped by a historic farm that is noted for its fence made of thousands of wheels and gears soldered together. It was a beautiful, blue-sky day, with big puffy clouds floating in the sky. The question came to mind, which way should I turn my camera? Did I want to convey the vast wheat fields with the fence as a strong foreground element (**Figure 4.19**)? Or, would turning the camera in a vertical format emphasizing the blue sky and puffy clouds better tell the story? Once again, either image works, but what was I trying to communicate in my image? My goal was to capture the wheel fence, which both images do quite well. So, it boils down to either more sky or more wheat fields. I felt that the wheat fields gave the image a greater sense of place, and I was still able to include some sky and clouds. In this case I prefer the horizontal composition (**Figure 4.20**).

ISO 200
1/250 sec.
f/11
90mm lens

**FIGURE 4.19**
A horizontal composition gives the image a feeling of width and expanse.

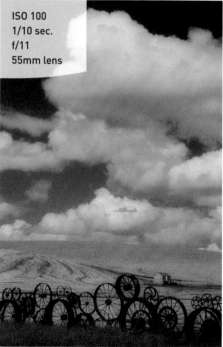

ISO 100
1/10 sec.
f/11
55mm lens

**FIGURE 4.20**
A vertical composition emphasizes the vastness of the sky rather than the fence and fields.

## VERTICAL VS. HORIZONTAL

Next time, study both sets of images and decide what you like about each image. Do you connect with the vertical or horizontal images in the two examples? There is usually no right or wrong answer, it simply depends on the subject and the feeling you choose to convey. Lines, shape, and form all change their appearance when the camera is turned from a horizontal to vertical format.

However, most times it's pretty obvious which way to turn your camera. When a grizzly bear is walking straight at the lens, I turn the camera to a vertical composition to fill the frame with the bear, centering it in the frame for increased impact (**Figure 4.21**). And when a sandhill crane with its wings fully extended flies by, I instinctively turn the camera to a horizontal composition to include it all, from wing tip to wing tip (**Figure 4.22**).

ISO 200
1/200 sec.
f/4
400mm lens

### FIGURE 4.21
A vertical composition was the obvious choice with this grizzly bear.

**FIGURE 4.22**
The position of
the wings and
the body posture
of the sandhill
crane make a
nice horizontal
composition.

ISO 200
1/1000 sec.
f/8
850mm lens

## LAYERS

Another effective use of lines and shapes is to compose an image using layering of
the landscape to create visual depth. Aerial perspective lends itself to this technique
(**Figure 4.23**). When the sun is dropping lower in the sky, partially backlighting the
scene, the distant mountains take on an ethereal look as they seem to fade away into
the distance. Layering is also achieved when there are repeating patterns, like the
rolling wheat fields photographed from a relatively high perspective. The undulating
hills with the shadow and light playing across them produce a unique layering effect
(**Figure 4.24**).

### LAYERING

I normally select a telephoto lens when capturing an image with the layered look. I feel
that the tighter composition lends itself nicely to an intimate landscape.

ISO 100
1/50 sec.
f/22
200mm lens

**FIGURE 4.23**
Using a long lens to compress the scene and dialing in minus exposure compensation to add drama to the layers create a very interesting effect called aerial perspective.

ISO 200
1/800 sec.
f/6.7
190mm lens

**FIGURE 4.24**
Shadow and light (Chapter 3) as well as color contrast (Chapter 5) all play important roles in creating the layered look in a composition.

# Chapter 4 Assignments

Before moving on to Chapter 5, take some time to complete the following assignments to gain a better grasp of lines, shape, and form and the role they play in composition.

### Lines

Using lines to lead to your subject, work a scene by shooting straight on with the lines moving horizontally through the image to see how a horizontal line can divide the frame and create a barrier between the viewer and the subject. Using the same subject, change position so that the line is moving in a diagonal direction towards the subject. For the final shot, shoot straight down a line towards your subject to see the dramatic impact that shooting directly towards the subject has on your images. Notice how changing your camera angle dramatically alters the effect of lines and their effect on the final composition.

### Curves

Go out and look for curves that lead your eye to your subject. Find a classic S-curve and use it to lead the viewer's eye to your subject. Note the softer approach of using curves as leading lines as opposed to the preceding assignment using straight lines.

### Vertical or Horizontal

The next time you are composing a scene, stop and ask yourself why you are composing it the way you are. Once you have captured the image in the orientation you first decided on, turn the camera to the opposite orientation (if you began with a horizontal position, turn the camera to a vertical position) and shoot the same scene. Compare the two images to see what qualities you like about each composition. You may be surprised that many scenes look as good or better when you turn the camera from one orientation to the other.

*Share your results with the book's Flickr group!*

*Join the group here: flickr.com/groups/composition_fromsnapshotstogreatshots*

5

ISO 200
1/125 sec.
f/8
24mm lens

# Color

## UNDERSTANDING COLOR AND ITS ROLE IN MAKING DYNAMIC IMAGES

Color plays a vital role in your photography. It can evoke reactions such as peace, fear, joy, anger, sadness, and so on. Understanding color and the message it sends can help you to achieve a better grasp of the images you make and their emotional impact on your viewers. How these colors are represented within a photograph evokes feelings in your viewers. The natural world is a cacophony of colors. It's these colors that first capture your viewer's attention as they blend together to make up the elements of an image.

# PORING OVER THE PICTURE

Secondary colors are made up of a mixture between two primary colors. Orange is a mix of red and yellow; green is a mix of blue and yellow; purple is a mix of red and blue. The combination of secondary colors in this photograph of a red-eyed tree frog blend together to create an image that portrays some of the vivid colors of nature.

An aperture of f/5.6 renders the subject sharp while throwing the background out of focus.

The background is made up of muted oranges and greens similar to the colors of the tree frog.

Green is a secondary color made up of a mixture of the primary colors blue and yellow.

Orange is a secondary color made up of a mixture of the primary colors red and yellow.

ISO 200
1/50 sec.
f/5.6
180mm lens

# PORING OVER THE PICTURE

Although most people don't think of black-and-white photographs as having color, black and white are colors, as are the variety of shades of gray. It's the tonalities of these shades of gray, black, and white that make up a black-and-white image. Without the bold colors, it's the subtle change in tonalities that give a black-and-white image impact.

A weathered old barn makes an excellent black-and-white subject, emphasizing the feeling of times long past.

ISO 200
1/500 sec.
f/8
20mm lens

Black, white, and shades of gray are all colors.

# COLOR WHEEL

All colors are made from a mixture of two or more of the three primary colors: red, yellow, and blue (**Figure 5.1**). (Remember the nursery school rhyme about primary colors?) Primary colors are the boldest of all colors and have the greatest impact on a photograph. The reflection of Portland illustrates this, as the flags stand boldly apart from the rest of the colors in the scene (**Figure 5.2**). Mixing two primary colors together produces secondary colors, such as red and yellow mixing to create orange, blue and red mixing to make purple, and blue and yellow mixing to make green (**Figure 5.3**). The secondary colors of green leaves and a purple dahlia bud complement each other (**Figure 5.4**). Taking it even further by mixing primary with secondary colors reveals tertiary colors, which provide an unlimited color palette to work with. The relationship of these colors affects the mood of your images.

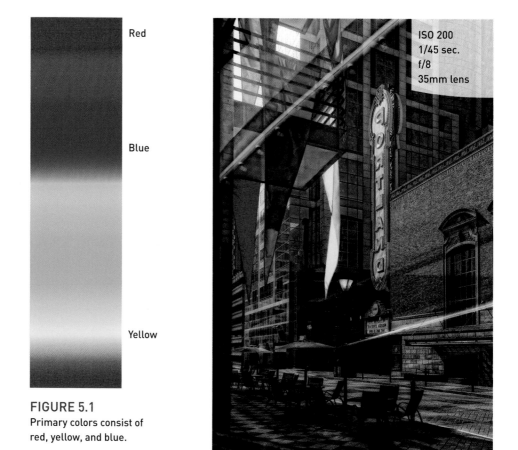

Red

Blue

Yellow

**FIGURE 5.1**
Primary colors consist of red, yellow, and blue.

ISO 200
1/45 sec.
f/8
35mm lens

**FIGURE 5.2**
Your eye goes to the primary colors in this image first.

Purple

Green

Orange

ISO 100
1/20 sec.
f/16
155mm lens

**FIGURE 5.3**
Secondary colors consist of
orange, green, and purple.

**FIGURE 5.4**
Secondary colors go together nicely in this image of a dahlia
bud among the green foliage.

A color wheel (**Figure 5.5**) is a good place to start to better understand colors, their
meaning, their relationship to each other, and their impact on your images.

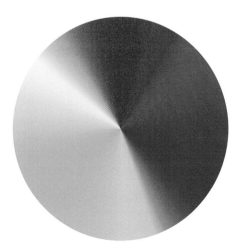

**FIGURE 5.5**
The color wheel illustrates
the relationship of colors
to each other.

# COMPLEMENTARY COLORS

Colors that are opposite each other on the color wheel are said to be complementary colors; their contrasting colors complement each other. The complementary color for red is green, for blue is orange, and for yellow is purple. Some common complementary colors in nature include the red of a ladybug in a complementary sea of green **(Figure 5.6),** and the cool blue tones of a late afternoon in winter reflected from the sky to the mountains to the snow-covered ground, emphasizing the feeling of coldness and offering a nice contrast to the warm colors of the orange snowplow in the foreground **(Figure 5.7).**

**FIGURE 5.6**
Red and green sit across the color scale from each other, making them complementary colors.

ISO 100
1/160 sec.
f/8
105mm lens

**FIGURE 5.7**
Blue and orange are complementary colors.

ISO 200
1/250 sec.
f/8
102mm lens

# EMOTION OF COLOR

Color is said to stir emotion. When you look at a photograph, do you feel anger, joy, peace, tension, or some other emotion? It is likely that if you look closely at the photograph and understand the emotion of color, you will find a link to the image and your feelings based on the colors that are represented within the image (**Figure 5.8**). What emotion do you feel when you look at the following photographs? Does your emotional response have to do with the colors of the image? Compare your emotional response to the description of the colors. Do they match? When you look at a beautiful green butterfly against the soft greens of foliage (**Figure 5.9**), do you feel the serenity and calm that green represents? Flowers are supposed to instill the feeling of youth and innocence; is that what you feel when you look at this dahlia (**Figure 5.10**)? Do you feel a slight chill when your eye lands on the image of the Arctic fox in winter (**Figure 5.11**)? If you do, I have been successful in my rendition of the scene. The yellow and orange buoys (**Figure 5.12**) work together because yellow is a primary color, and orange comes from mixing red with yellow. The splash of blue scattered throughout the image adds the contrast of a cool-toned color.

Red: aggression, strength, boldness

Purple: sophistication, royalty, religion

Blue: loyality, security, comfort

Green: money, nature, health

Yellow: brightness, spring, caution

Orange: warmth, energy, excitement

FIGURE 5.8
Emotional correlation
to colors.

**FIGURE 5.9**
Green: nature,
peace, calmness.

ISO 200
1/500 sec.
f/5.6
180mm lens

**FIGURE 5.10**
Green: nature,
peace, calmness.
Pink: femininity,
childlikeness,
health. White:
innocence, purity,
cleanliness.

ISO 200
1/20 sec.
f/22
160mm lens

ISO 200
1/320 sec.
f/8
550mm lens

**FIGURE 5.11**
White: innocence,
purity, cleanliness.
Blue: cold.

ISO 200
6 sec.
f/22
56mm lens

**FIGURE 5.12**
Red and yellow:
boldness, high
energy, passion.
Blue: cold.

# BLACK AND WHITE COLORS

As mentioned earlier, although they are not often considered colors, black, white, and all the shades of gray are indeed colors. And, like the vivid colors of a color wheel, black and white represent their own set of emotions (**Figure 5.13**). A dark and stormy afternoon at the coast rendered a flat, monochromatic image of the pounding waves. By converting the image to black-and-white infrared, I was able to convey the drama and power of the storm as the white waves crashed against the dark rocks (**Figure 5.14**).

Whenever I want to create a sense of age or history, I think black and white (**Figure 5.15**). In the not-so-distant past, our forebears had to render the world in black and white. It was through exposure (Chapter 3) and the enhancing of the tonal properties of a scene that they were able to bring life and emotion to their images.

White: purity, simplicity, cleanliness

Gray: cold, distinctiveness, businesslike quality

Black: class, drama, seriousness

ISO 100
1/60 sec.
f/8
200mm lens

**FIGURE 5.13**
Emotional correlation to black and white.

**FIGURE 5.14**
Black and white infrared brings the drama of a winter storm on the Oregon coast to life.

ISO 200
1/125 sec.
f/8
18mm lens

FIGURE 5.15
Black and white evoke age and history.

# COLORS AS PATTERNS

Color can be the subject, as in the reflection photograph in **Figure 5.16**, where the undulating colors blend, contrast, and complement each other in repeating patterns. Flowers are excellent examples of color patterns as petal upon petal repeats a color scheme unique to each and every flower. The colors can be bold, powerful, and passionate (**Figure 5.17**). Or, you can strip away the bold, warm colors and replace them with black and white and shades of gray to create an image of the same subject that imparts a totally different emotion. With no vivid colors to influence your feelings, it's the graphic nature of black and white that captures your attention in **Figure 5.18**.

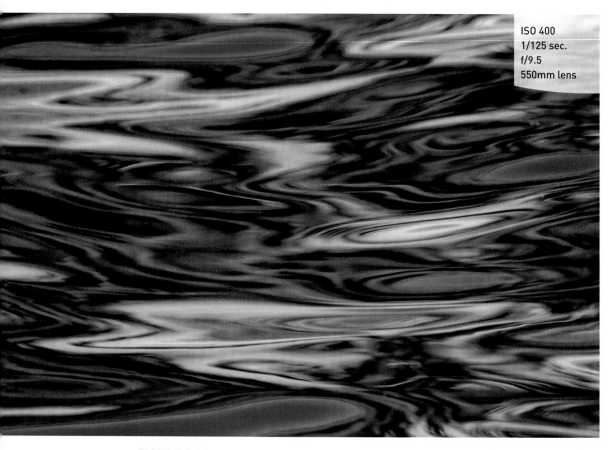

ISO 400
1/125 sec.
f/9.5
550mm lens

FIGURE 5.16
Warm and cool colors complement each other in this reflection.

ISO 100
1/60 sec.
f/16
105mm lens

**FIGURE 5.17**
Bold reds and yellows capture your
attention immediately.

ISO 100
1/60 sec.
f/16
105mm lens

**FIGURE 5.18**
Stripped of bold colors, the pattern becomes
even more graphic in black and white.

## COLORS AND WHITE BALANCE

Light has color, and as such influences the way your images look at any given time
of the day or night. The warm colors of first light or at sunset give a feeling of
warmth, as the sun baths the world in its golden glow (**Figure 5.19**). Twilight evokes
a completely different emotion with its cool tones. I have a feeling of peace and
contentment at the close of the day when the sun has dropped beneath the horizon,
taking with it the warm tones and leaving in their wake the cool blue of evening
(**Figure 5.20**).

**FIGURE 5.19**
Sunrise and sunset, with the sun low on the horizon, produce warm colors.

ISO 200
1/350 sec.
f/16
110mm lens

**FIGURE 5.20**
Twilight blue comes after the sun has set, taking the warm colors with it.

ISO 200
1/6 sec.
f/11
50mm lens

With the ability to control white balance in-camera I have even greater control over the emotional outcome of my images. I can warm up the cool tones of an overcast day by simply switching from the Auto white balance to Cloudy and bringing forth the warm colors (**Figure 5.21**).

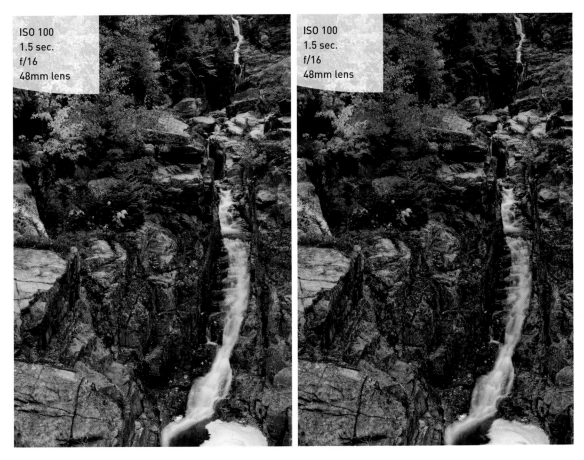

ISO 100
1.5 sec.
f/16
48mm lens

ISO 100
1.5 sec.
f/16
48mm lens

FIGURE 5.21
Auto white balance captures the cool tones of an overcast day (left). Cloudy white balance brings forth the warm colors that are subdued by an overcast sky (right).

# SIGNIFICANCE OF COLOR

Certain colors, when combined, trigger specific emotions in our hearts. What do you think of when you see the colors red, white, and blue together? I have a sense of patriotism when I see our flag (**Figure 5.22**). The changing colors of leaves as they transition from summer greens to the reds and yellows of fall give a sense of closure as one season comes to an end (**Figure 5.23**). For me, a rainbow signifies the end of a storm and a world freshly scrubbed and clean (**Figure 5.24**).

FIGURE 5.22
Red, white, and
blue convey a sense
of patriotism.

ISO 200
1/125 sec.
f/8
300mm lens

FIGURE 5.23
The reds and yellows as the foliage turns signal the end of summer and the beginning of fall.

ISO 100
1/30 sec.
f/8
26mm lens

ISO 200
1/180 sec.
f/11
52mm lens

FIGURE 5.24
Rainbows signify the end of a storm and a fresh new beginning.

# Chapter 5 Assignments

You should now have a much better understanding of color and how you can use it to convey emotion in your images. Take time to do the assignments before moving on to Chapter 6.

To get a better understanding of color and the role it plays in composition, complete the following assignments.

## Understanding the Emotion of Color

Review your top 20 favorite images with the color wheel in mind. Do most of your images contain the bold primary colors of the first order, or are you drawn to more moderate secondary colors? Do you feel the emotional impact that the dominant color within your image normally conveys? Based on your evaluation, what colors are you drawn to more often, and why? Are you drawn to the warmer end of the spectrum, where colors are bold and full of power and impact, or are you drawn to the cooler end of the spectrum, where there is a feeling of calm and peace?

## Black and White as Colors

Go in search of images that you feel will make good black-and-white photographs. Shoot in color and convert your images to black and white in the digital darkroom. Do they have the tonal range to make good black-and-white photographs? Study the images to see what works in black and white and what doesn't. Notice that increased contrast is necessary to capture the tonal ranges that make a good black-and-white image.

## White Balance and Its Influence on Color

The next time you are out photographing, dial in the different white balance settings so that you can compare the effect of the different settings on your image. Dialing in Cloudy on an overcast day adds warmth, whereas quite the opposite effect is achieved by dialing in Incandescent to cool down the scene. Try this in a variety of settings and light to get a good feel of how the white balance you select plays an important role in color.

*Share your results with the book's Flickr group!*

*Join the group here: flickr.com/groups/composition_fromsnapshotstogreatshots*

**6**

ISO 400
1/5 sec.
f/4
200mm lens

# Spatial Relationships

## THE WHAT, WHERE, WHEN, WHY, AND HOW THAT GO INTO THE MAKING OF A GOOD COMPOSITION

You've made a substantial journey, from the moment you select a lens (Chapter 1) to best represent the view you have in your mind's eye to deciding what the best exposure combination (Chapter 2) suits the moment. You have evaluated the light (Chapter 3), studied the scene from a variety of perspectives using leading lines to draw your viewer into the scene (Chapter 4), and either enhanced the colors or converted the image to black and white (Chapter 5). This chapter ties it all together with a look at special relationships: what you choose to include as well as what you exclude in your photographs, where you position yourself in relation to your subject, when is the best time to click the shutter, why you are drawn to the subject in the first place, and how to make it all come together in a photograph that speaks to the viewers, sharing with them your emotional connection to a moment in time.

# PORING OVER THE PICTURE

Background

Middle ground

Foreground

ISO 100
1/125 sec.
f/16
20mm lens

The steam hides much of the background, keeping the viewer's eye from wandering beyond the frame.

The vivid blue of the pool makes a nice contrast to the monochromatic tones of the scene.

The lifting fog swirls around the pools at West Thumb, in Yellowstone National Park. As the sun begins to burn away the fog, a beautiful blue pool becomes visible. A few moments later the fog lifts a bit more, revealing the snow-covered trees beyond the pool. Selecting an ultra-wide-angle lens to capture the entire scene before me, I moved in close to the snowy mounds in the foreground, giving the image a strong foundation that leads the viewer's eye to the pool in the middle ground and beyond to the trees in the background. The lifting fog continued to conceal the distant mountains in the far background, giving the image a more intimate feel.

# PORING OVER THE PICTURE

The slight color on the horizon conveys a sense of anticipation of the approaching dawn.

The soft light brings out the detail in the sandstone rocks and provides serenity to the scene.

ISO 200
1/15 sec.
f/8
38mm lens

On a trip to Arches National Park, I selected a wide-angle lens and moved in tight on North Window so I could use it to frame South Window beyond. I had to choose an aperture that would give me enough depth of field to render both foreground and background in sharp focus while keeping the shutter speed to a manageable setting for hand-holding the camera. Hand-holding the camera gave me the flexibility to move around and carefully choose my composition.

The strong foreground element of North Window invites the viewer to sit back and enjoy the scene beyond.

# POINT OF VIEW

When I first saw the Grand Canyon of the Yellowstone, with its sweeping view upriver to Lower Yellowstone Falls, I was totally overwhelmed at the view. Standing on the edge of the canyon, my eyes took in the entire scene from left to right and all that was in between. How could I compose the scene to share my emotional reaction to the moment—the overpowering sense of being very, very small? I could attach my widest-angle lens and include the canyon walls, leading me to the falls beyond to convey this sense (**Figure 6.1**). Moving in tighter on the canyon, I turned the camera to a vertical format to match the leading lines of the winding river to the falls (**Figure 6.2**). Wanting an even tighter view of the falls to capture the sheer power of the rushing water, I reached into my bag and pulled out my telephoto zoom to fill the frame with the falls (**Figure 6.3**). Each image captures a unique perspective of the scene. It's up to you to decide which composition best portrays your vision.

FIGURE 6.1
Using a wide-angle lens captures the sweeping view of the canyon and the falls.

ISO 200
1/8 sec.
f/22
32mm lens

ISO 200
1/20 sec.
f/22
70mm lens

ISO 200
1/30 sec.
f/22
170mm lens

**FIGURE 6.2**
Using a wide aperture, especially with a longer lens, blurs distracting background details.

**FIGURE 6.3**
Using a telephoto lens eliminates the surrounding landscape, filling the frame with the falls.

## VISUAL DEPTH

Visual depth is communicated in a variety of ways. It's the aperture you select that controls depth of field. Another way to capture a scene that has great visual depth is to find a scene with a strong foreground, middle ground, and background to lead the viewer through your image, pausing now and then to take in the details before moving deeper into the image. How do you create that visual depth to engage your viewers to the point where they simply get lost in your images? I find that moving in tight on the foreground with a wide-angle lens and a small aperture heightens the sense of depth in my images (**Figure 6.4**).

**FIGURE 6.4**
Fishing Cone in Yellowstone National Park, Wyoming, creates a strong foreground, with the vast, frozen expanse of Lake Yellowstone taking up the middle ground and the distant Absaroka Mountains in the background completing the composition.

ISO 100
1/30 sec.
f/22
36mm lens

Visual depth can be achieved with a telephoto lens shooting into the afternoon light creating an aerial-perspective feel as each progressive layer of mountains gets fainter and fainter, disappearing into the distant haze (**Figure 6.5**).

**FIGURE 6.5**
The Washer Woman in Canyonlands National Park, Utah, provides a strong graphic foreground element as the landscape recedes into the distance.

ISO 200
1/500 sec.
f/5.6
200mm lens

The effect of receding shapes, known as vanishing point, gives a sense of visual depth as each doorway becomes smaller the farther away it is from the camera (**Figure 6.6**).

**FIGURE 6.6**
Shooting down the hallway through door after receding door creates a sense of visual depth. A high ISO was required to hand hold the camera in low light.

ISO 800
1/6 sec.
f/8
66mm lens

# SCALE

I find that adding a person to a scene provides a sense of scale. Without the young man in red standing in the amphitheater at the base of Latourell Falls, you would have no idea of the size and power of the falls (**Figure 6.7**).

**FIGURE 6.7**
A person adds scale to the tight composition of this image of Latourell Falls in the Columbia Gorge, Oregon. His red T-shirt contrasts brightly with the green foliage.

ISO 200
1/2 sec.
f/16
50mm lens

# PERSPECTIVE

Many photographers have a tendency to shoot from eye level while in a standing position looking straight ahead. This works fine for many scenes, but it certainly restricts you from all the other points of view that are yours for the taking.

## LOOK UP, LOOK DOWN

Don't just look straight ahead; look up, look down. Don't stop there; get down or climb high if that's what it takes to get to eye level with your subject. When you wander through a forest, don't simply photograph the forest. Look up into the canopy of trees and capture the forest from a different perspective (**Figure 6.8**).

Raise your camera to the skies to capture birds in flight. Shooting up at a flying bird adds to the sense of place. It's a natural way to view birds and makes a good photograph (**Figure 6.9**).

ISO 200
1/2 sec.
f/22
16mm
Fisheye lens

FIGURE 6.9
Photographing birds in flight as they pass overhead increases the sense of looking upward.

ISO 200
1/1500 sec.
f/8
850mm lens

Don't stop now. You haven't looked down yet. The object you step on may well be a great photographic subject (**Figure 6.10**). I looked at several prints before deciding on this trio. Odd numbers have a sense of balance.

An approach from above afforded me a great view into an eagles nest. From the cover of the cliff, I was able to position myself to look over the edge towards the nest from a distance. An eagle chick with its crop full from a recent meal stared back at me (**Figure 6.11**). The higher perspective allowed me to look into the nest with an unobstructed view, which would not have been possible from another angle.

ISO 200
1/60 sec.
f/6.7
14mm lens

**FIGURE 6.10**
Tilting the camera at a slight angle created a diagonal path through the frame. A wide-angle lens allowed me to move in tight on the prints, capturing every detail in the cracked mud.

ISO 200
1/500 sec.
f/5.6
550mm lens

**FIGURE 6.11**
A downward camera angle provides a sense of perspective and scale to an eagle chick in its nest. Hand-holding the 200–400mm VR with a 1.4X teleconverter filled the frame as desired.

# GET UP, GET DOWN

At times, all it takes is to look up or down to find the composition you are searching for. Other times require you to become involved with your subject to the point where you get right down (or up) to its eye level for greater impact (**Figure 6.12**). When photographing shorebirds or other ground-dwelling birds, I often get down on my stomach to shoot at their eye level. A low perspective also renders the background a soft blur.

American skimmers nest in the sand. They sit on or near their eggs and chicks, providing the warmth they need as well as protecting them from the hot sun. By getting down at eye level with the parent and its chick, I was able to capture an intimate family portrait (**Figure 6.13**).

ISO 200
1/200 sec.
f/4
600mm lens

ISO 200
1/500 sec.
f/6.7
850mm lens

**FIGURE 6.12**
Shooting from a recessed blind put me right at ground level with this scaled quail. A wide aperture decreased the depth of field even further for a lovely soft blur in the background.

**FIGURE 6.13**
A ground pod allowed me to shoot right at eye level with the American skimmer and its chick.

Photographing birds in flight from a higher perspective completely changes the feel of an image. By shooting down or at eye level with a bird in flight, I am able to capture the top side of its wings, which is not an easy composition when shooting up at it. This angle adds to the sense of being at eye level with a bird in flight (**Figure 6.14**).

FIGURE 6.14
With my tripod raised to its full height, I was able to shoot at a downward angle at the great blue heron flying by.

ISO 400
1/500 sec.
f/4
600mm lens

# IN YOUR FACE, OR, ENVIRONMENTAL COMPOSITION

Filling the frame with your subject brings attention to each and every detail, giving the viewer a close-up glimpse of what you're shooting (**Figure 6.15**). A looser composition, on the other hand, one that includes the subject's environment, provides a greater sense of place. Close-ups provide great portraits, whereas environmental compositions provide information about where your subjects live and the conditions they must survive in. Wolves are typically shy creatures that try to avoid confrontations with humans, so it was a real treat to be able to focus my lens on this lone wolf emerging from the forest (**Figure 6.16**).

ISO 200
1/320 sec.
f/9
310mm lens

**FIGURE 6.15**
A close-up view of Denali enhances its majesty and power.

ISO 200
1/2 sec.
f/16
50mm lens

**FIGURE 6.16**
A lone wolf near a forest in Yellowstone communicates a solitary scene where the winters are harsh and survival can be a challenge.

While photographing the sunrise on a Hawaiian beach, I came across a monk seal taking a breather on the shore. I carefully approached, making sure not to scare it away or disturb it, and made the first composition with the seal, the beach, the ocean, and, oh yeah, a rainbow in the background (**Figure 6.17**). What a perfect setting for an environmental photograph. After capturing my fill of environmental compositions, I stealthily moved in closer, attaching my telephoto zoom to make a close-up portrait of the seal (**Figure 6.18**). It's important to capture tight compositions for detail as well as looser, more environmental poses to complete the story.

ISO 200
1/45 sec.
f/11
24mm lens

FIGURE 6.17
Including the environment in the scene adds a sense of place.

ISO 200
1/250 sec.
f/5.6
116mm lens

FIGURE 6.18
Moving in closer with a telephoto lens gives me a close-up view of a monk seal, with the background diffused to a soft blur.

# HORIZON LINE

Where do you place your horizon? Do you place the horizon low in the frame to capture the beautiful clouds that fill the sky (**Figure 6.19**)? Or, does the reflection of the clouds in the wet sand draw your camera downward to place the horizon high in the frame (**Figure 6.20**)? There are times when the right composition is to place the horizon line in the middle of the frame, dividing the image between the great sky and foreground (**Figure 6.21**); even though this breaks the rule of composition that states you cannot have the horizon line in the center. Take a look at the three horizon frames and decide for yourself which one you like best. There is no right or wrong answer; it's all a matter of personal preference.

FIGURE 6.19
A low horizon
emphasizes the sky.

ISO 100
1/80 sec.
f/11
17mm lens

ISO 100
1/60 sec.
f/11
17mm lens

**FIGURE 6.20**
A high horizon emphasizes the reflection in the wet sand.

ISO 100
1/60 sec.
f/11
17mm lens

**FIGURE 6.21**
A centered horizon divides the frame between the sky and reflection in the wet sand.

# RULE OF THIRDS

Where you place your subject in the frame affects the impact of the scene. The rule of thirds states that you should place your subject in one of the four corners that dissect the image into thirds when you divide the frame with three horizontal and three vertical sections (**Figure 6.22**). I say, if it works, go for it! Another rule states that your subject should not be in the center of the frame. Although that is good advice for most situations, one of the strongest compositions is one in which the subject is dead center, filling the frame (**Figure 6.23**). Talk about impact!

FIGURE 6.22
A black-throated sparrow fits into the upper right intersection of the rule-of-thirds grid.

ISO 200
1/250 sec.
f/5.6
850mm lens

FIGURE 6.23
Centering the owl
in the frame makes
for a dramatic
composition that
breaks the rules.

ISO 200
1/20 sec.
f/5.6
550mm lens

# Chapter 6 Assignments

The following exercises are just a start on your journey to better composition. Take time to complete the assignments before moving on to the next chapter. As you work through each assignment, you will gain a better understanding of what works and what doesn't when composing your photographs to achieve the greatest impact.

## Visual Depth

Using your widest lens, work a scene by moving in close to the foreground elements and shooting with a small aperture. Take one frame at the distance you feel most comfortable, and then take a step closer and shoot another frame. Take a couple of steps back and shoot one more frame. Compare the differences that moving just a few feet makes in your composition.

## Perspective

Find subjects that are low to the ground, such as children, some birds, pets, and so on. Shoot from your full height looking down on your subject, and then get down to your subject's eye level and take a few more shots. Compare the difference in perspective that can be gained by shooting from different heights.

## Horizon

When you have a scene that has an interesting foreground as well as an interesting sky, take three frames: one with the horizon low in the frame, emphasizing the sky; one with it high in the frame, emphasizing the foreground; and one with the horizon centered in the frame, dividing the image in two with equal parts sky and foreground. Which image has the strongest impact? Are more than one equally compelling? If so, why? This exercise will help you to see your compositions at the point of capture rather than later in the digital darkroom when it's too late.

*Share your results with the book's Flickr group!*

*Join the group here: flickr.com/groups/composition_fromsnapshotstogreatshots*

7

ISO 200
1/250 sec.
f/2.8
70mm lens

# Black and White

## LEARNING TO SEE IN BLACK AND WHITE

By John Batdorff

In the digital age, black-and-white photography is as popular as ever, and the good news is that it's never been easier to create stunning black-and-white images. Although the process of digital black-and-white photography is different from film, what makes a good image remains the same. We need to keep our eyes peeled for elements like tonal contrast, strong lines, patterns, shapes, and texture. We need to learn to see in grayscale. Postprocessing has also never been easier; we have access to amazing software that allows us to bring out the best in our black-and-white images. In this chapter, we'll go through my personal process for shooting black and white—from what I look for before I press the shutter button, to what I do for postprocessing, to my entire gear list for getting the perfect shot.

# PORING OVER THE PICTURE

Notice how I used the street lights and the fog to create a dramatic effect.

The trees create a stark, dark contrast to the bright lights and snow.

I was shoveling ice off my roof one winter night due to an unseasonably warm spell that hit the Midwest, causing all the snow to melt and creating tons of fog (and water that was leaking into my kitchen). As I was shoveling, I realized that I needed to get out there and see what the rest of the city looked like in this unusual situation. That's when this image caught my eye in a nearby park. The fog, lights, and snow created a compelling and mystical image. This was one of those moments when I said, "Stop what you're doing and get your camera." I've never regretted it.

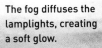

I had to shoot this at a high ISO of 1000 using a tripod and a cable release.

The fog diffuses the lamplights, creating a soft glow.

The footprints leave you with an eerie feeling and draw you into the image using leading lines.

ISO 1000
1/25 sec.
f/2.8
27mm lens

# PORING OVER THE PICTURE

I'm drawn to images that make me feel like I'm really, literally there and that convey a sense of honesty. A good black and white should tell a story and stand the test of time.

Packing light paid off. I shot this hand-held, without a tripod or any filters.

ISO 200
1/80 sec.
f/3.5
16mm lens

I later used Lightroom's Adjustment Brush to darken the clouds.

The silhouetted mountains are what make this image work.

# WHEN TO GO BLACK AND WHITE

I am asked this question a lot: "John, when do you decide to process an image as black-and-white?"

My family has been involved in the newspaper business for well over 100 years. I grew up reading a newspaper, and I've seen my share of black-and-white photos. My mind is constantly in grayscale mode. The question for me isn't when do I decide to shoot in black and white, but when do I decide an image will be processed as color. There's something timeless about a good black and white, and in my mind there's less to get wrong. Don't get me wrong—I shoot plenty of color images. But getting color right and not dating your work in the process can be difficult. For me, black and white just feels natural. Without a doubt, there are some shots that are better suited as black and whites. The following outlines a few of my thoughts on identifying and capturing those very images.

# LEARNING TO LIVE AND SEE IN A BLACK-AND-WHITE WORLD

I rarely think about color. Instead, I'm stripping down the image in my head and categorizing it by its strengths. It takes a lot of practice to learn to see in black and white, but it can be done. I recommend practicing as often as possible, and you'll see that you'll get better with time. The best part of this practice is that it will not only strengthen your black-and-white images, but your color images as well. Black-and-white photography gives us a chance to take away a very important element—color—and focus on the other elements that are harder to envision. The following are a few things to be on the lookout for when learning to see in black and white.

## TONAL CONTRAST

Tonal contrast can be broken down into three categories: high, normal, and low. A high-tonal-contrast image consists primarily of white and black with very little gray. A normal-tonal-contrast image consists of a balance of all three. A low-tonal-contrast image can appear very flat since there's little distinction between colors or tones within the image. I tend to enjoy images where the blacks are most certainly black and the whites are very white. Many of my images are of the high-tonal-contrast variety so that the other elements of the image, which I'll talk about next, come through even stronger (**Figure 7.1**).

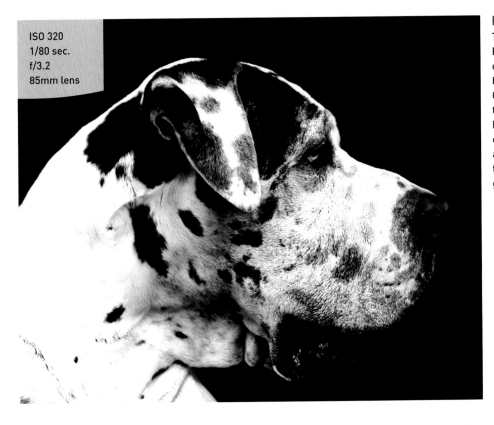

ISO 320
1/80 sec.
f/3.2
85mm lens

**FIGURE 7.1**
This image of Rodrigo is an example of very high tonal contrast. Check out how the whites and blacks are in strong contrast to one another, and how there's very little gray in the image.

The key to achieving this is to avoid colors with similar tonal ranges. For instance, if I'm shooting a dark red rose in front of dark green leaves, it's just not going to work as a black and white. When stripped of their color and examined as shades of gray, their tonal range is too similar; there's just not enough contrast there. If I were to shoot a white rose in front of dark green leaves, well, then I'd have the makings of a strong black-and-white image. Remember this when you are learning to see in black and white: Train your eye to look for variations in tone. Variations in color matter much less than variations in tone.

## TEXTURE

What the heck is texture? I know texture is one of those words that the artsy fartsy sorts love to throw around, and the definition can seem vague at best. It's real simple for me. If I see a barn and I can imagine running my hands over the aged, rough, splintered wood, that's texture. If I'm looking out over a field of wheat and I can imagine what it would feel like to run my hand over the top of the wheat, that's texture. It's something you can feel. Texture adds another dimension to an image, making a black-and-white image come to life and giving it an almost three-dimensional feeling. One of the best ways to show texture is with comparison. The smooth, puffy clouds in the sky countered by the old rough wood of a barn and the wispy grass provide the distinction among the textures that makes it visually appealing (**Figure 7.2**). If an image has too many similar textures, it gets too busy and becomes uninteresting. When playing with texture, work with contrasting textures within the same image to give it that extra something.

**FIGURE 7.2**
This image is almost three-dimensional. Here I tried to bring to life the textures in the barn, the clouds, and the grass so that it feels as though you're standing there and could touch the barn yourself.

ISO 160
1/125 sec.
f/8
16mm lens

## LIGHT

The golden hours—those first or last few hours of light during the day when the angle of the sun is low and the light is soft—are the magical hours to photograph textures. This is when scouting a location can truly pay off. If I find a location that has a lot of texture—for instance, a field of wheat planted on rolling hills—I make a mental note and come back to shoot it during the golden hours. And, yes, I'll even use my tripod (I'll discuss the use of tripods a little later).

The same lighting works great for portraits. The softer light of early morning and late afternoon shows more contrast and texture in a person's face. It can act to soften the skin or bring out the rough texture of sun-aged skin that has a real story to tell.

If your goal is to throw a lot of shadows or photograph something stark and barren, you'll occasionally want to shoot in the bright, harsh light of mid-afternoon. There is no such thing as bad light; you just have to know what the different types of light will do to your image and be ready to show up when you have the best light for the image that you want (**Figure 7.3**).

ISO 1000
1/25 sec.
f/2.8
27mm lens

FIGURE 7.3
What really made this image work for me was the incredible light. The park lights were diffused by the fog, creating a soft glow that silhouetted the trees perfectly.

## SHAPES AND PATTERNS

Shapes and patterns become even more evident in black-and-white photography. In fact, along with texture, they play the lead role. Keep your eyes peeled for repeating shapes, leading lines, and patterns. They make a big impact when you are viewing the landscape in black and white. For example, in **Figure 7.4**, the pillars create a very nice line for your eyes to follow. This line adds depth to the image while at the same time maintaining a solid frame. The pillars also have a strong shape and are arranged in a repeating pattern. Also, notice the light: When shooting architecture, I like to look for strong lines and shapes that are complemented by shadows that pull the viewers' eyes through a frame. If the pillars of the Agra Fort hadn't had strong shadows on the backside, they wouldn't have been nearly as effective at creating a strong leading line. It's key to keep your eye out for interesting light, such as strong shadows, when you're shooting lines, shapes, and patterns. As you can see, color doesn't matter in the image because the other elements are so strong. Preserving the color would only have taken something away from the final image.

**FIGURE 7.4**
This image of the Agra Fort in India caught my eye because of the strong lines, the shapes of the pillars, and the repeating pattern. What made it really great is the perfect lighting that created the dramatic shadows.

ISO 100
1/100 sec.
f/4
28mm lens

## PORTRAITS

I remember as a child looking at a black-and-white portrait my mother took of an oil-field worker. The image was extremely powerful. I couldn't stop staring at his face; I studied every little feature and found myself wondering what it was like to be him. A black-and-white portrait can be very powerful—once you strip an image of its color and free the mind of distractions, you truly begin to see things for what they are. I like to think of it as redirecting the visual conversation.

The Indian man in **Figure 7.5** is an excellent example. He is wearing a bright yellow turban, and the background is very colorful, which I found to be a distraction. To me, the story is in his face, not the colorful surroundings. With the color eliminated, the viewer is drawn into the man's face and eyes.

The Peruvian woman in **Figure 7.6** is wearing a bright traditional hat and clothing. When the image is converted to black and white, the focus falls off the clothing and is redirected to her eyes and the lines on her face. When you're composing a black-and-white image, always remember to ask yourself what the real story is. If color isn't the story, go ahead and leave it out. In doing so, you can make a good image really great.

ISO 200
1/80 sec.
f/4.5
63mm lens

FIGURE 7.5
India is such a colorful country, but in this image the color was too distracting, so converting it to black and white just felt natural.

ISO 200
1/200 sec.
f/9
70mm lens

FIGURE 7.6
This woman was going about her day on the streets of Cusco, Peru. She was dressed in traditional colorful Peruvian clothing, but what compelled me to photograph her was her face. I knew that converting to black and white would allow me to tell the story as I felt it.

## DRAMATIC LANDSCAPES

Learn to embrace nasty weather. If you follow my blog (batdorffphotography.com/blog), you know I love bad weather. Yep, it's official: I'm a storm chaser with a camera in tow. I'm a big fan of dramatic black-and-white landscapes, and nothing shouts "drama" louder than billowing dark clouds. I love it when the first word that comes to mind when I see clouds is "ominous." It doesn't get more dramatic than that.

Often when I'm out in the western United States shooting landscapes, I try to capitalize on the inclement weather. If the forecast calls for snow, rain, or better yet, severe thunderstorms, I'm ready to roll. Of course, you have to be careful not to put yourself in a precarious situation with lightning, but using some common sense can put you in a great spot when the amazing clouds come rolling in (**Figure 7.7**). Typically, I'll shoot with my 16–35mm lens so that I can adjust the focal range on the fly. And if I want the clouds even darker, I'll use my Lee Filters graduated neutral density filter.

A dramatic sky gives an extra "wow" factor to an already beautiful landscape. Remember to take the sky into consideration when shooting black and white. I'll discuss "active" skies in more detail later, but just think about the extra contrast and texture that you are putting into your image when the clouds are telling a story all by themselves. Active weather almost always makes for an extraordinary black-and-white landscape.

**FIGURE 7.7**
I was in the Tetons on my way to go backpacking when this storm rolled in. What drew me to this shot was the contrast between the dark clouds and the splinter of sunlight silhouetting the mountains.

ISO 200
1/80 sec.
f/3.5
16mm lens

# APPROACHING THE SHOT

Truth be told, many of my landscape images are taken while I'm on the road traveling across country. And they're often taken right off the highway (**Figure 7.8**). Just admit it: How often have you seen an amazing landscape right from the comfort of your car? Here's the key: stop and take the shot. I tell myself that life is short, and I want to remember this moment. To me, photography is more than just an art form, it's a documentation of our experiences. Remember that the only bad image is the one that's never taken. It seems almost too simple to say, but if you want to get great landscape shots, you first need to take the shots!

ISO 200
1/320 sec.
f/7.1
35mm lens

**FIGURE 7.8**
When I was driving through eastern Idaho one late summer afternoon, these wheat fields drew me in. The way the light was hitting the rolling hills and the texture of the wheat were so perfect I had to stop the car.

Before I bring out all my gear, I start off by viewing the scene through the camera. Whenever I approach a landscape image for the first time, I always check to see if what I'm seeing will translate well in the camera. Sometimes scenes just don't work. Any number of factors can prevent a good shot, but more often than not it's a depth-of-field or distortion issue. The subject can be too far away to translate well, or I just can't seem to get the right perspective to make it work. I might swap lenses to check focal length, but that's about it; once you break out the tripod, it's like agreeing to pick someone up at the airport—it's a commitment.

But what's the worst that can happen? You take a little extra time to take in a beautiful view. Despite all the cries from your family, pull over and at least take a look to see if you can get the shot. You'll be happier because you tried, and you can always bribe them with ice cream down the road.

# ONCE I'M COMMITTED: MY THOUGHT PROCESS

Once I commit to taking a photo, I try to create a vision for the final image. These are the steps that help me form that vision.

## WHAT IS THE ORIENTATION OF THE SHOT?

Will a vertical or horizontal orientation suit my subject? Where am I placing the subject in the frame? This is where the rule of thirds comes into play, big time. If I have an image that is symmetrical, typically I'll compose with the subject in the center of the frame. If I want to create a more dynamic feel, I'll place the subject on either side of the frame. In **Figure 7.9**, I wanted to create a pensive feel. I took a visual cue from the subject—the cowboy's hat, tipped down to the right, and his body language, which felt dramatic. The angle of his hat and also his demeanor supported the use of negative space, allowing me to create a more dramatic feeling in the final image.

FIGURE 7.9
This image of a dancer was taken in Mexico. He was a dramatic performer, and I wanted to capture that. I used negative space to help create a sense of movement and drama. This is also a high-tonal-contrast image; there is only stark black and white with very little gray.

ISO 5000
1/200 sec.
f/2.8
195mm lens

If you're unsure of your framing, look through the viewfinder both ways and see which orientation is more pleasing to your eye. Ask yourself, "What is it I'm trying to achieve?" Move the subject around the frame and take a gut check. You might not know exactly why (technically speaking) a certain orientation looks right, but chances are that what looks right to you is right. Trust your gut.

## SLOW DOWN

If there's one basic message I try to push in my seminars, it is this: Take it slow. There's no need to rush. Chances are, unless you're standing on the San Andreas Fault during an earthquake, nothing is going to move anytime soon. (But if you are, get to a safe place and then shoot like crazy!) Take your time. Ask yourself what it is that's drawn you to this spot? Is this the right time of day to be shooting? Will you have a chance to return?

## WHICH LENS WILL DO THE ORIENTATION JUSTICE?

Ninety percent of the time when I'm shooting landscapes, I'm using my 16–35mm (**Figure 7.10**). For portraiture I love my 85mm, and many people use a 50mm. You want to be able to fill the frame with your subject while deciding how much background or environmental information you want in the shot. Sometimes with a portrait you want to fill the frame entirely with a person's face; other times the photo tells a much stronger story when you leave in some part of the environment. Remember to think about what the story really is, and make sure you only put pertinent information in the frame, leaving out all the unimportant elements. In addition, with black-and-white photography, positioning a subject to enhance negative space can lead to a very powerful image. Having a stark black or pure white background for your subject can make for a great image. Remember this when choosing your lens and focal length. Remember, too, that black-and-white imagery is all about stripping down an image to tell a powerful story. Negative space can not only add tonal contrast to your image, but it can also add to the power of the story. A busy background or foreground only adds unnecessary information and clutters the story.

**FIGURE 7.10**
This image was taken on a bitterly cold winter day in Chicago. Aside from some brave runners, I was the only person at the lakeshore. The high contrast and negative space of the bright white snow versus the gray sky and water told a story of a cold, desolate pier. The strong lines leading into nowhere added to the story as well.

ISO 100
1/80 sec.
f/22
16mm lens

## DO I NEED MY TRIPOD AND CABLE RELEASE?

Not if I have good light and will be shooting at a fast enough shutter speed that it doesn't matter or that depth of field isn't critical. In reality, I prefer shooting without my tripod because it gives me the ability to move freely and frequently change my point of view to get it just right. Moving a tripod around can break my rhythm, so if it's not necessary, I'll avoid using it.

I do need my tripod and cable release if I'm shooting in a low-light situation and want to keep my ISO low so the image doesn't get grainy, or if I need to bracket for an HDR shot. When shooting in low light, you can choose to either slow down your shutter speed or increase your ISO. When you slow down your speed, you can easily get blur from camera shake, so a tripod is a must.

The other time I definitely need a tripod is if depth of field is critical and I want a super-sharp image. There is no way to hold your camera as steady as a tripod can, so sometimes you just have to break down and use it.

## DO I NEED MY GRADUATED NEUTRAL DENSITY FILTERS?

Not when the sky is perfect. In my images, I usually have "active clouds" that don't need to be enhanced. By "active clouds" I mean those that grab your attention. If you're saying, "Wow, look at that sky!" those are active clouds. A perfect blue sky can be equally as beautiful, but it doesn't offer much contrast when converted to black and white. A blue sky will be a solid tone, so a sky with active clouds creates a nice tonal and textural contrast.

I will use my graduated neutral density filters when I have a very dull or hazy sky that needs to be enhanced, or a very bright sky that needs to be darkened—or dark clouds that I want to make even darker.

## IMAGE STABILIZATION: ON OR OFF?

It's on if I'm hand-holding my camera. It's off when I'm shooting with a tripod.

# MY STANDARD CAMERA SETTINGS

Once I've committed to the shot, I need to decide on what camera settings I'll be using.

## ISO

I change my ISO according to available light and my aperture needs. In good light I typically shoot with an ISO of 100. I will push my ISO up to 1600 in low-light conditions if I'm shooting freehand. Otherwise, I'll use a tripod and try to keep my ISO at 400 and below. I'm not a huge fan of digital noise, and as you increase your ISO, it's more likely that you'll see noise. Sometimes a noisy photo is desirable, if you're going for that look. If not, this is another good time to bust out the tripod.

## APERTURE PRIORITY SHOOTING MODE

This is my primary shooting mode. The reason I love aperture priority is that it allows me to focus on my creativity. It's a gift from the camera gods, folks. Think about it. You set your ISO, and then all you need to worry about is your aperture. If I want a shallow depth of field (meaning things close to me in focus and the background blurry), I use a large aperture. If I want a deeper depth of field (meaning more in-focus details throughout the image), I use a smaller aperture (like f/16). The camera handles the rest. As you work the aperture, the camera adjusts the shutter speed accordingly. A general rule I follow is this: Don't hand-hold your camera at speeds below the focal length of the lens—for example, using an 120mm lens would mean not going slower than 1/120th of a second—and never go lower than 1/60th of a second unless you want a blurry image.

## METERING MODE

Eighty percent of my photography is shot in the evaluative metering mode because it takes into consideration the entire frame of the image. For my landscape images I use this mode almost exclusively.

If I'm shooting a portrait that is backlit, I'll use the partial metering mode (**Figure 7.11**).

**FIGURE 7.11**
This environmental portrait was shot in New Orleans' Jackson Square district. The trombone player was backlit, so using the partial metering mode helped me achieve the perfect exposure.

ISO 160
1/1000 sec.
f/3.5
70mm lens

## WHITE BALANCE

I'm a white-balance freak. I'm one of those people who would rather adjust the white balance up front in my camera than mess with it in postprocessing. You can either select from one of the many white-balance presets that come with your camera, or you can create a custom white balance. I use an ExpoDisc to create a custom white balance; another inexpensive option is a Lally cap. Having the correct white balance is key in reviewing your work on your LCD. If your white balance is way off, chances are that when you review your image on the camera's LCD, you're not getting the true picture. This can affect your exposure and other adjustments that you make on the fly.

Another important thing to remember is that getting the correct white balance isn't only for color photography. If your white balance is off, it could change the tonal range of the objects you're shooting. In turn, this can change the way the image looks when you convert to black and white. So take the time to adjust your white balance in the camera before taking the shot. You won't regret it.

## DO I NEED TO BRACKET THE EXPOSURE?

Bracketing the exposure is key when I'm just not sure where my exposure needs to be. I'm a control freak, and the only way you would get me to jump out of a plane is if I were equipped with a parachute, an emergency chute, and a safety net anxiously awaiting my arrival. Auto Exposure Bracketing (AEB) is a photographer's safety net for exposure. If you're not quite sure where you need to be on exposure, remember this: When in doubt, bracket about. You'll be dealing with a few extra files, but chances are you won't lose out on an image due to poor exposure.

I will bracket if after taking a few test shots and looking at the histogram, I'm still not sure about the exposure. A good histogram is as important in black-and-white photography as it is in color. Remember that when in doubt, bracket the shot.

If, after a few test shots, the exposure looks decent, I won't do any bracketing.

## HDR ISN'T ONLY FOR COLOR!

When most people think of high dynamic range (HDR), they tend to think of saturated color photos. But an HDR color photo converted to black and white can make for a unique look. Granted, on occasion HDR can be overdone, but I think you'll find in **Figure 7.12** it doesn't look fake. It can create a very dynamic photograph.

Here's the setup:

1. Place your camera on a tripod (yep, this is the time to use it).
2. Shoot in aperture priority mode to maintain the same depth of field.
3. Set your camera to continuous shooting mode.
4. Set your camera to bracketing mode, allowing for 3–5 images separated by +1 and –1 stops.
5. Lock your camera's mirror to reduce mirror shake.
6. Use a cable release to reduce hand shake.
7. Compose your image.
8. Take your shots.

How I process the image:

1. Import the photos into Adobe Lightroom.
2. Select the bracketed images and export them into Photomatix.
3. Create a color HDR.

Import the HDR back into Lightroom and convert it to black and white either manually or using a preset.

ISO 2000
1/8 sec.
f/3
16mm lens

**FIGURE 7.12**
The "Bean" is an often-captured image in Chicago. To give my version a unique look, I chose to shoot it at night and then convert it to black and white. This increased the contrast within the image. (This image is actually what I call a "dirty HDR." I used one image and created two virtual copies—at +1 and −1 exposures—and then merged them.)

# POSTPROCESSING FOR BLACK AND WHITE

Do you remember when you first started taking digital pictures? I do. I remember looking at my color images and saying, "Man, these look flat." So, like any beginner, I focused on one setting and one setting alone: Saturation. Guess what? My images were no longer flat—possibly a little cartoonish, but no one could call them flat.

The hard, cold fact is that to get good at anything it takes time and experimentation. If you're new to black and white, I have one word for you: contrast (**Figure 7.13**). If you use Lightroom, Photoshop, Aperture, or even free software like Picasa, they all have contrast adjustments. Start there.

**FIGURE 7.13**
If there's one word you should remember from this chapter, it's "contrast." If you're starting out, don't be afraid of the Contrast slider when processing your images. That is the single most important place to start your postprocessing for black-and-white images.

ISO 160
1/500 sec.
f/14
24mm lens

## SOFTWARE

I use two basic programs for all my black-and-white conversions: Adobe Photoshop Lightroom and Nik Software's Silver Efex Pro.

I start out by importing my raw files into Lightroom. I only worry about three basic adjustments at this stage. First, is my exposure where I want it to be? Second, I typically always add a little black into the photo at this stage with Lightroom's Blacks slider in the Develop module. If you want to take it up a level, focus on the tone curve. I like to work the Lights and Darks sliders in Lightroom. Third, I crop the image if needed. Then I export the photo into Nik Software's Silver Efex Pro. Now, some of you might be asking, "Why do you leave Lightroom?" Well, it's true, Lightroom does a great job with black-and-white conversion. But I'm a visual guy, and I love how Nik Software converts the black and white and provides you with several visual options that you can tailor to your taste.

# MY KIT

Many people think that in order to take a really good landscape shot they need to have a ton of gear. Well, in some cases, that may be true. But often, working with a simple pack can get the job done. To be totally honest, many of my shots are taken with my Canon 5D and my 16–35mm lens—no filters, no tripod, not even a lens hood. Getting a good shot isn't always about the equipment; it's simply about being in the right place at the right time and then knowing what to do when you're there.

Here are a few recommendations to help ensure you'll get the shot right:

- Invest in a bubble level. Even with a tripod, it's easy to set up on uneven ground. Nothing is worse than shooting a beautiful landscape image only to find that it's sloping to one side or the other.

- Use a cable release or remote trigger. Especially for long exposure settings, a cable release is key.

- Buy a tripod that you'll use. Listen, this isn't an inexpensive hobby you've taken on. It can suck your wallet dry, so invest in the things that make sense. A good tripod will set you back a few bucks, but like luggage, you'll have it for the rest of your life and you'll use it. I love my carbon-fiber Gitzo GT-1550 Traveler. Carbon fiber is strong enough to hold even the heaviest of lenses but light enough to put on my backpack for long backcountry excursions.

- Get a decent ball head for your tripod. I use a Really Right Stuff BH-40.

- Use an L-bracket, so when you change from portrait to landscape you don't have to recompose your image.

- Invest in a graduated neutral density filter. I use the LEE Filters system.

- Use a grid focusing screen. Folks, this is probably the one item I love the most. If your camera doesn't already have a grid focusing screen, consider picking one up. I use an Eg-D Precision Matte Focusing Screen for my Canon 5D Mark II. This is a great way to see the rules of thirds in-camera as you're composing your shot.

- **Travel light**. But no lighter! Leave the tripod behind. Yep, I said it. If you don't need it, don't bring it. I have the sexiest tripod known to humankind, but there are many moments that it simply gets in the way. Sometimes having the ability to move freely and unencumbered outweighs the benefits of a steady shot.

- **Buy quality glass**. Invest in a good lens. A quality lens improves the microcontrast of black-and-white images. You can really feel the textures when you have good contrast.

# BREAK THE RULES AND HAVE FUN

Much of what I know has come from years of experience. My photographic journey is probably much like yours. I've stumbled along the learning curve, picking up pieces of knowledge here and there in an effort to become better at my craft. Getting where I am today has required tons of practice, and most of all, dedication. I've learned many rules along the way for getting a great shot, but if there is one thing I've concluded, it's this: Break the rules!

Rules are wonderful. They provide order, secure us with a blanket of comfort from the unknown, and most important, they provide us with guidelines to break! Much of this book is dedicated to rules. Embrace them, learn from them. But remember to break them from time to time, too. Photography is about having fun and growing. If you're always preoccupied by rules, you'll fail to see the bigger picture, which is learning to experiment and create a style all your own. That's right: experimentation! Take a few risks. Dare I say it—try splitting a horizon or two. You'll never get better at this if you're not willing to make mistakes. I've failed miserably many times, but for every hundred mistakes I get one killer image! So take a few risks. Start by focusing on one rule or suggestion at a time, and have a little fun.

# Chapter 7 Assignments

Before you move on to the next chapter, be sure to complete the following assignments.

### Seeing the Light

Try photographing the same image three times: once in the morning, once during midday, and once in the evening. Then compare the light. You'll see the difference that the time of day can make on how an image looks. Seeing is believing!

### Mine Your Archive

Fire up your postprocessing software and start making black and whites today. Take some of your favorites shots and see how they look in black and white. Better yet, take a photograph that just didn't work in color and convert it to black and white. You might just surprise yourself—I know I have.

### Throw a Filter on It

If you want to get creative in-camera, throw a red filter on your lens. Red filters will add contrast to many black-and-white images, and can create very compelling pictures.

*Share your results with the book's Flickr group!*

*Join the group here: flickr.com/groups/composition_fromsnapshotstogreatshots*

8

ISO 200
1/3200 sec.
f/3.5
300mm
f/2.8 lens

# Sports and Composition

## A TOTALLY DIFFERENT ANIMAL

By Rick Rickman

I've been a sports photographer for 33 years now. It's one genre of photography that I truly love. It can be (and it has been for me) one of the most challenging genres to try to master; all the demands of photography come into play at such a high rate of speed.

When I was asked to write about sports and composition, I was a bit dubious at first. I wrestled with how to best describe the processes involved in making the decisions that affect the outcome and determine the success of the pictures produced. The compositional elements are all the same; we still have to think about the aspects of composition that have been discussed throughout this book. But the process of preparing for what to shoot in relation to the activity is so much more extensive when it comes to sports and action photography.

In the spirit of full disclosure, I'll admit that I decided that the best way I could come to terms with describing how composition works in relation to sports photography was to tell a few stories about how I've been able to capture some of my best images over the many years of my career. I hope you find the stories interesting and the lessons useful in the pursuit of your work with sports as well.

I had an idea that it would be fun to show a real sense of motion and excitement that exists at the start of any sprint race. I knew that when speed is involved, it can be fun to get that sense of movement that is so iconic to speed. I also had a real concern that the background was going to be an issue with a stopped action frame. I made a command decision to slow down the shutter and pan with the subject to make sure that the background didn't become an issue for what I knew had the potential to be an exciting image.

Lining up the starting line at an angle gave a view of the other runners in conjunction with Devers, which also helped.

The energy of the image was enhanced by the fact that the composition included a large group of runners.

The motion effect of the slow shutter added an air of excitement to the image.

ISO 200
1/80 sec.
f/5.6
200mm lens

# PORING OVER THE PICTURE

The image of the baseball player hiding behind his clothes in the locker before the game was one I had to have, and the light in the locker room was so low that I had to figure out how to make the picture work. It had such a funny twist to it that I knew the viewers of this story would appreciate the dilemma of this very nervous player. I ended up using a strobe to raise the light level to a usable level. I knew there was an element of risk using the strobe because it might bother the player, but taking the chance paid off. I tried a wide-angle lens first, but there were other players on either side of him that I found to be a distraction. I switched to an 85mm to eliminate the other players.

Using the strobe helped keep the quality of the image high.

Bouncing the flash off the ceiling helped even out the light, and using a slower shutter speed helped balance the strobe with the ambient light.

Using a wide-angle lens helped give the image a sense of place, but the players on either side of him were a distraction so I changed the lens to an 85mm to tighten up a bit and help the composition.

ISO 200
1/30 sec.
f/2.8
85mm lens

# LEARNING TO HANDLE THE COMPLEXITIES OF SPORTS PHOTOGRAPHY

When it comes to sports, there's so much more to think about. If you're shooting portraits, landscapes, still lifes, weddings, or your family members, things move at a much more manageable pace. There's often ample time to think about how the compositional elements within your frame are working together.

On the other hand, the reasons so many people are attracted to shooting sports are the very same reasons that it is, compositionally speaking, so taxing. The speed and motion of sports complicate factors that can be difficult to address if you aren't prepared. I refer to sports photography as "Potential Compositional Anarchy."

## ONE SIMPLE EXERCISE

Good sports photography is all about adapting to speed and motion. To prepare you a bit for what we are about to address, I'd like you to try an exercise that I repeatedly use to keep my eye sharp and my compositional reaction time tuned. It's a home shooting exercise that can help improve your images and your ability to compose at a high speed.

Take the longest lens you have—preferably a 200mm or longer lens—and go to the corner of a very busy intersection near your house. Stand on the corner of the intersection closest to oncoming traffic. Begin to focus on cars entering the intersection, keeping the face of the driver framed and focused in your viewfinder while tracking the car all the way through the intersection.

If you are able to keep the image of the driver's face framed well and in focus for at least four or five frames, you are doing well and sports photography will be easy for you. If, on the other hand, you have trouble framing and focusing during these attempts, it's a good idea to continue to try this exercise regularly until you can consistently deliver on those four or five frames.

I always suggest this exercise to photographers because it's a real-world example of what a photographer can expect to encounter when dealing with the challenges of sports photography. It's also a great tool to use to improve your hand-eye coordination—which will improve your ability to follow-focus—as well as your ability to frame the shot.

# DEALING WITH SPEED

In sports photography, one of the most important aspects of successful pictures is the photographer's sense of anticipation. A good sense of anticipation can be supplemented and accentuated by a working knowledge of the sport you're shooting. Staying tuned in to information of the sport or game can be important because any insight that puts you in a great location to make a unique image is a true advantage. Positioning is often one key to great pictures, and it improves your composition as well. Finding a location with a good background is essential. If a background is a problem, making an appropriate lens choice to help diminish the effect of a busy background is crucial. And there's another important element that so many photographers dismiss, but that I find to be immensely useful: intuition. Intuition is a key ingredient to success. In many cases, it isn't cultivated nearly as much as it should be.

I've been fortunate to cover 14 Olympic competitions in my career. In Athens in 2004, I had the great good fortune to be listening intently to the little intuitive voice in my head as it clearly told me that I needed to be close to the start of the women's 100 meter hurdles. I knew I was going to cover that event because one of my favorite women athletes, Gail Devers, was competing; it would probably be her last Olympic effort ever. Little did I know how important listening to that voice would be.

There's always an incredible amount of energy at any Olympic competition, but when your intuition is screaming at you to get to a certain place because something important is going to happen, it makes it that much more intense. I went to a shooting position just two hurdles down track from the starting area and lay out my camera gear.

In sports photography, there are so many things to think about compositionally, but one that is always essential is perspective. What are you trying to say with the image, and how should you shoot it to make the image best work? Perspective relates to everything in life; all our decisions are directly determined by how we choose to look at things. The same is true for photography! The angle of view we choose creates its own viewpoint and level of communication. That's perspective!

There are at least six distinct perspectives, or points of view, that always need to be considered in connection to compositions and how they relate to picture and storytelling communications. Those six points of view include wide view, medium view, tight view, high angles, low angles, and details. These elements of perspective are always running around in my head, and on this night at the Olympics I was calculating what I needed to do to create a variety of perspectives from this race.

I grabbed my 400mm lens and put on a 1.4 teleconverter because I wanted to be sure to get a very tight shot of Devers. She has extremely long fingernails, and the image in **Figure 8.1** always captivates people. As the competitors prepared to come to their starting blocks, I began to shoot Devers with the long lens.

**FIGURE 8.1**
The tight view.

ISO 400
1/400 sec.
f/4
400mm lens
with a 1.4
teleconverter

I kept telling myself that the long lens would help eliminate much of what could be a potentially distracting background, and it seemed to work. My mind was racing because I knew there were just a few minutes until the competitors would be called to their starting blocks. I wanted to be sure that I had the appropriate lens to shoot the first three hurdles of the race.

I chose to put a 70–200mm f/2.8 lens on the second camera body and a 200mm f/2 lens on yet a third camera body. I figured this combination would give me plenty of options, depending on what unfolded. There was one last thought that bounced through my head before the gun went off: What can I do to convey a sense of speed and motion in these images? I made a conscious decision to shoot at a slower shutter speed and pan with the action, which would also effectively help clean up a bad background by blurring it (**Figure 8.2**).

ISO 200
1/80 sec.
f/5.6
200mm lens

FIGURE 8.2
The medium view.
I decided to shoot
at a slow shutter
speed to enhance
the sense of speed,
as well as help
clean up a seriously
troublesome
background.

The gun went off. She approached the first hurdle and I knew something was wrong.
She began to pull up (**Figure 8.3**). The little voice in my head was screaming. All my
senses were lit up like fireworks on the fourth of July. When I'm in that state of
mind, it always seems like time actually slows down and things seem to move in slow
motion. I saw Devers wince and try to stop before she made contact with the first
hurdle in her lane, but she was unsuccessful and went down hard, grabbing the
cross-member of the hurdle (**Figures 8.4** and **8.5**).

As Devers collapsed to the track clutching the hurdle, my mind was in hyperdrive.
What did I just experience? Will this be a defining moment in this Olympic competition?
Did I make the right lens choices for the composition? I was pretty sure the images
were successful. Devers lay on the track for some time after the crash, and that image
was the one that most other photographers ended up with. I felt a huge smile cross
my face as I realized that there was only one other shooter of the 400 credentialed
photographers at these Olympics shooting this scene from my location—and the look
on his face told me he hadn't had such a great experience with this situation. A good
sense of anticipation and planning had helped me capture a classic Olympic moment
almost exclusively.

The one detail that is hard to imagine is the fact that the entire episode of Dever's
crash took place in less than three seconds. This is why dealing with the intricacies
of composition when shooting sports is such a different situation from other genres
of photography.

**FIGURE 8.3**
The low angle.

ISO 800
1/1000 sec.
f/2.8
175mm lens
(70–200mm
zoom)

**FIGURE 8.4**
The medium view.

ISO 800
1/1000 sec.
f/2.8
175mm lens

ISO 800
1/1000 sec.
f/2.8
175mm lens

**FIGURE 8.5**
Gail Dever's track career had come to an end as she lay under the hurdle in pain from her hamstring tear. Medical personnel came to her aid in just a few seconds, but her chance for a medal was gone.

# THE TWO MOST IMPORTANT QUESTIONS

I like to keep things simple. One of the most influential editors in my 33-year photographic career used to drum into my head the KISS theory of success: Keep It Simple Stupid. This little theory has helped me on so many occasions, and it's led me to understand that all any photographer has to do to really get the most from any given situation is ask two things of any scene: What am I seeing, and how do I make it work? The answers to these two questions are the compositional magic bullets that allow us to stay focused and think clearly as we shoot.

If you've been with your camera for any amount of time now, I know that you've experienced the following situation: You encounter a scene, something stops you, and the little voice in your head cries out, "Whoa dude, get your camera out, there's a picture here!" It's happened to you, right? Well, when that happens, the very next thing a photographer should do is ask, "What am I seeing?" This question creates a sense of focus that forces you to look closer at what it is in the scene that grabbed your attention. This is important; too often, novice photographers point their cameras toward what they believe to be the picture they think they want without thinking clearly about where the picture actually is in the context of the scene itself. Isolating what it is that you are subconsciously seeing is one of the most important aspects of great photography.

Once you've isolated what grabbed your attention, answering the second question—how do I make it work?—will help raise your pictures to an even higher, more insightful level. This question puts into play a series of thoughts that can make your next image very special indeed. Contemplating the answer to this question should get your mind racing. If you're attempting to find the successful solution, answering this question will put your head and feet in motion. How do I make what I'm seeing work in a best-case scenario?

This is the moment when all the synapses begin to fire and all the possible photographic techniques come into sharp focus. Questions will be rattling around in your skull. What's my best camera position? If I choose this camera position, which lens do I need to use? If I choose that lens, how should I frame this up? Is it best to use a rule-of-thirds composition or something else? All these questions fly through your mind in milliseconds. Suddenly, you begin to think logically about what it is you're going to do.

## THE ROAD TRIP TO ENLIGHTENMENT

Several years ago, I was asked by a popular publishing interest to follow a minor league baseball team for a few days for a book it was going to publish. The call came in at the last minute, and even though baseball isn't my favorite sport, I accepted the assignment. A mere five hours later I was on a plane to Salt Lake City to meet the members of a team I had never heard of and to be their best friend for three days. I'd never shot much baseball and was just a tad bit nervous about the whole situation.

When I landed in Salt Lake City, I was met by the sports information guy. As he quickly grabbed my bag, he told me that we were leaving on a bus to Medicine Hat, Canada, in 20 minutes, so I had to hurry—and, by the way, we would be on the bus for the better part of the day and night. I muttered to myself, "What a glamorous job I have..." as I headed out the baggage claim door with my cameras.

No sooner had I gotten to the parking lot of the ballpark than my bag was thrown into the baggage bay of the bus, and we were off to Medicine Hat for three days of on-the-road baseball.

The bus trip was one of the defining moments of my career because it was the first time that, on a daily basis, I had to ask myself the two important questions. I had been thrown into this assignment so quickly that I didn't have time to do my normal research, and I didn't really know anything about baseball. I was flying by the seat of my pants on a very important assignment.

I remember sitting at the back of the bus saying to myself, "This is a great story. I just have to figure out how to say what needs to be said about these guys so that everyone who sees these images will be able to feel what it's like to be part of this team." Pictures give visual voice to life's experiences, and we need to keep in mind that the way pictures communicate is through feeling. Acknowledging this and working with it gives us our best chance for success.

As the bus headed up the highway, I asked myself, "How do I make what I'm seeing here work?" As time and the trip grew longer, the players settled in and attempted to find ways to rest and relax. At one point, the catcher for the team, the Trappers, climbed into the luggage rack above the seats. My heart started to race. I reached into my bag and grabbed the 24mm lens—and my flash, because I knew I would need to balance the light outside the bus with the little amount of light that was visible in the luggage rack. I knew I had a picture, but the question was how to make the picture captivating. I needed to wait for a moment.

I stood in the aisle of the bus for a long time. The catcher began to snore. His mouth was open and he was drooling a bit. I needed to show a sense of environment, so I decided to use that ol' rule of thirds and fire off some frames. I got three shots before the catcher awoke and began to protest my photographing him this way. It didn't matter, though, because I knew I had one telling image (**Figure 8.6**).

ISO 200
1/60 sec.
f/4.0
18mm lens

**FIGURE 8.6**
A minor leaguer found a place to stretch out in the luggage rack of the bus as the team headed for Medicine Hat, Canada.

When the bus finally arrived at Medicine Hat, field preparation was just beginning. I was so glad to be off the bus that any excuse to move was the right one. I went out to visit with the groundskeepers. I watched as they prepped the field, and I began to see pictures everywhere. The one that really caught my eye was the detail of the well-worn, somewhat archaic equipment the field guys were using to line the bases.

Details are the descriptive adjectives of any picture story or essay. They help every story along. I loved the clean texture of the graveled ground, and all the pieces of equipment became graphic elements in the frame. That looming question came to mind again: How do I make this work? I began to think compositionally about the string as the leading line that seemed to tie all the graphic elements together. Then the only thing that remained was how to visually align the objects in the frame (**Figure 8.7**).

**FIGURE 8.7**
The equipment used in the minor leagues to line the field of play.

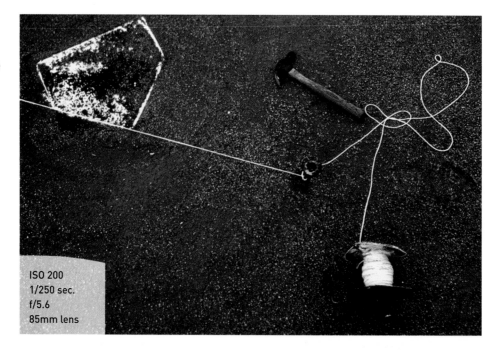

ISO 200
1/250 sec.
f/5.6
85mm lens

I took a few frames and turned around to see another fabulous scene unfolding behind me. Some of the guys from the Trappers were coming out for batting practice and warm-up. It was late in the day, and the light was fabulous. That infamous golden hour was upon us, and I was in heaven.

The scene was perfect. I had no doubt about what I was going to do. Sometimes the obvious choice is the best choice, and I decided to let the detail element of the old, worn bat rack become the picture's leading line element, which brought the eye directly to the silhouetted figures on the beautiful purple color palette of the wall.

The rich, warm, late afternoon light gave such a marvelous aesthetic to the image that all I really had to do was record the beauty of the scene (**Figure 8.8**). After I captured this image I realized that this was going to be an amazing story; most of what I was going to photograph for this story would have very little to do with the action of baseball; instead, it would concentrate on the kinds of things that fans might normally overlook. The answers to the question, How do I make this work? was finally starting to come into shape for me.

ISO 200
1/500 sec.
f/5.6
85mm lens

**FIGURE 8.8**
The shadow from the late afternoon hour projects the shadows of two players conversing just before the start of another inning of play.

I experience a great sense of tranquility when I finally realize that I have a plan for covering an assignment or a story. And from that tranquility comes a real sense of creative freedom. I stop worrying so much about what it is I'm doing, and I think more about what it is I'm seeing and experiencing in the midst of new and exciting things. This was one of those few times when the creative insecurity faded away. I was beginning to see pictures everywhere. When your mind clears and you begin to have a sense of focus for the story, it becomes much easier to see how things fit.

I began to look for those great moments that happen in any event. Sometimes they occur on the field, but many times they happen off the field. Capturing great moments is the key to good coverage of any story; the more of those moments you can find, the greater the level of success you will have with the overall package. Before the game began, the San Diego Chicken was getting the crowd warmed up and thrilling the spectators with the typical threats of baby cannibalism—a classic crowd pleaser.

Sometimes a great way to achieve a unique image is just to observe the subject for a while before you actually pull the trigger. I shot a few frames of the Chicken as he worked the crowd, but mostly I watched him perform. I began to notice a pattern to his antics.

The Chicken would work small sections of the crowd, playing to specific personalities. He would interact with the young kids and make them laugh. I watched the Chicken head toward a small group in a lower section of the stands where a mom had a young baby on her lap. I had seen him work with another baby earlier and knew that he would most likely do something with this little one, too.

That nagging question jumped into my head again: How would I make this scene work better than the one I missed earlier? It was almost subconscious now, but I began to look at the faces in the crowd as the Chicken approached the section. I saw a family behind the woman with the baby and figured that the young boy would be very interested in the big mascot. I lined up so I would be in position to see the young boy and the Chicken in my pictures, and then waited. I wanted to be able to see the Chicken and the faces near him, so I decided to use my 70–200mm lens with an aperture setting of f/4, which would give me a decent amount of depth of field. I knew the heads of the people would become shapes and repetition of form, but what I didn't know until the moment unfolded was that I would get such a great reaction from the young boy in the foreground (**Figure 8.9**). People often refer to good images as a result of luck, but I believe that luck happens because of good place-ment and preparation—with a fair share of anticipation thrown in for good measure.

The one image from the story that really converted me to infinite belief in the two-question scenario was a shot that I was able to get inside the locker room of the Trappers just before the game. The room was small and—as you might imagine—there was a lot going on. But the one thing that really caught my eye was a young man who, according to his teammates, always got exceptionally nervous before the beginning of each game. He was sitting in his locker behind his clothes, hiding his head and trying to calm down.

There were two other players on either side of him preparing for the game, but the picture I really wanted was just the young man hiding his head. The scene stopped me. I started to raise my camera and then realized that the lens I was using was too wide to create the isolated feeling of the scene I wanted to capture. The wide-angle lens would have shown too much of the room—with both players on either side of the hiding subject—and would have diminished the impact of a more meaningful picture.

ISO 500
1/500 sec.
f/2.8
300mm lens

FIGURE 8.9
The San Diego
Chicken entertains
the crowd by
devouring a small
bewildered child.

I quickly changed to an 85mm f/1.4 lens, which would give me a much tighter view of the man behind the clothes, concentrating the viewers' attention onto what I really wanted them to see. As I began to shoot, the two players on either side of the young man got up to go out to the field. So I backed up a little more and included the space of the lockers on either side of him; it felt like the added space would help enhance the feeling of isolation (**Figure 8.10**). It worked, and I came face to face with the fact that constantly asking those questions—What am I seeing? and How do I make it work?—makes all the difference in the world. In this case, the answer to those questions—the resulting picture—was quite nice.

**FIGURE 8.10**
A very nervous player tries to find some solitude behind his clothes in his locker just before the start of the game.

ISO 200
1/30 sec.
f/2.8
85mm lens

My favorite picture of the entire assignment came on the last day of my time with the Trappers. The team returned home for an evening game, and the weather was terrible. It was raining heavily and the winds were blowing as if they would become a tornado. However, an hour or so before game time the rain stopped and people filled the stands. The lights came on, and as the players took the field, the sun found an opening through the clouds just as it was beginning to sink below the horizon. The sky filled with the most vivid fuchsia color, one that defied description. It was as though the photographic gods had been waiting to see if I would give up on the day, and as a reward for putting up with the storm, they gave me a momentary present of ultimate beauty.

I was on the field when the color filled the sky, and I knew it would only be there for a very brief time. I quickly looked around to see what vantage points I could use to capture the beauty in the sky. For a moment I was a little panic-stricken because I could see the color begin to fade a bit. It was one of those times when if I didn't act quickly and correctly, I would lose a great moment.

I grabbed my camera and an 18mm lens. I raced into the stands and up to the announcer's booth. Before anyone could say a word I began to climb up the side of the booth using the conduit pole next to the booth's door. I got to the roof of the booth and shot off three frames. One turned out to be a bit out of focus. The second framed the shot a little too far to the left. The third had a good overall balance. I wanted the poles of the backstop to frame the field, and I wanted the leading lines of the ends of the grandstands at the field's edge to pull me out to the outfield and the mountains beyond. I feel like it worked; as you look at the image, it seems to have a fair sense of balance (**Figure 8.11**).

**FIGURE 8.11**
The last rays of the day turned the sky over the field a brilliant fuchsia as the earlier rainstorm cleared the valley.

ISO 200
1/60 sec.
f/5.6
18mm lens

# LEARNING LESSONS FROM YOUR MISTAKES

Photography is a wonderful developmental pursuit that can take you to great heights of self-expression, as long as you learn that any creative pursuit demands a sense of patience and persistence. There are stages of photography that we all go through, and the early ones can be the most taxing. No artist I know attained a position of great stature and recognition overnight. The creative process doesn't really kick in until you stop having to think about the fundamentals so intently.

It's when the fundamentals become rote that your mind can truly begin to embrace the aesthetic values of what you are seeing and to put all the principles discussed in this book to good use. One of the best ways to become better at anything is to practice, which means spending lots of time with the camera. Having said that, however, I must qualify it: Time spent with the camera isn't necessarily *quality* time spent.

If you go out and shoot pictures in the afternoon, and then go home and don't bother to spend the time examining the results of your work—by carefully deconstructing the pictures—the time spent is not quality time. Shooting the pictures is one thing. Examining your performance is something else.

In the initial learning stages, which are probably the most frustrating, you learn that there are so many factors that affect the quality of your pictures that it can be quite frustrating. This may be the stage you're in now. The next stage—the creative stage—is the one where you really don't need much help anymore; your pictures start coming from an inner place that speaks to you in unique and aesthetic ways. People will then come to you for advice and counsel.

If you want to get there, you can, but it will take some patience and concerted effort. One of the best ways I know to hasten your growth is to be with your images more often. Shoot your images, download them onto your computer, and examine their effectiveness. After all my years of shooting, I know that no image is perfect. They can all be better, and I spend a lot of time looking at them to see what I've done and what I could have done better. This is a great exercise that will definitely improve your composition.

## EVERY PICTURE CAN BE BETTER

Every time I come back from a shoot or an assignment, I immediately download my images and begin to look at what worked compositionally. For instance, after a day on the golf course I wanted to carefully look at what I didn't do so well in order to see where I could have improved.

I was kicking myself with the image in **Figure 8.12** because it could have been so much better had I just moved a bit to the right and gotten a little higher. Moving to the right would have put the shadow on the tree trunk a little deeper into the frame and allowed the viewer to see a bit more of the golfer on the right just past the tree. Getting a little higher would have given the golfer addressing the ball more separation from the background by placing him more solidly against the clean, dark, green grass of the next fairway. These are two simple fixes that would have made a great deal of difference to the final image.

Looking at **Figure 8.13**, I realized that I had cut off the entry to the island. And, had I taken advantage of the fact that the foursome's golf cart was parked at the edge of the bridge, it would have added another dimension to the image as well. Choosing a slightly wider lens would have given the image a greater sense of isolation, too. Simple improvements would have made a noticeable difference in the final image.

**FIGURE 8.12**
Golfers play a round late in the afternoon at Desert Hot Springs Resort in California.

ISO 200
1/250 sec.
f/9.0
17–55 mm lens

**FIGURE 8.13**
The Island Hole par three at Desert Hot Springs Resort is a favorite for many golfers who frequent the Palm Springs area.

ISO 100
1/500 sec.
f/5.6
85mm lens

## SIMPLE THINGS MAKE BIG DIFFERENCES

Each time you take the time to examine your shots, you refine your eye compositionally, and that process helps your growth. In the image of the basketball player (**Figure 8.14**), my conscious decision to place the player in the left third of the frame using the red color palette to the right as negative space worked, but making the silly mistake of cutting off the fingers of the player's left hand worked against the overall aesthetic value of the image. Just using a wider focal length lens would have corrected the problem and made for a better picture. In the image of the sprinter and her shadow on the track (**Figure 8.15**), the framing of the shot becomes a real distraction because of the upper-edge railing on the inside of the first lane, as well as the fact that I should have had the presence of mind to use a bit of a longer focal length to help me keep the hand of the shadow on the track in the frame.

ISO 400
1/500 sec.
f/2.8
200mm lens

**FIGURE 8.14**

A player in a local college tournament appears from behind a player in the foreground.

**FIGURE 8.15**
A sprinter heads for the tape in a national track and field competition in Sacramento, California, late in the afternoon.

ISO 200
1/2000 sec.
f/4.0
420mm lens

Learning to master composition means learning to become hyperfocused on the minute details within the viewfinder. It's making sure that you accurately see all those elements so that the construction of your pictures allows for the best possible images in any given situation. In sports, this process has to be faster and more accurate than in any other discipline of photography. To master it requires more practice and more attention on your part. Once you master the true art of managing sports compositions, everything else will seem like child's play; it will all seem like it's moving in slow motion.

# Chapter 8 Assignments

Be sure to complete the following assignments to help you become accustomed to speed and motion in your photography.

## Developing Visual Awareness

The idea in this exercise is to train yourself to see cleanly and compose pictures in a graphic context. A former editor of mine, whose voice still echoes in my head, used to preach endlessly at me. His mantra was this: "If you can't be good, be graphic!" It sounds silly and simplistic, but the premise is golden. The clutter of our busy world can create a visual nightmare for pictures, so we have to train our eyes to see and shoot cleanly. Your assignment is to go to the local park where kids play peewee football. Bring your camera and the longest lens you can get your hands on. It would be best to have at least a 200mm lens with a fast aperture (f/2, f/2.8 etc.). Shoot only the action of the kids' games using the fastest aperture available to you. Take the images home and review your shots. Look for the cleanest, tightest images you have, carefully examining the backgrounds in the photos. Were you able to shoot when the play was close and keep the images sharp? How well framed are the images? Do you notice that the tighter the images are, the cleaner the pictures look? Try to find at least five images that have well-framed subjects, diffused, pleasing backgrounds, and tight action. If you can't find at least five images, repeat the assignment again until you can.

## Controlling Your Compositions

Go to a local tennis club and shoot the action of people playing. In this exercise, use only manual focus and a long lens (preferably a 300mm or better). Shoot peak action moments, but put the subject in the left third of the frame of the viewfinder. Make sure you have ten sharp images that are peak action oriented. Once you have ten images in the left third quadrant of the frame, shoot ten more, putting the subject in the right third quadrant of the frame. Again, it's important to use manual focus. This exercise will help you develop the skill of conscious image placement and raise your awareness of the importance of compositional development.

## Shooting Traffic

See the first assignment at the beginning of the chapter in the section "One Simple Exercise."

*Share your results with the book's Flickr group!*

*Join the group here: flickr.com/groups/composition_fromsnapshotstogreatshots*

# 9

ISO 100
1/1000 sec.
f/4
Lensbaby
3G with 0.6X
wide-angle
conversion
lens

# Beyond the Rule of Thirds

## A BRIEF HISTORY, SOME PSYCHOLOGY, AND POSITIVE AND NEGATIVE SPACE

By David Brommer

I have a wonderful job. Aside from living a life of photography, I run a seminar program where I get to work with legendary photographers and also create photo programs. Lots of people show me their work, and I notice a recurring issue: They cut the scene in half. This is considered a cardinal sin in the world of photographic composition. And the more I look, the more base compositional problems I begin to notice. So I've done what any decent, self-respecting, photo guru would do—I created a program called, "Better Photographic Composition: Beyond the Rule of Thirds."

In this chapter, I'll illustrate a few key points that are not often spoken of in the conversation of composition. The topics will include a history of composition (I firmly believe you have to know where you came from to move forward), deconstruction of a photograph, psychology, contextual considerations of said photograph, and using positive and negative space in the photograph.

# PORING OVER THE PICTURE

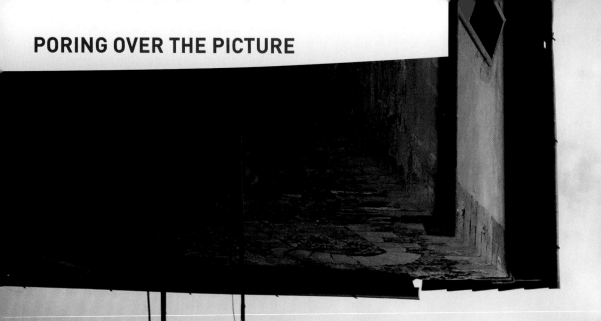

The wires break up the pattern and give the left side weight.

I travel to Italy every summer and always self-assign a project. This year I took a Leica M8.2 and a bag full of legendary Leica lenses. I concocted the plan on the plane ride leaving New York City: I would only point the camera up, and find compositions that were above. The narrow alleys of the old Italian towns provided wonderful experiments in composition and revealed seldom-seen perspectives.

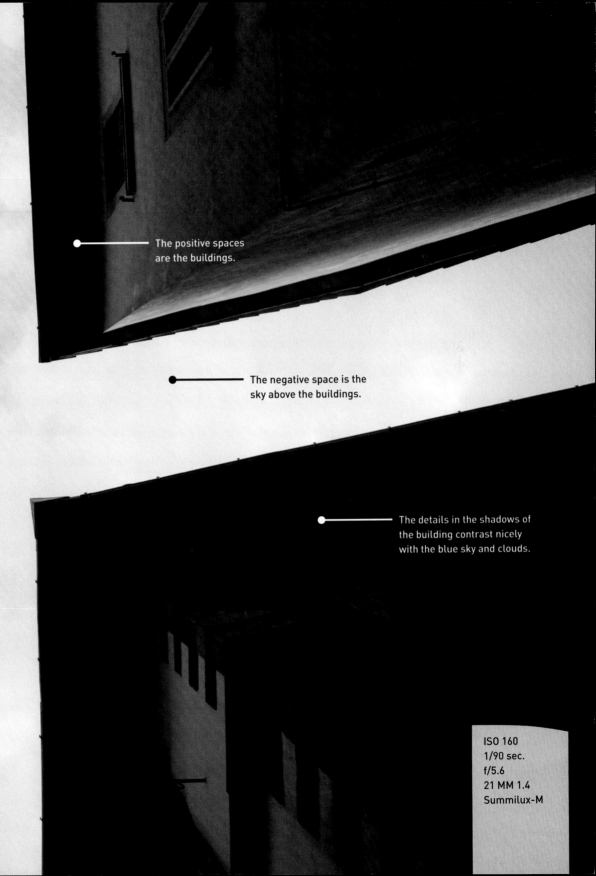

The positive spaces are the buildings.

The negative space is the sky above the buildings.

The details in the shadows of the building contrast nicely with the blue sky and clouds.

ISO 160
1/90 sec.
f/5.6
21 MM 1.4
Summilux-M

# PORING OVER THE PICTURE

The lines in the tiles are dynamic, like the word Imagine.

The shot is taken from a lower angle to accentuate the radiating lines.

Using a Lensbaby to shoot this well photographed New York landmark gives it a distinctive flavor.

The contrasting color palette of gray tiles against saturated flowers builds visual complexity.

The best part of working with an advanced camera like a DSLR is the control it provides over your image, allowing you to imagine limitless possibilities from lens selection to constructing perfect compositions.

ISO 200
1/125 sec.
f/4.0
Lensbaby
Control Freak

# WHERE DID COMPOSITION ORIGINATE?

Roughly 40,000 years ago, humans began to draw local fauna on cave walls. Most likely, this was done not for aesthetics but to create a record of what could be hunted in that region. This was practical art, which represented something quite significant. It explained an idea or concept beyond an elocution, in effect, telling a story with pictures instead of words. These petroglyphs would evolve into hieroglyphs where images and words intertwined to communicate various concepts about the afterlife. Throughout the later ages, painting would evolve, but realism would prove elusive.

We have very little record of painting at the start of the Common Era and leading up to the Middle Ages because it was a dark time of strife. Rome, the cultural capital of the world, had fallen to ruins, her art destroyed or lost. The paintings executed thereafter were mostly in the "Iconic" style of the Byzantine Empire. They were flat, used a narrow color palette, and were limited in scope and grandeur. However, the early Renaissance brought about much change, which can be attributed to one man, an Italian Florentine named Giotto di Bondone.

Giotto (1267–1337) was able to resurrect a quality of painting that had remained dormant since the onset of the Dark Ages. He was keen on reproducing nature in his paintings. His work included the use of perspective, a wide palette of colors, and most important, expressions on the faces of his subjects. Figures came alive and elements of design were incorporated—both practices that profoundly impacted art.

The lessons in this book are a direct result of Giotto's influence on aesthetics. Although Giotto painted in fresco and tempera during the early Renaissance, later the great artists of the middle and high Renaissance would study his works in churches throughout Italy. His use of perspective and realism would be key to our foundations of composition.

After Giotto, Leonardo da Vinci would paint his Last Supper, and all the lines in the painting converged on the right eye of the centrally placed Christ, in a harmony of figures and space unseen (and unpainted) before. Leonardo used draftsmanship and mathematics to achieve a complicated composition. Michelangelo would paint with such emotion and complicated compositions that it would seem he had a divine right to the brush and colors. It took five years for Michelangelo to complete the Sistine Chapel, and when he finished, he had created a massive storyboard under one roof telling nine stories from the Book of Genesis. Sandro Botticelli would be unafraid to use bold colors and elaborate compositions to illustrate both Christian and pagan themes. Caravaggio showed an appreciation for light and shadow. His ability to represent these elements in paint heavily influenced the Dutch and Flemish painters. The Western world would use these practices as a blueprint and foundation for artwork "rules" that would prevail until the present.

## THE HOCKNEY-FALCO THEORY

Advancing painting techniques of the old masters started a trend. Hyperrealism and accuracy started showing up in works as early as the mid-1400s on. Jan Vermeer (1632–1675), a Dutch painter, completed works that offered amazingly detailed perspectives of cityscapes—almost so perfect that they were "photographic" in their imitation of reality. Contemporary artist David Hockney and physicist Charles Falco proposed a theory that camera obscura and other optical devices were used to aid the painter in rendering a scene. In the case of Vermeer's "View of Delft" (1660–1661) (**Figure 9.1**), we see a perfect painting depicting his hometown of Delft taken across a river. Imagine that Vermeer walked about viewing his scene the same way photographers survey the best vantage point to shoot. Once the ideal location was found, Vermeer set up a tent of opaque material, used either a pinhole or a primitive piece of optics, placed his canvas opposite the aperture or lens, and traced the inverted "camera obscura" image as reference. He then took the canvas back to his studio and completed the painting.

FIGURE 9.1
"View of Delft,"
by Jan Vermeer.

Although the Hockney-Falco theory is very romantic to photographers, it is not without its detractors. In argument, and simply put, the old masters were that good. Never mind that Vermeer didn't make extensive preliminary perspective studies as precursors to his final paintings, or that certain specular highlights were painted by Jan Van Eyck, suggesting that convex mirrors were being used. The truth about what went on is lost in antiquity, but remains a bridge to the true invention of photography—where the image can be permanently fixed upon a material and subsequently duplicated.

## GOOD COMPOSITION IS IN OUR DNA!

A good compositional sense is hardwired into each of us. When composition works, it allows our minds to perceive an image with harmony, and we begin to like or dislike an image and subsequently have an emotional reaction (**Figure 9.2**). In nature, there are repeating aspects of perfection, such as in the spiral. The spiral can be manifested in the shell of a snail or the twist of our DNA. The spiral is, like the number three and our rule of thirds, an aspect deeply rooted in our psychology of imagery. When seeking out a great composition, keep your eyes open for spirals or circles (**Figure 9.3**). They can help you create wonderful compositions.

For many years I took it for granted that the old masters created the rules, but they didn't. Good old Giotto simply reestablished what was in our human heritage. Thus far I have spoken about Western considerations as they relate to art, but what about Eastern art? As image makers we know that the finesse of Japanese photographers certainly deserves admiration. I had the opportunity to view firsthand paintings by the Japanese painter Hiroshige (1797–1858), who worked in a style known as Ukiyo-e, a woodblock painting technique very common in Japan from the seventeenth through the twentieth century. Hiroshige was quite famous and prolific, and considered a master of this technique. Aside from the sheer beauty of his work, what stunned me were the compositional similarities to Western masters. Granted that sweeping waves, a traditional Japanese color palette, and images of Mount Fuji weren't to be found in the paintings produced in Florence during the mid-1500s, but Hiroshige adhered to compositional rules that were completely in line with Western masters. He never cut his horizon in two, he embraced the rule of thirds, and he used leading lines, as well as positive and negative space. Hiroshige lived in Edo, which is now Tokyo, and was most likely not exposed to Giotto or what was going on art-wise on the other side of the world. During his lifetime Japan, the holy empire of the east, was sealed off from the world due to political conditions and xenophobia. He never traveled off the island of Japan, and the odds of his being exposed to Western art

**ISO 200**
**4 sec.**
**f/32**
**8¼ inch Dagor lens (28mm equivalent 35mm)**

## FIGURE 9.2

The lines formed by the roof gutters lead the viewer to the center of the composition, not off to the right side. A small aperture gave me maximum depth of field, so everything in the image is sharp. Black and white is a good choice when shooting a medieval city such as Cortona.

**ISO 160**
**1/125 sec.**
**f/8.0**
**24 mm Leica Tri-Elmar**

## FIGURE 9.3

Try to incorporate a spiral element in your image. This arcade is the Galleria Vittorio Emanuele II in Milan.

culture were next to nil. From this I extrapolate that the rules of composition reside in our DNA. Humans comprise multiple races and nationalities, and no matter our color or creed, it seems that composition is inherent, like the spiral found inside a strand of DNA.

One thing that the painters had going for them was time. They were able to craft their paintings and build up perfection in their compositions. As photographers, we do not have that luxury; we must carefully find a correct vantage to lend the image its point of view. Paying close attention first to the corners is essential and can help you find just the right place to set up the camera (**Figure 9.4**). After establishing the subject, you must consider the corners of the image. This is when you notice that tree branch in the background cutting into your subject's head or that the left corner that is six stops brighter than anything else and will be distracting. Take your time and reflect on the entire frame so as to not make a compositional error that will make the image render poorly.

**FIGURE 9.4**
Elements in the foreground help define the complexity of the subject matter. Here the flags illustrate the political context of Election Night 2007.

ISO 100
1/4 sec.
f/16
8 ¼ Inch Dagor

Artists, be they painters or photographers, often work in a two-dimensional medium. We create flat artwork of a three-dimensional world. Even photographers who create 3-D work by utilizing stereoscopic techniques are still essentially making flat artwork. We have tools such as depth of field, perspective, and compression to capture reality in a photograph (**Figure 9.5**), and we do so with sometimes astonishing technical acumen. But what makes one photograph stand out from another? With the advent of digital photography and large-capacity memory cards, a tremendous volume of photographs are currently being captured. This poses some questions: What are we accomplishing with all this work being created? Do we make good, bad, or great photographs? And what constitutes "good" or "bad"?

ISO 800
1/100 sec.
f/14
95mm Fuji
Instax Instant
photograph

**FIGURE 9.5**
A reflecting pool can add dimension to your composition. Here I adjusted the camera so the reflection complemented the original, the Castello Sforza in Milan.

# DECONSTRUCTION AND PSYCHOLOGY OF A COMPOSITION

Our photographs are frequently classified as landscapes, portraits, wild life, still life, street shooting, fashion—the list goes on. I'm sure you are familiar with the type of photography you mostly engage in. However, let us break this down much further and deconstruct our image to its core. No matter the subject or the light it is photographed in, we seek a reaction to our image from our viewers. Garnering an emotional response is essential to the composition, or I should state, the psychological composition. Take for example a photograph of a lion: If the lion is sleeping, the reaction will be less enthusiastic than, say, if the lion were in mid-roar. The roaring lion will spark either fear or awe. *Playboy* magazine centerfolds seek to elicit lust; landscapes and street shooting seek to capture the spirit of a place; and a portrait of a bride seeks to impart her excitement about that special day. What are your subjects saying? A photograph either has a voice (**Figure 9.6**) or is silent. Silent photographs are the ones that are frequently edited out or are deleted.

**FIGURE 9.6**
I wanted the viewer to feel as though they were in the parade and sense the pride that the flag bearer has walking with his brothers in the Sikh Day Parade.

ISO 100
1/750 sec.
f/4.0
Lensbaby 3G

## STUDIUM AND PUNCTUM

To better understand a photograph, I'll borrow a lesson from Roland Barthe's seminal photography essay book, *Camera Lucida*. Barthe speaks about an image causing a reaction and attraction, and he classifies these responses in two categories, studium and punctum. Studium is Latin for a general "liking" or intellectual commitment to the image. To expand on Barthe's definitions, I'd like to add that images containing studium have compositional harmony that conveys the idea and allows a viewer to acknowledge the photograph at face value. The viewer's reaction is not a like or dislike but that a "notice" has occurred and some type of psychological judgment made. Studium at best is when the picture simply works but isn't going to win any contests (**Figure 9.7**). Not to diminish images that elicit studium, on the contrary, many stock images of travel and lifestyle, portraits, sports, street scenes, landscapes, and wild life fall into this category.

ISO 400
1/250 sec.
f/4.8
35mm lens

FIGURE 9.7
A simple composition of the Citroen 2CV.

Punctum, on the other hand, is a quality that transcends studium. An image with punctum penetrates the viewer's consciousness. If studium is talking, then punctum is a scream. Punctum is the most elusive to capture. Sometimes punctum occurs by accident; at other times you have to integrate elements and really think about your photograph to induce punctum. Eddie Adams's famous photograph of the Vietnamese general executing the North Vietnamese sniper contains punctum, but certainly not every frame Eddie captured in his tour of Vietnam was able to live up to that photograph. Punctum is the photographic Holy Grail; images that contain it win awards, sell on gallery walls, and are chosen to be magazine covers.

I present to you Fire Ball Bill (**Figure 9.8**), a contortionist and fire-breathing performance artist who is the perfect subject for an image with a bang. Shooting sequentially, I was able to capture Fire Ball Bill escaping from the confines of a straight jacket. His crazy clown makeup, his body language, and his bare feet all combine to make an image with a little shock and awe.

**FIGURE 9.8**
For this image, shooting in continuous drive mode with flash presented problems with the strobes keeping up with the camera. I used less flash power and moved the strobes closer to compensate. Less flash output allows the strobes to recharge quicker.

ISO 25
1/125 sec.
f/8.0
60 mm
Makro Planar

## HUMOR

Now that we are deep into emotional reactions to images, we have many options to stimulate an emotional response. Let's consider *humor,* which can be exploited to make a viewer chuckle and enjoy the image. Seek the punctum in your images, but don't overlook the studium. Studium is the concert performance leading up to the encore set. Poorly composed and ill-executed photographs will not get you paid nor make anyone admire your photography. Practice the lessons in this book and create a large body of work that qualifies as studium, and when an opportunity for punctum presents itself, you will be ready to capture one of those elusive photographs that becomes one of your *signature images.*

I like to call the image in **Figure 9.9** "double punctum." While walking through a large square I spotted the two beagles with their tails up and quickly ran up behind them to snap the shot with a Fuji Instax camera. Most dog lovers laugh when they see this image; it's fun and whimsical.

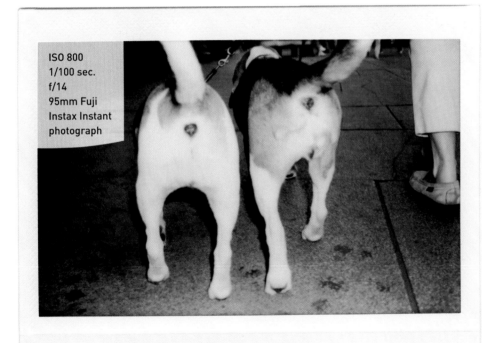

ISO 800
1/100 sec.
f/14
95mm Fuji
Instax Instant
photograph

**FIGURE 9.9**
Candid street shooting gives you less time to prepare the shot. Make sure your exposure and focus modes are preset so you don't miss the shot adjusting your camera.

# POSITIVE AND NEGATIVE SPACE

No matter whether you're an optimist or a pessimist, or whether you find that the viewfinder frame tends to be half full or half empty, incorporating positive and negative space is fundamental to good composition. Permit me to emphasize this element because it is critical to composition. Positive space is the part of the frame that is filled with something, such as lines, subjects, color, or shapes. The positive is surrounded by negative space, which is empty or void space, space around an object or form (**Figure 9.10**). Think of positive and negative space like yin and yang; the two are harmonious. The eye follows the negative space and is driven into the positive space like a highway drives into a city.

**FIGURE 9.10**
To capture the child's playful energy, I chose a lower shutter speed and panned the camera.

ISO 100
1/60 sec.
f/4
Lensbaby
3G with 0.6X
wide-angle
conversion
lens

Positive space does not hold the subject in it, it is the subject. As an eye traverses the image, it will stop on the aspects of positive space and contemplate. The viewer's mind will recognize and draw conclusions about what it perceives in this area of the composition and decide if it has studium enough to merit further attention. Negative space surrounding the positive is akin to a backdrop for the subject. Often, it will be a contrast or an opposite of the positive space. It is best when the negative space makes intrusions into the positive space. I like to call these intrusions "rivers" of negative space, and much like rivers across a landscape, they force the viewers' eyes to meander about the image, soaking up the details in different parts of the photograph.

Using negative space to surround a subject is always a good idea.

Take a look at **Figures 9.11** and **9.12**. At first they appear identical, but one has a compositional defect. After composing and taking the picture, I "chimped" (photographer slang for reviewing the image on the camera's LCD screen) and noticed I had ever so slightly broken up the negative space by touching leaves to the building. A strategic two steps to the left, and the next shot kept the building floating in the blue sky without interruption.

**FIGURE 9.11**
Keep and eye out for objects to frame your subject and occupy the foreground.

**FIGURE 9.12**
Reposition your camera to maximize the interaction of negative and positive space.

The foreground is another aspect to keep in mind. How does foreground play into the positive and negative space? Foreground can be considered positive space if it has details; foreground can also be considered negative space if it supports the main subject in a simplified graphic way (**Figure 9.13**). Integrating foreground is actually very important, because it can inform the viewer of scale, help establish the location of the shot, and also provide another element to work within the composition. Incorporating an element of foreground will also help build up the complexity of your image.

FIGURE 9.13 The original image was captured in color, but I found that a black and white treatment during postprocessing added to the mystery of the garden.

ISO 400
1/125 sec.
f/5.6
21 mm 3.2
Pentax AL lens

## BALANCE OF POSITIVE AND NEGATIVE SPACE

Harmony is achievable when the image has a fairly equal measure of positive space and negative space. Negative space is not always a sky or open background (**Figure 9.14**). Negative space can also be a texture or a repeating pattern, like a dense forest of pines, an ocean vista, or a wall of peeling paint. If the image has a limited color palette, and the negative space is the opposite of those colors, it can be more dramatic, like a slice of blue sky in a city scene of tan buildings. Think about looking up Fifth Avenue in New York City on a rainy day at 5 P.M. You will see a sea of black umbrellas, but the one red umbrella is what you really notice. Even though there may be 20 black umbrellas to the one red one, the red one is the one your eye will follow.

ISO 200
1/750 sec.
f/4
Lensbaby
3G with 0.6X
wide-angle
conversion
lens

**FIGURE 9.14**
To capture this
busy image, I shot
low to the ground
using the pavement
to frame the boxes
of balls and create
negative space.

You should be very conscious of positive and negative space, and try to lead the negative space into or surrounding the positive space whenever possible. Sometimes you will have to move to get the right angle, or you may have to adjust objects in the image to create a nice harmony of positive and negative space (**Figure 9.15**). When I shoot in the studio, I have no problem moving things around until they "fit" just right into the composition.

**FIGURE 9.15**
Here I positioned the roll of paper towels with a wire coat hanger to create positive and negative space. I turned the bucket so the handle stuck out in negative space.

ISO 25
1/125 sec.
f/8
60 mm
Makro Planar

## POSITIVE AND NEGATIVE SPACE IN PORTRAITS

My true passion in photography is portraits. I like a photograph to say something, and allowing a person to speak for me makes the most satisfying image. Years ago at a museum, I watched a video of a Helmut Newton interview, which made a lasting impression on me. It really married positive and negative space in the portrait as a method for my future compositions. He said he would ask his models to face him and give him a "western gunslinger" pose, which is characterized by arms dangling down a few inches from the sides of the torso, thumbs extended, and palms facing the hips. Aside from expressing an attitude, this pose allows the background to creep up the arms, terminating at the shoulder. It is a dynamic pose, which conveys energy and action. The eyes follow the arms and explore the body language. It's interesting to use the term body language, because if we are trying to have the image speak, visual linguistics are surely at play (**Figure 9.16**).

ISO 25
1/125 sec.
f/8
60 mm
Makro Planar

**FIGURE 9.16**
In this shot, I dodged the circle in the subject's shirt to make it brighter, forming negative space in a positive space.

If you don't have the luxury of a studio, there are other creative backgrounds you can utilize by limiting the depth of field and working with a portrait or telephoto lens. Shoot wide open, and focus on the eye of the subject (**Figure 9.17**). It is very important that you lock focus on the eyes. If the subject is skewed to you, focus on the eye closest to your lens. If the subject is facing straight at you, make sure you don't accidentally focus on the nose. Feel free to move up and shoot down so as to hide the horizon (by shooting higher than the subject, you will lose the horizon above the subject's head). Or place the subject at least five feet from a wall. Try to avoid having subjects right up against the wall so that depth of field can do its job and soften the wall, thus accentuating the subject.

**FIGURE 9.17**
The background of this shot is gray pavement, but using depth of field it appears as a seamless studio backdrop.

ISO 400
1/4000 sec.
f/1.2
85 mm 1.2
Canon L lens

Sometimes negative space can be very complicated to integrate. A trick used in **Figure 9.18** was to turn some of the subjects and cluttered background slightly out of focus using a shallower depth of field. The foreground with the interesting colored vegetables remains sharp, but the farther back the scene goes, the less is in focus.

ISO 200
1/30 sec.
f/8
21mm 3.2
Pentax AL

FIGURE 9.18
In this image of
colorful produce,
the figures have
complementary
gestures. Each
figure has what the
other is lacking
(heads or hands).

## THOUGHTS ON CROPPING AND PRINTING

When we go to print and have decided on using an established size, such as 8x10, 11x14, or 16x20, there will be a significant crop to most captured images. The great Ansel Adams was a proponent of previsualization when he made his photographs. Before he took the photograph, he would crop the image in the viewfinder the way he wanted the final print to look (**Figure 9.19**). I like to use all the space that I have on my sensor/film to capture the image, and sometimes the crop factor will negate my careful composition. That's why when I go to print, I choose a larger size paper than the size of my final image. I will fit the image on the paper without a crop and gain a wider border. I never print borderless because I'm afraid I'll lose a part of the composition, usually in the delicate negative space. Often with a modern, pigment-based inkjet printer, I will print on 13x19 paper, but the image may end up being 11x17 or slightly smaller. You can always trim the excess border, but when you use high-quality papers, that clean, white border containing your image can often be very pleasing.

**FIGURE 9.19**
I was drawn to
the corners of this
photograph. The
top was clean sky
and the bottom
was rough brick.
The texture of the
building's surface is
visually irresistible.

ISO 200
1/15 sec.
f/32
14 Inch Kodak
Ektar lens

# Chapter 9 Assignments

After completing the following assignments, you should have a better understanding of what reactions your images elicit and how to work with positive and negative space.

## Look at More Photo Books

For this assignment, you won't need your camera or lenses. Simply go to a good bookstore and spend some time perusing the photography books. You will notice that there will be a selection of the masters, as well as quite a few books by photographers you may not have heard of. I suggest you pick up a book by a photographer who has a similar style to your own and study those images. Just looking at more images will affect your photographic eye as much as creating images.

## Play "Stock Photographer"

Go to a market, mall, or amusement park and make images that reflect studium. Capture a sense of place, but use this mantra, "I will spend more time making fewer pictures." In other words, spend a good amount of time shooting, say, the roller coaster. Capture the essence by making abstract photos of the girders and supports, take a few portraits of the operators, and most of all, step behind the roller coaster where there aren't any people and capture a side that few see.

## Photograph Your Day

Load your camera with fresh film or a memory card and a charged battery, and leave it on your nightstand before you go to bed on a night before a workday. When you wake up, start shooting the light coming in your window. Keep the camera with you all day and document your day. That means photograph your breakfast, lunch, and dinner; photograph your commute; and photograph your co-workers. It is an interesting exercise and one that you will learn a lot from. You'll also come back with some great shots of just a regular day.

*Share your results with the book's Flickr group!*

*Join the group here: flickr.com/groups/composition_fromsnapshotstogreatshots*

10

ISO 100
1/1000 sec.
f/5.6
17–55mm lens

# The Compositional Dance

By Steve Simon

*I work from awkwardness. By that I mean I don't like to arrange things. If I stand in front of something, instead of arranging it, I arrange myself.*

*—Diane Arbus*

The sheer act of determining what is placed within the frame and what is left out—the organization of space—is one of the most important tasks we do when taking pictures. Composition is a bit like a dance: You move around the floor and try new angles to see what they look like so you can arrive at the best possible place to take the picture.

The more you work the scene, often the better the photographs become. Here are some strategies for finding your way to the best composition for any given shooting situation.

I was walking along the beach at Coney Island when I noticed this scene. The two guys lying in the foreground caught my eye. Everyone was resting, and no one seemed to notice me. So I got to work waiting, then shooting the scene, and then waiting for the boat to near the center of the frame at the horizon. Luckily, the arms of the man exercising seem to push your eye to the child running. In fact, all the arms of the individuals within the frame seem to work visually in concert as your eye roams around the scene. I took several shots, but this was my favorite.

The main subjects are all sitting in off-center areas of the frame for added emphasis.

I shot several frames of this scene hoping to get something like this where all arms are in interesting places—sometimes moving, sometimes pointing, but always connecting with each other as compositional elements.

Shooting a foreground, a middle ground, and background elements adds depth to the two-dimensional scene.

The clock-like circular composition moves my eye around the main elements in the scene in an endless loop.

400 ISO
1/1000 sec.
f/8
24mm lens

# PORING OVER THE PICTURE

It was an absolute downpour when I saw these kids heading home in the rain. I instantly knew there was potential for a great photo to be made. I pulled my car over, grabbed my camera, and ran to find an angle that would work. There was no time for an umbrella or camera cover, but my Nikon D2X was up to the task. I got as drenched as the kids and the shot I was after. I dried out, my camera did too, and I ended up with one of my favorite shots ever.

Because my 17–55mm lens wasn't the ideal lens in this situation and I needed to crop in, I made sure my ISO was low enough (200) to let me crop some and not exaggerate any digital noise that a higher ISO on my camera would have rendered.

The composition isn't perfect, especially with the wires at the top of the frame, but as often happens in my images, the content trumps perfection when it comes to composition. As a documentary journalist, I won't remove anything from the scene short of cropping or adjusting color and tones.

ISO 200
1/200 sec.
f/4.5
17–55mm lens

I composed the scene balancing the students with the large light area of the landscape.

I needed a fast enough shutter speed to freeze the students, and I cropped them on the extreme right as if they are walking out of the frame, which seems to bring the image to life.

# THE DANCE

The compositional dance is a game of inches. Look through the viewfinder to see how a slight movement can dramatically impact your final composition. This is important to know, because a slight movement can transform a good photograph into a great one.

It's not just you, the photographer, moving and changing the composition. In a world that never stops, a slight gesture can have a dramatic effect on the final photograph. Bend your knees, change the perspective, and change the juxtaposition of foreground subjects with the horizon (**Figures 10.1–10.4**).

**FIGURES 10.1 AND 10.2**
This image uses the horizon line to cut the image in half, something that is not often recommended, but the picture still works. There are no rules, only guides. A composition is successful when it works. Straightening the horizon, however, did help.

ISO 200
1/100 sec.
f/14
35mm lens

ISO 200
1/100 sec.
f/14
35mm lens

But the art of composition is not a science. Photography is personal. It takes a long time for photographers to learn to trust their intuition, especially when the creative process can feel so technical when using a camera. Your left brain is busy worrying about the camera settings like white balance, f-stops, and shutter speeds, and all your right brain wants to do is take pictures.

The guidelines for good composition are there for good reason: They often work. But for new photographers, they sometimes add to the left-brain dilemma with more dos and don'ts that can get in the way of seeing and feeling your compositions.

ISO 200
1/100 sec.
f/14
35mm lens

**FIGURES 10.3 AND 10.4**
Bend your knees and see how the subject changes position relative to other elements within the frame. I often go down low, to place a subject above the horizon line for a more dramatic and effective composition.

ISO 200
1/100 sec.
f/14
35mm lens

Therefore, it is important to learn and understand the rules and guides of composing through the viewfinder while determining how to put them to work for you. However, learning when to ignore them is key to your evolution as a photographer.

Before your left brain can be freed from the chains of technical constraint and before technique fades to the unconscious and becomes second nature as you explore your subjects with abandon in a beautiful dance of color, tones, and light—you have to pay your dues. That is, put in the time learning all you can from this book, and most important, through personal experience. When you do this and you persevere, I guarantee you will get to a place of photographic competence and satisfaction you can't even imagine right now.

Before I go further, it's worth mentioning that I've never been one to break down the component parts of an image, spill them on the floor, and scientifically analyze them. There is mystery and magic to the creative process that can't be articulated. Sometimes an image can adhere to all the rules and guides, and end up being perfectly boring.

The photographic process at its highest level is akin to a musician arranging notes that provoke emotions or a designer stimulating your senses. Personally, if I had to articulate what I do as I dance around the composition, I would say I'm trying to compose my pictures by arranging visual elements for maximum impact and communication.

We don't always do it on a conscious level, but with experience we learn to constantly scan the viewfinder, looking at the placement of lines and form, the balance of objects, the relationship with foreground and background elements, and the scale between them.

## WORK THE SCENE

Once your photograph is found, working the composition can be a very subtractive process as you eliminate clutter, cleaning up and organizing image elements to focus attention on what you deem important. Scan the edges of the frame to make sure you're not missing anything, and look for details that can be improved by cropping or inclusion within the frame (**Figures 10.5–10.10**).

Sometimes there is an energy and movement created with a good composition where the lines and curves of image elements keep the viewer's eye inside the frame. Then there's the content itself and what it might mean to—or how it will be interpreted by—the viewer.

ISO 200
1/200–1/640 sec.
f/4
35–60mm lens
and 24–70mm
zoom

## FIGURES 10.5–10.10

Working the scene. The first shot shown here was my starting point, but as Suzane Nyirabukara walked away from me toward her home in Kigali, Rwanda, I thought it was a more interesting shot from behind. I followed her, shooting and cleaning up the frame as I went.

# CHANGE YOUR VANTAGE POINT

As we wander through life, we see the world from perhaps our most common vantage point: standing up, eye-level, a distance from our subject that can be described as our comfort zone—not too close, not too far away. In the compositional dance, this is just the starting point for photography.

Filling the frame is often a good idea and can help define the focal point of your image or the point of interest that makes your photograph unique (**Figure 10.11**). My photographer friend Bill Durrence has a mantra that I also share because it helps many photographers find focus. Take the picture, and then move three steps closer. Take another, and then move three steps closer. Repeat. We need to shake ourselves out of our comfort zone (**Figures 10.12–10.14**).

**FIGURE 10.11**
Filling the frame by getting in close can add impact to your final composition. Mmmm, blueberry pie.

ISO 200
1/500 sec.
f/5.6
24mm lens

ISO 400
1/125–1/250 sec.
f/2.8
35–70mm lens

## FIGURES 10.12–10.14

By moving in three steps closer and then three steps closer, I ended up with a much more powerful image than the one I started with.

Show viewers of your work a new view of a common scene. Explore different points of view by getting down low, up high, in close, or in some other unexpected camera position. This is where the dance should take you.

*National Geographic* photographer Sam Abell spoke about how the photographic process is often a form of chaos with much that is out of your control. What you can control is the composition. Once selected, if life is moving about within the frame, with luck and timing all the forces combine to produce a great photograph.

# BE IN THE MOMENT

My best shooting experiences meld the physical—the act of shooting—with the mental and emotional (which becomes second nature with experience) to get to a place where I'm in a zone of concentration, where I'm in the moment. To be in the moment, I save my final editing decisions for when I'm home on my computer and don't look much at my image-review screen except to check exposure and focus (**Figures 10.15–10.17**). I find if I look at images of what I just shot, it takes me away from the dance and out of the moment, interrupting my concentration.

It helps me when I discipline myself to maintain my concentration. Sometimes photographers need a hand, but I much prefer to shoot alone. In my experience, my best shooting comes from a lone-wolf style, with just me or just me and my subject(s), which limits distractions.

We're constantly working in a kind of shorthand: Our eyes are open, but we may not see. If you've ever driven a car while deep in thought or perhaps while talking on your speakerphone, you understand auto-pilot mode. During this time, you often have little or no recollection of what you saw as you were driving—a bit scary, actually. We can function at both tasks because we look with our eyes, but we see with our brains. We're not really concentrating on what our eyes are showing us. We look at the road, the lights, and the other cars enough to safely get to where we need to go, but we're not seeing the way a photographer needs to see to do good work.

With our cameras we need to look, recognize, and see an almost infinite number of variables that can be included or excluded in the frame of our photograph.

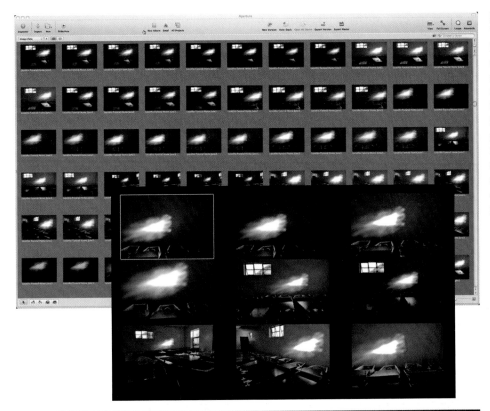

FIGURES
10.15–10.17
By being in the
moment and
concentrating while
moving around
to determine
the composition,
you can create
numerous options
and arrive at the
strongest image
at the end of the
process.

ISO 400
1/500 sec.
f/5.6
17–55mm lens

To get to that place, I can't just turn it on like the switch on my digital camera. I need to warm up. Athletes warm up. Musicians do, too. So why not photographers? For me, warming up means picking up my camera and shooting as soon as possible—shooting something, anything, as an icebreaker—not waiting for that perfect picture but working up to it by limbering up my photographic muscles physically and mentally.

Putting in years as a newspaper photographer, I often had to go out and find pictures. Inspired or not, it was my job. Those times when I waited for something better—instead of stopping and exploring a lesser photo opportunity and really working it—would often lead to regret, because the opportunities passed were better than the ones I ended up seeing.

## CHOICES AND LIMITATIONS

The compositional dance is about figuring out a way to compose the image within the viewfinder by moving yourself, which moves the smallest of details for maximum visual impact. You can make use of all photographic techniques to create the atmosphere or emotion you are feeling and want to transmit.

We have some control by choosing how we work. Different lenses, from wide-angle to telephoto, can change and alter shapes and relationships between foreground and background objects. Longer lenses give flatter, more compressed perspectives, whereas wide-angle lenses communicate intimate perspectives, which "read" in the final image (**Figure 10.18**).

So many of us use zooms these days, and for new photographers, I feel they present too many choices that add to the overwhelming number of decisions we already have to make. I suggest using fixed focal lenses when you hit the compositional dance floor, or shooting with zoom lenses racked to either extreme and moving yourself as Diane Arbus did. With experience, you will know when to finesse your compositions with slight adjustments of the zoom's focal length.

In the meantime, there are several other choices to make. Deciding which camera angle, shutter speed, aperture, distance, light, and moment the picture is taken can all have a profound effect on what will be emphasized and communicated in the final composition. Choosing selective focus or maximum depth of field, blurring through slow exposures or stopping the motion entirely, as well as determining sharpness and clarity can each tell a different story. We decide what story to tell.

ISO 640
1/25 sec.
f/2.8
28mm lens

By working through a number of these technical scenarios, you can later determine what resembles your vision of the scene best. Give yourself options. Try them all and learn. Working the scene makes editing more difficult, and that's a good thing. It forces you to choose between many strong images with subtle degrees of difference (**Figures 10.19 and 10.20**). With experience, you will have a clearer idea of which technical approaches to employ.

Even for experienced photographers, working the photo is all important. Sometimes in the field I think that one shooting situation or photo is going to be "the one," but it isn't. Even after a life of obsessing with photography, I'm never really sure which photograph will end up being the best. So, I advocate that you keep shooting as you dance with your camera—all the while feeling your way through, shooting on impulse, and taking chances. Your medium is digital, and you can always delete later, so shoot freely.

**FIGURES 10.19 AND 10.20**

We have so many technical choices to make. With experience, these choices become almost second nature and instantaneous. Selective focus and what to keep sharp is one such choice. Give yourself options in the field and edit later.

ISO 400
1/500 sec.
f/4
70mm lens

# HAVE PATIENCE

Learning and growing as a photographer is a lifelong process. Everything you experience in your life can be infused into the work you create. Patience is not only a virtue in life, but it can also be a huge asset for improving your work.

Life rarely gives you fully finished photographs suitable for framing. It's just not that easy. Maybe every picture you've ever taken could have been improved. If there's any truth to the preceding sentence, you might agree that working the photo a little more is a good idea.

All subjects are not created equal. But there are photographic gifts around every corner and infinite situations with visual potential waiting to be recognized. Confucius said, "Everything has its beauty, but not everyone sees it." When you're ready to see it, getting that shot requires preparation, eye to the viewfinder, moving and tweaking, and waiting for the moment to materialize. It also requires patience (**Figure 10.21**).

ISO 200
1/160 sec.
f/3.2
85mm lens

**FIGURE 10.21**
I waited all night for this picture. Knowing the balloons would be released from the ceiling of Madison Square Garden when George Bush and family walked onto center stage, I shot and waited and shot some more, eventually getting this image that shows Mr. Bush very prominently in the frame, even though he's a small figure in a complex image.

I'm a believer in a photographer's needing to get through a sheer volume of work to come out on the other side a stronger, more consistent photographer. But it's not just a quantity thing. The great Henri Cartier-Bresson reminded us that increased patience will lead to more great photographs:

> "Sometimes it happens that you stall, delay, wait for something to happen. Sometimes you have the feeling that here are all the makings of a picture—except for just one thing that seems to be missing. But what one thing? Perhaps someone suddenly walks into your range of view. You follow his progress through the viewfinder. You wait and wait, and then finally you press the button—and you depart with the feeling (though you don't know why) that you've really got something."

But it's not always easy being patient, and in a digital world, we don't have to be. Some of my colleagues have said that in the not-so-distant film past, they would work a little harder because they couldn't be sure until the film was developed that they got the shots they needed. Does the image-review screen keep you from working the situation to the max (**Figure 10.22**)? Is "good" good enough?

**FIGURE 10.22**
I try to limit my peeking at the image-review screen because I find it distracts me from the task at hand—making photographs. When there are kids in the area and they find out about the picture magically appearing on the screen, it can be a blessing or a curse as you continue to shoot, so be careful!

ISO 1000
1/60 sec.
f/5.6
28mm lens

## REVIEW YOUR WORK

During the many years that I worked as a photojournalist, I developed the habit of taking time at the end of every year to look back and pull out my best work to enter into various contests. Now, as a full-time freelance and documentary photographer, I continue this practice, which gives me a critical look back at the year that was. It's kind of a photographic road map from which I can update my portfolio, track my progress, and spot weaknesses that I can work to improve.

I look at the work and ask myself some questions. Did I work the image enough? Was I shooting from similar angles? Lens-to-subject distances? How can I make things better?

But the somewhat surprising and ultimately disappointing reality I find after completing this exercise is that when I pull out the best of my best from the year— those truly special, magical moments when something extraordinary happened in front of the camera—there are just not that many of them.

Learning to recognize "the magic" when it happens allows you to maximize those rare opportunities.

## FOLLOW THE MAGIC

The compositional dance includes a work ethic that you try and squeeze the best possible photo out of in every shooting situation. You should always work hard and long on every assignment or photographic opportunity. (If you're reading this book, you know it's really a labor of love that pays off in great photographs—and is always worth it.)

The picture of the young boy with the painting illustrates my point (**Figure 10.23**). I remember following two boys who were each carrying a painting, and their father was lagging behind outside the frame. I'm not unhappy with the resulting photograph, but the experience taught me a lesson. When the fast-moving boys turned the corner, I stopped shooting and went the other way. Why did I stop? I'm not really sure.

FIGURE 10.23
This picture taught me an important lesson about recognizing situations that are better than the ordinary and about working the scene until it goes away.

ISO 400
1/500 sec.
f/4
50mm lens

I figured I had a decent image. The fact that I didn't continue following and shooting this scene nags at me and reminds me not to take anything for granted. I pledged from that day forward that I wouldn't give up on a moment, on a potentially great photograph, if I don't have to—even if I think I may have something good. I didn't have to stop when those kids turned the corner. And although I had taken a picture I thought I liked, if there were better photographs to be had, I will never know.

So I now always follow the magic through until it goes away, the light fades, the subjects are tired, or the moment is gone. Photography is a passion and it's fun, but it's important to push limits, work a little harder, and see where it takes you. This is the compositional dance, too.

I always keep in mind what photographer Melissa Farlow once told me back in the days of film. She said that many times at the end of a shoot when it's late and she's tired and she thinks she has her picture, she will put one more roll into the camera. Sometimes that last roll pushes her to a place she could never have predicted, where those last photographs are better than anything she had taken previously. It's all about working the opportunities and taking chances (**Figure 10.24**).

ISO 1000
1/500 sec.
f/2.8
24mm lens

It's hard to get it right every time because there's a nearly infinite number of images we can make. The possibilities of a scene—including or cropping out elements—are virtually unlimited during the in-camera as well as the postprocessing stages (**Figures 10.25** and **10.26**). It helps to take a critical look at the work you do and think of how to make it better. Having a second set of eyes that can articulate and constructively criticize how images can be improved is huge.

And when it's possible, it has been my experience that going back for a second or third try can teach you much and yield spectacular results. You can move past your visual frustrations by learning from your mistakes and correcting them. There is no shame in admitting that your bar is raised very high. Let your subjects know what it is you are after, or that you want to try again. They will often appreciate (but not always understand) the extraordinary effort you are taking to get the best possible images.

**FIGURES 10.25 AND 10.26**

When it comes to fast-moving subjects in the field, just shoot, and perfect your composition with the second chance that postprocessing and the Crop tool provide.

ISO 200
1/200 sec.
f/4.5
17–55mm lens

## EXPERIENCE LEADS TO INTUITION

In the creative picture-taking process, the choices you make are often intuitive, but they come from experience. As we develop our critical-thinking skills, it gets easier to articulate our feelings about photographs and understand what others are saying about our work. It helps us to ask questions for a clearer understanding on how we can improve.

The more we study the acknowledged great photographs, the more we see the commonalities of strong images and the characteristics they share, as well as the picture components that make the images communicate so powerfully.

After years of teaching and shooting, I've come to the realization that spending time learning about composition, as you are doing with this book, can help you improve your photography and create images that communicate better. As your experience and confidence grow, many of these ideas and concepts get infused into your unconscious process and help you make good aesthetic picture-making decisions on instinct.

# Chapter 10 Assignments

By completing the following assignments, you'll be on your way toward improving your unique compositions.

### Getting Close

This assignment forces me out of my comfort zone and gives me ideas for future shoots. Set your lens to its minimum focusing distance and photograph 40 frames in close proximity to your main subject. It's not a lens-to-subject distance you've likely tried often, but it forces you to see in new ways with limited depth of field, even stopped down some. As always, pay attention to the entire frame and challenge yourself to include people as part of this assignment, giving them fair warning, of course, that you're about to get close.

### The Dance

By moving around with your eye to the viewfinder, shooting as you adjust your camera position, you can discover new and dynamic compositions that you never would have without the dance. Choose a subject and challenge yourself to take 40 completely different compositions of the same subject or scene. It will stretch your visual muscles and make it easier to try new angles on future shoots.

### Get Vertical

Too often photographers ignore the vertical composition, even when it might best communicate visually the scene you're recording. Set out to find some interesting subjects that work vertically, from buildings to portraits. Challenge yourself to continue shooting until you've shot 40 vertical frames that work. By completing this exercise, you'll be able to see vertical compositions more often. If you're one of those rare photographers who shoots mostly verticals, substitute the word horizontal for vertical and start shooting!

*Share your results with the book's Flickr group!*

*Join the group here: flickr.com/groups/composition_fromsnapshotstogreatshots*

# INDEX

3D Matrix Metering, 26
4/3 format cameras, 2, 3
600mm VR lens, 13

## A

Abell, Sam, 240
accessories, 20–22
action photography. See sports photography
Adams, Ansel, 225
Adams, Eddie, 216
Adobe Photoshop Lightroom, 172
Adobe RGB color space, 27
aerial perspective, 100, 101
AF 16mm f/2.8 Fisheye lens, 8
AF-ON (AEL/AFL) button, 28
AF-S 14-24mm f/2.8 lens, 10
AF-S 24-70mm f/2.8 lens, 10
AF-S 70-200mm f/2.8 VR II lens, 10
AF-S 200-400mm f/4 VR II lens, 10
AF-S 600mm f/4 VR lens, 13
Agra Fort, 159–160
angle of view, 8, 9
aperture, 41–47
    depth of field and, 41, 42, 44, 47
    ISO setting and, 41, 43, 46
    shutter speed and, 44–45, 49–53
    test assignment on, 53–54
aperture priority mode, 23–24, 167–168
Arbus, Diane, 229, 242
Arches National Park, 72, 130–131
architectural photography, 159–160
Auto Exposure Bracketing (AEB), 169

## B

backgrounds, blurring, 36–37, 43, 47, 50
backlighting subjects, 71–72
Barthe, Roland, 215
baseball photography, 188–196
Batdorff, John, 151
batteries, spare, 21
being in the moment, 240–242
black, emotion conveyed by, 116
black-and-white images, 151–175
    annotated examples of, 108–109, 152–155
    approach to shooting, 163–164
    assignments on shooting, 124, 175
    camera settings for, 167–169
    color tonalities in, 108–109, 116, 124

considerations on shooting, 164–167
contrast in, 156–157, 171–172
emotion conveyed by, 116–117
equipment for, 166–167, 173–174
HDR (high dynamic range) for, 170, 171
identifying photos for, 156
landscapes as, 162, 163–164
light in, 158–159
orientation of, 164–165
portraits as, 160–161
postprocessing software for, 171–172
shapes and patterns in, 159–160
texture in, 157–158
tonal range in, 156–157
blinkies, 27
blue, emotion conveyed by, 113, 115
blur
    background, 36–37, 43, 47, 50
    motion, 34–35, 46, 51
body language, 223
Botticelli, Sandro, 208
bracketing exposures, 169, 170
breaking the rules, 173
Brommer, David, 203
Bryce Canyon National Park, 97
bubble level, 173
Bush, George, 245

## C

cable release, 166, 173
Camera Lucinda (Barthe), 215
camera obscura, 209
cameras
    basic settings for, 23–29, 30, 167–169
    formats available for, 2–3
    key features of, 7
    working with DSLR, 207
    See also equipment
Canon cameras, 2, 26
Canyonlands National Park, 134
Caravaggio, 208–209
Cartier-Bresson, Henri, 246
chimping images, 219
close-up photography
    assignment on shooting, 251
    wildlife portraits as, 140, 142–143
color space, 27
color wheel, 111

colors, 105–124
    annotated examples of, 106–109
    assignments on using, 124
    black and white, 108–109, 116–117
    complementary, 112
    emotions conveyed by, 113–115, 116, 122
    as patterns, 118–119
    primary and secondary, 106, 107, 110–111
    significance of, 122–123
    white balance and, 119–121, 124
CompactFlash cards, 21
complementary colors, 112
composition
    black-and-white, 151–175
    choices made in, 242–244
    color used in, 105–124
    dance of, 229, 234–236, 251
    emotional responses to, 214–217
    exposure triangle and, 33–54
    hardwired into human DNA, 210–213
    historical origins of, 208–210
    lighting considerations for, 57–78
    lines, shapes, and patterns in, 81–102
    positive and negative space in, 218–226
    spatial relationships in, 127–148
    sports photography and, 177–201
    studium and punctum in, 215–216, 217
    vantage point in, 238–240
    working the scene for, 236–237, 243
concentration, 240, 241
Coney Island, 230–231
Confucius, 245
Conservatory of Flowers, 82–83
Continuous AF Dynamic setting, 24
Continuous High Advance setting, 24–25
contrast
    black-and-white images and, 156–157, 171–172
    tonal range and, 156–157
cool tones, 119, 121
corners of images, 212, 226
cropped sensors, 2, 3
cropping images, 225–226
curves, 81, 86–87, 102

**D**

depth, visual, 133–135, 148
depth of field
    aperture and, 41, 42, 44, 47
    explanation of, 44
    shutter speed and, 51
    tripod use and, 166
Devers, Gail, 183–187

diagonal lines, 91–92
diffused light, 67–68
digital cameras. See cameras
direction of light, 70–74
    assignment on, 78
    backlight, 71–72
    front light, 70–71
    sidelight, 73–74
dramatic landscapes, 162
Durrence, Bill, 238

**E**

emotion
    of black and white, 116
    of color, 113–115, 122, 124
    of composition, 214–217
environmental compositions, 140–142
equipment, 1–30
    accessories, 20–22
    assignments on, 29–30
    author's bag of, 6–7
    cameras, 2–3, 7
    filters, 16–19
    inventory of, 29
    landscape photography, 173–174
    lens shades, 15
    lenses, 4–5, 8–13
    teleconverters, 13–14
    traveling with, 174
evaluative metering mode, 26, 168
examining your shots, 196–200, 247
experience, 250–251
exposure, 33–54
    annotated examples of, 34–37
    aperture value and, 41–47
    assignments on, 53–54
    bracketing, 169, 170
    combining elements of, 38
    ISO setting and, 39–41
    shutter speed and, 48–53
exposure compensation, 74–77, 78
Exposure: From Snapshots to Great Shots
    (Revell), 33
exposure triangle, 38
eyes, focusing on, 224

**F**

Falco, Charles, 209
fall foliage, 122, 123
Farlow, Melissa, 248
fast shutter speeds, 48

File number sequence, 28
fill flash, 20, 21
filling the frame, 238
filters, 16–19
    graduated neutral density, 17–18, 162, 167, 173
    polarizing, 16–17
    red, for B&W images, 175
    variable-neutral density, 19, 51, 52
Fire Ball Bill, 216
fisheye lens, 8, 9
fixed focal lenses, 242
flash
    fill, 20, 21
    low-light, 180–181
flashlight/headlamp, 21
Flickr group for book, 30
focal length
    exercise on, 30
    sensor size and, 2
    teleconverters and, 13–14
focus
    continuous, 24
    portrait, 224
following the magic, 247–250
foregrounds, 220
forests, 84–85, 96
framing images, 95–96, 165, 238
front light, 70–71
f-stops, 41
full-frame sensors, 2, 3

**G**

gear. See equipment
getting up/down, 139–140
Giotto di Bodone, 208
Gitzo tripods, 21, 173
Golden Gate Bridge, 68–70
golden hours, 62–63, 158
graduated neutral density filter, 17–18, 162, 167, 173
Grand Canyon, 132–133
gray, emotion conveyed by, 116
green, emotion conveyed by, 113, 114
grid focusing screen, 173
grizzly bear, 36–37

**H**

hand-holding cameras, 167
HDR (high dynamic range) images, 170, 171
heads for tripods, 21, 22, 173
highlight warning, 27, 76, 77

high-tonal-contrast images, 156–157
Hiroshige, 210
historical photos, 116, 117
history of composition, 208–210
Hockney, David, 209
Hockney-Falco theory, 209–210
horizon line, 144–145, 148, 234
horizontal lines, 89
horizontal orientation, 97–100, 102, 164
Horsetail Falls, 63, 64
humor, 217

**I**

image stabilization, 167
image-review screen, 246
intuition, 250–251
ISO, 39–41
    aperture and, 41, 43, 46
    basic settings for, 29, 167
    black-and-white images and, 167
    noise and, 29, 39, 41
    test assignment on, 53

**J**

JPEG format, 26–27

**K**

KISS theory of success, 187

**L**

landscapes
    approach to shooting, 163–164
    black-and-white, 162, 163–164
    equipment for shooting, 173–174
    inclement weather and, 162
    lenses used for, 165
    metering mode for, 168
Latourell Falls, 136
layering effect, 100–101
L-brackets, 173
Leica lenses, 204
lens shades, 15
lenses, 4–5, 8–13
    angle of view for, 8, 9
    choosing use of, 242
    fisheye, 8, 9
    fixed focal, 242
    focal length exercise, 30
    importance of quality, 174

lenses *(continued)*
    orientation of shots and, 165–166
    telephoto, 13
    ultra-wide, 10
    zoom, 10–12
Leonardo da Vinci, 208
light, 57–78
    annotated examples of using, 58–61
    assignments on working with, 78
    black-and-white images and, 158–159, 175
    changing quality of, 68–70
    diffused, 67–68
    direction of, 70–74
    exposure compensation and, 74–77
    midday, 63, 65, 66
    overcast days and, 67–68
    quality and quantity of, 62–70
    sunrise and sunset, 62–63, 64
    window, 74–75
lighthouses, 62, 63, 68
lightning storms, 22
Lightning Trigger, 21–22
Lightroom application, 172
lines, 81, 88–92
    annotated examples of, 82–85
    assignment on using, 102
    diagonal, 91–92
    horizon, 144–145, 148, 234
    straight, 89–90
looking up/down, 136–138, 204–205
low-light situations
    flash used in, 180–181
    tripods used in, 166, 167
low-tonal-contrast images, 156

**M**

memory cards, 21
metering modes
    3D Matrix, 26
    evaluative, 26, 168
Michelangelo, 208
microfiber cloth, 21
midday light, 63, 65, 66
mid-range zoom lenses, 10, 11
Monument Valley, 71–72, 96
motion
    blurring, 34–35, 46, 51
    conveying a sense of, 178–179, 184–185
    dealing with speed and, 183–187
    exercise on shooting, 182
    shutter speed and, 48

*See also* sports photography
MP-1 equipment bag, 21

**N**

negative space. See positive and negative space
Newton, Helmut, 223
Nik Software, 172
Nikon cameras, 7
Nikon lenses, 8–13
noise in photos, 29, 39, 41
normal-tonal-contrast images, 156
numbering photos, 28
Nyirabukara, Suzane, 237

**O**

ocean waves, 58–59
orange, emotion conveyed by, 113
orientation of shots, 97–100, 102, 164–165, 251
overcast days, 67–68

**P**

painting
    Hockney-Falco theory of, 209–210
    origins of composition in, 208–209
partial metering mode, 168
patience, importance of, 245–246
patterns
    black-and-white photography and, 159–160
    colors as, 118–119
    composition using, 81, 93–94
perspective, 136–140
    assignment on, 148
    getting up/down for, 139–140
    looking up/down for, 136–138, 204–205
    sports photography and, 183–187
    vantage point and, 238–240
Peterson, Moose, 21
photography books, 227
Photoshop Lightroom, 172
pink, emotion conveyed by, 114
point of view, 132–133, 238–240
    *See also* perspective
polarizers, 16–17
portraits
    black-and-white, 160–161
    exposure compensation for, 74–75
    golden hours for shooting, 158
    lenses used for, 165
    metering mode for, 168
    positive and negative space in, 223–224
    wildlife close-ups as, 140, 142–143

positive and negative space, 218–226
  balance of, 220–222
  cropping/printing and, 225–226
  explanation of, 218–220
  portraits and, 223–224
postprocessing software, 171–172
previsualization, 225
primary colors, 106, 107, 110–111
printing images, 225–226
psychology of composition, 214–217
punctum, 216, 217
purple, emotion conveyed by, 113

## Q

quality/quantity of light, 62–70
  assignment on, 78
  changing light and, 68–70
  diffused light and, 67–68
  midday light and, 63, 65, 66
  sunrise/sunset light and, 62–63, 64

## R

rain
  photo of children in, 232–233
  protecting equipment from, 21
  See also weather considerations
rainbows, 122, 123
RAW format, 26–27
RAW + JPEG setting, 26
red, emotion conveyed by, 113, 115
red filters, 175
red-eyed tree frog, 106–107
reflections
  colors in, 110, 118
  composing images with, 213
  filter for removing, 16, 17
remote release, 21, 173
resolution, 41
Revell, Jeff, 33
reviewing your work, 196–200, 247
Rickman, Rick, 177
rule of thirds, 146

## S

scale, 136
S-curves, 81, 86–87
secondary colors, 106, 107, 110–111
sensors, size of, 2–3
sequence of images, 24–25

shadows
  layered look and, 100, 101
  midday light and, 63, 65
shapes
  black-and-white photography and, 159–160
  composition using, 81, 82–83
shutter speed, 48–53
  aperture and, 44–45, 49–53
  explanation of, 48
  fast vs. slow, 48–49
  polarizing filter and, 17
  test assignment on, 54
  Vari-ND filter and, 19, 51, 52
sidelight, 73–74
signature images, 217
Silver Efex Pro software, 172
Simon, Steve, 229
Singh-Ray Vari-ND filter, 19
skies
  dramatic landscapes and, 162
  graduated neutral density filters for, 162, 167
slot canyons, 66
slow shutter speeds, 49
slowing down, 165
software, postprocessing, 171–172
spatial relationships, 127–148
  annotated examples of, 128–131
  assignments on, 148
  horizon line and, 144–145
  perspective and, 136–140
  point of view and, 132–133
  scale and, 136
  subject placement and, 146–147
  visual depth and, 133–135
speed
  conveying a sense of, 184–185
  See also motion
spirals, 210, 211
sports photography, 177–201
  annotated examples of, 178–181
  assignments on shooting, 201
  conveying speed in, 184–185
  examining images of, 197–198
  exercise on adapting to, 182
  image fix examples, 197–200
  important questions to ask in, 187–195
  learning from your mistakes in, 196–200
  making simple improvements to, 199–200
  perspectives for composing shots in, 183–187
  weather conditions and, 195–196
  See also motion

stock photography, 227
storm chasing, 162
straight lines, 89–90
studium, 215, 217, 227
subject placement, 146–147
sunrise/sunset light, 62–63, 64, 120

## T

TC-14E II teleconverter, 13, 14
TC-17E II teleconverter, 13, 14
TC-20E III teleconverter, 14
Teardrop Arch, 96
teleconverters, 13–14
telephoto lenses
    600mm VR, 13
    layered look and, 100
    teleconverters for, 13–14
    zoom, 10, 11, 12
texture, 157–158
three-dimensional images, 158
tonal contrast, 156–157
traffic photography exercise, 182, 201
traveling with equipment, 174
tripods
    equipment recommendations, 21, 22, 173
    when to use, 166, 167

## U

ultra-wide lens, 10

## V

Van Eyck, Jan, 210
vanishing point, 135
vantage point, 238–240
variable-neutral density filter, 19, 51, 52
Vermeer, Jan, 209
vertical lines, 89
vertical orientation, 97–100, 102, 251
"View of Delft" (Vermeer), 209
visual awareness, 201
visual depth, 133–135, 148

## W

warm colors, 119–120, 121
waterfalls, 51–52, 64, 136
weather considerations
    landscape photography and, 162
    sports photography and, 195–196

wheat fields, 60–61, 98, 163
white, emotion conveyed by, 114, 115, 116
white balance
    choosing settings for, 169
    colors and, 119–121, 124
wide-angle lenses, 10, 242, 243
wildlife
    close-up portraits of, 140, 142–143
    environmental compositions of, 140–142
    lighting considerations for, 67, 71, 74, 76–77
Wimberely Head II, 21, 22
window light, 74–75
work ethic, 247
working the scene, 236–237, 243

## Y

yellow, emotion conveyed by, 113, 115
Yellowstone National Park, 70–71, 128–129, 134
Yosemite National Park, 63, 64

## Z

zoom lenses
    mid-range, 10, 11
    telephoto, 10, 11, 12
    ultra-wide, 10

# INVENTIONS
## That
## COULD HAVE
## CHANGED
## The World
## ...BUT DIDN'T!

*Joe Rhatigan*

• ILLUSTRATIONS BY ANTHONY OWSLEY •

imagine!
Publishing

An Imagine Book
Published by Charlesbridge
9 Galen Street
Watertown, MA 02472
617-926-0329
www.charlesbridge.com

KiwiCo special edition 2021
First paperback edition 2018
Text copyright © 2015 by Joe Rhatigan
Illustrations copyright © 2015 by Charlesbridge Publishing, Inc.
Interior and cover design: Melissa Gerber
Editing: Kate Hurley

ISBN 978-1-63289-064-1 (softcover)


Printed in China
(sc)  10 9 8 7 6 5 4 3 2

At the time of publication, all URLs printed in this book were accurate and active. Charlesbridge,
the author, and the illustrator are not responsible for the content or accessibility of any website.

# CONTENTS

**INTRODUCTION:** *If at First* ..................................... 4

**CHAPTER 1:** *Going Nowhere* ................................ 10

**CHAPTER 2:** *Easier, Quicker, Safer ... Weirder* ......... 26

**CHAPTER 3:** *Fun & Games* .................................. 44

**CHAPTER 4:** *Bringing up Baby ... & Fido* ............... 58

**RESOURCES** ...................................................... 76

**INDEX** ............................................................ 77

## If at First . . .

Take a look around you and try to count the number of inventions you see. Everything from the light you're using to read this book to the machines used to create this book was invented by someone who saw a problem and found a creative way to solve it. That's what inventions are: solutions to problems.

Some of these solutions have changed the world in fascinating ways. Before lightbulbs, people went to bed when it got dark outside. (There was nothing else to do.) Before the printing press, only a very few people had access to books. The very best inventions make you wonder how people ever lived without them.

There are a lot of great books about these incredible inventions and the fascinating people who made them. But this book has something else on its mind: What about the inventions that didn't change the world?

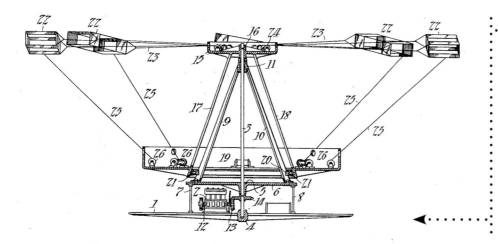

*Thomas Edison, perhaps the most famous inventor ever, is known for his more than one thousand patented inventions. He isn't, however, known for creating this flying machine, which he patented in 1910. Why? It didn't fly.*

The world is bursting with ideas. Unfortunately, not all of these ideas are good. For every amazing invention, there are thousands that are never produced, arrive too soon or too late to be of any use, or simply don't work. Some are too impractical, silly, or unwieldy. Others may be the next big thing . . . someday. In many ways, these flops can be just as fascinating as lightbulbs, cars, computers, and smartphones. Wacky, weird, wonderful, or just plain wrong, these are the inventions included in this book.

In some sense, you can say this book is about failure, but it's a kind of failure worth celebrating. The human race can't move forward without trying and sometimes not succeeding. Without these inventions that didn't work out, we probably wouldn't have the ones that did. So this book celebrates the flops and also-rans—the inventions that could have changed the world, should have made a difference, or would have astounded us all, but for one reason or another didn't.

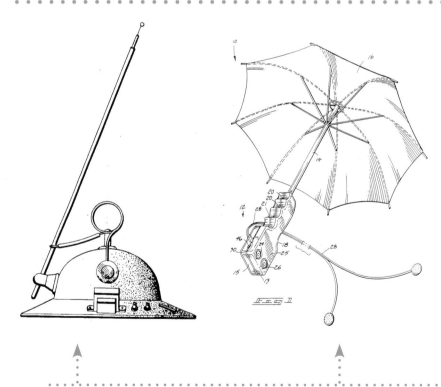

*There were dozens of failed inventions before personal sound systems succeeded, including the Radio Hat, patented by Olin Mumford in 1948, and the Umbrella with Removable Radio Handle, patented by Joseph Divine in 1989.*

# About the Illustrations in This Book

In order to get credit for an invention you come up with, you need to get it approved by your country's patent and trademark office. In order to do that, you have to fill out a patent application and provide compelling reasons why your invention should be granted a patent. Many times, inventors include illustrations of their ideas. The black-and-white illustrations in this book come straight from the patent applications inventors sent to the patent office. The numbers and arrows in many of these illustrations refer to written descriptions in the patents.

For instance, the illustration below is for U.S. Patent #1494508, issued to Henry Smith in 1924 for a cane with wheels. In Figure 6 at the top, the number 7 refers to an opening to receive number 8, the bolt.

My collaborator, Anthony Owsley, is responsible for the color illustrations. He worked hard to make sure the inventions he drew looked like the real ones—although he also had some fun along the way.

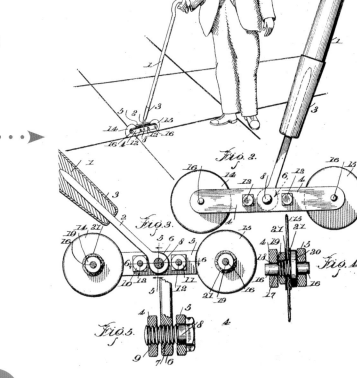

# The World of Inventions and Patents

Nobody knows who invented the wheel, the compass, or even mirrors. That's because people at the time didn't think to record that information anywhere. (Or writing hadn't been invented yet.) Beginning in 1790, if you created a device or procedure that was different and useful and you wanted to make sure nobody stole your idea, you could apply for a patent. According to the United States Patent and Trademark Office, a patent is "an intellectual property right granted by the government . . . to an inventor to exclude others from making, using, offering for sale, or selling the invention . . . for a limited time in exchange for public disclosure of the invention when the patent is granted." Simply put: If you write out an application, pay the fee, and then the government grants you a patent, nobody can steal or make money off your idea for twenty years. Meanwhile, your invention becomes public and anyone can look at your application, learn from it, and perhaps create new inventions based on it.

## FYI

The idea of patents has been around since the 1400s, and the first patent law in the United States was enacted in 1790. The United States Patent and Trademark Office grants more than 180,000 patents a year and so far has granted more than eight million patents. Meanwhile, the Canadian Patent Office examines more than 30,000 requests per year and has granted more than two million patents.

*The United States Patent and Trademark Office is headquartered in Alexandria, Virginia, and employs nearly ten thousand people.*

*The first U.S. patent was issued to Samuel Hopkins on July 31, 1790, for an improvement "in the making Pot ash and Pearl ash by a new Apparatus and Process." The patent was signed by President George Washington.*

N ot all patents are approved. In fact, in order for your invention to receive a patent, it has to pass three tests.

### Test #1: Is it novel?

In other words, is it new or does it have a new part that another inventor hasn't already thought of? You can't patent the paper clip because someone has already invented it. However, if you invent a paper clip that doubles as a nostril cleaner, you may be on your way to receiving a patent.

### Test #2: Is it useful?

Does your invention have a practical use and can someone actually create it? In other words, you can invent all the time machines you want, but until you can shake hands with George Washington, you can't patent it.

### Test #3: Is it inventive?

This means that your invention isn't obvious and couldn't have been thought of by just anyone with basic knowledge about the subject.

"The patent system added the fuel of interest to the fire of genius." ~Abraham Lincoln

lthough it's impossible to predict with certainty whether an invention will be the next great thing or a flop, these questions can help.

### Does it work?

This one is obvious.

### Does it do its job better and more cheaply than other inventions?

If something works better than your invention, nobody will want yours. Thomas Edison did not invent the lightbulb. He did, however, replace the oxygen in the bulb that others used in previous lightbulbs with gases that worked better. Also, he experimented with thousands of different filaments until he found the one that glowed the best and lasted the longest. Edison also invented the method of using the lightbulb in homes—making its use easy and affordable. That's why we remember his name and not those of his predecessors.

### Do people want it?

A great invention at the wrong time can fail just as easily as a horrible invention. Chester Carlson invented the photocopier in 1937. During the next seven years, his invention was turned down by more than twenty corporations. In fact, it took more than ten years for him to sell his idea and another ten before companies were buying Xerox machines, making Carlson a millionaire.

### Can you get the money to mass-produce and market your invention?

Many inventors have to rely on others to invest in (or pay for) producing their inventions in order to sell them. A great idea will just sit on a shelf without money to make it.

### Are you lucky?

It can't hurt to be lucky!

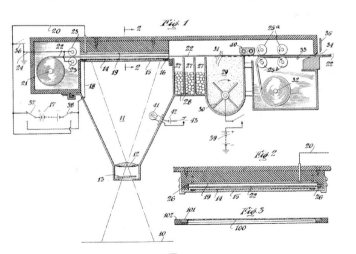

*Carlson's invention was a flop . . . until it wasn't.*

# CHAPTER 1

## Going Nowhere

**H**umans have always been fascinated with getting places quickly, efficiently, and in style. And for every mode of transportation you can think of, there are countless inventions that never quite took off. Imagine what your trip to school might be like if one of the following inventions had succeeded.

◄ • • • • • • • • • • • • • • • • • • • • • • • • • • • • • • • • • • • • • • • • • • • • • •

*The following inventions might get you where you want to go . . . but then again, perhaps they won't.*

• • • • • • • • • • • • • • • • • • • • • • • • • • • • • • • • • • • • • • • • • • ►

"Just because something doesn't do what you planned it to do doesn't mean it's useless."
~Thomas Edison

# The First American Horseless Carriage

As with many new inventions, the first person to do something isn't always the one who gets rich and famous. According to most historians, John W. Lambert invented and made the first gasoline automobile in America; however, not too many people know about him. The year was 1891, seventeen years before Henry Ford started producing his much more famous Model T car. Lambert's motorized tricycle had two speeds, no reverse gear, and three wooden wheels with steel rims. Although Lambert was never able to convince anyone to pay $585 for what he called the Buckeye Gasoline Buggy, Lambert and his horseless carriage were responsible for the first car accident. Lambert, out for a drive with a friend, hit a root sticking out of the ground. He lost control of the buggy and crashed into a post. Both driver and passenger had minor injuries.

# Ford's First

In 1896, Henry Ford designed and built his first automobile, which was called the Quadricycle because it ran atop four bicycle wheels. It had two gears and could reach speeds of twenty miles per hour. It couldn't, however, go in reverse. Ford only built three Quadricycles and sold one of them. It would take another twelve years of experimenting before Ford would find success with his Model T, but his success with this early model led him to found the Henry Ford Company, which would eventually make him the richest man in the world.

# Bike Inventions That Leave Us Flat

The bicycle in your garage isn't much different looking from the first bicycles in the late 1800s, but that doesn't mean there haven't been some strange two-wheeled inventions.

## Isn't It Dandy

The Dandy Horse or *Laufmaschine* ("running machine") was patented in 1818 in Mannheim, Germany, and is considered the first means of transportation using two wheels. In other words, it was the first bike. The Dandy Horse was very popular for a short time, until riders began hitting and hurting pedestrians. Within a year or so, the running machine and others like it were banned.

*Fig. 1.*

*Fig. 2.*

## Row, Row, Row Your Bike

Patented by Louis Burbank in 1900, this combination bicycle/rowing machine looks like great exercise . . . As long as you don't have to steer. The object of the invention was, according to the patent application, "to provide means whereby one may enjoy with a bicycle or similar vehicle exercise like that of rowing with a pair of sculls, which is adapted to develop the muscles of the arms and body as well as those of the legs."

## No Peaking

Theron Cherry, like most in the late 1800s, thought it improper for women to ride bicycles, lest their legs be viewed, causing scandal. This Screen for Ladies Bicycles, patented in 1896, protects a woman's feet and ankles from view when riding, and also keeps "the skirts from being blown about the limbs."

## No Frame Needed

A patent was issued to Justin W. Trenary in 2004 for this "body-connected bike." The Body Bike was meant for downhill racing cyclists who don't want to bother with gears, pedals, a frame, or even a seat. So far, it has not been produced. According to the patent application, "the body of the rider acts as a connecting means between the front and rear roller assemblies and allows high-performance riding."

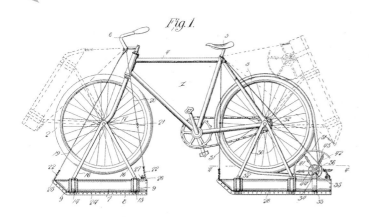

## Pedaling the Pond

This 1912 invention by Henry Munsen could supposedly travel on both land and water. The dotted lines in the illustration show where the metallic floats would be while riding on land. Once on the water, when you pedal, the rear wheel turns a paddle wheel, propelling you forward. Cables connect to the handlebars and front floats help with the steering.

## The Fliz

Before the modern bicycle was invented, similar contraptions were patented in which the rider had to walk or run while on top of the bike. These bicycles were called *velocipedes*, and they went out of favor once bicycles with pedals and chains became popular. Two German inventors, however, recently created the Fliz, a type of velocipede in which the rider is strapped to a frame between two wheels. You start it by running while holding on to the handlebars. Once you find yourself at the top of a hill, you can rest your feet on the back wheel. The Fliz was invented to encourage an alternative to driving.

# Is One Wheel Better Than Four?

**E**arly automobile inventors used carriages and coaches as inspiration for their designs, with some sort of compartment moving forward on top of four wheels. In the early 1930s, however, the British inventor Dr. John Purves decided to think outside the box by putting the car driver *inside* a single wheel. Purves invented a giant, ten-foot-tall, doughnut-shaped iron contraption that held a driver and three passengers. The Dynasphere, as Purves called his vehicle, reached speeds of up to twenty-five miles an hour during many demonstrations.

Unfortunately, those who watched this amazing wheel in action also noted the Dynasphere's driver had trouble steering, braking, and seeing the road in front of him. There was also a chance that the driver and his passengers would spin head over heels like a hamster that suddenly stops running in its wheel. These limitations kept the Dynasphere from ever appearing on our roads and highways.

*Online*
Watch the original Dynasphere in action: *bit.ly/1lo7NBK*

# Leg and Arm Powered

**T**ransporting yourself inside a wheel was a bad idea more than thirty years *before* the Dynasphere. With this contraption, patented by Thomas Tolson in 1897, you pedaled with your arms and legs and steered by leaning one way or the other.

# How High Can You Pedal?

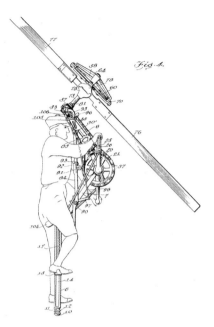

This flying machine, invented by Andrew Mraula, seems to have gotten its inspiration from the bicycle, as you pedal with your hands to turn the blades. Once the blades moved fast enough, you would be lifted into the air. Then you'd start pedaling for your life with your feet as well. Perhaps the best part of this scary contraption is you can fold it up when you're done and carry it on your back.

# Need a Lift?

This nifty contraption, patented by Harold Bush in 1969, is part pogo stick and part helicopter. By holding the upright support in your hands and pushing down on the foot pedals with your feet, you can propel yourself in a series of high jumps and gentle, blade-driven falls back to earth. According to the patent application, "substantial flights can be achieved by descending a hill and tilting the blades so that the angle of attack is such that the device is airborne for a substantial portion of the hill. The pivotable wheel can be replaced by a ski member during the wintertime to provide a year-round amusement device."

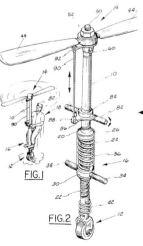

# The Jumping Balloon

The object of this invention, patented by Clarence Adams and others in 1925, was to produce a balloon "adapted to sustain the weight of a single passenger (who) with the aid of the balloon and propelling mechanism may perfect a jump from the ground to an altitude of several hundred feet. The balloon is particularly useful in jumping over buildings, trees, rivers, and chasms." The inventors imagined this device could be used to jump over buildings, trees, rivers, chasms, and more, as well as a neat way to take photographs and easily inspect rooftops.

# The Car That Flew

Imagine sitting in traffic. Suddenly, with a push of a button, your car lifts into the air and zooms away. That's one of the reasons many inventors have spent their lives trying to come up with a car that flies . . . or a plane that drives. One of the more famous of these attempts was the Aerocar, built in 1949 by Moulton Taylor, an aeronautical engineer from Oregon who wanted to create the only plane you could drive to the store. The Aerocar was a two-person, boxy vehicle with foldable wings that could be towed behind the car when driving. In fewer than five minutes, the driver could convert the car to a plane and be up, up, and away! In driving mode, the Aerocar could reach speeds up to sixty miles per hour. As a plane, it flew up to 110 miles per hour. Taylor couldn't attract enough investors in his invention, and even though he marketed it for several years, none were ever sold. He only ended up building six Aerocars, some of which are now in museums.

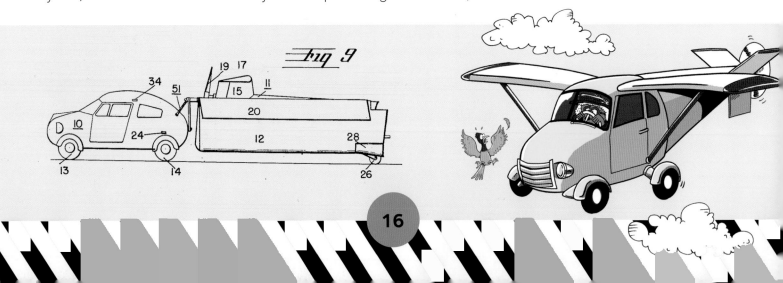

# An Airplane in Every Driveway

**H**enry Ford didn't invent the automobile, but his Model T and assembly line production method made the automobile cheap enough for people to actually buy. After this success, Ford wanted to create the Model T of the air. He called it the Flivver, and it was small enough to fit in the driveway and simple enough for anyone to fly. Prototypes were built in the mid-1920s, and the dream of highways in the sky seemed within reach.

During a test flight, the Flivver's engine stalled and crashed, killing the pilot and the whole project. It was later discovered that the crash was entirely avoidable, but Ford canceled the Flivver project anyway.

*The Ford Flivver after a test flight*

## Will It Change the World?

Several inventors have tried to turn Ford's dream of an airplane in every driveway into a reality. Using the Flivver as inspiration, Lewis Blomeley patented this one-seater airplane/motorcycle in 2013. This "roadable aircraft" has collapsible wings, with no parts having to be removed and left behind when converting from motorcycle to plane. Do you think it will change the world?

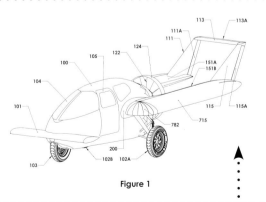

Figure 1

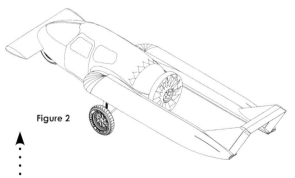

Figure 2

# The Falling Tailor

The airplane was a new invention during Franz Reichelt's lifetime, and many pilots died when their planes broke down in the air. The Austrian-born French tailor and inventor decided to invent a parachute coat that would provide a safe way for pilots to exit a plane and fall to the ground safely. Reichelt's final prototype was a twenty-pound, cloak-like garment that was deployed simply by extending your arms. Reichelt tested several prototypes with dummies, but in 1912, when he thought he had it right, he decided to test out his parachute coat himself . . . by jumping off the first deck of the Eiffel Tower (187 feet). Even though friends tried to stop him, Reichelt said, "I want to try the experiment myself and without trickery, as I intend to prove the worth of my invention." He jumped, and unfortunately, his invention wasn't worth much: the parachute failed to open and Reichelt plummeted to his death.

# Can Submarines Fly?

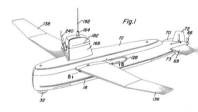

Imagine how incredible it would be to fly thousands of feet in the sky one instant, and then be underwater the next. Donald V. Reid, an engineer for an aircraft manufacturer, and his son, Bruce, decided to find out by building the first operational flying submarine they called the Reid Flying Submarine (the RFS-1, for short). Using leftover parts from crashed aircraft, Reid created several models before finally achieving flying and diving success in the early 1960s (patented in 1963). Unfortunately, the RFS-1 could only dive around twenty-five feet underwater, and it was so heavy that it could only fly for a few minutes at a time.

# The Car That Swam

For nearly thirty years, German inventor Hanns Trippel created dozens of designs for a car that was also a boat. Finally, in the early 1960s, the Amphicar was designed and marketed in the United States, although only around four thousand were ever produced. The main problem was that it wasn't a very good car, nor was it a very good boat. Plus, there wasn't that much demand for a swimming car.

## FYI ◄ ◄ ◄

President Lyndon Johnson owned an Amphicar and liked to trick friends by pretending the brakes stopped working as he headed for a lake. The car would enter the lake, and instead of sinking, it would begin swimming.

### Will It Change the World?

Bogdan Radu patented this flying, swimming, and driving vehicle in 2013. According to the patent, the vehicle stores its rotors (for flying) inside the body while the car is driving or in the water. When in the air, the rotors create the lift (sort of like a helicopter) to fly the vehicle. Radu invented the vehicle in order to "bypass congested roads, traverse water areas, and be able to fly over land or water." Do you think it will change the world?

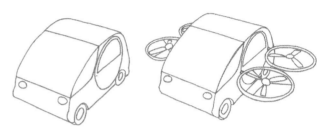

# Toot, Toot! Time to Fill the Tank

Although not as famous as Thomas Edison, Lee De Forest had more than 180 patents, and was the inventor of the Audion tube, the first electrical device that could amplify an electrical signal. This helped make radio broadcasting, television, and long-distance telephone service possible. Known as the father of radio and the grandfather of television, De Forest is not, however, known for his Indicating Device for Fluid Tanks (patented in 1925), a gas tank gauge that blew a whistle whenever a car's gas tank got low. Although it worked, consumers decided that a gas gauge on the dashboard was a better invention.

# Would You Like to Fly Like a Bird?

nventor W.F. Quinby was one of the many whose work with human flight led the way to hang gliders and eventually the first airplane, even though Quinby himself never got off the ground. Here are a few of his beautiful yet not-so-airworthy designs. (Due to Quinby's lack of understanding of how heavier-than-air flight was achieved, none of his inventions ever left the ground, and the inventor remained earthbound his entire life—even though it looks like he never gave up trying.)

## The Flying Apparatus

Flying Apparatus, patented in 1867, presents Quinby's idea of attaching wings to the arms, along with what look like feathers attached to the rear. Quinby stated, "This invention relates to a new and improved flying attachment, whereby a person will be enabled to fly or propel himself through the air similar to birds. In using this invention, a motion is given the arms and legs almost precisely like that in swimming, and the effect is nearly the same."

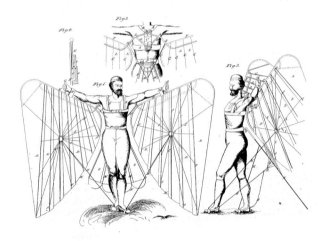

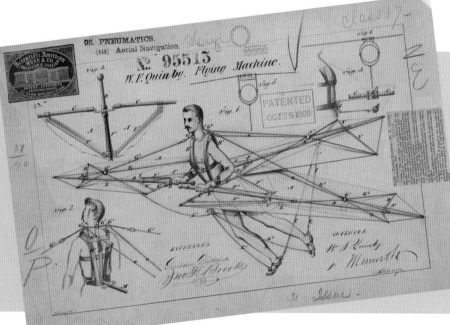

## The Flying Machine

Quinby continued his quest to fly with the Flying Machine, patented in 1869. This invention was "intended to provide an arrangement of temporary sails resembling the wings of birds, which may be readily connected to the body of a person."

## Improvement in Flying Apparatus

Quinby made further improvements to his flying designs in 1872. It doesn't look any safer! This improvement was to "support the flying apparatus entirely on the trunk of the operator and remove all weight from the arms and legs, so they will be free to give their entire strength to the operation."

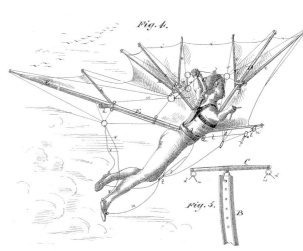

## Aerial Ship

In 1879, Quinby added a wheel and some kites. His Aerial Ship also didn't leave the ground.

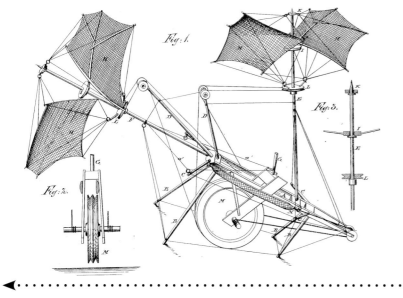

# Driving the Future

An architect, inventor, and scientist who explored possibilities about the future, Buckminster Fuller invented a car (patented in 1937) that looked and acted unlike any automobile then or now.

Built in time for the 1933 World's Fair in Chicago, the Dymaxion Car featured two wheels up front and one in back. Shaped like a gigantic eggplant, it was twice as long as a normal car and could fit eleven people. The steering wheel controlled the back wheel, which made it extremely easy to fit into small parking spaces and perform U-turns. Unfortunately, one of the Dymaxion Car prototypes crashed during the World's Fair, killing the driver and injuring two passengers. This crash was enough to scare off any investors in the project.

## FYI

The word *dymaxion* is a combination of the words *dynamic*, *maximum*, and *tension*.

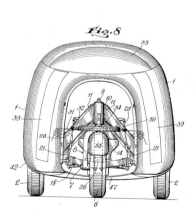

*Fig. 8*

*Only three Dymaxion cars were ever produced, with the only existing model now at the National Automobile Museum in Reno, Nevada. This photo is of a replica built in 2010 by Norman Foster, who used to work with Fuller.*

# Why Not Go Nuclear?

Once the automobile was established as the best way to get from one place to another, carmakers kept making their vehicles better, faster, and more reliable. Years of research and thousands of hours of experimentation have gone into each part of the cars we drive today. However, not every new idea is worth pursuing. One such not-so-hot idea was the Ford Nucleon. In 1958, the Ford Motor Company wanted to create a car that could go five thousand miles without having to refuel. Wouldn't that be wonderful?

What wasn't wonderful was the small nuclear reactor in the car's trunk. The idea for the Nucleon was scrapped once scientists realized the potential danger of highways jam-packed with vehicles that could cause radiation poisoning and mushroom cloud explosions.

# Rocket Packs for All!

Science fiction writers came up with the idea of a rocket-propelled lifting device for people way back in the 1920s. However, as of 2014, we still don't have a reliable jet pack we can use to lift ourselves off to school or work. In the 1960s, the Bell Aerospace Corporation developed the Rocket Pack for the U.S. Army to use, and although it worked rather well, the Army canceled the project since the belt could only keep a person in the air for about twenty seconds. More than fifty years and several more attempts later, we're still waiting for our rocket belts. The rocket pack on the right was patented in 1966 by John Hulbert and Wendell Moore. This design weighed sixty-eight pounds and could fly 300 feet in a circle at about twenty feet off the ground.

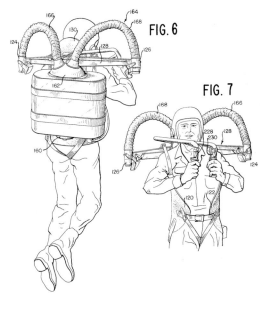

FIG. 6

FIG. 7

## Online
Go to this link to see the 1966 Rocket Pack in use: *http://bit.ly/1lJyB0M*

# No Wheels Needed

For a while during the middle of the last century, inventors thought the next great way to get around would be without wheels, and magazine articles announced that pretty soon we'd all be driving on air instead of on the ground. The vehicle that promised a world of no more potholes was the hovercraft, most versions of which looked like small flying saucers with motorcycle handlebars.

American inventor Charles Rhoades created one such device called the Hover Scooter, which rode six inches off the ground and could handle any terrain, including roads, grass, dirt, and even water. So why were the magazines wrong? Unfortunately, hovercrafts are hard to steer, and if you drive too fast, you may lose the air under you and end up back on the ground. But the worst news for hovercrafters is that the only way to stop one is to turn off the engine and then wait until you slow down. So unless hovercrafts come equipped with anchors, there won't be much demand for them any time soon.

## How Hovercrafts Work

Hovercrafts are simple devices that float on a cushion of air forced under the craft by a fan, providing the hovercraft the lift it needs to get off the ground. A skirt under the platform keeps the air beneath the craft. A motorized fan propels the vehicle forward, and rudders, such as the ones used to steer boats, are used for turning.

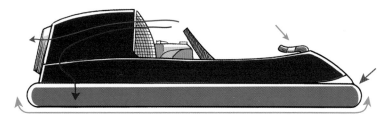

## Make Your Own Hovercraft

### What You Need

  A balloon

  A sports drink cap (that twists open and closed)

  Modeling clay or cyanoacrylate glue (such as Super Glue)

  A CD or DVD you don't need anymore

### What You Do

**1 .** Blow up the balloon and then attach it to the top of the closed drink cap.

**2 .** Roll a piece of the clay into a thin snake and press it around the hole in the CD. (If you're using glue instead, skip to the next step.)

**3 .** Press the drink cap onto the clay, making sure it's as airtight as possible. If you're using glue, place the drink cap over the hole in the CD and glue it into place, making sure to leave no space for air to escape.

**4 .** Open the drink cap and give your craft a gentle push.

**5 .** Next, try using different platforms, such as plastic plates, cardboard, or whatever else you find.

### Online

Watch the Hover Scooter online: *bit.ly/1ktqlz4*

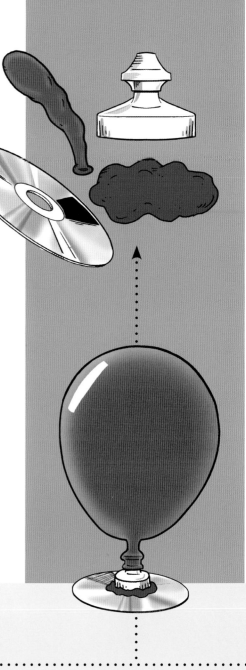

### Here's an Idea!

How about a car with bicycle parts attached so you can pedal home if you run out of gas?

# CHAPTER 2

## Easier, Quicker, Safer . . . Weirder

**P**eople invent things for many different reasons. Early in his career, Thomas Edison decided only to invent things that would make money. Other inventors want to be part of creating a better world in which everyday functions such as brushing your teeth are done more easily and quicker. When an inventor succeeds, we get electric toothbrushes. When an inventor fails, we get the incredibly strange inventions in this chapter.

"I have missed more than nine thousand shots in my career. I have lost almost three hundred games. On twenty-six occasions I have been entrusted to take the game-winning shot, and I missed. I have failed over and over and over again in my life. And that is why I succeed."
—Michael Jordan

*Imagine what life would be like if these inventions did change the world.*

# Concrete Dream Home

*Thomas Edison showing off a model of his concrete house design*

It would take a whole book to list all of Thomas Edison's accomplishments. Inventor, businessman, and hardworking genius, Edison developed the long-lasting lightbulb, and invented the phonograph (which recorded and played back sound) and the motion picture camera. He also made several innovations in electricity, concrete, and more. With more than a thousand patents to his name, Edison helped create the motion picture industry, the recorded music industry, the electronics industry, and more.

However, not every idea of Edison's was a smash hit. One of his failures included cement homes, complete with cement furniture and even pianos. In the early twentieth century, Edison wanted to provide cheap houses for low-income families, and he thought that creating homes from a single mold into which cement was poured would be a great idea. He dreamed of a future where millions of Americans lived in these practically indestructible, fireproof, and bug-proof homes that could be poured in a single day and ready to move into several days later. Nearly a dozen homes were built using this technique in 1917 in Union Township, New Jersey, where they are still lived in.

Unfortunately, the mold was too expensive for builders to afford. It included up to 2,300 different parts that needed to be put together before it could be used to pour the homes. Maybe if Edison's mold had been much simpler, you and all your friends would be living in concrete homes.

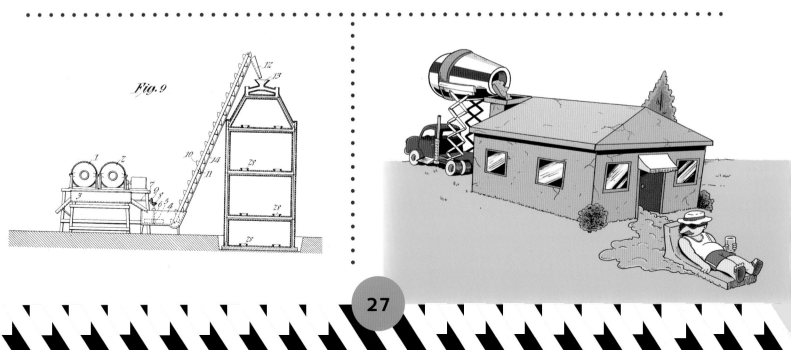

# Is It Possible to Talk to Ghosts?

**K**nown as the Wizard of Menlo Park (where his New Jersey laboratory was located), Thomas Edison would have had to be a real wizard to create an invention that would talk to the dead. But according to a magazine article from 1920, that's exactly what Edison was trying to do. In the article, Edison said, "I have been at work for some time building an apparatus to see if it is possible for personalities which have left this earth to communicate with us." There is no evidence the device was ever built or that, if it was built, it worked.

# How Powerful Is Your Voice?

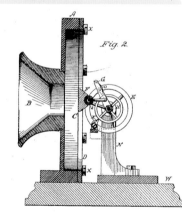

**P**atented in 1878, the Vocal Engine, or phonomotor, was one of Edison's weird failures. The Vocal Engine attempted to use the energy of voices to power a small engine. For instance, say your electric wall clock had stopped. All you would have to do to get it going again would be to speak into the mouthpiece (labeled B in the diagram to the right). Your voice vibrations would turn the wheel (labeled E), which, when connected to a belt, would drive a machine.

But one voice, no matter how much it is used, does not have enough energy to set anything in motion. According to author William M. Hartmann in his book *Signals, Sound, and Sensation*, it would take "one million people, all talking at once" to light a sixty-watt lightbulb.

# Eat 'n' Wash

Dishwashers have become a near necessity in today's kitchens. Since it was first invented in 1850, there have been many, many patents that improved dishwashers to the point where they are to-day. However, not every patent has been helpful. This 2000 patent by Harold DeHart combines the dining room table with the dishwasher so you would no longer have to "transport the dishes to and from the table." Simply eat and place the dirty dishes in the washer underneath the table.

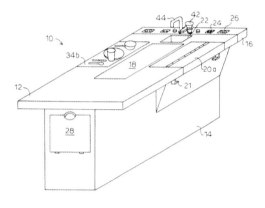

FYI

The first reliable dishwasher was invented in 1886 by Josephine Cochrane. She didn't have to wash dishes herself, but she invented her device to prevent her servants from chipping her dinnerware.

# Ejection Notice

Having trouble getting up in the morning? Do you simply ignore your alarm clock? Of course you do! That's why this bed was invented by George Seaman way back in 1892. The bed is wound sort of like a clock, and is attached to an alarm clock. Once the alarm goes off, the mechanism under the bed is triggered, and the bed's occupant is "spilled upon the floor." You will only oversleep once.

# All Snug on a Bouncing Rug

T he next time you're staying over at a friend's house and have to sleep on the floor, remember that in 1976, Donald Stephens knew your pain. He devised a rug with an inflatable backing that, when inflated, became a rug-covered mattress. Imagine the fun if we all had one of these!

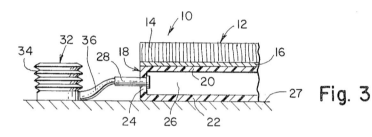

Fig. 3

# Bed in the Clouds

Y our bedroom only has so much space. Wouldn't it be great if you could store your bed somewhere until you needed it at night? How about the ceiling? This patented, but never produced, invention is basically a floating bed. Inventor William Calderwood imagined filling the mattress with helium so your bed would rise when you do. When you need it, simply reach up for the tether, pull it down, and hop on it before it floats back up. The inventor imagined that just about any piece of furniture could rest on the ceiling until needed.

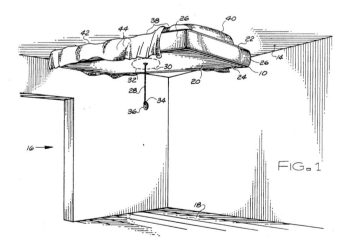

FIG. 1

# Ride and Watch

**H**ave you ever felt guilty for just sitting around watching TV instead of doing something like exercising? Have your parents ever told you to get off the couch and go outside and ride your bike? This invention, called 123GoTV, takes care of all that by making you ride a bike to power the TV. It's an exercise-activated switch that includes a bicycle mounted on a stand. When you pedal the bicycle, it sends a signal to the switch, which turns on the TV. Patented in 2011 by Margie Mullen, the 123GoTV was produced, and as of 2012, around fifty had been sold. For some reason, the 123GoTV is no longer for sale.

## Online

Watch an original TV commercial for 123GoTV here: *bit.ly/V23tAp*

# Dog Run

**Y**ou can burn a lot of calories jogging or walking, but your arms are just sort of hanging there while your legs do all the work. How rude! Inventor Richard Reinert decided to fix this "problem" with his 2001 invention, which is a treadmill for your legs *and* arms, "similar to four-footed animals." A belt around your waist holds you up as you bend over and gallop your way to fabulous fitness.

FYI

People started inventing exercise machines in the late 1800s, and one of the most successful inventors was Gustav Zander. He built dozens of machines, including this velocipede motion apparatus, to help people develop all the muscles of the body. Many of his basic designs are still in use today.

# Living in Bucky's World

*The Biosphere is a geodesic, dome-shaped museum dedicated to the environment in Montreal, Canada.*

**B**uckminster Fuller developed and improved several inventions, including the geodesic dome structure. Although originally invented after World War I by Walther Bauersfeld, the geodesic dome was perfected and patented by Fuller in the 1940s. The dome is constructed using a pattern of connected triangles to form a structure that encloses the greatest amount of space with the least amount of surface area and is quite strong. Fuller's domes have been used for auditoriums, weather observatories, storage facilities, museums, hotels, and sports stadiums.

However, Fuller's Dymaxion Houses never caught on. Like Edison before him (see page 27), Fuller wished to create a home that just about anyone could purchase. He designed a few different prototypes, all of which (with the proper project funding) could be ordered by mail and delivered to where you wanted to place it. The design included a round, aluminum-covered structure with a waterless toilet, a fogger instead of a shower, revolving dresser drawers and storage shelves, a water-recycling system, and more. One reason his homes never changed the world was that they looked so weird—as if they belonged in a science fiction movie, not in a neighborhood.

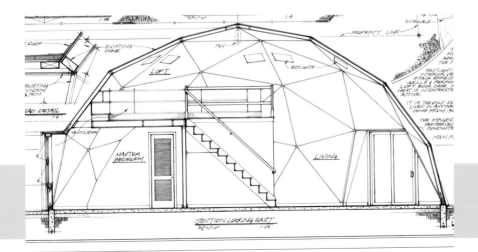

*Assembled in approximately seven hours on Tuesday, April 19, 1960, this was the plan for Buckminster and his wife's private residence, called the Dome Home. It was the only one ever built.*

*Online*

Go to the following link for more information on Bucky Fuller: *bit.ly/1nudWw0*

*Make Your Own Dome*

### What You Need

11 gumdrops or other soft candy

Toothpicks

Paper plate

### What You Do

1. Build a pentagon with 5 of the gumdrops and 5 of the toothpicks.
2. Using the gumdrops and toothpicks, build a triangle above each toothpick in the pentagon.
3. Connect the gumdrops of these new triangles with toothpicks.
4. Stick one toothpick in each of the gumdrops at the top of your structure. Lean them toward the center and then join them with a gumdrop. This is a simple dome. If you want to make a bigger structure, make your base larger and build around it.

# FYI ◀ ◀ ◀

Bucky Fuller felt that the death of his young daughter in 1922 was due, in part, to the damp and drafty home they lived in. He then had a vision in which he was floating above the ground bathed in a sphere of light. A voice told him that he belonged to the universe and that, if he applied himself, he could change the world. So began Fuller's journey to write, create, and invent.

*Would you want to live here? This is an early prototype of Fuller's Dymaxion House.*

# Food Flops

As we move faster, doing more and more, with barely any time to make our own meals, food companies and inventors have tried to come to the rescue with food that's easier, quicker, and, hopefully, delicious (although that doesn't always seem to matter). Here are a few tasty treats that didn't quite make it.

## Toasted

Toasters are mainly used for toasting bread. But that hasn't kept companies from trying to come up with other things that can be toasted. After the success of Pop-Tarts in the 1960s, inventors came up with Toaster Eggs, Toaster Chicken Patties, and Toaster French Fries—none of which succeeded. The best attempt, however, has to go to Reddi-Wip's Reddi-Bacon, which was precooked bacon in a foil pouch that you simply dropped in the toaster. Unfortunately, fat sometimes leaked from the pouch, causing a fire hazard.

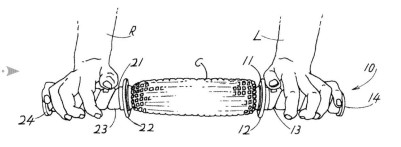

## Corn on the Hog

Tired of Junior not eating his veggies? How about attaching motorcycle handles to a corncob? This invention, if ever produced, would do much, much more. The handles, when activated, rotate the corn and make motorcycle noises. Although this patent was granted to Nicholas Kretschmer way back in 2001, this awesome invention has yet to be produced.

## Just in Case

For $81, you can now purchase an edible smartphone case. Made entirely of rice cake, the Senbei Rice Cracker Cover is made in Japan and is "great in an emergency when you are desperate for a snack." Unfortunately, the case will probably break if dropped, but you have five seconds to pick it up and eat it.

## Adult Baby Food

In 1974, Gerber released Gerber Singles, which were larger servings of their baby foods. These weren't for larger babies, though—they were aimed at college students, who were smart enough to veer away from this product.

## Ice Cream Drone

Is rotating your ice cream cone as you eat it too much effort? Well, with this invention, patented in 1999 by Richard Hartman, all you have to do is stick out your tongue and let the device do all the hard work for you as it turns the ice cream 'round and 'round.

## Food with Feet

This 1969 invention is for anyone who never understood why hot dogs are "dogs." It's a hot dog with dog legs. Unfortunately, inventor Edward Kiwala failed to invent the bun to go with these dogs.

*Fig. 1*

# Do Babies Need a Window View?

Living in a cramped apartment in a busy city? Do you feel like your baby needs more sunlight than she is getting? Try the Portable Baby Cage! Patented in the United States by Emma Reed in 1923, the Portable Baby Cage is exactly what it sounds like. Simply suspend the cage outside your window, make sure all the supports are in place, and drop the baby in. The baby is then free to take in the sights from the eighteenth floor. The inventor thought correctly that babies needed plenty of sunshine and fresh air to develop properly, but realized children born in crowded cities couldn't easily get either. Her portable cage provided both.

This device was used for a short time in crowded English cities before disappearing forever. No matter how safe this contraption actually was, it simply looked way too dangerous.

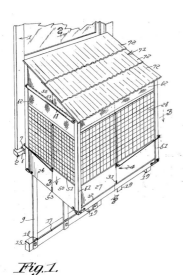

*Fig. 1.*

# Do Dogs Need Toy Dog Vacuums?

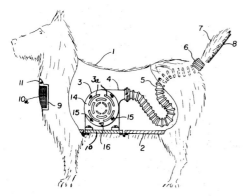

Most dogs don't like to take baths. Many also don't like getting their hair cut. They'll jump, whine, and sometimes even bite. This 1973 invention by A. Zaleski was meant to calm these poor creatures while they're being groomed. What is it? On the outside it's a realistic-looking toy dog. However, inside is a vacuum meant to suck up a real dog's recently cut hair from its body. Once a dog's hair has been cut, the groomer would turn on the vacuum dog and pull out its tail, which acts as the vacuum's suction hose. Since the vacuum is disguised as a dog, the real dog shouldn't freak out … unless seeing another dog's tail pulled from its body while making sucking sounds is something that would bother your dog. By the way, the tail end can be converted to a blow dryer as well.

# Putting the Kids to Work

With this invention, kids could start earning their keep before they're even out of diapers. This pedal-operated lawnmower, patented by Deanna Porath in 1984, combines exercise and mowing lawns into one fun activity. Although, if you're young enough to still be riding a tricycle, you're also probably young enough to get seriously hurt by this contraption.

# Is It a "Crush" or a "Bromb"?

Tolbert Lanston invented this combination comb and brush in 1871. This was designed "in such a manner that both operate on the hair at the same time." Unfortunately for the inventor, this combination just wasn't seen as needed.

# Baird's Bizarre Inventions

John Logie Baird was a Scottish scientist, engineer, and the inventor of the first television that transmitted a moving image. While considered one of the 100 Greatest Britons, this honor was not bestowed on him for his earlier, not-so-successful inventions. These unsuccessful inventions included: a glass razor, which although rust-resistant was not shatter-resistant; inflatable shoes; and the Baird under-sock, which was basically a sock you put on before you put on your socks for extra warmth.

PSSSH!

## FYI ◀ ◀ ◀ ◀

Tolbert Lanston became much better known as the inventor of a mechanical typesetting system to replace the difficult task of hand-setting every letter when printing a book.

# Out of the Fire, into More Trouble

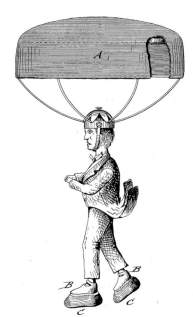

Inventing a useful means of escaping a dangerous fire inside a building is a noble cause. However, it's probably not such a great idea to invent something that could cause more harm than the fire.

## Safety Hat

Benjamin Oppenheimer's Improvement in Fire Escapes was patented in 1879, and the description of this contraption is best left to the inventor himself: "This invention relates to an improved fire escape or safety device, by which a person may safely jump out of the window of a burning building from any height, without injury and without the least damage, on the ground. It consists of a parachute attached, in suitable manner, to the upper part of the body, in combination with overshoes having elastic bottom pads of suitable thickness to take up the concussion with the ground."

## Safety Wings

In 1909, Pasquale Nigro, an Englishman living in Tennessee, thought wings would provide a better means of escaping a burning building. He stated that once the wearer strapped on the wings, "the air imprisoned beneath the fabric material [serves] to uphold the wearer and break the force of his fall."

Fig. 1.

### Will It Change the World?

This Fire Escape Parachute was patented in 1998 by Yu-Li Yu and has yet to be produced. Do you think it will change the world?

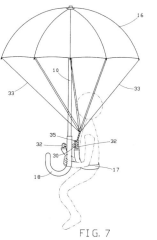

FIG. 7

## Rappel to Safety

This 1893 invention by Orville Matts was meant to be a portable device you bring with you when visiting a tall building. If the building catches on fire, you hook the device to a window ledge, snap the body belt around your body, place a foot in the stirrup, grasp the friction roller gripping device, and sail downward rapidly and safely—much as a cliff climber rappels down a slope.

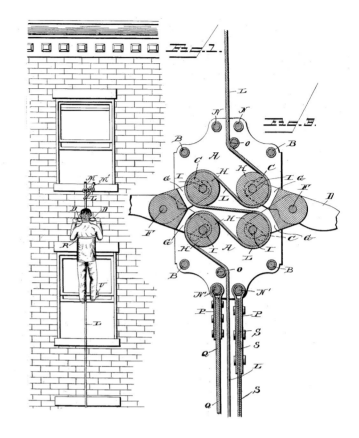

## FYI

Although fire escape chutes can be found on some old buildings, using a slide-type enclosure to quickly escape a building never really became all that popular. They certainly look like fun, though!

## Here's an Idea!

How about a building with fire escapes that double as a full playground for kids who don't live close to a park? If a fire ever breaks out in the building, the kids will know exactly how to escape.

# Lollipops for the Lazy

Even though the idea of putting food (especially sweets) on a stick has been around since the Middle Ages, the Bradley Smith Company of New Haven, Connecticut, was able to patent the term LollyPop in 1931, after producing the hard candy on a stick since 1908. Since then, inventors have been coming up with delivery devices for the delivery device—things that hold the stick that's holding the candy.

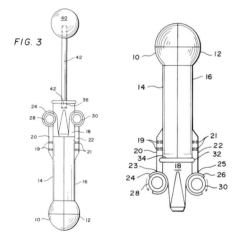

FIG. 3

## Pocket Pop

This device, patented by Thomas Coleman and three others in 1996, acts as a lollipop "stick" that also folds up over an unfinished pop, protecting it from dirt.

## Froggy-Pop

Peggy Levay patented this lollipop device in 1997. Put this contraption in your mouth and it looks like you're eating a frog, mouse, or other creepy critter.

## Fowl-lipop

The inventors of the Pocket Pop above also came up with this dandy in 2000. Why? Because everyone wants a "limp feeling" chicken lollipop.

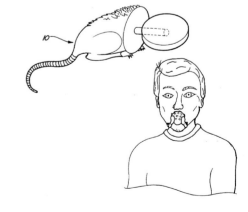

## Cell-ipop

Jules Schecter received a patent for this device in 1997. This contraption records and plays back messages. It rings. It also stores a lollipop antenna, which you can pull out of the phone when you need a treat.

## Pop and Pop

A patent was granted in 2003 to Al Cecere for this combination lollipop/drinking straw/ beverage bottle cap. You have to suck on the lollipop candy for a while before you can get to the drink. Then, you get to enjoy the drink and the pop at the same time.

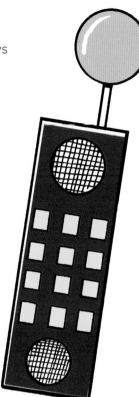

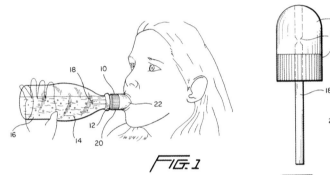

FIG. 1

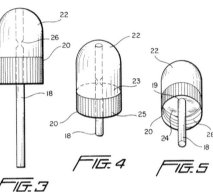

FIG. 3

FIG. 4

FIG. 5

## Jewel Pop

If you can't finish your lollipop in one sitting, you can use this device, patented in 1995 by Sandra J. Wyzykowski, to store … and wear … your candy until next time.

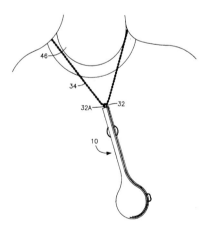

### Twin Spins

The Thomas Edisons of the lollipop world, Thomas Coleman and gang (see above), were granted a patent in 1997 for this device for when one lollipop just isn't enough. When turned on, the contraption spins the lollipops for you.

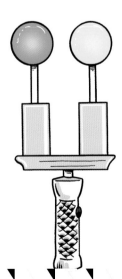

# Lady Edison Goes to the Beach

**B**eulah Louise Henry wasn't married to Thomas Edison, but she was called Lady Edison from the 1920s through the 1970s because of the number of useful items she invented. Over the course of her life, she patented more than forty inventions and had at least seventy more she never patented. Some of her inventions include a duplicating device for typewriters (it made up to four copies as you were typing) and baby dolls that could be bathed and whose eyes changed color, as well as innovations for sewing machines, can openers, and office machines.

*Henry with Miss Illusion, a doll with eyes that could change color and close*

As with the other great minds in this chapter, not all of Henry's inventions caught on. One such item was the Parasol Bag. The next time you're at the beach, think of how difficult it is to carry all your stuff as you plod along in the sand. You need your shoes, towel, book, beach blanket, sunscreen, chair, and umbrella. Henry came up with an umbrella that also doubled as a bag to carry all your stuff. Patented in 1926, the Parasol Bag failed to catch on, even though most beachgoers wouldn't mind having one.

# Two Ears Are Better Than One

**T**ired of passing the phone back and forth with his wife while talking to their son, Roger Heap invented and patented this contraption in 1952. The t-shaped plastic device fits over the earpiece of the (now old-fashioned) phone receiver, making three-way conversations simple and fun.

# Weird Beard

There are several inventions for making sure your sideburns, mustache, and beard are neat and even; however, this one, patented by Scott Bonge in 2011, takes all the guesswork out of crafting your goatee (a beard that only covers your chin). Adjust the shaving guide to the desired shape, place it in your mouth, clamp down on the mouthpiece, and shave away.

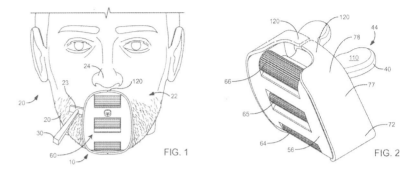

FIG. 1

FIG. 2

# How Will Your Hair Fare?

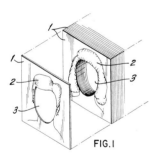

FIG.1

FIG.2

This 1992 invention, patented by Kim Jin, is for people who take great pains in selecting the proper hairstyle. Instead of imagining how a new look will look, simply stick your face in one of the cardboard hairstyles, check yourself out in the mirror, and decide if this is the new you. This invention would work for hairstyles or for people wishing for a wig or hairpiece.

## Here's an Idea!
How about a combination toothbrush, hairbrush, and ear cleaner?

# CHAPTER 3

## Fun & Games

We love to be entertained, and inventors are always looking for ways to show us a good time. They invent games, toys, sports, as well as new ways to experience movies and music. Only a very few of these ever make it to market, and of those, only a very few ever get noticed. The very best make the inventors millionaires. The rest end up in a book like this that celebrates how much fun these could have been … would have been … but sadly, aren't available for one reason or another.

"All I did was come up with what I thought was a fun idea [and] it just grew and grew and grew." -Ralph H. Baer, inventor of video games

*Have fun, but be warned: the toys, games, and overall fun in this chapter have not been tested. You may set yourself on fire at band practice, get smacked upside the head with a ball, or play with a doll so creepy it will disturb your dreams.*

# Can You Take Your Hamster with You?

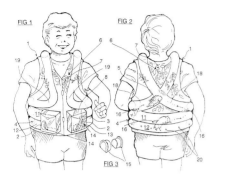

Dogs get to go on walks. Cats prowl around the yard or through the house. But what about hamsters, mice, and other little critters? They're stuck in cages! Inventor Brice Belisle tried to free these little guys to go where their owners go with this pet vest (patented in 1999) that's fun for you and your pet. With pet containers instead of pockets, and interlinking tubes that travel across the wearer's torso, the roving rodents could burrow, chase each other, eat, and look at the sights while you walk around town or sit in social studies class. Sadly, this invention was never produced.

# Make Yourself at Home

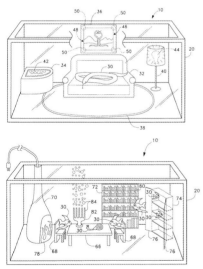

Feeling badly for your pet snake, fish, or other small pets for having to live among rocks, shells, and other annoying natural items? Well, give them the "human-like living quarters" of this 2001 invention by Olivia Terry and Lauren Dipolito. Your pet snake can lounge on a mini couch or sit by the fire. Or, your fish can enjoy a candlelight dinner before deciding what to read from the bookcase. Who said animals can't be sophisticated!?

## Here's an Idea!

How about an aquarium jacket? It will keep you warm and distracted . . . although it's also going to be quite heavy. And stay away from knives and other sharp objects. And don't fall down. And beware of cats and seagulls.

# The Screeching Toy

You have probably come across all sorts of toys, stuffed animals, and dolls that talk or otherwise make some sort of noise. Well, Thomas Edison was ahead of his time with his Talking Doll, which ended up a dismal failure back in 1890 (patented in 1888). Edison, working with other inventors, shrank his phonograph invention until it could fit into a toy doll. Kids whose parents could afford the $10 ($25 with a fancy dress) to purchase the doll (about one month's salary for most Americans back then) would turn a crank in the doll's back to hear a nursery rhyme.

There were so many things wrong with this poor doll that it's difficult to know where to start. First off, since the recording industry was still in its infancy, the recorded nursery rhymes were difficult to hear and many of them screeched and scared the children. Children also had to turn the crank at just the right speed, otherwise the rhyme would come out either sounding like the Chipmunks (too fast) or Charlie Brown's teacher (too slow). Also, the wax recordings wore out quickly, the dolls often arrived in stores already broken, and perhaps worst of all, the dolls' tin bodies were not cuddly at all. Edison later remarked that, "the voices of the little monsters were exceedingly unpleasant to hear." Of the 2,500 dolls produced, only five hundred were sold.

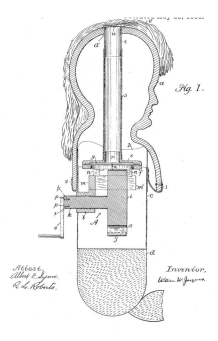

## Online
Hear what one of the dolls sounded like here: *1.usa.gov/1hFEJVD*

# Happy Face, Sad Face, Scary Face

Thomas Hong invented this re-configurable doll in 2008, and it comes with a blank face and plenty of lips, eyes, ears, and noses, which you can place on the face. Like a more cuddly Mr. Potato Head, this doll also has more expressions than the taters, although it's hard to tell what the doll in this illustration is feeling.

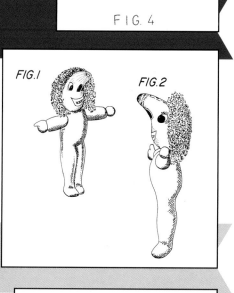

FIG. 4

# Banana Face

There isn't much information on the patent application for this 1992 doll designed by Otto Alber. It's just a doll with a banana for a nose and shrubbery for hair.

# Run the Other Way

When you see this doll coming your way, run! Patented in 1915 by Louis Aronson, it emits sounds and moves, much as Frankenstein's monster did. Simply press on its stomach, and prepare to be scared . . . very scared.

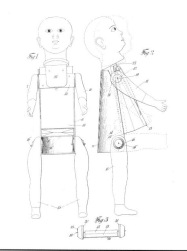

ny one of the following games could have become the next national pastime, as popular as baseball, tennis, or football. Unfortunately, for one reason or another, they didn't.

## Headaches Galore

In 1967, this patent was granted to Arthur Ryan, who took the saying "Just use your head" in a very different direction. The Head-Mounted Rebounding Device was invented to provide "enjoyable and beneficial physical activity . . . in which you project a ball . . . through the air without use of the hands."

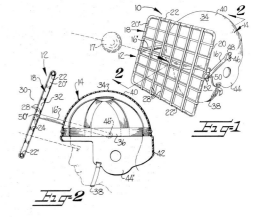

## Aim Carefully

Patented in 1989 by Wilfredo Diaz, this game/device is just like soccer or hockey, except the goal isn't on a poll or behind the goalie—it's between the goalie's legs. What could possibly go wrong with this setup!?

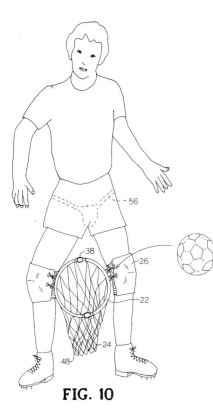

**FIG. 10**

## Soccer Knights

Here's another goal-protecting game, but this one uses shields to keep the ball from the goal. No lances required. R. Danford Lehman and Michael Williams patented this game in 1985.

## Waist-Ball Anyone?

W. Walker was granted a patent for this game in 1973. This is a game of skill in which "the first player manipulates his waist to swing the ball upwardly to the level of the second player's waist, and the second player manipulates his body to catch the ball in one of the openings of his device." It also seems like a good game for young people to "mix and communicate with each other."

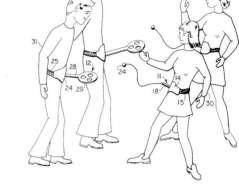

## Wrist-Ball

How about a game of what looks like wrist volleyball?
Patented in 1960 by Georgia Glintz, this device was created to develop "the coordination of muscles" and "skills in the judgment of distances."

## Hip Hip Game

Ralph Flanders patented this game in 1981. We have no idea what's going on with this contraption, so here's what the patent application says: "An exercise and game apparatus in which a ball having shafts attached thereto is rotatably mounted by the shafts within a hoop. Two attachment bars extend diametrically outwardly from the hoop and are secured to devices on belts around two people using the apparatus. Handles on the bars are provided to assist in steadying the apparatus as a revolving movement of the person's hips causes the ball to spin within the annular ring. Baskets may be provided on the attachment bars so that the people using the device can throw a ball back and forth, attempting to throw the ball into the basket on the opposite side of the hoop while continuing the hip movement necessary to keep the ball spinning."

## No Bounce, No Dunk

This creation, patented by John Blue in 1997, is one part basketball, one part badminton, and one part crazy fun. Called Air Ball by the inventor, the ball must be hit to your opponent's side without bouncing, and the object of the game is to get the ball into one of your opponent's nets.

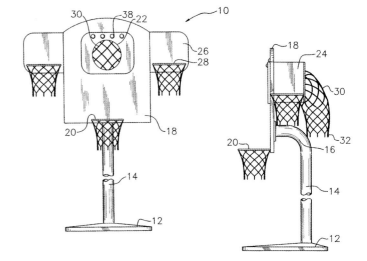

## Hand Hoops

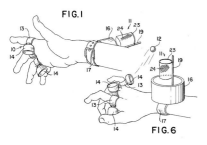

Who needs a court or a basketball hoop or even feet when you can play this basketball game with just one hand? Aida Sweeney and Patsy Boccardi patented this hand-version of basketball in 1964.

## Basket-Foot Ball

Harvey King, perhaps tired of having a plain-old basketball hoop in his driveway, patented this contraption in 2002. This novel backboard allows you to shoot a ball like a basketball or pass it through the top net like a football for more points.

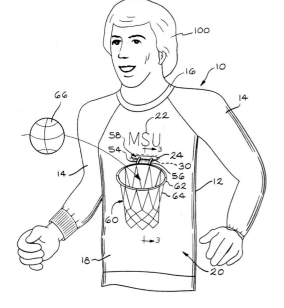

## A Sure-to-Get-Hurt Shirt

Kirk Bristor invented this shirt in 1993 so you could bring the game of basketball with you wherever you went. Just don't let anyone dunk on you.

# Two Noses Up

Imagine a car screeching to a halt in a cloud of burnt rubber and exhaust. Or a bad guy smoking a big cigar. When moviegoers walked into the Cinestage Theatre in Chicago to see the 1960 movie The Scent of Mystery, they were promised a movie that would not only show cars and cigars, but also let you smell them.

That's right: This mystery had action, suspense, and scents. The process of adding aroma to a movie was patented in 1956 and was at first called Scentovision and later changed to Smell-O-Vision. The invention included perfumes that were mechanically released during certain scenes in the movie. Fans would then blow the aromas into the theater. Unfortunately, most of the reviews of Smell-O-Vision were rotten. The contraption made a weird hissing noise, moviegoers in the back didn't smell the aromas until after the scene was over, and the odors didn't go away, they just mixed with the other odors, so soon the theater smelled like everything and nothing at the same time.

## FYI

Another smelly invention called AromaRama released aromas into a movie theater's air-conditioning system. It, too, failed to catch on. One magazine called the competing inventions the "Battle of the Smellies."

## Will It Change the World?

Dr. Kenichi Okada of Keio University in Tokyo is working on a desktop printer that will deliver odors instead of ink. Okada believes his invention could reinvent the way we view movies, TV shows, advertisements, and even old photographs. Do you think it will change the world?

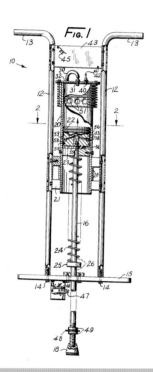

Fig. 1

peaking of pogo sticks, how about one that has a fully operational engine that runs on gasoline? This invention, patented by Gordon Spitzmesser in 1960, was called the Hop Rod, and the engine did the bouncing for you. All you had to do was stand on it and get bounced around. Even though advertisements said the Hop Rod was "extremely safe and harmless and tons of tremendous entertainment value," safety concerns kept it from being the biggest thing since the Hula-Hoop.

## Online

Check out the commercial for the Hop Rod here: *bit.ly/1hbyWbJ*

# Ski for Three

Fig. 1

harles Marsh patented this shuffling-type toy in 1976 to help kids develop teamwork and coordination. Races could have been fun, too.

# Cube-ism

Everybody wants to have fun, and there's no better way than inventing a game, toy, or idea that is so much fun that everybody wants to buy it. Imagine, for instance, being the inventor of Rubik's Cube, the three-dimensional puzzle game. Erno Rubik patented the device in 1983, and more than 350 million cubes have been bought. It was an instant sensation, and it continues to be popular more than thirty years later. Now, imagine being Larry Nichols, who patented a similar cube-like device in 1972. His toy looked like a Rubik's Cube, even though it was smaller, and you played with it in much the same way. However, it didn't catch on, even though it also looks like a lot of fun. He even tried suing Rubik and his toy company for patent infringement, but lost.

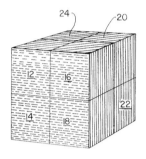

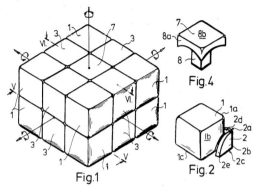

Nichols' Cube (left) vs.
Rubik's Cube (above)

## FYI

It took inventor Erno Rubik one month to solve his own invention.

# Is Your Playing Hot?

Burn down the house with this trumpet (patented in 1981 by Pat Vidas) that not only helps you play the hottest tunes, but also emits, upon request, a large, controlled flame. Whatever you do, make sure you're not a second-chair player!

# Food Should Be Fun

The inventors of the following foods think food should be exciting and fun. What do you think?

### What Color Is Your Ketchup?

Around 2000, Heinz, the condiment company, introduced EZ Squirt, a collection of colored ketchups, which included Blastin' Green, Funky Purple, Stellar Blue, and Mystery Color (which could be orange, teal, or purple). The ketchup came in squeezable containers so it was easy to "draw" wacky shapes and faces on your food. At first, these weirdly colored ketchups did okay, but eventually, families tired of purple fries and green burgers, and EZ Squirt was discontinued.

### Will It Change the World?

With his 2005 patent application, Daniel Witkowski wanted to make eating fun once again by turning your soup or cereal into a game of skill. With this invention, you can link noodle monkeys together, put together

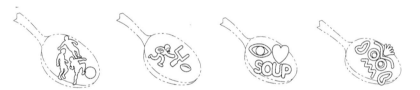

*Which is your favorite?*

a noodle puzzle, write a noodle sentence, create a noodle face, and more. Since "food is something to inspire imagination and provide entertainment," why not also make it interactive!? Do you think it will change the world?

# FYI ◀◀◀

Alphabet-shape pasta noodles have been a hit with kids and adults since the 1880s, when they were first introduced.

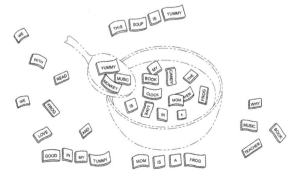

## Carbonated Milk

There's milk, there's soda, and for a short time in 2009, there was Vio, the world's first (and perhaps last) carbonated milk product. The makers of Vio called it "100-percent different," as well as "the world's first vibrancy drink." It contained 15 percent of your daily calcium and came in these fruity flavors: Citrus Burst, Very Berry, Peach Mango, and Tropical Colada. Unfortunately, it was full of sugar and didn't taste all that great.

## Really Hot Dog

The only thing better than a hotdog is a hotdog with the feet, tail, and head of a dog! Edward Coleman patented this novel idea in 1960. According to the patent application, "the parts may be readily detached from the edible frankfurter and the frankfurter may be eaten if desired."

## Eat Your Toys

Playing dolls can make a person very hungry. Valerie Gardner decided to help out these poor, hungry kids with this 1998 invention: clothing and other accessories for dolls that can be eaten.

## Hot Dog Pretzel on a Stick

Patented in 1990 by Robert M. Kempher, the hot dog pretzel on a stick was certainly meant for state fairs and carnivals. And although you can buy pretzel dogs in some grocery stores, you'll have to add your own stick.

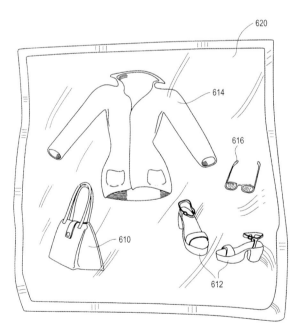

# Built for Two

Nobody would ever be cold or wet again if all our coats could expand into Double Coats. Patented in 1953 by Howard Ross, this coat was meant for people caught in a storm at outdoor sporting events. If Double Coats were around today, we'd wear them everywhere … wouldn't we? Imagine playing tag, jumping rope, and going through revolving doors in one of these!

# Forget the Suntan Lotion!

Patented in 1991 by Frederick Sevilla, this helium-filled sun shade will protect you from harmful ultraviolet rays. Simply attach the giant, flat, disc-shaped balloon to your clothing or your beach chair, and bring the shade with you wherever you go. Don't forget your helium tank!

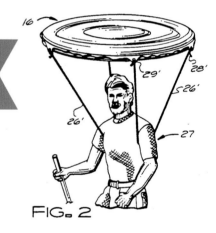

FIG. 2

# Who Needs Binoculars?

Although most people are perfectly okay watching birds and other flying critters from a distance, this 1999 invention by David Leslie guarantees you a front-row seat. Simply put this bird feeder contraption on your head—and whatever you do, don't sneeze!

# Fun in the Tub

After a fun-filled day, wouldn't it be awesome to take a nice bath? Around the late 1800s, rocking baths were all the rage. The thinking was that if you couldn't get to the beach and enjoy the ocean waves, you could create some of your own waves in the comfort of your home. Sitting in water wasn't just considered relaxing back then, however; it was also supposed to be good for your health. Known as hydropathy, this belief that water can cure ailments was quite popular for at least fifty years, with water cure centers opening in Europe and in the United States. To cash in on this craze, Richard Straube invented the bath on the left in 1899 so people could get the benefits of these water centers at home. This model, when emptied, could also be used as a rocking chair.

Unfortunately for rocking bathers, no matter what the advertisements said, water got everywhere. Otto Hensel came to the rescue in 1900 with the rocking bathtub on the right, which featured a neck curtain that kept the water where it belonged.

Even though rocking baths fell out of fashion fairly quickly, hydropathy, which is now called hydrotherapy, is still popular with physical therapists, who use water jets, whirlpool baths, hot tubs, mineral baths, and more to help their patients recover from injuries.

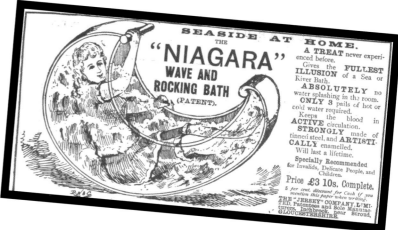

*An advertisement from September, 1891, extols the benefits of rocking in your bath.*

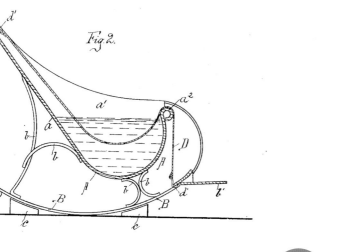

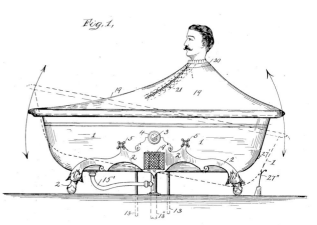

# CHAPTER 4

## Bringing up Baby . . . & Fido

The first thing you'll probably notice about the inventions in this chapter is that they don't make babies' and pets' lives any better—in fact, in some cases, they're dangerous. These inventions are for the people who have to take care of the babies and the pets: the parents. From toilet training and picking up pet poop to learning to walk and making sure you don't run away, the inventors of the following devices think they know how to enrich the lives of children, animals, and parents everywhere. What's interesting, however, is how similar many of the inventions for the babies are to the inventions for the pets.

*You and your animal friends will thank your parents for not using any of these contraptions!*

*"One of the things that really surprised us is that adult dogs behave toward their caregivers like human children do." –Dr. Lisa Horn, who studied how dogs treat their owners similar to the way young children treat their parents*

# Take a Stand

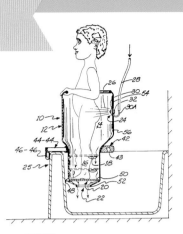

For most babies, bath time is fun time, with splashing, playing with toys, and getting your hair washed. But for parents who don't want to get wet, it can be a hassle. Jack Paden attempted to come to the rescue with this 1991 invention. It's a container you place in the bathtub that acts as a mini-shower for the child. Plop the kid in, hose him off, and you're done.

# Baby in a Bucket

Here's a similar invention, with a much more frightening illustration, patented in 2000 by Frances Tuoriniemi and two others. The invention is simply a long bucket a baby can practice standing in while immersed up to the waist in water. According to the patent application, "baby feels herself lighter in water and is encouraged to stand. If the baby loses balance the walls will support her from falling." The premise of the invention is that a parent can take the baby in a bucket into the shower with them.

# Got Soap?

Tired of chasing your dog or cat, holding him down, and spraying him with soap and water, all while getting bitten and scratched? Perhaps it's time for a Pet Shower. Patented in 1997 by Brian Moore, this device is a compartment that's hooked up to your home's water line. Simply put your pet inside the device, close the door (making sure your pet's head is sticking out), add soap, turn on the water, and sit back while Fido gets a shower he won't soon forget!

# Who Needs a Helping Hand?

Thomas V. Zelenka of Hanford, California, patented the Baby Patting Machine in 1971. According to patent documents, Zelenka wished to create something for those poor parents who "must resort to patting the baby to sleep by repeated pats upon the hind parts thereof." Instead of spending all that time patting their baby's bottom, parents need only install the mechanical arm with a soft pad at the end to do the patting for them. Good night, kid, and hello Netflix! This invention was never produced, most likely because too many things could go wrong leaving a baby alone with a machine like this, thus saving a generation of kids from weird dreams of getting spanked in their sleep.

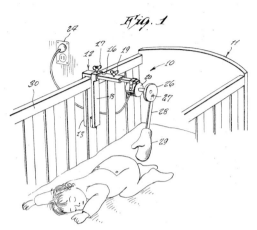

## Will It Change the World?

For parents who need an extra set of hands, they can now keep them free with a Zaky Infant Pillow. Invented by Yamile Jackson, these pillows are the shape, size, and weight of human hands, and if you put them in the clothes dryer for a few minutes, they'll even be warm. They're flexible and can go over, under, and around the baby, helping him feel comforted and supported while his parents nap in the next room. Yamile's 2008 patent application is still pending. Do you think it will change the world?

# Canine Petter

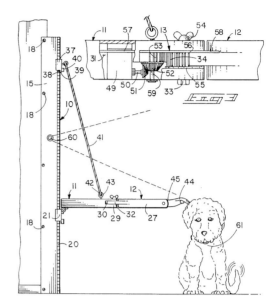

hat does your doggy do when you're not home? Who gives him attention? Doesn't he get lonely? To keep your pet from realizing he's alone when you're not around, Rita Della Vecchia invented this device in 1989, which gives your dog some loving when you're at school and your parents are at work. The application states that this invention "provides a mechanical device to simulate petting for pets without requiring human attention." When your pet walks onto the base, the petting and scratching machine turns on.

# Feline Scratcher

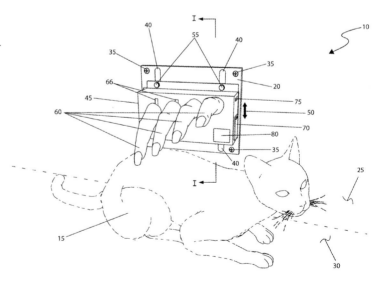

his scratcher, patented by Allison Schmuck in 2012 provides cats with four motion-activated fingers covered with a latex material so that they feel like real fingers. The device would be mounted on the wall, and when the cat came up to it, the fingers would start moving, giving the cat "entertainment, companionship, and solace when the owner is not present or available."

# Too Pooped to Walk Your Dog?

The worst part about walking your dog is when you have to pick up his business. Sure, you could just leave it there, but that's usually against the law, and it's gross. Some of the following inventions that attempt to make picking up dog poop less work should also be against the law!

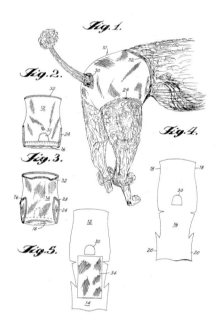

## Diaper Dandy

This doggy diaper, patented in 1965 by David Hersh, was intended to "prevent damage to household furnishings occasioned by their exposure to animal wastes and to conserve time and energy in housebreaking a dog."

## Keeping Them On

Dogs don't like diapers and tend to tear them off. This invention, patented in 2010 by Dorice Krenkel, includes two straps that help keep a dog's diaper in place.

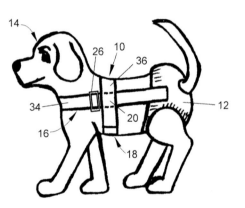

## Swish

This 2013 invention by Melvin Powell is like a game of basketball. It provides a net with a disposable bag that can be placed right where the dog is about to go. Aim correctly, and swish! Two points!

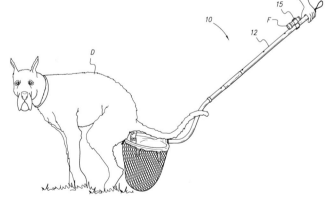

FIG. 1

## Going Just Like Us

This idea patented in 2004 by Chui-Wen Chiu was never created, and perhaps you can see why by looking at the illustration. This was proposed as a flat platform with side walls to protect the room the toilet is placed in. When flushed, water would rush over the platform, removing whatever was there. The patent didn't specify who would do the flushing, the dog or its owner.

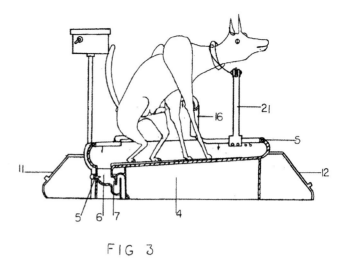

FIG 3

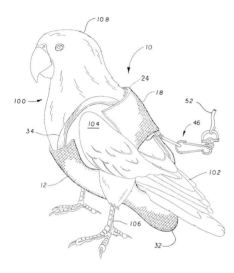

FIG. 1

## Polly Wants a Diaper

Patented in 1999 by Cely Giron and two others, this is a bird diaper for an un-caged pet bird. A removable leash is also included so the bird doesn't fly away for good once you put the diaper on him.

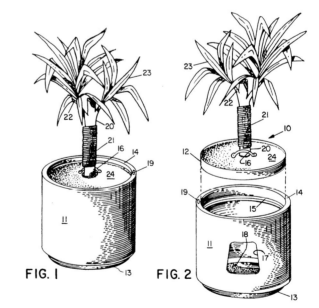

FIG. 1     FIG. 2

## Where Cats Plant Their Business

Tired of regular cat litter boxes that house-guests could stare and grimace at, Ronald Evans patented this device in 1993. It's a litter box disguised as a plant and flowerpot. The cat enters through a hole in the "pot" and does what he has to do while you enjoy the fake plant on top.

# The Scoop on Kids and Poop

**M**uch like pets, little kids are great to have around except for the whining and the pooping. Whereas we have to take care of animal poop all the time, children learn to do it themselves at some point. There are many inventions around to help this process.

## Encouraging Words

Learning to go to the bathroom by oneself is an important achievement in a little kid's life, and parents are usually very impatient to get the whole process over with so they don't have to change diapers anymore. Unfortunately for parents, neither of these inventions took off. The Automatic Talking Potty, invented by Glory Hoskins in 1996, senses when a child is sitting on the potty and then talks to him. One sample message could be, "Big boy (or girl), you have used the potty. Now it is time to go wash your hands. Very good."

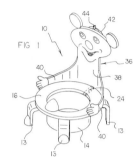

## Toilets in Disguise

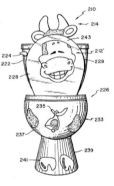

FIG.5

This invention by Joseph Lalicata, patented in 2007, is brilliant in its simplicity. Parents need only place decorative stickers of a cartoon figure on the lid, bowl, and bottom surface of a regular toilet bowl. The fun stickers will comfort kids when it's time to go (unless a goofy cow isn't comforting to you).

## Will It Change the World?

A company in Brooklyn, New York, thinks little kids will stick to potty training if they're properly amused. They created the iPotty, which is a plastic potty with a stand for an iPad. Although the iPotty has only been on sale since 2013, it has drawn a lot of attention, including from child experts who say that an iPad provides way too much stimulation for kids who should be paying attention to what they should be doing and where they should be doing it. Thankfully for anyone else in the family who wants to use the iPad, the iPotty comes with a removable touch screen cover to "protect the tablet against messy hands and smudges." Do you think it will change the world?

# Got It Covered

Have you ever seen how miserable dogs are when they have to walk in the rain? Have you ever smelled a wet dog? Yuck. Irinia Zhadan-Milligan and Yuri Zhadan came up with this dog umbrella and leash, which they patented in 2005. When it stops raining, the closed umbrella folds onto the leash.

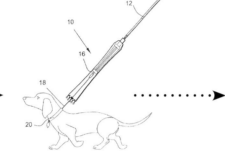

Fig.1

# Got It Way Covered

Meanwhile, this 1992 invention by Celess Antoine lets dogs do their business on rainy days while their owners stay inside. Simply attach the device to the dog's midsection, positioning the covering so the dog can breathe, and watch your pet frolic in the rain, dry as a bone.

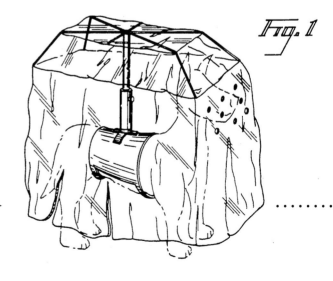

Fig. 1

# Put Your Baby to Work

In Japan, there is a fad called *chindogu*, which is the art of creating totally useless—and usually fake—inventions. *Chindogu* inventions include the butter stick (a glue-stick-like device filled with butter that you rub on bread), and the all-day tissue dispenser (a toilet roll attached to the top of a hat). One famous *chindogu* was a baby's Onesie outfit that also doubled as a floor mop, which let crawling babies help out with housework. Some people, finding the fake advertisement online, wanted one so badly that the kind folks at www.betterthanpants.com obliged, making it for real. So far, sales have been strong, but until someone proves that dust-covered babies are a good thing, this fad will fade quickly.

### Online
The Baby Mop in the news: *abcn.ws/1fFemia*

## FYI

*Chindogu* means "unusual or weird tool" in Japanese.

### Here's an Idea!
How about attaching a small vacuum to the baby so when he crawls on the carpet he can clean that, too?

# Dog Walks Man

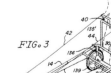

FIG. 3

This 2005 invention by Philip Kortuem is a dog-powered, human-controlled vehicle. The dog walks its owner, but the owner does the steering. It's great for Arctic exploring and racing, or for long walks around the park.

# Fetch! Sit! Carry!

**W**hy should you have to carry everything around with you when your perfectly capable dog can share the load? Sylvan Caditz patented this pet backpack in 1997.

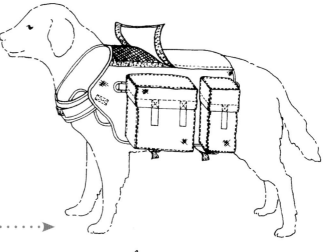

*Fig. 1.*

# Can Cats Flush?

**I**ndoor cats pretty much take care of themselves. Feed them and clean up their poop, and they're set. This invention, patented in 1972 by Michael Mcgee, teaches cats to use human toilets, eliminating the need for a litter box. The cat's potty training begins by first placing an oval-shaped litter box over the toilet bowl. When the cat gets used to this new arrangement, the first litter box is replaced with a box that has a hole in the bottom, so the cat's business falls into the toilet.

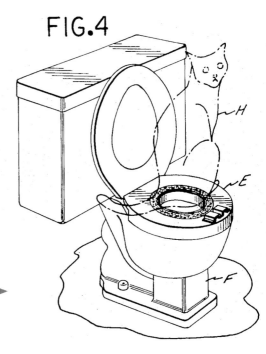

FIG.4

# The Wubby Wire

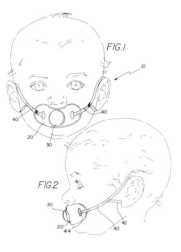

FIG.1

FIG.2

The illustration alone is enough to scare any parent away from this device, which is supposed to keep a pacifier in a baby's mouth (whether he wants it there or not). The Pacifier Securing System, which was patented in 2000 by Constance Chamberlain, includes a pacifier with adjustable straps that attach to the baby's ears, keeping the pacifier in his mouth and off the floor.

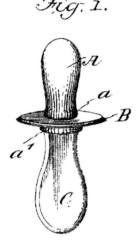

Fig. 1.

## FYI

Although homemade pacifiers have been used for centuries, the first patent for what could pass for today's design was issued in 1900 to Christian W. Meinecke from Jersey City, New Jersey. Meinecke patented at least three designs for pacifiers, one of which was meant to be a superior design to a pacifier patented by Thomas Borcher, also of Jersey City, New Jersey. Strange!

# Ears a Funny One

Animal ear protectors, patented in 1980 by James Williams, protect the ears of long-haired dogs from falling into their food while they eat. The dog's ears are pushed through two tubes, which keep the ears clean and out of the way.

## Will It Change the World?

With dog obesity becoming more of a problem, inventors are looking for ways owners can help their pets get more exercise without the owners having to exercise with them. One such invention is a toy gun that shoots doggy treats (or lion treats). This design, patented in 2013 by J. Clarke Anderson and two others, hasn't been produced yet; however, there are a few similar designs on the market. Do you think it will change the world?

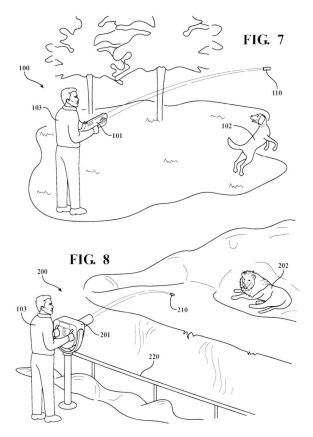

FIG. 7

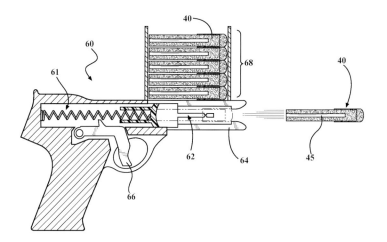

FIG. 8

# *Here Comes the Scary Face!*

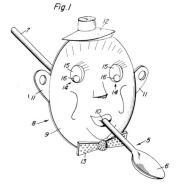

Fig.1

Parents will often play games with their babies to get them to eat their dinner. For children who are on to their parents' game of "open up, here comes the choo choo train," inventor John Wertz came up with this spoon in 1957. The face hides the parent's hand completely, making it look like a clown with a spoon in its mouth is heading straight for your mouth. Nothing scary about that, is there!?

# FYI: BABY WALKERS THROUGH THE YEARS

Inventors often come up with their ideas when they see someone else's invention and realize they can improve it. Even though most babies figure out the whole walking thing on their own, inventors have been trying to help them out for at least a hundred years. Check out how an idea in 1920 led to an invention in 2011.

*"A simple, cheaply constructed but thoroughly efficient device for assisting babies in walking." Patented in 1929 by Fred Stoll.*

*"An exercising device for an infant, which will enable it to practice walking without danger of overexertion or injury to its back or limbs." Patented in 1920 by John Bowden.*

*A device invented in the 1930s in Switzerland that, thankfully, never caught on.*

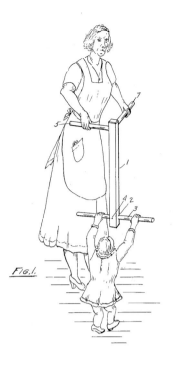

"A baby walking and balancing device."
Patented in 1951 by Joseph Spiteri.

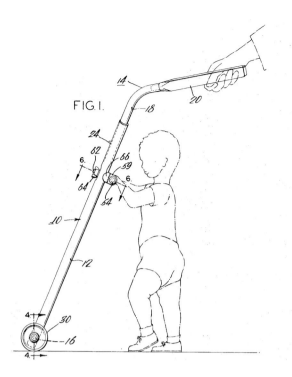

"Training device for aiding infants to walk."
Patented in 1970 by John Blank.

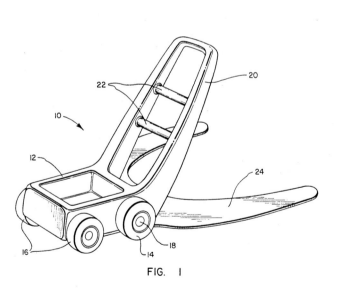

"Child walker-trainer." Patented in 1991 by
Lloyd Baum and Dan Fischer.

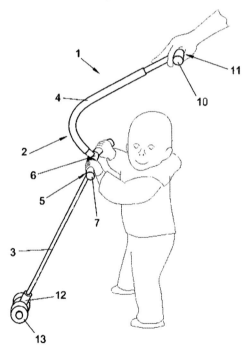

"A baby walking apparatus." Patented in
2011 by Antonio Peron.

# Just Hanging Around

There are many useful baby carriers on the market today, but only one that's designed for parents who need to use the bathroom. Whether at the mall, the doctor's office, or even at home, toddlers can get into all sorts of trouble while their parents are taking care of business. Fitted with two metal hooks that conveniently fit over door tops, the BabyKeeper lets a parent suspend their child from a bathroom door, preventing escapes. Patented in 2009 by Tonja King, this invention is a practical device for parents on the go. It hasn't really caught on, though, perhaps because the hanging child will most likely be staring right at their pottying parent? Then there's the slight chance the parent may forget the baby and leave her on the door . . .

# Hooked up

This 2010 patent from Louis and Karen Tompros is a "sling comprising a tail portion and two arm portions that support an infant when rings at the ends of the tail and arm are brought together at a single point above the infant. The rings are held together by a clamp, and the clamp allows the sling to be attached to a wall-mounted hook, a ceiling-mounted hook, a door-mounted hook and more."

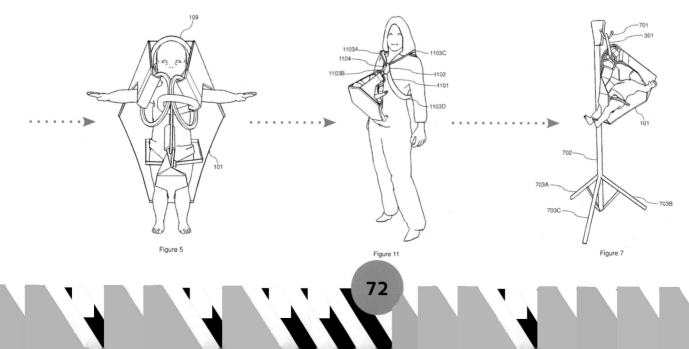

Figure 5          Figure 11          Figure 7

# Pockets for Your Pooch

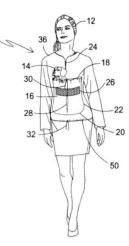

**W**ho needs a leash when you can wear your favorite pet inside your shirt? As long as you don't own a Rottweiler or a Great Dane, your pet can travel with you anywhere, while both of your arms remain free. Donna Samet patented this invention in 2007.

## Moo-ve It

**W**orried about the proper care and transport of newborn cows, Gerald Funk patented this carrier for calves in 1992. Calves can weigh up to 130 pounds at birth, and they often need to be transported to ensure their survival. This carrier not only does the trick, it also provides a "great deal of tender loving care."

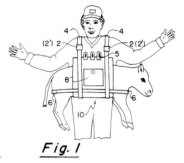

Fig. I

## Puppy Purse

**K**athy Manuel patented this small animal carrier in 1998. It's basically a dog vest with a strap. When it's time to go, simply pick the dog up by the strap and be on your way. If you place some pockets in the vest, your puppy becomes an instant purse on the run.

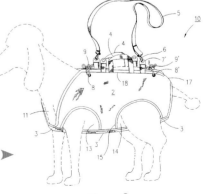

Fig. 6

# Short Leash on Life

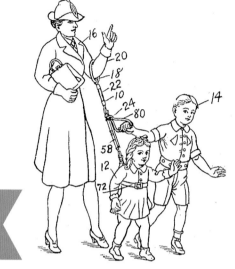

**A**lthough called a "device for use in guiding and supporting children," its more common name is a "leash." There are several patented children's leashes, but this 1940 invention by Edouard Nadeau is notable for its ability to tether one child while giving a slightly older child something to hold onto.

# Enjoying Your Ride?

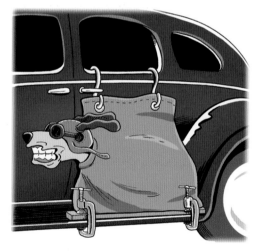

**H**ow does one solve the problem of dogs wanting to stick their heads out car windows? Here is one novel, if not extremely dangerous idea. A 1935 issue of *Popular Mechanics* proposed the Dog Sack, which places the dog outside the car completely, fastened to one of the car doors. The dog would rest his legs on running boards (small platforms) along both sides of old cars.

*In 1954, another inventor cut a hole in the trunk of his car for his dog to peek through.*

# The Dog Days ... and Hours

Fig.1

Since most animals live shorter lives as measured by human time, shouldn't animals have different watches? The inventors of this watch thought so. According to the 1991 patent application by Rodney Metts and Barry Thomas, "a dog that lives ten years has lived a full life; a man might live seventy-seven years . . . This invention is a watch made to run at a time different than human time." So a dog's watch would run seven times faster than a human's watch, since on average a human lives seven times longer than a dog. The usefulness of the watch, according to its inventors, is that pet owners can figure out how long human activities seem to their pets. For instance, "a one-hour ride in an automobile will register seven hours on a dog watch." The watch was never made, probably because it would be confusing for humans, and animals don't care about the time.

# We're Out of Time

Okay, technically, we're out of space; however, this dog has been keeping an eye on our progress and has informed us it's time to wrap things up here. We hope this book has inspired you as much as it has us. There are some crazy brilliant, crazy useful, and crazy-crazy inventions in this book, and there are millions more out there that should have changed the world, could have changed the world, would have changed the world . . . but for some reason or another, didn't. Some inventors gave up, while others went on to create something better. The human mind was made for solving problems, and these inventions prove that while not all the inventions we come up with change the world, they are certainly worth checking out because they may give us an idea that will change it. Good luck and thanks for reading this book!

## Will You Change the World?

See a problem out there that needs fixing? Why not invent something? Do your research to see what has already been invented, then come up with your own idea and test it out. If you're happy with the results, patent it. What do you think? Will you change the world?

# Resources

Most of the research for this book was done through Google's patents search engine, which is easy to use and quite fun. Check it out at www.google.com/patents.

There are lots of books about inventions and inventors; head to the local library and check them out!

For more information on how patents work, check out http://money.howstuffworks.com/patent.htm.

To read old magazine articles about inventions that could have changed the world but didn't, check out http://blog.modernmechanix.com/.

Interested in wacky inventions? Check out http://www.wackyinventions.com/.

To watch a documentary about failed inventions, check out http://topdocumentaryfilms.com/failed-inventions/.

To get more information on the United States Patent and Trademark Office, check out http://www.uspto.gov/patents/.

To search Canadian patents, check out http://brevets-patents.ic.gc.ca/opic-cipo/cpd/eng/introduction.html.

To search more than 32 million international patents, check out http://patentscope.wipo.int/search/en/search.jsf.

To access all of Thomas Edison's patent applications, check out http://edison.rutgers.edu/patenti1.htm.

For more information on Buckminster Fuller, check out https://bfi.org/about-fuller.

For more information on famous women inventors, check out http://www.women-inventors.com/.

To watch a documentary about inventions that changed the world, check out http://topdocumentaryfilms.com/inventions-changed-world/.

To find out about some kid inventors, check out http://www.cnbc.com/id/42497934#.

## PHOTO CREDITS

Page 7, bottom left: Wikipedia user Coolcaesar
Page 7, bottom right: Courtesy of the Chicago History Museum
Page 11, bottom: Public domain
Page 12, right: Public domain
Page 17, right: Library of Congress
Page 18, right: Public domain
Page 22, bottom: Wikipedia user Sicnag
Page 27, top right: Library of Congress

Page 28, bottom: Public domain; from the book *Scholar's ABC of Electricity* by William H. Meadowcroft, 1896
Page 31, right: Public domain
Page 32, left: meunierd / Shutterstock.com
Page 32, right: Wikipedia user Philipp Hienstorfer
Page 33, bottom: Library of Congress
Page 39, left: Library of Congress
Page 42, left: Library of Congress
Page 57, right: Public domain

# Subject Index

Airplanes, 16-18, 20
Antennas, 41
Applications, 6
Architects, 22
Aromas, 51
Automobiles, 11, 14, 17, 23

Babies, 36, 58, 59, 66, 68-72
Backpacks, 67
Balloons, 16, 25, 56
Balls, 48, 49
Baths, 57, 59
Baum, Frank L., 76
Beds, 29, 30
Bell Aerospace Corporation, 23
Belts, 39
Bicycles, 11-13, 15, 25, 31
Biosphere, 32
Birds, 20, 56
Boats, 18, 24
Books, 4, 5, 27, 37, 42
Brakes, 19
Brown, Charlie, 46
Brushes, 37, 43
Buggies, 11

Cages, 36, 45
Cameras, 27
Canada, 6, 7
   Montreal, 32
Canes, 6
Carriages, 11, 14
Carriers
   Baby, 72
   Dog, 73
Cars, 5, 11, 16, 22, 23, 25, 51, 74
Cats, 45, 59, 62, 63, 67
CDs, 25
Ceilings, 30
Chairs, 42, 57
Chicago, 22, 51
Chindogu, 66
Chipmonks, the, 46
Cleaners, nostril, 8
Clips, paper, 8
Clocks, 28, 29

Clouds, 30
Coats, 56
Combs, 37
Compasses, 7
Computers, 5
Connecticut, New Haven, 40
Corporations, 9
Couches, 31, 45
Cows, 73
Crashes, 11

Deaths, 17, 18, 22, 33
Diapers, 36, 61, 62, 64
Dishwashers, 29
Diving, 18, 24
Dogs, 36, 45, 58, 59, 61-63, 65, 67-69, 73, 74
Dolls, 42, 44, 46, 47, 55
Domes, geodesic, 32
Dusters, 66

Ears, 68
Electricity, 27
Energy, 28
Engineers, 16, 18
Engines, 28, 52
Europe, 57
Explosions, 23

Fans, 24
Filaments, 9
Fire escapes, 39
Fires, 38, 39, 44, 53
Floating, 33
Flying, 4, 16, 18-21, 23, 24
Food, 34
   Bacon, 34
   Chicken, 34
   Corn, 34
   Eggs, 34
   French fries, 34
   Hot dogs, 35, 55
   Ice cream, 35
   Ketchup, 54
   Lollipops, 40
   Noodles, 54
Ford Motor Corporation, 23

Games, video, 44
Gases
   Helium, 30, 56
   Oxygen, 9
Gasoline, 25, 52
Gauges, gas tank, 19
Gliders, 20

Hamsters, 45
Handlebars, 13
Hartmann, William M., 28
Hats, 38
Helicopters, 15
Henry Ford Corporation, 11
Homes
   Concrete, 27
   Domes, 32
Horn, Dr. Lisa, 58
Hovercrafts, 24, 25

Ideas, 5, 6
Illustrations, 6
Injuries, 11

Japan, 35, 66
Jogging, 31
Johnson, President Lyndon, 19
Jordan, Michael, 26
Jumping, 16, 38

Keio University, 51
Kitchens, 29

Lady Edison, 42
Leashes, 62, 65, 73, 74
Light, 4
Lightbulbs, 4, 5, 9, 27, 28
Lincoln, President Abraham, 9
Litter boxes, 62, 67

Machines
   Exercise, 31
   Flying, 15, 20, 21
   Office, 42
   Petting, 63
   Rowing, 12

Scratching, 63
Sewing, 42
Time, 8
Mannheim, Germany, 12
Mattresses, 30
Mice, 45
Milk, carbonated, 55
Mirrors, 7
Model T, 11, 17
Molds, 27
Money, 9, 26
Mops, 66
Movies, 32, 51
Museums, 16, 22, 32

National Automobile Museum, 22
Nevada, Reno, 22
New Jersey, Jersey City, 68
New Jersey, Union Township, 27
New York, Brooklyn, 64

Pacifiers, 68
Parachutes, 18, 38
Patents, 6-8
Pedals, 15, 25, 37
Photocopiers, 9
Photographs, 51
Pillows, 60
Playgrounds, 39
Pogo sticks, 15, 52
Poisoning, radiation, 23
Poop, 58, 61, 65
Press, printing, 4
Prototypes, 17, 18, 22, 32
Purses, 73

Radios, 5, 19
Razors, 37
Recycling, water, 32
Rhoades, Charles, 24
Rudders, 24
Rugs, 30

Saucers, flying, 24
School, 10
Scientists, 22, 23, 37
Shaving, 43
Shirts, 50
Shoes, 37
Showers, 32
Signals, electrical, 19
Sinking, 19
Smartphones, 5
Snakes, 45

Socks, 37
Spoons, 69
Sports
    Badminton, 50
    Baseball, 48
    Basketball, 50, 62
    Football, 48
    Soccer, 49
    Tennis, 48
Steering, 13, 14, 24
Submarines, 18
Swimming, 19, 20
System, sound, 5

Tables, 29
Telephones, 42
Television, 19, 31, 37, 51
Tennessee, 38
Toasters, 34
Toilet training, 58, 64
Toilets, 32, 62, 64, 67
Toothbrushes, electric, 26, 43
Treadmills, 31
Tricycles, 11, 37
Trumpets, 53
Typesetting, 37
Typewriters, 42

Umbrellas, 5, 42, 65
United States Army, 23
United States Patent and Trademark Office,
    6, 7

Vacuums, 36, 66
Vehicles, 23, 66
Velocipedes, 13
Vibrations, 28
Virginia, Alexandria, 7

Walkers, baby, 70, 71
Walking, 31
Washington, President George, 7, 8
Wheels, 6, 7, 11-14, 21, 22, 24, 28
Wings, 17
World War I, 32
World's Fair, 22

Xerox, 9

# Inventor Index

Adams, Clarence, 16
Alber, Otto, 47
Anderson, J. Clarke, 69
Antoine, Celess, 65
Aronson, Louis, 47

Baer, Ralph H., 44
Baird, John Logie, 37
Bauersfeld, Walther, 32
Baum, Lloyd, 71
Belisle, Brice, 45
Blank, John, 71
Blomeley, Lewis, 17

Blue, John, 50
Boccardi, Patsy, 50
Bonge, Scott, 43
Borcher, Thomas, 68
Bowden, John, 70
Bradley Smith Company, 40
Bristor, Kirk, 50
Burbank, Louis, 12
Bush, Harold, 15

Caditz, Sylvan, 67
Calderwood, William, 30
Carlson, Chester, 9
Cecere, Al, 41
Chamberlain, Constance, 68
Cherry, Theron, 12
Chiu, Chui-Wen, 62
Cochrane, Josephine, 29
Coleman, Edward, 55
Coleman, Thomas, 40, 41

De Forest, Lee, 19
DeHart, Harold, 29
Diaz, Wilfredo, 48
Dipolito, Lauren, 45
Divine, Joseph, 5

Edison, Thomas, 4, 9, 10, 19, 26-28, 41, 42, 46
Fischer, Dan, 71
Flanders, Ralph, 49

Ford, Henry, 11, 17
Foster, Norman, 22
Fuller, Buckminster, 22, 32, 33
Funk, Gerald, 73

Gardner, Valerie, 55
Giron, Cely, 62
Glintz, Georgia, 49

Harlev, Amos, 47
Hartman, Richard, 35
Hayes, Frances, 61
Heap, Roger, 42
Heinz, 54
Henry, Beulah Louise, 42
Hensel, Otto, 57
Hersh, David, 61
Hong, Thomas, 47
Hulbert, John, 23

Jackson, Yamile, 60
Jin, Kim, 43

Kempher, Robert M., 55
King, Harvey, 50
King, Tonja, 72
Kiwala, Edward, 35
Kortuem, Philip, 66
Krenkel, Dorice, 61
Kretschmer, Nicholas, 34

Lalicata, Joseph, 64
Lambert, John W., 11
Lanston, Tolbert, 37
Lehman, R. Danford, 49
Leslie, David, 56

Marsh, Charles, 52
Matts, Orville, 39
Mcgee, Michael, 67
Meinecke, Christian W., 68
Metts, Rodney, 74
Moore, Brian, 59
Moore, Wendell, 23

Mullen, Margie, 31
Mumford, Olin, 5
Munsen, Henry, 13

Nadeau, Edouard, 74
Nichols, Larry, 53
Nigro, Pasquale, 38

Okada, Dr. Kenichi, 51
Oppenheimer, Benjamin, 38

Paden, Jack, 59
Peron, Antonio, 71
Powell, Melvin, 62
Purves, Dr. John, 14

Quinby, W.F., 20, 21

Porath, Deanna, 37

Radu, Bogdan, 19
Reed, Emma, 36
Reichelt, Franz, 18

Reid, Donald V., 18
Reinert, Richard, 31
Ross, Howard, 56
Rubik, Erno, 53
Ryan, Arthur, 48

Samet, Donna, 73
Schecter, Jules, 41
Schmuck, Allison, 63
Seaman, George, 29
Sevilla, Frederick, 56
Smith, Henry, 6
Spiteri, Joseph, 71
Spitzmesser, Gordon, 52
Stephens, Donald, 30
Stoll, Fred, 70
Straube, Richard, 57
Sweeney, Aida, 50

Taylor, Moulton, 16

Terry, Olivia, 45
Thomas, Barry, 74
Tolson, Thomas, 14
Tompros, Karen, 72
Tompros, Louis, 72
Trenary, Justin W., 13
Trippel, Hanns, 18
Tuoriniemi, Frances, 59

Vecchia, Rita Della, 63
Vidas, Pat, 53

Walker, W., 49
Wertz, John, 69

Williams, James, 68
Williams, Michael, 49
Witkowski, Daniel, 54

Wyzykowski, Sandra J., 41

Yu, Yu-Li, 38

Zaleski, A., 36
Zander, Gustav, 31
Zhadan, Yuri, 65
Zhadan-Milligan, Irinia, 65

"Imagination has brought mankind through the Dark Ages to its present state of civilization. Imagination led Columbus to discover America. Imagination led Franklin to discover electricity. Imagination has given us the steam engine, the telephone, the talking-machine, and the automobile, for these things had to be dreamed of before they became realities. So I believe that dreams—daydreams, you know, with your eyes wide open and your brain-machinery whizzing—are likely to lead to the betterment of the world. The imaginative child will become the imaginative man or woman most apt to create, to invent, and therefore to foster civilization."

~L. Frank Baum, from his book, The Lost Princess of Oz

Monika Beisner's
# BOOK OF RIDDLES

# Monika Beisner's
# BOOK OF RIDDLES

A SUNBURST BOOK

FARRAR, STRAUS AND GIROUX

# For Johannes

When first I appear I seem mysterious,
But when I am explained I am nothing serious.

## 1

What is it?
It stands on one leg
With its heart in its head.

## 2

My tail is long, my coat is brown,
I like the country, I like the town.
I can live in a house or live in a
shed,
And I come out to play when you
are in bed.

## 3

What is it:
Has a mouth and does not speak,
Has a bed and does not sleep?

## 4

I sleep by day,
I fly by night.
I have no feathers
To aid my flight.

## 5

It has four legs and a foot
And can't walk.
It has a head
And can't talk.

## 6

My face is pale, and full and fair;
And round it beauty spots there are;
By day, indeed, I seem less bright,
I'm only seen sometimes at night.
And when the sun has gone to bed
I then begin to show my head.

## 7

Flip flop fleezy, .
When it is in, it is easy.
But when it is out,
It flops all about.
Flip flop fleezy.

## 8

I prefer a bed of lettuce to any other
kind,
And frolicking about is most often
on my mind.
My ears are long, and short my tail.
If you try to catch me you will fail.

## 9

My first is in ocean but never in sea,
My second's in wasp but never in
bee,
My third is in glider and also in
flight,
My whole is a creature that comes
out at night.

## 10

What force and strength cannot get through,
I, with a gentle touch, can do;
And many in the street would stand,
Were I not, as a friend, at hand.

## 11

My first is in chocolate but not in ham,
My second's in cake and also in jam,
My third at tea-time is easily found,
My whole is a friend who's often around.
What am I?

## 12

I saw a man in white,
He looked quite a sight.
He was not old,
But he stood in the cold.
And when he felt the sun
He started to run.
Who could he be?
Do answer me.

## 13

What lives in winter,
Dies in summer,
And grows with its root upwards?

## 14

My first is in window but not in pane,
My second's in road but not in lane,
My third is in oval but not in round,
My fourth is in hearing but not in sound,
My whole is known as a sign of peace,
And from Noah's Ark won quick release.

## 15

What has:
Six legs, two heads,
Four ears, two hands,
But walks
On four feet?

## 16

There dwell four sisters near this town,
In looks alike, and like in gown.
Round and round in a ring they run,
Chasing each other just for fun.
But even though they gather pace,
Between them there is equal space.

## 17

No head has he but he wears a hat.
No feet has he but he stands up
straight.
On him perhaps a fairy sat,
Weaving a spell one evening late.

## 18

I love to dance
And twist and prance,
I shake my tail,
As away I sail,
Wingless I fly
Into the sky.
What am I?

## 19

My first is in football but isn't in
shoot,
My second's in treasure but isn't in
loot,
My fourth is in swallow and so is my
third,
My whole on a Sunday is far and
wide heard.

## 20

Iron roof
Glass walls
Burns and burns
And never falls.

## 21

Its belly is linen
Its neck velvet
Its mouth music
Its tail a fork.

## 22

My second is performed by my first;
And, it is thought,
A thief by the marks of my whole
Might be caught.

## 23

Four stiff-standers,
Four dillydanders,
Two hookers,
Two lookers ,
And a flip-flap.

## 24

Two brothers we are, great burden
we bear
By which we are bitterly pressed;
In truth we may say, we are full all
the day,
But empty when we go to rest.

## 25

My teeth are sharp,
My back is straight,
To cut things up it is my fate.
What am I?

## 26

In marble walls as white as milk
Lined with a skin as soft as silk;
Within a fountain crystal clear
A golden apple does appear.
No doors there are to this
stronghold –
Yet thieves break in and steal the
gold.

## 27

Riddle me ree,
They grow on a tree,
Are smooth, red and shiny,
Not large but quite tiny.
Their hearts are of stone
When they are full grown.

## 28

As I was walking by Padston bay
Upon a cloudy summer's day,
I saw an object smooth and round
Which very sweet and fresh I found.
But as the outside was quite dry
No further use for it had I,
So I threw its skin away.

## 29

First I am as white as snow,
Then as green as grass I grow,
Next I am as red as blood,
Lastly I'm as black as mud.

## 30

There was a little green house;
And in the little green house
There was a little brown house;
And in the little brown house
There was a little yellow house;
And in the little yellow house
There was a little white house;
And in the little white house
There was a little white heart.

## 31

Brown are their toes,
Striped are their clothes,
Tell me this riddle
And you can pull my nose.

## 32

Old Mister Puddididdle
Played in the muddy puddle;
He had yellow socks and shoes
And a cap of greens and blues,
He was often in a muddle.
Now guess the riddle.

## 33

My first is a woman,
My second a bird,
My whole is an insect
I give you my word.

## 31

When she has a root
She has no leaves;
And when she pulls up her root,
The leaves appear.

## 35

Eight were standing
Two were cracking
Two were looking.

## 36

The greater it is
The less you see of it.

## 37

At night they come without being
fetched,
And by day they are lost without
being stolen.

## 38

Come up and let us go;
Go down and here we stay.

## 39

Long legs
Short thighs
Bald head
And bullet eyes.

## 40

I run smoother than any rhyme,
I love to fall but cannot climb.
I tremble at each breath of air,
And yet can heaviest burdens bear.

## 41

Who is he that runs without a leg
With his house on his back?

## 42

Me riddle, me racket,
Suppose I tell you this riddle,
And perhaps not;
There is something moves all day
And all night and never stops.

## 43

I come out of the earth,
I am sold in the market.
He who buys me cuts my tail,
Takes off my suit of silk,
And weeps beside me when I am
dead.

## 44

What has teeth
And can't bite?

## 45

My first is twice in apple
But not once in tart.
My second is in liver
But not in heart.
My third is in giant
And also in ghost.
Whole I'm best when I am roast.

## 46

Four fingers and a thumb,
Yet flesh and blood I have none.

## 47

Long pole, bushy tail.
What is it?

## 48

The sun bakes them
The hand breaks them
The foot treads them
The mouth tastes them.

## 49

He's a boastful, puffed-up fellow,
Wearing spurs; eyes gleaming yellow.
As he proudly struts about
He's in charge, there is no doubt.

## 50

My first is in bottle but isn't in milk,
My second's in satin but isn't in silk,
My third and my fourth are both in
a pair,
My fifth is in hope and also despair,
My last is in yellow but isn't in
pink,
My whole contains liquid for people
to drink.

## 51

What is it that leaps and runs
And has no feet?

## 52

Two little holes
In the side of a hill
Just as you come
To the cherry-red mill.

## 53

What runs round the garden without
moving?

## 54

My first is in fish and also in chips,
My second's in mouth but not in
lips,
My third is in ache but not in pain,
My fourth is my third all over again,
My fifth is in pupil but isn't in class,
My whole is a beast that feeds on
the grass.

## 55

A father's child
A mother's child
Yet no one's son.

## 56

My voice is tender
My waist is slender
I'm often invited to play.
Yet wherever I go
I must take my bow
Or else I have nothing to say.

## 57

We are a pair,
We can dart here and there,
Though we always stay in one place.
We can smile or shed tears,
Show our pleasure or fears,
And you'll find us on everyone's
face.

## 58

White and thin,
Red within,
With a nail at the end.

## 59

I'm very tempting, so it's said,
I have a shiny coat of red,
And my flesh is white beneath.
I smell so sweet,
Taste good to eat,
And help to guard your teeth.

## 60

I daily am in France and Spain,
At times do all the world explore,
Since time began I've held my reign,
And shall till time will be no more.
I never in my life have strolled
In garden, field, or city park,
Yet all of these are sad and cold
If I'm not there and it is dark.

## 61

Without a bridle, or a saddle,
Across a thing I ride a-straddle.
And those I ride, by help of me,
Though almost blind, are made to
see.

## 62

I open wide and tight I shut,
Sharp am I and paper cut –
Fingers too, so do take care,
I'm good and bad, so best beware.

## 63

What has black spots and a white
face,
Is fat not thin, and helps you to
win,
But tumbles all over the place?

## 64

I have no voice and yet I speak to
you,
I tell of all things in the world that
people do;
I have leaves, but I am not a tree,
I have pages, but I am not a bride or
royalty;
I have a spine and hinges, but I am
not a man or a door,
I have told you all,
I cannot tell you more.

## 65

There is a thing that nothing is,
And yet it has a name:
It's sometimes tall
And sometimes short,
It tumbles if we fall.
It joins our sport,
And plays at every game.

## 66

More eyes have I than I do need for
sight,
A cry have I that is both sharp and
clear,
A tail have I more fit for show than
flight,
Admired am I wherever I appear.

## 67

I move silently without wings,
Between silvery, silken strings,
And there stretched in the grass
You'll see my web as you pass.

## 68

No mouth, no eyes,
Nor yet a nose,
Two arms, two feet,
And as it goes,
The feet don't touch the ground,
But all the way the head runs round.

## 69

My first is in dog but isn't in cat,
My second's in glove but not in hat,
My third is in flame but isn't in
smoke,
My fourth is in jester but not in
joke.
My whole makes no fuss about what
it will eat,
And is known to be nimble on its
four feet.

## 70

What is it
That has teeth
And can't eat?

## 71

Mother and father, sister and
brother,
All running after one another,
Each pair running behind the other,
Bet they'll never catch each other.

## 72

I'm a busy active creature,
Full of mirth and play by nature;
Nimbly I skip from tree to tree,
To get the food that's fit for me;
Then let me hear, if you can tell,
What is my name and where I
dwell.

## 73

From house to house I go,
Sometimes narrow, sometimes wide.
And whether there's rain or snow
I always stay outside.

## 74

A very pretty thing am I,
Fluttering in the pale-blue sky.
Delicate, fragile on the wing,
Indeed I am a pretty thing.

## 75

Two bodies have I
Though both joined in one.
The more still I stand
The quicker I run.

## 76

Little Nancy Etticoat
Has a white petticoat
And a red nose.
She has no feet or hands;
The longer she stands
The shorter she grows.

## 77

What flares up
And does a lot of good,
And when it dies,
It's just a piece of wood?

## 78

High in the sky
I can see with my eye
White horses are grazing.
Isn't that amazing?

## 79

What is full of holes and holds
water?

## 80

Old Mother Twitchett has but one
eye,
And a long tail which she can let
fly,
And every time she goes over a gap,
She leaves a bit of her tail in a trap.

## 81

As black as ink and is not ink,
As white as milk and is not milk,
As soft as silk and is not silk,
And is a thief but does not know it.

## 82

The beginning of eternity,
The end of time and space,
The beginning of every end,
And the end of every place.

## 83

Look in my face, I am somebody;
Look in my back, I am nobody.

## 84

Headed like a thimble,
Tailed like a rat.
You may guess to Doomsday,
But you couldn't guess that.

## 85

You would scarcely believe
That one dwarf could heave
A whole mountain range
On our lawn. That's strange!

## 86

What is it that has four legs
And one back,
Yet can't walk?

## 87

My first is in wood but isn't in tree,
My second's in four and also in
three,
My third is in music and also in
tune,
My fourth is in May but isn't in
June.
My whole makes a noise
You can hear down the street.
What am I?

## 88

First you see me in the grass
Dressed in yellow gay;
Next I am in dainty white,
Then I fly away.

## 89

In spring I am gay
In handsome array;
In summer more clothing I wear;
When colder it grows
I fling off my clothes;
And in winter quite naked appear.

## 90

Hands she has but does not hold,
Teeth she has but does not bite,
Feet she has but they are cold,
Eyes she has but without sight.
Who is she?

## 91

As I went over Lincoln Bridge,
I met Mister Rusticap;
Pins and needles on his back,
A-going to Thorny Fair.

## 92

Its headscarf is red,
And it grows in the ground.
When it shakes its bald head,
You can hear a loud sound.

## 93

To cross the water I'm the way,
For water I'm above:
I touch it not and, truth to say,
I neither swim nor move.

## 94

Black within,
Red without,
Four corners round about.

## 95

Violet, indigo, blue and green,
Yellow, orange and red,
These are the colours you have seen
After the storm has fled.

## 96

What is the thing which,
Once poured out,
Cannot be gathered again?

## 97

Round as an apple,
Deep as a cup,
All the King's horses
Can't pull it up.

## 98

What is it
That makes tears without sorrow
And takes its journey to heaven?

## 99

As long as I live I eat,
But when I drink I die.

## 100

What is it?
The more you take from it,
The larger it gets.

## 101

What always goes to bed with his
shoes on?

# Answers

*page 5*
riddle

| | | | |
|---|---|---|---|
| 1 cabbage | 6 moon | 26 egg | 30 walnut |
| 2 mouse | 7 fish | 27 cherry | 31 bee |
| 3 river | 8 rabbit | 28 orange | 32 duck |
| 4 bat | 9 owl | 29 blackberry | 33 ladybird |
| 5 bed | | | |

| | | | |
|---|---|---|---|
| 10 key | 14 dove | 34 sailing ship | 39 frog |
| 11 cat | 15 horse and rider | 35 crab | 40 water |
| 12 snowman | 16 windmill | 36 darkness | 41 snail |
| 13 icicle | | 37 star | 42 sea |
| | | 38 anchor | |

| | | | |
|---|---|---|---|
| 17 toadstool | 21 swallow | 43 onion | 47 broom |
| 18 kite | 22 footstep | 44 comb | 48 grapes |
| 19 bell | 23 cow | 45 pig | 49 cockerel |
| 20 lantern | 24 pair of shoes | 46 gloves | 50 barrel |
| | 25 saw | | |

# Answers

| | | | |
|---|---|---|---|
| 51 ball | 56 violin | 75 hourglass | 80 needle and thread |
| 52 nose and mouth | 57 eyes | 76 candle | 81 magpie |
| 53 fence | 58 finger | 77 match | 82 letter E |
| 54 sheep | 59 apple | 78 clouds | 83 mirror |
| 55 girl | | 79 sponge | 84 pipe |

| | | | |
|---|---|---|---|
| 60 sun | 64 book | 85 mole | 89 tree |
| 61 spectacles | 65 shadow | 86 chair | 90 doll |
| 62 scissors | 66 peacock | 87 drum | 91 hedgehog |
| 63 dice | | 88 dandelion | 92 poppy |

| | | | |
|---|---|---|---|
| 67 spider | 71 four wheels | 93 bridge | 97 well |
| 68 wheelbarrow | 72 squirrel | 94 chimney | 98 smoke |
| 69 goat | 73 path | 95 rainbow | 99 fire |
| 70 rake | 74 butterfly | 96 rain | 100 ditch |
| | | | 101 horse |